MARTIN'S CONCISE
JAPANESE DICTIONARY

MARTIN'S CONCISE
JAPANESE DICTIONARY

ENGLISH–JAPANESE
JAPANESE–ENGLISH

*Fully Romanized
with Complete Kanji & Kana*

SAMUEL E. MARTIN

CHARLES E. TUTTLE COMPANY
Rutland, Vermont & Tokyo, Japan

Published by the Charles E. Tuttle Company, Inc.
of Rutland, Vermont & Tokyo, Japan
with editorial offices at
2-6 Suido 1-chome, Bunkyo-ku, Tokyo, Japan

© 1994 by Charles E. Tuttle Publishing Co., Inc.
All rights reserved

Library of Congress Catalog Card No. 93-60380
International Standard Book No. 0-8048-1912-2

First edition, 1994

Third printing, 1995

Printed in Singapore

CONTENTS

INTRODUCTION

This is a dictionary of spoken Japanese, in two parts: English-Japanese and Japanese-English. It aims to be of immediate use to the beginning student of Japanese who wants to know the meaning of an expression he has just heard or who seeks to express himself in ordinary, everyday situations. This is the place to look for the words to help you get a plumber, staples for your stapler, or sushi without the horseradish. It will also help you when you are groping for the appropriate form of a Japanese verb; here, too, you will find just which different verbs may converge in a given form, such as **itte,** which can mean 'going', 'needing', or 'saying'. The dictionary cannot take the place of a textbook or a reference grammar, but it can remind you of the important points made by those books.

If you are primarily interested in reading and writing Japanese, you will need other tools, but certain features of this work will be useful to you in unexpected ways. Japanese sentences can be written using only kana—all hiragana or all katakana or a mixture of the two, but the result is often hard to read because the Japanese do not traditionally use any device to separate words, such as the spaces we use in English. Japanese sentences written in romanized form (in any system) are easier to read because the spaces make the words stand out individually, and judiciously placed hyphens make the structure of compound words more accessible to the eye.

The Japanese normally write their sentences in a mixed script, using kanji (Chinese characters) for the more salient words, especially nouns, and hiragana as a kind of neutral background, appropriate for grammatical endings, particles, and the like. They also use kana as a kind of fallback, when they are uncertain or ignorant of the appropriate kanji. By using katakana for modern foreign words and other oddities, as well as kanji for the words made up of elements borrowed many years ago from China, a writer can make words stand out from the background in a way that partly makes up for the absence of spaces between them.

Unfortunately, the use of kanji tempts the writer into relying entirely on the eye, forgetting that texts might be read over the telephone or listened to in the dark. For this reason, words confusing to the ear should be avoided. As a result, written Japanese today is an artificial and unstandardized medium of communication, varying in complexity with each writer and every text. If you ask ten Japanese to write out a typical long sentence read aloud from a magazine or newspaper, you will probably find you have eight to ten different versions. Many writers feel free to create new words and abbreviations based solely on the meanings associated with the kanji, and with total disregard to whether the result is meaningful to the ear.

Yet all of that is a superstructure imposed on the basic language which underlies the written text, and the basic language is spoken Japanese. That is why it is necessary to approach the written language from a good knowledge of the sentence structure and vocabulary of the spoken language.

PRONUNCIATION

Because we are dealing with the spoken language, the words are given in romanized form. The system used is Hepburn Romanization, traditionally favored by foreigners, with the addition of a few marks to help with the pronunciation. If at first the marks bother you, just disregard them; later you will probably find the notations useful as a reminder of what you have heard.

Japanese phrases are accompanied by little tunes that help the hearer know what words a phrase contains. The tunes consist of a limited number of patterns of higher and lower pitch; each phrase has an inherent pattern. For example, a very common tune is rather monotonous: the pitch is slightly lower on the first syllable, then rises and stays on a plateau for the rest of the word or phrase:

kono kodomo wa nakanai

'this child does not cry'

Yokohama e iku

'goes to Yokohama'

A less common tune starts high and immediately falls, staying down till the end:

a⌐me desu 'it's rain'

Me⌐guro e mo iku 'goes to Meguro too'

Other tunes rise to a plateau and then fall at some point before the end:

Aka⌐saka 'Akasaka'

Ikebu⌐kuro 'Ikebukuro'

yasumima⌐shita 'rested'

When the accent, i.e., a fall of pitch, is on the last syllable, you sometimes cannot hear it unless another word, such as a particle, is attached:

hana (ga akai) 'the nose (is red)'

hana⌐ (ga akai) 'the flower (is red)'

When the change of pitch is within a long syllable, you will probably notice a rise or fall within the syllable, as shown by these place names:

Ōsaka = ₀osaka

Kyō⌐to = kyo⌐oto

Ryūkyū⌐ = ryuukyu⌐u

Daitō⌐-ku = daito⌐oku

When a word has more than one accent mark, that means the word has variant forms. Some people may say it with the fall at one of the syllables, others at a different syllable. When an accent mark appears in parentheses, the word is often phrased with the preceding word, which carries an accent. That accounts for the difference between **hi⌐rō shima(⌐)sụ** and **riyō shima⌐sụ**. The mark ⌐ᵕ⌐ instead of ⌐ is used when the word has a variant with no accent; some speakers let the word stay high to the end. What should you do? Imitate what you hear; the notation is just to let you know which of the standard tunes are in use for that word. The accent of a particular word, especially a verb form, may change in certain contexts, as explained in the grammars; the changes often involve an accent acquired or lost on the last syllable of the form. A compound word has an inherent tune that follows rules somewhat independent of those of the component elements.

Japanese speakers often reduce the short vowels **i** and **u** in certain words by devoicing (whispering) them or even suppressing them completely. The vowel reductions are a surface phenomenon, a kind of last-minute touch when you are about to speak your sentence, and they are ignored by the traditional writing system and most transcriptions. But there are many subtleties to the rules that call for i̥ and u̥ instead of i or u, and they often involve word boundaries and other grammatical factors. It isn't just a matter of "whisper i and u when they are between voiceless consonants (**p, t, k, f, s, h**)," though that is a good rule. You can have more than one whispered vowel in a word (**ki̥kima¬shi̥ta** 'I heard it') but not in successive syllables (**ki̥ki-tai** 'I want to hear it'). Usually it is the first of two susceptible syllables that are whispered, but not always, for syllables beginning with stops (**p, t, k**) are more resistant than those that begin with the affricates (**ch** and **ts**). And, syllables beginning with these affricates are more resistant than syllables that begin with fricatives (**f, h, s, sh**). In **reki̥shi̥-ka** 'historian' (from **reki̥shi** 'history') it is the second of the susceptible syllables that is whispered.

Another general rule is that i and u are unvoiced at the end of a word that has an inherent accent when that word ends a phrase or sentence. That is why we write all the polite nonpast forms as **...ma¬su̥**. The vowel will remain voiceless before a voiceless consonant (**dekima¬su̥ ka** 'Can you do it?) but usually will get voiced before a voiced consonant (**dekima¬su ga** 'I can, but'). For nouns, however, and for verb forms other than **...ma¬su̥**, we have not marked as voiceless such cases of final **...i** and **...u**, because so often they are followed by particles or other elements that begin with a voiced consonant. For example, by itself **ga¬su** 'gas' is pronounced **ga¬su̥** (and **da¬su** 'puts it out' is pronounced **da⌐su**) but the second syllable will be voiced in the more common phrases that you hear, such as **ga⌐su o tsuke⌐te kudasa(⌐)i** 'turn on the gas'.

When **shima⌐su** 'does' is attached to a noun that ends in a reducible syllable, we write the voiceless vowel: **insatsu** 'print-ing' becomes **insatsu shima⌐su** 'prints it'. (This dictionary does not always call your attention to regular situations that will bring back the voicing, as in **insatsu shite** 'printing it'.) At the beginning of a word (**kusa⌐** 'grass') or in the middle (**empi-tsu** 'pencil'), an unvoiced vowel remains unvoiced except when the syllables are recited, sounded out, or sung.

In using the traditional romanization, this dictionary follows the older practice of writing **-mm-**, **-mb-**, and **-mp-** in words now often written **-nm-**, **-nb-**, and **-np-**. The first letter represents a nasal syllable that takes its color from the sounds around it, so that before a sound made with the lips (**m**, **b**, **p**) it sounds like a long **m**. Before **f**, however, and in all other situa-tions, the syllable is represented with the letter **n**, so that 'pam-phlet' is **pa⌐nfure⌐tto**.

Many Japanese pronounced **fu** as **hu**. The syllable **hi** is often said as a palatal fricative (like German *ich*), and you may notice that quite a few speakers make it sound just like **shi**, especially when the **i** is devoiced; if your ears hear **shito**, be aware that it is very likely just a variant of **hito** 'person'. The lips are not much rounded for the Japanese vowel **u** and are totally disengaged in the syllables **su** and **tsu**, for which the tongue is moved quite far forward, so that the **u** sound is somewhere between **i** and **u**.

We have not shown the distinction between the two kinds of **g** that are used by many speakers because the present-day situation is in flux and the distinction, which carries little semantic weight, is missing in many parts of the country. The prestige pronunciation, however, favors a "softened" form of ...**g**... when it is felt to be internal to a word, or begins a particle, as in ... **ga**. The softened form is pronounced through the nose, like the *ng* at the end of English 'sing'. Some speakers use a murmured version of ...**g**..., a voiced fricative, instead of the nasal.

The long vowels **ō** and **ū** are written with a macron in virtually all cases, though they are functionally equivalent to double vowels **oo** and **uu** and are often so transcribed. The long vowels **ā** and **ē** are similar, but except in foreignisms, most cases of long **ē** are written as **ei**, following the practice of the hiragana orthography, which takes into account the fact that in some areas people pronounce **ei** as a diphthong, as once was true everywhere.

The long vowels are written in katakana with a bar (a dash) after the syllable; in hiragana they are written as double vowels **oo, uu, ii, ee, aa**, but for historical reasons most often the long **ō** is written **ou**. That is why when you use romanization to type your input for a Japanese word processor you have to write **ho u ho u** to produce the hiragana string that can be converted into the kanji deemed appropriate for the word **hōhō** 'method'. (But you input **Ōsaka** as **o o sa ka** because the first element of that name, the **ō** of **ōkíi** 'big', happens to be one of the handful of common exceptions.) We write the word for 'beer' as **bi͞iru** instead of putting a long mark over a single **i** both for esthetic reasons and for linguistic considerations: most cases of long **i** consist of two grammatically different elements, as in the many adjectives that end in **...i-i** or, less obviously, such nouns as **chi͞i** 'position'.

GRAMMAR

This dictionary differs from other dictionaries in a number of ways. The verb forms are cited primarily in the normal polite form (**...ma͞su**), for that is what the beginning student will most often hear and practice using at the end of sentences. Other common forms are also given, such as the plain nonpast (**...u** or **...ru**) and the gerund (**...te** or **...de**). The nonpast forms, whether plain or polite, refer to general, repeated, or future situations ('does' or 'will do'); they are also used for situations that started in the past but continue on into the present, such as 'I have been staying here since the day before yesterday' (**ototo͞i kara koko ni ima͞su**), or that have a result that lasts, such as 'I have gotten married' (**kekkon shite ima͞su**), another way to say 'I am married'.

The past forms ('did') are easily made: for the polite past, change **...ma͞su** to **...ma͞shita**, and for the plain, take the gerund and change its final **e** to **a**, with the result being **...ta** or **...da**. The plain nonpast form for NOUN **de͞su** 'it is [a matter of]' is **...da͞**, but that is replaced by **... no** or **... na** when the expression modifies a following noun. The choice of **... no** or **... na** depends on a number of factors that are described in grammars and textbooks. This dictionary gives the appropriate form in parentheses in many cases. The polite past of NOUN **de⌐su** is ... **de⌐shita**, the plain past is ... **da⌐tta** (even when the nonpast would change to **na** or **no**), and the gerund is ... **de⌐**. The form ... **ni**, in addition to its many uses as a particle ('to' 'at', 'for'), also functions as a form of ... **de⌐su**, the infinitive in the meaning 'so as to be', as in **jōzu⌐ ni narima⌐shita ne⌐** 'has gotten good at it'.

The infinitive form of verbs (**...i** or **...e**) in spoken Japanese is mainly used to form compounds, and many nouns are derived from infinitives by a change of accent, e.g., **yasumi⌐** 'vacation' or 'work break' from **yasu⌐mi** 'to rest'). The common nouns and infinitives derived in this manner are included in the Japanese–English dictionary. The polite negative nonpast forms of verbs are made by changing **...ma⌐su** to **...mase⌐n** and the past to **...mase⌐n deshita**, run together as if one word; the plain nonpast forms end in **...(⌐)nai** or **...a(⌐)nai** and the plain past forms end in **...na(⌐)katta** or **...a⌐na⌐katta**. The negative gerund is **...⌐na⌐ide** or **...a⌐na⌐ide**, as in **Isoga⌐naide kudasa(⌐)i** 'Don't go so fast', but before ... **mo** or ... **wa**, it is usually **...⌐na⌐kute** or **...a⌐na⌐kute**, as in **Isoga⌐nakute wa dame⌐ desu** 'You've got to go fast' and **Tabe⌐nakute mo i⌐i desu** 'We don't have to eat'. In the English–Japanese section, the citation form for verbs is the English infinitive ('to do' minus the 'to ...'), whereas most Japanese–English dictionaries use the plain nonpast as a citation form; do not confuse that with the English infinitive. This dictionary gives most English translations as third-person singular ('does'), but the Japanese verb itself is nonspecific with reference to person.

Adjectives are cited in the plain forms …a(˥)-i, …o(˥)-i, …u(˥)-i, and …i(˥)-i, for they are often used before a noun, where the plain form is most common. The polite forms appropriate at the end of a sentence end in …˥-i desu: …a˥i desu, …o˥i desu, …u˥-i desu, and …i˥i desu. The plain past is made by replacing -(˥)i with -ka˥tta, and the polite past, with -ka˥tta desu. (Do not confuse -˥i desu and -ka˥tta desu with NOUN de˥su, for which the past is NOUN de˥shita.) The infinitive ('so as to be') ends in -ku, as in sa˥muku narima˥shita 'it turned cold'. There are many adverbs derived from the adjective infinitive, such as ha˥yaku 'quickly' or 'early'. And the -ku combines with arimase˥n (plain form na˥i) to make the negative: sa˥muku arimase˥n 'it isn't cold', sa˥muku na˥i hi˥ ni wa 'on days that are not cold'. The past of the negative is -ku arimase˥n deshita (plain past -ku na˥katta). The gerund of the adjective ('being …' or 'is … and') ends in -kute, and the negative gerund, in -ku na˥kute.

But many Japanese words that translate as English adjectives belong to a different class of words and are treated more like nouns. For that reason they are sometimes called "adjectival nouns" or "nominal adjectives," but you may want to think of them simply as "na words," since they attach the word na ('that/who is …') when they modify a following noun: heya˥ ga shi˥zuka desu 'the room is quiet', shi˥zuka na heya˥ desu 'it is a quiet room'. As with nouns, the nonpast form of na words is … de˥su (plain form da˥ or nothing, but replaced by **no** or **na** before a noun), and the past is ... **de͞shita** (plain form ... **da͞tta**). The negative is ... **ja arimase͞n** (plain form ... **ja na͞i**), the negative past is ... **ja arimase͞n deshita** (plain form ... **ja na͞katta**); all are usually run together with the preceding word to make one long phrase. The gerund is ... **de͞**, as in **heya͞ ga shi͞zuka de ki͞rei desu** 'the rooms are quiet and clean' and **ki͞rei de shi͞zuka na heya͞** 'rooms that are quiet and clean'. The infinitive ... **ni** means 'so as to be ...' as in **shi͞zuka ni narima͞shita** 'became quiet' or '...ly' as in **shi͞zuka ni asonde ima͞su** 'is playing quietly'.

In a similar manner, Japanese nouns are often followed by some form of ... **de͞su** (often called the "copula"), replacing a more specific predicate. When the predicate is a verb or an adjective, the role of the noun is marked by a particle. Because the particles go on the end of the noun, they are sometimes called "postpositions," a kind of mirror image of English prepositions: **Kyo͞to kara Na͞ra e ikima͞shita** 'I went from Kyoto to Nara'. English subjects and objects are usually unmarked except by word order, but since that is not the case in Japanese, particles mark the subject and object: **Da͞re ga na͞ni o shima͞su ka** 'Who does what?' **Na͞ni o da͞re ga shima͞su ka** 'Just who does what?'

There is often little semantic need for such marking, for you can usually tell subjects and objects from the context: it is usually people who act and things that are acted upon. So if the particles ... **ga** and ... **o** are omitted, as is required when you attach ... **mo** 'also ..., even ...' or ... **wa** 'as for ...', you usually still know who is doing what: **Watashi mo kikima͞shita**

'I, too, heard it [as did others]', **Sore mo kịkimaˈshịta** 'I heard that too [as well as other things]'.

For many nouns in spoken Japanese, it is quite common to attach a personalizing prefix **o-**, which conveys a vague sense of 'that important thing'. The prefix is also used to make honorific or humble verb forms, with reference to the subject of a sentence. **O-teˈgami** often means '*your* letter', but does not tell us whether the reference is the letter *you* have written, or a letter that has been written *to you*; and it can mean just 'the letter' or 'letters', said with a personalizing touch much appreciated by women and children. Another prefix **go-** attaches to certain nouns (mostly of Chinese origin).

Although these personalized forms are ignored by most dictionaries, we have included many of them, because they are often irregular in accentuation or in some other way. Do not try to use the prefixes **o-** and **go-** with new nouns unless you find the forms in this dictionary or hear them from a Japanese speaker. Honorific and humble verb forms, however, can be made up rather freely, though for certain common verbs they are replaced by euphemisms or unrelated forms; for example, **osshaimaˈsụ** usually replaces **o-ii ni narimaˈsụ** 'deigns to say' as the honorific of **iimaˈsụ** 'says'.

KANJI & KANA

Japanese kanji and kana characters have been introduced into the original dictionary and can be found immediately after the romanized forms of the entries. The most contemporary renderings of kanji have been used, including the 1,945 characters from the *jōyō* kanji list. As it is unreasonable to attempt to convert all romanized words into kanji, kanji is provided only when it is commonly used by the Japanese. In some cases, the kana representation appears before the kanji, and in other cases, after. This means that in the former case kana is most commonly used but at times kanji may be preferable because it conveys the precise meaning of the original word. In the latter case this means that the word is usually written in kanji but kana may sometimes be substituted when the kanji is perceived as too difficult or too long to write.

Other dictionaries provide difficult kanji that are rarely used by native Japanese, but we have chosen to avoid this and focus on contemporary usage. It is possible to write "lemon" in kanji, for example, with the kanji 檸檬, but the katakana form レモン is much preferred.

Every effort has been made to reflect common usage of kanji and kana; thus the ordering of the kanji and kana that follows the romanization is based on frequency of usage. Centered dots mean "or," so **appearance** yōsu 様子・ようす indicates that 様子 is more frequently used but ようす is also an acceptable representation for **appearance**.   Kanji is of course important to clarify the exact meaning of the word; as the Japanese language contains many homonyms there is a certain amount of vagueness in the usage of kana, especially out of context.

In general, romanized words are not hyphenated unless the

hyphen represents a morpheme boundary within a compound. In addition, in this dictionary we have provided kanji and kana renderings for all forms of the romanized words offered, including constituent parts of words that are abbreviated by a hyphen or substituted by a swung dash. Although this takes up extra space, it will facilitate understanding of the exact forms of the relevant word.

GUIDE TO SYMBOLS

˥ A fall of pitch occurs after the marked syllable. When the accent is on the last syllable, the fall in pitch is sometimes not apparent unless another word follows it.

  a˥me rain

  ashi˥ foot, leg

⌐˥ The word is sometimes pronounced without an accent.

  da⌐˥iya schedule *(train)*

  funa⌐˥yoi seasick(ness)

(˥) The word has an accent that is not pronounced when the word follows a preceding, accented word.

  bon'ya˥ri shima(˥)su is absent-minded

  Isoga˥naide kudasa(˥)i Don't go so fast.

ā, ē, ō, ū, Vowels with macrons are pronounced twice as long as regular vowels.

  byōdō (na) equal

  kyūka vacation, furlough

  pēji page

  wā-puro word processor

i̱, u̱ These vowels are suppressed.

  hi̱to person, man, fellow, people

  suki̱-ma crack; opening; opportunity

Note: A fuller explanation of the symbols shown above can be found in the Introduction.

PART I
English–Japanese

— A —

a, an → **one** *(but usually omitted in Japanese)*

abacus soroban そろばん; ~ **rod** keta けた・桁

abalone a⌐wabi あわび・鮑・鰒

abandon sutema⌐su (suteru, sutete) 捨てます(捨てる, 捨てて)

abbreviate ryakushima⌐su (ryaku⌐su, ryaku⌐shite) 略します (略す, 略して)

abbreviation ryakugo 略語, shōryaku 省略

ability nō⌐ryoku 能力, ki⌐ryō 器量, utsuwa 器・うつわ, udema⌐e⌐ 腕前, tcmae (o-te⌐mae) 手前(お手前); *(function)* hataraki 働き; *(proficiency)* jitsuryoku 実力; *(talent)* sa⌐i 才

able → **can**

abnormal, abnormality ijō (na) 異常(な)

aboard: gets ~ norima⌐su (noru, notte) 乗ります(乗る, 乗って); **puts** ~ nosema⌐su (noseru, nosete) 乗せます(乗せる, 乗せて)

abolish haishi shima⌐su (suru, shite) 廃止します(する, して); yamema⌐su (yameru, yamete)

止めます(止める, 止めて)

abortion datai 堕胎, ninshin-chū⌐zetsu 妊娠中絶; **has an** ~ oroshima⌐su (oro⌐su, oro⌐shite) 下ろします(下ろす, 下ろして)

abound tomima⌐su (to⌐mu, to⌐nde) 富みます(富む, 富んで)

about *(an amount)* ya⌐ku ...約..., ... gu⌐rai ...位, ... hodo ...程, ...-ze⌐ngo ...前後, ...-ke⌐ntō ...見当; → **almost, around**

about *(a time)* ... go⌐ro (ni) ...頃 (に)

about *(concerning)* ... ni tsu⌐ite (no) ...ついて(の); **talk about** ... (no) koto⌐ o iima⌐su (yū, itte/ yutte) ...(の)ことを言います (言う, 言って/ゆって)

about to: is ~ **happen** (su)-ru tokoro⌐ desu (す)るところで す, (shi)-yō to shima⌐su (し)よ うとします, (shi)-sō de⌐su (し)そうです

about when itsu-goro いつ頃

above (no) ue⌐ (ni) ...(の)上 (に)

abreast: not ~ **of** ... ni uto⌐i ... に疎い・うとい

abroad gaikoku (de) 外国(で);

ka͞igai 海外

abrupt totsuzen (no) 突然（の）;
abruptly totsuzen 突然

absence, absent kesseki (no) 欠
席（の）; *(from home)* (o-)ru͞su
(no) （お）留守（の）

absentee kesse͞ki͞-sha 欠席者

absent-minded bon'ya͞ri
shima͞su (suru, shi̱te) ぼんや
りします（する、して）

absent-mindedly ukka͞ri うっか
り

absolute zettai (no) 絶対（の）

absolutely zettai ni 絶対に、
honto ni 本当に; ～ **cannot**
tōtei 到底 + NEGATIVE

absorbed *(fascinated)* utto͞ri (to)
うっとり（と）; **gets ～ in** ... ni
korima͞su (ko͞ru, ko͞tte) ...に
凝ります（凝る、凝って）

absorbent cotton dasshi͞-men 脱
脂綿

abstain from ... o yamema͞su ...
をやめます; **abstaining from**
(alcohol/tobacco) bu-chō͞hō
不調法

abstainer buchōhō-mono͞ 不調
法者

abstract chūshō-teki (na) 抽象的
（な）; *(summary)* yō͞shi 要旨

absurd baka-rashi͞i ばからしい

abundance to͞mi 富

abundant yu͞taka (na) 豊か（な）;
→ **abound**

abuse waru͞-kuchi 悪口/-guchi
悪口; → **scold, mistreat**

AC, alternating current kōryū 交
流

accede to ... ni ō-jima͞su (ō-
ji͞ru, ō͞-jite) ...に応じます
（応じる、応じて）

accent a͞kusento アクセント; →
pronunciation, dialect

accept ukema͞su (uke͞ru, u͞kete)
受けます（受ける、受けて）,
uke-torima͞su (-to͞ru,
-to͞tte) 受け取ります（取る、
取って）, uke-tsukema͞su
(-tsuke͞ru, -tsuke͞te) 受け付
けます（付ける、付けて）;
(consents) shōdaku shima͞su
(suru, shi̱te) 承諾します（する、
して）; ～ **a bill (of payment)**
tegata o hiki-ukema͞su
(-uke͞ru, -u͞kete) 手形を引き
受けます（受ける、受けて）

acceptance shōdaku 承諾;
(resignation) akirame 諦め

access: seeks ～ to ... ni sekkin o
hakarima͞su (haka͞ru,
haka͞tte) ...に接近を図ります
（図る、図って）

accessible *(easy to get to)* iki-
yasu͞i 行きやすい

accessory fuzoku (no) 付属（の）;
fuzoku͞-hin 付属品

accident ji͞ko 事故, deki͞goto 出
来事; *(disaster)* sōnan 遭難;
has an ～ sōnan shima͞su
(suru, shi̱te) 遭難します（する、
して）

accidental gūzen (no) 偶然（の）

accidentally gūzen ni 偶然に, hyo⌉tto ひょっと
accommodation *(place to stay)* tomaru tokoro⌉ 泊まる所; *(facilities)* se⌉tsubi 設備
accompany 1. (… to) issho ni ikima⌉sụ (iku, itte) (…と)一緒に行きます(行く, 行って); o-to⌉mo shima(⌉)sụ (suru, shịte) お供します(する, して); … ni tomonaima⌉sụ (tomona⌉u, tomona⌉tte) …に伴います(伴う, 伴って) **2. is accompanied by** *(= brings along)* … o tsurema⌉sụ (tsureru, tsurete) …を連れます(連れる, 連れて)
accomplice mikata 味方
accomplish 1. (shịte) shimaima⌉sụ (shimau, shimatte) (して)しまいます(しまう, しまって); hatashima⌉sụ (hata⌉su, hata⌉shịte) 果たします(果たす, 果たして); togema⌉sụ (toge⌉ru, to⌉gete) 遂げます(遂げる, 遂げて) **2.** *(attains)* …ni tas-shima⌉sụ (tas-su[⌉]ru, ta[⌉]s-shịte) …に達します(達する, 達して); … ga kanaima⌉sụ (kana⌉u, kana⌉tte) …がかないます(かなう, かなって)
accord (with) (… ni) kanaima⌉sụ (kana⌉u, kana⌉tte) (…に)かないます(かなう, かなって); (… to) itchị shima⌉sụ (suru, shịte) (…と)一致します(する, して)
accordance: in ~ with … ni ō[⌉]-jite …に応じて
accordingly shịtaga⌉tte したがって·従って
according to 1. *(relying on)* …ni yoru to …によると, … no hanashi⌉ de (wa) …の話で(は) **2.** *(in conformity with)* … ni shịtaga[⌉]tte …に従って
account *(bill)* kanjō⌉ (o-kanjō) 勘定(お勘定); *(credit)* tsụke⌉ つけ; *(bank account)* kōza 口座, yokin 預金
account: on ~ of … no se⌉i de … のせいで; → **because;** → **sake (for the)**
account: takes into ~ kō⌉ryo ni irema⌉sụ (ireru, irete) 考慮に入れます(入れる, 入れて)
accountant kaikei(-ga⌉kari) 会計(係), kaike⌉i-shi 会計士
accounts (o-)kaikei (お)会計
accumulate 1. *(it accumulates)* tsumorima⌉sụ (tsumoru, tsumotte) 積もります(積もる, 積もって), tamarima⌉sụ (tamaru, tamatte) たまります(たまる, たまって); tsumema⌉sụ (tsumeru, tsumete) つめます(つめる, つめて), atsumarima⌉sụ (atsuma⌉ru, atsuma⌉tte) 集まります(集まる, 集まって) **2.** *(accumulates it)* tsumima⌉sụ (tsumu, tsunde)

積みます（積む，積んで），tamemásu (tameru, tamete) ためます（ためる，ためて）; atsumemásu (atsu̅meru, atsu̅mete) 集めます（集める，集めて）

accurate seikaku (na) 正確（な）

accuse uttaemásu (utta⌐e⌐ru, utta⌐ete) 訴えます（訴える，訴えて）; *(criticizes)* hi̅nan shima(⌐)su̩ (suru, shite) 非難します（する，して）

accustom oneself to ... ni naremásu (nare̅ru, na̅rete) ... に慣れます（慣れる，慣れて）

accustomed jū̅rai no 従来の

ache 1. *(it aches)* itamimásu (ita̅mu, ita̅nde) 痛みます（痛む，痛んで）**2.** *(an ache)* itami̅ 痛み

achieve → **accomplish**

achievement *(work)* hataraki 働き

acid sa̅n 酸

acknowledge mitomemásu (mitomeru, mitomete) 認めます（認める，認めて）

acquaintance shiriai 知り合い; chi⌐jin 知人

acquaint oneself with (... o) shirimásu (shiru, shitte) (... を)知ります（知る，知って）; **is acquainted with** ... o shitte imásu (iru, ite) ...を知っています（いる，いて）

acquire → **get**

across ... (no) mukō⌐ (ni) ...（の）向こう（に），o-mu̅kō お向こう; **goes across** → **cross**

across: ~ the way mukō⌐ 向こう，mukō-gawa 向こう側; **cuts ~** yoko-girimásu (-gi̅ru, -gi̅tte) 横切ります（切る，切って）; **goes ~** ōdan shimásu (suru, shite) 横断します（する，して）

act 1. → **do 2.** *(deed)* shiwaza しわざ・仕業, okonai 行い, kō̅i 行為 **3.** *(of play)* maku̅ 幕; da̅n 段

acting 1. *(play ~)* e̅ngi 演技 **2.** → **temporary 3.** → **agent; ~ as agent** daikō 代行

action katsudō 活動; *(conduct)* okonai 行い; *(behavior)* kōdō 行動; → **activity**

active: is ~ katsuyaku shimásu (suru, shite) 活躍します（する，して）

activity katsudō 活動, katsuyaku 活躍; *(work)* hataraki 働き; *(agency)* kika̅n 機関; → **exercise; → movement**

actor yakusha 役者, haiyū 俳優

actress joyū 女優

actual jitchi (no) 実地（の）; **~ conditions** jissai 実際

actuality jitchi 実地

actually jitsu̅ wa 実は, jitsu ni̅ 実に

acupuncture ha̅ri はり・鍼

acute *(sharp)* surudo˥i 鋭い; *(severe)* hageshi˥i 激しい; *(sudden)* kyūsei (no) 急性(の)

ad → **advertisement**

adaptability yūzū 融通; **is adaptable** yūzū ga kikima˥su (kiku, kiite) 融通がききます(きく, きいて)

add kuwaema˥su (kuwae˥ru, kuwa˥ete) 加えます(加える, 加えて); *(supplements it with)* soema˥su (soeru, soete) 添えます(添える, 添えて); yosema˥su (yoseru, yosete) 寄せます(寄せる, 寄せて); *(attaches)* tsukema˥su (tsuke˥ru, tsuke˥te) 付けます(付ける, 付けて)

addict jōyō˥-sha 常用者

addition: house ~ tate-mashi 建て増し; **in** ~ **to** ... no hoka (ni) ...の他(に), [*bookish*] ... no ta˥ ni ...の他(に)

additionally hoka ni 他に; [*bookish*] ta˥ ni 他に

address tokoro 所, jūsho 住所; *(destination)* todoke-saki 届け先, (...) saki (...)先; *(house number)* banchi 番地; *(written)* tokoro-gaki 所書き, ate-na あて名・宛て名, banchi 番地; *(on envelope)* uwagaki 上書き; ~ **of contact** renraku-saki 連絡先

addressed to ...-ate (no) ...あて(の)・宛て(の)

adhesive tape nenchaku-te˥pu 粘着テープ; bansōkō ばんそうこう・絆創膏

adjacent 1. → **next 2. is** ~ **to** ... ni ses-shima˥su (ses-su˥ru, se˥s-shite) ...に接します(接する, 接して)

adjective keiyō˥shi 形容詞

adjoining → **next**

adjust totonoema˥su (totono˥e˥ru, totono˥ete) 整えます(整える, 整えて), chōsei/se˥iri/kagen shima˥su (suru, shite) 調整/整理/加減します(する, して)

adjustment chōsei 調整, se˥iri 整理, kagen 加減

administration *(of government)* gyōsei 行政; *(of business)* keiei 経営, ka˥nri 管理

admirable mi˥goto (na) 見事(な), rippa (na) 立派(な)

admirably mi˥goto ni 見事に, rippa ni 立派に

admiral ta˥ishō 大将; **(vice)** chū˥jō 中将; **(rear)** shō˥shō 少将

admire kanshin shima˥su (suru, shite) 感心します(する, して), homema˥su (home˥ru, ho˥mete) 褒めます(褒める, 褒めて)

admission *(to hospital)* nyūin 入院; *(to school)* nyūgaku 入学; *(to a place)* nyūjō 入場; ~ **fee** nyūjō˥-ryō 入場料; ~ **ticket**

nyūjō̄-ken 入場券
admit *(lets in)* irema̅su (ireru, irete) 入れます(入れる, 入れて), tōshima̅su (tō̄su, tō̄shite) 通します(通す, 通して); *(acknowledges)* mitome-ma̅su (mitomeru, mitomete) 認めます(認める, 認めて); *(confesses)* uchi-akema̅su (-ake⌐ru, -a⌐kete) 打ち明けます(明ける, 明けて)
adolescence seine⌐n-ki 青年期, seishu⌐n-ki 青春期, shishu⌐n-ki 思春期
adolescent seinen 青年
adopt *(a boy)* yōshi ni shima̅su (suru, shite) 養子にします(する, して); *(a girl)* yō̄jo ni shima̅su (suru, shite) 養女にします(する, して)
adopted *(son)* yōshi 養子; *(daughter)* yō̄jo 養女
adult otona おとな・大人, se⌐i-jin 成人
adultery kantsū 姦通
advance *(goes ahead)* susumima̅su (susumu, susunde) 進みます(進む, 進んで); *(advances it)* susumema̅su (susumeru, susumete) 進めます(進める, 進めて), *(lends money)* yūzū shima̅su (suru, shite) 融通します(する, して)
advance: in ～ sono ma̅e ni その前に; *(beforehand)* mae-mo⌐tte 前もって
advanced sale maeuri 前売り; **advanced-sale ticket** maeuri (-ki⌐ppu) 前売り(切符)
advantage 1. toku (o-toku) 得 (お得), *(benefit)* ri̅eki 利益; **takes ～ of** ... o riyō shima̅su (suru, shite) ...を利用します (する, して) **2.** *(merit)* chō̄sho 長所
advantageous yū̄ri (na) 有利(な), toku (na) 得(な)
adventure bōken 冒険
adverb fukushi 副詞
adversary aite̅ (o-aite) 相手(お相手)
advertisement kōkoku 広告
advice chūkoku 忠告; *(consultation)* sōdan 相談
adviser *(consultant)* komon 顧問
advocate tonaema̅su (tona̅e̅ru, tona̅ete) 唱えます(唱える, 唱えて)
aerial *(antenna)* antena アンテナ
aerogram(me) → **air letter**
affair 1. koto̅ 事, kotoga⌐ra⌐ 事柄, ji̅ken 事件 **2.** *(love ～)* ren'ai-ka̅nkei 恋愛関係, *(extramarital)* uwaki 浮気, yoro-meki⌐ よろめき; **has an ～** uwaki o shima̅su (suru, shite) 浮気をします(する, して), yoro-mekima̅su (-me̅ku, -me̅ite) よろめきます(めく, めいて)
affect → **influence**

affected kidotta … 気取った…;
is ~ kidotte imaꜜsu (iru, ite)
気取っています(いる、いて)

affection naꜛsakeꜛ (o-naꜜsake)
情け(お情け), aijō 愛情;
treats with ~ (… o) kawai-
garimaꜜsu (-gaꜜru, -gaꜜtte) (…
を)かわいがります(がる、が
って)

affiliate kamei shimaꜜsu (suru,
shite) 加盟します(する、して)

afflict kurushimemaꜜsu
(kurushimeꜜru, kurushiꜜmete)
苦しめます(苦しめる、苦し
めて)

affliction kurushiꜛmiꜛ 苦しみ

afford (jūbun na) kane ga
arimaꜜsu (aꜜru, aꜜtte) (十分な)
金があります(ある、あって);
yoyū ga arimaꜜsu (aꜜru, aꜜtte)
余裕があります(ある、あっ
て)

afraid: is ~ of … (… ga) kowaꜜi
desu (…が)怖いです, (… o)
kowagarimaꜜsu (kowagaꜜru,
kowagaꜜtte) (…を)怖がります
(怖がる、怖がって)

Africa Afurika アフリカ

after … karaꜜ …から、 … (no)
aꜜto de …(の)後で; **after doing** shiteꜜ kara してから、shita
nꜛto deꜛ した後で

after all kekkyoku 結局、tōꜜtō と
うとう; yappaꜜri やっぱり、
yappaꜜshi やっぱし; tsuꜜmari
つまり、tsumaꜜru tokoro つま

るところ, yō-suꜜru ni 要する
に; tsuꜛi-ni ついに

after a long time (of absence)
hisashi-buri ni 久しぶりに

after a meal shokugo 食後

after (a) while shibaꜜraku shite し
ばらくして

after-hours bar sunaꜜkku スナッ
ク

afternoon hiruꜜ kara 昼から、
goꜜgo 午後

aftershave (lotion) asutoriꜜnzen
アストリンゼン

aftertaste atoꜜ-aji 後味; **leaves a
bad ~** atoꜜ-aji ga waruꜜi 後味
が悪い

after the war seꜛngo (= sensō
no aꜜto) 戦後(=戦争の後)

afterward(s) aꜜto de 後で

After you! Dōꜜzo o-saki ni. どう
ぞお先に.

again mō ichi-do もう一度、mō
ik-kaꜜi もう一回; mata また・
又; arataꜜmete 改めて

against (in contrast to) …ni taꜜi-
shite …に対して; (contrary to)
…ni haꜜn-shite …に反して;
(opposing) …ni hantai/taikō
shite …に反対/対抗して; (run-
ning into) …ni butsukatte …
にぶつかって; (leaning on) …
ni motaꜜrete (no) …にもたれて
(の)

age 1, toshiꜜ 年、 **your age** o-toshi
お年; [bookish] nenrei 年齢;
(era) jidai 時代 **2.** (gets old)

toshi̇́ o torima̋su (tőru, tőtte) 年を取ります(取る, 取って), fukema̋su (fuke̋ru, fuke̋te) 老けます(老ける, 老けて)

agency dairi 代理, dairi̋-ten 代理店; *(commission)* tori-tsugi 取り次ぎ・取次; *(organization)* ki̖ka̋n 機関

agent dairi 代理, dairi̋-nin 代理人; *(proxy)* daikō̋-sha 代行者; *(broker)* burōka̋ ブローカー; *(ticket agent)* kippű-uri 切符売り

aggravating haradatashi̋i 腹立たしい

aggression shinryaku 侵略

agitated: gets ~ dōyō shima̋su (suru, shite) 動揺します(する, して); → **flustered**

agitation a̋ji アジ

ago ... ma̋e ni ...前に; **a little while ago** saki̖-hodo 先程, sa̋kki さっき

agony kurushi̋mi̋ 苦しみ

agree *(approves)* sansei shima̋su (suru, shite) 賛成します(する, して); *(concurs)* dōi shima̋su (suru, shite) 同意します(する, して); *(promises)* yakusoku shima̋su (suru, shite) 約束します(する, して); *(accords with)* ... ni kanaima̋su (kana̋u, kana̋tte) ...にかないます(かなう, かなって), ... to itchi̖ shima̋su (suru,

shite) ...と一致します(する, して); **~ with** *(in harmony)* ... to chōwa shima̋su (suru, shite) ...と調和します(する, して)

agreement *(promise)* yakusoku 約束; *(contract)* keiyaku 契約; *(treaty)* jō̋yaku 条約; *(understanding)* shōchi 承知; *(consensus)* itchi̖ 一致; *(harmony)* chōwa 調和

agriculture nō̋gyō 農業

ague okori̋ おこり

ahead saki (ni) (o-saki) 先(に)(お先); **gets ~** susumima̋su (susumu, susunde) 進みます(進む, 進んで)

ahead and behind ze̋n-go (ni) 前後(に)

aid → help

AIDS e̋izu, e̋zu エイズ, エーズ

ail → sick

aim nerai 狙い, me̋ate 目当て, me̋do 目度・目途, me̋yasu 目安, kentō̋ 見当; *(goal)* mokuteki 目的, *(direction)* hōshin 方針; *(target)* mato 的; **takes ~** kentō̋ o tsukema̋su (tsuke̋ru, tsuke̋te) 見当をつけます(つける, つけて)

aim at ... o neraima̋su (nerau, neratte) ...を狙います(狙う, 狙って); ... o megakema̋su (megake̋ru, mega̋kete) ...を目掛けます(目掛ける, 目掛けて)

air 1. kū'ki 空気 **2.** *(manner)* furi' ふり; *(appearance)* fū' 風; *(tune)* fushi' 節

air (= dry) it hoshima'su (ho'su, ho'shịte) 干します(干す, 干して)

air base kūgun-kị'chi 空軍基地

air conditioner kū'rā クーラー; ea-kon エアコン

air conditioning reibō(-sō'chi) 冷房(装置); ea-kon エアコン

airfield hịkō-jō 飛行場

air force kūgun 空軍

air letter kōkū-sho'kan 航空書簡

airline (company) kōkū-ga'isha 航空会社

airmail kōkū'-bin 航空便, kōkū-yū'bin 航空郵便; hịkō-bin 飛行便, hịkō-yū'bin 飛行郵便

airman kōkū'-hei 航空兵

airplane hịkō'-ki 飛行機

airport hịkō-jō 飛行場; kūkō 空港

airsick: gets ~ yoima'su (yo'u, yo'tte) 酔います(酔う, 酔って)

airsick(ness) hịkō-yoi 飛行酔い

aisle rōka 廊下, tsū'ro 通路

à la carte ippin-ryō'ri 一品料理

alarm keihō 警報

alarm clock meza'mashi 目覚し, mezamashi-do'kei 目覚し時計

album *(photograph)* shashin-chō 写真帳; *(stamp)* kịtte-chō 切手帳

alcohol arukōru アルコール

alcove *(in Japanese room)* tokonoma 床の間

alert (= alarm) keihō 警報

alien 1. yoso' (no) よそ(の) **2.** *(an alien)* → **foreigner**

alike onaji (yō' na) 同じ(ような)

alimony bekkyo-te'ate 別居手当

alive: is ~ i'kịte ima'su (iru, ite) 生きています(いる, いて); **keeps it ~** ikashima'su (ika'su, ika'shịte) 生かします (生かす, 生かして)

all minna' みんな・皆, ze'mbu 全部, su'bete 全て・すべて; *(everything)* i'ssa'i 一切; *(completely)* sụkka'ri すっかり; **~ (concerned/present)** ichidō 一同

all along *(from the beginning)* mo'to kara 元から

all day (long) ichinichi-jū 一日中

all directions shịhō' 四方, shi'hō 四方

allergy are'ru'gii アレルギー

alley ro'ji 路地; *(back street)* ura' 裏, ura-dō'ri 裏通り; *(side street)* yokochō 横町

alliance, allied rengō 連合

Allies (Allied) Rengō'-koku (no) 連合国(の)

alligator wa'ni わに・鰐

all kinds of sama'za'ma (na) さまざま(な)・様々(な), iroiro (na/no) いろいろ・色々 (な/の), shu'ju (no) 種々(の)

allot kubarima'su (kuba'ru, kuba'tte) 配ります(配る, 配って); **allotment** wariate 割り当て, wappu 割符; *(share)* buntan 分担

all over 1. *(= everywhere)* hō'bō ほうぼう・方々; ...-jū ...中 **2.** *(finished)* → end

allow 1. *(permits)* yurushima'su (yuru'su, yuru'shite) 許します(許す, 許して) **2.** → give

allowance *(bonus)* te'ate (o-te'ate) 手当(お手当); *(grant)* kyō'yo 供与

allowance: makes ~ for ... o kagen shima'su (suru, shite) ...を加減します(する, して)

all right *(OK)* daijō'bu (na) 大丈夫(な); *(permissible)* i'i いい・良い, yoroshii よろしい

all sides shihō 四方, shi'hō 四方

all the more issō いっそう・一層, na□o-sara なおさら・尚更

all the time zutto ずっと, sho'tchū/shi'jū しょっちゅう/始終; *(usually)* tsune□zu□ne 常々・常常

all the way: ~ to ... ma'de ...まで; **~ through** zutto ずっと

all together awa'sete 合わせて

almost hoto'ndo ほとんど・殆ど; daitai 大体; **~ all, ~ all the time** hoto'ndo ほとんど・殆ど; **~ every day** ma'inichi no yō ni 毎日のように

alone hito'ri (de) 一人[独り]で・ひとり(で)

along ... ni sotte ...に沿って; *(somewhere)* ... no do'ko ka (de) ...のどこか(で)

alongside ... no so'ba ...のそば

aloud ko'e o da'shite 声を出して

alphabet (ABC) ē-bii-shi'i エービーシー; **(Japanese)** kana かな・仮名

already mō もう, su'de-ni すでに・既に

also ... mo ...も, sono ue その上, ma'ta'-wa または・又は; yaha'ri やはり, yappa'ri やっぱり

altar saidan 祭壇; **household ~** *(Buddhist)* butsudan 仏壇, *(Shinto)* kami-dana 神棚

alter naoshima'su (nao'su, nao'shite) 直します(直す, 直して); aratamema'su (aratame'ru, arata'mete) 改めます(改める, 改めて)

alternate (with) kōtai shima'su (suru, shite) 交代[交替]します(する, して)

alternately kawaru-ga'waru 代わる代わる

alternating current kōryū 交流

alternation kōtai 交代・交替

alternative ... (no) hō' (ga) ...(の)方(が)

although ... no ni ...のに

altitude kō'do 高度

altogether ze'mbu de 全部で, minna' de みんなで・皆で;

(completely) mattaku まったく・全く

aluminum arumi(nyūmu) アルミ(ニューム)

alumni association dōsō-kai 同窓会

alumnus (of ...) (... no) sotsugyō(-sei) (...の)卒業(生), shusshin 出身

always itsu-mo いつも, *(usually)* fudan ふだん・普段; *(from the beginning)* moto kara 元から; **as** ~ aikawarazu 相変わらず

am → **is**

a.m. *(morning)* gozen 午前

amass tamemasu (tameru, tamete) ため[貯め・溜め]ます(ためる, ためて)

amateur amachua アマチュア; *(novice)* shiroto しろうと・素人

amazed: gets ~ akiremasu (akireru, akirete) 呆れます(呆れる, 呆れて)

ambassador taishi 大使

amber kohaku こはく・琥珀

ambition *(hope)* netsubō 熱望, yashin 野心; *(energetic spirit)* haki 覇気

ambulance kyūkyū-sha 救急車

America Amerika アメリカ, Beikoku 米国

American Amerika-jin アメリカ人

ammunition dan'yaku 弾薬

among ... no naka/uchi (ni) ... の中/内(に)

amount *(= sum)* gaku 額; *(large and/or small)* ~ tashō 多少

amount to (how much) (ikura/ o-ikura) ni narimasu (naru, natte) (いくら/おいくら)になります(なる, なって); **what it amounts to is ...** yōsuru ni 要するに

ample → **enough**

amplifier ampu アンプ

amulet o-mamori お守り

amusement asobi 遊び; nagusami 慰み

amusing omoshiroi おもしろい・面白い; *(funny)* okashii おかしい, kokkei (na) こっけい・滑稽(な)

an → **a**

analogy tatoe 例え・たとえ, tatoi たとい; ruiji 類似

analysis bunseki 分析

ancestor sosen 祖先, senzo 先祖

ancestry: of ... ~ ...-kei (no) ...系(の); **an American of Japanese** ~ Nikkei no Amerika-jin 日系のアメリカ人, (Amerika no) Nikkei-jin (アメリカの)日系人; **an American of German** ~ Doitsu-kei no Amerika-jin ドイツ系のアメリカ人

anchor ikari 錨・碇

ancient mukashi no 昔の, kodai no 古代の; ~ **days** mukashi 昔; ~ **times** kodai 古代

and ... *(including each item)* ...
to ...と; *(choosing typical
items)* ... ya ...や
and: (does/did) and VERB-te て;
VERB-ru˥/-ta˥ shi る/たし;
(is/was) and NOUN de で, AD-
JECTIVE˥-kute くて; NOUN da˥/
da˥tta shi だ/だったし, ADJEC-
TIVE-i˥/-ka˥tta shi い/かった
し
and also ... o˥nyobi ...及び
and now/then sa˥-te さて
and/or ma˥ta-wa または·又は
and others ...˥-ra ...ら; ... na˥do ...
など·等; sono˥-hoka その他·
そのほか, [*bookish*] sono˥-ta
その他
**and so forth/on, and the like,
and what-not** ... na˥do ...な
ど·等, ... na˥nka ...なんか
and yet sore de˥ mo それでも,
shika˥-mo しかも, sore na˥ no
ni それなのに
anew atara˥shiku 新しく,
arata˥mete 改めて, sa˥ra-ni さ
らに·更に
angel te˥nshi 天使
anger ikari˥ 怒り
angle ka˥kudo 角度, kaku˥ 角;
(viewpoint) ke˥nchi 見地
angry: gets ~ okorima˥su
(oko˥ru, oko˥tte) 怒ります(怒
る, 怒って), hara˥ o
tatema˥su (tate˥ru, ta˥tete) 腹
を立てます(立てる, 立てて)
animal dōbutsu 動物,

ke(da)mono け(だ)もの·獣
(1 ip-pi̠ki˥ 一匹, **2 ni̠˥-hiki**
二匹, **3 sa̠m-biki** 三匹, **how
many** na̠˥m-biki 何匹)
ankle ashi̠˥-ku̠bi 足首
anklets so̠kku̠su ソックス
annex *(building)* bekkan 別館,
(new) shinkan 新館; *(addition)*
tate-mashi 建て増し
annihilation zemmetsu 全滅
anniversary *(day)* kine˥m-bi 記念
日
announce *(inform)* shirasema˥su
(shiraseru, shirasete) 知らせま
す(知らせる, 知らせて);
(publish) happyō shima˥su
(suru, shite) 発表します(する,
して); *(wedding, etc.)* hi̠˥rō
shima(˥)su (suru, shite) 披露
します(する, して)
announcement happyō 発表
announcer anau˥nsā アナウン
サー
annoyance *(trouble)* me˥iwaku
迷惑
annoying urusa˥i うるさい,
yakamashi̠˥i やかましい,
me˥iwaku (na) 迷惑(な)
anonymous mumei (no) 無名(の)
another mō hito˥tsu もう一つ,
mō ichi-... もう一...; **~ person** mō hito˥ri もう一人; **~
place** yo˥so よそ, ta˥sho 他所;
~ time *(some other time)*
i̠˥tsu-ka いつか, izure いずれ
answer 1. *(an answer)* kota̠e˥ 答

え, henji' (o-henji) 返事(お返
事), [bookish] hentō' 返答
2. (answers) kotaema'su
(kota'e'ru, kota'ete) 答えます
(答える, 答えて); ～ **the
phone/door** denwa/toritsugi
ni dema'su (de'ru, de'te) 電話/
取り次ぎに出ます(出る, 出
て)

ant ari あり・蟻 (**1** ip-piki' 一匹,
2 ni'-hiki 二匹, **3** sa'm-biki 三
匹, **how many** na'm-biki 何匹)

antenna antena アンテナ

anthropology jinru'i-gaku 人類
学

anti-American hambei (no) 反米
(の)

antibiotic(s) kōsei-bu'sshitsu 抗
性物質

anticipate machima'su (ma'tsu,
ma'tte) 待ちます(待つ, 待っ
て), kitai shima'su (suru,
shite) 期待します(する, して);
(presume) yoso shima'su
(suru, shite) 予想します(する,
して)

anticipation → **expectation**; →
hope

anti-Communist hankyō (no) 反
共(の)

anti-diarrhetic geri-dome 下痢止
め

antidote dok(u)-ke'shi' 毒消し

antifreeze kōtōketsu'-zai 抗凍結
剤

antihistamine kōhisutami'n-zai

抗ヒスタミン剤

anti-Japanese hannichi (no) 反日
(の)

antique jidai-mono 時代物;
(curio) kottō'-hin 骨董品

antiseptic bōfu'-zai 防腐剤

antiwar hansen (no) 反戦(の)

antonym hantai-go 反対語

anxiety ki-zu'ka'i 気遣い; →
worry

anxious → **worried, worry**; →
eager

any ... ka ...か, ... mo ...も (but
often omitted); → **anything**

anybody hito 人, da're ka 誰か;
(**not ～**) dare mo 誰も; **～ (at
all)** da're de'mo 誰でも

anyhow (nevertheless) to'-ni-
kaku とにかく; (anyway) to'-
mo-kaku ともかく, nanibun
なにぶん・何分, na'ni-shiro 何
しろ

anyhow (at all) dō de'mo どう
でも

anyone → **anybody**

anyplace → **anywhere**

anything (something) na'ni ka 何
か (but often omitted); (**not
～**) nani mo 何も

anything (at all) na'n de'mo
何でも

any time i'tsu mo いつで
も

anyway → **anyhow**

anywhere (somewhere) do'ko ka
(...) どこか(...); **～ (at all)**
do'ko de'mo どこでも; **not**

~ → **nowhere**

apart: lives ~ bekkyo shima̅su
(suru, shite) 別居します(する,
して); ~ **from** ... ... wa betsu
to shite ...は別として; **quite**
~ **from** ... ... to̅ wa betsu
ni (shite) ...とは別に(して);
takes it ~ barashima̅su
(bara̅su, bara̅shite) ばらしま
す(ばらす, ばらして)

apartment (house) apa̅to アパー
ト, (luxury) ma̅nshon マン
ション; ~ **complex** danchi-
apa̅to 団地アパート

apiece ...̅zu̅tsu ...ずつ

apologize wabima̅su (wabiru,
wabite) わび[詫び]ます(わび
る, わびて), ayamarima̅su
(ayama̅ru, ayama̅tte) 謝りま
す(謝る, 謝って); **I apologize
(for what I did)** Suma̅nai
koto̅ o shima̅shita. すまない
[済まない]ことをしました.

apology wabi (o-wabi) わび・詫
び(おわび・お詫び), ayama̅ri̅
謝り

apparatus so̅chi 装置; ki̅gu 器具

apparent(ly) ... rashi̅i ...らしい

appeal (to one) pin-to kima̅su
(ku̅ru, kite̅) ぴんときます(く
る, きて)

appear (looks, seems) miema̅su
(mie̅ru, mi̅ete) 見えます(見
える, 見えて); (shows up)
dema̅su (de̅ru, de̅te) 出ます
(出る, 出て), arawarema̅su

(araware̅ru, arawa̅rete) 現わ
れます(現われる, 現われて),
(occurs) hassei shima̅su (suru,
shite) 発生します(する, し
て); ~ **on stage** bu̅tai ni dema̅su
(de̅ru, de̅te) 舞台に出ます(出
る, 出て), tōjō shima̅su
(suru, shite) 登場します(する,
して)

appearance yōsu 様子・ようす, ...
yō̅ ...様; (air, manner) ...fū̅ ...
風; (get-up, form) teisai 体裁;
(outer appearances) uwabe う
わべ・上辺, omote̅ 表; (shape)
kakkō かっこう・格好・恰好;
→ **personal** ~

appendicitis mōchō⌐-en 盲腸炎

appetite shokuyoku 食欲

appetizers (to go with drinks)
sakana さかな・肴; tsumami-
mono (o-tsu̅mami) つまみも
の(おつまみ)

apple ringo りんご・林檎 (**how
many** na̅n-ko 何個)

appliances (katei-)yō̅gu (家庭)
用具, katei-yō̅hin 家庭用品;
(electric) denki-yō̅hin 電気用
品

applicant mōshikomi̅-sha 申し
込み者, kibō̅-sha 希望者

application 1. (for a job, etc.)
mōshi-komi 申し込み, (claim)
mōshi-de 申し出; (for a per-
mit) shinsei-sho⌐ 申請書
2. (putting to use) ōyō 応用,
jitsuyō 実用

apply 1. *(it applies)* atarima`su (ataru, atatte) 当たります(当たる, 当たって); *(accordingly)* jun-jima`su (jun-ji⌐ru, jun⌐-jite) 準じます(準じる, 準じて) **2.** *(applies it)* atema`su (ateru, atete) 当てます(当てる, 当てて), tsukema`su (tsuke`ru, tsuke`te) 付けます(付ける, 付けて); ōyō shima`su (suru, shite) 応用します(する, して) **3.** *(applies for)* mōshi-komima`su (-ko⌐mu, -ko⌐nde) 申し込みます(込む, 込んで), *(claims)* mōshi-dema`su (-de⌐ru, -de⌐te) 申し出ます(出る, 出て)

appoint *(nominates)* mei-jima`su (mei-ji⌐ru, me⌐i-jite) 命じます(命じる, 命じて); *(designates)* shitei shima`su (suru, shite) 指定します(する, して)

appointed day ki`jitsu 期日

appointment *(prior arrangement)* uchi-awase 打ち合せ; *(engagement, date)* yakusoku 約束; *(to see doctor, ...)* yoyaku 予約

appreciate ariga`taku omoima`su (omo⌐u, omo⌐tte) ありがたく [有り難く]思います(思う, 思って), ka⌐nsha shima`su (suru, shite) 感謝します(する, して)

apprehensive kimi` ga waru`i 気味が悪い

apprentice deshi` 弟子; kozō` 小僧・こぞう

approach (... ni) chika-zukima`su (-zu⌐ku, -zu⌐ite) (... に)近付きます(付く, 付いて), yorima`su (yo`ru, yo`tte) 寄ります(寄る, 寄って); sekkin shima`su (suru, shite) 接近します(する, して)

approach: lets one ~ (... o) chika-zukema`su (-zuke`ru, -zu`kete) (...を)近付けます (付ける, 付けて)

approach to a shrine sandō 参道

appropriate 1. *(suitable)* teki-setsu (na) 適切(な), tekitō (na) 適当(な) **2.** *(sets it aside)* atema`su (ateru, atete) 当てます(当てる, 当てて) **3. → seize**

approve sansei shima`su (suru, shite) 賛成します(する, して)

approximately daitai 大体; ya`ku ... 約...; ... gu`rai ...位; ...-ze⌐ngo ...前後; ...-ke⌐ntō ...見当; ...-na`igai (de) ...内外(で)

apricot anzu あんず・杏; **Japanese ~** ume`/mme` うめ・梅

April Shi-gatsu` 四月・4月

apt to (do) (shi)-yasu`i (し)やすい・易い; tokaku (shima`su) とかく(します); e⌐te-shite

(shima̱sṵ) 得てして（します）
aquarium suizō̱k-kan 水族館,
　suizo̱kṵ-kan 水族館
Arab A̱rabu アラブ, *(person)*
　Arabu̱-jin アラブ人; **Arabian**
　(language) Arabia-go アラビ
　ア語
arch yumi-gata 弓形
archery *(the traditional art)*
　kyū̱dō 弓道, kyū̱jutsu 弓術
archipelago rettō 列島, ...-re̱ttō ...
　列島
architect kenchi̱ku-ka 建築家
architecture kenchi̱ku 建築
Arctic Hokkyoku 北極
are → **is**
area me̱nseki 面積; *(district)*
　chi̱hō̱ 地方; → **place**; →
　vicinity
argue kenka shima̱sṵ (suru,
　shi̱te) けんか［喧嘩］します（す
　る, して）; *(discusses, de-
　bates)* ron-jima̱sṵ (ron-ji̱ru,
　ro̱n-jite) 論じます（論ずる,
　論じて）
argument kenka けんか・喧嘩,
　kṵchi-ge̱nka 口げんか・口喧
　嘩; *(discussion)* ro̱n 論, ronsō
　論争; *(logic)* rikutsu 理屈
arise okima̱sṵ (oki̱ru, o̱ki̱te) 起
　きます（起きる, 起きて）;
　(happens) shō-jima̱sṵ (shō-
　ji̱ru, shō̱-jite) 生じます（生
　じる, 生じて）
ark shell *(= blood clam)* aka̱-gai
　赤貝

arm te̱ 手 *or (strictly)* ude̱ 腕
armpit waki no̱ shi̱ta 腋の下・脇
　の下; ~ **smell** *(body odor)*
　waki̱-ga わきが・腋臭
army gu̱ntai 軍隊; *(vs. navy)*
　riku̱gun 陸軍
around 1. (... no) mawari ni (...
　の）周りに; **goes ~** (... o)
　mawarima̱sṵ (mawaru,
　mawatte) (...を)回ります（回
　る, 回って）**2.** → **about, ap-
　proximately**
arrange 1. *(lines them up)*
　narabema̱sṵ (naraberu,
　narabete) 並べます（並べる,
　並べて）; ~ **themselves**
　narabima̱sṵ (narabu,
　narande) 並びます（並ぶ, 並
　んで）**2.** *(decides, sets)*
　kimema̱sṵ (kimeru, kimete)
　決めます（決める, 決めて）,
　(a meeting/consultation) uchi-
　awasema̱sṵ (-awase̱ru,
　-awa̱sete) 打ち合わせます（合
　わせる, 合わせて）**3.** *(puts
　together)* matomema̱sṵ
　(matomeru, matomete) まとめ
　まる（まとめる, まとめて）
arrange (flowers) *(hana̱* o)
　ikema̱sṵ (ike̱ru, i̱kete) （花
　を）生けます（生ける, 生けて）
arranged: gets ~ 1. *(is put
　together)* matomarima̱sṵ
　(matomaru, matomatte) まと
　まります（まとまる, まと
　まって）, *(as a set/array)*

soroima̍su (soro̍u, soro̍tte) 揃います(揃う, 揃って); *(gets decided/set)* kimarima̍su (kimaru, kimatte) 決まります (決まる, 決まって) **2. it has been arranged that** ... koto̍ ni natte ima̍su ...ことになって います

arranged marriage miai-ke̍kkon 見合い結婚

arrangement *(settlement)* kimari 決まり; *(adjustment)* se̍iri 整理; **flower ~** ike̍bana 生け 花・生花; **prior ~** uchi-awase 打ち合わせ

arrangements *(preparations)* ju̍mbi 準備, shitaku 支度・仕 度; *(plans)* te̍hazu 手はず・手 筈

array soro̍e̍ 揃え

arrest toraema̍su (tora̍e̍ru, tora̍ete) 捕えます(捕える, 捕 えて), tsukamaema̍su (tsukamaeru, tsukamaete) 捕 まえます(捕まえる, 捕まえ て), ta̍iho shima̍(ꜜ)su (suru, shite) 逮捕します(する, して)

arrival tōchaku 到着; ... cha̍ku ... 着

arrive (at) 1. (... ni) tsukima̍su (tsuku̍, tsu̍ite) (...に)着きま す(着く, 着いて), tōchaku shima̍su (suru, shite) 到着し ます(する, して), itarima̍su (itaꜜru, itaꜜtte) 至ります(至 る, 至って) **2.** *(is delivered)*

todokima̍su (todo̍ku, todo̍ite) 届きます(届く, 届い て)

arriving at (TIME/PLACE) ... cha̍ku (no) ...着(の)

arrogant gōman (na) 傲慢(な); **is/acts ~** ibarima̍su (iba̍ru, iba̍tte) 威張ります(威張る, 威張って)

arrow ya̍ 矢; *(sign)* ya-ji̍rushi 矢印

arrowroot kuzu くず・葛; **powdered ~** kuzuꜜko̍ꜜ くず 粉・葛粉

art bi̍jutsu 美術, geijutsu 芸術

article *(thing)* mono̍ 物, *(goods)* shina(-mono) 品(物); *(write-up)* ki̍ji 記事; *(scholarly)* rombun 論文

artificial jinkō (no) 人工(の)

artist geijutsu-ka 芸術家; *(painter)* gaka 画家

arts ge̍i 芸

as 1. *(like)* ... (no) yō̍ (ni) ...(の) よう(に) **2.** *(so as to be)* ... ni ... に **3.** *(in the role of)* ... to shite ...として **4. as usual/ever/ always** aikawarazu 相変わら ず

Asakusa Asakusa 浅草; **~ Park** Asakusa-kōen 浅草公園

ascertain tashikamema̍su (tashikame̍ru, tashika̍mete) 確かめます(確かめる, 確か めて)

ascetic practices shugyō 修行, gyō̍ 行

as far as ... is concerned ... ni
ka⌐kete wa ...にかけては

as for ... wa ...は

ashamed hazukashi⌐i 恥ずかしい;
(guilty-feeling) yamashi⌐i やま
しい・疚しい

ash(es) hai 灰; **volcanic ash**
kaza⌐m-bai 火山灰

ashtray hai-zara 灰皿, sara 皿

Asia(n) Aji(y)a (no) アジア［ヤ］
（の）; **an Asian** Aji(y)a⌐-jin ア
ジア［ヤ］人

aside from ... wa betsu to shite ...
は別として

ask (a favor of a person) (... ni ...
o) tanomima⌐su (tano⌐mu,
tano⌐nde) (...に...を)頼みます
(頼む, 頼んで), negaima⌐su
(negau, negatte) 願います(願
う, 願って); *(requires)*
motomema⌐su (motome⌐ru,
moto⌐mete) 求めます(求める,
求めて)

ask (a person a question) (... ni)
kikima⌐su (kiku, kiite) (...に)
聞きます(聞く, 聞いて),
tazunema⌐su (tazune⌐ru,
tazu⌐nete) 尋ねます(尋ねる,
尋ねて), ukagaima⌐su
(ukagau, ukagatte) 伺います
(伺う, 伺って)

aslant nana⌐me (no/ni) 斜め(の/
に)

as much as ... gu⌐rai ...位; ...
hodo ...程・ほど; ~ **one likes**
zombu⌐n (ni) 存分(に); ~

possible dekiru-dake 出来るだ
け・できるだけ

aspect yōsu 様子; *(grammatical)*
a⌐supe⌐kuto アスペクト

aspire → **hope**

aspirin asupi⌐rin アスピリン

as regards ... ni ka⌐kete wa ...に
かけては; ... ni ka⌐n-shite ...に
関して

assault → **attack**

assemble 1. *(they collect)*
atsumarima⌐su (atsuma⌐ru,
atsuma⌐tte) 集まります(集ま
る, 集まって), shūgō
shima⌐su (suru, shite) 集合し
ます(する, して); *(collects
them)* atsumema⌐su (atsu-
me⌐ru, atsu⌐mete) 集めます(集
める, 集めて) **2.** *(fits parts
together to make a whole)*
kumi-awasema⌐su (-awase⌐ru,
-awa⌐sete) 組合わせます
(合わせる, 合わせて), kumi-
tatema⌐su (-tate⌐ru, -ta⌐tete)
組み立てます(立てる, 立て
て)

assembly *(gathering)* shūgō 集合;
(parliament) kokkai 国会

assent nattoku shima⌐su (suru,
shite) 納得します(する, して);
→ **consent**

assert shuchō shima⌐su (suru,
shite) 主張します(する, して)

assertion shuchō 主張

assist → **help**

assistance sewa⌐ (o-se⌐wa) 世話

（お世話）; tetsuda'i (o-te'tsudai) 手伝い（お手伝い）

assistant joshu 助手

assistant professor jo-kyo'ju 助教授　　　　　　　「教授

associate professor jun-kyo'ju 準

associate with ... to tsuki-aima'su (-a'u, -a'tte) ...と付き合います（合う，合って）; ... to majiwarima'su (majiwa'ru, majiwa'tte) ...と交わります（交わる，交わって）; ... o chika-zukema'su (-zuke'ru, -zu'kete) ...を近付けます（付ける，付けて）

association 1. kyōkai 協会; *(academic)* gakkai 学会; *(guild, union)* kumiai 組合 **2.** *(social company)* tsuki-ai (o-tsuki'ai) 付き合い（お付き合い）**3.** *(of thought)* rensō 連想

as soon as ... (suru) to (su'gu) ...（する）と（すぐ）; (shite') kara su'gu （して）からすぐ; (VERB-i い)-shi'dai (ni) 次第（に）

assortment kumi-awase 組み合わせ, tori-awase 取り合わせ

assumed name kamei 仮名

asterisk hoshi-ji'rushi 星印

asthma zensoku 喘息

as to = as for; ～ **the matter at hand** sa'-te さて

astonished: gets ～ odorokima'su (odoro'ku, odoro'ite) 驚きます（驚く，驚いて）

astringent shibu'i 渋い; *(an ～)* asutori'nzen アストリンゼン

astronomy temmo'n-gaku 天文学

at ... de ...で; *(being located at)* ... ni ...に

at any rate to'-mo-kaku ともかく

at best se'izei せいぜい

at ease yukku'ri ゆっくり

atelier atori'e アトリエ

athlete se'nshu 選手, undō-ka 運動家

athlete's foot mizumushi 水虫, tamushi 田虫

athletic field undō-ba/-jō 運動場/場

athletics undō 運動, supo'tsu スポーツ; *(physical education)* ta'iiku 体育

athletic supporter sapo'tā サポーター

Atlantic Ocean Taise'iyō 大西洋

at last iyo'-iyo いよいよ, yōyaku ようやく, tsu'i-ni ついに; *(after difficulty)* yatto やっと

at least suku'na'ku-tomo 少なくとも, se'mete せめて

atmosphere (of a place) fun'i'ki 雰囲気

at most se'mete せめて, se'izei せいぜい

atom ge'nshi 原子; ～ **bomb** genshi-ba'kudan 原子爆弾;

atomic energy genshi̅-ryoku 原子力

at once sassoku̅ 早速・さっそく

at one time ka̅tsute かつて, ka̅tte かって

atrocious *(brutal)* zangyaku (na) 残虐(な)

atrocity zangyaku-ko̅i 残虐行為

attach 1. *(sticks on)* tsukema̅su (tsuke̅ru, tsuke̅te) 付けます (付ける, 付けて) **2.** *(adds)* soema̅su (soeru, soete) 添えます(添える, 添えて)

attachment(s) fuzoku 付属・附属, fuzoku̅-hin 付属品・附属品

attack 1. *(an attack)* ko̅geki 攻撃, shu̅geki 襲撃 **2.** *(makes an attack)* ko̅geki/shu̅geki shima̅su (suru, shite) 攻撃/襲撃します (する, して); semema̅su (seme̅ru, se̅mete) 攻めます (攻める, 攻めて)

attain → **reach**; → **accomplish**

attempt 1. tameshi̅ 試し, kokoro̅mi̅ 試み; kuwada̅te̅ 企て **2.** *(attempts it)* tameshima̅su (tame̅su, tame̅shite) 試します(試す, 試して), kokoromima̅su (kokoromi̅ru, kokoro̅mite) 試みます(試みる, 試みて); kuwadatema̅su (kuwadate̅ru, kuwada̅tete) 企てます(企てる, 企てて)

attendance shu̅sseki 出席; **office**

～ shukkin 出勤

attendant *(in charge)* ka̅kari 係, kakari̅-in 係員, ... -ga̅kari ...係; kyu̅ji 給仕; *(servant)* ko̅zukai 小使い → **clerk**

attention chu̅i 注意, ne̅n 念

attest sho̅mei shima̅su (suru, shite) 証明します(する, して); **attestation** sho̅mei 証明

attitude ta̅ido 態度, shisei 姿勢

attract hikima̅su (hiku, hiite) 引きます(引く, 引いて)

attractive *(nice-looking)* ki̅rei (na) きれい・綺麗(な); *(charming)* mi̅ryoku ga arima̅su (a̅ru, a̅tte) 魅力があります (ある, あって)

attractiveness *(= charm)* aikyo̅ あいきょう・愛嬌

auction seri̅ 競り・セリ

audience cho̅shu̅ 聴衆

auditorium kaido̅ 会堂, ko̅do̅ 講堂 「(さん)

aunt oba (san) おば・伯母・叔母

auspicious medeta̅i めでたい・日出度い

Australia Ō̅sutora̅ri(y)a オーストラリア[ヤ]

Australian *(person)* Ō̅sutorari-(y)a̅-jin オーストラリア[ヤ]人

authentic kakujitsu (na) 確実(な)

authentication: note of ～ sho̅me̅i-sho̅ 証明書

author cho̅sha 著者; → **writer**

authority *(expert)* ta̅ika 大家,

tsū 通, tsūji⌐n 通人; *(basis)*
ko⌐nkyo 根拠; **the authorities**
tōkyoku 当局, oka⌐mi お上;
**the authorities/people con-
cerned with … … no kanke⌐i-
sha** …の関係者

authorized kōnin (no) 公認(の)

automatic jidō-teki (na) 自動的
(な)

automatically jidō-teki ni 自動的
に; *(spontaneously)* hitori-de
ni ひとりでに・独りでに,
onozukara おのずから・自ず
から

automobile jidō⌐-sha 自動車
(**how many** na⌐n-dai 何台)

autumn a⌐ki 秋; **~ leaves**
mo⌐miji もみじ・紅葉; **~
period/term** shū⌐ki 秋期

autumnal equinox shūbun 秋分;
Autumnal Equinox Day
Shūbun no hi⌐ 秋分の日

available: ~ room(s) aki-beya/
-ma/-shitsu 空き部屋/間/室;
~ space ma 間; **~ taxi** kūsha
空車; **seats are ~**
suwarema⌐su (suwareru,
suwarete) 座れ[すわれ]ます
(座れる, 座れて)

avalanche nadare⌐ なだれ・雪崩;
(snowslide) yuki-na⌐dare 雪な
だれ

avenue tōri 通り, ōdo⌐ri 大通り,
kaidō⌐ 街道; michi 道

average 1. *(on the average)*
heikin 平均 **2.** *(ordinary)* nami

(no) 並(の), heibon (na) 平凡
(な) **3. averages it**
narashima⌐su (nara⌐su,
nara⌐shite) ならし[均し]ます
(ならす, ならして)

avoid sakema⌐su (sake⌐ru,
sa⌐kete) 避けます(避ける, 避
けて), yokema⌐su (yoke⌐ru,
yo⌐kete) よけます(よける, よ
けて)

await → wait for

awake *(comes awake)*
mezamema⌐su (mezame⌐ru,
meza⌐mete) 目覚めます(目覚
める, 目覚めて); **is awake**
(not asleep) nemurimase⌐n
(nemuranai) 眠りません(眠ら
ない)

award sho⌐ (o ju⌐yo shima(⌐)su;
suru, shite) 賞(を授与します;
する, して); *(gives)*
okurima⌐su (okuru, okutte) 贈
ります(贈る, 贈って)

awardee jushō⌐-sha 受賞者

away: away from home ru⌐su
(no) 留守(の); **right away**
su⌐gu すぐ; **go away** ikima⌐su
(iku, itte) 行きます(行く, 行
って); **run away** *(flees)*
nigema⌐su (nige⌐ru, ni⌐gete) 逃げ
ます(逃げる, 逃げて); **take
away** torimo⌐su (to⌐ru, to⌐tte)
取ります(取る, 取って)

awesome mono-sugo⌐i ものすご
い・物凄い

awful osoroshi⌐i 恐ろしい;

awfully → very

awkward mazu'i まずい; *(feels flustered)* terema'su (tere'ru, te'rete) 照れます(照れる, 照れて)

awl ki'ri 錐
awning hi-o'o'i 日覆い
ax o'no 斧
axis, axle jiku' 軸
azalea tsutsu'ji つつじ

— B —

baby 1. a'ka-chan 赤ちゃん, akambo 赤ん坊・赤んぼ 2. *(pampers one)* ama-yakashima'su (amayaka⌐su, amayaka⌐shite) 甘やかします(甘やかす, 甘やかして)

babysitter komo'ri 子守

bachelor dokushin 独身, hitori-mo'no' ひとり者・独り者

bachelor's degree ga'kushi 学士

back *(behind)* ... no ushiro (de/ni) ...の後ろ(で/に)

back *(of body)* senaka 背中, *(lower part)* koshi 腰; *(of room etc.)* o'ku 奥; *(reverse side)* ura' 裏; → support

back: go back modorima'su (modo'ru, modo'tte) 戻ります(戻る, 戻って); *(to one's usual place)* kaerima'su (ka'eru, ka'ette) 帰ります(帰る, 帰って) **I'll be right back** Cho'tto itte kima'su. ちょっと行って来ます. **Hello, I'm back** Tada'ima (kaerima'shita). ただいま(帰りました).

back and forth ze'ngo (ni) 前後 (に); **goes ~** kayoima'su (kayou, kayotte) 通います(通う, 通って)

backbone sebone 背骨

back door ura-guchi 裏口

backed up *(traffic)* jūtai shite ima'su (iru, ite) 渋滞しています(いる, いて)

back gate ura-mon 裏門

background haikei 背景

backing 1. *(support)* kōen 後援 2. → lining

backrest *(= legless chair)* za-isu 座椅子

back room (o-)na'ndo (お)納戸

back street ura-do'ri 裏通り

backwards *(contrariwise)* gyaku (ni) 逆(に)

bacon bē'kon ベーコン

bad waru'i 悪い, dame' (na) だめ・駄目(な); furyō (na) 不良(な); *(inept)* heta' (na) へた・下手(な)

bad: goes bad *(= rots, sours)* kusarima'su (kusa'ru,

kusa⌐tte) 腐ります(腐る, 腐って)

bad: too bad (= *regrettable*) zannen (na) 残念(な); ikemase⌐n (ikenai) いけません(いけない)

badger anaguma あなぐま・穴熊 (**not** ta⌐nuki たぬき・狸 **raccoon-dog**)

badminton: a kind of ~ hane⌐-tsuki⌐ 羽根突き

bad-tasting mazu⌐i まずい

bag 1. fukuro⌐ 袋; (*paper*) kami-bu⌐kuro 紙袋, (*plastic*) pori-bu⌐kuro ポリ袋 **2.** → **suitcase** **3.** → **handbag; purse**

baggage ni⌐motsu (o-ni⌐motsu) 荷物(お荷物)

bait esa⌐ えさ・餌

bake yakima⌐su (yaku, yaite) 焼きます(焼く, 焼いて); **gets baked** yakema⌐su (yakeru, yakete) 焼けます(焼ける, 焼けて)

baker, bakery, bakeshop pa⌐n-ya パン屋

baking yaki 焼き

balance (*equilibrium*) tsuriai 釣り合い

bald (*gets* ~) hagema⌐su (hage⌐ru, ha⌐gete) はげます・禿げます(はげる, はげて); (*is* ~) ha⌐gete ima⌐su (iru, ite) はげて[禿げて]います(いる, いて); ha⌐geta ... はげた[禿げた]...

baldness, bald spot ha⌐ge はげ・禿

bale tawara⌐ 俵

ball tama⌐ 玉, mari まり, bo⌐ru ボール

ballad min'yō 民謡

ballet ba⌐rē バレエ

balloon fūsen 風船, kikyū 気球; (*toy* ~) fūsen-dama 風船玉

ballot tōhyō 投票

ball park yakyū-jō 野球場, kyū-jō 球場

ballpoint pen bōru-pen ボールペン

bamboo take 竹 (1 i⌐p-pon 一本, 2 ni⌐-hon 二本, 3 sa⌐m-bon 三本, **how many** na⌐m-bon 何本)

bamboo blind misu みす・御簾

bamboo hat ka⌐sa 笠

bamboo shoot take-no-ko たけのこ・竹の子・筍

bamboo tea whisk chase⌐n 茶せん・茶筅

bambooware take-za⌐iku 竹細工

bamboo wind-chimes take-fu⌐rin 竹風鈴

ban kinshi 禁止; **bans it** kinshi shima⌐su (suru, shite) 禁止します(する, して)

band 1. (*group*) kumi⌐ 組; (*of musicians*) gakudan 楽団, hayashi⌐ (o-hayashi) はやし・囃し(おはやし・お囃し) **2.** (*watchband, etc.*) bando バンド

bandage hōtai 包帯

bandit zoku 賊

banjo: three-stringed ~ shamisen しゃみせん・三味線

bank 1. ginkō 銀行; ~ **account** yokin-ko⌐za 預金口座; ~

clerk ginkō-in 銀行員
2. *(riverbank)* kishi̱ 岸

bankbook kayoi 通い, tsūchō 通帳, yokin-tsū̄chō 預金通帳

bankruptcy hasan 破産; **goes bankrupt** hasan shima̱su (suru, shite) 破産します(する, して)

banquet enkai 宴会

bar *(for drinking)* saka-ba 酒場, bā̄ バー, *(neighborhood pub)* nomi̱-ya 飲み屋, *(after-hours)* suna̱kku スナック; *(iron)* (tetsu-)bō (鉄)棒; **a bar of soap** sekken i̱k-ko せっけん[石鹸]一個

barbarous yaban (na) 野蛮(な); **a barbarian** yaban-ji̱n 野蛮(人)

barbed wire yūshi̱-te̱ssen 有刺鉄線

barber(shop) tokoya 床屋, riha̱tsu̱-ten 理髪店, sampatsu-ya 散髪屋

bare 1. *(austere)* shibu̱i 渋い 2. → **naked** 3. → **reveal**

barefoot hadashi はだし・裸足

barely yatto やっと, yōyaku ようやく

bargain *(a real find)* horidashi-mono 掘出し物

bar hopping hashigo̱-zake はしご酒, hashigo はしご・梯子

bark *(of tree)* ki̱ no kawa̱ 木の皮; *(a dog barks)* hoema̱su (hoe̱ru, ho̱ete) 吠えます(吠える, 吠えて)

barley mu̱gi 麦, ō-mu̱gi 大麦

barn na̱ya 納屋

barracks he̱isha 兵舎

barracuda kamasu̱ かます

barrel taru 樽; ~ **hoop** taga̱ たが

base *(military)* ki̱chi̱ 基地; *(of a tree)* ne-moto̱ 根元

baseball yakyū 野球, bēsubo̱ru ベースボール; ~ **stadium** yakyū-jō 野球場, kyūjō 球場; ~ **team** na̱in ナイン

based on: is ~ ... ni motozukima̱su (motozu̱ku, motozu̱ite) ...に基づきます (基づく, 基づいて)

basement *(floor)* chikai 地階; *(room)* chika̱(-shitsu) 地下(室)

bash tatakima̱su (tata̱ku, tata̱ite) 叩きます(叩く, 叩いて)

bashful → **shy**

bashing tataki̱ 叩き

basic ki̱hon-teki (na) 基本的(な), kompon-teki (na) 根本的(な)

basin tarai たらい, hachi̱ 鉢; *(for washing face)* semme̱n-ki 洗面器

basis ki̱hon 基本, kompo̱n 基本; *(grounds)* ko̱nkyo 根拠

basket kago かご・籠

basking (in the sun) hinata-bo̱kko ひなたぼっこ

bass *(sea bass)* suzuki すずき・鱸

baste (with thread) shi̱-

tsukema⌐su (-tsuke⌐ru, -tsu⌐kete) 仕付けます(付ける, 付けて); **basting thread** shị-tsuke-i⌐to 仕付け糸

bat kō⌐mori こうもり; *(baseball)* ba⌐tto バット

bath 1. fu⌐ro (o-fu⌐ro) 風呂(お風呂), ba⌐su バス; yu⌐ (o-yu) 湯(お湯) **2. public ～** se⌐ntō 銭湯, yokujō 浴場; **Turkish ～** sa⌐una サウナ, sauna-bu⌐ro サウナ風呂

bath: taking a ～ nyūyoku 入浴; **takes a ～** fu⌐ro⌐ ni hairima⌐su (ha⌐iru, ha⌐itte) 風呂に入ります(入る, 入って), nyūyoku shima⌐su (suru, shite) 入浴します(する, して)

bath(house) attendant sentō no jūgyō⌐-in 銭湯の従業員

bathing mokuyoku 沐浴; **～ suit** mizu-gi 水着

bathrobe *(padded)* ta⌐nze⌐n 丹前 = dotera どてら; *(light)* yukata ゆかた・浴衣

bathroom 1. *(for bathing)* furo-ba⌐ (o-furoba) 風呂場(お風呂場), yokujō 浴場, ba⌐su バス = basu-rū⌐mu バスルーム **2.** *(toilet)* benjo⌐ 便所, to⌐ire (to⌐iretto) トイレ(トイレット), keshō⌐-shitsu 化粧室 (ㅇㅅ) tea⌐rai (お)手洗い

bathroom: goes to the ～ yō⌐ o tashima⌐su (tasu, tashite) 用を足します(足す, 足して)

bathtub yu⌐bune 湯舟, yokusō 浴槽

battery de⌐nchi 電池, ba⌐tterii バッテリー

battle sentō 戦闘

battledore hago⌐-i⌐ta 羽子板; **～ and shuttlecock (a kind of badminton)** hane⌐-tsuki⌐ 羽根突き

bay wa⌐n 湾, ura⌐ 浦

be → **is**; → **go**, → **come**

beach hama⌐ 浜, bi⌐ichi ビーチ; *(seashore)* kaigan 海岸

bead tama⌐ 玉; **(prayer) beads** juzu⌐ じゅず・数珠; **counting beads** → **abacus**

beam 1. *(crossbeam)* keta けた・桁; **under the ～** keta-shịta 桁下・けた下 **2.** *(～ of light)* kōsen 光線

bean mame⌐ 豆; *(soy beans)* da⌐izu 大豆

bean curd tōfu⌐ (o-tōfu) 豆腐(お豆腐); *(pot-boiled squares)* yu-dō⌐fu 湯豆腐; *(parboiled cubes)* yakko(-dō⌐fu) やっこ・奴(豆腐); *(broiled)* yaki-dō⌐fu 焼き豆腐; *(deep-fried)* abura⌐age 油揚げ

bean-curd lees o-kara おから, kara⌐ から

bean-flour threads harusame 春

bean jam/paste a⌐n(ko) あん(こ)・餡(こ); *(fermented)* mi⌐so (o-mi⌐so) みそ・味噌(おみそ・お味噌)

bear 1. *(animal)* ku⌐ma⌐ 熊

2. *(puts up with)* shinobima͡su (shino⌐ꜜbu, shino⌐ꜜnde) 忍びます(忍ぶ, 忍んで), taema͡su (tae͡ru, ta͡ete) 耐えます(耐える, 耐えて), shi͡mbō shima(͡)su (suru, shite) 辛抱します(する, して)
3. → carry **4.** → give birth
5. bears fruit minorima͡su (mino⌐ꜜru, mino⌐ꜜtte) 実ります(実る, 実って)

beard hige (o-hige) ひげ・髭(おひげ・お髭); *(chin-whiskers)* ago⌐ꜜ-hige あごひげ・あご髭

bearings: one's ～ hōgaku 方角

bear up *(stands firm)* gambarima͡su (gamba͡ru, gamba͡tte) がんばり[頑張り]ます(がんばる, がんばって)

beat 1. *(hits)* nagurima͡su (nagu͡ru, nagu͡tte) なぐり[殴り]ます(なぐる, なぐって); *(slaps)* hatakima͡su (hata͡ku, hata͡ite) はたきます(はたく, はたいて) **2.** *(defeats)* makashima͡su (makasu, makashite) 負かします(負かす, 負かして) **3.** *(heart throbs)* do͡kidoki shima͡su (suru, shite) どきどきします(する, して)

beat around the bush *(is non-committal)* hanashi͡ o bokashima͡su (boka͡su, boka͡shite) 話をぼかします(ぼかす, ぼかして)

beaten: gets ～ yararema͡su (yarareru, yararete) やられます(やられる, やられて)

beautiful utsukushi͡i 美しい, ki͡rei (na) きれい・綺麗(な), mi͡goto (na) 見事(な)

beauty parlor biyō͡in 美容院

because ... kara ...から, ... tame ...ため・為, ... mono ...もの, ... no de ...ので, ... yue͡ ni ...ゆえに・故に; **perhaps ～ of ...** (no) se͡i ka ...(の)せいか

beckoning tema͡neki 手招き

become (... ni, ...-ku) narima͡su (na͡ru, na͡tte) (...に, ...く)なります(なる, なって); [HONORIFIC] o-nari ni narima͡su (na͡ru, na͡tte) おなりになります(なる, なって)

become: is becoming to ... *(suits)* ... ni ni-aima͡su (-a͡u, -a͡tte) ...に似合います(合う, 合って)

bed toko (o-toko) 床(お床); *(Western)* be͡ddo (be͡tto) ベッド(ベット), shindai 寝台

bed: goes to ～ nema͡su (neru, nete) 寝ます(寝る, 寝て), yasumima͡su, (yasu͡mu, yasu͡nde) 休みます(休む, 休んで); **takes to one's ～** toko ni tsukima͡su (tsuku͡, tsu͡ite) 床に就きます(就く, 就いて)

bed-and-breakfast minshuku 民宿

bedclothes, bedding shi͡ngu 寝具, ya͡gu 夜具; *(Japanese quilt)* futon (o-fúto'n) 布団(お布団)

bedpan benki 便器; *(urinal)* shibin しびん; *(fecal)* oma⸢ru おまる

bedroom shinshitsu 寝室, né⸢-ma 寝間; ~ **community** beddo-ta⸢un ベッドタウン

bed sheet shi⸢itsu シーツ, shikifu 敷布

bee mitsu⸥-bachi 蜜蜂, hachi 蜂

beef gyūniku 牛肉

beef hash over rice hayashi-ra⸢isu ハヤシライス

beef slices dipped in hot broth shabu-shabu しゃぶしゃぶ

beefsteak sutēki ステーキ

beefsteak plant *(= perilla)* shiso しそ·紫蘇

been → **is**; → **go**, → **come**; **Where have you been?** Do⸢ko e itte kima⸥shita ka. どこへ行って来ましたか.

beer bi⸢iru ビール; **draft** ~ na⸢ma 生, nama-bi⸢iru 生ビール

beer bottle/can biirú⸥-bin/-kan ビール瓶/缶

beer hall biya-hó⸥ru ビヤホール

beeswax mitsurō みつろう·蜜蝋

beet bi⸢ito ビート

before (… no) má⸢e (ni) (…の)前(に); ~ **it happens** (shi)-nai uchi ni (し)ないうちに **Eat before you go** Ta⸢bete kara itte kudasa⸥i. 食べてから行って下さい.

before a meal shokuzen 食前

before and after ze⸢ngo (ni) 前後(に); ma⸢e mo a⸢to mo 前も後も

before anything else ma⸢zu まず·先ず

beforehand mae-mo⸢tte 前もって

before long ma-mo⸢-naku まもなく·間もなく, so⸢rosoro そろそろ; *(eventually)* yagate⸢ やがて

before the war senzen 戦前 (= sensō no ma⸢e 戦争の前)

beg tanomima⸢su (tano⸢mu, tano⸢nde) 頼みます(頼む, 頼んで), negaima⸢su (nega⸢u, nega⸢tte) 願います(願う, 願って)

beg: I beg your pardon, but … shitsu⸥rei desu ga …. 失礼ですが…, habakari-nagara … はばかりながら…

beggar kojiki⸢ こじき·乞食

begin *(it begins)* hajimarima⸢su (hajimaru, hajimatte) 始まります(始まる, 始まって); *(begins it)* hajimema⸢su (hajimeru, haji⸢mete) 始めます(始める, 始めて)

beginning hajime 始め, *(outset)* saisho 最初, ha⸢na はな; **from the or hajime (k)kara 始め(っ)から, mo⸢to kara もとから·元から, mo⸢to⸥-yori もとより·元より

begrudge uramima⸢su (ura⸢mu,

ura⌐nde) 恨みます(恨む, 恨ん
で)

behavior *(actions)* kōdō 行動,
(act) kō⌐i 行為; *(deportment)*
furu⌐ma⌐i ふるまい·振る舞
い; *(manners)* (o-)gyōgi (お)
行儀; *(attitude)* ta⌐ido 態度

behind (… no) ushiro (de/ni)
(...の)後ろ(で/に); *(the other
side)* ura⌐ 裏

behind: falls/gets ~ okurema⌐su
(okureru, okurete) 遅れます
(遅れる, 遅れて)

behind: gets left ~ nokorima⌐su
(noko⌐ru, noko⌐tte) 残ります
(残る, 残って); **leaves** ~
nokoshima⌐su (noko⌐su,
noko⌐shite) 残します(残す,
残して), *(forgets)* wasure-
mono o shima⌐su (suru, shite)
忘れ物をします(する, して)

being 1. *(in existence; person)*
sonzai 存在; **human** ~ ningen
人間 **2.** → **is 3. comes into** ~
seiritsu shima⌐su (suru, shite)
成立します(する, して)

being: … ~ **what it is (who one
is)** sasuga no … さすがの...

belch ge⌐ppu⌐ げっぷ, okubi
(o shima⌐su; suru, shite) おく
び(をします; する, して)

believe 1. ~ **(in)** (… o) shin-
jima⌐su (shin-ji⌐ru, shi⌐n-
jite) 信じます(信じる,
信じて) **2.** → **think**

bell *(large)* kane 鐘; *(small)* ri⌐n

鈴; *(doorbell)* be⌐ru ベル; *(temple bell)* tsurigane 釣り鐘

bellboy bōi ボーイ

bell pepper pi⌐iman ピーマン

belly hara⌐ 腹 「(おへそ)

bellybutton heso (o-heso) へそ

belong (to) (… ni) zoku-
shima⌐su (zoku-su⌐ru, zoku⌐-
shite) (...に)属します(属する,
属して)

belonging *(possessed)* shoyū (no)
所有(の); **belongings** mochi⌐-
mono 持ち物

below (… no) shita⌐ (ni) (...の)
下(に); *(less than)* …i⌐ka ...以
下, … mi⌐man ...未満

belt bando バンド, be⌐ruto ベ
ルト, o⌐bi 帯; *(sumo
wrestler's)* mawashi まわし·回
し; *(zone)* (chi)tai (地)帯; ~
line kanjō-sen 環状線

bend 1. *(it bends)* orema⌐su
(ore⌐ru, o⌐rete) 折れます(折れ
る, 折れて), *(curves)*
magarima⌐su (magaru,
magatte) 曲がります(曲がる,
曲がって), *(warps)* sorima⌐su
(so⌐ru, so⌐tte) 反ります(反る,
反って) **2.** *(bends it)* orima⌐su
(o⌐ru, o⌐tte) 折ります(折る,
折って), magema⌐su (mageru,
magete) 曲げます(曲げる, 曲
げて), sorashima⌐su (sora⌐su,
sora⌐shite) 反らします(反らす,
反らして)

beneath → **below**

benefit ri᷄eki 利益; (… no) tame᷄ (o-tame) (…の)為(お為)

Berlin Be᷄ruri᷄n ベルリン

berry ki᷄-no-mi 木の実 *(includes nuts, fruits)*; → **strawberry**; → **mulberry**

berth shindai 寝台; ~ **ticket** shinda᷄i-ken 寝台券

beset *(stricken)*: **gets ~** *(by illness)* yararema᷄su (yarareru, yararete) やられます(やられる, やられて)

beside … no so᷄ba (de/ni) …のそば(で/に), … no tonari (de/ni) …の隣り(で/に), … no waki (de/ni) …のわき(で/に)

besides sono ue᷄ ni その上に, (sono) hoka ni (その)他に

best ichiban i᷄i 一番いい[好い, 良い, 善い]; sairyō (no) 最良(の); *(highest)* saikō (no) 最高(の); *(top-class)* jōtō (no) 上等(の); *(special-quality)* tokkyu᷄ 特級; be᷄suto ベスト, ~ **ten** besuto᷄-te᷄n ベストテン

best: at best se᷄izei せいぜい; **Please give my best wishes to …** … ni yoroshiku (itte kudasa᷄i, o-tsutae kudasa᷄i) …によろしく・宜しく(言って下さい, お伝え下さい); **the best, one's best** saizen 最善

bet kakema᷄su (kake᷄ru, ka᷄kete) 賭けます(賭ける, 賭けて), kake᷄ o shima᷄su (suru, shite) 賭をします(する, して)

betray ura-girima᷄su (-gi᷄ru, -gi᷄tte) 裏切ります(切る, 切って); **betrayal** ura-gi᷄ri᷄ 裏切り

better mo᷄tto i᷄i もっといい[良い], (…) yo᷄ri i᷄i (…)よりいい, yori-i᷄i よりいい; *(preferable)* … (no hō᷄) ga i᷄i …(の方)がいい; **had better do it** shita hō᷄ ga i᷄i した方がいい, **had better not do it** shinai hō᷄ ga i᷄i しない方がいい

betterment zōshin 増進

between (… no) aida (ni) (…の)間(に); (…-) …᷄-kan (…)…間; ~ **acts** maku᷄ no aida 幕の間, makuai ni 幕あいに・幕間に・幕合に

beverage nomi᷄-mono 飲み物

beyond (… no) mukō᷄ (ni) (…の)向こう(に), o-mu᷄kō お向こう; ~ **expectations** zo᷄ngai 存外; ~ **remedy** shō (shi-yō) ga na᷄i しょう(しよう・仕様)がない

Bible Se᷄isho 聖書, Ba᷄iburu バイブル

bicycle jite᷄n-sha 自転車; ~ **race** keirin 競輪; ~ **shop** jiten-sha-ya 自転車屋

big ōki᷄i 大きい; *(spacious)* hiro᷄i 広い; **big brother** a᷄ni 兄, (o-)ni᷄i-san (お)兄さん; **big sister** ane 姉, (o-)ne᷄-san (お)姉さん

big hurry: in a ~ ō-i᷄sogi (de/no) 大急ぎ(で/の)

big shot ō-mono 大物
bill 1. (to pay) kanjō゙ (o-kanjō゙) 勘定（お勘定）; dempyō 伝票, o-aiso お愛想・おあいそ; daikin 代金, ...゙-dai ...代; (account) tsuke゙ つけ
2. (bank bill, check) tegata 手形 **3.** (currency note) (o-)satsu （お）札; **two ¥1000 bills** sen'e゙n-satsu nī゙-mai 千円札二枚 **4.** (handbill) bira びら・ビラ
billfold → wallet
billiards tama゙-tsukī゙ 玉突き
billion jū゙-oku 十億 (U.S.); chō゙ 兆, ī゙t-chō 一兆 (Britain)
billy-club kombō 棍棒
bind 1. tsuzurima゙su (tsuzu⌐ru, tsuzu⌐tte) 綴ります（綴る, 綴って） **2.** → tie
binding (a book) seihon 製本; (bound pages) tsuzuri⌐ 綴り
binoculars sōgan-kyō 双眼鏡
biological seibutsugaku-teki (na) 生物学的（な）
biologist seibutsuga゙ku-sha 生物学者
biology seibutsu゙-gaku 生物学
bird ko-tori 小鳥, tori 鳥 (**1** ichī゙-wa 一羽, **2** nī゙-wa 二羽, **3** sa゙m-ba 三羽, **6** ro゙p-pa 六羽, **10** jī゙p-pa 十羽, ...-wa ...羽; **how many** na゙m-ba 何羽)
birth (being born) umare/mmare 生まれ, [bookish] shussei 出生; (origin) hassei 発生

birth: give birth to ... o umima゙su (umu, unde) ...を生みます（生む, 生んで）, o-san shima゙su (suru, shite) お産します（する, して）
birthday tanjō゙bi (o-tanjō゙bi) 誕生日（お誕生日）
birthplace ko゙kyō 故郷
bit (a little) suko゙shi 少し; cho゙tto ちょっと
bite kamima゙su (ka゙mu, ka゙nde) かみます（かむ, かんで）, kami-tsukima゙su (-tsu⌐ku, -tsu⌐ite) かみつきます（つく, ついて）
bitter niga゙i 苦い; (harsh) hido゙i ひどい
bitter orange daida゙i だいだい・橙; **~ juice** po゙nsu ポン酢, ponzu゙ ポン酢
bivouac yaei 野営
black kuro゙i 黒い; ku゙ro (no) 黒(の); **jet ~** makku゙ro (na) 真っ黒(な); **~ person** kokujin 黒人; **~ tea** kō⌐cha 紅茶
blackboard kokuban 黒板
blackmail yusuri ゆすり
black mark batte゙n ばってん
black market yami-i⌐chi 闇市, yamī゙-i⌐chiba 闇市場
blade (razor) (kamiso゙ri゙ no) ha (かみそりの）刃; (sword) yaiba やいば・刃
blame 1. (censure) togame゙ (o-togame) とがめ（おとがめ）, hī゙nan 非難 **2.** (rebukes one)

togamema‾su (togame‾ru, toga‾mete) とがめます(とがめる, とがめて), hi‾nan shima(˥)su (suru, shite) 非難します(する, して); **I'm (the one who is) to blame** Watashi ga waru‾i no desu. わたしが悪いのです。 **3.** → **responsibility**

bland aji ga usui 味が薄い

blank 1. *(space)* kūsho 空所, yohaku 余白 **2.** *(form)* yōshi 用紙

blank: with a ～ look utsuro na hyōjō(˥) o mi‾sete うつろな表情を見せて

blanket mō‾fu 毛布, ketto(˥) ケット

bleed chi ga dema‾su (de‾ru, de‾te) 血が出ます(出る, 出て)

blemish kizu 傷

blender mi‾kisā ミキサー

blessing megumi 恵み

bless with ... o megumima‾su (megumu, megunde) ...を恵みます(恵む, 恵んで); **gets blessed with** ... ni megumarema‾su (megumareru, megumarete) ...に恵まれます(恵まれる, 恵まれて)

blind *(person)* mōjin(˥) 盲人; (= sunshade) hi o‾i 日覆い, hiyoke 日よけ

blindfold me-ka‾kushi 目隠し

blindly yatara ni やたらに

blink ma-ta‾taki/ma-ba‾taki

shima(˥)su (suru, shite) またたき/まばたきします(する, して)

blister mizu-bu‾kure 水膨れ; *(corn)* mame‾ まめ, soko-mame 底まめ

blizzard (ō-)fu‾buki (大)吹雪

block 1. city block: *The closest equivalent is* chōme(˥) 丁目, *a square of several blocks. For distances, use* ...˥-chō ...町: *It is three [stretches of] blocks from here.* Koko kara sa‾n-chō desu. ここから三町です。 *Or:* ... Michi o mittsu watarima‾su ... 道を三つ渡ります。 ... *You cross three streets.* **2. block of wood** kakuzai 角材 **3.** *(cloggs, impedes)* fusagima‾su (fusagu, fusaide) ふさぎます(ふさぐ, ふさいで)

blocked (off): gets ～ fusagarima‾su (fusagaru, fusagatte) ふさがります(ふさがる, ふさがって); **the road is ～** dō‾ro ga fusaga‾tte ima‾su 道路がふさがっています

blond kimpatsu (no) 金髪(の)

blood chi 血, ketsu(˥)eki 血液

blood pressure ketsuatsu 血圧; ～ **gauge** ketsuatsu‾kei 血圧計, **takes one's ～** ketsuatsu o hakarima‾su (haka‾ru, haka‾tte) 血圧を計ります(計る, 計って)

bloodshot: with ～ eyes chimaˈnako ni naˈtte 血眼になって

bloody chinamagusaˈi 血生臭い

bloom sakimaˈsu (saku, saite) 咲きます(咲く, 咲いて)

blossom → **bloom**; → **flower**

blot, blotch shimi しみ・染み, yogore 汚れ

blotter suitoriˈ-gami 吸い取り紙

blouse (of uniform) jaketsu ジャケツ; (woman's, child's) buraˈusu ブラウス; (coat) uwagi 上着

blow fukimaˈsu (fukuˈ, fuˈite) 吹きます(吹く, 吹いて); **blows one's nose** hana o kamimaˈsu (kamu, kande) 鼻をかみます(かむ, かんで)

blowfish fuˈgu ふぐ・河豚

blowout panku パンク

bludgeon kombō 棍棒

blue 1. aoˈi 青い; aˈo (no) 青(の) **2. dark (navy) blue** kon-iro (no) 紺色(の) **3. light (sky) blue** sora-iro (no) 空色(の)

bluejeans jii-pan ジーパン

blueprint ao-jaˈshin 青写真

blunder shippai 失敗; choˈmbo ちょんぼ; (faux pas) bu-saˈhō 不作法・無作法

blunt (dull-edged) kireˈnai 切れない; (dull-pointed) nibuˈi 鈍い; (rude) bu-saˈhō (na) 不作法・無作法(な); (curt) bu-aˈisō (na) 無愛想(な), bukkiˈraˈbō

(na) ぶっきらぼう(な)

blush akaku narimaˈsu (naˈru, naˈtte) 赤くなります(なる, なって)

board 1. (plank) iˈta 板 **2.** (meals) (o-)shokuji (お)食事 **3.** (gets on a train/bus) jōsha shimaˈsu (suru, shite) 乗車します(する, して), (a plane) tōjō shimaˈsu 搭乗します(する, して)

boarding area/place nori-ba 乗り場

boarding house geshuku-ya 下宿屋; (dormitory) kishuˈkuˈsha 寄宿舎, ryoˈ 寮

boarding pass tōjōˈ-ken 搭乗券

boast jiman shimaˈsu (suru, shite) 自慢します(する, して)

boat fuˈne (o-fune) 舟・船(お舟・お船); (small) kobune 小舟・小船, bōˈto ボート; (how many naˈn-seki 何隻)

bock beer kuro-biˈiru 黒ビール

body karada 体・身体; (collective ～, group) shūdan 集団; ～ **build** taikaku 体格; ～ **odor** wakiˈ-ga わきが・腋臭; ～ **temperature** taion 体温; ～ **weight** taijū 体重

bog down, gets bogged down ikizumarimaˈsu (-zumaˈru, -zumaˈtte) 行き詰まります(詰まる, 詰まって)

bog rhubarb fuki ふき・蕗

boil 1. boils water o-yu o wakashimaˈsu (wakasu,

wakashịte) お湯を沸かします
（沸かす，沸かして）; **water
boils** o-yu ga wakimạ́sụ
(waku, waite) お湯が沸きます
（沸く，沸いて） **2. boils (food)**
nimạ́sụ (niru, nite) 煮ます（煮
る，煮て），yudemạ́sụ
(yudéru, yụ́dete) ゆでます
（ゆでる，ゆでて）; *(soup,
rice)* takimạ́sụ (taku, taite) 炊
きます（炊く，炊いて） **3. it
boils** niemạ́sụ (nieru, niete) 煮
えます（煮える，煮えて）
**boil: what it boils down to (is
...)** yō-sụ́ru ni 要するに
boil (on skin) hare-mono はれも
の，dekị́-mọ́nọ́ (o-dẹ́ki) でき
もの（おでき）
boiled eggs yude-tạ́mago ゆで卵
boiled fish and vegetables
nishime 煮しめ，o-nị́shime お
煮しめ
boiled foods ni-mono 煮物;
(assorted) o-dẹ́n おでん，
dengạ́ku 田楽
boiled greens *(usually spinach,
served cold with seasoning)*
hịtashi-mọ́nọ́ ひたしもの
= o-hịtạ́shi おひたし
boiled water *(cooled for drinking)* yu-zạ̄mashi 湯冷まし
boiler bọ́irā ボイラー *(for
heating water)* yu-wạ́kashi 湯
沸かし; *(pot)* kama かま・釜，
nạ́be 鍋
boisterous yakamashị́i やかまし

い，sawagashị́i 騒がしい
bok choi *(Chinese cabbage)*
hakusạ́i 白菜
bold daitạ́n (na) 大胆（な），
yūkan (na) 勇敢（な），kịtsui き
つい
bolt *(of door)* kannụ́kị́ かん
ぬき・閂; *(of nut and bolt)*
bọ́ruto ボルト; *(of cloth)* ...
-maki ...巻き，-tan 反
bomb 1. *(a bomb)* bakudan 爆弾
2. *(bombing)* bakugeki 爆撃
3. *(bombs it)* bakugeki
shimạ́sụ (suru, shịte) 爆撃し
ます（する，して）
bomber bakugẹ́kị́-ki 爆撃機
bombing bakugeki 爆撃
bombshell hōdan 砲弾
Bon: the Bon Festival (o-)bọ́n
（お）盆，urạ́bon うら盆・盂
蘭盆
bond *(debenture)* saiken 債券
bone honẹ́ 骨
bonfire taki-bi たき火
bonito katsuo かつお・鰹; *(dried)*
katsuo-bushi かつお節・鰹節
bonnet → hat; → *(car)* hood
bonus *(wage)* bọ́nasu ボーナス，
shọ́yo 賞与 = shōyọ́-kin 賞
与金; *(extra)* omake おまけ
booboo chọ̄mbo ちょんぼ
book hạ́n 本 *(how many)* nạ́n-
satsu 何冊），shọ́motsu 書物;
(publications) shọ́seki 書籍;
~ of (commuting) tickets
kaisū́-ken 回数券

bookcase hoˈm-bako 本箱
book collection zōsho 蔵書, toˈsho 図書
booked up: gets ~ fusagarimaˈsu (fusagaru, fusagatte) ふさがります(ふさがる, ふさがって)
bookends hoˈn-tate 本立て
bookie kakeˈ-ya (san) 賭け屋(さん)
book(ing) yoyaku 予約; **books** (= reserves) yoyaku shimaˈsu (suru, shite) 予約します(する, して)
bookkeeper chōbo-gaˈkari 帳簿係
bookkeeping boˈki 簿記
bookmark shiori しおり
bookshelf hoˈn-dana 本棚
bookshop, bookstore hoˈn-ya 本屋, shoˈten 書店
boom (prosperity) keiki 景気; (fad) būˈmu ブーム; (sound) doˈn ドン
booster (of current) shōaˈtsu-ki 昇圧器
booth (selling things) baiten 売店; (in a tavern, etc.) boˈkkusu ボックス; (telephone) denwaˈ-shitsu 電話室, denwa-boˈkkusu 電話ボックス
boot(s) naga-gutsu 長靴, (rubber) gomuˈ-gutsu ゴム靴; **to boot** (= extra) omake (ni) おまけ(に)
border 1. (boundary) sakaˈi 境;

(of a district, etc.) kyōkai 境界; (of a country) kokkyō 国境; (edging) heriˈ へり・縁 **2. ~ on** ... ni ses-shimaˈsu (ses-suˈru, seˈs-shite) ...に接します(接する, 接して)
boring (dull) taikutsu (na) 退屈(な), tsumaraˈnai つまらない
born: gets ~ umaremaˈsu/ mmaremaˈsu (umareru/ mmareru, umarete/mmarete) 生まれます(生まれる, 生まれて); **~ in/of** ... no de/umare ...の出/生まれ, ...-uˈmare ...生まれ
borrow (from ...) (... ni) karimaˈsu (kariru, karite) (...に)借ります(借りる, 借りて); [HUMBLE] haishaku shimaˈsu (suru, shite) 拝借します(する, して)
bosom futokoro 懐
boss shuˈjin 主人; (head of company) shachō 社長; (ringleader) oˈyaˈ-bun 親分
botanical garden shokubutsuˈ-en 植物園
botch yari-sokonaimaˈsu (-sokonaˈu, -sokonaˈtte) やり損ないます(損なう, 損なって)
both ryōhō 両方, doˈchira mo どちらも; **~ ... and ...** ... mo ... mo ...も...も
both directions/sides ryōmeˈn 両面, ryō-gawa 両側

bother mendō˺ 面倒, me˺iwaku 迷惑; *(intrusion)* jama じゃま・邪魔; *(care)* sewa˺ (o-se˺wa, o-sewa-sama) 世話(お世話, お世話様), ya˺kkai (go-ya˺kkai) やっかい・厄介(ごやっかい・ご厄介); → **worry**

bother a person hito no jama o shima˺su (suru, shite) 人のじゃま[邪魔]をします(する, して)

bothersome mendō-kusa˺i 面倒くさい[臭い], (go-)ya˺kkai (na) (ご)やっかい・厄介(な); (o-)jama (na) (お)じゃま・邪魔(な)

bottle bi˺n 瓶; **a bottle of beer** bi˺iru i˺p-pon ビール一本; **1.8-liter bottle** *(of saké)* isshō˺-bin 一升瓶

bottle cap (bi˺n no) kya˺ppu (瓶の)キャップ, (bi˺n no) ōkan (瓶の)王冠

bottle opener sen-nu˹ki˺ 栓抜き

bottom soko 底; *(underneath)* shita 下, ... shita˺ ...下; *(buttock)* shiri˺ (o-shiri) 尻(お尻); *(bottommost, minimum, minimal)* saitei (no) 最低(の)

bottoms up *(toast)* kampai 乾杯

bounce hazumima˺su (hazumu, hazunde) 弾みます(弾む, 弾んで)

bound 1. → **bind**; ~ **pages** tsuzuri˹ 綴り 2. → **jump**

boundary saka˺i 境

bound for ...-iki (no) ...行き(の); **is bound for** ... e ikima˺su (iku, itte) ...へ行きます(行く, 行って)

bound to (do) kitto ... (suru) deshō きっと...(する)でしょう

bouquet hana˺-ta˺ba 花束

bourbon ba˺bon バーボン

bow *(archery or violin)* yumi˹ 弓; *(shape)* yumi-gata 弓形; *(of ribbon)* chō-mu˺subi ちょう結び・蝶結び

bow *(of head, etc.)* ji˹gi じぎ・辞儀 = o-jigi (o shima˺su; suru, shite) おじぎ・お辞儀(をします; する, して)

bowel movement tsū-ji (o-tsū˺-ji) 通じ(お通じ); **has a ~** tsū-ji ga tsukima˺su (tsuku˺, tsu˺ite) 通じがつきます(つく, ついて)

bowels: one's ~ move tsū-jima˺su (tsū-jiru, tsū-jite) 通じます(通じる, 通じて)

bowl wan (o-wan) 碗(お碗); *(ricebowl)* chawan (o-cha˺wan) 茶碗(お茶碗); *(basin, pot)* hachi˺ 鉢

bowlegged gani-mata (no) がにまた(の), wani˺ ashi (no) わに足(の)

bowl(ful) ...˹-hai ...杯 (1 i˺p-pai 一杯, 2 ni˺-hai 二杯, 3 sa˺m-bai 三杯)

bowl of rice with topping dom-buri (o-do'mburi) どんぶり・丼(おどんぶり・お丼), ...-don ...どん・丼

bow-wow! wa'n-wan ワンワン

box hako 箱; **box lunch** bentō 弁当, *(sold at station)* eki-ben 駅弁 「升

box: small measuring box masu'

boxing kentō 拳闘, bo'kushingu ボクシング; ~ **glove** gu'rabu グラブ

box office kippu-u'riba 切符売り場

boxtree, boxwood tsuge つげ

boy otoko'-no-ko 男の子, kodomo 子供, bō'ya 坊や, bo'tchan 坊ちゃん; *(= male)* otoko' 男; shōnen 少年; *(waiter)* bōi ボーイ

boy friend bōi-fure'ndo ボーイフレンド; ka're-shi 彼氏

Boys' Festival (5 May) Ta'ngo no sekku 端午の節句

bra, brassiere bura'jā ブラジャー

bracelet ude-wa 腕輪

brace oneself shimarima'su (shimaru, shimatte) 締まります(締まる, 締まって)

braces → suspenders

bracing *(refreshing)* sawa'yaka (na) さわやか・爽やか(な)

brag ho'ra o fukima'su (fuku', fu'ite) ほらを吹きます(吹く, 吹いて)

brag about jiman shima'su (suru, shite) 自慢します(する, して), hokorima'su (hoko'ru, hoko'tte) 誇ります(誇る, 誇って)

braid amima'su (a'mu, a'nde) 編みます(編む, 編んで)

brain(s) nō-mi'so 脳みそ, atama' 頭, zu'nō 頭脳

brake bure'ki ブレーキ, wa-dome' 輪留

branch 1. *(of tree)* eda 枝; *(of store)* shiten 支店; *(of rail line)* shisen 支線; *(of school)* ...'-kō ...校 **2. it branches off** wakarema'su (wakare'ru, waka'rete) 分かれます(分かれる, 分かれて)

brass shinchū 真ちゅう・真鍮

brassiere bura'jā ブラジャー

brat wampaku-kozō' わんぱく[腕白]小僧, gaki' がき・餓鬼

brave yūkan (na) 勇敢(な), tsuyo'i 強い

brazen zūzūshi'i ずうずうしい

brazier (o-)hi'bachi (お)火鉢

Brazil Burajiru ブラジル

bread pa'n パン, shoku-pa'n 食パン

bread crumbs pan-ko' パン粉, pan-ku'zu パンくず

bread flour pan-ko' パン粉

break: 1. a break *(rift or pause)* kire-me' 切れ目, *(rest)* yasumi' (o-yasumi) 休み(お休み), kyūkei 休憩 **2. it breaks**

kowarema͚su (koware͚ru, kowa͚rete) 壊れます(壊れる, 壊れて), *(in two)* orema͚su (ore͚ru, o͚rete) 折れます(折れる, 折れて), *(it splits)* warema͚su (wareru, warete) 割れます(割れる, 割れて), *(it smashes)* kudakema͚su (kudake͚ru, kuda͚kete) 砕けます(砕ける, 砕けて); *(it opens up, it dawns)* akema͚su (akeru, akete) 開け[明け]ます(開け[明け]る, 開け[明け]て)
3. breaks it kowashima͚su (kowa͚su, kowa͚shite) 壊します(壊す, 壊して), *(in two)* orima͚su (o͚ru, o͚tte) 折ります(折る, 折って), *(splits)* warima͚su (waru, watte) 割ります(割る, 割って), *(smashes it)* kudakima͚su (kuda͚ku, kuda͚ite) 砕きます(砕く, 砕いて)
breakable koware-yasu͚i 壊れやすい
break down 1. it breaks down *(crumbles)* kuzurema͚su (kuzure͚ru, kuzu͚rete) 崩れます(崩れる, 崩れて), *(stops working)* koshō shima͚su (suru, shite) 故障します(する, して) **2. breaks (demolishes) it** kuzushima͚su (kuzu͚su, kuzu͚shite) 崩します(崩す, 崩して)
breakdown koshō 故障

breakfast asa-han 朝飯, asa-go͚han 朝ご飯, asa-meshi 朝飯, chōshoku 朝食
break off *(ends it)* kirima͚su (ki͚ru, ki͚tte) 切ります(切る, 切って); *(it ends)* kirema͚su (kire͚ru, ki͚rete) 切れます(切れる, 切れて)
break out *(appears)* hassei shima͚su (suru, shite) 発生します(する, して); → **occur**
bream: sea ~ ta͚i たい・鯛
breast *(chest)* mune͚ 胸; *(woman's)* chichi͚ 乳, [*baby talk, slang*] o͚ppai おっぱい; **~ cancer** nyū͚-gan 乳がん・乳癌
breath i͚ki 息; **a breath** hito͚-iki 一息; **draws/takes one's last ~** i͚ki o hiki-torima͚su (-to͚ru, -to͚tte) 息を引き取ります(取る, 取って)
breathe i͚ki o shima͚su (suru, shite) 息をします(する, して); kokyū shima͚su (suru, shite) 呼吸します(する, して)
breathe a sigh of relief ho͚tto shima͚su (suru, shite) ほっとします(する, して)
breathe (it) in (... o) suima͚su (suu, sutte) (...を)吸います(吸う, 吸って)
breechcloth fundoshi ふんどし・褌
breeze (soyo͚)kaze (そよ)風; **shoots the ~** daberima͚su

(dabe'ru, dabe'tte) だべります
(だべる, だべって)

brewery jōzō-sho⌐¬ 醸造所

bribe(ry) wa'iro わいろ・賄賂

bric-a-brac oki-mono 置物

brick re'nga れんが・煉瓦

bride hana'-yome 花嫁, (o-)yome
(san) (お)嫁(さん)

bridegroom (hana-)mu'ko (o-
mu'ko san) (花)婿(お婿さん)

bridge hashi' 橋; *(iron)* tekkyō 鉄
橋

**bridge: the bridges on a Japanese
harp** koto⌐¬-ji 琴柱

bridle baroku 馬勒

brief *(short)* mijika'i 短い; *(simple)* kantan (na) 簡単(な);
briefly *(in brief)* zatto ざっと

briefcase kaban かばん

brigade ryo'dan 旅団

brigadier general daishō 代将,
ju'nshō 准将

bright akaru⌐¬i 明るい, *(sunny)*
hoga'raka (na) 朗らか(な),
(colorful) hana'yaka (na) 華や
か(な), *(gaudy)* hade' (na) は
で・派手(な); *(of spirit)* yōki
(na) 陽気(な)

bring *(a thing)* motte/to'tte
kima'su (ku'ru, kite') 持って/
取って来ます(来る, 来て);
(a person) tsurete kima'su
(ku'ru, kite') 連れて来ます(来
る, 来て). — *But* **"bring to
you/them"** … ikima'su (iku,
itte) …行きます(行く, 行って)

bring about okoshima'su
(oko'su, oko'shite) 起こしま
す(起こす, 起こして); shō-
jima'su (shō-ji'ru, shō⌐¬-jite)
生じます(生じる, 生じて);
genjitsu⌐¬-ka shima'su (suru,
shite) 現実化します(する, し
て)

bring close/near chika-
zukema'su (-zuke'ru, -zu'kete)
近付けます(付ける, 付けて),
yosema'su (yoseru, yosete) 寄
せます(寄せる, 寄せて)

bring up *(= rears)* sodatema'su
(sodate'ru, soda'tete) 育てま
す(育てる, 育てて);
yashinaima'su (yashinau,
yashinatte) 養います(養う,
養って); yōiku shima'su
(suru, shite) 養育します(する,
して); *(trains)* shitsukema'su
(shitsuke'ru, shitsu'kete) しつ
けます(しつける, しつけて)

brink kiwa' 際

Britain → England

British → English

brittle moro'i もろい

broad hiro'i 広い

broadcast hōsō (shima'su; suru,
shite) 放送(します; する, し
て)

broadcasting station hōsō'-
kyoku 放送局

brocade ni'shiki 錦

broil yakima'su (yaku, yaite) 焼
きます(焼く, 焼いて)

broiled foods yaki-mono 焼物; **broiled salt-coated fish** shio-ya⌐ki⌐ 塩焼き

broken (*not working*) dame⌐ desu̱ (da/na, de, ni) だめ[駄目]です(だ/な, で, に); koshō shi̱ta 故障した

brokenhearted: gets ~ shitsuren shima⌐su̱ (suru, shi̱te) 失恋します(する, して)

broker burō⌐kā ブローカー, naka⌐gai 仲買い, nakadachi⌐ 仲立ち

brokerage (*commission*) sa⌐ya さや

bronze seidō 青銅

brook ogawa 小川

broom hō⌐ki ほうき

broth shi̱⌐ru シール

brothel jorō-ya 女郎屋

brother otoko no kyō⌐dai 男の兄弟; (*older*) (o-)ni̱⌐i-san （お）兄さん, a⌐ni 兄; (*younger*) otōto⌐ 弟, otōto-san 弟さん

brother-in-law gi̱⌐ri no a⌐ni/otōto⌐ (kyō⌐dai) 義理の兄/弟(兄弟)

brothers and sisters kyō⌐dai 兄弟・きょうだい

brought up: gets ~ (*is reared*) sodachima⌐su̱ (soda⌐tsu, soda⌐tte) 育ちます(育つ, 育って)

brow (*eyebrow*) ma⌐yu 眉; (*forehead*) hi̱tai 額

brown cha-iro (no) 茶色（の）

brown bread kuro-pan 黒パン

bruise uchi̱⌐-ki̱⌐zu 打ち傷, uchi̱⌐-mi̱⌐ 打ち身, dabo⌐ku̱⌐-shō 打撲傷

brush bu̱⌐rashi ブラシ, hake⌐ はけ・刷毛; (*for writing or painting*) fude 筆

brush aside haraima⌐su̱ (hara⌐u, hara⌐tte) 払います(払う, 払って)

brushwood shiba 柴

brusque bu-a⌐isō (na) 無愛想(な), bukki̱⌐ra⌐bō (na) ぶっきらぼう(な)

Brussels sprouts me-kya⌐betsu 芽キャベツ

brutal mugo⌐i むごい, zankoku (na) 残酷(な), zangyaku (na) 残虐(な), zannin (na) 残忍(な)

bubble awa⌐ 泡, abuku⌐ あぶく; (*soap*) shabon-dama シャボン玉

bubble gum fūsen-ga⌐mu 風船ガム

bucket baketsu バケツ, o⌐ke 桶; (*rice*) (o-)hachi お鉢, (o-)hitsu おひつ・お櫃, meshi̱⌐-bitsu 飯びつ・飯櫃

buckle shimc⌐-gane 締め金, ba⌐kkuru バックル

buck private heisotsu 兵卒

buck tooth do⌐ppa 出っ歯, so⌐ppa 反っ歯

buckwheat chaff soba-gara そばがら

buckwheat noodles (o-)so⌐ba

（お）そば・（お）蕎麦

bud *(of leaf)* me⌐ (o-me) 芽（お芽）;
(of flower) tsubomi つぼみ・蕾

Buddha Hotoke-sa⌐ma 仏様,
(Sakyamuni) Sha⌐ka 釈迦 =
o-Shaka-sa⌐ma お釈迦様;
(= statue of ～) Butsu-zō 仏
像

Buddhism Bu⌐kkyō⌐ 仏教

Buddhist priest (o-)bō-san （お）
坊さん, bō⌐zu 坊主, sō⌐ryo 僧
侶

Buddhist temple tera⌐ 寺, o-tera
お寺

budding willow aoyagi 青やぎ・
青柳 = aoya⌐nagi 青柳

buddy → **friend**

budge → **move**

budget yosan 予算

bug mushi 虫 (1 ip-piki⌐ 一匹,
2 ni⌐-hiki 二匹, 3 sa⌐m-biki
三匹; **how many** na⌐m-biki 何
匹)

bugle rappa らっぱ

build *(erects)* tatema⌐su (tate⌐ru,
ta⌐tete) 建てます（建てる、建
てて）; *(creates)* tsukurima⌐su
(tsuku⌐ru, tsuku⌐tte) 造ります
（造る、造って）

build: body ～ taikaku 体格

building tate⌐-mo⌐no 建物,
bi⌐rudi⌐ngu ビルディング;
(public hall) kaikan 会館

building lot shiki-chi 敷地

bulb tama⌐ 玉; *(= light ～)*
denkyū 電球

bulge fukurami ふくらみ・膨ら
み

bulk kasa⌐ かさ; **in ～** ba⌐ra de ば
らで

bull *(= **bullshit**)* baka-/muda-
ba⌐nashi ばか/無駄話, *(brag-
ging)* ho⌐ra ほら; **shoots the ～**
daberima⌐su (dabe⌐ru,
dabe⌐tte) だべります（だべる、
だべって）, muda-ba⌐nashi o
shima⌐su (suru, shite) 無駄話
をします（する、して）　「ー

bulldozer burudō⌐za ブルドーザ

bullet tama⌐ 弾, dangan 弾丸

bulletin board keiji-ban 掲示板

bullet train (line) shinka⌐nsen 新
幹線; **... ～ station** shi⌐n ...⌐-
eki 新...駅

bum *(hobo)* furō⌐-sha 浮浪者,
ru⌐mpen ルンペン

bump *(swelling)* kobu⌐ こぶ・瘤;
(in road) dekoboko でこぼこ・
凸凹; **(with) bumps** bo⌐tsubo-
tsu (ga dekite) ぼつぼつ（がで
きて）

bump into ... ni butsukarima⌐su
(butsukaru, butsukatte) ...に
ぶつかります（ぶつかる、ぶ
つかって）; *(happens to meet)*
de-aima⌐su (-a⌐u, -a⌐tte) 出
会います（会う、会って）

bun: *(steamed)* manjū まんじゅ
う, *(pork-stuffed)* niku-man
肉まん, *(beanjam-stuffed)*
am-man あんまん

bunch *(cluster)* fusa⌐ 房; *(pile)*

yama 山; *(bundle)* ta'ba 束; *(group)* mure 群れ

bundle tsutsumi 包み; *(bunch)* ta'ba 束

bungle he'ma (o shima'su; suru, shite) へま(をします; する, して)

bunion mame まめ, soko-mame 底まめ

bunk *(bed)* shindai 寝台

burden ni 荷, *(on one's mind)* omo-ni 重荷

burdock (root) gobō ごぼう

bureau *(department)* kyo'ku 局, ...-kyoku ...局; *(chest)* tansu たんす

burglar dorobō 泥棒・どろぼう

burglar alarm bōham-be'ru 防犯 ベル

burial maisō 埋葬

buried → **bury**

burlesque sutori'ppu ストリップ

Burma Bi'ruma ビルマ

burn 1. *(it burns)* yakema'su (yakeru, yakete) 焼けます(焼 ける, 焼けて); *(fire burns)* moema'su (moeru, moete) 燃 えます(燃える, 燃えて) 2. *(burns it)* yakima'su (yaku, yaite) 焼きます(焼く, 焼いて); *(burns a fire; wood, coal)* takima'su (taku, taite) 焚きま す(焚く, 焚いて), *(burns a light)* tomoshima'su (tomo'su, tomo'shite) ともし[点し]ます (ともす, ともして)

burn: a burn (on the skin) yakedo やけど・火傷

burp ge'ppu (o shima'su; suru, shite) げっぷ(をします; する, して)

burst *(it bursts)* yaburema'su (yabure'ru, yabu'rete) 破れま す(破れる, 破れて), *(explodes)* bakuhatsu shima'su (suru, shite) 爆発します(する, して); *(bursts it)* yaburima'su (yabu'ru, yabu'tte) 破ります (破る, 破って)

burst out tobi-dashima'su (-da'su, -da'shite) 飛び出しま す(出す, 出して)

bury uzumema'su (uzumeru, uzumete) うずめます・埋めま す(うずめる, うずめて), umema'su/mmema'su (umeru/mmeru, umete/ mmete) 埋めます(埋める, 埋めて); **gets buried** uzumarima'su (uzumaru, uzumatte) うずまります・埋ま ります(うずまる, うずまっ て), umarima'su/mmarima'su (umaru/mmaru, umatte/ mmatte) 埋まります(埋まる, 埋まって)

bus ba'su バス (**how many** na'n-dai 何台)

bush kamboku 潅木・灌木

Bushido bushi'-dō 武士道

bush warbler ugu'isu うぐいす・ 鶯・鴬

business *(job)* shigoto (o-shi͡goto) 仕事(お仕事), *(line of trade)* shō͡bai 商売; *(office work)* ji͡mu 事務; *(transaction)* to͡ri͡-hiki 取り引き・取引; *(errand)* yōji 用事, (go-)yo͡ (ご)用, yō-ta͡shi͡ 用足し; *(enterprise)* ji͡gyō 事業, jitsugyō 実業; *(commerce)* shō͡gyō 商業; **having no ~** mu͡yō (no) 無用(の)

business concern kaisha 会社

business conditions keiki 景気

business hours eigyō-ji͡kan 営業時間

businessman jitsugyō-ka 実業家

business suit sebiro 背広

business trip shu͡tchō 出張

bus information booth ba͡su no annai-jo͡ バスの案内所

bus stop teiryū-jo͡ 停留所; (ba͡su no) nori-ba (バスの)乗り場

bust → burst

bustling nigi͡yaka (na) にぎやか(な)

busy isogashi͡i 忙しい, sewashi͡i せわしい; [*bookish*] tabō (na) 多忙(な); **gets ~** (= *work-jammed*) tsukaema͡su (tsuka͡e͡ru, tsuka͡ete) つかえます・支えます(つかえる, つかえて); *(in the midst of work)* shigoto-chū 仕事中, *(in conference)* kaigi-chū 会議中; **The line is busy** (O-)hanashi-chū de͡su. (お)話し中です.

but shika͡shi しかし, de͡ mo でも, da͡tte だって, tokoro͡-ga ところが; ... ga ...が, (...) ke͡redo(-mo) (...)けれど(も), ... tokoro͡ ga ...ところが; ippō 一方

butcher knife niku͡kiri-bo͡chō 肉切り包丁

butcher (shop) niku͡-ya 肉屋

butt 1. *(cigarette, cigar)* suigara 吸いがら **2. → buttock**

butter ba͡ta バタ, ba͡tā バター; **~ roll** bata-rō͡ru バタロール

butterfly chō͡ ちょう・蝶, chō͡chō ちょうちょう・蝶蝶, chō͡cho ちょうちょ

buttock shiri͡ (o-shiri) 尻(お尻), ketsu けつ

button 1. bo͡tan ボタン **2.** *(buttons it)* ... no bo͡tan o kakema͡su (kake͡ru, ka͡kete) ...のボタンをかけます(かける, かけて)

buy kaima͡su (kau, katte) 買います(買う, 買って); motomema͡su (motome͡ru, moto͡mete) 求めます(求める, 求めて)

buyer kai-te 買い手; *(professional)* ba͡iyā バイヤー

buy up kai-torima͡su (-to͡ru, -to͡tte) 買い取ります(取る, 取って)

buzzer bu͡zā ブザー

by *(no later than)* ... ma͡de ni ... までに; **by ... at the latest** ...

ma゛de ni wa ...までには
by: gets by *(lives)* kurashima゛su
(kurasu, kurashite) 暮らしま
す(暮らす, 暮らして)
by and by → **soon**
by chance hyo゛tto ひょっと,
gūzen ni 偶然に, futo ふと
bye(-bye) → **good-bye**
by far zutto ずっと; ha゛ruka (ni)
はるか(に)
by heart/memory so゛ra de そら
で·空で
by itself, by nature hitori-de ni
ひとりでに·独りでに,

motomoto もともと·元々,
mo゛to゛-yori もと[元]より
by (means of) ... de ...で
by oneself jibun de 自分で
bystander hata no mono゛ はた
[端]の者
by the way *(incidentally)* sore wa
so゛ to それはそうと, tokoro゛-
de ところで, chi⌐nami ni ち
なみに, tsuide ni ついでに,
toki゛ ni 時に
by (way of) ... o to゛tte ...を通っ
て; *(via)* ... ke⌐iyu (de/no) ...
経由(で/の)

— C —

cab → **taxi**
cabaret kya゛barē キャバレー
cabbage kya゛betsu キャベツ;
(Chinese) hakusa⌐i 白菜
cabin koya⌐ 小屋; *(mountain
lodge)* yama-goya 山小屋
cabinet *(government)* na゛ikaku
内閣
cable tsuna゛ 綱, kē゛buru ケーブ
ル; *(telegram)* kaigai-de゛mpō
海外電報 「ー
cable car kēburu゛-kā゛ ケーブルカ
cactus sabuten サボテン,
shaboten シャボテン
cafe *(coffee shop)* kōhi⌐i-ten コ
ーヒー店, kissa⌐-ten 喫茶店;
(restaurant) ryōri゛-ten 料理店

cage *(for bird)* kago かご·籠,
tori-kago 鳥かご·鳥籠; *(for
animal)* ori゛ おり·檻
cahoots: in ~ with ... to
takura゛nde ...と企んで
cake 1. kē゛ki ケーキ, (o-)ka゛shi
(お)菓子; *(Japanese)* o-ka゛shi
お菓子, wa-ga゛shi 和菓子;
(spongecake) kasutera カステ
ラ; *(rice)* mochi もち·餅
2. it (mud) cakes (doro゛ ga)
katamarima゛su (katamaru,
katamatte) (泥が)固まります
(固まる, 固まって)
3. → **bar (of soap)**
calamity saina゛n 災難, wazawai
災い

calculate keisan shima͏̄su (suru, shite) 計算します(する，して)

calculation keisan 計算

calculator keia͏̄n-ki 計算機

calendar koyomi͏̄ 暦; kare͏̄ndā カレンダー

calisthenics taisō 体操

call yobima͏̄su (yobu, yonde) 呼びます(呼ぶ，呼んで); *(phone)* denwa o shima͏̄su (suru, shite) 電話をします(する，して); (~ **on**) → **visit**; ~ **to mind** → **recall**

call 1. *(phone ~)* denwa 電話 **2.** *(visit)* hōmon 訪問, *(of solicitude)* (o-)mimai (お)見舞い

called: is ~ ... to iima͏̄su (yū, itte/yutte) ...と言います(言う，言って/ゆって); **a fish called carp** ko͏̄i to iū sakana こい[鯉]という魚

caller *(visitor)* raikyaku 来客

calligraphy sho͏̄dō 書道; *(handwriting practice)* shūji (o-shū͏̄ji) 習字(お習字)

calling card meishi 名刺

calling-card case meishi͏̄-ire 名刺入れ

callus ta͏̄ko たこ

calm *(quiet)* shi͏̄zuka (na) 静か(な), oda͏̄yaka (na) 穏やか(な), no͏̄doka (na) のどか(な); **gets calm** shizumarima͏̄su (shizuma͏̄ru, shizuma͏̄tte) 静まります(静まる，静まって);

calms, makes calm shizumema͏̄su (shizume͏̄ru, shizu͏̄mete) 静めます(静める，静めて); **calms down** *(= regains composure)* ochi-tsukima͏̄su (ochi-tsuku, ochi-tsuite) 落ち着きます(落ち着く，落ち着いて)

calmly ochi-tsuite 落ち着いて; *(unperturbed)* heiki de 平気で

came: → **come**

camel rakuda らくだ・駱駝

camellia tsu͏̄baki つばき・椿

camera shashi͏̄n-ki 写真機, ka͏̄mera カメラ

camp kya͏̄mpu (o shima͏̄su; suru, shite) キャンプ(をします; する，して); *(bivouac)* yaei 野営

campus kōtei 校庭, kya͏̄mpasu キャンパス; *(within the university)* daigaku͏̄-kōnai 大学構内

can 1. *(tin can)* ka͏̄n 缶 (**1** i͏̄p-pon 一本, **2** ni͏̄-hon 二本, **3** sa͏̄m-bon 三本, **how many** na͏̄m-bon 何本) **2. cans it** (ka͏̄n ni) tsumema͏̄su (tsume͏̄ru, tsu͏̄mete) (缶に)詰めます(詰める，詰めて)

can *(can do it)* (... ga) dekima͏̄su (deki͏̄ru, de͏̄kite) (...が)出来ます(出来る，出来て), (suru) koto͏̄ ga dekima͏̄su (する)事が出来ます; (... ga) kanaima͏̄su (kana͏̄u, kana͏̄tte)

(...が)叶います(叶う, 叶っ
て)

USAGE: Da⌐re ga(/ni) na⌐ni ga
dekima⌐su ka 誰が(/に)何が
出来ますか **Who can do
what?** NOTE: *A potential
("can") version of almost
every verb can be made by
replacing ...-ru ...る with ...
-(ra)reru ...(ら)れる, or ...-u ...
う with ...-eru ...える. Most of
the potentials will be found in
the Japanese-English section.
Some Japanese frown upon
the ...-reru ...れる forms, and
use only the longer ...-rareru...
られる; some use ...-areru ...
あれる (for ...-eru ...える) as
well as ...-rareru (= ...-reru) ...
られる(=...れる).*

can: can see (... ga) miema⌐su
(mie⌐ru, mi⌐ete) (...が)見えま
す(見える, 見えて); **can hear**
(... ga) kikoema⌐su (kikoeru,
kikoete) (...が)聞こえます(聞
こえる, 聞こえて)

Canada Ka⌐nada カナダ; **Cana-
dian** Kanada⌐-jin カナダ人

canal horiwari 掘り割り・掘割,
u⌐nga 運河

canary kanari(y)a カナリア[ヤ]

cancel tori-keshima⌐su (-ke⌐su,
-ke⌐shite) 取り消します(消す,
消して); keshima⌐su (kesu,
keshite) 消します(消す, 消し
て)

cancellation mark/stamp keshi-
in 消印

**cancelled flight, flight cancella-
tion** kekkō 欠航

cancer ga⌐n がん・癌; *(lung)* hai-
gan 肺がん・肺癌; *(stomach)*
i⌐-gan 胃がん・胃癌; *(breast)*
nyū⌐-gan 乳がん・乳癌

candidate kibō⌐-sha 希望者

candid(ly) o⌐pun (no/ni) オープ
ン(の/に); → **frank**

candle rōso⌐ku ろうそく

candy (o-)ka⌐shi (お)菓子,
kya⌐ndē キャンデー, *(wheat-
gluten)* ame あめ; **(how many
pieces** na⌐n-ko 何個)

candy store kashi⌐-ya 菓子屋

cane 1. *(walking stick)* sute⌐kki
ステッキ; *(staff)* tsu⌐e 杖
2. *(= rattan)* tō⌐ 籐

canned beer kam-bi⌐iru 缶ビール

canned (food) (... no) kan-
zu⌐me⌐ (...の)缶詰; **canned
pineapple** pai-kan パイ缶

cannon taihō 大砲

cannot dekimase⌐n (deki⌐nai) で
き[出来]ません(でき[出来]
ない); (shi)-kiremase⌐n
(-kire⌐nai) (し)切れません(切
れない); ~ **stand it** ga⌐man
dekimase⌐n (deki⌐nai) がまん
[我慢]でき[出来]ない), tamarimase⌐n
(tamaranai) たまりません(た
まらない)

can opener kan-ki⌐ri⌐ 缶切り

canvas (*material*) zuʼkku ズック；
~ **shoes** zukkuʼ-gutsu ズック
靴

cap 1. → **hat 2.** (*of a pen*)
kyaʼppu キャップ **3.** (*of a bottle*) kyaʼppu キャップ, ōkan
王冠 **4.** (*of a mushroom*) kaʼsa
かさ・笠

cape (*promontory*) miⁿsaki 岬

capital (*city*) shuʼfu 首府, shuʼtoʼ
首都, miyako 都

capital (*money*) shihon 資本

capitalism shihon-shuʼgi 資本主
義

capitalist shihon-ka 資本家

capsule kaʼpuseru カプセル

captain (*army*) taʼii 大尉; (*navy*)
daisa (*or* taisa) 大佐; (*airplane*) kichōʼ 機長; (*ship*)
seʼnchō 船長, (*warship*)
kaⁿnchō 艦長

caption midashi 見出し

capture toraemaʼsu (toraʼeru,
toraʼete) 捕らえます(捕らえ
る, 捕らえて)

car kuruma (o-kuʼruma) 車(お車),
jidōⁿ-sha 自動車 (**how many**
naʼn-dai 何台); **Car Number
(Six)** (roku)-gōʼsha (六)号車;
what (number) car nan-gōʼsha
何号車

caramel kyarameru キャラメル

car barn shaʼko 車庫

carbolic acid sekitan-san 石炭酸

carbonic acid tansan 炭酸「ター

carburetor kyabureʼtā キャブレ

card fuda 札, kāʼdo カード；
(*playing card*) toraʼmpu (ichiʼ-
mai) トランプ(一枚); (*calling
card, name card*) meishi 名刺;
(*postcard*) hagaki (o-haʼgaki)
はがき・葉書(おはがき・お葉
書); **New Year's card** nengaⁿ-
jō 年賀状; (**how many** naʼm-
mai 何枚)

cardboard bōru-gami ボール紙;
(*corrugated*) dam-bōʼru 段ボ
ール

care (*caution*) yōjin 用心, neʼn 念;
(*upkeep*) te-ireʼ 手入れ

care: take ~ of (*a person*) ... no
sewaʼ (o-seʼwa) o shimaʼsu
(suru, shite) ...の世話(お世
話)をします(する, して), ...
no mendōʼ o mimaʼsu (miʼru,
miʼte) ...の面倒を見ます(見る,
見て); (*a matter*) ... o shoʼri
shima(ⁿ)su (suru, shite) ...を
処理します(する, して)

career shokuʼgyō 職業; (*history*)
keireki 経歴, (*summary,
resume*) rireki 履歴

care for → **like, love, want;** →
look after

carefree kiraku (na) 気楽(な),
noʼnki (na) のんき(な)

careful (go-)teʼinei (na) (ご)丁寧
(な); **is ~** ki o tsukemaʼsu
(tsukeʼru, tsukeʼte) 気を付け
ます(付ける, 付けて); neʼn o
iremaʼsu (ireru, irete) 念を入
れます(入れる, 入れて);

chūi-buka'i 注意深い

careless muto'n-chaku/-jaku (na) 無頓着/着(な), zusan/ zuzan (na) ずさん/ずざん(な), zonza'i (na) ぞんざい(な), taiman (na) 怠慢(な), fuchū'i (na) 不注意(な)

carelessly (*casually*) muzo'sa ni 無造作に

carelessness fuchū'i 不注意, yudan 油断

caretaker (*while one is away*) rusu-ban 留守番

carp (*fish*) ko'i こい・鯉; ~ **streamers (for the Boys' Festival)** koi-no'bori こいのぼ り

carpenter da'iku 大工

carpet jū'tan じゅうたん・絨毯, kā'pe'tto カーペット

carrot ninjin にんじん・人参

carry motte/to'tte ikima'su (iku, itte) 持って/取って行きます (行く, 行って); (*loads aboard*) nosema'su (noseru, nosete) 載せます(載せる, 載 せて); (*conveys*) hakobima'su (hakobu, hakonde) 運びます (運ぶ, 運んで)

carry (*dangling from the hand*) sagema'su (sage'ru, sa'gete) 提 げます(提げる, 提げて)

carry on one's back/shoulders shoima'su (shou, shotte) しょ います(しょう, しょって), ninaima'su (nina'u, nina'tte) 担います(担う, 担って),

katsugima'su (katsu'gu, katsu'ide) 担ぎ[かつぎ]ます (担ぐ, 担いで); (*piggyback*) oima'su (o'u, o'tte) 負い ます(負う, 負って), obuima'su (obu'u, obu'tte) おぶ[負ぶ] います(おぶう, おぶって), o'mbu shima'(')su (suru, shite) おんぶ[負んぶ]します (する, して)

carry out (= *performs*) okonaima'su (okonau, okonatte) 行います(行う, 行って); (*brings about*) genjitsu'-ka shima'su (suru, shite) 現実化します(する, し て)

carsick: gets ~ yoima'su (yo'u, yo'tte) 酔います(酔う, 酔っ て)

cart te-gu'ruma 手車, kuruma 車

carton → box

cartoon manga 漫画・まんが

carve kizamima'su (kizamu, kizande) 刻みます(刻む, 刻 んで), horima'su (ho'ru, ho'tte) 彫ります(彫る, 彫っ て)

carving hori'-mo'no' 彫り物, chōkoku 彫刻; ~ **knife** nikukiri-bo'chō 肉切り包丁

case 1. (*situation*) ba(w)ai 場合, ... wa'ke ...訳, (*event*) ...da'n ... 段; (*matter*) koto' 事, (*particular instance*) ke'su ケース; ~ **by** ~ kēsu-bai-ke'su ケー

ス・バイ・ケース; **in that ~**
sonna̲ra そんなら; *(sore)* de̲
wa（それ）では, ja じゃ, jā
じゃあ **2.** *(box)* hako 箱

case: in ~ of ... ni sa̲i-shite ...に
際して; ... no baai/toki̲ ni ...
の場合/時に

cash (a check) genki̲n ni hi̲ki-
kaema̲su (-kae̲ru, -ka̲ete) 現
金に引き換えます（換える,
換えて）*or* shima̲su (suru,
shite) します（する, して）

cashbox kane-bako 金箱

cash envelope (registered mail)
genkin-ka̲kitome 現金書留

cashier kanjō-ga̲kari 勘定係,
suitō-ga̲kari 出納係, re̲ji レジ

cash (into smaller bills/coins)
komaka̲ku shima̲su (suru,
shite) 細かくします（する, し
て）, kuzushima̲su (kuzu̲su,
kuzu̲shite) くずします・崩し
ます（くずす, くずして）

cash (money) gen-nama 現なま,
genki̲n 現金, shōkin 賞金; **petty ~** sa̲sai na kane ささいな
金

cask taru たる・樽

castle (o-)shiro（お)城; ...-jō ...
城

casual nanige-na̲i 何気ない

casually *(effortlessly; carelessly)*
muzō̲sa ni 無造作に

casualty *(injury, damage)* hi̲gai
被害; *(victim)* higa̲i-sha 被害
者; *(dead and wounded)*
shishō̲-sha 死傷者

cat ne̲ko 猫 **(1** ip-pi̲ki̲ 一匹,
2 ni̲-hiki 二匹, **3** sa̲m-biki 三
匹, **how many** na̲m-biki 何匹)

catalog mokuroku 目録; *(directory)* meibo 名簿

catch *(= seizes)* tsukamaema̲su
(tsu̲kamaeru, tsu̲kamaete) 捕
まえます（捕まえる, 捕まえ
て）; torima̲su (to̲ru, to̲tte) 取
ります（取る, 取って）; *(= at-
tracts)* hikima̲su (hi̲ku, hiite)
引きます（引く, 引いて）

catch (a disease) (byōki ni)
kakarima̲su (kaka̲ru,
kaka̲tte)（病気に）かかります
（かかる, かかって）; **catch a
cold** kaze o hikima̲su (hi̲ku,
hiite) かぜ［風邪］をひきます
（ひく, ひいて）, [HONORIFIC]
kaze o o-meshi ni narima̲su
(na̲ru, na̲tte) かぜ［風邪］をお
召しになります（なる, なっ
て）

catch up (with) (... ni) oi-
tsukima̲su (-tsuku̲, -tsu̲ite)
(...に)追い付きます（付く,
付いて）

caterer, catering shop shidashi-
ya 仕出し屋

catering *(food delivered to
order)* (o-)demae（お)出前

caterpillar kemushi̲ 毛虫

catfish namazu なまず・鯰

Catholic Katori̲kku カトリック

cattle ushi 牛 **(how many** na̲n-tō
何頭)

cauldron kama かま・釜・罐

cause *(of an effect)* moto¬ 元, gen'in 原因; *(effect)* ... se¬i ... せい; *(source)* ta¬ne 種; *(reason)* wa¬ke 訳, riyū 理由; *(purpose, benefit)* tame ため・為¬

cause (one) concern/worry (... ni) shimpai o kakema¬su (kake¬ru, ka¬kete) (...に)心配をかけます(かける, かけて)

cause (one) trouble (... ni) me¬iwaku o kakema¬su (kake¬ru, ka¬kete) (...に)迷惑をかけます(かける, かけて)

cause (someone to do) ... ni sasema¬su (saseru, sasete) ...にさせます(させる, させて)

caution 1. yōjin 用心; *(precaution)* yo¬i 用意, ne¬n 念; **as (a word of) caution** nen no tame¬ (ni) 念のため[為](に) **2.** *(warns)* keikai shima¬su (suru, shite) 警戒します(する, して)

cautious yōjin-buka¬i 用心深い

cave hora-ana 洞穴・ほら穴, ho¬ra¬ 洞・ほら; ...-dō ...洞

caviar *(roe)* i¬kura イクラ; *(salmon/trout roe)* suji¬ko¬ 筋子, suzu¬ko¬ すずこ; *(cod roe)* tara¬ko¬ たらこ

cease yamima¬su (yamu, yande) 止みます(止む, 止んで), taema¬su (tae¬ru, ta¬ete) 絶えます(絶える, 絶えて)

cedar: cryptomeria, Japanese cedar sugi 杉

cede yuzurima¬su (yuzuru, yuzutte) 譲ります(譲る, 譲って)

ceiling tenjō(-i¬ta) 天井(板)

celebrate iwaima¬su (iwa¬u, iwa¬tte) 祝います(祝う, 祝って)

celebration *(party)* iwa¬i (o-iwai) 祝い(お祝い)

celery se¬rori セロリ; **Japanese ~** u¬do うど・独活

cellar *(storehouse)* kura 倉; *(basement)* chika¬-shitsu 地下室

cello che¬ro チェロ

cellophane se¬rohan セロハン

cement semento セメント; **~ floor** tataki¬ たたき・三和土

cemetery haka-ba¬ 墓場, bo¬chi 墓地

censor(ship) ken'etsu 検閲

censure 1. *(blame)* hi¬nan 非難 **2.** *(blames one)* hi¬nan shima(¬)su (suru, shite) 非難します(する, して), semema¬su (seme¬ru, se¬mete) 責めます(責める, 責めて)

cent se¬nto セント; **per cent** pāse¬nto パーセント

center mannaka 真ん中, chūō¬ 中央, chūshin 中心; *(institution)* se¬ntā センター

centimeter se¬nchi センチ,

senchi-mḗtoru センチメートル

centipede mukade むかで・百足

central mannaka no 真ん中の, chūshin no 中心の, chūō⌐ no 中央の; **~ office** hoⁿbu 本部

central area chūshiⁿ-chi 中心地

century hyakū-nen 百年, seⁱki 世紀

ceramics *(ceramic art)* tōgei 陶芸; *(ceramic ware)* tōⁱki 陶器; *(pottery)* yaki-mono 焼き物

cereal kokuⁱmotsu 穀物, kokuⁱrui 穀類

ceremony shikiⁱ 式

certain taⁱshika (na) 確か(な); kakujitsu (na) 確実(な); *(specific, particular)* aⁱru … ある…

certainly mochiⁱron もちろん; taⁱshika ni 確かに; maⁱsa-ni 正に

certainty kakujitsu 確実, kakujitsu-sei 確実性

certificate shōme⌐i-sho⌐ 証明書

certification shōmei 証明

certified kōnin (no) 公認(の); **~ public accountant (CPA)** kōnin-kaikeⁱishi 公認会計士

certify shōmei shimaⁱsu (suru, shite) 証明します(する, して)

cesspool osui-dame 汚水溜め, gesui-dame 下水溜め

Ceylon Se⌐iron セイロン = **Sri Lanka** Suriraⁿka スリランカ

chaff momigara もみ殻

chain kusari 鎖; **~ of islands** rettō 列島; **(linked) in a ~** tsunagatte つながって

chair isu 椅子・いす, koshi-kaⁱke 腰掛け

chalk chōⁱku チョーク **(1 piece of ~** iⁱp-pon 一本, **2** niⁱ-hon 二本, **3** saⁱm-bon 三本, **how many** naⁱm-bon 何本)

chamberpot oma⌐ru おまる

champagne shampaⁿ シャンパン, shampeⁿ シャンペン

championship yūshō 優勝

champion sumo wrestler ōⁱ-zeki 大関; **grand ~** yokozuna 横綱

chance *(opportunity)* kikaⁱi 機会, chaⁿsu チャンス; *(impulse)* hazumi 弾み; → **by chance**

change *(small money)* komakaⁱi kane 細かい金, kozeni 小銭; *(money returned)* o-tsuri お釣り・おつり, tsuri⌐-sen 釣り銭

change 1. a change kawari (o-kawari) 変わり(お変わり), heⁿka 変化; *(in health)* o-kawari お変わり; *(abnormality)* ijō 異常; *(of trains)* nori-kae 乗り換え; *(of clothing)* kigae 着替え **2. it changes** kawarimaⁱsu (kawaru, kawatte) 変わります(変わる, 変わって); heⁿka shima(⌐)su (suru, shite) 変化します(する, して); utsurimaⁱsu (utsuⁱru, utsu̱'tte) 移ります(移る, 移って) **3. changes it** kaema̱'su (kaeru, kaete) 変えます(変える, 変えて); aratamema̱'su (aratame̱ru, arata̱'mete) 改めます(改める, 改めて)

4. changes (clothes) kigaema̱'su (kiga̱'e̱ru, kiga̱'ete) 着替えます(着替える, 着替えて)

5. changes (train, bus, plane) nori-kaema̱'su (-ka̱'e̱ru, -ka̱'ete) 乗り換えます(換える, 換えて)

chant utaima̱'su (utau, utatte) 歌い[謡い]ます(歌[謡]う, 歌[謡]って)

chanting: ~ **Buddhist scriptures** shō̱'myō̱' 声明; ~ **a Noh libretto** utai 謡, o-u̱'tai お謡

character *(quality)* seishitsu 性質; *(personal traits)* seikaku 性格; *(written)* ji̱' 字, mo̱'ji 文字

characteristic 1. *(an earmark)* toku̱shoku 特色, *(a distin-guishing ~)* tokuchō 特徴 **2.** *(typical)* daihyō-teki (na) 代表的(な)

charcoal sumi̱' 炭, mokuta̱'n 木炭; **charcoal brazier** (o-)hi̱'bachi (お)火鉢

charge 1. *(an attack)* shūgeki 襲撃, *(attacks)* shūgeki shima̱'su (suru, shite) 襲撃します(する, して) **2.** *(fee)* ryō̱'kin 料金, daikin 代金, ...-ryō ...料, ...

-dai ...代; *(with fee)* yūryō (no) 有料(の); **no charge** mu̱'ryō (no) 無料(の); **Is there a charge?** Yūryō de̱'su ka. 有料ですか.

charge: *(teacher)* in ~ tannin 担任; **takes (is in) ~ of** ... o tannin shima̱'su (suru, shite) ...を担当します(する, して); **takes (is in) partial ~ of** ... o buntan shima̱'su (suru, shite) ...を分担します(する, して)

charge (how much) (i̱'kura) shima̱'su (suru, shite) (いくら)します(する, して)

charity hodoko̱'shi̱' 施し, jizen 慈善; *(mercy)* megumi 恵み

charm *(good-luck piece)* o-mamori お守り; *(attraction)* mi̱'ryoku 魅力, *(attrac-tiveness)* aikyō̱' あいきょう・愛敬・愛嬌

charming: is ~ mi̱'ryoku/aikyō̱' ga arima̱'su (a̱'ru, a̱'tte) 魅力/あいきょう[愛嬌・愛敬]があります(ある, あって)

chart zuhyō 図表, zu 図

chartered: ~ **accountant** kōnin-kaike̱'ishi 公認会計士; ~ **plane** chātā̱-ki チャーター機; ~ **bus** kashikiri-ba̱'su 貸し切りバス

chase oi-kakema̱'su (-kake̱'ru, -ka̱'kete) 追いかけます(かける, かけて), oima̱'su (ou, otte)

追います(追う, 追って)

chaste teisetsu (na) 貞節(な)

chat sekem-ba⌐nashi 世間話, tachi-ba⌐nashi (o shima⌐su; suru, shite) 立ち話(をします; する, して); zadan 座談

chatter shaberima⌐su (shabe⌐ru, shabe⌐tte) しゃべります(しゃべる, しゃべって)

chatterbox o-sha⌐beri おしゃべり

chauffeur okakae unte⌐n-shu 運転手

cheap yasu⌐i 安い; **cheaper by ¥100** hyakue⌐n-yasu 百円安

cheat (deceives) damashima⌐su (dama⌐su, dama⌐shite) だまします(だます, だまして), gomakashima⌐su (gomaka⌐su, gomaka⌐shite) ごまかし[誤魔化し]ます(ごまかす, ごまかして); (dissembles, shirks, tricks) zu⌐ru o shima⌐su ずるをします; (on her husband) futei o hatarakima⌐su (hataraku, hataraite) 不貞をはたらきます(はたらく, はたらいて)

check: (a) check (bank) kogi⌐tte 小切手, (chit) fuda 札, (receipt, stub) chi⌐kki チッキ

check: (the) check (restaurant bill) kanjō⌐ (o-kanjō) 勘定(お勘定), dempyō 伝票, aiso⌐ (aisō⌐) あいそ・愛想(愛想) = o-aiso/-aiso おあいそ・お愛想/愛想; **Check please!** O-ikura

de⌐su ka. おいくらですか.

check: checks it 1. (baggage) azukema⌐su (azuke⌐ru, azu⌐kete) 預けます(預ける, 預けて), chi⌐kki ni shima⌐su (suru, shite) チッキにします (する, して) **2.** (investigates) shirabema⌐su (shirabe⌐ru, shira⌐bete) 調べます(調べる, 調べて); (inspects) ke⌐nsa shima(⌐)su (suru, shite) 検査します(する, して); (compares) terashima⌐su (tera⌐su, tera⌐shite) 照らします(照らす, 照らして)

check in (registers) chekku⌐in/ kichō shima⌐su (suru, shite) チェックイン/記帳します(する, して)

checking account tōza-yo⌐kin 当座預金

check out (of hotel) chekkua⌐uto shima(⌐)su (suru, shite) チェックアウトします(する, して), hiki-haraima⌐su (-hara⌐u, -hara⌐tte) 引き払います(払う, 払って)

check room (= cloakroom) kurō⌐ku クローク; azukari-jo⌐ 預かり所

check-up ke⌐nsa 検査

cheek hoppe⌐ta ほっぺた, hō⌐ 頬・ほお

cheer hazumima⌐su (hazumu, hazunde) 弾みます(弾む, 弾んで)

cheerful kigen ga i`i 機嫌がいい, hoga`raka (na) 朗らか・ほがらか(な), yōki (na) 陽気(な)

cheese chi`izu チーズ

cheesecloth kanre`isha 寒冷紗

chef (of Japanese food) itamae (san) 板前(さん)

chemicals kagaku-se`ihin 化学製品; *(pharmaceuticals)* yakuhin 薬品, kagaku-ya`kuhin 化学薬品

chemistry ka`gaku 化学 = bake⌐gaku 化学

cherish chō`hō shima(⌐)su (suru, shite) 重宝します(する, して), chōhō-garima`su (-ga`ru, -ga`tte) 重宝がります(がる, がって), daiji` ni shima`su (suru, shite) 大事にします(する, して)

cherry *(tree)* sakura 桜; *(fruit)* sakurambo さくらんぼ・桜んぼ

cherry blossoms sakura no hana` 桜の花

chess shōgi 将棋; **chessboard** shōgi-ban 将棋盤

chest *(of body)* mune` 胸; *(box)* hako 箱; ~ **of drawers** tansu たんす・箪笥

chestnut kuri` 栗; *(roasted)* yaki⌐ guri 焼キ栗

chew kamima`su (ka`mu, ka`nde) 噛[咬]みます(噛[咬]む, 噛[咬]んで); shaburima`su (shaburu, shabutte) しゃぶり

ます(しゃぶる, しゃぶって); ~ **the fat** *(idly talk)* daberima`su (dabe`ru, dabe`tte) だべります(だべる, だべって)

chiao-tze *(jiǎozi)* gyōza 餃子・ぎょうざ・ギョーザ

chic otsu (na) おつ[乙](な)

chicken tori 鶏・とり, niwatori 鶏・にわとり; ~ **(etc.) dipped into hot broth** mizutaki 水炊き; ~ **shishkebab** yaki-tori 焼き鳥・やきとり, **(shop)** yakitori-ya 焼き鳥屋

chief *(head)* chō 長, chōkan 長官, *(ringleader)* o`ya`-bun 親分, *(main)* shuyō (na) 主要(な), o`mo na 主な, hon-... 本...

chiefly mo⌐ppara 専ら・もっぱら, o`mo ni 主に

child kodomo 子供・こども・子ども, ko 子; **your child** o-ko-san お子さん

childhood kodomo no toki` 子供の時

childish osana`i 幼い; kodomoppoi 子供っぽい

children kodomo`-tachi 子供達; **Children's Day (5 May)** Kodomo no hi` こどもの日・子供の日

chilled wheat-flour noodles hiya-mu`gi ひやむぎ・冷麦

chill it hiyashima`su (hiya`su, hiya`shite) 冷やします(冷やす, 冷やして)

chilly samu⌐i 寒い
chimney entotsu 煙突; ~ **pot** shabu-shabu しゃぶしゃぶ
chin ago⌐ あご・顎
China Chū⌐goku 中国; [*old-fashioned*] Shī⌐na 支那
china(ware) setomono 瀬戸物
Chinese (*language*) Chūgoku-go 中国語; (*person*) Chūgoku⌐-jin 中国人
Chinese: cabbage (*bok choi*) hakusa⌐i 白菜
  character kanji 漢字, ji⌐ 字
  cooking chūka-ryō⌐ri 中華料理
  egg rolls haru-maki 春巻
  fried rice chā⌐han チャーハン
  meatballs niku-da⌐ngo 肉団子
  noodles rā⌐men ラーメン; (*with tidbits*) gomoku-so⌐ba 五目そば
  pickles zāsai ザーサイ
  restaurant chūka-ryōrī⌐-ten 中華料理店
  word/vocabulary (*in Japanese*) kango 漢語
chip (*of wood*) ko⌐ppa⌐ 木っ端; (*crack*) kizu 傷
chisel no⌐mi のみ・鑿
chitbook kayoi 通い, tsūchō 通帳
chives asa⌐tsuki あさつき・浅葱
chlorine e⌐nso 塩素
chocolate chokorē⌐to チョコレート
chocolate bar ita-choko 板チョコ

chocolate milk choko-mi⌐ruku チョコミルク
chocolate shake choko-sē⌐ki チョコセーキ
choice (*selection*) sentaku 選択; (*best-quality*) jōtō (na) 上等 (な)
choir kō⌐rasu コーラス
choke (*he chokes*) i⌐ki ga tsumarima⌐su (tsuma⌐ru, tsuma⌐tte) 息が詰まります(詰まる, 詰まって); (*chokes him*) ... no i⌐ki o tomema⌐su (tomeru, tomete) ...の息を止めます(止める, 止めて)
cholera ko⌐rera コレラ
choose 1. erabima⌐su (era⌐bu, era⌐nde) 選びます(選ぶ, 選んで); sentaku shima⌐su (suru, shite) 選択します(する, して) **2.** (*decides on*) ... ni shima⌐su (suru, shite) ...にします(する, して)
choosy yorigo⌐nomi ga hageshi⌐i より好みが激しい, yorigo⌐nomi o shima⌐su (suru, shite) より好みをします(する, して)
chop 1. (*chops it*) kizamima⌐su (kizamu, kizande) 刻みます(刻む, 刻んで) **2.** (= *signature seal*) hanko⌐ はんこ, ha⌐n はん・判
chopped meat hiki-niku 挽き肉
chopping board manai⌐ta⌐ まないた・組

chopstick rest hashi-oki 箸置き
chopsticks (o-)hashi（お)箸;
　(throwaway) wari-bashi 割
　り箸 **(1 pair** ichi-zen 一膳)
chorus kōrasu コーラス
chow → **food**
chowder yose-nabe 寄せなべ・寄
　せ鍋
chow mein yaki-soba 焼きそば
Christ Kirisuto キリスト
Christian 1. Kirisuto-kyō no ...
　キリスト教の... **2. a ~**
　(Kirisuto-kyō no) shinja（キ
　リスト教の)信者
Christianity Kirisuto-kyō キリス
　ト教
Christmas Kurisumasu クリス
　マス
chrysanthemum kiku 菊; **(tasty**
　leaves of) a kind of ~
　shungiku 春菊
church kyōkai 教会
"cider" saidā サイダー *(fizzy*
　lcmon soda)
cigar shigā シガー, ha-maki 葉
　巻; **~ shop/store** tabako-ya
　たばこ屋
cigarette tabako たばこ, maki-
　tabako 巻きたばこ,
　shigaretto シガレット **(1** ip-
　pon 一本, **2** ni-hon 二本,
　3 sam-bon 三本, **how many**
　nam-bon 何本; **1 pack** hito-
　hako 一箱, **2** futa-hako 二箱,
　3 mi-hako 三箱, **how many**
　packs nam-pako 何箱)

cigarette/cigar butt suigara 吸い
　殻
cigarette case tabako-ire たばこ
　入れ
cigarette holder paipu パイプ,
　sui-kuchi 吸い口
cinch *(an easy thing to do)* wake
　mo nai (koto) わけもないこ
　と・訳もない事
cinder(s) moegara 燃え殻
cinema → **movies**
cinnamon nikke(i) 肉桂, nikki
　にっき
circle maru 丸, en 円, wa 輪;
　traffic ~ rōtarii ロータリー
circular kanjō (no) 環状(の)
circulate *(it circulates)*
　mawarimasu (mawaru,
　mawatte) 回ります(回る, 回
　って); *(circulates it)*
　mawashimasu (mawasu,
　mawashite) 回します(回す,
　回して)
circulation *(cyclc)* junkan 循環
circumference shui 周囲, shūhen
　周辺
circumstance ba(w)ai 場合; koto
　事, ... wake ...訳, ... tokoro ...
　所, ... shidai ...次第; jijō 事情;
　jotai 状態, jōkyo 状況; yoshi
　由; yōsu 様子; *(convenience)*
　tsugō (go-tsugō) 都合(ご都合)
circumstances *(details)* ikisatsu
　いきさつ・行きさつ・経緯
circus sakasu サーカス,
　kyokuba-dan 曲馬団

citizen shi⌐min 市民; (= **national**) kokumin 国民

citron yu⌐zu ゆず・柚

city machi⌐ 町, shi⌐ 市; (metropolis) to⌐shi 都市, tokai 都会; (within the city) shi⌐nai (no) 市内(の); ~ **dweller** toka⌐i-jin 都会人; ~ **office** shi-ya⌐kusho 市役所

civilian minkan (no) shi⌐min 民間(の)市民; (military employee) gu⌐nzoku 軍属

civilian clothes, civies shifuku 私服, heijō⌐-fuku 平常服

civilization bummei 文明, bu⌐nka 文化

claim 1. (demands) yōkyū/seikyū (shima⌐su; suru, shite) 要求/請求(します; する, して) **2.** (maintains) shuchō shima⌐su (suru, shite) 主張します(する, して), tonaema⌐su (tona⌐e⌐ru, tona⌐ete) 唱えます(唱える, 唱えて)

clam hama⌐guri はまぐり・蛤; **short-necked** ~ asari あさり・浅蜊; **blood(y)** ~ aka⌐-gai 赤貝

clamor (a clamor) sa⌐wagi 騒ぎ; (makes a clamor) sawagima⌐su (sawa⌐gu, sawa⌐ide) 騒ぎます(騒ぐ, 騒いで)

clan u⌐ji 氏

clap (one's hands) te⌐ o tatakima⌐su (tata⌐ku, tata⌐ite)

手を叩きます(叩く, 叩いて); ha⌐kushu shima⌐su (suru, shite) 拍手します(する, して)

clasp one's hands te⌐ o kumima⌐su (ku⌐mu, ku⌐nde) 手を組みます(組む, 組んで)

class ku⌐rasu クラス, kyū⌐ 級, (in school) gakkyū 学級; ~ **instruction** ju⌐gyō 授業

classmate dōkyū⌐-sei 同級生; (= former ~) dōki⌐-sei 同期生

class reunion dōsō⌐-kai 同窓会

classroom kyōshitsu 教室; ~ **teaching** ju⌐gyō 授業

clatter ga⌐tagata shima⌐su (suru, shite) がたがたします(する, して)

claw tsume⌐ 爪; (of crab) hasami⌐ はさみ・螯

claw hammer kugi-nu⌐ki⌐ 釘抜き

clay ne⌐ndo 粘土

clean 1. ki⌐rei (na) きれい[綺麗](な), seiketsu (na) 清潔(な); (fresh) sappa⌐ri shita さっぱりした **2. cleans it (up)** ki⌐rei ni shima⌐su (suru, shite) きれい[綺麗]にします(する, して), (tidies) katazukema⌐su (katazuke⌐ru, katazu⌐kete) 片付けます(片付ける, 片付けて), (sweeps) sōji shima⌐su (suru, shite) 掃除します(する, して)

cleaner(s) kuriiningu-ya クリーニング屋

cleaning *(dry)* (dorai-) kurī'ini'ngu（ドライ）クリーニング; *(sweeping up)* sōji (o-sō'ji) 掃除（お掃除）

cleaning person sōji'-fu 掃除夫

clear 1. *(bright)* akaru⌐i 明るい; *(sunny)* ha'rete ima'su 晴れています, hareta … 晴れた…; *(transparent)* tōmei (na) 透明（な）; *(evident)* aki'raka (na) 明らか（な）, *(obvious, explicit)* meihaku (na) 明白（な）; *(understood)* waka'tte ima'su 分かっています, waka'tta … 分かった…; *(easy to see)* mi-yasu'i 見やすい; *(easy to understand)* wakari-yasu'i 分かりやすい **2.** *(unimpeded)* jama ga na'i じゃま［邪魔］がない **3.** *(takes away from the table)* sagema'su (sage'ru, sa'gete) 下げます（下げる, 下げて） **4.** *gets clear (empty)* sukima'su (suku, suite) すきます（すく, すいて）

clear: gets ~ *(evident)* shirema'su (shireru, shirete) 知れます（知れる, 知れて）

clearly *(distinctly)* hakki'ri はっきり; *(obviously, explicitly)* meihaku ni 明白に

clear soup sui mono 吸い物; (o-)tsu'yu（お）つゆ

clear weather hare' 晴れ

cleaver hōchō 包丁, **(meat ~)** nikukiri-bo'chō 肉切り包丁

clerk *(in shop)* ten'in 店員; *(in office)* jimu'-in 事務員; *(in bank)* ginkō'-in 銀行員; *(errand-runner)* bōi ボーイ

clever rikō (na) 利口（な）; *(nimble with fingers)* ki'yō (na) 器用（な）; *(skilled)* jōzu' (o-jōzu) (na) じょうず・上手（おじょうず・お上手）（な）

cliff gake がけ・崖

climate kikō 気候

climax yama 山, chō'ten 頂点; *(= upshot)* shi'matsu 始末

climb noborima'su (noboru, nobotte) 登ります（登る, 登って）

clinic byōin 病院

clip 1. clips it tsumima'su (tsumu, tsunde) 摘みます（摘む, 摘んで）; kirima'su (ki'ru, ki'tte) 切ります（切る, 切って） **2. a clip** kuri'ppu クリップ; → **paperclip**

clippers hasami' はさみ・鋏; *(nail)* tsumeki'ri' 爪切り; *(barber's)* barikan バリカン

clipping *(from newspaper, etc.)* kirinuki 切り抜き

clique renchū/renjū 連中/連中, habatsu 派閥

cloak ma'nto マント; **cloakroom** kurō'ku クローク, azukari-jo⌐ 預かり所

clock tokei 時計; **clockspring** zemmai ぜんまい 「り(に)

clockwise migi-ma'wari (ni) 右回

clogged (up): gets ~
fusagarima'su (fusaga'ru,
fusaga'tte) ふさがります(ふ
さがる, ふさがって)

clogs 1. *(wooden shoes)* geta' げ
た・下駄 **2.** *(it clogs up, gets
clogged)* tsumarima'su
(tsuma'ru, tsuma'tte) 詰まりま
す(詰まる, 詰まって),
tsukaema'su (tsuka'e'ru,
tsuka'ete) つかえます(つかえ
る, つかえて)

close *(near)* chika'i 近い; *(intimate)* missetsu (na) 密接(な);
(humid) mushi-atsu'i 蒸し暑い

close 1. closes it *(= shuts)*
shimema'su (shime'ru,
shi'mete) 閉めます(閉める,
閉めて), *(a book, etc.)*
tojima'su (toji'ru, to'jite) 閉じ
ます(閉じる, 閉じて), ~
one's eyes me' o tsuburima'su
(tsuburu, tsubutte) 目をつぶ
ります(つぶる, つぶって);
(= obstructs) fusagima'su
(fusagu, fusaide) ふさぎます
(ふさぐ, ふさいで); *(=
ends)* owarima'su (owaru,
owatte) 終わります(終わる,
終わって) **2. it closes**
shimarima'su (shima'ru,
shima'tte) 閉まります(閉まる,
閉まって); → **end**

close = the end owari 終わり,
sue 末

close by so'ba (no ...) (o-soba)

そば(の...)(おそば)

closely pitta'ri ぴったり

closet oshi-ire 押し入れ,
(o-)na'ndo (お)納戸

clot *(a clot)* katamari 固まり・塊;
(it clots) katamarima'su
(katamaru, katamatte) 固まり
ます(固まる, 固まって)

cloth ori'-mo'no 織物, ki'ji 生
地, nuno 布; *(a piece of)* kire'
切れ, nuno-gire 布切れ; *(dustcloth)* zōkin ぞうきん・雑巾;
(dishcloth) fuki'n ふきん・布
巾; *(traditional wrapper)*
furoshiki ふろしき・風呂敷

clothes ki-mono 着物; fuku' 服,
(Western) yō-fuku (o-yō'fuku)
洋服(お洋服), *(Japanese)* wa-
fuku 和服

clothesbag *(for laundry)*
sentakumono-ire 洗濯物入れ

clothesbrush kimono-bu'rashi 着
物ブラシ

clothesline monohoshi-zuna 物
干し綱

clothes moth i'ga いが, shi'mi
衣魚・しみ

clothing shop yōfuku-ya 洋服屋

cloud ku'mo 雲

cloudy: gets ~ kumorima'su
(kumo'ru, kumo'tte) 曇りま
す・くもります(曇る, 曇っ
て); **~ weather** kumori' 曇り・
くもり

cloves chō'ji 丁字

club *(group; card suit)* ku'rabu

クラブ; *(stick)* kombō 棍棒・
こん棒

clue tega˥kari 手掛かり,
ito˥guchi 糸口

clumsy heta˥ (na) へた[下手](な),
bu-ki˥yō (na) 不器用(な)

cluster → bunch

clutch 1. *(grasps)* nigirima˥su
(nigiru, nigitte) 握ります(握
る, 握って), tsukamima˥su
(tsuka˥mu, tsuka˥nde) つかみ
ます(つかむ, つかんで)
2. *(of car)* kura˥tchi クラッチ,
(pedal) kuratchi-pe˥daru ク
ラッチペダル

CM → commercial (message)

coach 1. *(railroad)* kyakusha 客
車; *(director)* shidō˥-sha 指導
者, *(sports)* kō˥chi コーチ
2. *(coaches them)* shidō
shima˥su (suru, shite) 指導しま
す(する, して)

coal sekita˥n 石炭

coal mine tankō 炭鉱

coarse arai 荒い; so˥matsu (na)
粗末(な), ya˥kuza (na) やくざ
(な); zatsu-... 雑...

coast engan 沿岸, kaigan 海岸,
kishi˥ 岸

coat uwagi 上着, kō˥to コート;
(overcoat) gaitō 外套, ō˥bā オ
ーバー (*traditional Japanese*)
haori (o-ha˥ori) 羽織(お羽織)

coax odatema˥su (odateru,
odatete) おだてます(おだて
る, おだてて)

cobweb ku˥mo no su⌐ くもの巣,
kumo-no-su くもの巣; ku˥mo
no i˥to くもの糸

cocain koka˥in コカイン

cockle tori˥-gai とりがい

cockroach gokiburi ごきぶり

cocktail (party) ka˥kuteru (pātii)
カクテル(パーティー)

cocoa ko˥ko˥a ココア

coconut ko˥kona˥ttsu ココナッ
ツ; ~ palm ya˥shi やし・椰子

cocoon ma˥yu まゆ・繭

C.O.D. (collect on delivery)
daikin hiki-kae (de) 代金引き
換え(で)

code kō˥do コード; *(secret)* angō
暗号

cod (fish) ta˥ra たら・鱈

cod roe tara⌐ko⌐ たらこ・鱈子

co-ed jo(shi)-ga˥kusei 女(子)学
生, mechi-kō メチコ

coeducation da˥njo kyōgaku 男
女共学

co-existence kyōson 共存,
kyōzon 共存

coffee kōhi˥i コーヒー

coffee cup kōhii-ja˥wan/-ka˥ppu
コーヒー茶碗/カップ

coffee pot kōhii-po˥tto コーヒー
ポット

coffee shop/house kōhi⌐i-ten
コーヒー店, kissa⌐ten 喫茶
店

cog (wheel) ha-gu˥ruma 歯車

coin tama˥ 玉, kō˥ka 硬貨, ko˥in
コイン; *(brass or copper)*

dō̄ka 銅貨; *(¥10)* jū-en-dama
十円玉; *(¥100)* hyaku-en-dama
百円玉

coin dealer koi̅n-shō コイン商

coin locker koin-ro̅kkā コイン
ロッカー

cola kō̄ra コーラ

colander mizu-ko̅shi̅ 水こし・水
漉し; *(bamboo)* zaru̅ ざる

cold samu̅i 寒い; *(to touch)*
tsumeta̅i 冷たい

cold: catches a cold kaze o
hikima̅su (hiku, hiite) かぜ
[風邪]をひきます(ひく, ひ
いて), [HONORIFIC] kaze o o-
meshi ni narima̅su (na̅ru,
na̅tte) かぜ[風邪]をお召しに
なります(なる, なって)

cold: gets cold sa̅muku/
tsumeta̅ku narima̅su (na̅ru,
na̅tte) 寒く/冷たくなります
(なる, なって); samema̅su
(same̅ru, sa̅mete) 冷めます
(冷める, 冷めて); hiema̅su
(hie̅ru, hi̅ete) 冷えます(冷え
る, 冷えて)

coldhearted tsurena̅i つれない

cold medicine kaze-gu̅suri かぜ
[風邪]薬

cold water mizu 水, (o-)hi̅ya
(お)冷や・(お)ひや

coleslaw kyabetsu-sa̅rada キャ
ベツサラダ

collapse taorema̅su (taore̅ru,
tao̅rete) 倒れます(倒れる, 倒
れて); *(gets smashed)*

tsuburema̅su (tsubure̅ru,
tsuburete) つぶれます・潰れま
す(つぶれる, つぶれて)

collar ka̅rā カラー; *(of coat)* eri̅
えり・襟; *(of dog)* kubi-wa 首
輪

collate *(compares)* terashima̅su
(tera̅su, tera̅shite) 照らしま
す(照らす, 照らして),
terashi-awase̅masu
(-awase̅ru, -awase̅te) 照らし
合わせます(合わせる,合わせ
て)

colleague dōryō 同僚

collect 1. collects them
atsumema̅su (atsume̅ru,
atsu̅mete) 集めます(集める,
集めて), yosema̅su (yoseru,
yosete) 寄せます(寄せる, 寄
せて), *(completes a set)*
soroema̅su (soroe̅ru, soro̅ete)
揃えます(揃える, 揃えて);
(gathers up) shūshū shima̅su
(suru, shite) 収集します(する,
して); *(reaps, brings in)*
osamema̅su (osame̅ru,
osa̅mete) 納めます(納める,
納めて), *(levies taxes etc.)*
chōshū shima̅su (suru, shite)
徴収します(する, して); ~
tickets shūsatsu shima̅su
(suru, shite) 集札します(する,
して) **2. they collect** *(come
together)* atsumarima̅su
(atsuma̅ru, atsuma̅tte) 集ま
ります(集まる, 集まって)

collect call ryō⌐┐kin saki-ba⌐rai (no denwa) 料金先払い（の電話）

collection (of books) zōsho 蔵書

collection (of taxes etc.) chōshū 徴収

collect (on delivery), C.O.D. daikin hiki-kae (de) 代金引き換え（で）

collector shūshū-ka 収集家

college daigaku 大学; **college student** daiga⌐ku-sei 大学生

collide shōtotsu shima⌐su (suru, shite) 衝突します（する，して）

collision shōtotsu 衝突

colloquial (language, word) kōgo 口語; kōgo-teki (na) 口語的（な）

collusion: in ～ with ... to takura⌐nde ...と企んで

colonel taisa 大佐

colony shokumi⌐n-chi 植民地

color iro⌐ 色; ka⌐rā カラー; **what ～** nani-iro (no) 何色（の）, do⌐nna iro⌐ (no) どんな色（の）

colored paper iro⌐gami 色紙

colorful (bright) hana⌐yaka (na) 華やか（な）

column 1. ra⌐n 欄; (page ～) da⌐n 段; (numerical ～) keta けた・桁 **2. → pillar**

comb kushi⌐ くし，櫛

combination 1. kumi-awase 組み合わせ **2.** (union) gappei 合併, gōdō 合同

combine 1. (combines them) kumi-awasema⌐su (-awase⌐ru, -awa⌐sete) 組み合わせます（合わせる，合わせて）, awasema⌐su (awase⌐ru, awa⌐sete) 合わせます（合わせる，合わせて）; (dually serves as) kanema⌐su (kane⌐ru, ka⌐nete) 兼ねます（兼ねる，兼ねて） **2.** (they unite) gappei/gōdō shima⌐su (suru, shite) 合併/合同します（する，して）; **combined** gōdō no ... 合同の...

comb the hair kami⌐ o sukima⌐su (suku, suite) 髪をすきます（すく，すいて）, tokima⌐su (to⌐ku, to⌐ite) ときます・梳きます（とく，といて）, tokashima⌐su (toka⌐su, toka⌐shite) とかします・梳かします（とかす，とかして）

come kima⌐su (ku⌐ru, kite⌐) 来ます（来る，来て）; (I/we come to you) ikima⌐su (iku, itte) 行きます（行く，行って）

come back itte kima⌐su (ku⌐ru, kite⌐) 行って来ます（来る，来て）; kaerima⌐su (ka⌐eru, ka⌐ette) 帰ります（帰る，帰って）

come down kudarima⌐su (kudaru, kudatte) 下ります（下る，下って）; (on the price) makema⌐su (makeru, makete) 負けます（負ける，負けて）

come in hairima⌐su (ha⌐iru,

haʾitte) 入ります(入る, 入っ
て), haʾitte kimaʾsu (kuʾru,
kiteʾ) 入って来ます(来る,
来て)

come near yorimaʾsu (yoru,
yotte) 寄ります(寄る, 寄っ
て), chika-zukimaʾsu
(-zuʾku, -zuʾite) 近づきま
す(づく, づいて)

come off (button, etc.)
toremaʾsu (toreʾru, toʾrete)
取れます(取れる, 取れて);
nukemaʾsu (nukeru, nukete)
抜けます(抜ける, 抜けて);
hazuremaʾsu (hazureru,
hazurete) 外れます(外れる,
外れて)

come on, ... ! ~ saʾ さあ (urg-
ing an invitation)

come out demaʾsu (deʾru,
deʾte) 出ます(出る, 出て),
deʾte kimaʾsu (kuʾru, kiteʾ)
出て来ます(来る, 来て);
(appears) arawaremaʾsu
(arawareʾru, arawaʾrete) 現
れます(現れる, 現れて)

come to (= reach) ... ni
itarimaʾsu (itaʾru, itaʾtte) ...
に至ります(至る, 至って)

come to an end sumimaʾsu
(suʾmu, suʾnde) 済みます
(済む, 済んで),
owarimaʾsu (owaru, owatte)
終わります(終わる, 終
わって), tsukimaʾsu
(tsukiʾru, tsuʾkite) 尽き

ます(尽きる, 尽きて)

come to the end of (a street)
tsuki-atarimaʾsu (-ataru,
-atatte) 突き当たります
(当たる, 当たって)

come what may naʾn to itteʾ
mo 何と言っても

comedy kiʾgeki 喜劇

comet hōkiʾ-boshi ほうき星・彗
星

comfort 1. aⁿnraku 安楽,
kiraku 気楽 **2.** (consolation)
nagusame 慰め, ian 慰安; (consoles) nagusamemaʾsu
(nagusameⁿru,
nagusaⁿmete) 慰めます
(慰める, 慰めて)

comfortable 1. rakuʾ (na) 楽(な),
aⁿnraku (na) 安楽(な),
kiraku (na) 気楽(な); kimochi
ga iʾi 気持ちがいい **2.** → **relax**
3. (easy to wear) ki-yasuʾi 着や
すい, (easy to sit on) suwari-
yasuʾi 座りやすい・すわりやす
い

comic: ~ **book** manga-bon 漫画
本; ~ **storytelling** rakugo 落
語; ~ **storyteller** rakugo-ka 落
語家

comical → **funny**

comics manga 漫画・まんが

Coming-of-Age Day (January
15) Seⁿijin no hiʾ 成人の日

command 1. (a ~) meirei 命令;
saʾtaʾ さた・沙汰 **2.** (orders a
person) ...ni ii-tsukemaʾsu

(-tsukeˈru, -tsukeˈte) ...に言い付けます(付ける, 付けて), mei-jimaˈsu (mei-jiⁿru, meⁿi-jite) 命じます(命じる, 命じて) **3.** *(leads)* hikiimaˈsu (hikiiˈru, hikiˈite) 率います(率いる, 率いて)

commander shireˈi-kan 指令官; *(navy)* chūsa 中佐

commemoration kinen 記念; **commemorate** kinen shimaˈsu (suru, shite) 記念します(する, して)

commemorative stamp kinen-kiˈtte/-giˈtte 記念切手/切手

commencement *(ceremony)* sotsugyōˈ-shiki 卒業式

comment 1. *(explanation)* kaisetsu 解説 **2.** *(critique, opinion)* hyōron 評論 **3.** → **remark**

commentator 1. kaiseˈtsu-sha 解説者 **2.** *(critic)* hyōron-ka 評論家

comment on *(explains)* kaisetsu shimaˈsu (suru, shite) 解説します(する, して); *(criticizes)* hyōron shimaˈsu (suru, shite) 評論します(する, して)

commerce shōˈgyō 商業; *(trade)* bōeki 貿易

commercial *(message)* shiieˈmu (CM) シーエム

commission 1. *(handling charge)* tesūˈ-ryō 手数料; *(brokerage fee)* saˈya さや **2.** *(commissions ... to do it)* (sore o ... ni)

irai shimaˈsu (suru, shite) (それを...に)依頼します(する, して)

commit 1. *(entrusts)* yudanemaˈsu (yudaneˈru, yudaˈnete) ゆだねます・委ねます(ゆだねる, ゆだねて) **2.** *(perpetrates)* okashimaˈsu (okaⁿsu, okaⁿshite) 犯します(犯す, 犯して); hatarakimaˈsu (hataraku, hataraite) 働きます(働く, 働いて); → **do 3. commit oneself** → **promise**; → **say**

committee iˈn-kai 委員会; ~ **member(s)** ˈin 委員

commodity prices bukka 物価

common futsū (no) 普通(の), kyōtsū (no) 共通(の); *(average)* nami (no) 並(の); *(vulgar, popular)* zoku (na) 俗(な); *(is prevalent)* hayarimaˈsu (hayaˈru, hayaˈtte) はやります(はやる, はやって); *(is found everywhere)* zara-ni arimaˈsu (aˈru, aˈtte) ざらにあります(ある, あって)

commonplace heibon (na) 平凡(な)

common sense jōshiki 常識

communicate tsutaemaˈsu (tsutaⁿeˈru, tsutaⁿete) 伝えます(伝える, 伝えて); tsū-jimaˈsu (tsū-jiru, tsū-jite) 通じます(通じる, 通じて)

communicated: gets ~
tsutawarima͞su (tsutawa⌐ru,
tsutawa⌐tte) 伝わります(伝
わる, 伝わって)

communication *(traffic)* kōtsū
交通, ōrai 往来; *(message,
news)* ta⌐yori 便り, tsūshin 通
信

Communism kyōsan-shu⌐gi 共産
主義; **a Communist** kyōsan-
shugi⌐-sha 共産主義者

community sha⌐kai 社会; →
town, village

community college *(= junior college)* tanki-da⌐igaku 短期大学

commute kayoima͞su (kayou,
kayotte) 通います(通う, 通っ
て); **~ to work** tsūkin
shima͞su 通勤します

commuting: ~ to work tsūkin
通勤; **~ time** tsūkin-ji⌐kan 通
勤時間

companion nakama⌐ 仲間; tsure
(o-tsure) 連れ(お連れ), to⌐mo
(o-to⌐mo) 供(お供),
tomodachi 友達; aite⌐ (o-aite)
相手(お相手)

company *(firm)* kaisha 会社, ...⌐
-sha ...社; *(within the office/
company)* sha⌐nai (no) 社内
(の); *(group)* kumi⌐ 組;
(social) tsuki-ai 付き合い,
kōsai 交際; *(guests)* raikyaku
来客, (o-)kyaku (お)客, o-
kyaku-san/sa⌐ma⌐ お客さん/
様

company: keep one ~ ... to
tsuki-aima͞su (-a⌐u, -a⌐tte) ...と
付き合います(合う, 合って);
keep ~ with ... o chika-
zukema͞su (-zuke⌐ru, -zu⌐kete) ...
を近付けます(付ける, 付け
て)

comparatively hikaku-teki (ni)
比較的(に), wari ni 割に,
wariai (ni) 割合(に)

compare kurabema͞su
(kuraberu, kurabete) 比べま
す(比べる, 比べて), hikaku
shima͞su (suru, shite) 比較し
ます(する, して); taishō/
ta⌐ihi shima͞su (suru, shite)
対照/対比します(する, して);
(collates) terashima͞su
(tera⌐su, tera⌐shite) 照らしま
す(照らす, 照らして); **as
compared with** ... ni ta⌐i-shite ...
に対して

comparison hikaku 比較; taishō
対照, ta⌐ihi 対比

compass *(for directions)* rashim-
ban 羅針盤; *(for drafting)*
ko⌐mpasu コンパス

compassion na⌐sake⌐ (o-
na⌐sake) 情け(お情け)

compensate mukuima͞su 報いま
す, muku⌐iru 報いる; *(indem-
nifies)* hoshō shima͞su (suru,
shite) 補償します

compensation *(indemnity
money)* hoshō⌐-kin 補償金;
(allowance) kyō⌐yo 供与

compete kisoima‾su (kiso‾u, kiso‾tte) 競います（競う，競って）, kyōsō shima‾su (suru, shite) 競争します（する，して）

competency *(qualification)* shikaku 資格

competition kyōsō 競争; **competitor** kyōsō-a‾ite 競争相手

complain fuhei/mo‾nku o iima‾su (yū, itte/yutte) 不平/文句を言います（言う，言って/ゆって）; (guchi o) koboshima‾su (kobo‾su, kobo‾shite) （ぐち・愚痴を）こぼします（こぼす，こぼして）

complaint fuhei 不平, mo‾nku 文句, kogoto (o-ko‾goto) 小言（お小言）, guchi ぐち・愚痴; *(lawsuit)* uttae 訴え

complement, complete oginaima‾su 補います, ogina‾u 補う

complete 1. becomes ~ *(full)* michima‾su (michi‾ru, mi‾chite) 満ちます（満ちる，満ちて） **2.** *(exhaustive)* mō‾ra shita ... 網羅した... **3. completes it** kansei shima‾su (suru, shite) 完成します（する，して）; *(a set)* soroema‾su (soroe‾ru, soro‾ete) 揃えます（揃える，揃えて）

completely mattaku‾ 全く, to(t)temo とっ（っ）ても, sukka‾ri すっかり, sokku‾ri そっくり; (+ NEGATIVE) zenzen 全然; *(all)* ze‾mbu 全部, minna‾ みんな・皆; *(the whole ...)* ze‾n(-) ... 全...

completion kansei 完成

complexities *(details)* ikisatsu いきさつ・経緯

compliance: in ~ with ... ni ō‾-jite ...に応じて

complicated fukuzatsu (na) 複雑（な）, komi-i‾tta 込み入った, yaya(k)koshi‾i やや（っ）こしい, wazurawashi‾i 煩わしい; **gets ~** kojirema‾su (kojire‾ru, koji‾rete) こじれます（こじれる，こじれて）, motsurema‾su (motsure‾ru, motsu‾rete) もつれます（もつれる，もつれて）

complications *(details)* ikisatsu いきさつ・経緯; *(entanglements)* motsure‾ もつれ

compliment o-seji お世辞

comply with ... ni ō-jima‾su (ō-ji‾ru, ō‾-jite) ...に応じます（応じる，応じて）; ... o nattoku shima‾su (suru, shite) ...を納得します（する，して）

component se‾ibun 成分

compose *(writes)* tsuzurima‾su (tsuzu‾ru, tsuzu‾tte) 綴ります（綴る，綴って）, tsukurima‾su (tsuku‾ru, tsuku‾tte) 作ります（作る，作って）

composed *(unperturbed)* heiki (na) 平気（な）

composite sōgō-teki (na) 総合的
(な)

composition *(writing)* sakubun
作文; *(constituency)* kōsei 構
成

compound (word) fukugō-go 複
合語, jukugo 熟語

comprehend → **understand**; →
include; → **comprise**; → **consist of**

comprehension ri⌐kai 理解; *(=
~ ability)* rika¹i-ryoku 理解力

comprehensive *(composite)*
sōgō-teki (na) 総合的 (な)

comprise *(includes all items)*
mō¹ra shima(⌐)su (suru, shite)
網羅します(する, して)

compromise dakyō 妥協; *(makes
a compromise)* dakyō
shima¹su (suru, shite) 妥協し
ます(する, して)

compulsory *(stipulated)* kitei
(no) 規定(の); ~ **education**
gimu-kyō¹iku 義務教育

computation keisan 計算

compute keisan shima¹su (suru,
shite) 計算します(する, して)

computer kompyū¹tā コンピュ
ーター, keisa¹n-ki 計算機

comrade (…) dō¹shi (…)同志

conceal → **hide**; → **cover up**

conceited person tengu 天狗

concentrate shūchū shima¹su
(suru, shite) 集中します(する,
して)

concentration shūchū 集中

concept ga¹inen 概念, shisō 思想

concern 1. *(relevance)* kankei 関
係, *(interest)* kanshin 関心;
(worry) shimpai 心配;
(business) kaisha 会社
2. *(relates to)* … ni kan-
shima¹su (kan-su¹ru, ka¹n-shite)
…に関します(関する, 関し
て), *(centers on)* … o
megurima¹su (meguru,
megutte) …を巡ります(巡る,
巡って)

concerning … ni ka¹n-shite …に
関して, … o megutte …を巡っ
て

concert onga¹k(u)-kai 音楽会,
ensō¹-kai 演奏会

conclude *(brings to an end)*
sumashima¹su (suma¹su,
suma¹shite) 済まします(済ま
す, 済まして); *(ends a discussion)* ketsu⌐ron shima¹su
(suru, shite) 結論します(する,
して); *(finalizes)* seiritsu
shima¹su (suru, shite) 成立し
ます(する, して)

conclusion 1. *(of discussion)*
ketsu⌐ron 結論; **in ~**
ketsu⌐ron to shite 結論として
2. *(finalization)* seiritsu 成立

concoct koshiraema¹su
(koshiraeru, koshiraete) こし
らえます(こしらえる, こし
らえて)

concrete *(cement)* konkuri¹ito コ
ンクリート; *(not abstract)*

gutai-teki 具体的

concrete floor tataki たたき・三和土

concubine mekake (o-mekake) 妾 (お妾), nigō (san) 二号 (さん)

concur (agrees) dōi shimasu (suru, shite) 同意します(する, して)

concurrently serves as … o kanemasu (kaneru, kanete) …を兼ねます(兼ねる, 兼ねて)

condensed milk rennyū 練乳

condition (state) ari-sama 有様・ありさま, jōtai 状態, jijō 事情, jissai 実際, guai 具合, chōshi 調子; (weather) hiyori 日和; (stipulation) jōken 条件

condom sakku サック, kondōmu コンドーム

conduct (behavior) okonai 行い

conductor (train) shashō (san) 車掌 (さん); (orchestra) shiki-sha 指揮者

confections (o-)kashi (お)菓子

confer 1. hanashi-aimasu (-au, -atte) 話し合います (合う, 合って) **2. → grant**

conference (personal) sōdan 相談; (formal) kaigi 会議, taikai 大会; (discussion) kyōgi 協議, (negotiation) hanashi-ai 話し合い

confess 1. hakujō shima(')su (suru, shite) 白状します(する,

して); (= ～ sin) zange shima(')su (suru, shite) ざんげ・懺悔します(する, して) **2.** (frankly reveals) uchi-akemasu (-akeru, -akete) 打ち明けます(明ける, 明けて)

confession hakujō 白状; (of sins) zange ざんげ・懺悔

confidence shin'yō 信用, shinrai 信頼, tanomi 頼み; (self-～) jishin 自信; (secure feeling) anshin 安心

confidential naisho (no) 内緒 (の)

confirm (a reservation) (yoyaku o) kakunin shimasu (suru, shite) (予約を)確認します(する, して)

confirmation kakunin 確認

confluence gōryū 合流

conform (with/to) … ni shitagaimasu (shitagau, shitagatte) …に従います(従う, 従って), … ni motozukimasu (motozuku, motozuite) …に基づきます (基づく, 基づいて)

confront … ni tai-shimasu (tai-suru, tai-shite) …に対します(対する, 対して); … to tairitsu shimasu (suru, shite) …と対立します(する, して); (opposes) … ni taikō shimasu (suru, shite) …に対抗します(する, して)

confrontation taikō 対抗

Confucianism Ju゛kyō 儒教; **Confucius** Kōshi 孔子

confused: gets ~ komarima゛su (koma゛ru, koma゛tte) 困ります(困る, 困って), *(flustered)* awatema゛su (awateru, awatete) 慌てます(慌てる, 慌てて); *(all jumbled)* mechamecha めちゃめちゃ

confusion *(disorder)* konran 混乱, ko゛nzatsu 混雑

congeal 1. it congeals katamarima゛su (katamaru, katamatte) 固まります(固まる, 固まって) **2. congeals it** katamema゛su (katameru, katamete) 固めます(固める, 固めて)

conger eel anago あなご・穴子

congested (traffic) jūtai-jo゛tai 渋滞状態; **is ~** jūtai shite ima゛su 渋滞しています

congestion jūtai 渋滞

congratulation shuku゛ga 祝賀; **Congratulations!** O-medetō gozaima゛su. おめでとう［お目出度う］ございます.

congregate shūgō shima゛su (suru, shite) 集合します(する, して)

congress → diet; conference

congruence gōdō 合同

conjecture suisoku 推測, sas-shi (o-sasshi) 察し(お察し); *(guesses, supposes)* sas-shima゛su (sas-su゛ru, sa゛s-shite) 察します(察する, 察して)

conjunction setsuzo゛ku-shi 接続詞

connect (with) (... to) tsunagima゛su (tsunagu, tsunaide) (...と)つなぎます(つなぐ, つないで); ... to renraku shima゛su (suru, shite) ...と連絡します(する, して); tsū-jima゛su (tsū-jiru, tsū-jite) 通じます(通じる, 通じて)

connected: is ~ (with ...) (... to) tsunagarima゛su (tsunagaru, tsunagatte) (...と)つながります(つながる, つながって), (... ni) kan-shima゛su (kan-su゛ru, ka゛n-shite) (...に)関します(関する, 関して)

connection renraku 連絡; *(relevance)* kankei 関係; *(relation)* tsunagari つながり; *(link)* tsunagi つなぎ; *("pull", avenue of influence)* kone コネ; *(discussions)* kōshō 交渉

conscience ryo゛shin 良心

conscientious majime (na) まじめ・真面目(な); ryōshin-teki (na) 良心的(な)

consciousness i゛shiki 意識, obo゛e 覚え; **loses ~** i゛shiki o ushinaima゛su (ushinau, ushinatte) 意識を失います(失う, 失って)

conscription *(for military serv-*

ice) shōshū 召集・招集

consent shōchi/shōdaku/dōi shima˥su (suru, shite) 承知/承諾/同意します(する，して)，nattoku shima˥su (suru, shite) 納得します(する，して)；[HUMBLE] uketamawarima˥su (uketamawa˥ru, uketamawa˥tte) 承ります(承る，承って)

consequence → **result**

conservative hoshu-teki (na) 保守的(な)；shōkyoku-teki (na) 消極的(な)；*(moderate)* uchiwa (na) 内輪(な)

conserve *(saves)* setsuyaku shima˥su (suru, shite) 節約します(する，して)

conserves boiled down from fish or seaweed tsukuda-ni つくだ煮・佃煮

consider kangaema˥su (kanga˥e˥ru, kanga˥ete) 考えます(考える，考えて)；*(takes into account)* kō˥ryo ni irema˥su (ireru, irete) 考慮に入れます(入れる，入れて)

considerable, considerably sōtō 相当・そうとう，yohodo よほど・余程，yoppodo よっぽど

consideration *(being kind)* omoi-yari 思いやり；*(thought)* kō˥ryo 考慮，shi˥ryo 思慮；**takes into ~** kō˥ryo ni irema˥su (ireru, irete) 考慮に入れます(入れる，入れて)

consist of … kara na˥tte ima˥su (iru, ite) …から成っています(いる，いて)   「慰安

consolation nagusame 慰め，ian

console nagusamema˥su (nagusame˥ru, nagusa˥mete) 慰めます(慰める，慰めて)

consomme konsome コンソメ

consonant shion 子音，shiin 子音

conspicuous ichijirushi˥i 著しい；meda˥tta … 目立った…，meda˥tte ima˥su 目立っています

conspicuously ichijiru˥shiku 著しく；meda˥tte 目立って

constantly → **always**

constipation bempi 便秘

constituency *(composition)* kōsei 構成

constitute kōsei shima˥su (suru, shite) 構成します(する，して)

constitution 1. *(basic laws)* ke˥mpō 憲法；**Constitution (Memorial) Day (3 May)** Kempō-kine˥mbi 憲法記念日 **2.** *(physical)* taishitsu 体質

constrained kyū˥kutsu (na) 窮屈・きゅうくつ(な)

constricted place, waist kubire くびれ

construct → **build**

construction (work) kō˥ji 工事；**under ~** kōji-chū 工事中；*(building)* kensetsu 建設；*(constituency)* kōsei 構成

construe ka⌐ishaku shima(⌐)su
(suru, shite) 解釈します(する,
して)

consul ryō⌐ji 領事; **consul
general** sō-ryō⌐ji 総領事

consulate ryōji⌐-kan 領事館

consult (a person) ... to sōdan
shima⌐su (suru, shite) ...と相
談します(する, して)

consultant ko⌐mon 顧問, konsa⌐rutanto コンサルタント

consultation ukagai (o-ukagai)
伺い(お伺い), sōdan 相談;
(by appointment) uchi-awase
打ち合わせ

consumer shōhi⌐-sha 消費者

consumption, consuming shōhi
消費

contact 1. sesshoku 接触; **comes
in ~ (with ...)** (... ni)
furema⌐su (fureru, furete) (...
に)触れます(触れる, 触れて),
ses-shima⌐su (ses-su⌐ru, se⌐s-
shite) 接します(接する, 接し
て), sesshoku shima⌐su (suru,
shite) 接触します(する, して)
2. contacts (a person) ... to
renraku shima⌐su (suru, shite) ...
と連絡します(する, して), ...
ni aima⌐su (a⌐u, a⌐tte) ...に会い
ます(会う, 会って) **3. con-
tacts** = **contact lenses**

contact lenses kontakuto-re⌐nzu
コンタクトレンズ,
konta⌐kuto コンタクト;
wears ~ konta⌐kuto o shite

ima⌐su コンタクトをしていま
す

contagion densen 伝染; **con-
tagious disease** densem-byō 伝
染病

contain ... ga ha⌐itte ima⌐su (iru,
ite) ...が入っています(いる,
いて); ... o fukumima⌐su
(fuku⌐mu, fuku⌐nde) ...を含み
ます(含む, 含んで)

container ire-mono 入れ物, yō⌐ki
容器; (box) hako 箱; (for
transporting goods) ko⌐nte⌐na
コンテナ

contamination osen 汚染

contempt keibetsu 軽蔑

contented with ... de ma⌐nzoku
shima(⌐)su (suru, shite) ...で
満足します(する, して);
osamarima⌐su (osama⌐ru,
osama⌐tte) 治まります(治まる,
治まって)

contention araso⌐i 争い

contents naka⌐mi 中身, naiyō 内
容; (table of contents) mokuji
目次, midashi 見出し

contest konku⌐ru コンクール,
ko⌐ntesuto コンテスト; (com-
petition) kyōsō 競争; (sports)
kyō⌐gi 競技, (match) shō⌐bu 勝
負, (meet) shiai 試合

contiguous: is ~ to ... ni ses-
shima⌐su (sessu⌐ru, se⌐s-
shite) ...に接します(接する,
接して)

continent tairiku 大陸

continuation tsuzuki 続き

continue *(it continues)* tsuzukima̱su (tsuzuku, tsuzuite) 続きます(続く, 続いて); *(continues it)* tsuzukema̱su (tsuzukeru, tsuzukete) 続けます(続ける, 続けて)

continuously taema-na̱ku 絶え間なく, ta̱ezu 絶えず; *(without resting)* yasuma̱naide 休まないで; tsuzukete 続けて

contraceptive hini̱n-yaku 避妊薬, *(pills)* keikō-hini̱n-yaku 経口避妊薬; *(device)* hini̱n-gu 避妊具; *(condom)* sa̱kku サック, kondo̱mu コンドーム

contract 1. *(an agreement)* keiyaku 契約 **2.** *(agrees to undertake work)* ukeoima̱su (ukeo̱u, ukeo̱tte) 請け負います(請け負う, 請け負って)

contractor ukeoi̱-nin 請け負い人

contradict ... ni sakaraima̱su (sakara̱u, sakara̱tte) ...に逆らいます(逆らう, 逆らって); → **deny**

contradiction *(inconsistency)* mujun 矛盾

contradictory *(inconsistent)* mujun shi̱te ima̱su (iru, ite) 矛盾しています(いる, いて)

contrary hantai (no) 反対(の); gyaku (no) 逆(の); **acts con-** trary to *(goes against)* ... ni han-shima̱su (-suru, -shi̱te) ...に反します(する, して), ... ni sakaraima̱su (sakara̱u, sakara̱tte) ...に逆らいます(逆らう, 逆らって)

contrary to ... ni ha̱n-shi̱te ...に反して; **~ expectations** ka̱ette かえって

contrast taishō/ta̱ihi (shima̱su; suru, shi̱te) 対照/対比(します; する, して); *(compares)* kurabema̱su (kuraberu, kurabete) 比べます(比べる, 比べて); **in ~ to/ with** ... ni ta̱i-shi̱te ...に対して, ... ni ha̱n-shi̱te ...に反して

control shiha̱i/shi̱hai 支配/支配, ka̱nri 管理; *(of prices, etc.)* tōsei 統制; *(supervises it)* tori-shimarima̱su (-shima̱ru, -shima̱tte) 取り締まります(締まる, 締まって); *(restrains)* osaema̱su (osa̱e̱ru, osa̱ete) 抑えます(抑える, 抑えて); *(operates)* sōjū shima̱su (suru, shi̱te) 操縦します(する, して)

controversy ronsō 論争

convenience tsugō (go-tsugō) 都合(ご都合), tsuide ついで; bi̱n 便

convenience: at your ~ o-tsuide no se̱tsu おついでの節, o-tsuide no toki̱ ni おついでの時に

convenient be͞nri (na) 便利(な), be͞n ga i͞i 便がいい; cho͞ho͞ (na) 重宝(な); *(easy to arrange)* tsugō ga i͞i 都合がいい

convent shūdō-in 修道院

convention → **conference, meeting** ⌐(な)

conventional heibon (na) 平凡

conversation *(ordinary)* hanashi͞ 話, danwa 談話; *(in language class, etc.)* kaiwa 会話

conversion henkan 変換; **kana-to-kanji ~ key** henkan-ki͞i 変換キー

convert hiki-kaema͞su (-ka͞e͞ru, -ka͞ete) 引き換えます(換える, 換えて)

converter henka͞n-ki 変換器; *(AC-DC)* henryu͞-ki 変流器; *(transformer)* hen'atsu͞-ki 変圧器

conveys hakobima͞su (hakobu, hakonde) 運びます(運ぶ, 運んで)

cook 1. ryōri⌐-nin 料理人, ko͞kku(-san) コック(さん), *(Japanese chef)* itamae 板前 **2.** *(cooks it)* ryo͞ri shima(⌐)su (suru, shite) 料理します(する, して), *(boils it)* nima͞su (niru, nite) 煮ます(煮る, 煮て); *(rice, soup)* takima͞su (taku, taite) 炊きます(炊く, 炊いて) **3.** *(it boils)* niema͞su (nieru, niete) 煮えます(煮える, 煮えて)

cooked rice meshi͞ 飯, go͞han ご飯

cooking ryo͞ri 料理; **~ stove** re͞nji レンジ

cool suzushi͞i 涼しい; *(unperturbed)* heiki (na) 平気(な); **it cools off/down** samema͞su (same͞ru, sa͞mete) 冷めます (冷める, 冷めて), hiema͞su (hie͞ru, hi͞ete) 冷えます(冷える, 冷えて); *(cools it)* hiyashima͞su (hiya͞su, hiya͞shite) 冷やします(冷やす, 冷やして) ⌐足

coolie ni͞mpu 人夫, ni⌐nsoku 人

cooperation kyō⌐ryoku 協力; *(joint activity)* kyōdō 共同

cop → **policeman**

copper aka-gane あかがね・銅, dō͞ 銅

copula shitei-shi/keiji 指定詞/繋詞 (= de͞su, da͞, na͞, no͞, ni͞, de͞, ... です, だ, な, の, に, で, ...)

copy 1. *(of a book)* ...-bu ...部, ichi͞-bu 一部 **2.** *(photocopy)* ko͞pii コピー (**how many na͞m-mai** 何枚) **3.** *(reproduction)* fukusha 複写, fukusei 複製

copy *(copies it)* utsushima͞su (utsu͞su, utsu͞shite) 写します (写す, 写して), fukusha/fukusei shima͞su (suru, shite) 複写/複製します(する, して); *(makes a copy)* ko͞pii o torima̱su, (to̱ru, to̱tte) コピーをとります(とる, とって); *(imitates)* nisema̱su (niseru, nisete) 似せます(似せる, 似せて)

coral sa̱ngo さんご・珊瑚

cord himo ひも・紐, nawa̱ なわ・縄, ko̱do コード

cordial shi̱nsetsu (na) 親切(な)

core shi̱n しん・心・芯

cork ko̱ruku コルク, se̱n 栓, koruku̱-sen コルク栓

corkscrew koruku̱-nuki コルク抜き, sen-nu̱ki栓抜き

cormorant u う・鵜; **~ fishing** u̱kai 鵜飼い

corn 1. *(maize)* tō-mo̱rokoshi とうもろこし **2.** *(on skin)* uonome̱ 魚の目; *(callus)* ta̱ko たこ, *(bunion)* mame̱ まめ; soko-mame 底まめ

corner *(outside)* ka̱do 角; *(inside)* su̱mi 隅

cornstarch kōn-suta̱chi コーンスターチ, tōmorokoshi̱-ko とうもろこし粉

corporal go̱chō 伍長

corporation kabushiki-ga̱isha 株式会社, sha̱dan 社団; **public ~** kōdan 公団

corps gu̱ndan 軍団; **Marine Corps** kaiheitai 海兵隊; **Peace Corps** heiwa-bu̱tai 平和部隊; **medical corps** cisci-tai 衛生隊

corpse nakigara なきがら・亡骸, shitai 死体, shigai 死骸

corpsman *(medical)* eise̱i-hei 衛生兵

correct tadashi̱i 正しい; atarima̱su (ataru, atatte) 当たります(当たる, 当たって); *(corrects it)* naoshima̱su (nao̱su, nao̱shite) 直します(直す, 直して), aratamema̱su (aratame̱ru, arata̱mete) 改めます(改める, 改めて)

correcting, correction naoshi̱ 直し

correctly tada̱shiku 正しく

correspond (to ...) (... ni) taiō shima̱su (suru, shite) (...に)対応します(する, して)

correspondence *(messages)* tsūshin 通信; *(equivalence)* taiō 対応

corridor rōka 廊下

corrugated cardboard dam-bō̱ru 段ボール

cosmetics keshō̱ (o-keshō̱) 化粧(お化粧), keshō̱-hin 化粧品

cost 1. *(expense)* hi̱yō 費用 **2. it costs (how much)** (i̱kura) shima̱su (suru, shite) (いくら)します(する, して); *(requires)* yō-shima̱su (yō-su̱ru, yō̱-shite) 要します(要する, 要して)

cost: at any ~ na̱n to shite̱ mo 何としても

costly ⟩ expensive

cotton wata̱ 綿, momen 木綿; **ab-**

sorbent ~ dasshi̮-men 脱脂綿; ~-**padded (garment)** wata-i̮re̮ 綿入れ　　　　　「椅子

couch ne-isu 寝椅子, naga-isu 長

cough seki̮ o shima̮su (suru, shi̮te) 咳をします(する，して)

could → can; maybe

counsel 1. *(guide, coach)* shidō-sha 指導者 **2.** *(counsels them)* shidō shima̮su (suru, shi̮te) 指導します(する，して)

count kazoema̮su (kazoe̮ru, kazo̮ete) 数えます(数える，数えて); ~ **on one's fingers** yubi̮ o o̮tte kazoema̮su 指を折って数えます; **is counting on** ... o ate ni shi̮te ima̮su (iru, ite) ...を当てにしています(いる，いて)

counter (shop ~) uri-ba 売り場

counterclockwise hidari-ma̮wari (ni) 左回り(に)

counterfeit nisema̮su (niseru, nisete) 似せます(似せる，似せて); ~ **bill (currency)** nise-satsu 偽札・にせ札・贋札

countless kazoe-kire̮nai 数え切れない, musū̮ (no) 無数(の)

country kuni (o-kuni) 国(お国), ...-koku ...国; **how many countries** nan-ka̮koku 何カ国; *(countryside)* inaka い なか・田舎; *(outdoors)* ya̮gai 野外

county gu̮n 郡 *(U.S.);* shū̮ 州 *(Britain)*

couple → two; a couple *(husband and wife)* fū̮fu 夫婦, *(on a date)* abe̮kku アベック

coupon ticket kaisū̮-ken 回数券

course kō̮su コース; *(in school)* kamoku 科目; *(of action)* hōshin 方針; *(of time)* keika 経過; *(development)* nariyuki 成り行き・なりゆき

course: → of course

court 1. *(of law)* saiban-sho̮ 裁判所, hōtei 法廷 **2.** *(sports)* kō̮to コート **3.** *(imperial/ royal)* kyūtei 宮廷; ~ **dances and music** bu̮gaku 舞楽

courtesy reigi̮ 礼儀

cousin ito̮ko いとこ・従兄弟・従姉妹; **your ~** o-itoko-san お いとこさん

cover 1. *(lid)* fu̮ta ふた **2.** *(covers it)* ōima̮su (ō̮u = oo̮u, ō̮tte) 覆[おお]います(覆う= おおう，覆って); *(includes all items)* mō̮ra shima(̮)su (suru, shi̮te) 網羅します(する，して) **3.** ~ **with a roof** ... no ya̮ne o fu̮kima̮su (fu̮ku̮, fu̮ite) ...の屋根をふきます(ふく， ふいて) **4.** ~ **up** *(conceals)* fu̮sema̮su (fu̮se̮ru, fu̮se̮te) 伏せます(伏せる，伏せて)

cover charge *(restaurant)* seki̮-ryō 席料, sābisu̮-ryō サービス 料; *(admission)* nyūjō̮-ryō 入 場料　　　　　「何頭

cow ushi 牛 (**how many** na̮n-tō

coward okubyō-mo⌐no⌐ 臆病 ［憶病］者; **cowardice** okubyō⌐ 臆病·憶病; **cowardly** okubyō⌐ (na) 臆病·憶病(な)

crab kani かに·蟹 (**1** ip-piki⌐ 一 匹, **2** ni⌐-hiki 二匹, **3** sa⌐m-biki 三匹, **how many** na⌐m-biki 何 匹)

crack suki(-ma) 透き(間); *(wide)* ware-me 割れ目; *(fine)* hibi⌐ ひ び; *(flaw)* kizu 傷

crack: it cracks warema⌐su (wareru, warete) 割れます(割 れる, 割れて)

crackers kura⌐kkā クラッカー, bisuke⌐tto ビスケット

cradle yuri-kago ゆりかご·揺り 籠

crag iwa⌐ 岩

cram: crams it in tsumema⌐su (tsume⌐ru, tsu⌐mete) 詰めます (詰める, 詰めて); **it is crammed in** tsumarima⌐su (tsuma⌐ru, tsuma⌐tte) 詰まりま す(詰まる, 詰まって)

cram school ju⌐ku 塾

crane *(bird)* tsu⌐ru つる·鶴; *(machine)* kure⌐n クレーン

crash *(plane)* tsuiraku 墜落; *(collision)* shōtotsu 衝突

crass egetsuna⌐i えげつない

crate waku⌐ 枠, hako⌐ 箱

crater funka⌐-kō 噴火口

crawl haima⌐su (ha⌐u, ha⌐tte) は います·這います(はう, はっ て)

crawly mu⌐zumuzu (shima⌐su; suru, shite) むずむず(します; する, して)

crazy ki-chiga⌐i (no) 気違い·き ちがい(の); **is crazy about ...** ni muchū de⌐su ...に夢中です

cream kuri⌐imu クリーム; **cream puff** shū-kuri⌐imu シュークリ ーム

crease shiwa しわ·皺, *(pleat)* ori-me⌐ 折り目

create tsukurima⌐su (tsuku⌐ru, tsuku⌐tte) 造［創］ります(造 ［創］る, 造［創］って)

creature se⌐ibutsu 生物

credit shin'yō 信用; *(one's ～)* noren のれん·暖簾; *(on ～)* kake⌐ 掛け, **credit sales** kake-uri 掛け売り = uri-kake 売り 掛け; **buys it on ～ (on one's account)** tsuke⌐ de kaima⌐su (kau, katte) つけで買います (買う, 買って)

credit card kurejitto-kā⌐do クレ ジットカード

creepy mu⌐zumuzu (shima⌐su; suru, shite) むずむず(します; する, して)

crest: family ～ monshō 紋章, mo⌐n 紋

crested ibis to⌐ki とき·朱鷺

crevice ware-me 割れ目

crew (member) norikumi⌐in 乗 組員, *(of ship)* sen'in 船員

crime tsu⌐mi 罪, hanzai 犯罪

criminal *(culprit)* ha⌐nnin 犯人

crimson makkaˈ (na) 真っ赤(な)

cripple kataˈwa 片輪・かたわ, fuˈgu 不具; **is crippled** ashiˈ ga fuˈ-jiyū desu 脚が不自由です

crisis kyūˈ 急, *(critical moment)* kiˈkiˈ 危機

crisp paripari (no) パリパリ・ぱりぱり(の)

criterion *(standard of judgment)* monosaˈshiˈ ものさし・物差し・物指し

critic hihyō-ka 批評家, *(judge)* hihaˈn-sha 批判者; *(commentator)* hyōron-ka 評論家

critical *(judgmental)* (na) 批判的(な); ~ **moment** kiˈkiˈ 危機

criticism 1. hihyō 批評; *(unfavorable)* akuhyō 悪評, *(favorable)* kōhyō 好評 **2.** *(commentary)* hyōron 評論

criticize hihyō shimaˈsu (suru, shite) 批評します(する, して); *(judges)* hihan/hiˈhan shimaˈsu (suru, shite) 批判/批判します(する, して); *(comments on)* hyōron shimaˈsu (suru, shite) 評論します(する, して); *(censures)* sememaˈsu (semeˈru, seˈmete) 責めます(責める, 責めて)

crock tsubo つぼ・壷

crocodile waˈni わに・鰐

crop *(harvest)* minori 実り, shūkaku 収穫

cross 1. *(symbol)* jūˈji 十字;

(wooden) jūji-ka 十字架; *("X")* baˈtsu ばつ **(vs. maru** 丸 **"O") 2.** *(goes across)* watarimaˈsu (wataru, watatte) 渡ります(渡る, 渡って), yoko-girimaˈsu (-giˈru, -giˈtte) 横切ります(切る, 切って); *(a height, an obstacle)* koemaˈsu (koeru, koete) 越えます(越える, 越えて) **3.** *(crosses one's legs)* ashiˈ o kumimaˈsu (kuˈmu, kuˈnde) 脚を組みます(組む, 組んで)

crossbeam keta けた・桁

crossing *(street intersection)* kōsaˈ-ten 交差点; *(crossing over)* ōdan 横断

crossroads jūˈjiˈ-ro 十字路, tsuji 辻; → **intersection**

cross-talk comedy manzaˈi 漫才

crotch mataˈ また・股・又

crouch shagamimaˈsu (shagamu, shagande) しゃがみます(しゃがむ, しゃがんで); *(so as not to be seen)* mi o fusemaˈsu (fuseˈru, fuseˈte) 身を伏せます(伏せる, 伏せて)

crow kaˈrasu からす・烏・鴉

crowd gunshū 群衆, renjū/renchū 連中/連中; **in crowds** zoˈrozoro ぞろぞろ

crowded: gets ~ komimaˈsu (koˈmu, koˈnde) こみます・混みます(こむ, こんで); **is ~** koˈnde imaˈsu (iru, ite) こんで[混んで]います(いる, いて)

crown ōkan 王冠
Crown Prince Kōta'ishi 皇太子,
 Kōta'ishi-sama 皇太子様
crucian carp fu'na ふな・鮒
crude so'matsu (na) 粗末(な),
 zatsu (na) 雑(な)
cruel mugo'i むごい, tsurai つら
 い, hakujō (na) 薄情(な),
 zankoku (na) 残酷(な),
 zangyaku (na) 残虐(な);
 cruelly hi'doku ひどく
crumble *(it crumbles)*
 kudakema'su (kudake'ru,
 kuda'kete) 砕けます(砕ける,
 砕けて); *(crumbles it)*
 kudakima'su (kuda'ku,
 kuda'ite) 砕きます(砕く, 砕
 いて)
crumb(s) pan-ku'zu パンくず,
 pan-ko' パン粉
crush *(crushes it)* tsubushima'su
 (tsubusu, tsubushite) つぶし
 ます(つぶす, つぶして); *(it
 gets crushed)* tsuburema'su
 (tsuburu, tsuburete) つぶれ
 ます(つぶれる, つぶれて)
crust kawa' 皮
crutch matsuba-zu'e 松葉杖
cry nakima'su (naku, naite) 泣き
 ます(泣く, 泣いて); *(cries
 out)* sakebima'su (sake'bu,
 sake'nde) 叫びます(叫ぶ, 叫
 んで)
cryptomeria *(Japanese cedar)*
 sugi 杉
cuckoo ka'kkō かっこう・郭公;

(little) hototo'gisu ほととぎす
 ・時鳥
cucumber kyu'ri きゅうり;
 [*sushi-bar term*] kappa かっぱ
cuff ka'fusu カフス
culprit ha'nnin 犯人
cultural festival bunka'-sai 文化祭
culture *(refinement)* kyōyō 教養;
 (civilization) bu'nka 文化;
 Culture Day (3 November)
 Bu'nka no hi' 文化の日
cultured pearls yōshoku-shi'nju
 養殖真珠
cumquat kinka'n きんかん
cunning zuru'i ずるい
cup chawan (o-cha'wan) 茶碗(お
 茶碗), koppu コップ, *(with
 handle)* ka'ppu カップ; *(cup-
 ful)* ...'-hai ...杯 (**1** i'p-pai 一杯,
 2 ni'-hai 二杯, **3** sa'm-bai 三杯,
 how many na'm-bai 何杯)
cupboard *(enclosed shelves)* to-
 dana 戸棚; *(for dishes)*
 shokki-to'dana 食器戸棚;
 (closet) oshi-ire 押し入れ
curb *(of road)* michi/dō'ro no
 fuchi' 道/道路のふち → **side-
 walk**
cure naoshima'su (nao'su,
 nao'shite) 治します(治す, 治
 して)
curios kottō'-hin 骨董品, **an-
 tiques**
curiosity kōki'shin 好奇心
curious *(inquisitive)* mono'zuki'
 (na) 物好き(な); *(novel)*

mezurashi'i 珍しい; **I'm
curious about something**
Shiri-ta'i/Kiki-tai koto' ga
arima'su. 知りたい/聞きたい
事があります.

currency *(bill/note)* satsu
(o-satsu) 札(お札); shihei
紙幣, shi'hei 紙幣

current 1. *(present)* ge'nzai no …
現在の…, ge'n(-) … 現…; ~
address gen-ju'sho 現住所; ~
deposit tōza-yo'kin 当座預金
2. *(tide)* chōryū 潮流

curry karē カレー; *(with rice)*
karē-ra'isu カレーライス

curse 1. a curse noro'i のろい・
呪い **2. curses** *(utters a curse)*
noroima'su (noro'u, noro'tte)
のろい[呪い]ます(のろう,
のろって), *(reviles)*
nonoshirima'su (nonoshi'ru,
nonoshi'tte) ののしります(の
のしる, ののしって)

cursor kāsoru カーソル

curt bu-a'isō (na) 無愛想(な),
bukki'ra'bō (na) ぶっきらぼう
(な)

curtail herashima'su (herasu,
herashite) 減らします(減らす,
減らして)

curtain kā'ten カーテン, mado'-
kake 窓掛け; *(bamboo)* sudare
すだれ・簾; *(stage)* maku' 幕

curtain rod kāten-ro'ddo カーテ
ンロッド

curtain time kaien-ji'kan

開演時間

curve magari 曲がり; *(road)*
kā'bu カーブ; *(bend)* sori' そ
り・反り, *(arch)* yumi-gata 弓
形

curve: it curves magarima'su
(magaru, magatte) 曲がります
(曲がる, 曲がって); **curves it**
magema'su (mageru, magete)
曲げます(曲げる, 曲げて)

cushion *(seat)* zabu'ton 座布団;
(spread) shiki-mono 敷物

custard pu'ri'n プリン; *(from
fish broth and eggs)* chawan-
mushi 茶碗蒸し

custodian *(janitor)* ko'zukai 小使
い; kanri'-nin 管理人

custom shūkan 習慣

customary ju'rai no 従来の

customer (o-)kyaku (お)客, o-
kyaku-sa'ma' お客様; *(patron)*
toku'i 得意, tokui-saki 得意
先

customs *(place)* zeikan 税関;
(tariff) kanzei 関税, ze'i 税

cut kirima'su (ki'ru, ki'tte) 切り
ます(切る, 切って); *(mows)*
karima'su (karu, katte) 刈りま
す(刈る, 刈って); *(it cuts
well)* kirema'su (kire'ru,
ki'rete) 切れます(切れる, 切
れて); **cuts the price** benkyō
shima'su (suru, shite) 勉強し
ます(する, して),
makema'su (makeru, makete)
負けます(負ける, 負けて)

cut: a cut *(of cloth)* kireˈ 切れ；
(percentage) riˈtsu 率

cut across yoko-girimaˈsu (-giˈru,
-giˈtte) 横切ります(切る，
切って)

cut class saborimaˈsu (saboˈru,
saboˈtte) さぼります(さぼる，
さぼって)

cut (down) *(lessens)*
herashimaˈsu (herasu,
herashite) 減らします(減らす，
減らして)；*(reduces)*
tsuzumemaˈsu (tsuzumeˈru,
tsuzuˈmete) つづめます(つづ
める，つづめて)；*(dilutes)*
warimaˈsu (waru, watte) 割り
ます(割る，割って)

cute kawaiˈi かわいい・可愛い，
kawairashiˈi かわいらしい・
可愛らしい

cutlery haˈ-mono 刃物

cutlet kaˈtsu カツ；**pork ~** ton-
katsu とんかつ・豚カツ

cut off kirimaˈsu (kiˈru, kiˈtteˈ)
切ります(切る，切って)；
tachimaˈsu (taˈtsu, taˈtte) 裁ち
ます・断ちます・絶ちます(裁
[断・絶]つ，裁[断・絶]って)

cut out *(eliminates)* habukimaˈsu
(habuˈku, habuˈite) 省きます
(省く，省いて)

cuttlefish *(squid)* ika いか；**dried
~** surume するめ

cycle 1. → **bicycle 2.** *(circulation)* junkan 循環

cylinder tsuˈtsu 筒

cynical hiniku (na) 皮肉(な)

cypress hiˈnoki ひのき・檜

— D —

Dacron daˈkuron ダクロン

dairy (shop) gyūnyū-ya 牛乳屋

dam daˈmu ダム

damage 1. songai 損害；soˈn 損，
gaˈi 害，hiˈgai 被害
2. damages it itamemaˈsu
(itameˈru, itaˈmete) 傷めます
(傷める，傷めて)，
sokonaimaˈsu (sokonaˈu,
sokonaˈtte) 損ないます(損な
う，損なって)

damascene niˈeˈ にえ，zōgaˈn 象
眼・象嵌

damask doˈnsu どんす・緞子

Damn! Shimaˈtta! しまった!

damn (fool) ...-me ...め；**~ idiot**
baka-me ばかめ

damp shimeppoˈi 湿っぽい；
gets damp shimerimaˈsu
(shimeru, shimette) 湿ります
(湿る，湿って)，nuremaˈsu
(nureru, nurete) ぬれます・濡
れます(ぬれる，ぬれて)

dampen nurashimaˈsu (nurasu,

nurashite) ぬらします・濡らします(ぬらす, ぬらして), shimeshima'su (shimesu, shimeshite) 湿します(湿す, 湿して)

damp (hand-)towel shibori' 絞り, o-shi'bori おしぼり・お絞り

dampness shikki⁽ⁿ⁾ 湿気, shikke⁽ⁿ⁾ 湿気

dance odori (o shima'su; suru, shite) 踊り(をします; する, して); **dances** odorima'su (odoru, odotte) 踊ります(踊る, 踊って)

dandelion ta'mpopo たんぽぽ

dandruff fuke ふけ

dandy (fancy dresser) osha're おしゃれ

danger kiken 危険; (crisis) kyū 急; (fear/worry lest ...) ...osore'/shimpai ...恐れ/心配

dangerous abunai 危ない, kiken (na) 危険(な); yaba'i やばい; (delicate, ticklish) kiwado'i きわどい

dangle (dangles it) sagema'su (sage'ru, sa'gete) 下げます(下げる, 下げて), tarashima'su (tara'su, tara'shite) 垂らします(垂らす, 垂らして); (it dangles) tarema'su (tare'ru, ta'rete) 垂れます(垂れる, 垂れて)

dangling (idly) bu'rabura ぶらぶら

dare (to do) a'ete (shima'su) あえて(します)

dark 1. kurai 暗い; (color) ko'i

濃い COLOR NAME (no) (の) **2. the dark** higure 日暮れ, yami' 闇 **3. it gets dark** hi ga kurema'su (kureru, kurete) 日が暮れます(暮れる, 暮れて)

dark blue ko'n 紺 = kon-iro (no) 紺色(の)

darkness yami' 闇

darling kawai'i かわいい・可愛い, kawairashi'i かわいらしい・可愛らしい

data de'ta データ

date de'to デート; (of month) hizuke 日付; (complete) nenga'ppi 年月日; ~ **of birth** seinen-ga'ppi 生年月日

date (a couple) abe'kku アベック

date (engagement) yakusoku (o-yakusoku) 約束(お約束)

date (fruit) natsume なつめ

daughter musume (san) 娘(さん); (your) ojō'-san お嬢さん

dawn yoake' 夜明け

day hi 日, ... hi' ...日; (daytime) hiru' (o-hi'ru) 昼(お昼), hiru-ma' 昼間; **the ~ in question, that very ~** tōjitsu 当日; (fixed) ~ hinichi 日にち

day after tomorrow asa'tte あさって・明後日, myōgo'-nichi 明後日

day before last/yesterday ototo'i おととい・一昨日, issaku'-jitsu 一昨日

daydream bon'ya'ri shima'su ぼんやりします

day in and day out akete' mo

kurete⌐ mo 明けても暮れても

day off yasumi⌐ (no hi⌐) 休み（の日）, kyūjitsu 休日

days: 1 ichi-nichi⌐ 一日, **2** fu̱tsuka 二日, **3** mikka 三日, **4** yokka 四日, **5** itsu̱ka⌐ 五日, **6** muika 六日, **7** nanoka⌐ 七日, **8** yōka 八日, **9** kokonoka⌐ 九日, **10** tōka 十日; **14** jū⌐-yokka 十四日; **24** ni⌐-jū yokka 二十四日; (*others* ...-nichi ...日); **how many** na⌐n-nichi 何日

daytime hiru⌐ (o-hi⌐ru) 昼（お昼）, hiru-ma⌐ 昼間

dazed: gets ~ mayoima⌐su (mayo⌐u, mayo⌐tte) 迷います（迷う，迷って）

dazzling mabushi⌐i まぶしい・眩しい

DC, direct current chokuryū 直流

dead shinda ... 死んだ...; **~ person** shinda hito⌐ 死んだ人, shinin 死人; **is ~** shinde ima⌐su (iru, ite) 死んでいます（いる，いて）

deadline (shimekiri-)ki⌐gen（締め切り・〆切）期限, (shimekiri-)ki⌐jitsu（締め切り・〆切）期日

deaf (*person*) mimi⌐ no kikoenai hito 耳の聞こえない人; **is deaf** mimi⌐ ga fu⌐-jiyū desu 耳が不自由です

deal (*transaction*) to⌐ri-hi̱ki 取引

deal (*cards*) kubarima⌐su (kuba⌐ru, kuba⌐tte) 配ります（配る，配って）

deal: a good/great deal → lots, much

dealer (*retail outlet*) hamba⌐i-ten 販売店; (*seller of ...*) ...⌐-shō ...商, ...-ya ...屋

deal in (*sells*) urima⌐su (uru, utte) 売ります（売る，売って）, hambai shima⌐su (suru, shi̱te) 販売します（する，して）

deal with tori-atsukaima⌐su (-atsuka⌐u, -atsuka⌐tte) 取り扱います（扱う，扱って）; (*treats a person*) ashiraima⌐su (ashira⌐u, ashira⌐tte) あしらいます（あしらう，あしらって）; (*copes*) sho⌐ri/sho⌐bun/sho⌐chi shima(⌐)su (suru, shi̱te) 処理/処分/処置します（する，して）; (*disposes of a matter*) shi⌐matsu shima(⌐)su (suru, shi̱te) 始末します（する，して）

dear 1. (*beloved*) shi̱tashi⌐i 親しい, itoshi⌐i いとしい・愛しい, natsu̱kashi⌐i 懐かしい; **Dear Sir/Madam** Ha⌐ikei 拝啓; **Dear dear!** O⌐yaoya! おやおや!; **Dear me!** Ma⌐! まあ! **2. → expensive**

death shi⌐ 死

debate 1. tō⌐ron 討論, ronsō 論争 **2. debates it** ron-jima⌐su (ron ji⌐ru, ro⌐n jito) 論じます（論じる，論じて）

debt shakki⌐n 借金

decay kuchima⌐su (kuchi⌐ru, ku̱⌐chite) 朽ちます（朽ちる，

朽ちて); kusarima͞su
(kusa͞ru, kusa͞tte) 腐ります
（腐る，腐って）

decayed tooth mushi-ba 虫歯

deceive → **cheat**　　「12月

December Jūni-gatsu͞ 十二月·

decent: a ~ /**respectable** …
cho͞tto shita … ちょっとした…

decide kimema͞su (kimeru,
kimete) 決めます（決める，決
めて); kettei shima͞su (suru,
shite) 決定します（する，して）

decision kettei 決定

deck (of ship) kampa͞ n 甲板,
de͞kki デッキ; → **pack (of
cards)**

decline 1. (refuses) kotowari-
ma͞su (kotowa͞ru, kotowa͞tte)
断わります（断わる，断わっ
て) 2. (it fades) otoroema͞su
(otoro͞e͞ru, otoro͞ete) 衰え
ます（衰える，衰えて）

decorate kazarima͞su (kazaru,
kazatte) 飾ります（飾る，飾っ
て）

decoration kazari(-mono) 飾り
（物), sōshoku 装飾

decoy otori おとり

decrease (it decreases) herima͞su
(heru, hette) 減ります（減る,
減って); (decreases it)
herashima͞su (herasu,
herashite) 減らします（減ら
す，減らして）

deduct hikima͞su (hiku, hiite) 引
きます（引く，引いて）

deed (act) shiwaza 仕業, kō͞i 行
為

deep 1. fuka͞i 深い 2. (saturated
color) ko͞i 濃い; ~ **red**
makka͞ (na) 真っ赤(な)

deeply fuka͞ku 深く, (feeling
~) shimiji͞mi (to) しみじみ
（と）

deepness fuka͞sa 深さ; (of color)
ko͞sa 濃さ

deer shika͞ 鹿

defeat make 負け, shippai 失敗;
(defeats) makashima͞su
(makasu, makashite)
負かします（負かす，負かし
て), yaburima͞su (yabu͞ru,
yabu͞tte) 破ります（破る，
破って); (is defeated)
makema͞su (makeru, makete)
負けます（負ける，負けて),
mairima͞su (ma͞iru, ma͞itte)
参ります（参る，参って),
okure o torima͞su (to͞ru,
to͞tte) 遅れを取ります（取る，
取って）

defecate daibe͞n shima(͞)su
(suru, shite) 大便します（す
る，して); **defecation** daibe͞n
大便

defect kette͞ n 欠点, kizu͞ 傷

defend mamorima͞su (mamo͞ru,
mamo͞tte) 守ります（守る，
守って）

defer nobashima͞su (noba͞su,
noba͞shite) 延ばします（延ば
す，延ばして）

deficiency fusoku 不足
deficit (figures) aka-ji 赤字
definite ittei (no) 一定（の）
definitely *(firmly)* kippa'ri (to)
きっぱり（と）
defy ... ni sakaraima'su
(sakara'u, sakara'tte) ...に逆ら
います（逆らう，逆らって）
degree *(extent)* te'ido 程度, do'
度, kagen 加減; **... degrees ...**
-do ...度; *(school)* ga'ku'i 学位
delay *(delays it)* okurasema'su
(okuraseru, okurasete) 遅らせ
ます（遅らせる，遅らせて）;
(gets delayed) okurema'su
(okureru, okurete) 遅れます
（遅れる，遅れて）
delete tori-keshima'su (-ke'su,
-ke'shite) 取り消します（消
す，消して）
deletion tori-keshi 取り消し
deliberate *(intentional)* ko'i no
故意の
deliberately wa'za to わざと,
wa'zawaza わざわざ, ko'i ni
故意に
delicate *(fine)* bimyō (na) 微妙
（な）; *(ticklish)* kiwado'i きわ
どい
delicious oishi'i おいしい,
uma'i/mma'i うまい
delight: is delighted
yorokobima'su (yoroko'bu,
yoroko'nde) 喜びます（喜ぶ，
喜んで）; **with great delight** ō-
yo'rokobi de 大喜びで

delightful ureshi'i うれしい・嬉
しい
delimit kagirima'su (kagi'ru,
kagi'tte) 限ります（限る，限
って）
delirium uwagoto うわごと・う
わ言
deliver todokema'su (todoke'ru,
todo'kete) 届けます（届ける，
届けて）
delivered food (o-)demae （お)出
前
delivery haitatsu 配達;
restaurant ~ (service/person)
demae 出前, **(person)** dema'e'-
mochi 出前持ち
deluxe jō' 上, jōtō (no) 上等（の),
gō'ka (na) 豪華（な）
demand yōkyū/seikyū
(shima'su; suru, shite) 要求
/請求（します; する，して）;
motomema'su (motome'ru,
moto'mete) 求めます（求める，
求めて）
demand: is in ~ *(= sells)*
urema'su (ureru, urete) 売れま
す（売れる，売れて）
demanding *(overly strict)*
yakamashi'i やかましい
democracy minshu-shu'gi 民主主
義
demolishes kuzushima'su
(kuzu'su, kuzu'shite) 崩します
（崩す，崩して）; hakai
shima'su (suru, shite) 破壊し
ます（する，して）
denial uchi-keshi 打ち消し, hitei
否定
denomination → sect

dense ko⌐i 濃い, mi⌐tsu (na) 密
(な), missetsu (na) 密接(な)
dent kubomi 窪み・くぼみ
dentifrice ha-mi⌐gaki 歯磨き
dentist ha⌐-isha 歯医者
deny uchi-keshima⌐su (-ke⌐su,
-ke⌐shite) 打ち消します(消
す, 消して), hitei shima⌐su
(suru, shite) 否定します(す
る, して)
deodorant (personal) dasshū⌐-zai
脱臭剤; (household, etc.)
shūki-dome 臭気止め
departing at/from (TIME/PLACE)
… ha⌐tsu (no) …発(の)
department store depā⌐to デパー
ト
departure shuppatsu 出発;
TIME/PLACE ha⌐tsu (no …) 発
(の…); **point of ~** shup-
pa⌐tsu⌐-ten 出発点
dependence irai 依頼
depend on (… ni) tayorima⌐su
(tayo⌐ru, tayo⌐tte) (…に)頼り
ます(頼る, 頼って), irai
shima⌐su (suru, shite) 依頼し
ます(する, して); **it depends
(on …)** (… ni) yorima⌐su
(yoru, yotte) (…に)よります
(よる, よって), (NOUN,
VERB-i い)-shi⌐dai desu 次第で
す
depilatory datsumō⌐-zai 脱毛剤
deposit 1. azukema⌐su (azuke⌐ru,
azu⌐kete) 預けます(預ける,
預けて); (money) yokin/

chokin shima⌐su (suru, shite)
預金/貯金します(する, して);
tsumima⌐su (tsumu, tsunde) 積
みます(積む, 積んで)
2. → down payment
depressed (feeling) ki ga omoi 気
が重い
depressed: gets ~ (concave)
hekomima⌐su (hekomu,
hekonde) へこみます(へこ
む, へこんで)
depression (hard times) fuke⌐iki
不景気; (hollow) kubomi 窪
み・くぼみ
depth → deepness
derailed: is ~ dassen shima⌐su
(suru, shite) 脱線します(す
る, して); **derailment** dassen
脱線
descend kudarima⌐su (kudaru,
kudatte) 下ります(下る,
下って)
descendants shi⌐son 子孫
descent (going down) kudari 下
り
describe … (no koto⌐) o
kuwa⌐shiku iima⌐su (yū, itte/
yutte) …(の事)を詳しく言い
ます(言う, 言って/ゆって);
(explains it) setsumei shima⌐su
(suru, shite) 説明します(す
る, して); **→ relate**
description setsumei 説明
desert sa⌐baku 砂漠　「然(の)
deserved (proper) tōzen (no) 当
design (sketch) zuan 図案; (plans

it) hakarima̶su (haka̶ru, haka̶tte) 図ります(図る, 図って)

designate atema̶su (ateru, atete) 当てます(当てる, 当てて); shitei shima̶su (suru, shite) 指定します(する, して); → **name**

designation shitei 指定; → **name**

desirable nozomashi⌐i 望ましい, hoshi̶i 欲しい; **most ~** *(ideal)* motte-ko̶i (no) もってこい(の)

desire 1. a desire nozomi⌐ 望み, omo̶i 思い, ne̶n 念; *(hope)* kibō 希望 **2. desires it (… ga)** hoshi̶i (…が)欲しい; *(wants to do)* (shi)-ta̶i desu (し)たいです; *(hopes for)* nozomima̶su (nozo⌐mu, nozo⌐nde) 望みます(望む, 望んで)

desk tsukue 机, ta⌐ku 卓; *(desktop)* takujō 卓上; **~ lamp** sutando スタンド = denki-suta̶ndo 電気スタンド

despair, desperation zetsubō 絶望, ya̶ke やけ

desperately *(= hard)* isshō-ke̶mmei ni 一生懸命に; *(= out of despair)* ya̶ke ni na̶tte やけになって

despise keībetsu shima̶su (suru, shite) 軽蔑します(する, して)

despite (that) (sore na̶) no ni (それな)のに

dessert deza̶to デザート

destination iku tokoro̶ 行く所, mokuteki̶-chi 目的地; *(last stop)* shūten 終点

destiny u̶mmei 運命

destroy kowashima̶su (kowa̶su, kowa̶shite) 壊します(壊す, 壊して); hakai shima̶su (suru, shite) 破壊します(する, して); horoboshima̶su (horobo⌐su, horobo⌐shite) 滅ぼします(滅ぼす, 滅ぼして)

detach hanashima̶su (hana̶su, hana̶shite) 離します(離す, 離して)

detailed kuwashi̶i 詳しい; bisai (na) 微細(な); seimitsu (na) 精密(な)

details kuwashi̶i koto̶ 詳しい事, shōsai 詳細; *(complexities)* ikisatsu いきさつ・経緯

detect → **see**; → **smell**; → **hear**; → **discover**; → **discern**

detective tantei 探偵

deteriorate *(weather)* kuzurema̶su (kuzure̶ru, kuzu̶rete) 崩れます(崩れる, 崩れて)

determination *(decision)* kettei 決定; *(resolve)* ke̶sshi̶n 決心

determine (to do) kettei shima̶su (suru, shite) 決定します(する, して)

detest nikumima̶su (niku̶mu, niku̶nde) 憎みます(憎む, 憎んで)

detour mawari⌐-michi 回り道, ukai 迂回, tōma⌐wari 遠回り

develop 1. *(it unfolds)* hattatsu/hatten shima⌐su (suru, shite) 発達/発展します(する，して) **2.** *(processes film)* genzō shima⌐su (suru, shite) 現像します(する，して)

developing nation hatten tojō-koku 発展途上国

development hattatsu 発達, hatten 発展, *(process)* nariyuki 成り行き, *(course)* keika 経過; **housing ～** danchi 団地

deviate sorema⌐su (sore⌐ru, so⌐rete) それます・逸れます(それる，それて)

device *(gadget)* shikake 仕掛け; *(scheme)* kufū 工夫

devil oni⌐ 鬼, a⌐kuma 悪魔

devil's-tongue root made into gelatin strips konnya⌐ku⌐ こんにゃく

dew tsu⌐yu 露

diabetes tōnyō-byō 糖尿病

diagonal nana⌐me (no) 斜め(の)

diagram zu 図, zuhyō 図表, zukai 図解

dialect namari⌐ なまり・訛り, hōge⌐n 方言

dialogue (lines) seri⌐fu せりふ・台詞

diamond da⌐iya ダイヤ, daiyamo⌐ndo ダイヤモンド, kongō⌐-seki 金剛石

diapers oshi⌐me おしめ, omu⌐tsu 「おむつ

diarrhea geri 下痢

diary nikki 日記

dice saiko⌐ro さいころ

dictation kaki⌐tori 書き取り

dictator dokusa⌐i-sha 独裁者, wa⌐m-man ワンマン

dictionary jibiki⌐ 字引, jisho⌐ 辞書, ji⌐ten 辞典; **～ entry** midashi 見出し, midashi⌐-go 見出し語

did shima⌐shita (shita, shite) しました(した，して)

didn't shimase⌐n deshita (shina⌐katta, shina⌐ide) しませんでした(しなかった，しないで)

die 1. shinima⌐su (shinu, shinde) 死にます(死ぬ，死んで), naku-narima⌐su (-naru, -natte) 亡くなります(なる，なって); i⌐ki o hiki-torima⌐su (-to⌐ru, -to⌐tte) 息を引き取ります(取る，取って) **2.** → **dice**

diet kite⌐i-shoku 規定食, ...⌐-shoku ...食

Diet *(parliament)* kokkai 国会, gi⌐kai 議会; *(building)* (kokkai) giji-dō (国会)議事堂

differ kotonarima⌐su (kotona⌐ru, kotona⌐tte) 異なります(異なる，異なって); **～ in opinion** i⌐ken ga chigaima⌐su (chigau, chigatte) 意見が違います(違う，違って)

difference chigai 違い, sōi 相違, sa⌐ 差, sa⌐i (sa⌐-i) 差異(差異);

(a big ~) taˈisa 大差; *(differentiation)* kuˈbetsu 区別; *(price ~ , commission)* saˈya さや; **~ in time** jiˈsa 時差

difference: it makes no ~ kamaimaseˈn (kamawaˈnai, kamawaˈnaide) 構いません（構わない，構わないで）

different: is ~ chigaimaˈsu (chigau, chigatte) 違います（違う，違って）; kotonarimaˈsu (kotonaˈru, kotonaˈtte) 異なります（異なる，異なって）; **a ~ direction** tahōˈ 他方; **~ opinion/view** iken (go-iken) 意見（ご意見）

differentiation kuˈbetsu 区別

difficult muzukashii 難しい; koˈnnan (na) 困難（な）; *(hard to do)* shi-nikuˈi しにくい; *(requires much effort)* honeˈ ga oremaˈsu (oreˈru, oˈrete) 骨が折れます（折れる，折れて）

difficulty koˈnnan 困難; *(hardship)* kuˈrō 苦労; *(nuisance)* mendōˈ 面倒

difficulty: with ~ yatto やっと

diffusion fukyū 普及; **gets diffused** fukyū shimaˈsu (suru, shite) 普及します（する，して）

dig horimaˈsu (hoˈru, hoˈtte) 掘ります（掘る，掘って）

digest konashimaˈsu (konasu, konashite) こなします（こなす，こなして），shōka shimaˈsu (suru, shite) 消化し

ます（する，して）

digestion shōka 消化

dignity hin 品

digress soremaˈsu (soreˈru, soˈrete) それます・逸れます（それる，それて）

dike tsutsumiˈ 堤, dote 土手, teibō 堤防

dilapidated: gets ~ aremaˈsu (areru, arete) 荒れます（荒れる，荒れて）

dilemma tōwaku 当惑

diligent kimben (na) 勤勉（な）, mame (na) まめ（な）

diligently kimben ni 勤勉に; seˈsse-to せっせと

dilute *(dilutes it)* (mizu de) warimaˈsu (waru, watte) （水で）割ります（割る，割って）

dim 1. *(faint)* kaˈsuka (na) かすか（な）, *(dark)* kurai 暗い; **Dim your headlights.** Heddoraˈito o kuraku shite kudasaˈi. ヘッドライトを暗くして下さい。 **2.** *(gets dim)* kasumimaˈsu (kasumu, kasunde) かすみます・霞みます（かすむ，かすんで）

dime store komamoˈnoˈ-ya 小間物屋; **dime-store goods** komaˈ-mono 小間物

dimple eˈkubo えくぼ

dine shokuji shimaˈsu (suru, shite) 食事します（する，して）

diner *(dining car)* shokudōˈ-sha 食堂車

dining room shokudō 食堂
dinner *(meal)* shokuji 食事,
go'han ご飯; *(supper)* ban-
go'han 晩ご飯, yūshoku 夕食,
yū-han 夕飯, yū-meshi 夕飯
diploma menjō⌐ 免状
diplomacy gaikō 外交
diplomat *(= diplomatic official)*
gaikō'-kan 外交官; *(= diplo-
matic person)* gaikō-ka 外交
家
diplomatic gaikō-teki (na) 外交
的(な); gaikō no 外交の; ~
relations gaikō 外交
direct 1. chokusetsu (no) 直接
(の); **goes ~ (through to
destination)** tōshi' de ikima'su
通しで行きます **2.** *(tells the
way)* (michi o) oshiema'su
(oshieru, oshiete) (道を)教え
ます(教える, 教えて)
3. *(guides, coaches)* shidō
shima'su (suru, shite) 指導し
ます(する, して); *(a film)*
kantoku shima'su (suru, shite)
監督します(する, して)
direct current chokuryū 直流
direction hōkō 方向; kentō' 見当;
hōme'n 方面; ... (no) hō' ...
(の)方; hōgaku 方角
directions *(instructions)* shi'ji 指
示, oshie 教え; **gives ~ (to a
destination)** michi o
oshiema'su (oshieru, oshiete)
道を教えます(教える, 教え
て)

directly chokusetsu (ni) 直接(に),
zutto ずっと, jika-ni じかに,
(= immediately) su'gu すぐ,
(= shortly) ma-mo'-naku 間も
なく
director *(coach)* shidō'-sha 指導
者; *(of a film)* kantoku 監督
directory *(telephone)* denwa-chō
電話帳; *(list of names)* meibo
名簿
dirt yogore 汚れ; *(filth)* doro' 泥;
(grime) aka' あか・垢; *(soil)*
tsuchi' 土
dirty 1. kitana'i 汚い, fuketsu
(na) 不潔(な); **gets dirty**
yogorema'su (yogoreru,
yogorete) 汚れます(汚れる,
汚れて); **dirties it**
yogoshima'su (yogosu,
yogoshite) 汚します(汚す, 汚
して) **2.** *(~-minded)* e'tchi
(na) エッチ(な); ~ **story**
e'tchi na hanashi' エッチな話
disadvantage so'n 損; *(shortcoming)* kette⌐n 欠点, mainasu マ
イナス, ta'nsho 短所
disagreeable iya' (na) 嫌(な)
disappointed zannen (na) 残念
(な); **gets ~** gakka'ri
shima'su (suru, shite) がっか
りします(する, して)
disappointment shitsubō 失望;
(in love) shitsuren 失恋
disassemble barashima'su
(bara'su, bara'shite) ばらしま
す(ばらす, ばらして)

disaster sōnan 遭難, saina'n 災難, wazawai 災い; **has a ~** sōnan shima'su (suru, shite) 遭難します(する, して)

disastrous taihen (na) 大変(な)

discern 1. *(discriminates)* shikibetsu/bembetsu shima'su (suru, shite) 識別/弁別します(する, して) **2.** → **see**

discharge (from employment) ka'iko shima'(ꝿ)su (suru, shite) 解雇します(する, して)

disciple deshi' 弟子

discipline 1. ki'ritsu 規律; shi-tsuke しつけ・躾 **2.** *(drills, trains)* kitaema'su (kitae'ru, kita'ete) 鍛えます(鍛える, 鍛えて), *(brings up children, ...)* shitsukema'su (shitsuke'ru, shitsu'kete) しつけます(しつける, しつけて)

disconnect hazushima'su (hazusu, hazushite) 外します(外す, 外して), hanashima'su (hana'su, hana'shite) 離します(離す, 離して)

disconnected: gets ~ *(comes off)* hazurema'su (hazureru, hazurete) 外れます(外れる, 外れて)

discontent *(grumbling)* fuhei 不平 ꝿ(な)

discontented fuman (na) 不満

discount wari-biki 割引, ne-biki 値引き

discourage ki o kujikima'su (kuji'ku, kuji'ite) 気をくじきます(くじく, くじいて); **gets discouraged** ki ga kujikema'su (kujike'ru, kuji'kete) 気がくじけます(くじける, くじけて)

discourtesy bu'rei 無礼, shitsu'rei 失礼

discover *(finds)* mitsukema'su (mitsukeru, mitsukete) 見つけます(見つける, 見つけて), hakken shima'su (suru, shite) 発見します(する, して); → **find out**

discrepancy chigai 違い, sa'ꝿ 差, sōi 相違; *(gap)* zure' ずれ

discretion tsutsushimi'ꝿ 慎み, tego'koro 手心

discriminate *(distinguishes them)* mi-wakema'su (-wake'ꝿru, -wa'ꝿkete) 見分けます(分ける, 分けて), shikibetsu /bembetsu shima'su (suru, shite) 識別/弁別します(する, して)

discrimination sa'betsu 差別; ku'betsu 区別; *(distinguishing)* shikibetsu 識別, bembetsu 弁別

discuss *(talks it over)* hanashi-aima'su (-a'ꝿu, -a'ꝿtte) 話し合います(合う, 合って), sōdan shima'su (suru, shite) 相談します(する, して); *(debates, argues)* ron-jima'su (ron-ji'ꝿru, ro'ꝿn-jite) 論じます

（論じる，論じて）

discussion hanashi-ai 話し合い; hanashi 話; kyōgi 協議; *(argument)* rón 論, *(debate)* tō□ron 討論, ronsō 論争; *(roundtable ~)* zada'n-kai 座談会

disease byōki 病気

disembark jōriku shima'su (suru, shite) 上陸します(する，して)

disemploy ka'iko shima(□)su (suru, shite) 解雇します(する，して)

disgrace haji 恥; chijoku 恥辱, ojoku 汚辱; ~ **oneself** haji o kakima'su (ka'ku, ka'ite) 恥をかきます(かく，かいて)

disgraceful hazukashi'i 恥ずかしい

disgusted: gets ~ akirema'su (akireru, akirete) 呆れます(呆れる，呆れて); iya' ni narima'su (na'ru, na'tte) 嫌になります(なる，なって)

disgusting iya' (na) 嫌(な)

dish sara (o-sara) 皿(お皿); shokki 食器; **(how many** na'm-mai 何枚)

dishcloth fuki'n ふきん・布巾

dish cupboard shokki-to'dana 食器戸棚

dishearten → discourage

dishpan sara-arai-o'ke 皿洗い桶

dish rack shokki'-dana 食器棚

dishtowel fuki'n ふきん・布巾

disinfectant shōdoku'-yaku/-zai 消毒薬/剤

dislikable niku'i 憎い, iya' (na) 嫌(な)

dislike ... ga kirai de'su (iya' desu) ...が嫌いです(嫌です)，... o iya-garima'su (-ga'ru, -ga'tte) ...を嫌がります(がる，がって)

dismal *(gloomy)* uttōshi'i うっとうしい

dismiss *(from employment)* ka'iko shima(□)su (suru, shite) 解雇します(する，して)

dismissal *(from employment)* ka'iko 解雇, *(of servant)* hima 暇

disobey ... ni somukima'su (somu'ku, somu'ite) ...に背きます(背く，背いて)

disorder konran 混乱, ko'nzatsu 混雑, midare' 乱れ, yami' 闇; **in disorder** mechamecha めちゃめちゃ

disorderly rambō (na) 乱暴(な)

dispatched from/at (PLACE/TIME) ... ha'tsu (no) ...発(の)

dispensary yakkyoku 薬局

disperse *(= they scatter)* chirima'su (chiru, chitte) 散ります(散る，散って)

display → show

displease fu-yu'kai ni shima'su (suru, shite) 不愉快にします(する，して)

displeased, displeasing fu-yu'kai

(na) 不愉快（な）

dispose of shi̥matsu shima(ꜜ)su
(suru, shi̥te) 始末します（す
る，して）; sho̞ri shima(ꜜ)su
(suru, shi̥te) 処理します（す
る，して）

disposition 1. seishi̥tsu 性質;
(nature) taꜜchi たち・質, shoꜜ
性; *(temperament)* teꜜnsei 天性;
(attitude) taꜜido 態度 **2.** *(dealing with)* sho̞ri 処理, sho̞bun
処分, sho̞chi 処置

dispute arasoꜜi 争い, tōꜜron 討
論, sōꜜron 争論

dissatisfied fuman (na) 不満（な）

dissertation rombun 論文, *(for a
degree)* gakui-roꜜmbun 学位論
文, *(doctoral)* hakase-roꜜmbun
博士論文

dissipation dōraꜜku 道楽

dissolve *(dissolves it)*
tokashimaꜜsu (tokaꜜsu,
tokaꜜshi̥te) 溶かします（溶か
す，溶かして）; *(it dissolves)*
tokemaꜜsu (tokeꜜru, toꜜkete) 溶
けます（溶ける，溶けて）

distance kyo̞ri 距離

distant *(far)* tōi 遠い, haꜜruka
(na) はるか・遥か（な）; *(gets
distant)* hedatarimaꜜsu
(hedataꜜru, hedataꜜtte) 隔たり
ます（隔たる，隔たって）

**distilled liquor (from yam or
rice)** shōchūꜜ 焼酎

distilled water jōryūꜜ-sui 蒸留水

distinctly hakkiꜜri はっきり

distinguish *(discriminates)* mi-
wakemaꜜsu (-wakeꜜru,
-waꜜkete) 見分けます（分け
る，分けて）, shi̥kibetsu/
bembetsu shimaꜜsu (suru,
shi̥te) 識別/弁別します（する，
して）

distort yugamemaꜜsu
(yugameꜜru, yugaꜜmete) ゆ
がめます・歪めます（ゆがめる，
ゆがめて）; **gets distorted**
yugamimaꜜsu (yugaꜜmu,
yugaꜜnde) ゆがみます・歪みま
す（ゆがむ，ゆがんで）

distortion yugamiꜜ ゆがみ・歪
み

distress 1. nayamiꜜ 悩み,
kurushiꜜmiꜜ 苦しみ
2. *(afflicts)* kurushimemaꜜsu
(kurushimeꜜru, kurushiꜜmete)
苦しめます（苦しめる，苦し
めて）; **gets distressed**
kurushimimaꜜsu (kurushiꜜmu,
kurushiꜜnde) 苦しみます（苦し
む，苦しんで）

distribute kubarimaꜜsu (kubaꜜru,
kubaꜜtte) 配ります（配る，
配って）; wakemaꜜsu (wakeꜜru,
waꜜkete) 分けます（分ける，
分けて）

district chihōꜜ 地方; hōmeꜜn 方面,
...-nūꜜmen ...方面

disturb (... no) jama o shimaꜜsu
(suru, shi̥te) (...の)じゃま[邪
魔]をします（する，して）

disturbance *(intrusion)* (o-)jama

(お)じゃま・邪魔; *(unrest)* sōdō 騒動; *(strife)* arasoi 争い, ran 乱

disused fuyō (no) 不要(の)

ditch mizo 溝; hori 堀

dive (under) mogurimasu (moguru, mogutte) 潜ります (潜る, 潜って)

diver moguri 潜り; *(woman pearl ~)* ama 海女

diverse samazama (na) さまざま・様々(な)

divide *(divides it)* warimasu (waru, watte) 割ります(割る, 割って), wakemasu (wakeru, wakete) 分けます(分ける, 分けて); *(it divides)* waremasu (wareru, warete) 割れます(割れる, 割れて); wakaremasu (wakareru, wakarete) 分かれます(分かれる, 分かれて)

divide roughly (into main categories) taibetsu shimasu (suru, shite) 大別します(する, して)

dividing line wake-me 分け目

diving (under) moguri 潜り

division bu 部; *(army)* shidan 師団; *(branching)* wakare 分かれ

divorce rikon 離婚; **gets divorced from ... to** rikon shimasu (suru, shite) ...と離婚します(する, して)

do shimasu (suru, shite) します

(する, して); yarimasu (yaru, yatte) やります(やる, やって); nashimasu (nasu, nashite) なします(なす, なして); *(performs)* okonaimasu (okonau, okonatte) 行います(行う, 行って); [HONORIFIC] nasaimasu (nasaru, nasatte/ nasutte, nasaimashite) なさいます(なさる, なさって/ なすって, なさいまして); [HUMBLE, DEFERENTIAL] itashimasu (itasu, itashite, itashimashite) 致します(致す, 致して, 致しまして)

do: do it *(deprecating object)* yarakashimasu (yarakasu, yarakashite) やらかします(やらかす, やらかして)

do: do it over (again) yarinaoshimasu (-naosu, -naoshite) やり直します(直す, 直して)

docile sunao (na) すなお・素直(な)

dock dokku ドック

doctor 1. *(physician)* (o-)isha (san) (お)医者(さん), sensei 先生 **2.** *(Ph.D.)* hakase 博士

doctoral dissertation hakase-rombun 博士論文

doctor's office *(clinic)* byōin 病院

doctrine shugi 主義

document shorui 書類

dodge *(turns it aside)* sorashima⌐su (sora⌐su, sora⌐shite) そらします・逸らします(そらす, そらして)

does → **do; doesn't** → **don't**

dog inu⌐ 犬 (**1** ip-piki⌐ 一匹, **2** ni⌐-hiki 二匹, **3** sa⌐m-biki 三匹, **how many** na⌐m-biki 何匹)

dog tag *(= dog license)* inu⌐ no kansatsu 犬の鑑札; *(= name tag)* nafuda 名札

doll ningyō (o-ningyō) 人形(お人形); **festival** ~ hina-ni⌐ngyō ひな人形

dollar do⌐ru ドル

Doll's Festival (3 March) Hina-ma⌐tsuri ひな祭り

domestic *(not foreign)* koku⌐nai (no) 国内(の); *(domestically made)* kokusan (no) 国産(の)

domesticate narashima⌐su (nara⌐su, nara⌐shite) 慣らします(慣らす, 慣らして)

done *(ready)* dekima⌐shita 出来ました, de⌐kite ima⌐su (iru, ite) 出来ています(いる, いて); *(finished)* (shi)-te shimaima⌐shita (shimatta, shimatte) (し)てしまいました(しまった, しまって)

half-done *(cooked medium)* han-yake no 半焼けの

underdone *(cooked rare)* nama-yake no 生焼けの, *(beef)* re⌐a レア

well-done yo⌐ku yaketa 良く焼

けた, *(beef)* ue⌐rudan ウェルダン

donkey ro⌐ba ろば

don't shimase⌐n (shinai, shina⌐ide) しません(しない, しないで)

don't (do it)! (shite⌐ wa) dame⌐ desu (/da) (しては)だめです(/だ), ikemase⌐n (/ikenai) いけません(/いけない); (shi)-na⌐ide kudasai (し)ないで下さい

Don't be shy/reticent Go-enryo na⌐ku. ご遠慮なく.

Don't feel you have to rush Go-yukku⌐ri. ごゆっくり.

Don't go to any trouble O-kamai na⌐ku. お構いなく.

Don't worry about it Go-shimpai na⌐ku. ご心配なく.

doodling rakugaki 落書き

door to 戸, do⌐a ドア; *(hinged)* hiraki-do 開き戸; *(opaque sliding)* fusuma⌐ ふすま・襖; ~ **wing,** ~ **of a gate** tobira 扉

doorbell ri⌐n 鈴, be⌐ru ベル

doorknob hiki-te 引き手

dope *(narcotic)* mayaku 麻薬

dormitory kishu⌐ku⌐sha 寄宿舎, ryō⌐ 寮

dot ten 点, cho⌐bo ちょぼ, po⌐chi ぽち, po⌐tsu ぽつ; *(with)* **dots** bo⌐tsubotsu ぽつぽつ

double 1. ba⌐i (no) 倍(の), *(two-layer)* ni-jū (no) 二重(の); ~ **boiler** nijū-na⌐be 二重鍋;

~ **(room)** da¯buru ダブル＝
daburu-rū¯mu ダブルルーム;
~ **(-size) drink** da¯buru ダブル;
~ **s** *(tennis)* da¯burusu ダブル
ス **2. doubles it** (... o) ba⌐ɹ¯i ni
shima¯su (suru, shite) (...を)
倍にします(する，して)

double bed daburu-be¯ddo ダブ
ルベッド

double-breasted suit da¯buru ダ
ブル

double-check ne¯n o oshima¯su
(osu, oshite) 念を押します(押
す，押して)

double-cross 1. *(treachery)* ura-
gi⌐ɹri⌐ɹ 裏切り **2.** *(betrays)*
ura-girima¯su (-gi¯ru, -gi¯tte) 裏
切ります(切る，切って)

double plug *(two-way socket)*
futamata-soke¯tto 二又ソケッ
ト

double suicide shinjū 心中

doubt *(a doubt)* gimon 疑問,
utagai 疑い, fushin 不審;
(doubts it) utagaima¯su
(utagau, utagatte) 疑います
(疑う，疑って), fushin ni
omoima¯su (omo¯u, omo¯tte)
不審に思います(思う，思っ
て)

douche chūsu¯i-ki 注水器

dough nama-pan 生パン, neri¯-
ko¯ 練り粉

dove ha¯to 鳩

down shita e 下へ; **down** *(=
lower in price by)* ¥100

hyakue¯n-yasu 百円安

get down orima¯su (ori¯ru,
o¯rite) 下ります(下りる，
下りて)

go down kudarima¯su
(kudaru, kudatte) 下ります
(下る，下って),
sagarima¯su (saga¯ru,
saga¯tte) 下がります(下が
る，下がって)

hang down tarema¯su (tare¯ru,
ta¯rete) 垂れます(垂れる，
垂れて), sagema¯su
(sage¯ru, sa¯gete) 下げます
(下げる，下げて)

lie down nema¯su (neru, nete)
寝ます(寝る，寝て)

take down oroshima¯su
(oro¯su, oro¯shite) 下ろしま
す(下ろす，下ろして)

down payment atama-kin 頭金

downpour gō¯u 豪雨; **local ~**
shūchū-gō¯u 集中豪雨

downtown hanka-gai 繁華街

doze u¯touto shima(⌐)su (suru,
shite) うとうとします(する，
して)

dozen (ichi-)dā¯su (一)ダース,
jū-ni¯ 十二・12

Dr. ... ... sense¯i ...先生

draft *(military conscription)*
shōshū (shima¯su; suru, shite)
召集(します; する，して)

draft (beer) na¯ma 生, nama-
bi¯iru 生ビール

drag hipparima¯su (hip-

pa⌐ru, hippa⌐tte 引っ張ります（引っ張る, 引っ張って）, **hikima⌐su (hiku, hiite)** 引きます（引く, 引いて）, **hiki-zurima⌐su (-zuru, -zutte)** 引きずります（ずる, ずって）

dragnet te⌐ha⌐i 手配; **sets up a ～** te⌐ha⌐i shima(⌐)su (suru, shite) 手配します（する, して）

dragon ryū⌐ 竜·龍

dragonfly tombo とんぼ

drain 1. *(kitchen)* gesui 下水; *(ditch)* mizo 溝 **2. it drains off** hakema⌐su (hake⌐ru, ha⌐kete) はけます（はける, はけて）; **it drains well** hake⌐ ga i⌐i de⌐su はけがいいです

drain pipe to⌐i 樋

drama engeki 演劇, ge⌐ki 劇

Dramamine dorama⌐min ドラマミン

draperies tam-mono 反物

drapes kā⌐ten カーテン

draw 1. *(a picture)* egakima⌐su (ega⌐ku, ega⌐ite) 描きます（描く, 描いて） **2.** *(= pulls)* hikima⌐su (hiku, hiite) 引きます（引く, 引いて） **3.** *(water etc.)* kumima⌐su (kumu, kunde) 汲みます（汲む, 汲んで）

draw an underline kasen o hikima⌐su (hiku, hiite) 下線を引きます（引く, 引いて）

drawer *(of desk, etc.)* hiki-dashi 引き出し

drawers *(underwear)* zubo⌐n-shita ズボン下, zurō⌐su ズロース, momohiki 股引き

drawing *(diagram)* zu 図; *(picture)* e⌐ 絵

drawing room (= *parlor*) kyakuma 客間

draw near → approach

dreadful osoroshi⌐i 恐ろしい, sugo⌐i すごい·凄い

dream yume⌐ (o mima⌐su; mi⌐ru, mi⌐te) 夢（を見ます; 見る, 見て）

dreary uttōshi⌐i うっとうしい

dregs ka⌐su かす; ori おり

dress 1. ki-mono (o kima⌐su; kiru, kite) 着物（を着ます; 着る, 着て）; yō-fuku 洋服, fuku⌐ 服, *(woman's)* wampi⌐isu ワンピース, do⌐resu ドレス **2.** *(dresses vegetables, fish)* aema⌐su (ae⌐ru, a⌐ete) あえます·和えます（あえる, あえて）

dressmaker yōsa⌐i-shi 洋裁師, doresu-mē⌐kā ドレスメーカー

dressmaking yōsai 洋裁

dried 1. hoshi⌐-... 干し...; **～ persimmons** hoshi⌐-gaki 干し柿 **2. → dry**

dried bonito fish katsuo-bushi かつおぶし·鰹節

dried gourd strips kampyō⌐ かんぴょう

drill *(tool)* ki⌐ri きり·錐; *(practice)* do⌐ri⌐ru ドリル, (o-)

ke̅iko (お)けいこ・稽古;
(study) renshū 練習

drill *(training)* ku̅nren 訓練;
(trains) nerima̅su (ne̅ru,
ne̅tte) 練ります(練る, 練っ
て), ku̅nren shima̅su (suru,
shite)訓練します(する, して),
(disciplines) kitaema̅su
(kitae̅ru, kita̅ete) 鍛えます
(鍛える, 鍛えて)

drink nomima̅su (no̅mu,
no̅nde) 飲みます(飲む, 飲ん
で); **has a drink** i̅p-pai
nomima̅su/yarima̅su 一杯飲
みます/やります;
[HONORIFIC] meshiagarima̅su
(meshiagaru, meshiagatte)
召し上がります(召し上がる,
召し上がって); [HUMBLE]
itadakima̅su (itadaku,
itadaite) いただきます・頂き
ます(いただく, いただいて)

drink *(= beverage)* nomi̅-mono
飲み物

drinkable: is ~ nomema̅su
(nome̅ru, no̅mete) 飲めます
(飲める, 飲めて)

drinking water nomi̅-mizu 飲み
水

drip tarema̅su (tare̅ru, ta̅rete)
垂れます(垂れる, 垂れて)

drive (a car) unten shima̅su
(suru, shite) 運転します(す
る, して)

drive: what one is driving at
nerai ねらい・狙い

drive-in nori-komi 乗り込み

driver unte̅n-shu 運転手

driveway shadō 車道

drizzle kosame 小雨; *(on-and-
off)* shigure 時雨

droll yu̅kai (na) 愉快(な); →
funny

droop naema̅su (nae̅ru, na̅ete)
萎えます・なえます(萎える,
萎えて)

drop 1. *(drops it)* otoshima̅su
(oto̅su, oto̅shite) 落とします
(落とす, 落として), *(lets it
fall, spills)* tarashima̅su
(tara̅su, tara̅shite) 垂らしま
す(垂らす, 垂らして) **2.** *(it
drops)* ochima̅su (ochi̅ru,
o̅chite) 落ちます(落ちる, 落
ちて) **3.** *(a drop)* tsu̅bu 粒,
tama̅ 玉; *(counting)* ...-teki ...
滴

drop in yorima̅su (yoru, yotte)
寄ります(寄る, 寄って)

drop off *(a person from a
vehicle)* oroshima̅su (oro̅su,
oro̅shite) 降ろします(降ろ
す, 降ろして)

drown obore-jini shima̅su (suru,
shite) おぼれ[溺れ]死にしま
す(する, して)

drowse u̅touto shima()su
(suru, shite) うとうとします
(する, して)

drudging (away) a̅kuseku あく
せく

drug kusuri (o-kusu̅ri) 薬(お薬),

yakuhin 薬品

druggist kusuri-ya (san) 薬屋(さん)

drugstore kusuri-ya 薬屋, yak-kyoku 薬局

drum taiko (o-taiko) 太鼓(お太鼓), *(large)* ō-da͞iko 大太鼓; *(hourglass-shaped)* tsuzumi͞ 鼓, *(small)* ko-tsu͞zumi 小鼓

drunk: gets ~ yopparaima͞su (yopparau, yopparatte) 酔っぱらいます・酔っ払います(酔っぱらう, 酔っぱらって); yoima͞su (yo͞u, yo͞tte) 酔います(酔う, 酔って)

dry *(it dries)* kawakima͞su (kawa͞ku, kawa͞ite) 乾きます(乾く, 乾いて); *(dries it)* kawakashima͞su (kawaka͞su, kawaka͞shite) 乾かします(乾かす, 乾かして), *(foodstuff)* hoshima͞su (ho͞su, ho͞shite) 干します(干す, 干して)

dry cleaning dorai-kuri͞iniŋgu ドライクリーニング

dry goods tam-mono 反物, gofuku⁽ⁿ⁾-mono 呉服物; **~ store** gofuku-ya 呉服屋

dry land oka おか・陸

dry milk kona-mi͞ruku 粉ミルク

dually serves as ... o kanema͞su (kane͞ru, ka͞nete) ...を兼ねます(兼ねる, 兼ねて)

dub *(names)* nazukema͞su (nazuke͞ru, nazu͞kete) 名付けます(名付ける, 名付けて)

duck *(wild)* ka͞mo かも・鴨, *(tame)* ahiru あひる; *(canvas)* zu͞kku ズック

dude osha͞re おしゃれ

due to → **because; →** **supposed to**

dull nibu͞i 鈍い, noro͞i のろい; *(uninteresting)* taikutsu (na) 退屈(な), *(long-winded)* kudo͞i くどい; *(dull-witted)* wakari͞ ga waru͞i 分かりが悪い

dump *(discards)* sutema͞su (suteru, sutete) 捨てます(捨てる, 捨てて); *(dump site)* sute-ba 捨て場

dumpling dango (o-dango) だんご・団子(お団子); *(large stuffed bun)* manjū まんじゅう・饅頭; *(small meat-stuffed crescent)* gyōza ぎょうざ・餃子

dune sakyū 砂丘

dung kuso͞ くそ・糞, fu͞n ふん・糞

dupe ka͞mo カモ・鴨

duplicate *(= double)* ni-jū (no) 二重(の); **→** **copy**

during (...) no aida (ni) (...)の間(に); **~ the war** senji-chū 戦時中

dust 1. *(in air)* hokori͞ ほこり・埃, *(on ground, floor, etc.)* chiri ちり・塵; *(in house)* gomi͞ ごみ **2.** *(dusts it)* hatakima͞su (hata͞ku, hata͞ite) はたきます

（はたく，はたいて）
dustbin gomi﹃-bako ごみ箱
dustcloth zōkin ぞうきん・雑巾
duster hataki﹄ はたき
dustpan chiri-to﹄ri﹄ ちり取り・塵取り
Dutch Ora﹃nda no オランダの;
(language) Oranda-go オランダ語; *(person)* Oranda﹄-jin オランダ人
Dutch treat wari-kan 割り勘
duty 1. *(obligation)* gi﹄mu 義務
2. *(function)* yakume﹄ (o-yakume) 役目（お役目）, yaku﹄ (o-yaku) 役（お役）, hombun 本分; *(job post)* tsutome﹄ (o-tsutome) 務め（お務め）, yaku﹄

(o-yaku) 役（お役）; *(work, service)* ki﹄mmu 勤務; **those on ~** kimmu﹄-sha 勤務者; **the person on duty** to﹄ban (o-to﹄ban) 当番（お当番） **3.** *(import tax)* kanzei 関税, yunyū-zei 輸入税
duty: → off duty
dwarf trees bonsai 盆栽
dwindle herima﹄su (heru, hette) 減ります（減る，減って）, suku﹄na﹄ku narima﹄su (na﹄ru, na﹄tte) 少なくなります（なる，なって）
dye (it) soma﹄su (someru, somete) 染めます（染める，染めて）
dysentery se﹄kiri 赤痢

— E —

each [NUMBER, QUANTITY +]
...﹄zu﹄tsu ...ずつ; *(every)* mai-... 毎..., ka﹄ku(-) ... (goto ni) 各...（毎に）, ... goto ni ...毎に
each other o-tagai ni お互いに; [VERB-i い]-aima﹄su (-au/-a﹄u, -atte/-a﹄tte) 合います（合う/合う，合って/合って）
eagerly ne﹄sshi﹄n ni 熱心に
eager to (do) ze﹄-hi (shi)-tai ぜひ［是非］（し）たい, (shi)-tagarima﹄su (-taga﹄ru, -taga﹄tte) （し）たがります（たがる，たがって）

eagle washi わし・鷲
ear mimi﹄ 耳; **earache** mimi(﹃) no itami﹄ 耳の痛み
earlier *(= former)* ma﹄e no ... 前の...; [*bookish*] ze﹄n(-) ... 前...
early haya﹄i (ha﹄yaku) 早い（早く）; *(in good time)* hayame﹃ ni 早めに; **~ years** *(growing up)* sodachi﹄ (o-sodachi) 育ち（お育ち）
earn kasegima﹄su (kase﹄gu, kase﹄ide) 稼ぎます（稼ぐ，稼いで）
earnest majime (na) まじめ・真面

目（な）, *(serious)* honki (no) 本気（の）

earnings *(income)* shūnyū 収入

earpick mimi-ka⌐ki¬ 耳かき

earpieces *(of glasses frame)* tsuru⌐ つる

earring i⌐yaringu イヤリング, mimi-ka⌐zari 耳飾り, mimi-wa 耳輪

earth tsuchi¬ 土, tochi 土地; **the Earth** chikyū 地球

earthenware do⌐¬ki 土器; ~ **pan** hōro⌐ku¬ ほうろく・焙烙

earthquake jishin 地震

ease *(comfort)* raku¬ 楽; **at ease** jiyū¬ (ni) 自由（に）, yukku¬ri ゆっくり; ~ **it** yasumema⌐su (yasume¬ru, yasu¬mete) 休めます（休める, 休めて）

easily 1. taya¬suku たやすく, wa⌐ke-naku わけなく, muzō⌐sa ni 無造作に; assa⌐ri (to) あっさり（と） **2. →** undoubtedly

easily broken koware-yasu⌐i 壊れやすい

easily intoxicated sake ni yowa¬i 酒に弱い

east higashi⌐¬ 東, tō-... 東...; *(the east)* tōhō 東方, *(the eastern part)* tō¬bu 東部

East Asia Higashi-A⌐ji(y)a 東アジア［ヤ］, Tō¬a 東亜

east coast higashi-ka⌐igan 東海岸

easterly (wind) higashi-yori (no kaze) 東寄り（の風）

easy 1. yasashii やさしい・易しい, tayasu¬i たやすい, wa⌐ke-nai わけない, muzō⌐sa (na) 無造作（な）; ~ **(to do)** (shi)-yasu¬i （し）やすい, (shi)-i¬i （し）いい; ~ **to get to** iki-yasu¬i 行きやすい, ~ **to understand** wakari-yasu¬i 分かりやすい **2. →** comfortable

easygoing no⌐nki (na) のん気（な）, kiraku (na) 気楽（な）

easy money abuku⌐-ze¬ni あぶく銭

eat tabema⌐su (tabe¬ru, ta¬bete) 食べます（食べる, 食べて）, kuima⌐su (ku¬u, ku¬tte) 食います（食う, 食って）; *(has a meal)* shokuji shima⌐su (suru, shite) 食事します（する, して）; [HONORIFIC] meshiagarima⌐su (meshiaga⌐¬ru, meshiaga⌐¬tte) 召し上がります（召し上がる, 召し上がって）; [HUMBLE] itadakima⌐su (itadaku, itadaite) いただきます・頂きます（いただく, いただいて）

eat-in kitchen dii-kē¬ (DK) ディーケー, dainingu-ki¬tchin ダイニングキッチン

eaves noki 軒

echo hibiki¬ 響き, kodama こだま 小魂, hankyō 反響, *(it echoes)* hibikima⌐su (hibi¬ku, hibi¬ite) 響きます（響く, 響いて）

éclair shū-kuri¬imu シュークリ

economical keizai-teki (na) 経済
的（な）
economics ke̜izai 経済; *(science/
study)* keiza̜i-gaku 経済学
economize on ... o ken'yaku/
setsuyaku shima̜su (suru, shite)
...を倹約/節約します（する，し
て），shimema̜su (shime̜ru,
shi̜mete) 締めます（締める，締
めて）
economizing setsuyaku 節約
ecstasy muchū 夢中
edge fuchi̜ ふち・縁, hashi 端 =
hashikko/hajikko 端っこ/端
っこ, ha̜na 端, *(rim)* heri̜ へり
・縁, *(brink)* kiwa̜ 際, *(end)*
tamoto̜ たもと・袂, *(nearby)*
so̜ba そば; *(of knife)* ha 刃
educate *(rears)* sodatema̜su
(sodate̜ru, soda̜tete) 育てま
す（育てる，育てて）; → **teach**
education kyōiku 教育; *(learning)* gaku̜mon 学問, *(culture)*
kyōyō 教養; *(bringing up)*
yōiku 養育; **Ministry of Education** Mombu̜-shō 文部省
educational background
gakureki 学歴
eel unagi (o-u̜na) うなぎ・鰻（お
うな）; *(conger eel)* anago あな
ご・穴子; **broiled eel** kabayaki
蒲焼き, *(on rice in a lacquered
box)* una̜-jū うな重; *(on a
bowl of rice)* una-don うな丼
effect *(result)* kekka 結果;
(cause) ... (no) se̜i ...（の）せい;

(effectiveness) ki̜ki-me 効き目,
shirushi しるし, kō̜ka 効果;
(gist) mune̜ 旨; **in ~** yō-su̜ru
ni 要するに
effect: has/takes ~ kikima̜su
(kiku, kiite) 効きます（効く，
効いて）
effective yūkō (na) 有効（な）
efficiency nō̜ritsu 能率
efficient nōritsu-teki (na) 能率的
（な）
effort hone-o̜ri (o-honeori) 骨
折り（お骨折り）, do̜ryoku 努
力; ku̜rō (go-ku̜rō) 苦労（ご苦
労）; **with much ~**
sekkaku̜ せっかく; **requires
much ~** hone̜ ga orema̜su
(ore̜ru, o̜rete) 骨が折れます
（折れる，折れて）
effortless muzō̜sa (na) 無造作
（な）; **effortlessly** muzō̜sa ni
無造作に
egg tama̜go (o-ta̜mago, o-
ta̜ma) 卵・玉子（お卵・お玉子，
お玉）**(how many** na̜n-ko 何
個）
eggplant na̜su なす・茄子,
na̜subi なすび
egg rolls haru-maki 春巻
eggshell tama̜go no kara 卵の
殻
ego ji̜ga 自我
eight hachi̜ 八・8, yattsu̜ 八つ；
(8-oared racing boat) e̜ito/ē̜to
エイト/エート; **8 days** yōka
八日

eight: small things, pieces haˈk-ko 八個; **long things** haˈp-pon 八本; **flat things** hachiˈ-mai 八枚; **small animals/fish/bugs** hap-piki̱ˈ 八匹; **large animals** haˈt-tō 八頭; **birds** haˈp-pa 八羽; **machines/vehicles** hachiˈ-dai 八台; **books/magazines** has-satsu 八冊

eight degrees hachiˈ-do 八度

eighteen jū-hachiˈ 十八・18

eighth hachi-bammeˈ (no) 八番目(の), yattsu-meˈ (no) 八つ目(の); **the ~ day** yōka-meˈ 八日目, **(of the month)** yōka 八日

eight hundred hap-pyakuˈ 八百・800

eight thousand has-seˈn 八千・8,000

eight times hachiˈ-doˈ 八度, hak-kaˈi 八回, hap-peˈn 八遍

eighty hachi-jūˈ 八十・80; **~ thousand** hachi-maˈn 八万・80,000

either one doˈchira deˈ mo どちらでも

elapse tachimaˈsu (taˈtsu, taˈtte) 経ちます(経つ, 経って), hemaˈsu (heˈru, heˈte) 経ます(経る, 経て), keika shimaˈsu (suru, shi̱te) 経過します(する, して)

elastic *(material)* = **rubber** goˈmu ゴム; **~ band** wa-gomu 輪ゴム

elbow hijiˈ 肘・肱

eldest son chōˈnaˈn 長男

elect erabimaˈsu (eraˈbu, eraˈnde) 選びます(選ぶ, 選んで)

election seˈnkyo 選挙

electric: ~ appliances denki-kiˈgu 電気器具 = denki-yōˈhin 電気用品, **~ heater** denki-su̱tōˈbu 電気ストーブ, **~ hot plate** denki-koˈnro 電気こんろ[コンロ], **~ shaver** denki-kaˈmisori 電気かみそり, **~ vacuum cleaner** denki-sōjiˈki 電気掃除機

electric car deˈnsha 電車

electric fan sempūˈ-ki 扇風機

electrician denki-ya (san) 電気屋(さん)

electric(ity) deˈnki (no) 電気(の)

electric wire densen 電線

electron(ic) deˈnshi (no) 電子(の)

elegance hin 品, (o-)jōhiˈn (お)上品, fūˈryū 風流

elegant fūˈryū (na) 風流(な), yūˈbi (na) 優美(な), (o-)jōhiˈn na (お)上品な

element yōˈso 要素

elementary (primary) school shōgaˈkkō 小学校; **~ student** shōgaˈku-sei 小学生

elephant zōˈ 象

elevator erebeˈta = リフト

eleven jū-ichiˈ 十一・11

eliminate habukimaˈsu (habuˈku, habuˈite) 省きます(省く, 省いて), nozokimaˈsu (nozoku,

nozoite) 除きます(除く、除いて); ha'ijo shima('sụ (suru, shịte) 排除します(する、して)
elimination ha'ijo 排除
elite ichiryū (no) 一流(の)
else hoka (no/ni) 他(の/に); **or ~** ma'ta'-wa または・又は、sore-to'mo それとも; **somewhere ~** yoso' (no) よそ(の)
embankment teibō 堤防、tsụtsumi' 堤
embarrass komarasema'sụ (komarase'ru, komara'sete) 困らせます(困らせる、困らせて)、kurushimema'sụ (kurushime'ru, kurushi'mete) 苦しめます(苦しめる、苦しめて); **~ oneself** haji' o kakima'sụ (ka'ku, ka'ite) 恥をかきます(かく、かいて)
embarrassed: gets ~ komarima'sụ (koma'ru, koma'tte) 困ります(困る、困って)、kurushimima'sụ (kurushi'mu, kurushi'nde) 苦しみます(苦しむ、苦しんで); **feels ~** terema'sụ (tere'ru, te'rete) 照れます(照れる、照れて)、kimari ga waru'i (desụ) きまりが悪い(です); **is ~** (= **ashamed, shy**) hazukashi'i 恥ずかしい
embarrassment tōwaku 当惑; koma'ru koto' 困る事; haji' 恥
embassy taishi'-kan 大使館
embroidery shishū 刺しゅう・刺

emerge dema'sụ (de'ru, de'te) 出ます(出る、出て); **emergence** de 出
emergency hijō (no baai) 非常(の場合)、(temporary) rinji 臨時; (crisis) kyū' 急、ki'ki' 危機; **~ exit** hijō'-guchi 非常口
emergency brake hijō-burē'ki 非常ブレーキ
emergency phone hijō-de'nwa 非常電話
emery board tsume-ya'suri 爪やすり
emotion kanjō 感情; (feeling) kandō 感動、kangeki 感激
Emperor Tennō'(-sama) 天皇(様)、**His Majesty the ~** Tennō-he'ika 天皇陛下
emphasis kyōchō 強調
emphasize kyōchō shima'sụ (suru, shịte) 強調します(する、して)
empire te'ikoku 帝国
employ tsụkaima'sụ (tsụkau, tsụkatte) 使います(使う、使って)、yatoima'sụ (yato'u, yato'tte) 雇います(雇う、雇って); **is employed** tsụto'mete ima'sụ (iru, ite) 勤めています(いる、いて)
employee jūgyō'-in 従業員; (of a company) sha'-in 社員、kaisha'-in 会社員
employment (use) shiyō 使用; (hiring) koyō 雇用、yato'i 雇い; (job) tsụtome' (o-tsụtome) 勤め(お勤め); **finding ~**

shūshoku 就職; **place of** ～
tsutome-saki 勤め先; **seeking**
～ kyūshoku 求職

Empress Kōgō(-sama) 皇后(様);
Her Majesty the ～ Kōgō-
heika 皇后陛下

empty 1. kara (no) 空(の),
karappo (no) 空っぽ(の);
(with nothing in it) nani mo
haitte inai … 何も入っていな
い…; *(hollow)* utsuro (na) 虚
ろ(な); *(futile)* munashii 空
しい・虚しい; *(is vacant)* aite
imasu (iru, ite) 空いています
(いる, いて); **gets empty**
akimasu (aku, aite) 空きます
(空く, 空いて), sukimasu
(suku, suite) すきます・空きま
す(すく, すいて) **2. empties
it** akemasu (akeru, akete) 空
けます(空ける, 空けて);
(drinks to the bottom) kampai
shimasu (suru, shite) 乾杯し
ます(する, して)

empty aki-… 空き… : ～ **bottle**
aki-bin 空き瓶; ～ **box** aki-
bako 空き箱; ～ **can** aki-kan
空き缶; ～ **house** aki-ya 空き
家; ～ **room/office** aki-ma 空
き間, aki-shitsu 空き室

enclose *(in envelope)* dōfū
shimasu (suru, shite) 同封し
ます(する, して)

encounter … ni de-aimasu (-au,
-atte) …に出会います(会う,
会って)

encourage susumemasu
(susumeru, susumete) 勧めま
す(勧める, 勧めて)
hagemashimasu (hagemasu,
hagemashite) 励まします(励
ます, 励まして)

encouragement shōrei 奨励

encroach upon okashimasu
(okasu, okashite) 侵します
(侵す, 侵して)

end *(the ending)* owari 終わり,
o-shimai おしまい, *(close)* sue
末; *(of street)* tsuki-atari 突き
当たり; *(edge)* hashi 端 =
hashikko/hajikko 端っこ/端
っこ, tamoto 袂; *(purpose)*
mokuteki 目的

end *(it ends, ends it)* owarimasu
(owaru, owatte) 終わります
(終わる, 終わって); *(comes
to an end)* sumimasu (sumu,
sunde) 済みます(済む, 済ん
で), *(runs out)* tsukimasu
(tsukiru, tsukite) 尽きます
(尽きる, 尽きて)

end: goes to the ～ *(of a road,
etc.)* tsuki-atarimasu (-ataru,
-atatte) 突き当たります(当た
る, 当たって)

end: to the (very) ～ aku-made
(mo) あくまで(も)

endeavor tsutomemasu
(tsutomeru, tsutomete) 努め
ます(努める, 努めて),
doryoku shima(")su (suru,
shite) 努力します(する, して)

end of the year kure 暮れ, nem-matsu 年末

endorse → sign; → support

end up (doing) shite shimaima͡su (shimau, shimatte) してしまいます(しまう, しまって)

endurance (*patience*) shi͡mbō 辛抱

endure (*puts up with*) shi͡mbō shima(⌐)su (suru, shite) 辛抱します(する, して)

enema kanchō 浣腸・灌腸

enemy teki 敵

energetic ge͡nki (na) 元気(な), enerugi͡sshu (na) エネルギッシュ(な); (*vigorous*) sek-kyoku-teki (na) 積極的(な)

energetically ge͡nki ni 元気に, ikio͡i yo͡ku 勢いよく

energy ikio͡i 勢い; ene͡ru͡gii エネルギー; (*pep*) ge͡nki (o-ge͡nki) 元気(お元気)

engage 1. (*hires a professional*) tanomima͡su (tano͡mu, tano͡nde) 頼みます(頼む, 頼んで) **2. ~ in** (*an activity*) ... ni jū͡ji shima(⌐)su (suru, shite) ...に従事します(する, して)

engaged: gets ~ (*booked up, occupied*) fusagarima͡su (fusaga͡ru, fusaga͡tte) ふさがります(ふさがる, ふさがって)

engaged (*to be married*) kon'yaku shite ima͡su (iru, ite) 婚約しています(いる, いて)

engagement (*date*) yaku͡soku 約束

engine 1. kika͡n 機関, (*automobile*) e͡njin エンジン; **the ~ starts** e͡njin ga kakarima͡su (kaka͡ru, kaka͡tte) エンジンがかかります(かかる, かかって), **starts the ~** e͡njin o kakema͡su (kake͡ru, ka͡kete) エンジンをかけます(かける, かけて) **2.** → fire engine

engineer gi͡shi 技師; **engineering** kō͡gaku 工学

England Igirisu イギリス, Eikoku 英国

English (*language*) Eigo 英語; (*person*) Igirisu͡-jin イギリス人

English-Japanese ei-wa 英和; **~ dictionary** eiwa-ji͡ten 英和辞典

engrave chōkoku shima͡su (suru, shite) 彫刻します(する, して)

engraving chōkoku 彫刻; → woodblock print

engrossed: gets ~ in ... ni muchū ni narima͡su (na͡ru, na͡tte) ...に夢中になります(なる, なって); ... ni korima͡su (ko͡ru, ko͡tte) ...に凝ります(凝る, 凝って)

enjoy tanoshimima͡su (tanoshi͡mu, tanoshi͡nde) 楽しみます(楽しむ, 楽しんで); enjo͡i shima(⌐)su (suru, shite)

エンジョイします（する，して）; ~ **the company of** ... to tsuki-aima͡su (-a͡u, -a͡tte) ...と付き合います（合う，合って）

enjoyable tanoshi͡i 楽しい

enjoyment tanoshi͡mi͡ 楽しみ, enjo͡i エンジョイ

enlargement zōdai 増大

enlightenment satori 悟り

enliven ikashima͡su (ika͡su, ika͡shite) 生かします（生かす，生かして）

enormous bakudai (na) ばく大・莫大（な）, bōdai (na) 膨大（な）; taihen (na) 大変（な）

enough jūbu͡n (na) 十分（な）; tappu͡ri たっぷり; ke͡kkō 結構; **is ~** tarima͡su (tariru, tarite) 足ります（足りる，足りて）; **gets (more than) ~ of** akima͡su (aki͡ru, a͡kite) 飽きます（飽きる，飽きて）

enroll (in school) nyūgaku shima͡su (suru, shite) 入学します（する，して）

ensign (naval officer) shō͡i 少尉

entangled: gets ~ kojirema͡su (kojire͡ru, koji͡rete) こじれます（こじれる，こじれて）, motsurema͡su (motsure͡ru, motsu͡rete) もつれます（もつれる，もつれて）

entanglement motsure͡ もつれ

enter ... (no naka) ni hairima͡su (ha͡iru, ha͡itte) ...（の中）に入ります（入る，入って）; (ap-

pears on stage) tōjō shima͡su (suru, shite) 登場します（する，して）

entering: ~ a country nyūkoku 入国; **~ a hospital** nyūin 入院; **~ a school** nyūgaku 入学; **~ a company** nyūsha 入社

enterprise ji͡gyō 事業

entertain gochi͡sō shima͡su (suru, shite) ごちそう［ご馳走］します（する，して）

entertainer geinō͡-jin 芸能人

entertainment nagusami 慰み

enthusiastic ne͡sshi͡n (na) 熱心（な）; **enthusiastically** ne͡sshi͡n ni 熱心に

entire zentai no 全体の; **~ surface** zemme͡n 全面; **throughout the ~** ... ...-jū ...中

entirely zenzen 全然; sokku͡ri そっくり; → **all;** → **completely**

entrance iriguchi 入口, kuchi 口; (front entryway) ge͡nkan 玄関; **~ gate** (wicket) ki͡do 木戸

entranced: gets ~ with ... ni muchū ni narima͡su (na͡ru, na͡tte) ...に夢中になります（なる，なって）

entrance exam (school) nyūgaku-shike͡n 入学試験; (company) nyūsha-shike͡n 入社試験

entrust (one with it) (sore o ... ni) azukema͡su (azuke͡ru, azu͡kete) （それを...に）預けます（預ける，預けて）; yudanema͡su (yudane͡ru,

yuda｢nete) 委ねます(委ねる,
委ねて); makasema｢su
(makase｢ru, maka｢sete) 任せま
す(任せる, 任せて);
tanomima｢su (tano｢mu,
tano｢nde) 頼みます(頼む, 頼
んで); irai shima｢su (suru,
shite) 依頼します(する, して)

entry 1. dictionary ~ midashi 見
出し, midashi⌐-go 見出し語
2. ~ upon the stage tōjō 登場
3. → enter 4. → entrance

envelope fūtō 封筒 (**how many**
na｢m-mai 何枚)

enviable/envious netamashi｢i ね
たましい・妬ましい,
urayamashi｢i うらやましい・
羨ましい

environment kankyō 環境

environs shūhen 周辺

envy urayamima｢su (uraya｢mu,
uraya｢nde) うらやみ[羨み]ま
す(うらやむ, うらやんで),
netamima｢su (neta｢mu,
neta｢nde) ねたみ[妬み]ます
(ねたむ, ねたんで)

epidemic ryūkō-byō 流行病;
densem-byō 伝染病

equal byōdō (na) 平等(な); (*on
an equal level*) taitō (no) 対等
(の); (*equivalent to*) ...to
hitoshi｢i ...と等しい; (*extends
to*) ... ni oyobima｢su (oyobu,
oyonde) ...に及びます(及ぶ,
及んで); (*constitutes*) ... de｢su
(da｢/na｢/no｢, de｢, ni｢) ...です

(だ/な/の, で, に)

equilibrium tsuriai 釣り合い

equipment (*apparatus*) sō｢chi 装
置, (*facilities*) se｢tsubi 設備

equivalence taiō 対応

equivalent taitō (no) 対等(の):
~ to ... to hitoshi｢i ...と等し
い; ... ni taiō shima｢su (suru,
shite) ...に対応します(する,
して)

era jidai 時代; ...-ji｢dai ...時代

erase keshima｢su (kesu, keshite)
消します(消す, 消して),
tori-keshima｢su (-ke⌐su,
-ke⌐shite) 取り消します(消
す, 消して)

eraser (*pencil*) keshi-gomu 消し
ゴム; (*blackboard*) kokuba｢n-
fuki 黒板拭き

erasure tori-keshi 取り消し

erect tatema｢su (tate｢ru, ta｢tete)
立てます(立てる, 立てて)

erotic iroppo｢i 色っぽい,
kōshoku (na) 好色(な), e｢ro
(na) エロ(な)

err ayamarima｢su (ayama｢ru,
ayama｢tte) 誤ります(誤る,
誤って)

errand yōji 用事, tsukai 使い,
yō-ta｢shi 用足し; **~ runner** o-
tsukai (san) お使い(さん)

error machigai 間違い; ayama｢ri｢
誤り; **is in ~** machigaema｢su
(machiga｢u, machiga｢tte) 間違
えます(間違う, 間違って)

erupt funka shima｢su (suru,

shịte) 噴火します(する, して)

eruption funka 噴火; *(= skin ~)* hasshin 発疹

escape nigemaʹsu (nigeʹru, niʹgete) 逃げます(逃げる, 逃げて); nukemaʹsu (nukeru, nukete) 抜けます(抜ける, 抜けて)

escape: a convenient ~ watari ni fuʹne 渡りに船

esoteric *(mysterious)* shimpị-teki (na) 神秘的(な)

especially tokubetsu ni 特別に, koʹto-ni ことに・殊に; toriwake とりわけ; sekkakuʹ せっかく

essays zuihitsu 随筆

essential *(necessary)* hịtsuyō (na) 必要(な)

establish tatemaʹsu (tateʹru, taʹtete) 建てます(建てる, 建てて); okoshimaʹsu (okoʹsu, okoʹshịte) 起こします(起こす, 起こして)

establishment 1. *(founding)* sōritsu 創立 **2.** *(facility)* shị⌐seʹ⌐tsu 施設 **3.** → com- pany

esteem sonkei 尊敬

estimate 1. *(an estimatc)* mi- tsumori 見積もり, kentōʹ 見当, suitei 推定, *(forecast)* yosoku 予測 *2. (cstimatcs it)* mi- tsumorimaʹsu (-tsumo⌐ru, -tsumo⌐tte) 見積もります(積 もる, 積もって), *(makes a guess)* kentōʹ o tsukemaʹsu

(tsukeʹru, tsukeʹte) 見当をつ けます(つける, つけて), *(in- fers)* suitei shimaʹsu (suru, shịte) 推定します(する, して), *(forecasts)* yosoku shimaʹsu (suru, shịte) 予測します(する, して)

estimation *(inference, presump- tion)* suitei 推定; → **judgment**

estrange: gets estranged hedatarimaʹsu (hedataʹru, hedataʹtte) 隔たります(隔た る, 隔たって); **estranges them** hedatemaʹsu (hedateʹru, hedaʹtete) 隔てます(隔てる, 隔てて); **estranged** utoʹi うと い・疎い

ethics riʹnri 倫理, shūʹshin 修身

etiquette reigiʹ 礼儀, echikeʹtto エチケット

etymology gogen 語源

Europe Yōroʹppa ヨーロッパ, Ōʹshū 欧州; **~ and America** Ō⌐-Bei 欧米, Seʹiyō 西洋

evacuate *(gets repatriated)* hịki- agemaʹsu (-ageʹru, -aʹgete) 引 き揚げます(揚げる, 揚げて)

evacuation *(repatriation)* hịki- age 引き揚げ

evacuee *(repatriated)* hịkiageʹ- sha 引き揚げ者

evaluation score hyōten 評点

evaporated milk eba-miʹruku エ バミルク

even *(smooth, flat)* taira (na) 平 ら(な)

even ... ... mo ...も; ~ **doing (if it does)** (shị)-te⌉ mo/(shị)-ta⌉tte (し)ても/(し)たって; ~ **being (if it is)** ADJECTIVE -⌉kụte mo/-⌉kụtatte くても/くたって, NOUN de⌉ mo/da⌉tte でも/だって

evening ban 晩, yūgata 夕方, yoi 宵; ~ **paper** yūkan 夕刊; ~ **performance** yo⌉ru no bu⌉ 夜の部

evening meal yūshoku 夕食

even so (sore) de⌉ mo (それ)でも

event koto⌉ 事; *(incident)* ji⌉ken 事件; *(case)* da⌉n 段; *(ceremony)* gyō⌉ji⌉ 行事; *(game)* kyō⌉gi⌉ (no shu[⌉]moku) 競技(の種目)

eventually *(come what may)* na⌉n to itte⌉ mo 何と言っても; → **finally, at last**

ever 1. *(always)* i⌉tsu-mo いつも; **as** ~ aikawarazu 相変わらず **2.** *(once)* i⌉tsụ-ka いつか, ... koto⌉ ga arima⌉sụ (a⌉ru, a⌉tte) ... 事があります(ある, あって) **3. wh...ever** ittai ... ?! いったい·一体...?!; **Wherever have you been?** Ittai do⌉ko e itte kima⌉shịta ka. いったい[一体]どこへ行って来ましたか.

ever since ... i⌉rai ...以来

ever so many i⌉kutsu mo いくつも, na⌉n-COUNTER mo 何 COUNTER も

ever so much i⌉kura mo いくらも; dō⌉mo どうも

every ... do⌉no ... de⌉ mo どの...でも; ... goto (ni) ...ごと·毎(に), mai-... 毎...

everybody minna⌉ みんな·皆, mina⌉-san 皆さん; da[⌉]re de[⌉] mo 誰でも

every chance one gets koto a⌉ru go⌉to (ni) 事あるごと(に)

every day ma⌉inichi 毎日, hi[⌉]-goto (ni) 日毎(に), hi⌉bi 日々; **almost** ~ ma⌉inichi no yō⌉ ni 毎日のように

everyday ... *(daily)* ma⌉inichi no ... 毎日の...; *(usual)* fu⌉dan no ... 普段の...; ~ **clothes** fuda⌉n-gi⌉ 普段着

every Jane and Mary Miichan-hā⌉chan (Mi⌉i-chan Hā⌉-chan) ミーちゃんハーちゃん(みいちゃん　はあちゃん), Miihā⌉-zoku ミーハー族·みいはあ族

every month mai-tsụki 毎月, maigetsu 毎月

every morning ma⌉i-asa 毎朝

every night ma[⌉]i-ban 毎晩, ma[⌉]i-yo 毎夜

every other ··· ichi-... oki ni 一...「おきに

everyplace → **everywhere**

every station ka[⌉]ku-eki 各駅

everything minna⌉ みんな·皆, ze⌉mbu 全部, na[⌉]n de[⌉]mo 何でも, i⌉ssa⌉i 一切; mono⌉goto 物事

every time maido 毎度; ~ **that** ... tabi⌉ (ni) ...度(に)

every week maishū 毎週

everywhere do⌐ko de⌐mo どこ でも, do⌐ko ni mo どこにも, hō⌐bō 方々·ほうぼう

every which way hō⌐bō 方々·ほ うぼう

every year mai-toshi 毎年, mainen 毎年

evidence shōko 証拠; *(basis)* ko⌐nkyo 根拠

evil 1. → **bad 2. an** ~ a⌐ku⌐ 悪; ~ **spirit** a⌐kuma 悪魔

exact *(detailed)* kuwashi⌐i 詳しい, komaka⌐i 細かい; *(correct)* seikaku (na) 正確(な)

exactly chōdo ちょうど·丁度, mattaku⌐ 全く, pitta⌐ri ぴった り, hakki⌐ri はっきり; ma⌐sa-ni まさに·正に; ... dake⌐ ...だ け

exaggerate kochō shima⌐su (suru, shite) 誇張します(する, して)

exaggerated ōgesa (na) 大げさ (な), (go-)ta⌐isō (na) (ご)大層 (な)

exaggeration kochō 誇張; *(bragging)* ho⌐ra ほら

examination *(test)* shike⌐n (o-shike⌐n) 試験(お試験); *(inquiry)* chō⌐sa 調査; *(inspection)* ke⌐nsa 検査; *(medical)* shinsatsu 診察

examine *(investigates)* shirabema⌐su (shirabe⌐ru, shira⌐bete) 調べます(調べる,

調べて); *(medically)* mima⌐su (mi⌐ru, mi⌐te) 診ます(診る, 診 て), shinsatsu shima⌐su (suru, shite) 診察します(する, して); ~ **tickets** *(at wicket)* kaisatsu shima⌐su (suru, shite) 改札し ます(する, して); *(aboard)* kensatsu shima⌐su (suru, shite) 検札します(する, して)

example re⌐i 例, ichi-rei 一例, tato⌐e 例え·たとえ, tato⌐i 例い; **for** ~ tato⌐eba 例えば· たとえば; **follows (learns from) the** ~ **of ...** o mi-naraima⌐su (-nara⌐u, -nara⌐tte) ...を見習います (習う, 習って)

exam room/place shiken-jō 試験 場

excavates horima⌐su (ho⌐ru, ho⌐tte) 掘ります(掘る, 掘っ て)

exceed sugima⌐su (sugi⌐ru, su⌐gite) 過ぎます(過ぎる, 過 ぎて), chōka shima⌐su (suru, shite) 超過します(する, して); koshima⌐su (kosu, koshite) 超 します(超す, 超して)

exceedingly mo⌐tto⌐mo 最も, go⌐ku ごく·極, taihen 大変, hijō ni 非常に

excel sugurema⌐su (sugure⌐ru, sugu⌐rete) 優れます(優れる, 優れて)

excellent sugu⌐reta 優れた, ke⌐kkō (na) 結構(な); **is ex-**

cellent sugu͡rete ima͡su (iru, ite) 優れています(いる, いて)

except (for) ... no hoka ...の他, ... i͡gai ...以外

exception reigai 例外; **without ~** (= all) i͡ssa͡i 一切

excess chōka 超過, kajō 過剰; (leeway, margin) yoyū 余裕; **is in ~** amarima͡su (ama͡ru, ama͡tte) 余ります(余る, 余って)

excessive yokei (na) 余計(な), hō⌐ɪgai (na) 法外(な); (extreme) kageki (na) 過激(な), kyokuta͡n na 極端な

excessively ya͡ke ni やけに, (extremely) kyokuta͡n ni 極端に

exchange (tori-)kaema͡su (kaeru, kaete) (取り)替えます(替える, 替えて), hiki-kaema͡su (-ka͡e͡ru, -ka͡ete) 引き換えます(換える, 換えて), kōkan shima͡su (suru, shite) 交換します(する, して)

excited: gets excited ki ga tachima͡su (ta͡tsu, ta͡tte) 気が立ちます(立つ, 立って); nes-shima͡su (nes-su⌐ɪru, ne͡s-shite) 熱します(熱する, 熱して); **is excited** kōfun shite ima͡su (iru, ite) 興奮しています(いる, いて)

excitement kōfun 興奮

exclude ha͡ijo shima(⌐ɪ)su (suru, shite) 排除します(する, して)

exclusion ha͡ijo 排除

excrement daibe͡n 大便, kuso͡ 糞・くそ

excursion ensoku 遠足, yūran 遊覧

excuse ii-wake 言い訳, mōshi-wake 申し訳; (pretext) kōjitsu 口実; **makes excuses** (apologizes) ii-wake o shima͡su (suru, shite) 言い訳をします(する, して), (declines) kotowarima͡su (kotowa͡ru, kotowa͡tte) 断ります(断る, 断って)

excuse: a convenient ~ watari ni fu͡ne 渡りに舟

Excuse me Sumimase͡n. すみません; Oso͡re-irimasu. 恐れ入ります; Dō͡mo. どうも; Gomen nasa͡i. ごめんなさい; Shitsu͡rei shima(⌐ɪ)su. 失礼します. **Excuse me but I'll be on my way** Sore de͡ wa shitsu͡rei shima(⌐ɪ)su. それでは失礼します. **Excuse me for having interrupted/bothered you** O-jama shima͡shita. おじゃま[お邪魔]しました. **Excuse me for interrupting/bothering you (but)** O-jama deshō͡ ga ... おじゃま[お邪魔]でしょうが.... **Excuse me for being the first to leave** O-saki ni shitsu͡rei shima(⌐ɪ)su. お先に失礼します. **Excuse me for going first** O-saki ni. お先に.

exempt: tax-exempt menzei (no)

免税(の); **is exempt from … o** manukarema͞su (manukare͞ru, manuka͞rete) …を免れます(免れる, 免れて)

exercise (*physical*) undō 運動, (*callisthenics*) taisō 体操; (*study*) renshū 練習, (*practice*) do͞ri͞ru ドリル, (o-)ke͞iko (お)稽古・けいこ

exerts oneself tsutomema͞su (tsutome͞ru, tsuto͞mete) 努めます(努める, 努めて); tsukushima͞su (tsuku͞su, tsuku͞shite) 尽くします(尽くす, 尽くして)

exhaust haiki 排気; (*fumes*) haiki-ga͞su 排気ガス; **exhaust fan** haiki͞-sen 排気扇

exhaust it tsukushima͞su (tsuku͞su, tsuku͞shite) 尽くします(尽くす, 尽くして); (*runs out of*) kirashima͞su (kira͞su, kira͞shite) 切らします(切らす, 切らして)

exhaustive mo͞ra shite ima͞su 網羅しています(いる, いて), mo͞ra shita … 網羅した…

exhibition tenji͞-kai 展示会, tenra͞n-kai 展覧会, hakura͞n-kai 博覧会; (*display*) mise-mo͞no͞ 見せ物

exhibit it misema͞su (mise͞ru, mi͞sete) 見せます(見せる, 見せて); shuppin shima͞su (suru, shite) 出品します(する, して)

exhibitor shuppi͞n-sha 出品者

exist sonzai shima͞su (suru, shite) 存在します(する, して)

existence sonzai 存在, seizon 生存; (*or nonexistence*) u͞mu 有無

exit de͞-guchi 出口; **north/ south/east/west ~** kita-/ minami-/higashi-/nishi-guchi 北/南/東/西口

exorbitant hō͞gai (na) 法外(な)

expand → **develop**; → **grow**; → **spread**

expansion → **development**; → **growth**

expect (*awaits*) ma͞tte ima͞su (iru, ite) 待っています(いる, いて), kitai shima͞su (suru, shite) 期待します(する, して); (*anticipates*) yosō shima͞su (suru, shite) 予想します(する, して)

expect: as we might ~ sasuga (ni) さすが(に)

expectably … hazu de͞su …はずです

expectation mikomi 見込み, tsumori (o-tsumori) つもり (おつもり), ate 当て, yosō 予想, yotei 予定; kitai 期待; … hazu …はず

expect to (do) … (suru) tsumori de͞su …(する)つもりです

expediency, expedient ri͞nki (no) 臨機(の)

expense hi͞yō 費用; …͞-hi …費

expensive (ne ga) taka˼i（値が）高
い

experience 1. keiken 経験, *(personal)* taiken 体験; *(a sometime happening)* …koto˼ …事;
(professional) shokureki 職歴
2. *(experiences, undergoes)*
keiken shima˼su (suru, shite)
経験します（する，して），…
me˼ ni aima˼su (a˼u, a˼tte) …目
に遭います（遭う，遭って）

experiment jikken (o shima˼su;
suru, shite) 実験（をします；
する，して）; *(test)* shike˼n
(o-shike˼n) 試験（お試験），
tameshi˼ 試し; 〜 **with** … o
tameshima˼su (tame˼su,
tame˼shite) …を試します（試
す，試して）

expert jōzu˼ (na) じょうず・上手
（な），tassha (na) 達者（な）; **an
expert** meiji˼n 名人, tsū˼ 通,
tsūji˼n 通人, *(veteran)*
ku˼rōto くろうと・玄人,
(specialist) semmon-ka 専門家

expire keika shima˼su (suru,
shite) 経過します（する，して）

explain setsumei shima˼su (suru,
shite) 説明します（する，して）;
tokima˼su (to˼ku, to˼ite) 説き
ます（説く，説いて）;
ka˼ishaku shima˼su (suru,
shite) 解釈します（する，して）

explanation setsumei 説明; *(interpretation)* ka˼i-shaku 解釈; *(excuse)* ii-wake 言い訳

explanatory notes hanrei 凡例

explicit meihaku (na) 明白（な）;
explicitly meihaku ni 明白に

explode bakuhatsu shima˼su
(suru, shite) 爆発します（する，
して）　　　　　　　「爆発

exploding, explosion bakuhatsu

export 1. = **exporting** yushutsu
輸出; 〜 **goods** yushutsu˼-hin
輸出品 **2. exports it** yushutsu
shima˼su (suru, shite) 輸出し
ます（する，して）

expose (a secret) barashima˼su
(bara˼su, bara˼shite) ばらしま
す（ばらす，ばらして）

exposition 1. *(a fair)* hakura˼n-
kai 博覧会 **2.** *(explanation)*
ka˼ishaku 解釈

expound ka˼ishaku shima(˼)su
(suru, shite) 解釈します（する，
して）

express 1. *(train, bus)* kyūkō 急
行 **2.** *(puts into words)* ii-
arawashima˼su (-arawa˼su,
-arawa˼shite) 言い表します
（表す，表して）, *(tells)* iima˼su
(yū, itte/yutte) 言います（言う，
言って/ゆって）

express agent unsō-ya 運送屋

expression *(way of saying)* ii-
kata 言い方, *(phrase)*
hyōge˼n 表現; *(on face)*
hyōjō˼ 表情, kao 顔; **has/
wears an 〜 of** … (no) kao o
shite ima˼su (iru, ite) …（の）
顔をしています（いる，いて）

expressly state utaima‸su (utau, utatte) うたいます(うたう, うたって)

extend *(extends it)* nobashima‸su (noba‸su, noba‸shite) 延ばします(延ばす, 延ばして), enchō shima‸su (suru, shite) 延長します(する, して); *(it extends)* nobima‸su (nobi‸ru, no‸bite) 伸びます(伸びる, 伸びて), *(reaches)* oyobima‸su (oyobu, oyonde) 及びます(及ぶ, 及んで)

extension *(cord)* tsugitashi‸-kō‸do 継ぎ足しコード, enchō-kō‸do 延長コード; *(phone line, inside)* naisen 内線, *(outside)* gaisen 外線

extent ka‸giri‸ 限り; hodo 程; ku‸rai 位; kagen 加減; → **scope**; → **degree**

extent: to what ~ do‸nna ni どんなに; **to this** ~ konna ni こんなに; **to that** ~ sonna ni そんなに, anna ni あんなに

exterior ga‸ibu 外部, gaime⌐n 外面

external soto-gawa (no) 外側(の); ga‸ibu/gaime⌐n (no) 外部/外面(の); gai-... 外...

extinguish keshima‸su (kesu, keshite) 消します(消す, 消して); **gets extinguished** kiema‸su (kieru, kiete) 消えます(消える, 消えて)

extinguisher → **fire extinguisher**

extol utaima‸su (utau, utatte) うたいます(うたう, うたって)

extortion yusuri ゆすり

extra yobun (no/ni) 余分(に/の), betsu (no/ni) 別(の/に); *(special)* tokubetsu (no) 特別(の); (~ *charge*) betsu-dai/-ryō‸kin 別代/料金; *(bonus)* omake おまけ; **throws it in** ~ soema‸su (soeru, soete) 添えます(添える, 添えて)

extraordinary rinji (no) 臨時(の)

extravagance muda-zu‸kai 無駄使い, rō⌐hi 浪費

extravagant zeita‸ku‸ (na) ぜいたく・贅沢(な); ogorima‸su (ogoru, ogotte) 奢ります(奢る, 奢って)

extreme kyokuta‸n (na) 極端(な); *(radical)* kageki (na) 過激(な)

extremely hijō ni 非常に, kiwa‸mete 極めて, hanahada 甚だ・はなはだ, go‸ku ごく・極, shi⌐goku しごく, itatte 至って, kyokuta‸n ni 極端に, to(t)temo と(っ)ても, mono-su‸go‸ku 物凄く・ものすごく, zu‸ibun 随分・ずいぶん; *(more than one might expect)* nakanaka なかなか・中中

extremists kageki-ha 過激派

exultant *(proud)* toku⌐i (na) 得意(な)

eye me‸ (o-me) 目・眼(お目・お眼); **(of a needle)** me‸do めど・針孔

eyebrow ma‸yu(ge) 眉(毛)

eye doctor me⌐-isha 目医者・眼医
eye drops me-gu⌐suri 目薬　└者
eyeglasses me⌐gane 眼鏡・めがね;
puts on (wears) ～ me⌐gane o kakema⌐su (ka⌐kete ima⌐su) 眼

鏡をかけます(かけています)
eyelash ma⌐tsuge まつげ・睫
eyelid ma⌐buta まぶた・目蓋・瞼
eye lotion me-gu⌐suri 目薬
eyesight shi⌐ryoku 視力

— F —

fabric ori⌐-mo⌐no 織物, ki⌐ji 生地
face 1. kao 顔, tsura⌐ つら・面;
(= one's honor) taime⌐n 体面 **2.** (front) shōme⌐n 正面
3. (faces it) mukima⌐su (muku, muite) 向きます(向く, 向いて); atarima⌐su (ataru, atatte) 当たります(当たる, 当たって)
face powder oshiroi おしろい・白粉
facility, facilities shi⌐se⌐tsu 施設, se⌐tsubi 設備; be⌐n 便
facing mukō⌐ (o-mu⌐kō) no 向こう(お向こう)の
fact koto⌐ 事, ji⌐jitsu 事実; **in ～** jitsu⌐ wa 実は, jissai (wa) 実際(は), iyo⌐-iyo いよいよ, jitai 事態
faction habatsu 派閥
factory kōba⌐ 工場 = kōjō⌐ 工場; ～ **worker** kōin 工員, shokkō 職工
fade samema⌐su (same⌐ru, sa⌐mete) さめます(さめる, さ

めて), asema⌐su (ase⌐ru, a⌐sete) あせます(あせる, あせて); (grows weak)
otoroema⌐su (otoro⌐e⌐ru, otoro⌐ete) 衰えます(衰える, 衰えて); (vanishes) kiema⌐su (kieru, kiete) 消えます(消える, 消えて)
fail shippai shima⌐su (suru, shite) 失敗します(する, して); (exam) ochima⌐su (ochi⌐ru, o⌐chite) 落ちます(落ちる, 落ちて), rakudai shima⌐su (suru, shite) 落第します(する, して); (is wide of the mark) hazurema⌐su (hazureru, hazurete) 外れます(外れる, 外れて); (engine etc. breaks down) koshō shima⌐su (suru, shite) 故障します(する, して)
fail: without ～ ze⌐-hi ぜひ・是非
failure shippai 失敗; (exam) rakudai 落第; **power ～** teiden 停電
faint 1. (dim) ka⌐suka (na) かすか[微か](な) **2.** (loses con-

sciousness) ki o ushinaima͞su (ushinau, ushinatte) 気を失い ます(失う，失って)

fair *(market)* i͞chi 市, i͞chi-ba͞ 市 場; *(temple festival)* e͞n-nichi 縁日

fair *(just, impartial)* kōhei (na) 公平(な); *(sunny)* ha͞rete ima͞su (ha͞reta ...) 晴れて います(晴れた...); ~ **weather** hare͞ 晴れ, (o-)te͞nki (お)天気

fairly *(rather)* ka͞nari かなり, sōtō 相当, zu͞ibun 随分・ず いぶん; ~ **well** *(sufficiently)* ke͞kkō 結構

faithful seijitsu (na) 誠実(な), makoto (no) 誠(の)

fake nise (no) 偽・にせ(の), inchiki (na) いんちき・イン チキ(な); *(thing)* nise-mono 偽物・にせもの

fall *(autumn)* a͞ki 秋

fall 1. *(it falls)* ochima͞su (ochi͞ru, o͞chite) 落ちます(落 ちる，落ちて), okkochima͞su (okkochi͞ru, okko͞chite) 落っ こちます(落っこちる，落っ こちて) 2. *(falls and scatters)* chirima͞su (chiru, chitte) 散り ます(散る，散って)

fall behind okurema͞su (okureru, okurete) 遅れます (遅れる，遅れて); okure o torima͞su (to͞ru, to͞tte) 後れを 取ります(取る，取って)

fall down taorema͞su (taore͞ru,

tao͞rete) 倒れます(倒れる，倒 れて), korobima͞su (korobu, koronde) 転びます(転ぶ，転 んで)

fall in love with ... ni horema͞su (horeru, horete) ...にほれ[惚 れ]ます(ほれる，ほれて)

false *(falsehood)* u͞so うそ・嘘, itsuwa⌐ri⌐ 偽り・いつわり; *(fake)* nise (no) 偽・にせ(の), *(artificial)* jinzō (no) 人造(の)

false teeth ire-ba 入れ歯

falter yoro-mekima͞su (-me͞ku, -me͞ite) よろめきます(めく， めいて), yo͞royoro shima͞su (suru, shite) よろよろします (する，して)

fame 1. *(reputation)* hyōban 評 判 2. → **honor**

familiar shitashi͞i 親しい; → **ac- customed**; → **know**

family uchi 家, ... uchi͞ (o-uchi) ... 家(お家); ka͞zoku 家族, *(household)* katei 家庭; *(clan)* u͞ji 氏, ...⌐-ke ...家; ~ **crest** mo͞n 紋 = monshō 紋章

family circle uchiwa 内輪

family inn minshuku 民宿, minka͞n-shuku 民間宿

family name *(= surname)* se͞i 姓, u͞ji 氏, ka͞mei 家名, *(as writ- ten)* myō͞ji 名字・苗字

family room: Japanese ~ cha- no-ma (o-chanoma) 茶の間 (お茶の間)

famous yūmei (na) 有名(な),

na-daka'i 名高い; **gets ~**
shirerema'su (shirareru,
shirarete) 知られます(知られ
る，知られて)，yūmei ni
narima'su (na'ru, na'tte) 有名
になります(なる，なって)

fan ōgi' 扇; (*folding*) sensu 扇子，
o-sensu お扇子; (*flat*) uchi'wa
うちわ; (*electric*) sempū-ki 扇
風機

fan (*enthusiast*) fu'an ファン，
fa'n ファン; ...-zuki ...好き

fancy (*high-grade*) kōkyū (no) 高
級(の)，**~ goods** kōkyū'-hin
高級品; **~ dresser** osha're お
しゃれ

fan shell (*a kind of scallop*)
taira'-gai 平貝，taira-gi' たいら
ぎ・玉珧

far tōi 遠い，ha'ruka (na) はるか
・遥か(な); ha'ruka (ni) はる
か・遥か(に); **how far** dono-
gurai どの位，do'ko made ど
こまで; **as far as it goes** ichiō
一応; **by far** zutto ずっと，
ha'ruka (ni) はるか・遥か(に)

farce: traditional Noh ~
kyōge'n 狂言

fare (*fee*) ryō'kin 料金，
(*transportation*) u'nchin 運賃

Far East kyokutō 極東

farewell wakare' (o-wakare) 別れ
(お別れ); **~ party** sōbe'tsukai 送別会

farm nōjō' 農場; **~ house/
family** no'ka 農家; **~ land**

no'chi 農地

farmer hyakushō' 百姓，no'fu 農
夫，no'ka 農家，nōmin 農民

farming nō'gyō 農業

far-off tōi 遠い，ha'ruka (na) は
るか・遥か(な)

farsighted (*presbyopic*) rōgan 老
眼，enshi 遠視; (*forward-look-
ing*) mae-muki (no) 前向き(の)

fart onara (o shima'su; suru,
shite) おなら(をします; する，
して); he' (o hirima'su; hi'ru,
hi'tte) へ・屁(をひります; ひ
る，ひって)

fascinated utto'ri (to) うっとり
(と); **is ~** utto'ri shima(')su
(suru, shite) うっとりします
(する，して)

fashion (=*way*) (...) fū' (...)

fashion: is in ~ hayarima'su
(haya'ru, haya'tte) はやり[流
行]ます(はやる，はやって)

fashionable hayari (no) はやり
[流行り](の)，ryūkō (no) 流
行(の); haikara (na) ハイカラ
(な)，sumā'to (na) スマート
(な)

fast ha'yaku 速く; haya'i 速い;
(*clock runs fast*) susunde
ima'su (iru, ite) 進んでいます
(いる，いて)

fasten 1. (*firmly attaches*)
tomema'su (tomeru, tomete)
留めます(留める，留めて)
2. (*tightens, secures*)
shimema'su (shime'ru,

shiꜜmete) 締めます(締める，締めて); **Fasten your seat belts.** Shiito-beꜜruto o shiꜜmete kudasa(⎤)i. シートベルトを締めて下さい.

fastidious → **choosy**

fat (*grease*) abura あぶら・脂, (*lard, blubber*) shibō 脂肪; (*cooking*) heꜜtto ヘット

fat (*gets fat*) futorimaꜜsu (futoꜜru, futoꜜtte) 太ります(太る，太って)，koemaꜜsu (koeꜜru, koꜜete) 肥えます(肥える，肥えて); (*is fat*) futoꜜtte imaꜜsu (iru, ite) 太っています(いる，いて); (*plump*) futoꜜi 太い

fate uꜜn 運, uꜜmmei 運命

father otoꜜsan お父さん, chichiꜜ 父, chichi-oya 父親

Father (*Reverend*) ...shiꜜmpu san ...神父さん

father-in-law giꜜfu 義父

fatty aburakkoꜜi 脂っこい; ~ **tuna** toꜜro とろ

faucet jaguchi 蛇口

fault 1. (*defect*) kizu きず; (*shortcoming*) taꜜnsho 短所; (*guilt*) tsuꜜmi 罪; (*cause*) ...seꜜi ...せい 2. at ~ waruꜜi 悪い; **it is my** ~ watashi ga waruꜜi/waꜜrukatta わたしが悪い./悪かった 3. **finds fault with** togamemaꜜsu (togameꜜru, togaꜜmete) とがめ[咎め]ます(とがめる，とがめて)

faux pas bu-saꜜhō 無作法・不作法

favor 1. (*kindness*) shiꜜnsetsu (go-shiꜜnsetsu) 親切(ご親切)，(*goodwill*) kōꜜi 好意; (*request*) o-negai お願い 2. **does a** ~ kōꜜi o misemaꜜsu (miseꜜru, miꜜsete) 好意を見せます(見せる，見せて); **does me/us the** ~ **of ...ing** ...te kudasaimaꜜsu (kudasaꜜru, kudasaꜜtte) / kuremaꜜsu (kureru, kurete) ...て下さいます(下さる，下さって)/くれます(くれる，くれて) 3. **favors** (*a choice*) ...(no) hoꜜ ga iꜜi to omoimaꜜsu (omoꜜu, omoꜜtte) ...(の)方がいいと思います(思う，思って)

favorite daꜜi-suki (na) 大好き(な), (ichiban) sukiꜜ (na) (一番)好き(な); konomiꜜ (o-konomi) no ... 好み(お好み)の...; tokuꜜi (na/no) 得意(な/の)

fear 1. (*a fear*) osoreꜜ 恐れ, shimpai 心配 2. **fears it** osoremaꜜsu (osoreꜜru, osoꜜrete) 恐れます(恐れる，恐れて); kowagari maꜜsu (kowagaꜜru, kowagaꜜtte) 怖がります(怖がる，怖がって); (*worries about*) shimpai shimaꜜsu (suru, shite) 心配します(する，して)

fearful osoroshiꜜi 恐ろしい

feat waza 業; (*deed*) shiwaza 仕業

feather hane 羽; ke 毛
February Ni-gatsu˥ 二月・2月
feces kuso˥ くそ・糞, fu˥n ふん・糞; be˥n 便 = daibe˥n 大便
fee ryō˥kin 料金; ...˥-ryō ...料; (remuneration) sharei 謝礼, rei 礼
feeble → weak
feed tabesasema˥su (tabesase˥ru, tabesa˥sete) 食べさせます（食べさせる, 食べさせて）; [inelegant] kuwasema˥su (kuwase˥ru, kuwa˥sete) 食わせます（食わせる, 食わせて）
feel (by touch) sawarima˥su (sawaru, sawatte) さわり［触り］ます（さわる, さわって）; (by emotion) kan-jima˥su (kan-jiru, kan-jite) 感じます（感じる, 感じて）; (thinks) omoima˥su (omo˥u, omo˥tte) 思います（思う, 思って）, zon-jima˥su (zon-ji˥ru, zo˥n-jite) 存じます（存じる, 存じて）; (body reaction) moyōshima˥su (moyō˥su, moyō˥shite) 催します（催す, 催して）
feel: it feels good/bad kimochi ga i˥i/waru˥i 気持ちがいい/悪い
feeling kimochi 気持ち, kanji 感じ, ki 気, ne˥n 念; (sense) kimi˥ 気味; koko˥ro (o-kokoro) 心（お心）, omo˥i 思い; (mood) kokoro-mochi˥ 心持ち,

ki˥bun 気分; (one's view) i˥kō 意向; (health) (karada no) guai 〔体の〕具合; (compassion) na˥sake˥ (o-na˥sake) 情け（お情け）, ni˥njō 人情
fellow hito 人, ... hito˥ ...人; mono 者, ya˥tsu やつ・奴; **fellow ... ...** dō˥shi ...同士
female onna˥ (no hito) 女（の人）, josei 女性; ~ ... (she-animal) ... no mesu˥ ...の雌
female impersonator (in Kabuki) onna-gata 女形 = o˥ya˥ma おやま・女形
female student jo(shi)-ga˥kusei 女(子)学生
fence kaki˥ne 垣根, (wall) hei 塀
fencing: the art of ~ (with bamboo swords) ke˥ndō 剣道
fermented: ~ bean paste mi˥so (o-mi˥so) みそ・味噌（おみそ・お味噌）; ~ **soy beans** nattō˥ 納豆
fern shi˥da しだ; **royal ~ (= osmund)** zemmai ぜんまい
ferry (them over) watashima˥su (watasu, watashite) 渡します（渡す, 渡して）
ferryboat watashi-bu˥ne 渡し舟〔船〕
festers umima˥su うみます・膿みます, u˥mu うむ・膿む
festival matsuri˥ (o-matsuri) 祭り（お祭り）
feudal lord daimyō˥ (o-daimyō) 大名（お大名）

feudal *(period, system)* hōken (-ji̅dai, -se̅ido) 封建（時代，制度）

fever netsu̅ (o-ne̅tsu) 熱（お熱）

few suko̅shi (no) 少し（の）; sukuna̅i 少ない; **a few →** **several**

few: a few days ago sendatte̅ せんだって·先だって, senjitsu 先日

fewer (yori) sukuna̅i （より）少ない

fib u̅so うそ·嘘

fiber se̅n'i 繊維; *(line)* su̅ji 筋; *(staple fiber)* su̅fu スフ; **synthetic →** kasen 化繊

fickle uwaki (na) 浮気（な）

fiction shōsetsu 小説

field *(dry)* hatake 畑; *(moor)* no̅hara 野原, no̅ 野, ha̅rappa 原っぱ; *(rice paddy)* ta̅ 田, tambo 田んぼ; *(specialty)* semmon 専門; *(out in the field)* ya̅gai 野外

field study/trip/work kengaku 見学

fierce hageshi̅i 激しい, sugo̅i すごい·凄い

fifteen ju̅-go 十五·15

fifth go-bamme̅ (no) 五番目（の）, itsutsu-me̅ (no) 五つ目（の）; **the ~ day** itsuka-me̅ 五日目, **(of the month)** itsuka̅ 五日

fifth floor go-kai 五階

fifty go-ju̅ 五十·50; **~ thousand** go-ma̅n 五万·50,000

fig ichi̅jiku いちじく

fight tatakaima̅su (tatakau, tatakatte) 戦います（戦う，戦って）; **→ argue**

figure → **count; number; think;** **shape; body; being, person;** **diagram**

file 1. *(nail file, etc.)* yasuri̅ やすり 2. **→ folder**

file *(grinds)* surima̅su (su̅ru, sutte̅) すります（する，すって）

filet *(of pork etc.)* hire ヒレ

fill 1. ippai ni shima̅su (suru, shite) 一杯にします（する，して）; mitashima̅su (mita̅su, mita̅shite) 満たします（満たす，満たして）; **fills the tank,** **fills it up** man-tan ni shima̅su 満タンにします 2. *(fulfills)* konashima̅su (konasu, konashite) こなします（こなす，こなして）, **~ an order** chū̅mon o konashima̅su 注文をこなします

fill in *(information)* kaki-irema̅su (-ire̅ru, -i̅rete) 書き入れます（入れる，入れて）

filling station → **gas station**

film fuirumu フィルム, fui̅rumu フイルム; *(movie)* e̅iga 映画

filter f(u)i̅rutā フィルター（フイルター）; *(filters it)* koshima̅su (kosu, koshite) こします（こす，こして）

filthy → **dirty**

fin hire ひれ

final sa⌐igo (no) 最後（の）, saishū (no) 最終（の）

finalization seiritsu 成立; **gets finalized** seiritsu shima⌐su (suru, shite) 成立します（する, して）

finance 1. kin'yū 金融; ke⌐izai 経済; zaisei 財政; (= *financial circles*) zaikai 財界; **Ministry of Finance** Ōkura⌐-shō 大蔵省 2. = **financing** yūzū 融通; **finances it** yūzū shima⌐su (suru, shite) 融通します（する, して）

financial circles zaikai 財界

find 1. mitsukema⌐su (mitsukeru, mitsukete) 見つけます（見つける, 見つけて） 2. **a find** (*bargain*) horidashi-mono 掘り出し物

find fault with togamema⌐su (togame⌐ru, toga⌐mete) とがめ［咎め］ます（とがめる, とがめて）

find out (*hears*) (... ga) mimi⌐ ni hairima⌐su (ha⌐iru, ha⌐itte) (... が) 耳に入ります（入る, 入って）; (... ga) wakarima⌐su (waka⌐ru, waka⌐tte) (...が) 分かります（分かる, 分かって）

fine 1. (*small/detailed*) komaka⌐i 細かい, (*minute*) bisai (na) 微細（な）, (*delicate*) bimyō (na) 微妙（な） 2. → **OK, good, splendid, fair** 3. (*penalty*) bakkin 罰金

finger yubi⌐ 指; **fingernail** (yubi(⌐) no) tsume (指の) つめ·爪

fingerprint shimon 指紋

finish 1. → **end** 2. (*finishes ...ing*) ...te shimaima⌐su (shimau, shimatte) ...てしまいます（しまう, しまって）

fir mo⌐mi もみ

fire 1. hi⌐ 火, (*accidental*) ka⌐ji 火事, kasai 火災; (*bonfire*) taki-bi たき火 2. = **lays off** (*disemploys*) kubi ni shima⌐su (suru, shite) 首にします（する, して）, kotowarima⌐su (kotowa⌐ru, kotowa⌐tte) 断ります（断る, 断って）, ka⌐iko shima(⌐)su (suru, shite) 解雇します（する, して）; **got fired** kubi ni narima⌐shita 首になりました

fire alarm kasai-ke⌐ihō 火災警報; (*device*) kasai-hōchi⌐ki 火災報知器

fire department shōbō-sho⌐ 消防署

fire engine shōbō⌐-sha 消防車

fire extinguisher shōka⌐-ki 消火器

fire fighter shōbō⌐-shi/-fu 消防士/夫

fire fighting shōbō 消防

fire house/station shōbō-sho⌐ 消防署

fireman → **fire fighter**

fireplug shōka⌐-sen 消火栓

firewood taki-gi 薪・たきぎ, maki まき・薪

fireworks ha⌐na-bi 花火

firm 1. jōbu (na) 丈夫(な); *(hard)* katai 固い・硬い・堅い **2.** *(business)* → **company**

firmly jōbu ni 丈夫に; kataku 固く・硬く・堅く; *(securely)* chan-to ちゃんと; *(resolutely)* shikka⌐ri しっかり; *(def-initely)* kippa⌐ri (to) きっぱり(と)

first hajime (no) 初め(の), saisho (no) 最初(の); *(number one)* ichi⌐-ban 一番, da⌐i-ichi 第一; *(first of all)* ma⌐zu まず・先ず; *(ahead of others)* saki (ni) 先(に)

first aid ōkyū-te⌐ate 応急手当; **first-aid kit** kyūkyū⌐-bako 救急箱

first class ik-kyū 一級; *(ticket, seat)* it-tō⌐ 一等; *(hotel, school)* ichiryū (no) 一流(の)

first day of the month tsuitachi⌐ 一日・ついたち

first day of the year ganjitsu 元日, gantan 元旦

first floor ik-kai 一階

first generation is-sei 一世

first-rate ichiryū (no) 一流(の), paripari (no) ぱりぱり(の); jōtō (no) 上等(の)

first-run movie rōdo-shō⌐ ロードショー ⌐(の)

first time haji⌐mete (no) 初めて

first volume *(of a set of 2 or 3)* jō-kan 上巻, jō⌐ 上

first-year student ichine⌐n-sei 一年生

fish sakana (o-sakana) 魚(お魚), uo 魚 (**1** ip-pi⌐ki⌐ 一匹, **2** ni⌐-hiki 二匹, **3** sa⌐m-biki 三匹, **how many** na⌐m-biki 何匹); **sliced raw ~** sashimi 刺身・さしみ

fish *(angles)* tsurima⌐su (tsuru, tsutte) 釣ります(釣る, 釣って)

fishballs *(for soup)* tsumi-(i)re 摘みれ・つみれ

fish cake *(steamed)* kamaboko かまぼこ; *(boiled)* hampe⌐n はんぺん; *(broiled)* chikuwa ちくわ・竹輪; *(deep-fried)* Sa-tsuma⌐-age さつま[薩摩]揚げ

fish dealer/market sakana-ya 魚屋

fisherman ryō⌐shi 漁師, gyo⌐fu 漁夫

fishhook tsuriba⌐ri 釣り針

fishing *(as sport)* (sakana⌐-)tsuri (魚)釣り, ryō⌐ 漁; *(business)* gyo⌐gyō 漁業

fish meal soboro そぼろ

fishy *(= questionable)* kusa⌐i 臭い; **fishy-smelling** namagusa⌐i 生臭い

fist ko⌐bushi こぶし・拳; genko げんこ, genkotsu げんこつ・拳骨

fit 1. *(= suitable)* te⌐kigi (no)

適宜(の); **fits … nicely** … ni yo͞ku aima͞su (a͞u, a͞tte) …に良く合います(合う, 合って)
2. fits it to … ni ate-hamema͞su (-hame͞ru, -ha͞mete) …に当てはめます(はめる, はめて)

five go͞ 五・5; itsu͞tsu 五つ, itsu͞tsu 五つ; f(u)a͞ibu ファイブ(ファイブ); **~ days** itsu-ka͞ 五日

five: small things, pieces go͞-ko 五個; **long things** go-hon 五本; **flat things** go-mai 五枚; **small animals/fish/bugs** go͞-hiki 五匹; **large animals** go-tō 五頭; **birds** go͞-wa 五羽; **machines/vehicles** go-dai 五台; **books/magazines** go͞-satsu͞ 五冊

five degrees go͞-do 五度

five floors/stories go-kai 五階

five hundred go-hyaku͞ 五百・500

five o'clock go͞-ji 五時・5時; **~ shadow** bushō͞-hige 無精ひげ・不精ひげ

five thousand go-se͞n 五千・5,000

five times go-do͞ 五度, go-ka͞i 五回, go-he͞n 五遍

five years go-nen 五年, gone͞n-kan 五年間; **~ old** itsu͞tsu 五つ, go͞-sai 五歳

fix (*repairs*) naoshima͞su (nao͞su, nao͞shite) 直します(直す, 直して); (*makes*)

tsukurima͞su (tsuku͞ru, tsuku͞tte) 作ります(作る, 作って); (*prepares*) sonaema͞su (sona͞eru, sona͞ete) 備えます(備える, 備えて); (*settles*) sadamema͞su (sadame͞ru, sada͞mete) 定めます(定める, 定めて)

fix (= *plight*) hame͞ 羽目

fixed (*settled*) ittei (no) 一定(の); (*periodic*) te͞iki (no) 定期(の); tei-… 定…

fixed: gets fixed (*repaired*) naorima͞su (nao͞ru, nao͞tte) 直ります(直る, 直って); (*settled*) sadamarima͞su (sadama͞ru, sadama͞tte) 定まります(定まる, 定まって)

fixedly (*staring*) jitto じっと

fixture ki͞gu 器具

flag hata͞ 旗; (*national*) kokki 国旗

flannel ne͞ru ネル

flap (*of envelope, etc.*) futa ふた・蓋

flashing pika͞pika ぴかぴか

flashlight kaichū-de͞ntō 懐中電灯, dentō 電灯

flashy hade͞ (na) はで・派手(な)

flat taira (na) 平ら(な), hirattai 平ったい; (*flavorless*) ajike-na͞i 味気ない

flat = **flat tire** panku パンク; **gets a ~** panku o shima͞su (suru, shite) パンクをします(する, して)

flatfish ka⌐rei かれい・鰈

flathead *(fish)* ko⌐chi こち・鯒

flat land heichi 平地

flatter o-seji o iima⌐su (yū, itte/ yutte) お世辞をいいます(言う, 言って/ゆって); goma o surima⌐su (su⌐ru, sutte⌐) ごま[胡麻]をすります(する, すって)

flattery o-seji お世辞; goma-su⌐ri⌐ ごま[胡麻]すり

flatulate he⌐ o hirima⌐su (hi⌐ru, hi⌐tte⌐) 屁をひります(ひる, ひって)

flatulence onara おなら, he⌐ へ・屁

flavor 1. aji 味 = fū⌐mi⌐ 風味; *(seasoning)* cho⌐mi 調味, kagen 加減 **2.** *(seasons it)* ... ni aji o tsukema⌐su (tsuke⌐ru, tsuke⌐te) ...に味を付けます(付ける, 付けて)

flavorless ajike-na⌐i 味気ない

flavor sprinkles (to top rice) furi-kake ふりかけ

flaw kizu 傷, *(defect)* kette⌐n 欠点

flax asa⌐ 麻

flea nomi⌐ のみ・蚤

flee nigema⌐su (nige⌐ru, ni⌐gete) 逃げます(逃げる, 逃げて)

fleeting *(transitory)* haka⌐nai はかない

flesh nikutai 肉体

flies → **fly**

flight (number …) ...⌐-bin ...便

flint (for lighter) (ra⌐itā no) ishi⌐ (ライターの)石

float *(it floats)* ukabima⌐su (ukabu, ukande) 浮かびます(浮かぶ, 浮かんで), ukima⌐su (uku, uite) 浮きます(浮く, 浮いて); *(floats it)* ukabema⌐su (ukaberu, ukabete) 浮かべます(浮かべる, 浮かべて)

flock 1. mure⌐ 群れ **2. they flock together** muragarima⌐su (muraga⌐ru, muraga⌐tte) 群がります(群がる, 群がって)

flood kō⌐zui 洪水, ō⌐mi⌐zu⌐ 大水

floor yuka 床, *(story)* (-)kai 階, **What floor?** na⌐n-gai/-kai 何階/階 (**1** ik-kai 一階, **2** ni-kai 二階, **3** san-gai 三階); **mezzanine** (～) chū-ni⌐-kai 中二階

floor lamp (denki-)suta⌐ndo (電気)スタンド

floor mat(ting) tatami 畳

floor space tate⌐-tsubo 建て坪

florist, flower shop hana⌐-ya 花屋

flounder hirame ひらめ・平目

flour kona⌐ 粉, ko⌐ 粉; *(wheat)* meriken-ko メリケン粉

flourish sakaema⌐su (saka⌐e⌐ru, saka⌐ete) 栄えます(栄える, 栄えて)

flourishing nigi⌐yaka (na) にぎやか[賑やか](な)

flow 1. it flows nagarema⌐su

(nagare⌐ru, naga⌐rete) 流れます(流れる, 流れて) **2.** *(outflow)* de 出, nagare 流れ

flow: lets it flow nagashima⌐su (naga⌐su, naga⌐shite) 流します(流す, 流して)

flower hana⌐ (o-hana) 花(お花)

flower arrangement o-hana お花, *(arranging)* ike⌐bana 生け花; *(in a tall vase)* nage-ire 投げ入れ, *(in a low basin)* moribana 盛り花

flower bud tsubomi つぼみ・蕾

flower cards (game) hana⌐-fuda 花札, hana-ka⌐ruta 花かるた

flowerpot ueki⌐-bachi 植木鉢

flower vase kabin 花瓶, ka⌐ki 花器

flower viewing hana-mi⌐ (o-hanami) 花見(お花見)

flu infurue⌐nza インフルエンザ

fluent ryū⌐chō (na) 流ちょう[流暢](な); sawa⌐yaka (na) さわやか(な); *(= can speak it fluently)* jiyū⌐ ni hanasema⌐su (hanase⌐ru, hana⌐sete) 自由に話せます(話せる, 話せて)

fluorescent light keikō-tō 蛍光灯

flush (the toilet) to⌐ire o) suisen shima⌐su (suru, shite) (トイレを)水洗します(する, して)

flush toilet suisen-be⌐njo/-to⌐ire 水洗便所/トイレ

flustered: gets ~ awatema⌐su (awateru, awatete) あわてます(あわてる, あわてて); **feels**

~ terema⌐su (tere⌐ru, te⌐rete) 照れます(照れる, 照れて); **a person easily ~** awate-mono あわて者

flute fue 笛

flute: vertical bamboo ~ shaku⌐hachi 尺八

flutter: one's heart flutters do⌐kidoki shima(⌐)su (suru, shite) どきどき[ドキドキ]します(する, して)

fly 1. *(insect)* hae はえ・ハエ・蝿 **(1** ip-pi⌐ki 一匹, **2** ni⌐-hiki 二匹, **3** sa⌐m-biki 三匹, **how many** na⌐m-biki 何匹) **2. your ~ is open** *(unzipped/unbuttoned)* sha⌐kai no ma⌐do ga aite ima⌐su 社会の窓が開いています = cha⌐kku ga aite ima⌐su チャックが開いています

fly *(moves in air)* tobima⌐su (tobu, tonde) 飛びます(飛ぶ, 飛んで); **(flies it)** tobashima⌐su (tobasu, tobashite) 飛ばします(飛ばす, 飛ばして), **flies a kite** ta⌐ko o agema⌐su (ageru, agete) 凧を揚げます(揚げる, 揚げて); *(pilots)* sōjū shima⌐su (suru, shite) 操縦します(する, して); *(goes by plane)* hikō⌐-ki de ikima⌐su (iku, itte) 飛行機で行きます(行く, 行って)

foam → bubble

focus *(camera)* pi⌐nto ピント; *(focal point)* shō⌐ten 焦点

fog kiri 霧; **foggy** kiri ga fuka'i 霧が深い

fold shiwa しわ・皺, ori-me' 折り目; *(folds it)* orima'su (o'ru, o'tte) 折ります(折る, 折って), *(folds it up)* tatamima'su (tatamu, tatande) 畳みます(畳む, 畳んで); *(it folds)* orema'su (ore'ru, o'rete) 折れます(折れる, 折れて); **folds one's arms** ude' o kumima'su (ku'mu, ku'nde) 腕を組みます(組む, 組んで)

folder: file ~ kami-ba'sami 紙挟み

folding money satsu 札, o-satsu お札

fold up (ori-)tatamima'su (tatamu, tatande) (折り)畳みます(畳む, 畳んで)

folkcraft mingei 民芸, minge[ⁿ]i-hin 民芸品

folks → people; parents; family

folk song min'yō 民謡

follow *(follows it)* ... no a'to o tsukema'su (tsuke'ru, tsuke'te) ...のあとをつけます(つける, つけて); *(adheres to)* ... ni tsukima'su (tsuku', tsu'ite) ...に付きます(付く, 付いて), *(conforms to)* ... ni shitagaima'su (shitaga[ⁿ]u, shitaga[ⁿ]tte) ...に従います(従う, 従って); *(runs along)* ... ni soima'su (sou, sotte) ...に沿います(沿う, 沿って); **~ the**

example of o mi-naraima'su (-nara[ⁿ]u, -nara[ⁿ]tte) ...を見習います(習う, 習って)

follower *(subordinate)* ko'-bun 子分

following tsugi' (no) 次(の)

fond of → like

food tabe-mo'no' 食べ物, go'han 御飯・ごはん, shoku'motsu 食物; *(meal)* shoku[ⁿ] 食, **(Western)** yō-shoku 洋食; **(Japanese)** wa-shoku 和食

food boiled with (or poured over) rice meshi'-mono 飯物

food cooked and served in a pan nabe'-mono 鍋物

food delivered to order demae (o-demae) 出前(お出前)

food fried in batter tempura てんぷら・天麩羅

food(stuff) → groceries

fool ba'ka ばか・馬鹿, to'mma とんま・頓馬

foolish baka-rashi'i ばか[馬鹿]らしい, ba'ka (na) ばか[馬鹿]な

foot ashi' 足; *(of a mountain)* fumoto' ふもと・麓; **at the foot of** ... no fumoto' (de) ...のふもと[麓](で)

footprint ashi-a'to 足跡

foot sore (from shoe rubbing) kutsu-zu[ⁿ]re[ⁿ] 靴ずれ・靴擦れ

footstool ashinose'-dai 足乗せ台

for ... (no) tame' (ni) ...(の)ため(に); ... ni (wa) ...に(は); ...

ni toʾtte ...にとって; ... no ... ...
の...; *(for the use of)* ...-yō
(no) ...用(の); *(suitable for)* ...
-muki (no) ...向き(の); *(bound
/intended for)* ...-muke (no)
...向け(の)

**for: do it for me/us, they do it
for you** ...te kuremaʾsu
(kureru, kurete) ...てくれます
(くれる, くれて)/
kudasaimaʾsu (kudasaʾru,
kudasaʾtte, kudasuʾtte) くださ
います(くださる, くださっ
て, くだすって); **do it for
you/them, you do it for them** ...te
agemaʾsu (ageru, agete) ...てあ
げます(あげる, あげて)/
sashi-agemaʾsu (-ageru, -agete)
さしあげます(-あげる, あげ
て)

for a long time (now) zutto maʾe
kara ずっと前から

for a while shibaʾraku しばらく;
hitoʾmazu ひとまず 「辛抱

forbearance shiʾmbō しんぼう・

forbid kin-jimaʾsu (kin-jiⁿru,
kiⁿn-jite) 禁じます(禁じる,
禁じて)

force 1. *(power)* jitsuryoku 実力
2. forces one (to do) muʾri ni
(*or* shiʾite) sasemaʾsu (saseru,
sasete) 無理に[強いて]させま
す(させる, させて)

forcible gōin (na) 強引(な); **forcibly** gōin ni 強引に, shiʾite 強
いて

foreboding yokan 予感

forecast yohō 予報, yosoku 予測;
weather ~ tenki-yoʾhō 天気予
報; **forecasts** *(predicts,
estimates)* it yosoku shimaʾsu
(suru, shite) 予測します(する,
して)

forehead hitai 額

foreign gaikoku (no) 外国(の),
gai-... 外..., *(Western)* yō-...
洋...

foreigner gaijin 外人, gaikokuʾ-
jin 外国人

forest mori 森, *(grove)* hayashiⁿ
林

forever iʾtsu mo いつも

for example tatoʾeba 例えば

forge 1. *(a signature, document,
etc.)* nisemaʾsu (niseru, nisete)
似せます(似せる, 似せて)
2. *(tempers metal)* kitaemaʾsu
(kitaeʾru, kitaete) 鍛えます
(鍛える, 鍛えて)

forgery *(making a fake copy)*
gizō 偽造; *(a fake)* nise-mono
偽物

forget wasuremaʾsu (wasureru,
wasurete) 忘れます(忘れる,
忘れて); **don't forget to do it**
wasurenaʾide shite kudasai 忘
れないでして下さい

forgive yurushimaʾsu (yuruʾsu,
yuruʾshite) 許します(許す, 許
して)

for instance tatoʾeba 例えば

fork 1. f(u)ōku フォーク(フォ

ーク), hō‾ku ホーク **2.** *(forking, branching)* wakare‾ 分かれ, mata‾ 又・叉

forked *(bifurcate)* futamata (no) 二叉[股](の)

form katachi 形, *(pattern)* kata‾ 型, *(figure)* su‾gata (o-su‾gata) 姿(お姿), kakkō 格好・恰好; nari‾ (o-na‾ri) なり(おなり), *(style)* ta‾i 体; *(appearance)* teisai 体裁; *(blank paper)* yō‾shi 用紙; *(document)* sho‾rui 書類

form *(creates it)* nashima‾su (na‾su, na‾shite) 成します(成す, 成して), tsukurima‾su (tsuku‾ru, tsuku‾tte) 作ります (作る, 作って)

formal, formality seishiki (na) 正式(な); keishiki 形式; *(procedure, red tape)* te-tsu‾zuki 手続き

format teisai 体裁

formation *(getting formed)* seiritsu 成立

formed: gets ~ *(organized)* seiritsu shima‾su (suru, shite) 成立します(する, して)

former ma‾e no 前の; mo‾to no もと[元]の; [bookish] ze‾n(-) ... 前...; **the former** ze‾nsha 前者

formerly mo‾to wa もと[元]は; ka‾tsute かつて, ka‾tte かって

Formosa Taiwa‾n 台湾

for sure kanarazu 必ず, ze‾-hi 是非・ぜひ, ta‾shika ni 確かに;

(not forgetting) wasurena‾ide 忘れないで

for the first time haji‾‾mete 初めて

for the most part taigai 大概・たいがい, ōkata おおかた・大方

for the reason that ... to iu riyū de ...という理由で, ... yue‾ ni ... 故に・ゆえに

for the time being tōbun 当分, hito‾mazu ひとまず

fortuitous *(accidental)* gūzen (no) 偶然(の)

fortunate saiwai (na) 幸い(な); **fortunately** saiwai ni 幸いに

fortune *(property)* za‾isan 財産; *(luck)* u‾n 運, u‾mmei 運命; *(good luck)* saiwai 幸い, shiawase 幸せ; *(written)* (o-) mikuji (お)みくじ

fortuneteller urana‾i 占い = urana‾i‾-sha 占い者

fortunetelling urana‾i 占い

forty yo‾n-jū 四十・40, shi-jū‾ 四十

forty thousand yom-ma‾n 四万・40,000

forward 1. *(ahead)* ma‾e e/ni 前へ/に; **goes ~** susumima‾su (susumu, susunde) 進みます (進む, 進んで) **2.** *(pushy)* bu-e‾nryo (na) 無遠慮な

forwarding agent unsō-ya 運送

foster yashinaima‾su (yashinau, yashinatte) 養います(養う, 養って)

foster parent sodate-no-oya⌐ 育
ての親, sato-oya 里親

foul → **dirty**

found → **find; gets found**
mitsukarima⌐su (mitsukaru,
mitsukatte) 見つかります(見
つかる, 見つかって); →
establish

foundation *(base)* kiso⌐ 基礎,
(basis) kompo⌐n 根本, kihon
基本; *(non-profit organi-
zation)* zaidan 財団

fountain funsui 噴水

fountain pen manne⌐n-hitsu 万年
筆

four yo⌐n 四・4, shi⌐ 四・4,
yottsu⌐ 四つ; *(4-oared racing
boat)* f(u)o⌐a フォア(フオア);
number four yo-ban 四番
(also yo⌐m-ban) 四番

four: small things, pieces yo⌐n-
ko 四個; **long things** yo⌐n-hon
四本; **flat things** yo⌐m-mai (yo-
mai) 四枚(四枚); **machines/
vehicles** yo⌐n-dai 四台; **books/
magazines** yo⌐n-satsu 四冊

four-and-a-half mat area yojō⌐-
han 四畳半

four animals/fish/bugs yo⌐n-
hiki 四匹; *(large animals)*
yo⌐n-tō 四頭

four birds shi⌐-wa 四羽, yo⌐n-wa
四羽

four cupfuls yo⌐n-hai 四杯

four days yokka 四日, yokka⌐-
kan 四日間

four degrees yo⌐n-do 四度

four floors/stories yon-kai 四階

fourfold, four times doubled
yom-bai 四倍

four hours yo-ji⌐kan 四時間

four hundred yo⌐n-hyaku 四百・
400

four minutes yo⌐m-pun 四分・4
分 *(also* yo⌐n-fun 四分・4 分)

four months yon-ka⌐getsu 四ヶ
月, yonkagetsu⌐-kan 四ヶ月間

four o'clock yo⌐-ji 四時・4 時

four or five shi-go-... 四, 五...

four people yo-ni⌐n 四人

fourteen jū-yo⌐n 十四・14, jū-shi⌐
十四・14; **14 days** jū-yokka 十
四日; **14th (day of month)** jū-
yokka 十四日

fourteen people jū⌐yo-nin 十四人

fourteenth jūyo(m)-bamme⌐ (no)
十四番目(の); **the ~ day**
jūyokka-me⌐ 十四日目, **(of the
month)** jū⌐-yokka 十四日

fourteen years, the year 14 jū⌐yo-
nen 十四年

fourth yo-bamme⌐ (no) 四番目
(の) *(also* yom-bamme⌐ 四番
目), yottsu-me⌐ (no) 四つ目(の);
the ~ day yokka-me⌐ 四日目,
(of the month) yokka 四日

fourth floor yon-kai 四階

four thousand yon-se⌐n 四千・
4,000

fourth time yondo-me⌐ 四度目,
yonkai-me⌐ 四回目 「年生

fourth-year student yone⌐n-sei 四

four times yoⁿ-do 四度, yoⁿ-kaⁱi 四回, yoⁿ-heⁱn 四遍

four years yo-nen 四年, yoneⁿn-kan 四年間; **~ old** yottsuⁱ 四つ, yoⁿn-sai 四歳

four yen yoⁿ(n)-en 四円

fox ki̯tsune きつね・狐

fragile koware-yasuⁱi 壊れやすい; *(thing)* koware-moⁿnoⁿ 壊れ物

frail moroⁱi もろい・脆い; yowaⁱi 弱い

frame wakuⁱ 枠, fu̯chiⁱ ふち・縁, kamachiⁱ かまち・框; *(of picture)* gaku-buchi 額縁; *(of glasses)* meⁱgane no fu̯chiⁱ 眼鏡の縁

framework kumi-tate 組み立て, honeguⁿmiⁿ 骨組み

France Furansu フランス

frank sotchoku (na) 率直(な), assaⁱri shi̯ta … あっさりした…; *(unreserved)* enryo ga naⁱi 遠慮がない, e̯nryo shinai 遠慮しない, bu-eⁱnryo (na) 無遠慮(な); *(uninhibited)* sappaⁱri shi̯ta … さっぱりした…

frankly sotchoku ni 率直に, assaⁱri (to) あっさり(と); *(unreservedly)* enryo shinaⁱide 遠慮しないで

frantically chi-maⁱnako ni naⁱtte 血眼になって

fraud saⁱgi 詐欺, i̯ⁿnchi̯ki いんちき

free *(gratis)* taⁱda (no) ただ(の),

(as part of the service) saⁱbisu サービス; *(no fee/charge)* muⁿryō (no) 無料(の); *(unrestrained)* jiyūⁱ (na) 自由(な); *(unbusy)* hima (na) 暇(な)

free: sets free *(releases)* hanashimaⁱsu (hanaⁱsu, hanaⁱshi̯te) 放します(放す, 放して); → **liberate**

freedom jiyūⁱ 自由

freelance (work), freelancing jiyūⁱ-gyō 自由業

freely jiyūⁱ ni 自由に

free parking muryō-chūⁱsha 無料駐車

free (unreserved) seat jiyūⁱ-seki 自由席

freeway kōsoku-dōⁱro 高速道路

freeze *(it freezes)* kōrimaⁱsu (kōru, kōtte) 凍ります(凍る, 凍って); *(freezes it)* kōrasemaⁱsu (kōraseru, kōrasete) 凍らせます(凍らせる, 凍らせて)

French: *(language)* Furansu-go フランス語; *(person)* Furansuⁱ-jin フランス人

French beans (= kidney beans) iⁱngen いんげん・隠元 = ingeⁱm-mame 隠元豆

frequently → **often**

fresh atarashiⁱi 新しい, shinsen (na) 新鮮(な); **fresh from …** …-tate (no) …たて(の), …-aⁱgari (no) …上がり(の)

freshman ichine'n-sei 一年生
friction masatsu 摩擦
Friday Kin'yō'bi 金曜日
fried burdock root and carrot strips *(served cold)* kimpira きんぴら・金平
fried eggs medama-yaki 目玉焼
fried rice chā'han チャーハン, yaki-meshi 焼き飯
fried shrimp *(in batter)* ebi-ten えび[海老]天, *(in bread crumbs)* ebi-fu'rai えび[海老]フライ
friend tomodachi (o-tomodachi) 友達(お友達); to'mo' (o-to'mo) 友(お友), *(pal)* nakama' (o-nakama) 仲間(お仲間); *(accomplice)* mikata 味方
friendship *(keeping company)* tsuki-ai (o-tsuki'ai) 付き合い (お付き合い)
frightened → afraid
frightful kowa'i 怖い・こわい
fritters kakiage かき揚げ
frog 1. kaeru かえる・蛙 2. *(pinholder for flowers)* ke'nzan 剣山
from ... kara ...から; **from now on** kore kara これから, ko'ngo 今後 **from ... to ...** ... kara ... ma'de ...から...まで, [*bookish*] ... na'ishi ... ...ないし...
front ma'e 前, *(ahead)* saki (o-saki) 先(お先); zempō' 前方;

(side) omote' 表, *(surface)* shōme'n 正面, zemme'n 前面; ~ **gate/entrance** seimon 正門, omote-mon 表門
front desk furonto フロント
frost shimo' 霜
frown niga'i kao o shima'su (suru, shite) 苦い顔をします (する, して)
frozen: is ~ kōtte ima'su 凍っています (→ kōrima'su 凍ります)
frugal tsumashi'i つましい, ken'yaku (na) 倹約(な), shi'sso (na) 質素(な)
fruit 1. kuda'mono 果物; ki'-no-mi 木の実, mi 実; ~ **market** kudamo'no'-ya 果物屋 2. *(product, outcome)* sambutsu 産物; → result; → crop
frustrate yaburima'su (yabu'ru, yabu'tte) 破ります(破る, 破って), zasetsu sasema'su (saseru, sasete) 挫折させます (させる, させて); *(a plan)* kujikima'su (kuji'ku, kuji'ite) くじきます・挫きます(くじく, くじいて)
frustrated: gets ~ yaburema'su (yabure'ru, yabu'rete) 破れます(破れる, 破れて), zasetsu shima'su (suru, shite) 挫折します(する, して); *(a plan)* kujikema'su (kujike'ru, kuji'kete) くじけます・挫けます(くじける, くじけて)

frustration zasetsu 挫折; *(feeling of ~)* zasetsu゙-kan 挫折感

fry agema゙su (ageru, agete) 揚げます(揚げる, 揚げて); *(pan-fries, sautés)* itamema゙su (itame゙ru, ita゙mete) 炒めます (炒める, 炒めて)

frying pan age-nabe 揚げ鍋; furai-pan フライパン

fuel nenryō゙ 燃料; *(firewood)* taki-gi たきぎ・薪; *(gasoline)* gasorin ガソリン

Fujiyama Fu゙ji(-san) 富士(山)

fulfill konashima゙su (konasu, konashite) こなします(こなす, こなして); → **accomplish; a desire is fulfilled** nozomi⌐ ga kanaima゙su (kana゙u, kana゙tte) 望みが叶います(叶う, 叶って)

full ippai (no) いっぱい[一杯] (の); *(of people)* man'in (no) 満員(の)

full: gets full michima゙su (michi゙ru, mi゙chite) 満ちます (満ちる, 満ちて)

full stop *(= period)* shūshi゙-fu 終止符

full tank man-tan 満タン

fully tappu゙ri たっぷり; ma゙n(-) ... 満... maru(-) ... まる...; *(appreciating)* shimiji゙mi (to) しみじみ(と); ~ **maturing** enjuku 円熟

fun omoshiro゙i (koto゙) おもしろい[面白い](こと); asobi 遊び

function yakume゙ (o-yakume) 役目(お役目); hataraki 働き

fund shiki゙n 資金, *(capital)* shihon 資本

fundamental kompo⌐n-teki (na) 根本的(な), kihon-teki (na) 基本的(な)

funeral (o-)sōshiki (お)葬式

funnel jō゙go じょうご, [*bookish*] rō゙to ろうと・漏斗

funny okashi゙i おかしい, oka゙shi na おかしな; *(comical)* kokkei (na) こっけい・滑稽(な), *(droll)* yu゙kai (na) 愉快(な), *(strange)* he゙n (na) 変(な), fushigi (na) 不思議(な)

fur ke-gawa 毛皮

furlough hima 暇

furnace ro 炉; kamado かまど; dambō(-sō゙chi) 暖房(装置)

furnish *(provides)* sonaema゙su (sona゙e゙ru, sona゙ete) 備えます (備える, 備えて)

furnished *(with household goods)* kagu-tsuki (no) 家具付き(の)

furniture ka゙gu 家具; ~ **store** kagu゙-ya 家具屋

further 1. hoka (ni) 他(に); *(more)* mō suko゙shi もう少し, mo゙tto もっと **2.** *(advances it)* susumema゙su (susumeru, susumete) 進めます(進める, 進めて)

fuse hyu゙zu ヒューズ

fusion gōdō 合同

fuss sa⌐wagi 騒ぎ, ō-sa⌐wagi 大騒ぎ 「→ **choosy**
fussy ki-muzukashi⌐i 気難しい;
futile muda (na) 無駄(な), munashi⌐i 空しい・虚しい

future shō⌐rai 将来, mi⌐rai 未来, saki (o-saki) 先(お先); ze⌐nto 前途, sue 末; **in the ~** ko⌐ngo 今後; **in the near ~** chika⌐i uchi⌐ ni 近いうちに

— G —

gaffe bu-sa⌐hō 無作法・不作法
gain 1. toku (o-toku) 得(お得), *(income)* shotoku 所得 **2. → get**
gale bōfū⌐ 暴風
gallop kakema⌐su (kake⌐ru, ka⌐kete) 駆けます(駆ける, 駆けて)
galoshes ama⌐-gutsu 雨靴
gambling kake⌐(goto) 賭け事, tobaku とばく・賭博, bakuchi ばくち・博奕
game asobi 遊び, gē⌐mu ゲーム; *(athletic)* kyō⌐gi 競技
gang renchū/renjū 連中/連中
gangway tara⌐ppu タラップ
gap suki-ma 透き間・隙間, suki 透き・隙; ware-me 割れ目, kire-me⌐ 切れ目; zure⌐ ずれ, gya⌐ppu ギャップ
garage ga⌐rē⌐ji ガレージ, sha⌐ko 車庫
garbage gomi⌐ ごみ, *(kitchen waste)* nama-gomi 生ごみ; ~ **bag** gomi-bu⌐kuro ごみ袋; ~ **bin/can** gomi⌐-bako ごみ箱;

~ **collector** gomi⌐-ya (san) ごみ屋(さん); ~ **dump** gomi-suteba⌐ ごみ捨て場
garden niwa (o-niwa) 庭(お庭)
gardener ueki-ya 植木屋
garlic ninniku にんにく
garnishings *(to go with sashimi)* tsuma⌐ つま
garter gā⌐tā ガーター
gas 1. *(natural)* ga⌐su ガス; ~ **bill** gasu⌐-dai ガス台; ~ **range** gasu-re⌐nji ガスレンジ **2.** *(a gas, vapor)* kitai 気体 **3.** *(gasoline)* gasorin ガソリン; ~ **pedal** kasoku-pe⌐daru 加速ペダル, a⌐kuseru アクセル; **steps on the ~** a⌐kuseru o fumima⌐su (fumu, funde) アクセルを踏みます(踏む, 踏んで) 「会社
gas company gasu-ga⌐isha ガス
gas(oline) station gasorin-suta⌐ndo ガソリンスタンド
gasp aegima⌐su (ae⌐gu, ae⌐ide) あえぎ[喘ぎ]ます(あえぐ, あえいで)

gate mo⌐n 門, *(gateway)* deiri⌐guchi 出入り口; *(of shrine)* torii 鳥居; *(front)* omote-mon 表門, *(back)* ura-mon 裏門, *(main = front)* seimon 正門; *(at airport terminal)* gēto ゲート

gatekeeper mo⌐mban 門番

gather *(they gather)* atsumari-ma⌐su (atsuma⌐ru, atsu-ma⌐tte) 集まります(集まる, 集まって), *(to make a set)* soroima⌐su (soro⌐u, soro⌐tte) 揃います・そろいます(揃う, 揃って), *(congregate)* shūgō shima⌐su (suru, shite) 集合します(する, して); *(gathers them)* atsumema⌐su (atsu-me⌐ru, atsu⌐mete) 集めます (集める, 集めて), yosema⌐su (yoseru, yosete) 寄せます(寄せる, 寄せて)

gather *(plucks, clips)* tsumima⌐su (tsumu, tsundc) 摘みます(摘む, 摘んで)

gathering shūgō 集合; ~ **place** tamari-ba たまり場

gaudy hade⌐ (na) はで・派手(な)

gauze gā⌐ze ガーゼ

gave → **give**

gaze at mi-tsumema⌐su (-tsume⌐ru, -tsu⌐mete) 見つめ ます(つめる, つめて), nagamema⌐su (nagame⌐ru, naga⌐mete) 眺めます(眺める, 眺めて)

gay akaru⌐i 明るい, yu⌐kai (na) 愉快(な); *(homosexual)* ho⌐mo (no) ホモ(の)

gear gi⌐(y)a ギア[ヤ], ha-gu⌐ruma 歯車; **high** ~ kōsokugi⌐(y)a 高速ギア[ヤ], **low** ~ teisoku-gi⌐(y)a 低速ギ ア[ヤ]

gearshift hensoku-re⌐bā 変速レ バー

gecko ya⌐mori やもり・守宮

geisha girl geisha 芸者

gelatine zera⌐chin ゼラチン; *(from tengusa 天草 seaweed)* kante⌐n 寒天

gem hōseki 宝石; **gem dealer** hōseki⌐-shō 宝石商

gender se⌐i 性

general *(over-all)* ippan (no) 一 般(の); *(common)* kyōtsū (no) 共通(の); **in** ~ , **generally** daitai 大体・だいたい, taigai 大概・たいがい, ichiō 一応・い ちおう; **the** ~ **public** taishū 大衆; ~ **remarks** *(outline)* sō⌐ron 総論

general *(army)* ta⌐ishō 大将; **ma-jor** ~ shō⌐shō 少将

generally zentai ni 全体に; daitai 大体・だいたい, taigai 大概・た いがい

generation: ~ **after** ~ , **for generations** da⌐idai 代々

generator hatsude⌐n-ki 発電機

generous kimae ga⌐i⌐i 気前がいい, kandai (na) 寛大(な)

genius tensai 天才

gentle yasashii 優しい, *(well-behaved)* otonashi⌐i おとなしい, *(docile)* su⌐nao (na) すなお [素直](な); *(calm)* oda⌐yaka (na) 穏やか(な)

gentleman da⌐nshi 男子, shi⌐nshi 紳士; *(middle-aged man)* oji-san おじさん, *(old man)* oji⌐i-san おじいさん

gently yasashiku 優しく, otona⌐shiku おとなしく

genuine hontō (no) 本当(の), hom-mono (no) 本物(の), makoto (no) 真(の)

geoduck *(surf clam)* miru⌐-gai みる貝

geographical chiri-teki (na) 地理的(な), chiri-jō (no) 地理上(の)

geography chi⌐ri 地理; *(study/science)* chiri⌐-gaku 地理学

geology *(of a place)* chi⌐shitsu 地質; *(study/science)* chishitsu⌐-gaku 地質学

germ saikin 細菌, baikin ばい菌

German *(language)* Doitsu-go ドイツ語; *(person)* Doitsu⌐-jin ドイツ人

Germany Do⌐itsu ドイツ

gesture te⌐mane 手まね; mi⌐buri 身振り; dō⌐sa 動作

get *(receives)* moraima⌐su (morau, moratte) もらいます (もらう, もらって), [HUMBLE] itadakima⌐su (itadaku,

itadaite) いただき[頂き]ます (いただく, いただいて), [HONORIFIC] o-morai ni narima⌐su (na⌐ru, na⌐tte) おもらいになります(なる, なって); **gets (someone) to do it** (hito ni) shite moraima⌐su (morau, moratte) (人に)して もらいます(もらう, もらって); → **obtain, buy, become, go, suffer, ...** ; [*bookish*] ema⌐su (e⌐ru, e⌐te) 得ます(得る, 得て)

get down *(descends)* orima⌐su (ori⌐ru, o⌐rite) 降ります(降りる, 降りて); *(crouches)* mi o fusema⌐su (fuse⌐ru, fuse⌐te) 身を伏せます(伏せる, 伏せて)

get in *(enters)* hairima⌐su (ha⌐iru, ha⌐itte) 入ります(入る, 入って); *(gets it in)* irema⌐su (ireru, irete) 入れます(入れる, 入れて)

get into a vehicle (... ni) norima⌐su (noru, notte) (... に)乗ります(乗る, 乗って)

get off *(gets down)* orima⌐su (ori⌐ru, o⌐rite) 降ります(降りる, 降りて)

get old toshi⌐ o torima⌐su (to⌐ru, to⌐tte) 年を取ります (取る, 取って), fukema⌐su (fuke⌐ru, fuke⌐te) 老けます・ ふけます(老ける, 老けて)

get out *(leaves)* dema⌐su

(de̅ru, de̅te) 出ます(出る,
出て); *(gets it out)*
dashima̅su (da̅su, da̅shite)
出します(出す, 出して)

get out of the way dokima̅su
(doku, doite) どきます(ど
く, どいて), nokima̅su
(noku, noite) のきます(の
く, のいて)

get to be → become

get up *(arises)* okima̅su
(oki̅ru, o̅ki̅te) 起きます(起
きる, 起きて)

getting aboard (into a car, etc.)
jōsha 乗車

getting a job shūshoku 就職

Getting off! Orima̅su! 降ります!

get-together party konshi̅n-kai
懇親会

get-up *(appearance)* teisai 体裁

ghastly sugo̅i すごい・凄い,
sugo̅ku waru̅i すごく[凄く]
悪い

ghost yu̅rei 幽霊; *(goblin)*
oba̅ke お化け, bake-mo̅no̅
化け物; **hungry/begging ~**
gaki̅ がき・餓鬼

giant kyojin 巨人, ō̅toko 大男;
the Giants Kyo̅jin 巨人

gift (o-)miyage (お)みやげ[土産];
~ shop miyagemono-ya みや
げ[土産]物屋; **→ present**

gigantic bōdai (na) 膨大(な)

ginger shōga しょうが・生姜;
Japanese ~ (buds) myōga み
ょうが・茗荷; **pickled ~** su-

shō̅ga 酢しょうが, ga̅ri がり

gingko *(tree)* ichō いちょう・銀
杏; **~ nuts** ginna̅n ぎんなん・
銀杏

girder keta けた・桁; **under the
~** keta-shita けた下・桁下

girdle o̅bi 帯, koshi-o̅bi 腰帯

girl musume (san) 娘(さん);
onna̅-no-ko 女の子

girl friend gāru-fure̅ndo ガール
フレンド; ka̅no-jo 彼女

gist mune̅ 旨; yō̅ 要, yō̅shi 要旨,
yōte̅n 要点, yōryō̅ 要領

give:
1. *(they to you/me, you to
   me)* kurema̅su (kureru,
   kurete) くれます(くれる,
   くれて), kudasaima̅su
   (kudasa̅ru, kudasa̅tte) 下さ
   います(下さる, 下さって)
2. *(I to you/them, you to
   them, they to them)*
   agema̅su (ageru, agete) あ
   げます(あげる, あげて),
   yarima̅su (yaru, yatte) やり
   ます(やる, やって); [HUM-
   BLE, DEFERENTIAL] sashi-
   agema̅su (-age̅ru, -a̅
   gcte) 差し上げます(上げる,
   上げて)
3. *(provides)* ataema̅su
   (ataeru, ataete) 与えます
   (与える, 与えて),
   motasema̅su (motase̅ru,
   mota̅sete) 持たせます(持た
   せる, 持たせて); **~ mer-**

cifully *(in charity)*
megumima'su (megumu,
megunde) 恵みます(恵む,
恵んで)

4. *(entrusts temporarily)*
azukema'su (azuke'ru,
azu'kete) 預けます(預ける,
預けて)

5. *(a party, etc.)*
moyōshima'su (moyō⌐su,
moyō⌐shite) 催します(催
す, 催して)

give birth to ... o umima'su
(umu, unde) ...を生み[産み]
ます(生む, 生んで)

give in/up *(cedes, concedes)*
yuzurima'su (yuzuru, yuzutte)
譲ります(譲る, 譲って)

give up (on) ... o akiramema'su
(akirame'ru, akira'mete) ...を
諦めます(諦める, 諦めて)

gizzard suna-bu'kuro 砂袋

glacier hyōga 氷河

glad ureshi'i うれしい・嬉しい; **is
glad** yorokobima'su
(yoroko'bu, yoroko'nde) 喜び
ます(喜ぶ, 喜んで)

gladly yoroko'nde 喜んで

glare at ... o niramima'su
(nira'mu, nira'nde) ...をにら
み[睨み]ます(にらむ, にら
んで)

glaring *(= dazzling)* mabushi'i
まぶしい・眩しい

glass *(the substance)* garasu ガラ
ス; *(the container)* koppu コッ

プ, gu'rasu グラス

glass = **glassful** ...'-hai ...杯
(1 i'p-pai 一杯, **2** ni'-hai 二杯,
3 sa'm-bai 三杯, **how many**
na'm-bai 何杯)

glasses me'gane めがね・眼鏡

gleam, glitter kagayakima'su
(kagaya'ku, kagaya'ite) 輝きま
す(輝く, 輝いて); **glittering**
pika'pika ぴかぴか

globe *(shape)* tama' 玉; *(map)*
chikyū'-gi 地球儀

gloomy uttōshi'i うっとうしい,
kurai 暗い, yūutsu (na) 憂うつ
[憂鬱](な), inki (na) 陰気(な)

glorious hana'yaka (na) 華やか
(な)

glory me'iyo 名誉

gloss *(shine)* tsuya つや・艶

glove tebu'kuro 手袋; *(baseball,
boxing)* gu'rabu グラブ

glow hikarima'su (hika'ru,
hika'tte) 光ります(光る, 光っ
て)

glue 1. nikawa にかわ・膠
2. *(glues it)* nikawa de
tsukema'su (tsuke'ru, tsuke'te) に
かわで付けます(付ける, 付
けて), tsugima'su (tsugu,
tsuide) 接ぎます(接ぐ, 接い
で)

glum shibu'i 渋い, inki (na) 陰気
(な)

glut kajō 過剰 　　　　「米

glutinous rice mochi-gome もち

glutton(ous) ku'i-shi'mbō (na) 食

いしん坊(な)

gnarl fushi¯ 節

gnaw kajirima¯su (kaji¯ru,
 kaji¯tte) かじります(かじる,
 かじって)

go ikima¯su (iku, itte) 行きます
 (行く, 行って)

  go against … ni somukima¯su
 (somu¯ku, somu¯ite) …に背
 きます(背く, 背いて); …
 ni han-shima¯su (han-su¯ru,
 ha¯n-shite) …に反します(反
 する, 反して); **goes ~ the
 stream = goes upstream**
 sakanoborima¯su
 (sakanobo¯ru, sakanobo¯tte)
 さかのぼります・溯ります
 (さかのぼる, さかのぼっ
 て)

  go ahead = all clear (to
 driver) ōrai オーライ

  go around magarima¯su
 (magaru, magatte) 曲がりま
 す(曲がる, 曲がって); (=
 revolves) mawarima¯su
 (mawaru, mawatte) 回りま
 す(回る, 回って)

  go away ikima¯su (iku, itte) 行
 きます(行く, 行って);
 sarima¯su (sa⌐ru, sa⌐tte)
 去ります(去る, 去って)

  go back modorima¯su
 (modo¯ru, modo¯tte) 戻りま
 す(戻る, 戻って),
 kaerima¯su (ka¯eru, ka¯ette)
 帰ります(帰る, 帰って)

  go back and forth kayoima¯su
 (kayou, kayotte) 通います
 (通う, 通って)

  go back (in time) to … ni
 sakanoborima¯su
 (sakanobo¯ru, sakanobo¯tte)
 …にさかのぼります・溯り
 ます(さかのぼる, さかの
 ぼって)

  go down orima¯su (ori¯ru,
 o¯rite) 下ります(下りる, 下
 りて); kudarima¯su
 (kudaru, kudatte) 下ります
 (下る, 下って); sagari-
 ma¯su (saga¯ru, saga¯tte) 下
 がります(下がる, 下がっ
 て); (on the price)
 makema¯su (makeru,
 makete) 負けます(負ける,
 負けて); (dwindles)
 herima¯su (heru, hette) 減り
 ます(減る, 減って)

  go forward susumima¯su
 (susumu, susunde) 進みま
 す(進む, 進んで)

  go home kaerima¯su (ka¯eru,
 ka¯ette) 帰ります(帰る, 帰
 って)

  go in hairima¯su (ha¯iru,
 ha¯itte) 入ります(入る, 入
 って), ha¯itte ikima¯su (iku,
 itte) 入って行きます(行く,
 行って)

  go out dema¯su (de¯ru, de¯te)
 出ます(出る, 出て), de¯te
 ikima¯su (iku, itte) 出て行き

ます(行く, 行って); *(of
the house)* dekakema´su
(dekakeru, dekakete) 出か
けます(出かける, 出かけ
て), gaishutsu shima´su
(suru, shite) 外出します(す
る, して); *(appears)*
arawarema´su (araware´ru,
arawa´rete) 現れます(現れ
る, 現れて); *(lights, fire,
etc.)* kiema´su (kieru, kiete)
消えます(消える, 消えて)

go over *(exceeds)* sugima´su
(sugi´ru, su´gite) 過ぎます
(過ぎる, 過ぎて), chōka
shima´su (suru, shite) 超過
します(する, して);
koshima´su (kosu, koshite)
超[越]します(超[越]す,
超[越]して)

go to *(= reaches)* itarima´su
(ita⌐ru, ita⌐tte) 至ります
(至る, 至って)

go to bed yasumima´su
(yasu´mu, yasu´nde) 休みま
す(休む, 休んで), nema´su
(neru, nete) 寝ます(寝る,
寝て)

go too far (to excess) do o
sugoshima´su (sugo´su,
sugo´shite) 度を過ごします
(過ごす, 過ごして)

go too fast *(clock)*
susumima´su (susumu,
susunde) 進みます(進む,
進んで)

go to the end of (a street)
tsuki-atarima´su (-ata´ru,
-ata´tte) 突き当たります
(当たる, 当たって)

go to (= start) work shūgyō
shima´su (suru, shite) 就業
します(する, して)

go up agarima´su (agaru,
agatte) 上がります(上がる,
上がって), noborima´su
(noboru, nobotte) 上ります
(上る, 上って)

go upstream sakanoborima´su
(sakanobo´ru, sakanobo´tte)
さかのぼります・溯ります
(さかのぼる, さかのぼっ
て)

Go *(board game)* go´ 碁, i´go 囲
碁

goal mokuteki 目的, ate 当て;
(destination) mokuteki´-chi 目
的地; *(sports)* gō´ru ゴール

goat ya´gi やぎ・山羊

gobang *(simplified version of
Go)* gomoku-na´rabe 五目並
べ

go-between *(intermediary)*
nakadachi 仲立ち; *(match-
maker)* nakō´do 仲人

goblin *(long-nosed)* tengu 天狗・
てんぐ

Go board go-ban 碁盤

goby ha´ze はぜ

God, gods ka´mi(-sama) 神(様)

godown *(storeroom)* kura´ 蔵・倉

Goh = Go *(game)* go´ 碁, i´go 囲
碁

gold ki̅n 金; **(color)** = **golden** kin-iro (no) 金色(の)

Golden Week (29 April − 5 May) gōruden-ui̅iku/-wi̅iku ゴールデンウイーク/ウィーク

goldfish ki̅ngyo 金魚

gold lacquer kim-ma̅kie 金蒔絵

golf go̅rufu ゴルフ

golf course gorufu-jō ゴルフ場

gone → **go; is gone** itte ima̅su (iru, ite) 行っています(いる, いて)

gonorrhea rimbyō りん病・淋病

good i̅i いい・良い・好い・善い, yo̅i 良い・好い・善い; **good at** (… ga) uma̅i/mma̅i (…が) うまい, jōzu̅ (na) (o-jōzu) じょうず[上手](な)(お上手), tassha (na) 達者(な)

Good morning O-hayō (gozaima̅su). おはよう[お早う]ございます. **Good afternoon** Konnichi wa. こんにちは・今日は. **Good evening** Komban wa. こんばんは・今晩は. **Good night** O-yasumi nasa̅i. おやすみ[お休み]なさい.

good: a good deal yohodo よほど・余程, yoppodo よっぽど; u⌐nto うんと; takusa̅n (no) たくさん・沢山(の)

good: for the good of … no tame̅ (o-tame) ni …のため[為] (お為)に

good-bye sayona⌐ra さよなら, sayōna̅ra さようなら; sore de̅ wa それでは; Go-kigen yō̅. ごきげんよう.

good fortune saiwai 幸い

good heavens/grief mā̅ まあ

good-looking ki̅rei (na) きれい [綺麗](な)

good-luck piece o-mamori お守り

good offices: through the ~ of … no assen de …のあっせん[斡旋]で

goods shina(-mono) 品(物); *(merchandise)* shō⌐hin 商品

goodwill kō̅i 好意, kokoro-zashi⌐ 志, shi̅nsetsu (go-shi̅nsetsu) 親切(ご親切)

goof *(blunder)* cho̅mbo ちょんぼ・チョンボ; **goofs off** → **loaf**

goose gachō がちょう・鵞鳥

gorgeous rippa (na) 立派(な); hana̅yaka (na) 華やか(な)

gossip 1. uwasa うわさ・噂; muda-/baka-ba̅nashi 無駄/ばか話 **2.** *(a gossip)* osha̅beri おしゃべり

gourd hyōta̅n ひょうたん・瓢箪; **sponge ~** hechima へちま・糸瓜

gourd strips (dried) kampyō⌐ かんぴょう・干瓢

govern osamema̅su (osame̅ru, osa̅mete) 治めます(治める, 治めて)

government se̅ifu 政府; *(cabinet)* na̅ikaku 内閣; *(nation)* kuni (no) 国（の）, *(national)* kokuritsu (no) 国立（の）; *(the authorities)* to̅kyoku 当局, oka̅mi お上; ~ **office** (o-)yakusho （お）役所; ~ **official** yakunin 役人

government worker/employee ko̅mu̅-in 公務員

governor chi̅ji 知事

grab → **seize**

graceful yu̅bi (na) 優美（な）

grade *(class)* kyu̅ 級, gakkyū 学級; *(step)* da̅n 段; *(evaluation score)* hyōten 評点; *(academic record)* seiseki 成績

gradually danda̅n だんだん, sukoshi̅ zu̅tsu 少しずつ, so̅rosoro そろそろ; *(finally)* yōyaku ようやく

graduate sotsugyō shima̅su (suru, shite) 卒業します（する, して）; a ~ sotsugyo̅-sei 卒業生, (~ of …) … no de …の出

graduate school daigaku̅-in 大学院

graduate student daigaku̅n-sei 大学院生

graft *(bribery)* wa̅iro 賄賂・わいろ

graft *(attaches)* tsugima̅su (tsugu, tsuide) 接ぎます（接ぐ, 接いで）

grain 1. (a ~) tsu̅bu 粒
2. *(cereal)* koku̅motsu 穀物,

koku̅rui 穀類 **3.** *(texture)* kime̅ きめ・木目

gram gu̅ramu グラム

grammar bumpō 文法

grand subarashi̅i すばらしい, era̅i 偉い, sōdai (na) 壮大（な）

grandchild mago̅ (o-mago-san) 孫（お孫さん）

grandfather oji̅i-san おじいさん, so̅fu 祖父

grandmother oba̅-san おばあさん, so̅bo 祖母

grandstand *(seats)* kanra̅n-seki 観覧席

grand total sōkei 総計

granite kakō̅-gan かこう岩・花崗岩, mikage̅-ishi みかげ石・御影石

grant 1. *(allowance)* kyo̅yo 供与 **2.** *(grants it)* kyo̅yo shima(⌐)su (suru, shite) 供与します（する, して）

grapefruit gurēpufuru̅tsu グレープフルーツ; natsu-mi̅kan 夏みかん・夏蜜柑

grapes budō ぶどう・葡萄

grasp tsukamima̅su (tsuka̅mu, tsuka̅nde) つかみます（つかむ, つかんで）; nigirima̅su (nigiru, nigitte) 握ります（握る, 握って）

grass ku̅sa 草; *(lawn)* shibafu 芝生

grated radish oroshi̅ おろし・下ろし, daikon-o̅roshi 大根おろし［下ろし］

grated yam tororo とろろ

grateful arigata'i ありがたい・有り難い; **I am ~** arigata'ku/ari'gatō zon-jima'su (zon-ji'ru, zo'n-jite) ありがたく[有り難く]/ありがとう[有り難う]存じます(存じる, 存じて); **feels ~ /obliged** kyōshu̱ku shima'su (suru, shi̱te) 恐縮します(する, して)

grater oroshi'-gane 下ろし金

gratis → **free**

gratitude ka'nsha 感謝

gratuity kokoro-zuke'' 心付け

grave (tomb) haka' (o-haka) 墓 (お墓); **graveyard** haka-ba' 墓場, bo'chi 墓地

grave (serious) omoi 重い, shinkoku (na) 深刻(な)

gravel jari 砂利

gravy tare'' たれ; sō'su (o-sō'su) ソース(お ソース); shi'ru 汁

gray hai-iro (no) 灰色(の), nezumi-iro (no) ねずみ色(の); gure'' no グレーの

gray hair shiraga' 白髪・しらが

gray mullet bora ぼら

graze surema'su (sure'ru, su'rete) すれます(すれる, すれて); kasumema'su (kasume''ru, kasu''mete) かすめます(かすめる, かすめて)

grease abura 脂・油

greasy aburakko'i 脂っこい; kudo'i くどい

great dai- 大...; (superior) era'i

偉い; → **big**; → **good**; → **grand**

great: a ~ difference taisa 大差; **a ~ many/much** ta'isō (na) たいそう・大層(な); **a ~ war** taisen 大戦

greatly u'nto うんと; → **extremely**

Greece Gi'risha ギリシャ

greed yokuba'ri'' 欲張り, yoku'' 欲

greedy ku'i-shi'mbō (na) 食いしん坊(な); yokubarima'su (yokuba'ru, yokuba'tte) 欲張ります(欲張る, 欲張って); **~ person** yokuba'ri'' 欲張り

Greek Girisha-go ギリシャ語

green 1. mi'dori (no) 緑(の), ao'i 青い; guri'in (no) グリーン(の) **2.** (inexperienced) osana'i 幼い

Green Car (deluxe coach) guri'in-sha グリーン車

greengrocer aomo'no-ya 青物屋, yao-ya 八百屋

green light (signal) ao-shi'ngō 青信号

green onion nira'' にら・韭; naga-ne''gi 長ねぎ[葱], ne''gi ねぎ・葱; (= chives, scallion) asa'tsuki あさつき・浅葱

green pepper pi'iman ピーマン

greens ao''-mono 青物, na''ppa 菜っ葉, na'' (o-na) 菜(お菜); (boiled) hi̱tashi-mo''no'' 浸し物 = o-hi̱ta'shi お浸し・おひたし

green tea (o-)cha（お）茶; **a cup of** ～ *(in a sushi bar)* (o-)agari（お）上がり

Green Window *(for special train tickets)* mi˺dori no mado˺-guchi みどりの窓口

greet *(welcomes, receives)* de-mukaema˺su (-mukae⌐ru, -muka⌐ete) 出迎えます(迎える, 迎えて)

greeting a˺isatsu あいさつ・挨拶; re˺i 礼

grief nageki˺ 嘆き

grieve nagekima˺su (nage˺ku, nage˺ite) 嘆きます(嘆く, 嘆いて); koko˺ro o itamema˺su (itame˺ru, ita˺mete) 心を痛めます(痛める, 痛めて)

grill yakima˺su (yaku, yaite) 焼きます(焼く, 焼いて), aburima˺su (abu˺ru, abu˺tte) あぶります(あぶる, あぶって)

grind surima˺su (su˺ru, su˺tte˺) すります(する, すって); *(into powder)* hikima˺su (hiku, hiite) ひきます(ひく, ひいて); *(grinds it up)* konashima˺su (konasu, konashi˺te) こなします(こなす, こなして); → **sharpen**; → **polish**

grip nigirima˺su (nigiru, nigitte) 握ります(握る, 握って)

gripe *(complaint)* guchi ぐち・愚痴; *(complains)* guchi o koboshima˺su (kobo˺su,

kobo˺shite) ぐち[愚痴]をこぼします(こぼす, こぼして), gu˺zuguzu iima˺su (yū, itte/yutte) ぐずぐず言います(言う, 言って/ゆって), boyakima˺su (boya˺ku, boya˺ite) ぼやきます(ぼやく, ぼやいて)

groan *(a groan)* umeki˺/mmeki˺ うめき; *(groans)* umekima˺su/mmekima˺su (ume˺ku/mme˺ku, ume˺ite/mme˺ite) うめきます(うめく, うめいて)

groceries shokuryō⌐-hin 食料品, shokuhin 食品

grocery: ～ **(store)** shokuryō-hi⌐n-ten/-ya 食料品店/屋; ～ **bill** shokuryōhi⌐n-ya no tsuke˺ 食料品屋のつけ

groin mata˺ 股

grope sagurima˺su (sagu⌐ru, sagu⌐tte) 探ります(探る, 探って); **groper** *(molester)* chikan 痴漢

gross *(crass)* egetsuna˺i えげつない

ground *(land)* tochi 土地, ji˺ 地; *(earth)* tsuchi˺ 土; *(surface)* ji˺men 地面

ground floor ik-kai 一階

ground meat hiki-niku 挽き肉

grounds *(= reason)* riyū 理由, yue˺ 故

group gurū˺pu グループ, dantai 団体; shūdan 集団; *(class)* ku˺rasu クラス; *(throng,* *flock)* mure⌐ 群れ

grove hayashi⌐ 林

grow 1. *(it grows)* seichō shima¬su (suru, shite) 成長します(する, して); *(gets big)* o¬kiku/o¬ku narima¬su (na¬ru, na¬tte) 大きく/多くなります(なる, なって); *(increases)* fuema¬su (fue¬ru, fu¬ete) 増えます(増える, 増えて); *(teeth, hair, mold, ...)* haema¬su (hae¬ru, ha¬ete) 生えます(生える, 生えて); *(appears)* hassei shima¬su (suru, shite) 発生します(する, して); *(develops)* hatten shima¬su (suru, shite) 発展します(する, して)
2. *(grows it) (a plant)* uema¬su (ueru, uete) 植えます(植える, 植えて), *(a crop)* tsukurima¬su (tsuku¬ru, tsuku¬tte) 作ります(作る, 作って); *(hair, teeth, ...)* hayashima¬su (haya¬su, haya¬shite) 生やします(生やす, 生やして)

grow *(= becomes)* (... ni, ...-ku) narima¬su (na¬ru, na¬tte) (...に, ...く)なります(なる, なって)

growing up seichō 成長; sodachi¬ (o-sodachi) 育ち(お育ち)

growl *(a growl)* unari⌐ うなり・唸り; *(growls)* unarima¬su (una¬ru, una¬tte) うなり[唸り]ます(うなる, うなって)

grow late (yo¬ ga) fukema¬su (fuke¬ru, fuke¬te) (夜が)更けます(更ける, 更けて)

growth seichō 成長; *(increase)* zō⌐ka 増加; *(development)* hatten 発展

grow thick(ly) shigerima¬su (shige¬ru, shige¬tte) 茂り[繁り]ます(茂[繁]る, 茂[繁]って)

grow up sodachima¬su (soda¬tsu, soda¬tte) 育ちます(育つ, 育って); seichō shima¬su (suru, shite) 成長します(する, して)

grow weak otoroema¬su (otoro¬e¬ru, otoro¬ete) 衰えます(衰える, 衰えて)

grudge urami⌐ 恨み

gruel *(rice)* (o-)kayu (お)かゆ[粥]

grumble boyakima¬su (boya¬ku, boya¬ite) ぼやきます(ぼやく, ぼやいて), gu¬zuguzu iima¬su (iu/yū, itte/yutte) ぐずぐず言います(言う/ゆう, 言って/ゆって), koboshima¬su (kobo¬su, kobo¬shite) こぼします(こぼす, こぼして)

grumbling fuhei 不平

guarantee hoshō 保証; **letter of ~** hoshō⌐-sho⌐ 保証書

guard 1. ba¬n 番, mo¬mban 門番; *(vigilance)* keikai 警戒
2. guards it mamorima¬su (mamo¬ru, mamo¬tte) 守りま

す(守る, 守って); **guards against** ... o keikai shimaʹsu (suru, shite) ...を警戒します (する, して)

guardian spirit (= *tutelary deity*) ujiⁿ-gaⁿmi 氏神

guess (*conjecture*) sas-shi (o-sasshi) 察し(お察し), suisoku 推測, (*estimate*) kentōʹ 見当; (*guesses*) sas-shimaʹsu (sas-suʹru, saʹs-shite) 察します(察する, 察して), suisoku shimaʹsu (suru, shite) 推測します(する, して), kentōʹ o tsukemaʹsu (tsukeʹru, tsukeʹte) 見当をつけます(つける, つけて); (*correctly*) sas-shi ga tsukimaʹsu (tsukuʹ, tsuʹite) 察しがつきます(つく, ついて), atemaʹsu (ateru, atete) 当てます(当てる, 当てて)

guest (o-)kyaku (お)客, o-kyaku-san/-saʹma お客さん/様; (*caller*) raikyaku 来客

guest house minshuku 民宿

guest room kyakuma 客間

guidance annaʹi (go-annai) 案内 (ご案内); (*direction, counseling*) shidō 指導

guide 1. (*person*) annai-gaʹkari 案内係, annaⁿi-nin 案内人, annaʹi-sha 案内者, gaʹido ガイド; (*coach, counsel*) shidōʹ-sha 指導者; (*book*) annaⁿi-sho 案内書, (*travel*) ryokō-aʹnnai 旅行案内; (*visual*) meʹate 目当

て, meⁿyasu 目安 **2.** (*guides them*) annaʹi shima(ʹ)su (suru, shite) 案内します(する, して), michibikimaʹsu (michibiʹku, michibiʹite) 導きます(導く, 導いて); (*directs, counsels*) shidō shimaʹsu (suru, shite) 指導します(する, して)

guild (*union*) kumiai 組合

guilt tsuⁿmi 罪

guilty-feeling yamashiⁿi やましい

gulf waⁿn 湾

gull kamome かもめ・鴎

gullible baka-shōʹjiki (na) ばか正直(な)

gulp: with a ~ guⁿtto ぐっと; **gulps down** guⁿtto nomi-komimaʹsu (-koⁿmu, -koⁿnde) ぐっと飲み込みます(込む, 込んで)

gum (*chewing*) gaʹmu ガム; (*mucus from eye*) me-yani 目やに; (*teethridge*) haʹguki 歯茎

gun jūʹ 銃, teppō 鉄砲

gunpowder kayaku 火薬

gush wakimaʹsu (waku, waite) わき[湧き・涌き]ます(わく, わいて)

guts harawaⁿtaⁿ はらわた・腸・腑, wataʹ わた・腸; → **courage**

gutter (*ditch*) dobu どぶ; (*drain pipe*) toⁿi 樋

guy yaʹtsu やつ・奴

gymnasium taiⁿkuʹ-kan 体育館, jiʹmu ジム

gymnastics taisō 体操

— H —

haberdashery *(notions)* koma⌐-mono 小間物, yōhin 洋品; *(shop)* komamo⌐no⌐-ya 小間物屋, yōhi⌐n-ten 洋品店

habit shūkan 習慣; *(bad habit)* ku̱se̱⌐ 癖

had → **have**; gets ~ (by …) (…ni) yararema⌐su̱ (yarareru, yararete) (…に)やられます（やられる, やられて）

hail arare/hyō⌐ (ga furima⌐su̱; fu̱⌐ru, fu̱⌐tte⌐) あられ・霰/ひょう・雹(が降ります; 降る, 降って)

hair *(on head)* kami⌐ 髪; *(general)* ke 毛

haircut rihatsu 理髪, sampatsu 散髪; gets/gives a ~ rihatsu/sampatsu shima⌐su̱ (suru, shi̱te) 理髪/散髪します(する, して)

hairdresser → **beauty parlor**; → **barber(shop)**

hair oil kami-a̱⌐bura 髪油, pomā⌐do ポマード; *(stick pomade)* chi̱⌐kku チック

hairspring zemmai ぜんまい

half hambu̱⌐n 半分; half a … han-… 半…, … no hambu̱⌐n …の半分; and a half …-ha̱⌐n …半

half a day han-nichi⌐ 半日

half a month han-tsu̱ki⌐ 半月

half a week sa̱⌐n-yokka 三, 四日 *(= 3 or 4 days)*

half a year han-toshi⌐ 半年, ha̱⌐n-nen 半年, han-ka̱⌐nen 半か年

halfbeak *(fish)* sa̱⌐yori さより

half-done *(meat)* han'yake (no) 半焼け(の)

halfhearted ii-kagen (na) いい加減(な)

hall *(building)* kaikan 会館; *(lecture hall)* kōdō 講堂; *(entrance)* ge̱⌐nkan 玄関

halt → **stop**

ham ha̱⌐mu ハム; **ham and eggs** hamu-e̱⌐ggu/-e̱⌐kku ハムエッグ/エック; **ham sandwich** hamu-sa̱⌐ndo ハムサンド

hamburger *(sandwich)* hambā⌐gā ハンバーガー; *(ground beef)* hambā⌐gu ハンバーグ

hammer 1. kanazuchi⌐ かなづち・金槌, ha̱⌐mmā/ha̱⌐mma ハンマー/ハンマ, tsu̱chi⌐ 槌, *(small)* ko̱⌐zuchi 小槌; **claw ~** kuginu⌐ki⌐ 釘抜き 2. *(= hits)* uchima̱⌐su̱ (u̱⌐tsu, u̱⌐tte) 打ちます(打つ, 打って)

hand te̱⌐ 手; *(of clock)* ha̱⌐ri 針

hand: has on hand (in stock) mochi-awasema͟su (-awase͟ru, -awa͟sete) 持ち合わせます(合わせる, 合わせて)

handbag handoba͟ggu (handoba͟kku) ハンドバッグ(ハンドバック), tesage͟ 手提げ

handball te͟-mari 手まり

handbill bira びら・ビラ

handbrake saido-bure͟ki サイドブレーキ

handcrafted tesei no 手製の

hand down tsutaema͟su (tsutae͟ru, tsutaete) 伝えます(伝える, 伝えて); **gets handed down** tsutawarima͟su (tsutawa͟ru, tsutawa͟tte) 伝わります(伝わる, 伝わって)

handicapped (physically) karada ga fu͟-jiyū (na) 体が不自由(な); ～ **person** (shintai-)shōga͟i-sha (身体)障害者

handiwork te-za͟iku 手細工, saiku͟ 細工

handkerchief ha͟nkachi ハンカチ

handle totte͟ 取っ手, handoru ハンドル, tsuru͟ つる・鉉

handle it tori-atsukaima͟su (-atsuka͟u, -atsuka͟tte) 取り扱います(扱う, 扱って); *(copes with it)* sho͟ri shima͟su (suru, shite) 処理します(する, して); *(uses a tool)*

tsukaima͟su (tsukau, tsukatte) 使います(使う, 使って); *(controls)* sōjū shima͟su (suru, shite) 操縦します(する, して); *(receives)* …ni ses-shima͟su (ses-su͟ru, se͟s-shite) …に接します(接する, 接して); → **sell**; → **touch**

Handle With Care Kowaremono-chu͟i 壊れ物注意

handling tori-atsukai 取り扱い; *(operation)* sōjū 操縦; ～ **charge** tesu͟-ryō 手数料

hand luggage te-ni͟motsu 手荷物

hand over watashima͟su (watasu, watashite) 渡します(渡す, 渡して); torima͟su (toru, totte) 取ります(取る, 取って); **(to me)** yokoshima͟su (yokosu, yokoshite) よこします(よこす, よこして)

handshake a͟kushu 握手

hand towel te-nugui (o-te͟nugui) 手ぬぐい・手拭い(お手ぬぐい), tefuki͟ (o-te͟fuki) 手ふき・手拭き(お手ふき); *(damp)* (o-)shi͟bori (お)絞り・(お)しぼり

handy be͟nri (na) 便利(な)

handyman *(or his shop)* benri-ya 便利屋

hang 1. it hangs kakarima͟su (kaka͟ru, kaka͟tte) 掛かります(掛かる, 掛かって) **2. hangs it** kakema͟su (kake͟ru, ka͟kete) 掛けます(掛ける, 掛けて),

(suspends it) tsurima'su (tsuru, tsutte) 吊ります(吊る, 吊って)

hang down 1. it hangs down tarema'su (tare'ru, ta'rete) 垂れます(垂れる, 垂れて); sagarima'su (saga'ru, saga'tte) 下がります(下がる, 下がって) **2. hangs it down** sagema'su (sage'ru, sa'gete) 下げます(下げる, 下げて); **hangs one's head** utsumukima'su (utsumu⌐ku, utsumu⌐ite) うつむきます・俯きます(うつむく, うつむいて)

hanger ha'ngā ハンガー

hanging scroll → scroll

hang in there gambarima'su (gamba'ru, gamba'tte) がんばり[頑張り]ます(がんばる, がんばって)

hangout tamari-ba 溜まり場

hang up (phone) (denwa o) kirima'su (ki'ru, ki'tte') (電話を)切ります(切る, 切って)

haphazard ii-kagen (na) いい加減(な)

happen okorima'su (oko'ru, oko'tte) 起こります(起こる, 起こって); ~ **to see/observe** mi-ukema'su (-uke⌐ru, -u⌐kete) 見受けます(受ける, 受けて); ~ **to see/meet** de-aima'su (-a'u, -a'tte) 出会います(会う, 会って)

happening *(incident)* deki'goto 出来事, ji'hen 事変; *(event)* koto' 事

happi coat hante'n 半天, happi はっぴ・法被

happiness kōfuku 幸福, shiawase 幸せ・しあわせ

happy ureshi'i うれしい・嬉しい, yu'kai (na) 愉快(な), kōfuku (na) 幸福(な), shiawase (na) 幸せ・しあわせ(な); *(cheerful)* yōki (na) 陽気(な); *(auspicious)* medeta'i めでたい・目出度い; *(is delighted)* yorokobima'su (yoroko'bu, yoroko'nde) 喜びます(喜ぶ, 喜んで); → **lucky** 「気(な)

happy-go-lucky no'nki (na) のん

Happy New Year Shi'nnen/Akema'shite o-medetō gozaima'su. 新年/あけ[明け]ましておめでとう[お目出度う]ございます.

harakiri seppuku 切腹

harbor → **port**

hard katai 固い・硬い・堅い; *(difficult)* muzukashii 難しい, *(hard to do)* shi-niku'i しにくい; *(onerous)* kurushi'i 苦しい, *(trying)* tsurai つらい・辛い; *(requires much effort)* hone' ga orema'su (ore'ru, o'rete) 骨が折れます(折れる, 折れて); *(cruelly, terribly)* hi'doku ひどく; *(intently)* shikiri-ni しきりに

hard: (working ~) yo'ku 良く;
(laboriously) a'kuseku あくせ
く, se'sse-to せっせと;
(zealously) ne'sshi'n ni 熱心に;
(seriously) majime ni まじめ
[真面目]に

hard cash genki'n 現金, shōkin
正金

harden 1. it hardens
katamarima'su (katamaru,
katamatte) 固まります(固ま
る, 固まって) **2. hardens it**
katamema'su (katameru,
katamete) 固めます(固める,
固めて)

hardly hoto'ndo ほとんど・殆ど
+ NEGATIVE

hard of hearing, hard to hear
mimi' ga tōi 耳が遠い

hardship ko'nnan 困難, ku'rō 苦
労

hard times fuke'iki 不景気

hardware 1. kanamono 金物;
(items) tekki 鉄器, tekki'-rui
鉄器類; *(store)* kanamono-ya
金物屋; → **houseware 2. (computer ~)** hādowe'a ハードウ
ェア

hard work ku'rō (go-ku'rō) 苦労
(ご苦労)

hardworking kimben (na) 勤勉
(な)

hare usagi うさぎ・兎

harm ga'i 害, songai 損害;
(harms it) sokonaima'su
(sokona'u, sokona'tte) 損ない

ます(損なう, 損なって);
without ~ (incident) buji (ni)
無事(に); **it will do no ~ to
(do it)** (shi)-te' mo motomoto
de'su (し)てももともとです

harmony chōwa 調和; **is in ~
with ...** to chōwa shima'su
(suru, shite) ...と調和します
(する, して)

harp *(Japanese)* (o-)ko'to (お)琴;
(Western) hā'pu ハープ

harsh *(cruel)* zankoku (na) 残酷
(な)

harvest minori 実り, shūkaku 収
穫; *(harvests it)* osamema'su
(osame'ru, osa'mete) 収めます
(収める, 収めて), shūkaku
shima'su (suru, shite) 収穫し
ます(する, して)

has → have

hash: beef ~ over rice hayashi-
ra'isu ハヤシライス

haste isogi' 急ぎ

hasten → hurry

hasty *(hurried)* isogi' no 急ぎの;
(rash) keisotsu (na) 軽率(な)

hat bōshi (o-bo'shi) 帽子(お帽子);
bamboo ~ ka'sa 笠

hatchet nata なた, o'no 斧, te'-
o'no 手斧

hate (... ga) iya' desu (...が)嫌
です; (... ga) kirai desu (...
が)嫌いです; (... o)
nikumima'su (niku'mu,
niku'nde) (...を)憎みます(憎
む, 憎んで)

haughty gōman (na) 傲慢(な); **is/acts ~** ibarima̗su (iba̗ru, iba̗tte) 威張ります(威張る, 威張って)

haute couture (= *high fashion*) ōtokuchūru オートクチュール

have (… ga) arima̗su (a̗ru, a̗tte) (...が)あります(ある, あって), (… o) mo̗tte ima̗su (iru, ite) (...を)持っています (いる, いて); *(keeps, retains)* kakaema̗su (kakae̗ru, kaka̗ete) 抱えます(抱える, 抱えて)

USAGE: Da̗re ga(/ni) na̗ni ga arima̗su ka 誰が(/に)何があ りますか **Who has what?**

have: ~ someone do it (hito ni sore o) sasema̗su (saseru, sasete) (人にそれを)させます (させる, させて), *(as a favor)* shite moraima̗su (morau, moratte) してもらい ます(もらう, もらって); **~ it done** *(by someone unwantedly)* (hito ni sore o) sarema̗su (sareru, sarete) (人にそれを) されます(される, されて)

have no (… ga) arimase̗n (na̗i, na̗kute) (...が)ありません(な い, なくて)

have to → must

Hawaii Ha̗wai ハワイ

hawk taka たか・鷹

hay magusa まぐさ・秣; **~ fever** kafu̗n-shō 花粉症, are̗ru̗gii アレルギー

haze mo̗ya もや・靄, *(mist)* kasumi かすみ・霞

hazy: gets ~ kasumima̗su (kasumu, kasunde) かすみま す・霞みます(かすむ, かすん で)

he ka̗re 彼, ano̗-hito あの人 *(but use name, title, or role; often omitted)*; (= *that guy*) ya̗tsu やつ・奴, yakko san やっこさん

he-… *(animal)* … no osu̗ ...の雄

head atama̗ 頭, kashira̗ (o-kashira) 頭(お頭); *(brains)* zu̗nō 頭脳; *(leader)* kashira̗ 頭, chō̗ 長, *(of a school)* kōchō 校長

headache zutsū 頭痛; **have a ~** zutsū ga shima̗su (suru, shite) 頭痛がします(する, して), atama̗ ga ita̗i 頭が痛い

head for … ni mukaima̗su (mukau, mukatte) ...に向かい ます(向かう, 向かって); … o mezashima̗su (meza̗su, meza̗shite) ...を目指します (目指す, 目指して)

heading *(caption)* midashi 見出 し

headland mi̗saki 岬

headlight(s) heddora̗ito ヘッド ライト; **turns the ~ on/off** heddora̗ito o tsukema̗su/ keshima̗su ヘッドライトをつ

けます/消します
headline midashi 見出し
head over heels massaꞋka-sama
ni まっさかさまに・真っ逆様
に
headquarters hoꞋmbu 本部,
shireꞋi-bu 指令部, *(building)*
shireꞋi-kan 指令官
health kenkō 健康, **(one's ~)**
karada 体・身体; **(state of
one's ~)** (go-)kigen（ご）機嫌,
(o-)kagen（お）加減; *(hygiene,
sanitation)* eisei 衛生; **~ service** *(= clinic)* byōin 病院
healthy kenkō (na) 健康(な),
geꞋnki (na) 元気(な), tassha
(na) 達者(な), mame (na) ま
め(な); *(sturdy)* jōbu (na) 丈
夫(な); *(good for one's
health)* karada ni iꞋi 体にいい
heap yamaꞋ 山, *(one)* hitoꞋ-yama
一山
heap it up morimaꞋsu (moru,
motte) 盛ります(盛る, 盛っ
て)
hear kikimaꞋsu (kiku, kiite) 聞き
ます(聞く, 聞いて); [HUM-
BLE] ukagaimaꞋsu (ukagau,
ukagatte) 伺います(伺う, 伺
って), uke-tamawarimaꞋsu
(uke-tamawaⁿru, uke-
tamawaⁿtte) 承ります(承る,
承って)
hearer kiki-te 聞き手
heart shinzō 心臓; *(as seat of
emotions)* kokoꞋro (o-kokoro)

心（お心）; *(the very center)*
chūshin 中心; *(core, spirit)*
shiꞋn 芯; *(mind)* muneꞋ 胸,
omoꞋi 思い; *(spirit)* ki 気
heart: by ~ *(= from memory)*
soꞋra de 空で
heartfelt kokoꞋro kara (no) 心か
ら(の)
heartless mujō (na) 無情(な),
hakujō (na) 薄情(な)
heat 1. aꞋtsu-sa 熱さ・暑さ, netsuꞋ
熱 **2. heats it** aꞋtsuku shimaꞋsu
(suru, shite) 熱くします(する,
して), nes-shimaꞋsu
(nes-suⁿru, neꞋs-shite) 熱し
ます(熱する, 熱して); →
warm it up 3. it heats up
aꞋtsuku narimaꞋsu (naru,
natte) 熱く[暑く]なります(な
る, なって), nes-shimaꞋsu
(nes-suⁿru, neꞋs-shite) 熱
します(熱する, 熱して)
heater sutoꞋbu ストーブ, hiꞋitā
ヒーター, kanetsuꞋ-ki 加熱器
heating *(of room, etc.)* dambō 暖
房; **traditional quilt-covered
~ device** kotatsu (o-koꞋtatsu,
o-koꞋta) こたつ(おこたつ, お
こた)
heating rice wine o-kan お燗,
kaꞋn 燗
heaven teꞋn 天; *(sky)* soꞋra 空;
(paradise) teꞋngoku 天国
heavy omoi 重い; *(onerous)*
kurushiꞋi 苦しい
heavy rain ō-aꞋme 大雨; *(torren-*

tial downpour) gō̄u 豪雨
heavy snow ō-yuki⌐ 大雪
heckling ya⌐ji やじ・野次
hedge ike⌐gaki 生け垣
heel kakato かかと・踵
height ta⌐kasa 高さ; *(stature)* se⌐i 背・せい = se⌐ 背
hell jigoku⌐ 地獄
hello *(on phone)* mo⌐shi-moshi もしもし; *(shouting at door)* Gomen kudasa⌐i ごめん下さい; *(on encounter)* ā ああ + NAME *and/or* TITLE; yā やあ; Go-kigen yō̄ ごきげんよう.
help 1. *(assistance)* tetsuda⌐i (o-te⌐tsudai) 手伝い（お手伝い）; *(good offices)* assen あっせん・斡旋, sewa⌐ 世話, **with the ~ of** ... no assen/sewa⌐ de ...のあっせん/世話で **2.** *(assists)* tetsudaima⌐su (tetsuda⌐u, tetsuda⌐tte) 手伝います（手伝う, 手伝って）; *(rescues)* tasukema⌐su (tasuke⌐ru, tasuke⌐te) 助けます（助ける, 助けて）, *(saves)* sukuima⌐su (sukuu, sukutte) 救います（救う, 救って）
helper joshu 助手; **household helper** o-te⌐tsudai (san) お手伝い（さん）
helping: a second ~ (of rice, etc.) o-ka⌐wari お代わり
hem suso 裾
hemorrhoids ji 痔・ぢ
henchman ko⌐-bun 子分

hepatitis kan'en 肝炎
her → **she; herself** → **oneself**
herb kusa⌐ 草; hā̄bu ハーブ
here koko ここ; kochira こちら, kotchi⌐ こっち; **is here** kite⌐ ima(⌐)su (iru, ite) 来ています（いる, いて）
　Here! *(answering roll call)* Ha⌐i! はい!
　Here (you are)! Ha⌐i (kore de⌐su)! はい（これです）!
here and there achi⌐-ko⌐chi あちこち; *(various places)* tokorodo⌐koro ところどころ・所々
herpes hōshin 疱疹, he⌐rupesu ヘルペス
herring ni⌐shin にしん・鰊
hers *(= of her)* → **she**
hesitate tameraima⌐su (tamera⌐u, tamera⌐tte) ためらいます（ためらう, ためらって）; chū̄cho shima(⌐)su (suru, shite) ちゅうちょ［躊躇］します（する, して）; enryo shima⌐su (suru, shite) 遠慮します（する, して）
hey! o⌐i! おい!, mo⌐shi-moshi! もしもし!, ano ne⌐! あのね!
hi! yā̄ やあ!; → **hello**; → **hey**
Hibiya Hibiya 日比谷; **~ Park** Hibiya-kō̄en 日比谷公園
hiccup sha⌐kkuri しゃっくり
hide *(hides it)* kakushima⌐su (kaku⌐su⌐, kaku⌐shite) 隠しま

す(隠す, 隠して); *(it hides)*
kakurema'su (kakure'ru,
kaku'rete) 隠れます(隠れる,
隠れて)

high taka'i 高い; kō-... 高...;
highest *(maximum, top)* saikō
(no) 最高(の), saijō (no) 最上
(の); **higher by ¥100**
hyakue'n-daka 百円高; **the
highest** *(degree)* saikō-ge'ndo
最高限度

high: ~ **(barometric) pressure**
kō-ki'atsu 高気圧; ~ **blood
pressure** kō-ke'tsu'atsu 高血圧

highball haibō'ru ハイボール;
(of shōchū 焼酎*)* chū-hai 酎杯
・チュー杯; *(whisky-and-
water)* mizuwari 水割り

highbrow interi インテリ

high-class *(high-grade/-ranking)*
kōkyū (na) 高級(な);
(fashionable) haikara (no) ハ
イカラ(の)

high degree kō'do 高度

highest ichiban taka'i 一番高い,
saikō (no) 最高(の); ichiban
ue 一番上, saijō (no) 最上(の)

high fashion ōtokuchū'ru オート
クチュール

high gear kōsoku-gi'(y)a 高速ギ
ア[ヤ]

highhanded gōin (na) 強引(な);
highhandedly gōin ni 強引に

highpoint chō'te'n 頂点

highrise kōsō (no) 高層(の)

high school kōtō-ga'kkō 高等学

校; ~ **student** kōkō'-sei 高校
生

high sea taika⌐i 大海 *(also
daika⌐i 大海)*

high speed kōsoku 高速

highway kaidō⌐ 街道, kokudō
国道, kōdō 公道; *(expressway)*
kōsoku-dō'ro 高速道路

hijack nottorima'su (notto'ru,
notto'tte) 乗っ取ります(乗っ
取る, 乗っ取って)

hijacker nottori'-han 乗っ取り犯

hijacking nottori-ji'ken 乗っ取
り事件

hike, hiking ha'iki'ngu (o
shima'su; suru, shite) ハイキ
ング(をします; する, して)

hill *(slope)* saka'坂; *(small mountain)* oka 丘, koyama 小山

hilt tsuka'柄

him → **he; himself** → **oneself**

hinder samatagema'su
(samatage⌐ru, samata⌐gete) 妨
げます(妨げる, 妨げて)

hindrance sashitsukae 差し支え;
(o-)jama (お)じゃま[邪魔];
koshō 故障; shōgai 障害

hinge chō-tsu'gai ちょうつがい・
蝶番; **hinged door** hiraki'-do
開き戸

hint 1. hi'nto ヒント, hono-
mekashi'ほのめかし, anji
暗示 **2.** *(hints it)* hono-
mekashima'su (-meka'su,
-meka'shite) ほのめかします
(めかす, めかして), anji

shima'su (suru, shite) 暗示し
ます(する, して)

hip *(buttock)* shiri' (o-shiri) 尻
(お尻), *(thigh)* mo'mo もも・
股; *(loins)* koshi 腰

hiragana hira'ga'na' ひらがな・平
仮名

hire yatoima'su (yato'u, yato'tte)
雇います(雇う, 雇って); *(a
professional)* tanomima'su
(tano'mu, tano'nde) 頼みます
(頼む, 頼んで)

Hiroshima Hiroshima 広島; ~
Station Hiroshima'-eki 広島駅

his *(= of him)* → **he**

historian rekishi-ka 歴史家

history rekishi 歴史; **one's personal** ~ rireki 履歴, *(written)*
rire[ʃ]ki[ʃ]-sho 履歴書

hit butsukema'su (butsukeru,
butsukete) ぶつけます(ぶつ
ける, ぶつけて), uchima'su
(u'tsu, u'tte) 打ちます(打つ,
打って); *(strike)* tatakima'su
(tata'ku, tata'ite) 叩きます(叩
く, 叩いて); atema'su (ateru,
atete) 当てます(当てる, 当て
て), atarima'su (ataru, atatte)
当たります(当たる, 当たっ
て)

hit: a hit hi'tto' ヒット; atari 当
たり

hit: gets ~ *(= robbed, beset,
wounded, killed)* yararema'su
(yarareru, yararcte) やられま
す(やられる, やられて)

hitherto ju̅'rai 従来

hit home *(with/to one)* pin-to
kima'su (ku'ru, kite') ぴんと
きます(くる, きて)

hoard takuwaema'su
(takuwa[ʃ]e[ʃ]ru, takuwa[ʃ]ete)
蓄えます(蓄える, 蓄えて)

hobby shu'mi 趣味; ohako おは
こ・十八番

hobo furo̅-sha 浮浪者, ru̅'mpen
ルンペン

hoe kuwa くわ・鍬

Hokkaido Hokka'ido̅ 北海道

hold (te' ni) mochima'su (mo'tsu,
mo'tte) (手に)持ちます(持つ,
持って), mo'tte ima'su (iru,
ite) 持っています(いる, いて);
(in arms) dakima'su (daku,
daite) 抱きます(抱く, 抱いて),
(or under the arm) kakaema'su
(kakae[ʃ]ru, kaka[ʃ]ete) 抱えま
す(抱える, 抱えて); *(an open
umbrella)* sashima'su (sa'su,
sa'shite) 差します(差す, 差し
て); *(keeps in reserve)* to'tte
okima'su (oku, oite) 取って置
きます(置く, 置いて); *(gives
an event)* moyōshima'su
(moyō[ʃ]su, moyō[ʃ]shite) 催し
ます(催す, 催して); ~ **in the
mouth** fukumima'su
(fuku'mu, fuku'nde) 含みます
(含む, 含んで)

hold: a hold *(place to hold on)*
tega'kari 手掛かり

hold back *(hesitates)* enryo (go-

enryo) shima̱su (suru, shite)
遠慮(ご遠慮)します(する,
して)

hold it up sashi-agema̱su
(-ageᴺru, -aᴺgete) 差し上げ
ます(上げる, 上げて)

hole ana̱ 穴; *(opening)* kuchi 口

hole-punch ki̱ri きり・錐

holiday yasumi̱ 休み, kyūjitsu
休日; *(official)* saijitsu 祭日

Holland Oraᴺnda オランダ

hollow *(empty)* utsuro (na) うつ
ろ(な); *(a dent)* kubomi くぼ
み・窪み; **gets ～** hekomima̱su
(hekomu, hekonde) へこみま
す・凹みます(へこむ, へこん
で)

home uchi 家, ... uchi̱ (o-uchi) ...
家(お家); *(one's residence)*
jitaku 自宅; *(household)* katei
家庭; *(of a product/crop)*
sa̱nchi 産地; **～ and abroad**
na̱igai 内外; **(one's) ～ area**
kuni (o-kuni) 国(お国), inaka
いなか・田舎; **goes ～**
kaerima̱su (ka̱eru, ka̱ette) 帰
ります(帰る, 帰って)

home appliances katei-yo̱gu/
-yo̱hin 家庭用具/用品

homeland so̱koku 祖国,
bo̱koku 母国

homely *(ugly)* bu-ki̱ryō (na) 無
器量[不器量](な)

homemade tesei (no) 手製(の),
tezu̱kuri (no) 手作り(の)

homesick (uchi ga) natsukashi̱i

(家が)懐かしい

hometown ko̱kyō 故郷; inaka い
なか・田舎; sato (o-sato) 里(お
里)

homework shukudai 宿題

homosexual ho̱mo ホモ, dōse̱i-
ai (no) 同性愛(の)

honest shōji̱ki̱ (na) 正直(な),
katagi (na) 堅気(な); *(proper)*
tadashi̱i 正しい; *(earnest)* majime (na) まじめ[真面目](な)

honestly shōji̱ki̱ ni 正直に

honewort mitsuba 三つ葉

honey mi̱tsu 蜜, hachi-mitsu 蜂
蜜

Hong Kong Ho̱nko̱n ホンコン・
香港

Honolulu Honoruru ホノルル

honor me̱iyo 名誉; *(= "face")*
taimeᴺn 体面; *(sense of
obligation)* giri̱ (o-giᴺri) 義理
(お義理); *(shame)* re̱nchi 廉
恥, *(sense of shame)* renchi̱-
shin 廉恥心

honorific (word) keigo 敬語
HONORIFIC PREFIX o- お・御;
go- ご・御; *(for a few words)*
on- 御, mi- み・御, o-mi- おみ,
gyo- 御

Honshu Ho̱nshū 本州

hood *(of car)* bonne̱tto ボン
ネット

hoodlum yotamono よたもの;
chimpira ちんぴら

hoof hizume ひづめ・蹄

hook kagi̱ かぎ・鈎; *(snap)*

ho˥kku ホック; *(fish ~)* tsuriba[˥]ri 釣り針
hookey: plays ~ saborima˥sụ (sabo˥ru, sabo˥tte) さぼ[サボ]ります(さぼる, さぼって), zuru-ya˥sumi shima(˥)sụ (-suru, -shite) ずる休みします(する, して)
hoop: a barrel ~ taga˥ たが
hope 1. a hope nozomi[˥] 望み, kibō 希望, *(anticipation)* mikomi 見込み, *(ambition)* kokoro-zashi[˥] 志 **2. hopes for** nozomima˥sụ (nozo[˥]mu, nozo[˥]nde) 望みます(望む, 望んで), kibō shima˥sụ (suru, shịte) 希望します(する, して) **I hope that …** (VERB-(r)u う(る)/ADJECTIVE-i い/NOUN da˥ だ) to i˥i desụ (ga ne˥) といいです(がね)
horizon *(sea)* suihei-sen 水平線, *(land)* chịhei-sen 地平線
horizontal suihei (no) 水平(の)
horn *(of animal)* tsuno˥ 角; *(of car)* keiteki 警笛; *(music)* ho˥run ホルン
hornet suzume˥-bachi すずめばち·雀蜂
horrible osoroshi˥i 恐ろしい
horse uma˥/mma˥ 馬 **(how many** na˥n-tō 何頭)
horse mackerel a˥ji あじ·鯵
horse racing keiba 競馬
horseradish wa˥sabi わさび·山葵
hose hō˥su ホース; → **stockings**
hospital byōin 病院; **~ admission** nyūin 入院; **is in the ~** nyūin shịte ima˥sụ (iru, ite) 入院しています(いる, いて)
hospital head/director i˥nchō 院長
hospitality ashira[˥]i あしらい
host shu˥jin 主人, te˥ishu 亭主
hostelry minshụku 民宿
hostess onna-shu˥jin 女主人; ho˥sụtesu ホステス
hot 1. atsu˥i 熱い·暑い; **gets ~** nes-shima˥sụ (nes-su[˥]ru, ne[˥]s-shịte) 熱します(熱する, 熱して) **2.** *(pungent, spicy)* karai からい·辛い
hot air *(idle talk)* baka-/muda-ba˥nashi ばか/無駄話
hotel ho˥teru ホテル; **~ bill** hoteru˥-dai ホテル代
hot plate *(electric)* denkị-ko˥nro 電気こんろ, *(gas)* gasụ-ko˥nro ガスこんろ
hot spring onsen 温泉; **hot-spring cure** tōji 湯治
hot water o-yu お湯, yu˥ 湯
hot-water bottle yu-ta˥mpo 湯たんぽ
hour ji[˥]kan (o-ji˥kan) 時間(お時間)
house uchi 家, … uchi˥ (o-uchi) … 家(お家), ie˥ 家 **(1** i˥k-ken 一軒, **2** ni˥-ken 二軒, **3** sa˥n-gen 三軒, **how many** na˥n-gen 何軒); taku 宅, …-ya …家; **your ~** o-taku お宅

house: rental house (= *house for rent or rented house*) kashi-ya 貸家

house addition/extension tate-mashi 建て増し

house dust gomi ごみ

housefly hae はえ・蠅

household katei 家庭; shotai 所帯; **~ altar** (*Buddhist*) butsudan 仏壇, (*Shinto*) kami-dana 神棚; **~ helper** otetsudai (san) お手伝い(さん)

housekeeper kasei-fu 家政婦

housekeeping kasei 家政, shotai 所帯

house rent ya-chin 家賃

housesit: is housesitting (for) (... no) kawari ni sunde imasu (...の)代わりに住んでいます

housesite shiki-chi 敷地

houseware ara-mono 荒物; **~ dealer/store** aramono-ya 荒物屋

housewife shufu 主婦

housing development danchi 団地

how dō どう, [DEFERENTIAL] ikaga いかが・如何

How are you (feeling)? Go-kigen (wa) ikaga desu ka. ご機嫌(は)いかが[如何]ですか. O-genki desu ka. お元気ですか.

how come dō-shite どうして

How do you do? (*on first being introduced*) Hajimemashite.

初めまして.

however keredo(mo) けれど(も), shikashi しかし, de mo でも, datte だって, tokoro-ga とこ ろが, tadashi ただし・但し; (*to be sure*) motto mo もっと も

how far/long dono-gurai どの位

how many ikutsu (o-ikutsu) い くつ(おいくつ); nan-... 何..., iku-... いく・幾...

how many: small things, pieces nan-ko 何個; **long things** nam-bon 何本; **flat things** nam-mai 何枚; **small animals/ fish/bugs** nam-biki 何匹; **large animals** nan-tō 何頭; **birds** nam-ba 何羽; **machines, vehicles** nan-dai 何台; **books, magazines** nan-satsu 何冊

how many days nan-nichi 何日

how many people nan-nin 何人 nam-mei 何名

how many times nan-do 何度, nan-kai 何回, nam-ben 何遍 (= *how manyfold*); nam-bai 何杯

how many years nan-nen 何年 **~ old** ikutsu (o-ikutsu) いく つ(おいくつ), nan-sai 何歳

how much ikura (o-ikura) いく ら(おいくら), dono-gurai と の位, ika-hodo いか程; donna ni どんなに

how old ikutsu (o-ikutsu) いく つ(おいくつ); nan-sai 何歳

how true naru-hodo (so゜ desu ne゜) なるほど[成る程](そうですね)

hug daki-shimema゜su (-shime゜ru, -shi゜mete) 抱き締めます(締める, 締めて)

huge kyodai (na) 巨大(な), bakudai (na) 莫大(な)

huh?! ho゜ra! ほら!

human being ningen 人間; ji゜nrui 人類

human feelings/nature ni゜njō 人情

humble (modest) kenson (na) 謙遜(な)

humid (in summer) mushi-atsu゜i 蒸し暑い, (gets sultry) mushima゜su (mu゜su, mu゜shite) 蒸します(蒸す, 蒸して); (in winter) shimeppo゜i 湿っぽい

humidity shikki゜ 湿気 (also shikke゜) 湿気), shitsu゜do 湿度

humiliating kuyashi゜i 悔しい

humor yū゜moa ユーモア

hundred hyaku゜ 百・100, **how many hundred** na゜mbyaku (-...) 何百(...)

hundred million o゜ku 億

hundred thousand jū-ma゜n 十万・100,000

hungry: gets ~ o-naka ga sukima゜su (suku, suite) おなかがすきます(すく, すいて)

hunt(ing) ka゜ri 狩り, ryō゜ (o

shima゜su; suru, shite) 猟(をします; する, して); → **look for**

hurray! banza゜i! 万歳!

hurricane bōfū゜ 暴風

hurry isogima゜su (iso゜gu, iso゜ide) 急ぎます(急ぐ, 急いで); tobashima゜su (tobasu, tobashite) 飛ばします(飛ばす, 飛ばして)

hurt 1. it hurts (= is painful) ita゜i 痛い **2. gets hurt** kega゜ o shima゜su (suru, shite) けが[怪我]をします(する, して) **3.** (injures) itamema゜su (itame゜ru, ita゜mete) 傷めます(傷める, 傷めて); (damages) sokonaima゜su (sokona゜u, sokona゜tte) 損ないます(損なう, 損なって)

husband otto 夫, shu゜jin 主人, danna-san/-sama 旦那さん/様, te゜ishu 亭主, ha゜zu ハズ; **your ~** go-shu゜jin ご主人; **my ~** otto 夫, shu゜jin 主人, taku 宅

husband and wife fū゜fu 夫婦; **both ~** fūfu-tomo 夫婦共

hut koya゜ 小屋

hydrant → **fireplug**

hydrogen su゜iso 水素

hygiene eisei 衛生

hypothesis katei 仮定

— I —

I watashi わたし・私, watakushi わたくし・私; [HUMBLE] temae 手前; *(mostly male)* bo⌐ku ぼく・僕; *(male, unrefined)* ore おれ・俺; *(mostly female)* atashi あたし

...-ic, ...-ical ...-teki (na) ...的 (な)

ice kōri 氷

iceberg hyō⌐zan 氷山

icebox reizō⌐ko 冷蔵庫

ice cream aisu-kuri⌐imu アイスクリーム

icicle tsurara つらら・氷柱

idea kanga⌐e 考え, omo⌐i 思い; *(opinion)* i⌐ken 意見, *(your ~)* go-i⌐ken ご意見; aide⌐a アイデア; *(intention, aim)* nerai 狙い; → **rough ~**

ideal risō-teki (na) 理想的(な); *(most desirable)* motte-ko⌐i (no) もってこい(の)

identical hitoshi⌐i 等しい; → **same**

identified: gets ~ shirema⌐su (shireru, shirete) 知れます(知れる, 知れて)

idiot ba⌐ka ばか, to⌐mma とんま

idle *(is lazy)* namakema⌐su (namake⌐ru, nama⌐kete) 怠けます(怠ける, 怠けて); *(useless, unavailing)* muda (na) 無駄(な); **~ talk** baka-/muda-ba⌐nashi ばか/無駄話

idly bu⌐rabura ぶらぶら

if mo⌐shi ... (shi)-ta⌐ra もし... (し)たら; ... (no) ba(w)ai ... (の)場合; **~ by any chance** ma⌐n'ichi 万一; **if you prefer/ like** nan-na⌐ra なんなら

if I remember rightly ta⌐shika 確か

if you don't mind yoroshika⌐ttara よろしかったら・宣しかったら; nan-na⌐ra なんなら

if you don't want to/if you like nan-na⌐ra なんなら

ignition (switch) sui⌐tchi スイッチ; **turns on the ~** sui⌐tchi o irema⌐su (ireru, irete) スイッチを入れます(入れる, 入れて)

ignore mu⌐shi shima(⌐)su (suru, shite) 無視します(する, して)

ill → **sick; bad**

illegal fuhō (na) 不法(な)

illicit: anything ~ yami⌐ 闇

illness byōki 病気

ill-tempered iji⌐ ga waru⌐i 意地が悪い

illuminate terashima⌐su (tera⌐su, tera⌐shite) 照らします(照らす, 照らして)

illustration zukai 図解, ira⌐sụto
  イラスト
ill will urami⌐ 恨み
image zō⌐ 像; *(psychological,
  social)* imē⌐ji イメージ
imagination sōzō 想像
imagine sōzō shima⌐sụ (suru,
  shịte) 想像します(する, して);
  → **suppose, think**
imitate ... no mane o shima⌐sụ
  (suru, shịte) ...のまね[真似]
  をします(する, して), ... o
  manema⌐sụ (maneru, manete) ...
  をまね[真似]ます(まねる,
  まねて); nisema⌐sụ (niseru,
  nisete) 似せます(似せる, 似
  せて)
imitation 1. *(man-made)* jinzō
  (no) 人造(の); *(fake)* nise (no)
  偽(の), nise-mono 偽物
  2. *(mimicry)* mane まね・真似
immediate tossa (no) とっさ(の);
  → **direct**
immediately su⌐gu (ni) すぐ(に),
  sassoku⌐ 早速・さっそく, jiki
  (ni) じき(に), ta⌐dachi-ni 直ち
  に・ただちに, tachimachi (ni)
  たちまち(に), tossa ni とっさ
  (に); *(without waiting)*
  mata⌐naide 待たないで
immense ta⌐i-shịta 大した;
  bakudai (na) 莫大(な)
immigrant(s) imin 移民
immigration *(entry)* nyūkoku 入
  国; **immigration control office**
  nyūkoku-kanri-jimu⌐sho 入国

管理事務所
imminent tossa (no) とっさ(の)
immoderately mu⌐yami ni むや
  みに
immoral fu-dō⌐toku (na) 不道徳
  (な); **immorality** fu-dō⌐toku
  不道徳
impartial kōhei (na) 公平(な),
  kōsei (na) 公正(な); **impartiality** kōsei 公正
impatient ki ga mijika⌐i 気が短い
impediment koshō 故障, shōgai
  障害; *(hindrance)* sashitsụkae
  差し支え
imperial te⌐ikoku (no) 帝国(の);
  imperialism teikoku-shu⌐gi 帝
  国主義
impertinent namaiki (na) 生意気
impetus hazumi 弾み ⌐(な)
implement *(tool)* yō⌐gu 用具; *(apparatus)* ki⌐gu 器具
imply 1. fụkumima⌐sụ (fụku⌐mu,
  fụku⌐nde) 含みます(含む, 含
  んで) **2.** → **hint**
impolite bu⌐rei (na) 無礼(な),
  shịtsu⌐rei (na) 失礼(な)
import yunyū shima⌐sụ (suru,
  shịte) 輸入します(する, して);
  (goods) yunyū⌐-hin 輸入品
importance: a matter of ~ da⌐iji
  大事, jūda⌐i-ji 重大事
important jūyō (na) 重要(な),
  taisetsu (na) 大切(な), jūdai
  (na) 重大(な), *(precious)*
  daiji⌐ (na) 大事(な); ta⌐i-shịta
  (koto⌐) 大した(事); omoi 重い

impose it kuwaema⌐su
(kuwae⌐ru, kuwa⌐ete) 加え
ます(加える, 加えて)
impossible deki⌐nai 出来ない,
fुka⌐nō (na) 不可能(な); **impossible!** ma⌐saka まさか
impression inshō 印象
impressive inshō-teki (na) 印象
的(な)
improve 1. *(it improves)*
naorima⌐su (nao⌐ru, nao⌐tte) 直
ります(直る, 直って), yo⌐ku
narima⌐su (na⌐ru, na⌐tte) 良く
なります(なる, なって)
2. *(improves it)*
naoshima⌐su (nao⌐su,
nao⌐shite) 直します(直す,
直して), yo⌐ku shima⌐su
(suru, shite) 良くします(す
る, して)
impulse hazumi 弾み
in ... de ...で, *(located in)* ...ni
...に; *(inside)* ...no na⌐ka (de/
ni) ...の中(で/に); *(resident
in)* zai-... 在...
comes in (... ni) ha⌐itte
kima⌐su (ku⌐ru, ki⌐te) (...に)
入って来ます(来る, 来て)
goes in (... ni) hairima⌐su
(ha⌐iru, ha⌐itte) ...に入ります
(入る, 入って), ha⌐itte
ikima⌐su (iku, itte) 入って行き
ます(行く, 行って)
lets/puts in (... ni) irema⌐su
(ireru, irete) (...に)入れます
(入れる, 入れて)

inadvertently tsu⌐i つい
inadvisable mazu⌐i まずい
inbound (to Tōkyō) nobori (no)
上り(の)
incense kō⌐ 香; (o-)se⌐nko (お)線
香, se⌐nkō 線香
incessantly shikiri-ni しきりに
inch (...-)i⌐nchi (...)インチ;
(Japanese) (...-)su⌐n (...)寸
incident ji⌐hen 事変, ji⌐ken 事件
incidentally *(by the way)* sore wa
sō⌐ to それはそうと, tokoro⌐-
de ところで, chi⌐nami ni ち
なみ[因み]に, tsuide ni つい
でに, toki⌐ ni 時に
inclination katamu⌐ki⌐ 傾き;
(intention) ikō 意向
include irema⌐su (ireru, irete) 入
れます(入れる, 入れて),
komema⌐su (kome⌐ru,
ko⌐mete) 込めます(込める,
込めて), fुkुmema⌐su
(fुkुme⌐ru, fुkु⌐mete) 含め
ます(含める, 含めて);
(covers all items) mō⌐ra
shima(⌐)su (suru, shite) 網羅し
ます(する, して)
including ... o irete/fुkु⌐mete ...
を入れて/含めて; ...-tsुki ...
付き
income sho⌐toku 所得, shūnyū
収入; **~ tax** shotoku⌐-zei 所得
税
inconsistency mujun 矛盾
inconsistent: is ~ mujun shite
ima⌐su (iru, ite) 矛盾していま
す(いる, いて)

inconvenience *(trouble taken)* tesū̄ (o-tesū) 手数(お手数), tḙ́kazu 手数

inconvenient fu̇́ben (na) 不便(な); fu̇́-jiyū (na) 不自由(な)

increase 1. *(it increases/increases it)* mashimáṣu (masu, mashite) 増します(増す, 増して); *(it/they increase)* fuemáṣu (fue̊ru, fu̇́ete) 増えます(増える, 増えて), *(increases it/them)* fuyashimáṣu (fuyá̇su, fuyá̇shite) 増やします(増やす, 増やして) **2.** *(an increase)* mashi 増し; zō̄ka 増加, zōdai 増大, zōshin 増進

increasingly masū̄-masu ますます・益々

incur kōmurimáṣu (kōmu̇́ru, kōmu̇́tte) 被ります・こうむります(被る, 被って)

indecent gehi̇́n (na) 下品(な); *(obscene)* waisetsu (na) わいせつ・猥褻(な)

indeed honto ni ほんとに・本当に, jitsu̇́ ni 実に; ittai いったい・一体; *(of course)* mo̊́ttomo もっとも・最も; *(as we might expect)* sasuga (ni) さすが(に)

indefinite fu̇tei (no) 不定(の)

indemnify hoshō shimá̇su (suru, shite) 保証します(する, して)

indemnity baishō̄-kin 賠償金, hoshō̄-kin 補償金

independence dokuritsu 独立

independent dokuritsu shita ... 独立した...; **is ~** dokuritsu shite imá̇su (iru, ite) 独立しています(いる, いて)

index sakuin 索引, midashi 見出し

India Ĩndo インド; **Indian** Indō̄-jin インド人, **(American ~)** Ĩnde(y)an インデア[ヤ]ン

India ink sumī̄ 墨; **~ painting** sumī̄-e 墨絵

indicate shimeshimáṣu (shime̊su, shime̊shite) 示します(示す, 示して); sashimáṣu (sá̇su, sá̇shite) 指します(指す, 指して); shiteki shimá̇su (suru, shite) 指摘します(する, して), shi̇́ji shimá̇(̄)ṣu (suru, shite) 指示します(する, して)

indication shi̇́ji 指示, *(token, sign)* shirushi しるし・印

indifferent to ... ni mu-ká̇nshin (no) ...に無関心(の)

indigestion fu̇shō̄ka 不消化, shōka-fu̇́ryō 消化不良

indignant: gets ~ fungai shimá̇su (suru, shite) 憤慨します(する, して), ikidōrimá̇su (ikidō̊ru, ikidō̊tte) 憤ります(憤る, 憤って)

indignation fungai 憤慨, ikidōri̊ 憤り

indirect kansetsu no 間接の; **indirectly** kansetsu ni 間接に

indiscriminate yatara na やたら
な
indiscriminately yatara ni やたら
に, mu⌐yami ni むやみに
individual kojin-teki (na) 個人的
（な）; *(a person)* ko⌐jin 個人
individually betsu-betsu ni 別々
に
Indonesia Indone⌐shi(y)a インド
ネシア［ヤ］; **Indonesian**
(language) Indoneshi(y)a-go
インドネシア［ヤ］語, *(person)*
Indoneshi(y)a⌐-jin インドネシ
ア［ヤ］人
indoors uchi (no na⌐ka) de/ni 家
（の中）で/に
indoor shoes uwabaki 上履き
industrious kimben (na) 勤勉（な）
industry kō⌐gyō 工業, sangyō 産
業
in effect yō-su⌐ru ni 要するに
inept heta⌐ (na) へた［下手］（な）
inevitable yondokoro-na⌐i よん
どころない・拠ん所無い
inevitably kanarazu 必ず; na⌐n
to shite⌐ mo 何としても
inexpert heta⌐ (na) へた［下手］な
infant yō⌐ji 幼児, shō⌐ni 小児
infantile paralysis shōni-ma⌐hi 小
児麻痺
infect utsushima⌐su (utsu⌐su⌐,
utsu⌐shite) 移します（移す, 移
して）
infection = infectious disease
densem-byō 伝染病
infer suitei shima⌐su (suru, shite)
推定します（する, して）
inference suitei 推定
inferior: is ～ ochima⌐su
(ochi⌐ru, o⌐chite) 落ちます（落
ちる, 落ちて), otorima⌐su
(oto⌐ru, oto⌐tte) 劣ります
（劣る, 劣って）; yuzurima⌐su
(yuzuru, yuzutte) 譲ります（譲
る, 譲って）, makema⌐su
(makeru, makete) 負けます
（負ける, 負けて）
inflation infure インフレ
influence *(effect)* eikyō 影響, ...
se⌐i ...せい・所為; *(power)*
se⌐iryoku 勢力
influential yūryoku (na) 有力（な）
influenza → **flu**
inform kikasema⌐su (kikaseru,
kikasete) 聞かせます（聞かせ
る, 聞かせて), shirasema⌐su
(shiraseru, shirasete) 知らせま
す（知らせる, 知らせて),
tsugema⌐su (tsugeru, tsugete)
告げます（告げる, 告げて）;
(instructs) oshiema⌐su
(oshieru, oshiete) 教えます（教
える, 教えて）; *(tells)* mimi⌐ ni
irema⌐su (ireru, irete) 耳に入
れます（入れる, 入れて）
informal hi-kō⌐shiki (no) 非公式
（の）
information jōhō 情報, shirase
知らせ; *(guidance)* anna⌐i 案内;
(reception desk) uke-tsuke 受
付
infrequent tama no たまの,

mare⌐ na まれ[稀]な; **infre-quently** tama ni たまに, mare⌐ ni まれ[稀]に

ingredient (*component*) se⌐ibun 成分; (*raw material*) zairyō⌐ 材料

inherit (*succeeds to*) tsugima⌐su (tsugu, tsuide) 継ぎます(継ぐ, 継いで)

injection chūsha 注射

injure itamema⌐su (itame⌐ru, ita⌐mete) 傷めます(傷める, 傷めて); (*damages it*) sokonaima⌐su (sokona⌐u, sokona⌐tte) 損ないます(損なう, 損なって)

injury kega⌐ けが・怪我; (*damage*) ga⌐i 害, hi⌐gai 被害

ink i⌐nki インキ, i⌐nku インク; **India ink, ink stick** sumi⌐ 墨

inkstone suzuri⌐ 硯; ~ **case** suzuri⌐-bako 硯箱

inlaid work zōga⌐n 象眼・象嵌

inland (*domestic*) koku⌐nai (no) 国内(の); (*internal to Japan*) na⌐ichi (no) 内地(の)

Inland Sea Seto-na⌐ikai 瀬戸内海

...-in-law giri⌐ no ... 義理の...

inlet (*opening*) kuchi 口

inn (*Japanese-style*) ryokan 旅館; yado-ya 宿屋, ya⌐do (o-yado) 宿(お宿)

inner moat uchi-bori 内堀

innocent (*naive*) mu⌐jaki (na) 無邪気(な); (*not guilty*) mu⌐zai (no) 無罪(の)

innumerable musū⌐ (no) 無数(の), kazoe-kire⌐nai 数え切れない

inoculation yobō-chū⌐sha 予防注射

inordinate hō⌐gai (na) 法外(な)

in other words suna⌐wachi すなわち・即ち

in particular to⌐ku-ni 特に, toriwake とりわけ

in pieces mechamecha めちゃめちゃ

inquire toima⌐su (to⌐u, tō⌐te) 問います(問う, 問うて); → **ask**

inquiry (o-)toiawase (お)問い合わせ; (o-)ukagai (お)伺い; (*survey*) chō⌐sa 調査

inquisitive mono⌐zuki⌐ (na) 物好き(な)

inquisitiveness kōki⌐shin 好奇心

in rapid succession zo⌐kuzoku 続々

insane ki̠-chiga⌐i (no) 気違い(の); **goes** ~ ki ga kuruima⌐su (kuru⌐u, kuru⌐tte) 気が狂います(狂う, 狂って)

insect konchū 昆虫, mushi 虫 (1 ip-piki⌐ 一匹, 2 ni⌐-hiki 二匹, 3 sa⌐m-biki 三匹, **how many** na⌐m-biki 何匹)

insecticide bōchū⌐-zai 防虫剤

insect repellent mushi-yo⌐ke⌐ 虫よけ

insert sashi̠-komima⌐su (-ko⌐mu, -ko⌐nde) 差し込

みます(込む, 込んで); *(puts it between)* hasamima̱su (hasa̱mu, hasa̱nde) 挟みます (挟む, 挟んで)

in short tsu̱mari つまり, yō-su̱ru ni 要するに

inside (... no) na̱ka (de/ni) (...の)中(で/に), ...-nai ...内; *(among)* (... no) uchi̱ (de/ni) (...の)内(で/に); **the inside** uchi-gawa 内側, uchiwa 内輪, *(back/deep inside)* o̱ku 奥; **is inside** ha̱itte ima̱su (iru, ite) 入っています(いる, いて)

inside and out na̱igai 内外

inside corner su̱mi 隅

insipid ajike-na̱i 味気ない

inspect ke̱nsa/kansatsu shima̱su (suru, shite) 検査/監察します(する, して)

inspection ke̱nsa 検査, kansatsu 監察

install sonaema̱su (sona̱e̱ru, sona̱ete) 備えます(備える, 備えて)

installation shi̱se̱tsu 施設

installment(s) wappu 割賦; *(monthly payments)* geppu 月賦

installment savings tsumitate̱-kin 積立金

instance *(example)* tato̱e 例え, tato̱i 例い, re̱i 例, ichi-rei 一例; **for ~** tato̱eba 例えば

instant *(moment)* shunkan 瞬間, se̱tsuna せつな・刹那; **in an ~**

tachimachi (ni) たちまち(に), su̱gu すぐ, tossa ni とっさに; **(at) the ~ that ...** totan ni 途端に

instantly tachimachi (ni) たちまち(に)

instead (sono) kawari ni (その)代わりに

institute *(research)* kenkyū-jo̱ 研究所; **~ director** shochō 所長

institution shi̱se̱tsu 施設

instruct → **teach**

instruction oshie 教え; shidō 指導

instructions *(directions)* sa̱shizu 指図, shi̱ji 指示; *(written explanation)* setsume̱i-sho̱ 説明書

instructor kyō̱shi 教師, sense̱i 先生

instrument *(implement)* yō̱gu 用具; *(instrumentality)* kika̱i 機械, kika̱n 機関; *(musical)* gakki 楽器

insufficiency fu̱soku 不足, ...-bu̱soku ...不足

insufficient tarimase̱n (tarinai) 足りません(足りない)

insulate zetsuen shima̱su (suru, shite) 絶縁します(する, して)

insult 1. bujoku 侮辱 **2.** *(insults one)* bujoku̱ shima̱su (suru, shite) 侮辱します(する, して)

insurance hoken 保険

insure (it) (... ni) hoken o

kakema̱su (kake̱ru, ka̱kete)
(...に)保険をかけます(かけ
る, かけて)

intact sono mama̱ (de/no) その
まま(で/の)

intellectual(s), intelligentsia
interi インテリ

intelligence *(information)* jōhō
情報; → **knowledge**

intelligent wakari̱ ga i̱i 分かりが
いい, rikō 利口(な)

intend to (do) (suru) tsumori
de̱su (する)つもりです

intent mune̱ 旨; → **intention**

intention tsumori (o-tsumori) つ
もり(おつもり), i̱to 意図,
i̱shi 意志, kokoro-zashi 志;
(aim) nerai 狙い

intentionally takura̱nde 企んで;
→ **[on] purpose**

intently shikiri-ni しきりに; jitto
じっと

intercourse *(social)* shakō 社交;
(sexual) seikō 性交

interest *(on money)* risoku 利息,
ri̱shi 利子, ri̱ 利; *(pleasure)*
kyo̱mi 興味, shu̱mi 趣味;
(relevance) kankei 関係, *(con-cern)* kanshin 関心

interesting omoshiro̱i おもしろ
い・面白い, kyōmi-buka̱i 興味
深い; **(Oh?) How interesting!**
Sō̱ desu ka. そうですか。

interfere jama ni narima̱su
(na̱ru, na̱tte) じゃま[邪魔]に
なります(なる, なって),

jama o shima̱su (suru, shite)
じゃま[邪魔]をします(する,
して), kanshō shima̱su (suru,
shite) 干渉します(する, して)

interference jama じゃま・邪魔;
(meddling) kanshō 干渉

interjection *(word)* kantō̱shi 間
投詞

intermediary nakadachi̱ 仲立ち

intermission *(between acts)*
makuai 幕あい・幕間

internal 1. uchi (no) 内(の),
na̱ibu (no) 内部(の), nai-teki
(na) 内的(な); ~ **evidence**
nai-teki shō̱ko 内的証拠 **2.** *(to
the nation)* koku̱nai (no) 国内
(の), na̱ichi (no) 内地(の)
3. *(within the office/com-pany)* sha̱nai (no) 社内(の)

international kokusai-teki (na)
国際的(な); *(worldwide)*
sekai-teki (na) 世界的(な)

interpret tsū̱yaku shima̱su
(suru, shite) 通訳します(する,
して); *(explains, construes)*
ka̱ishaku shima̱su (suru, shite)
解釈します(する, して)

interpretation tsū̱yaku 通訳; *(ex-planation, construal)*
ka̱ishaku 解釈

interpreter tsū̱yaku 通訳

interrupt *(with a remark)* (... no
hanashi̱ ni) sashide̱guchi o
shima̱su (suru, shite) (...の話
に)差し出口をします(する,
して)

interruption shadan 遮断;
(suspension) teishi 停止;
(remark) sashide⌐guchi 差し
出口

intersect yoko-girima´su (-gi´ru,
-gi´tte) 横切ります(切る,
切って); **intersecting** ōdan
横断

intersection (of streets) kōsa⌐-
ten 交差点, yotsu-kado 四つ
角　　　　　　　　　「間隔

interval aida 間, ma 間; kankaku

interview kaiken 会見; taimen 体
面, (meeting with) menkai 面
会; **interviewing** (questioning)
shimon 試問

intestines harawa⌐ta⌐ はらわた
・腸, wata´ わた・腸, chō´ 腸

intimate shitashi´i 親しい;
missetsu (na) 密接(な)

in time (eventually) yagate⌐ や
がて

intolerable tamarimase´n
(tamaranai) たまりません(た
まらない); **intolerably** ya´ke
ni やけに

**intoxicated → drunk; is easily in-
toxicated** sake ni yowa´i 酒に
弱い

intoxication yoi 酔い

intramural kō´nai (no) 校内(の)

intransitive verb jidō´shi 自動詞

intricate komi-i⌐tta 込み入った

introduce shōkai shima´su (suru,
shite) 紹介します(する, して);
Let me ~ you Go-shōkai

shima´su. ご紹介します.

introduction shōkai (go-shōkai)
紹介(ご紹介)

intrusive (o-)jama (na) (お)じゃ
ま[邪魔](な)

intuition chokkan 直観・直感

in vain munashi⌐i 空しい・虚し
い, muda (na/ni) 無駄(な/に)

invalid (not valid) mukō (na) 無
効(な); (ill person) byōnin 病
人

invention hatsumei 発明

inventory mokuroku 目録

invest oroshima´su (oro´su,
oro´shite) 下ろします(下ろす,
下ろして); tō⌐shi shima´su
(suru, shite) 投資します(する,
して)

investigate shirabema´su
(shirabe´ru, shira´bete) 調べま
す(調べる, 調べて);
kiwamema´su (kiwame´ru,
kiwa´mete) 究めます(究める,
究めて)

investigation shirabe´ (o-shirabe)
調べ(お調べ), chōsa 調査

investment tō⌐shi 投資

invisible (me´ ni) miemase´n
(mie´nai) (目に)見えません
(見えない)

invitation sasoi 誘い, shō´tai
(shō´dai) 招待(招待); (card)
shōta´i-jō (shōda´i-jō) 招待状
(招待状)

invite yobima´su (yobu, yonde)
呼びます(呼ぶ, 呼んで),

sasoima῀su (sasou, sasotte) 誘
います(誘う, 誘って),
manekima῀su (mane῀ku,
mane῀ite) 招きます(招く, 招
いて), shōtai shima῀su (suru,
shite) 招待します(する, して),
mukaema῀su (mukaeru,
mukaete) 迎えます(迎える,
迎えて); [HONORIFIC] o-meshi
ni narima῀su (na῀ru, na῀tte) お
召しになります(なる, なっ
て)

involuntary mu-i῀shiki (no/na)
無意識(の/な)

iodine yō῀do ヨード

Ireland Airura῀ndo アイルラン
ド

iris shō῀bu しょうぶ・菖蒲

Irish potato jagaimo (o-ja῀ga)
じゃがいも(おじゃが)

iron *(metal)* tetsu 鉄; *(clothes
iron)* airon アイロン; **irons a
shirt** wai-shatsu ni airon o
kakema῀su (kake῀ru, ka῀kete)
ワイシャツにアイロンをかけ
ます(かける, かけて)

iron bar tetsu-bō 鉄棒

iron bridge tekkyō 鉄橋

irregular fuki῀so῀ku (na) 不規則
(な)

irrelevant to ... to mu-ka῀nkei
(no) ...と無関係(の)

irresponsible mu-se῀kinin (na) 無
責任(な)

**irritate: gets irritated / is irri-
tating** shaku ni sawarima῀su

(sawaru, sawatte) しゃく[癪]
にさわります(さわる, さ
わって)

is (am, are, be):
1. *(it is)* ... de῀su (da῀/no῀/
na῀, de῀, ni῀) です(だ/の/な,
で, に); [DEFERENTIAL] ...
de gozaima῀su (de
gozaima῀shite) ...でござい
ます(でございまして),
[HONORIFIC] ... de
irasshaima῀su (de irassha῀ru,
de irassha῀tte/ira῀shite) ...で
いらっしゃいます(でい
らっしゃる, でいらっ
しゃって/いらして)
2. *(there is; it is there)*
arima῀su (a῀ru, a῀tte) ありま
す(ある, あって);
[DEFERENTIAL] gozaima῀su
(gozaima῀shite) ございます
(ございまして)
3. *(person is there)* ima῀su
(iru, ite) います(いる, いて),
[DEFERENTIAL/HUMBLE]
orima῀su (o῀ru, o῀tte/
orima῀shite) おります(おる,
おって/おりまして),
[HONORIFIC] irasshaima῀su
(irassha῀ru, irassha῀tte/
ira῀shite/irasshaima῀shite)
いらっしゃいます(いらっ
しゃる, いらっしゃって/
いらして/いらっしゃいま
して)
4. *(is doing)* ...te ima῀su (iru,

ite) ...ています(いる, いて),
...te orima'su (o'ru, o'tte/
orima'shite) ...ております
(おる, おって/おりまして),
...te irasshaima'su
(irassha'ru, irassha'tte/
ira'shite/irasshaima'shite) ...
ていらっしゃいます(い
らっしゃる, いらっしゃっ
て/いらして/いらっしゃい
まして) = ...te oide ni
narima'su (na'ru, na'tte/
narima'shite) ...おいでにな
ります(なる, なって/なり
まして)

I see! naru-hodo なるほど・成る
程

island shima' 島; **(group of)
islands** ...-sho'tō ...諸島,
(archipelago) rettō 列島,
...-re'ttō ...列島

(-)ism shu'gi 主義

isn't (aren't) 1. *(it isn't)* ... ja
arimase'n (ja na'i, ja na'kute) ...
じゃありません(じゃない,

じゃなくて) **2.** *(there isn't)*
arimase'n (na'i, na'kute) あり
ません(ない, なくて)

issue *(publishes)* hakkō shima'su
(suru, shite) 発行します(する,
して); → **put out**

it sore それ *(but usually omitted)*

Italian *(language)* Itari(y)a-go イ
タリア[ヤ]語; *(person)*
Itari(y)a'-jin イタリア[ヤ]人

Italy Itari(y)a イタリア[ヤ]

itch(y) kai'i かいい, kayu'i かゆ
い・痒い; mu'zumuzu むずむ
ず

item kōmoku 項目, shu'moku
種目

itinerary nittei 日程

itself sore ji'shin/ji'tai それ自身/
自体; ... ~ **(as we might expect)** sasuga no ... さすがの...;
... **(in)** ~ ... sono-mo'no' ...そ
のもの, (sore) ji'tai (それ)自
体; **of/by** ~ hitori-de ni ひと
りでに・独りでに

ivory zōge' 象牙

ivy tsuta' つた・蔦

— **J** —

jacket uwagi 上着; jaketsu ジャ
ケツ, ja'ke'tto ジャケット;
traditional workman's ~
hante'n 半天, happi 法被

jade hisu'i ひすい・翡翠, hi'sui
ひすい・翡翠

jail keimu'-sho 刑務所, rōgoku
牢獄, [*uncommon*] ori' おり・
檻

jam *(to eat)* ja'mu ジャム

janitor ko'zukai 小使い, yōmu'-
in 用務員; kanri'-nin 管理人

January Ichi-gatsu⌐ 一月・1 月, Shōgatsu⌐ 正月

Japan Niho⌐n 日本, Nippo⌐n 日本; **made in Japan** Nihon-sei (no) 日本製(の), kokusan (no) 国産(の)

Japan Airlines (JAL) Nihon Kōkū(-Ga⌐isha) 日本航空(会社), Ja⌐ru ジャル

Japan-bashing Nihon-ta⌐taki 日本叩き[たたき]

Japanese *(language)* Nihon-go 日本語

Japanese *(of Japan)* Niho⌐n no 日本の; wa-... 和..., nichi-... 日...

Japanese *(person)* Nihon-ji⌐n 日本人

Japanese cakes/sweets wa-ga⌐shi 和菓子

Japanese celery u⌐do うど・独活

Japanese clothes wa-fuku 和服

Japanese cuisine kappō 割烹, Nihon-ryō⌐ri 日本料理

Japanese-English wa-ei 和英; ~ **dictionary** waei-ji⌐ten 和英辞典

Japanese food wa-shoku 和食

Japanese ginger (buds) myōga みょうが・茗荷

Japanese grapefruit (= pomelo) natsu-mi⌐kan 夏みかん・夏蜜柑

Japanese harp (o-)ko⌐to (お)琴

Japanese music hōgaku 邦楽; *(traditional to the imperial court)* ga⌐gaku 雅楽, *(and dances)* bu⌐gaku 舞楽

Japanese noodles (wheat-flour) udon (o-u⌐don) うどん(おうどん)

Japanese paper wa⌐shi 和紙

Japanese parsley seri⌐ せり・芹

Japanese pepper (mild) sanshō さんしょう・山椒

Japanese restaurant kappō⌐-ten 割烹店, ryōri⌐-ya 料理屋

Japanese-style room wa-shitsu 和室, Nihom-ma 日本間

Japanese wrestling sumō 相撲

Japan Travel Bureau (JTB) (Nihon) Kōtsū-Kō⌐sha (日本)交通公社

jar *(with a large mouth)* kame⌐ かめ・瓶; *(with a small mouth)* tsubo つぼ・壷; *(glass)* garasu⌐-bin ガラス瓶, bi⌐n びん・瓶

jargon semmon-go 専門語

jaundice ōdan 黄疸

jaw ago⌐ あご・顎

jealous: gets ~ (yaki-mo⌐chi⌐ o) yakima⌐su (yaku, yaite) (焼きもちを)焼きます(焼く, 焼いて)

jealousy yaki-mo⌐chi⌐ 焼きもち, shitto⌐ 嫉妬

jelly ze⌐rii ゼリー, je⌐rii ジェリー

jellyfish ku⌐rage くらげ・水母

jerk: with a ~ gu⌐tto ぐっと

jet black makku⌐ro (na) 真っ黒(な)

jet (plane) jettō-ki ジェット機;
jet lag jisa-boke 時差ぼけ
Jew Yudaya-jin ユダヤ人
jewel hōseki 宝石, tama 玉;
jeweler hōseki-shō 宝石商
job shigoto (o-shigoto) 仕事(お
仕事), tsutome (o-tsutome)
勤め(お勤め), (place)
tsutome-saki 勤め先; **getting a**
~ shūshoku 就職; ~ **hunting**
kyūshoku 求職; ~ **transfer**
tenkin 転勤, tennin 転任
jockstrap (athletic supporter)
sapōtā サポーター; (loin-
cloth) sarumata 猿股, fun-
doshi ふんどし・褌
jog(ging) jogingu (o shimasu;
suru, shite) ジョギング(をし
ます; する, して), marason
マラソン
join (joins them together)
awasemasu (awaseru,
awasete) 合わせます(合わせ
る, 合わせて), (grafts, glues)
tsugimasu (tsugu, tsuide) 接ぎ
ます(接ぐ, 接いで); (enters) ...
ni hairimasu (hairu, haitte) ...
に入ります(入る, 入って);
(in cooperation) tsukimasu
(tsuku, tsuite) 付きます(付く,
付いて); ~ (forces) gōdō
shimasu (suru, shite) 合同し
ます(する, して)
joint 1. a joint fushi 節; (of two
bones) kansetsu 関節; (of
pipe; seam) tsugi-me 接ぎ目

2. (combined) gōdō no ... 合同
の...
joke jōdan 冗談, share しゃれ
joss stick (o-)senko (お)線香,
senkō 線香
journalist shimbun-kisha 新聞
記者, kisha 記者
journey tabi 旅; → **trip**
joy yorokobi 喜び
Judaism Yudaya-kyō ユダヤ教
judge hanji 判事, saiban-kan 裁
判官; (gives judgment)
handan shima(.)su (suru,
shite) 判断します(する, して),
(criticizes) hihan/hihan
shimasu (suru, shite) 批判/批
判します(する, して)
judgment handan 判断;
(criticism) hihan/hihan 批判/
批判
judo, jujitsu jūdō 柔道; ~ **out-
fit/suit** jūdō-gi 柔道着
juggler tejina-shi 手品師; **jugglery** tejina 手品
juice jūsu ジュース; shiru 汁;
~ **of bitter orange** ponsu ポ
ン酢, ponzu ポン酢
July Shichi-gatsu 七月・7月
jumble konzatsu 混雑
jumbo shrimp kuruma-ebi 車え
び[海老]
jump tobimasu (tobu, tonde) 跳
びます(跳ぶ, 跳んで); **jumps
out** tobi-dashimasu (-dasu,
-dashite) 飛び出します(出す,
出して)

June Roku-gatsu 六月・6 月

jungle mitsurin 密林, ja'nguru ジャングル; ～ **gym** janguru-ji'mu ジャングルジム

junior (younger) toshi-shita (no) 年下(の); (colleague, fellow student) kōhai 後輩; (3rd-year student) sanne'n-sei 三年生

junior college tanki-da'igaku 短期大学

junior high school chūga'kkō 中学校; ～ **student** chūga'ku-sei 中学生

junk ku'zu くず, kuzu⌐-mono くず物, garakuta がらくた, sute-mono 捨て物

junkyard sute-ba⌐ 捨て場

just (exactly) chōdo ちょうど・丁度, ma'sa-ni まさに・正に; (only) …dake' …だけ, (merely) ta'da ただ; **just a moment** cho'tto ちょっと; **just did it** (shi)-ta ba'kari desu (し)たばかりです

just now tatta-i'ma たった今, tada'ima ただ今・只今, tsu'i imashi'gata つい今しがた

just right pitta'ri ぴったり; uttetsuke (no) うってつけ (の); **is just right for me** watashi ni pitta'ri desu わたし[私]にぴったりです

just the (one/thing/ticket, …) uttetsuke (no) うってつけ(の)

juvenile delinquent chimpira ちんぴら・チンピラ

— **K** —

kana kana かな・仮名

karate (weaponless self-defense) karate 空手; ～ **outfit/suit** karate'-gi' 空手着

katakana kata'ka'na カタカナ・かたかな・片仮名

keenly (feels) shimiji'mi (to) しみじみ(と)

keep tamochima'su (tamo'tsu, tamo'tte) 保ちます(保つ, 保って); (retains) kakaema'su (kakae⌐ru, kaka⌐ete) 抱えます(抱える, 抱えて); (takes in trust) azukarima'su (azuka'ru, azuka'tte) 預かります(預かる, 預かって); (raises animals) kaima'su (ka'u, ka'tte) 飼います(飼う, 飼って)

keep away from yokema'su (yoke'ru, yo'kete) よけます (よける, よけて)

keep company with (… o) chika-zukema'su (-zuke'ru, -zu'kete) (…を)近付けます(付ける, 付けて)

keep cool (calms down) ochi-

tsukima'su (-tsuku, -tsuite) 落
ち着きます(着く, 着いて)

keep doing (shi)-te ima'su (iru,
ite) (し)ています(いる, いて);
(shi)-tsuzukema'su
(-tsuzuke'ru, -tsuzu'kete) (し)
続けます(続ける, 続けて)

keg taru たる・樽

kelp ko'mbu 昆布; **~ flakes**
tororo-ko'mbu とろろ昆布

kerosene tōyu 灯油, sekiyu 石油;
~ heater sekiyu-suto'bu 石油
ストーブ

ketchup kecha'ppu ケチャップ

kettle (teakettle) yakan やかん,
yu-wa'kashi 湯沸かし;
(cauldron) kama かま・釜

key kagi' 鍵, ki'i キー; **keyhole**
kagi-ana 鍵穴

"key money" (to obtain rental
lease) kenri[□]-kin 権利金

kick kerima'su (ke'ru, ke'tte) 蹴
ります(蹴る, 蹴って);
ketchaima'su (ke'tchau,
ke'tchatte) 蹴っちゃいます
(蹴っちゃう, 蹴っちゃって)

kid kozo' 小僧; → **child**; **kids**
oneself about ... (underestimates) ... o amaku mima'su
(mi'ru, mi'te) ...を甘く見ます
(見る, 見て)

kidding: no kidding! ma'saka ま
さか

kidnap yūkai shima'su (suru,
shite) 誘拐します(する, して)

kidney jinzō 腎臓

kidney beans i'ngen いんげん・隠
元, inge'm-mame 隠元豆

kill koroshima'su (korosu,
koroshite) 殺します(殺す, 殺
して); [slang] barashima'su
(bara'su, bara'shite) ばらしま
す(ばらす, ばらして)

killed: gets ~ korosarema'su
(korosareru, korosarete) 殺さ
れます(殺される, 殺されて),
yararema'su (yarareru,
yararete) やられます(やられ
る, やられて)

kiln kama かま・釜

kilo(gram/meter/watt/liter)
ki'ro キロ

kimono 1. (= bathrobe) ta'nze'n
丹前, (light) yukata ゆかた・浴
衣, (to sleep in) ne-maki ねま
き・寝巻き **2.** (Japanese attire)
wa-fuku 和服, ki-mono 着物;
(long-sleeved) furisode[□] 振り
袖

kind (variety) shu'rui 種類, te' 手;
a kind of ... no i's-shu ...の一
種 (= i's-shu no ... 一種の...);
all kinds of shu'ju (no) 種々
(の), iroiro (na/no) 色々(な/
の); **kinds of ...**-rui ...類

kind (nice) (go-)shi'nsetsu (na)
(ご)親切(な)

kindergarten yōchi'-en 幼稚園

kindling taki-tsuke たきつけ

kindly (does) (shi)-te kurema'su
(kureru, kurete)/
kudasaima'su (kudasa'ru,

kudasa⌐tte/kuda⌐sutte) （し）て
くれます（くれる，くれて）/
下さいます（下さる，下さっ
て/下すって）

kindness o⌐n (go-o⌐n) 恩（ご恩），
kokoro-zashi⌐ (o-
kokorozashi) 志（お志），
shi⌐nsetsu (go-shi⌐nsetsu) 親切
（ご親切）

king ō⌐ 王，ō-sama 王様

kiosk (selling things) baiten 売店

kiss ki⌐(s)su キ（ッ）ス，seppun
(shima⌐su; suru, shite) 接吻
（します；する，して）

kit (of tools) yō⌐gu 用具; ～ **bag**
yōgu-bu⌐kuro 用具袋

kitchen daidokoro 台所，katte 勝
手; ～ **door** katte-guchi 勝手
口; ～ **range/stove** kamado か
まど; ～ **sink** nagashi⌐ 流し;
～ **utensils** daidokoro-/katte-
dō⌐gu 台所/勝手道具

kitchenware ara⌐-mono 荒物

kite ta⌐ko 凧・たこ; **flies a ～**
ta⌐ko o agema⌐su (ageru,
agete) 凧を揚げます（揚げる，
揚げて）; **kite-flying** tako⌐-a⌐ge⌐
凧揚げ

kitten kone⌐ko 小猫

Kleenex (tissue) tisshu-pē⌐pā
ティッシュペーパー; hana-
gami 鼻紙，chiri-gami ちり紙

knack kotsu⌐ こつ; yōryō⌐ 要領

knapsack ryu⌐kku リュック，
ryukkusa⌐kku リュックサック，
rando⌐seru ランドセル

knead nerima⌐su (ne⌐ru, ne⌐tte)
練ります（練る，練って）

knee hiza ひざ・膝

knew → know

knife na⌐ifu ナイフ; (big) hōchō
包丁，(carving) nikukiri-
bō⌐chō 肉切り包丁

knit amima⌐su (a⌐mu, a⌐nde) 編み
ます（編む，編んで）

knitted goods meriyasu メリヤ
ス，ami⌐-mono 編み物

knob (bump) kobu⌐ こぶ，(gnarl)
fushi⌐ 節; (doorknob) hiki-te
引き手

knock (hits) nagurima⌐su
(nagu⌐ru, nagu⌐tte) 殴ります
（殴る，殴って）

knock down taoshima⌐su (tao⌐su,
tao⌐shite) 倒します（倒す，倒
して）

knock (on door) (to o)
tatakima⌐su (tata⌐ku, tata⌐ite)
（戸を）叩きます（叩く，叩い
て），no⌐kku shima(⌐)su (suru,
shite) ノックします（する，し
て）

knot musubi(-me) 結び（目）;
(gnarl) fushi⌐ 節

know ... o shitte ima⌐su (iru, ite) ...
を知っています（いる，いて），
[DEFERENTIAL] zon-jima⌐su
(zon-ji⌐ru, zo⌐n-jite) 存じま
す（存じる，存じて），
[HONORIFIC] go-zo⌐nji (de⌐su,
ni narima⌐su) ご存じ（です，
になります）; (understands)...ga

wakarima᷉su (waka᷉ru,
waka᷉tte) ...が分かります(分
かる, 分かって); **doesn't
know** shirimase᷉n (shiranai,
shirana᷉ide) 知りません(知ら
ない, 知らないで),
wakarimase᷉n (wakara᷉nai,
wakara᷉naide) 分かりません
(分からない, 分からないで)
USAGE: **knows** shitte ima᷉su
知っています; **doesn't know**
shirimase᷉n 知りません
knowledge chi᷉shiki 知識; *(learning)* gaku᷉mon 学問
knowledgeable about ... ni
kuwashi᷉i ...に詳しい
known: gets ~ shirema᷉su
(shireru, shirete) 知れます(知
れる, 知れて), *(widely)*
shirarema᷉su (shirareru,
shirarete) 知られます(知られ

る, 知られて); **~ as ...** *(=
so-called)* iwa᷉yu᷉ru ... いわゆ
る...
Kobe Kō᷉be 神戸; **~ Station**
Kōbe᷉-Eki 神戸駅; **the port of
~** Kōbe᷉-kō 神戸港
Korea Ka᷉nkoku 韓国 [*preferred
in South Korea*], Chōse᷉n 朝鮮
[*preferred in North Korea*]
Korean *(person)* Kankoku᷉-jin 韓
国人, Chōsen-ji᷉n 朝鮮人
Korean (language) Kankoku-go
韓国語, Chōsen-go 朝鮮語
Kurile (Islands) Chishi᷉ma 千島,
Chishima-re᷉ttō 千島列島
Kyoto Kyō᷉to 京都; **~ Station**
Kyōto᷉-eki 京都駅
Kyotoite Kyōto᷉-jin 京都人
Kyoto-style cooking/dishes Kyō-
ryō᷉ri 京料理
Kyushu Kyū᷉shū 九州

— L —

lab ra᷉bo ラボ; *(language
laboratory)* eru-e᷉ru エルエル
("LL"); *(research)* kenkyū-
jo⌐ 研究所; *(testing)* shiken-
jo⌐ 試験所
label re⌐tteru レッテル, *(tag)*
fuda 札
labor rōdō 労働; **~ union** rōdō-
ku᷉miai 労働組合; **Labor
Thanksgiving Day (23**

November) Kinrō-ka᷉nsha no
hi᷉ 勤労感謝の日
laborer rōdō᷉-sha 労働者
laboriously a᷉kuseku あくせく
lace 1. rē᷉su レース, mō᷉ru モー
ル **2.** → **shoelace**
lack 1. *(shortage)* fusoku 不足
2. *(is not available)* ...ga
arimase᷉n (na᷉i) ...がありませ
ん(ない)

USAGE: Da⌐re ga(/ni) na⌐ni ga arimase⌐n ka 誰が(/に)何がありませんか **Who lacks (is missing) what?**

lacquer 1. urushi 漆, nuri 塗り; (~ ware) nuri-mono 塗り物, shikki 漆器; (raised ~) maki⌐-e 蒔絵 **2. (lacquers it)** nurima⌐su (nuru, nutte) 塗ります(塗る, 塗って)

lad shōnen 少年

ladder hashigo はしご・梯子

ladle hishaku ひしゃく; (large wooden) sha⌐kushi しゃくし・杓子

ladle it kumima⌐su (kumu, kunde) 汲みます(汲む, 汲んで)

lady fujin 婦人, o⌐ku-san/-sama 奥さん/様; (young) ojō⌐-san お嬢さん, (middle-aged) oba (-san) おば(さん), (old) obā⌐-san おばあさん; → **woman**

ladykiller, ladies' man onna-ta⌐rashi 女たらし

lag 1. (a lag) okure 遅れ **2.** (lags behind) okurema⌐su (okureru, okurete) 遅れます(遅れる, 遅れて)

lake mizuu⌐mi 湖, ...⌐-ko ...湖; **lakeside** ko⌐han 湖畔; **lakeshore** ko⌐gan 湖岸; **lake trout** masu⌐ ます・鱒

lamb ko-hi⌐tsu⌐ji 子羊; (meat, includes mutton) yōniku 羊肉

lame ashi⌐ ga fu⌐-jiyū (na) 足が不自由(な); see **cripple(d)**

lament nagekima⌐su (nage⌐ku, nage⌐ite) 嘆きます(嘆く, 嘆いて); **lamentation** nageki⌐ 嘆き

lamp ra⌐mpu ランプ; dentō 電灯・電燈; **desk/floor** ~ sutando スタンド = denki-suta⌐ndo 電気スタンド

land riku⌐ 陸, oka 丘, ji⌐ 地; (a piece of ~) tochi 土地; → **country**; → **earth**; → **place**

land (comes ashore) jōriku shima⌐su (suru, shite) 上陸します(する, して); (from the air) chakuriku shima⌐su (suru, shite) 着陸します(する, して)

landlady oka⌐mi おかみ・女将, okami-san おかみさん・女将さん

landlord ō⌐ya (san) 大家(さん), ya⌐nushi 家主, shu⌐jin 主人, te⌐ishu 亭主; (rental manager) kanri⌐-nin 管理人

landowner ji-nushi 地主

landscape fū⌐kei 風景

landslide ji-su⌐beri 地滑り

lane (traffic, swim) kō⌐su コース; (path) ko⌐michi 小道; **Lanes Merge** "Gōryū chu⌐i" "合流注意"

language 1. kotoba⌐ 言葉・ことば, ge⌐ngo 言語; ...-go ...語; **what** ~ nani-go 何語; **how many languages** nan-ka⌐kokugo 何カ国語; ~ **learning** go⌐gaku 語学 **2.** (= foreign language) gaikoku-go 外国語; **How many languages do you know?** Gaikoku-go wa i'kutsu dekima'su ka. 外国語はいくつできますか.

lantern *(of paper)* chōchi'n ちょうちん・提灯; *(traditional night-light)* andon あんどん・行灯

lap hiza ひざ・膝

lapse keika shima'su (suru, shite) 経過します(する, して)

large ōki'i 大きい, o'ki-na 大きな; *(wide, spacious)* hiro'i 広い

large crowd ōze'i 大勢

large number tasu' 多数

large quantity taryō 多量, tairyō'[i] 大量

large-size (model) ōgata 大型

lasso nage-nawa 投げ縄, wa'na わな・罠

last 1. *(final)* owari no 終わりの, sa'igo no 最後の; *(the tail end)* bi'ri (no) びり(の), ketsu (no) けつ(の) **2.** *(the preceding ...)* kono ma'e no この前の, sen-... 先..., sa'[i]ru 去る (+ DATE)

last: at last tō'tō とうとう, yatto (no koto' de) やっと(のことで), iyo'-iyo いよいよ, tsu'i-ni ついに, yōyaku ようやく

last: it lasts mochima'su (mo'tsu, mo'tte) 持ちます(持つ, 持って)

last day (of month) misoka みそ

か・晦日; *(of year)* ō-mi'soka 大みそか・大晦日

last month se'ngetsu 先月

last night kinō no ban きのう［昨日］の晩, saku'ban 昨晩, yūbe' ゆうべ・昨夜

last stop shūten 終点

last time ko'ndo 今度, kono ma'e この前

last volume (of a set of 2 or 3) ge-kan 下巻, ge' 下

last week senshū 先週

last year kyo'nen 去年

late osoi (osoku) 遅い(遅く); *(lags, fails to be on time)* okurema'su (okureru, okurete) 遅れます(遅れる, 遅れて); **is too ~ (for it)** ma ni aimase'n (awa'nai, awa'naide) 間に合いません(合わない, 合わないで); **till ~** osoku' made 遅くまで; **till ~ at night** yo'ru osoku' made 夜遅くまで, shi'n'ya made 深夜まで; **the night grows ~** yo' ga fukema'su (fuke'ru, fuke'te) 夜が更けます(更ける, 更けて)

lately kono-aida' この間, konaida' こないだ, chika'goro 近頃, saikin 最近

later: does for ~ (shi)-t[e] okima'su (-t[e] oku, -t[e] o'ite) (し)と[てお]きます(と[てお]く, と[てお]いて)

later (on) a'to (de) 後(で); a'to

no ... 後の..., [*bookish*] kō̄(-) ... 後...
latest (*newest*) saishin (no) 最新 (の); **at the latest** ... ma̱de ni wa ...まで[迄]には, osoku̱tomo 遅くとも
Latin Raten-go ラテン語; ~ **letters** rōma̱-ji ローマ字
latrine → **toilet**
latter a̱to no ... 後の..., [*bookish*] kō̄(-) ... 後...; **the latter** kō̱sha 後者
laugh, laugh at (... o) waraima̱su (warau, waratte) (...を)笑います(笑う, 笑って)
laughter warai 笑い
launch ra̱nchi ランチ
launder sentaku̱ shima̱su (suru, shite) 洗濯します(する, して)
laundry sentaku(-mono) 洗濯(物), o-se̱ntaku お洗濯; (*a laundry*) sentaku-ya 洗濯屋, kuriininguya クリーニング屋
laurel gekkei 月桂, gekke̱i-ju 月桂樹
lava yō̱gan 溶岩
lavatory (*to wash up in*) semmen-jo̱ 洗面所; → **bathroom, toilet**
law hōritsu 法律, hō 法; (*rule*) hōsoku 法則; (*science/study*) hōgaku 法学; → **...-in-law**
lawn shiba 芝, shibafu 芝生
lawn mower shibakari̱-ki 芝刈り機

lawsuit soshō 訴訟; uttae 訴え
lawyer bengo̱shi 弁護士
lax yuru̱i 緩い
laxative gezai 下剤, kudashi (-gu̱suri) 下し(薬)
lay (*puts*) okima̱su (oku, oite) 置きます(置く, 置いて); (*did lie down*) nema̱shita (neta) 寝ました(寝た)
lay it: ~ **face down** fusema̱su (fuse̱ru, fuse̱te) 伏せます(伏せる, 伏せて); ~ **on its side** nekashima̱su (nekasu, nekashite) 寝かします(寝かす, 寝かして)
layman monga̱i-kan 門外漢
layout (*format*) teisai 体裁
lazy: gets ~ namakema̱su (namake̱ru, nama̱kete) 怠けます(怠ける, 怠けて); ~ **person** namake-mo□no□ 怠け者; (*shirks*) okotarima̱su (okotaru, okotatte) 怠ります (怠る, 怠って)
lead (*metal*) namari 鉛
lead (*guides them*) anna̱i shima(□)su (suru, shite) 案内します(する, して), michibikima̱su (michibi̱ku, michibi̱ite) 導きます(導く, 導いて); (*coaches them*) shidō shima̱su (suru, shite) 指導します(する, して); (*commands them*) hiki-ima̱su (hiki-i̱ru, hiki̱-ite) 率います(率いる, 率いて)

leader chō 長; *(director, coach)* shidō-sha 指導者

leadership *(guidance)* shidō 指導

leading *(= chief)* shuyō (na) 主要(な)

leaf happa 葉っぱ, ha 葉; **how many leaves** na¬m-mai 何枚

leaflet bira びら・ビラ

leak 1. it leaks morima¬su (mo¬ru, mo¬tte) 漏ります(漏る, 漏って), morema¬su (more¬ru, mo¬rete) 漏れます(漏れる, 漏れて) **2. leaks it** morashima¬su (mora¬su, mora¬shite) 漏らします(漏らす, 漏らして)

lean: ~ against ... ni motarema¬su (motare¬ru, mota¬rete) ...にもたれます(もたれる, もたれて); **~ toward** ... no hō ni katamukima¬su (katamu¬ku, katamu¬ite) ...の方に傾きます(傾く, 傾いて); **(to one side)** kata-yorima¬su (-yo¬ru, -yo¬tte) 片寄ります(寄る, 寄って)

lean (meat/fish) aka-mi 赤身

lean out of ... kara noridashima¬su (-da¬su, -da¬shite) ...から乗り出します(出す, 出して)

leap → **jump; leap year** urū-doshi うるう[閏]年

learn naraima¬su (nara¬u, nara¬tte) 習います(習う, 習って), manabima¬su (manabu, manande) 学びます(学ぶ, 学んで); *(finds out)* shirima¬su (shiru, shitte) 知ります(知る, 知って), *(hears)* ... ga mimi¬ ni hairima¬su (ha¬iru, ha¬itte) ...が耳に入ります(入る, 入って)

learning gaku¬mon 学問, ga¬ku 学; *(study of a basic subject)* gakushū 学習

least *(smallest)* saishō (no) 最小(の)

least: at least suku¬na¬ku-tomo 少なくとも, se¬mete せめて; *(anyway)* to¬-ni-kaku とにかく

leather kawa 皮・革

leave dema¬su (de¬ru, de¬te) 出ます(出る, 出て); sarima¬su (sa¬ru, sa¬tte) 去ります(去る, 去って); *(for a far place)* tachima¬su (ta¬tsu, ta¬tte) 発ちます(発つ, 発って); *(to go home)* kaerima¬su (ka¬eru, ka¬ette) 帰ります(帰る, 帰って); *(withdraws)* hiki-agema¬su (-age¬ru, -a¬gete) 引き揚げます(揚げる, 揚げて), hiki-torima¬su (-to¬ru, -to¬tte) 引き取ります(取る, 取って) *(~ one's seat)* se¬ki o hazushima¬su (hazusu, hazushite) 席を外します(外す, 外して)

leave it behind nokoshima¬su

(noko͞'su, noko'shite) 残します(残す, 残して); *(forgetfully)* wasure-mono o shima'su (suru, shite) 忘れ物をします(する, して)

leave it empty akema'su (akeru, akete) 空けます(空ける, 空けて)

leave it intact *(untouched)* sono mama' ni shima'su (suru, shite) そのままにします(する, して)

leave it undone shina'ide okima'su (oku, oite) しないでおきます(おく, おいて)

leave out *(skips)* nukashima'su (nukasu, nukashite) 抜かします(抜かす, 抜かして)

leave-taking itoma⌐ (o-itoma) 暇(お暇)

leavings nokori-mo⌐no⌐ 残り物

lecherous suke͞'bē (na) すけべな・助平(な), kōshoku (na) 好色(な)

lecture kōgi⌐ 講義, *(talk)* kōen 講演; ~ **platform** endan 演壇, kōdan 講壇

lecturer *(instructor)* kō͞'shi 講師

leech hi͞'ru ひる・蛭

leek nira⌐ にら・韮; ne͞'gi ねぎ・葱 (= naga-ne⌐gi 長ねぎ[葱])

leeway yoyū 余裕, yo⌐chi 余地

left 1. *(not right)* hidari (no) 左の **2.** → **leave 3.** → **rest**

left behind: gets ~ nokorima'su (noko͞'ru, noko'tte) 残ります(残る, 残って)

left-handed (person) hidari⌐-kiki/-giki (no) 左利き/利き(の); gi͞'tcho (no) ぎっちょ(の)

left over: gets ~ *(in excess)* amarima'su (ama͞'ru, ama'tte) 余ります(余る, 余って); → **left behind**

leftover nokori͞' 残り; *(surplus)* amari͞' 余り

leftovers nokori-mo⌐no⌐ 残り物

leg ashi͞' 脚, *(shin)* sune͞' すね・脛・臑; (1 i͞'p-pon 一本, 2 ni͞'-hon 二本, 3 sa͞'m-bon 三本, **how many** na͞'m-bon 何本)

legend mukashi-ba͞'nashi 昔話, densetsu 伝説, monoga͞'tari 物語

leisure hima 暇, ma 間; re͞'jā レジャー

lemon re⌐mon レモン; **lemonade** remo͞'n-sui レモン水, remone͞'do レモネード; ~ **soda** ramune ラムネ

lend kashima'su (kasu, kashite) 貸します(貸す, 貸して); **lends money** *(finances it)* yūzū shima'su (suru, shite) 融通します(する, して)

length na͞'gasa 長さ

lengthen (mo'tto) na͞'gaku shima'su (suru, shite) (もっと)長くします(する, して);

(prolongs it) nobashimásu (nobásu, nobáshite) 伸ばします(伸ばす, 伸ばして); enchō shimásu (suru, shite) 延長します(する, して)

lengthwise táte (no/ni) 縦(の/に)

lenient yuru̯i ゆるい・緩い; amai 甘い

lens re̅nzu レンズ (**how many** na̅n-ko 何個)

leopard hyō̄ ひょう・豹

less (yori) sukuna̯i (より)少ない; *(minus)* mainasu マイナス

lessen suku̯na̯ku/chi̅isaku shimásu (suru, shite) 少なく/小さくします(する, して); herashimásu (herasu, herashite) 減らします(減らす, 減らして)

lesson …́-ka …課; **takes lessons (in)** (… o) naraimásu (nara̯u, nara̅tte) (…を)習います(習う, 習って)

less than (…) i̅ka (…)以下, … mi̅man …未満

let: lets (one) do it (… ni sore o) sasemásu (saseru, sasete) (…にそれを)させます(させる, させて), yurushimásu (yuru̅su, yuru̅shite) 許します(許す, 許して); *(as a favor)* (… ni sore o) sasete (…にそれを)させて + GIVE

let approach yosemásu (yoseru, yosete) 寄せます(寄せる, 寄せて)

let fly tobashimásu (tobasu, tobashite) 飛ばします(飛ばす, 飛ばして)

let get away nigashimásu (niga̅su, niga̅shite) 逃がします(逃がす, 逃がして)

let go *(releases)* hanashimásu (hana̅su, hana̅shite) 放します(放す, 放して)

let in iremásu (ireru, irete) 入れます(入れる, 入れて)

let off/out *(of a vehicle)* oroshimásu (oro̅su, oro̅shite) 降ろします(降ろす, 降ろして)

let through/in tōshimásu (tō̅su, tō̅shite) 通します(通す, 通して)

let me see *(= well now)* sā̄ さあ; Sō̄ desu ne. そうですね。

let's (do it) (shi)-mashō̄ (し)ましょう

letter tegami (o-te̅gami) 手紙(お手紙), *(news)* ta̅yori 便り; *(of alphabet)* mo̅ji 文字, *(character)* ji̅ 字; ~ **of guarantee** hoshō̄-sho 保証書; ~ **of recommendation** suise̅n-jō 推薦状

lettuce re̅tasu レタス

level *(flat)* taira (na) 平ら(な); *(extent)* te̅ido 程度; *(standard; water level)* suijun 水準

lever teko てこ・挺子, re̅bā レバー

Levi's → bluejeans

levy chōshū shima˺su (suru, shite) 徴収します(する, して); **levying** chōshū 徴収

lewd suke˺bē (na) すけべい·助平 (な)

liable to (do) → **apt to**

liaison renraku 連絡

liar uso˺-tsuki うそつき

liberate kaihō shima˺su (suru, shite) 解放します(する, して); **liberation** kaihō 解放

librarian tosho-ga˺kari 図書係, toshoka˺n-in 図書館員

library *(building)* tosho˺-kan 図書館; *(room)* tosho˺-shitsu 図書室, *(home study)* shosai 書斎, *(collection)* zōsho 蔵書

lice shirami しらみ·虱

license me˺nkyo 免許, menkyo⌐-shō/-jō 免許証/状; menjō⌐免状; ~ **(tag)** kansatsu 鑑札; **(car)** ~ **plate** na˺mbā ナンバー, nambā-pure˺to ナンバープレート

lick namema˺su (name˺ru, na˺mete) なめます(なめる, なめて)

lid futa ふた·蓋 **(how many** na˺m-mai) 何枚

lie *(falsehood)* u˺so うそ·嘘, itsuwa⌐ri 偽り

lie (down) nema˺su (neru, nete) 寝ます(寝る, 寝て)

lieutenant *(1st Lt, Lt JG)* chū˺i 中尉; *(2nd Lt)* shō˺i 少尉; *(navy full)* da˺ii (ta˺ii)

大尉(大尉)

lieutenant colonel chūsa 中佐

lieutenant commander shōsa 少佐

life i˺nochi 命, se⌐ime⌐i 生命; *(daily living)* seikatsu 生活; *(lifetime)* shō˺gai 生涯, isshō 一生, yo⌐ 世; **brings ~ to ...** o ikashima˺su (ika˺su, ika˺shite) ...を生かします(生かす, 生かして)

lift 1. mochi-agema˺su (-age⌐ru, -a⌐gete) 持ち上げます(上げる, 上げて), agema˺su (ageru, agete) 上げます(上げる, 上げて) **2.** → **elevator**

light 1. hikari˺ 光, *(ray)* kōsen 光線; *(electric)* de˺nki 電気, dentō 電灯; **in the ~ of ...** ni tera˺shite ...に照らして **2. lights it up** terashima˺su (tera˺su, tera˺shite) 照らします(照らす, 照らして)

light *(not heavy)* karui 軽い; *(bright)* akaru⌐i 明るい; *(pale)* usui 薄い; *(simple)* assa˺ri shita ...あっさりした...; ~ **place** akarumi 明るみ; ~ **soup** (o)tsu˺yu (お)つゆ; ~ **rain** kosame 小雨

lightbulb denkyū 電球

lighter *(cigarette)* ra˺itā ライター

lighthouse tōdai 灯台

lighting *(illumination)* shōmei 照明; ~ **fixtures** shōmei-ki˺gu 照明器具

lightning inabi⌐kari 稲光, ina⌐zuma 稲妻

like: would like → want, wish

like *(is fond of)* ... ga suki⌐ desu ... が好きです, ... o sukima⌐su (suku⌐, su⌐ite) ...を好きます (好く, 好いて), ... o konomima⌐su (kono⌐mu, kono⌐nde) ...を好みます (好む, 好んで)

like *(similar)* ... no yō⌐ (na) ...の様 (な); *(is similar to)* ... ni nite ima⌐su (iru, ite) ...に似ています (いる, いて)

likely ari-sō⌐ (na) ありそう (な); (shi)-sō⌐ (na) (し)そう (な), (shi)-yasu⌐i (し)やすい

likely = probably ta⌐bun たぶん・多分

like(ly) as not taigai 大概

likely to (do) (shi)-yasu⌐i (し)やすい

like that sō (sō⌐ + PARTICLE/ de⌐su) そう (そう +PARTICLE/ です); sonna ... そんな...; ā (ā⌐ + PARTICLE/de⌐su) ああ (ああ+PARTICLE/です), an-na ... あんな...

like this kō (kō⌐ + PARTICLE/ de⌐su) こう (こう +PARTICLE/ です); konna ... こんな...

liking: a ~ , a fancy shikō 志向, konomi⌐ (o-konomi) 好み (お好み)

lily yuri ゆり・百合

lime 1. *(fruit)* ra⌐imu ライム

(1 i⌐k-ko 一個) **2.** *(mineral)* se⌐kkai 石灰

limit 1. ka⌐giri⌐ 限り, seige⌐n 制限; ge⌐ndo 限度; hodo 程; ha⌐n'i 範囲 **2. limits (delimits) it** kagirima⌐su (kagi⌐ru, kagi⌐tte) 限ります (限る, 限って); *(restricts)* gentei shima⌐su (suru, shite) 限定します (する, して), seige⌐n shima(⌐)su (suru, shite) 制限します (する, して)

limitation gentei 限定, seige⌐n 制限

limousine for hire ha⌐iyā ハイヤー

line se⌐n 線, re⌐tsu 列, *(of letters)* gyō⌐ 行; *(plot)* su⌐ji 筋; *(in a play)* seri⌐fu せりふ・台詞; **the line is busy** (o-)hanashi-chū desu (お)話し中です; *(of work)* shoku⌐gyō 職業, gyō⌐ 業

lined garment awase⌐ あわせ・袷

linen a⌐ma 亜麻, rinneru リンネル

line up *(they line up)* narabima⌐su (narabu, narande) 並びます (並ぶ, 並んで); *(lines them up)* narabema⌐su (naraberu, narabete) 並べます (並べる, 並べて)

linguistics *(language learning)* go⌐gaku 語学; *(science of language)* gengo⌐-gaku 言語学

lining ura⌐ 裏; *(material)*

ura-ji 裏地

link 1. wa⌐ 輪 **2. links them** tsunagima⌐su (tsunagu, tsunaide) つなぎます(つなぐ, つないで)

linked: is ~ (with …) (… to) tsunagarima⌐su (tsunagaru, tsunagatte) (…と)つながります(つながる, つながって)

lion ra⌐ion ライオン, shi⌐shi しし・獅子

lip kuchibiru くちびる・唇

lipstick kuchi-beni 口紅

liquid ekitai 液体; mizu 水

liquor (o-)sake (お)酒, *(Western)* yōshu 洋酒; *(distilled from yam or rice)* shōchū⌐ 焼酎

lisp shita⌐ ga motsurema⌐su (motsure⌐ru, motsu⌐rete) 舌がもつれます(もつれる, もつれて)

list *(of items)* hyō 表, mokuroku 目録, ri⌐suto リスト; *(of names)* meibo 名簿; *(lists them)* hyō ni shima⌐su (suru, shite) 表にします(する, して), *(puts it in a list)* (ri⌐suto ni) irema⌐su (ireru, irete) (リストに)入れます(入れる, 入れて)

listen kikima⌐su (kiku, kiite) 聞きます(聞く, 聞いて); [HUMBLE] uketamawarima⌐su (uketamawa⌐ru, uketamawa⌐tte) 承ります(承る, 承って)

listener kiki-te 聞き手

lit: is ~ tsu⌐ite ima⌐su (iru, ite) ついています・点いています (いる, いて) (→ tsukima⌐su つきます・点きます)

liter ri⌐ttoru リットル

literary 1. *(language/word)* bungo 文語; bungo-teki (na) 文語的(な) **2.** *(literature)* bu⌐ngaku (no) 文学(の)

literature bu⌐ngaku 文学

litter 1. *(= rubbish)* ku⌐zu くず・屑, kuzu⌐-mono くず物・屑物, garakuta がらくた **2.** *(= stretcher)* ta⌐nka 担架

little *(in size)* chiisa⌐i 小さい, chi⌐isa-na 小さな; chiccha⌐i ちっちゃい, chi⌐tcha-na ちっちゃな; *(in quantity)* sukuna⌐i 少ない, suko⌐shi (no) 少し(の)

little: a ~ suko⌐shi 少し, *(somewhat)* ya⌐ya やや; **a ~ at a time** sukoshi⌐-zu⌐tsu 少しずつ

little: a ~ while ago saki-hodo 先程, sa⌐kki さっき

little by little sukoshi⌐ zu⌐tsu 少しずつ; so⌐rosoro そろそろ

live *(resides)* su⌐nde ima⌐su (iru, ite) 住んでいます(いる, いて); *(is alive)* i⌐kite ima⌐su (iru, ite) 生きています(いる, いて); *(gets along)* kurashima⌐su (kurasu, kurashite) 暮らします (暮らす, 暮らして)

live: lets/makes it ~

ikashima῀su (ika῀su, ika῀shite)
生かします(生かす, 生かし
て)

lively *(cheerful)* yōki (na) 陽気
(な), *(peppy)* ge῀nki (na) 元気
(な), *(flourishing)* nigi῀yaka
(na) 賑やか(な)

live-out kayoi (no) 通い(の)

liver kimo῀ 肝, kanzō 肝臓; *(as
food)* re῀bā レバー

living costs seikatsu῀-hi 生活費

living room i῀ma῀ 居間, zashiki῀
(o-zashiki) 座敷(お座敷)

lizard tokage とかげ

loach dojō どじょう

load ni῀motsu (o-ni῀motsu) 荷物
(お荷物), ni῀ 荷

load it *(piles it on)* tsumima῀su
(tsumu, tsunde) 積みます(積
む, 積んで), *(puts it aboard)*
nosema῀su (noseru, nosete) 載
せます(載せる, 載せて)

loaf *(around)* bu῀rabura
shima῀su (suru, shite) ぶらぶ
らします(する, して); *(on
the job)* saborima῀su (sabo῀ru,
sabo῀tte) さぼります(さぼる,
さぼって)

loaf (of bread) katamari 固まり・
塊, hito῀-ka῀tamari 一固まり
[塊]

loan → lend

lobby ro῀bii ロビー

lobster ise῀-ebi 伊勢えび[海老]

local chihō῀ no 地方の; *(of the
city)* machi῀ no 町の, *(within
the city)* shi῀nai (no) 市内の

local downpour shūchū-gō῀u 集
中豪雨

local specialty me῀ibutsu 名物

local telephone call shinai-
de῀nwa 市内電話

local train kakueki-te῀isha (no
re῀ssha) 各駅停車(の列車);
(= non-express) futsū-de῀nsha
普通電車

location i῀chi 位置

lock 1. jō(-mae) 錠(前) **2. locks
(a door)** (to ni) kagi῀ o
kakema῀su (kake῀ru, ka῀kete)
(戸に)鍵を掛けます(掛ける,
掛けて); *(shuts it)* shimema῀su
(shime῀ru, shi῀mete) 閉めます
(閉める, 閉めて) **3. it locks**
kagi῀ ga kakarima῀su (kaka῀ru,
kaka῀tte) 鍵が掛かります(掛
かる, 掛かって), *(it shuts)*
shimarima῀su (shima῀ru,
shima῀tte) 閉まります(閉まる,
閉まって)

lodging(-house) geshuku(-ya) 下
宿(屋)

log maruta 丸太 **(1** i῀p-pon 一本,
2 ni῀-hon 二本, **3** sa῀m-bon 三
本, **how many** na῀m-bon 何本)

logic ro῀nri 論理, rikutsu 理屈;
logical ronri-teki (na) 論理的
(な)

loincloth fundoshi ふんどし・褌,
sarumata 猿股, koshi-maki 腰
巻き

loin(s) koshi 腰

London Ro゛ndon ロンドン

lonely hitori-bo゛tchi ひとりぼっち・独りぼっち, sabishi゛i 寂しい・淋しい, wabishi゛i わびしい・侘びしい, kokoro-boso゛i 心細い

long naga゛i (na゛gaku) 長い（長く）; **how long (a time)** dono-gurai どの位

long: before ~ ma-mo゛-naku 間もなく, so゛rosoro そろそろ, yagate[ ] やがて

long ago mukashi 昔; su゛de-ni 既に

long and slender/narrow hoso゛i 細い

long awaited machidōshi゛i 待ち遠しい

long before daibu ma゛e ni だいぶ［大分］前に; su゛de-ni 既に

long distance chō-kyo゛ri 長距離

longer mo゛tto (na゛gaku) もっと（長く）; **no ~ = not any ~** mo゛ もう ＋ NEGATIVE

long-nosed goblin tengu 天狗

longsighted → farsighted

longsleeved kimono furisode[ ] 振り袖

long time: after a ~ (of absence) hisashi-buri ni 久しぶりに; **for a ~** na゛gaku 長く, naga゛i aida 長い間, (~ **now)** ma゛e kara 前から

long-winded kudo゛i くどい

loofah → luffa

look (*appearance*) yōsu 様子;

(*personal appearance*) ki゛ryō 器量, kao 顔; (*a look in one's eyes*) me゛-tsuki 目付き

look: it looks like (as though) ... yō゛/mi゛tai desu (da/na, de, ni) ... よう／みたいです（だ／な, で, に）: NOUN / NOUN da゛tta だった ～, VERB-(r)u/-ta う［る］/た ～, ADJECTIVE-i/-ka゛tta い/かった ～

look after ... no sewa゛ o shima゛su (suru, shite) ...の世話をします（する, して）, ... no mendō゛ o mima゛su (mi゛ru, mi゛te) ...の面倒を見ます（見る, 見て）, (*a matter*) sho゛ri shima゛su (suru, shite) 処理します（する, して）; (*takes over*) hiki-torima゛su (-to゛ru, -to゛tte) 引き取ります（取る, 取って）

look around for, shop around for busshoku shima゛su (suru, shite) 物色します（する, して）

look (at) (... o) mima゛su (mi゛ru, mi゛te) (...を)見ます（見る, 見て）, [HUMBLE] haiken shima゛su (suru, shite) 拝見します（する, して）, [HONORIFIC] goran ni narima゛su (na゛ru, na゛tte) ご覧になります（なる, なって）

look down utsumukima゛su (utsumu[ ]ku, utsumu[ ]ite) うつむきます・俯きます（うつむく, うつむいて）

look for 1. *(searches)* sagashima͏̀su (sagasu, sagashi͏̀te) 捜し[探し]ます(捜す・探す, 捜し[探し]て); motomema͏̀su (motome͏̀ru, moto͏̀mete) 求めます(求める, 求めて), tazunema͏̀su (tazune͏̀ru, tazu͏̀nete) 尋ねます(尋ねる, 尋ねて), ukagaima͏̀su (ukagau, ukagatte) 伺います(伺う, 伺って) **2.** *(expects)* machima͏̀su (ma͏̀tsu, ma͏̀tte) 待ちます(待つ, 待って)

look out on, look to ... o nozomima͏̀su (nozo͏◌̚mu, nozo͏◌̚nde) ...を望みます(望む, 望んで)

look up (a word) hikima͏̀su (hi͏̀ku, hiite) 引きます(引く, 引いて)

loom hata͏̀ 機

loop wa͏̀ 輪; *(shape)* kanjō 環状; ~ **line** kanjō-sen 環状線

loose yuru͏̀i ゆるい・緩い, ba͏̀ra (de) ばら(で); **lets it loose** *(releases)* hanashima͏̀su (hana͏̀su, hana͏̀shite) 放します(放す, 放して)

loose: gets/comes ~ zurema͏̀su (zure͏̀ru, zu͏̀rete) ずれます(ずれる, ずれて), *(slack)* tarumima͏̀su (tarumu, tarunde) たるみ[弛み]ます(たるむ, たるんで)

loquat bi͏̀wa びわ・枇杷

lord *(feudal)* daimyō͏̀ (o-daimyō)

大名(お大名)

Los Angeles Rosanze͏̀rusu ロサンゼルス, Ro͏◌̚su ロス

lose nakushima͏̀su (nakusu, nakushi͏̀te) なくします(なくす, なくして), ushinaima͏̀su (ushinau, ushinatte) 失います(失う, 失って); *(gets defeated)* makema͏̀su (makeru, makete) 負けます(負ける, 負けて), mairima͏̀su (ma͏̀iru, ma͏̀itte) 参ります(参る, 参って)

lose color (iro͏̀ ga) samema͏̀su (same͏̀ru, sa͏̀mete) 色がさめます(さめる, さめて)

lose consciousness ki/i͏̀shiki o ushinaima͏̀su (ushinau, ushinatte) 気/意識を失います(失う, 失って)

lose patience shibire͏̀ o kirashima͏̀su (kira͏̀su, kira͏̀shite) しびれを切らします(切らす, 切らして)

loss 1. songai 損害, sonshitsu 損失 **2.** *(defeat)* make͏̀ 負け, shippai 失敗

lost: it gets ~ naku-narima͏̀su (-naru, -natte) なくなります(なる, なって); **a person gets ~** (michi ni) mayoima͏̀su (mayo͏̀u, mayo͏̀tte) (道に)迷います(迷う, 迷って)

lost child ma͏̀igo 迷子

lot *(in a lottery)* ku͏̀ji くじ; *(vacant land)* aki-chi 空き地;

parking lot chūsha-jō 駐車場

lot: a lot, lots *(= much/many)*
takusa⌐n (no) たくさん[沢山]
(の), ō⌐i (= oo⌐i) 多い(=多い),
ō⌐ku no 多くの; ō⌐ku 多く,
ta⌐bun ni 多分に; yo⌐ku よく

lottery takara⌐-kuji 宝くじ,
fukubiki 福引

lotus hasu はす・蓮; **lotus root**
renkon れんこん・蓮根

loud *(noise)* ōki⌐i 大きい, ō⌐ki-na
大きな; taka⌐i 高い; *(color)*
hade⌐ (na) はで[派手](な)

loud: in a ~ voice ō⌐go⌐e de 大声
で

loudspeaker kakuse⌐i-ki 拡声器,
supi⌐ikā スピーカー

lounge *(room)* kyūke⌐i-shitsu 休
憩室, keshō⌐-shitsu 化粧室;
(chair) ne-isu 寝椅子

louse → **lice**

love ko⌐i 恋, ren'ai 恋愛; **~ marriage** ren'ai-ke⌐kkon 恋愛結婚

love ai-shima⌐su (ai-su⌐ru, a⌐i-
shite) 愛します(愛する, 愛し
て); kawai-garima⌐su (-ga⌐ru,
-ga⌐tte) かわい[可愛]がりま
す(がる, がって); → **like**

love: falls in ~ (with) ... ni
horema⌐su (horeru, horete) ...
に惚れ[ほれ]ます(惚れる,
惚れて)

loveable kawai⌐i かわいい・可愛
い, kawairashi⌐i かわいらしい
・可愛らしい   「係

love affair ren'ai-ka⌐nkei 恋愛関

lover koibito 恋人, i⌐i-hi⌐to いい
人; *(devotee of …)* (... no)
aikō-ka (...の)愛好家, ...-zuki
...好き

lovers' suicide shinjū 心中

low *(short)* hiku⌐i 低い; *(cheap)*
yasu⌐i 安い

low: ~ (barometric) pressure
tei-ki⌐atsu 低気圧; **~ blood
pressure** tei-ke⌐tsu⌐atsu 低血圧;
~ gear teisoku-gi⌐(y)a 低速ギ
ア[ヤ]

lower shita (no) 下(の); **lower
(= cheaper) by ¥100**
hyakue⌐n-yasu 百円安

lower it sagema⌐su (sage⌐ru,
sa⌐gete) 下げます(下げる, 下
げて), oroshima⌐su (oro⌐su,
oro⌐shite) 下ろします(下ろす,
下ろして)

lower one's eyes me⌐ o fusema⌐su
(fuse⌐ru, fuse⌐te) 目を伏せま
す(伏せる, 伏せて),
utsumukima⌐su (utsumu⌐ku,
utsumu⌐ite) うつむきます・
俯きます(うつむく, うつむ
いて)

lower part of the back koshi 腰

lowest *(minimum, minimal)*
sa⌐ika (no) 最下(の), *(bottom)*
saitei (no) 最低(の); **the ~
(degree)** saitei-ge⌐ndo 最低限
度

lowly iyashi⌐i 卑しい

low voice kogoe 小声

luck u⌐n 運, u⌐mmei 運命;

shiawase 幸せ
luckily u̅n-yoku 運良く
lucky u̅n ga i̅i 運がいい;
shiawase (na) 幸せ(な);
(strikes it lucky) tsu̅ite ima̅su
(iru, ite) ついています(いる、
いて)
luffa *(= sponge gourd)* hechima
へちま・糸瓜
luggage (te-)ni̅motsu (手)荷物、
tema̅wari 手回り、temawari[ⁿ]
-hin 手回り品
lukewarm nuru̅i ぬるい
lumber zaimoku 材木、za̅i 材
lump katamari 固まり・塊
lunch hiru-go̅han (hiru̅, o-hi̅ru)

昼ご飯(昼、お昼)、chūshoku
昼食、ra̅nchi ランチ; *(box)*
bentō̅ (o-bentō) 弁当(お弁
当)
luncheon special ranchi-sā̅bisu
ランチサービス
lung cancer hai-gan 肺がん・肺
癌
lungs hai 肺
lure *(= decoy)* otori おとり
lute bi̅wa 琵琶
luxury, luxurious zeita̅ku̅ (na)
ぜいたく[贅沢](な); *(de
luxe)* gō̅ka (na) 豪華(な)
luxury goods, luxuries zeitaku[ⁿ]-
hin ぜいたく[贅沢]品

— M —

machine kika̅i 機械 (**how many**
na̅n-dai 何台)
machine gun kikan-jū 機関銃
mackerel saba さば・鯖; sawara
さわら・鰆; ~ **pike** samma さ
んま・秋刀魚
mad 1. *(= insane)* ki̅-chiga̅i (no)
気違い(の); *(goes mad)* ki ga
kuruima̅su (kuru̅u, kuru̅tte)
気が狂います(狂う、狂って)
2. gets mad *(= angry)*
okorima̅su (oko̅ru, oko̅tte)
怒ります(怒る、怒って)
Madam o̅ku̅-san/-sama 奥さん/
様

made → **make**
made in ...-sei ...製; ~ **Japan**
Nihon-sei (no) 日本製(の)
Maestro ... sense̅i ...先生
magazine zasshi 雑誌 (**how many**
na̅n-satsu 何冊)
magic (tricks) te̅jina 手品; **magician** tejina̅-shi 手品師
magnet ji̅shaku 磁石; **magnetic**
ji̅ki (no) 磁気(の)
magnificent subarashi̅i
すばらしい; sōdai (na) 壮大
(な)
mahjong mā[ⁿ]jan マージャン・
麻雀; ~ **parlor** mājan-ya マー

ジャン[麻雀]屋; ~ **tile** pa˺i
パイ

maid(-servant) ote˺tsudai (san)
お手伝い(さん), mē˺do メイ
ド; **maid's room** ote˺tsudai san
no heya お手伝いさんの部屋,
jochū-beya 女中部屋

mail 1. yūbin 郵便 **2.** *(mails it)*
dashima˺su (da˺su, da˺shite) 出
します(出す, 出して)

mail box yūbi˺m-bako 郵便箱,
po˺suto ポスト

mail drop po˺suto ポスト

mailman, mail deliverer yūbin-
ya (san) 郵便屋(さん)

main o˺mo na 主な, shuyō na 主
要な; hon-... 本...

mainly o˺mo ni 主に

main road to a shrine omote-
sa˺ndō 表参道

main route hondō 本道

main street ōdō˺ri 大通り

maintain *(preserves)* ho˺shu
shima(˺)su (suru, shite) 保守
します(する, して); *(sup-
ports)* shi˺ji/i˺ji shima(˺)su
(suru, shite) 支持/維持します
(する, して); *(insists)* shuchō
shima˺su (suru, shite) 主張し
ます(する, して)

maintenance *(preservation)*
ho˺shu 保守; *(support)* shi˺ji 支
持, *(upkeep)* i˺ji 維持

major *(army)* shōsa 少佐; *(line/
field/study)* semmon 専門;
(study) senkō (shima˺su; suru,

shite) 専攻(します; する, し
て); → **main**, → **big**

major city shuyō-to˺shi 主要
都市

major general shō˺shō 少将

majority dai-bu˺bun 大部分,
tasū˺ 多数

make *(does)* shima˺su (suru,
shite) します(する, して);
(creates) tsukurima˺su
(tsuku˺ru, tsuku˺tte) 作ります
(作る, 作って), *(concocts)*
koshiraema˺su (koshiraeru,
koshiraete) こしらえます(こ
しらえる, こしらえて)

make a fire (hi˺ o) takima˺su
(taku, taite) (火を)焚きま
す(焚く, 焚いて)

make a living kurashima˺su
(kurasu, kurashite) 暮らし
ます(暮らす, 暮らして)

make do (with ...) (... de) ma-
ni-awasema˺su (-awase˺ru,
-awa˺sete) (...で)間に合わ
せます(合わせる, 合わせ
て)

make good, make up for ... o
oginaima˺su (ogina˺u,
ogina˺tte) ...を補います(補
う, 補って)

make money *(profit)* (kane o)
mōkema˺su (mōke˺ru,
mō˺kete) (金を)もうけ[儲
け]ます(もうける, もうけ
て)

make one do (... ni ... o)

sasema´su (saseru, sasete)
(...に...を)させます(させ
る、させて)
make sure tashikamema´su
(tashikame´ru,
tashika´mete) 確かめます
(確かめる、確かめて)
make the most of ... o
ikashima´su (ika´su,
ika´shite) ...を生かします
(生かす、生かして)
make-believe mise-kake (no) 見
せかけ(の)
maker (*manufacturer*) mḗkā
メーカー、seizō-moto 製造元
makeshift ma-ni-awase 間に合わ
せ
makeup keshō´ (o-keshō) 化粧
(お化粧)、mēkya´ppu メーキ
ャップ; (*cosmetics*) keshō⌐-
hin 化粧品; (*structure*)
kumi-tate 組み立て、kōzō 構
造
makeup exam tsui-shike´n 追試
験、sai-shike´n 再試験
male otoko´ 男、dansei 男性;
(*animal*) (... no) osu´ (...の)雄;
~ **and female** da´njo 男女
malfunction koshō 故障
malice a´ku´i 悪意
malignant akushitsu (na) 悪質
(な)
man 1. (*male*) otoko´ 男、otoko
no hito´/kata´ 男の人/方、
da´nshi 男子、(*middle-aged*)
oji-san おじさん、(*old*) oji´i-

san おじいさん、(*young*)
o-ni´i-san お兄さん
2. (*person*) hito 人、... hito´
...人
manage (*treats*) tori-
atsukaima´su (-atsuka⌐u,
-atsuka⌐tte) 取り扱います
(扱う、扱って); (*copes with*)
sho´ri shima(⌐)su (suru, shite)
処理します(する、して);
(*runs a business*) keiei
shima´su (suru, shite) 経営し
ます(する、して); (*a team*)
kantoku shima´su (suru, shite)
監督します(する、して)
management keiei 経営; (*control*) shiha´i 支配、shi´hai 支配;
(*handling*) tori-atsukai 取り扱
い
manager shiha´i-nin/-sha 支配人
/者、kanri⌐-nin 管理人、
ma´nḗjā マネージャー;
(*sports*) kantoku 監督
manage to do dō´ ni ka shima´su
(suru, shite) どうにかします
(する、して); konashima´su
(konasu, konashite) こなしま
す(こなす、こなして)
Manchuria Ma´nshū 満州
mandarin orange → **tangerine**
Manila Ma´nira マニラ
manipulate sōjū shima´su (suru,
shite) 操縦します(する、して)
mankiller (= *seductress*) otoko-
ta´rashi 男たらし
manner (of doing) yari-kata やり

方, shi-kata 仕方; furi ふり; (fashion) (...) fū (...)風

manners gyōgi 行儀, sahō 作法; → **etiquette**

mantis shrimp shako しゃこ・蝦蛄

manufacture seisan/seizō shimasu (suru, shite) 生産/製造します(する, して), tsukurimasu (tsukuru, tsukutte) 作[造]ります(作[造]る, 作[造]って)

manuscript genkō 原稿

many takusan no たくさん[沢山]の, ōku no 多くの; **are/has many** ... ga ōi ...が多い; **how many** ikutsu いくつ, nan-... 何...

map chizu 地図, (diagram) zu 図 (**how many** nam-mai 何枚)

maple kaede かえで・楓, momiji もみじ・紅葉

marathon marason マラソン

marbles o-hajiki おはじき

march kōshin (shimasu; suru, shite) 行進(します; する, して)

March San-gatsu 三月・3月

margin (white space) yohaku 余白; (leeway) yoyū 余裕, yochi 余地; (price difference) saya さや・鞘

marijuana marifana マリファナ

marine(s), Marine Corps kaiheitai 海兵隊, rikusentai 陸戦隊

mark 1. (sign) (o-)shirushi（お)印, kigō 記号
2. (vestige) konseki 痕跡; **leaves a** ~ konseki o nokoshimasu (nokosu, nokoshite) 痕跡を残します(残す, 残して)
3. (score point) ten 点, (score) tensū 点数; (school grades) seiseki 成績
4. (makes a mark on) ... ni shirushi/kigō/ten o tsukemasu (tsukeru, tsukete) ...に印/記号/点を付けます(付ける, 付けて)

market ichi(-ba) 市(場), shijō 市場, māketto マーケット; **vegetable** ~ yaoya 八百屋

marriage kekkon 結婚; ~ **proposal** endan 縁談

marry (... to) kekkon shimasu (suru, shite) (...と)結婚します(する, して)

Mars kasei 火星; **Martian** kasei-jin 火星人

marsh numa 沼

martial arts bujutsu 武術, budō 武道; ~ **hall** dōjō 道場

marvelous suteki (na) すてき[素敵](な), sugoi すごい・凄い

mask men 面, masuku マスク; (Noh drama) nō-men 能面

mass (Buddhist) hōji 法事, (Catholic) misa ミサ

mass (lump) katamari 固まり・塊;

(people) taishū 大衆, kōshū 公衆, minshū 民衆; **~ com-munications** masu-komi マスコミ; **~ meeting** taikai 大会

massage massāji マッサージ, amma あんま・按摩; *(rubs with both hands)* momima̱su (momu, monde) 揉みます・もみます(揉む, 揉んで)

masseur amma あんま・按摩, massāji̱-shi マッサージ師

massive bōdai (na) 膨大(な)

master *(of house/shop)* shu̱jin 主人, danna-san/-sama 旦那さん/様; *(owner)* (mochi̱-)nushi (持ち)主; *(college degree)* shū̱shi 修士; *(maestro)* sense̱i 先生

masterpiece kessaku 傑作

master's thesis shūshi-ro̱mbun 修士論文

masturbate ji̱i/shuin o shima̱su (suru, shite) 自慰/手淫をします(する, して), [*vulgar*] senzuri o kakima̱su (ka̱ku, ka̱ite) せんずりをかきます(かく, かいて)

mat shiki-mono 敷物, ma̱tto マット; *(Japanese floor)* tatami 畳, *(thin)* goza̱ ござ・茣蓙; **(how many** na̱m-mai 何枚)

match 1. *(sports)* shiai 試合, kyo̱gi 競技; *(contest)* sho̱bu 勝負 **2.** *(matches, equals, is a match for)* ... ni kanaima̱su (kana̱u, kana̱tte) ...にかない

ます(かなう, かなって), ... **to** yo̱ku aima̱su (a̱u, a̱tte) ...とよく合います(合う, 合って)

matchbook ma̱tchi マッチ (**1** hito̱tsu 一つ; **how many** i̱kutsu いくつ)

matchbox matchi̱-bako マッチ箱

match(es) *(for fire)* ma̱tchi マッチ; (**1** i̱p-pon 一本, **2** ni̱-hon 二本, **3** sa̱m-bon 三本; **how many** na̱m-bon 何本)

material *(cloth)* ki̱ji 生地; *(raw ~)* zairyō̱ 材料, za̱i 材; *(topic)* ta̱ne 種; → **substance**

material *(= physical)* busshitsu-teki 物質的

materialism busshitsu-shu̱gi 物質主義

materialize genjitsu□-ka shima̱su (suru, shite) 現実化します(する, して)

materials zairyō̱ 材料, genryō̱ 原料, shi̱ryō 資料

mathematics sūgaku 数学; **mathematician** sūga̱ku-sha 数学者

matinee ma̱chi̱nē マチネー; hiru(□) no bu̱ 昼の部

matter 1. koto̱ 事; *(from the eye)* me-yani̱ (ga dema̱su; de̱ru, de̱ te) 目やに(が出ます; 出る, 出て) **2. (something that is) the ~** *(= amiss, wrong)* ijō 異常, *(hitch)* koma̱ru tokoro̱ 困るところ, *(bad aspect/point/*

thing) waru⌐i tokoro⌐/ten/
koto⌐ 悪いところ/点/事;
What's the matter? Do⌐ shita n
desu ka. どうしたんですか.
3. It doesn't matter.
Kamaimase⌐n. 構いません.
mature: matures seijuku
shima⌐su (suru, shite) 成熟し
ます(する, して); **fully
matures** enjuku shima⌐su
(suru, shite) 円熟します(する,
mausoleum ryo⌐ 陵   └して)
maximal, maximum *(= greatest)*
saidai (no) 最大(の); *(=
highest)* saikō (no) 最高(の)
maximum (degree) saidai-ge⌐ndo
最大限度
May Go⌐-gatsu 五月・5 月
may *(perhaps)* ...ka⌐ mo
shiremase⌐n ...かもしれません;
(it is OK to do) (shi)-te⌐ mo i⌐i
desu (し)てもいいです
maybe (ta⌐bun) ... deshō⌐ (多分)
...でしょう, ... ka⌐ mo
shiremase⌐n ...かもしれません;
hyo⌐tto shita⌐ra ひょっとし
たら; aru⌐i-wa あるいは・或い
mayor shichō⌐ 市長   └は
me watashi わたし・私,
watakushi わたくし・私;
(usually male) bo⌐⌐ku ぼく・僕,
[*unrefined*] ore おれ・俺
meager sukuna⌐i 少ない,
toboshi⌐⌐i 乏しい
meal (o-)shokuji (o shima⌐su;
suru, shite) (お)食事(をしま

す; する, して), go⌐han /
meshi⌐ (o tabema⌐su; tabe⌐ru,
ta⌐bete) ご飯/飯(を食べます;
食べる, 食べて); **(1** is-shoku⌐
一食, **2** ni⌐-shoku 二食, **3** sa⌐n-
shoku 三食)
meal: a set/complete ~ teishoku
定食; **a set ~ (of house
choices)** se⌐tto セット, kō⌐su
コース; **with meals (included)**
shoku(ji)-tsuki (no) 食(事)付
き(の)
meal ticket shokken 食券 **(how
many** na⌐m-mai 何枚)
mean: it means ... ... to iu i⌐mi
desu ...という意味です; ... o
i⌐mi shima(⌐)su (suru, shite) ...
を意味します(する, して);
what I mean is ... ii-tai koto⌐
wa ... 言いたい事は...
meaning i⌐mi 意味, wa⌐ke 訳;
(significance) i⌐gi 意義; *(what
one wants to say)* ii-tai koto⌐
言いたい事   ┌(な)
meaningless mu-i⌐mi (na) 無意味
means 1. shu⌐dan 手段, shi-kata
仕方, shi-yō 仕様; **by all
means** ze⌐-hi 是非・ぜひ; **by
some means (or other)** na⌐n to
ka shite 何とかして
2. → **mean**
mean(-spirited) iji⌐ ga waru⌐i 意
地が悪い; → **stingy**
meanwhile sono-uchi (ni) そのう
ち(に); *(on the other hand)*
ippō⌐ 一方

measure 1. → a means **2.** *(ruler)*
monosa⌐shi⌐ 物差し
3. measures it hakarima⌐su
(haka⌐ru, haka⌐tte) 計ります
(計る, 計って)
measurement(s) sumpō 寸法
meat niku⌐ (o-ni⌐ku) 肉(お肉);
grilled ~ slices yaki-niku 焼肉
meatballs *(Chinese)* niku-da⌐ngo
肉団子
meat cleaver nikukiri-bō⌐chō 肉
切り包丁
meat grinder hikiniku⌐-ki 挽き肉
機
mechanic *(car repairman)* shūri⌐-
kō 修理工
mechanical kikai-teki (na) 機械
的(な)
meddle o-se⌐kkai o shima⌐su お
せっかい[お節介]をします
meddling o-se⌐kkai おせっかい・
お節介; kanshō 干渉; sewa⌐ (o-
se⌐wa, o-sewa-sama) 世話(お
世話, お世話様)
mediation *(good offices)* asscn
あっせん・斡旋
medic *(hospital orderly; medical
corpsman)* eise⌐i-hei 衛生兵
medical corps eisei-tai 衛生隊
medical department i⌐ka 医科
medical examination shinsatsu
診察
medicine kusuri (o-kusu⌐ri) 薬
(お薬), yaku⌐zai 薬剤; *(doc-
toring)* i⌐gaku 医学, i-... 医...
meditation mokusō 黙想;

shugyō 修行, gyō⌐ 行; *(Zen)*
zaze⌐n 座禅
medium chū(-) 中; → **medium-
rare**
medium-fat (pink) tuna chū-toro
中とろ
medium-rare (meat) han-yake 半
焼け　　　　　　　「型
medium-size (model) chūgata 中
meek su⌐nao (na) すなお[素直]
(な)
meet 1. *(sees a person)* ...ni
aima⌐su (a⌐u, a⌐tte) ...に会いま
す(会う, 会って); *(welcomes)*
... o mukaema⌐su (mukaeru,
mukaete) ...を迎えます(迎え
る, 迎えて), ... o de-
mukaema⌐su (-mukae⌐ru,
-muka⌐ete) ...を出迎えます
(迎える, 迎えて); *(happens
to ~)* de-aima⌐su (-a⌐u,
-a⌐tte) 出会います(会う, 会っ
て), *(encounters)* ses-shima⌐su
(ses-su⌐ru, se⌐s-shite) 接しま
す(接する, 接して) **2.** *(they
assemble)* atsumarima⌐su
(atsuma⌐ru, atsuma⌐tte) 集まり
ます(集まる, 集まって),
shūgō shima⌐su (suru, shite) 集
合します(する, して)
meeting 1. ka⌐i 会; *(mass ~)*
taikai 大会; *(conference)*
ka⌐igi 会議 **2.** *(interview)*
menkai 面会; *(of prospective
bride and groom)* miai 見合い
3. *(by prior arrangement)*

uchi-awase 打ち合わせ
melancholy yūutsu (na) 憂うつ·憂鬱（な）
mellow (= gets mellow) enjukụ shima̱sụ (suru, shite) 円熟します（する，して）
melon me̱ron メロン; u̱ri 瓜
melt (it melts) tokema̱sụ (toke̱ru, to̱kete) 溶けます（溶ける，溶けて）; (melts it) tokashima̱sụ (toka̱su, toka̱shite) 溶かします（溶かす，溶かして）
member me̱mbā メンバー, kai-in 会員; (ichi⌐)-in （一）員
memo(randum) me̱mo メモ
memorial service (100 days after the death) hya̱kkanichi 百か日
memorize ankị shima̱sụ (suru, shite) 暗記します（する，して）
memory obo̱e 覚え, mono-o̱boe 物覚え, kioku 記憶, (~ capacity) kioku̱-ryoku 記憶力; (a recollection) omoide 思い出; **by/from memory** so̱ra de そらで, anki shite 暗記して
men → man
mending naoshi̱ 直し; → repair
mend it naoshima̱sụ (nao̱su, nao̱shite) 直します（直す，直して）, tsụkuroima̱sụ (tsụkuro̱u, tsụkuro̱tte) 繕います（繕う，繕って）
men's bath otoko-yu 男湯
menstruation gekkei 月経

menswear otoko-mono 男物
mental se̱ishin (no) 精神（の）; **mentality** shi̱nri 心理
mention 1. ... ni furema̱sụ (fureru, furete) ...に触れます（触れる，触れて）; [bookish] ... ni genkyū shima̱sụ (suru, shite) ...に言及します（する，して） **2.** → say
Don't mention it. Dō̱ itashima(⌐)shite. どういたしまして.
menu konda⌐te⌐ 献立, me̱nyū メニュー
merchandise shō⌐hin 商品
merchant shō̱nin 商人
mercy megumi 恵み
mere honno ... ほんの...; ta̱da ただ; [bookish] ta̱n naru ... 単なる...
merely ta̱da ただ, tatta たった; [bookish] ta̱n ni 単に
merge (they unite) gappei shima̱sụ (suru, shite) 合併します（する，して）; (they flow together) gōryū shima̱sụ (suru, shite) 合流します（する，して）; **Lanes Merge (Ahead), Merge (Lanes)** ''Gōryu chū̱i'' "合流注意"
merger gappei 合併; (confluence) gōryū 合流
merit (strong point) chō̱sho 長所
merry yu̱kai (na) 愉快（な）, (bustling) nigi̱yaka (na) にぎやか［賑やか］（な）; **Merry**

Christmas. Kuri̇̄su̇̄masu o-medetō (gozaima̍su̇̄) クリスマスおめでとう[お目出度う](ございます).

mess (*disorder*) konran 混乱; (*predicament*) koma̍tta koto 困った事, (*plight*) (kurushi̍i) hame̍ (苦しい)羽目; (*bungle*) he̍ma へま・ヘマ; **makes a damn mess of it** he̍ma o yarakashima̍su̇̄ へま[ヘマ]をやらかします

It's a mess. Taihen de̍su̇̄ ne̍. 大変ですね.

I'm in a mess. Koma̍tte ima̍su̇̄. 困っています.

message kotozu̇̄ke ことづけ・言付け, kotozu̇̄te ことづて・言伝て, me̍ssēji メッセージ, tsutae (o-tsutae) 伝え(お伝え), sa̍ta̍ (o-sa̍ta) さた[沙汰](おさた)

messenger tsukai 使い

messy kitana̍i 汚い

metal kane 金, ki̍nzoku 金属

meter 1. (*of length*) mētoru メートル **2.** (*device*) ke̍iki 計器, mē̍tā メーター

method shi̇̄-kata 仕方, shi-yō 仕様, hōhō 方法, ... hō̍ ...法

metro(politan) (*run by Tokyo*) toei 都営

mezzanine (*floor*) chū-ni̍-kai 中二階

microcomputer mai-kon マイコン

microscope kembi-kyō 顕微鏡

middle na̍ka 中, mannaka 真ん中, chūshin 中心; naka̍ba̍ 半ば; (*medium*) chū̍ 中

middle age chūnen 中年; **middle-aged person** chūnem-mono 中年者

middle of the night yonaka̍ 夜中

middle school (*junior high*) chūga̍kkō 中学校

middle volume (*of a set of three*) chū-kan 中巻, chū̍ 中

midget chi̍bi ちび

midnight ma-yo̍naka 真夜中

midst (... no) sa̍ichū (...の)最中

midsummer/midyear (*gift*) (o-)chūgen (お)中元

might → **perhaps**; → **power**

mild yawaraka̍i 柔らかい

mildew kabi かび

military: ~ **base** ki̍chi̍ 基地; ~ **occupation** senryō 占領; ~ **officer** shō̍kō 将校; ~ **person** gunjin 軍人; ~ **uniform** gumpu̇̄ku 軍服

milk mi̍ruku ミルク, gyūnyū 牛乳; **mother's** ~ chichi̍ 乳, [*baby talk, slang*] o̍ppai おっぱい

milkshake miruku̇̄-sē̍ki ミルクセーキ

millet a̍wa あわ・粟

million hyaku-ma̍n 百万・1,000,000

mimic ... no mane (o shima̍su̇̄; suru, shi̇̄te) ...のまね[真似]

（をします; する, して）

mimicry mane まね・真似

minced meat hiki-niku 挽き肉

mincing (fish/meat) tataki⌐ 叩き, ...-ta⌐taki ...叩き

mind koko⌐ro (o-kokoro) 心（お心）, omo⌐i 思い, se⌐ishin 精神; mune⌐ 旨・むね; ki 気; kokoro-zashi⌐ 志, *(what one has in mind)* tsumori (o-tsumori) つもり（おつもり）, ikō 意向; **one's right ~** shō⌐ki 正気; **if you don't ~** nan-na⌐ra なんなら, yoroshika⌐ttara よろしかったら・宜しかったら **Never mind.** Kamaimase⌐n. 構いません. **Do you mind?** I⌐i desu ka. いいですか.

mind: bears/keeps in ~ fukumima⌐su (fuku⌐mu, fuku⌐nde) 含みます（含む, 含んで）; oboema⌐su (oboe⌐ru, obo⌐ete) 覚えます（覚える, 覚えて）

mine *(my)* wata(ku)shi no わた（く）し［私］の

mine *(coal, etc.)* kō⌐zan 鉱山

minimal, minimum *(= smallest, least)* saishō no 最小の; *(= lowest)* saitei (no) 最低（の）, sa⌐ika (no) 最下（の）

minimum (degree) saishō-ge⌐ndo 最小限度

minister *(pastor)* bo⌐kushi 牧師; *(cabinet)* da⌐ijin 大臣

Ministry ...⌐-shō ...省; **~ of Education** Mombu⌐-shō 文部省; **~ of Foreign Affairs** Gaimu⌐-shō 外務省; **~ of Trade and Industry** Tsūshō-sangyō⌐-shō 通商産業省; **~ of Finance** Ōkura⌐-shō 大蔵省

minus mainasu マイナス

minute ...⌐-fun ...分 **(1** i⌐p-pun 一分, **3** sa⌐m-pun 三分, **4** yo⌐m-pun 四分, **6** ro⌐p-pun 六分, **8** ha⌐p-pun 八分, **10** ji⌐p-pun 十分; **how many** na⌐m-pun 何分）

minute: in a ~ su⌐gu (ni) すぐ（に）; tada⌐ima ただ今・只今

minute *(fine, detailed)* bisai (na) 微細（な）, seimitsu (na) 精密（な）

mirror 1. kagami⌐ (o-kagami) 鏡（お鏡） **2.** *(= reflects it)* utsushima⌐su (utsu⌐su, utsu⌐shite) 映します（映す, 映して）

miscarriage ryū⌐zan 流産

miscellaneous sama⌐za⌐ma (na) 様々・さまざま（な）, zatta (na) 雑多（な）; **~ goods** zakka 雑貨

mischief itazura いたずら

mischievous wa⌐mpaku na 腕白な; **~ child** wampaku-mono⌐ 腕白者

miserable wabishi⌐i わびしい・侘びしい; nasake-na⌐i 情けない

misfortune fukō⌐ 不幸, wazawai 災い

mishap kega' (o-ke'ga) けが・怪
我（おけが・お怪我）, wazawai
災い; → **accident**

misrepresent gomakashima'su
(gomaka'su, gomaka'shite) ご
まかします（ごまかす, ごま
かして）

miss 1. *(a miss)* mi'su ミス;
(goes wide of the mark)
hazurema'su (hazureru,
hazurete) 外れます（外れる,
外れて）, *(fails)* shippai
shima'su (suru, shite) 失敗し
ます（する, して）; *(is not in
time for)* (... ni) ma ni
aimase'n (awa'nai, awa'naide)
(...に)間に合いません（合わ
ない, 合わないで）**2.** *(yearns
for)* ...ga natsukashi'i ...が懐
かしい; *(feels lonely without)*
...ga inakute/na'kute sabishi'i
...がいなくて/なくて寂しい

Miss ... san ...さん, ... san no
ojo'-san ...さんのお嬢さん

missing: (it) is ~ arimase'n (na'i,
na'kute) ありません（ない, な
くて）; **(he) is ~** imase'n (inai,
ina'ide) いません（いない, い
ないで）

Who is missing what? Da're
ga(/ni) na'ni ga arimase'n
ka. 誰が(/に)何がありませ
んか.

Who is missing? Da're ga
(ki'te') imase'n ka? 誰が（来
て）いませんか?

missionary senkyo'shi 宣教師

mist kasumi かすみ・霞, kiri き
り・霧, mo'ya もや・靄

mistake machiga'i 間違い,
ayama'ri' 誤り, mi'su ミス,
misute'ku ミステーク; *(makes
a mistake)* machigaima'su
(machiga'u, machiga'tte) 間違
います（間違う, 間違って）,
ayamarima'su (ayama'ru,
ayama'tte) 誤ります（誤る,
誤って）; **mistakes it**
machigaema'su (machiga'e'ru,
machiga'ete) 間違えます（間違
える, 間違えて）

mistreat gyakutai shima'su
(suru, shite) 虐待します（する,
して）

mistress 1. *(Madam)* o'ku-san/
-sama 奥さん/様 **2.** *(lover)*
ka'no-jo 彼女; *(concubine)*
mekake' (o-mekake) 妾（お妾）,
ni'go' (san) 二号（さん）, *(of
American serviceman)* o'nrii
オンリー

misty: gets ~ kasumima'su
(kasumu, kasunde) かすみま
す・霞みます（かすむ, かすん
で）

misunderstand gokai shima'su
(suru, shite) 誤解します（する,
して）

mix *(mixes it in with)* (... ni sore
o) mazema'su (maze'ru,
ma'zete) (...にそれを)混ぜま
す（混ぜる, 混ぜて）; *(it*

mixes) mazarima͡su (maza͡ru, maza͡tte) 混ざります(混ざる, 混ざって), majirima͡su (maji͡ru, maji͡tte) 混じります(混じる, 混じって)

mixed bathing kon'yoku 混浴

mixing one's foods/drinks cha͡mpon ちゃんぽん

mixture *(assortment)* kumi-awase 組み合わせ

moan nagekima͡su (nage͡ku, nage͡ite) 嘆きます(嘆く, 嘆いて)

moat hori͡ 堀; **inner ~** uchi-bori 内堀, **outer ~** soto-bori 外堀

model mohan 模範, teho͡n (o-tehon) 手本(お手本); *(mold)* mokei 模型; *(type)* kata͡ 型, ...-gata ...型, ...-kei ...型; mo͡deru モデル

moderate *(reasonable)* kakkō (na) 格好(な); *(properly limited/restrained)* ii-kagen (na) いい加減(な); *(conservative)* uchiwa (na) 内輪(な)

moderate it kagen shima͡su (suru, shite) 加減します(する, して)

moderation te͡kido 適度, hodo 程; do 度; kagen 加減

modern ge͡ndai no 現代の

modern drama shingeki 新劇

modernization genda͡i-ka 現代化

modest kenson (na) 謙遜(な), hikaeme͡ (no) 控え目(の),

uchiwa (na) 内輪(な); *(small)* ō͡kiku na͡i 大きくない; ~ **taste(s)** wabi͡ わび・侘び

moist → damp; **→** wet

moisten shimeshima͡su (shime͡su, shime͡shite) 湿します(湿す, 湿して)

mold 1. *(pattern)* kata͡ 型; *(model)* mokei 模型 **2.** (= mould) *(growth)* kabi かび; **is moldy** kabi ga ha͡ete ima͡su かびが生えています

mole *(on skin)* hokuro ほくろ; *(rodent)* mogura もぐら

molester *(sexual)* chikan 痴漢・ちかん

moment *(instant)* shunkan 瞬間, se͡tsuna せつな・刹那; **just a ~** cho͡tto ちょっと; **on the spur of the ~** toki͡ no hazumi de 時の弾みで; **(at) the ~ that** ... totan ni ...とたん[途端]に

momentum hazumi 弾み

Monday Getsuyo͡bi 月曜日; **Monday-Wednesday-Friday** ge͡s-su͡i-kin 月水金

money (o-)kane (お)金; **→** cash; **→** finance

money-changer = money-changing machine ryōgae͡-ki 両替機

money changing/exchange ryō͡gae 両替

money market kin'yū-shi͡jō 金融市場

money offering (to a shrine) saise͡n (o-saisen) さい銭・賽

銭（おさい銭）

money order kawase 為替;
(postal) yūbin-ga⌐wase 郵便為
替

Mongolia Mongoru モンゴル,
Mō⌐ko 蒙古; **Mongolian
chimney pot** shabu-shabu
しゃぶしゃぶ

monk (Buddhist) bō⌐zu 坊主, o-
bō-san お坊さん; **young ～**
kozō⌐ 小僧, kozō-san 小僧さ
ん

monkey sa⌐ru (o-saru) 猿（お猿）

monorail monorē⌐ru モノレール

monster kaibutsu 怪物, kaijū 怪
獣

month tsuki⌐ 月, ...-getsu ...月;
how many months nan-
ka⌐getsu 何ヵ月

month after next sara⌐igetsu 再
来月

month before last sense⌐n-getsu
先々月

monthly maigetsu (no) 毎月（の）;
～ installments/payments
geppu 月賦; **～ salary** gekkyū
月給

mood ki⌐bun 気分, kokoro-
mochi⌐ 心持ち; (go-)kigen
（ご）機嫌

moody kigen ga waru⌐i 機嫌が悪
い

moon tsuki⌐ 月, o⌐-tsuki-sama お
月様

moonfaced woman oka⌐me おか
め［亀］

moonlight night tsuki⌐-yo 月夜

moonrise tsuki(⌐) no de 月の出

moon viewing tsuki-mi⌐ (o-
tsukimi) 月見（お月見）

mop mo⌐ppu モップ

moral dōtoku-teki (na) 道徳的
（な）

morality, morals dōtoku 道徳;
(= ethics) shū⌐shin 修身

more mo⌐tto もっと, mō
suko⌐shi もう少し, mō もう＋
NUMBER; **(some ～)** sa⌐ra-ni さ
らに・更に; **a little ～** mō
suko⌐shi もう少し, **a lot ～**
mo⌐tto takusa⌐n もっとたくさ
ん［沢山］; **all the ～ ... , still/
much ～ ...** issō ...一層・いっ
そう, na⌐o-sara なおさら・尚
更

more: (the more ...) the more ...
(...-e⌐ba/ ...-ke⌐reba/ ... na⌐ra
...えば/...ければ/...なら) ...
hodo/dake ...程/だけ (issō ...
一層・いっそう...)

more and more masu⌐-masu ます
ます・益々, iyo⌐-iyo いよいよ

more or less tsu⌐mari つまり;
tashō 多少

moreover sono ue(⌐ ni) その上
（に）, mata⌐ 又・また, na⌐o 尚・
なお, shika⌐-mo しかも, ko⌐to-
ni ことに・殊に

more than: ～ anything na⌐ni
yori mo 何よりも; **～ enough**
tappu⌐ri たっぷり; **～ we
might expect** nakanaka なか

なか・中々

morning aˈsa 朝, goⁿzen 午前;
Good morning. O-hayō
(gozaimaˈsu). おはよう[お早
う](ございます).

morning meal chōshoku 朝食 =
asa-han 朝飯

morning paper chōkan 朝刊

morphine moruhine モルヒネ

mortar uˈsu うす・臼; suriˈbachi
すり鉢

mortifying kuyashiˈi 悔しい

Moscow Moⁿsukuwa モスクワ

mosquito ka 蚊

mosquito net kaya かや・蚊帳

moss kokeⁿ こけ・苔

most ichiban 一番, moˈtto mo 最
も; **most of the** ... no dai-
buˈbun ...の大部分; **at ~**
ōˈkute 多くて, seˈmete せめて,
seˈizei せいぜい; **for the ~
part** ōkata おおかた, taigai 大
概・たいがい, ōˈku 多く; **the
~** (= largest) saidai (no) 最大
(の)

most recent (+ DATE) saⁿru ...
去る...

moth ga が・蛾; (clothes moth)
iˈga いが・衣蛾, shiˈmi しみ・
衣魚, mushi 虫

mothballs nafutaⁿrin ナフタリ
ン, shimi-yoⁿkeⁿ しみ[衣
魚]よけ, mushi-yoⁿkeⁿ 虫よ
け, bōchū-zai 防虫剤

mother okaˈ-san お母さん, haˈha
母, haha-oya 母親; ofukuro お

ふくろ・お袋

mother country boˈkoku 母国,
soˈkoku 祖国

mother-in-law giˈbo 義母

mother's milk chichiˈi 乳; [baby
talk] oˈppai おっぱい

motion ugoki 動き; moˈshon モ
ーション; **~ sickness** yoi 酔い

motivation, motive dōⁿki 動機

motor hatsudōˈ-ki 発動機, moˈtā
モーター; → **automobile**; **~
pool** (mōtā-)pūˈru (モーター)
プール

motorcycle ōtoˈbai オートバイ
(how many naˈn-dai 何台)

motto hyōgo 標語

mould → **mold**

mound tsukaˈ 塚; (burial ~)
ryōˈ 陵

mount ... ni norimaˈsu (noru,
notte) ...に乗ります(乗る,
乗って); (sits astride) ... ni
matagarimaˈsu (matagaˈru,
matagaˈtte) ...にまたがります
(またがる, またがって)

mountain yamaˈ 山; ...ˈ-san ...山

mountain-climber tozaˈn-sha 登
山者

mountain-climbing yama-
noˈbori 山登り, toⁿzan 登山;
~ rope zaˈiru ザイル

mountain lodge yama-goya 山小
屋

mountain pass tōgeˈ 峠

mountain range sammyaku 山脈

Mount Fuji Fuˈji-san 富士山

mouse nezumi ねずみ・鼠, hatsuka-neˈzumi 二十日ねずみ[鼠]

mousetrap nezumiˈ-tori ねずみ[鼠]取り[捕り]

mouth kuchi 口

mouth organ: 17-reed ~ shōˈ 笙

movable type katsuji 活字

move 1. *(it moves)* ugokimaˈsu (ugoˈku, ugoˈite) 動きます(動く, 動いて); *(moves it)* ugokashimaˈsu (ugokaˈsu, ugokaˈshite) 動かします(動かす, 動かして) **2.** *(moves residence)* utsurimaˈsu (utsuˈru, utsuˈtte) 移ります(移る, 移って), *(changes residence)* hikkoshimaˈsu (hikkoˈsu, hikkoˈshite) 引っ越します(引っ越す, 引っ越して); *(moves into an apartment)* nyūkyo shimaˈsu (suru, shiite) 入居します(する, して)

movement ugokiˈ 動き; katsudō 活動; undō 運動; *(gesture)* miˈburi みぶり・身振り, dōˈsa 動作

mover *(household* ~ *)* hikkoshi-ya 引っ越し屋, (hikkoshi no) unsō-ya (引っ越しの)運送屋

movie(s) eˈiga 映画; **movie theater** eigaˈ-kan 映画館; **movie projector** eishaˈ-ki 映写機

moving *(one's household)* hikkoshi 引っ越し; ~ **van**

hikkoshi-toraˈkku 引っ越しトラック; ~ **man** → **mover**

mow karimaˈsu (karu, katte) 刈ります(刈る, 刈って)

moxibustion (o-)kyū (お)きゅう・(お)灸

MP (military patrol) keˈmpei 憲兵

Mr. ... san ...さん; **Mrs.** ... san (no oˈku-san) ...さん(の奥さん); **Mr. and Mrs.** ... fusaˈi ...夫妻; **Ms.** ... san ...さん, ...joˈshi ...女史

much takusaˈn (no) たくさん[沢山](の), ōˈku (no) 多く(の), uˈnto うんと; **is/has much** ... ga ōˈi ...が多い; **not (very) much** ammari あんまり + NEGATIVE; **how much** iˈkura (o-ikura) いくら(おいくら), dono-gurai どの位

much: as ~ **as** ... guˈrai ...位, ... no yōˈ ni ...のよう[様]に; **as** ~ **as one likes** (omoˈu) zombuˈn ni (思う)存分に

much: → **how much**

much more moˈtto takusaˈn もっとたくさん[沢山], zutto ōˈku ずっと多く; *(still more)* issō いっそう・一層, naˈo-sara なおさら・尚更

muck → **mud**

mucus *(nasal)* hana 鼻

mud doroˈ 泥

muddy doro-daˈrake (no) 泥だらけ(の); **gets** ~ nigorimaˈsu

(nigóru, nigótte) 濁ります
（濁る，濁って）

mudfish dojō どじょう・泥鰌

mugged: gets ~ *(robbed)* gōtō ni
yararemásu (yarareru,
yararete) 強盗にやられます
（やられる，やられて）

muggy mushi-atsúi 蒸し暑い

mulberry kúwa くわ・桑

multiply *(grow)* fuemásu
(fuéru, fúete) 増えます（増え
る，増えて）; **(3 by 5** sán ni gó
o) kakemásu (kakéru,
kákete) （3に5を）掛けます・
（掛ける，掛けて）

municipal shí (no) 市（の），
shíritsu (no) 市立（の），
kōritsu (no) 公立（の），
(urban) shínai (no) 市内（の）

murder satsujin 殺人, hito-
góroshi 人殺し; → **kill**

murmur → **whisper**

muscle kínniku 筋肉, súji 筋;
(power) kínryoku 筋力,
chikará 力

museum hakubútsu-kan 博物館;
(art gallery) bijútsu-kan 美術
館

mushroom kínoko きのこ・茸;
(thumb-like) matsutake 松茸,
matsudake 松茸; *(large
brown)* shíitake 椎茸; *(straw)*
enokí-dake えのき［榎］茸,
enokí-take えのき［榎］茸

music óngaku 音楽, *(traditional
to the imperial court)* gágaku
雅楽

musical: ~ instrument gakki 楽
器; **~ score** gakufu 楽譜

musician ongak(u)-ka 音楽家

must (do) (shi)-nákereba
narimasén (し)なければなり
ません; **must not (do)** (shi)-
téwa ikemasén （し）てはいけ
ません

mustache kuchi-hige 口ひげ
［髭］

mustard karashi からし・芥子;
(horseradish) wásabi わさび・
山葵

mutton → **lamb**

mutual o-tagai (no) お互い（の）;
[*bookish*] sōgo (no) 相互（の）

mutually o-tagai ni お互いに;
[*bookish*] sōgo ni 相互に

my wata(ku)shi no わた（く）し
［私］（の）; **my wife** kánai 家内

My my! My goodness! Sore wa
sore wa それはそれは

myopic kingan (no) 近眼（の），
kinshi (no) 近視（の）

myself jibun 自分, (watakushi)
jíshin （私）自身; **by ~** jibun
jíshin de 自分自身で

mysterious *(strange)* fushigi (na)
不思議（な）; *(esoteric)* shimpi-
teki (na) 神秘的（な）

mystery himitsu 秘密, nazo 謎

myth shinwa 神話

— N —

Nagasaki Naga┐saki 長崎; ~
  City Nagasa┐ki┐-shi 長崎市; ~
  Prefecture Nagasa┐ki┐-ken 長
  崎県
nail kugi 釘; *(finger, toe)* tsume
  爪
nail clippers tsumeki┐ri┐ 爪切り
naive mu┐jaki (na) むじゃき・無
  邪気(な), soboku (na) 素朴
  (な)
naked hadaka (no) 裸(の); →
  nude
name namae (o-namae) 名前(お
  名前), (o-)na (お)名; *(calls)* (...
  to) yobima┐su (yobu, yonde)
  (...と)呼びます(呼ぶ, 呼ん
  で), *(dubs)* nazukema┐su
  (nazuke┐ru, nazu┐kete) 名付け
  ます(名付ける, 名付けて);
  (says the name of) ... no
  namae o iima┐su (yū, itte/
  yutte) ...の名前を言います(言
  う, 言って/ゆって)
name: list of names meibo 名簿
name card meishi 名刺
nameless mumei (no) 無名(の)
namely suna┐wachi すなわち・即
  ち
name plate/tag nafuda 名札
name seal/stamp ("chop")
  hanko┐ はんこ・判こ

nap hiru-ne (o shima┐su; suru,
  shite) 昼寝(をします; する,
  して)
napkin na┐puki┐n ナプキン,
  fuki┐n ふきん・布巾
narcotic(s) mayaku 麻薬
narrow sema┐i 狭い; hoso┐i 細い
nasal mucus hana 鼻; → **snivel**
nasty iya (na) 嫌(な), akuratsu
  (na) 悪らつ・悪辣(な)
nation kuni (o-kuni) 国(お国),
  ko┐kka 国家, *(= people)*
  kokumin 国民; **how many nations** nan-ka┐koku 何か国
national kuni no 国の; koku-...
  国..., kokuritsu (no) 国立(の)
national defense kokubō 国防
**National Foundation Day (11
  February)** Kenkoku-ki┐nen no
  hi 建国記念の日
nationality kokuseki 国籍
national(s) kokumin 国民
nation-wide ze┐nkoku (no) 全国
  (の)
native place kuni (o-kuni) 国(お
  国)
natural 1. shizen (no, [= *spontaneous*] na) 自然(の, な);
  te┌nnen (no) 天然(の) **2.** *(proper, deserved)* tōzen (no) 当然
  (の) **3.** *(to be expected)* ...

(suru) mono˼ desu ...(する)も
のです

natural gas ga˼su ガス

naturally shizen ni 自然に; *(by nature)* motomoto もともと・元々; → **spontaneously**; → **of course**

nature 1. shizen 自然 **2.** seishitsu 性質, shō˼ 性, se˼i 性; *(quality)* shitsu˼ 質; *(disposition)* ta˼chi たち・質

nature: by ~ mo˼to˼-yori もとより, motomoto もともと・元々; **human ~** ni˼njō 人情

naughty wa˼mpaku (na) 腕白 (な), itazura (na) いたずら (な); **naughty child** wampaku-mono˼ 腕白者, itazura˼kko いたずらっ子

nauseate: feels nauseated haki-ke˼ (o moyōshima˼su; moyō˼su, moyō˼shite) 吐き気 (を催します; 催す, 催して); → **queasy**

navel (o-)heso (お)へそ

navigate kō˼kai shima˼su (suru, shite) 航海します(する, して)

navy ka˼igun 海軍

near chika˼i 近い

near(by) so˼ba (o-soba) そば(お そば); chika˼ku 近く

nearly hoto˼ndo ほとんど・殆ど; ma˼zu まず; ho˼bo ほぼ

nearsighted *(myopic)* kingan (no) 近眼(の), kinshi (no) 近 視(の)

neat *(tidy)* kichi˼n-to shite ima˼su (iru, ite) きちんとしています (いる, いて); *(attractive)* ki˼rei (na) きれい[綺麗](な)

necessarily kanarazu 必ず

necessary hitsuyō (na) 必要(な), *(needed)* nyūyō (na) 入用(な); ... ga irima˼su (iru, itte) ...が要 ります(要る, 要って)

necessity hitsuyō 必要

neck kubi 首; *(of a bottle)* kubire くびれ

necklace kubi-ka˼zari 首飾り, ne˼kkuresu ネックレス

necktie ne˼kutai ネクタイ; **puts on (wears) a ~** ne˼kutai o musubima˼su (musubu, musunde) ネクタイを結びま す(結ぶ, 結んで) *or* shima˼su (suru, shite) します(する, し て)

need: is in ~ *(of help)* komarima˼su (koma˼ru, koma˼tte) 困ります(困る, 困 って)

need: needs to do (... ga) irima˼su (iru, itte) (...が)要り ます(要る, 要って), (... o) yō-shima˼su (yō-su˼ru, yō˼-shite) (...を)要します(要する, 要して); *(necessity)* hitsuyō 必 要; *(poverty)* hinkon 貧困, fu˼-jiyū 不自由; **needs not do** (shi)-na˼kute mo i˼i desu (し)なく てもいいです

USAGE: Who needs what?

Da̅re ga(/ni) na̅ni ga irima̅su ka 誰が(/に)何が要りますか.

needle ha̅ri 針; **sewing needle** nu̅i̅bari 縫い針

needlework hari-shi̅goto 針仕事, ha̅ri 針 = o-hari お針

need to do (suru) hitsuyō ga arima̅su (a̅ru, a̅tte) (する)必要があります(ある, あって), (shi)-na̅kereba narimase̅n (し)なければなりません

needy mazushi̅i 貧しい, fu̅-jiyū (na) 不自由(な), hinkon (na) 貧困(な)

negation uchi-keshi 打ち消し, hitei 否定

negative shōkyoku-teki (na) 消極的(な)

neglect (disregards) mu̅shi shima(̅)su (suru, shi̅te) 無視します(する, して); (leaves undone) (shi)-na̅ide okima̅su (oku, oite) (し)ないでおきます(おく, おいて); (shirks) okotarima̅su (okotaru, okotatte) 怠ります(怠る, 怠って); **~ to write/visit** (go-)busata shima̅su (suru, shi̅te) (ご)無沙汰します(する, して)

neglectful taiman (na) 怠慢(な); **I have been ~ (in not keeping in touch with you).** Go-busata itashima̅shi̅ta. ご無沙汰致しました.

negligence (carelessness) yudan 油断

negligent taiman (na) 怠慢(な)

negotiate hanashi-aima̅su (-a̅u, -a̅tte) 話し合います(合う, 合って)

negotiation hanashi-ai 話し合い, kōshō 交渉

Negro Kokujin 黒人

neighborhood ki̅njo 近所; **~ bar** nomi̅-ya 飲み屋

neighbor(ing) tonari (no) 隣り(の)

neither … nor … mo … mo … も…も + NEGATIVE

neither one do̅chira (no …) mo どちら(の…)も + NEGATIVE

nephew oi おい・甥; **your ~** oigo-san 甥子さん

nerve shi̅nkei 神経; **gets on one's nerves** shi̅nkei ni sawarima̅su (sawaru, sawatte) 神経に障ります(障る, 障って)

nervous 1. shinke̅i-shitsu (na) 神経質(な) **2.** (feels self-conscious) agarima̅su (agaru, agatte) 上がります(上がる, 上がって) **3.** (gets agitated) dōyō shima̅su (suru, shi̅te) 動揺します(する, して); → **flustered 4.** (feeling apprehensive) kimi̅ ga waru̅i 気味が悪い; → **worried**

nest su̅ 巣

nested boxes jūbako (o-jū̅) 重箱 (お重)

net ami 網; *(= net price)* seˈika
正価 (¥ …)　　　　　　「(の)

neutral(ity) chūritsu (no) 中立

never kesshite 決して +
NEGATIVE; **has never (done)**
(shi)-ta kotoˈ ga arimaseˈn
(naˈi) (し)た事がありません
(ない); **never (does)** (su)-ru
kotoˈ ga arimaseˈn (naˈi) (す)
る事がありません(ない)

never mind kamaimaseˈn
(kamawaˈnai) 構いません(構
わない)

nevertheless sore naˈ no ni それ
なのに, toˈ-ni-kaku とにかく

new atarashiˈi 新しい; shiˈn(-) ...
新...

newest saishin (no) 最新(の)

newly ataraˈshiku 新しく,
arataˈmete 改めて

news nyūˈsu ニュース, tsūshin
通信; *(newspaper item)* kiˈji 記
事; *(word from)* taˈyori 便り,
shōsoku 消息, saˈtaˈ (o-saˈta)
沙汰(お沙汰)

**newsboy/newsgirl = news ven-
dor** shimbun-uˈriko 新聞売り
子, uriko 売り子

newspaper shimbun 新聞; *(morning)* chōkan 朝刊, *(evening)*
yūkan 夕刊; *(company)*
shimbuˈn-sha 新聞社; **~ bill**
shimbuˈn-dai 新聞代; **~ re-
porter** shimbun-kiˈsha 新聞記者

newsstand shimbun-uˈriba 新聞
売り場

new year shiˈnnen 新年; **Happy
~ .** (Shiˈnnen/Akemaˈshite)
o-medetō (gozaimaˈsu) (新年/
明けまして)おめでとう[お目
出度う](ございます).

New Year's (day) ganjitsu 元日,
gantan 元旦; o-Shōgatsu お正
月

New Year's eve ō-miˈsoka 大み
そか[晦日]; **~ party** bōneˈn-
kai 忘年会

New York Nyūyoˈku ニューヨー
ク

New Zealand Nyūjiiraˈndo ニュ
ージーランド; **New Zealander**
Nyūjiirandoˈ-jin ニュージー
ランド人

next *(in time/order)* tsugiˈ (no)
(o-tsuˈgi) 次(の)(お次),
(date etc.) yoˈku(-) ... 翌...; *(=
the next one)* tsugiˈ 次 = tsugiˈ
no 次の; *(= going on to the
~)* tsuzukete 続けて

next: ~ to *(in space)*, **~ door to**
... no tonari (no) ...の隣り(の);
~ on the left/right hidari-/
migi-doˈnari (no) 左/右隣り
(の); **~ after/to ...** *(in importance)* ... ni tsuˈide (no) ...に次
いで(の)

next month raˈigetsu 来月

next time koˈndo 今度, kono-
tsuˈgiˈ この次

next year rainen 来年

next week raishū 来週

nibble kajirimaˈsu (kajiˈru,

kaji⌐tte) かじります(かじる、
かじって)

nice → **good**; → **delicious**; →
fair; → **kind**; → **delicate**

nice weather (i⌐i) te⌐nki (いい)天
気

nick kizamima⌐su (kizamu,
kizande) 刻みます(刻む、刻
んで)

niece me⌐i めい・姪; **your ~**
me⌐igo-san めいごさん・姪子
さん

night yo⌐ru 夜, yo⌐ 夜; ban 晩;
(at) ~ ya⌐kan 夜間, **late at
~** yo⌐ru osoku 夜遅く,
shi⌐n'ya 深夜; **~ before last**
issaku⌐-ban/ya 一昨晩/夜;
the ~ before (… no) ze⌐n'ya
(…の)前夜; **one night** hito⌐-
ban 一晩, **two nights** futa⌐-ban
二晩

night: night(s) of lodging …-
haku …泊 (**1** ip-paku 一泊, **2**
ni-haku 二泊, **3** sam-paku 三
泊); **How many nights will you
stay?** Na⌐m-paku shima⌐su ka.
何泊しますか.

nightclub *(cabaret)* kya⌐barē
キャバレー

night duty tomari 泊まり

night game (of baseball) na⌐itā ナ
イター

**night-light (traditional paper-
covered)** andon あんどん・行
灯

night train yo⌐-gi⌐sha 夜汽車

night watchman yo-ma⌐wari 夜
巡り

Nikko Ni⌐kkō 日光

nimble ki⌐yō (na) 器用(な)

nine kyū⌐ 九・9, ku⌐ 九・9,
koko⌐notsu 九つ; na⌐in ナイン;
~ days kokonoka⌐ 九日・9
日

nine: small things, pieces kyū⌐-ko
九個; **long things** kyū⌐-hon 九
本; **flat things** kyū⌐-mai 九枚;
small animals/fish/bugs kyū⌐-
hiki 九匹; **large animals** kyū⌐-
tō 九頭; **birds** kyū⌐-wa 九羽;
machines/vehicles kyū⌐-dai 九
台; **books/ magazines** kyū⌐-
satsu 九冊

nine degrees kyū⌐-do 九度

nine hundred kyū⌐-hyaku 九百・
900

nineteen jū⌐-ku 十九・19, jū-kyū⌐
十九・19

nine thousand kyū-se⌐n 九千・
9,000

nine times kyū⌐-do 九度, kyū⌐-
ka⌐i 九回, kyū⌐-he⌐n 九遍

ninety kyū⌐-jū 九十・90, ku-jū⌐
九十; **~ thousand** kyū-ma⌐n
九万・90,000

ninja ni⌐nja 忍者; **ninjitsu** ni⌐njut-
su 忍術

ninth kyū-bamme (no) 九番目
(の)・9番目(の)ku-bamme⌐
(no) 九番目(の), kokonotsu-
me⌐ (no) 九つ目(の); **the ~
day** kokonoka-me⌐ 九日目・9

日目, *(of the month)*
kokonoka⌐ 九日・9日

no iie いいえ *(or just say the
negative verb)*; **no charge/fee**
mūryō (no) 無料(の); **No
parking** chūsha kinshi 駐車禁
止; **No passing** oi-koshi kinshi
追越し禁止; **No smoking**
kin'en 禁煙; **No trespassing**
tachiiri kinshi 立ち入り禁止

no: No, thank you. Kē kkō desu.
結構です。

nobody dare mo 誰も ＋ NEGA-
TIVE

nod unazukima su (unazu⌐ku,
unazu⌐ite) うなずきます(う
なずく, うなずいて)

no doubt *(surely)* kitto きっと

no good tsumara nai つまらない;
dame (na) だめ[駄目](な);
furyō (na) 不良(な); *(futile)*
muda (na) 無駄(な); *(worth-
less)* ya kuza (na) やくざ(な)

Noh *(Japanese classical theater)*
nō⌐ 能, o-nō お能; **traditional
~ farce** kyōge n 狂言

noise oto 音; *(unwanted)* sōon
騒音, *(static)* zatsuon 雑音;
(boisterous) sa wagi 騒ぎ

noisy yakamashi i やかましい,
sōzōshi i 騒々しい

No kidding! ma saka まさか

no later than ... ma de ni wa ...ま
でには

nominate mei-jima su
(mei-ji⌐ru, me i-jite) 命じ

ます(命じる, 命じて)

noncommittal *(beats around the
bush)* hanashi o bokashima su
(boka su, boka shite) 話をぼ
かします(ぼかす, ぼかして)

nondrinker *(sake no)* buchōhō-
mono⌐ (酒の)不調法者

none *(nothing)* nani mo 何も ＋
NEGATIVE; *(not even one)*
hitotsu mo 一つも ＋
NEGATIVE, *(person)* hitori mo
一人も ＋ NEGATIVE

no need to worry daijō bu (na)
大丈夫(な)

nonetheless sore na no ni それな
のに

nonsense baka na koto ばかな
こと; baka-ba nashi ばか話;
detarame でたらめ

nonsmoker *(tabako no)*
buchōhō-mono⌐ (たばこの)
不調法者

no(n)-smoking car kin'e n-sha 禁
煙車   「漢

nonspecialist monga i-kan 門外

non-stop (flight) mu-cha kuriku
(no) 無着陸(の)

**nonverbal communication: (a
talent for ~)** hara⌐ gei 腹芸

noodles me n(-rui) めん[麺](類);
(o-)so ba (お)そば・蕎麦;
(Japanese wheat-flour) udon
(o-u don) うどん・饂飩(おう
どん), *(thin)* so men そうめん,
(chilled) hiya-mu gi 冷や麦;
(Chinese) rā men ラーメン,

men めん·麺
noodle shop soba˥-ya そば[蕎麦]屋, o-sobaya おそば[蕎麦]屋; udon-ya うどん屋
noon hiru˥ (o-hi˥ru) 昼(お昼); *(exactly noon)* shō˥go 正午
nope iya いや, n˥n ううん
no place = nowhere
norm *(standard)* kịkaku 規格
normal → usual
north kịta[˥] 北, hoku-... 北...; *(the north)* hoppō 北方, *(the northern part)* ho˥kubu 北部; ~ **and south** na˥mboku 南北
North America Kita-A˥merika 北アメリカ, Hoku-Bei 北米
northeast hokụtō 北東
northerly (wind) kịta-yori (no kaze) 北寄り(の風)
North Pole Hokkyoku 北極
northwest hokụsei 北西
nose hana (o-hana) 鼻(お鼻)
nosebleed hanaji 鼻血
not: does not VERB-mase˥n (-nai, -na˥ide) ません(ない, ないで)
not: is not ADJECTIVE-ku arimase˥n (-ku na˥i, -ku na˥kụte) くありません(くない, くなくて); NOUN ja arimase˥n (ja na˥i, ja na˥kụte) じゃありません(じゃない, じゃなくて)
not as/so much as ··· ... hodo ... ほど·程 + NEGATIVE
not at all 1. sappa˥ri さっぱり; kesshịte 決して + NEGATIVE
2. *(you're welcome)* dō˥ itashima(˥)shịte どういたしまして
notch *(makes a notch)* kizamima˥sụ (kizamu, kizande) 刻みます(刻む, 刻んで)
note *(memorandum)* me˥mo メモ; *(reminder)* chū˥i 注意; *(bill)* tegata 手形; **→ letter; → notice, explanatory notes; → sound**
notebook nō˥to ノート, nōtobu˥kku ノートブック
note pad memo-chō メモ帳
nothing nani mo 何も + NEGATIVE; ~ **(at all)** nan to mo 何とも + NEGATIVE
nothing: there is ~ like (better than) ... ni kagirima˥sụ (kagi˥ru, kagi˥tte) ...に限ります(限る, 限って)
notice ... ni ki ga tsụkima˥sụ (tsụku˥, tsu˥ite) ...に気が付きます(付く, 付いて), kizukima˥sụ (-zu˥ku, -zu˥ite) 気付きます(付く, 付いて); *(notification)* shirase (o-shirase) 知らせ(お知らせ), todoke˥ (o-todoke) 届け(お届け), tsūchi 通知; *(reminder)* chū˥i 注意
notice: without ~ mu[˥]dan de 無断で; kotowa˥ri˥ mo na˥ku 断りもなく
notification → notice
notify shirasema˥sụ (shiraseru,

shirasete) 知らせます(知らせ
る，知らせて)，tsūchi
shima'su (suru, shite) 通知し
ます(する，して)；
todokema'su (todoke'ru,
todo'kete) 届けます(届ける，
届けて)

notion → **idea**；→ **concept**

notions (haberdashery) koma⌐-
mono 小間物

not working properly guai ga
waru'i 具合が悪い

not yet ma'da まだ ＋ NEGATIVE
NON-PAST (... -mase'n ...ませ
ん，...-nai ...ない)

noun meishi 名詞

nourish yashinaima'su
(yashinau, yashinatte) 養いま
す(養う，養って)

no use dame' (na) だめ[駄目](な)

novel (fiction) shōsetsu 小説；
(curious) mezurashi'i 珍しい

novelist sa⌐kka 作家

November Jūichi-gatsu 十一月・

now i'ma 今, (already) mō' もう；
from now on kore kara これか
ら，ko⌐ngo 今後；**just now**
tada'ima ただ今，tsu'i ima-
shi'gata つい今しがた；**until
now** ima-ma'de 今まで；**well
now** (sore) ja (それ)じゃ，ja'
じゃあ，de' wa では，sa'-te さ
て；**now that** ... i'jō ...以上；
now then, and now sa'-te さて

now and then tama ni たまに

No way! tonde-mo arimase'n

(na'i) とんでもありません(な
い)

nowhere doko (de/ni/e) mo どこ
(で/に/へ)も ＋ NEGATIVE

nuclear ka'ku (no) 核(の)

nude ratai (no) 裸体(の)，nū'do
ヌード；**(picture)** ratai-ga 裸体
画；→ **naked**

nuisance mendō' 面倒

numb mu-ka'nkaku (na) 無感覚
(な)；**goes/gets ~**
shibirema'su (shibire'ru,
shibi'rete) しびれます(しびれ
る，しびれて)

number ka'zu 数，sū' 数，ba'n 番，
...'-ban ...番；**(written
numeral)** sūji 数字；**(assigned)**
bangō' 番号，**(on an athlete)**
ze'kken ゼッケン；**(large and/
or small)** tashō 多少

number: a ~ of ... i'kutsu ka no
... いくつかの...，nan-
COUNTER ka no ... 何 COUNTER
かの...，sū-COUNTER no ... 数
COUNTER の...；**the ~ of days**
nissū' 日数，hinichi 日にち；
the ~ of people ni'nzu 人数，
ni'nzū 人数

number one ichi'-ban 一番

numbers: in large ~ ōze'i 大勢，
do'ndon どんどん，zo'rozoro
ぞろぞろ

numbness shibire' しびれ

numeral sūji 数字，sū' 数

numerous → **many**

nun a'ma 尼

nurse 1. kango⌐-fu 看護婦
2. *(nurses a patient)* ka⌐ngo shima(⌐)su (suru, shite) 看護します(する, して)
nursery school *(pre-kindergarten)* hoiku⌐-en 保育園

nursing *(a patient)* ka⌐ngo 看護
nuts na⌐ttsu ナッツ, kurumi⌐ くるみ・胡桃, ke⌐nka 堅果; ki⌐-no-mi 木の実 *(includes fruits and berries)*, mi 実
nylon na⌐iron ナイロン

— O—

oath chika⌐i 誓い
obedient su⌐nao (na) すなお[素直](な)
obey *(a person)* (... ga) yū koto⌐ o kikima⌐su (kiku, kiite) (...が)言う事を聞きます(聞く, 聞いて)
object taishō 対象; *(thing)* mono⌐ 物; *(objective, goal)* mokuteki 目的, ate 当て; *(aim)* nerai 狙い
object to *(opposes)* ... ni hantai shima⌐su (suru, shite) ...に反対します(する, して)
obligation *(duty)* gi⌐mu 義務, *(responsibility)* sekinin 責任; *(sense of ~)* giri⌐ (o-gi⌐ri) 義理(お義理); *(for a kindness)* o⌐n (go-o⌐n) 恩(ご恩)
obliged 1. becomes ~ (to ... for help) (... no) sewa⌐ ni narima⌐su (naru, natte) (...の)世話になります(なる, なって); **I'm much obliged for all your help.** Iroiro o-se⌐wa ni

narima⌐shita. いろいろ[色々]お世話になりました.
2. feels ~ (grateful) kyōshuku shima⌐su (suru, shite) 恐縮します(する, して)
oblique *(diagonal)* nana⌐me (no) 斜め(の), *(slanting)* hasu (no) はす(の)
obliquely nana⌐me ni 斜めに, hasu ni はすに
oboe-like instrument *(in gagaku* 雅楽*)* hichi⌐riki ひちりき・篳篥
obscene waisetsu (na) わいせつ・猥褻(な)
obscure *(unknown)* fumei (no) 不明(の); *(unrenowned)* mumei (no) 無名(の); → **dark**
observation kansatsu 観察, kansoku 観測
observatory *(astronomical)* temmon-dai 天文台; *(weather station)* sokkō-jo⌐ 測候所,

kishō-dai 気象台; *(sightseeing)* tembō-dai 展望台

observe 1. *(happens to see)* mi-ukema̱su (-uke⌐ru, -u⌐kete) 見受けます（受ける，受けて）
2. *(watches)* kansatsu/kansoku shima̱su (suru, shite) 観察/観測します（する，して）
3. → **say**

observer kansatsu̱-sha 観察者

obstacle → **hindrance**

obstruct *(hinders)* samatage-ma̱su (samatage⌐ru, samata⌐gete) 妨げます（妨げる，妨げて）; **gets obstructed** *(clogged)* tsukaema̱su (tsuka̱e̱ru, tsuka̱ete) つかえます（つかえる，つかえて）

obstruction tsuka̱e̱ つかえ

obtain te̱ ni irema̱su (ireru, irete) 手に入れます（入れる，入れて）; → **get**

obvious meihaku (na) 明白（な）

obviously *(clearly)* meihaku (ni) 明白（に）; → **certainly, of course**

occasion *(time)* toki̱ 時, *(event)* se̱tsu 節, sa̱i 際, ori̱ 折, ji̱-setsu 時節; *(opportunity)* kika̱i 機会; tsuide ついで; *(circumstance)* ba(w)ai 場合; **on the ~ of** ... ni sa̱i-shite ...に際して

occasional *(infrequent)* tama no

たまの

occasionally tamatama たまたま; tama ni たまに

Occident Se̱iyō 西洋; **Occidental** yō-... 洋...

occupation *(job)* shoku̱gyō 職業, shoku̱⌐ 職; *(military)* senryō 占領

occupied 1. *(toilet, etc.)* shiyō-chū 使用中; **(I'm in here)** Ha̱itte ima̱su 入っています
2. *(a seat)* **(They're coming!)** Kima̱su 来ます
3. → **busy**

occupied: gets ~ *(booked up)* fusagarima̱su (fusagaru, fusagatte) ふさがります（ふさがる，ふさがって）

occur okorima̱su (oko̱ru, oko̱tte) 起こります（起こる，起こって）, hassei shima̱su (suru, shite) 発生します（する，して）

occurrence hassei 発生

ocean taiyō 大洋, taika⌐i/daika⌐i 大海/大海

o'clock ...̱-ji ...時 (**4 ~** yo̱-ji 四時）

October Jū-gatsu̱ 十月・10月

octopus ta̱ko たこ・蛸; **baby ~** i̱idako いいだこ・飯蛸

oculist me̱-isha 目[眼]医者

odd *(peculiar)* he̱n (na) 変（な）; *(strange)* fushigi (na) 不思議（な）

odor → **smell**

of ... ... no ...の

of course mochi⌐ron もちろん, mo⌐tto⌐mo もっとも

off ... (= offshore from) ... no oki ...の沖

off: time off yasumi⌐ 休み; **off** (= down in price by) ¥100 hyakue⌐n-yasu 百円安

off: (turns) off (light, radio, etc.) ... o keshima⌐su (kesu, keshite) ...を消します(消す, 消して); **(button, etc.) comes off** torema⌐su (tore⌐ru, to⌐rete) 取れます(取れる, 取れて), (slips off) nukema⌐su (nukeru, nukete) 抜けます(抜ける, 抜けて); **gets off (a vehicle)** orima⌐su (ori⌐ru, o⌐rite) 降ります(降りる, 降りて); **takes off (clothes, shoes)** nugima⌐su (nu⌐gu, nu⌐ide) 脱ぎます(脱ぐ, 脱いで)

off and on: does/is ~ ...-ta⌐ri/ ...-ka⌐ttari/... da⌐ttari shima⌐su (suru, shite) ...たり/...かった り/...だったりします(する, して)

off duty (taxi) kaisō(-chū) 回送 (中); **~ taxi** kaisō⌐-sha 回送 車

offend 1. (violates) ... ni ihan shima⌐su (suru, shite) ...に違 反します(する, して)
2. → displease **3. →** anger

offense: takes ~ shaku ni sawarima⌐su (sawaru, sawatte)

しゃく[癪]に障ります(障る, 障って)

offensive: ... is ~ ... ga shaku ni sawarima⌐su (sawaru, sawatte) ...がしゃく[癪]に障ります (障る, 障って)

offer mōshi⌐-komi 申し込み; (makes an offer) mōshi⌐-komima⌐su (-ko⌐⌐mu, -ko⌐⌐nde) 申し込みます(込 む, 込んで)

offering mōshi⌐-de 申し出, mōshi⌐-komi 申し込み; (public) mōshi⌐-ire 申し入れ

office (business) jimu⌐-sho 事務 所; (government) (o-)yakụsho (お)役所; (within the company) sha⌐nai 社内; (job) shokụ⌐ 職, tsutome⌐ (o-tsụtome) 勤め(お勤め), (post) yakụ⌐ (o-yaku) 役(お役); (place of employment) tsụtome-saki 勤め先

office attendance shụkkin 出勤

office boy/girl kyū⌐ji 給仕

office clerk/worker jimu⌐-in 事 務員

officer (military) shō⌐kō 将校; **police ~** oma⌐wari-san おまわ り[お巡り]さん, keikan 警官

office work ji⌐mu 事務

official (public) ōyake (no) 公 (の); (a government official) yakunin 役人

offing, offshore oki 沖

Off Limits ''Tachiiri kinshi'' "立

ち入り禁止"

off the rack (ready to wear) puretapo⌐rute プレタポルテ

off the track: gets ~ dassen shima⌐su (suru, shite) 脱線します(する, して)

often yo⌐ku よく, tabitabi たびたび, shi⌐bashiba しばしば, se⌐sse-to せっせと

ogre oni⌐ 鬼

oh a⌐ ああ; **oh?** so⌐ desu ka そうですか; **oh??** a⌐ra⌐ あら; **oh well** ma⌐ まあ

oil abura 油, *(petroleum, machine oil)* sekiyu 石油; *(for lubricating cars)* o⌐iru オイル; **hair ~** poma⌐do ポマード

ointment nuri-gu⌐suri 塗り薬

O.K. 1. i⌐i desu いいです; *(I approve)* sansei (de⌐su) 賛成(です); *(safe; functioning)* dai-jo⌐bu (na) 大丈夫(な) **2. O.K.!** Yo⌐shi! よし!

Okinawa Okinawa 沖縄; Ryūkyū⌐ 琉球

old 1. *(not new)* furu⌐i 古い, *(from way back)* mukashi kara⌐ no 昔からの; kyū⌐(-) …旧… **2.** *(not young)* toshi-to⌐tta 年取った, rō-… 老…; *(old person)* rōji⌐n 老人

old: gets old toshi⌐ o torima⌐su (to⌐ru, to⌐tte) 年を取ります(取る, 取って), fukema⌐su (fuke⌐ru, fuke⌐te) 老けます(老ける, 老けて)

old: how old i⌐kutsu (o-ikutsu) いくつ(おいくつ), na⌐n-sai 何歳; *(age)* toshi⌐ 年 「(の)

older ue 上＝toshi-ue (no) 年上

older brother a⌐ni 兄; (o-)ni⌐i-san (お)兄さん

older sister ane 姉; (o-)ne⌐-san (お)姉さん

oldest ichiban (toshi-)ue (no) 一番(年)上(の)

old person toshiyo⌐ri⌐ (o-toshiyori) 年寄り(お年寄り), rōji⌐n 老人; *(man)* oji⌐i-san おじいさん, *(woman)* oba⌐-san おばあさん

olive ori⌐ibu オリーブ

...ology ...-gaku ...学

omelet omuretsu オムレツ; **~ wrapped around rice mixed with tidbits** omu-ra⌐isu オムライス

omen engi 縁起, zenchō 前兆

omit otoshima⌐su (oto⌐su, oto⌐shite) 落とします(落とす, 落として), habukima⌐su (habu⌐ku, habu⌐ite) 省きます(省く, 省いて), nokema⌐su (nokeru, nokete) のけ[除け]ます(のける, のけて), nukima⌐su (nuku, nuite) 抜きます(抜く, 抜いて), nozokima⌐su (nozoku, nozoite) 除きます(除く, 除いて); *(skips)* tobashima⌐su (tobasu, tobashite) とばします・飛ばします(とばす, とば

して); *(curtails)*
ryakushima̱su (ryaku̱su̱,
ryaku̱shite) 略します(略す,
略して)

omit: gets omitted ochima̱su
(ochi̱ru, o̱chite) 落ちます(落
ちる, 落ちて); nukema̱su
(nukeru, nukete) 抜けます(抜
ける, 抜けて); morema̱su
(more̱ru, mo̱rete) 漏れます
(漏れる, 漏れて)

on ... de ...で, *(located)* ... ni ...
に; *(atop)* ... no ue (de/ni) ...
の上(で/に)

on: has/puts on (clothes, etc.) →
wear

on: turns on (light, radio, etc.) ...
o tsukema̱su (tsuke̱ru,
tsuke̱te) ...を付けます(付け
る, 付けて)

once ichi-do̱ 一度, ik-ka̱i 一回;
ichiō 一応; *(sometime)* i̱tsu ka
いつか; ~ **did** shita koto̱ ga
arima̱su (a̱ru, a̱tte) した事が
あります(ある, あって)

once in a while tama ni たまに

one ichi̱ 一; hi̱totsu 一つ; hito-...
一..., ichi-... 一...; wa̱n ワン;
(person) hito̱ri (o-hito̱ri) 一
人(お一人), ichi̱-mei 一名; ~
of a pair, the other ~ kata̱hō
片方, kata̱ppō 片っ方,
kata̱ppo 片っぽ

one: small thing, piece i̱k-ko 一
個; **long thing** i̱p-pon 一本;
flat thing ichi̱-mai 一枚; **small**

animal/fish/bug ip-piki̱ 一匹;
large animal i̱t-tō 一頭; **bird**
ichi̱-wa 一羽; **machine/vehi-
cle** ichi̱-dai 一台; **book/
magazine** is-satsu̱ 一冊

one after another tsugi̱-tsugi ni
次々に, zo̱kuzoku 続々

one and the same hito̱tsu 一つ

one day ichi-nichi̱ 一日; *(a certain day)* a̱ru hi ある日; *(someday)* ichijitsu̱ 一日

one o'clock ichi̱-ji 一時

one-room (studio) apartment
wan-rū̱mu ワンルーム

oneself jibun 自分; wa̱re 我; ~
(as we might expect) sasuga no
... さすがの...

one side ippō̱ 一方

one time ichi-do̱ 一度, ik-ka̱i 一
回, ip-pe̱n 一遍

one-time ichi̱-ji (no) 一時(の);
ka̱tsute (no) かつて(の), i̱zen
(no) 以前(の)

one-way *(ticket)* katamichi
(-ki̱ppu) 片道(切符); *(traffic)*
ippō-tsū̱kō 一方通行

one word ichi̱-go 一語

one year ichi̱-nen 一年,
ik-ka̱nen 一か年; ~ **old**
hito̱tsu 一つ, i̱s-sai 一歳

onion *(green)* ne̱gi ねぎ・葱,
naga-ne̱gi 長ねぎ[葱],
nira̱ にら・韮; *(round bulb)*
tama-ne̱gi 玉ねぎ[葱]

only ta̱da ... ただ..., tatta ...
たった...; ... dake̱ ...だけ, ...

ba⌐kari ...ばかり; ... ni
sugi⌐nai (sugimase⌐n) ...に過ぎ
ない(過ぎません)
on the way tochū 途中
on the whole daitai だいたい・大
open 1. opens it akema⌐su
(akeru, akete) 開けます(開け
る, 開けて), *(opens it up)*
hirakima⌐su (hira⌐ku, hira⌐ite)
開きます(開く, 開いて);
(begins it) hajimema⌐su
(hajimeru, hajimete) 始めます
(始める, 始めて) **2. it opens**
akima⌐su (aku, aite) 開きます
(開く, 開いて); *(it begins)*
hajimarima⌐su (hajimaru,
hajimatte) 始まります(始ま
る, 始まって), *(a place, an
event)* o⌐pun shima(⌐)su (suru,
shite) オープンします(する,
して), kaijō shima⌐su (suru,
shite) 開場します(する, し
て), *(a shop/business)*
kaiten shima⌐su (suru,
shite) 開店します(する, し
て)
open(ly) *(publicly)* kōzen (no/to)
公然(の/と), ōyake (no/ni) 公
(の/に); *(candid)* o⌐pun (na/
ni) オープン(な/に),
sotchoku (na/ni) 率直
(な/に)
opener *(can)* kan-ki⌐ri⌐ 缶切り;
(bottle) sen-nu⌐ki⌐ 栓抜き
opening 1. *(inlet)* kuchi 口
2. *(gap)* suki(-ma) 透き(間)・

隙(間) **3.** *(of a place)* kaijō 開
場, o⌐pun オープン; ~ **ceremo-
ny** kaijō-shiki 開場式; ~ **time**
kaijō-ji⌐kan 開場時間
open space hi⌐ro⌐-ba 広場
open to the public kōkai (no) 公
開(の); **opens it to the public**
kōkai shima⌐su (suru, shite) 公
開します(する, して)
opera ka⌐geki 歌劇, o⌐pera オペ
ラ
operate *(machinery)* sōjū
shima⌐su (suru, shite) 操縦し
ます(する, して); *(vehicle)*
unten shima⌐su (suru, shite) 運
転します(する, して);
(business) keiei shima⌐su
(suru, shite) 経営します(する,
して)
operation *(surgical)* shu⌐jutsu 手
術; *(driving)* unten 運転;
(handling) sōjū 操縦; *(management)* keiei 経営; *(working)*
hataraki 働き
operator 1. *(telephone)* kōka⌐n-
shu 交換手 **2.** *(vehicle)* unte⌐n-
shu 運転手 **3.** *(business)* keie⌐i-
sha 経営者
operator-only *(bus)* wa⌐m-man
ワンマン
opinion i⌐ken (go-i⌐ken) 意見(ご
意見), kanga⌐e 考え,
(outlook) mikomi 見込み,
(observation) kansoku 観測;
(= public ~) yo⌐ron 世論
opium a⌐hen アヘン・阿片
opponent *(sports)* aite⌐ (o-aite)

相手（お相手）; *(rival)* teki 敵

opportunity kikaˈi 機会; *(opening)* suki(-ma) 透き（間）・隙（間）; *(opportune time)* jiˈki 時機, jiˈsetsu 時節; *(convenience)* tsugō 都合, tsuide ついで

oppose ... ni hantai shimaˈsu (suru, shite) ...に反対します（する，して），... o kobamimaˈsu (kobaˈmu, kobaˈnde) ...を拒みます（拒む，拒んで）; *(resists)* ... ni hankō shimaˈsu (suru, shite) ...に反抗します（する，して）; *(confronts)* ... ni tai-shimaˈsu (tai-suˈru, taˈi-shite) ...に対します（対する，対して），... to tairitsu shimaˈsu (suru, shite) ...と対立します（する，して），... ni taikō shimaˈsu (suru, shite) ...に対抗します（する，して）; *(faces)* ... ni mukaimaˈsu (mukau, mukatte) ...に向かいます（向かう，向かって）

opposite *(facing)* mukōˈ (no) (o-muˈkō) 向こう（の）（お向こう）; *(contrary)* gyaku (no) 逆（の），*(opposing)* hantai (no) 反対（の）

opposite side hantai-gawa 反対側, mukō-gawa 向こう側

opposition *(resistance)* hankō 反抗; *(confrontation)* taikō 対抗; **in ~ to** ... ni taikō shite ...に対抗して

oppress appaku shimaˈsu (suru, shite) 圧迫します（する，して）; **oppression** appaku 圧迫

optimism rakkan 楽観; **optimistic** rakkan-teki (na) 楽観的（な）

optional zuˈii (na) 随意（な）

or ... ka ...か; maˈtaˈ-wa または・又は

oral 1. kuchi no 口の, kuchi karaˈ no 口からの; keikō(-) 経口; **~ contraceptive** keikō-hiniˈn'yaku 経口避妊薬 **2.** *(verbal)* kōtō (no) 口頭（の）; **~ examination** kōtō-shiˈmon 口頭試問

orange oreˈnji オレンジ; *(Mandarin orange, tangerine)* miˈkan (o-miˈkan) みかん・蜜柑（おみかん）; *(bitter)* daidaˈi だいだい・橙

orange drink oreˈnji オレンジ; **orange soda pop** jūˈsu ジュース; **orange juice** orenji-jūˈsu オレンジジュース

orchid raˈn 蘭

order tsuide 次いで, juˈnjo 順序, jun 順; **alphabetical ~** ABC-jun エービーシー［ＡＢＣ］順; *(turn)* jumban 順番; *(grade, step)* daˈn 段, dankai 段階; *(procedure)* teˈjun 手順; *(rule)* kimari 決まり; *(command)* meirei 命令

order *(clothes, meal, etc.)* chūˈmon shimaˈsu (suru,

shite) 注文します(する, して);
(a person to do something)
... ni ii-tsuke̲ma̲ʾsu̲ (-tsuke̲ʾru,
-tsu̲ke̲ʾte) ...に言い付けます
(付ける, 付けて), mei-
jima̲ʾsu̲ (mei-ji̲ʾru, me̲ʾi-jite)
命じます(命じる, 命じて)
order: puts in ~ *(tidies up)*
katazukema̲ʾsu̲ (katazuke̲ʾru,
katazu̲ʾkete) 片付けます(片付
ける, 片付けて); *(arranges as
a set)* soroema̲ʾsu̲ (soroe̲ʾru,
soro̲ʾete) 揃えます・そろえま
す(揃える, 揃えて)
ordinarily heizei 平生, futsū 普
通, fu̲ʾdan 普段・ふだん
ordinary futsū (no) 普通(の),
tsūjō (no) 通常(の), tsu̲ʾne
(no) 常(の), fu̲ʾdan (no) 普段・
ふだん(の); ta̲ʾda (no) ただ
(の); *(average)* nami (no) 並
(の)
or else sore-to̲ʾmo それとも,
ma̲ta̲ʾ-wa または・又は, aru̲ʾi-
wa あるいは・或いは
organization *(setup)* so̲ʾshiki 組
織; *(structure)* kumi-tate 組み
立て, kōzō 構造; *(group)*
dantai 団体
organize *(sets up)* kumi-
tatema̲ʾsu̲ (-tate̲ʾru, -ta̲ʾtete)
組み立てます(立てる, 立て
て)
Orient Tōʾyō 東洋
origin kiʾgen 起源, gen'in 原因,
moto̲ʾ 元, okoriʾ 起こり,

hassei 発生; *(historical ~)*
engi 縁起; *(a person's origins)*
de 出
originally mo̲ʾto wa 元は・もとは,
motomoto 元々・もともと,
ho̲ʾnrai 本来, ga̲ʾnrai 元来,
ze̲ʾntai 全体; *(in itself)* jitai 自
体
ornament kazari(-mono) 飾り
(物), *(decoration)* sōshoku 装
飾, *(bric-a-brac)* oki-mono 置
物
orphan ko̲ʾji 孤児; **orphanage**
koji̲ʾ-in 孤児院
or something (like it) ... to̲ʾ ka ...
とか
Osaka Ōsaka 大阪; **~ Station**
Ōsaka̲ʾ-eki 大阪駅; **Osakan**
Ōsaka̲ʾ-jin 大阪人
other hoka (no) 他(の), betsu
(no) 別(の); *[bookish]* ta̲ʾ (no)
他(の); **~ companies/news-
papers** ta̲ʾsha 他社; → **every
other**
the ~ fellow aite̲ʾ (o-aite) 相手
(お相手)
the ~ side sempō 先方
on the ~ hand tahōʾ de wa 他
方では
the ~ day kon[o]aida̲ʾ こない
だ[この間]
other than ... yo̲ʾri ...より
otherwise sa̲ʾ-mo na̲ʾkereba さも
なければ, sōʾ ja na̲ʾi to そう
じゃないと
ouch! ita̲ʾi! 痛い!

ought to (do) (shi)-ta hō̱ ga ī̱i deshō（し）た方がいいでしょう，[*bookish*] (su)-ru be̱ki desu（す）るべきです

our(s) watakushi̱-tachi no わたくし[私]達の, wata̱shi̱-ta̱chi no わたし[私]達の

out so̱to e 外へ; (*away from home*) (o)-ru̱su (desu)（お）留守（です）, gaishutsu-chū (de̱su) 外出中（です）
　come/go out (... kara) dema̱su (de̱ru, de̱te) (...から)出ます（出る, 出て）
　let out (of a vehicle) oroshima̱su (oro̱su, oro̱shite) 降ろします（降ろす, 降ろして）

out (*baseball*) a̱uto アウト

outbound (from Tokyo) kudari 下り

outbreak toppatsu 突発; hassei 発生

outcome shi̱matsu 始末; (*result*) se̱ika 成果; (*product*) sambutsu 産物

outdoors so̱to (de/ni/e) 外（で/に/へ）; ya̱gai (de/no) 野外（で/の）; noten (de/no) 野天（で/の）; ~ **bath** noten-bu̱ro 野天風呂

outer: ~ **appearance** uwabe うわべ・上辺; ~ **lane/track** auto-kō̱su アウトコース; ~ **moat** soto-bori 外堀; ~ **side/surface** omote̱ 表; ~ **space**

u̱chū 宇宙

outfit: judo ~ jūdō̱-gi 柔道着; **karate** ~ karate̱-gi̱ 空手着

outflow de 出

outing (*picnic etc.*) ensoku 遠足

outlet 1. de̱guchi 出口; (*for water/emotion/goods*) hake̱-kuchi/-guchi はけ口/口; (*sales* ~) ure-kuchi 売れ口; (*store*) hamba̱i-ten 販売店 **2.** (*electric* ~) ko̱nse̱nto コンセント; (*plug*) sashi̱-komi 差し込み, pu̱ra̱gu プラグ

outlook mikomi 見込み, mitōshi 見通し

out loud ko̱e o da̱shite 声を出して

out of order: gets ~ kuruima̱su (kuru̱u, kuru̱tte) 狂います（狂う, 狂って）

out of place ba-chi̱gai (no) 場違い（の）; **slips** ~ zurema̱su (zure̱ru, zu̱rete) ずれます（ずれる, ずれて）

out of service kaisō(-chū) 回送（中）; **a car** ~ kaisō̱-sha 回送車

out of the way: gets ~ dokima̱su (doku, doite) どきます・退く（どく, どいて）, nokima̱su (noku, noite) のきます・退きます（のく, のいて）

out of touch with ... ni uto̱i ...に疎い・うとい

outrage rambō 乱暴; → **indignation**

outrageous tonde-mo na˺i とん
    でもない, tonda とんだ
outset *(beginning)* ha˺na はな・端,
    saisho 最初
outside so˺to (de/ni) 外(で/に);
    the outside soto-gawa 外側,
    hata はた・端, ga˺ibu 外部,
    gaime⌐n 外面
outside corner ka˺do 角
outside of *(other than)* ... no
    hoka ...の他, ... i˺gai ...以外
outsider *(stranger)* yoso˺ no hito˺
    よその人, yoso-mono よそ者,
    tanin 他人; hata no mono˺ 端
    の者, monga˺i-kan 門外漢
outskirts *(of city)* shi˺gai 市外,
    (to˺shi no) shūhen (都市の)周
    辺
outstanding meda˺tta ... 目立っ
    た..., meda˺tte ima˺su 目立っ
    ています
outstandingly meda˺tte 目立って
outward appearance mikake 見
    かけ
outwardly mikake wa 見かけは
outwitted: gets ~ (u˺maku)
    yararema˺su (yarareru,
    yararete) (うまく)やられます
    (やられる, やられて)
oven te˺mpi 天火, kama かま・窯,
    kamado かまど・竈
over *(above)* ... no ue˺ (de/ni) ...
    の上(で/に); *(more than)* ...
    i˺jō ...以上; → **overly**
over *(finished)* ... o (shi)-te
    shimatta ...を(し)てしまった,

... o (shi)-chatta ...を(し)ちゃ
    った; owarima˺shita (owatta,
    owatte) 終わりました(終わっ
    た, 終わって)
over: leaves ~ nokoshima˺su
    (noko˺su, noko˺shite) 残しま
    す(残す, 残して)
over: 1. over(does) (shi)-
    sugima˺su (-sugi˺ru, -su˺gite)
    (し)過ぎます(過ぎる, 過ぎ
    て); mu˺ri ni shima˺su (suru,
    shite) 無理にします(する, し
    て) **2. does it over** (shi)-
    naoshima˺su (-nao˺su,
    -nao˺shite) (し)直します(直
    す, 直して)
over again = again
overall *(composite)* sōgō-teki
    (na) 総合的(な)
overcharge (for) borima˺su
    (bo˺ru, bo˺tte) ぼります(ぼる,
    ぼって), fukkakema˺su
    (fukkake˺ru, fukka˺kete) ふっ
    かけます(ふっかける, ふっか
    けて); **gets overcharged for**
    ... o borarema˺su (borare˺ru,
    bora˺rete) ...をぼられます(ぼ
    られる, ぼられて),
    fukkakcrarcma˺su
    (fukkakerare˺ru,
    fukkakera˺rete) ふっかけられ
    ます(ふっかけられる, ふっ
    かけられて)
overcoat gaitō 外套, o˺ba オー
    バー
overdo (it) mu˺ri o shima˺su 無理

をします, (sore o) mu˺ri ni shima˺su (suru, shi̱te) (それを)無理にします(する, して)

overflow afurema˺su (afure˺ru, afu˺rete) あふれ[溢れ]ます (あふれる, あふれて)

overlap daburima˺su (dabu˺ru, dabu˺tte) だぶります(だぶる, だぶって)

overly ammari あんまり; ... -sugima˺su (-sugi˺ru, -su˺gite) ... 過ぎます(過ぎる, 過ぎて); ~ **strict** yakamashi˺i やかましい

overquilt kake-bu˺ton 掛け布団

overseas ka˺igai 海外

oversee kantoku shima˺su (suru, shi̱te) 監督します(する, して)

overseer kantoku 監督

overshoes ama˺-gutsu 雨靴, ōbāshū˺zu オーバーシューズ

overtake ... ni oi-tsu̱kima˺su (-tsu̱ku˺, -tsu˺ite) ...に追い付きます(付く, 付いて)

over there mukō˺ (o-mu˺kō) 向こう(お向こう); (where you are) soko そこ, sochira/sotchi˺ そちら/そっち; (where they are) asoko/asu̱ko あそこ/あすこ, achira/atchi˺ あ

ちら/あっち

overthrow taoshima˺su (tao˺su, tao˺shi̱te) 倒します(倒す, 倒して)

overtime: runs ~ ji˺kan ga ō˺bā shima(˺)su (suru, shi̱te) 時間がオーバーします(する, して); ~ **work** zangyō 残業

overwork mu˺ri o shima˺su (suru, shi̱te) 無理をします(する, して)

owe (a person money) (hi̱to ni kane o) karite ima˺su (iru, ite) (人に金を)借りています(いる, いて)

owing to ... (no) se˺i de ...(の)せいで; → **because**

owl fu̱ku˺rō ふくろう・梟

own (possesses) mo˺tte ima˺su (iru, ite) 持っています(いる, いて); (one's own) jibun no 自分の, shoyū no 所有の

owner (mochi˺-)nushi (持ち)主; (master) shu˺jin 主人; (landowner) ji-nushi 地主

ox(en) ushi 牛; **how many oxen** na˺n-tō 何頭

oxygen sa˺nso 酸素

oyster (u˺mi no) ka˺ki (海の)かき・牡蠣

— P —

Pacific Ocean Taiheˈiyō 太平洋

pacifier *(for baby)* o-shaˈburi お
しゃぶり

pacify shizumemaˈsu
(shizumeˈru, shizuˈmete) 静め
ます・鎮めます(静[鎮]める，
静[鎮]めて)；*(soothes)*
nadamemaˈsu (nadameˈru,
nadaˈmete) なだめます・宥め
ます(なだめる，なだめて)；
(suppresses an uprising)
osamemaˈsu (osameˈru,
osaˈmete) 収めます(収める，
収めて)

pack 1. *(of cards)* (toraˈmpu)
hitoˈ-kumi (トランプ)一組
2. *(= package)* *(of cigarettes)*
(tabako) hitoˈ-hako (たばこ)
一箱

pack 1. *(one's bags)* ni-zuˈkuri o
shimaˈsu (suru, shiˈte) 荷造り
をします(する，して) **2.** *(=
wraps it up)* tsutsumimaˈsu
(tsutsuˈmu, tsutsuˈnde) 包みま
す(包む，包んで)，hōsō
shimaˈsu (suru, shiˈte) 包装し
ます(する，して)

package kozuˈtsumi 小包；→
packet

packet (kogata) hōsōˈ-butsu (小
型)包装物

pad *(= note ~)* memo-chō メ
モ帳

padded: ~ **garment** wata-iˈreˈ 綿
入れ；~ **bathrobe** taˈnzeˈn 丹
前 = dotera どてら；~ **quilt**
futon (o-futoˈn) 布団(お布団)

page pēji ページ

pagoda tōˈ 塔

pain 1. itamiˈ 痛み；*(suffering)*
kurushiˈmiˈ 苦しみ **2.** *(distresses)* kurushimemaˈsu
(kurushimeˈru, kurushiˈmete)
苦しめます(苦しめる，苦し
めて) **3. takes (great) pains**
honeˈ o orimaˈsu (oˈru, oˈtte)
骨を折ります(折る，折って)

painful itaˈi 痛い；kurushiˈi 苦し
い，tsurai 辛い

paint penki (o nurimaˈsu; nuru,
nutte) ペンキ(を塗ります；塗
る，塗って)

painter *(artist)* gaka 画家；*(housepainter)* penki-ya ペンキ屋

painting *(picture)* eˈ 絵，...-ga ...
画

pair (it-)tsui (一)対；*(of footwear)* is-soku 一足；→ **two**

pal nakamaˈ (o-nakama) 仲間
(お仲間)

palace *(in Tokyo)* kōˈkyo 皇居；
(in Kyoto) goˈsho 御所；*(in*

general) kyūden 宮殿

pale 1. *(color)* usui COLOR (no) 薄い COLOR (の) **2.** *(face)* kao ga ao¹i 顔が青い; **turns pale** kao ga a¹oku narima¹su (na¹ru, na¹tte) 顔が青くなります(なる, なって)

palm *(tree)* ya¹shi やし・椰子; *(of hand)* te¹-no¹-hira 手のひら

pamper amayakashima¹su (amayaka¹su, amayaka¹shite) 甘やかします(甘やかす, 甘やかして)

pamphlet pa¹nfure¹tto パンフレット; *(leaflet, handbill)* bira びら・ビラ

pan na¹be (o-nabe) 鍋(お鍋); *(earthenware)* hōro¹ku¹ ほうろく・焙烙

pan: food cooked and served in a ～ nabe¹-mono 鍋物

pancake: seasoned ～ okonomi-yaki お好み焼き

pan-fry itamema¹su (itame¹ru, ita¹mete) 炒めます(炒める, 炒めて)

pant *(for breath)* aegima¹su (ae¹gu, ae¹ide) あえぎ[喘ぎ]ます(あえぐ, あえいで)

panties zurōsu ズロース, pa¹ntii パンティー

pantry *(dish cupboard)* shokki-to¹dana 食器戸棚; *(room)* shokki¹-shitsu 食器室

pants zubo¹n ズボン, *(slacks)* sura¹kkusu スラックス,

pa¹ntsu パンツ; *(underpants)* zubo¹n-shita ズボン下; *(women's)* pa¹ntaron パンタロン, *(underpants)* zurō¹su ズロース

paper 1. kami¹ 紙; *(blank)* yō¹shi 用紙, *(squared)* genkō-yō¹shi 原稿用紙; *(tissues)* chiri-gami ちり紙; *(Japanese)* wa¹shi 和紙 **2.** *(newspaper)* shimbun 新聞, *(morning)* chōkan 朝刊, *(evening)* yūkan 夕刊 **3.** *(research report)* happyō 発表, kenkyū-ha¹ppyō 研究発表 **4.** → document

paper: colored ～ iro¹gami 色紙

paper bag kami-bu¹kuro 紙袋

paperclip kami-ba¹sami 紙挟み, kuri¹ppu クリップ

paperfolding (art) ori¹gami 折り紙・おりがみ

paper-hanger/-repairer hyōgu-¹ya 表具屋

paper money shihei/shi¹hei 紙幣/紙幣; *(currency bills)* ...¹-satsu ...札 **(two $100 bills** hyakudoru¹-satsu ni¹-mai 百ドル札二枚)

paperweight bunchin 文鎮

paradise te¹ngoku 天国

paralysis ma¹hi 麻痺; **infantile** ～ *(polio)* shōni-ma¹hi 小児麻痺

parasol (umbrella) hi-ga¹sa 日傘

parcel kozu¹tsumi 小包; **parcel post** kozutsumi-yū¹bin 小包郵便

pardon yurushima¹su (yuru¹su,

yuru̱shite) 許します(許す, 許
して)

Pardon me! Shi̱tsu̱rei
shima(⌐)su. 失礼します;
Sumimase̱n. すみません; Go-
men kudasa̱i. ごめん下さい.

pare *(peels it)* mukima̱su (muku,
muite) むきます(むく, むい
て)

paregoric geri-dome 下痢止め

parent oya̱ 親, **your** ~ oyago-
san 親御さん; **parents** oya̱-
tachi 親達, *(= father and
mother)* ryo̱shin 両親, **your**
~s go-ryo̱shin ご両親

parent and child o̱yako 親子

Paris Pa̱ri(i) パリ(ー)

park kōen 公園; *(a car)* chūsha
shima̱su (suru, shite) 駐車し
ます(する, して)

parking chūsha 駐車; ~ **lot**
chūsha-jō 駐車場, pū̱ru プー
ル; **No** ~ chūsha kinshi 駐車
禁止; **free** ~ muryō-chū̱sha
無料駐車; **pay** ~ yūryō-
chū̱sha 有料駐車

parliament → **diet**

parlor *(drawing room)* kyakuma
客間; **mahjong** ~ mājan-ya
マージャン[麻雀]屋

parrot ōmu おうむ・鸚鵡

parsley: Japanese ~ seri̱ せり・

part 1. *(portion)* bu̱bun 部分, ichi̱-bu 一
部; *(portion)* bu̱n 分, *(section)*
bu̱ 部 **2.** *(passage of a text)* ...
tokoro̱ ...所; **this** ~ koko ここ

3. *(parting of hair)* wake-me
分け目 **4.** *(role)* yakuwa⌐ri⌐
役割, yaku̱ (o-yaku) 役
(お役)

part: I for my part watashi wa
watashi de わたし[私]はわた
し[私]で

part *(= divides it)* wakema̱su
(wake̱ru, wa̱kete) 分けます
(分ける, 分けて); *(= they
separate)* wakarema̱su
(wakare̱ru, waka̱rete) 別れま
す(別れる, 別れて)

participant sanka̱-sha 参加者

participate sa⌐nka shima̱su
(suru, shite) 参加します(する,
して) 「詞

particle *(auxiliary word)* joshi 助

particular 1. *(especial)* tokubetsu
no 特別の; *(separate)* betsu no
別の; *(peculiar)* to̱kushu na 特
殊な, tokuyū no 特有の
2. *(specific)* a̱ru ... ある...,
kore to yū ... これと言う...;
→ **choosy**

particular: in ~ to̱ku-ni 特に,
toriwake とりわけ

particularly: not ~ betsu ni 別に
+ NEGATIVE

particulars → **details**

parting *(separating)* wakare̱ (o-
wakare) 別れ(お別れ)

partition shi̱kiri 仕切り 「手)

partner aite̱ (o-aite) 相手(お相

part-time work aruba̱ito アルバ
イト

part with ... o hanashima῁su
(hana῁su, hana῁shite) ...を離し
ます(離す, 離して)

party 1. enkai 宴会, pā῁tii パーテ
ィー, ...-kai 会; → **recep-
tion 2. political** ~ seitō 政党

pass 1. *(commuter ticket)* teiki῁-
ken 定期券 **2.** *(mountain pass)*
tōge῁ 峠, ...-tō῁ge ...峠 **3.** *(sexual overture)* mō῁shon モー
ション; **makes a pass at** ... ni
mō῁shon o kakema῁su
(kake῁ru, ka῁kete) ...にモー
ションをかけます(かける,
かけて)

pass *(goes past)* ...o tōrima῁su
(tō῁ru, tō῁tte) ...を通ります(通
る, 通って); *(exceeds)*
sugima῁su (sugi῁ru, su῁gite) 過
ぎます(過ぎる, 過ぎて);
(hands over) watashima῁su
(watasu, watashite) 渡します
(渡す, 渡して); *(hands
around)* mawashima῁su
(mawasu, mawashite) 回しま
す(回す, 回して); *(salt,
sugar, etc.)* torima῁su (to῁ru,
to῁tte) 取ります(取る, 取って);
(exam) (shike῁n ni) gōkaku
shima῁su (suru, shite) (試験
に)合格します(する, して),
(shike῁n o) pa῁su-shimasu
(pa῁su-suru, pa῁su-shite) (試験
を)パスします(パスする, パ
スして)

pass: *(time passes)* tachima῁su

(ta῁tsu, ta῁tte) 経ちます(経つ,
経って), hema῁su (he῁ru,
he῁te) 経ます(経る, 経て),
keika shima῁su (suru, shite) 経
過します(する, して);
(passes time) sugoshima῁su
(sugo῁su, sugo῁shite) 過ごしま
す(過ごす, 過ごして)

pass: (overtake and) pass *(a vehicle)* ... o oi-koshima῁su (oi-
ko῁su, oi-ko῁shite) ...を追い越
します(追い越す, 追い越し
て); **No Passing** oi-koshi
kinshi 追い越し禁止

pass: pass it on tsutaema῁su
(tsutae□e῁ru, tsutae□ete) 伝え
ます(伝える, 伝えて);
is passed on tsutawarima῁su
(tsutawa□ru, tsutawa□tte) 伝
わります(伝わる, 伝わって)

passage tsūkō 通行; *(thoroughfare)* tōri῁ 通り, tsū῁ro 通路,
(corridor) rōka 廊下; *(of text)*
... tokoro῁ ...ところ, issetsu□
一節

passbook kayoi 通い, tsūchō 通
帳

passenger jōkyaku 乗客,
ryokyaku 旅客; ~ **car**
(automobile) jōyō῁-sha 乗用車,
(train) kyakusha 客車; ~
ticket jōsha῁-ken 乗車券

passer-by tsūkō-nin 通行人

pass out 1. *(loses consciousness)*
i῁shiki o ushinaima῁su
(ushinau, ushinatte) 意識を失

いstandaards (失う, 失って)

2. → **distribute**

passport ryoken 旅券, pasupo̅'to
パスポート

past *(the ~)* ka'ko 過去; *(... ~
the hour)* ...-(fu̅'n-)sugi ...(分)
過ぎ

paste nori のり・糊; *(pastes it)* ...ni
nori̅ o tsukema'su (tsuke̅'ru,
tsuke̅'te) ...にのりを付けます
(付ける, 付けて)

pastime do̅ra'ku̅ (o-do̅raku̅') 道
楽(お道楽); goraku 娯楽,
shu̅'mi 趣味

pastor bo̅'kushi 牧師

pastry (o-)ka'shi (お)菓子

pat nadema'su (nade̅'ru, na̅'dete)
なで[撫で]ます(なでる, な
でて)

patch 1. *(patches it)* (... ni) tsugi
o atema'su (ateru, atete) (...
に)継ぎを当てます(当てる,
当てて), tsuzurima'su
(tsuzu̅'ru, tsuzu̅'tte) つづり
[綴り]ます(つづる, つづっ
て); *(a patch)* tsugi 継ぎ

2. → **field**

path ko̅'michi 小道, michi 道

patience ga'man 我慢; **loses ~**
shibire̅' o kirashima'su
(kira̅'su, kira̅'shite) しびれを
切らします(切らす, 切らし
て)

patient 1. *(puts up with it)*
ga'man shima(̅)su (suru,
shite) 我慢します(する, して);

(has patience) gaman-zuyo̅'i 我
慢強い, **2.** *(medical)* kanja 患者,
(ill person) byo̅nin 病人

patiently jitto じっと; ga'man
shite 我慢して

patrolman ju̅'nsa 巡査

patron *(customer, client)* toku̅'i
得意

pattern pata̅'n/pata̅'n パターン/
パタン, moyo̅ 模様, teho̅'n (o-
teho̅n) 手本(お手本), kata' 型,
gara 柄

paulownia (tree/wood) kiri 桐

pause *(rest)* yasumi̅' (o-yasumi)
休み(お休み); *(break in talk
etc.)* kire-me̅' 切れ目

pavement *(roadway)* shado̅ 車道;
(walkway) hodo̅ 歩道

pawn *(something pawned)*
shichi̅' 質

pawnbroker/pawnshop shichi̅'-
ya' 質屋

pay *(one's wage)* kyu̅'ryo̅ (o-
kyu̅'ryo̅) 給料(お給料), ho̅kyu̅
俸給

pay *(not free)* yu̅ryo̅ (no) 有料
(の)

pay: pays (out) haraima'su
(hara̅'u, hara̅'tte) 払います(払
う, 払って), dashima'su
(da̅'su, da̅'shite) 出します(出
す, 出して); *(taxes)*
osamema'su (osame̅'ru,
osa̅'mete) 納めます(納める,
納めて); **pays attention to** ...
ni chu̅'i o haraima'su (hara̅'u,

hara'tte) ...に注意を払います
(払う, 払って), ... ni ne'n o
irema'su (ireru, irete) ...に念を
入れます(入れる, 入れて);
pays compliments o-seji o
iima'su (yū, itte/yutte) お世辞
を言います(言う, 言って/ゆ
って); **pays one's share**
buntan shima'su (suru, shite)
分担します(する, して)

payday kyūryō'-bi 給料日

payment shiharai 支払い, *(of
taxes)* nōzei 納税

pay parking yūryō-chū'sha 有料
駐車

pay phone aka-de'nwa 赤電話

pay raise be'a ベア

peace heiwa 平和; **~ of mind**
anshin 安心

Peace Corps heiwa-bu'tai 平和部
隊; **(member)** heiwa-buta'i-in
平和部隊員

peaceful *(calm)* oda'yaka (na) 穏
やか(な), no'doka (na) のど
か[長閑か](な)

peach momo もも・桃

peacock kujaku くじゃく・孔雀

peak itadaki 頂, chōjō' 頂上;
mine' 峰; *(highpoint)* chō'ten
頂点

peanuts Nanki'n-mame 南京豆,
pi'ina'tsu ピーナツ

pear nashi' なし・梨

pearl shinju 真珠

pearl diver *(woman)* a'ma 海女

Pearl Harbor Shinju'-wan 真珠
湾

peas e'ndō えんどう・豌豆,
endō'-mame えんどう豆・豌豆
豆

pebble koishi 小石; jari 砂利

peck (at) (... o) tsu(t)tsukima'su
(tsu(t)tsu'ku, tsu(t)tsu'ite) (...
を)つ(っ)つきます(つ(っ)つ
く, つ(っ)ついて)

peculiar okashi'i おかしい,
ki'myō (na) 奇妙(な), he'n
(na) 変(な); → **particular**

pedal pe'daru ペダル; → **gas
pedal**

pediatrician shōnika'-i 小児科医,
shōni-ka 小児科

pediatrics shōni-ka 小児科

peek (... o) nozokima'su
(nozoku, nozoite) (...を)のぞ
き[覗き]ます(のぞく, のぞ
いて)

peel 1. *(rind)* kawa' 皮 **2. peels it ...**
no kawa' o mukima'su (muku,
muite) ...の皮をむきます(む
く, むいて); **peels it off**
hagima'su (ha'gu, ha'ide) はぎ
[剥ぎ]ます(はぐ, はいで); **it
peels off** hagema'su (hage'ru,
ha'gete) はげ[剥げ]ます(はげ
る, はげて)

peep (at/into) → **peek**

peephole nozoki⌐-ana のぞき
[覗き]穴

peeping Tom nozoki-ya のぞき
[覗き]屋

peewee chi'bi ちび, chibi-me ち
びめ

peg kugi くぎ・釘

Peking Pe̱kin ペキン・北京

pen pe̱n ペン; *(ballpoint)* bōru-pen ボールペン; *(fountain)* manne̱n-hitsu 万年筆

penalty *(fine)* bakkin 罰金

pencil empitsu 鉛筆 (**1** i̱p-pon 一本, **2** ni̱-hon 二本, **3** sa̱m-bon 三本, **10** ji̱p-pon 十本; **how many** na̱m-bon 何本)

penetrate tōrima̱su (tō̱ru, tō̱tte) 通り[透り]ます(通[透]る, 通[透]って), tōshima̱su (tō̱su, tō̱shite) 通し[透し]ます(通[透]す, 通[透]して); *(soaks in, permeates)* shimima̱su (shimiru, shimite) 染みます(染みる, 染みて); *(violates)* okashima̱su (oka⌐su, oka⌐shite) 犯します(犯す, 犯して)

peninsula hantō 半島

penis pe̱nisu ペニス, inkei 陰茎, dankon 男根, mara̱ まら; *[baby talk]* (o-)chi̱mpo （お）ちんぽ, (o-)chi̱nko （お）ちんこ

pension nenkin 年金, taishoku-neṉkin 退職年金

people hito 人, … hito̱ …人; hito̱-tachi 人達; hito̱bito 人々, *(at large)* se̱ken 世間; *(of a nation)* kokumin 国民; *(populace, civilians)* minshū 民衆; *[counted]* …(⌐)-nin …人, *[bookish]* …⌐-mei …名 (**how many** na̱n-nin 何人; **1 person** hito̱ri 一人, **2** futari̱ 二人, **3** san-ni̱n 三人, **4** yo-ni̱n 四人, **5** go-ni̱n 五人, **10** jū̱-nin 十人, **14** jū̱yo-nin 十四人, **100** hyaku̱-nin 百人)

people/authorities concerned with … … no kanke̱i-sha …の関係者

pep ge̱nki 元気

pepper *(black)* koshō̱ こしょう・胡椒, *(Japanese mild)* sanshō さんしょう・山椒; *(green/bell)* pi̱iman ピーマン

peppermint hakka はっか・薄荷

pepper sprout ki̱-no-me 木の芽, ko̱nome 木の芽

peppery kara̱i 辛い

percent (…-)pāse̱nto （…）パーセント; **ten ～** ichi̱-wari 一割, **one ～** ichi̱-bu 一分, **eleven ～** ichi̱-wari ichi̱-bu 一割一分

percentage wari 割, wariai 割合; ri̱tsu 率

perfect 1. kanzen (na) 完全(な), mattaku̱ (no) 全く(の) **2. perfects it** kansei shima̱su (suru, shite) 完成します(する, して)

perfect circle, perfectly round mammaru (no) 真ん丸・まんまる(の)

perfectly kanzen ni 完全に, mattaku̱ 全く, maru de まるで, pitta̱ri ぴったり; → **absolutely, totally**

perform okonaima̱su (okonau,

okonatte) 行います(行う, 行って); ~ **an operation** shu'jutsu shima(')su (-suru, -shite)手術します(する, して)

performance 1. *(realization)* jikkō 実行 **2.** *(daytime/evening ~)* (hiru'/yo'ru no) bu' (昼/夜の)部 **3.** *(artistic)* e'ngi 演技; → **show**

performance: beginning a ~ kaien 開演 **during the ~** kaien-chū 開演中

performer engi'-sha 演技者

perfume kōsui 香水

perfunctory ii-kagen (na) いい加減(な)

perhaps ... ka' mo shiremase'n/ wakarimase'n (shirenai/ wakara'nai) ...かも知れません /分かりません(知れない/分からない), ta'bun ... deshō 多分...でしょう; ma'zu まず

peril kiken 危険

perilla shiso しそ・紫蘇

period *(of time)* kika'n 期間, *(limit)* ki'gen 期限; *(era)* jidai 時代, ...-ji'dai ...時代; *(punctuation)* shūshi'-fū 終止符

periodic te'iki (no) 定期(の)

perish horobima'su (horobi'ru, horo'bite) 滅びます(滅びる, 滅びて)

permanent residence ho'nseki 本籍; **place of ~** honse'ki'-chi 本籍地

permanent wave pa'ma パーマ

permission kyo'ka 許可; **without ~** mu'dan de 無断で, kotowa'ri' mo na'ku 断りもなく

permissive amai 甘い

permit → **allow**; → **permission**; → **license**

pernicious akushitsu (na) 悪質(な)

perpendicular suichoku (no) 垂直(の)

perpetrate okashima'su (oka'su, oka'shite) 犯します(犯す, 犯して)

perplexed: gets ~ komarima'su (koma'ru, koma'tte) 困ります(困る, 困って); mayoima'su (mayo'u, mayo'tte) 迷います(迷う, 迷って)

perseverant gaman-zuyo'i 我慢強い; **perseverance** ga'man 我慢

persevere ga'man shima'su (suru, shite) 我慢します(する, して)

persimmon (ki' no) kaki (木の)柿

person hito 人, ... hito' ...人; *(honored)* ...kata' (o-kata) ...方(お方); ... mono' ...者, ...ya'tsu ...やつ・奴; ko 個, te 手; ...'-jin ...人, ...-'nin ...人; ...'-sha ...者; hito'ri 一人; *(being)* sonzai 存在; → **people**

personage ji'mbutsu 人物; *(being)* sonzai 存在

personal kojin-teki (na) 個人的(な); *(for one's own use)*

jibun-yō (no) 自分用(の)

personal appearance nariꜜ (o-naꜜri) なり(おなり); kiꜜryō 器量

personal business jibun no yōꜜ 自分の用, shiyō 私用

personal computer paso-kon パソコン

personal effects temaꜜwari 手回り, temawariꜜ-hin 手回り品

personal experience taiken 体験

personal history rireki 履歴; rireꜜkiꜜ-shoꜜ 履歴書

personally jiꜜka-ni じか[直]に

personnel (section) jinji-ka 人事課

person-to-person call shimei-tsuꜜwa 指名通話

perspire → **sweat**

persuade settoku shimaꜜsu (suru, shite) 説得します(する, して); (… ni sore o) nattoku sasemaꜜsu (…にそれを)納得させます

persuasion settoku 説得; → **belief**

pertain to … ni kan-shimaꜜsu (kan-suꜜru, kaꜜn-shite) …に関します(関する, 関して)

pessimism hikan 悲観; **pessimistic** hikan-teki (na) 悲観的(な)

pet peꜜtto ペット; *(strokes, pats)* nademaꜜsu (nadeꜜru, naꜜdete) なで[撫で]ます(なでる, なでて)

petrol → **gasoline**

petroleum sekiyu 石油

petticoat koshi-maki 腰巻き

petty saꜜsai (na) ささい[些細](な), sasaꜜyaka (na) ささやか(な); ~ **cash** saꜜsai na kane ささいな金

pharmaceuticals yakuꜜzai 薬剤

pharmacy yakkyoku 薬局

pheasant kiji きじ・雉

phenomenon genshō 現象

Philippines F(u)iꜜriꜜ(p)pin フィリ[フイリ](ッ)ピン, Hiꜜriꜜ(p)-pin ヒリ(ッ)ピン

philosopher tetsugaꜜkuꜜ-sha 哲学者; **philosophy** tetsuꜜgaku 哲学

phone → **telephone**

phonograph chikuoꜜn-ki 蓄音機

phony nise (no) にせ・偽(の)

photograph 1. shashin 写真 **(how many** naꜜm-mai 何枚); ~ **of a wanted criminal** tehai-shaꜜshin 手配写真 **2. takes a** ~ **of** … no shashin o torimaꜜsu (toꜜru, toꜜtte) …の写真を撮ります(撮る, 撮って)

photographer shashin-ka 写真家

phrase moꜜnku 文句, kuꜜ 句

physical karada (no) 体(の), shiꜜntai (no) 身体(の)

physical exam shintai-keꜜnsa 身体検査

physical exercises taisō 体操

physician isha 医者, o-isha (san) お医者(さん)

physicist butsuriga˺kŭ-sha 物理
学者; **physics** butsuri˺-gaku 物
理学

physiology seiri 生理; **physiologi-
cal** seiri-teki (na) 生理的(な)

physique taikaku 体格

pick → **choose**; *(plucks)*
tsumima˺su (tsumu, tsunde) 摘
みます(摘む, 摘んで); **picks
it up** ... o hiroima˺su (hirou,
hirotte) ...を拾います(拾う,
拾って); tsumamima˺su
(tsumamu, tsumande) つまみ
ます(つまむ, つまんで);
picks one's pocket surima˺su
(su˺ru, su˺tte˺) すります(する,
すって)

pickle 1. tsukemono 漬物; (o-)
shinko (お)しんこ[新香];
(Chinese) zāsai ザーサイ
2. pickles it tsukema˺su
(tsukeru, tsukete) 漬けます(漬
ける, 漬けて)

pickled daikon (radish)
takŭ˺(w)an たくあ[わ]ん

pickled ginger ga˺ri ガリ, su-
shō˹ga 酢しょうが[生姜]

pickled plum/apricot ume-
boshi/mme-boshi 梅干し・う
めぼし

pickpocket su˺ri すり

picnic ensoku 遠足, pi˺kuni˺kku
ピクニック; ~ **boxes** jūbako
(o-jū˹) 重箱(お重)

picture e˹ 絵; *(photo)* shashin 写
真; *(diagram, drawing)* zu 図;

~ **book** e-ho˹n 絵本; ~ **postcard** e-ha˺gaki 絵葉書; **the ~
quality** utsuri˹ 映り

picture: takes a ~ shashin o
torima˺su (to˺ru, to˺tte) 写真を
撮ります(撮る, 撮って);
utsushima˺su (utsu˺su˺,
utsu˺shite) 映します(映す, 映
して)

pie pa˺i パイ

piece: (one) ~ (i˺k)-ko (一)個,
(hito˹)-tsu (一)つ; *(a cut)* kire˹
切れ, hito˺-kire 一切れ

pier sambashi 桟橋, hato-ba 波
止場

pierce tōshima˺su (tō˺su, tō˺shite)
通します(通す, 通して)

pig buta 豚

pigeon ha˺to 鳩

pile 1. *(stake)* ku˺i くい・杭
2. *(heap)* (hito˹)-yama (一)
山

pile 1. piles them up
kasanema˺su (kasaneru,
kasanete) 重ねます(重ねる,
重ねて); **they pile up**
kasanarima˺su (kasanaru,
kasanatte) 重なります(重なる,
重なって) **2. piles it up**
tsumima˺su (tsumu, tsunde) 積
みます(積む, 積んで),
morima˺su (moru, motte) 盛り
ます(盛る, 盛って)

piles → **hemorrhoids**

pill *(medicine)* kusuri (o-kusu˺ri)
薬(お薬), *(specifically)*

gan'yaku 丸薬, jōzai 錠剤

pillar hashira 柱 (**1** i'p-pon 一本, **2** ni'-hon 二本, **3** sa'm-bon 三本; **how many** na'm-bon 何本)

pillow ma'kura まくら・枕 (**how many** na'm-mai 何枚)

pilot *(plane captain)* kichō' 機長

pimp po'mbiki ぽん引き, po'mpiki ぽん引き

pimple ni'kibi にきび, deki'-mo'no' (o-de'ki) できもの・出来物（おでき）

pin *(for hair)* pi'n ピン; *(for sewing)* ha'ri 針; tome-ba'ri 留め針

pinball (machine) pachinko パチンコ

pincers yattoko やっとこ

pinch tsunerima'su (tsune'ru, tsune'tte) つねります（つねる, つねって）

pine (tree) ma'tsu (no ki') 松（の木）

pineapple paina'ppuru パイナップル; **canned ～** pai-kan パイ缶

pinholder *(frog for flowers)* ke'nzan 剣山

pink momo-iro (no) 桃色（の）, pi'nku (no) ピンク（の）

pin money ko'zukai 小遣い

pin shell *(a kind of scallop)* taira'-gai 平貝, taira-gi たいらぎ・玉珧

pipe pa'ipu パイプ; *(tube)* tsutsu' 筒, ku'da 管

pipsqueak chi'bi ちび, chibi-me ちびめ

pirate kaizoku 海賊

piss → urine; urinate

pissoir → urinal

pistol pisutoru ピストル, kenjū 拳銃

pitcher: saké ～ *(decanter)* tokkuri とっくり・徳利; **water ～** mizusa'shi 水差し

pith shi'n 芯

pitiful, pitiable kawai-sō' (na) かわいそう（な）, ki-no-do'ku' (na) 気の毒（な）

pity *(pities)* dōjō shima'su (suru, shite) 同情します（する, して）; *(it is a pity)* zannen (na) 残念（な）

pizza pi'za ピザ

place tokoro' 所, basho 場所; *(assigned seat)* se'ki (o-se'ki) 席（お席）; *(for something)* ba 場, ...-ba ...場; *(to put something)* oki-ba 置き場; **how many places** nan-ka'sho 何か所・何箇所; **→ put**

place: out of ～, not from the right/best ～ ba-chi'gai (na/no) 場違い（な/の）

place: takes the ～ of ... ni kawarima'su (kawaru, kawatte) ...に代わります（代わる, 代わって）; **takes ～ → happen**

place of employment tsutome-saki 勤め先

plain 1. *(not gaudy)* jimi̱ (na) 地味(な), *(simple, frugal)* shi̱sso (na) 質素(な) **2.** *(flat land)* heiya 平野, heichi 平地

plainly *(clearly)* hakki̱ri (to) はっきり(と); *(simply)* assa̱ri (to) あっさり(と)

plan keikaku shima̱su (suru, shite) 計画します(する, して); kikaku (kikaku shima̱su; suru, shite) 企画(企画します; する, して); kuwada̱te̱ (kuwadatema̱su; kuwadate̱ru, kuwada̱tete) 企て(企てます; 企てる, 企てて); *(schedule)* yotei (shima̱su; suru, shite) 予定(します; する, して); *(scheme)* takurami̱ たくらみ・企み, *(devises)* takuramima̱su (takura̱mu, takura̱nde) たくらみ[企み]ます(たくらむ, たくらんで); *(intention)* tsumori (o-tsumori) つもり(おつもり), i̱to 意図

plane → **airplane**; **~ crash** tsuiraku 墜落

planetarium puranetaryū̱mu プラネタリューム, tenshō̱gi 天象儀

plank i̱ta 板

plant 1. *(a plant)* shoku̱butsu 植物; *(herb)* kusa̱ 草, *(shrub)* ki̱ 木, *(garden/potted)* ueki 植木 **2.** *(factory)* kōjō̱ 工場 **3.** *(plants it)* uema̱su (ueru,

uete) 植えます(植える, 植えて) 「草

plantain ōbako おおばこ・車前

plaster 1. sekkō 石こう[膏]; **adhesive plaster** bansōkō ばんそうこう・絆創膏 **2.** *(stucco)* shikkui しっくい・漆喰

plastic pura̱suchi̱kku プラスチック; *(vinyl)* bi̱niru/bini̱iru ビニル/ビニール; *(polyethylene)* pori(-) ポリ; **~ bag** pori-bu̱kuro ポリ袋

plate sara (o-sara) 皿(お皿); shokki 食器

platform 1. *(at station)* hō̱mu ホーム, nori-ba 乗り場; **~** *(non-passenger)* **ticket** nyūjō̱-ken 入場券 **2.** *(lecture ~)* endan 演壇, kōdan 講壇

play asobima̱su (asobu, asonde) 遊びます(遊ぶ, 遊んで); *(a game)* shima̱su (suru, shite) します(する, して); *(a stringed instrument)* hikima̱su (hiku, hiite) 弾きます(弾く, 弾いて); **~ hookey** → **hookey**

play *(drama)* shibai 芝居, engeki 演劇

player *(sports)* se̱nshu 選手

playground undō-jō 運動場

playing cards tora̱mpu トランプ

play it safe daiji̱ o torima̱su (to̱ru, to̱tte) 大事をとります(とる, とって)

plaza hi̱ro̱-ba̱ 広場

pleasant tanoshi⌐i 楽しい,
omoshiro⌐i おもしろい・面白
い, ureshi⌐i うれしい・嬉しい

Please ... do⌐zo ... どうぞ..., ...
te kudasa⌐i ...て下さい, o-
negai shima⌐su お願いします;
... te chōda⌐i ...てちょうだい

pleasure tanoshi⌐mi⌐ (o-
tanoshimi) 楽しみ(お楽しみ)

pleat ori-me⌐ 折り目

plectrum bachi⌐ ばち・撥

pledge chika⌐i 誓い; *(swears it)*
chikaima⌐su (chika⌐u,
chika⌐tte) 誓います(誓う,
誓って); → **promise**

plentiful yu⌐taka (na) 豊か(な)

plenty takusa⌐n たくさん・沢山

pliers *(pincers)* yattoko やっと
こ・鋏, pe⌐nchi ペンチ

plight *(one gets into)* hame⌐ は
め・羽目

plot *(story line)* su⌐ji 筋; *(scheme,
trick)* kciryaku 計略,
hakarigo⌐to⌐ はかりごと・謀

plow 1. *(a plow)* suki すき・鋤
2. *(plows it)* tagayashima⌐su
(tagaya⌐su, tagaya⌐shite) 耕し
ます(耕す, 耕して),
sukima⌐su (suku, suite) すき
[鋤き]ます(すく, すいて)

pluck tsumima⌐su (tsumu,
tsunde) 摘みます(摘む, 摘ん
で)

plug se⌐n 栓; *(electricity)*
pu⌐ra⌐gu プラグ, sashi-
komi 差し込み, ko⌐nse⌐nto

コンセント

plum 1. su-momo すもも・李
2. *(= Japanese apricot)* ume/
mme 梅; **pickled** ～ ume-
boshi/mme-boshi 梅干し; ～
tree ume/mme 梅; ～ **wine**
ume-shu/mme-shu 梅酒

plumber suidō-ya (san) 水道屋
(さん); suidō⌐-kyoku 水道局

plumbing suidō (no se⌐tsubi) 水
道(の設備); ～ **service** suidō
水道

plump futo⌐i 太い

plunder ubaima⌐su (uba⌐u,
uba⌐tte) 奪います(奪う, 奪っ
て)

plus purasu プラス

p.m. *(afternoon)* go⌐go 午後

pneumonia haien 肺炎

poached eggs otoshi-ta⌐mago 落
とし卵[玉子]

pocket poke⌐tto ポケット;
kaichū (no) 懐中(の)

pocketbook handoba⌐ggu ハンド
バッグ; → **purse**

pocket money ko⌐zukai 小遣い

pod sa⌐ya さや

poem shi 詩, uta⌐ (o-uta) 歌(お歌);
→ **verse**

poet shijin 詩人

point ten 点, *(points obtained)*
tokute⌐n 得点; *(in a statement)* fushi⌐ 節; *(gist)* yōte⌐n
要点; *(tip, end)* saki 先

point *(= puts a point on)*
togarashima⌐su (togara⌐su,

togara'shite) とがらし[尖ら
し]ます(とがらす, とがらし
て)

point: to the ~ tekisetsu (na/ni)
適切(な/に)

point at/to ... o sashima'su
(sa'su, sa'shite) ...を指します
(指す, 指して)

pointed: gets ~ togarima'su
(toga'ru, toga'tte) とがり[尖
り]ます(とがる, とがって)

point of departure shuppa'tsu-
ten 出発点

point out shiteki shima'su (suru,
shite) 指摘します(する, して);
shi'ji shima(')su (suru, shite)
指示します(する, して)

poison doku' 毒

poke tsukima'su (tsuku, tsuite)
突きます(突く, 突いて); **~**
fun at karakaima'su
(karaka'u, karaka'tte) からか
います(からかう, からかっ
て)

pole (rod) bō 棒, sao' さお・竿;
telephone/light ~ denchū 電
柱

police keisatsu 警察; **~ box**
kōban 交番; **~ station**
keisatsu-sho[ ] 警察署

policeman oma'wari-san お巡り
[おまわり]さん, keikan 警官,
ju[ ]nsa 巡査

policy hōshin 方針, tate'mae 建
て前, (political) seisaku 政策;
makes ... one's ~ ... o

tate'mae to shima'su (suru,
shite) ...を建て前とします(す
る, して)

polio shōni-ma'hi 小児麻痺

polish (shines) migakima'su
(migaku, migaite) 磨きます
(磨く, 磨いて); (grinds)
togima'su (to'gu, to'ide) 研ぎ
ます(研ぐ, 研いで)

polished rice haku'mai 白米

polite te'inei (na) (go-te'inei) 丁
寧(な)(ご丁寧), (well-
behaved) otonashi'i おとなし
い, reigi-tadashi'i 礼儀正しい

politely te'inei ni 丁寧に,
otona'shiku おとなしく,
yasashiku 優しく

politics seiji 政治

pollution osen(-kō'gai) 汚染(公
害)

polyethylene pori(-) ポリ

polyvinyl bi'niru ビニル, bini'iru
ビニール

pomade pomā'do ポマード

pomelo (Japanese) natsu-mi'kan
夏みかん・夏蜜柑

pond ike' 池

pool (swimming/motor ~)
pū'ru プール; **swimming ~**
suiei-jō 水泳場, pū'ru プール

poor (needy) bi'mbō (na) 貧乏
(な), mazushi'i 貧しい; (clumsy) heta' (na) へた[下手](な);
(bad) waru'i 悪い; (pitiful)
kawaisō' (na) かわいそう[可
哀相](な)

pop 1. = **soda water 2.** *(it pops)*
hajikema͏̄su (hajike͏̄ru,
haji͏̄kete) はじけます(はじけ
る, はじけて) **3.** *(pops it)*
hajikesasema͏̄su
(hajikesase͏̄ru, hajikesa͏̄sete)
はじけさせます(はじけさせ
る, はじけさせて)

popcorn poppuko͏̄n ポップコー
ン

popular 1. ninki ga arima͏̄su
(a͏̄ru, a͏̄tte) 人気があります
(ある, あって); hayarima͏̄su
(haya͏̄ru, haya͏̄tte) はやり[流
行り]ます(はやる, はやって);
urema͏̄su (ureru, urete) 売れま
す(売れる, 売れて); *(a per-
son is well liked)* motema͏̄su
(mote͏̄ru, mo͏̄tete) もてます
(もてる, もてて) **2.** taishū
(no) 大衆(の); zoku (na) 俗
(な)

popularity ninki 人気; ryūkō 流
行

popularization fukyū 普及; **gets
popularized** fukyū shima͏̄su
(suru, shite) 普及します(する,
して)

population 1. jinkō 人口; ni͏̄nzu
人数, ni͏̄nzū 人数
2. *(populace)* → **people**

porcelain setomono 瀬戸物, ji͏̄ki
磁器

porch 1. *(entrance hall)* ge͏̄nkan
玄関 **2.** *(veranda)* engawa 縁側

pork buta-niku 豚肉

pork cutlet ton-katsu 豚カツ・と
んかつ

**pork meatballs steamed in thin
pastry** shūmai シューマイ・焼
売

porno film poruno-e͏̄iga ポルノ
映画, pinku-e͏̄iga ピンク映画

pornography po͏̄runo ポルノ,
shunga 春画

porridge (o-)kayu (お)かゆ[粥]

port minato 港; **Port of
(Yokohama)** (Yokohama͏̄)-kō
(横浜)港

**portable shrine (for festival
parades)** mi͏̄koshi (o-
mi͏̄koshi) みこし[神輿](おみ
こし)

porter po͏̄tā ポーター; *(redcap)*
akabō 赤帽

portion bu͏̄bun 部分, bu͏̄n 分,
ichi͏̄-bu 一部, wari-mae 割り
前; *(serving)* ...-nimmae ...人
前

portrait shozō-ga 肖像画, zo͏̄ 像

position 1. i͏̄chi 位置 **2.** *(status,
rank)* chi͏̄i 地位 **3.** → **place**; →
job

positive 1. sekkyoku-teki (na) 積
極的(な) **2.** → **sure**

possess 1. → **have**; → **own**
2. sonaema͏̄su (sona͏̄e͏̄ru,
sona͏̄ete) 備えます(備える,
備えて)

possessed shoyū (no) 所有(の);
possession *(thing owned)*
shoyū͏̄-butsu/-hin 所有物/品

possibility kanō-sei 可能性

possible kanō (na) 可能(な); is ~ dekima⌐su (deki⌐ru, de⌐kite) でき[出来]ます(できる, できて), kanaima⌐su (kana⌐u, kana⌐tte) かない[叶い]ます(かなう, かなって)

possibly hyo⌐tto shita⌐ra ひょっとしたら; aru⌐i-wa あるいは・或いは

post 1. → **mail** 2. → **pole, stake** 3. *(duty)* yaku⌐ (o-yaku) 役(お役), *(station, seat)* se⌐ki (o-se⌐ki) 席(お席)

postage yūbin-ryō⌐kin 郵便料金, yūsō⌐-ryō 郵送料; ~ **stamp** ki⌐tte⌐ 切手, yūbin-ki⌐tte/-gi⌐tte 郵便切手/切手

postal: ~ **savings** yūbin-cho⌐kin 郵便貯金; ~ **transfer** yūbin-fu⌐rikae 郵便振替

postcard hagaki (o-ha⌐gaki) 葉書(お葉書); *(picture)* e-ha⌐gaki 絵葉書

posterity shi⌐son 子孫

postman yūbin-ya (san) 郵便屋(さん)

post office yūbi⌐n-kyoku 郵便局

posture shisei 姿勢

postwar se⌐ngo (no) 戦後(の)

pot 1. *(piece of pottery)* yaki-mono 焼き物 2. *(for cooking)* kama かま・釜; *(pan)* na⌐be (o-nabe) 鍋(お鍋) 3. *(for plants)* hachi⌐ 鉢; **potted plant** hachi-ue⌐ 鉢植え, hachi⌐-mono 鉢

物, ueki 植木

potage *(thick soup)* pota⌐ju ポタージュ

potato po⌐te⌐to ポテト; *(Irish)* jagaimo (o-ja⌐ga) じゃが芋(おじゃが); *(sweet)* imo⌐ (o-imo) 芋(お芋), Satsuma-imo さつま[薩摩]芋; *(baked sweet potato)* yaki-imo 焼き芋

potato starch kataku⌐ri⌐ko 片栗粉

potter's wheel ro⌐kuro ろくろ・轆轤

pottery yaki-mono 焼き物, tō⌐ki 陶器

pound *(weight or money)* po⌐ndo ポンド; **pounds it** tatakima⌐su (tata⌐ku, tata⌐ite) 叩きます(叩く, 叩いて)

pounding tataki⌐ 叩き

pour tsugima⌐su (tsugu, tsuide) つぎ[注ぎ]ます(つぐ, ついで), sosogima⌐su (soso⌐gu, soso⌐ide) 注ぎます(注ぐ, 注いで)

pouring the rice wine (o-)shaku (お)酌

pout fukurema⌐su (fukureru, fukurete) ふくれます(ふくれる, ふくれて)

poverty hinkon 貧困

powder kona⌐ (o-ko⌐na) 粉(お粉); *(face)* oshiroi おしろい・白粉

powdered arrowroot kuzu⌐ko⌐ くず粉 「粉薬

powdered medicine kona-gu⌐suri

powdered milk kona-mi⌐ruku 粉
ミルク

power chikara⌐ 力, jitsuryoku 実
力; *(energy, influence)*
se⌐iryoku 勢力; *(electricity)*
de⌐nki 電気

power failure/outage teiden 停
電

powerful yūryoku (na) 有力(な)

power line densen 電線

practical jitchi (no) 実地(の)

practically taigai 大概・たいがい

practical use jitsuyō 実用

practice *(drill)* renshū 練習;
(artistic) (o)-ke⌐iko (お)けいこ
[稽古]; *(realization)* jikkō 実
行, *(reality)* jissai 実際; *(habit)*
shūkan 習慣

practice: (putting to) ~ jitchi 実
地; **puts to practice** jisshii⌐
shima⌐su (suru, shite) 実施し
ます(する, して)

praise 1. *(homage)* home-ko⌐toba
ほめ[褒め]言葉, home⌐ ほめ・
褒め **2.** *(lauds)* homema⌐su
(home⌐ru, ho⌐mete) ほめ[褒
め]ます(ほめる, ほめて)

prank itazura いたずら・悪戯

prawn kuruma⌐-ebi 車えび[海老]

pray inorima⌐su (ino⌐ru, ino⌐tte)
祈ります(祈る, 祈って)

prayer inori⌐ (o-inori) 祈り(お祈
り)

preach se⌐kkyo⌐ shima⌐su
(suru, shite) 説教します(する,
して), tokima⌐su (to⌐ku, to⌐ite)
説きます(説く, 説いて)

preacher bo⌐kushi (san) 牧師
(さん)

prearrange uchi-awasema⌐su
(-awase⌐ru, -awa⌐sete) 打ち合
わせます(合わせる, 合わせ
て)

precaution *(care)* yō⌐jin 用心,
ne⌐n 念; *(prevention)* yobō 予
防; **as a** ~ nen no tame⌐ (ni) 念
の為(に)

precedent senrei 先例, zenrei 前
例, re⌐i 例

precious taisetsu (na) 大切(な),
daiji⌐ (na) 大事(な); oshi⌐i 惜
しい

precipice zeppeki 絶壁

precipitate *(rains, snows)*
furima⌐su (fu⌐ru, fu⌐tte) 降り
ます(降る, 降って)

precipitous kyū (na) 急(な),
kewashi⌐i 険しい

precise seimitsu (na) 精密(な)

precisely ... ko⌐so ...こそ;
kichi⌐n-to きちんと; seimitsu
ni 精密に

predict yogen shima⌐su (suru,
shite) 予言します(する, して)

prediction *(weather, etc.)* yohō
予報

prefectural kenritsu (no) 県立
(の), kōritsu (no) 公立(の)

prefecture ke⌐n 県, ...⌐-ken ...県;
prefecture office ke⌐nchō 県
庁

prefer ... no hō⌐ ga suki⌐ desu ...

の方が好きです;
konomima'su (kono'mu,
kono'nde) 好みます(好む, 好ん
で)

preferably isso いっそ, mu'shiro
むしろ

prefix settō[ﾛ]-go/-ji 接頭語/辞

pregnancy (gets pregnant)
ninshin (shima'su; suru, shite)
妊娠(します; する, して)

prejudice henken 偏見

pre-kindergarten hoiku'-en 保育
園

premeditation ka'ku'go 覚悟

premium (bonus) omake おまけ

premonition yokan 予感

preparation(s) yō'i 用意, ju'mbi
準備; shitaku したく・支度;
(anticipatory steps) yo'bi 予備;
(advance study) yoshū 予習;
(provisions) sona'e' 備え

prep(aratory) school yobi-kō 予
備校

prepare 1. ... no yō'i/ju'mbi o
shima'su (suru, shite) ...の用
意/準備をします(する, して)
2. *(arranges)* ...no shitaku o
shima'su (suru, shite) ...のし
たく[支度]をします(する,
して) **3.** *(studies ahead)* yoshū
shima'su (suru, shite) 予習し
ます(する, して) **4.** *(readies
it)* totonoema'su (totono'e'ru,
totono'ete) 整えます(整える,
整えて) **5.** *(makes it)*
tsukurima'su (tsuku'ru,

tsuku'tte) 作ります(作る, 作
って) **6.** *(sets up, provides)*
mōkema'su (mōke'ru,
mo'kete) 設けます(設ける,
設けて)

prepared: is ~ for *(resigned to)*
ka'ku'go shima([ﾛ])su (suru,
shite) 覚悟します(する, して)

prescribe 1. *(prescribes medicine)* shohō shima'su (suru,
shite) 処方します(する, して)
2. *(stipulates)* kitei shima'su
(suru, shite) 規定します(する,
して)

prescription shohō 処方; (~
slip) shohō-sen 処方せん[箋]

present *(gift)* okuri-mono 贈り物,
pure'zento プレゼント; o-rei
お礼; kokoro-zashi[ﾛ] (o-
kokorozashi) 志(お志); *(as a
souvenir)* (o-)miyage (お)みや
げ[土産], [*baby talk*] o-mi'ya
おみや; *(midyear)* (o-)chūgen
(お)中元, *(year-end)* (o-)seibo
(お)歳暮

present *(the present time)* ge'nzai
現在; i'ma (no) 今(の);
ko'ndo (no) 今度(の); hon-...
本..., kon-... 今...; **at ~** i'ma
wa 今は; **up to the ~** ima-
ma'de 今まで; **the ~ condi-
tions/state** genjō 現状

present *(in attendance)* shusseki
(no) 出席(の)

present *(gives)* agema'su (ageru,
agete) あげます(あげる, あげ

て), sashi-agema｀su (-age⌐ru,
-a⌐gete) 差し上げます(上げ
る, 上げて); okurima｀su
(okuru, okutte) 贈ります(贈
る, 贈って)

presently 1. (= by and by) i｀ma
ni 今に; → **soon**　**2.** (= at
present) i｀ma wa 今は

preserve tamochima｀su
(tamo｀tsu, tamo｀tte) 保ちます
(保つ, 保って); ho｀shu
shima(⌐)su (suru, shite) 保守
します(する, して)

president (of a nation) daito⌐ryō
大統領; (of a company)
shachō 社長; (of a school)
gakuchō 学長

pressed: feels ~ aserima｀su
(ase｀ru, ase｀tte) 焦ります(焦る,
焦って)

press (on) oshima｀su (osu,
oshite) 押します(押す, 押し
て)

pressure atsuryoku 圧力; appaku
圧迫; **puts ~ on** appaku
shima｀su (suru, shite) 圧迫し
ます(する, して)

prestige me｀iyo 名誉

presumably ... hazu dc｀su (da｀,
de｀) ...はずです(だ, で)

presume suitei/yosō shima｀su
(suru, shite) 推定/予想します
(する, して); → **think**

presumption suitei 推定, yosō 予
想

pret à porter (ready to wear)

puretapo｀rute プレタポルテ

pretend ... (no) furi｀ o shima｀su
(suru, shite) ...(の)ふりをし
ます(する, して)

pretend(ed) (sham) mise-kake
(no) 見せかけ(の)

pretense furi｀ ふり

pretext kōjitsu 口実

pretty ki｀rei (na) きれい[綺麗]
(な); → **fairly, rather**

prevent (hinders) (... no) jama o
shima｀su (suru, shite) (...の)
じゃま[邪魔]をします(する,
して); (thwarts) habamima｀su
(haba｀mu, haba｀nde) 阻みます
(阻む, 阻んで); (blocks)
fusegima｀su (fuse｀gu, fuse｀ide)
防ぎます(防ぐ, 防いで),
(wards off) yobō shima｀su
(suru, shite) 予防します(する,
して)

prevention yobō 予防

previous ma｀e no 前の; **~ ap-
pointment/engagement**
sen'yaku 先約, sashitsukae 差
し支え

prewar senzen (no) 戦前(の)

price nedan (o-ne｀dan) 値段(お
値段), ne｀ 値; (the set/regular/
net price) teika 定価; **commodity prices** bukka 物価

price difference/differential
sa｀ya さや

price rise ne-age 値上げ

price tag shō-fuda⌐ 正札

pride hokori⌐ 誇り, jiman 自慢;

toku⌐i 得意

priest *(Christian)* shi⌐mpu (san) 神父(さん), bo⌐kushi 牧師; *(Buddhist)* bo⌐zu 坊主, so⌐(ryo) 僧(侶); *(Shinto)* ka⌐n-nushi 神主

primarily ga⌐nrai 元来, ze⌐ntai 全体

primary election yobi-se⌐nkyo 予備選挙

primary school → **elementary school**

prime minister sōri-da⌐ijin 総理大臣, shushō 首相

prince miya 宮, miya sama 宮様

princess hi⌐me 姫, o-hi⌐me sama お姫様

principal 1. *(head of a school)* kōchō 校長 **2.** *(main)* o⌐mo na 主な

principally o⌐mo ni 主に, mo⌐ppara もっぱら・専ら

principle *(policy)* tate⌐mae 建て前; *(doctrine)* shu⌐gi 主義

print *(woodblock)* mokuhan (-ga) 木版(画), hanga 版画

print *(prints it)* insatsu shima⌐su (suru, shite) 印刷します(する, して), surima⌐su (su⌐ru, su⌐tte) 刷ります(刷る, 刷って); *(puts it in print)* katsuji ni shima⌐su (suru, shite) 活字にします(する, して)

printed matter insatsu⌐-butsu 印刷物 「ち合わせ

prior arrangement uchi-awase 打

prison → **jail**

private *(use)* jibun-yō (no) 自分用(の), shiyō (no) 私用(の); *(undisturbed)* jama sarenai じゃま[邪魔]されない; *(confidential)* naisho⌐ (no) 内緒(の), *(secret)* himitsu (no) 秘密(の); *(within the family)* uchiwa 内輪; *(privately established)* watakushi⌐-ritsu 私立, shi⌐ritsu (no) 私立(の), watakushi-setsu 私設, shisetsu (no) 私設(の)

private railroad shitetsu 私鉄

private talk naisho(⌐) no hanashi⌐ 内緒の話, naisho-ba⌐nashi 内緒話

prize 1. shō⌐ 賞, ...-shō ...賞, *(object)* shōhin 賞品, *(money)* shōkin 賞金; ～ **contest** konkū⌐ru コンクール **2.** *(reward)* go-hō⌐bi ごほうび・ご褒美

prize *(prizes it)* daiji⌐ ni shima⌐su (suru, shite) 大事にします(する, して)

probably ta⌐bun 多分・たぶん, oso⌐raku 恐らく・おそらく, ōkata おおかた・大方, taigai 大概・たいがい; ... (suru⌐/ shita⌐) deshō⌐ ...(する/した)でしょう

problem mondai 問題

procedure *(formalities)* te-tsu⌐zuki 手続き; *(program)* te⌐jun 手順

process 1. *(method)* yari-kata や

り方, hōhō 方法 *(course, stage)* katei 過程; *(development)* nariyuki 成り行き
2. *(handles)* sho⌝ri shima(⌝)sụ (suru, shịte) 処理します(する, して); *(industrially treats)* kakō shima⌝sụ (suru, shịte) 加工します(する, して)

produce 1. *(produces it)* … ga dekima⌝sụ (deki⌝ru, de⌝kịte) …ができ[出来]ます(できる, できて), … o tsụkurima⌝sụ (tsụku⌝ru, tsụku⌝tte) …を作ります(作る, 作って), … o seizō/seisakụ shima⌝sụ (suru, shịte) …を製造/制作します(する, して); *(brings it about)* … o shō-jima⌝sụ (shō-ji[⌝]ru, shō[⌝]-jite) …を生じます(生じる, 生じて)
2. → **product**

product sambutsu 産物

production *(manufacture)* seisan 生産, seizō 製造

profession *(vocation)* shoku⌝gyō 職業

professional *(an expert)* ku⌝rō⌝to くろうと·玄人, pu⌝ro プロ

professional experience shokureki 職歴

professional wrestling puro-resu プロレス

professor kyō[⌝]ju 教授

proficiency jitsuryoku 実力

profit 1. ri⌝eki 利益; toku (o-toku) 得(お得); *(interest)* ri⌝ 利 **2.** *(makes a profit)* mōkema⌝sụ (mōke⌝ru, mō⌝kete) もうけ[儲け]ます(もうける, もうけて)

profitable yū⌝ri (na) 有利(な), toku (na) 得(な); uma⌝i/mma⌝i うまい; wari ga i⌝i 割がいい

program *(TV, etc.)* bangu[⌝]mi[⌝] 番組, purogu⌝ramu プログラム; *(plan)* keikaku 計画, *(itinerary, routine)* nittei 日程; *(procedure)* te[⌝]jun 手順

programmer purogura⌝mā プログラマー

progress 1. shi⌝mpo 進歩; keika 経過 **2.** *(it progresses)* sụsumima⌝sụ (sụsumu, sụsunde) 進みます(進む, 進んで), shi⌝mpo shima(⌝)sụ (suru, shịte) 進歩します(する, して)

prohibit kinshị shima⌝sụ (suru, shịte) 禁止します(する, して)

project (a picture) utsụshima⌝sụ (utsụ⌝su⌝, utsu⌝shịte) 映します(映す, 映して)

projector *(movie)* eisha⌝-ki 映写機

prolong → **lengthen**

prominent ichijirushi⌝i 著しい

prominently ichijiru⌝shịku 著しく

promise 1. (o-)yakụsoku (お)約束, yakụsokụ-goto 約束事; *(outlook)* mikomi 見込み

2. promises it yakusoku shima‛su (suru, shite) 約束します(する, して)

promontory mi⌐saki 岬

promotion shōrei 奨励; *(betterment, increase)* zōshin 増進

prompt sassoku‛ (no) 早速(の), tossa (no) とっさ(の)

promptly sassoku‛ 早速, tossa ni とっさに

pronoun daime⌐ishi 代名詞

pronounce hatsuon shima‛su (suru, shite) 発音します(する, して)

pronunciation hatsuon 発音

proof shōko 証拠, shōmei 証明

proofread kōsei shima‛su (suru, shite) 校正します(する, して)

prop *(a support)* sasa⌐e⌐ 支え; **props it (up)** sasaema‛su (sasa⌐e⌐ru, sasa⌐ete) 支えます(支える, 支えて)

propaganda senden 宣伝

propane puro‛pan プロパン; ~ **gas** puropan-ga‛su プロパンガス

proper *(appropriate)* tekitō (na) 適当(な), chanto shita ちゃんとした; *(expected, deserved)* tōzen 当然; *(correct)* tadashi‛i 正しい

properly tada‛shiku 正しく; tekitō ni 適当に; chanto ちゃんと

property *(fortune)* za⌐isan 財産; → **belongings**; → **land**

proportion ri‛tsu 率

proposal mōshi-komi 申し込み, mōshi-de 申し出; *(public)* mōshi-ire 申し入れ; *(of marriage)* endan 縁談; kyūkon 求婚

propose teian shima‛su (suru, shite) 提案します(する, して); mōshi-komima‛su (-ko⌐mu, -ko⌐nde) 申し込みます(込む, 込んで), mōshi-dema‛su (-de⌐ru, -de⌐te) 申し出ます(出る, 出て); *(publicly)* mōshi-irema‛su (-ire⌐ru, -i⌐rete) 申し入れます(入れる, 入れて); *(marriage)* kyūkon shima‛su (suru, shite) 求婚します(する, して)

proprietor keie‛i-sha 経営者

prosecutor ke‛nji 検事

prospect(s) ze‛nto 前途; *(outlook)* mikomi 見込み, mitōshi 見通し

prosper sakaema‛su (saka‛e‛ru, saka‛ete) 栄えます(栄える, 栄えて)

prosperity *(relative business conditions)* keiki 景気; *(good business conditions)* kō-ke‛iki 好景気

prosperous sakan (na) 盛ん(な)

prostitute baishu‛n-fu 売春婦, jōrō 女郎, joro‛ 女郎

prostitution baishun 売春; **house of** ~ baishun-ya‛do 売春宿

protect mamorima‛su (mamo‛ru,

mamoˈtte) 守ります(守る, 守って); *(safeguards)* hoˈgo shima(ˈ)su (suru, shite) 保護します(する, して)

protein tampakuˈ-shitsu たんぱく[蛋白]質

protest koˈgi (shima(ˈ)su; suru, shite) 抗議(します; する, して)

protrude tsuki-demaˈsu (-deˈru, -deˈte) 突き出ます(出る, 出て), tobi-dashimaˈsu (-daˈsu, -daˈshite) 跳び[飛び]出します(出す, 出して)

protruding tooth deˈppa 出っ歯, soˈppa 反っ歯

proud 1. tokuˈi (na) 得意(な) **2. is proud of** ... o jiman shimaˈsu (suru, shite) ...を自慢します(する, して)

prove shōmei shimaˈsu (suru, shite) 証明します(する, して)

proverb kotowazaˈ ことわざ・諺

provide *(provides one with)* motasemaˈsu (motaseˈru, motaˈsete) 持たせます(持たせる, 持たせて); → **give**; → **prepare**

provide a treat gochisō shimaˈsu (suru, shite) ごちそう[ご馳走]します(する, して)

provided taˈdashi ただし・但し; → **if**

province *(of old Japan)* (... no) kuni (...の)国; *(modern*

prefecture) keˈn 県, ...ˈ-ken ...県; *(of Canada)* shūˈ 州, ...ˈ-shū ...州; *(region)* chihōˈ 地方

provision *(supply)* kyōkyū 供給; *(allowance)* teˈate (o-teˈate) 手当(お手当); *(stipulation)* jōkeˈn 条件; *(preparations)* sonaˈe 備え

provoke: gets provoked / is provoking shaku ni sawarimaˈsu (sawaru, sawatte) しゃく[癪]に障ります(障る, 障って)

prowess *(ability)* udemaˈeˈ 腕前, temae (o-teˈmae) 手前(お手前)

prudence tsutsushimiˈ 慎しみ・つつしみ

pseudo-... ese-... えせ..., gi-... 偽...

psyche seˈishin 精神

psychologist shinrigaˈkuˈ-sha 心理学者

psychology shiˈnri 心理; *(science /study)* shinriˈ-gaku 心理学

public kōshū (no) 公衆(の); kōkai (no) 公開(の); ōyake (no) 公(の); *(open)* kōzen (no) 公然(の), *(officially established)* kōritsu (no) 公立(の); *(society)* yo-noˈ-naka 世の中, yoˈ 世, seˈken 世間

publication shuppan 出版; *(things)* shuppaˈn-butsu 出版物; *(publishing)* hakkō 発行; *(books)* shoˈseki 書籍 「浴場

public bath seˈntō 銭湯, yokujō

public corporation kōdan 公団
public hall kaikan 会館
publicity senden 宣伝
public opinion yo⌐ron 世論,
se⌐ron 世論
public park kōen 公園
publish arawashima⌐su
(arawa⌐su, arawa⌐shite) 著しま
す(著す, 著して), shuppan
shima⌐su (suru, shite) 出版し
ます(する, して), hakkō
shima⌐su (suru, shite) 発行し
ます(する, して); *(puts it in a
newspaper)* nosema⌐su
(noseru, nosete) 載せます(載
せる, 載せて); → **announce**
publisher shuppa⌐n-sha 出版者·
出版社, hakkō⌐-sha 発行者;
shuppan-moto 出版元
pucker: puckers it up
tsubomema⌐su (tsubomeru,
tsubomete) つぼめます(つぼ
める, つぼめて); **it puckers
up** tsubomarima⌐su
(tsubomaru, tsubomatte) つぼ
まります(つぼまる, つぼま
puckery shibu⌐i 渋い ⌐って)
puff: cream puff shū-kuri⌐imu
シュークリーム
puffer *(fish)* fu⌐gu ふぐ·河豚
puke → **vomit**
pull hipparima⌐su (hippa⌐ru, hip-
pa⌐tte) 引っ張ります(引っ張
る, 引っ張って), hikima⌐su
(hiku, hiite) 引きます(引く,
引いて)

pull *(= connections)*: **has pull
(with …)** (… ni) ko⌐ne o
tsuke⌐te ima⌐su (iru, ite) (…に)
コネを付けています(いる,
いて), ko⌐ne ga arima⌐su (a⌐ru,
a⌐tte) コネがあります(ある,
あって)
pull up *(refloats it)* hiki-
agema⌐su (-age⌐ru, -a⌐gete) 引
き上げます(上げる, 上げて)
pulse myaku⌐ 脈, myakuhaku 脈
拍
pulverize konashima⌐su (konasu,
konashite) こなします(こな
す, こなして)
pumice karuishi 軽石
pump po⌐mpu ポンプ ⌐瓜
pumpkin kabocha かぼちゃ·南
pun share しゃれ·洒落, jiguchi
地口, goro-a⌐wase ごろ[語呂]
合わせ
punctually kichi⌐n-to きちんと
punctuation kugiri⌐ 区切り
puncture *(of tire)* panku パンク
pungent kara⌐i からい·辛い
punish bas-shima⌐su (bas-su⌐ru,
ba⌐s-shite) 罰します(罰する,
罰して) ⌐ラ
punk chimpira ちんぴら·チンピ
pupil *(student)* se⌐ito 生徒; *(apprentice, disciple)* deshi⌐ 弟子
puppet show ningyō-shi⌐bai 人形
芝居; *(traditional)* bu⌐nraku 文
puppy koinu 子犬 ⌐楽
purchase → **buy**
pure junsui (na) 純粋(な), ju⌐n

(na) 純(な); *(clean)* seiketsu (na) 清潔(な)

purgative gezai 下剤, kudashi (-gu̱ʼsuri) 下し(薬)

purge tsuihō 追放

purple muraʼsaki (no) 紫(の)

purport muneʼ 旨

purpose *(intention)* tsumori (o-tsumori) つもり(おつもり), iʼto 意図, kokoro-zashiʼ 志; *(goal)* mokuteki 目的

purpose: for the ~ of ... (no) tameʼ (ni) ...(の)ため[為](に); **on ~** waʼza-to わざと, waʼzawaza わざわざ, ito-teki ni 意図的に, takuraʼnde たくらんで・企んで; **serves a ~ →** **useful** 「まぐち

purse saifu 財布, gamaguchi が

pursue oimaʼsu (ou, otte) 追います(追う, 追って)

pus umiʼ うみ・膿

Pusan Fuʼzan 釜山

push oshimaʼsu (osu, oshiʼte) 押します(押す, 押して); *(thrusts)* tsukimaʼsu (tsuku, tsuite) 突きます(突く, 突いて)

push a good thing too far zu ni norimaʼsu (noru, notte) 図に乗ります(乗る, 乗って)

pushy zūzūshiʼi ずうずうしい・図々しい, bu-eʼnryo (na) 無遠慮(な)

put okimaʼsu (oku, oite) 置きます(置く, 置いて)

put aboard nosemaʼsu (noseru, nosete) 載せます(載せる, 載せて)

put aside toʼtte okimaʼsu (oku, oite) 取っておきます(おく, おいて)

put away shimaimaʼsu (shimau, shimatte) しまいます(しまう, しまって)

put in iremaʼsu (ireru, irete) 入れます(入れる, 入れて); **~ a call** denwa o iremaʼsu (ireru, irete) 電話を入れます(入れる, 入れて)

put in order soroemaʼsu (soroeʼru, soroʼete) 揃えます(揃える, 揃えて); *(tidies it up)* katazukemaʼsu (kata-zukeʼru, katazuʼkete) 片付けます(片付ける, 片付けて)

put in print katsuji ni shimaʼsu (suru, shite) 活字にします(する, して)

put into words ii-arawashimaʼsu (-arawaʼsu, -arawaʼshite) 言い表します(表す, 表して)

put it another way ii-kaemaʼsu (-kaeʼru, -kaʼete) 言い換えます(換える, 換えて)

put it on its side nekashimaʼsu (nekasu, nekashite) 寝かします(寝かす, 寝かして)

put it together *(assembles it)* kumi-tatemaʼsu (-tateʼru, -taʼtete) 組み立てます(立てる, 立てて)

put it to use yaku¹ ni tatema¹su (tate¹ru, ta¹tete) 役に立てます (立てる, 立てて)

put on → wear; ~ airs kidorima¹su (kidoru, kidotte) 気取ります(気取る, 気取って)

put one on top of another kasanema¹su (kasaneru, kasanete) 重ねます(重ねる, 重ねて)

put out dashima¹su (da¹su, da¹shite) 出します(出す, 出して); *(extinguishes)* keshima¹su (kesu, keshite) 消します(消す, 消して)

put pressure on appaku shima¹su (suru, shite) 圧迫します(する, して)

put to bed/sleep nekashima¹su (nekasu, nekashite) 寝かします(寝かす, 寝かして)

put together awasema¹su (awase¹ru, awa¹sete) 合わせます(合わせる, 合わせて); *(sets up)* kumima¹su (ku¹mu, ku¹nde) 組みます(組む, 組んで)

put up: puts someone up overnight tomema¹su (tomeru, tomete) 泊めます(泊める, 泊めて)

put up with ga¹man shima(¬)su (suru, shite) 我慢します(する, して); shinobima¹su (shino[¬]bu, shino[¬]nde) 忍びます(忍ぶ, 忍んで), taema¹su (tae¹ru, ta¹ete) 耐えます(耐える, 耐えて), shi¹mbō shima(¬)su (suru, shite) 辛抱します(する, して); sumashima¹su (suma¹su, suma¹shite) 済まします(済ます, 済まして) 「ズル

puzzle nazo なぞ・謎, pa¹zuru パ

puzzling yayakoshi¹i ややこしい

— Q —

quail uzura うずら・鶉

qualification(s) *(competency)* shikaku 資格

qualified *(suitable)* teki-shima¹su (teki-su¹ru, teki¹-shite) 適します(適する, 適して) 「(な)

qualitative shitsu-teki (na) 質的

quality shitsu[¬] 質, hin 品,

hinshitsu 品質; shina 品; shō¹ 性; *(best ~)* tokkyū (no) 特級 (の) 「(な)

quantitative ryō-teki (na) 量的

quantity ryō¹ 量; ta¹ka¹ 多寡; *(large)* taryō 多量, tairyō 大量; *(large and/or small)* tashō 多少

quarrel kenka (shima'su; suru, shite) けんか[喧嘩](します; する, して); → **argument**; → **dispute**

quarter (*district*) hōme'n 方面, ...-hō'men ...方面

quay hato-ba 波止場

queasy (*feels nauseated*) mu'kamuka shima'su (suru, shite) むかむかします(する, して), haki-ke' ga shima'su 吐き気がします, haki-ke' o moyōshima'su (moyō[ⁿ]su, moyō[ⁿ]shite) 吐き気を催します(催す, 催して)

queen joō' 女王

queer he'n (na) 変(な), okashi'i おかしい; (*wondrous*) myō' (na) 妙(な)

question shitsumon 質問; (*problem*) mondai 問題; (*doubt, query*) gimon 疑問

questionable ayashi'i 怪しい, ikagawashi'i いかがわしい; (*fishy*) kusa'i くさい・臭い

questioning (*interviewing*) shimon 試問

question mark gimo'n-fu 疑問符

queue re'tsu 列; **forms a ~** re'tsu o tsukurima'su (tsukuru, tsukutte) 列を作ります(作る, 作って)

quick haya'i 速い・早い; **quickly** ha'yaku 速く・早く

quick-witted wakari' ga haya'i 分かりが早い

quiet 1. shi'zuka (na) 静か(な), oda'yaka (na) 穏やか(な), no'doka (na) のどか(な); **gets quiet** shizumarima'su (shizumaru, shizumatte) 静まります(静まる, 静まって)

2. quiets it, makes it quiet shizumema'su (shizumeru, shizumete) 静めます(静める, 静めて)

quietly shi'zuka ni 静かに; jitto じっと

quilt (*padded*) futon (o-futo'n) ふとん・布団(お布団); **bottom ~** shiki-bu'ton 敷布団; **top ~** kake-bu'ton 掛け布団, ya'gu 夜具

quinine kini'ine キニーネ, ki'na キナ

quirk kuse' 癖

quit yamema'su (yameru, yamete) やめ[止め, 辞め]ます(やめる, やめて)

quite sōtō 相当, daibu だいぶ・大分, zu'ibun ずいぶん・随分; (*rather*) ii-kagen いい加減; (*completely*) mattaku' 全く; → **very**; → **almost**

quite a ... cho'tto shita ... ちょっとした...

quite so naru-hodo なるほど・成る程

quota wariate 割り当て

quotation in'yō 引用

quote in'yō shima'su (suru, shite) 引用します(する, して)

— R —

rabbit usagi うさぎ・兎

raccoon dog ta⌐nuki たぬき・狸

race kyōsō 競争, rē⌐su レース; *(bike)* keirin 競輪; *(horse)* keiba 競馬

race *(of people)* jinshu 人種, mi⌐nzoku 民族; *(the human ~)* ji⌐nrui 人類

race: races the engine e⌐njin o fukashima⌐su (fuka⌐su, fuka⌐shite) エンジンを吹かします(吹かす, 吹かして)

racetrack keiba-jō 競馬場

rack tana 棚

radiator *(in house, etc.)* dambō (-sō⌐chi) 暖房(装置); *(car)* rajiē⌐tā ラジエーター

radical *(extremist)* kageki (na) 過激(な); **the radicals** kageki-ha 過激派

radio ra⌐njio ラジオ

radish *(the giant white)* daikon 大根; **~ pickles** taku⌐(w)an たくあ[わ]ん, *(radish, etc.)* (o-)shinko (お)しんこ[新香]

raffle fukubiki 福引き

raft ikada いかだ・筏

rag bo⌐ro ぼろ; ku⌐zu くず・屑; *(dust cloth)* zōkin ぞうきん・雑巾

rage abarema⌐su (abareru, abarete) 暴れます(暴れる, 暴れて), arema⌐su (areru, arete) 荒れます(荒れる, 荒れて)

ragpicker kuzu-hi⌐roi くず拾い・屑拾い, bata⌐ya ばた屋

raid 1. *(attacking)* shūgeki 襲撃, kōgeki 攻撃; *(bombing)* bakugeki 爆撃 **2.** *(raids it)* shūgeki/kōgeki/bakugeki shima⌐su (suru, shite) 襲撃/攻撃/爆撃します(する, して); *(invades, make a raid on)* fumi-komima⌐su (-ko⌐mu, -ko⌐nde) 踏み込みます(込む, 込んで)

railroad, railway tetsudō 鉄道; **~ line/track** se⌐nro 線路; **~ station** e⌐ki 駅, sutē⌐nshon ステーション

rain 1. a⌐me 雨; **light ~** kosame 小雨; **heavy ~** ō-a⌐me 大雨, gō⌐u 豪雨 **2.** *(it rains)* a⌐me ga furima⌐su (fu⌐ru, fu⌐tte) 雨が降ります(降る, 降って)

rainbow niji⌐n 虹

rain check: takes a ~ enryo shite okima⌐su (oku, o⌐ite) 遠慮しておきます(おく, おいて)

rainshoes ama⌐-gutsu 雨靴

rain shutters ama⌐do 雨戸

rainy season *(in Japan)* tsuyu つ

ゆ・梅雨, nyūbai 入梅
raise 1. agema'su (ageru, agete)
あげ［上げ, 挙げ, 揚げ］ます
（あげる, あげて）, *(arouses)*
okoshima'su (oko'su,
oko'shite) 起こします（起こす,
起こして）; *(increases)*
mashima'su (masu, mashite)
増します（増す, 増して）,
(price, wage, fee) hiki-
agema'su (-age'ru, -a'gete) 引
き上げます（上げる, 上げて）;
(erects) tatema'su (tate'ru,
ta'tete) 立てます（立てる, 立
てて）**2.** *(fosters, nourishes)*
yashinaima'su (yashinau,
yashinatte) 養います（養う,
養って）; *(rears a child)*
sodatema'su (sodate'ru,
soda'tete) 育てます（育てる,
育てて）; *(keeps animals, etc.)*
kaima'su (ka'u, ka'tte) 飼いま
す（飼う, 飼って）
raise: is raised *(reared)*
sodachima'su (soda'tsu,
soda'tte) 育ちます（育つ,
育って）
raised lacquer maki'-e 蒔絵
raising silkworms yōsan 養蚕
raisin(s) hoshi-bu'dō 干しぶどう
［葡萄］
rake kumade'⌐ くまで・熊手;
(rakes them up) kaki-
atsumema'su (-atsume'ru,
-atsu⌐mete) かき集めます
（集める, 集めて）

ramp surō'pu スロープ, ra'mpu
ランプ
rampage abarema'su (abareru,
abarete) 暴れます（暴れる, 暴
れて）
ran → run
random yatara (na) やたら（な）;
randomly yatara ni やたらに
range *(kitchen)* kamado かまど・
竈, re'nji レンジ; *(gas)* gasu-
re'nji ガスレンジ; *(mount-
ains)* sammyaku 山脈; *(scope)*
han'i 範囲
rank kurai 位, …'-i …位; chi'i 地
位
rape 1. *(plant)* na'ppa 菜っ葉, o-
na お菜, na' 菜 **2.** *(forcible intercourse)* gōkan 強姦; **rapes**
gōkan shima'su (suru, shite)
強姦します（する, して）
rapid → fast; in ～ succession
zo⌐kuzoku ぞくぞく・続々
rapids *(river)* kyūryū 急流
rare *(infrequent)* mare⌐ (na) ま
れ［稀］（な）, *(precious,
curious)* mezurashi'i 珍しい;
(uncooked) na'ma no 生の, *(little cooked)* nama-yake (no) 生
焼け（の）, re'a (no) レア（の）
rarely mare⌐ ni まれ［稀］に; *(occasionally)* tama ni たまに
rash *(skin)* hasshin 発疹; *(hasty)*
keisotsu (na) 軽率（な）, me'tta
(na) めった（な）, mukō'-mizu
(na) 向こう見ず（な）
rasp yasuri⌐ やすり

rat nezumi ねずみ・鼠

rate 1. *(ratio)* ri˺tsu 率, *(percentage)* wariai 割合; *(charge)* ryō˺kin 料金 **2.** *(estimates it)* mi-tsumorima˺su (-tsumo˺ru, -tsumo˺tte) 見積ります(積もる, 積もって) **3.** → **at any rate**

rather mu˺shiro むしろ; *(preferably)* isso いっそ; *(fairly)* ka˺nari かなり, ii-kagen いい加減; → **quite, relatively, somewhat**

ration haikyū 配給; *(rations it)* haikyū shima˺su (suru, shi̱te) 配給します(する, して)

rational gōri-teki (na) 合理的(な)

rationalization gōri˺-ka 合理化; **rationalize** gōri˺-ka shima˺su (suru, shi̱te) 合理化します(する, して)

rattan tō˺ 藤

rattle ga˺ragara narima˺su (naru, natte) がらがら鳴ります(鳴る, 鳴って); *(clatters)* ga˺tagata shima˺su (suru, shi̱te) がたがたします(する, して)

raving uwagoto うわごと

raw na˺ma (no, de) 生(の/で); **sliced ~ fish** sashimi˺ (o-sashimi) 刺身(お刺身)

raw material zairyō˺ 材料

raw silk ki˺-ito 生糸

ray kōsen 光線

razor kamiso˺ri˺ かみそり・剃刀;

~ blade kamiso˺ri˺ no ha かみそりの刃

razor shell *(a kind of scallop)* taira˺-gai 平貝, taira-gi たいらぎ・玉珧

re-... sai-... shima˺su (suru, shi̱te) 再...します(する, して); mō ichi-do ... shima˺su (suru, shi̱te) もう一度...します(する, して); *(improves)* (shi)-naoshima˺su (-nao˺su, -nao˺shi̱te) (し)直します(直す, 直して)

reach *(it is delivered)* todokima˺su (todo˺ku, todo˺ite) 届きます(届く, 届いて); *(it extends to)* ... ni oyobima˺su (oyobu, oyonde) ...に及びます(及ぶ, 及んで), nobima˺su (nobi˺ru, no˺bite) 伸びます(伸びる, 伸びて); *(arrives at)* ... ni tsukima˺su (tsuku˺, tsu˺ite) ...に着きます(着く, 着いて); *(achieves)* ... ni tas-shima˺su (tas-su˺ru, ta˺s-shi̱te) ...に達します(達する, 達して)

reaction *(response)* hannō 反応; *(repercussion)* handō 反動

reactionary handō-teki (na) 反動的(な); **the reactionaries** handō-ha 反動派

read yomima˺su (yo˺mu, yo˺nde) 読みます(読む, 読んで)

reader *(person)* do˺kusha 読者; *(book)* tokuhon 読本

readily wa̱ke-naku 訳なく, muzo̱sa ni 無造作に

ready 1. (yo̱i ga) de̱kite ima̱su (iru, ite) (用意が)出来ています(いる, いて), dekima̱shita 出来ました; *(is arranged)* totonoima̱su (totono̱u, totono̱tte) 整います(整う, 整って)
2. *(easy)* wa̱ke-nai 訳ない

ready it *(provides)* sonaema̱su (sona̱e̱ru, sona̱ete) 備えます(備える, 備えて), *(arranges it)* totonoema̱su (totono̱e̱ru, totono̱ete) 整えます(整える, 整えて)

ready money genki̱n 現金, gen-nama 現なま

ready to wear (off the rack) puretapo̱rute プレタポルテ

real 1. hontō no 本当の; → **genuine; the real thing** hom-mono 本物 **2.** *(actual)* genjitsu (no) 現実(の)

real estate fudō̱san 不動産

realistic genjitsu̱-teki (na) 現実的(な)

reality jissai 実際; genjitsu 現実

realization 1. jikkō 実行; gen-jitsu̱-ka 現実化 **2.** → **understanding, enlightenment**

realize 1. *(comprehends)* ... ga wakarima̱su (waka̱ru, waka̱tte) ...が分かります(分かる, 分かって), satorima̱su (sato̱ru, sato̱tte) 悟ります

(悟る, 悟って) **2.** *(carries out)* genjitsu̱-ka shima̱su (suru, shite) 現実化します(する, して); → **accomplish; a desire is realized** nozomi̱ ga kanaima̱su (kana̱u, kana̱tte) 望みが叶い[かない]ます(叶う, 叶って)

really hontō/honto (ni) 本当/ほんと(に), jitsu̱ (ni) 実(に); **Really??** *(= No kidding!)* ma̱saka まさか

reap osamema̱su (osame̱ru, osa̱mete) 収めます(収める, 収めて), shūkaku̱ shima̱su (suru, shite) 収穫します(する, して)

reaped: gets ~ osamarima̱su (osama̱ru, osama̱tte) 収まります(収まる, 収まって), shūkaku̱ sarema̱su (sareru, sarete) 収穫されます(される, されて)

rear 1. → **back, behind**; → **tail end 2.** → **raise**

rear admiral shō̱shō 少将

rearview mirror bakku-mi̱rā バックミラー

reason wa̱ke わけ・訳, riyū 理由; *(what is sensible)* dōri̱ 道理; *(logic)* rikutsu 理屈; *(meaning)* yo̱shi 由; *(grounds)* yue̱ 故, ko̱nkyo 根拠; **for the ~ that ...** to iu riyū de ...という理由で, ... yue̱ ni ...故[ゆえ]に

reasonable *(natural, proper)*

atarimae (no) 当たり前(の);
(rational) gōri-teki (na) 合理的
(な); → **moderate**; → **suitable**; → **sensible**

rebel (against) … ni
somukima͞su (somu͞ku,
somu͞ite) …に背き[そむき]ま
す(背く，背いて), hangyaku
shima͞su (suru, shite) 反逆し
ます(する，して)

rebellion hangyaku 反逆

rebuke togame͞ (o-togame) とが
め・咎め(お咎め); *(blames)*
togamema͞su (togame͞ru,
toga͞mete) とがめ[咎め]ます
(とがめる，とがめて)

recall *(remembers)* omoi-
dashima͞su (-da[ⁿ]su,
-da[ⁿ]shite) 思い出します(出
す，出して)

receipt uke-tori 受け取り,
ryōshū[ⁿ]-sho[ⁿ] 領収書, juryō͞-
shō 受領証, *(check)* chi͞kki
チッキ

receive moraima͞su (morau,
moratte) もらいます(もらう，
もらって), ukema͞su (uke͞ru,
u͞kete) 受けます(受ける，受
けて), uke-torima͞su (-to[ⁿ]ru,
-to[ⁿ]tte) 受け取ります(取る，
取って), uke-tsukema͞su
(-tsuke[ⁿ]ru, -tsuke[ⁿ]te) 受け
付けます(付ける，付けて);
hiki-torima͞su (-to͞ru, -to͞tte)
引き取ります(取る，取って);
ses-shima͞su (ses-su[ⁿ]ru, se[ⁿ]s-

shite) 接します(接する，接し
て)

receiver *(telephone)* juwa͞-ki 受
話器

recently saikin (ni) 最近(に),
kono-goro この頃, chika͞goro
近頃; *(a few days ago)* sen-
datte͞ 先立って, senjitsu 先日

receptacle yō͞ki 容器, utsuwa 器

reception rese͞pushon レセプ
ション; *(get-together party)*
konshi[ⁿ]n-kai 懇親会; *(welcome
party)* kange͞i-kai 歓迎会;
(farewell party) sōbe͞tsu͞-kai
送別会; *(engagement, wed-
ding, etc.)* hirō͞-kai 披露会,
hirō͞-en 披露宴

recess yasumi͞ 休み; *[bookish]*
kyūkei 休憩

recession fuke͞iki 不景気

reciprocal o-tagai (no) お互い
(の); *[bookish]* sō͞go (no) 相
互(の)

reciprocally o-tagai ni お互いに;
[bookish] sō͞go ni 相互に

recite utaima͞su (utau, utatte)
歌います(歌う，歌って);
tonaema͞su (tona͞e͞ru,
tona͞ete) 唱えます(唱える，
唱えて)

reckless mubō 無謀(na) 無謀(な),
mu͞cha (na) むちゃ[無茶](な),
me͞tta (na) めった[滅多](な),
yatara (na) やたら(な),
mukō͞-mizu (na) 向こう見ず
(な); **recklessly** yatara ni やた

らに, mu'yami ni むやみ[無闇]に, mukō'-mizu ni 向こう見ず(に)

recognize mitomema'su (mitomeru, mitomete) 認めます(認める, 認めて)

recommend susumema'su (susumeru, susumete) 勧め[薦め]ます(勧め[薦め]る, 勧め[薦め]て)

recommendation suisen 推薦, (letter) suise'n-jō 推薦状

reconfirmation sai-ka'kunin 再確認

reconfirm reservations yoyaku o sai-ka'kunin shima('')su (suru, shite) 予約を再確認します(する, して)

record (phonograph) rekō'do レコード; (results, marks) seiseki 成績; (historic) kiroku 記録

record: records it (sound) rokuon shima'su (suru, shite) 録音します(する, して); (event) kiroku shima'su (suru, shite) 記録します(する, して)

recorder rokuo'n-ki 録音機

record player chikuo'n-ki 蓄音機

recover kaifuku shima'su (suru, shite) 回復します(する, して)

recovery kaifuku 回復

recreation goraku 娯楽; ian 慰安; re'jā レジャー, rekurie'shon レクリエーション

recuperate → **recover**

recuperation → **recovery**

red akai 赤い; a'ka (no) 赤(の); **deep** ～ makka' (na) 真っ赤(な); **the** ～ (deficit figures) aka-ji 赤字

red bean azuki' あずき・小豆; **soup with** ～ **paste** shiruko□ (o-shiruko) 汁粉(お汁粉)

redcap akabō 赤帽

Red Cross Sekijū'ji 赤十字

red light (signal) aka-shi'ngō 赤信号

redo = do it over (again) yari-naoshima'su (-nao'su, -nao'shite) やり直します(直す, 直して)

red (= pay) **phone** aka-de'nwa 赤電話, akai denwa 赤い電話

red snapper ta'i たい・鯛

reduce → **lessen**; → **lower**; → **shorten**; (curtails) habukima'su (habu'ku, habu'ite) 省きます(省く, 省いて); (summarizes) tsuzumema'su (tsuzume'ru, tsuzu'mete) つづめます・約める(つづめる, つづめて); (loses weight) yasema'su (yaseru, yasete) やせ[痩せ]ます(やせる, やせて)

Reduce Speed "So'kudo oto'se" "速度落とせ"

reduction → **discount**

reed o'gi おぎ・荻

reel 1. (spool) ito□maki 糸巻き;

(frame) waku 枠 **2.** *(reels it)* kurimaꜜsu (kuꜜru, kuꜜtte) 繰ります(繰る, 繰って) **3.** → **stagger**

reentry (into the country) sainyū̄koku 再入国

refer to ... ni furemaꜜsu (fureru, furete) ...に触れます(触れる, 触れて); [*bookish*] ... ni genkyū shimaꜜsu (suru, shite) ...に言及します(する, して)

refined *(genteel)* (o-)jōhiꜜn (na) (お)上品(な)

refinement hin 品, jōhiꜜn 上品; *(culture)* kyōyō 教養

refinery *(oil)* seiyu-sho▯ 製油所

reflect *(mirrors it)* utsushimaꜜsu (utsuꜜsu, utsuꜜshite) 写します(写す, 写して); **gets reflected** utsurimaꜜsu (utsuꜜru, utsuꜜtte) 映ります(映る, 映って)

reflection utsuriꜜ 写り; *(consideration)* kōꜜryo 考慮

refloat hiki-agemaꜜsu (-ageꜜru, -aꜜgete) 引き上げます(上げる, 上げて)

reform *(starts a new life)* kōsei shimaꜜsu (suru, shite) 更生します(する, して); **reformation** kōsei 更生

refrain from ... o enryo shimaꜜsu (suru, shite) ...を遠慮します(する, して)

refreshing sawaꜜyaka (na) さわやか(な)

refreshments *(food)* tabe-moꜜnoꜜ

食べ物; *(drink)* nomiꜜ-mono 飲み物; *(tea)* o-cha お茶

refrigerate hiyashimaꜜsu (hiyaꜜsu, hiyaꜜshite) 冷やします(冷やす, 冷やして)

refrigerator reizōꜜko 冷蔵庫 (**how many** naꜜn-dai 何台)

refugee hinaꜜn-sha 避難者

refund harai-modoshi 払い戻し, henkin 返金; *(refunds it)* harai-modoshimaꜜsu (-modo▯su, -modo▯shite) 払い戻します(戻す, 戻して), henkin shimaꜜsu (suru, shite) 返金します(する, して)

refusal kotowaꜜriꜜ 断り; kyoꜜhi 拒否

refuse kotowarimaꜜsu (kotowaꜜru, kotowaꜜtte) 断ります(断る, 断って); kyoꜜhi shima(▯)su (suru, shite) 拒否します(する, して); *(rejects it)* kobamimaꜜsu (kobaꜜmu, kobaꜜnde) 拒みます(拒む, 拒んで)

refuse *(waste)* kuꜜzu くず・屑, kuzu▯-mono くず物・屑物; rōzu ローズ・蘆頭

regard → **look at**; **think**

regarding, in/with regard to ... ni taꜜi-shite (tai-suꜜru ...) ...に対して(対する...), ... ni tsuꜜite (no) ...について(の)

regardless → **nevertheless**; **(doesn't) matter**

Regards to ... ni yoroshiku (itte

kudasa⌐i, o-tsutae kudasa⌐i) ...
によろしく[宜しく](言って
下さい、お伝え下さい)

regeneration kōsei 更生

region chihō⌐ 地方, chi⌐iki 地域

register *(of names)* meibo 名簿

register *(checks into hotel)*
chekku⌐i⌐n shima(⌐)su (suru,
shite) チェックインします(す
る、して); *(enrolls, signs up)*
tōroku shima⌐su (suru, shite)
登録します(する、して); ~
a letter tegami o kaki-tome ni
shima⌐su (suru, shite) 手紙を
書留にします(する、して)

registered (mail) kaki-tome 書留

registration tōroku 登録, tō⌐ki 登
記

regret 1. kō⌐kai 後悔 **2.** *(regrets
it)* kō⌐kai shima(⌐)su (suru,
shite) 後悔します(する、して),
uramima⌐su (ura⌐mu, ura⌐nde)
恨みます(恨む、恨んで); **I
regret that ...** zannen/ikan
na⌐gara ... 残念/遺憾ながら...

regrettable oshi⌐i 惜しい,
zanne⌐n (na) 残念(な)

regrettably zannen na⌐gara 残
念ながら

regular *(usual)* futsū no 普通の,
(ordinary) nami no 並の;
(periodic/scheduled) te⌐iki no
定期の

regulate *(adjusts)* totonoema⌐su
(totono⌐e⌐ru, totono⌐ete) 整え
ます(整える、整えて)

regulation kiso⌐ku 規則, kitei 規
定; kimari 決まり

rein(s) ta⌐zuna 手綱・たづな

reject kobamima⌐su (koba⌐mu,
koba⌐nde) 拒みます(拒む、拒
んで); kyo⌐hi shima(⌐)su
(suru, shite) 拒否します(する、
して)

rejoice yorokobima⌐su
(yoroko⌐bu, yoroko⌐nde) 喜び
ます(喜ぶ、喜んで)

relate 1. *(tells)* katarima⌐su
(kataru, katatte) 語ります(語
る、語って), nobema⌐su
(nobe⌐ru, no⌐bete) 述べます
(述べる、述べて) **2.** *(is con-
nected/relevant to)* ... ni kan-
shima⌐su (kan-su⌐ru, ka⌐n-
shite) ...に関します(関する、
関して)

relation(ship) kankei 関係;
tsunagari つながり; na⌐ka 仲

relative *(person)* shi⌐nrui 親類,
shinseki 親戚

relatively wari(ai) ni 割(合)に,
hikaku-teki ni 比較的に

relative merits yū⌐retsu 優劣

relax *(loses tension)* tarumima⌐su
(tarumu, tarunde) たるみ[弛
み]ます(たるむ、たるんで);
(gets comfortable)
kutsurogima⌐su (kutsuro⌐gu,
kutsuro⌐ide) くつろぎ[寛ぎ]
ます(くつろぐ、くつろいで);
(rests oneself) yasumima⌐su
(yasu⌐mu, yasu⌐nde) 休みます

(休む, 休んで); *(enjoys oneself)* asobima͘su (asobu, asonde) 遊びます(遊ぶ, 遊んで)

release → **let go; announce**

relevance renraku 連絡, kanren 関連; **is relevant to** ... ni kanren shima͘su (suru, shite) ...に関連します(する, して)

reliability shinrai-sei 信頼性

reliable *(steady)* te-gata͘i 手堅い; *(trustworthy)* shinrai deki͘ru 信頼できる, **is highly ~** shinrai-sei ga taka͘i 信頼性が高い

reliance ate 当て, ta͘nomi 頼み, shinrai 信頼

relief *(rescue)* kyū͘jo 救助; *(from worry)* anshin 安心; **breathes a sigh of ~** ho͘tto͘ shima͘su (suru, shite) ほっとします(する, して)

relieve 1. is relieved anshin shima͘su (suru, shite) 安心します(する, して); *(gets saved)* tasu̧karima͘su (tasu̧ka͘ru, tasu̧ka͘tte) 助かります(助かる, 助かって) **2. relieves oneself** *(= goes to the bathroom)* yō͘ o tashima͘su (tasu, tashite) 用を足します(足す, 足して)

religion shū͘kyō 宗教, ...-kyō ...教

relish: small dish of ~ su-no-mono 酢の物

rely on ... ni tayorima͘su (tayo͘ru, tayo͘tte) ...に頼ります(頼る, 頼って), *(requests)* tanomima͘su (tano͘mu, tano͘nde) 頼みます(頼む, 頼んで), irai shima͘su (suru, shite) 依頼します(する, して)

remain *(gets left behind)* nokorima͘su (noko͘ru, noko͘tte) 残ります(残る, 残って); *(is in excess)* amarima͘su (ama͘ru, ama͘tte) 余ります(余る, 余って); *(stops)* todomarima͘su (todoma͘ru, todoma͘tte) とどまります(とどまる, とどまって); *(stays)* ima͘su (iru, ite) います(いる, いて), *(rather than go)* ikimase͘n (ikanai, ikana͘ide) 行きません(行かない, 行かないで)

remainder *(leftover)* nokori͘ 残り, *(surplus)* amari͘ (o-a͘mari) 余り(お余り); a͘to no (mono͘, hito͘, ...) 後の(物, 人, ...)

remaining: the ~ ... a͘to/nokori(͘) no ... 後/残りの...

remains *(= what remains)* nokori-mo͘no͘ 残り物

remark 1. a remark kotoba͘ 言葉, ... (yū/itta) koto͘ ...(言う/言った)事; **uncalled-for ~** sashide͘guchi 差し出口 **2.** → **say**

remarkable ijō 異常 (na) (な); ichijirushi͘i 著しい

remember *(recalls)* omoi-dashima'su (-da⌐su, -da⌐shite) 思い出します(出す, 出して); *(retains in memory)* obo'ete ima'su (iru, ite) 覚えています(いる, いて)

Remember me to ... ... ni yoroshiku (itte kudasa'i, o-tsutae kudasa'i) ...によろしく[宜しく](言って下さい, お伝え下さい) 「意

reminder hi'nto ヒント, chu'i 注

remind one of ... ... o omowasema'su (omowase'ru, omowa'sete) ...を思わせます(思わせる, 思わせて)

remissness yudan 油断

remit sōkin shima'su (suru, shite) 送金します(する, して)

remittance sōkin 送金 「ン

remote control rimo-kon リモコ

remove torima'su (to'ru, to'tte) 取ります(取る, 取って), nozokima'su (nozoku, nozoite) 除きます(除く, 除いて); sarima'su (sa⌐ru, sa⌐tte) 去ります(去る, 去って); ha'ijo shima(⌐)su (suru, shite) 排除します(する, して); → **take off**; → **omit**; → **move** *(house)*

remuneration sharei 謝礼

renew kōshin shima'su (suru, shite) 更新します(する, して)

renewal kōshin 更新

rent *(cost)* kari'-chin 借り賃,

(house) ya'-chin 家賃; *(rents it out to)* kashima'su (kasu, kashite) 貸します(貸す, 貸して); *(rents it from)* karima'su (kariru, karite) 借ります(借りる, 借りて)

rented/rental house kashi-ya 貸家

rented/rental room kashi-ma 貸間

rental car renta'ka' レンタカー

reorder *(adjusts)* se'iri shima(⌐)su (suru, shite) 整理します(する, して)

reorganize → reorder

repaint nuri-kaema'su (-ka'e'ru, -ka'ete) 塗り替えます(替える, 替えて)

repair 1. *(repairing)* naoshi' 直し, shu'ri 修理, shūzen 修繕, tsukuro'i 繕い; *(upkeep, care)* te-ire' 手入れ **2.** *(repairs it)* naoshima'su (nao'su, nao'shite) 直します(直す, 直して); tsukuroima'su (tsukuro'u, tsukuro'tte) 繕います(繕う, 繕って); shu'ri/ shūzen shima'su (suru, shite) 修理/修繕します(する, して); *(it gets repaired)* ... ga naorima'su (nao'ru, nao'tte) ...が直ります(直る, 直って), *(gets it repaired)* ... o nao'shite moraima'su (morau, moratte) ...を直してもらいます(もらう, もらって)

repairman shūrī-kō 修理工, shūzen-kō 修繕工

reparation (*provision*) teate (o-teate) 手当て（お手当て）; (*money*) baishō-kin 賠償金

repatriate hikiage-sha 引き揚げ者; **gets repatriated** hiki-agema'su (-age'ru, -a'gete) 引き揚げます（揚げる, 揚げて）

repatriation hiki-age 引き揚げ

repay (*compensates*) mukuima'su (mukui'ru, muku'ite) 報います（報いる, 報いて）

repeat mō ichi-do iima'su (yū, itte/yutte) もう一度言います（言う, 言って/ゆって）; kuri-kaeshima'su (-kae'su, -ka'eshite) 繰り返します（返す, 返して）

repeatedly (*often*) shi'bashiba しばしば; (*ever so many times*) na'n-do/-kai mo 何度/回も

repel (*water, etc.*) hajikima'su (haji'ku, haji'ite) 弾きます（弾く, 弾いて）

repercussion handō 反動

rephrase ii-kaema'su (-kae'ru, -ka'ete) 言い換えます（換える, 換えて）

replace torikaema'su (torikaeru, torikaete) 取り換えます（取り換える, 取り換えて）

replacement torikae 取り換え

replica fukusei 複製

reply → **answer**

report 1. (*notice*) shirase (o-shirase) 知らせ（お知らせ）, tsūchi 通知, todoke' (o-todoke) 届け（お届け）; (*announcement*) hōkoku 報告, (*message*) tsutae' (o-tsutae) 伝え（お伝え）; (*research paper*) happyō 発表; (*claim*) mōshi-de 申し出 2. (*announces*) hōkoku shima'su (suru, shite) 報告します（する, して）, (*relays, tells*) tsutaema'su (tsutaeru, tsutaete) 伝えます（伝える, 伝えて）, (*is reported*) tsutawarima'su (tsutawaru, tsutawatte) 伝わります（伝わる, 伝わって）, (*notifies*) todokema'su (todoke'ru, todo'kete) 届けます（届ける, 届けて）; (*presents research*) happyō shima'su (suru, shite) 発表します（する, して）; (*claims*) mōshi-dema'su (-de'ru, -de'te) 申し出ます（出る, 出て）; → **inform**; → **tell**

report card seiseki-hyō 成績表

reportedly ... sō' desu ...そうです

reporter shimbun-ki'sha 新聞記者, kisha' 記者

report for work shukkin shima'su (suru, shite) 出勤します（する, して）

representative daihyō 代表,

daihyṓ-sha 代表者; *(typical, model)* daihyō-teki (na) 代表的(な); → **agent**

repress osaema'su (osa'e'ru, osa'ete) 抑えます(抑える, 抑えて)

reprint fukusei/fukusha (shima'su; suru, shite) 複製/複写(します; する, して)

reproach hi'nan shima(¬)su (suru, shite) 非難します(する, して), semema'su (seme'ru, se'mete) 責めます(責める, 責めて)

reproduce *(replicates/copies it)* fukusei/fukusha shima'su (suru, shite) 複製/複写します(する, して)

reproduction *(replication)* fukusei 複製, *(copy)* fukusha 複写

reprove togamema'su (togame'ru, toga'mete) とがめ[咎め]ます(とがめる, とがめて)

reputation hyōban 評判

request 1. nega'i 願い, tanomi' 頼み, irai 依頼; *(a demand)* yōkyū 要求, seikyū 請求; *(requesting)* ko'i 請い 2. *(asks a favor)* negaima'su (nega'u, nega'tte) 願います(願う, 願って), tanomima'su (tano'mu, tano'nde) 頼みます(頼む, 頼んで), irai shima'su (suru, shite) 依頼します(する, して);

(demands) seikyū shima'su (suru, shite) 請求します(する, して)

require 1. *(demands)* yōkyū shima'su (suru, shite) 要求します(する, して) 2. → **need**; → **take** *(time/money)*; → **stipulate**

requirement yōkyū 要求; *(qualification)* shikaku 資格

rescue tasukema'su (tasuke'ru, tasuke'te) 助けます(助ける, 助けて), sukuima'su (sukuu, sukutte) 救います(救う, 救って); kyū'jo shima'su (suru, shite) 救助します(する, して)

research kenkyū (shima'su; suru, shite) 研究(します; する, して); *(investigation)* chō'sa 調査

resemblance ruiji 類似

resemble ... ni nite ima'su (iru, ite) ...に似ています(いる, いて), nima'su (niru, nite) 似ます(似る, 似て); ... ni/to ruiji shima'su (suru, shite) ...に/と類似します(する, して); **closely ~** ... ni/to ni-kayoima'su (-kayo'u, -kayo'tte) ...に/と似通います(通う, 通って)

resent fungai shima'su (suru, shite) 憤慨します(する, して); ikidōrima'su (ikidō'ru, ikidō'tte) 憤ります(憤る, 憤って); uramima'su (ura'mu,

ura﹁nde) 恨みます(恨む, 恨ん
で)

resentment fungai 憤慨,
ikidōri﹁ 憤り, urami﹁ 恨み

reservation *(booking)* yoyaku 予
約, mōshi-komi 申し込み

reserve *(reticence)* enryo 遠慮;
shows ~ enryo shima﹁su
(suru, shite) 遠慮します(する,
して)

reserve *(spare)* yo﹁bi (no) 予備
(の); **~ fund** tsumitate﹁-kin
積立金

reserve *(makes a reservation)*
yoyaku shima﹁su (suru, shite)
予約します(する, して),
mōshi-komima﹁su (-ko﹁mu,
-ko﹁nde) 申し込みます(込む,
込んで); *(puts aside, holds)*
to﹁tte okima﹁su (oku, oite)
取って置きます(置く, 置い
て)　　　　　　　　　「席

reserved seat(s) shite﹁i-seki 指定

reserves *(reserve forces)* yobi-tai
予備隊

reservoir chosu﹁i-chi 貯水池,
jōsu﹁i-chi 浄水池

reside → **live**

residence 1. *(place)* su﹁ma﹁i (o-
su﹁mai) 住まい(お住まい),
jū﹁sho 住所, jūtaku 住宅;
one's ~ (home) jitaku 自宅
2. *(residing)* zairyū 在留;
status of ~ zairyū-shi﹁kaku
在留資格; **permanent ~**
ho﹁nseki 本籍, *(place)*

honse﹁ki﹁-chi 本籍地

resident *(person)* kyojū﹁-sha 居住
者; *(apartment tenant)*
nyūkyo﹁-sha 入居者

resident in ... zai-... 在...

resign (a job) (shigoto o)
yamema﹁su (yameru, yamete)
(仕事を)辞めます(辞める,
辞めて), jishoku shima﹁su
(suru, shite) 辞職します(する,
して)

resignation 1. *(quitting a job)*
jishoku 辞職 **2.** *(acceptance)*
akirame 諦め, ka﹁ku﹁go 覚悟

resigned: is resigned to ... o
ka﹁ku﹁go shima(﹁)su (suru,
shite) ...を覚悟します(する,
して), akiramema﹁su
(akirame﹁ru, akira﹁mete) 諦めま
す(諦める, 諦めて)

resin yani﹁ やに, *(pine)* matsu-
yani 松やに

resist ... ni hankō/teikō shima﹁su
(suru, shite) ...に反抗/抵抗し
ます(する, して),
kobamima﹁su (koba﹁mu,
koba﹁nde) 拒みます(拒む, 拒
んで)

resistance hankō 反抗, teikō 抵
抗

resolutely shikka﹁ri しっかり

resolution *(premeditation)*
ka﹁ku﹁go 覚悟

resolve *(determination)* ke﹁sshi﹁n
決心; **resolves to do** (shiyō to)
ke﹁sshi﹁n shima(﹁)su (suru,

shi̱te) （しようと）決心します
（する，して）

resolved: is ~ (to do) ka̱ku̱go
shima(˥)su̱ (suru, shi̱te) 覚悟
します（する，して）

resound *(echo)* hibikima̱su
(hi̱bi̱ku, hibi̱ite) 響きます（響
く，響いて）

respect 1. sonkei 尊敬, uyama˥i
敬い，**2.** sonkei shima̱su (suru,
shi̱te) 尊敬します（する，して）;
uyamaima̱su (uyama̱u,
uyama̱tte) 敬います（敬う，敬
って），ogamima̱su (oga̱mu,
oga̱nde) 拝みます（拝む，拝
んで）**3.** → **with respect to**

respectable katagi (na) 堅気（な）;
(proper) chanto shita ... ちゃ
んとした...; *(considerable)*
cho̱tto shi̱ta ... ちょっとした...

respect for the aged keirō 敬老;
**Respect-for-the-Aged Day (15
September)** Keirō no hi˥ 敬老
の日

respective sore˥zo̱re no ... それ
ぞれの..., ono̱ono no ... 各々
［おのおの］の...; **respectively**
sore˥zo̱re それぞれ, ono̱ono
各々・おのおの

respiration kokyū 呼吸

respond kotaema̱su (kota̱e̱ru,
kota̱ete) 答えます（答える，
答えて）; ō-jima̱su (ō-ji˥ru,
ō˥-jite) 応じます（応じる，応
じて）

response kota̱e̱ 答え

responsibility sekinin 責任;
(charge) tantō 担当; *(cause)*
gen'in 原因

responsible for *(is in charge of)* ...
o tantō shi̱te ima̱su (iru, ite) ...
を担当しています（いる，い
て）; *(is the cause of)* ... no
gen'in desu ...の原因です

responsible person sekini̱n-sha
責任者; *(the one in charge)*
tantō˥-sha 担当者

rest 1. *(a break/pause)* yasumi˥
(o-yasumi) 休み（お休み），
kyūkei 休憩 **2. the rest** *(remainder)* nokori˥ 残り;
(thereafter) sore kara a̱to (wa)
それから後（は）**3.** *(takes a
rest)* yasumima̱su (yasu̱mu,
yasu̱nde) 休みます（休む，休
んで）

restaurant re˥su̱toran レストラ
ン, shokudō 食堂; ryōri˥-ten/
-ya 料理店/屋

restless ochi-tsu̱kimase̱n
(-tsu̱kanai) 落ち着きません
（着かない）

restrain osaema̱su (osa̱e̱ru,
osa̱ete) 抑えます（抑える，抑
えて）; **properly restrained** ii-
kagen (na) いい加減（な）

restrict seige̱n/gentei shima̱su
(suru, shi̱te) 制限/限定します
（する，して）; **restriction**
seige̱n 制限, gentei 限定

restricted fu̱-jiyū (na) 不自由（な）

rest room keshō˥-shi̱tsu 化粧室,

(o-)tea˺rai（お）手洗い；→
toilet

result kekka 結果；*(outcome)*
se˺ika 成果；*(marks, grades)*
seiseki 成績

retail ko-uri 小売り；*(retails it)*
ko-uri shima˺su (suru, shite)
小売りします（する，して）

retain *(keeps it)* kakaema˺su
(kakae˺ru, kaka˺ete) 抱えま
す（抱える，抱えて）

retentiveness (of memory)
kioku˺-ryoku 記憶力

reticence enryo (go-enryo) 遠慮
（ご遠慮）

retire 1. *(from job)* intai/
taishoku shima˺su (suru, shite)
引退/退職します（する，して）
2. *(withdraws)* shirizokima˺su
(shirizo˺ku, shirizo˺ite) 退きま
す（退く，退いて）；hiki-
torima˺su (-to˺ru, -to˺tte) 引き
取ります（取る，取って）

retirement intai 引退, taishoku
退職；~ **allowance** taishoku˺-
kin 退職金；~ **pension**
taishoku-ne˺nkin 退職年金

retreat shirizokima˺su
(shirizo˺ku, shirizo˺ite) 退きま
す（退く，退いて）

retribution bachi˺ 罰・ばち

return *(reverses direction)*
modorima˺su (modo˺ru,
modo˺tte) 戻ります（戻る，
戻って）；*(goes back/home)*
kaerima˺su (ka˺eru, ka˺ette) 帰

ります（帰る，帰って）；
*(comes back to where one is
now)* itte kima˺su (ku˺ru, kite˺)
行って来ます（来る，来て）；
~ **from abroad** kikoku
shima˺su (suru, shite) 帰国し
ます（する，して）

return it kaeshima˺su (ka˺esu,
ka˺eshite) 返します（返す，返
して）；modoshima˺su
(modo˺su, modo˺shite) 戻しま
す（戻す，戻して）

reveal morashima˺su (mora˺su,
mora˺shite) 漏らします（漏ら
す，漏らして）；*(shows)*
arawashima˺su (arawa˺su,
arawa˺shite) 現（わ）します（現
（わ）す，現（わ）して）；*(makes
it public)* aki˺raka ni shima˺su
(suru, shite) 明らかにします
（する，して）

revenge (… no) fukushū o
shima˺su (suru, shite) (…の)復
讐をします（する，して）

revenue stamp shūnyū-i˺nshi 収
入印紙

revere uyamaima˺su (uyama˺u,
uyama˺tte) 敬います（敬う，敬

reverence uyama˺i 敬い ⌐って）

Reverend … bo˺kushi …牧師, …
shi˺mpu …神父

reverse hantai 反対；*(back;
lining)* ura˺ 裏

revert modorima˺su (modo˺ru,
modo˺tte) 戻ります（戻る，
戻って）

review 1. *(study)* fukushū 復習; *(studies it)* fukushū shima῾su (suru, shite) 復習します(する, して) **2.** *(criticism)* hihyō 批評, *(commentary)* hyōron 評論; *(criticizes it / comments on it)* hihyō/hyōron shima῾su (suru, shite) 批評/評論します(する, して)

reviewer hyōron-ka 評論家

revival *(regeneration)* kōsei 更生; → **recover**

revive *(brings back to life)* ikashima῾su (ika῾su, ika῾shite) 生かします(生かす, 生かして)

revoke tori-keshima῾su (-ke῎su, -ke῎shite) 取り消します(消す, 消して)

revolt somukima῾su (somu῎ku, somu῎ite) 背きます(背く, 背いて)

revolution *(political)* kakumei 革命; *(revolving)* kaiten 回転

revolve mawarima῾su (mawaru, mawatte) 回ります(回る, 回って), kaiten shima῾su (suru, shite) 回転します(する, して)

revolver pisutoru ピストル

reward shōkin 賞金, shō῎yo 賞与; sharei 謝礼; (go-)hō῎bi (ご)ほうび・褒美

rewards and punishments shō῎-batsu 賞罰

rewrite (it) kaki-naoshima῾su (-nao῎su, -nao῎shite) 書き

直します(直す, 直して), kaki-kaema῾su (-kae῎ru, -kae῎ete) 書き換えます(換える, 換えて)

rhubarb: bog ~ fuki ふき・蕗

ribbon himo ひも・紐, ri῎bon リボン

rice kome῎ (o-kome) 米(お米); *(cooked)* go῎han ご飯, meshi῎ 飯, *(on plate)* ra῎isu ライス; *(at store)* o-kome お米; *(hulled)* kome῎ 米, *(unhulled)* momi῎ もみ・籾; *(unpolished)* ge῎mmai 玄米, *(polished)* haku῎mai 白米; *(plant)* i῎ne 稲

rice: Chinese fried rice chā῎han チャーハン・炒飯

riceball musubi (o-mu῎subi) むすび・結び(おむすび・お結び); nigiri-meshi にぎり[握り]飯, o-ni῎giri おにぎり・お握り; ~ **lunch(box)** makuno῎uchi 幕の内

rice boiled in a soup zōsui 雑炊

rice boiled with red beans sekiha῎n (o-se῎kihan) 赤飯(お赤飯)

rice bowl chawan (o-cha῎wan) 茶碗(お茶碗)

rice bucket/tub meshi῎-bitsu 飯びつ[櫃] (= o-hitsu おひつ[櫃] = o-hachi お鉢)

rice cake mochi 餅

rice cakes boiled with vegetables zōni῎ (o-zōni) 雑煮・ぞうに(お雑煮)

rice-cracker cubes/tidbits arare
あられ

rice crackers se⌐mbe(i) せんべ
(い)・煎餅, o-se⌐n おせん

rice curry (= *rice with curry*)
karē-ra⌐isu カレーライス

rice dealer kome⌐-ya (o-komeya)
米屋(お米屋)

rice field ta⌐ 田, tambo 田んぼ・
たんぼ

rice gruel/porridge (o-)kayu
(お)かゆ[粥]

rice paper (*stationery*) ha⌐nshi 半
紙

rice planting taue⌐ 田植え

**rice seasoned with sweetened
vinegar** su⌐shi すし・鮨・寿司,
sushi⌐ すし・鮨・寿司

rice straw wa⌐ra わら・藁

**rice topped with chicken and
onion cooked in egg** oyako-
do⌐mburi 親子どんぶり[丼]

rice topped with something dom-
buri (o-do⌐mburi) どんぶり・
丼(おどんぶり・お丼)

rice wine → saké

**rice with hot tea and flavorings
poured over it** (o-)chazuke
(お)茶漬け

rich (*wealthy*) kanemo⌐chi⌐ (no)
金持ち(の), yū⌐fuku (na) 裕
福(な); (*abundant*) yu⌐taka
(na) 豊か(な), hō⌐fu (na) 豊
富(な); **is rich/abundant in** ...
ni tomima⌐su (to⌐mu, to⌐nde) ...
に富みます(富む, 富んで)

ricksha jinri⌐ki⌐sha 人力車

riddle nazo 謎

ride 1. ... ni norima⌐su (noru,
notte) ...に乗ります(乗る,
乗って), ... ni notte ikima⌐su
(iku, itte) ...に乗って行きます
(行く, 行って); (*sits astride*)
matagarima⌐su (mataga⌐ru,
mataga⌐tte) またがり[跨り]ま
す(またがる, またがって)
2. gives a ride to ... o
nosema⌐su (noseru, nosete) ...
を乗せます(乗せる, 乗せて)

ridge (of roof) mune 棟

rifle shōjū 小銃, raifuru⌐-jū ライ
フル銃, teppō 鉄砲

right (*not left*) migi (no) 右(の);
(*correct*) tadashi⌐i (tada⌐shiku)
正しい(正しく), i⌐i (yo⌐ku) い
い(良く); (*privilege*) ke⌐nri 権
利

right: just ~ pitta⌐ri ぴったり

right: That's right Sō⌐ desu. そう
です. **You are so right.** Naru-
hodo. なるほど・成る程.

right away (*at once*) sassoku⌐ 早
速

right-handed migi-kiki (no) 右利
き(の)

right mind: in one's ~ shō⌐ki
(no) 正気(の)

right or wrong ze⌐-hi 是非

rim heri⌐ へり・縁, fuchi⌐ ふち・縁

ring (*on finger*) yubi-wa 指輪;
(*circle*) wa⌐ 輪, maru 丸・円

ring (*a bell sounds*) narima⌐su

(naru, natte) 鳴ります(鳴る、鳴って); *(sounds a bell)* narashima᷄su (narasu, narashite) 鳴らします(鳴らす、鳴らして)

ringleader oꞌyaꞌ-bun 親分

ring-shaped kanjō (no) 環状(の)

ringworm tamushi⌐ たむし・田虫、mizumushi 水虫

riot bōdō 暴動、sōꞌdō 騒動

ripen: it gets ripe jukushima᷄su (jukuꞌsu, jukuꞌshite) 熟します(熟す、熟して)、seijuku shima᷄su (suru, shite) 成熟します(する、して); minorima᷄su (mino⌐ru, mino⌐tte) 実ります(実る、実って)

ripped off: gets ~ *(overcharged)* borarema᷄su (borareꞌru, boraꞌrete) ぼられます(ぼられる、ぼられて)、*(robbed)* yararema᷄su (yarareru, yararete) やられます(やられる、やられて)

rise *(gets up)* okima᷄su (okiꞌru, oꞌkite) 起きます(起きる、起きて); *(goes up)* agarima᷄su (agaru, agatte) 上がります(上がる、上がって)、*(climbs, sun rises)* noborima᷄su (noboru, nobotte) 登り[昇り]ます(登[昇]る、登[昇]って); *(stands up)* tachi-agarima᷄su (-aga⌐ru, -aga⌐tte) 立ち上がります(上がる、上がって);

(looms) sobiema᷄su (sobieꞌru, sobiꞌete) そびえます・聳えます(そびえる、そびえて)

rise: gives ~ to ... o okoshima᷄su (okoꞌsu, okoꞌshite) ...を起こします(起こす、起こして)、shō-jima᷄su (shō-ji⌐ru, shō⌐-jite) 生じます(生じる、生じて)

rise *(in price, wage, fee)* hiki-age 引き上げ

rival teki 敵

rivalry kyōsō 競争; **in ~ with ...** ni taikō shite ...に対抗して

river kawaꞌ 川・河

river trout aꞌyu あゆ・鮎、aꞌi あい

road michi 道、dōꞌro 道路、**(main ~)** kaidō⌐ 街道; *(= road-way)* shadō 車道; *(roadside)* tsuji 辻、michibata 道端

road-show attraction rōdo-shō ロードショー

roadside michibata 道端、tsuji 辻

roadsign dōro-hyōꞌshiki 道路標識

roar 1. *(a roar)* unariꞌ うなり・唸り **2.** *(roars)* unarima᷄su (unaꞌru, unaꞌtte) うなり[唸り]ます(うなる、うなって) **3.** *(rumbles)* todorokima᷄su (todoroꞌku, todoroꞌite) とどろき[轟き]ます(とどろく、とどろいて)

roast 1. yaki-... 焼き...、...-yaki ...焼き; *(cut of meat)* rōꞌsu ロース; rōꞌsuto ロースト; **~ beef/**

chicken rōsuto-bīfu/-chīkin ローストビーフ/チキン
2. *(roasts it)* yakima̅su (yaku, yaite) 焼きます(焼く, 焼いて); irima̅su (i̅ru, i̅tte) いり[炒り]ます(いる, いって)

roasted chestnuts yaki⌐-guri 焼き栗

rob *(steals)* nusumima̅su (nusu̅mu, nusu̅nde) 盗みます(盗む, 盗んで); *(plunders)* ubaima̅su (uba̅u, uba̅tte) 奪います(奪う, 奪って); *(robs it of ...)* kasume-torima̅su (-to̅ru, -to̅tte) かすめ取ります(取る, 取って); **gets robbed (hit with a robbery)** (gōtō ni) yararema̅su (yarareru, yararete) (強盗に)やられます(やられる, やられて)

robber gōtō 強盗, dorobō どろぼう・泥棒; zoku 賊

robbery gōtō 強盗

rock *(stone)* ishi̅ 石, *(crag)* iwa̅ 岩

rock *(it rocks)* yurema̅su (yureru, yurete) 揺れます(揺れる, 揺れて)

rod sao̅ さお・竿; *(curtain, etc.)* ro̅ddo ロッド

roe *(caviar):* salmon ~ i⌐kura イクラ, *(salmon/trout)* suji⌐ko⌐ すじこ・筋子, suzu⌐ko⌐ すずこ; cod ~ tara̅ko たらこ・鱈子

role yakuwa⌐ri⌐ 役割, yaku̅ (o-

yaku) 役(お役); tsutome̅ (o-tsutome) 務め(お務め)

roll 1. *(it rolls)* korogarima̅su (korogaru, korogatte) 転がります(転がる, 転がって), *(= sways)* yurema̅su (yureru, yurete) 揺れます(揺れる, 揺れて); *(rolls it)* korogashima̅su (korogasu, korogashite) 転がします(転がす, 転がして); *(rolls it up)* makima̅su (maku, maite) 巻きます(巻く, 巻いて)
2. *(bread)* maki-pan 巻きパン, rōru ロール＝rōru-pa⌐n ロールパン, (batā-)rōru (バター)ロール **3. a roll (of toilet paper)** (toiretto-pe̅pā) hito̅-maki (トイレットペーパー)一巻; ~ **of (currency) bills** satsu-ta⌐ba 札束 **4.** *(list of names)* meibo 名簿

roller rō̅rā ローラー; **roller-skates/-skating** rōra-sukē̅to ローラースケート

romanization rōma̅-ji ローマ字
Rome Rō̅ma ローマ

roof 1. ya̅ne 屋根; *(rooftop floor)* okujō 屋上 **2. roofs a house** uchi no ya̅ne o fukima̅su (fuku⌐, fu⌐ite) 家の屋根をふき[葺き]ます(ふく, ふいて)

room 1. heya̅ (o-heya) 部屋(お部屋), (....-)ma (...)間; ...̅-shitsu ...室; *(tatami room)* zashiki̖ (o-zashiki̖) 座敷（お座敷）; *(small Japanese room)* yo-jō̖-han 四畳半 **2.** *(extra space)* yo̖chi 余地, *(leeway)* yoyū 余裕

room and board geshuku 下宿

rooming/boarding house geshuku-ya 下宿屋

roommate dōshitsu̖-sha 同室者

room number heya̖ no bangō̖ 部屋の番号; **Room No. 3** san-gō̖shitsu 三号室

room service rūmu-sā̖bisu ルームサービス

rooms for rent kashi-ma 貸間

root ne̖ 根, **near the ~** ne-moto̖ 根元; *(cause)* gen'in 原因

rope nawa̖ 縄・繩, tsuna̖ 綱; **mountain-climbing ~** za̖iru ザイル

rose bara (no hana̖) ばら［薔薇］（の花）

rosy momoiro (no) 桃色（の）

rot kuchima̖su (kuchi̖ru, ku̖chite) 朽ちます（朽ちる, 朽ちて）, kusarima̖su (kusa̖ru, kusa̖tte) 腐ります（腐る, 腐って）

rotary → **traffic circle**

rotate kaiten shima̖su (suru, shite) 回転します（する, して）; **rotation** kaiten 回転

rouge be̖ni べに・紅

rough *(coarse; wild)* arai 荒い, zatsu-... 雑...; *(in texture)* za̖razara (shita ...) ざらざら

（した...）; *(bumpy)* dekoboko no でこぼこ・凸凹の; *(rambunctious)* rambō (na) 乱暴（な）; *(approximate)* ōyoso no おおよその; *(sloppy)* zonzai (na) ぞんざい（な）

rough: gets ~ arema̖su (areru, arete) 荒れます（荒れる, 荒れて）

rough idea: gets a ~ of it kentō̖ ga tsukima̖su (tsuku̖, tsu̖ite) 見当がつきます（つく, ついて）

roughly oyoso およそ; zatto ざっと; ho̖bo ほぼ; ...-ke̖ntō ...見当

roughneck abare-mono 暴れ者

round marui 丸い; **~ thing** tama̖ 玉・珠

roundabout → **traffic circle**

roundtable discussion zada̖n-kai 座談会

round trip (ticket) ōfuku (-ki̖ppu) 往復（切符）

rouse okoshima̖su (oko̖su, oko̖shite) 起こします（起こす, 起こして）

route se̖n 線

row *(line)* re̖tsu 列, narabi 並び, *(of trees)* namiki 並木; **are in a row** narande ima̖su (iru, ite) 並んでいます（いる, いて）; **(linked) in a row** tsunagatte つながって

row (a boat) kogima̖su (ko̖gu, ko̖ide) こぎ［漕ぎ］ます（こぐ, こいで）

rub 1. *(rubs it)* kosurima̅sụ
(kosu̅ru, kosụtte̅) こすりま
す(こする, こすって),
surima̅sụ (su̅ru, sụtte̅) 擦り
ます(擦る, 擦って), masatsu
shima̅sụ (suru, shịte) 摩擦し
ます(する, して); *(with both
hands)* momima̅sụ (momu,
monde) もみ[揉み]ます(もむ,
もんで) **2.** *(it rubs)* surema̅sụ
(sure̅ru, su̅rete) 擦れます(擦
れる, 擦れて)

rubber go̅mu ゴム; *(condom)*
sa̅kku サック

rubber band wa-gomu 輪ゴム

rubbish gomi̅ ごみ; ku̅zu くず・
屑, kuzu⌐-mono くず物・屑物,
garakụta がらくた, sụte-
mono 捨て物; ~ **collector**
gomi̅-ya (san) ごみ屋(さん)

rudder ka̅ji かじ・舵

rude bu̅rei (na) 無礼(な); bu-
e̅nryo (na) 無遠慮(な)

ruffian abare-mono 暴れ者

rug shịki-mono 敷物, jū̅tan じゅ
うたん・絨毯

ruin 1. ruins it dame̅ ni shima̅sụ
(suru, shịte) だめ[駄目]にし
ます(する, して) **2. goes to
~** arema̅sụ (areru, arete) 荒
れます(荒れる, 荒れて)

ruined: gets ~ dame̅ ni
narima̅sụ (na̅ru, na̅tte) だめ
[駄目]になります(なる,
なって)

ruin one's health karada o

kowashima̅sụ (kowa̅su,
kowa̅shịte) 体をこわします(こ
わす, こわして)

rule *(regulation)* kịso̅ku 規則,
kịtei 規定; *(law)* hōsoku 法則,
hō̅ 法

ruler *(to measure with)* jo̅gi 定規,
(foot rule) monosa̅shị 物差し

rumble todorokima̅sụ
(todoro̅ku, todoro̅ite) とどろ
き[轟き]ます(とどろく, と
どろいて)

rumor uwasa うわさ・噂

run 1. hashirima̅sụ (hashi̅ru,
hashị̅tte) 走ります(走る,
走って), *(gallops)* kakema̅sụ
(kake̅ru, ka̅kete) 駆けます
(駆ける, 駆けて); ~**s a
marathon** marason o shima̅sụ
(suru, shịte) マラソンをしま
す(する, して) **2.** *(connects)*
tsū-jima̅sụ (tsū-jiru, tsū-jite)
通じます(通じる, 通じて)
3. *(operates a machine)* unten
shima̅sụ (suru, shịte) 運転し
ます(する, して)
4. *(manages, operates a
business)* keiei shima̅sụ (suru,
shịte) 経営します(する, して)

run:

　run along(side) soima̅sụ (sou,
　　sotte) 沿います(沿う, 沿っ
　　て)

　run away *(flees)* nigema̅sụ
　　(nige̅ru, ni̅gete) 逃げます
　　(逃げる, 逃げて),

ochima'sụ (ochi'ru, o'chite)
落ちます(落ちる, 落ちて);
(from home) (uchi o) tobi-
dashima'sụ (-da'sụ,
-da'shịte) (家を)飛び出しま
す(出す, 出して), iede⎡⎤
shima'sụ 家出します

run fast *(timepiece)*
sụsumima'sụ (sụsumu,
sụsunde) 進みます(進む,
進んで)

run into 1. → **collide 2.** →
meet 3. *(comes to the end of
a street)* tsụki-atarima'sụ
(-ataru, -atatte) 突き当たり
ます(当たる, 当たって)

run out 1. *(dashes out)* tobi-
dashima'sụ (-da'sụ,
-da'shịte) 跳び[飛び]出しま
す(出す, 出して) **2. it runs
out** *(stock is exhausted)*
kirema'sụ (kire'ru, kị'rete)
切れます(切れる, 切れて),
(gets used up) tsụkima'sụ
(tsụki⎡⎤ru, tsụ'ki⎡⎤te) 尽き
ます(尽きる, 尽きて)
3. runs out of it … o
kirashima'sụ (kira'sụ,
kira'shịte)…を切らします
(切らす, 切らして), … o
tsụkushima'sụ (tsụku'sụ,
tsụku'shịte) …を尽くします
(尽くす, 尽くして); *(it
sells out)* uri-kirema'sụ
(-kire'ru, -kị'rete) 売り切れ
ます(切れる, 切れて)

run over 1. *(a person)*
hịkima'sụ (hịku, hiite) ひき
ます・轢きます(ひく, ひい
て); **gets run over by** … ni
hịkarema'sụ (hịkareru,
hịkarete) …にひかれ[轢か
れ]ます(ひかれる, ひかれ
て) **2.** → **exceed**

run overtime ji⎡⎤kan ga o'bā
shima'sụ (suru, shịte) 時間
がオーバーします(する,
して)

run slow *(it lags)* okurema'sụ
(okureru, okurete) 遅れま
す(遅れる, 遅れて)

runaway iede-nin 家出人

running water suidō 水道

runt *(deprecating a short person)*
chị'bi ちび, chibi-me ちびめ

runway to the stage (in Kabuki)
hana'-michi 花道

rural inaka no いなか[田舎]の

rush isogima'sụ (iso'gu, iso'ide)
急ぎます(急ぐ, 急いで); ō-
i'sogi de shima'sụ (suru, shịte)
大急ぎでします(する, して)

rush: with a ~ *(suddenly)*
do⎡⎤tto どっと

rushed: feels ~ aserima'sụ
(ase'ru, ase'tte) 焦ります(焦る,
焦って)   ⎡アワー

rush hour rasshu-a'wā ラッシュ

Russia Ro'shi(y)a ロシア[ヤ];
   (Soviet Union) So'ren ソ連

Russian Roshi(y)a'-jin ロシア
[ヤ]人; *(language)* Roshi(y)a-

go ロシア[ヤ]語
rust sabi˩ さび・錆; *(it rusts)*
sabima˩su (sabi˩ru, sa˩bite) さ
び[錆び]ます(さびる, さび
て)

rustic ya˩bo (na) やぼ[野暮](な)
rustproof sabi˩nai さび[錆び]な
い
rut wa⌐-dachi わだち・轍
Ryukyu (islands) Ryūkyū˩ 琉球

— S —

sack fukuro˩ 袋
sacrifice gisei 犠牲; **makes a ~
(scapegoat) of** ... o gisei ni
shima˩su (suru, shite) ...を犠
牲にします(する, して); **is
sacrificed** gisei ni narima˩su
(na˩ru, na˩tte) 犠牲になります
(なる, なって)
sad kanashii 悲しい
saddle kura˩ くら・鞍
safe 1. *(harmproof)* anzen (na)
安全(な); *(reliable)* dai-jō˩bu
(na) 大丈夫(な), jōbu (na) 丈
夫(な); *(steady)* te-gata⌐i 手
堅い; *(certain)* ta˩shika (na) 確
か(な)
2. *(strongbox)* ki˩nko 金庫
safe: to be on the ~ side nen no
tame˩ (ni) 念のため[為](に);
plays it ~ daiji˩ o torima˩su
(to˩ru, to˩tte) 大事をとります
(とる, とって)
safeguard ho˩go shima(⌐)su
(suru, shite) 保護します(する,
して)
safe(ly) *(harmfree, without inci-*

dent) bu˩ji (ni) 無事(に); *(for
sure)* chanto ちゃんと,
ta˩shika (ni) 確か(に)
safety pin anze˩m-pi˩n 安全ピン
said iima˩shita (itta/yutta) 言い
ました(言った/ゆった) →
say
sail 1. ho⌐ 帆 2. *(makes a
voyage)* kō⌐kai shima˩su
(suru, shite) 航海します(する,
して)
sailor funa˩nori 船乗り, su˩ifu 水
夫; *(member of the crew)*
sen'in 船員; *(navy enlisted person)* su˩ihei 水兵
saké *(rice wine)* (o-)sake (お)酒,
Nihon-shu 日本酒; **sweet ~
(for cooking)** mirin みりん・味
醂; **~ bottle/pitcher** *(=
decanter)* tokkuri とっくり・
徳利; **~ cup** (o-)cho˩ko (お)
ちょこ, sakazuki⌐ (o-
sakazuki) 杯(お杯); **~ of-
fered to the gods** mi⌐ki 神酒
= o-miki お神酒・おみき
sake: for the sake of ... no tame˩

(o-tame) ni ...のため[為](お
ため)に

salad sa⌐rada サラダ

salary hōkyū 俸給, (o-)kyū⌐ryō
(お)給料, sa⌐rarii サラリー;
(monthly) gekkyū 月給

sale hambai 販売; *(special)* uri-
dashi 売り出し, (...-)sē⌐ru
(...)セール; **~ goods/item,
(something) for ~** uri-mono
売り物

sales agency hambai-moto 販売
元

**salesclerk, salesperson (salesgirl/
saleswoman/salesman)** ten'in
店員, uriko 売り子

sales outlet hamba⌐i-ten 販売店

sales volume hamba⌐i-daka 販売
高

saliva tsubaki⌐ つばき・唾, tsu⌐ba⌐
つば・唾

salmon sa⌐ke さけ・鮭, sha⌐ke
しゃけ・鮭; **~ roe** i⌐kura イク
ラ; suji⌐ko⌐ すじこ・筋子,
suzu⌐ko⌐ すずこ

salt shio⌐ 塩, o-shi⌐o お塩; **table
~** shoku⌐en 食塩

salty shio-kara⌐i 塩辛い, shop-
pa⌐i しょっぱい

salvage hiki-age 引き揚げ

same onaji ... 同じ..., *[bookish]*
dō⌐(-) ... 同...; onaji yō⌐ (na/
ni) 同じ様(な/に); **one and
the ~** hito⌐tsu 一つ; **~ period**
dō⌐ki 同期; **~ time** dō⌐ji 同
時

sample 1. mihon 見本
2. *(samples = tries doing)*
(shi)-te mima⌐su (mi⌐ru, mi⌐te)
(し)てみます(みる, みて)

samurai (warrior) samurai 侍,
bu⌐shi 武士; **way of the ~**
bushi⌐-dō 武士道

sand suna 砂; **~ dune** sakyū 砂
丘

sandal sa⌐ndaru サンダル;
straw sandals zōri (o-zō⌐ri) 草
履・ぞうり(お草履)

sandalwood byakudan びゃくだ
ん・白壇

sandbag suna-bu⌐kuro 砂袋

sandpaper sandopē⌐pā サンド
ペーパー, kami-ya⌐suri 紙やす
り, yasuri⌐-gami やすり紙

sandwich sandoi⌐tchi サンドイッ
チ; ...-sa⌐ndo ...サンド

sane shō⌐ki (no) 正気(の)

San Francisco Sanfuranshi⌐suko
サンフランシスコ

sanitary cisei teki (na) 衛生的(な);
~ belt gekkei-tai 月経帯; **~
napkin** (seiri-yō no) na⌐puki⌐n
(生理用の)ナプキン

sanitation eisei 衛生

sarcasm, sarcastic hiniku (na) 皮
肉(な)

sardine iwashi いわし・鰯; *(baby)*
shi⌐rasu しらす・白子; *(large,
usually dried)* urume(-i⌐washi)
うるめ(いわし)・潤目(鰯)

sash *(girdle)* o⌐bi 帯; *(military)*
suka⌐fu スカーフ; *(window-*

sash) mado-waku 窓枠, saˈsshu サッシュ, saˈsshi サッシ

satin shuˈsu しゅす・繻子, saˈten サテン

satisfactory yoroshii よろしい・宜しい, maˈnzoku (na) 満足 (な)

satisfied: gets ～ maˈnzoku shima(ˈ)su (suru, shite) 満足 します(する, して)

satisfy maˈnzoku sasema(ˈ)su (saseru, sasete) 満足させます (させる, させて); *(fulfills)* mitashima(ˈsu (mitaˈsu, mitaˈshite) 満たします(満た す, 満たして)

saturated koˈi 濃い

Saturday Doyōˈbi 土曜日; **Saturday-Sunday** dō-nichi 土日

sauce sōˈsu (o-sōˈsu) ソース(お ソース); *(cooking)* tareˈ たれ; **soy sauce** (o-)shōyu (お)しょ うゆ[醤油]

saucer koˈ-zara (o-koˈzara) 小 皿(お小皿), sara (o-sara) 皿 (お皿); *(for cup)* ukeˈ-zara 受 け皿

saurel aˈji あじ・鯵

saury-pike kamasu かます・魳

sausage sōˈsēˈji ソーセージ

sauté itamema(ˈsu (itameˈru, itaˈmete) 炒めます(炒める, 炒めて)

savage yaban (na) 野蛮(な); **a** ～ yaban-jiˈn 野蛮人

save *(saves up, hoards)* taku-waema(ˈsu (takuwaˈeˈru, takuwaˈete) 蓄えます(蓄 える, 蓄えて), *(deposits money)* chokin shima(ˈsu (suru, shite) 貯金します(する, して); *(accumulates)* tamema(ˈsu (tameru, tamete) ため[溜め]ます(ためる, た めて); *(curtails, omits)* habukima(ˈsu (habuˈku, habuˈite) 省きます(省く, 省 いて); *(economizes on)* setsuyaku shima(ˈsu (suru, shite) 節約します(する, し て), ken'yaku shima(ˈsu (suru, shite) 倹約します(する, して); → **rescue**

savings takuwaˈeˈ 蓄え; (～ **account)** chokin 貯金; **install- ment** ～ tsumitateˈ-kin 積立 金

savings account yokin-kōˈza 預 金口座, tsumitate-choˈkin 積 立貯金; ～ **book** yokin-tsūˈchō 預金通帳

saw *(tool)* nokogiˈriˈ のこぎり・鋸; *(saws it)* nokogiˈriˈ de hikima(ˈsu (hiku, hiite) のこぎ り[鋸]で引きます(引く, 引 いて)

saw *(did see)* mima(ˈshita (miˈta) 見ました(見た); *(met a per- son)* ... ni aima(ˈshita (aˈtta) ... に会いました(会った)

say it another way ii-kaema(ˈsu

(-kae⌐ru, -ka⌐ete) 言い換えま
す(換える, 換えて)
say (that ...) (... to) iima⌐su (yū,
itte/yutte) (...と) 言います(言
う, 言って/ゆって); [HUM-
BLE] mōshima⌐su (mō⌐su,
mō⌐shite/mōshima⌐shite) 申し
ます(申す, 申して/申しまし
て), mōshi-agema⌐su
(-age⌐ru, -a⌐gete) 申し上げ
ます(上げる, 上げて); [HONO-
RIFIC] osshaima⌐su (ossha⌐ru,
ossha⌐tte/osshaima⌐shite) おっ
しゃいます(おっしゃる,
おっしゃって/おっしゃいま
して)
say there! mo⌐shi-moshi! もしも
し!
scald 1. *(mark on the skin)*
yakedo やけど・火傷
2. *(scalds)* yakima⌐su (yaku,
yaite) 焼きます(焼く, 焼いて),
(gets scalded) yakema⌐su
(yakeru, yakete) 焼けます(焼
ける, 焼けて)
scales *(weighing)* hakari⌐ 秤・はか
り; *(fish)* u⌐roko うろこ・鱗
scallion asa⌐tsuki あさつき・浅葱
scallop(s) hotate⌐-gai はたて「帆
立」貝; *(pin/razor/fan shell)*
taira⌐-gai 平貝, taira-gi たいら
ぎ・玉珧
scandal ojoku 汚辱; sukya⌐ndaru
スキャンダル
scanty toboshi⌐i 乏しい
scapegoat → **sacrifice**

scar kizu-ato 傷跡
scarce sukuna⌐i 少ない,
toboshi⌐i 乏しい
scarcity *(shortage)* fusoku 不足;
(... ga) sukuna⌐i koto⌐ (...が)
少ない事
scare odorokashima⌐su
(odoroka⌐su, odoroka⌐shite)
驚かします(驚かす, 驚かし
て)
scarf suka⌐fu スカーフ
scatterbrain awate-mono 慌て
者
scatter (them) chira(ka)shima⌐su
(chira(ka)su, chira(ka)shite)
散ら(か)します(散ら(か)す,
散ら(か)して)
scene shi⌐in シーン; da⌐n 段;
ba⌐men 場面; *(sight)* ari⌐-
sama 有り様・ありさま
scenery ke⌐shiki 景色, fu⌐kei 風景,
(view) nagame⌐ 眺め
schedule yotei (shima⌐su; suru,
shite) 予定(します; する, し
て); *(daily routine)* nittei 日程;
(train) da⌐iya ダイヤ; *(timetable)* jikan-hyō 時間表; *(list)*
hyō 表
scheduled *(= periodic)* te⌐iki
(no) 定期(の)
scheme *(plan)* keikaku 計画;
(device) kufū 工夫; *(plot,
trick)* keiryaku 計略,
hakarigo⌐to はかりごと・
謀
scholar gakusha 学者; **scholarly**

society gakkai 学会

school gakkō 学校; **primary ~** shōga⌐kkō 小学校, **middle** *(junior high)* **~** chūga⌐kkō 中学校; **high ~** kōtō-ga⌐kkō 高等学校; **tutoring/cram ~** ju⌐ku 塾

school grounds kōtei 校庭

school hours jugyō-ji⌐kan 授業時間

schoolteacher gakkō no sense⌐i 学校の先生

school uniform gakuse⌐i-fuku 学生服

school year gakunen 学年

science ka⌐gaku 科学, sa⌐iensu サイエンス, *(study)* ga⌐ku 学

scientific kagaku-teki (na) 科学的(な)

scientist *(saiensu no)* kaga⌐ku-sha (サイエンスの)科学者

scissors hasami⌐ はさみ・鋏 (**how many pairs** na⌐n-chō 何丁)

scold shikarima⌐su (shikaru, shikatte) しかり[叱り]ます (しかる, しかって)

scolding kogoto (o-ko⌐goto) 小言 (お小言), o-shikari おしかり [叱り]; *(abuse)* waru⌐-kuchi/ -guchi 悪口/口

scoop 1. hishaku ひしゃく; *(one scoopful)* hito⌐-mori 一盛り 2. *(scoops it up)* kumima⌐su (kumu, kunde) くみ[汲み]ます(くむ, くんで), sukuima⌐su (sukuu, sukutte)

すくいます(すくう, すくって)

scope ha⌐n'i 範囲

scorch 1. *(scorches it)* kogashima⌐su (koga⌐su, koga⌐shite) 焦がします(焦がす, 焦がして) 2. *(it gets scorched)* kogema⌐su (koge⌐ru, ko⌐gete) 焦げます(焦げる, 焦げて)

score *(game)* toku⌐ten 得点, *(makes a ~)* ten o torima⌐su (to⌐ru, to⌐tte) 点を取ります(取る, 取って); *(~ points)* tensū⌐ 点数; *(musical ~)* gakufu 楽譜

scoundrel yarō⌐ 野郎

scrambled eggs iri-ta⌐mago いり卵・炒り卵, sukuramburu-e⌐ggu スクランブルエッグ

scrap ku⌐zu くず・屑, danpen 断片, kuzu⌐-mono くず物・屑物; *(refuse)* sute-mono 捨て物

scrape kosurima⌐su (kosu⌐ru, kosu⌐tte) こすります(こする, こすって)

scratch *(scratches it)* (hik-) kakima⌐su (ka⌐ku, ka⌐ite) (ひっ)かきます(かく, かいて); *(a scratch)* kizu 傷

scream *(kyatto)* sakebima⌐su (sake⌐bu, sake⌐nde) (きゃっと)叫びます(叫ぶ, 叫んで); *(a scream)* himei 悲鳴

screen *(folding)* byōbu びょうぶ・屏風; *(movie, TV, computer)*

ga⌐men 画面, sukuri⌐in スク
リーン; → **window screen**

screen door ami⌐-do 網戸

screw ne⌐ji ねじ

screwdriver neji-ma⌐washi ねじ
回し

scribbling rakugaki 落書き

scroll maki-mono 巻物; *(hanging)* kake⌐-mono 掛け物,
kake⌐jiku 掛軸, kake⌐ji 掛け字

scrubbing brush tawashi たわし

sea u⌐mi 海, ...⌐-kai ...海; **high
sea** taika⌐i (daika⌐i) 大海(大
海); **Inland Sea** Seto-na⌐ikai
瀬戸内海, **Sea of Japan**
Niho⌐n-kai 日本海

sea bass suzuki すずき・鱸

sea bream ta⌐i たい・鯛

seadiver: woman ~ a⌐ma 海女

seagull kamome かもめ・鷗

seal *(animal)* aza⌐rashi あざらし・
海豹

seal *(for stamping one's name)*
ha⌐n はん・判, hanko⌐ はんこ・
判こ, i⌐n 印

seal a letter tegami no fu⌐ o
shima⌐su (suru, shite) 手紙の
封をします(する, して)

seam nui-me⌐ 縫い目, tsugi-me
接ぎ目

seamail funa⌐bin 船便

seaman su⌐ifu 水夫; *(navy)*
su⌐ihei 水兵

search: ~ **for** *(seeks)* ... o
sagashima⌐su (sagasu,
sagashite) ...を探し[捜し]ま

す(探[捜]す, 探[捜]して); **a**
~ **for a criminal** te⌐ha⌐i 手配

seashore kaigan 海岸

seasick: gets ~ *(fu⌐ne ni)*
yoima⌐su (yo⌐u, yo⌐tte) (船に)
酔います(酔う, 酔って)

seasickness funa⌐yoi 船酔い

seaside umibe 海辺

season 1. kise⌐tsu 季節; shi⌐izun
シーズン; ji⌐ki 時季; ji⌐setsu 時
節 **2.** *(flavors it)* ... ni aji o
tsukema⌐su (tsuke⌐ru, tsuke⌐te)
...に味を付けます(付ける,
付けて)

seasoning *(food)* cho⌐mi 調味, aji
味; kagen 加減

season ticket teiki⌐-ken 定期券

seat se⌐ki (o-se⌐ki) 席(お席),
zaseki 座席, koshi-ka⌐ke⌐ 腰掛
け; *(bottom, butt)* shiri⌐ (o-
shiri) 尻(お尻); **Are there
seats (available)?**
Suwarema⌐su ka. 座れますか.

seat belt zaseki-be⌐ruto 座席ベル
ト

seat number zaseki-ba⌐ngō 座席
番号

sea urchin u⌐ni うに・海胆

seaweed kaisō 海藻; *(green)* nori⌐
のり・海苔; waka⌐me わかめ・
若布; *(kelp)* ko⌐mbu 昆布

seaweed-gelatin strips tokoroten
ところてん

seaweed-rolled sushi nori⌐-maki
のり巻き; *(with cucumber)*
kappa-maki かっぱ巻き;

(with tuna) tekka-maki 鉄火巻き

second 1. ni-bamme⌐ (no) 二番目（の）, futatsu-me⌐ (no) 二つ目（の）; **the ~ day** futsuka-me⌐ 二日目, **(of the month)** futsuka 二日 **2.** *(of a minute)* ichi⌐-byō 一秒

second class ni-tō 二等

second-class: ~ **car** nitō⌐-sha 二等車; ~ **seat** nitō⌐-seki 二等席; ~ **ticket** nitō⌐-ken 二等券

second floor ni-kai (o-ni⌐kai) 二階（お二階）

second generation ni⌐-sei 二世

secondhand chū⌐ko/chūburu (no) 中古/中古（の）, furu⌐i 古い; *(goods)* chūko⌐-hin 中古品

second helping o-ka⌐wari お代わり

second time nido-me⌐ 二度目, nikai-me⌐ 二回目

secret 1. a ~ himitsu 秘密 **2. the secret (= trick to it)** ta⌐ne 種 **3.** *(= confidential)* naisho⌐ (no) 内緒（の）

secretary sho⌐ki 書記; *(private)* hisho⌐ 秘書

sect shū⌐ha 宗派

section bu⌐ 部; ka⌐ 課, ...⌐-ka ...課; *(area)* chi⌐ku 地区

section manager ka-chō 課長

sector *(area)* chi⌐ku 地区

secure 1. is ~ chanto shite ima⌐su (iru, ite) ちゃんとして

います（いる, いて）**2. feels ~** anshin shima⌐su (suru, shite) 安心します（する, して）**3. → get**

securely chanto ちゃんと; *(firmly)* shikka⌐ri しっかり

security *(stock, bond)* shō⌐ken 証券; *(secure feeling)* anshin 安心

security deposit *(for rental)* shiki⌐-kin 敷金

sediment ka⌐su かす; ori おり

seduce tarashi-komima⌐su (-ko⌐mu, -ko⌐nde) たらし込みます（込む, 込んで）, yūwaku shima⌐su (suru, shite) 誘惑します（する, して）

seducer onna-ta⌐rashi 女たらし

seduction yūwaku 誘惑

seductress otoko-ta⌐rashi 男たらし

see 1. mima⌐su (mi⌐ru, mi⌐te) 見ます（見る, 見て）; [HONORIFIC] goran ni narima⌐su (na⌐ru, na⌐tte) ご覧になります（なる, なって）; [HUMBLE] haiken shima⌐su (suru, shite) 拝見します（する, して）**2.** *(meets a person)* ... ni aima⌐su (a⌐u, a⌐tte) ...に会います（会う, 会って）; [HUMBLE] o-me ni kakarima⌐su (kaka⌐ru, kaka⌐tte) お目にかかります（かかる, かかって）**3.** *(understands)* wakarima⌐su (waka'ru, waka'tte) 分かります(分かる, 分かって); **I see!** Naru-hodo! なるほど・成る程! **4. see one off** (mi-)okurima'su (okuru, okutte) (見)送ります(送る, 送って)

seed ta'ne 種

seedling na'e 苗

seeing-eye dog mōdō-ken 盲導犬

seek 1. busshoku shima'su (suru, shite) 物色します(する, して); → **search (for) 2.** → **aim at**

seemingly (outwardly) mikake wa 見かけ・見掛けは

seem (like) ... to miema'su (mie'ru, mi'ete) ...と見えます(見える, 見えて), ... (no) yō' desu ...(の)よう[様]です, ... rashi'i desu ...らしいです

seize tsukamima'su (tsuka'mu, tsuka'nde) つかみます(つかむ, つかんで), toraema'su (tora'eru, tora'ete) 捕らえます(捕らえる, 捕らえて), tsukamaema'su (tsukamaeru, tsukamaete) 捕まえ[つかまえ]ます(捕まえる, 捕まえて); (plunders) ubaima'su (uba'u, uba'tte) 奪います(奪う, 奪って); (illegally takes over) nottorima'su (notto'ru, notto'tte) 乗っ取ります(乗っ取る, 乗っ取って)

seizure (illegal takeover) nottori-ji'ken 乗っ取り事件

seldom me'tta ni めった[滅多]

に + NEGATIVE, hoto'ndo 殆ど・ほとんど + NEGATIVE; (infrequently) tama ni たまに

select → **choose; selection** → **choice**

selective buying (of stocks, ...) busshoku-gai 物色買い

self jibun (go-jibun) 自分(ご自分); ji-... 自...; onore 己; ji'ko 己

self-confidence jishin 自信

self-conscious: feels ~ agarima'su (agaru, agatte) 上がり[あがり]ます(上がる, 上がって)

self-defense: weaponless ~ art jū'dō 柔道, karate 空手, aiki'-dō 合気道

Self-Defense Forces Jiei-tai 自衛隊

selfish katte (na) 勝手(な), jibun-ka'tte/-ga'tte (na) 自分勝手/勝手(な), waga-ma'ma' (na) わがまま(な)

sell 1. sells it urima'su (uru, utte) 売ります(売る, 売って) **2. it sells (well)** (yo'ku) urema'su (ureru, urete) (良く)売れます(売れる, 売れて); hakema'su (hake'ru, ha'kete) はけます(はける, はけて), hake' ga i'i desu はけがいいです

seller uri-te 売り手; (dealer) hamba'i-nin 販売人

sell out uri-kirema'su (-kire'ru, -ki'rete) 売り切れます(切れる,

切れて）; **sellout** uri-kire 売り
切れ

sell retail ko-uri shimáʼsu (suru,
shíte) 小売りします（する，し
て）

sell wholesale oroshiⁿ-uri
shimáʼsu (suru, shíte) 卸売り
します（する，して）

semester gakki 学期

semicircle hanshū 半周

seminar zéʼmi ゼミ, zemináʼru ゼ
ミナール

send okurimáʼsu (okuru, okútte)
送ります（送る，送って），
yarimáʼsu (yaru, yatte) やりま
す（やる，やって）, yosemáʼsu
(yoseru, yosete) 寄せます（寄
せる，寄せて）; (a telegram)
uchimáʼsu (úʼtsu, úʼtte) 打ちま
す（打つ，打って）; (a person)
ikasemáʼsu (ikaseru, ikasete)
行かせます（行かせる，行か
せて）

send here yokoshimáʼsu
(yokóʼsu, yokoʼshite) よこし
［寄越し］ます（よこす，よこ
して）

send-off (farewell) sōbetsu 送別,
~ **party** sōbéʼtsu-kai 送別会

senior (older) toshi-ue (no) 年上
（の）; (colleague, fellow student) sempai 先輩; (4th-year
student) yonéⁿ-sei 四年生; ~
essay gakushi-roʼmbun 学士論
文

senior high school kōtō-gaʼkkō

高等学校, kō-kō 高校; ~ **stu-
dent** kōkōʼ-sei 高校生

sensation (feeling) kimochi 気持
ち・気持, kimíʼ 気味; (sense)
kankaku 感覚; (excitement)
senséʼshon センセーション

sense séʼnsu センス; → **feel(ing)**;
→ **meaning**; → **significance**;
→ **reason**; → **consciousness**

sense: common ~ jōshiki 常識;
~ **of honor** taimen 体面,
renchíʼ-shin 廉恥心; ~ **of obligation** giri (o-giⁿri) 義理（お
義理）

senses: come to one's senses
(recovers consciousness) ki ga
tsukimáʼsu (tsukúʼ, tsúʼite) 気
が付きます（付く，付いて），
nemuri kara samemáʼsu
(saméʼru, sáʼmete) 眠りから覚
めます（覚める，覚めて）

sensibility kankaku 感覚

sensible gōri-teki (na) 合理的（な），
atarimae (no) 当たり前（の）;
what is ~ dōríʼ 道理

sentence (written) buʼnshō 文章;
(spoken) kotoʼ 事, kotobaʼ 言
葉; (linguistic) seʼntensu セン
テンス

sentimental senchiméʼntaru na
センチメンタルな

Seoul Sóʼuru ソウル

separate 1. (different) betsu (no)
別（の） **2.** (separates them)
wakemáʼsu (wakéʼru, waʼkete)
分けます（分ける，分けて）;

(gets them apart) hedatema⌐su (hedate⌐ru, heda⌐tete) 隔てます(隔てる, 隔てて) **3.** *(they separate)* wakarema⌐su (wakare⌐ru, waka⌐rete) 分かれ[別れ]ます(分かれ[別れ]る, 分かれ[別れ]て); *(gets distant)* hanarema⌐su (hanare⌐ru, hana⌐rete) 離れます(離れる, 離れて)

separate bill betsu-dai/-ryō⌐kin 別代/料金

separated: is *(= lives)* ~ **from** ... **to** bekkyo shima⌐su (suru, shite) ...と別居します(する, して)

separate it (from) ... o hanashima⌐su (hana⌐su, hana⌐shite) ...を離します(離す, 離して)

separately: quite separately from ... to⌐ wa betsu ni (shite) ...とは別に(して)

September Ku-gatsu⌐ 九月・9月

sequel tsuzuki 続き

sequence *(order)* ju⌐njo 順序, ze⌐ngo 前後

sergeant gu⌐nsō 軍曹

sericulture yōsan 養蚕

series (hito⌐-)tsuzuki (一)続き

serious majime (na) まじめ[真面目](な); *(in earnest)* honki (no) 本気(の), *(not joking)* jōda⌐n ja arimase⌐n (na⌐i) 冗談じゃありません(ない); *(heavy, grave)* omoi 重い,

jūdai (na) 重大(な), shinkoku (na) 深刻(な); taihen (na) 大変(な), ta⌐i-shita ... 大した...

seriously: takes it ~ ... o honki ni shima⌐su (suru, shite) ...を本気にします(する, して)

sermon se⌐kkyō⌐ 説教

servant meshi-tsu⌐kai 召し使い; shiyō⌐-nin 使用人; yōmu⌐-in 用務員, ko⌐zukai 小使い; *(slave)* yakko やっこ・奴

serve (a meal) dashima⌐su (da⌐su, da⌐shite) 出します(出す, 出して); **meals are served** shokuji ga dema⌐su (de⌐ru, de⌐te) 食事が出ます(出る, 出て)

serve a purpose yaku⌐ ni tachima⌐su (ta⌐tsu, ta⌐tte) 役に立ちます(立つ, 立って), yaku-dachima⌐su (-da⌐tsu, -da⌐tte) 役立ちます(立つ, 立って)

serve the purpose mokuteki ni kanaima⌐su (kana⌐u, kana⌐tte) 目的にかないます(かなう, かなって)

serve the rice wine, pour the saké (o-)shaku o shima⌐su (suru, shite) (お)酌をします(する, して)

service *(in restaurant, etc.)* sā⌐bisu サービス; *(maintenance and repair)* afutā-sā⌐bisu アフターサービス; *(utility)* yaku⌐ (o-yaku) 役(お役); *(armed forces)* gu⌐ntai 軍

隊; *(duty, work)* kiˀmmu 勤務
service charge tesūˀ-ryō 手数料
serviceman, service personnel
   1. *(military)* gunjin 軍人
   2. → repairman
service station → gas station
servicing afutā-sāˀbisu アフター
   サービス
… serving(s) … -niˀmmae …人前
serving the rice wine (o-)shaku
   (お)酌
sesame goma ごま・胡麻
set 1. *(collection)* kumiˀ 組, hitoˀ-
   kumi 一組; *(array)* soroi 揃い;
   makes (up) a set soroimaˀsu
   (soroˀu, soroˀtte) 揃い[そろ
   い]ます(揃う, 揃って),
   makes into a set soroemaˀsu
   (soroeˀru, soroˀete) 揃え[そろ
   え]ます(揃える, 揃えて)
   2. *(hair)* seˀtto セット **3. sets
   it** *(puts it there)* okimaˀsu
   (oku, oite) 置きます(置く, 置
   いて) **4.** → sit; → settle; →
   decide
set aside atemaˀsu (ateru, atete)
   当てます(当てる, 当てて)
set free hanashimaˀsu (hanaˀsu,
   hanaˀshite) 放します(放す,
   放して)
set meal teishoku 定食
set off/out *(departs)*
   dekakemaˀsu (dekakeru,
   dekakete) 出かけます(出かけ
   る, 出かけて)
set price teika 定価

set series of chef's choices kōˀsu
   コース
settle *(decides it)* kimemaˀsu
   (kimeru, kimete) 決めます(決
   める, 決めて), *(fixes)*
   sadamemaˀsu (sadameˀru,
   sadaˀmete) 定めます(定める,
   定めて); *(completes)*
   matomemaˀsu (matomeru,
   matomete) まとめます(まと
   める, まとめて); *(disposes
   of)* shiˀmatsu shima(ˀ)su
   (suru, shite) 始末します(する,
   して); *(solves, resolves)*
   kaiketsu shimaˀsu (suru, shite)
   解決します(する, して);
   (gets relaxed/calm) ochi-
   tsukimaˀsu (-tsuku, -tsuite) 落
   ち着きます(着く, 着いて);
   ~ down/in osamarimaˀsu
   (osamaˀru, osamaˀtte) 収[治・
   納]まります(収[治・納]まる,
   収[治・納]まって)
settled 1. ittei (no) 一定(の)
   2. gets ~ kimarimaˀsu
   (kimaru, kimatte) 決まります
   (決まる, 決まって),
   sadamarimaˀsu (sadamaˀru,
   sadamaˀtte) 定まります(定ま
   る, 定まって);
   matomarimaˀsu (matomaru,
   matomatte) まとまります(ま
   とまる, まとまって)
settlement kimari 決まり;
   kaiketsu 解決
settling accounts keˀssan 決算

set up tatema̱su (tate̱ru, ta̱tete) 立てます（立てる，立てて）; *(provides)* mōkema̱su (mōke̱ru, mō̱kete) 設けます（設ける，設けて）; *(assembles)* kumi-tatema̱su (-tate⌐ru, -ta⌐tete) 組み立てます（立てる，立てて）

setup kumi-tate 組み立て

seven na̱na 七・7, shichi̱ 七・7, nana̱tsu 七つ・7つ; se̱bun セブン; ~ **days** nanoka⌐ 七日・7日

seven: small things, pieces nana̱-ko 七個; **long things** nana̱-hon 七本; **flat things** nana̱-mai 七枚; **small animals/fish/bugs** nana̱-hiki 七匹; **large animals** nana̱-tō 七頭; **birds** nana̱-wa 七羽; **machines/vehicles** nana̱-dai 七台; **books/magazines** nana̱-satsu 七冊

seven degrees nana̱-do 七度

seven floors/stories nana-kai 七階

seven hundred nana̱-hyaku 七百・700

seven people nana̱-nin 七人, nana̱-mei 七名

seventeen jū-na̱na 十七・17, jū-shichi̱ 十七・17

seventh nana-bamme̱ (no) 七番目（の）, nanatsu-me̱ (no) 七つ目（の）; **the ~ day** nanoka-me̱ 七日目・7日目, **(of the month)** nanoka⌐ 七日・7日

seventh floor nana-kai 七階

seven thousand nana-se̱n 七千・7,000

seven times nana̱-do 七度, nana̱-ka̱i 七回, nana̱-he̱n 七遍; *(= sevenfold)* nana-bai 七倍

seventy nana̱-jū 七十・70, shichi-jū̱ 七十・70; ~ **thousand** nana-ma̱n 七万・70,000

seven years nana̱-nen 七年, nanane̱n-kan 七年間; ~ **old** nana̱tsu 七つ・7つ, nana̱-sai 七歳

several futatsu̱-mi(t)tsu (no) 二つ三つ（の）, ni̱-san (no) 二三（の）, jakkan (no) 若干（の）, i̱kutsu ka (no) いくつか（の）; sū-... 数...（~ **days** sū⌐-jitsu 数日, ~ **people** sū⌐-nin 数人, ~ **years** sū⌐-nen 数年）

severally sore̱zo̱re それぞれ, ono̱ono 各々・おのおの

severe kibishi̱i 厳しい; kitsui きつい; *(terrible)* hido̱i ひどい

sew nuima̱su (nu̱u, nu̱tte) 縫います（縫う，縫って）; ~ **together/up** tsuzurima̱su (tsuzu⌐ru, tsuzu⌐tte) 綴ります（綴る，綴って）

sewage gesui 下水, osui 汚水; ~ **treatment plant** gesui shori-jō 下水処理場

sewing machine ミシン mi̱shin **(how many** na̱n-dai 何台）

sewing needle nuʾiʾbari 縫い針

sex seʾi 性, seʾkkusu セックス; *(the erotic)* iroʾ 色, eʾro エロ; **has sex** seʾkkusu o shimaʾsu (suru, shite) セックスをします(する, して), [*vulgar*] yarimaʾsu (yaru, yatte) やります(やる, やって)

sexual sei-teki (na) 性的(な); **makes a ~ overture** *(= pass)* moʾshon o kakemaʾsu (kakeʾru, kaʾkete) モーションをかけます(かける, かけて)

shad kohada こはだ

shade kaʾge 陰; *(of trees)* kiʾ no kaʾge 木の陰, koʾkaʾge 木陰; **window shade** (maʾdo no) hiyoke (窓の)日よけ

shadow kaʾge 影, *(from sunlight)* hi-kage 日影; *(of a person)* kaʾge-boʾshi 影法師

shady *(questionable)* ayashiʾi 怪しい, ikagawashiʾi いかがわしい

shake 1. *(shakes it)* furimaʾsu (furu, futte) 振ります(振る, 振って); yusuburimaʾsu (yusuburu, yusubutte) 揺すぶります(揺すぶる, 揺すぶって) **2.** *(it shakes)* furuemaʾsu (furueru, furuete) 震えます(震える, 震えて), *(sways)* yuremaʾsu (yureru, yurete) 揺れます(揺れる, 揺れて) **3.** = **milkshake** (mirukuʾ-)seʾki (ミルク)セーキ

shake hands aʾkushu shima(ʾ)su (suru, shite) 握手します(する, して)

shake out haraimaʾsu (haraʾu, haraʾtte) 払います(払う, 払って)

shall: 1. Shall I/we do it? Shimashoʾ ka. しましょうか. **2.** → **will**

shallow asai 浅い; **shallows** asase 浅瀬

sham mise-kake (no) 見せかけ(の)

shame hazukashiʾi (kotoʾ) 恥ずかしい(事), hajiʾ 恥; *(scandal)* ojoku 汚辱 **That's a shame.** Sore wa ikemaseʾn ne. それはいけませんね.

shameful nasake-naʾi 情けない

shameless zūzūshiʾi ずうずうしい・図々しい

shampoo kami-aʾrai 髪洗い, shaʾmpū/shaʾmpu シャンプー/シャンプ

Shanghai Shaʾnhaʾi シャンハイ・上海

shape katachi 形, kataʾ 型; *(figure)* suʾgata (o-suʾgata) 姿(お姿), kakkō かっこう・格好・恰好; *(condition)* guai 具合

shapely kakkō gaʾiʾi かっこう[格好・恰好]がいい

share 1. *(portion)* buʾn 分, wari-mae 割り前; *(allotment)* bun-tan 分担; **one's ~ (of expenses)** dashi-mae 出し前

2. → **divide**; → **Dutch**
3. **shares in = pays/does one's share** buntan shima͞su (suru, shite) 分担します(する，して)

shark same さめ・鮫, fuka⌐ ふか・鱶

sharp surudo͞i 鋭い; (clever) rikō (na) 利口(な)

sharp: gets sharp (pointed) togarima͞su (toga͞ru, toga͞tte) 尖り[とがり]ます(尖る，尖って)

sharpen (pencil) kezurima͞su (kezuru, kezutte) 削ります(削る，削って), togarashima͞su (togara͞su, togara shite) 尖らし[とがらし]ます(尖らす，尖らして); (blade) togima͞su (to͞gu, to͞ide) 研ぎます(研ぐ，研いで)

shave hige o sorima͞su (so͞ru, so͞tte) ひげを剃ります(剃る，剃って)

shaver (electric) denki-ka͞misori 電気かみそり

shaving cream higesori-yō kuri͞imu ひげ剃り用クリーム

she ka͞no-jo 彼女, ano͞-hito あの人, ano͞-ko あの子 (but use name, title, or role; often omitted)　　　　　　　　「雌

she-… (animal) … no mesu͞ …の

sheath sa͞ya さや・鞘

shed na⌐ya 納屋; (storehouse) mono-o͞ki͞ 物置; (hut) koya⌐ 小屋

sheep hitsuji 羊

sheet (of paper, glass, etc.) (ichi͞)-mai (一)枚; (bed ~) shi͞itsu シーツ, shikifu 敷布

shelf tana 棚; **enclosed shelves** to-dana 戸棚

shell kara 殻; (of shellfish) ka͞i 貝, kai-gara 貝殻; (of tortoise etc.) kōra 甲羅; **eggshell** tama⌐go no kara 卵[玉子]の殻; **bombshell** hōdan 砲弾

shellfish ka͞i 貝, …-gai …貝

Shiba Shi͞ba 芝; ~ **Park** Shiba-Kō͞en 芝公園

Shibuya Shibuya 渋谷; ~ **Station** Shibuya͞-Eki 渋谷駅

shield 1. ta͞te 盾 2. (protects) ho͞go shima(⌐)su (suru, shite) 保護します(する，して); (covers) ōima͞su 覆い[おおい]ます (ō⌐u 覆う・おおう = oo⌐u 覆う・おおう, ō⌐tte 覆って・おおって)

shift 1. (it shifts) utsurima͞su (utsu͞ru, utsu͞tte) 移ります(移る，移って); (shifts/changes it) ten-jima͞su (ten-ji⌐ru, te⌐n-jite) 転じます(転じる，転じて) 2. (alternates) kōtai shima͞su (suru, shite) 交替します(する，して)

Shikoku Shiko͞ku 四国

Shimbashi Shi͞mbashi 新橋; ~ **Station** Shimbashi͞-Eki 新橋駅

shin sune͞ すね・脛・臑

shine 1. (gloss) tsuya つや・艶

2. *(it shines)* hikarima⌐su (hika⌐ru, hika⌐tte) 光ります（光る，光って）, *(gleams)* kagayakima⌐su (kagaya⌐ku, kagaya⌐ite) 輝きます（輝く，輝いて）; *(the sun)* terima⌐su (te⌐ru, te⌐tte) 照ります（照る，照って）; *(polishes it)* migakima⌐su (migaku, migaite) 磨きます（磨く，磨いて）

shine on *(illuminates)* ... o terashima⌐su (tera⌐su, tera⌐shite) ...を照らします（照らす，照らして）

shingle i⌐ta 板; **shingles a roof** i⌐ta de ya⌐ne o fukima⌐su (fuku⌐, fu⌐ite) 板で屋根をふき［葺き］ます（ふく，ふいて）

shingles (= *herpes zoster*) obijō-hō⌐shin 帯状疱疹

Shinjuku Shinjuku/Shinjuku 新宿/新宿; ~ **Station** Shinjuku⌐-eki 新宿駅

Shinto(ism) Shi⌐ntō/Shi⌐ndō 神道/神道

Shinto music and dances ka⌐gura 神楽

Shinto shrine (o-)miya （お）宮, ji⌐nja 神社

ship fu⌐ne 船・舟, **(steamship)** kisen 汽船, ...-sen ...船; **(how many** na⌐n-seki 何隻, na⌐n-sō 何艘）

ship *(loads/carries)* nosema⌐su (noseru, nosete) 載せます（載

せる，載せて）

ship building zōsen 造船

ship's crew (member) sen'in 船員

shipwreck nampa 難破, sōnan 遭難

shipyard zōsen-jo⌐ 造船所

shirk okotarima⌐su (okotaru, okotatte) 怠ります（怠る，怠って）, zurukema⌐su (zuruke⌐ru, zuru⌐kete) ずるけます（ずるける，ずるけて）

shirt wai-shatsu ワイシャツ; *(undershirt)* sha⌐tsu シャツ; **(how many** na⌐m-mai 何枚）

shishkebab: chicken ~ (shop) yakitori(-ya) 焼き鳥(屋)

shit → **dung, feces**; → **defecation**; → **defecate**

shiver zotto shima⌐su (suru, shite) ぞっとします（する，して）; **with a ~** zotto ぞっと

shock sho⌐kku ショック; **the oil ~** oiru-sho⌐kku オイルショック

shocking tonde-mo nai ... とんでもない...; tonda ... とんだ...

shoe kutsu⌐ 靴, *(outdoor shoes)* shita-baki 下履き; **(1 pair is-soku⌐** 一足, **2 ni⌐-soku** 二足, **3 sa⌐n-zoku/-soku** 三足/足; **how many na⌐n-zoku/-soku** 何足/足）

shoe box *(at entryway)* geta-bako げた［下駄］箱

shoehorn kutsu-be⌐ra 靴べら

shoelace kutsu⌐-himo 靴ひも［紐］

shoe-repair(er) kutsu-naoshi 靴
直し

shoeshine kutsu-migaki 靴磨き

shoe shop/store kutsu-ya 靴屋

shoesole kutsu(ꜜ) no ura 靴の裏,
kutsu-zoko 靴底

shogunate bakufu 幕府;
bakufu-jidai 幕府時代

shoot uchimasu (utsu, utte) 撃
ちます(撃つ, 撃って), (ar-
row) irimasu (iru, itte) 射り
ます(射る, 射って); (~ **to**
death) uchi-koroshimasu
(-korosu, -koroshite) 撃
ち殺す(殺す, 殺して),
barashimasu (barasu,
barashite) ばらします(ばら
す, ばらして)

shooting star nagare-boshi 流れ
星

shop (store) mise 店, uri-ba 売り
場, shōten 商店; ...-ya ...屋, ...
-ten ...店; (1 ik-ken 一軒, 2 ni
-ken 二軒, 3 san-gen 三軒;
how many nan-gen 何軒)

shop (does the shopping; buys)
kai-mono shimasu (suru,
shite) 買い物します(する, し
て)

shop around for ... o busshoku
shimasu (suru, shite) ...を物
色します(する, して)

shopboy (apprentice) kozō 小僧

shop clerk ten'in 店員

shop curtain noren のれん・暖簾

shopgirl uriko 売り子, (joshi-)

ten'in (女子)店員

shopkeeper mise(ꜜ) no hito 店の
人; ...-ya (san) ...屋(さん)

shoplift kapparaimasu (kap-
parau, kapparatte) かっぱ
らいます(かっぱらう, かっ
ぱらって), mambiki o
shimasu (suru, shite) 万引き
[まんびき]をします(する,
して); **shoplifting, shoplifter**
mambiki 万引き・まんび
き

shopping kai-mono 買い物,
shoppingu ショッピング; ~
bag shoppingu-baggu ショッ
ピングバッグ; ~ **center** shop-
pingu-sentā ショッピングセ
ンター

shopping area, shop street(s)
shōten-gai 商店街

shore kishi 岸; (seashore) kaigan
海岸, (seaside) umibe 海辺;
(lakeshore) kogan 湖岸

shore patrol kempei 憲兵

short (not long) mijikai 短い;
(not tall) (se ga) hikui (背が)
低い; (deficient) ... ga
tarimasen (tarinai) ...が足り
ません(足りない)

short: in ~ tsumari つまり, yōsuru ni 要するに

shortage fusoku 不足, ...
-busoku ...不足; **water ~**
mizu-busoku 水不足

shortchange tsuri-sen o
gomakashimasu (gomakasu,

gomaka॒shite) 釣り銭をごま
かします(ごまかす, ごまか
して)

short circuit shō॒to ショート
shortcoming ta॒nsho 短所
shortcut chika॒-michi 近道
shorten miji॒ka॒ku shima॒su
(suru, shite) 短くします(する,
して); chijimema॒su
(chijimeru, chijimete) 縮
めます(縮める, 縮めて);
herashima॒su (herasu,
herashite) 減らします(減らす,
減らして); (abbreviates)
ryakushima॒su (ryaku॒su॒,
ryaku॒shite) 略します(略す,
略して)
shorthand sokki 速記
shortly ma-mo॒-naku 間もなく,
chika॒ku 近く
short-necked clam asari あさり・
浅蜊
shorts 1. (outerwear) shōto-
pa॒ntsu ショートパンツ
2. (undershorts) zubo⌐n-
shita ズボン下
shortsighted (myopic) kinshi
(no) 近視(の), kingan (no) 近
眼(の); (not thinking ahead)
shō॒rai o kangaemase॒n
(kangae॒nai) 将来を考えませ
ん(考えない)
shortstop shō॒to ショート
short story shō॒to ショート
should → **ought**
shoulder 1. ka॒ta 肩 2. (carries on

shoulders) shoima॒su (shou,
shotte) しょいます(しょう,
しょって)
shout (calls out) sakebima॒su
(sake॒bu, sake॒nde) 叫びます
(叫ぶ, 叫んで); tonaema॒su
(tona॒e॒ru, tona॒ete) 唱えます
(唱える, 唱えて); (yells)
donarima॒su (dona॒ru,
dona॒tte) どなります・怒鳴り
ます(どなる, どなって)
shovel sha॒beru シャベル
show 1. (display) mie॒ 見え・見栄
2. (an exhibit) mise-mo॒no॒ 見
せ物 3. → **movie**; → **play**
show 1. (displays it) misema॒su
(mise॒ru, mi॒sete) 見せます(見
せる, 見せて); [HUMBLE] o-
me ni kakema॒su (kake॒ru,
ka॒kete) お目にかけます(かけ
る, かけて) 2. (reveals)
arawashima॒su (arawa॒su,
arawa॒shite) 表します(表
す, 表して); (indicates)
shimeshima॒su (shime⌐su,
shime⌐shite) 示します(示す,
示して) 3. (tells) oshiema॒su
(oshieru, oshiete) 教えます
(教える, 教えて)
shower 1. (bath) sha॒wā シャ
ワー; (takes a shower) sha॒wā
o abima॒su (abiru, abite) シャ
ワーを浴びます(浴びる, 浴び
て) 2. rain ~ yūdachi 夕立;
sudden ~ niwaka-a॒me にわ
か雨

show in *(usher)* tōshima'su (tō'su, tō'shite) 通します(通す, 通して)

show up arawarema'su (araware'ru, arawa'rete) 現れます(現れる, 現れて); *(comes)* miema'su (mie'ru, mi'ete) 見えます(見える, 見えて)

showy hana'yaka (na) 華やか・はなやか(な), hade' (na) はで[派手](な)

shrimp 1. ebi えび・海老; *(batter-fried)* ebi-ten えび天; *(fried in bread crumbs)* ebi-fu'rai えびフライ **2. giant ~** (= **prawn**) kuruma'-ebi 車えび・車海老 **3. tiny ~** shiba⁽ⁿ⁾ebi 芝えび・芝海老 **4. mantis ~** sha'ko しゃこ・蝦蛄

shrine *(Shinto)* (o-)miya (お)宮; ji'nja 神社, *(large)* jingū' 神宮

shrink chijimima'su (chijimu, chijinde) 縮みます(縮む, 縮んで), tsuzumarima'su (tsuzuma'ru, tsuzuma'tte) つづまり[約まり]ます(つづまる, つづまって)

shudder zotto shima'su (suru, shite) ぞっとします(する, して); **with a shudder** zotto ぞっと

shuffle cards tora'mpu o kirima'su (ki'ru, ki'tte') トランプを切ります(切る, 切って)

shut 1. *(shuts it)* shimema'su (shime'ru, shi'mete) 閉めます(閉める, 閉めて); *(a book, etc.)* tojima'su (toji'ru, to'jite) 閉じます(閉じる, 閉じて) **2.** *(it gets shut)* shimarima'su (shima'ru, shima'tte) 閉まります(閉まる, 閉まって); *(it puckers up)* tsubomarima'su (tsubomaru, tsubomatte) つぼまります(つぼまる, つぼまって)

shut one's eyes me' o tsuburima'su (tsuburu, tsubutte) 目をつぶります(つぶる, つぶって)

shutter *(camera, etc.)* sha'ttā シャッター; *(house)* yoroi⁽ⁿ⁾-do よろい[鎧]戸, *(rain shutters)* ama'do 雨戸

shuttlecock hane 羽根, hago⁽ⁿ⁾ 羽子; *see* **battledore**

shut up *(not speak)* damarima'su (dama'ru, dama'tte) 黙ります(黙る, 黙って)

shy uchiki (na) 内気(な), hazukashi'i 恥ずかしい; **acts ~** hanikamima'su (hanika'mu, hanika'nde) はにかみます(はにかむ, はにかんで), enryo shima'su (suru, shite) 遠慮します(する, して)

shyness enryo (go-enryo) 遠慮(ご遠慮)

Siberia Shiberi(y)a シベリア[ヤ]

sick byōki (no) 病気(の); → **queasy**

sickly byōki-gachi (na) 病気がち
(な)

sickness byōki 病気

side 1. yoko 横 2. *(beside, near-by)* so¯ba そば・側・傍, *(off to the side)* hata 端 3. *(of body)* waki¯ わき・脇

that side achira-gawa あちら
側

this (my/our) side kochira-gawa こちら側

your side sochira-gawa そちら
側

which side dochira-gawa どち
ら側

both sides ryō-gawa 両側

one side … the other side ippō¯
… (mō) ippō¯ 一方…(もう)一
方

side dish *(to go with the rice)* (o-)
sai (お)菜; okazu おかず

side job, sideline aruba¯ito アル
バイト

side street yokochō 横町

sidetracked: gets ~ dassen
shima¯su (suru, shite) 脱線し
ます(する, して)

sidewalk hodō 歩道, jindō 人道

sideways, sidewise yoko (no/ni)
横(の/に)

sieve, sifter furui ふるい・篩,
zaru¯ ざる

sight *(scene)* ari[¯]-sama ありさ
ま・有り様; *(scenery)* ke¯shiki
景色; *(eyesight)* shi¯ryoku 視力;
sees the sights kembutsu

shima¯su (suru, shite) 見物し
ます(する, して)

sightseeing kembutsu 見物,
kankō 観光; **~ bus/train**
kankō-ba¯su/-re¯ssha 観光バ
ス/列車

sightseer kankō¯-kyaku 観光客

sign 1. *(symptom)* (o-)shirushi
(お)しるし[徴]; *(omen)* zen-
chō 前兆 2. *(signboard)* kamban 看板 3. *(marker)* hyōshi¯ki
標識 4. *(symbol)* kigō 記号
5. *(writes one's name)* shomei
shima¯su (suru, shite) 署名し
ます(する, して)

signal shingō 信号

signature shomei 署名

signboard (o-)kamban (お)看板,
tate¯-fuda 立て札

significance i¯gi 意義

silent: is ~ *(not speak)*
damarima¯su (dama¯ru,
dama¯tte) 黙ります(黙る,
黙って)

silk ki¯nu 絹; **raw ~** ki¯-ito 生糸

silkworm (o-)ka¯iko (お)蚕; **raising silkworms, silk farming**
yōsan 養蚕

sill: (window/door) ~ (ma¯do/
to no) shikii (窓/戸の)敷居

sillago *(fish)* kisu[¯] きす・鱚

silly girl(s) Miichan-hā¯chan
(Mi¯i-chan Hā¯-chan) ミーちゃ
んハーちゃん(ミーちゃん
ハーちゃん), Miihā¯-zoku
ミーハー族

silver giˈn 銀; *(color)* gin-iro (no) 銀色(の)

Silver Week (around 3 November) shirubā-uˈiku/ wiˈiku シルバーウイーク/ ウィーク

similar onaji yoˈ (na) 同じよう ［様］(な), hitoshiˈi 等しい, nita 似た, ruiji no 類似の

similarity ruiji 類似

simile tatoˈeˈ 例え, tatoˈiˈ 例い

simple kantan (na) 簡単(な), tan- jun (na) 単純(な), shiˈmpuru (na) シンプル(な); *(easy)* waˈke-nai 訳ない; *(plain)* assaˈri shita あっさりした; *(frugal)* shiˈsso (na) 質素(な); *(naive)* soboku (na) 素朴(な); *(tastefully restrained)* shibuˈi 渋い; ~ **(modest) tastes** wabiⁿ わび・佗び

simplehearted tanjun (na) 単純 (な)

simple-minded tanjun (na) 単純 (な); (o-)medetaˈi (お)めでた い［目出度い］

simply 1. kantan ni 簡単に; *(easi- ly)* waˈke-naku 訳なく; assaˈri (to) あっさり(と) **2.** *(merely)* taˈda ただ, ... ni sugimaseˈn (sugiˈnai) ...に過ぎません(過 ぎない)

simultaneous dōⁿji (no) 同時 (の); ~ **translation** dōji- tsuˈyaku 同時通訳

sin tsuˈmi 罪

since 1. ... kara ...から; (sono) aˈto (その)後, sono-go その後; (...) iˈrai (...)以来 **2.** → **because**

sincere makoto (no) 誠(の), sei- jitsu (na) 誠実(な); *(heartfelt)* koˈkoro kara (no) 心から(の)

sing utaimaˈsu (utau, utatte) 歌 います(歌う, 歌って)

single *(for one person)* hitoˈri no 一人［独り］の; *(unmarried)* hitori-moˈnoˈ 独り者, dokushin 独身; ~ **(room)** shiˈnguru シングル＝ shinguru-rūˈmu シングルルー ム

sink *(in kitchen)* nagashiˈ 流し; *(it sinks)* shizumimaˈsu (shizumu, shizunde) 沈みます (沈む, 沈んで); *(sinks it)* shizumemaˈsu (shizumeru, shizumete) 沈めます(沈める, 沈めて)

sip suimaˈsu (suu, sutte) 吸いま す(吸う, 吸って)

sister onna(ⁿ) no kyoˈdai 女のき ょうだい; *(older)* ane 姉, (o-) neˈ-san (お)姉さん; *(younger)* imōtoˈ 妹, (o-)imōto-san (お) 妹さん

sister-in-law giriˈ no ane/imōtoˈ 義理の姉/妹 *(older/younger)*

sit *(especially Japanese-style)* suwarimaˈsu (suwaru, suwatte) 座ります・すわりま す(座る, 座って), *(on a* *cushion)* shikima῁su (shiku, shiite) 敷きます(敷く, 敷いて); *(in chair)* (koshi-)kakema῁su (kake῁ru, ka῁kete) (腰)掛けます(掛ける, 掛けて)

sit astride ... ni matagarima῁su (mataga῁ru, mataga῁tte) ...に跨がり[またがり]ます(跨がる, 跨がって)

site *(building lot)* shiki-chi 敷地

sit-in *(strike)* suwarikomi(-su῁to) 座り込み(スト)

situation jōtai 状態, jōkyō 状況・情況, ji῁tai 事態; *(circumstance)* ba(w)ai 場合; *(standpoint)* tachi-ba 立場; *(stage)* kurai 位; *(location)* i῁chi 位置

six roku῁ 六・6, muttsu῁ 六つ; shi῁kkusu シックス

six: small things, pieces ro῁k-ko 六個; **long things** ro῁p-pon 六本; **flat things** roku῁-mai 六枚; **small animals/fish/bugs** rop-piki῁ 六匹; **large animals** roku῁-tō 六頭; **birds** ro῁p-pa 六羽; **machines/vehicles** roku῁-dai 六台; **books/magazines** roku῁-satsu῁ 六冊

six days muika 六日・6日

six degrees roku῁-do 六度

six hundred rop-pyaku῁ 六百・600

six people roku῁-nin 六人

sixteen jū-roku῁ 十六・16

sixth roku-bamme῁ (no) 六番目

(の), muttsu-me῁ (no) 六つ目 (の); **the ~ day** muika-me῁ 六日目, **(of the month)** muika 六日

six thousand roku-se῁n 六千・6,000

sixth time rokudo-me῁ 六度目, rokkai-me῁ 六回目

six times roku῁-do 六度, rok-ka῁i 六回, rop-pe῁n 六遍; *(= sixfold)* roku-bai 六倍

sixty roku-jū῁ 六十・60; **~ thousand** roku-ma῁n 六万・60,000

six years roku῁-nen 六年, rokune῁n-kan 六年間; **~ old** muttsu῁ 六つ, roku῁-sa῁i 六歳

size ōkisa 大きさ, sa῁izu サイズ; *(model)* kata῁ 型, ...-gata ...型

skate, skating suke῁to (o shima῁su; suru, shite) スケート(をします; する, して); suberima῁su (sube῁ru, sube῁tte) 滑ります(滑る, 滑って)

sketch zuan 図案

skewer yaki-gushi 焼き串

ski, skiing suki῁i (o shima῁su; suru, shite) スキー(をします; する, して)

skill udema῁e῁ 腕前; o-te῁mae おてまえ・御手前

skillful jōzu῁ (na) (o-jōzu) じょうず[上手](な)(おじょうず), uma῁i/mma῁i うまい, ta῁kumi (na) 巧み(な); *(proficient)* tassha (na) 達者(な); *(nimble)* ki῁yō (na) 器用(な)

skim *(grazes)* kasumema̱su
(kasumeꞋru, kasuꞋmete) か
すめ[掠め]ます(かすめる、
かすめて); **~ off** kasume-
torima̱su (-toꞋru, -toꞋtte) かす
め[掠め]取ります(取る、
取って)

skim milk dasshiꞋ-nyū 脱脂乳

skin 1. hiꞋfu/hifu 皮膚/皮膚; *(of
animal, potato, ...)* kawaꞋ 皮
2. *(pares/peels it)* mukima̱su
(muku, muite) むきます(むく、
むいて)

skinflint keꞋchimbo けちんぼ

skip *(leaves out)* nukashima̱su
(nukasu, nukashite) 抜かしま
す(抜かす、抜かして)、
tobashima̱su (tobasu,
tobashite) 飛ばします(飛ばす、
飛ばして)

skip school gakkō o saborima̱su
(saboꞋru, saboꞋtte) 学校をさぼ
ります(さぼる、さぼって)、
zuru-ya̱sumi shima(Ꞌ)su ずる
休みします、zurukema̱su
(zurukeꞋru, zuruꞋkete) ずる
けます(ずるける、ずるけて)

skirt sukāꞋto スカート、tsumaꞋ つ
ま・褄; *(of mountain)* su̱so す
そ・裾

sky soꞋra 空; *(heaven)* teꞋn 天;
(blue, empty) aozoꞋra 青空

skyscraper kōsō-biꞋru 高層ビル

slack yuruꞋi 緩い・弛い; **gets ~**
tarumima̱su (tarumu,
tarunde) たるみ[弛み]ます

(たるむ、たるんで)

slacks suraꞋkkusu スラックス

slander waruꞋ-kuchi/-guchi 悪口
/口、hibō ひぼう・誹謗

slang zokugo 俗語

slant 1. katamuꞋki 傾き
2. *(leans)* katamukima̱su
(katamuꞋku, katamuꞋite) 傾き
ます(傾く、傾いて)

slanting nanaꞋme (no) 斜め(の)、
hasu (no) はす[斜](の)

slant line shasen 斜線

slap hatakima̱su (hataꞋku,
hataꞋite) はたき[叩き]ます
(はたく、はたいて); *(one's
face)* ... no kao o uchima̱su
(uꞋtsu, uꞋtte) ...の顔を打ちま
す(打つ、打って)、... ni biꞋnta
o harima̱su (haru, hatte) ...に
びんたを張ります(張る、張っ
て)、... biꞋnta o kuwasema̱su
(kuwaseꞋru, kuwaꞋsete) ...
びんたを食わせます(食わせ
る、食わせて)

slave dorei 奴隷; yakko やっこ・奴

sled soꞋri そり・橇

sleep 1. *(= sleeping)* nemuri 眠
り、ne 寝、suimin 睡眠; **not
enough ~** ne-buꞋsoku 寝不足
2. *(sleeps)* nemurima̱su
(nemuru, nemutte) 眠ります
(眠る、眠って); yasumima̱su
(yasuꞋmu, yasuꞋnde) 休みます
(休む、休んで); *(goes to bed)*
nema̱su (neru, nete) 寝ます
(寝る、寝て)

sleep: (a leg, etc.) goes to ~ *(gets numb)* shibirema̱su (shibire̱ru, shibi̱rete) しびれます・痺れる(しびれる, しびれて)

sleeping car shinda̱i-sha 寝台車

sleeping pill suimi̱n-zai 睡眠剤, suimi̱n-yaku 睡眠薬

sleepy nemui 眠い

sleeve (o-)sode (お)袖; *(end of kimono sleeve)* tamoto̱ 袂; ~ **cord** tasuki̱ たすき

slender hoso̱i 細い

slice → **cut; piece**

slick subekko̱i すべっこい・滑っこい

slide suberima̱su (sube̱ru, sube̱tte) 滑ります(滑る, 滑って)

sliding panel/door 1. *(translucent)* shōji (o-shō̱ji) 障子(お障子) **2.** *(opaque)* fusuma̱ ふすま・襖

slight cho̱tto shita … ちょっとした…

slip → **slide**

slip out of place zurema̱su (zure̱ru, zu̱rete) ずれます(ずれる, ずれて)

slippers suri̱ppa スリッパ, uwabaki うわばき・上履き

slippery subekko̱i すべっこい・滑っこい; **Slippery (Area)** "Surippu-ji̱ko ō̱shi [= ō̱i]" "スリップ事故多し[=多い]"

slippery-slide suberi̱-dai すべり台・滑り台, o-su̱beri お滑り

slipshod zusan/zuzan (na) ずさん/ずざん[杜撰](な)

slogan surō̱gan スローガン, hyōgo 標語

slope saka̱ 坂

sloppy zonza̱i (na) ぞんざい(な), zusan/zuzan (na) ずさん/ずざん[杜撰](な)

slot kuchi 口, ana̱ 穴

slot machine *(vending machine)* (jidō-)hamba̱i-ki (自動)販売機; *(gambling)* (jidō-)tobaku̱-ki (自動)賭博機

slovenly zonza̱i (na) ぞんざい(な)

slow osoi 遅い, surō̱ (na) スロー(な); *(sluggish)* noro̱i のろい, yuru̱i 緩い; *(clock runs slow)* okurete ima̱su (iru, ite) 遅れています(いる, いて)

slow(ly) yukku̱ri ゆっくり; *(tardily, late)* osoku 遅く

slug (coin) tama̱ 玉

sluggish noro̱i のろい

slum himmi̱n-kutsu/-gai 貧民窟/街

sly zuru̱i ずるい; ~ **person** ta̱nuki たぬき・狸

small *(little)* chiisa̱i/chitcha̱i 小さい/ちっちゃい, chi̱isa-na/chi̱tcha-na … 小さな/ちっちゃな…, ko-… 小…; *(fine)* komaka̱i 細かい; *(small-scale)* sasa̱yaka (na) ささやか(な)

small boat kobune 小舟

small change komaka̱i kane 細

かい金, ko-zeni 小銭; o-tsuri
お釣り・おつり, tsuri⌐-sen 釣
り銭

small hammer ko⌐zuchi 小槌・こ
づち

smallpox tennentō 天然痘

**small restaurant (Japanese tradi-
tional)** koryōri⌐-ya 小料理屋

small-size (model) kogata (no) 小
型(の)

smart (*intelligent*) atama⌐ ga i⌐i
頭がいい, rikō (na) 利口(な);
(*stylish*) sumā⌐to (na) スマー
ト(な), iki (na) いき[粋](な)

smart (*it smarts*) shimima⌐su
(shimiru, shimite) 染みます
(染みる, 染みて)

smash 1. (*breaks it*)
kowashima⌐su (kowa⌐su,
kowa⌐shite) 壊します(壊す, 壊
して), kudakima⌐su (kuda⌐ku,
kuda⌐ite) 砕きます(砕く, 砕
いて); (*crushes it*)
tsubushima⌐su (tsubusu,
tsubushite) 潰し[つぶし]ます
(潰す, 潰して) 2. (*it breaks*)
kowarema⌐su (koware⌐ru,
kowa⌐rete) 壊れます(壊れる,
壊れて), kudakema⌐su
(kudake⌐ru, kuda⌐kete) 砕けま
す(砕ける, 砕けて); (*it
crushes*) tsuburema⌐su
(tsubureru, tsuburete) 潰れ[つ
ぶれ]ます(潰れる, 潰れて)

smell 1. (*odor*) nio⌐i におい・臭い
・匂い 2. (*it smells*) nioima⌐su

(nio⌐u, nio⌐tte) におい[臭い・
匂い]ます(におう, におって),
nio⌐i ga shima⌐su (suru, shite)
におい[臭い・匂い]がします
(する, して) 3. (*smells it*)
kagima⌐su (kagu, kaide) 嗅ぎ
ます(嗅ぐ, 嗅いで)

smelly kusa⌐i 臭い・くさい

smile ni⌐koniko shima⌐su (suru,
shite) にこにこします(する,
して)

smoke kemuri 煙

smoker (*person who smokes*)
tabako⌐-nomi たばこ飲み,
kitsue⌐n-sha 喫煙者

smokestack entotsu 煙突

smoke (tobacco) tabako o
nomima⌐su (no⌐mu, no⌐nde) た
ばこを飲み[呑み]ます(飲
[呑]む, 飲[呑]んで),
suima⌐su (suu, sutte) 吸います
(吸う, 吸って); kitsuen
shima⌐su (suru, shite) 喫煙し
ます(する, して)

smoking kitsuen 喫煙; ～ pro-
hibited kin'en 禁煙

smoky kemui 煙い・けむい,
kemutai 煙たい・けむたい

**SMON (subacute myelo-optico
neuropathy)** su⌐mon スモン,
sumon-byō スモン病

smooth name⌐raka (na) 滑らか・
なめらか(な), (*flat*) taira (na)
平ら(な), (*slippery*) subekko⌐i
滑っこい・すべっこい

smoothe narashima⌐su (nara⌐su,

nara⌐shite) ならし[均し]ます
（ならす，ならして）; *(pats)*
nadema⌐su (nade⌐ru, na⌐dete)
なで[撫で]ます（なでる，な
でて）

smorgasbord ("Viking")
ba⌐ikingu バイキング

smudge yogore 汚れ

smuggle mitsuyu shima⌐su (suru,
shite) 密輸します（する，して）

snack keishoku 軽食, karu⌐i
mono⌐/tabe-mo⌐no⌐/shokuji
軽い物/食べ物/食事; *(mid-
afternoon)* o-sa⌐nji お三時, o-
ya⌐tsu おやつ・お八つ

snackshop suna⌐kku スナック

snake he⌐bi 蛇

snap 1. *(it snaps)* hajikema⌐su
(hajike⌐ru, haji⌐kete) はじけ
[弾け]ます（はじける，はじ
けて）**2.** *(snaps it)* hajikima⌐su
(haji⌐ku, haji⌐ite) はじき[弾
き]ます（はじく，はじいて）

snapping turtle suppon すっぽん

sneakers zukku⌐-gutsu ズック靴
= zu⌐kku no kutsu⌐ ズックの
靴

sneeze kusha⌐mi (o shima⌐su;
suru, shite) くしゃみ（をしま
す; する，して）

snivel hana はな・涕・鼻 = hana-
mizu⌐ 鼻水

snore ibiki⌐ (o kakima⌐su; ka⌐ku,
ka⌐ite) いびき・鼾（をかきます;
かく，かいて）

snoring (away) gū⌐gū ぐうぐう

snow yuki⌐ (ga furima⌐su; fu⌐ru,
fu⌐tte) 雪（が降ります; 降る，
降って）

snowslide yuki-na⌐dare 雪なだれ,
nadare⌐ なだれ・雪崩

snowstorm fu⌐buki 吹雪・ふぶき

snow white masshi⌐ro (na) 真っ
白・まっしろ(な)

so 1. *(like that)* sō⌐ そう (sō そう
+ VERB), *(like this)* kō⌐ こう
(kō こう + VERB) **2.** *(that
much)* sonna ni そんなに,
(this much) konna ni こんなに
3. *(and so)* ... kara ...から, ...
-te ...て (...-kute ...くて, ... de
...で); da⌐ kara (sa) だから（さ）

soak 1. soaks it tsukema⌐su
(tsukeru, tsukete) 漬けます
（漬ける，漬けて）**2. it soaks**
tsukarima⌐su (tsukaru,
tsukatte) 漬かります（漬かる，
漬かって）**3. it soaks in**
shimima⌐su (shimiru, shimite)
染みます（染みる，染みて）

so-and-so 1. da⌐redare だれだれ
・誰々, da⌐resore だれそれ・誰
それ; ya⌐tsu やつ・奴; *(scoun-
drel)* yarō⌐ 野郎 **2.** na⌐ninani
なになに・何々

soap sekken 石けん・石鹸,
shabon シャボン

soap bubble shabon-dama シャ
ボン玉

soap opera hōmu-do⌐rama ホー
ムドラマ

so as to be NOUN ni に, ADJEC-

TIVE-ku く; ... yō ̄ ni ...よう
[様]に
sober *(in one's right mind)*
shō ̄ki (no) 正気(の); *(plain)*
jimi ̄ (na) 地味(な)
so-called iwayuru いわゆる
soccer sa ̄kkā サッカー「がいい
sociable aiso ̄ ga i ̄i あいそ[愛想]
social sha ̄kai (no) 社会(の); ~
company tsuki-ai (o-tsuki ̄ai)
付き合い（お付き合い）, *(=
~ intercourse/relations)*
kōsai 交際; ~ **standing**
mi ̄bun 身分, shakai-teki chi ̄i
社会的地位
socialism shakai-shu ̄gi 社会主義
socialist shakaishugi ̄-sha 社会主
義者
social science(s) shakai-ka ̄gaku
社会科学
society sha ̄kai 社会; *(association)* kyōkai 協会, *(scholarly)*
gakkai 学会; ...-kai ...会
socket soke ̄tto ソケット; **two-
way** ~ futamata-soke ̄tto 二
又ソケット
socks kutsu ̄-shita ̄ 靴下, *(anklets)* so ̄kkusu ソックス, *(split-
toe)* ta ̄bi たび・足袋; **(1 pair**
is-soku ̄ 一足, **2** ni ̄-soku
二足, **3** sa ̄n-zoku/-soku 三足/
足; **how many** na ̄n-zoku/
-soku 何足/足)
soda water tansa ̄n-sui 炭酸水;
so ̄da ソーダ, soda ̄-sui ソーダ
水

soft yawaraka ̄i 柔らかい; ~ **ice
cream** so ̄futo ソフト, sofuto-
kuri ̄imu ソフトクリーム
software sofutowe ̄a ソフトウェ
ア
soil *(earth)* tsuchi ̄ 土, tochi 土地;
(makes it dirty) yogoshima ̄su
(yogosu, yogoshite) 汚します
（汚す, 汚して）; *(gets dirty)*
yogorema ̄su (yogoreru,
yogorete) 汚れます（汚れる,
汚れて）
sojourn taizai (shima ̄su; suru,
shite) 滞在（します; する, し
て）
sold → **sell**; ~ **out** uri-kire (no)
売り切れ(の)
soldier heitai 兵隊, gunjin 軍人
sole 1. *(fish)* shita-bi ̄rame 舌平
目 **2.** *(of foot)* ashi ̄ no ura ̄
足の裏; *(of shoe)* kutsu ̄ no
ura ̄ 靴の裏, kutsu-zoko 靴底
3. → **only (one)**
solicitude omoi-yari 思いやり;
thanks to your ~ okage-sama
de おかげ[お蔭]さまで; **a
visit of** ~ (o-)mimai （お）見舞
い
solid *(firm)* katai 固い・硬い・堅
い; *(a solid)* kotai 固体, rittai
立体
solid-color mu ̄ji (no) 無地(の)
solstice → **summer** ~ , **winter**
~
solution kaiketsu 解決
solve 1. tokima ̄su (to ̄ku, to ̄ite)

解きます(解く, 解いて); **gets solved** tokema῀su (toke῀ru, to῀kete) 解けます(解ける, 解けて) **2.** kaiketsu shima῀su (suru, shite) 解決します(する, して)

some (*a little*) suko῀shi 少し (*but often omitted*); (*certain*) na῀n-ra῀ ka no ... 何らかの... (*a certain amount*) i῀kura ka (no) いくらか(の), (*a certain number*) i῀kutsu ka (no) いくつか(の); tashō (no) 多少(の)

some (*particular*) a῀ru ... ある...; **~ people** a῀ru hito ある人, ...hito῀ mo arima῀su (a῀ru, a῀tte) ...人もあります(ある, あって)

somebody → someone

someday izure いずれ, i῀tsu-ka いつか; [*bookish*] ichijitsu῀ 一日

somehow dō῀ ni ka どうにか; (*vaguely*) dō῀mo どうも; **~ or other** na῀n to ka shite 何とかして, (*necessarily*) dō-shite῀ mo どうしても

someone da῀re ka 誰か; (...) hito (...)人; **~ or other** da῀redare だれだれ・誰々, da῀resore だれそれ・誰それ

some other time izure いずれ

something na῀ni ka 何か; (...) mono῀ (...)物; **~ or other** na῀ninani なになに・何々; **~ to drink** nomi῀-mono 飲み物; **~ to talk about** hanashi῀ 話

something the matter, something wrong ijō 異常

sometime i῀tsu ka いつか; izure いずれ

sometimes tokidoki⌐ 時々, toki῀ ni 時に; (*occasionally*) tama ni たまに...; ... (suru) koto῀ ga arima῀su (a῀ru, a῀tte) ...(する)事があります(ある, あって); **~** (*intermittently*) **does/is** ...-ta῀ri / ...-ka῀ttari / ... da῀ttari shima῀su (suru, shite) ...たり/...かったり/...だったりします (する, して)

somewhat suko῀shi 少し, cho῀tto ちょっと; → somehow

somewhere do῀ko ka どこか; **~ else** yoso῀ よそ; **~ or other** do῀kodoko どこどこ, do῀kosoko どこそこ

son musuko 息子; (*your son*) bo῀tchan 坊ちゃん; **eldest son** chō῀na῀n 長男

song uta῀ (o-uta) 歌(お歌)

son-in-law mu῀ko (o-mu῀ko-san) 婿(お婿さん)

soon ma-mo῀-naku 間もなく, mō⌐ (su῀gu) もう(すぐ), jiki ni じき[直]に

soon: as soon as ... (suru) to (su῀gu) (する)と(すぐ); (shite῀) kara su῀gu (して)からすぐ; (VERB-i)-shi῀dai (ni) (VERB い)次第(に)

soot su῀su すす・煤

soothe shizumema῀su

(shizumeru, shizumete) 静め
ます・鎮めます(静[鎮]める,
静[鎮]めて), nadamema´su
(nadame´ru, nada´mete) なだ
め[宥め]ます(なだめる, な
だめて)

sophisticated dora⌐i (na) ドライ
(な)

sophomore nine´n-sei 二年生

sore ita´i 痛い; (a sore spot) ita´i
tokoro´ 痛い所, (from shoe
rubbing) kutsu-zu⌐re⌐ 靴ず
れ; → **boil**; → **wound**

sorry (for you/him) ki-no-do´ku´
desu 気の毒です

Sorry! Sumimase´n. すみません。

sort (kind) shu´rui 種類, i´s-shu
一種

so-so ma´-mā まあまあ

so to speak i⌐wa⌐ba いわば・言
わば

soul se´ishin 精神, ta´mashii 魂;
(= person) hito 人, ningen 人
間

sound 1. (noise) oto´ 音; ne 音;
onkyō 音響 **2. it sounds**
narima´su (naru, natte) 鳴りま
す(鳴る, 鳴って), (makes an
animal sound) nakima´su
(naku, naite) 鳴きます(鳴く,
鳴いて) **3. sounds it**
narashima´su (narasu,
narashite) 鳴らします(鳴らす,
鳴らして)

sound asleep gussu´ri ぐっすり,
gu´gū (nemutte ima´su) ぐうぐ

う(眠っています)

sound out (a person) dashin
shima´su (suru, shite) 打診し
ます(する, して)

soup sū´pu スープ, shi´ru 汁;
(Japanese clear) sui-mono 吸
い物, (o-)tsu´yu (お)つゆ[汁];
(Japanese dark) miso-shi´ru み
そ[味噌]汁; (sweet redbean-
paste) shiruko⌐ (o-shiruko)
汁粉・しるこ(お汁粉・おしる
こ); (thick Western) potā´ju
ポタージュ; (thin Western)
konsome コンソメ

soup stock dashi だし

sour suppa´i 酸っぱい・すっぱい;
it sours kusarima´su (kusa´ru,
kusa´tte) 腐ります(腐る, 腐
って)

source moto⌐ もと・元; ta´ne 種;
okori´ 起こり

south minami 南, nan-... 南...;
(the south) nampō 南方, (the
southern part) na´mbu 南部

southeast nantō 南東; **southwest**
nansei 南西

southerly minami-yori (no kaze)
南寄り(の風)

souvenir (o-)miyage (o-mi´ya)
(お)みやげ[土産](おみや),
miyage-mono みやげ[土産]物;
kine⌐n-hin 記念品

Soviet So´ren/So´bi´e´to (no) ソ
連/ソビエト(の); (= ~
citizen) Sore´n-jin ソ連人,
Sobieto´-jin ソビエト人; ~

Union Sōren ソ連
sow (seeds) makimasu (maku, maite) まき[蒔き]ます(まく, まいて)
soy bean daizu 大豆; fermented ~ nattō 納豆
soybean meal/flour kinako きなこ・黄な粉
soy sauce (o-)shōyu（お）しょうゆ[醤油]; (in sushi restaurant) murasaki 紫
spa tōji-ba 湯治場
space (available) ma 間; (between) aida 間; (outer space) uchū 宇宙; (room, leeway) yochi 余地; → blank (space)
Spain Supein スペイン
span (stretches over it) ... ni matagarimasu (matagaru, matagatte) ...に跨がり[またがり]ます(跨がる, 跨がって)
Spaniard, Spanish (person) Supein-jin スペイン人
Spanish (language) Supein-go スペイン語
spare 1. (reserve) yobi (no) 予備（の）2. (leeway, surplus) yoyū 余裕; ~ time hima 暇 3. → save
spark hibana 火花
sparrow suzume 雀・すずめ
speak hanashimasu (hanasu, hanashite) 話します(話す, 話して)
speaker → loudspeaker
speaking of ... ... wa ...は; ... no koto/hanashi desu ga ...の事/話ですが
spear yari 槍
special tokubetsu (no) 特別（の）; betsu (no) 別（の）, toku-... 特...; (peculiar) tokushu (no) 特殊（の）; (favorite) tokui (na/no) 得意（な/の）; (emergency) rinji (no) 臨時（の）
special class tokkyū 特級
special delivery sokutatsu 速達
special express (train) tokkyū 特急; special-express ticket tokkyū-ken 特急券
special feature/quality tokushoku 特色, tokuchō 特徴・特長
specialist semmon-ka 専門家; (medical) semmon-i 専門医
special lunch ranchi-sābisu ランチサービス
special second class toku-nitō 特二等
specialty semmon 専門, (forte) tokui 得意, (trick) ohako おはこ・十八番
species of ... ...-rui ...類; a ~ ... no is-shu ...の一種
specific (particular) kore to iū ... これという
speculation (venture) yama やま
speech hanashi 話, kotoba 言葉, kuchi 口; (public) enzetsu 演説, kōen 講演
speed hayasa 速さ, sokudo 速度, supiido スピード; (hour-

ly) ji⌐soku 時速

spell (ji⌐ o) tsuzurima⌐su (tsuzu⌐ru, tsuzu⌐tte) (字を) 綴り[つづり]ます(綴る, 綴って)

spellbound: is ~ utto⌐ri shima⌐su (suru, shịte) うっとりします(する, して)

spelling tsuzuri⌐ 綴り・つづり, supe⌐ringu スペリング; *(way written)* kaki-ka⌐ta⌐ 書き方, *(letters)* ji⌐ 字

spend tsukaima⌐su (tsukau, tsukatte) 使います(使う, 使って), *(pays)* dashima⌐su (da⌐su, da⌐shịte) 出します(出す, 出して); *(uses time)* okurima⌐su (okuru, okutte) 送ります(送る, 送って)

sphygmomanometer ketsuatsụ-kei 血圧計

spice kō⌐ryō 香料, chōmi(-ryō) 調味(料)

spiced saké (o-)to⌐so (お)とそ・屠蘇

spicy karai からい・辛い

spider ku⌐mo くも・蜘蛛; **~ web → cobweb**

spill *(it spills)* koborema⌐su (kobore⌐ru, kobo⌐rete) こぼれます(こぼれる, こぼれて); *(spills it)* koboshima⌐su (kobo⌐su, kobo⌐shịte) こぼします(こぼす, こぼして), tarashima⌐su (tara⌐su, tara⌐shịte) 垂らします(垂らす, 垂らして)

spinach hōre⌐nsō ほうれん草; *(boiled and seasoned)* o-hịta⌐shi おひたし・お浸し

spine sebone 背骨

spinning bōseki 紡績; **~ mill** bōseki-kō⌐jō 紡績工場

spirit se⌐ishin 精神, koko⌐ro (o-kokoro) 心(お心), ta⌐mashii 魂; kokoro-mochi⌐ 心持ち; ki 気

spit *(skewer)* kushi⌐ 串, yaki-gushi 焼き串

spit 1. *(spittle)* tsu⌐ba つば・唾, tsubaki⌐ つばき・唾 **2.** *(spits out)* (tsu⌐ba o) hakima⌐su (ha⌐ku, ha⌐ite) (つばを)吐きます(吐く, 吐いて)

spite: in spite of ... (na⌐) no ni ...(な)のに

splendid rippa (na) 立派(な), subarashi⌐i すばらしい, sụteki (na) すてき・素敵(な), mi⌐goto (na) 見事(な), sakan (na) 盛ん(な), ke⌐kkō (na) 結構(な)

splendidly rippa ni 立派に, subara⌐shịku すばらしく

split 1. *(splits it)* sakima⌐su (sa⌐ku, sa⌐ite) 裂きます(裂く, 裂いて), warima⌐su (waru, watte) 割ります(割る, 割って); *(divides it)* wakema⌐su (wake⌐ru, wa⌐kete) 分けます(分ける, 分けて) **2.** *(it splits)* sakema⌐su (sake⌐ru, sa⌐kete) 裂けます(裂ける, 裂けて),

warema‸su (wareru, warete) 割
れます(割れる, 割れて); *(it
separates)* wakarema‸su
(wakare‸ru, waka‸rete) 別れま
す(別れる, 別れて)
splitting the bill wari-kan 割り勘
split-toe socks ta‸bi たび・足袋
spoil 1. spoils it wa‸ruku (dame‸
ni) shima‸su (suru, shite) 悪く
(駄目に)します(する, して);
itamema‸su (itame‸ru,
ita‸mete) 傷めます(傷める,
傷めて) **2. it gets spoiled**
wa‸ruku narima‸su (na‸ru,
na‸tte) 悪くなります(なる,
なって), itamima‸su (ita‸mu,
ita‸nde) 傷みます(傷む, 傷ん
で) **3. it spoils** *(sours)*
kusarima‸su (kusa‸ru,
kusa‸tte) 腐ります(腐る,
腐って); *(rots)* itamima‸su
(ita‸mu, ita‸nde) 傷みます(傷
む, 傷んで)
spoil a person's mood ki‸bun o
kowashima‸su (kowa‸su,
kowa‸shite) 気分を壊します(壊
す, 壊して)
**spoke → speak; spoken
language** kōgo 口語
sponge kaimen 海綿, suponji ス
ポンジ; **~ gourd** hechima へ
ちま・糸瓜
spongecake kasutera カステラ
spontaneously hitori-de ni 独り
でに・ひとりでに, onozukara
自ずから・おのずから

spool ito‸maki 糸巻き
spoon supū‸n スプーン, sa‸ji‸ (o-
sa‸ji) さじ・匙(お匙); **(1** i‸p-
pon 一本, **2** ni‸-hon 二本,
3 sa‸m-bon 三本; **how many**
na‸m-bon 何本)
spoonful (hito‸)-saji (一)匙・さ
じ; **how many spoonfuls** na‸n-
saji 何匙
sport(s) supō‸tsu スポーツ, undō
運動; **Sports Day (10 October)**
Ta‸iiku no hi‸ 体育の日
spot 1. ten 点; *(spotted)* madara
(no) まだら[斑](の), *(blot)*
shimi 染み・しみ, **(with) spots**
bo‸tsubotsu ぼつぼつ・ボツボ
ツ **2.** *(place)* basho 場所
sprain (an ankle) (ashi‸ o)
kujikima‸su (kuji‸ku, kuji‸ite)
(足を)挫き[くじき]ます(挫
く, 挫いて); **gets a sprained
ankle** ashi‸ ga kujikema‸su
(kujike‸ru, kuji‸kete) 足が挫け
[くじけ]ます(挫ける, 挫け
て)
spread 1. *(spreads it)*
hirogema‸su (hirogeru,
hirogete) 広げます(広げる,
広げて), *(diffuses it)*
hiromema‸su (hirome‸ru,
hiro‸mete) 広めます(広める,
広めて); *(spreads it out)*
nobashima‸su (noba‸su,
noba‸shite) 伸ばします(伸ば
す, 伸ばして), nobema‸su
(nobe‸ru, no‸bete) 伸べます

(伸べる, 伸べて); (spreads it on) harima'su (haru, hatte) 張ります(張る, 張って)
2. (it spreads) hirogarima'su (hirogaru, hirogatte) 広がります(広がる, 広がって), (it gets diffused) hiromarima'su (hiroma'ru, hiroma'tte) 広まります(広まる, 広まって), fukyū shima'su (suru, shite) 普及します(する, して); (it spreads out) nobima'su (nobi'ru, no'bite) 伸びます(伸びる, 伸びて)

spread: a spread shiki-mono 敷物

spring (season) ha'ru 春; (device) bane(-ji'kake) ばね(仕掛け), (of clock) zemmai ぜんまい

spring: hot spring onsen 温泉

spring → jump

spring forth (gushes) wakima'su (waku, waite) わき[湧き]ます(わく, わいて)

spring from ... kara okorima'su (oko'ru, oko'tte) ...から起こります(起こる, 起こって)

springtime ha'ru 春

sprinkle it furi-kakema'su (-kake'ru, -ka'kete) 振りかけます(かける, かけて)

sprout(s) → pepper sprout

spy supa'i スパイ

square shikaku' (no) 四角(の), shikaku'i 四角い; kaku' 角; (plaza) hi'ro'-ba' 広場

squared paper genkō-yō'shi 原稿用紙

squat shagamima'su (shagamu, shagande) しゃがみます(しゃがむ, しゃがんで)

squeeze tsubushima'su (tsubusu, tsubushite) 潰し[つぶし]ます(潰す, 潰して); (squeezes out) shiborima'su (shibo'ru, shibo'tte) 絞ります(絞る, 絞って)

squid ika いか・烏賊

squilla (mantis shrimp) sha'ko しゃこ・蝦蛄

squirrel ri'su りす・栗鼠

Sri Lanka Surira'nka スリランカ

stab (tsuki-)sashima'su (sa'su, sa'shite) (突き)刺します(刺す, 刺して)

stadium kyōgi-jō 競技場; (baseball ~) yakyū-jō 野球場, kyūjō 球場

stage bu'tai 舞台; (of a process) dankai 段階

stage fright: gets ~ agarima'su (agaru, agatte) 上がります(上がる, 上がって)

stagger yoro-mekima'su (-me'ku, -me'ite) よろめきます(めく, めいて)

staggered work hours jisa-shu'kkin 時差出勤 「ろ(と)

staggering yo'royoro (to) よろよ

stain shimi 染み・しみ; (paints it) nurima'su (nuru, nutte) 塗り

ます(塗る，塗って); *(soils it)*
yogoshima̍su (yogosu,
yogoshi̱te) 汚します(汚す，汚
して)，*(gets soiled)* yogore-
ma̍su (yogoreru, yogorete)
汚れます(汚れる，汚れて)
stairs, stairway kaidan 階段，
(wooden) hashigo-dan はしご
stake *(post)* ku̍i 杭 ┃[梯子]段
stale *(not fresh)* furu̍i 古い
stalk ku̱ki̍ 茎
stamp 1. *(postal)* ki̱tte̍ 切手
(**how many** na̍m-mai 何枚)；
~ **album** ki̱tte-chō 切手帳
2. *(seal)* i̍n 印; *(cancellation
mark)* keshi-in 消印
stand 1. *(sales booth)* uri-ba 売り
場, baiten 売店, su̱tando スタ
ンド **2.** *(stands up)* tachima̍su
(ta̍tsu, ta̍tte) 立ちます(立つ，
立って); **stands it up**
tatema̍su (tate̍ru, ta̍tete) 立
てます(立てる，立てて)
3. stands it *(tolerates)* ga̍man
shima(̄)su (suru, shi̱te) 我慢
します(する，して),
koraema̍su (kora e̍ru, kora e̍te)
こらえます(こらえる，こら
えて), taema̍su (tae̍ru, ta e̍te)
耐えます(耐える，耐えて),
shi̍mbō shima(̄)su (suru,
shi̱te) 辛抱します(する，して)
stand against *(= opposes)* ... ni
taikō shima̍su (suru, shi̱te) ...
に対抗します(する，して)
standard 1. hyōjun 標準; ~

Japanese hyōjun-go 標準語
2. a ~ me̍ʼyasu 目安; ki̱kaku
規格
standardize tōitsu shima̍su
(suru, shi̱te) 統一します(する，
して); ki̱kaku̍-ka shima̍su
(suru, shi̱te) 規格化します(す
る，して); **standardization**
ki̱kaku̍-ka 規格化; tōitsu 統
一
standee tachimi no kyaku 立ち見
の客; **sees it as a** ~ tachimi
shima̍su (suru, shi̱te) 立ち見
します(する，して)
stand firm gambarima̍su
(gamba̍ru, gamba̍tte) がん
ばり[頑張り]ます(がんばる，
がんばって) ┌見席
standing room tachimi̍-seki 立ち
stand out (prominently) medachi-
ma̍su (meda̍tsu, meda̍tte)
目立ちます(目立つ，目立って)
standpoint tachi-ba 立場
stand still tachi-domarima̍su
(-doma̍ru, -doma̍tte) 立ち
止まります(止まる，止まっ
staple fiber su̍fu スフ ┃て)
staple (of stapler) ha̍ri 針
stapler ho̍chikisu ホチキス
star hoshi 星; *(symbol)* hoshi-
ji̍rushi 星印; *(actor)* su̱tā̍ ス
ター, hana̍gata 花形
starch 1. *(laundry)* nori̍ 糊・のり,
No starch please. Nori̍ zuke̍
kinshi. 糊付け禁止. **2.** *(food)*
dempun でんぷん・澱粉;

potato ~ kataku῀ri῀ko 片栗粉;
→ **cornstarch**

stare (at) (… o) ji῀ro-jiro
mima῀su (mi῀ru, mi῀te) (…を)
じろじろ見ます(見る, 見て);
mi-tsumema῀su (-tsume◌ru,
-tsu῀mete) 見詰め[見つめ]ます
(詰める, 詰めて), nagame-
ma῀su (nagame῀ru, naga῀mete)
眺めます(眺める, 眺めて)

start 1. *(it starts)* hajimarima῀su
(hajimaru, hajimatte) 始まり
ます(始まる, 始まって);
(sets out) dema῀su (de῀ru,
de῀te) 出ます(出る, 出て);
from the start hajime kara 始
めから, ho῀nrai 本来 **2.** *(starts
it)* hajimema῀su (hajimeru,
hajimete) 始めます(始める,
始めて), *(starts doing it)* shi-
hajimema῀su (-hajime῀ru,
-haji῀mete) し始めます(始め
る, 始めて); **it starts to rain**
a῀me ga furi-hajimema῀su
(-hajime◌ru, -haji◌mete) 雨
が降り始めます(始める, 始め
て), a῀me ni narima῀su (na῀ru,
na῀tte) 雨になります(なる,
なって); **starts the engine** →
engine 3. → **startle** 「演
starting a performance kaien 開
startle bikku῀ri sasema῀su (saseru, sasete) びっくりさせます
(させる, させて); **gets startled**
bikku῀ri shima῀su (suru, shite)
びっくりします(する, して)

start off/out *(departs)* dekake-
ma῀su (dekakeru, dekakete) 出
かけます(出かける, 出かけて)
starve uema῀su (ue῀ru, u῀ete) 飢え
ます(飢える, 飢えて)
state 1. *(of the U.S.)* shū῀ 州, …῀
-shū …州; *(status)* bu῀n 分; ~
of affairs jōkyō 状況, ji῀tai 事
態; → **condition**; → **nation**
2. expressly states utaima῀su
(utau, utatte) うたい[謳い]ま
す(うたう, うたって); → **say**
static (noise) zatsuon 雑音
station 1. *(rail)* e῀ki 駅, su̱te῀shon
ステーション **2.** → **gas station**
stationery *(letter paper)* binsen
便箋; *(writing supplies)*
bumbo῀-gu 文房具; *(shop)*
bumbōgu-ya 文房具屋
stationmaster ekichō 駅長; ~'s
office ekichō῀-shi̱tsu 駅長室
statistics tōkei 統計
statue zo῀ 像, *(bronze)* dōzō 銅像
stature (= height) se῀i/se῀ 背/背
status bu῀n 分, *(social, personal)*
mi῀bun 身分, *(position)* chi῀i
地位; **the status quo** genjō 現
状
stay 1. ima῀su (iru, ite) います
(いる, いて), [DEFERENTIAL/
HUMBLE] orima῀su (o῀ru, o῀tte/
orima῀shi̱te) おります(おる,
おって/おりまして),
[HONORIFIC] irasshaima῀su
(irassha῀ru, irassha῀tte/
ira῀shi̱te/irasshaima῀shi̱te) い

らっしゃいます(いらっしゃ
る, いらっしゃって/いらして/
いらっしゃいまして) = oide
ni narima̅su (na̅ru, na̅tte/
narima̅shite) おいでになりま
す(なる, なって/なりまして)
2. todomarima̅su (todoma̅ru,
todoma̅tte) とどまり[止ま
り・留まり]ます(とどまる, と
どまって); *(overnight)* toma-
rima̅su (tomaru, tomatte) 泊
まります(泊まる, 泊まって)

stay: a stay (away from home)
taizai 滞在; **stays** taizai
shima̅su (suru, shite) 滞在し
ます(する, して)

stay away (from school, etc.)
yasumima̅su (yasu̅mu, yasu̅-
nde) 休みます(休む, 休んで)

stay up: ~ **all night** tetsuya
shima̅su (suru, shite) 徹夜し
ます(する, して); ~ **late** yo̅
o fukashima̅su (fuka̅su,
fuka̅shite) 夜を更かします
(更かす, 更かして), yo̅
fu̅ka̅shi o shima̅su (suru,
shite) 夜更しをします(する,

steadily jitto じっと   して)

steady katagi (na) 堅気(な), te-
gata̅i 手堅い

steak su̅te̅ki ステーキ, *(beefsteak)* bifu̅teki ビフテキ

steak sandwich teki̅-sa̅ndo テキ
サンド

steal nusumima̅su (nusu̅mu,
nusu̅nde) 盗みます(盗む, 盗

んで), kapparaima̅su
(kappara̅u, kappara̅tte)
かっぱらいます(かっぱらう,
かっぱらって)

stealth(y espionage): the art of
~ ni̅njutsu 忍術; **a master of**
~ ni̅nja 忍者

steam jo̅ki 蒸気, yu̅ge 湯気;
(steams food) fukashima̅su
(fuka̅su, fuka̅shite) ふかしま
す(ふかす, ふかして)

steamed bun manjū まんじゅう
・饅頭; *(stuffed with bean jam)*
am-man あんまん, *(ground
pork)* niku-man 肉まん

**steamed custard (from fish broth
and eggs)** chawan-mushi 茶碗
蒸し   「まぼこ

steamed fish cake kamaboko か

steamed foods mushi̅-mono 蒸

steamship ki̅sen 汽船   し物

steel hagane 鋼・はがね, kōtetsu
鋼鉄, tetsu 鉄

steep *(precipitous)* kyū (na) 急
(な), kewashi̅i 険しい

steering wheel handoru ハンドル

stem *(of plant)* ku̅ki 茎

step 1. *(walk)* arukima̅su (aru̅-
ku, aru̅ite) 歩きます(歩く,
歩いて); → **measure**; → **stage**
2. steps into/on fumi-komi-
ma̅su (-ko̅mu, -ko̅nde) 踏み
込みます(込む, 込んで); **steps
on the gas** a̅kuseru o fumi-
ma̅su アクセルを踏みます

stepchild mama-ko まま[継]子

stepfather mama-chichi まま
［継］父 ［［継］母
stepmother mama-haha まま
steps → **stairs** ［立体（の）
stereo(phonic/scopic) rittai (no)
stereo (sound/player) sutereo ス
stew shichū シチュー ⌐テレオ
steward bōi ボーイ, kyūji 給仕,
ho'suto ホスト, suchuwā'do
スチュワード
stewardess ho'sutesu ホステス,
suchuwā'desu スチュワーデス
stick 1. *(club)* bō(-kkire) 棒（っ切
れ）; *(staff)* tsu'e 杖 *or (cane)*
sute'kki ステッキ **2.** *(of gum,
candy, etc.)* ...ichi'-mai ...一枚,
(of yakitori, etc.) i'p-pon 一本
3. *(of hair-grease)* chi'kku
チック (i'p-pon) 一本
stick 1. *(it sticks to)* ... ni
kuttsukima'su (kuttsu'ku,
kuttsu'ite) ...にくっつきます
（くっつく，くっついて）
2. *(sticks it on)* tsukema'su
(tsuke'ru, tsuke'te) 付けます
（付ける，付けて），*(pastes it
on)* harima'su (haru, hatte) 貼
ります（貼る，貼って）
stickiness nebari' 粘り
stick out → **protrude**; *(sticks
it out)* tsuki-dashima'su (-da'su,
-da'shite) 突き出します（出す，
出して）
sticky: is ~ ne'baneba shima'su
(suru, shite) ねばねばします
（する，して）

sticky water from boiling rice o-
ne'ba おねば
stiff 1. → **hard 2.** *(shoulder) gets*
~ *(kata' ga)* korima'su (ko'ru,
ko'tte) 肩が凝ります（凝る，
凝って）; ~ **shoulder, stiffness of shoulder** kata(ー) no
kori 肩の凝り
still *(yet)* ma'da まだ; *(but)* (sore)
de' mo （それ）でも; **still better**
issō/na'o i'i 一層［いっそう］/
尚［なお］いい; **still more**
mo'tto もっと; na'o 尚・なお;
issō 一層・いっそう
still → **quiet**; **Stand still!**
Ugoka'naide kudasai. 動かな
いで下さい.
stimulate unagashima'su
(unaga'su, unaga'shite) 促しま
す（促す，促して）
stimulation shigeki 刺激
sting sashima'su (sa'su, sa'shite)
刺します（刺す，刺して）
stingy ke'chi (na) けち（な）; ~
person ke'chimbo けちんぼ
stinking kusa'i 臭い
stipulate kitei shima'su (suru,
shite) 規定します（する，して）
stipulation kitei 規定; → **provision**; → **condition**
stir it kaki-mawashima'su
(-mawaーsu, -mawaーshite)
かき回します（回す，回して）
stir up *(fans, incites)* aorima'su
(ao'ru, ao'tte) あおり［煽り］ま
す（あおる，あおって）

stock *(financial)* kabu 株; *(soup)* dashi だし; *(on hand)* mochi-awase (no) 持ち合わせ(の)

stock: has in ~ (on hand) mochi-awasema͞su (-awase͞ru, -awa͞sete) 持ち合わせます(合わせる, 合わせて)

stockings kutsu-shita 靴下; **(1 pair** is-soku 一足, **2** ni-soku 二足, **3** sa͞n-zoku/-soku 三足/足; **how many pairs** na͞n-zoku/-soku 何足/足)

stomach i-bu͞kuro 胃袋, i 胃; *(strictly, belly)* o-naka おなか, hara 腹; **~ band** hara-maki 腹巻き 「胃癌

stomach cancer i-gan 胃がん・

stomach trouble: develops ~ o-naka o kowashima͞su (kowa͞su, kowa͞shite) おなかを壊します(壊す, 壊して)

stone ishi 石

stone lantern tōrō 灯籠

stop 1. *(it comes to rest)* tomarima͞su (tomaru, tomatte) 止まります(止まる, 止まって), todomarima͞su (todoma͞ru, todoma͞tte) とどまり[止まり・留まり]ます(とどまる, とどまって), → **stand still;** *(it ceases)* yamima͞su (yamu, yande) 止みます(止む, 止んで) **2.** *(stops it)* tomema͞su (tomeru, tomete) 止めます(止める, 止めて),

todomema͞su (todome͞ru, todo͞mete) とどめ[止め]ます(とどめる, とどめて), yoshima͞su (yo͞su, yo͞shite) よします(よす, よして); *(stops doing)* ... o yamema͞su (yameru, yamete) ...を止めます(止める, 止めて)

3. *(halting place)* teiryū-jo 停留所 「電

stoppage of electricity teiden 停

stopped up: gets ~ fusagarima͞su (fusaga͞ru, fusaga͞tte) ふさがります(ふさがる, ふさがって) 「cork) se͞n 栓

stopper *(cork)* kuchi 口; *(plug,*

stopping *(of a vehicle)* teisha 停車

stop up fusagima͞su (fusagu, fusaide) ふさぎます(ふさぐ, ふさいで)

store *(shop)* mise 店 「倉・蔵

storeroom (= **storehouse**) kura

storm a͞rashi 嵐, bōfū 暴風; *(rages)* abarema͞su (abareru, abarete) 暴れます(暴れる, 暴れて)

story hanashi 話; → **floor**

storyteller hanashi-ka はなし家・噺家

stove suto͞bu ストーブ, **(kitchen)** kamado かまど・竈, kama かま・釜, re͞nji レンジ; *(portable cooking)* ko͞nro コンロ

straddle ... ni matagarima͞su

(mataga⌐ru, mataga⌐tte) ...に跨
がり[またがり]ます(跨がる,
跨がって)

straight massu⌐gu (na) まっすぐ・
真っ直ぐ(な)

straighten it up *(tidies it)*
katazukema⌐su (katazuke⌐ru,
katazu⌐kete) 片付けます(片付
ける, 片付けて)

strain 1. *(tension)* kinchō 緊張
2. *(forces)* mu⌐ri ni shima⌐su
(suru, shite) 無理にします(す
る, して); *(filters)* koshima⌐su
(kosu, koshite) こし[漉し]ま
す(こす, こして), *(through
cloth)* shiborima⌐su (shibo⌐ru,
shibo⌐tte) 絞ります(絞る, 絞
って)

strait(s) kaikyō 海峡

strange he⌐n (na) 変(な), fushigi
(na) 不思議(な); *(peculiar)*
ki⌐myō (na) 奇妙(な), okashi⌐i
おかしい; *(wondrous)* myō⌐
(na) 妙(な); *(alien)* yoso⌐ (no)
よそ(の); *(unknown)* shiranai
知らない

stranger *(unknown person)*
shiranai hito⌐ 知らない人;
(outsider) yoso⌐ no hito⌐ よそ
の人, tanin 他人

strap himo ひも・紐; *(to hang on
to)* tsuri-kawa 吊り革; *(watchband, etc.)* bando バンド

straw wa⌐ra わら・藁, mugi-
wa⌐ra 麦わら[藁]; *(to drink
with)* suto⌐rō ストロー

straw bag tawara⌐ 俵

strawberry i⌐chigo いちご・苺

straw mushrooms enoki⌐-take え
のき茸・榎茸, enoki⌐-dake え
のき茸・榎茸

straw raincoat mi⌐no みの・蓑

straw sandals zōri (o-zō⌐ri) 草履
(お草履)

**straw wrapping, straw-wrapped
package** tsuto⌐ つと・苞

stray *(digresses)* sorema⌐su
(sore⌐ru, so⌐rete) 逸れ[それ]ま
す(逸れる, 逸れて)

stream nagare⌐ 流れ; **in streams**
zo⌐rozoro ぞろぞろ

streamline (procedures, ...)
gōri⌐-ka shima⌐su (suru, shite)
合理化します(する, して)

street michi 道, tōri⌐ 通り, shadō
車道, tsuji 辻; **(on) the ~**
gaitō (de) 街頭(で)

streetcar de⌐nsha 電車

strength tsu⌐yosa 強さ, *(power)*
chikara⌐ (o-chikara) 力(お力);
(real ~) jitsuryoku 実力; *(of
saturation)* ko⌐sa 濃さ

strengthen (it) tsu⌐yoku shima⌐su
(suru, shite) 強くします(する,
して), katamema⌐su
(katameru, katamete) 固めま
す(固める, 固めて)

stretch *(stretches it)*
nobashima⌐su (noba⌐su,
noba⌐shite) 伸ばします(伸ば
す, 伸ばして); *(it stretches)*
nobima⌐su (nobi⌐ru, no⌐bite)
伸びます(伸びる, 伸びて),

(taut) harima̅su (haru, hatte)
張ります(張る, 張って)

stretcher ta̅nka 担架

stretch over *(extends over)* ... ni
matagarima̅su (mataga̅ru,
mataga̅tte) ...に跨がり[また
がり]ます(跨がる, 跨がって)

strew chirashima̅su (chirasu,
chirashite) 散らします(散ら
す, 散らして)

stricken area higa̅i-chi 被害地

strict *(severe)* kibishi̅i 厳しい,
katai 固い・堅い, yakamashi̅i
やかましい; *(precise)*
gemmitsu (na) 厳密(な)

stride over matagima̅su
(mata̅gu, mata̅ide) 跨ぎ[また
ぎ]ます(跨ぐ, 跨いで)

strife araso̅i 争い, so̅dō 騒動

strike 1. *(job action)* suto̅ スト,
sutora̅iki ストライキ; *(base-
ball)* sutora̅iku ストライク
2. → **hit**

striking *(outstanding)*
ichijirushi̅i 著しい

strikingly ichijiru̅shiku 著しく

string *(thread)* i̅to 糸; *(cord)*
himo ひも・紐; *(of violin or
bow)* tsuru̅ つる・弦

string: (linked) in a ~ tsunagatte
つながって

string up *(suspends)* tsurima̅su
(tsuru, tsutte) 吊ります(吊る,
吊って)

stripe shima̅ しま・縞

striptease, strip show sutori̅ppu

ストリップ

strive tsutomema̅su (tsutome̅ru,
tsuto̅mete) 努めます(努める,
努めて), do̅ryoku shima(̅)su
(suru, shite) 努力します(する,
して), tsukushima̅su
(tsuku̅su, tsuku̅shite) 尽くし
ます(尽くす, 尽くして)

stroke nadema̅su (nade̅ru,
na̅dete) なで[撫で]ます(なで
る, なでて)

stroll sampo (shima̅su; suru,
shite) 散歩(します; する, し
て)

strong tsuyo̅i 強い; *(coffee, etc.)*
ko̅i 濃い; *(influential)*
yūryoku (na) 有力(な)

strong point *(merit)* cho̅sho 長所

strong wind ō-ka̅ze̅ 大風

structure kōzō 構造; *(setup)*
kumi-tate 組み立て; *(system)*
so̅shiki 組織

struggle *(contention)* araso̅i 争
い; **~ for** *(contends)* ... o
arasoima̅su (araso̅u,
araso̅tte) ...を争います(争う,
争って)

stub *(check)* chi̅kki チッキ

stucco shikkui しっくい・漆喰

stuck: gets stuck *(clogged)*
tsumarima̅su (tsuma̅ru,
tsuma̅tte) 詰まります(詰まる,
詰まって)

stuck-up *(affected)* kidotte
ima̅su 気取っています,
kidotta ... 気取った...

student gakusei 学生, ...-̄-sei ... 生, *(pupil)* se̊ito 生徒; ~ **between schools** rōnin 浪人; **a ~ of the teacher's, one of the teacher's students** sense̊i no oshie⌐go 先生の教え子; **the student of English [in general]** Eigo (no) gakushū⌐-sha 英語(の)学習者

studio *(private)* atori⌐e アトリエ; *(public)* suta⌐jio スタジオ

studio apartment wan-rū⌐mu 「ワンルーム」「家

studious person benkyō-ka 勉強

study 1. benkyō 勉強; gakushū 学習; *(studies it)* benkyō shimåsu (suru, shi̊te) 勉強します(する, して), manabimåsu (manabu, manande) 学びます(学ぶ, 学んで), *(is tutored/taught)* osowarimåsu (osowaru, osowatte) 教わります(教わる, 教わって); *(a basic subject)* gakushū shimåsu (suru, shi̊te) 学習します(する, して)
2. *(room)* shosai 書斎
3. → **research**; → **science**

study: ~ by observation, field ~ kengaku 見学

stuff 1. *(thing)* mono̊ 物
2. *(crams)* tsumemåsu (tsume̊ru, tsůmete) 詰めます(詰める, 詰めて)

stumble tsuma-zukimåsu (tsuma-zuku, tsuma-zuite)

つまずきます・躓きます(つまずく, つまずいて)

stump *(tree)* kiri⌐-kabu 切り株

stumped: is stumped mairimåsu (måiru, måitte) 参ります(参る, 参って); → **perplexed**

stunt ge̊i 芸; **horseback stunts** kyokuba 曲馬

stupid båka (na) ばか(な); *(rustic)* yåbo (na) 野暮(な)

sturdy jōbu (na) 丈夫(な)

style 1. ... fū̊ ...風, ...-fū ...風; **Japanese ~** Nihon-fū (no) 日本風(の) **2.** *(form)* tåi 態

stylish sumåto (na) スマート(な), iki (na) いき[粋](な), otsu (na) 乙(な)

styptic pencil chi-dome 血止め

subject *(topic)* mondai 問題, *(of conversation)* wadai 話題; tånc 種; *(school)* kamoku 科目; *(grammar)* shůgo 主語

subjective shukan-teki (na) 主観的な; **subjectivity** shukan 主観

submarine sensu⌐i-kan 潜水艦

submissive sůnao (na) すなお[素直](な)

subordinate bůka 部下, *(follower)* ko̊-bun 子分

subscribe yoyaku shimåsu (suru, shi̊te) 予約します(する, して), mōshi-komimåsu (-ko⌐mu, -ko⌐nde) 申し込みます(込む, 込んで)

subscription yoyaku 予約

subsequently tsu⌐ide 次いで; →

later; → **next**

substance (*material*) busshitsu 物質

substantial 1. (*concrete*) gutaiteki (na) 具体的 (な) **2.** → **considerable**

substitute kawari (o-ka'wari) 代わり (お代わり) 「(な)

subtle (*delicate*) bimyō (na) 微妙

subtract hikima'su (hiku, hiite) 引きます (引く, 引いて)

suburb kō'gai 郊外, shi'gai 市外, (*outskirts*) basue 場末; (*bedroom community*) beddota'un ベッドタウン

subway chika'-tetsu 地下 (鉄)

succeed (*is successful*) seikō shima'su (suru, shite) 成功します (する, して); (*succeed to*) tsugima'su (tsugu, tsuide) 継ぎます (継ぐ, 継いで)

success: making a ～ out of life shusse 出世

successful uma'i/mma'i うまい; **is ～ → succeed; successfully** u'maku うまく

succession: in ～ tsu'ide 次いで, tsuzuite 続いて; tsunagatte つながって; tsuzukete 続けて

such sonna そんな, sono yō' na そのよう [様] な, sō yū そうゆう; (*like this*) konna こんな, kono yō' na このよう [様] な, kō yū こうゆう

such-and-such a place do'kodoko どこどこ,

do'kosoko どこそこ

suck suima'su (suu, sutte) 吸います (吸う, 吸って); shaburima'su (shaburu, shabutte) しゃぶります (しゃぶる, しゃぶって)

sucker (*dupe*) ka'mo かも・鴨

sudden (*unexpected*) totsuzen (no) 突然 (の), ni'waka にわか; (*urgent*) kyū (na) 急 (な)

suddenly fui ni 不意に, totsuzen 突然; (*unexpectedly*) ni'waka ni にわかに, (*immediately*) tachimachi (ni) たちまち (に); (*urgently*) kyū ni 急に; (*with a rush*) do'tto どっと; (*with a jerk/gulp*) gu'tto ぐっと; (*with a sudden start of surprise*) hatto (shite) はっと (して)

sudden shower yūdachi 夕立

sue uttaema'su (utta'e'ru, utta'ete) 訴えます (訴える, 訴えて)

suet he'tto ヘット

suffer kurushimima'su (kurushi'mu, kurushi'nde) 苦しみます (苦しむ, 苦しんで), nayamima'su (naya'mu, naya'nde) 悩みます (悩む, 悩んで), wazuraima'su (wazurau, wazuratte) 煩い [わずらい] ます (煩う, 煩って); (*incurs*) kōmurima'su (kōmu'ru, kōmu'tte) 被り [こうむり] ます (被る, 被って),

ukema'su (uke'ru, u'kete) 受け
ます(受ける, 受けて)
suffer from ... o wazuraima'su
(wazurau, wazuratte) ...を煩
い[わずらい]ます(煩う,
煩って); → **incur**
suffering kurushi'mi 苦しみ,
nayami' 悩み
suffice, sufficient tarima'su
(tariru, tarite) 足ります(足り
る, 足りて)
suffix setsubi'-go/-ji 接尾語/辞
sugar sato' (o-sato) 砂糖(お砂糖)
suggest(ion) → **propose (proposal)**; → **hint**
suicide jisatsu 自殺
suit 1. yō-fuku (o-yō'fuku) 洋服
(お洋服), fuku' 服, *(business)*
sebiro 背広, *(esp. woman's)*
sū'tsu スーツ, *(two-piece)* tsū-
pi'isu ツーピース **2.** *(of playing cards)* kumi' 組
suit 1. *(matches with)* ...ni
aima'su (a'u, a'tte) ...に合いま
す(合う, 合って); **suits one's
taste** kuchi ni aima'su 口に合
います **2.** *(is becoming to)* ...ni
ni-aima'su (-a'u, -a'tte) ...に似
合います(合う, 合って)
suitable fusawashi'i ふさわしい,
tekitō (na) 適当(な), te'kigi
(na) 適宜(な); *(moderate)*
kakkō (na) 格好(な); **is ~**
teki-shima'su (teki-su'ru,
teki'-shite) 適します(適する,
適して)

suitable: the most ~ uttetsuke
(no) うってつけ(の)
suitably fusawa'shiku ふさわし
く, tekitō ni 適当に
suitcase kaban かばん・鞄,
sūtsuke'su スーツケース; *(lug-
gage)* (te-)ni'motsu (手)荷物
sulk fukurema'su (fukureru,
fukurete) 膨れます(膨れる,
膨れて)
sullen face butchō-zura 仏頂面
sultry mushi-atsu'i 蒸し暑い;
gets sultry mushima'su (mu'su,
mu'shite) 蒸します(蒸す, 蒸
して)
sum 1. ga'ku 額 **2. to ~ it up** yōsu'ru ni 要するに
sumac ha'ze はぜ
summarize yōyaku shima'su
(suru, shite) 要約します(する,
して), tsumamima'su
(tsumamu, tsumande) つまみ
ます(つまむ, つまんで),
tsuzumema'su (tsuzume'ru,
tsuzu'mete) つづめ[約め]ます
(つづめる, つづめて)
summary taiyō 大要, yōyaku 要
約, *(gist)* yō'shi 要旨; **in ~** yōsu'ru ni 要するに
summer natsu 夏; **~ gift** (o-)
chūgen (お)中元; **~ period/
term** ka'ki 夏期; **~ school**
kaki-ga'kkō 夏期学校; **~
solstice** geshi 夏至; **~ vaca-
tion/holidays** natsuya'sumi 夏
休み

summit itadaki 頂, chōjō 頂上, mine⌐¬ 峰

summon yobima⌐su (yobu, yonde) 呼びます(呼ぶ, 呼んで)

sumo → **wrestling, wrestler**

sun o-hi-sama お日様, hi 日, ta⌐iyō 太陽, o-te⌐nto-sama おてんとさま・お天道様

sunbathing hinata-bo⌐kko ひなた[日向]ぼっこ

sunburn hiyake 日焼け

Sunday Nichiyō⌐bi 日曜日

sundry zatta (na) 雑多(な); **sundries** zakka 雑貨

sunny *(room, etc.)* hiatari⌐¬ ga i⌐i 日当りがいい

sunrise hinode 日の出

sunset hinoiri 日の入り, nichibotsu 日没; *(time)* higure 日暮れ

sunshade hiyoke 日よけ

sunshine hinata ひなた・日向, ni⌐kkō 日光

superfluous yokei (na) 余計(な); *(surplus)* kajō (no) 過剰(の)

superintendent kantoku 監督

superior 1. ue (no) 上(の), meue⌐¬ (no) 目上(の); **(a superior)** meue⌐¬ no hito⌐ 目上の人 **2.** era⌐i 偉い; masarima⌐su (masa⌐¬ru, masa⌐¬tte) 勝ります(勝る, 勝って)

supermarket sū⌐pā スーパー, sūpā-mā⌐ketto スーパーマーケット

supervise kantoku shima⌐su (suru, shite) 監督します(する, して)

supervisor kantoku 監督

supper ban-go⌐han 晩ご飯, yūshoku 夕食, yū-han 夕飯

supplement ogina⌐i 補い, zō⌐ho 増補

supplies for ... ...-yō⌐hin ...用品

supply(ing) kyōkyū 供給; **supplies it** kyōkyū shima⌐su (suru, shite) 供給します(する, して); → **provide**; → **give**; → **sell**

support 1. *(approval)* sansei 賛成; *(backing, help)* kōen 後援, *(aid)* e⌐njo 援助 **2.** *(props it)* sasaema⌐su (sasae⌐¬ru, sasa⌐¬ete) 支えます(支える, 支えて); *(endorses)* shi⌐ji shima⌐su (suru, shite) 支持します(する, して)

supporter: athletic ~ *(= jockstrap)* sapō⌐tā サポーター

suppose ... to shima⌐su (suru, shite) ...とします(する, して); → **think**; → **imagine**

supposition katei 仮定; *(conjecture)* suisoku 推測

suppress appaku shima⌐su (suru, shite) 圧迫します(する, して); **suppression** appaku 圧迫

surcharge mashi 増し

sure ta⌐shika (na) 確か(な)

sure: for sure kanarazu 必ず, ta⌐shika ni 確かに, ze⌐-hi ぜひ・是非

sure: makes sure tashikamema̅su (tashikame̅ru, tashika̅mete) 確かめます(確かめる, 確かめて); **to make sure** nen no tame̅ (ni) 念のため[為](に)

sure: to be sure (= **of course**) mo̅tto̅mo もっとも; → **of course**

surely kitto きっと

surf yose-nami 寄せ波; **surfing** nami-no⌐ri⌐ 波乗り; **surfboard** naminori-i̅ta 波乗り板

surface me̅n 面, hyo̅me̅n 表面; **(top)** uwabe うわべ・上辺; **entire ~** zemme⌐n 全面

surf clam (geoduck) miru̅-gai みる貝

surgeon geka̅-i 外科医

surgery (= surgical operation) shu̅jutsu 手術; (as a medical specialty) geka 外科

surmisal suisoku 推測; **surmise** suisoku shima̅su (suru, shite) 推測します(する, して)

surpass sugurema̅su (sugure̅ru, sugu̅rete) 優れ[すぐれ]ます (優れる, 優れて), nukima̅su (nuku, nuite) 抜きます(抜く, 抜いて), masarima̅su (masa⌐ru, masa⌐tte) 勝ります(勝る, 勝って)

surplus yoyū 余裕; kajō (no) 過剰(の)

surprised: gets ~ bikku̅ri shima̅su (suru, shite) びっく

りします(する, して), odorokima̅su (odoro̅ku, odoro̅ite) 驚きます(驚く, 驚いて)

surrender kōfuku/kōsan (shima̅su; suru, shite) 降伏/降参(します; する, して)

surround kakomima̅su (kakomu, kakonde) 囲みます (囲む, 囲んで); (centers on) megurima̅su (meguru, megutte) 巡ります(巡る, 巡って)

surrounding 1. the ~ ... shūhen no ... 周辺の...; **surroundings** shū̅i 周囲 **2.** (centering on) ... o megutte ...を巡って

sushi (o-)su̅shi (お)すし[寿司・鮨], sushi̅ すし・寿司・鮨

sushi: 1. covered with fish tidbits chirashi̅-zushi 散らしずし[鮨] **2. in a bag of aburage** (fried bean curd) inari̅-zushi いなりずし・稲荷鮨 **3. rolled in seaweed** nori̅-maki のり巻き; (with cucumber) kappa (-maki) かっぱ(巻き); (around tuna tidbit) tekka (-maki) 鉄火(巻き) **4. hand-packed into small balls** (Tokyo style) nigiri̅-zushi 握りずし[鮨] **5. pressed with marinated fish in squarish molds** (Osaka style) oshi⌐-zushi 押しずし[鮨]

sushi bar sushi̅-ya (o-sushiya) す

し[寿司・鮨]屋（おすし屋）

suspect 1. utagaima'su (utagau, utagatte) 疑います（疑う、疑って）**2. a suspect** yōgi'-sha 容疑者

suspend 1. *(hangs it)* tsurima'su (tsuru, tsutte) 吊ります（吊る、吊って）**2.** *(stops in the midst)* chūshi shima'su (suru, shite) 中止します（する、して）

suspenders zubo'n-tsuri ズボン吊り

suspension *(stoppage)* teishi 停止、*(abeyance)* chūshi 中止

suspicious fushigi (na) 不思議（な）、ayashi'i 怪しい、ikagawashi'i いかがわしい

sustain *(incurs)* kōmurima'su (kōmu'ru, kōmu'tte) 被り[こうむり]ます（被る、被って）

sutra *(Buddhist scripture)* o-kyō お経、kyōten 経典

swab *(scrub)* tawashi たわし、*(mop)* mo'ppu モップ；*(cotton)* wata' 綿、*(sponge)* suponji スポンジ；*(earpick)* mimi-ka'ki 耳かき

swagger ibarima'su (iba'ru, iba'tte) 威張ります（威張る、威張って）

swallow *(the bird)* tsubame つばめ・燕；*(ingests)* nomi-komima'su (-ko'mu, -ko'nde) 呑み込みます（込む、込んで）

swamp numa' 沼

swan hakuchō 白鳥

sway 1. *(it sways)* yurema'su (yureru, yurete) 揺れます（揺れる、揺れて）**2.** *(sways it)* yusuburima'su (yusuburu, yusubutte) 揺すぶります（揺すぶる、揺すぶって）、yurima'su (yuru, yutte) 揺ります（揺る、揺って）

swear 1. *(vows)* chikaima'su (chika⌐u, chika⌐tte) 誓います（誓う、誓って）**2.** *(reviles)* nonoshirima'su (nonoshi'ru, nonoshi'tte) ののしります（ののしる、ののしって）

sweat a'se (ga dema'su; de'ru, de'te) 汗（が出ます；出る、出て）

sweater sē'tā セーター（**how many** na'm-mai 何枚）

sweep sōji shima'su (suru, shite) 掃除します（する、して）；hakima'su (ha'ku, ha'ite) 掃きます（掃く、掃いて）

sweeper sōji'-ki 掃除機

sweeping sōji (o-sō'ji) 掃除（お掃除）

sweet amai 甘い

sweet and sour pork su⌐-buta 酢豚

sweetfish *(river trout)* a'yu あゆ・鮎、a'i あい

sweetheart i'i-hito いい人、koibito 恋人

sweet potato → potato 　　　「酢

sweet rice wine mirin みりん・味

sweet roll with beanjam inside
ampa⌐ɪ⌐n あんパン
sweets *(pastry, candy)* (o-)kaˈshi
（お）菓子
swell *(splendid)* suteki (na) すて
き［素敵］（な）, *(terrific)* sugoˈi
すごい・凄い
swelling hare-mono 腫れ物;
dekiˈ-moˈnoˈ (o-deˈki) できも
の・出来物（おでき）; *(bump)*
kobuˈ こぶ・瘤
swell (up) haremaˈsu (hareru,
harete) 腫れ［はれ］ます（腫れ
る, 腫れて）; fukuramimaˈsu
(fukuramu, fukurande) 膨らみ
［ふくらみ］ます（膨らむ,
膨らんで）, fukuremaˈsu
(fukureru, fukurete) 膨れ［ふ
くれ］ます（膨れる, 膨れて）;
ōˈkiku narimaˈsu (naˈru,
naˈtte) 大きくなります（なる,
なって）; → **increase**
swim oyogimaˈsu (oyoˈgu,
oyoˈide) 泳ぎます（泳ぐ, 泳い
で）
swimming oyogiˈ 泳ぎ, suiei 水
泳; **swimming pool** suiei-jō 水
泳場, pūˈru プール
swim suit mizu-gi 水着, suieˈi-giˈ
水泳着
swing 1. *(it swings)* yuremaˈsu
(yureru, yurete) 揺れます（揺
れる, 揺れて） **2.** *(swings it)*
yusuburimaˈsu (yusuburu,
yusubutte) 揺すぶります（揺
すぶる, 揺すぶって）,

yurimaˈsu (yuru, yutte) 揺りま
す（揺る, 揺って） **3.** *(a swing)*
buˈranko ぶらんこ
swing: gets into the ～ of things
chōshi ni norimaˈsu (noru,
notte) 調子に乗ります（乗る,
乗って）, chōshi ga demaˈsu
(deˈru, deˈte) 調子が出ます（出
る, 出て）
swipe kapparaimaˈsu
(kappara⌐u, kappara⌐tte)
かっぱらいます（かっぱらう,
かっぱらって）; nusumimaˈsu
(nusuˈmu, nusuˈnde) 盗みます
（盗む, 盗んで）
Swiss Suˈisu no スイスの; *(per-son)* Suisuˈ-jin スイス人
switch suiˈtchi スイッチ; →
change; → **turn on/off**
Switzerland Suˈisu スイス
sword katanaˈ 刀; tsurugiˈ 剣;
yaiba やいば・刃
sword battle chambara ちゃんば
ら
swordfish kaˈjiki かじき・旗魚
sword-guard tsuˈba つば・鍔
syllable onsetsu 音節
symbol shōchō 象徴; *(mark)*
kigō 記号
symmetry tsuriai 釣り合い; taiō
対応
sympathize with ... ni dōjō
shimaˈsu (suru, shiˈte) ...に同
情します（する, して）; *(takes
into consideration)* ... o
kumimaˈsu (kumu, kunde) ...

を汲みます（汲む，汲んで）;
sas-shima'su (sas-su'ru,
sa's-shite) 察します（察する，
察して）

sympathy dōjō 同情, sas-shi (o-
sasshi) 察し（お察し）

symptom *(sign)* (o-)shirushi （お）
しるし［徴］; *(unusual state)*
ijō 異常

synonym dōi-go 同意語, dōgi-go
同義語

synthesis sōgō 総合

synthesized *(composite)* sōgō-
teki (na) 総合的（な）

synthetic fiber kasen 化繊

syphilis ba'idoku 梅毒

syringe *(for injections)* chūsha'-
ki 注射器; *(for water)* chūsu'i-
ki 注水器

syrup shi'ro'ppu シロップ

system so'shiki 組織, se'ido 制
度, taikei 体系

— **T** —

tab ta'bu タブ; → bill

table tēburu テーブル, ta'ku 卓;
(dinner table) shokutaku 食卓,
(low meal table) (shoku)zen
(o-zen, go'-zen) （食）膳（お膳，
ご膳）; *(list)* hyō 表, *(inventory)* mokuroku 目録

tablecloth tēburu'-kake テーブ
ル掛け

table d'hôte *(meal of the house/
day)* teishoku 定食

table salt shoku'en 食塩,
shokutaku'-en 食卓塩

tablespoon ō-saji 大さじ・大匙

tablet *(pill)* jōzai 錠剤; *(note
pad)* memo-chō メモ帳

tableware shokki 食器

tack 1. a tack byō' びょう・鋲
2. tacks it on the wall ... o
kabe ni byō' de tomema'su

(tomeru, tomete) ...を壁に
びょう［鋲］で留めます（留め
る，留めて）**3. tacks it (with
thread)** shi-tsukema'su
(-tsuke'ru, -tsu'kete) 仕付けま
す（付ける，付けて）

tacking (with thread) shi-tsuke
仕付け; **tacking thread**
shitsuke-i'to 仕付け糸

tag fuda 札; **(baggage/package
～)** ni'-fuda 荷札

tail shippo' しっぽ・尻尾, o' 尾;
the ～ end bi'ri びり, ketsu け
つ・尻   「ya 洋服屋

tailor shitate-ya 仕立屋, yōfuku-
Taiwan Taiwa'n 台湾; **a Taiwanese** Taiwa'n-jin 台湾人

take torima'su (to'ru, to'tte) 取り
ます（取る，取って）, totte/
motte ikima'su (iku, itte) 取っ

て/持って行きます(行く, 行
って); hipparima'su (hip-
pa'ru, hippa'tte) 引っ張ります
(引っ張る, 引っ張って); *(re-
quires)* yō-shima'su (yō-su'ru,
yō'-shite) 要します(要する,
要して); *(requires time/
money)* (ji'kan/kane ga)
kakarima'su (kaka'ru,
kaka'tte) (時間/金が)かかり
ます(かかる, かかって); *(in-
curs)* ukema'su (uke'ru,
u'kete) 受けます(受ける, 受
けて); *(accepts; understands)*
uke-torima'su (-to'ru,
-to'tte) 受け取ります(取る,
取って); ~ **it seriously** honki
ni shima'su (suru, shite) 本
気にします(する, して); ~
one's blood pressure ketsuatsu
o hakarima'su (haka'ru,
haka'tte) 血圧を計ります(計
る, 計って)

take: ~ **a bath** fu'ro' ni
hairima'su (ha'iru, ha'itte) 風
呂に入ります(入る, 入って);
~ **a shower** sha'wā o abima'su
(abiru, abite) シャワーを浴び
ます(浴びる, 浴びて); ~
medicine kusuri o nomima'su
(no'mu, no'nde) 薬を飲みます
(飲む, 飲んで); ~ **a picture**
shashin o torima'su (to'ru,
to'tte) 写真を撮ります(撮る,
撮って), utsushima'su
(utsu'su', utsu'shite) 写します

(写す, 写して); ~ **Japanese
(as a course)** Nihon-go o
torima'su (to'ru, to'tte) 日本語
をとります(とる, とって)

take advantage of ... o riyō
shima'su (suru, shite) ...を利
用します(する, して); ~ **a
person** zu ni norima'su (noru,
notte) 図に乗ります(乗る,
乗って)

take aim nerai o tsukema'su
(tsuke'ru, tsuke'te) 狙いをつ
けます(つける, つけて)

take apart barashima'su
(bara'su, bara'shite) ばらしま
す(ばらす, ばらして)

take away totte ikima'su (iku,
itte) 取って行きます(行く,
行って); *(confiscates,
deprives of)* tori-agema'su
(-age'ru, -a'gete) 取り上げま
す(上げる, 上げて);
(clears from table) sagema'su
(sage'ru, sa'gete) 下げます(下
げる, 下げて)

take care of 1. *(handles)* ... o
sho'ri shima'su (suru, shite) ...
を処理します(する, して)
2. *(~ a person)* ... no sewa'
o shima'su (suru, shite) ...の
世話をします(する, して),
... no mendō' o mima'su
(mi'ru, mi'te) ...の面倒をみま
す(みる, みて)

Take care (of yourself). O-daiji
ni! お大事に!

take charge of … o hiki-ukema'su (-uke'ru, -u'kete) …を引き受けます(受ける, 受けて), tannin/tantō shima'su (suru, shite) 担任/担当します(する, して)

take down oroshima'su (oro'su, oro'shite) 下ろし[降ろし]ます(下ろす, 下ろして)

take effect *(is effective)* kikima'su (kiku, kiite) 効きます(効く, 効いて)

take fright kowagarima'su (kowaga'ru, kowaga'tte) 怖がり[こわがり]ます(怖がる, 怖がって)

take in(to) irema'su (ireru, irete) 入れます(入れる, 入れて); **takes into consideration/account** kō'ryo ni irema'su (ireru, irete) 考慮に入れます(入れる, 入れて)

take in trust azukarima'su (azuka'ru, azuka'tte) 預ります(預かる, 預って)

Take it easy. 1. Go-yukku'ri. ごゆっくり. **2.** → **good-bye**

take off 1. *(removes)* hazushima'su (hazusu, hazushite) 外します(外す, 外して); *(clothes, shoes, etc.)* nugima'su (nu'gu, nu'ide), 脱ぎます(脱ぐ, 脱いで)
2. *(airplane)* ririku shima'su (suru, shite) 離陸します(する, して)

take-off *(of an airplane)* ririku 離陸

take offense shaku ni sawarima'su (sawaru, sawatte) しゃく[癪]にさわり[障り]ます(さわる, さわって)

take over hiki-torima'su (-to'ru, -to'tte) 引き取ります(取る, 取って); *(illegally seizes)* nottorima'su (notto'ru, notto'tte) 乗っ取ります(乗っ取る, 乗っ取って)

takeover *(illegal seizure)* nottori-ji'ken 乗っ取り事件

take pains hone' o orima'su (o'ru, o'tte) 骨を折ります(折る, 折って)

take refuge hi'nan shima(')su (suru, shite) 避難します(する, して)

take responsibility for … o hiki-ukema'su (-uke'ru, -u'kete) …を引き受けます(受ける, 受けて), … no sekinin o oima'su (o'u, o'tte) …の責任を負います(負う, 負って)

take revenge fukushū shima'su (suru, shite) 復讐します(する, して)

take time off yasumima'su (yasu'mu, yasu'nde) 休みます(休む, 休んで)

take up tori-agema'su (-age'ru, -a'gete) 取り上げます(上げる, 上げて) 「語

tale hanashi' 話, monoga'tari 物

talent sa⁽ˀ⁾inō 才能, saˀi 才; *(personality)* ta⁽ˀ⁾rento タレント

talisman (of a shrine) o-fuda お札

talk 1. hanashiˀ 話; *(conference, discussion)* hanashi-ai 話し合い, *(consultation)* sōdan 相談; → **speech 2.** *(speaks)* hanashimaˀsụ (hanaˀsu, hanaˀshịte) 話します(話す, 話して); ~ **together** hanashi-aimaˀsụ (-a⁽ˀ⁾u, -a⁽ˀ⁾tte) 話し合います(合う, 合って)

tall takaˀi 高い; *(of body height)* seˀ ga takaˀi 背が高い

tame it narashimaˀsụ (naraˀsu, naraˀshịte) 馴らします(馴らす, 馴らして)

tangerine *(Mandarin orange)* miˀkan (o-miˀkan) みかん·蜜柑(おみかん)

tangible gutai-teki (na) 具体的(な)

tangle *(entanglement)* motsure⁽ˀ⁾ もつれ·縺れ

tangled *(complicated)* yaya(k)koshiˀi やや(っ)こしい; → **entangled**

tape 1. tēˀpu テープ; himo ひも·紐 **2.** → **adhesive tape**

tape recorder tēpu-rekōˀdā テープレコーダー

tapping *(medical exam)* dashin 打診

target mato 的; *(goal)* mokụhyō 目標

task shigoto 仕事

taste *(flavor)* aji 味; *(has flavor)* aji ga shimaˀsụ (suru, shịte) 味がします(する, して); *(liking)* shuˀmi 趣味, konomiˀ (o-konomi) 好み(お好み); **simple (modest) tastes** wabi⁽ˀ⁾ わび·侘び

taste *(tastes it)* ajiwaimaˀsụ (ajiwa⁽ˀ⁾u, ajiwa⁽ˀ⁾tte) 味わいます(味わう, 味わって), namemaˀsụ (nameˀru, naˀmete) なめ[舐め]ます(なめる, なめて); *(tries eating it)* taˀbete mimaˀsụ (miˀru, miˀte) 食べてみます(みる, みて)

tasty oishii おいしい, umaˀi/mmaˀi うまい

tatami room zashịkiˀ (o-zashịki) 座敷(お座敷)

tattoo ire-zumi 入れ墨·刺青

taught → **teach; is taught** osowarimaˀsụ (osowaru, osowatte) 教わります(教わる, 教わって)

taut: stretched ~ pin-to hatta ピンと張った

tavern nomiˀ-ya 飲み屋

tax zeˀi 税, zeikin 税金; ~ **(revenue) stamp** shūnyū-iˀnshi 収入印紙

tax-free menzei (no) 免税(の); ~ **goods** menze⁽ˀ⁾i-hin 免税品

taxi taˀkụshii タクシー, kuruma (o-kuˀruma) 車(お車); ~ **stand** (taˀkụshii no) tamari-ba

(タクシーの)溜まり場; ~ **station** (ta῀kushii no) nori-ba (タクシーの)乗り場

TB kekkaku (= hai-ke῀kkaku) 結核(=肺結核), haibyō 肺病

tea cha 茶; *(green)* ryoku-cha 緑茶, o-cha お茶, *(coarse)* bancha 番茶; *(black)* kō῀cha 紅茶; *(powdered green, for tea ceremony)* matcha 抹茶; *(weak powdered)* usu-cha (o-u῀su) 薄茶(お薄); **a cup of green tea** [*sushi bar term*] agari 上がり

tea: makes ~ o-cha o irema῀su (ireru, irete) お茶を入れます (入れる, 入れて)

teacake cha-ga῀shi 茶菓子

tea canister/caddy cha-ire῀ 茶入れ

tea ceremony o-cha お茶, cha-no-yu 茶の湯, sa῀dō 茶道; ~ **procedures** temae (o-te῀mae) 点前(お点前)

teach oshiema῀su (oshieru, oshiete) 教えます(教える, 教えて)

teacher sense῀i 先生; *(schoolteacher)* gakkō no sense῀i 学校の先生, *(instructor)* kyō῀shi 教師

teaching kyō῀ju 教授, oshie 教え; **classroom** ~ ju῀gyō 授業; ~ **hours** jugyō-ji῀kan 授業時間

teaching materials kyōzai 教材

teacup yunomi῀ 湯飲み, yunomi-ja῀wan 湯飲み茶碗; *(also ricebowl)* chawan (o-cha῀wan) 茶碗(お茶碗)

teakettle yakan やかん, yuwa῀kashi 湯沸し

team chi῀imu チーム; **teamwork** chiimu-wa῀ku チームワーク

team up (with) (... to) kumima῀su (ku῀mu, ku῀nde) (...と)組みます(組む, 組んで)

teapot do-bin どびん・土瓶, kyūsu きゅうす・急須, cha-bin ちゃびん・茶瓶

tear *(in eye)* na῀mida 涙

tear (tore, torn) 1. *(tears it)* sakima῀su (sa῀ku, sa῀ite) 裂きます(裂く, 裂いて), yaburima῀su (yabu῀ru, yabu῀tte) 破ります(破る, 破って) **2.** *(it tears)* sakema῀su (sake῀ru, sa῀kete) 裂けます(裂ける, 裂けて), yaburema῀su (yabure῀ru, yabu῀rete) 破れます(破れる, 破れて)

tearoom kissa῀-ten 喫茶店; *(for tea ceremony)* (o-)chashitsu (お)茶室

tea scoop (for tea ceremony) chashaku 茶杓

tease *(pokes fun at)* karakaima῀su (karaka῀u, karaka῀tte) からかいます(からかう, からかって); *(torments)* ijimema῀su

(ijimeru, ijimete) いじめます
（いじめる，いじめて）

teaspoon sa̅ji̅ (o-sa̅ji) さじ・匙
（おさじ），ko-saji 小さじ・小
匙，cha-saji 茶さじ・茶匙

tea whisk (for tea ceremony)
chase̅n 茶筅

technical term semmon-go 専門
語

technician gijutsu-ka 技術家

technique gi̅jutsu 技術

teeth → tooth

teething ring osha̅buri おしゃぶ
り

telegram dempō (o uchima̅su;
u̅tsu, u̅tte) 電報（を打ちます；
打つ，打って）

telephone, telephone call denwa
(o-de̅nwa) 電話（お電話）；
telephones (… ni) denwa o
kakema̅su (kake̅ru, ka̅kete) /
shima̅su (suru, shite) (…に)
電話をかけます（かける，か
けて）／します（する，して）

telephone book/directory
denwa-chō 電話帳

telephone booth denwa̅-shitsu
電話室，denwa-bo̅kkusu 電話
ボックス

telephone line denwa-sen 電話線

telephone number denwa-ba̅ngō
電話番号

telephone operator (denwa-)
kōka̅n-shu （電話）交換手

telephone wire(s) denwa-sen 電
話線

telescope bōenkyō 望遠鏡

television te̅rebi テレビ，
terebi̅jon テレビジョン

tell iima̅su (yū, itte/yutte) 言い
ます（言う，言って／ゆって）；
(informs one of) … no mimi̅
ni irema̅su (ireru, irete) …の
耳に入れます（入れる，入れ
て），… ni kikasema̅su
(kikaseru, kikasete) …に聞か
せます（聞かせる，聞かせて），
… ni tsugema̅su (tsugeru,
tsugete) …に告げます（告げる，
告げて）；*(instructs)*
oshiema̅su (oshieru, oshiete)
教えます（教える，教えて）；
(relates) nobema̅su (nobe̅ru,
no̅bete) 述べます（述べる，述
べて）；katarima̅su (kataru,
katatte) 語ります（語る，語っ
て）

tell on (=tattle) ii-tsukema̅su
(-tsuke̅ru, -tsu̅kete) 言い付け
ます（付ける，付けて）

temper 1. *(disposition)* iji̅ 意地；
ta̅chi たち・質，te̅nsei 天性，
ta̅ido 態度 **2.** *(forges metal)*
kitaema̅su (kitae̅ru, kita̅ete)
鍛えます（鍛える，鍛えて）

temperament te̅nsei 天性

temperature o̅ndo 温度；*(of
body)* taion 体温；*(fever)*
netsu̅ (o-ne̅tsu) 熱（お熱）

temple tera̅ 寺，o-tera お寺；…̅
-ji …寺

temple bell tsurigane 釣り鐘

temple fair e˺nnichi 縁日
temple gate sammon 山門
temporary rinji (no) 臨時(の), tōza (no) 当座(の); *(passing)* ichi˺ji (no) 一時(の), ichiji-teki (na) 一時的(な); *(tentative)* kari (no) 仮(の), ka-... 仮...
tempt sasoima˺su (sasou, sasotte) 誘います(誘う, 誘って)
temptation sasoi 誘い, yūwaku 誘惑
ten jū˺ 十・10, tō˺ 十・10; **ten days** tōka 十日・10日
ten: small things, pieces ji˺k-ko 十個; **long things** ji˺p-pon 十本; **flat things** jū˺-mai 十枚; **small animals/fish/bugs** jip-pi˺ki 十匹; **large animals** ji˺t-tō 十頭; **birds** ji˺p-pa 十羽; **machines/ vehicles** jū˺-dai 十台; **books/ magazines** jis-satsu˺ 十冊
tenant *(of apartment, room)* magari˺-nin 間借人, nyūkyo˺-sha 入居者
ten degrees jū˺-do 十度
tend (to do/happen) yo˺ku ... (shima˺su) よく...(します); (shi)-yasu˺i desu (し)やすいです
tendency keikō 傾向
tender → gentle, soft; → hurt
tenderness na˺nsake˺ (o-na˺sake) 情け(お情け)
tendon su˺ji 筋
tenement house naga-ya 長屋

tennis te˺nisu テニス
tense: is ~ *(taut)* hatte ima˺su (iru, ite) 張っています(いる, いて); *(strained)* kinchō shite ima˺su (iru, ite) 緊張しています(いる, いて)
tension kinchō 緊張
tent te˺nto テント
tentative ichiō (no) 一応(の), kari (no) 仮(の)
tenth jū-bamme˺ (no) 十番目(の), tō-me˺ (no) 十目(の); **the ~ day** tōka-me˺ 十日目, **(of the month)** tōka 十日・10日; **~ floor** jik-kai 十階
ten thousand ma˺n 万・10,000, ichi-ma˺n 一万・10,000
ten-thousandfold (ichi)mam-bai (一)万倍
ten times jū-do˺ 十度, jik-ka˺i 十回, jip-pe˺n 十遍; *(= tenfold)* jū-bai 十倍
ten years jū˺-nen 十年; **~ old** tō˺ 十, ji˺s-sai 十歳
term *(period)* kika˺n 期間, *(time limit)* ki˺gen 期限; *(of school)* gakki 学期; *(technical word)* semmon-go 専門語, yōgo 用語; *(stipulation)* jōke˺n 条件
terminal (place), terminus shūten 終点
terms *(between people)* na˺ka 仲; **they are on good/bad ~** na˺ka ga i˺i/waru˺i desu 仲がいい/悪いです
terrible (mono-)sugo˺i (もの)す

ごい・(物)凄い, taihen (na) 大
変(な); *(severe)* hido⌐i ひどい;
(frightening) osoroshi⌐i 恐ろし
い; *(shocking)* tonde-mo na⌐i
とんでもない, tonda とんだ

terribly su⌐go⌐ku すごく・凄く,
mono-su⌐go⌐ku ものすごく・物
凄く, taihen 大変, hi⌐doku ひ
どく; osoro⌐shiku 恐ろしく;
(extremely, completely)
to(t)temo と(っ)ても;
(unbearably) ya⌐ke ni やけに

terrific sugo⌐i すごい・凄い,
kowa⌐i こわい・怖い

territory ryo⌐do 領土, ryo⌐chi 領
地

terrorism, terrorist te⌐ro テロ

test 1. shike⌐n (o-shike⌐n) 試験
(お試験), te⌐suto テスト;
(check of blood, etc.) ke⌐nsa
検査; → **trial**; → **experiment**
2. → **try**

testament *(will)* yuigon 遺言; **the
Old/New Testament** Kyū-/
Shin-yaku 旧/新約

testicle(s) kōgan 睾丸, kin-
ta⌐ma⌐/kinda⌐ma⌐ 金玉/金玉

test tube shike⌐n-kan 試験管

text(book) te⌐ki⌐suto テキスト,
kyōka⌐-sho 教科書

textile ori⌐-mo⌐no 織物

texture ji⌐ 地 = ori-ji 織地; kime⌐
きめ・肌理

...th ...-me⌐ (no) ...目(の); **fifth**
itsutsu-me⌐ 五つ目

than ... ... yo⌐ri ...より

thank o-rei o iima⌐su (yū, itte/
yutte) お礼を言います(言う,
言って/ゆって)

thanks *(gratitude)* ka⌐nsha (no
kotoba⌐) 感謝(の言葉); (o-)rei
(お)礼

thanks to your solicitude okage-
sama de お蔭さまで

Thank you. Ari⌐gatō gozaima⌐su.
ありがとう[有り難う]ござい
ます; Dō⌐mo. どうも;
Sumimase⌐n. すみません;
Oso⌐re-irimasu. 恐れ入ります.

Thank you for the hard work.
Go-ku⌐rō-sama (deshita). ご苦
労さま(でした).

Thank you for the treat.
Gochisō-sama (de⌐shita). ご馳
走[ごちそう]さま(でした).

"thank-you money" *(to obtain
rental)* rei-kin 礼金

that ... sono ... その...; *(over
there; obvious)* ano ... あの...;
(said/thought that) ... to ...と;
(= which/who) − *not
translated*

that: that is to say suna⌐wachi す
なわち・即ち

thatch 1. ka⌐ya かや・茅, *(straw)*
wa⌐ra わら・藁, *(grass)* kusa⌐ 草
2. thatches a roof ka⌐ya/
wa⌐ra/kusa⌐ de ya⌐ne o
fukima⌐su (fuku, fu⌐ite) か
や/わら/草で屋根をふきます
(ふく, ふいて)

that extent: to ~ sonna ni そん

なに; anna ni あんなに
that kind of sono/ano yō̄ na そ
の/あのよう[様]な, sō/ā yū
そう/ああゆう, sonna/anna
そんな/あんな
that (one) sore それ, soitsu そい
つ, (of two) sochira/sotchī̄ そ
ちら/そっち; (over there; ob-
vious) are あれ, (of two)
achira/atchī̄ あちら/あっち;
that damn one soitsu そいつ,
aitsu あいつ, kyā̄tsu きゃつ
that place 1. soko そこ, sono
tokorō その所; sochira/sot-
chī̄ そちら/そっち **2.** (over
there; obvious) asoko あそこ,
asu̱ko あすこ; achira/atchī̄ あ
ちら/あっち
that side achira-gawa あちら側
that sort of → that kind of
that's right sō̄ (desu) そう(です)
that time sono to̱kī̄ その時, tō̄ji
当時
that very day tōjitsu 当日
that way (like that) sō̄ そう (sō̄
そう + PARTICLE or de̱su で
す); (over there; obvious) ā̄ あ
あ (ā̄ ああ + PARTICLE or
de̱su です); (that direction)
sochira/sotchī̄ そちら/そっち,
(over there; obvious) achira/
atchī̄ あちら/あっち
thaw (it thaws) tokema̱su
(toke̱ru, to̱kete) 溶けます(溶
ける/溶けて); (thaws it)
tokashima̱su (toka̱su,

toka̱shi̱te) 溶かします(溶か
す, 溶かして)
the (usually not translated); ano ...
あの..., hon- 本...
theater (building) gekijō̄ 劇場,
za̱ 座; (drama) engeki 演劇,
(play) shibai 芝居, (traditional) Kabuki 歌舞伎; **~ people**
engeki̱-jin 演劇人; **the
Kabuki ~** (building) Kabuki-
za 歌舞伎座
theft nusumi̱ 盗み, tōnan 盗難
them, they (people) ano̱hi̱to-
tachi あの人達, ka̱re-ra 彼ら
(or name/title/role + -tachi
達・たち); (things) sore̱-ra そ
れら
theme (topic) tē̱ma テーマ;
(composition) sakubun 作文
then (at that time) sono to̱kī̄ そ
の時, tō̄ji 当時; (after that)
sore kara それから; (in that
case) sore na̱ra それなら, son-
na̱ra そんなら; **and/well then**
sa̱-te さて
theory ri̱nron 理論, ...-ron ...論
there soko そこ; (over there)
asoko あそこ, asu̱ko あすこ
therefore da̱ kara (sa) だから(さ);
(accordingly) shi̱tagā̄tte した
がって・従って
there is/are ... ... ga arima̱su
(a̱ru, a̱tte) ...があります(あ
る, あって), [DEFERENTIAL]
gozaima̱su (gozaima̱shi̱te) ご
ざいます(ございまして)

there is/are no ... ... ga(/wa) arimase͞n (na͞i, na͞kute) ...が(/は)ありません(ない, なくて)

thermometer ondo⌐-kei 温度計; *(room)* kanda͞n-kei 寒暖計; *(body)* taio⌐n-kei 体温計, taio͞n-ki 体温機

thermos bottle maho͞-bin 魔法びん・魔法瓶

these ... kono ... この...; ~ **(ones)** kore͞-ra これら; ~ **damn ones** koitsu͞-ra こいつら

thesis rombun 論文, gakui-ro͞mbun 学位論文; **master's** ~ shūshi-ro͞mbun 修士論文

they → **them**

thick atsui 厚い, buatsu͞i 分厚い・部厚い, atsubotta⌐i 厚ぼったい; **(and round)** futo͞i 太い; *(dense, close)* ko͞i 濃い, mi͞tsu (na) 密(な), missetsu (na) 密接(な); *(greasy)* kudo͞i くどい

thicket yabu やぶ・薮

thief dorobō どろぼう・泥棒; zoku 賊

thigh mo͞mo もも・股

thimble yubi-nu͞ki͞ 指ぬき

thin usui 薄い; **(and round)** hoso͞i 細い

thin: gets thin *(loses weight)* yasema͞su (yaseru, yasete) やせ[痩せ]ます(やせる, やせて)

thing mono͞ 物, ya͞tsu やつ・奴; *(fact, matter)* koto⌐ 事; **things** mono͞goto 物事

thing: just the thing *(ideal)* motte-ko͞i (no) もってこい(の)

think (that ...) (... to) omoima͞su (omo͞u, omo͞tte) (...と)思います(思う, 思って), kangaema͞su (kanga͞e͞ru, kanga͞ete) 考えます(考える, 考えて); [DEFERENTIAL] zon-jima͞su (zon-ji⌐ru, zo͞n-jite) 存じます(存じる, 存じて)

third sam-bamme͞ (no) 三番目(の), mittsu-me͞ (no) 三つ目(の); **the ~ day** mikka-me͞ 三日目, **(of the month)** mikka 三日・3日; **third or fourth** san-yo-bamme͞ (no) 三, 四番目(の)

third class san-tō 三等

third floor san-gai 三階

third generation sa͞n-sei 三世

third time sando-me͞ 三度目, sankai-me͞ 三回目

third-year student sanne͞n-sei 三年生

thirsty no͞do ga kawakima͞shita (kawa͞ita) のど[喉]が渇きました(渇いた)

thirteen jū⌐-san 十三・13

thirty sa͞n-jū 三十・30

thirty or forty san-shi-jū⌐ 三, 四十; ~ **thousand** san-yo-man 三, 四万

thirty percent sa͞n-wari 三割 =

sanjip-pāse̅nto 三十パーセント・30%

this ... kono ... この...

this afternoon kyō̅ no go̅go 今日の午後

this evening ko̅mban 今晩

this extent: to ~ konna ni こんなに

this kind of kono yō̅ na このよう［様］な, kō yū こうゆう, konna こんな

this month kongetsu 今月

this morning ke̅sa 今朝; kyō̅ no a̅sa 今日の朝

this much konna ni こんなに

this (one) kore これ, hon-... 本...; *(of two)* kochira/kotchi̅ こちら/こっち; **this damn one** koitsu こいつ

this place koko ここ, kono tokoro̅ この所; kochira/kotchi̅ こちら/こっち

this side kochira-gawa こちら側; **~ of ...** no temae ...の手前

this sort of → this kind of

this time ko̅ndo 今度, i̅ma 今, kono tabi̅ このたび［度］

this way *(like this)* kō こう (kō̅ こう + PARTICLE *or* de̅su です); *(this direction)* kochira/kotchi̅ こちら/こっち

this week konshū 今週

this year kotoshi 今年

thong *(on geta* 下駄*)* hanao 鼻緒

thorn toge̅ とげ・棘

thorough tettei-teki (na) 徹底的

(な); *(detailed)* seimitsu (na) 精密(な)

thoroughfare tsū̅ro 通路, ōrai 往来

those → them

those ... sono ... その..., ano ... あの...; **~ (ones)** sore̅-ra それら, are̅-ra あれら; **~ damn ones** soitsu̅-ra そいつら, aitsu̅-ra あいつら; **~ present** shu̅sse̅ki̅-sha 出席者

those days tō̅ji 当時

though de̅ mo でも, ke̅redo (mo) けれど(も)

thought 1. kanga̅e 考え, omo̅i 思い; shisō 思想 **2. → think**

thought(fulness) shi̅ryo 思慮

thousand se̅n 千・1,000, is-se̅n 一千・1,000; **a thousand yen** sen-en 千円・1,000円

thousandfold sem-bai 千倍

thread i̅to 糸

threaten odo(ka)shima̅su (odo(ka)su, odo(ka)shi̅te) 脅(か)します(脅(か)す, 脅(か)して)

three san 三・3 , mittsu̅ 三つ; san-... 三..., mi-... 三...; suri̅i スリー; *(people)* san-ni̅n 三人, [*bookish*] sa̅m-mei 三名

three: small things, pieces san̅-ko 三個; **long things** sa̅m-bon 三本; **flat things** sa̅m-mai 三枚; **small animals/fish/bugs** sa̅m-biki 三匹; **large animals** sa̅n-tō 三頭; **birds** sa̅m-ba 三

羽; **machines/vehicles** saˈn-dai 三台; **books/magazines** saˈn-satsu 三冊

three days mikka 三日; **~ from now** shiasaˈtte しあさって·明々後日; **the first ~ of the new year** sangaˈnichi 三が日

three days ago mikka maˈe 三日前; saki-ototoˈi さきおととい·一昨々日, issakuᵤ-sakuˈ-jitsu 一昨々日

three-dimensional rittai (no) 立体(の)

three floors/stories san-gai 三階

three hundred saˈm-byaku 三百·300

three nights ago mikka maˈe no ban 三日前の晩; issakuᵤ-sakuˈ-ban/-ya 一昨々晩/夜

three or four san-shi- 三, 四, *except for:* **~ hours** san-yo-jiˈkan 三, 四時間, **o'clock** saˈn-ji ka yoˈ-ji 三時か四時, **people** san-yo-niˈn 三, 四人, **servings** san-yo-nimmae 三, 四人前, **times** san-yo-do 三, 四度, **times as much** san-yo-bai 三, 四倍 = sam-bai ka yo(m)-bai 三倍か四倍, **yen** san-yoˈ-en 三, 四円

three or four days san-yokka 三, 四日

three or four hundred san-shiᵤ-hyaku 三, 四百 = saˈmbyakuᵤ ka yoˈnhyaku 三百か四百

three times saˈn-doˈ 三度, saˈn-kaˈi 三回, saˈm-beˈn 三遍

three thousand san-zeˈn 三千·3,000

three years san-nen 三年, sanneˈn-kan 三年間; **~ ago** san-nen maˈe 三年前, saki-otoˈtoshi さきおととし·一昨々年, issakuᵤ-sakuˈ-nen 一昨々年; **~ old** mittsuˈ 三つ, saˈn-sai 三歳

threshold shikii 敷居

thrifty tsumashiˈi つましい·倹しい, ken'yaku (na) 倹約(な), komakaˈi 細かい

thrill suˈriˈru スリル; *(is thrilled)* zotto shimaˈsu (suru, shite) ぞっとします(する, して)

thrive sakaemaˈsu (sakaˈeˈru, sakaˈete) 栄えます(栄える, 栄えて); uremaˈsu (ureru, urete) 売れます(売れる, 売れて)

throat noˈdo のど·喉

throb doˈkidoki shimaˈsu (suru, shite) どきどきします(する, して)

throng 1. ōzeˈi 大勢; *(flock)* mureˈ 群れ **2. they throng together** muragarimaˈsu (muragaˈru, muragaˈtte) 群がります(群がる, 群がって)

through 1. *(putting ~)* ... o toˈshite ...を通して; *(coming ~)* ... o toˈtte ...を通って; *(via)* ... o heˈte ...を経て; ...

keˈiyu (de/no) ...経由(で/の)
2. *(throughout)* ...-jū ...じゅう・中; ... no aida-jū ...の間じゅう[間中] **3.** *(by means of)* ...de ...で, ... o tsukatte ...を使って **4.** *(extending ~)* ...ni kaˈkete ...にかけて **5.** *(is finished)* dekimaˈshita 出来ました, (shi)-te shimaimaˈshita (し)てしまいました

through: all the way ~ zutto ずっと; **gets ~** tsū-jimaˈsu (tsū-jiru, tsū-jite) 通じます(通じる, 通じて)

throughout (the entire PLACE/TIME) ...-jū ...じゅう・中; **~ the world** sekai-jū 世界じゅう[中]

through ticket tōshi-giˈppu 通し切符

throw nagemaˈsu (nageˈru, naˈgete) 投げます(投げる, 投げて); **~ away** sutemaˈsu (suteru, sutete) 捨てます(捨てる, 捨てて); **~ in extra** soemaˈsu (soeru, soete) 添えます(添える, 添えて); **~ into disorder** midashimaˈsu (midaˈsu, midaˈshite) 乱します(乱す, 乱して)

throwaway sute-mono 捨て物; **~ chopsticks** wari-baˈ⌐shi 割りばし[箸]

throw up → vomit

thrust tsukimaˈsu (tsuku, tsuite) 突きます(突く, 突いて)

thumb oya-yubi 親指
thumbprint boin 母印・拇印 「鋲
thumbtack gabyō 画びょう・画
thunder kaminaˈri (ga narimaˈsu; naru, natte) 雷(が鳴ります; 鳴る, 鳴って)
Thursday Mokuyōˈbi 木曜日
thwart habamimaˈsu (habaˈmu, habaˈnde) 阻みます(阻む, 阻んで)

ticket kippu 切符, chikeˈtto チケット; ...ˈ-ken ...券; **just the ~** *(ideal)* motte-koˈi (no) もってこい(の), *(most suitable)* uttetsuke (no) うってつけ(の)

ticket agency: theater ~ purē-gaˈido プレーガイド **("Play Guide")**

ticket book *(for commuting)* kaisūˈ-ken 回数券

ticket collecting shūsatsu 集札

ticket examining *(at wicket)* kaisatsu 改札, *(aboard)* ken-satsu 検札

ticket seller kippuˈ-uri 切符売り

ticket vending machine kembaˈi-ki 券売機 「札口

ticket wicket kaisatsu⌐-guchi 改

tickle kusugurimaˈsu (kusuguru, kusugutte) くすぐります(くすぐる, くすぐって)

ticklish kusuguttaˈi くすぐったい; *(delicate)* kiwadoˈi 際どい

tide shioˈ 潮; chōryū 潮流

tidy kiˈrei (na) きれい(な); **tidies**

it up katazukemaＳsu
(katazukeＳru, katazuＳkete) 片
付けます(片付ける，片付け
て); **it gets tidy** katazukimaＳsu
(katazuＳku, katazuＳite) 片付き
ます(片付く，片付いて)

tie musubimaＳsu (musubu,
musunde) 結びます(結ぶ，結
んで); *(fastens)* tsunagimaＳsu
(tsunagu, tsunaide) つなぎま
す(つなぐ，つないで); *(=
necktie)* neＳkutai ネクタイ

tie up *(binds)* shibarimaＳsu
(shibaＳru, shibaＳtte) 縛ります
(縛る，縛って)

tiff mome-goto もめ事・揉め事

tiger tora 虎

tight *(tight-fitting)* kitsui きつい;
(hard) katai 堅い; *(skimpy)*
semaＳi 狭い; → **drunk**

tighten, tighten up on
shimemaＳsu (shimeＳru,
shiＳmete) 締めます(締める，
締めて)

tile 1. *(roof)* kawara 瓦; ~
-roofed kawara-buki (no) 瓦
ぶき・瓦葺き(の) **2.** *(floor,
wall)* taＳiru タイル **3. tiles a
roof** kawara de yaＳne o
fukimaＳsu (fukuꞁ, fuꞁite)
瓦で屋根をふき[葺き]ます
(ふく，ふいて)

time tokiＳ (... toＳkiＳ) 時(...時)，
jiꞁkan (o-jiＳkan) 時間(お時間)，
jiꞁbun 時分; *(specified)*
jiＳkoku 時刻; *(season)* jiＳki 時

期; *(opportunity)* jiＳki 時機，
(appropriate occasion) jiＳsetsu
時節; *(free)* hima 暇, ma 間;
(taken up) temaＳ (o-teＳma) 手
間(お手間); *(interval, time
while ...)* aida 間

time = occasion tabiＳ たび・度，
oriＳ 折, saＳi 際, tokoroＳ ところ;
how many times naＳn-do 何度，
naＳn-kai 何回, naＳm-beＳn 何遍
(1 ip-peＳn 一遍, **2** ni-heＳn 二
遍, **3** saＳm-beＳn 三遍); **how
many times doubled** nam-bai
何倍; **this/next time** koＳndo
今度

time = what time naＳn-ji 何時;
Do you have/know the time?
NaＳn-ji ka wakarimaＳsu ka. 何
時か分かりますか.

time: at one ~ kaＳtsute かつて，
kaＳtte かって; **at the time of ...**
ni saＳi-shite ...に際して; **for
the ~ being** tōbun 当分, iＳma
no tokoroＳ wa 今のところは;
in time yagate やがて; **is in
time (for ...)** (... ni) ma ni
aimaＳsu (aＳu, aＳtte) (...に)間に
合います(合う，合って); *(the
trend of)* **the times** jiꞁsei (go-
jiＳsei) 時勢(ご時世)

time deposit teiki-yoＳkin 定期預 ⌐金
time difference jiＳsa 時差 ⌐金
time off yasumiＳ 休み
timepiece tokei 時計
time schedule jikoku-hyō 時刻表
timetable jikan-hyō 時間表

timid *(shy)* uchiki (na) 内気(な), *(cowardly)* okubyō (na) 臆病・憶病(な)

tin buriki ブリキ, suzu すず・錫

tip 1. *(money)* chippu チップ, kokoro-zuke 心付け, chadai 茶代; *(point)* saki 先 **2. it tips over** hikkuri-kaerimasu (-kaeru, -kaette) ひっくり返ります(返る, 返って), **tips it over** hikkuri-kaeshimasu (-kaesu, -kaeshite) ひっくり返します(返す, 返して)

tire *(of wheel)* taiya タイヤ

tired: gets ~ tsukaremasu (tsukareru, tsukarete) 疲れます(疲れる, 疲れて), kutabiremasu (kutabireru, kutabirete) くたびれます(くたびれる, くたびれて); **gets tired of** ... ni akimasu (akiru, akite) ...に飽きます(飽きる, 飽きて); **dead ~** ku(t)takuta く(っ)たくた

tissue tisshu-pēpā ティッシュペーパー; hana-gami 鼻紙, chiri-gami ちり紙

title *(of book, article, ...)* hyōdai 表題・標題, midashi 見出し; *(of anything, esp. movie, person, athlete)* taitoru タイトル; **~ page** tobira 扉

to ... ni ...に, ... e ...へ

toast tōsuto トースト; ("bottoms up") kampai 乾杯

toast *(toasts it)* yakimasu (yaku, yaite) 焼きます(焼く, 焼いて)

toasted rice-cake yaki-mochi 焼き餅

toaster tōsutā トースター

tobacco tabako たばこ; **~ shop** tabako-ya たばこ屋

to boot *(= extra)* omake (ni/no) おまけ(に/の)

today kyō 今日

toe ashi no yubi 足の指; *(toe-tip)* tsumasaki つま先・爪先

together issho ni いっしょ[一緒]に, tomo ni 共に

toilet toire トイレ, toiretto トイレット; keshō-shitsu 化粧室, tearai (o-tearai) 手洗(お手洗), benjo 便所; go-fujō ご不浄 [*used mostly by older women*]

toilet paper toiretto-pēpā トイレットペーパー, chiri-gami ちり紙

token *(sign, indication)* shirushi (o-shirushi) しるし・印・徴(おしるし)

Tokyo Tōkyō 東京; **~ Station** Tōkyō-eki 東京駅; **the metropolis of ~** Tōkyō-to 東京都

Tokyoite Tōkyō-jin 東京人

Tokyo Metro (train) toden 都電; **(Line)** Toei-sen 都営線

Tokyo University Tōkyō-Daigaku 東京大学, Tō-dai 東大

told → **tell**

tolerate ga˥man shima(˥)su
(suru, shi̱te) 我慢します(する,
して)

tomorrow ashita˥ あした・明日,
asu˥ 明日; [*bookish*] myo̱˥nichi
明日

tomorrow morning ashita(˥) no
a˥sa あした[明日]の朝;
[*bookish*] myōchō 明朝

tomorrow night ashita(˥) no ban
あした[明日]の晩; [*bookish*]
myo̱˥ban 明晩

tongs (*for fire*) hi̱˥-bashi 火ばし
[箸]

tongue shi̱ta˥ 舌; **barbed/spiteful**
~ dokuzetsu 毒舌

tonight ko̱˥mban 今晩; ko̱˥n'ya
今夜

too (*also*) ... mo ...も; (*overly*)
ammari あんまり, ...
-sugima˥su (-sugi̱˥ru, -su̱˥gi̱te)
...すぎます(すぎる, すぎて)

too bad zannen (na) 残念(な);
(*in commiseration*) ikemase̱˥n
(ikenai) いけません(いけない)

took → **take**

tool dōgu˥ (o-dōgu) 道具(お道具),
yo̱˥gu 用具, utsuwa 器

tool box dōgu(˥)-bako 道具箱,
yōgu(˥)-bako 用具箱

too many/much: is ~
amarima˥su (ama˥ru, ama˥tte)
余ります(余る, 余って); ō-
sugima˥su (-sugi̱˥ru, -su̱˥gi̱te)
多すぎます(すぎる, すぎて)

tooth ha˥ 歯; **protruding (buck)**

~ de̱˥ppa 出っ歯

toothache ha-ita 歯痛; **has a ~**
ha˥ ga ita˥i 歯が痛い

tooth brush ha-bu̱˥rashi 歯ブラ
シ

toothpaste neri-hami̱˥gaki 練り
歯磨き; (*or* **toothpowder**) ha-
mi̱˥gaki 歯磨き

toothpick tsuma-yo̱˥ji つまよう
じ・爪揚枝, yōji ようじ・揚枝

top ue 上; (*top side*) jōme̱˥n 上
面; (*highest part*) teppe̱˥n てっ
ぺん, (*summit*) chōjo̱˥ 頂上;
(*topmost, best*) saijō (no) 最上
(の), saikō (no) 最高(の)

top (*toy*) ko̱˥ma こま・独楽; **top-
spinning** koma-ma˥washi こま
[独楽]回し

topcoat ō˥bā オーバー

topflight (*elite*) ichiryū (no) 一流
(の)

topic daimoku 題目, da˥i 題;
ta˥ne 種; (*of talk*) wadai 話題;
(*problem*) mondai 問題

topmost saijō (no) 最上(の)

tops (*best*) saikō (no) 最高(の),
saijō (no) 最上(の)

torch ta˥imatsu たいまつ・松明;
→ **flashlight**

tore, torn → **tear**

torment 1. (*suffering*) nayami̱˥ 悩
み; (*teasing*) ijime いじめ・苛
め 2. → **tease**

torrential downpour go̱˥u 豪雨

tortoise ka˥me 亀; ~ **shell**
bekkō(˥) べっこう・鼈甲

toss → **throw**

tot chi'bi ちび

total ze'mbu (de/no) 全部(で/の), ze'n(-)... 全...; *(sum)* gōkei 合計, *(grand total)* sōkei 総計; *(absolute)* zettai (no) 絶対(の)

totter yoro-mekima'su (-me'ku, -me'ite) よろめきます(めく, めいて); **tottering** yo'royoro (to) よろよろと

touch sawarima'su (sawaru, sawatte) 触ります(触る, 触って); ... ni (te' o) furema'su (fureru, furete) ...に(手を)触れます(触れる, 触れて), ... ni tsukima'su (tsuku', tsu'ite) ...に付きます(付く, 付いて); atema'su (ateru, atete) 当てます(当てる, 当てて); *(comes in contact with)* ses-shima'su (ses-su⌐ru, se⌐s-shite) 接します(する, して), sesshoku shima'su (suru, shite) 接触します(する, して)

touch: gets in ~ with ... to renraku shima'su (suru, shite) ...と連絡します(する, して); **touches upon** ... ni furema'su (fureru, furete) ...に触れます(触れる, 触れて), [*bookish*] ... ni genkyū shima'su (suru, shite) ...に言及します(する, して); **out of ~ with** ... ni uto'i ...に疎い・うとい

tough katai 固い・堅い; → **hard**; → **strong**

tour ryokō (shima'su; suru, shite) 旅行(します; する, して); *(sightseeing)* kankō 観光, tsu'ā ツアー; *(official, duty)* shutchō 出張

tourist kankō'-kyaku 観光客

tourist home minshuku 民宿

tournament taikai 大会

tow hikima'su (hiku, hiite) 引[曳]きます(引[曳]く, 引[曳]いて)

toward ... no hō' e ...の方へ; *(towards, confronting)* ... ni ta'i-shite ...に対して, tai-... 対...

towel te-nugui (o-te'nugui) 手拭い・てぬぐい(お手拭い), ta'oru タオル, fuki'n 布きん・ふきん; **hand ~** tefuki' (o-te'fuki) 手拭き(お手拭き), *(damp)* o-shi'bori おしぼり・お絞り

tower tō' 塔

to wit suna'wachi すなわち・即ち

town machi' 町, tokai 都会

tow truck re'kkā レッカー, rekkā'-sha レッカー車

toy omo'cha おもちゃ・玩具

trace *(clue)* tega'kari 手掛かり, ate 当て; *(vestige)* konseki 痕跡

trace it back to sore o ... ni sakanoborima'su (sakanobo'ru, sakanobo'tte) それを...にさかのぼり[遡り]ます(さかのぼる, さかのぼって)

tracing paper torepe トレペ

(= torēshingu-pēˈpā トレーシングペーパー)

track *(railtrack)* seˈnro 線路; *(for running)* toraˈkku トラック

Track Number (Six) (roku)-bansen (六)番線; **what (number) track** nam-bansen 何番線

trade *(international)* bōeki 貿易; *(business)* shōˈbai 商売, *(commerce)* shōˈgyō 商業; *(transaction)* toˈriˈ-hiki 取り引き; *(exchanges A for B)* A o B to kōkan shimaˈsu (suru, shite) AをBと交換します(する, して)

trader *(merchant)* shōˈnin 商人; *(international)* bōēˈkiˈ-shō 貿易商

tradition dentō 伝統; *(legend)* densetsu 伝説

traditional dentō-teki (na) 伝統的な; *(accustomed)* jūˈrai no 従来の

traffic kōtsū 交通; ōrai 往来

traffic circle rōˈtarii ロータリー

traffic jam kōtsū-jūˈtai 交通渋滞

traffic sign kōtsū-hyōˈshiki 交通標識

traffic signal kōtsū-shiˈngō 交通信号

tragedy hiˈgeki 悲劇

tragic aeˈnaˈi あえない・敢えない; **tragically enough** aeˈnaku mo あえなくも・敢えなくも

train 1. deˈnsha 電車; reˈnssha 列車; *(nonelectric/steam)* kishaˈ 汽車 **2.** *(drills)* kuˈnren shima(ˈ)su (suru, shite) 訓練します(する, して), *(practices)* renshū shimaˈsu (suru, shite) 練習します(する, して); *(brings up children, disciplines)* shitsukemaˈsu (shitsukeˈru, shitsuˈkete) しつけ[躾け]ます(しつける, しつけて)

training kuˈnren 訓練; *(practice)* renshū 練習; *(imparting discipline)* shitsuke しつけ・躾; *(in ascetic practices)* shugyō 修行

train wreck ressha-jiˈko 列車事故

tramp *(= vagrant)* furōˈ-sha 浮浪者, ruˈmpen ルンペン

trance: in a ~ muchū (no/de) 夢中(の/で)

tranquil noˈdoka (na) のどか・長閑(な)

transacting *(= dealing with)* shoˈri 処理

transaction tori-atsukai 取扱い; *(business)* toˈriˈ-hiki 取り引き

transfer *(trains, etc.)* nori-kaemaˈsu (-kaeˈru, -kaˈete) 乗り換えます(換える, 換えて); *(job)* tennin (shimaˈsu; suru, shite) 転任(します; する, して), ten-jimaˈsu (ten-jiˈru, teˈn-jite) 転じます(転じる, 転じて); *(transfers it)*

utsushima̲su (utsu̲su̲,
utsu̲shite) 移します(移す,
移して)

transformer hen'a̲tsu̲-ki 変圧器

transit tsūkō 通行

transitive verb tado̲shi 他動詞

transitory hakana̲i はかない

translate yaku̲shima̲su
(yaku̲su̲, yaku̲shite) 訳しま
す(訳す, 訳して), hon'yaku̲
shima̲su (suru, shite) 翻訳し
ます(する, して); **(Japanese
into English)** Nihon-go o Eigo
ni naoshima̲su (nao̲su,
nao̲shite) 日本語を英語に直
します(直す, 直して)

translation hon'yaku 翻訳;
translator hon'ya̲ku̲-sha 翻訳
者

transmit tsutaema̲su
(tsuta[ꓤ]e[ꓤ]ru, tsuta[ꓤ]ete) 伝え
ます(伝える, 伝えて), tsū-
jima̲su (tsū-jiru, tsū-jite) 通じ
ます(通じる, 通じて)

transmitted: gets ~
tsutawarima̲su (tsutawa[ꓤ]ru,
tsutawa[ꓤ]tte) 伝わります(伝
わる, 伝わって)

transom window (opening) ramma 欄間

transparent tōmei (na) 透明(な)

transport(ation) unsō 運送,
umpan 運搬, yusō 輸送;
(traffic) kōtsū 交通

trap 1. wa̲na わな・罠 **2.** *(traps
it)* wa̲na ni kakema̲su

(kake̲ru, ka̲kete) わな[罠]に
かけます(かける, かけて);
(gets trapped) wa̲na ni
kakarima̲su (kaka̲ru,
kaka̲tte) わな[罠]にかかりま
す(かかる, かかって)

trash ku̲zu くず・屑, kuzu[ꓤ]-
mono くず物・屑物; *(scrap,
junk)* sute-mono 捨て物; ~
box gomi[ꓤ]-bako ごみ箱; ~
collector gomi̲-ya (san) ごみ
屋(さん)

travel ryokō (shima̲su; suru,
shite) 旅行(します; する, し
て)

traveler ryokō̲-sha 旅行者,
ryok(y)aku 旅客

traveler's check ryokō-kogi̲tte
旅行小切手, ryokōsha-yō
kogi̲tte 旅行者用小切手

tray (o-)bon (お)盆; *(dining
tray, low meal table)* (o-)zen
(go̲-zen) (お)膳(ご膳); →
ash tray

treachery ura-gi[ꓤ]ri[ꓤ] 裏切り;
(treason) ya[ꓤ]shin 野心

treasure takara̲ (o-takara) 宝(お
宝), takara-mo[ꓤ]no 宝物[ꓤ]

treat gochisō (shima̲su; suru,
shite) ごちそう[ご馳走](しま
す; する, して); *(pays the
bill)* ogorima̲su (ogoru,
ogotte) おごります(おごる,
おごって); *(medically)* chiryō
shima̲su (suru, shite) 治療し
ます(する, して); → **handle**

treatise rombun 論文, ro˥n 論
treatment te˥ate (o-te˥ate) 手当(お手当); *(handling)* tori-atsụkai 取り扱い; *(reception)* taigū 待遇; *(medical)* chiryō 治療
treaty jō[˥]yaku 条約
tree ki˥ 木 (**1** i˥p-pon 一本, **2** ni˥-hon 二本, **3** sa˥m-bon 三本; **how many** na˥m-bon 何本)
tree-ears (an edible fungus) kị-ku˥rage きくらげ·木耳
trefoil leaves mitsuba 三つ葉
tremor yure 揺れ
trend *(tendency)* keikō 傾向, *(inclination)* katamu[˥]ki[˥] 傾き, chōshi 調子; *(current)* chōryū 潮流; *(movement)* ugoki˥ 動き
trespass: No Trespassing "Tachiiri kinshi" "立ち入り禁止"
trespass (on) fumi-komima˥sụ (-ko˥mu, -ko˥nde) 踏み込みます(込む, 込んで)
trial *(legal)* sa˥iban 裁判; *(test)* shịke˥n (o-shịke˥n) 試験(お試験), *(trying)* tameshi˥ 試し, kokoro[˥]mi[˥] 試み
triangle sa˥nkaku 三角
tribe: the ~ (group, gang) of ... ...-˥zoku ...族
trick 1. *(feat)* waza 業, ge˥i 芸, *(one's favorite ~)* ohako おはこ·十八番; *(move)* te˥ 手; *(knack)* kotsu˥ こつ·コツ·骨, te˥guchi 手口; *(plot, scheme)* keiryaku 計略, hakarigo[˥]to[˥] 謀·はかりごと **2.** → **cheat**
trick to it *(= the secret of it)* ta˥ne 種
tricky zuru˥i ずるい
tricycle sanri˥n-sha 三輪車
trifling sa˥sai (na) ささい[些細](な)
trigger hịkigane 引き金
trip ryokō 旅行; *(business ~)* shụtchō 出張
triple sam-bai 三倍
trite heibon (na) 平凡(な)
trivial tsumara˥nai つまらない; cho˥tto shịta ちょっとした; sa˥sai (na) ささい[些細](な); → **unimportant**
troops gu˥ntai 軍隊, gu˥n 軍; *(detachment)* bu˥tai 部隊
tropic(s) nettai(-chị˥hō˥) 熱帯(地方)
trouble *(inconvenience)* te˥ka˥zu 手数, tesū˥ (o-tesū) 手数(お手数); *(time taken up)* tema˥ (o-te˥ma) 手間(お手間); *(nuisance)* (go-)me˥iwaku (ご)迷惑, mendō˥ 面倒, *(care)* sewa˥ (o-se˥wa, o-sewa-sama) 世話(お世話, お世話様); *(bother)* (go-)ya˥kkai (ご)やっかい·厄介; *(difficulty)* ko˥n-nan 困難, koma˥ru tokoro˥ 困るところ; *(ailment)* wazurai 煩い·わずらい, byōki 病気; → **worry**
trouble: goes to much ~ hone˥ o

orima︀su (o︀ru, o︀tte) 骨を折り
ます(折る, 折って)

**trouble: is troubled by (an ail-
ment), has trouble with** ... o
wazuraima︀su (wazurau,
wazuratte) ...を煩います(煩う,
煩って)

troublesome (go-)me︀iwaku (na)
(ご)迷惑(な); (go-)ya︀kkai
(na) (ご)やっかい・厄介(な);
wazurawashi︀i 煩わしい

trough shell aoyagi あおやぎ・青
柳

trousers zubo︀n ズボン

trout masu︀ ます・鱒

truck tora︀kku トラック; *(3-
wheeled)* ōto-sa︀nrin オート三
輪

true honto/hontō (no) ほんと/
本当(の); **how true** naru-hodo
なるほど・成る程

truly honto ni ほんとに・本当に,
makoto ni 誠に, jitsu︀ ni 実に

trumpet torampe︀tto トランペッ
ト, rappa らっぱ

trumpet-shell ho︀ra ほら・法螺 =
hora︀-gai ほら貝・法螺貝

trunk *(of tree)* mi︀ki 幹; *(of
elephant)* hana 鼻; *(baggage;
car ~)* tora︀nku トランク

trunks *(sports/swim)* (undō-/
suiei-)pa︀ntsu (運動/水泳)パ
ンツ

trust 1. ta︀nomi 頼み, irai 依頼;
shin'yō 信用, shinrai 信頼, ate
当て; anshin 安心 **2.** *(trusts*

them) shin'yō shima︀su (suru,
shite) 信用します(する, して),
shin-jima︀su (shin-ji︀ru,
shi︀n-jite) 信じます(信じる,
信じて)

trust: gives in ~ azukema︀su
(azuke︀ru, azu︀kete) 預けます
(預ける, 預けて); **takes in ~**
azukarima︀su (azuka︀ru,
azuka︀tte) 預かります(預かる,
預かって)

truth shi︀njitsu 真実, honto no
koto︀ ほんと[本当]の事

try tameshima︀su (tame︀su,
tame︀shite) 試します(試す,
試して); kokoromima︀su
(kokoromi︀ru, kokoro︀mite)
試みます(試みる, 試みて)

try (doing) (shi)-te mima︀su
(mi︀ru, mi︀te) (し)てみます
(みる, みて)

try (to do) (shi)-yō/(ya)r-ō to
shima︀su (suru, shite) (し)よ
う/(や)ろうとします(する,
して)

try hard(er) gambarima︀su (gam-
ba︀ru, gamba︀tte) がんばり[頑
張り]ます(がんばる, がんば
って); do︀ryoku shima︀su
(suru, shite) 努力します(する,
して) 「い

trying *(hard to bear)* tsurai つら

Tsukuba Tsuku︀ba つくば・筑波;
~ University Tsukuba-
Da︀igaku 筑波大学

tub o︀ke 桶; *(basin)* tarai たらい;

(bathtub) yu'bune 湯船; *(rice tub)* o-hachi お鉢, o-hitsu おひつ・お櫃, meshi⌐ン⌐-bitsu 飯びつ・飯櫃

tube ku'da 管, ka'n 管; *(flexible, squeezable, inflatable)* chū'bu チューブ; **test tube** shike⌐ン⌐-kan 試験管; **TV tube** buraun-kan ブラウン管

tuberculosis kekkaku (= hai-ke'kkaku) 結核(=肺結核), haibyō 肺病

Tuesday Kayō'bi 火曜日; **Tuesday-Thursday** Kā⌐ン⌐-Moku 火木

tug at hipparima'su (hippa'ru, hippa'tte) 引っ張ります(引っ張る, 引っ張って) 「船

tugboat hiki-fune 引き船・曳き

tumble korogarima'su (korogaru, korogatte) 転がります(転がる, 転がって); taorema'su (taore'ru, tao'rete) 倒れます(倒れる, 倒れて), korobima'su (korobu, koronde) 転びます(転ぶ, 転んで)

tumult sō'dō 騒動

tuna maguro まぐろ・鮪; *(fatty)* to'ro とろ・トロ, *(pink, medium-fat)* chū-toro 中とろ・中トロ, *(red, unfatty)* aka-mi 赤身; *(canned tunafish)* tsu'na ツナ

tunafish sandwich tsuna-sa'ndo ツナサンド

tune chōshi 調子, fushi' 節

tunnel tonneru トンネル

turban shell, turbo sa'zae さざえ・栄螺; **~ cooked in its shell** tsubo-yaki つぼ焼き・壷焼き

turbot karei かれい・鰈

turf shiba 芝

turkey shichimen-chō 七面鳥

Turkey To'ruko トルコ; **Turkish bath** sauna-bu⌐ン⌐ro サウナ風呂, sa'una サウナ

turn *(order)* jumban 順番

turn 1. *(changes directions)* magarima'su (magaru, magatte) 曲がります(曲がる, 曲がって); *(goes round)* mawarima'su (mawaru, mawatte) 回ります(回る, 回って) **2.** *(makes it go round)* mawashima'su (mawasu, mawashite) 回します(回す, 回して); *(directs one's face/ eyes/attention to)* ... ni mukema'su (mukeru, mukete) ...に向けます(向ける, 向けて)

turn aside *(diverts)* sorashima'su (sora'su, sora'shite) 逸らし[そらし]ます(逸らす, 逸らして)

turn into 1. (= *becomes*) (NOUN ni に, ADJECTIVE-ku く) narima'su (na'ru, na'tte) なります(なる, なって) **2.** (= *makes it into*) (NOUN ni に, ADJECTIVE-ku く) shima'su (suru, shite) します(する, して)

turnip kabu かぶ・蕪, kabura かぶら・蕪

turn loose nigashima̲su (niga̲su, niga̲shite) 逃がします(逃がす, 逃がして)

turn off (light, radio, etc.) ... o keshima̲su (kesu, keshite) ...を消します(消す, 消して); **~ the ignition** sui̲tchi o kirima̲su (ki̲ru, ki̲tte) スイッチを切ります(切る, 切って)

turn on (light, etc.) ... o tsukema̲su (tsuke̲ru, tsuke̲te) ...を付けます(付ける, 付けて); **~ the ignition** sui̲tchi o irema̲su (ireru, irete) スイッチを入れます(入れる, 入れて)

turn up (*it gets found*) mitsukarima̲su (mitsukaru, mitsukatte) 見付かります(見付かる, 見付かって); **~ one's nose at** ... o hana de ashiraima̲su (ashira̲u, ashira̲tte) ...を鼻であしらいます(あしらう, あしらって)

turtle ka̲me 亀; (*snapping*) suppon すっぽん

tutelary deity (= *guardian spirit*) uji̲-ga̲mi 氏神

tutor kyo̲shi 教師

tutoring school ju̲ku 塾

TV te̲rebi テレビ; **~ tube** buraun-kan ブラウン管

twelve jū-ni̲ 十二・12

twentieth nijū-bamme̲ (no) 二十番目(の); **the ~ day** hatsuka-me̲ 二十日目, **(of the month)** hatsuka 二十日・20日

twenty ni̲-jū 二十・20, futa̲-jū 二十; **(20 years old)** ha̲tachi 二十歳・20歳, ni̲ji̲s-sai 二十歳・20歳

twenty-four days, 24th (day of month) ni̲-jū yokka 二十四日・24日

twenty thousand ni-ma̲n 二万・20,000, futa-ma̲n 二万・20,000

twice (*two times*) ni-do̲ 二度, ni-ka̲i 二回; (*double*) ni-bai 二倍

twin(-bed) room tsu̲in ツイン, tsuin-rū̲mu ツインルーム

twin beds tsuin-be̲ddo ツインベッド

twine 1. → **string 2.** (*twists*) yorima̲su (yo̲ru, yo̲tte) よります(よる, よって)

twins futago 双子・ふたご

twist nejirima̲su (neji̲ru, neji̲tte) ねじります(ねじる, ねじって), hinerima̲su (hine̲ru, hine̲tte) ひねります(ひねる, ひねって), yorima̲su (yo̲ru, yo̲tte) よります(よる, よって); **gets twisted** (*entangled*) kojirema̲su (kojire̲ru, koji̲rete) こじれます(こじれる, こじれて)

two ni̲ 二・2, futatsu̲ 二つ・2つ; futa-... 二..., ni-... 二....; tsū̲ ツー; (*people*) futari̲ (o-futari) 二人(お二人), [*bookish*] ni̲-mei 二名

two: small things, pieces nī-ko 二個; **long things** nī-hon 二本; **flat things** nī-mai 二枚; **small animals/fish/bugs** nī-hikī 二匹; **large animals** nī-tō 二頭; **birds** nī-wa 二羽; **machines/vehicles** nī-dai 二台; **books/magazines** nī-satsu 二冊

two days futsuka 二日

two degrees nī-do 二度

two hundred nī-hyaku 二百・200, futā-hyaku 二百・200

two-piece woman's suit tsū-pīisu ツーピース

two thousand ni-sēn 二千・2,000, futa-sēn 二千・2,000

two times ni-dō 二度, ni-kāi 二回, ni-hēn 二遍

two-way socket futamata-sokētto 二又ソケット

two-way traffic ryōmen-tsūkō 両面通行

two-year college tanki-dāigaku 短期大学

two years nī-nen 二年, ninēn-kan 二年間; ~ **old** futatsu 二つ, nī-sai 二歳

type tāipu タイプ, (sort) shūrui 種類; (model) katā 型, ...-gata ...型; (print) katsuji 活字

type(write) tāipu (taipurāitā) de uchimāsu (ūtsu, ūtte) タイプ (タイプライター)で打ちます (打つ, 打って)

typewriter taipurāitā タイプライター, tāipu タイプ; (how many) nān-dai 何台)

typhoon taifū 台風

typical daihyō-teki (na) 代表的 (な); (usual) futsū (no) 普通 (の)

— U —

Ueno Ueno 上野; ~ **Park** Ueno-Kōen 上野公園; ~ **Station** Uenō-Eki 上野駅

ugly minikūi 醜い; mazūi まずい; ~ **woman** būsu ぶす

uh ē-to ええと; **uh ...** anō あのう...; **uh-huh** n̄ ん; **uh-uh** = **huh-uh** n̄n んん

ulcer (gastric) ikāiyō 胃潰瘍

umbrella kāsa かさ・傘, ama-gāsa 雨傘; (parasol) hi-gāsa 日傘; (oilpaper) ban-gāsa 番傘, kara-kāsa 唐傘; (western-style) kōmori こうもり = kōmori-gāsa こうもり傘, yō-gāsa 洋傘

unanticipated omowānu ... 思わぬ...

unavoidable yamu-o-ēnai やむを得ない

unbusy hima (na) 暇(な)

unbutton … no bo⌐n̩tan o hazushima̍su (hazusu, hazushi̍te) …のボタンを外します(外す, 外して); **comes unbuttoned** akima̍su (aku, aite) 空きます(空く, 空いて), … no bo⌐n̩tan ga hazurema̍su (hazureru, hazurete) …のボタンが外れます(外れる, 外れて)

uncalled-for yokei (na) 余計(な)

uncanny ayashi⌐n̩i 怪しい, sugo̍i すごい・凄い

uncertain futei (no) 不定(の); ayashi⌐n̩i 怪しい

unchaste futei (na) 不貞(な)

uncle oji(-san) おじ[叔父, 伯父](さん)

unclean fuketsu (na) 不潔(な)

uncomfortable kimochi ga waru̍i 気持が悪い; *(to wear)* ki-niku̍i 着にくい; *(constrained)* kyūkutsu (na) 窮屈(な)

uncommon mezurashi̍i 珍しい

unconcerned 1. → **calm** 2. ~ **with** … ni mu-ka̍nshin (na) …に無関心(な)

unconditional mu-jō̍ken (no) 無条件(の); **unconditionally** mu-jō̍ken de 無条件で

unconnected with … to mu-ka̍nkei (no) …と無関係(の)

unconscious i̍shiki fumei (no) 意識不明(の); *(involuntary)* mu-i̍shiki (no/na) 無意識(の/な)

uncooked na̍ma (no) 生(の)

uncork (… no se̍n o) nukima̍su (nuku, nuite) (…の栓を)抜きます(抜く, 抜いて); (… no kuchi o) akema̍su (akeru, akete) (…の口を)空けます(空ける, 空けて)

uncultivated *(wild)* yama̍ no 山の

undecided *(indefinite)* futei (no) 不定(の)

under … no shita̍ (de/ni/no) …の下(で/に/の); *(the tutelage of)* … no moto̍ (de) …の下(で)

underdone nama-yake (no) 生焼け(の)

underestimate *(= kids oneself about)* amaku mima̍su (mi̍ru, mi̍te) 甘く見ます(見る, 見て)

undergo *(experiences)* keiken shima̍su (suru, shite) 経験します(する, して); … me̍ ni aima̍su (a̍u, a̍tte) …目に会います(会う, 会って)

undergraduate *(student)* daiga̍ku-sei 大学生

underground chika̍ (no) 地下(の); → **subway**

underline kasen (o hikima̍su; hiku, hiite) 下線(を引きます; 引く, 引いて)

underpants zubo⌐n̩-shita ズボン下

undershirt sha̍tsu シャツ

understand (… ga) wakarima⌐su (waka⌐ru, waka⌐tte) (…が)分かります(分かる, 分かって); (… o) ri⌐kai shima⌐su (suru, shite) (…を)理解します(する, して)

  USAGE: Da⌐re ga(/ni) na⌐ni ga wakarima⌐su ka 誰が(/に)何が分かりますか **Who understands what?**

understanding ri⌐kai 理解, *(ability)* rika⌐i-ryoku 理解力; → **agreement**

understood: is ~ tsū-jima⌐su (tsū-jiru, tsū-jite) 通じます(通じる, 通じて)

undertake kuwadatema⌐su (kuwadate⌐ru, kuwada⌐tete) 企てます(企てる, 企てて)

undertaker *(funeral director)* sōgi-ya 葬儀屋

undertaking shigoto 仕事; *(enterprise)* ji⌐gyō 事業, kuwada⌐te⌐ 企て

underwear shita-gi 下着, hada-gi⌐ 肌着; *(underpants)* shita-baki 下穿き, pa⌐ntsu パンツ, *(women's drawers)* zurō⌐su ズロース, *(panties)* pa⌐ntii パンティー

undeserving mottai-na⌐i もったいない

undisturbed sono mama⌐ (de/no) そのまま(で/の)

undo hazushima⌐su (hazusu, hazushite) 外します(外す, 外して); *(unties)* hodokima⌐su (hodo⌐ku, hodo⌐ite) ほどきます(ほどく, ほどいて), tokima⌐su (to⌐ku, to⌐ite) 解きます(解く, 解いて)

undone: comes ~ tokema⌐su (toke⌐ru, to⌐kete) 解けます(解ける, 解けて); **leaves it** ~ shina⌐ide okima⌐su (oku, oite) しないでおきます(おく, おいて)

undoubtedly utagai na⌐ku 疑いなく, ta⌐shika ni 確かに, kitto きっと

undress ki-mono o nugima⌐su (nu⌐gu, nu⌐ide) 着物を脱ぎます(脱ぐ, 脱いで)

unduly yatara ni やたらに

uneasiness shimpai 心配

uneasy shimpai (na) 心配(な), fuan (na) 不安(な)

unemployed: ~ **person** shitsu-gyō⌐-sha 失業者; ~ **samurai** rōnin 浪人

unemployment shitsugyō 失業

uneven dekoboko (no) でこぼこ・凸凹(の)

unexpected i⌐ngai (na) 意外(な), *(sudden)* ni⌐waka (no) にわか(の); *(but welcome)* mezurashi⌐i 珍しい

unexpectedly i⌐ngai ni 意外に, futo ふと, *(suddenly)* ni⌐waka ni にわかに

unfair fu⌐-kō⌐hei (na) 不公平(な); *(unjustified)* futō (na) 不当(な)

unfaithful *(to her husband)* futei
(na) 不貞(な)

unfasten hazushima̱su (hazusu,
hazushite) 外します(外す, 外
して)

unfatty tuna maguro (no) aka-mi
(まぐろ[鮪]の)赤身

unfazed *(by ...)* (...-te̱ mo) dō-
jimase̱n (dō-ji̱nai, dō-
ji̱na̱ide) (...ても)動じません
(動じない, 動じないで);
heiki (na) 平気(な)

unfeeling hakujō (na) 薄情(な)

unfixed futei (no) 不定(の)

unfortunate *(unlucky)* fuko̱ (na)
不幸(な); *(regrettable, in-
opportune)* ainiku (na) あいに
く(な); → **pitiful**

unfortunately ainiku あいにく

unhandy fu̱ben (na) 不便(な)

unhappy *(gloomy)* inki (na) 陰気
(な), *(moody)* kigen ga waru̱i
機嫌が悪い, *(dissatisfied)*
fuman (na) 不満(な)

unhealthy *(bad for one's health)*
karada ni waru̱i 体に悪い;
(sickly) byōki-gachi (na) 病気
がち(な)

unhulled rice momi̱ もみ・籾

unification tōitsu 統一; **unify**
tōitsu shima̱su (suru, shite) 統
一します(する, して)

uniform seifuku 制服; *(military)*
gumpuku 軍服; *(school)*
gakuse̱i-fuku 学生服

unimportant *(matter)* mondai ni

nara̱nai 問題にならない

unintentionally tsu̱i つい

union *(labor)* kumiai 組合, rōdō-
ku̱miai 労働組合; *(alliance)*
rengō 連合; *(joint)* kyōdō 共同;
(merger) gappei 合併, gōdō 合
同

unique yu̱iitsu (no) 唯一(の)

unit ta̱n'i 単位; *(military)* bu̱tai
部隊

unite *(they merge)* gappei/gōdō
shima̱su (suru, shite) 合併/合
同します(する, して); *(com-
bines dual functions as)* ... o
kanema̱su (kane̱ru, ka̱nete) ...
を兼ねます(兼ねる, 兼ねて)

United Nations Kokusai-Re̱ngō
国際連合

United States Amerika
(-Gasshū̱koku) アメリカ(合
衆国)

universe u̱chū 宇宙

university daigaku 大学

unjustified futō (na) 不当(な)

unkind fu-shi̱nsetsu (na) 不親切
(な); → **mean**

unknown fumei (no) 不明(の);
shiranai 知らない

unless (shi)-na̱kereba (し)なけ
れば, (shi)-nai to (し)ないと

unlikely ari-so̱ mo na̱i ありそう
もない; (shi)-sō mo na̱i (し)
そうもない

unload oroshima̱su (oro̱su,
oro̱shite) 降ろします(降ろす,
降ろして)

unlock ... no kagi⌐ o akema⌐su (akeru, akete) ...の鍵を開けます(開ける，開けて)

unlocked: comes ~ ... (no kagi⌐ ga) akima⌐su (aku, aite) ...(の鍵が)開きます(開く，開いて)

unluckily u⌐n-waruku 運悪く

unlucky u⌐n ga waru⌐i 運が悪い; *(fails to strike it lucky)* tsu⌐ite imase⌐n (inai, ina⌐ikute) ついていません(いない，いなくて)

unmarried hitori-mo⌐no⌐ 独り者, dokushin 独身

unnatural fu-shi⌐zen (na) 不自然(な)

unnecessary, unneeded iranai いらない, mu⌐nyō (no) 無用(の), fuyō (no) 不要(の); *(superfluous)* yokei (na) 余計(な)

unoccupied *(free of business)* hima (na) 暇(な)

unofficial hi-kō⌐shiki (no) 非公式(の)

unperturbed heiki (na) 平気(な)

unpleasant iya⌐ (na) 嫌(な); fu-yu⌐kai (na) 不愉快(な)

unpolished rice ge⌐mmai 玄米

unprofitable wari ga waru⌐i 割が悪い

unreasonable mu⌐ri (na) 無理(な); mu⌐cha (na) むちゃ[無茶](な); hido⌐i ひどい

unrelated (to ...) (... to⌐ wa) muka⌐nkei (no) (...とは)無関係(の)

unreliable ayashi⌐i 怪しい, detarame (na) でたらめ(な)

unreserved *(= frank; rude)* bu-e⌐nryo (na) 無遠慮(な)

unreserved seat(s) jiyū⌐-seki 自由席

unrest sō⌐dō 騒動

unsafe *(troubled)* bussō⌐ (na) 物騒(な)

unsavory rumors tokaku no uwasa とかくのうわさ[噂]

unscrupulous akuratsu (na) 悪らつ(な)・悪辣(な)

unseemly, unsightly migurushi⌐i 見苦しい

unsentimental dora⌐i (na) ドライ(な)

unshapely kakkō ga waru⌐i かっこう[格好・恰好]が悪い

unskillful heta⌐ (na) へた[下手](な), mazu⌐i まずい

unsociable bu-a⌐isō (na) 無愛想(な)

unsophisticated mu⌐jaki (na) 無邪気・むじゃき(な), soboku (na) 素朴(な)

untasty mazu⌐i まずい

untidy kitana⌐i 汚い

untie tokima⌐su (to⌐ku, to⌐ite) 解きます(解く，解いて), hodokima⌐su (hodo⌐ku, hodo⌐ite) ほどきます(ほどく，ほどいて)

until ... ma⌐de ...まで・迄; **~ now** ima-ma⌐de 今まで[迄]

untouched sono mama⌐ (de/no)

そのまま（で/の）

unusual *(abnormal)* ijō (na) 異常
（な）; *(extreme)* hijō (na) 非常
（な）; *(novel)* kawatta 変わっ
た, mezurashiꜜi 珍しい

unusually mezuraꜜshiku 珍しく;
(extremely) hijō ni 非常に

unwell: feeling ～ kimochi ga
waruꜜi 気持ちが悪い

unwilling (to do) (shi)-taku
arimaseꜜn (naꜜi, naꜜkute)（し
たくありません（ない, なく
て）

unzipped: comes ～ (chaꜜkku ga)
akimaꜜsu (aku, aite)（チャッ
クが）空きます（空く, 空いて）

up (… no) ueꜜ e (…の)上へ; **up**
(= higher by) ¥100 hyakueꜜn-
daka 百円高

bring up *(trains)* shitsuke-
maꜜsu (shitsukeꜜru,
shitsuꜜkete) しつけ[躾け]
ます（しつける, しつけ
て）, *(rears)* sodatemaꜜsu
(sodateꜜru, sodaꜜtete) 育て
ます（育てる, 育てて）

get up okimaꜜsu (okiꜜru,
oꜜkite) 起きます（起きる,
起きて）; *(gets one up)*
okoshimaꜜsu (okoꜜsu,
okoꜜshite) 起こします（起こ
す, 起こして）

go up agarimaꜜsu (agaru,
agatte) 上がります（上がる,
上がって）, noborimaꜜsu
(noboru, nobotte) 上り[昇

り]ます（上[昇]る, 上[昇]っ
て）

make up for oginaimaꜜsu
(oginaꜜu, oginaꜜtte) 補います
（補う, 補って）

upbringing shitsuke しつけ・躾;
sodachiꜜ 育ち

up-front money atama-kin 頭金

upkeep iꜜji 維持, *(expense)* ijiꜜ-hi
維持費; *(care, repair)* te-ireꜜ 手
入れ

upon → on

upper ue (no) 上（の）

upping the (base) pay beꜜa ベア
= bēsu-aꜜppu ベースアップ

upright katai 堅い; → **honest**

upset *(it overturns)* hikkuri-
kaerimaꜜsu (-kaeꜜru, -kaꜜette)
ひっくり返ります（返る, 返
って）, *(overturns it)* hikkuri-
kaeshimaꜜsu (-kaeꜜsu,
-kaeshite) ひっくり返します
（返す, 返して）; → **spill**

upset *(disturbs)* midashimaꜜsu
(midaꜜsu, midaꜜshite) 乱しま
す（乱す, 乱して）; *(is dis-
turbed)* midaremaꜜsu
(midareꜜru, midaꜜrete) 乱れま
す（乱れる, 乱れて）, *(gets
nervous)* dōyō shimaꜜsu
(suru, shite) 動揺します（する,
して）

upset: has an upset stomach (o-
naka no) guai ga waruꜜi（おな
かの）具合が悪い

upshot shiꜜmatsu しまつ・始末

upside down sakasa(ma) 逆さ（ま）, abekobe あべこべ

upstairs ni-kai 二階, o-ni'kai (de/ni, e/ni, no) お二階（で/に，へ/に，の）

up-to-date *(modern)* ge'ndai (no) 現代（の）; *(latest)* saishin (no) 最新（の）

up to now jū'rai 従来, ima-ma'de 今まで［迄］

uptown (Tokyo) ya[ ]ma-te[ ] 山手, yama-no[ ]-te 山手・山の手

up until (…) i'zen (…)以前

upwards of (…) i'jō (…)以上

urban shi'nai (no) 市内（の）; ~ **prefecture** fu' 府 (Kyōto'-fu 京都府, Ōsaka'-fu 大阪府)

urbanite toka'i-jin 都会人

urge susumema'su (susumeru, susumete) 勧めます（勧める，勧めて）; unagashima'su (unaga'su, unaga'shite) 促します（促す，促して）

urgency shikyū 至急

urgent kyū (na) 急（な）, shikyū (no) 至急（の）; ~ **business** kyūyō 急用

urgently kyū ni 急に, shi̱kyū (ni) 至急（に）

urinal *(place)* shōben-jo[ ] 小便所; *(thing)* shōbe'n-ki 小便器, *(bedpan)* shibin しびん・溲瓶

urinate shōbe'n shima([ ])su (suru, shi̱te) 小便します（する，して）

urine shōbe'n 小便; [*baby talk*]

(o-)shi̱'kko （お）しっこ

us, we wata'shi̱'-ta'chi わたしたち［私達］, watakushi̱'-tachi わたくしたち［私達］; ware-ware われわれ・我々

U.S. Amerika アメリカ, Bei-koku 米国; Bei-… 米…, …-Bei …米

use *(the use)* shiyō 使用, *(for the use of)* …-yō …用; *(service)* (go-)yō （ご）用, yaku' (o-yaku) 役（お役）; *(utilization)* riyō 利用; *(putting to use)* ōyō 応用

use tsukaima'su (tsukau, tsukatte) 使います（使う，使って）, mochiima'su (mochii[ ]ru, mochi[ ]ite) 用います（用いる，用いて）; *(makes use of)* riyō shima'su (suru, shi̱te) 利用します（する，して）

used *(= secondhand)* chū[ ]ko (no) 中古（の）, furu'i 古い

used to: gets ~ … ni narema'su (nare'ru, na'rete) …に慣れます（慣れる，慣れて）

used to (do) (shi̱)-ta mono'/mo'n desu (し)たもの/もんです

useful yaku' ni tachima'su (ta'tsu, ta'tte) 役に立ちます（立つ，立って）, yaku-dachima'su (-da'tsu, -da'tte) 役立ちます（立つ，立って）; chō'hō (na) 重宝（な）

useless muda (na) 無駄（な）; mu'yō (no) 無用（の）, fuyō (no) 不用（の）

user tsukau hito｀ 使う人, shiyō｀-sha 使用者

usher toritsugi 取り次ぎ; annai-ga｀kari 案内係, anna⌐i-nin 案内人; *(ushers one)* anna｀i shima(⌐)su (suru, shite) 案内します(する, して)

U.S.S.R. So｀ren ソ連

usual futsū (no) 普通(の), i｀tsu-mo (no) いつも(の), heizei (no) 平生(の), fu｀dan (no) 普段(の); tsūjō (no) 通常(の), tsu｀ne (no) 常(の); **as ~** i｀tsu-mo no yō｀ ni いつものよう[様]に, aikawarazu 相変らず

usually futsū 普通・ふつう, taitei たいてい, i｀tsu mo いつも, heizei 平生, fu｀dan 普段・ふだん

utensil utsuwa 器; ...-yōhin ...用品

utility jitsuyō 実用

utility (bills) kōkyō-ryō｀kin 公共料金

utilization riyō 利用

utilize riyō shima｀su (suru, shite) 利用します(する, して)

utmost: to the ~ a｀ku｀-made (mo) あくまで(も); **does one's ~** saizen o tsukushima｀su (tsuku｀su, tsuku｀shite) 最善を尽くします(尽くす, 尽くして)

utter → **speak, say; ~ a curse** noroima｀su (noro｀u, noro｀tte) 呪います(呪う, 呪って)

utterly mattaku 全く, sukka｀ri すっかり, zenzen 全然; **~ exhausted** ku(t)takuta く(っ)たくた

U-turn yūtā｀n ユーターン・Uターン; **makes a ~** yūtā｀n shima(⌐)su (suru, shite) ユーターン[Uターン]します(する, して)

— V —

vacant 1. *(open)* aite ima｀su (iru, ite) 空いています(いる, いて) **2.** *(hollow)* utsuro (na) うつろ・虚ろ(な)

vacant ... aki-... 空き...; **~ car (available taxi)** kūsha 空車; **~ house** aki-ya 空き家; **~ lot** aki-chi 空き地; **~ room(s)** aki-ma 空き間, **~ room/of-fice** aki-shitsu 空き室

vacate akema｀su (akeru, akete) 空けます(空ける, 空けて)

vacation yasumi｀ 休み, kyūka 休暇

vaccine wa⌐kuchin ワクチン

vacuum bottle mahō｀-bin 魔法瓶

vacuum cleaner denki-sōji｀ki 電気掃除機

vagabond, vagrant furō-sha 浮浪者

vague aimai (na) あいまい(な)・暧昧(な); ii-kagen (na) いい加減(な)

vaguely aimai ni あいまいに・暧昧に; *(somehow)* dō-mo どうも

vain *(conceited)* unubore ga tsuyoi うぬぼれが強い; *(ineffectual)* muda (na) 無駄(な)

valid yūkō (na) 有効(な)

valley tani(-ma) 谷(間)

valuable taisetsu (na) 大切(な), kichō (na) 貴重(な); → **expensive**

valuables kichō-hin 貴重品

value 1. kachi 価値, neuchi 値打ち **2. values (cherishes) it** chōhō shima(-)su (suru, shite) 重宝します(する, して), chōhō-garimasu (-garu, -gatte) 重宝がります(がる, がって)

valued chōhō (na) 重宝(な); → **valuable**

valve ben 弁

vanilla banira バニラ

vanish *(from sight)* mienaku narimasu (naru, natte) 見えなくなります(なる, なって); *(from existence)* naku narimasu (naru, natte) なくなります(なる, なって); *(gets extinguished)* kiemasu (kieru, kiete) 消えます(消える, 消えて)

vapor kitai 気体; → **steam**

various iroiro (na/no) いろいろ[色々](な/の), ironna いろんな; ~ **places** tokorodokoro ところどころ・所々; ~ **(and nefarious)** tokaku no とかくの

varnish nisu ニス = wanisu (o nurimasu; nuru, nutte) ワニス(を塗ります; 塗る, 塗って); nuri 塗り

vase bin 瓶; *(for flowers)* kabin 花瓶, kaki 花器

vast bakudai (na) 莫大な

vaudeville (theater) yose 寄席

vegetable yasai (o-yasai) 野菜(お野菜); *(greens)* ao-mono 青物, nappa 菜っ葉, na (o-na) 菜(お菜)

vegetarian saishoku-sha 菜食者; ~ **cuisine** shōjin-ryōri 精進料理

vehicle nori-mono 乗り物, kuruma (o-kuruma) 車(お車), ...-sha ...車; **(how many** nan-dai 何台)

velvet birōdo ビロード

vending machine hanbai-ki 販売機; **ticket** ~ kembai-ki 券売機   ⌐**dealer**

vendor uriko 売り子; → **seller,**

venereal disease seibyō 性病

vengeance fukushū 復讐

ventilation kanki 換気; = ~ **system** kanki-sōchi 換気装置

venture *(speculation, wild guess)*

yama⌐ やま・山
veranda engawa 縁側
verb dōshi 動詞 ⌐頭(の)
verbal (= *spoken*) kōtō (no) 口
verification shōmei 証明
verify shōmei shima⌐su (suru, shite) 証明します(する, して)
vermifuge mushi-ku⌐dashi 虫下し, kudashi 下し
vernal equinox shumbun 春分; **Vernal Equinox Day** Shumbun no hi⌐ 春分の日
versatility yūzū 融通; **is versatile** yūzū ga kikima⌐su (kiku, kiite) 融通がききます(きく, きいて)
verse shi 詩; (*17-syllable*) ha⌐iku⌐ 俳句, hokku⌐ 発句; (*31-syllable*) wa⌐ka 和歌, ta⌐nka 短歌; (*longer*) chō⌐ka 長
versus tai-... 対... ⌐歌
vertical ta⌐te (no) 縦(の), suichoku (no) 垂直(の); **vertically** ta⌐te ni 縦に, suichoku ni 垂直に
very zu⌐ibun ずいぶん・随分, taihen たいへん・大変, totemo とても, hijō ni 非常に, ta⌐isō たいそう・大層, go⌐ku ごく; **the very + NOUN = the NOUN itself** ... sono-mo⌐no⌐ ...そのもの
very beginning/first saisho (no/ni) 最初(の/に) ⌐中(の)
very middle mannaka (no) 真ん
very well (= *satisfactory*)

vest chokki チョッキ
vestige konseki 痕跡
veto kyo⌐hi 拒否; (*rejects it*) kyo⌐hi shima(⌐)su (suru, shite) 拒否します(する, して)
vexatious kuyashi⌐i 悔しい
via ... ke⌐iyu (de) ...経由(で); ... o tō⌐tte ...を通って, ... o he⌐te ...
vibration shindō 振動 ⌐を経て
vice waru⌐i shūkan 悪い習慣, akufū 悪風
vice admiral chū⌐jō 中将
vice-president (*of company*) fuku-sha⌐chō 副社長; (*of nation*) fuku-daitō⌐ryō 副大統領
vice versa hantai ni 反対に, gyaku ni 逆に
vicinity fuki⌐n 付近, ki⌐njo 近所, chika⌐ku 近く, ... hen ...辺
vicious waru⌐i 悪い, hido⌐i ひどい
victim (*of sacrifice*) gise⌐i-sha 犠牲者, (*of injury*) higa⌐i-sha 被害者; **falls ~ to** ... no gisei ni narima⌐su (na⌐ru, na⌐tte) ...の犠牲になります(なる, なって) ⌐sha 優勝者
victor shōri⌐-sha 勝利者, yūshō-
victory shōri 勝利, yūshō 優勝; **wins the ~** yūshō shima⌐su (suru, shite) 優勝します(する,
vie → compete ⌐して)
view 1. (*scenery*) nagame⌐ 眺め 2. (*gazes at*) nagamema⌐su

(nagame⌐ru, naga⌐mete) 眺め
ます(眺める, 眺めて) **3.** →
opinion; → **outlook**; → **look**;
→ **standpoint**

view: in ~ of ... ni tera⌐shite ...
に照らして, ... o kanga⌐ete ...
を考えて

viewpoint ke⌐nchi 見地, mi-ka⌐ta⌐
見方, tachi-ba 立場

vigilance keikai 警戒

vigor ge⌐nki 元気

vigorous sakan (na) 盛ん(な);
sekkyoku-teki (na) 積極的(な);
→ **energetic**; → **healthy**;
strong

villa bessō⌐ 別荘

village mura⌐ 村; ...⌐-son ...村;
sato 里

vine tsuru⌐ つる・蔓

vinegar o-su お酢, su⌐ 酢

vinyl bi⌐niru ビニル, bini⌐iru ビ
ニール

violate okashima⌐su (oka⌐su,
oka⌐shite) 犯します(犯す,
犯して); yaburima⌐su
(yabu⌐ru, yabu⌐tte) 破ります
(破る, 破って); ... ni ihan
shima⌐su (suru, shite) ...に違
反します(する, して), ... ni
somukima⌐su (somu⌐ku,
somu⌐ite) ...に背きます(背く,
背いて)

violation ihan 違反

violence (*brute force*) bō⌐ryoku
暴力

violent (*severe*) hageshi⌐i 激しい;
(*unruly*) rambō⌐ (na) 乱暴(な);
mu⌐ri (na) 無理(な)

violet sumire すみれ・菫

violin baiorin バイオリン

virgin (*female*) sho⌐jo 処女,
oboko(-mu⌐sume) おぼこ(娘),
ki-mu⌐sume 生娘; (*male*) dōtei
童貞

virtue bi⌐ntoku 美徳, toku 徳

virus bi⌐irusu ビールス

visa bi⌐za ビザ, [*bookish*] sashō
査証

visible (me⌐ ni) miema⌐su (mie⌐ru,
mi⌐ete) (目に)見えます(見え
る, 見えて)

vision (*eyesight*) shi⌐ryoku 視力

visit hōmon shima⌐su (suru,
shite) 訪問します(する, して);
asobi ni ikima⌐su (iku, itte) 遊
びに行きます(行く, 行って),
tazunema⌐su (tazune⌐ru,
tazu⌐nete) 訪ねます(訪ねる,
訪ねて); [HUMBLE]
ukagaima⌐su (ukagau,
ukagatte) 伺います(伺う,
伺って), mairima⌐su (ma⌐iru,
ma⌐itte) 参ります(参る, 参っ
て)

visit: a visit hōmon 訪問, (o-)
asobi (お)遊び, (o-)ukagai
(お)伺い; (**of solicitude**) (o-)
mimai (お)見舞い; (*interview*)
menkai 面会

visiting card meishi 名刺

visitor o-kyaku (お)客, o-
kyaku-san/-sa⌐ma⌐ お客さん/
様; raikyaku 来客; (*solicitous*)
mima⌐i-kyaku 見舞い客; (*for
interview*) menkai-nin 面会人

vitamin(s) bita⌐nmin ビタミン;

(= ~ **pills**) bitami⌐n-zai ビ
タミン剤

vocabulary kotoba¹ 言葉, go⌐i 語
彙, tango 単語

vocation shoku¹gyō 職業

vogue ryūkō 流行

voice ko⌐e 声

void → **invalid**

volcanic ash kaza¹m-bai 火山灰

volcano ka¹zan 火山

volleyball barēbo¹ru バレーボー
「ル

volt bo⌐ruto ボルト

voltage converter hen'a¹tsu-ki 変
圧器

volume (book) ho¹n 本, ...-bon ...
本; (of a set) (da¹i ...¹-) kan
(第...)巻; (quantity) ryō¹ 量

voluntary (optional) zu⌐ii (na)
随意(な)

vomit 1. he¹do へど・反吐
2. modoshima¹su (modo¹su,
modo¹shite) 戻します(戻す,
戻して), (he¹do o) hakima¹su
(ha¹ku, ha¹ite) (へどを)吐き
ます(吐く, 吐いて);
komamo¹no¹-ya o hirogema¹su
(hirogeru, hirogete) 小間物屋
を広げます(広げる, 広げて)

vote tōhyō shima¹su (suru, shite)
投票します(する, して)

vow → **pledge**

vowel boin 母音, boon 母音

voyage kō⌐kai 航海; **makes a ~**
kō⌐kai shima¹su (suru, shite)
航海します(する, して)

vulgar gehi¹n (na) 下品(な),
iyashi¹i 卑しい; (mundane)
zoku (na) 俗(な)

— W —

wag furima¹su (furu, futte) 振り
ます(振る, 振って)

wage chi¹ngin 賃金; → **salary**

waist koshi 腰 (= loins),
(specifically) koshi no kubire
腰のくびれ; kubire くびれ

waiter, waitress kyū¹ji 給仕;
(waiter) uē¹tā ウエーター; bōi
(san) ボーイ(さん); (waitress)
uē¹toresu ウエートレス

Waiter!/Waitress! Cho¹tto
(sumimase¹n)! ちょっと(すみ

ません)!; Sumimase¹n! すみ
ません!

wait for ... o machima¹su
(ma¹tsu, ma¹tte) ...を待ちます
(待つ, 待って)

waiting a long time machidōshi¹i
待ち遠しい　　　　　「合室

waiting room machia¹i-shitsu 待

wake up me¹ ga samema¹su
(same¹ru, sa¹mete) 目が覚めます
(覚める, 覚めて), (rises)
okima¹su (oki¹ru, o¹kite) 起き

ます(起きる, 起きて);
(wakes a person up) … o
okoshima⌐su (oko⌐su,
oko⌐shite) …を起こします(起
こす, 起こして)

walk arukima⌐su (aru⌐ku, aru⌐ite)
歩きます(歩く, 歩いて),
aru⌐ite ikima⌐su (iku, itte) 歩い
て行きます(行く, 行って);
(stroll) sampo (shima⌐su; suru,
shite) 散歩(します; する, し
て); **goes for a ~** sampo ni
ikima⌐su (iku, itte) 散歩に行き
ます(行く, 行って)

walking stick *(= cane)* suṭe⌐kki
ステッキ, tsu⌐e 杖

walk(way) hodō 歩道, jindō 人
道

wall *(of house)* kabe 壁; *(around
courtyard, etc.)* hei 塀・へい

wallet saifu 財布, gamaguchi が
ま口, *(billfold)* satsu-i⌐re⌐ 札
入れ

walnut kurumi⌐ くるみ・胡桃

wander samayoima⌐su
(samayo⌐u, samayo⌐tte) さまよ
います(さまよう, さまよっ
て)

want 1. … ga irima⌐su (iru, itte) …
が要ります(要る, 要って), …
ga hoshi⌐i desu …が欲しいで
す; *(looks for, seeks to buy)*
motomema⌐su (motome⌐ru,
moto⌐mete) 求めます(求める,
求めて) **2. wants to do (it)** (…
ga) shi-ta⌐i desu (shi-tai, shi-

ta⌐kute) (…が)したいです(し
たい, したくて), (… o) shi-
tagarima⌐su (shi-tagaru, shi-
taga⌐tte) (…を)したがります
(したがる, したがって);

wants to have (it) done (by …)
(… ni) … o shi-te morai-ta⌐i
desu (morai-tai, morai-
ta⌐kute) (…に)…をしてもら
いたいです(もらいたい, も
らいたくて)

3. → need, poverty

USAGE: **Who wants what?**
Da⌐re ga(/ni) na⌐ni ga
irima⌐su (hoshi⌐i desu) ka 誰
が(/に)何が要ります(欲し
いです)か **Who wants to do
what?** Da⌐re ga na⌐ni o(/ga)
shita⌐i desu ka 誰が何を
(/が)したいですか

want: does as one wants katte ni
shima⌐su (suru, shite) 勝手に
します(する, して)

**wanted criminal: photograph of
~** tehai-sha⌐shin 手配写真

war sensō 戦争, ra⌐n 乱; **after/
since the ~** se⌐ngo (no) 戦後
(の); **(after) the end of the
war** shūsen(-go) 終戦(後);
before the war senzen (no) 戦
前(の); **during the war** senji-
chū 戦時中

war: a great ~ taisen 大戦;
world ~ sekai-ta⌐isen 世界大
戦; **World War II** Da⌐i ni⌐-ji
Sekai-Ta⌐isen 第二次世界大戦

warbler: bush warbler ugu⌐isu う
ぐいす・鶯・鶯　　　　「区
ward *(city district)* ku⌐区, ...⌐-ku ...
ward office ku-ya⌐kusho 区役所
ware saiku⌐ 細工; *(ceramic
ware)* tō⌐ki 陶器, setomono 瀬
戸物, ...-yaki ...焼き
warehouse sō⌐ko 倉庫, kura⌐ 倉
warm attaka⌐i あったかい・温か
い・暖かい, atataka⌐i 温かい・
暖かい; *(lukewarm liquids)*
nuru⌐i ぬるい
warmhearted kokoro⌐ ga
atataka⌐i 心が温かい, atsui 厚
い・篤い
warmheartedness atsu-sa 厚さ・
篤さ; ni⌐njō 人情
warm it up at(a)tamema⌐su
(at(a)tame⌐ru, at(a)ta⌐mete)
あっため[温め・暖め]ます
(あっため[温め・暖め]る,
あっため[温め・暖め]て), nes-
shima⌐su (nes-su⌐ru, ne⌐s-
shite) 熱します(熱する, 熱
して); **warms the rice wine**
ka⌐n (o-kan) o tsukema⌐su/
shima⌐su 燗(お燗)をつけま
す/します　　　　「さ
warmth *(heat)* a⌐tsu-sa 熱さ・暑
warn keikoku shima⌐su (suru,
shite) 警告します(する, して)
warning keikoku 警告; *(alert)*
keihō 警報; *(notice)* kotowa⌐ri⌐
断り
warp 1. sori⌐ そり・反り **2.** *(it
warps)* sorima⌐su (so⌐ru, so⌐tte)

そり[反り]ます(そる, そっ
て); *(warps it)* sorashima⌐su
(sora⌐su, sora⌐shite) そらし[反
らし]ます(そらす, そらして),
yugamema⌐su (yugame⌐ru,
yuga⌐mete) 歪め[ゆがめ]ま
す(歪める, 歪めて)
3. gets warped *(distorted)*
yugamima⌐su (yuga⌐mu,
yuga⌐nde) 歪み[ゆがみ]ます
(歪む, 歪んで); *(crooked)*
kuruima⌐su (kuru⌐u, kuru⌐tte)
狂います(狂う, 狂って)
warp *(vertical threads)* tate-ito
縦糸・経糸
warranty hoshō 保証
warrior samurai 侍, bu⌐shi 武士
warship gunkan 軍艦
wartime se⌐nji 戦時
was ... de⌐shita (... da⌐tta) ...で
した(...だった); arima⌐shita
(a⌐tta) ありました(あった);
ima⌐shita (ita) いました(いた);
→ **is**
wash araima⌐su (arau, aratte) 洗
います(洗う, 洗って); *(laun-
der)* sentaku shima⌐su (suru,
shite) 洗濯します(する, して)
wash: the wash(ing) sentaku (o-
se⌐ntaku) 洗濯(お洗濯),
sentaku-mono 洗濯物
wash basin semme⌐n-ki 洗面器
washcloth *(hand towel)* te-nugui
手拭い, *(dishcloth)* fuki⌐n ふ
きん・布巾
washer *(washing machine)*

senta'ku'-ki 洗濯機

Washington Washi'nton ワシントン

washroom (o-)tea'rai（お）手洗い

wasn't ... ja arimase'n deshita (... ja na'katta) ...じゃありませんでした(...じゃなかった); arimase'n deshita (na'katta) ありませんでした(なかった); imase'n deshita (ina'katta) いませんでした(いなかった); → **isn't**

waste 1. (trash) ku'zu 屑・くず, kuzu⌐-mono 屑物・くず物; (refuse; damaged goods) rōzu ローズ **2.** (wastes it) muda ni shima'su (suru, shite) 無駄にします(する，して); (is extravagant with) muda-zu'kai shima'su (suru, shite) 無駄使いします(する，して), rō⌐hi shima'su (suru, shite) 浪費します(する，して) **3. falls to** ~ arema'su (areru, arete) 荒れます(荒れる，荒れて)

wastebasket kuzu'-kago くずかご・屑籠　　　　　　　　「い

wasteful mottai-na'i もったいな

wastepaper kamiku'zu 紙くず・紙屑; ~ **basket** kamikuzu'-kago 紙くずかご・紙屑籠

watch 1. (timepiece) tokei 時計 **2.** (looks at/after) mima'su (miru, mite) 見ます(見る，見て); (guards it) ... no ba'n o shima'su (suru, shite) ...の番

をします(する，して) **3.** (observes) kansatsu shima'su (suru, shite) 観察します(する，して)

watch for neraima'su (nerau, neratte) 狙います(狙う，狙って); ~ **a chance** kika'i o ukagaima'su (ukagau, ukagatte) 機会を窺い[うかがい]ます(窺う，窺って)

watchful: keeps a ~ **eye (on the situation)** (jōkyō o) ukagaima'su (ukagau, ukagatte) (状況・情況を)窺い[うかがい]ます(窺う，窺って)

watchman banni'n 番人; (gate-keeper) mo'mban 門番; **night** ~ yo-ma'wari 夜回り　「よ!

Watch out! Abunai yo! 危ない

watch out for (guards against) keikai shima'su (suru, shite) 警戒します(する，して)

Watch your step! Ashi-mo'to' ni ki o tsuke'te! 足元に気を付けて!

water mizu 水; **hot** ~ o-yu お湯, yu' 湯; **drinking** ~ nomi'-mizu 飲み水, o-hi'ya お冷や

waterfall taki 滝　　　「おひや

water imp kappa かっぱ・河童

water level suihei 水平

watermelon suika すいか・西瓜

water pistol mizu-de'ppo 水鉄砲

water pitcher mizu-sa'shi' 水差し

water pressure (is good/bad) suidō no de (ga i'i/waru'i

desu) 水道の出(がいい/悪い
です)

waterproof bōsui (no) 防水(の)

water service, waterworks suidō
水道; **Waterworks Bureau**
suidō-kyoku 水道局

wave 1. nami͞ 波 **2.** *(permanent)*
pā͞ma パーマ **3.** *(waves a
hand)* te͞ o furima͞su (furu,
futte) 手を振ります(振る, 振
って)

wax mitsurō みつろう・蜜蝋, rō͞
ろう・蝋

way michi 道; *(method)* shi-kata
仕方, shi-yō 仕様, yari-kata や
り方; *(means)* shu͞dan 手段;
(manner) tō͞ri 通り, *(fashion)*
fū͞ 風, *(trick)* te͞guchi 手口

way: by way of ... → **via**

way: gets in the way (o-)jama ni
narima͞su (na͞ru, na͞tte) (お)
じゃま[邪魔]になります(な
る, なって), (o-)jama o
shima͞su (suru, shite) (お)じゃ
ま[邪魔]をします(する, し
て); **gets out of the way**
dokima͞su (doku, doite) どき
ます・退きます(どく, どいて),
nokima͞su (noku, noite) のき
ます・退きます(のく, のいて);
on the way tochū (de) 途中(で)

way: way of ...ing VERB INFINI-
TIVE + -kata 方; **~ of saying/
telling/putting it** ii-kata 言い
方   「っと前

way back (before) zutto ma͞e ず

wayside michibata 道端; gaitō 街
頭

we, us wata͞shi͞-ta͞chi わたした
ち・私達, watakushi͞-tachi わ
たくしたち・私達; ware-ware
われわれ・我々

weak yowa͞i 弱い; fu͞-jiyū (na)
不自由(な); *(coffee, etc.)* usui
薄い

weak: grows weak otoroema͞su
(otoro͞e͞ru, otoro͞ete) 衰えま
す(衰える, 衰えて)

weak point *(shortcoming)*
ta͞nsho 短所

wealth to͞mi 富, za[?]isan 財産,

wealthy → **rich**   └za͞i 財

wear *(on body)* kima͞su (kiru,
kite) 着ます(着る, 着て),
(a pin, ornament, etc.)
tsukema͞su (tsuke͞ru, tsuke͞te)
付けます(付ける, 付けて),
(necktie, belt) shimema͞su
(shime͞ru, shi͞mete) 締めます
(締める, 締めて); *(on legs or
feet)* hakima͞su (haku, haite)
はきます(はく, はいて); *(on
head)* kaburima͞su (kabu͞ru,
kabu͞tte) かぶります(かぶる,
かぶって); *(on hands, fingers)*
hamema͞su (hameru, hamete)
はめます(はめる, はめて);
(in general) shima͞su (suru,
shite) します(する, して)

wear [HONORIFIC] o-meshi ni
narima͞su (na͞ru, na͞tte) お召
しになります(なる, なって)

wear it there/here ki̱te (haite, kabu̱tte, ...) ikima̱su/kima̱su (iku/ku̱ru, itte/ki̱te⌐) 着て(はいて, かぶって, ...)行きます/来ます(行く/来る, 行って/来て)

weary 1. → **tired 2. wearies (of ...)** (... ni) akima̱su (aki̱ru, a̱kite) (...に)飽きます(飽きる, 飽きて)

weather te̱nki (o-te̱nki) 天気(お天気); hiyori 日和

weather forecast tenki-yo̱hō 天気予報

weather observatory/station sokkō-jo⌐ 測候所

weave orima̱su (o̱ru, o̱tte) 織ります(織る, 織って)

Weaver Star: the Festival of the ~ Tanabata 七夕 **(7 July)**

web → **cobweb, spiderweb**

wedding kekkon 結婚, *(ceremony)* kekko̱n-shiki 結婚式

Wednesday Suiyo̱bi 水曜日

weed ku̱sa̱ 草, zassō 雑草

week shūkan 週間; shū̱ 週, ...⌐-shū ...週; **how many weeks** nan-shū̱kan 何週間

week after next saraishū 再来週

week before last sense̱n-shū 先々週

weekend shūmatsu 週末

weep nakima̱su (naku, naite) 泣きます(泣く, 泣いて); *(laments)* nagekima̱su (nage̱ku, nage̱ite) 嘆きます(嘆く, 嘆いて)

weigh 1. it weighs ... (...) no mekata ga ... arima̱su (a̱ru, a̱tte) (...の)目方が...あります(ある, あって); **How much does it (do you) weigh? (...)** no mekata ga dono-gurai arima̱su ka (...の)目方がどの位ありますか **2. weighs it (... no)** mekata o hakarima̱su (haka̱ru, haka̱tte) (...の)目方を量り[測り]ます(量[測]る, 量[測]って)

weight mekata 目方, omosa 重さ, jūryo̱ 重量; *(of body)* taijū 体重; *(object)* omoshi 重し

weight-lifting jūryō-age 重量挙げ; **weight-lifter** jūryōage-se̱nshu 重量挙げ選手

weight/weighing scales hakari⌐ はかり・秤

weird ayashi⌐i 怪しい, fushigi (na) 不思議(な), sugo̱i すごい・凄い; *(feeling)* kimi̱ ga waru̱i 気味が悪い

welcome 1. *(a welcome)* mukae 迎え **2.** *(it is welcome)* nozomashi⌐i 望ましい, arigata̱i ありがたい・有り難い **3.** *(welcomes one)* ... o mukaema̱su (mukaeru, mukaete) ...を迎えます(迎える, 迎えて), ... o de-mukaema̱su (-mukae⌐ru, -muka⌐ete) ...を出迎えます(迎える, 迎えて)

Welcome! Yo̱ku irasshaima˺shita! よくいらっしゃいました!; Yō˺ koso! ようこそ!; Irasshaima˺se! いらっしゃいませ!

welcome: You're welcome! Dō˺ itashima˺shite. どういたしまして.

Welcome back/home! O-kaeri nasa˺i. お帰りなさい.

welfare fuku˺shi 福祉; ~ **policy** fukushi-se˺isaku 福祉政策

well (for water) i˺do 井戸; (good, nicely) yo˺ku よく・良く; (healthy) ge˺nki (na) 元気(な); (splendid) rippa (na/ni) 立派(な/に); **gets well** naorima˺su (nao˺ru, nao˺tte) 治り[直り]ます(治[直]る, 治[直]って)

well: ~ **(come on)** sā˺ さあ; ~ **now/then** (sore) de˺ wa (それ)では, (sore) ja (それ)じゃあ, jā˺ じゃあ, sa˺te さて; ē-to ええと; tokoro˺-de ところで; (= let me think) sō˺ desu ne˺ そうですね; (maybe) mā˺ まあ

well: very ~ (satisfactory) yoroshii よろしい・宜しい

well-behaved otonashi˺i おとなしい

well-liked: is ~ motema˺su (mote˺ru, mo˺tete) もてます(もてる, もてて)

well versed in tsū-ji(tei)ma˺su (tsū-ji(tei)ru, tsū-ji(tei)te) 通じ(てい)ます(通じ(てい)る, 通じ(てい)て)

went → **go**

were → **is**

west nishi 西, sei-... 西...; (the west) seihō 西方, (the western part) se˺ibu 西部, (the Occident) Se˺iyō 西洋, (Europe and America) Ō˹-Bei 欧米; **Western Japan** Ka˺nsai 関西

westerly (wind) nishi-yori (no kaze) 西寄り(の風)

western paper yōshi 洋紙

western-style (Occidental) Seiyō-fū 西洋風, yō-fū 洋風; yō-... 洋...; ~ **building** yōkan 洋館; ~ **room** yō-ma 洋間; ~ clothes yō-fuku˺ 洋服

wet 1. nureta ... ぬれた・濡れた (moist) shimetta 湿った, shimeppo˹i 湿っぽい **2. it gets wet** nurema˺su (nureru, nurete) 濡れます(濡れる, 濡れて) **3. makes it wet** nurashima˺su (nurasu, nurashite) 濡らします(濡らす, 濡らして), (dampens it) shimeshima˺su (shimesu, shimeshite) 湿します(湿す, 湿して)

whale kujira くじら・鯨

wharf hato-ba 波止場

what? na˺ni 何・なに [na˺n 何 before t, d, n]; na˺n no ... 何の..., na˺ni-... 何... [before any sound]; (which) do˺no ... どの...; (in what way) dō˺ どう

what ... (one/fact that) ...(no)

monoˉ/kotoˉ ...(の)物/事, ...ˉno
...の

what color nani-iro 何色, doˉnna
iroˉ どんな色

what day *(of the week)* nan-yoˉbi
何曜日; *(of the month)* naˉn-
nichi 何日

whatever naˉn deˉn mo 何でも;
naˉni (ga/o) ...-teˉ mo 何(が/
を)...ても

what kind of dono yoˉ na どのよ
う[様]な, doˉ yū どうゆう,
doˉnna どんな

what language nani-go 何語

what month naˉn-gatsu 何月

what nationality naniˉ-jin 何人

what part *(= where)* doˉko どこ;
~ **of Kyoto** Kyoˉto no doˉko
京都のどこ

what place doˉko どこ, doˉno
tokoroˉ どの所; doˉchira どち
ら, doˉtchi どっち

what's-his/her-name daˉredare
だれだれ・誰々, daˉresore だれ
それ・誰それ

what's-it(s-name) naˉninani 何々

what sort of → **what kind of**

what time naˉn-ji 何時

what university nani-daˉigaku 何
大学   「し

what with (the fact that) ... shi ...

what year naˉn-nen 何年

wheat komuˉgi 小麦; muˉgi 麦

wheedle tarashi-komimaˉsu
(tarashi-koˉn mu, tarashi-
koˉn nde) たらし込みます(た

らし込む, たらし込んで)

wheel waˉ 輪, sharin 車輪; *(steer-*
ing wheel) handoru ハンドル

when? iˉtsu いつ; **about** ~ itsu-
goro いつ頃

when ... *(the time that ...)* ...
(no) toˉkiˉ ...(の)時; *(where-*
upon) ... (suru) to ...(する)
と, (shi)-taˉra ...(し)たら,
... (shi)-ta toˉkiˉ ...(し)た時;
(and then) (shi)-te (し)て,
(shi)-teˉ kara (し)てから,
(shi)-te sore kara (し)てそれ
から; *(on the occasion of)*
... ni saˉi-shite ...に際して

where? doˉko どこ; [DEFEREN-
TIAL] doˉchira どちら

where ... *(the place that ...)* ...
(no) tokoroˉ ...(の)所; *(and*
there) ...-te soko (de/ni) ...て
そこ(で/に)

whereabouts shozai 所在

whereupon 1. → **when** ... **2.** ...
tokoroˉ ga ...ところが

whether ... ka doˉ ka ...かどうか

which ... **1.** *(of two)* doˉchira/
doˉtchi no ... どちら/どっち
の... *(or* ... no doˉchira/doˉtchi
...のどちら/どっち*); (of more*
than two) doˉno ... どの... *(or*
... no doˉre ...のどれ*) 2. (=*
that ...) — *not translated*
3. *(= and that)* (shi)-te sore
(ga/o) (し)てそれ(が/を)

which damn (one) doˉitsu どいつ

which (one) *(of two)* doˉchira/

do˥tchi どちら/どっち; *(of more than two)* do˥re どれ
while ... (no) aida ...(の)間; ... (shi)-nagara ...(し)ながら
while: (for) a while shiba˥raku しばらく; **a little while ago** saki̥-hodo 先程, sa˥kki さっき
whip mu˥chi (de uchima˥su̥; u˥tsu, u˥tte) むち[鞭](で打ちます; 打つ, 打って)
whipping cream nama-kuri˥imu 生クリーム
whirlpool uzu˥-maki 渦巻き·うずまき, u˥zu 渦
whirlwind sempū[˥] 旋風, tsumuji˥-kaze˥ つむじ風
whisky ui˥su̥˥ki˥i ウイスキー, wi˥su̥kii ウィスキー; ~ **and water** mizuwari 水割り
whisper *(a whisper)* kogoe 小声, sasayaki[˥] ささやき·囁き; *(whispers it)* sasayakima˥su̥ (sasaya[˥]ku, sasaya[˥]ite) ささやき[囁き]ます(ささやく, ささやいて), mimiu[˥]chi̥[˥] shima˥su̥ (suru, shi̥te) 耳打ちします(する, して)
whistle fue 笛; *(with lips)* ku̥chi-bu[˥]e (o fu̥kima˥su̥; fu̥ku˥, fu˥ite) 口笛(を吹きます, 吹く, 吹いて); *(steam)* ki̥teki 汽笛
white shiro˥i 白い; shi˥ro (no) 白(の); howa˥ito (no) ホワイト(の); **snow** ~ masshi˥ro (na) 真っ白(な); **the** ~ **of an egg** shi˥ro˥mi 白身
whitebait shi[˥]rasu しらす·白子
who? da˥re 誰; [DEFERENTIAL] do˥nata どなた, do˥chira (sama) どちら(様)
who ... 1. *(= that ...) – not translated* **2.** *(= and he/she/they)* ... (shi̥)-te sono˥-hi̥to ga ...(し)てその人が
whole zentai (no) 全体(の); ze˥n(-)... 全...; **the whole thing** *(= all of it)* ze˥mbu 全部
whole: one's ~ life isshō 一生
wholesale o˥roshi˥ (de) 卸し(で); **(selling ~)** oroshi[˥]-uri 卸し売り
wholly zentai ni 全体に
whore jōro˥ 女郎, jorō˥ 女郎; → **prostitute**
whorehouse jorō-ya 女郎屋, baishu˥n-yado 売春宿
whose? da˥re no 誰の
whose ... 1. *(= and his/her/their)* ... (shi̥)-te sono˥-hi̥to no ...(し)てその人の **2.** *(not translated)*
why? dō˥ shi̥te どうして, na˥ze なぜ, dō˥ どう; **that's why** da˥ kara (sa˥) だから(さ)
wicker trunk kō˥ri/ko˥ri 行李/行李
wicket ki˥do 木戸; **(ticket)** kaisatsu-guchi 改札口; *(window)* mado˥-guchi 窓口, ... -guchi ...口
wide (haba ga) hiro˥i (幅が)広い
widow mibō˥-jin 未亡人, yamome やもめ
widower otoko-ya˥mome 男やもめ

width hi̲'rosa 広さ, haba 幅;
yoko 横

wife *(your/his)* o̲'ku-san/-sama
奥さん/様; *(my)* ka̲'nai 家内,
sa̲'i 妻; wa̲'ifu ワイフ, tsu̲'ma
妻, nyo̲'bo/nyo̲'bō にょうぼ/
女房

wig katsura かつら・鬘

wild *(disorderly)* rambō (na) 乱
暴(な); *(rough)* arai 荒い;
(roughneck) abare-mono 暴れ
者; *(not cultivated)* yama̲' no
山の, yasei no 野性の

wild: gets wild arema̲'su (areru,
arete) 荒れます(荒れる, 荒れ
て)

wild duck ka̲'mo かも・鴨 ⌐て)

wild goose ga̲'n がん・雁

wild person abare-mono 暴れ者

will *(intention)* i̲'shi 意志, omo̲'i
思い; *(testament)* yuigon 遺言

will be ... ... de̲'su (da̲'/no̲'/na̲',
de̲', ni̲') ...です(だ/の/な, で,
に)

will do shima̲'su (suru, shi̲te) し
ます(する, して)

willow yanagi 柳; **budding ~**
aoyagi 青柳 = ao-ya̲'nagi 青柳

win *(game/war)* ... ni
kachima̲'su (ka̲'tsu, ka̲'tte) ...
に勝ちます(勝つ, 勝って);
(prize) jushō shima̲'su (suru,
shi̲te) 受賞します(する, して),
... o torima̲'su (to̲'ru, to̲'tte) ...
を取ります(取る, 取って);
→ **victory**

wind *(breeze)* kaze 風

Windbreaker (jacket) ja̲'mpā
ジャンパー

wind-chimes fūrin 風鈴

wind it (around/up) makima̲'su
(maku, maite) 巻きます(巻く,
巻いて); *(reel)* kurima̲'su
(ku̲'ru, ku̲'tte̲') 繰ります(繰る,
繰って)

window ma̲'do 窓; *(opening,
wicket)* mado̲'-guchi 窓口;
transom ~ ramma 欄間

windowpane mado-ga̲'rasu 窓ガ
ラス

window screen bōchū-ami 防虫
網, mushiyoke⌐-ami 虫よけ
網 ⌐パー

windshield wiper wa̲'ipā ワイ

wind up *(= concludes it)*
musubima̲'su (musubu,
musunde) 結びます(結ぶ, 結
んで); *(ends up doing)* (shi̲)-te
shimaima̲'su (shimau,
shimatte) (し)てしまいます
(しまう, しまって)

windy kaze ga tsuyo̲'i 風が強い

wine 1. wa̲'in ワイン, budō̲'-shu
ぶどう[葡萄]酒 **2.** → **rice
wine, saké**

wine cup *(= saké cup)*
sakazuki⌐ (o-sakazuki) 杯(お
杯), cho̲'ko ちょこ, o-cho̲'ko
おちょこ

wing *(of bird or plane)* tsu⌐'basa
翼; *(of insect)* hane 羽・羽根・
翅; *(of door/gate)* tobira 扉

wink ma-ba̲'taki まばたき,

uīnku/wīnku (shima(ⁿ)sụ;
suru, shite) ウインク/ウイン
ク(します; する, して)

winner *(victor)* shōrī-sha 勝利者,
yūshō̄-sha 優勝者; *(awardee)*
jushō̄-sha 受賞者

winter fuyū 冬; ~ **solstice** tōji
冬至

wipe fukimāsụ (fuku, fuite) 拭
きます(拭く, 拭いて); ~
away nuguimāsụ (nugūu,
nugūtte) 拭います(拭う, 拭
って)

wire harigane 針金; *(electric)*
densen 電線, *(telephone line)*
denwa-sen 電話線; →
telegram

wisdom chiē 知恵

wise kashikōi 賢い, kemmei (na)
賢明(な)

**wish: ~ (please send) my best
wishes to** ... .. ni (dō̄zo)
yoroshiku ...に(どうぞ)よろ
しく[宜しく]

wish for ... ga hoshīi desụ
(hoshīi, hōshikute) ...が欲し
いです(欲しい, 欲しくて)

wish that ... : ~ **(it does)** (shi)-
tāra īi desụ (ga) (し)たら良
いです(が); ~ **(it had done)**
(shi)-tāra yōkatta desụ (ga)
(し)たら良かったです(が) *or*
yōkatta no ni 良かったのに

wish to do (shi)-tāi desụ (shị-tai,
shị-tākute) (し)たいです(し
たい, したくて)

wish to have it done (shi)-te
morai-tāi desụ (し)てもらい
たいです

wisteria fuji ふじ・藤

wit yū̄moa ユーモア

with ... **to** ...と, ... **to issho ni** ...
と一緒に; *(by using)* ... **de** ...
で; *(with ... attached/includ-
ed)* ... **ga tsūita** ...が付いた,
...-tsuki (no) ...付き(の); **with
its being** ... **de** ...で

with: ~ bath basu-tsuki (no) バ
ス付き(の)

  ~ **difficulty** yatto やっと

  ~ **forethought** takurānde た
くらん[企ん]で

  ~ **great delight** ō-yōrokobi
de 大喜びで

  ~ **meals (included)** shoku(ji)-
tsuki (no) 食(事)付き(の);

  ~ **much devotion/effort (but)**
sekkakū せっかく

  ~ **a shudder/shiver** zotto
ぞっと

withdraw 1. *(leaves)* hịki-
agemāsụ (-agēru, -āgete) 引
き上げます(上げる, 上げて),
hịki-torimāsụ (-tōru, -tōtte)
引き取ります(取る, 取って)
2. *(takes out money)* yokin o
oroshimāsụ (orōsu, orōshite)
預金を下ろします(下ろす,
下ろして)

wither karemāsụ (kareru,
karete) 枯れます(枯れる, 枯
れて), naemāsụ (naēru,

naｴete) 萎え[なえ]ます(萎え
る, 萎えて)
within (...) iｷnai (...)以内; ...ｴ
-nai ...内; ... no naｴka (de/ni/
no) ...の中(で/に/の)
within the city shiｷnai 市内
within the metropolis (of Tokyo)
toｷnai 都内
within the office/company
shaｷnai (no) 社内(の)
without *(excluding)* ... no hoka
ni ...のほか[他・外]に; *(not
having)* ... ga naｴi to ...がない
と, ... ga naｴku(te) ...がなく
(て), ... naｴshi ni ...なしに;
(omitting) ...-nuki (de/no) ...
抜き(で/の)
without exception *(= all)* reigai
naｴku 例外なく, iｷssaｷi いっさ
い・一切
without fail zeｴ-hi 是非・ぜひ
without interruption taema-
naｴku 絶え間なく, taｴezu 絶え
ず
without notice/permission
muｷdan de 無断で
with respect to ... ni kaｴkete wa ...
にかけては; ... ni kaｴn-shite ...
に関して
witness *(in court)* shōnin 証人
wolf oｴkami おおかみ・狼
woman onnaｴ 女, onna(ｷ) no
hitoｴ/kataｴ 女の人/方; josei 女
性, joｴshi 女子; *(lady)* fujin 婦
人; okaｴmi おかみ・内儀 「し
womanizer onna-taｴrashi 女たら

women's bath onna-yu 女湯
women's language (terms) josei-
go 女性語
womenswear onna-mono 女物
wonder 1. I wonder ... ka shira ...
かしら, ... ka ne ...かね **2. it
is no wonder that** ... ... no mo
muｷri wa arimaseｷn (naｴi) ...の
も無理はありません(ない)
wonderful subarashiｷi すばらし
い, suｷteki (na) すてき・素敵
(な), sugoｴi すごい・凄い;
(delightful) ureshiｷi うれしい・
嬉しい; *(wondrous)* fushigi
(na) 不思議(な), myoｴ (na) 妙
(な)
won't do shimaseｷn (shinai,
shinaｴide) しません(しない,
しないで); **it ~ ikemaseｷn**
(ikenai, ikenaｴide) いけません
(いけない, いけないで),
dameｴ desu (da/na, de, ni) だ
めです(だ/な, で, に)
wood kiｷ 木, mokuｷzai 木材,
(lumber) zaimoku 材木; →
firewood
woodblock print mokuhan-ga 木
版画, hanga 版画
wooden bucket oｴke 桶
wooden shoes getaｴ げた・下駄
wooden stairs hashigo-dan はし
ご[梯子]段
woods *(forest)* mori 森
woof *(horizontal threads)* yoko-
ito 横糸
wool uｴru ウール, ke 毛, keito 毛

糸, yōmō 羊毛

woolen goods, woolens ke-o⌐ri⌐mono 毛織物

word 1. kotoba⌐ 言葉, tango 単語; ...-go ...語; *(one's words/speech)* ku̇chi 口; *(written characters)* ji⌐ 字; *(compound word)* jukugo 熟語 **2.** *(news)* ta⌐yori 便り, shōsoku 消息

word processor wā-puro ワープロ

wore → **wear**

work 1. hataraki 働き; *(job)* shigoto (o-shi⌐goto) 仕事(お仕事); *(operations)* sa⌐gyō 作業 **2.** *a work (of literature or art)* saku̇hin 作品 **3.** *(does work)* shigoto o shima⌐su (suru, shi̇te) 仕事をします(する, して); *(labors)* hatarakima⌐su (hataraku, hataraite) 働きます (働く, 働いて); ki⌐mmu shima(⌐)su (suru, shi̇te) 勤務します(する, して); *(is employed at/by)* ... ni tsu̇to⌐mete ima⌐su (iru, ite) ...に勤めています(いる, いて); *(hires oneself out for pay)* kasegima⌐su (kase⌐gu, kase⌐ide) 稼ぎます(稼ぐ, 稼いで) **4.** → **study**

work: construction ~ kō⌐ji 工事; **work in progress** kōji-chū 工事中

work: it works *(is effective)* kikima⌐su (ki̇ku, kiite) 効きます(効く, 効いて)

work = workmanship saiku⌐ 細工

work as (a ...) *(... o)* tsu̇tomema⌐su (tsu̇tome⌐ru, tsu̇to⌐mete) *(...を)* 務めます(務める, 務めて)

worker *(laborer)* rōdō⌐-sha 労働者, kōin 工員, shokkō 職工; *(person on duty)* kimmu⌐-sha 勤務者

working hataraki 働き; *(= duty, job)* tsu̇tome⌐ (o-tsu̇tome) 勤め(お勤め); *(= operating)* unten 運転, sa⌐gyō 作業; ~ **hours** sagyō-ji⌐kan 作業時間, kimmu-ji⌐kan 勤務時間

workman *(a day laborer)* kō⌐fu 工夫, ni⌐mpu 人夫, ni⌐nsoku 人足; *(factory)* kōin 工員, shokkō 職工

workpants *(tight-fitting)* momohiki 股引き・ももひき

world se⌐ka⌐i 世界; *(at large)* yo⌐ 世, *(people)* se⌐ken 世間; ~ **war** sekai-ta⌐isen 世界大戦

worldwide sekai-teki (na) 世界的(な), sekai-jū 世界中

worm mushi 虫; ~ **remedy** mushi-ku⌐dashi 虫下し

worry 1. shimpai 心配, ki-zu⌐ka⌐i 気遣い, wazurai 煩い・わずらい **2.** **worries (about ...)** *(... o)* shimpai shima⌐su (suru, shi̇te) *(...を)* 心配します(する, して), wazuraima⌐su

(wazurau, wazuratte) 煩い[わ
ずらい]ます(煩う, 煩って);
ki-zukaima'su (-zuka'u,
-zuka'tte) 気遣います(遣う,
遣って); kokoro' o
itamema'su (itame'ru,
ita'mete) 心を痛めます(痛め
る, 痛めて)

Don't worry about it. Go-
shimpai na'ku. ご心配なく.

worse mo'tto waru'i もっと悪い;
otorima'su (oto⌐ru, oto⌐tte)
劣ります(劣る, 劣って); **is
no ~ off even if ...** ...-te' mo
motomoto de'su ...てももとも
と[元々]です

worsen *(illness gets worse)*
kojirema'su (kojire'ru,
koji'rete) こじれます(こじれ
る, こじれて)

worship ogamima'su (oga'mu,
oga'nde) 拝みます(拝みます,
拝んで)

worst ichiban waru'i 一番悪い;
saiaku (no) 最悪の; *(lowest)*
saitei (no) 最低の

worth → value

worthless ya'kuza (na) やくざ
(な), tsumara'nai つまらない

would → perhaps

would like → want, wish

wound 1. *(injury)* kizu 傷, kega'
けが・怪我 2. *(gets wounded)*
kizu-tsukima'su (-tsu'ku',
-tsu'ite) 傷付きます(付く,
付いて), yararema'su

(yarareru, yararete) やられま
す(やられる, やられて); *(in-
jures)* kizu-tsukema'su
(-tsuke'ru, -tsu'ke'te) 傷付けま
す(付ける, 付けて)

wound it: → **wind it**

wrap tsutsumima'su (tsutsu'mu,
tsutsu'nde) 包みます(包む,
包んで), hōsō shima'su (suru,
shite) 包装します(する, して);
(something around it)
makima'su (maku, maite) 巻
きます(巻く, 巻いて)

wrapper (traditional cloth)
furoshiki ふろしき・風呂敷

wreath hanawa 花輪; **~ shell**
sa'zae さざえ・栄螺

wreck 1. *(accident)* ji'ko 事故,
(collision) shōtotsu 衝突; *(shipwreck)* nampa 難破, sōnan 遭
難; *(train wreck)* ressha-ji'ko
列車事故, sōnan 遭難; *(the
wreckage)* zangai 残骸
2. *(ruins it)* kowashima'su
(kowa'su, kowa'shite) 壊しま
す(壊す, 壊して); **wrecks a
car** kuruma o kowashima'su
車を壊します

wrecker *(tow truck)* re'kkā レッ
カー, rekkā'-sha レッカー車

wrench re'nchi レンチ, supa'na
スパナ

wrestler: sumo ~ sumō'-to'ri 相
撲取り, o-sumō-san お相撲さ
ん; *(ranking)* seki-to'ri 関取;
(champion) ō'-zeki 大関;

(grand champion) yokozuna 横綱

wrestler's belt (loincloth) mawashi まわし・回し

wrestling re̅suringu レスリング; *(professional)* puro-resu プロレス; *(Japanese)* sumō 相撲・すもう

wrestling ring *(sumo)* dohyō 土俵

wrestling tournament basho 場所; **grand ~** ō-zu̅mō 大相撲

wretch ya̅tsu やつ・奴

wretched nasake-na̅i 情けない

wring (out) shiborima̅su (shibo̅ru, shibo̅tte) 絞ります (絞る, 絞って)

wrinkle shiwa しわ・皺; *(it wrinkles)* shiwa ga dekima̅su (deki̅ru, de̅kite) しわ[皺]ができます(できる, できて)

wrist te̅-kubi 手首, ude̅-kubi 腕首

wristwatch ude-do̅kei 腕時計

write kakima̅su (ka̅ku, ka̅ite) 書きます(書く, 書いて); *(composes)* tsukurima̅su (tsuku̅ru, tsuku̅tte) 作ります(作る, 作って), tsuzurima̅su (tsuzu̅ru, tsuzu̅tte) 綴ります(綴る, 綴って); *(publishes)* arawashima̅su (arawa̅su, arawa̅shite) 著します(著す, 著して)

writer sa̅kka 作家, cho̅sha 著者; *(the author)* hi̅ssha 筆者, hissha 筆者

writing *(written characters)* mo̅ji 文字, ji̅ 字; **~ a composition/theme** sakubun 作文

writing brush fude 筆

writing paper binsen 便せん・便箋

written explanation setsume̅i-sho̅ 説明書

wrong *(mistaken)* machiga̅tta 間違った, *(is in error)* machigaema̅su (machiga̅u, machiga̅tte) 間違えます(間違う, 間違って); *(different)* chigatta 違った; *(wrongful)* waru̅i 悪い; *(amiss)* (… no) guai ga waru̅i (...の)具合が悪い; **something ~** ijō 異常, *(malfunction)* koshō 故障

wry shibu̅i 渋い, niga̅i 苦い; **~ face** shibu̅i/niga̅i kao 渋い/苦い顔

— **X** —

X *(symbol "wrong")* ba̅tsu ばつ・バツ, batte̅n ばってん・罰点

X-ray ekkusu-sen エックス線, rento̅gen レントゲン = rentogen-sen レントゲン線

— Y —

yam imoˉ (o-imo) 芋(お芋)

yard niwa 庭

yard goods gofukuˉ-mono 呉服
物

yarn (ke-)ito (毛)糸

yawn akubi o shimaˉsu (suru,
shite) あくび[欠伸]をします
(する, して)

yeah un うん ＝ んん

year toshiˉ 年; neˉn 年, ...-nen ...
年; **years old** ...-sai ...歳 *or*
NUMBER: **1-10** hitoˉtsu 一つ・ひ
とつ—toˉ 十・とお, **11-19** jū-
ichiˉ 十一・11—jūˉ-ku 十九・
19, **20** haˉtachi 二十・二十歳・
20歳, **21-29** niˉ-jū ichiˉ 二十一
・21—kuˉ 九・9 , **30** saˉn-jū 三
十・30, **44** yoˉn-jū yoˉn 四十四
・44; **how many years old**
iˉkutsu (o-ikutsu) いくつ(お
いくつ)・幾つ(お幾つ), naˉn-
sai 何歳

year after next sarainen 再来年

year before last otoˉtoshi おとと
し・一昨年, issakuˉ-nen 一昨年

year-end kure (no) 暮れ(の),
nemmatsu (no) 年末(の); ～
party bōneˉn-kai 忘年会; ～
gift (o-)seibo (お)歳暮

year period neˉndo 年度

yell wamekimaˉsu (wameˉku,
wameˉite) わめき[喚き]ます

(わめく, わめいて); → **shout**

yellow kiiroi 黄色い; kiiro (no)
黄色(の)

yellowtail (*fish*) buˉri ぶり・鰤,
(*baby*) inada いなだ, (*young*)
hamachi はまち

yen eˉn 円, ...-en ...円

yes haˉi はい, eˉ ええ; sōˉ desu そ
うです; (*or just say the verb*)
**Yes, I see./Yes, I will (comp-
ly).** Wakarimaˉshita. わかりま
した.
Yes, sir/ma[d]am. Shōchi
shimaˉshita. 承知しました.
**I can't be saying yes all the
time.** Sōˉ-sō iˉi kao mo
dekimaseˉn (dekiˉnai). そうそ
ういい顔もできません(でき
ない).

yesterday kinōˉ きのう・昨日

yet maˉda まだ; **and yet** sore deˉ
mo それでも, shikaˉ-mo しか
も; → **but**

yew nirc にれ・楡

yield 1. (*product; income*) agari
上がり **2.** (*gives in/up*)
yuzurimaˉsu (yuzuru, yuzutte)
譲ります(譲る, 譲って)

Yokohama Yokohama 横浜; **the
port of ～** Yokohamaˉ-kō 横
浜港

yolk (of egg) kimi 黄身

yonder achira あちら, atchi あっち

you anata あなた, anta あんた *(but use* NAME, TITLE, *or* ROLE *whenever possible)*; sochira (sama) そちら(様); o-taku お宅 = o-taku sama お宅様; *(intimate)* kimi 君; *(condescending)* omae お前・おまえ

you all mina-san 皆さん・みなさん, anata-tachi あなた達[たち], anata-gata あなた方

young 1. waka i 若い, **(very ~)** osana i 幼い; ~ **boy** shōnen 少年, ~ **girl** shōjo 少女; ~ **novelist** wakate-sakka 若手作家 **2. the young →** youth

younger toshi-shita (no) 年下(の); ~ **brother** otōto 弟, *(your)* otōto-san 弟さん; ~ **sister** imōto 妹, *(your)* (o-)imōto-san (お)妹さん

youngest ichiban waka i 一番若い, (toshi-)shita (no)

(年)下(の)

young lady ojō-san お嬢さん; musume 娘

young man seinen 青年

young person → youth

youngster 1. *(= young boy)* shōnen 少年 **2.** *(= young girl)* shōjo 少女

young writer wakate-sakka 若手作家

your(s) anata no あなたの; (NAME, TITLE, ROLE) no の; o-... お・御..., go-... ご・御...

You're welcome Dō itashimashite! どういたしまして!

yourself (go-)jibun (ご)自分; anata あなた *(or* NAME, TITLE, ROLE) jishin 自身

youth *(young person)* wakamono 若者, seinen 青年, jakunem-mono 若年者; *(when young)* waka i toki(ー) 若い時, seine n-ki 青年期

youth hostel yūsu-hosuteru ユースホステル

You've got me Shimatta! しまった!

— Z —

zebra shima uma/shima mma しまうま・縞馬

zero re i 零, ze ro ゼロ; *(written symbol)* maru 丸

zip [ZIP] code yūbim-bango 郵便番号

zipper cha kku チャック, ji ppā ジッパー

zone chita i 地帯, ku iki 区域, ta i 帯, ...-tai ...帯

zoo dōbutsu -en 動物園

zoology dōbutsu -gaku 動物学

PART II
Japanese–English

— A —

ā ああ like that, that way

a¹ ああ oh; yes; [+ NAME and/or TITLE] hello *(on encounter)*

abarema¹su 暴れます, **abareru** 暴れる rages, storms, rampages

abare-mono 暴れ者 ruffian, roughneck, wild person

abe¹kku アベック a couple (on a date)

abekobe あべこべ upside down

abima¹su 浴びます, **abiru** 浴びる bathes oneself in; douses

abuku¹ あぶく・泡 bubble; **abuku¹-ze¹ni** あぶく[泡]銭 easy money

abunai 危ない dangerous

abura あぶら・油・脂 oil, fat, grease 「bean curd

abur(a)a¹ge 油揚げ deep-fried

aburakko¹i 油っこい・脂っ濃い greasy, fatty

aburima¹su あぶり[炙り]ます, **abu¹ru** あぶる・炙る grills

abu¹tte あぶって・炙って → **aburima¹su** あぶります・炙ります 「there

achi¹-ko¹chi あちこち here and

achira あちら **1.** that one (of two) over there, the other one (over there) **2.** over there,

yonder **3.** he/him, she/her, they/them

achira-gawa あちら側 that (his/her/their) side

a¹e 会え → **aema¹su** 会えます [infinitive]; → **aima¹su** 会います [imperative] meet them!

a¹eba 会えば → **aima¹su** 会います (if one meet)

aegima¹su あえぎ[喘ぎ]ます, **ae¹gu** あえぐ・喘ぐ gasps, pants (for breath)

ae¹ide あえいで・喘いで → **aegima¹su** あえぎます・喘ぎます

aema¹su, ae¹ru 1. 和えます, 和える dresses (vegetables, fish) **2.** 会えます, 会える can meet

ae¹-mono 和え物 boiled or salt-rubbed fish and vegetables mixed with a dressing

ae¹nai 和えない・会えない = **aemase¹n** 和えません; 会えません (not dress … ; cannot meet)

ae¹na¹i あえない・敢えない tragic, sad; **ae¹naku mo** あえなくも・敢えなくも tragically enough

ae¹reba 和えれば・会えれば, **ae¹rya** 和えりゃ・会えりゃ →

aema͞su 和えます; 会えます
(if one dress …; if one can
meet)

a͞ete 1. 和えて・会えて →
aema͞su 和えます・会えます
2. あえて・敢えて ～ …
(shima͞su) あえて[敢えて]…
（します）dares (to do)

afurema͞su あふれ[溢れ]ます,
afure͞ru あふれ[溢れ]る
overflows

Afurika アフリカ Africa

afutā-sā͞bisu アフターサービス
service *(maintenance and
repair)*, servicing

agari 上がり **1.** a cup of green tea
(in a sushi bar) **2.** rise **3.** yield,
product; income **4.** finishing,
(resulting) finish **5.** → **agari-
ma͞su** 上がります [infinitive]

…-a͞gari (no) …上がり（の）
fresh from …, right after … ;
byōki-a͞gari no hi͞to 病気上が
りの人 a person just out of
sickbed; **ame-a͞gari no michi**
雨上がりの道 the road right
after the rain

agarima͞su 上がります・あがり
ます, **agaru** 上がる・あがる
1. goes up, rises **2.** feels self-
conscious, nervous; gets stage
fright

agatte 上がって・あがって →
agarima͞su 上がります・あが
ります

age 上げ・揚げ → **agema͞su** 上

げます・揚げます **1.** [infini-
tive] **2.** [imperative] **age ro**
上げろ・揚げろ, **age͞ yo** 上げ
よ・揚げよ

agema͞su, ageru 1. 上げます, 上
げる raises up; gives **2.** 揚げま
す, 揚げる fries

age-nabe 揚げ鍋 frying pan

age(ra)rema͞su, age(ra)reru 1. 上
げ(ら)れます, 上げ(ら)れる
can raise/give **2.** 揚げ(ら)れ
ます, 揚げ(ら)れる can fry

agere͞ba 上げれば・揚げれば,
agerya 上げりゃ・揚げりゃ →
agema͞su 上げます/揚げます
(if one raise/give/fry)

age͞ ya shinai 上げやしない・揚
げやしない = **age͞ wa shinai**
上げはしない・揚げはしない
= **agenai** 上げない/揚げない
(not raise/give/fry)

age͞ yo 上げよ・揚げよ →
agema͞su 上げます・揚げます
[imperative]

ageyō͞ 上げよう = **agemashō͞** 上
げましょう (let's give it!)

ago͞ あご・顎 jaw, chin

ago͞-hige あごひげ・顎ひげ
beard, (chin-)whiskers

a͞hen アヘン・阿片 opium

ahiru あひる・家鴨 duck *(tame)*

a͞i 1. 愛 love **2.** あい = **a͞yu** あ
ゆ・鮎 **3.** 会い・合い →
aima͞su 会い[合い]ます

aida 間 interval, space; between;
⌐while

aide͞a アイデア idea

aijō 愛情 affection

ai-kagi 合鍵 duplicate key

aikawarazu あいかわらず・相変わらず as usual/ever/always; ～ **ge゛nki desu** 相変わらず元気です I stay well (as always)

aiki゛-dō 合気道 aikido, an art of weaponless defense

aikō-ka 愛好家 lover (devotee of …)

aikyō゛ あいきょう・愛敬・愛矯 charm, attractiveness; ～ **ga arima゛su** あいきょう[愛敬, 愛矯]があります is nice, attractive, charming

aimai (na) あいまい・曖昧(な) vague

aima゛su, a゛u: … ni ～ 1. 会います, 会う:…に会います meets; sees (a person) **2.** 合います, 合う:…に合います matches with; **kuchi ni ～** 口に合います suits one's taste; **(… ni) ma ni ～** (…に)間に合います is in time (for …)

…-aima゛su …合います, **-au/-a゛u** 合う/合う [verb infinitive +] (to) each other

ainiku あいにく unfortunately; ～ **(na)** あいにく(な) regrettable

airon アイロン iron(ing)

Airura゛ndo アイルランド Ireland

ai-sa゛nai 愛さない = **ai-shimase゛n** 愛しません (not love)

a゛isatsu (go-a゛isatsu) あいさつ・挨拶(ごあいさつ・御挨拶) greeting; **(…) ni a゛isatsu shima(゛)su** (…)にあいさつ[挨拶]します greets

ai-shima゛su 愛します, **-su゛ru** 愛する loves

a゛i-shite 愛して → **ai-shima゛su** 愛します

aiso゛ あいそ・愛想, **aisō゛** あいそう・愛想 = **o-aiso** おあいそ, **o-aisō** お愛想 (restaurant) bill, check ⌐sociable

aiso゛ ga i゛i あいそ[愛想]がいい

aisu-kuri゛imu アイスクリーム ice cream

aite 開いて (→ **akima゛su** 開きます) coming open; ～ **ima゛su** 開いています is open, 空いています vacant, empty

aite゛ (o-aite) 相手(お相手) the other fellow; companion, partner; adversary, opponent

aitsu あいつ that damn one; **aitsu゛-ra** あいつら those damn ones

a゛izu 合図 signal, sign

aji 味 taste; flavor, seasoning; ～ **ga shima゛su** 味がします(する, して) it tastes (has flavor); ～ **ga usui** 味が薄い bland

a゛ji 1. あじ・鯵 horse mackerel, saurel **2.** アジ agitation

A゛jia アジア Asia; **Ajia゛-jin** アジア人 an Asian

ajike-na̍i 味気ない insipid, flavorless, flat

ajiwaema̍su 味わえます, **ajiwae⌐ru** 味わえる can taste it

ajiwaima̍su 味わいます, **ajiwa⌐u** 味わう tastes it

a̍ka 赤 red (color)

aka̍ あか・垢 dirt, grime

akabō 赤帽 redcap, porter

a̍ka-chan 赤ちゃん・あかちゃん baby

aka-de̍nwa 赤電話 red (= pay) phone

aka̍-gai 赤貝 ark shell, blood(y) clam

aka-gane あかがね・銅 copper

akai 赤い red; **akaku narima̍su** 赤くなります gets red, blushes

aka-ji 赤字 red letters, deficit figures; ～ **ni narima̍su** 赤字になります goes/gets in the red

akambo あかんぼ・赤ん坊, **akambō** 赤ん坊 baby

aka-mi 赤身 lean (meat/fish); unfatty (red) tuna

akanai 開かない = **akimase̍n** 開きません (not open)

akaru⌐i 明るい bright, light, clear, gay

akarumi 明るみ a light place; the (open/bright) light

aka-shi̍ngō 赤信号 red light (signal)

ake 開け → **akema̍su** 開けます:

1. [infinitive] **2.** [imperative] **ake ro̍** 開けろ, **ake̍ yo** 開けよ open it!

ake̍ba 開けば → **akima̍su** 開きます (if it come open)

akema̍shite o-medetō (gozaima̍su) 明けましておめでとう(ございます)! Happy New Year!

akema̍su, akeru 1. 開けます, 開ける opens it; 空けます, 空ける leaves empty, vacates **2.** 明けます, 明ける (it/dawn) breaks, it opens up, (the day/year) begins

ake(ra)rema̍su 開け(ら)れます, **ake(ra)reru** 開け(ら)れる can open it

akere̍ba 開ければ, **akerya** 開けりゃ → **akema̍su** 開けます (if one open it)

akete 明けて → **akema̍su** 明けます; **akete̍ mo kurete̍ mo** 明けても暮れても day in and day out

ake̍ ya shinai 開けやしない = **ake̍ wa shinai** 開けはしない = **akenai** 開けない (not open it)

ake̍ yo 開けよ → **akema̍su** 開けます (open it!)

akeyō̍ 開けよう = **akemashō̍** 開けましょう (let's open it!)

aki 開き → **akima̍su** 開きます (comes open)

a̍ki 1. 秋 autumn, fall **2.** 飽き →

akimaꞌsụ 飽きます (wearies of)

aki- 空き empty, vacant: **aki-bako** 空き箱 empty box, **aki-beya** 空き部屋 empty room, **aki-bin** 空き瓶 empty bottle; **akị-chi** 空き地 vacant lot (land); **akị-kan** 空き缶 empty can; **aki-ma** 空き間 vacant/available room(s); **aki-shitsu** 空き室 empty room/office; **aki-ya** 空き家 vacant/empty house

akimaꞋsụ 飽きます, **akiꞋru** 飽きる wearies (gets tired) of; gets enough of

akimaꞋsụ, aku 1. 開きます, 開く it opens, comes open; it comes unbuttoned/unzipped/unlocked 2. 空きます, 空く it gets empty, vacant

akiꞋnai 飽きない = **akimaseꞋn** 飽きません (not weary of)

akiꞋraka 明らか clear (evident); ～ **ni shimaꞋsụ** 明らかにします makes it public, reveals, explains

akirame 諦め resignation, acceptance

akiramemaꞋsụ 諦めます, **akirameꞋru** 諦める: ... o ～ ... を諦めます gives up (on), resigns oneself to

akire あきれ・呆れ → **akiremaꞋsụ** あきれます・呆れます

akiremaꞋsụ あきれます・呆れま

す, **akireru** あきれる・呆れる gets amazed; gets disgusted

akirete あきれて・呆れて → **akiremaꞋsụ** あきれます・呆れます

akịꞋru 飽きる = **akimaꞋsụ** 飽きます (wearies of)

aꞋkịte 飽きて → **akimaꞋsụ** 飽きます (wearies of)

aku 開く = **akimaꞋsụ** 開きます (it opens)

aꞋkụ 悪 an evil; an evil person

akubi あくび・欠伸 yawn(ing); ～ **o shimaꞋsụ** あくび［欠伸］をします yawn(s)

akụfū 悪風 vice

akụhyō 悪評 criticism (unfavorable)

aꞋkụi 悪意 ill will, malice

aku-juꞋnkan 悪循環 vicious circle

aꞋkuma 悪魔 devil, evil spirit

aꞋkụ-made (mo) あくまで(も) to the (very) end; to the utmost

akuratsu (na) 悪らつ・悪辣(な) unscrupulous, foul, nasty, mean

aꞋkụseku あくせく laboriously, (working) hard, drudging (away)

aꞋkụsento アクセント accent

aꞋkụseru アクセル gas pedal; ～ **o fumimaꞋsụ** アクセルを踏みます steps on the gas

aꞋkụseꞋsari(i) アクセサリ（ー） an

accessory

akushịtsu (na) 悪質(な) malignant, pernicious, vicious

a̍kụshu 握手 handshake; ～ **shima⌐sụ** 握手します shakes hands

a⌐kụta 芥・あくた dirt, rubbish

akya 開きゃ 1. = **ake̍ba** 開けば (if it come open) 2. ～ **shinai** 開きゃしない = **aki̍ ya/wa shinai** 開きや/はしない = **akanai** 開かない (not come open)

a̍kya shinai 飽きゃしない = **a̍ki ya/wa shinai** 飽きや/はしない = **aki̍nai** 飽きない (not weary of)

a̍ma 1. 亜麻 linen 2. 尼 nun 3. 海女 woman seadiver, pearl diver

ama⌐chua アマチュア amateur

ama̍do 雨戸 rain shutters

ama-ga̍sa 雨傘 umbrella

ama̍-gutsu 雨靴 overshoes, rainshoes, galoshes

amai 甘い sweet; lenient, permissive

amaku mima̍sụ (mi̍ru) 甘く見ます(見る) kids oneself about ... , underestimates

amari̍ (o-a̍mari) 余り(お余り) remainder, surplus

ama̍ri 余り → **amarima̍sụ** 余ります [infinitive]

amarima̍sụ 余ります, **ama̍ru** 余る is left over, remains, is in ex-

cess, is too much/many

ama̍tte 余って → **amarima̍sụ** 余ります

amayakashima̍sụ 甘やかします, **amayaka⌐su** 甘やかす pampers, babies

ame あめ・飴 candy

a̍me 雨 rain; ～ **ga furima̍sụ** 雨が降ります it rains; ～ **ni narima̍sụ** 雨になります it turns/starts to rain

a̍me 編め 1. → **amema̍sụ** 編めます [infinitive] 2. → **amima̍sụ** 編みます [imperative] knit it!

a̍meba 編めば → **amima̍sụ** 編みます (if one knit it)

amema̍sụ 編めます, **ame̍ru** 編める can knit

Amerika アメリカ America, U.S.(A.); ～**-Gasshū̍koku** アメリカ合衆国 United States of America; **Amerika̍-jin** アメリカ人 an American

ami̍ 網 net

a̍mi 編み → **amima̍sụ** 編みます

ami̍-do 網戸 screen door

amima̍sụ 編みます, **a̍mu** 編む knits, braids

ami̍-mono 編み物 knitting, knitted goods

amma あんま・按摩 masseur, massage

am-man あんまん steamed bun stuffed with bean jam

ammari あんまり too much,

overly; + NEGATIVE not (very) much

amō 編もう = **amimashō** 編みましょう (let's weave it!)

ampa⌐n あんパン sweet roll with bean jam inside

a⌐mpu アンプ amplifier

a⌐mya 編みゃ 1. = **a⌐meba** 編めば (if one knit) 2. ~ **shinai** 編みゃしない = **a⌐mi ya/wa shinai** 編みや/はしない = **ama⌐nai** 編まない (not knit)

a⌐n あん・餡 = **a⌐nko** あんこ・餡子 bean jam/paste

ana⌐ 穴 hole; slot

anago 穴子 conger eel

anaguma 穴熊 badger

ana⌐ta あなた you; ~**-tachi** あなた達, **anata⌐-ga⌐ta** あなた方 you (all); ~ **ji⌐shin** あなた自身 yourself; ~ **no** あなたの your(s)

anau⌐nsā アナウンサー announcer

andon あんどん・行灯 traditional paper-covered night-light

ane 姉 older sister

a⌐ngai 案外 1. unexpectedly (much) 2. contrary to expectations 3. ~ **(na)** 案外（な）unexpected

angō 暗号 (secret) code

a⌐ni 兄 older brother

anji 暗示 a hint; ~ **shima⌐su** 暗示します hints, suggests

anki 暗記 memorizing; **anki shima⌐su** 暗記します memorizes; **anki shi̱te** 暗記して by/from memory

a⌐nko あんこ・餡子 bean jam/paste

anna ... あんな... that kind of ...; ~ **ni** あんなに to that extent

anna⌐i (go-annai) 案内（ご案内）guidance, information; ~ **shima(⌐)su** 案内します guides, leads, ushers; **annai-ga⌐kari** 案内係, **anna⌐i-nin** 案内人, **anna⌐i-sha** 案内者 guide (person), usher; **anna⌐i-sho⌐** 案内書 guide(book); **annai-jo⌐** 案内所 information booth/desk

ano あの that (over there; *known to you and me*); **ano⌐-hito** あの人 he/him, she/her; **ano⌐ hito-tachi** あの人達 they/them; **ano⌐-ko** あの子 she/her, he/him

anō あのう uh ...

ano ne⌐ あのね say (there); hey

a⌐nraku 安楽 comfort; ~ **(na)** 安楽（な）comfortable, easy

anshin 安心 peace of mind; relief; security; confidence, trust; ~ **shima⌐su** 安心します doesn't worry, relaxes (one's anxieties), is relieved (of worry) ⌐you

a⌐nta あんた = **ana⌐ta** あなた

antena アンテナ antenna, aerial

anze̅m-pin 安全ピン, **anzem-pi̅n** 安全ピン safety pin

anzen (na) 安全（な）safe *(harm-proof)*

anzu あんず・杏 apricot

a̅o 青 blue, green (color)

ao̅ 会おう ＝ **aimasho̅** 会いましょう (let's meet!)

ao̅gi 扇ぎ・仰ぎ → **aogima̅su** 扇ぎます・仰ぎます

aogima̅su, ao̅gu 1. 扇ぎます, 扇ぐ fans; fans oneself 2. 仰ぎます, 仰ぐ looks up at/to; respects

ao̅i 青い blue, green

ao̅ide 扇いで・仰いで → **aogima̅su** 扇ぎます・仰ぎます

ao-ja̅shin 青写真 blueprint

ao̅-mono 青物 greens; **aomo̅no̅-ya** 青物屋 green-grocer

aorima̅su あおります・煽ります, **ao̅ru** あおる・煽る fans; stirs up, incites

ao-shi̅ngō 青信号 green light (signal)

ao̅tte あおって・煽って → **aorima̅su** あおります・煽ります

aoyagi 青柳 trough shell; (＝ **ao-ya̅nagi** 青柳) budding willow

aozo̅ra 青空 (blue, empty) sky

apa̅to アパート apartment (house)

appaku 圧迫 pressure; oppression, suppression; **appaku̧**

shima̅su 圧迫します puts pressure on; oppresses, suppresses

a̅ra̅ あら oh?? *(shows surprise, amazement)*

A̅rabu アラブ, **Arabu̅-jin** アラブ人 an Arab; **Arabu-go** アラブ語 Arabian (language)

araema̅su 洗えます, **araeru** 洗える can wash

arai 1. 荒い rough, coarse 2. 洗い → **araima̅su** 洗います [infinitive]

araima̅su 洗います, **arau** 洗う washes

ara̅-mono 荒物 housewares, kit-chenware; **aramo̅no̅-ya** 荒物屋 housewares dealer/shop

arao̅ 洗おう → **araimasho̅** (let's wash it!)

arare あられ・霰 1. (＝ **hyo̅** ひょう・雹) hail; ～ **ga furima̅su** あられ［霰］が降ります it hails 2. rice-cracker cubes (tidbits)

a̅rashi 嵐 storm

araso̅i 争い controversy, con-tention, struggle; argument, dispute, quarrel; strife, dis-turbance

araso̅i 争い → **arasoima̅su** 争います [infinitive]

arasoima̅su 争います, **araso̅u** 争う struggles/contends for; argues, quarrels

araso̅tte 争って → **arasoima̅su** 争います

aratemema'su 改めます, **aratame'ru** 改める changes, alters, corrects ⌐again

arata'mete 改めて newly, anew;

arawarema'su 表れ[現れ]ます, **araware'ru** 表れ[現れ]る appears, shows up, comes out

arawashima'su, arawa'su 1. 表します・現します, 表す・現す shows, reveals 2. 著します, 著す publishes, writes

are 1. あれ that one (over there; *known to you and me*); **are'-ra** あれら those, they/them 2. 荒れ → **arema'su** 荒れます [infinitive]

arema'su 荒れます, **areru** 荒れる goes to ruin, falls to waste, gets dilapidated; gets rough/wild; rages

arere'ba 荒れれば, **arerya** 荒れりゃ → **arema'su** 荒れます (if it rage; if ...) ⌐hay fever

are'ru'gii アレルギー allergy;

arete 荒れて → **arema'su** 荒れます

ari あり・蟻 ant

a'ri あり → **arima'su** あります

arigata'i ありがたい・有り難い appreciated, welcome; grateful

ari'gatō (gozaima'su) ありがとう[有り難う](ございます) thank you

arima'shita ありました there was, we had; it was (located)

arima'su あります, **a'ru** ある

there is, we've got; it is (located); **da're ga(/ni) na'ni ga arima'su ka** 誰が(/に)何がありますか who has what?

a'ri mo shinai ありもしない nor is there, there even/also isn't

ari⌐-sama ありさま・有り様 condition, state; scene, sight

ari-sō' (na) ありそう(な) likely; **ari-sō' mo na'i** ありそうもない unlikely

a'ri wa/ya shinai ありは/やしない = **na'i** ない = **arimase'n** ありません (is not)

arō' あろう [literary] = **a'ru darō'** あるだろう = **a'ru deshō'** あるでしょう probably is

a'ru ... ある... (a) certain ... , some ... ; ~ **hi** ある日 one (a certain) day

a'ru ある → **arima'su** あります

aruba'ito アルバイト a side job, a sideline, part-time work

aru'ite 歩いて → **arukima'su** 歩きます

aru'i-wa あるいは・或いは or else; maybe, possibly

arukima'su 歩きます, **aru'ku** 歩く walks

arukō' 歩こう = **arukimashō'** 歩きましょう (let's walk!)

arukōru アルコール alcohol

arumi(nyū'mu) アルミ(ニューム) aluminum ⌐for that)

arya ありゃ = **are wa** あれは (as

a⌐rya ありゃ **1.** = **a⌐reba** あれば (if there be) **2.** ~ **shinai** ありゃしない = **a⌐ri wa shinai** ありはしない = **na⌐i** ない (is not)

asa⌐ 麻 flax, linen

a⌐sa 朝 morning; **asa-han** 朝飯, **asa-go⌐han** 朝ご飯, **asa-meshi** 朝飯 breakfast

asai 浅い shallow

Asakusa 浅草 Asakusa; ~ **-Kō⌐en** 浅草公園 Asakusa Park

asari あさり・浅蜊 short-necked clam

asa-se 浅瀬 shallows

asa⌐tsuki あさつき・浅葱 scallion, green onion; chives

asa⌐tte あさって・明後日 day after tomorrow

a⌐se 汗 sweat; ~ **ga dema⌐su** 汗が出ます sweats

a⌐se あせ・褪せ → **asema⌐su** あせます・褪せます

asema⌐su あせます・褪せます, **ase⌐ru** あせる・褪せる fades

ase⌐nai あせない・褪せない = **asemase⌐n** あせません・褪せません (not fade)

asera⌐nai あせらない・焦らない = **aserimase⌐n** あせりません・焦りません (not feel rushed)

ase⌐ri あせり・焦り → **aserima⌐su** あせります・焦ります

aserima⌐su あせります・焦ります, **ase⌐ru** あせる・焦る feels rushed/pressed

ase⌐ru あせる・褪せる → **asema⌐su** あせます・褪せます

ase⌐ru あせる・焦る → **aserima⌐su** あせります・焦ります

a⌐sete あせて・褪せて → **asema⌐su** あせます・褪せます

ase⌐tte あせって・焦って → **aserima⌐su** あせります・焦ります

ashi⌐ 足・脚 foot, leg; **ashi-a⌐to** 足跡 footprint; **ashi⌐-dai** 足台 = **ashinose⌐-dai** 足乗せ台 footstool; **ashi⌐-ku⌐bi** 足首 ankle

ashi-mo⌐to⌐ 足元: ~ **ni ki o tsuke⌐te yo** 足元に気を付けてよ Watch your step!

ashira⌐i あしらい treatment, hospitality, service

ashira⌐i あしらい → **ashiraima⌐su** あしらいます

ashiraima⌐su あしらいます, **ashira⌐u** あしらう handles, manages, deals with; receives (a guest); **hana de** ~ 鼻であしらいます turns up one's nose at (a person)

ashira⌐tte あしらって → **ashiraima⌐su** あしらいます

ashirawa⌐nai あしらわない = **ashiraimase⌐n** あしらいません

ashita⌐ あした・明日 tomorrow

asobi 遊び **1.** fun, amusement; a game, play; a visit **2.** → **asobima⌐su** 遊びます

asobima⌐su 遊びます, **asobu** 遊

ぶ has fun, plays; visits

asoko あそこ, **asuko** あすこ (that place) over there; that place *(known to you and me)*

assa⎤ri (to) あっさり（と）simply, plainly; easily; frankly; ∼ **shi̱ta …** あっさり（と）した… simple, plain, light, easy; frank

assen あっせん・斡旋 mediation; good offices, help (= **sewa⎤** 世話); recommendation (= **suisen** 推薦); **… no assen de …** のあっせん［斡旋］で through the good offices of … , with the help of …

asu⎤ あす・明日 = **ashi̱ta** あした・明日 tomorrow

a⎤su̱pe⎤ku̱to アスペクト aspect *(grammatical)*

asupi⎤rin アスピリン aspirin

asutori⎤nzen アストリゼン astringent; aftershave (lotion)

ataema⎤su 与えます, **ataeru** 与える gives, provides

atama⎤ 頭 head

atama-kin 頭金 down payment, up-front money; deposit

atarashi⎤i 新しい new; fresh; **atara⎤shiku** 新しく newly, anew, freshly

atari 当たり 1. a hit 2. → **atarima⎤su** 当たります [infinitive]

atarimae (no) 当たり前（の）reasonable, natural, proper;

suitable, sensible

atarima⎤su 当たります, **ataru** 当たる hits, faces; applies; is correct

atashi あたし *(mostly female)* = **watashi** わたし・私 I/me

at(a)taka⎤i あったかい（あたたかい）・温かい・暖かい warm

atatamema⎤su 温めます・暖めます, **atatame⎤ru** 温める・暖める warms it up

atatte 当たって → **atarima⎤su** 当たります

atchi⎤ あっち = **achira** あちら

ate 当て 1. reliance, trust; **… o ate ni shi̱te ima⎤su** …を当てにしています is counting on … 2. anticipation, expectation 3. goal, object 4. (= **tega⎤kari** 手掛かり) clue, trace 5. → **atema⎤su** 当てます [infinitive]; [imperative] **ate ro** 当てろ, **ate⎤ yo** 当てよ

…-ate (no) …宛て（の）addressed to …

ate-hamema⎤su 当てはめます, **-hame⎤ru** 当てはめる applies, conforms, adapts, fits (it to); **… ni ate-ha⎤mete** …に当てはめて in conformity/accordance with …

atema⎤su 当てます, **ateru** 当てる guesses; hits; sets aside, appropriates, designates; touches; addresses

ate-na 宛て名 address

atenai 当てない ＝ **atemaseˈn** 当
てません (not guess)

ate(ra)remaˈsu 当て(ら)れます,
ate(ra)reru 当て(ら)れる can
guess/hit/ ...

aˈto 後 after(wards), later; ～ **no** ...
後の... the remaining ... ; ...
shita ～ **de** ...した後で ...
after doing

ato⁻-aji 後味 aftertaste; ～ **ga**
waruˈi 後味が悪い leaves a
bad aftertaste

atori⁻e アトリエ studio, work-
shop, atelier

atsubottai 厚ぼったい thick (＝
buatsui ぶ厚い・分厚い)

atsui 厚い thick (＝ **atsubottai** 厚
ぼったい, **buatsui** ぶ厚い・分
厚い)

atsuˈi 暑い・熱い hot; **aˈtsuku**
shimaˈsu 熱くします makes it
hot

atsumarimaˈsu 集まります,
atsumaˈru 集まる meet, assemble; it accumulates

atsumeˈmasu 集めます,
atsumeˈru 集める collects,
gathers, accumulates

atsuryoku 圧力 pressure

atsusa 厚さ thickness

aˈtsusa 暑さ・熱さ heat, warmth

aˈtta 1. あった ＝ **ariˈmashita** あ
りました 2. 会った ＝
aimaˈshita 会いました

attakaˈi あったかい・暖かい・温
かい ＝ **atatakaˈi** 暖[温]かい

warm

attamemaˈsu あっためます・暖め
ます・温めます, **attameˈru** あ
っためる・暖める・温める
warms it up

aˈtte 1. あって → **arimaˈsu** あり
ます 2. 会って → **aimaˈsu** 会
います

aˈu 合う・会う ＝ **aimaˈsu** 合いま
す・会います

aˈuto アウト out *(baseball)*;
auto-kōˈsu アウトコース
outer lane/track

awa あわ・泡 bubble; foam

aˈwa あわ・粟 millet

aˈwabi あわび・鮑・鰒 abalone

awaˈnai 合わない・会わない ＝
aimaseˈn 合いません・会いま
せん

awaseˈ 1. 袷・あわせ a lined garment 2. **awaˈse** 合わせ →
awasemaˈsu 合わせます [in-
finitive]

awasemaˈsu 合わせます,
awaseˈru 合わせる puts
together, combines, joins

awaˈsete あわせて・合わせて all
together (→ **awasemaˈsu** 合せ
ます)

awatadashiˈi あわただしい・慌た
だしい hurried, flustered, confused

awatemaˈsu あわてます・慌てま
す, **awateru** あわてる・慌てる
gets flustered/confused

awate-mono あわて者・慌て者 a

person easily flustered; a scatterbrain

aˈya 会や **1.** = **aˈeba** 会えば (if one meet) **2.** ~ **shinai** 会やしない = **aiˈ wa shinai** 会いはしない = **awaˈnai** 会わない (not meet)

ayamaˈri 1. 誤り error, mistake **2.** 謝り apology

ayamaˈri 誤り・謝り → **ayamarimaˈsu** 誤ります・謝ります [infinitive]

ayamarimaˈsu, ayamaˈru 1. 誤ります, 誤る errs, makes a mistake **2.** 謝ります, 謝る apologizes

ayamaˈtte 誤って・謝って → **ayamarimaˈsu** 誤ります・謝ります

ayashiˈ⁻i あやしい・怪しい questionable, suspicious, shady; uncertain; unreliable; uncanny, weird

aˈyu あゆ・鮎, **aˈi** あい sweetfish, river trout

ā yū ("iu") ああゆう(いう) ... that kind/sort of ... (= **anna** あんな)　　　　⌐*(animal)*

azaˈrashi あざらし・海豹 seal

azukaremaˈsu 預かれます, **azukareˈru** 預かれる can take in trust

azukaˈri 預り → **azukarimaˈsu** 預ります　　　　　⌐room

azukari-jo⁻ 預かり所 check

azukarimaˈsu 預かります, **azukaˈru** 預かる takes in trust

azuˈke 預け → **azukemaˈsu** 預けます

azukemaˈsu 預けます, **azukeˈru** 預ける gives in trust, entrusts, checks, deposits

azuke(ra)remaˈsu 預け(ら)れます, **azuke(ra)reˈru** 預け(ら)れる can give in trust

azukiˈ あずき・小豆 red beans

— B —

...-ba ...ば [emphatic] (if) indeed: **...** **naˈra(~)** ...なら(ば) if; **...** **daˈttara(~)** ...だったら (ば); **...-kaˈttara(~)** ...かったら(ば) if/when it is (or was); **...-taˈra(~)** ...たら(ば) if/when it does (or did)

ba 場 place *(for something)*

baˈ バー bar *(for drinking)*

baai 場合, **bawai** 場合 situation, case, circumstance, occasion; **...** **(no)** ~ ...(の)場合 if

baˈbon バーボン bourbon

bachiˈ 1. 撥 plectrum **2.** ばち・罰 retribution

ba-chiˈgai (na/no) 場違い(な/の)

1. out of place **2.** not from the right/best place

ba⌐i 倍 double; ~ **ni narima⌐su** 倍になります it doubles; ~ **ni shima⌐su** 倍にします doubles it

...-bai ...倍 ... times, ...-fold

Ba⌐iburu バイブル Bible

ba⌐idoku 梅毒 syphilis

baikin ばい菌・黴菌 germ

ba⌐ikingu バイキング smorgasbord ("Viking")

baiorin バイオリン violin

baishō⌐-kin 賠償金 indemnity, reparation

baishun 売春 prostitution; **baishun-ya⌐do** 売春宿 house of prostitution; **baishu⌐n-fu** 売春婦 prostitute

baiten 売店 booth, kiosk, stand (*selling things*)

ba⌐iyā バイヤー buyer (*professional*)

ba⌐ka ばか・馬鹿 fool, idiot; ~ **(na)** ばか・馬鹿(な) foolish, stupid

baka-ba⌐nashi ばか話・馬鹿話 nonsense; (= **muda-ba⌐nashi** 無駄話) idle talk; gossip; hot air, bull

baka-me ばかめ[奴] damn (fool) idiot

baka-rashi⌐i ばか[馬鹿]らしい absurd, foolish

... ba⌐kari ...ばかり, **... ba⌐kkari** ...ばっかり, **... ba⌐kkashi** ...ばっ

かし only, just

baka-shō⌐jiki (na) ばか[馬鹿]正直(な) gullible

bake⌐gaku 化け学・化学 chemistry

bake-mo⌐no⌐ 化け物 ghost (= **o-ba⌐ke** お化け・おばけ)

baketsu バケツ bucket

bakkin 罰金 fine, penalty

bakku-mi⌐rā バックミラー rear-view mirror

ba⌐kkuru バックル buckle

bakuchi ばくち・博打 gambling

bakudai (na) ばくだい[莫大](な) immense, vast, huge, enormous

bakudan 爆弾 bomb

ba⌐kufu 幕府 (**bakufu-ji⌐dai** 幕府時代) (the time of) the shogunate

bakugeki 爆撃 bombing; **bakugeki shima⌐su** 爆撃します bombs it

bakuge⌐ki⌐-ki 爆撃機 bomber

bakuhatsu 爆発 explosion, exploding; burst(ing)

ba⌐men 場面 scene

...-bamme⌐ (no) ...番目(の) NUMERAL-th

bam-meshi 晩飯 evening meal (dinner/supper)

ban 晩 evening, night; (**hito⌐-ban** 一晩 one night, **futa⌐-ban** 二晩 two nights, **i⌐ku-ban** いく晩・幾晩 how many nights)

ba⌐n 番 **1.** guard, watch **2.** number; (**ichi⌐-ban** 一番

number one, **naˉm-ban** 何番
what number)

ban-cha 番茶 coarse green tea

banchi 番地 address *(house number)*; **nam-baˉnchi** 何番地
what house/lot number

bando バンド strap, band
(watchband, etc.); belt

bane(-jiˉkake) ばね(仕掛け)
spring (device)

ban-gaˉsa 番傘 *(oilpaper)* umbrella

bangoˉ 番号 number *(assigned)*

ban-goˉhan 晩ご飯・晩御飯 evening meal (dinner/supper)

banguˉmiˉ 番組 program *(TV, etc.)*

baˉnira バニラ vanilla

banniˉn 番人 watchman

...-bansen ...番線 track number
... ; **nam-bansen** 何番線 what
(number) track?

bansōkō ばんそうこう・絆創膏
adhesive plaster/tape

banzaˉi! 万歳・ばんざい
hurray!

baˉra (de) ばら・バラ(で) (in)
bulk; loose, separately

bara (no hanaˉ) ばら[薔薇]の花
rose

barashimaˉsu ばらします,
baraˉsu ばらす 1. exposes (a
secret) 2. takes it apart,
disassembles 3. kills, shoots
(to death)

baˉrē バレエ ballet

barēboˉru バレーボール volleyball

barikan バリカン clippers
(barber's)

baroku 馬勒 bridle

basho 場所 1. place 2. a (two-week) sumo tournament;
natsu-baˉsho 夏場所 the summer sumo tournament

bas-shimaˉsu 罰します, **-suˉru**
罰する punishes

baˉsu バス 1. bus 2. bath, (basu-
rūˉmu) バスルーム bathroom;
basu-tsuki バス付き with bath

basue 場末 suburb *(outskirts)*

baˉta バタ, **baˉtā** バター butter;
bata-rōˉru バタロール (butter)
roll

bataˉya ばた屋 ragpicker

baˉtsu ばつ・バツ cross (= X
"wrong")

batteˉn ばってん・罰点 X
("wrong"), a black mark

baˉtterii バッテリー battery

baˉtto バット bat *(baseball)*

bawai 場合 = **baai** 場合

beˉa ペア = **bēsu-aˉppu** ベース
アップ upping/raising the
base pay; a pay raise

beˉddo ベッド, **beˉtto** ベット bed
(Western)

beddo-taˉun ベッドタウン
bedroom community, suburb

Bei-... 米..., **...-Bei** ...米
America(n)

Beikoku 米国 = **Amerika** アメ

リカ America

... be̱ki ...べき: suru ~ desu̱ するべきです ought to [bookish]

bekkan 別館 annex (building)

bekkō⁽ʼ⁾ べっこう・鼈甲 tortoise shell

bekkyo 別居 separate living; ~ -te̱ate 別居手当 alimony; ~ shima̱su (suru) 別居します (する) lives apart (separately), ... to ~ ...と別居します is separated from ...

be̱kon ベーコン bacon

bembetsu 弁別 discriminating; bembetsu shima̱su 弁別します discriminates, discerns, distinguishes

bempi 便秘 constipation

be̱n 1. 弁 valve 2. 便 facilities, convenience; ~ ga i̱i 便がいい convenient; (= daiben 大便) feces

...-be̱n ...遍 = ...-he̱n ...遍 (counts times)

be̱nchi ベンチ bench

bengo̱shi 弁護士 lawyer

be̱ni 紅 rouge

benjo̱ 便所 toilet

benki 便器 bedpan

benkyō 勉強 study, (mental) work; cutting a price; ~-ka 勉強家 a studious person, a good student; ~ shima̱su 勉強します studies; cuts the price

be̱nri (na) 便利(な) handy, convenient

benri-ya 便利屋 handyman (or his shop)

bentō̱ (o-bentō) 弁当(お弁当) box lunch

be̱ru ベル bell, doorbell

Be̱ruri̱n ベルリン Berlin

be⁽ʼ⁾ruto ベルト belt (= bando バンド)

bessō̱ 別荘 villa

bēsubō̱ru ベースボール baseball

be̱suto ベスト best; besuto̱-te̱n ベストテン best ten

betsu-betsu (na/no) 別々(な/の) separate, individual

betsu-dai 別代 extra (charge), separate bill

betsu (na/no) 別(な/の) separate, special, particular; ~ (no) 別(の) other; extra; ... wa betsu to shi̱te ...は別として apart/aside from ... , except for ...

betsu ni 別に 1. [+ NEGATIVE] not particularly 2. ... to̱ʼ wa ~ (shi̱te) とは別に(して) quite apart/separately from ...

be̱tto ベット = be̱ddo ベッド bed

bifu̱teki ビフテキ beafsteak

bi̱ʼichi ビーチ beach

bi̱ʼiru ビール beer; nama-bi̱ʼiru 生ビール draft beer; biiru̱ʼ-bin ビール瓶 beer bottle; biiru̱ʼ-

kan ビール缶 beer can

bi'irusu ビールス virus

bi'ito ビート beet

bi'jutsu 美術 art; biju'tsu'-kan 美術館 museum (art gallery)

bikku'ri shima(ˉ)su びっくりします gets startled

bi'mbō (na) 貧乏(な)poor (needy)

bimyō (na) 微妙(な) delicate, subtle, fine, nice

bi'n びん・瓶 bottle; jar; (= kabin 花瓶) vase

...ˉ-bin 便 flight (number) ...

bi'niru ビニル, bini'iru ビニール vinyl, polyvinyl; plastic

binsen 便箋 (letter-)writing paper, stationery

bi'nta びんた slapping (a person's face); ... ni ~ o harima'su/kuwasema'su ...にびんたをはります/くわせます slaps ...

bira びら・ビラ leaflet, handbill, pamphlet

bi'ri (no) びり(の) the last, the tail end, the rear

birōdo ビロード velvet

bi'ru(di'ngu) ビル(ディング) building

Bi'ruma ビルマ Burma

bisai (na) 微細(な) minute, detailed, fine

bisuke'tto ビスケット crackers

bita⌐min ビタミン vitamin(s), bitami⌐n-zai ビタミン剤

vitamin pills

bi⌐toku 美徳 virtue

bi'wa 1. びわ・枇杷 loquat 2. びわ・琵琶 lute

biya-hō'ru ビヤホール beer hall

biyō'in 美容院 beauty parlor

bi'za ビザ visa

bō 棒 pole (rod); (= bō-kkire 棒っきれ) stick, club; (= tetsu-bō 鉄棒) (iron) bar

bo'chi 墓地 cemetery, graveyard

bōchū-ami 防虫網 window screen

bōchū̄-zai 防虫剤 insecticide; mothballs

bōdai (na) ぼうだい(な)・膨大(な) enormous, gigantic, massive

bōdō 暴動 riot

bōeki 貿易 commerce, trade; bōe'ki'-shō 貿易商 trader; bōeki shima'su 貿易します conducts foreign trade

bōenkyō 望遠鏡 telescope

bōfū̄ 暴風 storm, gale, hurricane

bōfu⌐-zai 防腐剤 antiseptic (substance)

bōham-be'ru 防犯ベル burglar alarm

bōi ボーイ (bell)boy, waiter, steward, clerk (errand runner)

bōi-fure'ndo ボーイフレンド boyfriend

boin 1. 母印 thumbprint 2. 母音 (= boon 母音) vowel

bo̅irā ボイラー boiler

bokashima'su ぼかします, **boka'su** ぼかす: hanashi' o ~ 話をぼかします beats around the bush, is noncommittal

bōken 冒険 adventure

bo̅ki 簿記 bookkeeping

bō(-kkire) 棒(っきれ) stick (club)

bo̅kkusu ボックス booth (in a tavern etc.); denwa ~ 電話ボックス phone booth (= denwa̅-shitsu 電話室)

bo̅koku 母国 mother country, homeland

bo̅ku ぼく・僕 (usually male) I/me; bo̅ku-ra ぼくら・僕ら, bo̅ku-ta̅chi ぼくたち・僕たち we/us

bo̅kushi 牧師 (Christian) minister, preacher, pastor, priest; Reverend

bo̅kushingu ボクシング boxing

bon (o-bon) 盆(お盆) tray

bo̅n 盆, **o-bo̅n** お盆 the Bon Festival (Buddhist All Saints Day) = ura̅bon 盂蘭盆・うら盆

...-bon ...本 book, volume, text

...-bon ...本 (counts long things): → sa̅m-bon 三本, → se̅m-bon 千本, → ma̅m-bon 万本, → na̅m-bon 何本

bo̅nasu ボーナス (wage) bonus

bōne̅n-kai 忘年会 year-end (New Year's eve) party

bonne̅tto ボンネット (car) hood, bonnet

bonsai 盆栽 dwarf trees (in pots)

bon'ya̅ri shima(̅)su ぼんやりします is absent-minded, daydreams

boon 母音 vowel (= boin 母音)

bora ぼら・鯔 gray mullet

borarema̅su ぼられます, **borare̅ru** ぼられる gets overcharged (ripped off)

borima̅su ぼります, **bo̅ru** ぼる overcharges

bo̅ro ぼろ・ボロ rag

bo̅ru ボール ball

bōru-gami ボール紙 cardboard

bōru-pen ボールペン ballpoint pen

bo̅ruto ボルト bolt (of nut and bolt); volt

bo̅ryoku 暴力 violence (brute force)

bō-san 坊さん = o-bō-san お坊さん Buddhist monk

bōseki 紡績 spinning; **bōseki-kō̅jō** 紡績工場 spinning mill

bōshi (o-bo̅shi) 帽子(お帽子) hat

bōsui (no) 防水(の) waterproof

bo̅tan ボタン button

bo̅tchan 坊っちゃん boy, (your) son

bō̅to ボート boat

bo̅tsubotsu ぼつぼつ 1. (= so̅rosoro そろそろ) little by little, gradually; (leave) before long **2.** (with) dots, spots, bumps

bo͞tta ぼった = **borima͞shita** ぼりました; **bo͞tte** ぼって → **borima͞su** ぼります

bo͞ya 坊や boy

boyakima͞su ぼやきます, **boya͞ku** ぼやく grumbles, complains

bo͞zu 坊主 Buddhist monk or priest

bu͞ 部 **1.** (...͞-bu ...部) part, division, section **2.** performance; **hiru no bu͞** 昼の部 matinee; **yo͞ru no bu͞** 夜の部 evening performance

...͞-bu 1. ...分 (1–9) percent: **sa͞n-wari sa͞n-bu** 三割三分 = **sa͞njū sam-pāse͞nto** 三十三 [33]パーセント 33 percent **2.** ...部 copies (of a book); **ichi͞-bu** 一部 one copy

bu-a͞isō (na) 無愛想(な) unsociable, blunt, brusque, curt

buatsui ぶ厚い・分厚い thick (= **atsubottai** 厚ぼったい)

bu͞bun 部分 part, portion

bu-cho͞hō 不調法 **1.** a gaffe, a blunder; **~ o shima͞su** 不調法をします makes a blunder **2.** **~ (na)** 不調法(な) awkward, clumsy, impolite; abstaining (from alcohol/tobacco); **(sake/tabako wa) ~ desu** (酒/タバコは)不調法です I don't drink/smoke.

buchōhō-mono 不調法者 abstainer; **(sake no ~** 酒の不調法者**)** nondrinker, teetotaler; **(tabako no ~** タバコの不調法者**)** nonsmoker

bu͞dō ぶどう・葡萄 grapes

bu͞dō 武道 (= **bu͞jutsu** 武術) martial arts

budō͞-shu ぶどう[葡萄]酒 wine

bu-e͞nryo (na) 不遠慮(な) unreserved, frank, forward, pushy, rude

bu͞gaku 舞楽 traditional court dances and music

buji (ni) 無事(に) safe(ly) *(without incident)*

bujoku 侮辱 insult(ing); **bujoku shima͞su** 侮辱します insults

bu͞jutsu 武術 martial arts

bu͞ka 部下 a subordinate

bu-ki͞ryō (na) 不器量(な) homely, ugly

bu-ki͞yō (na) 不器用(な) clumsy

bukka 物価 commodity prices

bukki͞ra͞bō (na) ぶっきらぼう(な) blunt, brusque, curt

Bu͞kkyō 仏教 Buddhism

bumbō͞-gu 文房具 stationery supplies; **bumbōgu-ya** 文房具屋 stationery shop

bummei 文明 civilization

bumpō 文法 grammar

bumpō͞-gu 文房具 = **bumbō͞-gu** 文房具

bu͞mu ブーム boom *(fad)*

bu͞n 分 part, portion, share;

state, status

...-bun ...分 NUMERAL-th: **hachi-bun no ichi** 八分の一 one-eighth

bunchin 文鎮 paperweight

bu˺ngaku 文学 literature

bungo 文語 literary language/word; ～**-teki (na)** 文語的(な) literary

bu˺nka 文化 culture, civilization; **Bunka no hi˺** 文化の日 Culture Day (3 November); **bunka˺-sai** 文化祭 cultural festival

bu˺nraku 文楽 puppet show (traditional)

bunseki 分析 analysis

bu˺nshō 文章 (written) sentence

buntan 分担 (taking) partial charge; allotment, share; ～ **shima˺su** 分担します takes partial charge of, shares in; pays/does one's share

bu˺rabura ぶらぶら idly dangling, idling; ～ **shima˺su** ぶらぶらします loafs (around)

bura˺jā ブラ(ジャー) bra(ssiere)

Burajiru ブラジル Brazil

bu˺ranko ぶらんこ a swing

bu˺rashi ブラシ brush

buraun-kan ブラウン管 TV tube

bura˺usu ブラウス blouse

bu˺rei 無礼 discourtesy; ～ **(na)** 無礼(な) impolite, rude

bure˺ki ブレーキ brake

bu˺ri ぶり・鰤 yellowtail (fish);

cf. **hamachi** はまち・鮸, **inada** いなだ

buriki ブリキ tin

buro˺kā ブローカー agent, broker

bu˺rubon ブルボン = **ba˺bon** バーボン

burudo˺za ブルドーザー bulldozer

bu-sa˺hō 無作法・不作法 1. a social gaffe, a faux pas 2. ～ **(na)** 無作法・不作法(な) rude, blunt

bu-sata ぶさた・無沙汰 neglecting to write/visit; **(go)** ～ **shima˺su** (ご)ぶさたします・(ご)無沙汰します neglects to write/visit

bu˺shi 武士 warrior, samurai; **bushi˺-dō** 武士道 Bushido, the way of the samurai

bushō˺-mo˺no˺ 無精者 sluggard, sloven

bushō˺ (na) 無精・不精(な) lazy; slovenly; ～**-hige** 無精ひげ a three-day beard, a five-o'clock shadow

...-bu˺soku ...不足 shortage; **ne** ～ 寝不足 not enough sleep

busshitsu 物質 matter, substance; ～**-teki (na)** 物質的(な) material; ～**-shu˺gi** 物質主義 materialism

busshoku 物色 looking around for; ～**-gai** 物色買い selective buying (of stocks, ...);

busshoku shima͞su 物色します looks/shops around for, seeks

bussō͞ (na) 物騒(な) troubled, unsafe, dangerous

bu͞su ぶす an ugly woman

buta ぶた・豚 pig

bu͞tai 1. 舞台 stage **2.** 部隊 detachment of troops, unit, outfit

buta-niku 豚肉 pork

butchō-zura 仏頂面 a sullen face

butsudan 仏壇 household altar *(Buddhist)*

butsukarima͞su ぶつかります, **butsukaru** ぶつかる collides with, runs into

butsukema͞su ぶつけます, **butsukeru** ぶつける hits

butsuri͞-gaku 物理学 physics; **butsuriga͞ku-sha** 物理学者 physicist

Butsu-zō 仏像 Buddha *(statue)*

bu͞zā ブザー buzzer

byakudan 白壇 sandalwood

byō͞ 1. 秒 a second (of time) **2.** びょう・鋲 a tack; (= **gabyō** がびょう・画鋲) a thumbtack ⌈*(folding)*

byōbu びょうぶ・屏風 screen

byōdō (na) 平等(な) equal

byōin 病院 hospital; clinic, doctor's office, health service

byōki (no) 病気(の) sick, ill; sickness, illness; **〜-gachi (na)** 病気がち(な) sickly, unhealthy

byōnin 病人 an invalid, a patient

— C —

cha 茶 (= **o-cha** お茶) tea, green tea

...cha ...ちゃ = **...te̅wa** ...ては

cha-bin 茶瓶 teapot

chadai 茶代 tip *(money)*

...chae ...ちゃえ = **-te shimae** てしまえ [imperative]

cha-ga͞shi 茶菓子 tea cake

chā͞han チャーハン・炒飯 (Chinese) fried rice

...chai ...ちゃい = **-te shimai** てしまい [infinitive]

...chaima͞su ...ちゃいます = **-te shimaima͞su** てしまいます ⌈dy

cha-ire͞ 茶入れ tea canister/cad-

cha-iro (no) 茶色(の) brown

cha͞kku チャック zipper

... cha͞ku (no) ...着(の) arriving at (TIME/PLACE)

chakuriku 着陸 landing, touching ground; **chakuriku shima͞su** 着陸します lands

chambara ちゃんばら sword battle

cha‌mpon ちゃんぽん alternating, skipping back and forth, mixing one's drinks/foods

... (-)chan ...ちゃん [baby talk] = ... (-)san ...さん [title]

cha-no-ma (o-chanoma) 茶の間（お茶の間）Japanese family room

cha-no-yu 茶の湯 tea ceremony

cha‌nsu チャンス chance

chanto ちゃんと safe(ly) *(without incident)*, firmly, securely; ～ shita ちゃんとした proper, secure

cha-saji 茶匙 teaspoon

chase⌐n 茶筅 bamboo tea whisk (for tea ceremony)

chashaku 茶杓 tea scoop (for tea ceremony)

chashitsu 茶室 (o-chashitsu) お茶室 tearoom (for tea ceremony)

chātā‌-ki チャーター機 chartered plane

...chatta ...ちゃった = -te shimatta てしまった = -te shimaima‌shita てしまいました

...chau ...ちゃう = -te shimau てしまう = -te shimaima‌su てしまいます

chawan (o-cha‌wan) 茶碗（お茶碗）rice bowl; tea cup

chawan-mushi 茶碗蒸し a steamed cup of custard from fish broth and eggs with tidbits

chazuke 茶漬け, **o-chazuke** お茶漬け a bowl of rice with hot tea and flavorings poured over it

chekkua‌uto チェックアウト check-out; ～ shima(⌐)su チェックアウトします checks out

chekku‌in チェックイン check-in; ～ shima(⌐)su チェックインします checks in

che‌ro チェロ cello

chi 血 blood; ～ ga dema‌su 血が出ます bleeds

chi‌bi ちび midget; (tiny) tot

chibi-me ちびめ runt, peewee, pipsqueak

chichi‌ 1. 父 father (= chichi-oya 父親) 2. 乳 breasts; mother's milk

chi-dome 血止め styptic pencil

chie‌ 知恵 wisdom

chigai 違い 1. difference, discrepancy 2. → chigaima‌su 違います

chigaima‌su 違います, **chigau** 違う is different; is wrong; is not like that

chigatte 違って → chigaima‌su 違います

chihei-sen 地平線 horizon (on land)

chihō‌ 地方 area, region, province, district; ～ no 地方の local

chi‌i 地位 rank, position, status

chi‌iki 地域 region

chiィimu チーム team; chiimu-waィku チームワーク team-work

chiisaィi 小さい, chiィisa-na (...) 小さな(...) little, small

chiィizu チーズ cheese

chiィji 知事 governor

chijimemásu 縮めます, chijimeru 縮める shortens it

chijimimásu 縮みます, chijimu 縮む it shrinks

chiⁿjin 知人 an acquaintance (= shiriai 知り合い)

chijoku 恥辱 disgrace, shame

chikaィ 地下 underground; (= ~-tetsu 地下鉄) subway; (= ~-shitsu 地下室) basement

chikaィgoro 近頃 lately, recently

chikai 地階 basement

chikaⁿi 誓い vow, pledge, oath

chikaィi 近い near, close by; ~ uchiィ ni 近いうちに in the near future

chikaⁿi 誓い → chikaimásu 誓います

chikaimásu 誓います, chikaⁿu 誓う swears, vows, pledges

chikaィku 近く 1. vicinity 2. near-by 3. shortly

chikaィ-michi 近道 short cut

chikan 痴漢・ちかん (sexual) molester, groper

chikaraィ (o-chikara) 力(お力) power, strength

chika-zukemásu 近付けます, -zukeru 近付ける lets one ap-proach, brings close; associ-ates (keeps company) with; can approach it

chika-zukimásu 近付きます, -zuku 近付く approaches, draws/comes near

chikeィtto チケット ticket

chiィkki チッキ check, receipt, stub; luggage; ~ ni shimásu チッキにします checks it

chiィkku チック stick hair-grease, pomade

chiィkuィ 地区 section, sector (area)

chikuoⁿn-ki 蓄音機 phonograph, record player

chikuwa ちくわ・竹輪 broiled fish cake

chikyū 地球 the Earth; chikyū́-gi 地球儀 globe

chi-maィnako ni naィtte 血眼にな って with bloodshot eyes; fran-tically

chimpira ちんぴら・チンピラ a punk; hoodlum; juvenile delin-quent

chiィmpo (o-chiィmpo) ちんぽ(お ちんぽ) penis [baby, informal talk]

chinamagusaィi 血生臭い bloody

chiィngin 賃金 wage

chiィnko (o-chiィnko) ちんこ(おち んこ) penis [baby talk]

chiィppu チップ tip (money)

chira(ka)shimásu 散ら(か)しま す, chira(ka)su 散ら(か)す scatters, strews

chirashi-zushi 散らしずし[鮨] sushi rice covered with fish tidbits

chireba 散れば → **chirima´su** 散ります (if they scatter)

chiri 1. ちり・塵 dust *(on ground, floor, etc.)* 2. 散り → **chirima´su** 散ります

chi´ri 地理 the geography, the lay of the land

chiri´-gaku 地理学 (the study/science of) geography

chiri-gami ちり紙 tissues (Kleenex) or toilet paper

chiri-jō (no) 地理上(の) geographical

chirima´su 散ります, **chiru** 散る they disperse, scatter, fall about

chiri-teki (na) 地理的(な) geographical

chiri-to´ri´ ちり[塵]取り dustpan

chirya 散りゃ 1. = **chire´ba** 散れば (if they scatter) 2. ~ **shinai** 散りゃしない = **chiri´ wa shinai** 散りはしない = **chiranai** 散らない (not scatter)

chiryō 治療 treatment *(medical)*

chi´shiki 知識 knowledge

Chishi´ma 千島, **Chishima-re´ttō** 千島列島 the Kurile Islands

chi⌐shitsu 地質 the geology (of a place); **chishitsu´-gaku** 地質学 geology

chita⌐i 地帯 zone

chitcha´i ちっちゃい = **chiisa´i** 小さい little 「ます

chitte 散って → **chirima´su** 散り

chitto´-mo ちっとも + NEGATIVE not a bit, not in the least

chi´zu 地図 map

chō´ 腸 intestines

chō´ ちょう・蝶 = **chō⌐chō** ちょうちょう・蝶々, **chō⌐cho** ちょうちょ・蝶々 butterfly

(...-)chō´ 1. (...) 丁 block (or block area) of a city 2. (...)長 head, chief, leader 3. (...)兆 trillion *(American)* = billion *(British)*

chō´bo ちょぼ a dot

chōbo-ga´kari 帳簿係 bookkeeper

chōchi´n ちょうちん・堤灯 lantern *(of paper)*

chōda´i ちょうだい・頂戴 please; ~ **shima´su** ちょうだい[頂戴]します I (humbly) get

chōdo ちょうど exactly, just

chō´hō (na) ちょうほう(な)・重宝(な) useful, convenient, valued; ~ **shima(´)su** 重宝します, **chōhō-garima´su** 重宝がります values, cherishes, makes full use of

chō´ji 丁字 cloves

chōjō´ 頂上 top, summit, peak

chōka 超過 excess; ~ **shima´su** 超過します exceeds, goes/runs over (= **sugima´su** 過ぎます)

chō̄ka 長歌 poem *(longer)*

chōkan 1. 朝刊 morning paper 2. 長官 chief *(head)*

chokin 貯金 deposit, savings; ~ shima̍su 貯金します deposits (money), saves

chokkan 直感 intuition

chokki チョッキ vest

cho̍ko ちょこ, o-cho̍ko おちょこ saké cup

chōkoku 彫刻 carving, engraving; chōkoku shima̍su 彫刻します engraves

choko-mi̍ruku チョコミルク chocolate milk

chokore̍to チョコレート chocolate

choko-se̍ki チョコセーキ chocolate (milk)shake

chō̄ku チョーク chalk

chokuryū 直流 DC, direct current

chokusetsu (ni) 直接(に) direct(ly)

chō-kyo̍ri 長距離 long distance

cho̍mbo ちょんぼ・チョンボ a booboo, a goof, a blunder

(...-)chōme⁽ⁿ⁾ (...) 丁目 (...-th) block (of city)

chō̄mi 調味 seasoning *(food)*; (= chōmi̍-ryō 調味料) spice

chō-mu̍subi 蝶結び bow (of a ribbon)

chō̍na̍n 長男 eldest son

chōryū 潮流 current, tide; trend

cho̍sa 調査 examination, investigation, inquiry, research, survey

chōsei 調整 adjustment; ~ shima̍su 調整します adjusts it

Chōse̍n 朝鮮 *(preferred in North Korea)* = Ka̍nkoku 韓国 Korea; Chōsen-go 朝鮮語 Korean *(language)*; Chōsen-ji̍n 朝鮮人 Korean *(person)*

cho̍sha 著者 writer, author

chōshi 調子 tune; condition; trend; ~ ni norima̍su 調子に乗ります, ~ ga dema̍su 調子が出ます gets into the swing of things

chō̍sho 長所 strong point, advantage, merit

chōshoku 朝食 morning meal, breakfast (= asa-han 朝飯)

chō⁽ⁿ⁾shu 聴取 listening (to radio); chōshu̍-sha 聴取者 (radio) listener

chōshū 1. 聴衆 audience 2. 徴収 collection (of taxes, etc.), levying; ~ shima̍su 徴収します collects, levies

chosu̍i-chi 貯水池 reservoir

chō̍te̍n 頂点 climax, peak, highpoint

chō-tsu̍gai 蝶つがい・蝶番 hinge

cho̍tto ちょっと just a little; somewhat; just a minute

cho̍tto shita ... ちょっとした... 1. slight, trivial 2. quite a ... , a decent/respectable ...

chōwa 調和 harmony, agree-

ment; **... to ~ shimás̄u** ...と
調和します is in harmony
(agrees) with

chū 中 1. middle; medium 2. =
chū-kan 中巻 middle volume
(of a set of three)

chū́bu 1. 中部 middle (part)
2. チューブ tube

chūburu (no) 中古(の) secondhand

chū́cho ちゅうちょ・躊躇 hesita-
tion; **~ shimá(́)su** ちゅうち
ょします・躊躇します hesi-
tates

chūga̋kkō 中学校 middle school
(junior high school)

chūga̋ku-sei 中学生 junior high
school student

chūgata 中型 medium-size
(model)

chūgen 中元 = **o-chūgen** お中元
midsummer gift

Chū́goku 中国 China; **Chūgoku-
go** 中国語 Chinese language;
Chūgokú-jin 中国人 a Chinese

Chūgoku-chi̋hō 中国地方 the
Chugoku area of Japan
(*Hiroshima, etc.*)

chū-hai 酎ハイ a *shōchū* highball

chū́i 1. 注意 attention; note,
notice, reminder 2. 中尉 1st
lieutenant; lieutenant j.g.

chūi-buka̋i 注意深い careful

chū́jō 中将 vice admiral

chū-kan 中巻 middle volume (of
a set of three)

chūka-ryṓri (-ryōrí-ten) 中華料
理(料理店) Chinese cooking
(restaurant)

chūkoku 忠告 advice

chū⊓ko (no) 中古(の) secondhand; **chūko⊓-hin** 中古品
secondhand goods

chū⊓mon 注文 an order; **~
shimá̄su** 注文します orders
(*clothes, meal, etc.*)

chūnen 中年 middle age, **~ (no)**
中年(の) middle-aged;
chūnem-mono 中年者 a middle-aged person

chū-ni̋-kai 中二階 mezzanine
(floor)

chūō⊓ 中央 the center; **~ (no)**
中央(の) central; **Chūō-sen** 中
央線 the Chuo Line

chūritsu 中立 neutral(ity)

chūsa 中佐 lieutenant colonel;
(*navy*) commander

chūsha 1. 駐車 parking; **~-jō** 駐
車場 parking lot/garage; **~
kinshi** 駐車禁止 No Parking
2. 注射 injection

chūshá-ki 注射器 syringe (*for injections*)

chūshi 中止 suspension (*abeyance*); **chūshi shimá̄su** 中止
します suspends, stops (in
the midst)

chūshin 中心 center, heart, middle; **~ (no)** 中心(の) central

chūshi̅n-chi 中心地 central area
chūshoku 昼食 lunch
chūshō-teki (na) 抽象的（な）
 abstract

chūsu̅i-ki 注水器 douche, syringe *(for water)*
chū-toro 中とろ・中トロ
 medium-fat (pink) tuna

— D —

... da ...だ: *see* ... -ta た
... da̅ ...だ = ... de̅su ...です is;
 it is
daberima̅su だべります,
 dabe̅ru だべる shoots the
 breeze/bull, chews the fat
 (idly talks)
dabe̅tte だべって →
 daberima̅su だべります
dabo̅ku̅-shō 打撲傷 bruise
daburima̅su ダブります,
 dabu̅ru ダブる gets doubled,
 overlaps, repeats, is repeated
 (by mistake)
da̅buru ダブル 1. = daburu-
 ru̅mu ダブルルーム a double
 (room) 2. double(-size) drink
 3. double-breasted suit 4. ~
 su *(tennis)* doubles
daburu-be̅ddo ダブルベッド
 double bed
dabu̅tte ダブって →
 daburima̅su ダブります
da̅ ga だが but
da̅i 第 + NUMBER number ... ;
 (= ...-bamme̅ ...番目)
 NUMERAL-th (Separate word

except when attached to a
 single-unit numeral: da̅i-san
 no ie̅ 第三の家 house number
 three)
da̅i 題 = daimoku̅ 題目 topic
dai (o-dai) 代（お代）, ...-dai ...
 代 charge *(fee)*, bill
... dai ...だい: da̅re/na̅n ~ 誰/
 何だい who/what is it?
...-dai ...台 (counts mounted
 machines, vehicles)
daibe̅n 大便 defecation, bowel
 movement, feces; ~ shi-
 ma̅su 大便します defecates
daibu 大分・だいぶ quite
dai-bu̅bun 大部分 most, the majority
daida̅i だいだい・橙 the bitter
 orange
da̅idai 代々 generation after
 generation, for generations
daidokoro 台所 kitchen; ~
 -do̅gu 台所道具 kitchen utensils
daigaku 大学 college, university;
 daigaku̅-nai 大学内 campus;
 daiga̅ku-sei 大学生 college stu-

dent, undergrad(uate)

daigaku⌐-in 大学院 graduate school; **daigakuⁿn-sei** 大学院生 graduate student

da⌐i-go 第五 five; (= **go-bamme⌐** 五番目) fifth

daihyō 代表 representative; **daihyō-sha** 代表者 a representative (person); **daihyō-teki (na)** 代表的（な）representative, typical, model

da⌐i-(ichi) 第（一）number (one)

da⌐ii 大尉 navy lieutenant *(also* **ta⌐ii** 大尉*)*

da⌐i-ichi 第一 number one; (= **ichi-bamme⌐** 一番目) first

da⌐iji 大事 a matter of importance; ~ **o torima⌐su** 大事をとります plays it safe

daiji⌐ (na) 大事（な）important, precious; **karada o ~ ni shite kudasa⌐i** 体を大事にして下さい take good care of yourself

da⌐ijin 大臣 minister *(cabinet)*

dai-jo⌐bu (na) 大丈夫（な）OK, all right; safe (and sound); no need to worry

da⌐i-jū 第十 number ten; (= **jū-bamme⌐** 十番目) tenth

daika⌐ⁿi 大海 = **taikai** 大海 ocean, high sea

daikin 代金 the price/charge, the bill; ~ **hiki-kae (de)** 代金引換え（で）C.O.D., collect (on delivery)

daikō 代行 acting as agent;

daikō⌐-sha 代行者 agent

daikon 大根 giant white radish; ~**-o⌐roshi** 大根下ろし grated radish

da⌐iku 大工 carpenter

da⌐i-ku 第九 (= **da⌐i-kyū** 第九) number nine; (= **kyū-bamme⌐** 九番目) ninth

daime⌐ishi 代名詞 pronoun

daimoku⌐ⁿ 題目 topic

daimyō⌐ (o-daimyō) 大名（お大名）feudal lord

da⌐i-nana 第七 seven; (= **nana-bamme⌐** 七番目) seventh

da⌐i-ni 第二 number two; (= **ni-bamme⌐** 二番目) second

dainingu-ki⌐tchin (DK) ダイニングキッチン（DK）a combined diningroom-kitchen, an eat-in kitchen

da⌐i no ... 大の..., **dai-...** 大... big, great

dairi 代理 agent (= **dairi⌐ⁿ-nin** 代理人); agency (= **dairi⌐-ten** 代理店)

da⌐i-roku 第六 number six; (= **roku-bamme⌐** 六番目) sixth

daisa 大佐 navy captain *(also* **taisa** 大佐*)*

da⌐i-san 第三 number three; (= **sam-bamme⌐** 三番目) third

da⌐i-shi 第四 = **da⌐i-yon** 第四

da⌐i-shichi 第七 = **da⌐i-nana** 第七

dai-shō 代将 brigadier general

da⌐i-suki (na) 大好き（な）

favorite

daitai だいたい・大体 in general, on the whole, approximately, almost

daita￢n (na) 大胆（な）bold

daite 抱いて → **dakima￢su** 抱きます

daitō￢ryō 大統領 president *(of a nation)*

da￢iya ダイヤ schedule *(train)*; diamond

daiyamo￢ndo ダイヤモンド diamond

da￢i-yon 第四 number four; (= **yom-bamme￢** 四番目) fourth

da￢izu 大豆 soy beans

...￢-daka ...高 1. quantity, volume; sum 2. higher by ... **hyakue￢n-daka** 百円高 up ¥100

dakanai 抱かない = **dakimase￢n** 抱きません (not hold in arms)

da￢ kara (sa) だから（さ）and so; therefore; that's why

dake 抱け 1. → **dakema￢su** 抱けます [infinitive] 2. → **dakima￢su** 抱きます [imperative] **dake(￢ yo)** 抱け（よ）

... dake￢ ...だけ only, just; ... **(-ta) dake￢ de** ...（た）だけで just from (having done it)

dakema￢su 抱けます, **dakeru** 抱ける can hold in the arms

dakenai 抱けない = **dakemase￢n** 抱けません (cannot hold in arms) 「けます

dakete 抱けて → **dakema￢su** 抱

daki 抱き → **dakima￢su** 抱きます [infinitive]

dakima￢su 抱きます, **daku** 抱く holds in the arms

daki-shimema￢su 抱き締めます, **-shime￢ru** 抱き締める hugs

da￢kuron ダクロン Dacron

dakyō 妥協 compromise

damarima￢su 黙ります, **dama￢ru** 黙る is silent; shuts up

damashima￢su だまします・騙します, **dama￢su** だます・騙す deceives, cheats

dama￢tte 黙って → **damarima￢su** 黙ります

dambō 暖房 heating (of room, house); ～**-sō￢chi** 暖房装置 heating device, radiator; ～ **-se￢tsubi** 暖房設備 heating (equipment)

dam-bō￢ru ダンボール・段ボール corrugated cardboard

dame￢ (na) だめ［駄目］な no good, no use, won't; bad, broken, malfunctioning; don't!

dame￢ ni narima￢su だめ［駄目］になります gets ruined, spoiled

dame￢ ni shima￢su だめ［駄目］にします ruins it, spoils it

da￢mu ダム dam

da￢n 段 step(s); grade, order; (page) column; scene, act; (... ～ ...段) case, event

danchi 団地 housing develop-

ment; **~-apāto** 団地アパート
apartment complex

danda[ ]n だんだん・段々
gradually

dangan 弾丸 bullet

dango (o-dango) だんご・団子
（おだんご・お団子）dumpling

da[ ]njo 男女 male and female; **~
kyōgaku** 男女共学 coeduca-
tion

dankai 段階 stage *(of a process)*

dankon 男根 penis

danna-san/-sama 旦那さん/様
husband; master (of the
house/shop)

dansei 男性 male

da[ ]nshi 男子 gentleman

dantai 団体 organization, group

danwa 談話 conversation

dan'yaku 弾薬 ammunition

...da[ ]ra ...だら: *see* **...-ta[ ]ra** ...た
ら

da[ ]re 誰 who; **da[ ]re no** 誰の
whose; **da[ ]re de[ ] mo** 誰でも
anybody (at all), everybody

da[ ]redare 誰々・だれだれ someone or other, so-and-so,
what's-his/her-name

da[ ]re ka 誰か somebody, someone

dare mo 誰も (not) anybody; [+
NEGATIVE] nobody

da[ ]resore 誰それ・だれそれ
someone or other, so-and-so,
what's-his/her-name 「り

...da[ ]ri ...だり: *see* **...-ta[ ]ri** ...た

... darō ...だろう = **... deshō** ...
でしょう probably, probably
(it) is; I think; don't you
think?

dasa[ ]nai 出さない =
dashimase[ ]n 出しません (not
put out; not ...)

da[ ]seba 出せば → **dashima[ ]su** 出
します (if one put out; if ...)

da[ ]sha 出しゃ 1. = **da[ ]seba** 出せ
ば 2. **~ shinai** 出しゃしない
= **da[ ]shi ya/wa shinai** 出しや/
はしない = **dasa[ ]nai** 出さない

dashi[ ] だし・出汁 soup stock

da[ ]shi 出し → **dashima[ ]su** 出し
ます

dashi-mae 出し前 (one's) share
(of expenses)

dashima[ ]su 出します, **da[ ]su** 出す
puts out; serves (food/drink);
produces; pays; spends; mails;
begins

dashin 打診 (medical examination by) percussion, tapping;
sounding a person out; **~
shima[ ]su** 打診します sounds
(a person) out

dassen 脱線 derailment; **~
shima[ ]su** 脱線します is de-
railed; gets off the track, gets
sidetracked

dasshi[ ]-men 脱脂綿 absorbent
cotton

dasshi[ ]-nyū 脱脂乳 skim milk

dasshū[ ]-zai 脱臭剤 deodorant
(personal)

datai 堕胎 abortion

datsumō-zai 脱毛剤 depilatory

... da[˥]tta ...だった = **... de[˥]shita** ...
でした was; it was

... da[˥]ttara ...だったら if/when it
is (or was)

... da[˥]ttari (shima[˥]su/desu) ...だ
ったり(します/です) being
representatively/sometimes/
alternately ... ; ~ **... ja na[˥]kat-
tari** ...だったり...じゃなかっ
たり (is) off and on, some-
times is and sometimes
isn't

da[˥]tte だって = **de[˥] mo** でも but;
however, even so, though

... da[˥]tte ...だって = **... de[˥] mo** ...
でも even being ... ; ... or
something

de 出 1. a person's origins
(birthplace, family, school);
(**... no** ~ ...の出) born in/of
... , a graduate of ... 2. (out)-
flow; **suidō no de ga i[˥]i** 水道の
出がいい has good water pres-
sure 3. emergence, appearance; **tsuki(˥) no de** 月の出
moonrise

de[˥] 出 → **dema[˥]su** 出ます:
1. [infinitive] 2. [imperative];
~ **ro/yo** 出ろ/よ out!

...de ...で: *see* **...-te** ...て

... de[˥] ...で (happening) at, in,
on; with, by (means of),
through

... de[˥] ...で is/was and; being, its

being; with (its being)
[COPULA GERUND]

... de arima[˥]su ...であります
= **... de[˥]su** ...です

... de arimase[˥]n ...でありませ
ん = **... ja arimase[˥]n** ...じゃ
ありません

... de gozaima[˥]su ...でござい
ます [DEFERENTIAL] = **...
desu** ...です is; it is (, sir/
ma'am)

... de gozaimashō[˥] ...でござい
ましょう = **... deshō[˥]** ...で
しょう probably is; I think
it is (, sir/ma'am)

... de ima[˥]su ...でいます stays
/keeps (goes on) being ... ;
**Niho[˥]n wa i[˥]tsu made "sen-
shin-ko[˥]kka" de irareru[˥] ka**
日本はいつまで「先進国家」
でいられるか How long can
Japan remain an "Ad-
vanced Nation"?

... de orima[˥]su ...でおります
[DEFERENTIAL, HUMBLE] (I/
we) stay/keep (go on) be-
ing ...; **Minna ge[˥]nki** ~ みん
な[皆]元気でおります. We
are all keeping well

de-aima[˥]su 出会います, **-a[⌐]u** 出
会う: **... ni** ~ ...に出会います
encounters, meets, happens to
see/meet, runs/bumps into

de-a[˥]tte 出会って → **de-aima[˥]su**
出会います

de-awa[˥]nai 出会わない = **de-**

aimase̅n 出会いません (not en-counter)

de̅guchi 出口 exit, outlet

deiri[¯]guchi 出入り口 gate(way)

dekake 出掛け → **dekakema̅su** 出掛けます

dekakema̅su 出掛けます, **dekakeru** 出掛ける starts off/out, departs

de̅ki でき・出来 → **dekima̅su** でき[出来]ます

deki̅goto 出来事・できごと happening, accident

dekima̅su でき[出来]ます, **deki̅ru** でき[出来]る can (do), is possible; is produced; is done, finished, through, ready; **Da̅re ga(/ni) na̅ni ga dekima̅su ka** 誰が(/に)何ができ[出来]ますか Who can do what?

deki̅-mo-no̅ (o-de̅ki) できもの[出来物](おでき) swelling, sore, boil, pimple

deki̅nai でき[出来]ない impossible; = **dekimase̅n** でき[出来]ません (cannot)

deki̅ru でき[出来]る = **dekima̅su** でき[出来]ます

dekiru-dake できる[出来る]だけ as much as possible

de̅kki デッキ deck

dekoboko (no) でこぼこ・凸凹(の) 1. bump(y), rough (road) 2. uneven(ness), imbalance

demae (o-demae) 出前(お出前)

catering, food delivered to order, restaurant delivery (service/person); **dema̅e-mochi** 出前持ち restaurant delivery person

dema̅su 出ます, **de̅ru** 出る goes/comes out, emerges, appears; is served; leaves, starts

de̅mbu 1. でんぶ・田麩 sweet cooked ground fish **2.** 臀部 buttock, hips

de̅mo でも but, however, even so, though

... de̅mo ...でも even/also (being) ... , even if it be; ... or something; **gaka de̅mo sak[¯]ka de̅mo arima̅su** 画家でも作家でもあります is both a painter and a writer

dempō 電報 telegram; **~ o uchima̅su** 電報を打ちます sends a telegram

dempun でんぷん・澱粉 starch (for cooking); **dempu̅n-shitsu (no)** でんぷん[澱粉]質(の) starchy

dempyō 伝票 check (restaurant bill)

de-mukaema̅su 出迎えます, **-mukae[¯]ru** 出迎える meets, greets, welcomes

... de na̅i ...でない = **... ja na̅i** ...じゃない

de̅nai 出ない = **demase̅n** 出ません (not go/come out; ...)

de[¯]nchi 電池 battery

denchū 電柱 telephone/light pole

denga⌐ku 田楽, **o-de⌐n** おでん assorted boiled foods

de⌐nki 電気 electricity, power; lights; **denki-ga⌐isha** 電気会社 power/light company; ~ **-suta⌐ndo** 電気スタンド desk/ floor lamp; ~**-sutō⌐bu** 電気ストーブ electric heater; ~ **-yō⌐hin** 電気用品 = **denki-ki⌐gu** 電気器具 electrical appliances; **denki-ka⌐misori** 電気かみそり electric shaver; ~ **-ko⌐nro** 電気こんろ[焜炉]hot plate; ~**-sōji⌐ki** 電気掃除機 vacuum cleaner

denki-ya (san) 電気屋(さん) electrician

denkyū 電球 light bulb

densen 1. 電線 electric wire, power line **2.** 伝染 contagion; **densem-byō** 伝染病 contagious/infectious/communicable disease, epidemic

densetsu 伝説 tradition (legend)

de⌐nsha 電車 electric car, streetcar, train

de⌐nshi (no) 電子(の) electron-(ic)

dentō 1. 電灯 lamp, light, flashlight **2.** 伝統 tradition; ~**-teki (na)** 伝統的(な) traditional

denwa (o-de⌐nwa) 電話(お電話) telephone (call), **akai** ~ 赤い 電話 red (= pay) phone; ~ **ni dema⌐su** 電話に出ます answers the phone; ~ **o kakema⌐su/shima⌐su** 電話をかけます/します makes a phone call

denwa 電話; ~**-ba⌐ngō** 電話番号 telephone number; ~ **-bo⌐kkusu** 電話ボックス = **denwa⌐-shitsu** 電話室 phone booth; ~**-chō** 電話帳 telephone book/directory; ~ **-kōka⌐nshu** 電話交換手 telephone operator; ~**-sen** 電 話線 phone line, telephone wire(s)

depa⌐to デパート department store

de⌐ppa 出っ歯 protruding tooth, bucktooth

de⌐reba 出れば → **dema⌐su** 出ます (if one go/come out; if ...)

de⌐ ro 出ろ → **dema⌐su** 出ます [imperative]

de⌐ru 出る = **dema⌐su** 出ます (goes out, comes out, leaves, starts)

de⌐rya 出りゃ = **de⌐reba** 出れば (if one go/come out; ...)

deshi⌐ (o-deshi) 弟子(お弟子) apprentice, disciple

... de⌐shita ...でした **1.** was; it was **2.** **...-mase⌐n deshita** ...ま せんでした didn't

... dcshō⌐ ...でしょう probably, probably (it) is; I think; don't you think?

... de̅ su ...です, **da**̕ だ is, has been (and still is), will be; it is

de̅ ta 出た = **dema̅shi̱ta** 出ました (emerged)

de̅ ta データ data

detarame でたらめ nonsense; ~ **(na)** でたらめ(な) irresponsible, unreliable

de̅ te 出て → **dema̅su** 出ます [gerund]; ~ **kima̅su** 出て来ます, ~ **ku̅ru** 出て来る comes out; ~ **ikima̅su** 出て行きます, ~ **iku** 出て行く goes out

de̅ to デート date (time; engagement)

de̅ wa では (= **ja** じゃ) well then; in that case; and so; and now

... de̅ wa ...では (with) its being, it is and; if it be; ~ **arimase̅n (na̅i)** ...ではありません(ない) = **ja arimase̅n** じゃありません

de̅ ya/wa shinai 出や/はしない = **de̅nai** 出ない, (not come out)

de̅ yo 出よ → **dema̅su** 出ます [imperative]

deza̅to デザート dessert

di... ディ... → **ji...** ジ...

dii-ke̅ ディーケー (= **DK**) → **dainingu-ki̅tchin** ダイニングキッチン

do 度 degree; moderation; ~ **o sugoshima̅su** 度を過ごします goes too far, goes to excess

...-do ...度 times (occasions)

...-do ...度 degrees

do̅ どう how, why; (in) what (way)

do̅ 銅 copper (= **aka-gane** あかがね·銅)

do̅(-) 同... ... the same ... [bookish] = **onaji** 同じ

...-dō ...洞 cave

do̅a ドア door

do-bin 土瓶 teapot

dobu どぶ·溝 gutter

dōbutsu 動物 animal; **dōbutsu̅-en** 動物園 zoo; **dōbutsu̅-gaku** 動物学 zoology

do̅chira どちら which one (of the two); [DEFERENTIAL] where = **do̅ko** どこ, who = **da̅re** 誰

do̅chira de̅ mo どちらでも either one of the two

dochira-gawa どちら側 which one

do̅chira ka どちらか one of the two

dochira mo どちらも 1. [not] either one; neither one 2. both

do̅chira sama どちら様 [DEFERENTIAL] who (are you)

do̅ de̅ mo どうでも anyhow (at all)

dōfū shima̅su 同封します encloses (in envelope)

dōgi-go 同義語, **dōi-go** 同意語 synonym

dōgu̅ (o-dōgu) 道具(お道具)

tool; **dōgu**⌐-**bako** 道具箱 tool box

dohyō 土俵 sumo-wrestling ring

dōi shimaᵈsu 同意します agrees, concurs, consents

Dōʼ itashima(⌐)shite. どういたしまして. You're welcome.

doite どいて → **dokima**ʼsu どきます

doʼitsu どいつ which damn one

Doʼitsu ドイツ Germany; **Doitsu-go** ドイツ語 German language; **Doitsuʼ-jin** ドイツ人 a German; **Doitsu-kei** ドイツ系 of German ancestry

dō⌐**ji** 同時 1. ~ **(no)** 同時(の) simultaneous; **dōji-tsū**ʼyaku 同時通訳 simultaneous translation 2. ... **to** ~ **ni** ...と同時に at the same time as ... ; while ..., on the other hand 3. at a (single) time, at one time

dō-jimaʼsu 動じます, **dō-ji**⌐**ru** 動じる gets agitated, upset; (... -**te**ʼ **mo**) **dō-jimase**ʼn (...ても) 動じません is unfazed (by)

dojō どじょう・泥鰌 loach, mudfish

dōjō 同情 sympathy, compassion; (... **ni**) ~ **shima**ʼsu (...に)同情します sympathizes (with ...)

dō⌐**jō** 道場 martial arts hall

... **dōʼ ka** ...どうか (whether ...) or not   ⌐*copper)*

dōʼka どうか・銅貨 coin *(brass or*

dokanai どかない・退かない = **dokimase**ʼn どきません・退きません (not get out of the way)

doke どけ・退け 1. → **dokema**ʼsu どけます・退けます [infinitive] 2. → **dokima**ʼsu どきます・退きます [imperative] **doke(**⌐**yo)** どけ(よ)・退け(よ) get out of the way!

doki どき・退き → **dokima**ʼsu どきます・退きます [infinitive]

do⌐**ki** 土器 earthenware

dō⌐**ki** 動機 motivation, motive

doʼki 同期 the same period

doʼkidoki shima(ʼ**)su** どきどきします one's heart throbs (beats, flutters)

dokimaʼsu どきます・退きます, **doku** どく・退く gets out of the way

dōkiʼ-sei 同期生 (former) classmate

duk-keʼshiʼ 毒消し antidote

doʼkku ドック dock

doʼko どこ where, what part/place; **do**⌐**ko de**⌐ **mo** どこでも anywhere at all; **Doʼko e ikima**ʼsu **ka?** どこへ行きますか Where (to what place) are you going? **Doʼko o (= doʼno michi o) ikima**ʼsu **ka?** どこを(どこの道を)行きますか What path will you take? **Doʼko kara kima**ʼshita **ka?** どこから来ましたか Where did you come from?

do̱kodoko どこどこ somewhere or other

do̱ko ka どこか somewhere

do̱ko made どこまで where to; how far

doko mo どこも + NEGATIVE nowhere, (not) anywhere

do̱kosoko どこそこ somewhere or other, such-and-such a place

doku どく・退く = dokima̱su どきます・退きます

doku̱ 毒 poison; dok(u)-ke̱shi̱ 毒消し antidote

dokuritsu 独立 independence; ～ shite ima̱su 独立しています, ～ shita ... 独立した... independent

dokusa̱i-sha 独裁者 dictator

do⌐kusha 読者 reader (person)

dokushin 独身 single, unmarried, bachelor

dokutoku (no) 独特(の) characteristic, peculiar, unique

dokuzetsu 毒舌 a barbed/spiteful tongue

dōkyū̱-sei 同級生 classmate

domburi (o-do̱mburi) 丼(お丼) a bowl of rice with some kind of topping

...-do̱mo ...共 (makes humble plurals); watakushi-do̱mo わたくしども・私共 we/us

do̱mo どうも 1. thank you 2. ex-cuse me 3. ever so much 4. somehow, vaguely

do̱n どん boom (sound)

...-don ...丼 = domburi 丼・どんぶり: see ten-～ 天丼, una～ うな丼・鰻丼

donarima̱su どなります・怒鳴ります, dona̱ru どなる・怒鳴る shouts, yells

do̱nata どなた [DEFERENTIAL] = da̱re 誰 who

do̱ndon どんどん one right after another, in large numbers

dō-nichi 土日 Saturday and Sunday

dō̱ ni ka どうにか somehow; ～ shima̱su どうにかします manages to do

do̱nna ... どんな... what kind of ... ; ～ iro̱ どんな色 what color; ～ ni どんなに to what extent, how much

do̱no ... どの... which ... (of more than two)

dono-gurai どの位 how much/far/long

do̱nsu どんす・緞子 damask

dorai-kuri̱ini̱ngu ドライクリーニング dry cleaning

dora⌐i (na) ドライ(な) dry; modern, sophisticated, unsentimental

dōra̱ku 道楽 1. dissipation 2. (o-dōraku⌐ お道楽) pastime, hobby

dorama̱min ドラマミン Dramamine

do̅ re どれ which one (*of more than two*); **do̅ re ka** どれか some/any one of them; **do̅re de̅ mo** どれでも whichever/any of them; **dore mo** どれも (not) any of them

dorei 奴隷 slave

do̅ resu ドレス dress

doresu-me̅ kā ドレスメーカー dressmaker

do̅ri̅ 道理 reason (*what is sensible*)

...-do̅ri ...通り avenue; just as (according with); **jikan ~ (ni)** 時間通り(に) on time

do̅ri̅ru ドリル drill (*tool; practice*)

doro̅ 泥 mud; muck (filth, dirt); **doro-da̅rake (no)** 泥だらけ (の) muddy

do̅ro 道路 road; **do̅ro-hyo̅ shiki** 道路標識 roadsign

dorobo̅ 泥棒 thief, robber, burglar

do̅ru ドル dollar

do̅ryo̅ 同僚 colleague

do̅ryoku 努力 effort; **do̅ryoku shima̅su** 努力します makes an effort, tries (hard), endeavors, strives

do̅ sa 動作 (body) movements, gestures

do̅se̅i-ai (no) 同性愛(の) homosexual

do̅shi 動詞 verb

... do̅ shi ...同士・同志 fellow ...; comrade

Do̅ shima̅shita ka どうしましたか. What happened? What did you do?

do̅ -shite どうして why; how; **~ mo** どうしても, **do̅-shite̅ mo** どうしても one way or another, somehow or other

do̅shitsu̅-sha 同室者 roommate

do̅so̅ -kai 同窓会 alumni association; class reunion

do̅ tchi どっち = **do̅ chira** どちら which one (of the two)

dote 土手 dike

do̅tei 童貞 virgin (*male*)

dotera どてら padded bathrobe (= **tanzen** 丹前)

do̅toku 道徳 morals, morality; **~ -teki (na)** 道徳的(な) moral

do̅tto どっと suddenly, with a rush; **~ waraima̅su** どっと笑います everybody laughs

do̅yo̅ 1. **~ (no)** 同様(の) the same 2. 動揺 agitation, unrest; **~ shima̅su** 動揺します is agitated (nervous)

Doyo̅ bi 土曜日 Saturday

do̅ yū ("iu") ... どうゆう(いう)... what kind/sort of ... (= **do̅nna ...** どんな...)

do̅zo どうぞ please

do̅zo̅ 銅像 statue (*bronze*)

dy... → j...

dz... → z...

— E —

e 1. 絵 picture, painting, drawing 2. 得 → **emaꜜsu** 得ます [infinitive]

eꜜ? え? eh? what?

ēꜜ ええ 1. yes 2. [dialect] = **iꜜi** いい (good)

... e ...へ to (a place); [*replaces* ... **ni** ...に *before* ... **no** ...の...] to (a person)

ea-kon エアコン air conditioning/conditioner

eba-miꜜruku エバミルク evaporated milk

ebi えび・海老 shrimp; **kurumaꜜ-ebi** 車えび[海老] prawn; **iseꜜ-ebi** 伊勢えび[海老] lobster; **shibaꜜ-ebi** 芝えび[海老] tiny shrimp

ebi-fuꜜrai えび[海老]フライ shrimp fried in bread crumbs

ē-bii-shiꜜi エービーシー・ABC alphabet (ABC)

ebi-ten えび[海老]天 batter-fried shrimp

echiꜜketto エチケット etiquette

eda 枝 branch

eda-mame 枝豆 green soy beans to be boiled, podded and eaten as appetizers

egaꜜite 描いて → **egakimaꜜsu** 描きます

egakimaꜜsu 描きます, **egaꜜku** 描く draws (a picture)

egetsunaꜜi えげつない crass, gross

e-haꜜgaki 絵葉書 picture postcard

e-hoꜜn 絵本 picture book

eꜜiga 映画 movie, film; **eigaꜜ-kan** 映画館 movie theater

Eigo 英語 English

eigyō 営業 (running a) business; **~-jiꜜkan** 営業時間 business hours

Eikoku 英国 = **Igirisu** イギリス England

eikyō 影響 influence

eisei 衛生 hygiene, health, sanitation; **eiseꜜi-hei** 衛生兵 medic, hospital orderly/corpsman; **eisei-tai** 衛生隊 medical corps; **eisei-teki (na)** 衛生的(な) sanitary

eishaꜜ-ki 映写機 movie projector

eꜜito/ēꜜto エイト/エート eight; 8-oared racing boat

ei-wa 英和 English-Japanese; **eiwa-jiꜜten** 英和辞典 English-Japanese dictionary

eꜜizu エイズ AIDS

eꜜki 駅 railroad station

eki-ben 駅弁 box lunches sold at

railroad stations

ekichō 駅長 stationmaster;
ekichō̄-shitsu 駅長室 station-master's office

ekitai 液体 liquid

ekkusu-sen エックス[X]線 X-ray

e̅kubo えくぼ dimple

ema̅su 得ます, **e̅ru** 得る
[bookish] gets; can do

empitsu 鉛筆 pencil

e̅n 円 circle

e̅n 円, **...-en** ...円 yen (¥)

e̅nai 得ない = **emase̅n** 得ません (not get; cannot)

enchō 延長 extension; **~-kō̄do**
延長コード extension cord; **~
shima̅su** 延長します extends,
lengthens, prolongs

endan 1. 縁談 marriage proposal
2. 演壇 lecture platform

e̅ndō えんどう・豌豆, **endō̄-
mame** えんどうまめ・豌豆豆
peas

ene̅ru̅gii エネルギー energy

ene̅rugi̅sshu (na) エネルギッシュ(な) energetic

engan 1. 沿岸 the coast 2. **~
(no)** 遠眼(の) = **enshi** 遠視
farsighted (presbyopic)

engawa 縁側 veranda, porch

engeki 演劇 drama, play;
engeki̅-jin 演劇人 theater people

engi 縁起 1. omen, luck 2. (his-torical) origin

e̅ngi 演技 performance; acting;
engi̅-sha 演技者 performer

e̅njin エンジン engine (of
automobile); **~ ga
kakarima̅su** エンジンがかか
ります the engine starts, **~ o
kakema̅su** エンジンをかけま
す starts the engine; **~ o
fukashima̅su** エンジンを吹か
します races the engine

enjo 援助 support (aid)

enjo̅i shima(ー)su エンジョイし
ます enjoys

enjuku 円熟 fully maturing;
enjuku shima̅su 円熟します
fully matures; mellows

enkai 宴会 party; banquet

e̅nnichi 縁日 a temple fair
(festival)

enoki̅-dake えのき茸・榎茸,
enoki̅-take えのき茸・榎茸
straw mushrooms

enryo (go-enryo) 遠慮(ご遠慮)
reticence, social reserve,
shyness; **~ ga na̅i** 遠慮がない
frank; **~ shima̅su** 遠慮しま
す hesitates, holds back, is
shy, **(... o ~ shima̅su** ...を遠
慮します) refrains from; **~
shite okima̅su** 遠慮しておき
ます takes a rain check,
declines for now

enshi 遠視 farsighted (pres-byopic)

e̅nso 塩素 chlorine

ensō̄-kai 演奏会 concert

ensoku 遠足 picnic, outing

entotsu 煙突 chimney, smoke-stack

enzetsu 演説 speech *(public)*

erabima̱su 選びます, **era̱bu** 選ぶ chooses, selects, elects

era̱i 偉い great, grand, superior

e̱reba 得れば → **ema̱su** 得ます (if one get)

erebē̱ta エレベーター elevator

eri̱ えり・襟 collar *(of coat)*

e̱ro (na) エロ (な) erotic

e̱ru 得る → **ema̱su** 得ます (gets)

eru-e̱ru エルエル・LL ("LL") language lab(oratory)

esa̱ えさ・餌 bait

ese-... えせ...・似非... pseudo-...

e̱tchi (na) エッチ (な) dirty-minded; **~ na hanashi̱** エッチな話 a dirty (an off-color) story

e̱te 得て → **ema̱su** 得ます (gets)

e̱te-shi̱te えてして・得てして usually; **~ shima̱su** えてしてします is apt to do it

e̱to エート = **e̱ito** エイト eight; 8-oared racing boat ⌜see

ē-to えーと well now, uh, let me

e̱zu 得ず = **e̱naide** 得ないで (not getting; unable); → **ema̱su** 得ます

e̱zu エーズ AIDS

— **F** —

fa..., fi..., fo... → **f(u)a..., f(u)i..., f(u)o...**

fu ふ・麸 pieces of dried wheat gluten

fu̱ 府, **...-fu** ...府 an urban prefecture (Kyoto or Osaka)

fū̱ 封 sealing; **tegami no fū̱ o shima̱su** 手紙の封をします seals a letter

... fū̱ ...風, **...-fū** ...風 air; way, fashion, manner; style

f(u)a̱ibu ファ[フア]イブ five

fu̱an ファン, **fua̱n** ファン fan *(enthusiast)*

fuan (na) 不安 (な) uneasy

fu̱ben (na) 不便 (な) inconvenient, unhandy

fu̱bo 父母 father and mother, one's parents

fu̱buki 吹雪 snowstorm

fuchi̱ 縁 edge, rim, frame

fuchū̱i 不注意 carelessness; **~ (na)** 不注意 (な) careless

fuda ふだ・札 label, tag, card, check; **(o-fuda** おふだ・お札) talisman (of a shrine)

fu̱dan (ni) ふだん・普段 (に) usually, ordinarily, always; **~ (no)** ふだん・普段 (の) usual, ordinary, everyday

fuda**n-gi** ふだん［普段］着 every-
　day clothes
fude 筆 writing brush
fudō**□san** 不動産 real estate
fu-do**toku** 不道徳 immorality;
　～ **(na)** 不道徳（な）immoral
fue 笛 whistle; flute
fue 増え → **fuema**su 増えます
fuema**su** 増えます, **fue**ru 増え
　る multiply; grows in quanti-
　ty/number, gets bigger,
　swells, increases
fue**reba** 増えれば, **fue**rya 増え
　りゃ → **fuema**su 増えます (if
　they grow, …)
fu**ete** 増えて → **fuema**su 増え
　ます
fū**fu** 夫婦 husband and wife,
　Mr. and Mrs., (married) cou-
　ple; **fūfu-tomo** 夫婦共 both
　husband and wife
fu**gu** 1. ふぐ・河豚 blowfish,
　puffer 2. 不具 cripple
fuhei 不平 discontent, grumbl-
　ing
fuhō **(na)** 不法（な）illegal
fui ni ふいに・不意に suddenly
F(u)iri**(p)pin** フィリ［フイリ］
　（ッ）ピン, **Hi**ri**(p)pin** ヒリ
　（ッ）ピン Philippines
fuirumu フィルム, **f(u)i**rumu
　フィ［フイ］ルム film
f(u)iruta フィ［フイ］ルター
　filter
fuji ふじ・藤 wisteria
fujin 婦人 lady

Fu**ji(-san)** 富士（山）Mount
　Fuji, Fujiyama
fu**-jiyū (na)** 不自由（な）inconve-
　nient, restricted; needy; weak
fuka**□** ふか・鱶 shark
fuka**i** 深い deep; **fuka**ku 深く
　deeply
fukanai 拭かない = **fukimase**n
　拭きません (not wipe)
fuka**□nai** ふかない・葺かない =
　fukimasen ふきません・葺き
　ません (not roof)
fuka**nai** 吹かない = **fukimase**n
　吹きません (not blow)
fuka**nō (na)** 不可能（な）impossi-
　ble
fuka**sa** 深さ deepness, depth
fukashima**su, fuka**su 1. 蒸かし
　ます, 蒸かす steams (food)
　2. 吹かします, 吹かす
　smokes 3. e**njin o ～** エンジン
　を吹かします, 吹かす races
　the engine 4. 更かします, 更
　かす **yo**o **o ～** 夜を更かします,
　更かす stays up late
fuke 1. ふけ dandruff
　2. 拭け → **fukema**su 拭けま
　す (can wipe) [infinitive]
　3. 拭け → **fukima**su 拭きま
　す (wipes) [imperative] wipe
　it
fu**ke** 吹け → **fukima**su 吹きま
　す (blows) [imperative]
fuke 更け・老け・吹け →
　fukemasu 更けます; 老けま
　す; 吹けます (grows late;

ages; can blow) [infinitive]

fuke̅ba 拭けば・ふけば・吹けば → **fukima̅su** 拭きます/ふきます/吹きます (if one wipe/roof/blow)

fu̅kei 風景 scenery, landscape

fuke̅iki 不景気 depression, recession, hard times

fukema̅su 拭けます, **fukeru** 拭ける can wipe

fukema̅su, fuke̅ru 1. 更けます, 更ける (**yo ga ~** 夜が更けます, 更ける) (the night) grows late **2.** 老けます, 老ける gets old, ages **3.** 吹けます, 吹ける can blow

fukenai 拭けない = **fukemase̅n** 拭けません (cannot wipe)

fuke̅nai 更けない・老けない・吹けない = **fukemase̅n** 更けません; 老けません; 吹けません (not grow late; not age; cannot blow)

fuke̅reba 更ければ・吹ければ, **fuke̅rya** 更けりゃ・吹けりゃ → **fukema̅su** 更けます; 吹けます (if it grow late; if one can blow)

fukete 拭けて → **fukema̅su** 拭けます (wipes)

fuke̅te 更けて・老けて・吹けて → **fukema̅su** 更けます; 老けます; 吹けます (grows late; ages; can blow)

fuketsu (na) 不潔(な) unclean, dirty, filthy

fuki 1. ふき・蕗 bog rhubarb **2.** 拭き → **fukima̅su** 拭きます (wipe)

fuki̅ 吹き → **fukima̅su** 吹きます (blow) [infinitive]

fukima̅su 拭きます, **fuku** 拭く wipes

fukima̅su ふきます・葺きます, **fuku̅** ふく・葺く: **... no ya̅ne o ~** ...の屋根をふきます covers with a roof, roofs (**kawara de ~** 瓦でふきます tiles a roof, **i̅ta de ~** 板でふきます shingles, **ka̅ya/kusa̅/wa̅ra de ~** かや[茅]/草/わら[藁]でふきます thatches)

fukima̅su 吹きます, **fuku̅** 吹く blows

fuki̅n 1. 布きん napkin, towel, cloth, washcloth, dishcloth **2.** 付近 vicinity

fuki̅so̅ku (na) 不規則(な) irregular

fukkakema̅su ふっかけます, **fukkake̅ru** ふっかける overcharges; **... o fukkakerema̅su** ...をふっかけられます gets overcharged for

fuko̅ 不幸 misfortune; **~ (na)** 不幸(な) unfortunate, unlucky; **~ ni (mo)** 不幸に(も) unfortunately

fu-ko̅hei (na) 不公平(な) unfair

fuku 拭く → **fukima̅su** 拭きます (wipes)

fuku̅ 1. 服 clothes, suit, dress

uniform **2.** 吹く = **fu̱kima⌐su**
吹きます (blows)
fu̱kubiki 福引 lottery; raffle
fu̱ku-daitō⌐ryō 副大統領 vice-
president *(of nation)*
fu̱kugō-go 複合語 compound
(word)
fu̱ku⌐me 含め **1.** → **fu̱kume-**
ma⌐su 含めます [infinitive]
2. → **fu̱kumima⌐su** 含みます
[imperative]
fu̱kumema⌐su 含めます,
fu̱kume⌐ru 含める includes
fu̱kumima⌐su 含みます,
fu̱ku⌐mu 含む holds in the
mouth; contains; implies;
bears/keeps in mind
fu̱kurami 膨らみ・ふくらみ
bulge
fu̱kuramima⌐su 膨らみ[ふくら
み]ます, **fu̱kuramu** 膨らむ・ふ
くらむ swells up
fu̱kurema⌐su 膨れ[ふくれ]ます,
fu̱kureru 膨れる・ふくれる
swells up; pouts, sulks
fu̱kuro⌐ 袋 bag, sack
fu̱ku⌐rō ふくろう・梟 owl
fu̱kusei 複製 replica, reproduction, reprint; ~ **shima⌐su** 複製
します reproduces, reprints
fu̱kusha 複写 reproduction,
copy, reprint; ~ **shima⌐su** 複
写します copies (reproduces)
it
fu̱ku-sha⌐chō 副社長 vice-president *(of company)*

fu̱kushi 副詞 adverb
fu̱ku⌐shi 福祉 welfare; **fu̱kushi-**
se⌐isaku 福祉政策 welfare
policy
fu̱kushū 1. 復習 review (study)
2. 復讐 revenge, vengeance
fu̱kushū shima⌐su 1. 復習します
reviews (study) **2.** 復讐します
takes revenge, revenges
fu̱kuzatsu (na) 複雑(な) complicated
fu̱kya 1. 拭きゃ・ふきゃ・吹きゃ
= **fu̱ke⌐ba** 拭けば/ふけば/吹
けば (if one wipe/roof/blow)
2. ~ **shinai** = **fu̱ki⌐ ya/wa**
shinai 拭きゃ[ふきゃ・吹き
ゃ]しない=拭き[ふき・吹き]
や/はしない (not wipe), = **fu̱kanai** 拭か
ない (not wipe), = **fu̱ka⌐nai**
ふかない・葺かない (not roof),
= **fu̱ka⌐nai** 吹かない (not
blow)
fu̱kyū 普及 diffusion, popularization; ~ **shima⌐su** 普及しま
す gets diffused (spread,
popularized)
fuman 不満 discontent; ~ **(na)**
不満(な) discontented, dissatisfied, unhappy
fumanai 踏まない = **fumima-**
se⌐n 踏みません (not tread)
fume 踏め **1.** → **fumema⌐su** 踏め
ます [infinitive] **2.** → **fumi-**
ma⌐su 踏みます [imperative]
fume(⌐ yo) 踏め(よ) tread it!
fume⌐ba 踏めば → **fumima⌐su** 踏

みます (if one tread)

fumei (no) 不明（の）unknown, obscure

fumema̍su 踏めます, **fumeru** 踏める can tread

fumi 踏み → **fumima̍su** 踏みます [infinitive]

fū̍mi 風味 flavor

fumi-komima̍su 踏み込みます, **-ko̍mu** 踏み込む 1. steps into/on 2. trespasses (on); raids

fumima̍su 踏みます, **fumu** 踏む steps on, treads

fumoto̍ ふもと・麓 foot (of a mountain)

fumya 踏みゃ 1. = **fume̍ba** 踏めば (if one tread) 2. ~ **shinai** 踏みゃしない = **fumi̍ ya/wa shinai** 踏みや/はしない = **fumanai** 踏まない (not tread)

fu̍n ふん・糞 feces, dung

...̍-fun ...分 minute(s)

fu̍na ふな・鮒 crucian carp

funaᵈbin 船便 seamail

funa̍nori 船乗り sailor, crew (member)

funaᵈyoi 船酔い seasick(ness)

funde 踏んで → **fumima̍su** 踏みます

fundoshi ふんどし・褌 loincloth, breechcloth

fu̍ne (o-fune) 船・舟（お船・お舟）boat, ship

fungai 憤慨 indignation, resentment; ~ **shima̍su** 憤慨します gets indignant, resents

fun'i̍ki 雰囲気 atmosphere (of a place)

funka 噴火 eruption; **funkaᵈ-kō** 噴火口 crater; ~ **shima̍su** 噴火します erupts

funsui 噴水 fountain

f(u)o̍a フォ［フオ］ア four; 4-oared racing boat

f(u)o̍ku フォ［フオ］ーク = **hō̍ku** ホーク fork

furai-pan フライパン frying pan

furanai 振らない = **furimase̍n** 振りません (not wave)

fura̍nai 降らない = **furimase̍n** 降りません (not precipitate)

Furansu フランス France; ~ **-go** フランス語 French; **Furansu̍-jin** フランス人 a French person

fure 振れ 1. → **furema̍su** 振れます [infinitive] 2. → **furima̍su** 振ります [imperative]

fure(˥yo) 振れ（よ）wave it!

fure̍ba 振れば → **furima̍su** 振ります (if one wave it)

fu̍reba 降れば → **furima̍su** 降ります (if it rain/snow)

furema̍su, fureru 1. 触れます, 触れる（... **ni** ~ ...に触れます）touches, comes in contact with; touches upon, mentions, refers to 2. 振れます, 振れる（... **o/ga** ~ ...を/が振れます）can wave it, can shake it

fure(ra)rema̍su 触れ（ら）れます, **fure(ra)reru** 触れ（ら）れる can

touch

furete 触れて・振れて →
furema'su 触れます・振れます

furi 振り → **furima'su** 振ります
(waves) [infinitive]

furi 1. ふり・振り manner, air,
pretense 2. 降り the rain/
snow, the downpour

fu'ri 降り → **furima'su** 降ります
(rains/snows) [infinitive]

furi-kae 振替 transfer (of funds)

furikae-cho'kin 振替貯金 postal
transfer; **furikaechokin-kō'za**
振替貯金口座 a postal transfer
account

furi-kake ふりかけ・振り掛け
flavor sprinkles (to top rice)

furi-ka'ke ふりかけ・振り掛け
→ **furi-kakema'su** ふりかけま
す・振り掛けます

furi-kakema'su ふりかけます・
振り掛けます, **-kake'ru** ふり
かける・振り掛ける sprinkles
it

furima'su 振ります, **furu** 振る
waves, shakes, wags it

furima'su 降ります, **fu'ru** 降る it
precipitates (rains, snows)

fūrin 風鈴 wind-chimes

furisode[ ] ふりそで・振り袖
long-sleeved kimono

fu'ro' (o-fu'ro) 風呂（お風呂)
bath; ～ **ni hairima'su** 風呂に
入ります takes a bath

furo-ba' (o-furoba) 風呂場（お風
呂場) bathroom

furonto フロント front desk

furō'-sha 浮浪者 vagabond,
vagrant, tramp

furoshiki ふろしき・風呂敷 a
cloth wrapper

furu 振る = **furima'su** 振ります
(waves)

fu'ru 降る = **furima'su** 降ります
(rains, snows)

furue 震え → **furuema'su** 震え
ます

furuema'su 震えます, **furueru** 震
える it shakes

furui ふるい・篩 sieve, sifter

furu'i 古い old (not new), stale
(not fresh); secondhand, used

furu[ ]**ma**[ ]**i** 振る舞い behavior
(*deportment*)

furū'tsu フルーツ fruit

furya 振りゃ 1. = **fure'ba** 振れ
ば (if one wave it) 2. ～ **shinai**
振りゃしない = **furi'ya/wa**
shinai 振りや/はしない =
furanai 振らない (not wave)

fu'rya 降りゃ 1. = **fu'reba** 降れ
ば (if it rain/snow) 2. ～
shinai 降りゃしない = **fu'ri**
ya/wa shinai 降りや/はしな
い = **fura'nai** 降らない (not
rain/snow)

furyō (na) 不良（な) bad, no
good

fū'ryū (na) 風流（な) elegant

fusa' 房 bunch (*cluster*)

fusagarima'su ふさがります・塞
がります, **fusagaru** ふさがる・

塞がる gets blocked (off), clogged/stopped up; gets occupied, booked up, engaged

fusagima'su ふさぎます・塞ぎます, **fusagu** ふさぐ・塞ぐ stops up, closes, blocks

fusa'i 夫妻 Mr. and Mrs.; husband and wife

fusaide ふさいで・塞いで → **fusagima'su** ふさぎます・塞ぎます

fusawashi'i ふさわしい・相応しい suitable, worthy; becoming; **fusawa'shiku** ふさわしく・相応しく suitably

fusegima'su 防ぎます, **fuse'gu** 防ぐ prevents; defends, protects

fuse'ide 防いで → **fusegima'su** 防ぎます

fusema'su 伏せます, **fuse'ru** 伏せる covers (up), conceals; lays it face down; **mi o ~** 身を伏せます gets down, crouches (so as not to be seen); **me' o ~** 目を伏せます lowers one's eyes

fūsen 風船 balloon; **~-dama** 風船玉 toy balloon; **~-ga'mu** 風船ガム bubble gum

fushi' 節 joint; gnarl, knot, knob; tune, air; point (in a statement)

fushigi (na) 不思議（な）strange, mysterious; wonderful; suspicious, odd, funny, weird

fushin 1. 不審 doubt, suspicion; **~ (na)** 不審（な）doubtful, suspicious **2.** 普請 building (construction), repairs; **~ shima'su** 普請します builds, makes repairs

fu-shi'nsetsu (na) 不親切（な）unkind

fu-shi'zen (na) 不自然（な）unnatural

fusho'ka 不消化 indigestion

fusoku 不足 shortage, insufficiency, deficiency, scarcity, lack

fusuma' ふすま・襖 opaque sliding panel/door

futa ふた・蓋 lid, cover; flap (of envelope, etc.)

futa-... 二.... two; **futa'-ban** ふた晩・二晩 two nights

futago 双子・ふたご twins

futa'-hyaku 二百・200 = **ni-hyaku** 二百・200 two hundred

futa'-jū 二十・20 = **ni'-jū** 二十・20 twenty

futa-ma'n 二万・20,000 = **ni-ma'n** 二万・20,000 twenty thousand

futamata' (no) 二又・二叉（の）forked, bifurcate(d); **futamata-soke'tto** 二又［二叉］ソケット two-way socket, double plug

futari' (**o-futari**) 二人・ふたり（お二人・おふたり）two persons

futa-se'n 二千・2,000 = **ni-se'n**

二千・2,000 two thousand

futatsu⌐ 二つ・2つ・ふたつ two; two years old

futatsu⌐-mi(t)tsu 二つ三つ two or three

futei 1. ~ (no) 不定(の) un-fixed, uncertain, indefinite, undecided **2. ~ (na)** 不貞(な) unchaste, unfaithful (to her husband); **~ o hatarakima⌐su** 不貞を働きます cheats on her husband   ⌐chance

futo ふと unexpectedly; by

futō (na) 不当(な) unfair, un-justified

fūtō 封筒 envelope

futo⌐i 太い fat, plump, thick (and round)

futokoro ふところ・懐 bosom

futon (o-futo⌐n) 布団(お布団) padded quilt

futorima⌐su 太ります, **futo⌐ru** 太る gets fat; **futo⌐tte ima⌐su** 太っています is fat

futsū 普通・ふつう usual(ly),

regular(ly), ordinar(il)y, typical(ly); **~ -de⌐nsha** 普通電車 local (= nonexpress) train

futsuka 二日・2日・ふつか two days; 2nd day (of month)

futsū-yo⌐kin 普通預金 (ordinary) savings account

fuyashima⌐su 増やします・ふやします, **fuya⌐su** 増やす・ふやす increases it/them

fuyō (no) 不要・不用(の) useless, disused, unneeded

fuyu⌐ 冬 winter

fu-yu⌐kai (na) 不愉快(な) un-pleasant, displeasing, dis-pleased; **~ ni shima⌐su** 不愉快にします displeases, offends

fuyu-ya⌐sumi 冬休み winter break/vacation

Fu⌐zan 釜山 Pusan

fuzoku 付属・附属 attachment, belonging, accessory; **fuzoku⌐-hin** 付属品 attach-ments, accessories

— **G** —

ga が・蛾 moth

... ga ...が PARTICLE: marks sub-ject (WHO does, WHAT is), but marks also object of **arima⌐su** あります (has WHAT), **irima⌐su** いります・要ります (needs/

wants WHAT), **wakarima⌐su** 分かります (understands WHAT), and **dekima⌐su** できます・出来ます (can do WHAT)

... ga ...が but; and

...-ga ...画 painting, picture

gabyō 画鋲 thumbtack

gachō がちょう・鵞鳥 goose

ga⌐gaku 雅楽 music traditional to the imperial court

ga⌐i 害 damage, harm, injury

gai-... 外... external, foreign; **...-gai** ...外 outside (of)

...-gai ...貝 shell(fish)

ga⌐ibu 外部 the outside, the exterior; ～ **(no)** 外部（の）external

ga⌐ido ガイド guide

gaijin 外人 foreigner (usually American or European)

gaikō 外交 diplomacy, diplomatic relations; ～**-ka** 外交家 diplomat(ic person); **gaikō⌐-kan** 外交官 diplomat(ic officer); ～**-teki (na)** 外交的（な）diplomatic

gaikoku 外国 foreign (countries); ～**-go** 外国語 foreign language(s); **gaikoku⌐-jin** 外国人 foreigner

gaime⌐n 外面 the outside, the exterior; ～ **(no)** 外面（の）external

Gaimu⌐-shō 外務省 Ministry of Foreign Affairs

ga⌐inen 概念 concept

gaisen 外線 outside line/extension *(phone)*

...-ga⌐isha ...会社 company (= **kaisha** 会社)

gaishutsu 外出 going out; ～**-chū de⌐su** 外出中です is out; ～

shima⌐su 外出します = **dekakema⌐su** 出掛けます goes out

gaitō 1. 外套 coat, overcoat **2.** 街頭 the street, the wayside

gaka 画家 painter, artist

...-ga⌐kari ...係 attendant (in charge)

gake 崖 cliff

gaki⌐ 餓鬼 hungry/begging ghost; ガキ・がき・餓鬼 brat

gakkai 学会 scholarly society, association

gakka⌐ri shima(⌐)su がっかりします is disappointed, discouraged

gakki 1. 学期 term *(of school)*; semester **2.** 楽器 musical instrument

gakkō 学校 school

gakkyū 学級 class/grade in school

ga⌐ku 学 learning, study, science; **...⌐-gaku** ...学 ...-ology

ga⌐ku 額 amount, sum

gaku-buchi 額縁 frame *(of picture)*

gakuchō 学長 president of a school (college/university)

gakudan 楽団 band (of musicians)

gakufu 楽譜 musical score

ga⌐ku⌐i 学位 academic degree; **gakui-ro⌐mbun** 学位論文 thesis, dissertation

gaku⌐mon 学問 knowledge, learning, education

gakunen 学年 the school year

gakureki 学歴 educational background

gakusei 学生 student; **gakuse⌐i-fuku** 学生服 school uniform

gakusha 学者 scholar

ga⌐kushi 学士 bachelor's degree; **gakushi-ro⌐mbun** 学士論文 senior essay

gakushū 学習 study, learning; ~ **shima⌐su** 学習します studies, learns (a basic subject)

gakushū-sha 学習者 the student of a subject (in general); **Eigo no** ~ 英語の学習者 the student of English

gamaguchi がま口 purse, pocketbook, wallet

ga⌐man がまん・我慢 patience, perseverance; ~ **dekimase⌐n** がまん[我慢]できません can't stand it; ~ **shima(⌐)su** がまん[我慢]します is patient, puts up with, stands, tolerates, perseveres; **gaman-zuyo⌐i** がまん[我慢]強い patient, persevering

gambarima⌐su がんばります・頑張ります, **gamba⌐ru** がんばる・頑張る stands firm, bears up, hangs in there; tries hard(er)

ga⌐men 画面 screen (movie, TV, computer)

ga⌐mu ガム (chewing) gum

ga⌐n 1. がん・癌 cancer **2.** がん・雁 wild goose

gani-mata (no) がにまた・蟹股（の）bowlegged

ganjitsu 元日, **gantan** 元旦 New Year's day, first day of the year

ga⌐nnen 元年 the first year of an era; Year One

ga⌐nrai 元来 originally, primarily

gantan 元旦 = **ganjitsu** 元日

gan'yaku 丸薬 pill

gappei 合併 merger, combination, union; ~ **shima⌐su** 合併します (they) merge, unite, combine

gara 柄 pattern

ga⌐ragara がらがら rattling; ~ **narima⌐su** がらがら鳴ります it rattles

garakuta がらくた junk

garasu ガラス glass (the substance); **garasu⌐-bin** ガラス瓶 glass jar

ga⌐rē⌐ji ガレージ garage

ga⌐ri ガリ pickled ginger slices (= **su-shō⌐ga** 酢生姜)

gāru-fure⌐ndo ガールフレンド girlfriend

gasorin ガソリン gasoline; ~ **-suta⌐ndo** ガソリンスタンド gas(oline)/service station

ga⌐su ガス (natural) gas; **gasu⌐-dai** ガス代 gas bill; **gasu-ga⌐isha** ガス会社 gas company; **gasu-ko⌐nro** ガスこんろ

(gas) hot plate; **gasu-re⌉nji** ガスレンジ gas range
...-gata ...型 type, model; size
...-ga[⌉]ta ...方 [HONORIFIC PLURAL] esteemed (persons)
gā⌉tā ガーター garter
ga⌉tagata shima⌉sụ (suru) がたがたします(する) clatters, rattles
...-gatsu ...月 month of the year *(name)*
gā⌉ze ガーゼ gauze
ge⌉ 下 = **ge-kan** 下巻 last volume (of a set of 2 or 3)
gehi⌉n (na) 下品(な) vulgar
ge⌉i 芸 arts, accomplishments; tricks, stunts
geijutsu 芸術 art(s); **geijutsụ-ka** 芸術家 artist
geinō⌉-jin 芸能人 entertainer
geisha 芸者 a geisha girl
geka 外科 surgery (as a medical specialty); **geka⌉-i** 外科医 surgeon
ge-kan 下巻 last volume (of a set of 2 or 3)
ge⌉ki 劇 play, drama
gekijō 劇場 theater
gekkei 月経 menstruation; ~ **-tai** 月経帯 sanitary belt
gekkei 月桂 = **gekke⌉i-ju** 月桂樹 laurel
gekkyū 月給 monthly salary
ge⌉mmai 玄米 unpolished rice
gemmitsu (na) 厳密(な) strict
gē⌉mu ゲーム game
ge⌉n(-) ... 現... present, current; **gen-jū⌉sho** 現住所 current address
ge⌉ndai 現代 the present; ~ **(no)** 現代(の) modern, up-to-date; **genda[⌉]i-ka** 現代化 modernization
ge⌉ndo 限度 limit; **saidai-/saikō-** ~ 最大/最高限度 the maximum/highest (degree); **saishō-/saitei-** ~ 最小/最低限度 the minimum/lowest (degree)
ge⌉ngo 言語 language; **gengo⌉-gaku** 言語学 linguistics
gen'in 原因 cause, origin, root
genjitsu 現実 actuality, reality; ~ **(no)** 現実(の) actual, real; **genjitsụ-teki (na)** 現実的(な) realistic
genjitsụ[⌉]-ka shima⌉su 現実化します realizes, materializes, brings about, carries out
genjō 現状 the present conditions/state, the status quo
ge⌉nkan 玄関 porch, veranda; entrance (hall)
ge⌉nki (o-ge⌉nki) 元気(お元気) energy, vigor, pep; ~ **(na)** 元気(な) healthy, well, cheerful, vigorous
genki⌉n 現金, **gen-nama** 現なま cash (on hand), ready money; **genkin-ka⌉kịtome** 現金書留 cash envelope (registered mail)
genko げんこ·拳固, **genkotsu** げんこつ·拳骨 fist

genkō 原稿 manuscript; ~
-yō⌐shi 原稿用紙 squared
paper

genkyū shima⌐su (suru) 言及しま
す(する) [bookish] = (... ni)
furema⌐su (...に)触れます refers to ... , mentions ... 「金

gen-nama 現なま = **genki⌐n** 現

genryō 原料 (raw) materials

ge⌐nshi 原子 atom; **genshi-
ba⌐kudan** 原子爆弾 atomic
bomb; **genshi⌐-ryoku** 原子力
atomic energy

genshō 現象 phenomenon

gensoku 原則 a basic principle, a
rule; **gensoku to shite** 原則と
して as a rule

gentei 限定 limitation; ~
shima⌐su 限定します limits,
restricts

ge⌐nzai 現在 the present (time);
~ **(no)** 現在(の) current, present

genzō shima⌐su 現像します
develops (film)

geppu 月賦 monthly install-
ments/payments

ge⌐ppu⌐ げっぷ belch; ~ **o
shima⌐su** げっぷをします
belches, burps

geri 下痢 diarrhea

geri-dome 下痢止め anti-diarrhetic, paregoric

geshi 夏至 summer solstice

geshuku 下宿 lodgings, room
(and board); ~-**ya** 下宿屋

rooming/boarding house

ge⌐s-su⌐i-kin 月水金 Monday-
Wednesday-Friday

gesui 下水 sewage; (kitchen)
drain; ~-**dame** 下水溜め
cesspool; ~ **shori-jō** 下水処理
場 sewage treatment plant

geta⌐ 下駄 wooden clogs (shoes);
geta-bako 下駄箱 shoe box (at
entryway)

...-getsu ...月 month

Getsuyō⌐bi 月曜日 Monday

gezai 下剤 laxative

gi-... 偽... pseudo-...

gi⌐bo 義母 mother-in-law

gi⌐fu 義父 father-in-law

giji-dō 議事堂 (= **kokkai** ~ 国
会議事堂) Diet building

gi⌐jutsu 技術 technique; **gijutsu-
ka** 技術家 technician

gi⌐kai 議会 the Japanese Diet
(= parliament)

gimon 疑問 question, doubt;
gimo⌐n-fu 疑問符 question
mark

gi⌐mu 義務 duty, obligation;
gimu-kyō⌐iku 義務教育 compulsory education

gi⌐n 銀 silver

gin-iro (no) 銀色(の) silver (col-
or)

ginkō 銀行 bank; **ginkō⌐-in** 銀行
員 bank clerk

ginna⌐n ぎんなん・銀杏 gingko
nuts

girī (o-gi⌐ri) 義理(お義理)

obligation, sense of obligation, honor

giri¹ no ... 義理の... ...-in-law

Gi¹risha ギリシャ・ギリシア Greece; **Girisha-go** ギリシャ語 Greek

gisei 犠牲 a sacrifice; **... o ~ ni shima¹su** ...を犠牲にします makes a sacrifice/scapegoat of ... ; **~ ni narima¹su** 犠牲になります falls a victim, is sacrificed; **gise¹i-sha** 犠牲者 victim

gi¹shi 技師 engineer

gi¹tcho (no) ぎっちょ(の) left-handed (person)

gi¹(y)a ギア[ヤ] gear

gizō 偽造 forgery

go¹ 1. 五・5 five 2. 碁 (= **i¹go** 囲碁) the board game Go

go-... ご・御... HONORIFIC (personalizing) PREFIX (cf. **o-** お・御)

...-go ...語 language; word(s)

go-bamme¹ (no) 五番目(の) fifth

go-ban 1. 五番 number five 2. 碁盤 a Go board

gobō ごぼう・牛蒡 burdock (root)

Go-busata itashima¹shita. ご無沙汰致しました. I have been neglectful (of keeping in touch with you).

gochisō ごちそう・ご馳走 treat (of food); **~-sama** ご馳走さま・ごちそうさま. Thank you

for the treat (the reply is **o-so¹matsu-sama** お粗末さま); **~ shima¹su** ご馳走[ごちそう]します provides a treat

go¹chō 伍長 corporal (army)

go-dai 五台 five machines/vehicles

go-do¹ 五度 five times

go¹-do 五度 five degrees

gōdō 合同 combination, union, fusion; congruence; **~ no** 合同の combined, united, joint; **~ shima¹su** 合同します they combine, unite, join (forces)

Go-enryo na¹ku. ご遠慮なく. Don't be shy/reticent.

go-fujō ご不浄 [*used mostly by older women*] = **to¹ire** トイレ (toilet)

gofuku 呉服: **gofu̱ku⁽ ⁾-mono** 呉服物 yard/dry goods; **gofuku-ya** 呉服屋 dry goods store

go⁽ ⁾gaku 語学 language learning

Go¹-gatsu 五月・5月 May

gogen 語源 etymology

go¹go 午後 afternoon, p.m.

go¹han ご飯・御飯 cooked rice; meal, dinner; food

go¹-hiki 五匹 five animals/fish/bugs

go-hon 五本 five long things

go-hyaku¹ 五百・500 five hundred

go¹i 語彙 vocabulary (item)

gōin (na) 強引(な) forcible, highhanded; **~ ni** 強引に forcibly, highhandedly

go-ishi 碁石 a Go stone (= piece)

go-jibun ご自分 (you) yourself

go-ji‌sei ご時世 → **ji‌sei** 時世

go-jū‌ fifty 五十・50

gō‌ka (na) 豪華(な) luxurious, de luxe

gokai 誤解 misunderstanding; ~ **shima‌su** 誤解します misunderstands

go-kai 五階 five floors/stories; fifth floor

go-ka‌i 五回 five times

gōkaku 合格 passing (an exam); **(shiken ni) gōkaku shima‌su** (試験に)合格します passes (an exam)

gōkan 強姦 rape; ~ **shima‌su** 強姦します rapes

gōkei 合計 total (sum)

gokiburi ごきぶり cockroach

go-kigen ご機嫌 → **kigen** 機嫌

go‌-ko 五個 five small things

go‌ku ごく・極 very, exceedingly

Go-ku‌rō-sama (deshi‌ta). ご苦労さま[様](でした). Thank you for the hard work.

goma ごま・胡麻 sesame (seeds); ~ **o surima‌su (su‌ru)** ごま[胡麻]をすります(する) grinds sesame; flatters

go-mai 五枚 five flat things

gomakashima‌su ごまかします・誤魔化します, **gomaka‌su** ごまかす・誤魔化す deceives,

cheats, misrepresents; **tsuri‌-sen o** ~ 釣り銭をごまかし[誤魔化し]ます shortchanges

go-ma‌n 五万・50,000 fifty thousand

gōman (na) 傲慢(な) haughty, arrogant

goma-su‌ri‌ ごますり flattery

go-me‌iwaku ご迷惑・御迷惑 → **me‌iwaku** 迷惑

Gomen kudasa‌i. ごめん下さい・御免下さい. 1. Hello— anybody home? 2. Good-bye. (on phone) 3. Excuse me for interrupting.

Gomen nasa‌i. ごめんなさい・御免なさい. Excuse me.

gomi‌ ごみ trash, rubbish, garbage, (house) dust; **gomi‌-bako** ごみ箱 trash box, garbage can, dustbin; **gomi-bu‌kuro** ごみ袋 garbage bag; **gomi-suteba‌** ごみ捨て場 garbage dump

gomi‌-ya (san) ごみ屋(さん) trash/garbage collector

gomoku-na‌rabe 五目並べ gobang (a simplified version of the board game Go)

gomoku-so‌ba 五目そば Chinese noodles with a variety of tidbits

go‌mu ゴム rubber; **gomu‌-gutsu** ゴム靴 rubber boots

go-nen 五年 the year 5; (= **gone‌n-kan** 五年間) five years

go-ni̅n 五人 five people

go-o̅n ご恩 your kindness, my obligation to you

goraku 娯楽 entertainment, amusement, recreation

goran ni narima̅su (na̅ru) ご覧 になります（なる） [HONORIFIC] (you) look, see, try

go̅ri 合理 accordance with reason; **～-teki (na)** 合理的 （な） rational, reasonable, sensible

go̅ri⌐-ka 合理化 rationalization (= making it reasonable); streamlining; **～ shima̅su** 合 理化します makes it reasonable, rationalizes; streamlines (procedures, ...)

goro-a̅wase 語呂合わせ pun

... go̅ro (ni) ...ごろ[頃]（に）(at) about *(a time)*

go̅ru ゴール goal *(sports)*

go̅ruden-ui̅iku/-wi̅iku ゴールデ ンウイーク/ウィーク Golden Week (29 April – 5 May)

go̅rufu ゴルフ golf; **gorufu-jo̅** ゴルフ場 golf course

go-ryo̅shin ご両親 your parents

go̅ryū 合流 merger, confluence; **～ shima̅su** 合流します merges, joins; **"Go̅ryū chū̅i"** "合流注意" Lanes Merge (Ahead), Merge (Lanes)

go̅-sai 五歳 five years old

go-sa̅ta ご沙汰 → **sa̅ta** 沙汰

go̅-satsu 五冊 five books

go-se̅n 五千・5,000 five thousand

...-go̅sha ...号車 train car number ... ; **nan-go̅sha** 何号車 what (number) car

Go-shimpai na̅ku. ご心配［御心 配］なく. Don't worry about it.

go-shi̅nsetsu ご親切 → **shi̅nsetsu** 親切

go̅sho 御所 palace *(in Kyoto)*

go-shu̅jin ご主人 your husband

go-te̅inei ごていねい・ご丁寧 → **te̅inei** ていねい・丁寧

go-to̅ 五頭 five horses/oxen

go̅tō 強盗 robber; robbery

... go̅toku (ni) ...ごとく［如く］ （に）[literary] = ... yo̅ (ni) ... よう［様］（に）like

... go̅to (ni) ...ごと［毎］（に） every ... ; **koto a̅ru ～** 事ある ごと［毎］（に）every chance one gets

go-tsugō ご都合 → **tsugō** 都合

go̅u 豪雨 heavy rain, (torrential) downpour; **shūchū-～** 集中豪 雨 local downpour, locally heavy rain

go̅-wa 五羽 five birds

go-yo̅ ご用 your business

Go-yukku̅ri. ごゆっくり. Take it easy. Don't feel you have to rush.

goza̅ ござ・茣蓙 thin floor mat

gozaima̅shi̅te ございまして →

gozaima´su ございます

gozaimasho´ ございましょう =
gozaima´su deshō ございます
でしょう = **a´ru deshō** あるで
しょう

gozaima´su ございます [DEFER-
ENTIAL] = **arima´su** あります

go⌐zen 午前 morning, a.m.

go´-zen ご膳 low meal table, dining tray

go-zo´n-ji (de´su, ni narima´su)
ご存知(です, になります)
[HONORIFIC] knows; **go-zo´n-ji
(ja) arimase⌐n** ご存知(じゃ)あ
りません doesn't know

guai 具合 condition, shape, feelings (of health); ~ **ga waru´i**
具合が悪い is out of order, is
not working properly, is not
feeling good/right, is upset

guchi 愚痴・ぐち complaint,
gripe; ~ **o koboshima´su
(kobo´su)** 愚痴[ぐち]をこぼ
します(こぼす) complains,
gripes

...-guchi ...口 **1.** window, wicket
2. exit/entrance

gū´gū ぐうぐう snoring (away);
(= ~ **nemutte** ぐうぐう眠っ
て) sound asleep

gumpuku 軍服 military uniform

gu´n 1. 軍 army, troops **2.** 郡
county

gu⌐ndan 軍団 corps

gunjin 軍人 soldier, military person

gunkan 軍艦 warship

gunshū 群衆 crowd

gu´nsō 軍曹 sergeant

gu´ntai 軍隊 troops, army;
(armed) service (forces)

gu⌐nzoku 軍属 civilian attached
to the military

gu´rabu グラブ (baseball, boxing) glove

... gu´rai ...位・ぐらい about (an
amount); at least

(-)gu´ramu グラム gram(s)

gu´rasu グラス glass (the container)

gurē´ (no) グレー(の) gray

gurēpufurū´tsu グレープフルー
ツ grapefruit

guri´in (no) グリーン(の)
green; **gurii´n-sha** グリーン車
the Green Car (first-class
seats)

gurū´pu グループ group

gussu´ri ぐっすり sound asleep,
(sleeping) soundly

gutai-teki (na) 具体的(な) concrete, substantial, tangible,
material

gu⌐tto ぐっと with a jerk/gulp,
suddenly

gūzen (no) 偶然(の) accidental,
fortuitous; **gūzen ni** 偶然に
accidentally, by chance

gu´zuguzu iima´su (yū) ぐずぐず
言います(言う) complains,
grumbles

gyaku (no/ni) 逆(の/に) opposite, contrary, backwards

gyakutai shima`su 虐待します
mistreats

gya`ppu ギャップ gap

gyo- 御 (for a few words) = **go-**

gyō 1. 行 line (of letters); **sa`-gyō**
さ行 the **sa-shi-su-se-so**（さし
すせそ）line of the kana
chart 2. 行 (= **shugyō** 修行)
ascetic practices, meditation
3. 業 (= **shoku`gyō** 職業) line
of work

gyo`fu 漁夫 fisherman

gyōgi (o-gyōgi) 行儀（お行儀）
behavior, manners

gyo□gyō 漁業 fishing (*business*)

「ご・御

gyo`ji 行事 ceremony, event

gyōsei 行政 administration (*of
government*)

gyōza ぎょうざ・餃子 *chiao-tze
(jiaozi),* crescent-shaped
dumpling stuffed with ground

gyūniku 牛肉 beef ⌐pork, etc.

gyūnyū 牛乳 = **mi`ruku** ミルク
(cow's) milk; **～-ya** 牛乳屋
dairy (*shop*)

— H —

ha 葉 (= **happa** 葉っぱ) leaf

ha` 1. 歯 tooth 2. 刃 edge (*of
knife*), blade (*of razor*)

hā はあ [DEFERENTIAL] yes

haba 幅 width

habakari-na`gara ... はばかりな
がら... I beg your pardon, but ...

habamema`su 阻めます,
habame`ru 阻める can prevent/
thwart

habamima`su 阻みます,
haba`mu 阻む prevents,
thwarts

haba`nde 阻んで →
habamima`su 阻みます

habatsu 派閥 faction, clique

hā`bu ハーブ herb(s)

habu`ite** 省いて → **habukima`su

省きます

habukima`su** 省きます, **habu`ku
省く cuts out, reduces, saves,
eliminates, omits

ha-bu`rashi 歯ブラシ tooth
brush

Hā`-chan ハーちゃん →
Miichan-～ ミーちゃんハー
ちゃん

hachi 蜂 (= **mitsu`-bachi** 蜜蜂)
bee

hachi` 1. 八・8 eight 2. 鉢 bowl,
basin, pot, (**o-hachi** お鉢) rice
bucket/tub

hachi`-do` 八度 eight times

hachi`-do 八度 eight degrees

hachi-ma`n 八万・80,000 eighty
thousand

hachi-mitsu 蜂蜜 honey
hachi-mono 鉢物, **hachi-ue**⌐ 鉢植え potted plant
hada-gi 肌着 underwear
hadaka (no) 裸・はだか（の）naked
hadashi はだし・裸足 barefoot
hade (na) はで[派手]（な）gaudy, showy, flashy, bright, loud (color)
hādowe'a ハードウェア (computer) hardware
hae はえ・蝿 (house)fly
ha'e 1. 生え・這え → **haema'su** 生えます・這えます [infinitive] **2.** 這え・はえ → **ha'u** 這う・はう [imperative] crawl!
ha'eba 這えば・はえば → **haima'su** 這います・はいます (if one crawl)
haema'su, hae'ru 1. 生えます, 生える (tooth, hair, mold, …) grows **2.** 這えます・はえます, 這える・はえる can crawl
hagaki (o-ha'gaki) はがき・葉書（おはがき[葉書]）postcard
hagane はがね・鋼 steel
ha'ge 1. はげ・禿 bald spot, baldness **2.** 励 → **hagemashima'su** 励まします
hagemashima'su, hagema'su 励まします, 励ます encourages
hagema'su 励ます = **hagemashima'su** 励まします (encourages)
hagema'su, hage'ru 1. はげ[剥

げ]ます, はげ[剥げ]る it peels off **2.** はげ[禿げ]ます, はげ[禿げ]る gets/goes bald; **ha'gete ima'su** はげて[禿げて]います is bald; **ha'geta …** はげた・禿げた... bald
hageshi'i 激しい violent, severe, fierce, acute
hagima'su はぎ[剥ぎ]ます, **ha'gu** はぐ・剥ぐ peels it off
hago⌐ 羽子 shuttlecock
hago'-i'ta 羽子板 battledore
ha'guki 歯茎 gum (teethridge)
ha'guruma 歯車 cog(wheel), gear
ha'ha 母, **haha-oya** 母親 mother
hai 1. 灰 ashes **2.** 肺 lungs **3.** はい = **hae** はえ・蝿 (housefly)
ha'i 1. はい yes; here you are! **2.** 這い・はい → **haima'su** 這います・はいます
…'-hai …杯 cupful(s), bowlful(s)
haibō'ru ハイボール highball
haibyō 肺病 tuberculosis, TB
haien 肺炎 pneumonia
hai-gan 肺癌・肺がん lung cancer
hai-iro (no) 灰色（の）gray
ha'ijo 排除 removal, elimination, exclusion; ～ **shima(')su** 排除します removes, eliminates, excludes
haikara ハイカラ fashionable, high-class
haikei 背景 background
ha'ikei 拝啓 Dear Sir/Madam
haiken shima'su (suru) 拝見しま

す(する) [HUMBLE] (I) look at, see

haiki 排気 exhaust; **haiki-ga̅ su** 排気ガス exhaust (fumes); **haikī-sen** 排気扇 exhaust fan

ha̅iki̅ngu ハイキング hike, hiking; ~ **o shima̅su** ハイキングをします hikes

ha̅⌐iku⌐ 俳句 short (17-syllable) poem

haikyū 配給 rationing; ~ **shima̅su** 配給します rations

haima̅su 這います・はいます, **ha̅u** 這う・はう crawls

ha̅ire 入れ 1. → **hairema̅su** 入れます [infinitive] 2. → **hairima̅su** 入ります [imperative] enter!

hairema̅su 入れます, **haire̅ru** 入れる can enter

hairima̅su 入ります, **ha̅iru** 入る: (... **ni**) ~ (...に)入ります enters (...); **ha̅itte ima̅su** 入っています is inside

ha̅-isha 歯医者 dentist

haishaku shima̅su (suru) 拝借します(する) [HUMBLE] (I) borrow

haishi shima̅su (suru) 廃止します(する) abolishes

ha-ita 歯痛 toothache

haitatsu 配達 delivery

haite はいて → **hakima̅su** はきます (wears); ~ **ikima̅su/kima̅su** はいて行きます/来ます wears them there/here

ha̅ite 吐いて → **hakima̅su** 吐きます (vomits)

ha̅iyā ハイヤー limousine for hire

haiyū 俳優 actor

hai-zara 灰皿 ash tray

haji̅ 恥 shame; embarrassment; ~ **o kakima̅su (ka̅ku)** 恥をかきます(かく) disgraces/embarrasses oneself

hajikema̅su はじけ[弾け]ます, **hajike̅ru** はじける・弾ける it pops, snaps

hajiki̅ はじき = **o-ha̅jiki** おはじき marbles

hajikima̅su はじき[弾き]ます, **haji̅ku** はじく・弾く snaps it; repels it (water, ...)

hajikko 端っこ・はじっこ = **hashikko** 端っこ・はしっこ

hajimarima̅su 始まります, **hajimaru** 始まる it begins (starts)

hajime 始め 1. the beginning; in the beginning; ~ **no** 始めの the first ... 2. → **hajimema̅su** 始めます

Hajimema̅shite. 初めまして. How do you do? *(on being introduced)*

hajimema̅su 始めます, **hajimeru** 始める begins (starts) it

hajime(ra)rema̅su 始め(ら)れます, **hajime(ra)reru** 始め(ら)れる can begin it

hajimete 始めて → **hajimema̅su** 始めます

haji‐mete 初めて for the first time

haka‐ (o-haka) 墓（お墓）grave *(tomb)*

haka-ba‐ 墓場 graveyard, cemetery

hakai 破壊 destruction, demolition; ～ **shima‐su** 破壊します destroys, demolishes

hakanai はかない ＝ **hakimase‐n** はきません (not wear)

hakana‐i はかない・儚い fleeting, transitory

haka‐nai 吐かない・掃かない ＝ **hakimase‐n** 吐きません；掃きません (not vomit; not sweep)

haka‐re 測れ・量れ 1. → **hakarema‐su** 測れます・量れます 2. → **hakarima‐su** 測ります・量ります [imperative] measure it!

hakarema‐su 測れます・量れます, **hakare‐ru** 測れる・量れる can measure/weigh

hakari‐ はかり・秤 (weighing/ weight) scales

haka‐ri 測り・量り・図り → **hakarima‐su** 測ります・量ります・図ります [infinitive]

hakarigo‐to‐ 謀 plot, trick, scheme

hakarima‐su, haka‐ru 1. 測ります, 測る measures 2. 量ります, 量る weighs 3. 図り［謀り］ます, 図［謀］る plans, designs; plots

ha‐kase 博士 doctor (Ph.D.); **hakase-ro‐mbun** 博士論文 doctoral dissertation

haka‐tte 測って・量って・図って → **hakarima‐su** 測ります・量ります・図ります

hake はけ 1. → **hakema‐su** はけます (can wear) [infinitive] 2. → **hakima‐su** はきます [imperative] wear it!

hake‐ 1. はけ・刷毛 brush 2. はけ・捌け ～ **ga i‐i de‐su** はけ［捌け］がいいです it drains/ sells well

ha‐ke 1. 捌け・吐け・掃け → **hakema‐su** 捌けます；吐けます；掃けます (drains off; can vomit; can sweep) [infinitive] 2. 吐け・掃け [imperative] vomit! sweep!

hake‐ba はけば → **hakima‐su** はきます (if one wear)

hake‐-kuchi/-guchi はけ［捌け］口／口 outlet (for water/emotion/goods)

hakema‐su はけます, **hakeru** はける can wear

hakema‐su, hake‐ru 1. はけ［捌け］ます, はけ［捌け］る it drains off; it sells (well) 2. 吐けます, 吐ける can vomit 3. 掃けます, 掃ける can sweep

hakere‐ba はければ, **hakerya** はけりゃ → **hakema‐su** はけます (if one can wear)

hake̅reba はけ［捌け］れば・吐ければ・掃ければ, **hake̅rya** はけりゃ・吐けりゃ・掃けりゃ → **hakema̅su** はけ［捌け］ます・吐けます/掃けます (if it drain off; if one can vomit/sweep)

hakete はけて → **hakema̅su** はけます (can wear)

ha̅kete 吐けて・掃けて → **hakema̅su** 吐けます; 掃けます (can vomit; can sweep)

haki はき → **hakima̅su** はきます (wears)

ha̅ki 1. 覇気 ambition *(energetic spirit)* **2.** 吐き・掃き → **hakima̅su** 吐きます; 掃きます (vomits; sweeps)

haki̅-ke̅ 吐き気 nausea; ～ **ga shima̅su** 吐き気がします, ～ **o moyōshima̅su** 吐き気を催します feels nauseated/queasy

hakima̅su はきます, **haku** はく wears (on feet or legs), puts/slips on (shoes, socks, pants)

hakima̅su, ha̅ku 1. 吐きます, 吐く vomits, spits out **2.** 掃きます, 掃く sweeps

hakka はっか・薄荷 peppermint

hak-ka̅i 八回 eight times

hakken 発見 discovery; ～ **shima̅su** 発見します discovers

hakki̅ri はっきり plainly, clearly, distinctly, exactly

ha̅kko 八個 eight small things

hakkō 発行 publication; **hakkō̅-sha** 発行者 publisher; ～

shima̅su 発行します publishes, issues

hako 箱 box, case, chest, container

hakō̅ はこう = **hakimasho̅** はきましょう (let's wear it!)

hakō̅ 吐こう = **hakimasho̅** 吐きましょう (let's spit it out!)

hakobi 運び → **hakobima̅su** 運びます

hakobima̅su 運びます, **hakobu** 運ぶ carries, conveys

hakonde 運んで → **hakobima̅su** 運びます

...-haku ...泊, **...-paku** ...泊 (counts nights of lodging)

haku はく = **hakima̅su** はきます (wears)

ha̅ku 吐く・掃く = **hakima̅su** 吐きます; 掃きます (vomits; sweeps)

hakubu̅tsu̅-kan 博物館 museum

hakuchō 白鳥 swan

ha̅kujō 白状 confession; ～ **shima(̅)su** 白状します confesses

hakujō (na) 薄情（な）unfeeling, heartless, cruel

haku̅mai 白米 polished rice

hakura̅n-kai 博覧会 exhibition, exposition

hakusa̅┐i 白菜 Chinese cabbage, bok choi

ha̅kushu shima(̅)su (suru) 拍手します（する）claps one's hands

hakya はきゃ 1. = **hake⌐ba** はけ
ば (if one wear) 2. ~ **shinai**
はきゃしない = **haki⌐ ya/wa
shinai** はきや/はしない =
hakanai はかない (not wear)

ha⌐kya 吐きゃ・掃きゃ 1. =
ha⌐keba 吐けば/掃けば (if one
vomit/sweep) 2. ~ **shinai** 吐
きゃしない・掃きゃしない =
ha⌐ki ya/wa shinai 吐き・掃き
や/はしない = **haka⌐nai** 吐か
ない/掃かない (not vomit/
sweep)

hama⌐ 浜 beach

hamachi はまち・魬 young
yellowtail (*cf.* **bu⌐ri** ぶり・鰤,
inada いなだ)

hama⌐guri はまぐり・蛤 clam

ha-maki 葉巻 cigar

hambā⌐gā ハンバーガー a hamburger

hambā⌐gu ハンバーグ hamburger (meat)

hambai 販売 sale; **hamba⌐i-ki** 販
売機 vending machine; **ham-
ba⌐i-daka** 販売高 sales
volume; **hambai-moto** 販売元
sales agency; **hamba⌐◻i-nin** 販
売人 seller, dealer; **hamba⌐i-
ten** 販売店 sales outlet; ~
shima⌐su (suru) 販売します
（する）deals in, sells

hambei (no) 反米（の）anti-
American

hambu⌐n 半分 half

hame はめ → **hamema⌐su** はめま

hame⌐ はめ plight, fix (one gets
into)

hamema⌐su はめます, **hameru** は
める wears (on fingers, hands)

hame(ra)rema⌐su はめ（ら）れま
す, **hame(ra)reru** はめ（ら）れ
る can wear (on fingers,
hands)

ha-mi⌐gaki 歯磨き dentifrice; (=
neri-hami⌐gaki 練り歯磨き)
toothpaste

ha⌐mmā ハンマー, **ha⌐mma** ハン
マ hammer

ha⌐-mono 刃物 cutlery, knives

hampe⌐n はんぺん・反平 boiled
fish cake

ha⌐mu ハム ham; **hamu-e⌐ggu/
-e⌐kku** ハムエッグ/エック
ham and eggs; **hamu-sa⌐ndo** ハ
ムサンド ham sandwich

ha⌐n 半 half (= **hambu⌐n** 半分):
han-... 半... half a ... ; **...-ha⌐n** ...
半 and a half

ha⌐n 判 = **hanko⌐** 判こ a "chop"
= a seal (to stamp name)

hana (o-hana) 鼻（お鼻）1. nose;
trunk (of elephant) 2. nasal
mucus, snivel; ~ **o kamima⌐su
(kamu)** 鼻をかみます（かむ）
blows one's nose

hana⌐ (o-hana) 花（お花）flower;
flower arrangement

ha⌐na はな・端 beginning, outset;
edge

ha⌐na-bi 花火 fireworks

hana⌐-fuda 花札, **hana-ga⌐ruta** 花

がるた (the game of) flower
cards

hana-gami 鼻紙 Kleenex, tissues

hanaˈgata 花形 a star (in a
theatrical production)

hanahada はなはだ・甚だ ex-
tremely

hanaji 鼻血 nosebleed

hana-miˈ (o-hanami) 花見（お花
見）flower viewing

hanaˈ-michi 花道 the runway to
the stage (in Kabuki)

hana-mizuꟷ 鼻水 snivel

hana-muˈko 花婿 bridegroom

hanao 鼻緒 thong (on geta)

hanaremaˈsu 離れます,
hanareˈru 離れる separates,
becomes distant

hanasaˈnai 話さない, etc. =
hanashimaseˈn 話しません,
etc, (not speak; not ...)

hanasemaˈsu 話せます,
hanaseˈru 話せる can speak

hanaseˈnai 話せない, etc. =
hanasemaseˈn 話せません,
etc. (cannot speak; ...)

hanaˈsha 話しゃ, etc. 1. =
hanaˈseba 話せば, etc. (if one
speak; if ...) 2. ~ **shinai** 話し
ゃしない = **hanaˈshi ya/wa
shinai** 話しや/はしない =
hanasaˈnai 話さない, etc. (not
speak; not ...)

hanashiˈ 話 talk, story, tale,
speech, conversation; something to talk about; ... no

~ **de (wa) ... soˈ desu** ...の話
で(は)...そうです according
to what ... says ...

hanashi-ai 話し合い conference,
discussion, negotiation

hanashi-aꟷi 話し合い →
hanashi-aimaˈsu 話し合いま
す [infinitive]

hanashi-aimaˈsu 話し合います,
-aꟷu 話し合う talk
together, discuss, confer,
negotiate

hanashi-ka はなし家・噺家
storyteller

hanashimaˈsu, hanaˈsu 1. 話しま
す, 話す speaks, talks 2. 放し
ます, 放す lets loose, lets go,
sets free 3. 離します, 離す
separates from, parts with;
detaches, disconnects

hanaˈ-taˈba 花束 bouquet

hanawa 花輪 wreath

hanaˈ-ya 花屋 florist, flower
shop

hanaˈyaka (na) はなやか(な)・華
やか(な) colorful, showy,
gorgeous, glorious, bright

hanaˈ-yome 花嫁 bride

haˈndaˈn 判断 judgment; ~
shima(ꟷ)su 判断します judges,
gives judgment

handō 反動 reaction, repercussion; ~**-teki (na)** 反動的(な)
reactionary; ~**-ha** 反動派 the
reactionaries

handobaˈggu (handobaˈkku) ハ

ンドバッグ(ハンドバック)
handbag, pocketbook

handoru ハンドル steering
wheel; handle

hane 羽 feather; wing; 羽根 shuttlecock

hane̅-tsuki̅ 羽根突き battledore
and shuttlecock (a kind of badminton)

hanga 版画 woodblock print

ha̅nga̅ ハンガー hanger

hangyaku 反逆 rebellion;
hangyaku̅ shima̅su 反逆しま
す rebels; **hangya̅ku̅-sha** 反逆
者 rebel

ha̅n'i 範囲 scope, range, limits;
(... no) han'i̅-gai/-nai (...の)
範囲外/内 beyond/within the
limits (of ...)

hanikamima̅su はにかみます,
hanika̅mu はにかむ acts shy,
is bashful

ha̅nji 判事 judge

ha̅nkachi ハンカチ handkerchief

han-ka̅nen 半か年 half a year

hanko̅ 判こ a "chop" = signature seal, name stamp

hanko̅ 反抗 opposition, resistance; **... ni ~ shima̅su** ...に反
抗します opposes, resists

hankyō 1. 反響 echo **2. ~ (no)**
反共(の) anti-Communist

ha̅n-nen 半年 half a year

han-nichi̅ 半日 half a day, a
half-day

hannichi (no) 反日(の) anti-
Japanese

ha̅nnin 犯人 criminal, culprit

hannō 反応 reaction, response

hanrei 凡例 explanatory notes
(on how to use a reference
work)

ha̅nsa (na) はんさ[煩瑣](な)
troublesome, complicated

hansen (no) 反戦(の) antiwar

ha̅nshi 半紙 rice paper (stationery)

ha̅n-shi 反し → **han-shima̅su** 反
します [infinitive]

han-shima̅su 反します, **-su̅ru** 反
する is contrary (to), goes
against, opposes; **... ni ha̅n-
shite** ...に反して contrary to,
against, in contrast with

hanshū 半周 semicircle

hantai 反対 opposite, contrary,
reverse; **~-gawa** 反対側 opposite side; **~-go** 反対語 antonym; **~ ni** 反対に vice versa; **~ shima̅su (suru)** 反対し
ます(する) opposes

hante̅n 半天・半纏 traditional
workman's jacket, happi coat

hantō 半島, **...-ha̅ntō** ...半島
peninsula

han-toshi̅ 半年 half a year

han-tsuki̅ 半月 half a month

han'yake (no) 半焼け(の)
medium-rare (meat), half-
done

hanzai 犯罪 crime

haō 這おう・はおう = **haimashō** 這いましょう・はいましょう (let's crawl!)

haori (o-haori) 羽織（お羽織） traditional Japanese coat

happa 葉っぱ leaf

hap-pa 八羽 eight birds

hap-peン 八遍 eight times

happi 法被 = **hanteン** 半天・半纏 traditional workman's jacket, *happi* coat

hap-piki 八匹 eight animals/fish/bugs

hap-pon 八本 eight long things

hap-pun 八分 eight minutes

hap-pyaku 八百・800 eight hundred

happyō 発表 announcement, publication; (research) paper; ～ **shimaす** 発表します announces, publishes

hāpu ハープ harp *(Western)*

hara (o-hara) 腹（お腹） 1. belly, stomach 2. mind, heart; ～ **ga tachimaす** 腹が立ちます = ～ **o tatemaす** 腹を立てます gets angry; ～ **ga ōkii** 腹が大きい is big-hearted; ～ **o kimemaす** 腹を決めます makes up one's mind; ... **no** ～ **o yomimaす** ...の腹を読みます reads the mind of ...

hara 原, **harappa** 原っぱ field

haradatashii 腹立たしい aggravating

hara-e 払え 1. → **haraemaす** 払えます [infinitive] 2. → **haraimaす** 払います [imperative] pay!

haraemaす 払えます, **haeru** 払える 1. can pay 2. can brush aside, can shake out

hara-gei 腹芸 (a talent for) nonverbal communication

haraimaす 払います, **harau** 払う 1. pays 2. brushes aside, shakes out

harai-modoshi 払い戻し a refund; **harai-modoshi** 払い戻し → **harai-modoshimaす** 払い戻します [infinitive]

harai-modoshimaす 払い戻します, **harai-modoす** 払い戻す refunds

hara-maki 腹巻き stomach band

haratte 払って → **haraimaす** 払います

harau 払う = **haraimaす** 払います (pays; ...)

harawanai 払わない = **haraimaseン** 払いません (not pay; not ...)

harawaта はらわた・腸 intestines

haraya 払や 1. = **haraeba** 払えば → **haraimaす** 払います (if one pay; if ...) 2. ～ **shinai** 払やしない = **harai ya/wa shinai** 払いや/はしない = **harawanai** 払わない (not pay; not ...)

hare 1. 腫れ・貼れ, etc. →

harema'su 腫れます; 貼れま
す, etc. (swells; can paste; …)
[infinitive] **2.** 貼れ →
harima'su 貼ります [impera-
tive] paste it!

hare' 晴れ fair (clear) weather

ha're 晴れ → **harema'su** 晴れま
す (clears up)

hare'ba 貼れば・張れば →
harima'su 貼ります/張ります
/張ります (if one paste/
spread/stretch it)

harema'su, hareru 1. 腫れます,
腫れる swells up **2.** 貼れます,
貼れる can paste **3.** 張れます,
張れる can spread/stretch it

harema'su 晴れます, **hare'ru** 晴
れる *(weather)* clears up;
ha'rete ima'su 晴れています is
clear/fair/sunny　⌈*(on skin)*

hare-mono 腫れ物 swelling, boil

harere'ba 腫れれば, **harerya** 腫
れりゃ → **harema'su** 腫れます
(if it swell)

hare'reba 晴れれば, **hare'rya** 晴
れりゃ → **harema'su** 晴れます
(if it clear up)

hari 貼り・張り → **harima'su** 貼
ります・張ります [infinitive]

ha'ri 1. 針 needle, pin; (= **o-hari**
お針) needlework; hand (of
clock); a staple (of stapler)
2. はり・鍼 acupuncture

harigane 針金 wire

harima'su, haru 1. 貼ります, 貼
る sticks on, pastes **2.** 張りま

す, 張る spreads/stretches it

hari-shi'goto 針仕事 needlework

haru 貼る・張る = **harima'su** 貼
ります・張ります

ha'ru 春 spring(time)

ha'ruka (ni) はるか・遥か(に)
far (off); long ago; by far; ~
(na) はるか・遥か(な) distant,
far

haru-maki 春巻 Chinese egg rolls

harusame 春雨 bean-flour
threads; "nylon noodles"

haru-ya'sumi 春休み spring
break/vacation

harya 貼りゃ・張りゃ **1.** =
hare'ba 貼れば・張れば (if one
paste/spread/stretch it) **2.** ~
shinai 貼りゃしない/張りゃ
しない = **hari'ya/wa shinai**
貼りや/はしない・張りや/は
しない = **haranai** 貼らない/
張らない (not paste/spread/
stretch it)

hasa'me 挟め **1.** → **hasamema'su**
挟めます [infinitive] **2.** →
hasamima'su 挟みます [imper-
ative]

hasamema'su 挟めます,
hasame'ru 挟める can insert
(put between)

hasami' 1. はさみ・鋏 scissors,
clippers **2.** はさみ・螯 pincer(s),
claw (of crab)

hasa'mi 挟み → **hasamima'su** 挟
みます [infinitive]

hasamima'su 挟みます, **hasa'mu**

挟む inserts, puts between;
ha¹shi de ~ 箸で挟みます
picks it up with chopsticks

hasan 破産 bankruptcy; ~
shima¹su (suru) 破産します
（する）goes bankrupt

hashi 端 (= **hashikko** 端っこ・は
しっこ) edge, end

hashi¹ 橋 bridge

ha¹shi 箸・はし (= **o-ha¹shi** お箸)
chopsticks

hashigo はしご・梯子 ladder,
stairs; (= **hashigo¹-zake** はし
ご[梯子]酒) bar hopping; ~
-dan はしご[梯子]段 wooden
stairs

hashikko 端っこ・はしっこ,
hajikko 端っこ・はじっこ
edge, end

hashi¹-o¹ki 箸置き chopstick rest

hashira 柱 pillar, post

hashi¹re 走れ 1. → **hashirema¹su**
走れます [infinitive] 2. →
hashirima¹su 走ります [impera-
tive] run!

hashirema¹su 走れます,
hashire¹ru 走れる can run

hashirima¹su 走ります, **hashi¹ru**
走る runs ⌈走ります

hashi¹tte 走って → **hashirima¹su**

hassei 発生 outbreak, occurrence, origin, birth, growth;
~ **shima¹su** 発生します
breaks out, occurs, appears,
grows ⌈sand

has-se¹n 八千・8,000 eight thou-

hasshin 発疹 (skin) rash

hasu 1. はす・蓮 lotus 2. ~ **(no)**
斜・はす(の) oblique, slant-
ing; ~ **ni** 斜に・はすに ob-
liquely

hata 端・はた the (out)side; ~
no mono¹ 端の者 outsider(s),
bystanders; (... **no**) ~ **de** (...
の)端で off to the side (of); ~
kara 端から from the outside,
to an outsider

hata¹ 1. 旗 flag 2. 機 loom

ha¹tachi 二十歳・はたち 20 years
old

hata¹ite はたいて →
hatakima¹su はたきます

hatake 畑 field *(dry)*

hata¹ke はたけ 1. →
hatakema¹su はたけます [in-
finitive] 2. → **hatakima¹su** は
たきます [imperative] slap/
dust it!

hatakema¹su はたけます,
hatake¹ru はたける can slap; can
dust

hataki¹ はたき duster

hata¹ki はたき → **hatakima¹su**
はたきます [infinitive]

hatakima¹su はたきます,
hata¹ku はたく slap, beat;
dust

hatarakema¹su 働けます,
hatarakeru 働ける can work

hataraki 働き work(ing), activity, operation, function; ability; achievement

hatarakima゛su 働きます, **hataraku** 働く works, labors; commits (a crime)

hatasema゛su 果たせます, **hatase゛ru** 果たせる can accomplish

hatashima゛su 果たします, **hata゛su** 果たす accomplishes

ha゛to はと・鳩 pigeon, dove

hato-ba 波止場 pier, wharf, quay

hatsude゛n-ki 発電機 generator

hatsudō゛-ki 発動機 motor

hatsuka 二十日 20 days; 20th of the month; ~**-me** 二十日目 the 20th day; ~**-ne゛zumi** 二十日ねずみ[鼠] mouse

hatsumei 発明 invention

... ha゛tsu (no) ...発（の）departing at/from (TIME/PLACE); dispatched from/at (PLACE/TIME)

hatsuon 発音 pronunciation; ~ **shima゛su (suru)** 発音します（する）pronounces

hattatsu 発達 development; **hattatsu shima゛su (suru)** 発達します（する）it develops

hatte 張って → **harima゛su** 張ります; **hatte ima゛su** 張っています is tense, taut

ha゛tte 這って・はって → **haima゛su** 這います・はいます; **ha゛tte ima゛su** 這って[はって]います is crawling

hatten 発展 development, expansion, growth; ~ **tojō゛-koku** 発展途上国 developing nation; ~ **shima゛su (suru)** 発展します（する）develops, expands, grows ⌜etc.⌝

ha゛t-tō 八頭 eight (horses/oxen,

hatto (shite) はっと（して）with a sudden start (of surprise)

Ha゛wai ハワイ Hawaii

hawa゛nai 這わない・はわない = **haimase゛n** 這いません・はいません (not crawl)

ha゛ya 這や・はや 1. = **ha゛eba** 這えば・はえば (if one crawl) 2. ~ **shinai** 這や[はや]しない = **ha゛i ya/wa shinai** 這い[はい]や/はしない = **hawa゛nai** 這わない・はわない (not crawl) ⌜ly

haya゛i 速い・早い, fast, quick; ear-

ha゛yaku 速く・早く (so as to be) fast/early; ~**-tomo** 早くとも at the earliest

hayame⌐ ni 早め・早目に early *(in good time)*

hayari (no) はやり[流行り]（の）fashionable

hayarima゛su はやり[流行り]ます, **haya゛ru** はやる・流行る gets popular, comes into fashion, spreads; *(disease)* spreads rapidly, is fast-spreading

ha゛yasa 速さ speed

hayashi ハヤシ; ~ **ra゛isu** ハヤシライス beef hash over rice

hayashi⁽ⁿ⁾ 林 forest, grove

hayashi⁽ⁿ⁾ **(o-hayashi)** はやし[囃し](おはやし) (musical) band

haya⁽ⁿ⁾**shi** はやし・生やし・囃し → **hayashima**⁽ⁿ⁾**su** はやします・生やします・囃します

hayashima⁽ⁿ⁾**su, haya**⁽ⁿ⁾**su** 1. はやします・生やします, はやす・生やす grows it (hair, teeth); lets it grow (sprout) 2. はやし[囃し]ます, はや[囃]す (musically) accompanies

haya⁽ⁿ⁾**tte** はやって・流行って → **hayarima**⁽ⁿ⁾**su** はやり[流行り]ます

ha⁽ⁿ⁾**ze** 1. はぜ・沙魚 goby *(fish)* 2. はぜ・黄櫨 sumac *(plant)*

ha⁽ⁿ⁾**zu** ハズ husband

... hazu de⁽ⁿ⁾**su** ...はずです presumably, expectably; ought to, should

... hazu ga/wa arimase⁽ⁿ⁾**n (na**⁽ⁿ⁾**i)** ...はずが/はありません(ない) there is no reason to expect/think that ...

hazukashi⁽ⁿ⁾**i** 恥ずかしい ashamed; embarrassed, shy; shameful, disgraceful

hazumi 弾み 1. impetus, momentum; impulse; chance; **toki no ~ de** 時の弾みで on the spur of the moment 2. → **hazumima**⁽ⁿ⁾**su** 弾みます

hazumima⁽ⁿ⁾**su** 弾みます, **hazumu** 弾む bounces (back); cheers

hazurema⁽ⁿ⁾**su** 外れます, **hazureru** 外れる gets disconnected, comes off, misses, fails

hazushima⁽ⁿ⁾**su** 外します, **hazusu** 外す disconnects, takes off, undoes, unfastens; **se**⁽ⁿ⁾**ki o ~** 席を外します leaves one's seat

he 1. 屁・へ flatulence, fart; **~ o hirima**⁽ⁿ⁾**su (hi**⁽ⁿ⁾**ru)** 屁をひります(ひる) flatulates, farts 2. 経 → **hema**⁽ⁿ⁾**su** 経ます (pass) [infinitive]

hē? へえ? really?? No kidding!

he⁽ⁿ⁾**bi** へび・蛇 snake

hechima へちま・糸瓜 sponge gourd, luffa (loofah)

hedatarima⁽ⁿ⁾**su** 隔たります, **hedata**⁽ⁿ⁾**ru** 隔たる is distant, is estranged

hedatema⁽ⁿ⁾**su** 隔てます, **hedate**⁽ⁿ⁾**ru** 隔てる estranges them, separates them, gets them apart

heddora⁽ⁿ⁾**ito** ヘッドライト headlight(s)

he⁽ⁿ⁾**do** へど・反吐 vomit

hei 塀 wall, fence

heibon (na) 平凡(な) commonplace, conventional

heichi 平地 flat land; (= **heiya** 平野) plain

heijō⁽ⁿ⁾**-fuku** 平常服 civilian clothes, civies ⌈rage

heikin 平均 average, on the ave-

heiki (na) 平気(な) calm, composed, cool, unperturbed, unfazed; **~ de** 平気で calmly

he⁽ⁿ⁾**isha** 兵舎 barracks

heisotsu 兵卒 buck private

heitai 兵隊 soldier

heiwa 平和 peace; ～-bu⌐tai 平和部隊 Peace Corps; ～-buta⌐i-in 平和部隊員 Peace Corps member

heiya 平野 plain *(flat land)*

heizei 平生 usually, ordinarily, generally

hekomima⌐su へこみます・凹みます, **hekomu** へこむ・凹む gets hollow, depressed; **hekonde ima⌐su** へこんで[凹んで]います is hollow, depressed

he⌐ma へま・ヘマ bungle, mess

hema⌐su 経ます, **he⌐ru** 経る passes (by), elapses

... hen ...辺 vicinity, neighborhood

...-he⌐n ...遍 (counts times)

henai 経ない = **hemase⌐n** 経ません (not pass)

hen'a⌐tsu-ki 変圧器 voltage converter, transformer

henji⌐ (o-henji) 返事（お返事） answer

he⌐nka 変化 change; **... ni ～ shima(⌐)su** ...に変化します it changes into ...

henkan 変換 conversion; **henka⌐n-ki** 変換器 converter; **henkan-kī⌐i** 変換キー the kana-to-kanji conversion key (on a Japanese word processor)

henken 偏見 prejudice

henkin 返金 refund; ～ **shima⌐su** 返金します refunds

he⌐n (na) 変・ヘン（な) strange, odd, peculiar, funny, queer

henryū⌐-ki 変流器 converter *(AC-DC)*

hensoku-re⌐bā 変速レバー gearshift
                                      「返事

hentō⌐ 返答 [bookish] = **henji⌐**

heranai 減らない = **herimase⌐n** 減りません (not decrease)

herashima⌐su 減らします, **herasu** 減らす decreases it, cuts it down, shortens, lessens, curtails

here⌐ba 減れば → **herima⌐su** 減ります (if it decrease)

heri 減り 1. a decrease 2. → **herima⌐su** 減ります

heri⌐ 縁・へり border, edge, rim

herima⌐su 減ります, **heru** 減る decreases, dwindles, goes down

he⌐rupesu ヘルペス herpes

herya 減りゃ 1. = **here⌐ba** 減れば (if it decrease) 2. ～ **shinai** 減りゃしない = **heri⌐ ya/wa shinai** 減りや/はしない = **heranai** 減らない (not decrease)

heso (o-heso) へそ（おへそ） navel, bellybutton

heta⌐ (na) へた[下手]（な) unskillful, inept, clumsy, poor, bad, inexpert; **heta⌐ o suru to**

へたをすると if you are
unlucky, if you are not careful

he'ta 経た = hema'shita 経まし
た (passed)

he'te 経て → hema'su 経ます
(pass); ... o ~ ...を経て by
way of (through, via) ...

hetta 減った = herima'shita 減
りました (decreased)

hette 減って → herima'su 減り
ます

he'tto ヘット fat (cooking), suet

heya' (o-heya) 部屋(お部屋)
room

hi 日 sun (= o-hi-sama お日様)

hi 日, ... hi' ...日 day

hi' 火 fire

...'-hi ...費 expense

hiatari 日当たり exposure to
the sun, sunniness; ~ ga i'i 日
当たりがいい is sunny

hi'bachi (o-hi'bachi) 火鉢(お火
鉢) charcoal brazier

hi'bana 火花 spark

hi'-bashi 火箸 tongs (for fire)

hibi' ひび・罅 crack (fine)

hi'bi 日々 every day

hibi'ite 響いて → hibikima'su 響
きます

hibiki' 響き echo; → hibikima'su
響きます

hibikima'su 響きます, hibi'ku 響
く echoes, resounds

Hibiya 日比谷 Hibiya; ~-Kō'en
日比谷公園 Hibiya Park

hibō 誹謗 slander

hichiriki ひちりき・篳篥 an
oboe-like reed instrument (in
gagaku)

hidari 左 left; ~-do'nari 左隣り
next (door) on the left;
hidari-kiki/-giki (no) 左利き/
利き(の) left-handed (person);
~-ma'wari (ni) 左回り(に)
counterclockwise

hido'i ひどい severe, unreasonable, terrible, vicious, bitter

hi'doku ひどく hard, cruelly, terribly

hi'e 冷え → hiema'su 冷えます

hiema'su 冷えます, hie'ru 冷え
る gets cold

hie'reba 冷えれば, hie'rya 冷え
りゃ → hiema'su 冷えます (if
it get cold)

hi'ete 冷えて → hiema'su 冷えま
す

hifu' 皮膚, hi'fu 皮膚 skin

higai 被害 damage, injury,
casualty; higa'i-chi 被害地
stricken area; higa'i-sha 被害
者 victim

hi-ga'sa 日傘 parasol (umbrella)

higashi 東 east; higashi-guchi
東口 the east exit/entrance;
higashi-yori (no kaze) 東寄り
(の風) easterly (wind);
higashi-ka'igan 東海岸 east
coast

hige (o-hige) ひげ・髭(おひげ)
beard; (= kuchi-hige 口ひ

げ・口髭) mustache; ～ **o hayashima̅su** ひげ[髭]を生やします grows a beard/mustache; ～ **o sorima̅su** ひげ[髭]を剃ります shaves

hi̅geki 悲劇 tragedy

higesori-yō kuri̅imu ひげ[髭]剃り用のクリーム shaving cream

hi̅[ꓯ]-goto (ni) 日毎(に) every day

higure 日暮れ sunset *(time);* the dark

hi̅[ꓯ]han 批判 judgment, criticism; **hihan-teki (na)** 批判的(な) critical; **hiha̅n-sha** 批判者 critic, judge; ～ **shima̅su** 批判します judges, criticizes

hihyō 批評 criticism, review; ～ **-ka** 批評家 critic, reviewer; ～ **shima̅su** 批評します criticizes, reviews

hiita 引いた = **hikima̅shita** 引きました (pulled)

hi̅itā ヒーター heater

hiite 引いて → **hikima̅su** 引きます (pulls)

hiji̅ ひじ・肘 elbow

hijō 非常 1. emergency; ～ **-bure̅ki** 非常ブレーキ emergency brake; ～ **-de̅nwa** 非常電話 emergency phone; **hijō[ꓯ]-guchi** 非常口 emergency exit; ～ **no baai** 非常の場合 in (the) event of emergency 2. ～ **(na)** 非常(な) unusual, extreme

hijō ni 非常に extremely

hikaeme[ꓯ] (no) 控え目(の) modest

hi̅-kage 日陰 shadow *(from sunlight)*

hikaku 比較 comparison; **hikaku-teki ni** 比較的に relatively, comparatively

hikan 悲観 pessimism; ～ **-teki (na)** 悲観的(な) pessimistic

hikanai 引かない = **hikimase̅n** 引きません (not pull)

hikarema̅su 引かれます, etc., **hikareru** 引かれる, etc. gets pulled (out), gets ... ; **tora̅kku ni** ～ トラックに引かれ[轢かれ]ます gets run over by a truck

hikari̅ 光 light; → **hikarima̅su** 光ります

hikarima̅su 光ります, **hika̅ru** 光る it shines, glows

hike 引け 1. → **hikema̅su** 引けます [infinitive] 2. → **hikima̅su** 引きます [imperative] pull!

hike̅ba 引けば → **hikima̅su** 引きます (if one pull)

hikema̅su 引けます, **hikeru** 引ける can pull

hikerya 引けりゃ → **hikema̅su** 引けます (if one can pull)

hiki- 引き PREFIX ("pull/take and")

...-hiki ...匹 (counts small animals, fish, insects)

hiki-age 1. 引き上げ・引き揚げ refloating; salvage 2. 引き揚げ evacuation, repatriation 3. 引き上げ rise/hike (in price, wage, fee)

hiki-agema̱su, -age̱ru 1. 引き上げます, 引き上げる pulls up; refloats 2. 引き揚げます, 引き揚げる withdraws, leaves; evacuates, gets repatriated 3. 引き上げます, 引き上げる raises (price, wage, fee)

hikiage̱-sha 引き揚げ者・引揚げ者 evacuee, repatriate

hikidashi 引き出し drawer

hiki-fune 引き船・曳き船・引き舟 tugboat

hikigane 引き金 trigger

hiki-haraima̱su 引き払います, -hara̱u 引き払う checks out (of hotel)

hikiima̱su 率います, hikii̱ru 率いる leads, commands

hiki̱ite 率いて → hikiima̱su 率います

hiki-kaema̱su 引き換えます, -ka̱e̱ru 引き換える exchanges, converts

hikima̱su, hiku 引きます, 引く pulls (out); draws; drags, tugs; catches; attracts 2. 引き[轢き]ます, 引く[轢く] runs over (a person) 3. 挽きます, 挽く saws 4. 引きます, 引く subtracts; deducts; looks up a word 5. 弾きます, 弾く

plays (a stringed instrument) 6. 碾きます, 碾く grinds (into powder)

hiki-niku 挽き肉 chopped/minced/ground meat

hikiniku̱-ki 挽き肉機 meat grinder

hiki-te 引き手 doorknob

hiki-torima̱su 引き取ります, -to̱ru 引き取る 1. leaves, withdraws, retires 2. takes over, looks after, receives 3. i̱ki o ～ 息を引き取ります takes/draws one's last breath, dies

hiki-ukema̱su 引き受けます, -uke̱ru 引き受ける undertakes, takes charge of, takes responsibility for; guarantees; tegata o ～ 手形を引き受けます accepts a bill (of payment)

hiki-zurima̱su 引きずります, -zuru 引きずる drags

hik-kakima̱su 引っかきます, -ka̱ku 引っかく scratches it

hikkoshi 引っ越し moving (house)

hikko̱shi 引っ越し → hikkoshima̱su 引っ越します [infinitive]

hikkoshima̱su 引っ越します, hikko̱su 引っ越す moves (house)

hikkoshi-tora̱kku 引っ越しトラック moving van

hikkoshi-ya 引っ越し屋 (house)

mover, moving man

hikkuri-kaerima͏̀su 引っくり返ります, **-ka͏̀eru** 引っくり返る it tips (over)

hikkuri-kaeshima͏̀su 引っくり返します, **-ka͏̀esu** 引っくり返す upsets (overturns) it

hikō 1. 飛行 flying (a plane); ～ **shima͏̀su** 飛行します flies (a plane) **2.** 引こう = **hikimasho͏̀** 引きましょう (let's pull!)

hikō-bin 飛行便, **hikō-yu͏̀bin** 飛行郵便 airmail

hikō-jō 飛行場 airfield, airport

hikō͏̀-ki 飛行機 airplane

hi-kō͏̀shiki (no) 非公式(の) unofficial, informal

hikō-yoi 飛行酔い airsick(ness)

hiku 引く = **hikima͏̀su** 引きます

hiku͏̀i 低い low, short

hikya 引きゃ **1.** = **hike͏̀ba** 引けば (if one pull) **2.** ～ **shinai** 引きゃしない = **hiki͏̀ ya/wa shinai** 引きや/はしない = **hikanai** 引かない (not pull)

hima 1. 暇 time; leisure, spare time; furlough, leave; dismissal (of servant) **2.** ～ **(na)** 暇(な) at leisure, unoccupied, unbusy, free (of business); slow (business)

hi͏̀me 姫, **o-hi͏̀me sama** お姫様 princess

himei 悲鳴 a scream

himitsu (no) 秘密(の) secret, mystery

himmi͏̀n-kutsu/-gai 貧民窟/街 slum

himo ひも・紐 string, cord, tape, strap, ribbon

himokawa(-u͏̀don) 紐革(うどん) long thin udon (served cold)

hin 品 quality; elegance, refinement, dignity

hina-ma͏̀tsuri ひな祭り the Dolls Festival (3 March)

hi͏̀nan 1. 非難 blame, reproach; ～ **shima(͏̀)su** 非難します blames, reproaches **2.** 避難 taking refuge; **hina͏̀n-sha** 避難者 refugee

hina-ni͏̀ngyō ひな人形 (festival) dolls

hinata 日なた・日向 sunshine; ～ **-bo͏̀kko** 日なた[日向]ぼっこ sunbathing, basking (in the sun)

hinerima͏̀su 捻ります・ひねります, **hine͏̀ru** 捻る・ひねる twists

hine͏̀tte 捻って・ひねって → **hinerima͏̀su** 捻ります・ひねります

hinichi 日にち (fixed) day; number of days

hiniku 皮肉 sarcasm; ～ **(na)** 皮肉(な) sarcastic, cynical

hinin 避妊 contraception; **hini͏̀n-gu** 避妊具 contraceptive *(device)*; **hini͏̀n-yaku** 避妊薬 contraceptive drug/pill

hinkon 貧困 poverty; ～ **(na)** 貧困(な) needy

hinode 日の出 sunrise

hinoiri 日の入り sunset

hiⁿnoki ひのき・檜・桧 cypress

hinshitsu 品質 quality

hiˈnto ヒント hint, reminder

hi-oˈiˈ 日覆い awning, sunshade, blind

hipparimaˈsu 引っ張ります, **hippaˈru** 引っ張る pulls, drags, tugs (at), takes

hiraˈgaˈnaˈ ひらがな・平仮名 hiragana (the roundish Japanese letters)

hiraˈite 開いて → **hirakimaˈsu** 開きます

hirakiˈ-do 開き戸 hinged door

hirakimaˈsu 開きます, **hiraˈku** 開く opens up

hirame ひらめ・平目 flounder

hiraˈnai ひらない = **hirimaseˈn** ひりません (not ...)

hira(t)tai 平(っ)たい flat

hire 1. ひれ・鰭 fin 2. ヒレ filet (of pork, etc.)

hirimaˈsu ひります, **hiˈru** ひる discharges (excretes) from the body; **heˈ** o ～ 屁をひります flatulates, farts

Hiˈriˈ(p)pin ヒリ(ッ)ピン = **F(u)iˈriˈ(p)pin** フィ[フイ]リ(ッ)ピン Philippines

hiˈro-baˈ 広場 a square, a place, an open space

hiroe 拾え 1. → **hiroemaˈsu** 拾えます [infinitive] 2. → **hiroimaˈsu** 拾います [impera-

tive] pick it up

hiroemaˈsu 拾えます, **hiroeru** 拾える can pick it up

hiroˈ-en 披露宴 reception (engagement, wedding, etc.)

hirogarimaˈsu 広がります, **hirogaru** 広がる it spreads, widens

hirogemaˈsu 広げます, **hirogeru** 広げる spreads/widens it

hiroi 拾い → **hiroimaˈsu** 拾います [infinitive]

hiroˈi 広い wide, broad; big (room, etc.)

hiroimaˈsu 拾います, **hirou** 拾う picks it up

hiroˈ-kai 披露会 reception (engagement, wedding, etc.)

hiromarimaˈsu 広まります, **hiromaˈru** 広まる it spreads, gets diffused

hiromemaˈsu 広めます, **hiromeˈru** 広める spreads/diffuses it

hiˈrosa 広さ width

Hiroshima 広島 Hiroshima; **Hiroshimaˈ-Eki** 広島駅 Hiroshima Station

hiˈrō shima(ˈ)su (suru) 披露します(する) announces (wedding, etc.)

hirotte 拾って → **hiroimaˈsu** 拾います

hirowanai 拾わない = **hiroimaseˈn** 拾いません (not pick up)

hiru⌐ (o-hi̋ru) 昼（お昼）daytime, noon (～ kara 昼から after noon); (= hiru-go⌐han 昼ご飯) lunch; hiru(⌐) no bu⌐ 昼の部 matinee

hi̋ru ひる・蛭 leech

hiru-go⌐han 昼ご飯 noon meal, lunch

hiru-ma⌐ 昼間 daytime

hiru-ne 昼寝 nap

hiru-su⌐gi̋ 昼過ぎ afternoon

hisashi-buri ni 久しぶりに after a long time (of absence)

hishaku ひしゃく・柄杓 scoop, ladle

hisho⌐ 秘書, hi̋sho 秘書 secretary (private)

hi̋ssha 筆者, hissha 筆者 the writer/author

hisu⌐i ひすい・翡翠, hi̋sui ひすい・翡翠 jade

hitai 額・ひたい forehead, brow

hitashi-mo⌐no⌐ 浸し物 = o-hita̋shi お浸し・おひたし

hitei 否定 denial; ～ shima̋su 否定します denies

hito 人, ... hito⌐ ...人 person, man, fellow, people; someone, somebody

hito-... 一... one; hito⌐-ban 一晩 one night

hito-a⌐nshin 一安心 a relief (from worry)

hito⌐-ban 一晩 one night

hito⌐bito 人々 people (in general)

hito-go⌐roshi 人殺し murder

hito⌐-hako 一箱 one boxful

hito⌐-iki 一息 a breath

hito⌐-ka⌐tamari 一固まり・一塊 one lump/loaf

hito⌐-kire 一切れ (one) piece (a cut)

hito⌐-koto 一言 a word

hito⌐-kumi 一組 a set (collection)

hito⌐-maki 一巻き one (roll, volume, bolt of cloth)

hito⌐mazu ひとまず for a while; for the time being

hito⌐-mori 一盛り scoop (one scoopful)

hito⌐ri (o-hito⌐ri) 一人（お一人）one person; (～ de ひとりで・独りで) alone; hitori-bo⌐tchi (no) ひとりぼっち・独りぼっち（の）lonely; hitori-mo⌐no⌐ 独り者 single (unmarried) person

hitori-de ni ひとりでに・独りで に by/of itself, spontaneously, automatically

hito⌐-saji 一匙 one spoonful

hitoshi̋i 等しい equal, identical, similar

hito⌐-tachi 人達 people

hito⌐tsu ひとつ・一つ one; one year old; one and the same

hito⌐-yama 一山 one heap/bunch

hitsuji 羊 sheep

hitsuyō 必要 necessity, need; ～ (na) 必要（な）necessary, essential

hi̋tte ひって → hirima̋su ひり⌐ます

hi̥'tto' ヒット a hit

hi̥'ya (= **o-hi̥'ya**) 冷や(お冷や) cold water

hiyake 日焼け sunburn

hiya-mu'gi 冷や麦・ひやむぎ chilled wheat-flour noodles (*cf.* **sō'men** そうめん)

hiyashima'su 冷やします, **hiya'su** 冷やす cools it off, refrigerates, chills

hiya-ya'kko 冷ややっこ cold bean curd

hi̥'yō 費用 cost, expense

hiyoke 日よけ sunshade, blind, awning

hiyori 日和 weather (conditions)

hiza 膝・ひざ knee, lap

hizuke 日付 date *(of month)*

hizume ひづめ・蹄 hoof

ho' 帆 sail

hō? ほお? oh??

hō 法 law (= **hōritsu** 法律); rule (= **hōsoku** 法則); method (= **hōhō** 方法)

hō' ほお・頬 (= **hoppe'ta** ほっぺた) cheek

... hō' ...方 alternative, the one (of two) that ... ; ~ **ga i'i desu** ...方がいいです ... is better

hōbi ほうび・褒美 (= **go-hō'bi** ごほうび・ご褒美) prize, reward

ho'bo ほぼ nearly; roughly

hō'bō 方々 everywhere, all over, every which way

ho'chikisu ホチキス stapler

hōchō 包丁 knife *(big)*; butcher knife; (= **nikukiri-bō'chō** 肉切り包丁) cleaver

hōdan 砲弾 bombshell

(...) hodo (...)程・ほど extent; limits; moderation; approximate time; about (as much as), (not) so much as; the more ... the more

hōdō 歩道 walk(way), pavement, sidewalk

hodo'ite ほどいて → **hodokima'su** ほどきます

hodo'ke ほどけ 1. → **hodokema'su** ほどけます [infinitive] 2. → **hodokima'su** ほどきます [imperative] undo/untie it!

hodokema'su ほどけます, **hodoke'ru** ほどける can undo, can untie

hodokima'su ほどきます, **hodo'ku** ほどく undoes, unties

hodoko'shi' 施し charity

hoema'su 吠えます, **hoe'ru** 吠える (dog) barks

hoe(ra)rema'su 吠え(ら)れます, **hoe(ra)re'ru** 吠え(ら)れる can bark

hō'fu (na) 豊富(な) rich

hō'gai (na) 法外(な) exorbitant, inordinate, excessive

hōgaku 1. 方角 direction, one's bearings 2. 邦楽 Japanese music hō̅⌐gaku 法学 (science/study of) law

hoga'raka (na) 朗らか・ほがらか (な) bright, sunny; cheerful

hōge̅n 方言 dialect

ho̅'go 保護 protection; ～ shima(⌐)su 保護します protects, safeguards, shields

hōhō 方法 method, process

hoiku'-en 保育園 nursery school, pre-kindergarten

hōji 法事 mass (Buddhist)

hoka ほか・外・他 other, in addition to, other than

hoken 保険 insurance; ... ni ～ o kakema'su ...に保険をかけます insures; ～-ga'isha 保険会社 insurance company

hōken 封建 feudal(ism); ～ -ji'dai 封建時代 feudal period; ～-se'ido 封建制度 feudal system

hō̅⌐ki ほうき・箒 broom

hōki'-boshi ほうき星・箒星 comet

Hokka'ido̅ 北海道 Hokkaido

ho̅'kku ホック hook (snap)

hokku⌐ 発句 (a kind of) haiku, short poem

Hokkyoku 北極 North Pole, Arctic

hōkō 方向 direction

hōkoku 報告 report; hōkoku shima'su 報告します reports

hokorema'su 誇れます, hokore'ru 誇れる can brag

hokori ほこり dust (in the air)

hokori⌐ 誇り pride, boast; → hokorima'su 誇ります

hokorima'su 誇ります, hoko'ru 誇る brags about/of

hoku-... 北... north (= kita no ... 北の...)

ho̅'ku ホーク = f(u)o̅'ku フォ [フオ]ーク fork

Hoku-Bei 北米 = Kita-A'merika 北アメリカ North America

ho'kubu 北部 the north, the northern part

hokuro ほくろ・黒子 mole (on skin)

hokusei 北西 northwest

hokutō 北東 northeast

hōkyū 俸給 pay, wages, salary

ho'm-bako 本箱 bookcase

ho'mbu 本部 central office, headquarters

ho⌐mbun 本分 one's duty

home̅ ほめ・褒め praise (= home-ko'toba ほめ[褒め]言葉)

ho'me ほめ・褒め → homema'su ほめ[褒め]ます [infinitive]

homema'su ほめ[褒め]ます, home'ru ほめ[褒め]る praises, admires

hōme̅n 方面, ...-ho̅'men ...方面 direction, quarter, district

hom-mono 本物 the real thing; ～ no 本物の genuine

ho'mo (no) ホモ(の) homosexual, gay

hōmon 訪問 visit, call; ～ **shima‌su** 訪問します visits, calls on

hō‌mu ホーム platform *(at station)*

hōmu-do‌rama ホームドラマ soap opera

ho‌n 本 book

hon-... 本... main; chief; this; the; the present

...‌-hon ...本 (counts long objects)

hō‌n ホーン horn

ho‌n-dana 本棚 bookshelf

hondō 本道 the main route

hone‌ 骨 bone; ～ **o orima‌su (o‌ru)** 骨を折ります（折る） takes (great) pains, goes to much trouble; ～ **ga orema‌su (ore‌ru)** 骨が折れます（折れる） requires much effort, is hard/difficult

honegu‌mi 骨組み framework

hone-o‌ri (o-honeori) 骨折り（お骨折り） effort

honki (no/de) 本気（の/で） serious(ly), (in) earnest; **... o ～ ni shima‌su** ...を本気にします takes it seriously

Ho‌nkon ホンコン・香港 Hong Kong

honno ... ほんの... just a little, a mere/slight ...

honomekashi‌ ほのめかし・仄めかし a hint

honomekashima‌su ほのめかし［仄めかし］ます, **honomeka‌su** ほのめかす・仄めかす hints

Hono‌ruru ホノルル Honolulu

ho‌nrai 本来 originally, from the start

ho‌nseki 本籍 permanent residence; **honse‌ki‌-chi** 本籍地 place of permanent residence

Ho‌nshū 本州 Honshu

ho‌n-tate 本立て bookends

hontō/honto (no) 本当/ほんと（の） true, real, genuine; **(～ no koto)** 本当の事 truth; ～ **ni** 本当に really, truly, indeed

ho‌n-ya 本屋 bookshop

hon'yaku 翻訳 translation; **hon'ya‌ku‌-sha** 翻訳者 translator; **hon'yaku shima‌su** 翻訳します translates

hoppe‌ta ほっぺた cheek

hoppō 北方 the north

ho‌ra 洞 = **hora-ana** 洞穴 cave

ho‌ra ほら・法螺 trumpet-shell; exaggeration, bragging, bull; ～ **o fukima‌su (fuku‌)** ほらを吹きます（吹く） brags

ho‌ra! ほら！ huh?! what's that?!

hora-ana 洞穴 cave

hora‌-gai ほら［法螺］貝 trumpetshell

hora‌nai 掘らない = **horimase‌n** 掘りません (not dig)

hore ほれ・惚れ → **horema‌su** ほれます・惚れます (falls in

love)

ho͞re 掘れ 1. → horema͞su 掘れ
ます (can dig) 2. → horima͞su
掘ります [imperative] dig!

ho͞reba 掘れば → horima͞su 掘
ります (if one dig)

horema͞su ほれます・惚れます,
horeru ほれる・惚れる: ... ni
~ ...にほれ[惚れ]ます falls
in love (with)

horema͞su 掘れます, ho͞reru 掘
れる can dig

horenai ほれない・惚れない =
horemase͞n ほれません・惚れ
ません (not fall in love)

hore͞nai 掘れない = horemase͞n
掘れません (cannot dig)

hōre͞nsō ほうれん草 spinach

horete ほれて・惚れて →
horema͞su ほれます・惚れます
(falls in love)

ho͞rete 掘れて → horema͞su 掘
れます (can dig)

hori͞ 堀 ditch, moat

ho͞ri 掘り → horima͞su 掘りま
す [infinitive]

horidashi-mono 掘り出し物 a
bargain, a real find

horima͞su 掘ります, ho͞ru 掘る
digs, carves; excavates

hori͞-mo͞no 彫物 a carving

hōritsu 法律 law

horiwari 掘り割り・堀割り canal

horobima͞su 滅びます,
horobi͞ru 滅びる perish

horoboshima͞su 滅ぼします,

horobo͞su 滅ぼす destroy

hōro͞ku ほうろく・焙烙 earthen-
ware pan

ho͞run ホルン horn (music)

ho͞rya 掘りゃ 1. = ho͞reba 掘れ
ば (if one dig) 2. ~ shinai 掘
りゃしない = ho͞ri ya/wa
shinai 掘りや/はしない =
hora͞nai 掘らない (not dig)

hosa͞nai 干さない =
hoshimase͞n 干しません (not
dry it)

ho͞seba 干せば → hoshima͞su 干
します (if one dry it)

hōseki 宝石 jewel, gem; hōseki͞-
shō 宝石商 jeweler, gem dealer

hosema͞su 干せます, hose͞ru 干
せる can dry it

hose͞nai 干せない = hosemase͞n
干せません (cannot dry it)

ho͞sete 干せて → hosema͞su 干
せます

ho͞sha 干しゃ 1. = ho͞seba 干せ
ば (if one dry it) 2. ~ shinai
干しゃしない = ho͞shi ya/wa
shinai 干しや/はしない =
hosa͞nai 干さない (not dry it)

hoshi 星 star

ho͞shi 干し → hoshima͞su 干し
ます [infinitive]

hoshi-bu͞dō 干しぶどう[葡萄]
raisin(s)

hoshi͞-gaki 干し柿 dried persimmons

hoshi͞i 欲しい is desired/desir-
able; desires, wants

hoshi-jiˈrushi 星印 star *(symbol)*, asterisk (*)

hoshimaˈsu 干します, **hoˈsu** 干す dries it; airs it

hōshin 1. 方針 policy, course (of action), aim *(direction)* **2.** 疱疹 herpes

hoˈshite 干して → **hoshimaˈsu** 干します

hoshō 1. 保証 guarantee, warranty; **hoshō⁽ⁿ⁾-sho⁽ⁿ⁾** 保証書 letter of guarantee **2.** 補償 compensating; **hoshō⁽ⁿ⁾-kin** 補償金 compensation (money), indemnity; ～ **shimaˈsu** 補償します compensates, indemnifies

hoˈshu 保守 maintenance, upkeep; **hoˈshu shima(ˈ)su** 保守します maintains, preserves

hoshu-teki (na) 保守的 (な) conservative

hosoˈ 干そう = **hoshimashoˈ** 干しましょう (let's dry it!)

hōsō 1. 放送 broadcasting; **hōsōˈ-kyoku** 放送局 broadcasting station; ～ **shimaˈsu** 放送します broadcasts **2.** 包装 packing, wrapping; ～ **shimaˈsu** 包装します packs, wraps

hōsōˈ-butsu 包装物 package, packet; **kogata (no)** ～ 小型 (の) 包装物 small packet (under 1 kg)

hosoˈi 細い slender; narrow; thin

(and round)

hōsoku 法則 rule(s), law(s)

hosonagaˈi 細長い long and slender/narrow

hoˈsu 干す = **hoshimaˈsu** 干します (dries it)

hoˈsu ホース hose

hoˈsutesu ホステス hostess; stewardess

hoˈsuto ホスト host; steward

hōtai 包帯 bandage

hotateˈ-gai 帆立貝 scallop(s)

hōtei 法廷 law court

hoˈteru ホテル hotel

Hotoke-saˈma ほとけ様・仏様 Buddha

hotoˈndo ほとんど・殆ど almost (all), nearly; almost all the time; + NEGATIVE hardly (ever), seldom

hototoˈgisu ほととぎす・時鳥 (little) cuckoo

hoˈtto shimaˈsu ほっとします breathes a sigh of relief

howaˈito (no) ホワイト (の) white

hu... → fu...

hyaˈkkanichi 百か日 a memorial service 100 days after the death

hyakuˈ 百・100 hundred

hyakuˈ-do 百度 a hundred times

hyakuˈ-do 百度 a hundred degrees

hyakuˈ-doru 百ドル a hundred dollars; **hyakudoruˈ-satsu** 百

ドル札 a hundred-dollar bill

hyaku-en-dama 百円玉 hundred-yen coin

hyaku-ma'n 百万・1,000,000 million

hyaku'-nen 百年 the year 100; (= **hyakune'n-kan** 百年間) a century

hyakushō' 百姓 farmer

hyō 表 table, schedule, list; ~ **ni shima'su** 表にします lists

hyō' 1. ひょう・豹 leopard 2. ひょう・雹 (= **arare** あられ・霰) hail

hyōban 評判 reputation, fame

hyōdai 表題・標題 title (of book, article, …)

hyō'ga 氷河 glacier

hyōge[ ]n 表現 expression (words)

hyōgo 標語 slogan; motto

hyōgu-ya 表具屋 paper-hanger/-repairer

hyōjō[ ] 表情 expression

(on face)

hyōjun 標準 standard

hyōjun-go 標準語 standard Japanese

hyōme'n 表面 surface

hyōron 評論 criticism, comment(ary); ~**-ka** 評論家 critic, commentator, reviewer; ~ **shima'su** 評論します criticizes, comments on, reviews

hyōshiki 標識 sign, mark(er); **kōtsū-hyō'shiki** 交通標識 traffic sign; **dōro-hyō'shiki** 道路標識 road sign

hyōta'n ひょうたん・瓢箪 gourd

hyōten 評点 evaluation score, grade

hyo'tto ひょっと accidentally, by chance; **hyo'tto shita[ ]ra** ひょっとしたら maybe, possibly

hyō'zan 氷山 iceberg

hyū'zu ヒューズ fuse

— I —

i い → **ima'su** います (be, stay): 1. [infinitive] 2. [imperative]: **i yo** いよ = **i ro'** (**yo**) いろ（よ） stay here!

i 胃 = **i-bu'kuro** 胃袋 stomach

i-… 医… medicine, medical, doctoring

…-i 1. …位 rank, grade 2. …医 doctor, (= **semmo'n-i** 専門医) medical specialist

ian 慰安 consolation, comfort; recreation

ibarima'su 威張ります, **iba'ru** 威張る is/acts arrogant,

haughty; swaggers

ibiki いびき・鼾 snore; ～ **o kakima´su** いびき[鼾]をかきます snores

i-bu´kuro 胃袋 stomach

icha いちゃ = **ite´ wa** いては

ichi 一・1 one

i´chi 1. 位置 position, location, situation **2.** 市 = **i´chi-ba** 市場 market, marketplace

ichiban 一番 most; ～ **i´i** 一番いい best

ichi´-ban 一番 number one; first

ichi´-bu 一部 a part, portion; a copy (of a book)

ichi´-byō 一秒 a second (1/60 minute)

ichi´-dai 一台 one (machine, vehicle)

ichi-do´ 一度 one time

ichi´-do 一度 one degree

ichidō 一同 all (who are concerned/present)

Ichi-gatsu´ 一月・1月 January (= **Shōgatsu´** 正月)

i⌐chigo いちご・苺 strawberry

ichi´-go 一語 one word

ichi⌐-in 一員 a member

ichi´-ji 一時 one o'clock; ～ **(no)** 一時(の) one-time, temporary

ichi´jiku いちじく・無花果 fig

ichijirushi´i 著しい conspicuous, prominent, remarkable, striking

ichijiru´shiku 著しく conspicuously, prominently, remarkably,

strikingly

ichiji-teki (na) 一時的(な) temporary

ichijitsu´ 一日 one day; someday

ichi´-mai 一枚 a sheet; one (flat object)

ichi-ma´n 一万・10,000 ten thousand

ichi´-mei 一名 [bookish] = **hito´ri** 一人 one person

ichi´-nen 一年 the year 1; (= **ichine´n-kan** 一年間) one year; **ichine´n-sei** 一年生 first-year student, freshman

ichi-nichi 一日 one day; **ichinichi-jū** 一日中 all day long

ichiō 一応 in general, as far as it goes; once; ～ **(no)** 一応(の) tentative

ichi-rei 一例 an example

ichiryū (no) 一流(の) first-rate, topflight, elite

ichi´-wa 一羽 one (bird)

ichi´-wari 一割 ten percent

ichō いちょう・銀杏 gingko (tree)

i´do 井戸 a well

ie 1. 言え → **iema´su** 言えます (can say) [infinitive] **2.** 言え → **iima´su** 言います [imperative] say it! **3.** いえ = **iie** いいえ no

ie´ 家 a house

ie´ba 言えば → **iima´su** 言います (if one say)

iede⌐ 家出 running away from

home; **iede-nin** 家出人 a
runaway; **～ shima̅su** 家出し
ます runs away
iema̅su 言えます, **ieru** 言える
can say/tell
ì̅ga 衣蛾 clothes moth
ì̅gai (na) 意外(な) unexpected;
～ ni 意外に unexpectedly
(...) ì̅gai (...)以外 outside (of
...), except (for) ...
ì̅gaku 医学 medicine, medical
science/studies
ì̅-gan 胃癌 stomach cancer
ì̅gi 意義 significance, sense,
meaning
Igirisu イギリス England (=
Eikoku 英国); **Igirisu̅-jin** イギ
リス人 an English person
ì̅go 囲碁 the board game Go
(...) ì̅go (...)以後 afterward,
from ... on
ihan 違反 violation, offense; **(...
ni) ～ shima̅su** (...に)違反し
ます violates, offends
(against) ...
ii 言い → **iima̅su** 言います (say)
[infinitive]
ì̅i いい good; OK, right, correct
[NEGATIVE **yo̅ku arimase̅n** 良
くありません; PAST **yo̅katta
desu** 良かったです]
ii-arawashima̅su 言い表(わ)し
ます, **-arawa̅su** 言い表(わ)す
expresses, puts into words
ì̅idako いいだこ・飯蛸 baby octopus

iie いいえ no
ì̅i-hito いい人 sweetheart, lover
ii-kaema̅su 言い換えます, **ii-
kae̅ru** 言い換える rephrases,
puts/says it another way
ii-kagen 1. いい加減 rather,
quite, pretty **2. ～ (na)** いい加
減(な) moderate, properly
limited/restrained; perfunctory, halfhearted, indifferent,
vague, haphazard
ii-kata 言い方 way of saying/tell-
ing/putting it, expression
iima̅su 言います, **yū ("iu")** ゆ
う(言う) says, tells; expresses
iima̅shita 言いました said
ì̅i mo shimase̅n (shinai) 言いも
しません(しない) nor say;
not say even/too
ì̅in 委員 committee member(s);
ì̅n-kai 委員会 committee
ii-tai 言いたい wants to say; **～
koto̅** 言いたい事 what one
means to say
ii-tsukema̅su 言い付けます,
-tsuke̅ru 言い付ける com-
mands, orders; tells on (= tat-
tles)
ii-wake 言い訳 explanation, excuse
ì̅i ya/wa shinai 言いや/はしな
い = **iwanai** 言わない (not
say)
ijì̅ 意地 temper, disposition; **～
ga waru̅i** 意地が悪い ill-
tempered, mean(-spirited)

i⌉ji 維持 maintenance, upkeep, support; ~ **shima(⌉)sụ** 維持します maintains, supports
iji⌉-hi 維持費 upkeep (expense)
ijime いじめ·苛め **1.** teasing, torment **2.** → **ijimema⌉sụ** いじめます·苛めます [infinitive]
ijimema⌉sụ いじめます·苛めます, **ijimeru** いじめる·苛める teases, torments
ijō 異常 **1.** something unusual/wrong *(the matter)*, change, abnormality, symptom **2.** ~ **(na)** 異常(な) abnormal; unusual; remarkable
(...) i⌉jō (...)以上 above, over, upwards of; now that ... ; the above; that's it! *(end of message/speech)* = thank you (for your attention)
ika いか·烏賊 cuttlefish, squid
i⌉ka 医科 medical department
(...) i⌉ka (...)以下 below (...), less than ...
ikada いかだ·筏 raft
ika⌉ga いかが·如何 how (about it)? [DEFERENTIAL] = **dō⌉** どう
ikagawashi⌉i いかがわしい suspicious, questionable, shady
ika-hodo いかほど = **i⌉kura** いくら; = **dono-gurai** どの位
ika⌉iyō 胃潰瘍 *(gastric)* ulcer
ikanai 行かない = **ikimase⌉n** 行きません (not go)
ikan na⌈⌉gara ... 遺憾ながら... (though) I regret it ...
ikarema⌉sụ 行かれます, **ikareru** 行かれる **1.** (= **ikema⌉sụ** 行けます) can go **2.** [passive] has them go (to one's distress); [HONORIFIC] goes (= **irasshaima⌉sụ** いらっしゃいます)
ikari いかり·錨 anchor
ikari⌈⌉ 怒り anger
ikasema⌉sụ 行かせます, **ikaseru** 行かせる sends *(a person)*; lets *(a person)* go
ikashima⌉sụ 生かします, **ika⌉su** 生かす lets/makes it live, brings life to, enlivens; keeps it alive; revives; makes the most of
ike 行け **1.** → **ikema⌉sụ** 行けます (can go) [infinitive] **2.** → **ikima⌉sụ** 行きます [imperative] go!
ike⌉ 池 pond
i⌉ke 生け → **ikema⌉sụ** 生けます (arrange flowers) [infinitive]
ike⌉ba 行けば → **ikima⌉sụ** 行きます (if one go)
ike⌉bana 生け花 flower arrangement
ike⌈⌉gaki 生け垣 hedge
ikemase⌉n, ikenai 1. いけません, いけない it won't do; you mustn't; don't **2.** いけません, いけない (that's) too bad **3.** 行けません, 行けない = **ikaremase⌉n** 行かれません

can't go **4.** 生けません，生け
ない **(ike̒nai)** not arrange
flowers

ikema̒su 行けます，**ikeru** 行ける
= **ikarema̒su** 行かれます，
ikareru 行かれる can go

ikema̒su 生けます，**ike̒ru** 生け
る arranges (flowers)

iken 1. 異見 different opinion/
view; **go-iken** ご異見 your dif-
fering view **2.** いけん・行けん
= **ikenu** いけぬ・行けぬ =
ikenai いけない・行けない =
ikemase̒n いけません・行けま
せん

i̇ken 意見 opinion, idea; **go-
i̇ken** ご意見 your opinion

ikenai いけない・行けない =
ikemase̒n いけません；行け
ません (it won't do; too bad;
can't go)

ike̒nai 生けない = **ikemase̒n** 生
けません (not arrange flow-
ers)

ike(ra)rema̒su 生け(ら)れます，
ike(ra)re̒ru 生け(ら)れる can
arrange (flowers)

ike̒reba 生ければ → **ikema̒su**
生けます (if one arrange flowers)

ikete 行けて → **ikema̒su** 行けま
す (can go)

i̇kete 生けて → **ikema̒su** 生けま
す (arrange flowers)

iki 1. ~ **(na)** いき[粋](な)
smart, stylish **2.** 行き →

ikima̒su 行きます (goes)

i̇ki 1. 息 breath; ~ **o shima̒su**
息をします breathes **2.** 生き
→ **ikima̒su** 生きます (lives)
[infinitive]

...-iki (no) ...行き(の) bound
for ...

ikidōri[n] 憤り indignation,
resentment

ikidōrima̒su 憤ります，**ikidō̒ru**
憤る gets indignant, resents

ikima̒su 行きます，**iku** 行く goes

ikima̒su 生きます，**iki̒ru** 生きる
lives

iki̒ mo shimase̒n (shinai) 行きも
しません(しない) nor goes

i̇ki mo shimase̒n (shinai) 1. 息も
しません(しない) nor
breathes **2.** 生きもしません
(しない) nor lives

iki̒nai 生きない = **ikimase̒n** 生
きません (not live)

ikio̒i 勢い energy; ~ **yo̒ku** 勢い
良く energetically

iki̒reba 生きれば，**iki̒rya** 生き
りゃ → **ikima̒su** 生きます (if
one live)

iki̒ru 生きる → **ikima̒su** 生きま
す (lives)

ikisatsu いきさつ・経緯 details,
circumstances, complexities;
complications

iki-tai 行きたい wants to go

i̇kite 生きて → **ikima̒su** 生きま
す (lives); ~ **ima̒su** 生きてい
ます is alive

iki̍ wa/ya shinai 行きは/やしな
い = ikanai 行かない (not go)

i̍ki wa/ya shinai 生きは/やしな
い = iki̍nai 生きない (not
live)

iki-yasu̍i 行きやすい accessible,
easy to get to

ikiyo̍ 生きよう = ikimasho̍ 生
きましょう (let's live!)

iki-zumarima̍su 行き詰まりま
す, -zuma̍ru 行き詰まる gets
bogged down

ik-kai 一階 one floor/story; first
floor, ground floor

ik-ka̍i 一回 one time, once

i̍k-ken 一軒 one house/building

i̍k-ko 一個 one (piece, small object)

ik-kyū 一級 first class

ikō 行こう = ikimasho̍ 行きま
しょう (let's go!)

ikō 意向 one's mind, inclination,
intention; one's views, feelings

iku 行く = ikima̍su 行きます
(goes)

i̍ku-... いく・幾... = na̍n-... 何...
how many ...

i⁽ⁿ⁾kura イクラ salmon roe
(caviar)

i̍kura (o-ikura) いくら(おいく
ら) how much; ～ ka いくら
か some, a little; ～ mo いくら
も ever so much, (+ NEGA-
TIVE) not very much

i̍kutsu (o-ikutsu) いくつ(おいく
つ) how many, how old; ～

-ka いくつか several, a number
of; ～ mo いくつも ever so
many, (+ NEGATIVE) not very
many

ikya 行きゃ 1. = ike̍ba 行けば
(if one go) 2. ～ shinai 行きゃ
しない = iki̍ ya/wa shinai 行
きや/はしない = ikanai 行か
ない (not go)

i̍kya shinai 生きゃしない = i̍ki
ya/wa shinai 生きや/はしな
い = iki̍nai 生きない (not
live)

i̍ma̍ 居間 living room (Western-
style)

i̍ma 今 now, this time; ～ wa 今
は at present; ～ no tokoro̍
wa 今のところは for the time
being

ima-ma̍de 今まで until now, up
to the present (time)

i̍ma ni 今に before long, soon,
by and by, presently

ima̍su います・居ます, iru いる・
居る is, stays

imē̍ji イメージ (psychological/
social) image

i̍mi 意味 meaning; ... to yū ～
desu ...とゆう意味です, ... o
～ shima(̍)su ...を意味します
it means ...

imin 移民 immigrant(s)/
emigrant(s)

imo̍ (o-imo) 芋(お芋) yam;
potato

i̍ mo shinai い[居]もしない nor

stay/be; not even/also stay or be

imōto 妹, **(o-)imōto-san** （お）妹さん younger sister

i͞n 印 seal, stamp

inabi͞kari 稲光 lightning

inada いなだ baby yellowtail (*cf.* **hamachi** はまち・魬, **buri** ぶり・鰤)

inai いない・居ない ＝ **imase͞n** いません・居ません (not stay)

(...) i͞nai (...)以内 within

inaka いなか・田舎 country(side); one's home area (hometown); ~ **no** いなか［田舎］の rural

inari͞-zushi 稲荷鮨［寿司］ sushi in a bag of *aburage* (fried bean-curd)

ina͞zuma 稲妻 lightning

(...-)i͞nchi (...)インチ inch(es)

i͞nchiki (na) いんちき（な） fake, fraud(ulent)

i͞nchō 院長 hospital head/director

i͞nde(y)an インデア［ヤ］ン (American) Indian

i͞ndo インド India; **Indo͞-jin** インド人 an (India) Indian

Indone͞shi(y)a インドネシア［ヤ］ Indonesia; **Indoneshi(y)a-go** インドネシア［ヤ］語 Indonesian *(language)*, **Indoneshi(y)a͞-jin** インドネシア［ヤ］人 an Indonesian

i͞ne 稲 rice plant

infure インフレ inflation

infurue͞nza インフルエンザ flu, influenza

i͞ngen 隠元 ＝ **inge͞m-mame** 隠元豆 kidney beans, French beans

inkei 陰茎 penis

inki (na) 陰気（な） gloomy, glum

i͞nki インキ, **i͞nku** インク ink

i͞nochi 命 one's life

inori͞ (o-inori) 祈り（お祈り） prayer

ino͞ri 祈り → **inorima͞su** 祈ります

inorima͞su 祈ります, **ino͞ru** 祈る prays

insatsu 印刷 printing; **insatsu͞-butsu** 印刷物 printed matter; **insatsu shima͞su** 印刷します prints

inshō 印象 impression; ~**-teki (na)** 印象的（な） impressive

intai 引退 retirement; ~ **shima͞su** 引退します retires

interi インテリ intellectual; highbrow

inu͞ 犬 dog

in'yō 引用 quoting, quotation; ~ **shima͞su** 引用します quotes

iō 言おう ＝ **iimashō** 言いましょう (let's say it!)

ippai (no) いっぱい［一杯］（の） full

i͞p-pai 一杯 a cupful, a glassful; a drink

ip-paku 一泊 one night's

lodging/stay

ippan (no) 一般（の）general, overall; ～**-teki (na)** 一般的（な）general

ip-peˉn 一遍 one time

ip-piki̱ 一匹 one (small animal, fish)

ippin-ryōˉri 一品料理 à la carte dishes

ippōˉ 一方 1. one side, (**mō ～** もう一方) the other side 2. on the other hand, but, meanwhile

iˉp-pon 一本 one (long object)

ippō-tsūˉkō 一方通行 one-way (traffic)

iˉp-pun 一分 one minute

irai 依頼 request; dependence, reliance; trust, commission; **(sore o ... ni) ～ shimaˉsu** (それを...に) 依頼します requests (it of ...); depends/relies (on ...) for; entrusts (...) with, commissions (... to do it)

(...) iˉrai (...) 以来 (ever) since ...

iranai いらない・要らない ＝ **irimaseˉn** いりません・要りません (not need)

iraˉnai 炒らない・射らない ＝ **irimaseˉn** 炒りません; 射りません (not roast; not shoot)

iraremaˉsu いられます・居られます, **irareru** いられる・居られる can stay/be

irasshaˉi いらっしゃい ＝ **irasshaimaˉse** いらっしゃいま

せ → **irasshaimaˉsu** いらっしゃいます [imperative]; Welcome!

irasshaimaˉsu いらっしゃいます・居らっしゃいます, **irasshaˉru** いらっしゃる・居らっしゃる [HONORIFIC] 1. comes 2. goes 3. stays, is

irasshaˉri いらっしゃり・居らっしゃり → **irasshaimaˉsu** いらっしゃいます・居らっしゃいます [infinitive]

iraˉshite いらして ＝ **irasshaˉtte** いらっしゃって (→ **irasshaimaˉsu** いらっしゃいます)

iraˉsuto イラスト illustration

ire 入れ → **iremaˉsu** 入れます (puts in) 1. [infinitive] 2. [imperative] **ire roˉ** 入れろ, **ireˉ yo** 入れよ put it in!

iˉre 1. 炒れ・射れ → **iremaˉsu** 炒れます; 射れます (can roast; can shoot) [infinitive] 2. 射れ・炒れ → **irimaˉsu** 射ります; 炒ります [imperative] shoot!; roast it!

ire-ba 入れ歯 false teeth

ireˉba 1. いれば・居れば → **imaˉsu** います・居ます (if one be/stay) 2. いれば・要れば → **irimaˉsu** いります・要ります (if one need/want)

iˉreba 1. 炒れば 2. 射れば → **irimaˉsu** 炒ります; 射ります (if one roast; if one shoot)

iremaˉsu 入れます, **ireru** 入れる

puts in, lets in, admits; includes; **o-cha o ~** お茶を入れます makes tea; **denwa o ~** 電話を入れます puts in a call

irema̍su, ire̍ru 1. 炒れます, 炒れる can roast **2.** 射れます, 射れる can shoot

ire-mono 入れ物 container

irenai 入れない = **iremase̍n** 入れません (not put/let in)

ire̍nai 炒れない/射れない = **iremase̍n** 炒れません/射れません (cannot roast/shoot)

irere̍ba 入れれば, **irerya** 入れりゃ → **irema̍su** 入れます (if one put/let in)

ire̍reba 炒れれば・射れれば, **ire̍rya** 炒れりゃ・射れりゃ → **irema̍su** 炒れます/射れます (if one can roast/shoot)

ireta 入れた = **irema̍shita** 入れました (put/let in)

ı̄reta 炒れた・射れた = **irema̍shita** 炒れました/射れました (could roast/shoot)

irete 入れて → **irema̍su** 入れます (puts/lets in); **... o ~** ...を入れて including

ı̄rete 炒れて・射れて → **irema̍su** 炒れます/射れます (can roast/shoot)

ireyo̍ 入れよう = **iremasho̍** 入れましょう (let's put it in!)

ire-zumi 入れ墨・文身・刺青 tattoo

iri いり・要り → **irima̍su** いります

す/要ります (needs/wants)

ı̄ri 炒り・射り → **irima̍su** 炒ります; 射ります (roasts; shoots)

iriguchi 入口, **irikuchi** 入口 entrance

irima̍su, iru 1. います・要ります, いる・要る is necessary; needs, wants; **Da̍re ga(/ni) na̍ni ga irima̍su ka** 誰が(/に)何がいりますか Who needs what? **2.** 入ります, 入る = **hairima̍su** 入ります enters

irima̍su, ı̄ri 1. 炒ります, 炒る roasts **2.** 射ります, 射る shoots

iri-ta̍mago 炒り卵 scrambled eggs

iri-yō (na) 入り用(な) = **nyūyō (na)** 入用(な) needed

iro̍ 色 color; sex

i ro̍ (yo) いろ(よ)・居ろ(よ) stay!

iro̍ 炒ろう・射ろう = **irimasho̍** 炒りましょう/射りましょう (let's roast/shoot!)

iro̍gami 色紙 colored paper

iroiro (no/na) いろいろ[色々] (の/な) various

ironna ... いろんな... various

iroppo̍i 色っぽい erotic

iru 1. いる・居る = **ima̍su** います・居ます (is, stays) **2.** いる・要る = **irima̍su** いります・要ります (needs)

ı̄ru 炒る・射る = **irima̍su** 炒り

ます; 射ります (roasts; shoots)

irya 1. いりゃ・居りゃ; 要りゃ = **ire｀ba** いれば・居れば; 要れ ば (if be/stay; if need) **2.** ~ **shinai** いりゃ[要りゃ]しない = **iri｀ ya/wa shinai** いり[要 り]や/はしない = **iranai** いら ない・要らない (not need)

i｀rya 1. 炒りゃ・射りゃ = **i｀reba** 炒れば; 射れば (if one roast; if one shoot) **2.** ~ **shinai** 炒り ゃしない・射りゃしない = **i｀ri ya/wa shinai** 炒りや/はしな い・射りや/はしない = **ira｀nai** 炒らない; 射らない (not roast; not shoot)

ise⌐ɭ-ebi 伊勢えび[海老] lobster

isha 医者, **o-isha (san)** お医者(さ ん) doctor, physician

ishi｀ 石 stone, rock

i｀shi 意志 will, intention

i｀shiki 意識 consciousness; ~ **o ushinaima｀su** 意識を失います loses consciousness, passes out; ~ **fumei (no)** 意識不明 (の) unconscious

isogashi｀i 忙しい busy

isogi｀ 急ぎ haste; ~ **(no)** 急ぎ (の) hasty, hurried, urgent

iso｀gi 急ぎ → **isogima｀su** 急ぎま す

isogima｀su 急ぎます, **iso｀gu** 急ぐ hurries, rushes

iso｀ida 急いだ = **isogima｀shita** 急ぎました

iso｀ide 急いで → **isogima｀su** 急 ぎます

i｀ssa｀i いっさい・一切 all, every- thing, without exception

i｀s-sai 一歳 one year old (= **hito｀tsu** 一つ)

issaku｀ 一昨: ~**-ban/-ya** 一昨晩 /夜 night before last; ~**-jitsu** 一昨日 day before yesterday, ~**-nen** 一昨年 year before last

issaku-saku｀ 一昨々: ~**-ban/-ya** 一昨々晩/夜 three nights ago; ~**-jitsu** 一昨々日 three days ago; ~**-nen** 一昨々年 three years ago

is-satsu｀ 一冊 one (book, maga- zine)

i｀s-sei 一世 first generation (Japanese emigrant); ... the First

is-se｀n 一千 one thousand

issetsu⌐ɭ 一節 passage (of text)

issho (ni) 一緒(に) together

isshō 一生 one's whole life

i｀s-shō 一升 1.8 liters; **isshō｀-bin** 一升瓶 a 1.8-liter bottle (of saké)

isshō-ke｀mmei ni 一生懸命 desperately; very hard

i｀s-shu 一種 a kind, a sort

isso いっそ rather, preferably

issō いっそう・一層 all the more ... , still/much more ... ; ~ **i｀i** いっそう[一層]いい still bet- ter

isu いす・椅子 chair

i'ta 板 board, plank

ita-choko 板チョコ chocolate bar

itadaite いただいて・頂いて, **itadakima'shite** いただきまして・頂きまして → **itadakima'su** いただきます・頂きます

itadaki 1. 頂・いただき peak, summit (= **chōjō'** 頂上) **2.** いただき・頂き → **itadakima'su** いただき[頂き]ます [infinitive]

itadakima'su いただき[頂き]ます, **itadaku** いただく・頂く (I/we humbly) receive, eat, drink

i-tai いたい・居たい wants to stay

ita'i 痛い painful, hurting, sore

itamae 板前 chef (of Japanese food)

ita'me 痛め・傷め・炒め → **itamema'su** 痛めます・傷めます・炒めます **1.** [infinitive] **2.** [imperative] ~ **yo** 痛めよ・傷めよ・炒めよ, **itame'ro** 痛めろ・傷めろ・炒めろ

itamema'su, itame'ru 1. 痛めます・傷めます, 痛める・傷める hurts, injures; damages, spoils it; **koko'ro o** ~ 心を痛めます worries (oneself), grieves **2.** 炒めます, 炒める (pan-)fries, sautés

itami' 痛み an ache, a pain

ita'mi 傷み・痛み → **itamima'su**

傷みます・痛みます [infinitive]

itamima'su, ita'mu 1. 傷みます, 傷む it spoils, rots **2.** 痛みます, 痛む it aches

itarima'su 至ります, **ita⌐ru** 至る arrives (at), reaches (to), goes/comes (to)

Itari(y)a イタリア[ヤ] Italy; ~**-go** イタリア[ヤ]語 Italian *(language)*; **Itari(y)a'-jin** イタリア[ヤ]人 an Italian

itashima'su 致します・いたします, **ita⌐su** 致す・いたす [HUMBLE/DEFERENTIAL] do(es)

itatte 至って・いたって extremely   「ります

ita⌐tte 至って → **itarima'su** 至

itazura いたずら・悪戯 mischief, prank

itazura'kko いたずらっこ・悪戯っ子 naughty child

itcha いっちゃ・行っちゃ = **itte' wa** いっては・行っては

itchaima'shita = **itte shimaima'shita 1.** 行っちゃいました＝行ってしまいました＝ **ikima'shita** 行きました (went) **2.** 言っちゃいました＝言ってしまいました＝ **iima'shita** 言いました (said)

itchaima'su, itchau = **itte shimaima'su 1.** 行っちゃいます, 行っちゃう＝行ってしまいます **2.** 言っちゃいます, 言っちゃう＝言ってしまいます

itchatta = **itte shimatta** = **itta**
1. 行っちゃった＝行ってしま
った＝行った (went) 2. 言っ
ちゃった＝言ってしまった＝
言った (said)

itchau = **itte shimau** 1. 行っちゃ
う＝行ってしまう 2. 言っち
ゃう＝言ってしまう

itchi 一致 agreement, consensus;
(... **to**) **itchi shimaˈsu** (...と)
一致します agrees/accords
(with) 「居ます

ite いて・居て → **imaˈsu** います・

iˈto 1. 糸 thread, yarn, string
2. 意図 intention, plan, purpose

itoˈko いとこ・従兄弟・従姉妹
cousin; **o-itoko-san** おいとこ
さん your cousin

itoma[ ] (**o-itoma**) 暇 (お暇)
1. leave-taking, farewell; (**o-**)
~ (**ita**)**shimaˈsu** (お)暇 (致)し
ます I will take my leave
2. = (**hima** 暇) free time;
leave of absence

ito[ ]**-maki** 糸巻き spool; reel

itoshiˈi 愛しい dear *(beloved)*

ito-teki ni 意図的に on purpose

iˈtsu いつ when; **i**[ ]**tsu de**[ ] **mo**
いつでも any time (at all)

itsu-goro いつ頃 about when

itsuka[ ] 五日 five days; fifth day
(of month)

iˈtsu-ka いつか sometime 「ever

iˈtsu made mo いつまでも for-

iˈtsu-mo いつも always, usually;

~ **no** いつもの usual

itsuˈtsu 五つ, **itsuˈtsu** 五つ five;
five years old

itsuwa[ ]**ri**[ ] 偽り falsehood, lie

itta 1. 行った → **ikimaˈsu** 行きま
す (went) 2. 言った → **iimaˈsu**
言います (said)

iˈtta 炒った・射った → **irimaˈsu**
炒ります・射ります

ittai ... いったい[一体]... on
earth, ... indeed, ... ever ... !

itte 1. 行って → **ikimaˈsu** 行きま
す (goes) 2 言って →
iimasu 言います (says) 3. 要っ
て・入って → **irimaˈsu** いり
[要り]ます; 入ります (needs;
enters)

iˈtte 炒って・射って → **irimaˈsu**
炒ります; 射ります (roasts;
shoots) 「definite

ittei (no) 一定(の) fixed, settled,

Itte(i)rassha[ ]**i/irasshaima**[ ]**se.** 行
って(い)らっしゃい/いらっ
しゃいませ。 Good-bye! *(said
to those departing home)*

Itte kimaˈsu/mairimaˈsu. 行って
きます/参ります。 Good-bye!
(said to those staying home)

it-tō[ ] 一等 first, first class; **ittō**[ ]**-
seki/-sha** 一等席/車 first-class
seat/car

iˈt-tō 一頭 one *(large animal)*

it-tsui 一対 a pair

iu 言う・いう = **yū** ゆう =
iimaˈsu 言います

iwa[ ] 岩 rock, crag

i⌐wa⌐ba いわば so to speak
iwa⌐i (o-iwai) 祝い・(お祝い) celebration; → **iwaima⌐su** 祝います 「celebrates
iwaima⌐su 祝います, **iwa⌐u** 祝う
iwanai 言わない = **iimase⌐n** 言いません (not say)
iwashi いわし・鰯 sardine
i⌐ wa shinai いは[居は]しない = **inai** いない・居ない (not stay/be) 「ます
iwa⌐tte 祝って → **iwaima⌐su** 祝い
iwawa⌐nai 祝わない → **iwaⅰmase⌐n** 祝いません (not celebrate)
iwa⌐yu⌐ru いわゆる so-called, what is known as
iya いや (usually male) no, nope
iya 言や 1. = **ie⌐ba** 言えば (if one say) 2. ~ **shinai** 言やしない = **i⌐ ya/wa shinai** 言いや/はしない = **iwanai** 言わない (not say)

iya⌐ (na) 嫌(な) unpleasant; disagreeable; disliked; disgusting, nasty
iya-garima⌐su 嫌がります, **-ga⌐ru** 嫌がる dislikes, hates
i⌐yaringu イヤリング earring
iyashi⌐i 卑しい lowly, vulgar
i⌐ ya shinai いや[居や]しない = **i⌐ wa shinai** いは[居は]しない = **inai** いない・居ない (not stay/be)
i yo いよ・居よ = **i ro⌐ (yo)** いろ(よ)・居ろ(よ) stay!
iyō 1. いよう・居よう = **imashō⌐** いましょう・居ましょう (let's stay!) 2. → **iō** 言おう = **iimashō⌐** 言いましょう (let's say it!)
iyo⌐-iyo いよいよ 1. at last 2. in fact 3. more and more
(...) i⌐zen (...)以前 before, up until ... , ago 「someday
izure いずれ some other time;

— J —

ja じゃ, **ja⌐** じゃあ = **de⌐ wa** では well, well then; in that case; (well) now
...ja ...じゃ = **...de⌐ wa** ...では
...ja arimase⌐n じゃありません, **...ja na⌐i** じゃない it is not; it is not a case of
...jae ...じゃえ = **...de⌐ shimae** ...

でしまえ [imperative]: **no⌐njae** 飲んじゃえ drink it up!
jagaimo じゃが芋 (Irish) potato (**o-ja⌐ga** おじゃが)
jaguchi 蛇口 faucet
...jai ...じゃい = **...de shimai** ...でしまい [infinitive]
jaketsu ジャケツ, **ja⌐ke⌐tto** ジャ

ケット jacket, blouse

jakkan (no) 若干(の) some (amount of), several

jakunem-mono 若年者 = **wakamono** 若者 the young, a youth

jama (o-jama) じゃま[邪魔](おじゃま・お邪魔) disturbance, hindrance, obstacle; **~ (na)** じゃま・邪魔(な) intrusive, bothersome; **~ ni narima'su** じゃま[邪魔]になります, **~ o shima'su** じゃま[邪魔]をします gets in the way, becomes a bother

ja'mpā ジャンパー Windbreaker (jacket)

ja'mu ジャム jam *(to eat)*

... ja na'i ...じゃない = **... ja arimase'n** ...じゃありません (it) is not; **~ to** ...じゃないと unless it be

... ja na'kereba/na'kerya ...じゃなければ/なけりゃ unless it be; **~ narimase'n** ...じゃなければ/なけりゃなりません must (has to) be

... ja na'ku(te) ...じゃなく(て) (it) is not and/but; without being

... ja na'kute mo ...じゃなくても even if it not be; **~ i'i desu** ...じゃなくてもいいです it need not be

... ja na'kute wa ...じゃなくては not being, without being; un-

less it be; **~ ikemase'n** ...じゃなくてはいけません it must (has to) be

ja'nguru ジャングル jungle; **janguru-ji'mu** ジャングルジム jungle gym

jari 砂利 gravel, pebbles

Ja'ru ジャル JAL (= Japan Airlines)

je'rii ジェリー jelly

jetto'-ki ジェット機 jet (plane)

ji 痔・ぢ hemorrhoids

ji' 1. 字 a letter (symbol); a Chinese character 2. 地 land, ground; texture; fabric

ji-... 自... self; one's own

...-ji 1. ...時 o'clock 2. ...寺 temple *(name)*

jibiki' 字引き dictionary

jibun 自分 oneself; myself; alone; **~-ka'tte/-ga'tte (na)** 自分勝手/勝手(な) selfish; **~ de** 自分で by oneself, in person; **~ no** 自分の (one's) own; **go-jibun** ご自分 yourself

ji⌐bun 時分 time

jidai 時代, **...-ji'dai** ...時代 age, period, era, time; **jidai-mono** 時代物 antique

jidō(-) 自動 automatic; **~-hamba'i-ki** 自動販売機 vending machine; **~-teki (na)** 自動的(な) automatic; **~-tobaku'-ki** 自動賭博機 slot machine

jidō⌐-sha 自動車 automobile

jidō'-shi 自動詞 intransitive verb

Jiei-tai 自衛隊 Self-Defence Forces

ji'ga 自我 ego

ji⌐gi 辞儀 = **o-jigi** お辞儀 (polite bow)

jigoku⌐ 地獄 hell

jiguchi 地口 pun

ji'gyō 事業 enterprise, business, undertaking

ji'hen 事変 incident, happening

ji'i 自慰 masturbation; ~ **shima'su** 自慰します masturbates

jii-pan ジーパン bluejeans, Levi's

ji'jitsu 事実 fact

jijō 事情 circumstances; conditions

ji⌐kan 時間 time (**o-ji'kan** お時間); hour(s); ~ **ga kakarima'su** 時間がかかります it takes time; **jikan-dō'ri (no/ni)** 時間通り(の/に) on time

jikan-hyō 時間表 timetable, schedule

ji'ka-ni じかに・直に directly; personally

ji'ken 事件 incident, event, affair

ji'ki 1. 時期 time; season 2. 時機 opportune time, opportunity 3. 磁器 porcelain 4. ~ **(no)** 磁気(の) magnetic

jiki (ni) じき(に)・直(に) immediately; soon

jik-kai 十階 ten floors/stories; tenth floor

jik-ka'i 十回 ten times

jikken 実験 experiment

ji'k-ko 十個 ten small things

jikkō 実行 performance; practice; realization

ji'ko 1. 事故 accident 2. 自己 self

ji'koku 時刻 time (specified); **jikoku̇-hyō** 時刻表 time schedule

jiku̇ 軸 axis, axle

jiman 自慢 pride, boast; ~ **shima'su** 自慢します boasts, brags about

ji'mbutsu 人物 personage

ji'men 地面 ground (surface)

jimi' (na) 地味(な) plain, sober

ji'mu 1. 事務 business, office work; **jimu̇-in** 事務員 office clerk; **jimu̇-sho** 事務所 office 2. ジム gym(nasium)

...⌐-ji'n ...人 person

jindō 人道 walk(way), sidewalk

jingū 神宮 (large) Shinto shrine

ji'nja 神社 Shinto shrine

jinji-ka 人事課 personnel (section)

jinkō 1. 人口 population 2. 人工 (~ **no** 人工の) artificial

jinri'ki'sha 人力車 ricksha

ji'nrui 人類 human beings, the human race; **jinru̇i-gaku** 人類学 anthropology

jinshu 人種 race (peoples)

ji-nushi 地主 landowner

jinzō 1. 腎臓 kidneys 2. ~ **(no)**

人造(の) artificial, imitation, false *(man-made)*

jíp-pa 十羽 ten birds

jíppā ジッパー zipper

jip-peꜜn 十遍 ten times

jíp-pon 十本 ten long things

jíp-pun 十分 10 minutes

jíꜜrojiro mimaꜜsu (mìꜜru) じろじろ見ます(見る) stares at

jíꜜsa 時差 difference in time; **jisa-boke** 時差ぼけ jet lag; **jisa-shuꜜkkin** 時差出勤 staggered work hours

jisatsu 自殺 suicide

jiꜛsei 1. 時勢 (the trend of) the times **2.** 時世 **(go-jíꜜsei** ご時世) the times

jíꜜsetsu 時節 season; (appropriate) time, occasion, opportunity

jíꜜshaku 磁石 magnet

jishin 1. 地震 earthquake **2.** 自信 self-confidence/-assurance; **～ o moꜜtte ... (shimaꜜsu)** 自信を持って...(します) (does it) with confidence

jíꜜshin 自身 oneself; myself

jíꜜsho 辞書 dictionary

jishoku shimaꜜsu 辞職します resigns (a position)

jiꜛsoku 時速 (hourly) speed

jissai 実際 actual conditions, reality; in practice; in fact, really

jíꜜs-sai 十歳 ten years old

jis-satsuꜜ 十冊 ten books

ji-suꜜberi 地滑り landslide

jitai 自体 in fact, in itself, originally

jíꜜtai 1. 事態 situation, state of affairs **2.** 自体 itself

jitaku 自宅 one's home, one's residence

jiꜛten 辞典 dictionary

jiteꜛn-sha 自転車 bicycle; **jiten-sha-ya** 自転車屋 bicycle shop/dealer

jitsuꜜ 実 truth; truly, really; **～ ni** 実に actually, indeed; **～ wa** 実は to tell the truth, actually, in fact

jitsugyō 実業 business, enterprise; **～-ka** 実業家 businessman

jitsuryoku 実力 (real) strength, ability, proficiency; force, power

jitsuyō 実用 practical use/application, utility

jitto じっと intently, steadily, fixedly (staring); quietly, patiently

jíꜜt-tō 十頭 ten horses/oxen

jiyūꜜ 自由 freedom; **～ (na)** 自由(な) free; fluent, at ease; **～ ni** 自由に freely; fluently; **～ -gyō** 自由業 freelancing, freelance work; **～-seki** 自由席 unreserved seat

jizen 慈善 charity

jō 錠 1. = **jō-mae** 錠前 lock; ...
no ~ o oroshima̍su ...の錠を
下ろします locks up 2. = **jō-
zai** 錠剤 pill

jō 上 1. (= **jōtō** 上等) deluxe
2. (= **jō-kan** 上巻) first
volume (of a set of 2 or 3)

...⌐-jō 1. ...畳 (counts room sizes
by mat) 2. ...城 castle (name)

jōbu (na) 丈夫・じょうぶ(な)
sturdy, firm, healthy; (= **dai-
jō̍bu** 大丈夫・だいじょうぶ)
safe

jochū 女中 maid-servant; ~
-beya 女中部屋 maid's room

jōda̍n 冗談 joke

jo-ga̍kusei 女学生 = **joshi-
ga̍kusei** 女子学生 female student, co-ed

jō̍gi 定規 ruler (to measure with)

jogingu ジョギング jog(ging);
~ **o shima̍su** ジョギングをし
ます jogs

jō̍go じょうご・漏斗 funnel

jōhi̍n (o-jōhi̍n) 上品(お上品)
elegance, refinement; ~ **(na)**
上品(な) elegant, refined

jōhō 情報 information, intelligence

jō-kan 上巻 first volume (of a set
of 2 or 3)

jōke⌐n 条件 condition, term,
stipulation, provision

jō̍ki 蒸気 steam

jōkyaku 乗客 passenger

jōkyō 状況・情況 situation, circumstances, state of affairs

jo-kyō̍ju 助教授 assistant professor

jō-mae 錠前 lock

jōme⌐n 上面 top (top side)

joō̍ 女王 queen

jōriku 上陸 disembarking, landing; **jōriku shima̍su** 上陸しま
す lands, disembarks, comes
ashore

jōro̍ 女郎, **jorō̍** 女郎 whore,
prostitute; **jorō-ya** 女郎屋
whorehouse, brothel

jōryū̍-sui 蒸留水 distilled water

josei 女性 woman, female; ~
-go 女性語 women's language
(terms)

jōsha 乗車 getting into a car,
boarding; **jōsha̍-ken** 乗車券
passenger ticket

joshi 助詞 particle (auxiliary
word)

(...) jo̍shi (...)女史 lady,
woman; Madame (...)

jōshiki 常識 common sense

joshu 助手 helper, assistant

jōsu̍i-chi 浄水池 reservoir

jōtai 状態 condition, situation,
state, circumstances

jōtō (no) 上等(の) the best,
first-rate, deluxe

jō⌐yaku 条約 treaty, agreement

jōyō̍-sha 1. 乗用車 passenger car
2. 常用者 addict

joyū 女優 actress

jōzai 錠剤 pill, tablet

jōzō-sho 醸造所 brewery

jōzu じょうず・上手, **o-jōzu (na)** おじょうず[上手]（な） skilled, clever, good at

jū 1. 十・10 ten **2.** 銃 gun

...-jū ...じゅう・中 throughout the (entire) ...

jū-bai 十倍 ten times, tenfold

jūbako (o-jū) 重箱（お重） nested boxes; picnic boxes

jū-bamme 十番目 tenth

jūbun (na) じゅうぶん[十分・充分]（な） enough, sufficient

jūdai (na) 重大（な） serious *(heavy, grave);* important; **jūdai-ji** 重大事 a matter of importance

jū-do 十度 ten times

jū-do 十度 ten degrees

jūdō 柔道 judo, jujitsu (an art of weaponless defense); **jūdō-gi** 柔道着 judo outfit/suit

jū-en-dama 十円玉 ten-yen coin

Jū-gatsu 十月・10月 October

jū-go 十五・15 fifteen

jugyō 授業 class instruction, classroom teaching; **jugyō-ji-kan** 授業時間 school/ teaching hours; **~ shima()su** 授業します teaches (class)

jūgyō 従業 employment; **~ shima su** 従業します is employed; **jūgyō-in** 従業員 employee

jū-hachi 十八・18 eighteen

jū-ichi 十一・11 eleven

Jūichi-gatsu 十一月・11月 November

jūji 1. 十字 a cross *(symbol);* **jū-ji-ka** 十字架 a cross *(wooden)* **2.** 従事 engaging in (an activity); **... ni ~ shima su** ...に従事します engages in ...

jūji-ro 十字路 crossroad(s)

juku 塾 a cram school, a tutoring school

jū-ku 十九・19 nineteen

jukugo 熟語 a compound word

jukushima su 熟します, **juku su** 熟す ripen, get ripe

Jukyō 儒教 Confucianism

jū-kyū 十九・19 nineteen

jū-man 十万・100,000 a hundred thousand ⌈turn

jumban 順番 (place in) order,

jumbi 準備 preparation(s), arrangements

jun 順 order; **~ ni** 順に in order

jun (na) 純（な） pure

jū-nana 十七・17 seventeen

junchō (na) 順調（な） smooth(ly going)

jū-ni 十二・12 twelve

Jūni-gatsu 十二月・12月 December

jun-jima su 準じます, **-ji-ru** 準じる applies correspondingly (to); is made to accord (with)

junjo 順序 order, sequence

junkan 循環 circulation; cycle

jun-kyō ju 準教授 associate pro-

fessor
ju⌐nsa 巡査 policeman, patrolman
junshō 准将 brigadier general
junsui (na) 純粋 (な) pure
jū-o⌐ku 十億 a thousand million; (U.S.) a billion
jū⌐rai 従来 up to now, hitherto; ~ no 従来の traditional, accustomed, customary
jū-roku⌐ 十六・16 sixteen
jūryō⌐ 重量 weight; jūryō-age 重量挙げ weight-lifting; jūryōage-se⌐nshu 重量挙げ選手 weight-lifter
juryō⌐-shō 受領証 receipt
jū-san 十三・13 thirteen
jū-shi⌐ 十四・14 fourteen
jū⌐sho 住所 residence, address
jushō 受賞 winning an award; ~ shima⌐su 受賞します wins; jushō⌐-sha 受賞者 winner, awardee

jū⌐su ジュース 1. juice 2. orange soda pop
jūtai 渋滞 congestion; ~-jō⌐tai 渋滞状態 congested (traffic); ~ shite ima⌐su 渋滞していま す is congested (backed up)
jūtaku 住宅 residence
jū⌐tan じゅうたん・絨毯 rug, carpet
juwa⌐-ki 受話器 (telephone) receiver
ju⌐yo 授与 awarding, conferring; ~ shima(⌐)su 授与します awards, confers
jū⌐yō (na) 重要 (な) important
jū-yokka 十四日 14 days; 14th day (of month)
jū-yo⌐n 十四・14 fourteen
jū⌐yo-nen 十四年 the year 14; (= jūyone⌐n-kan 十四年間) 14 years
jū⌐yo-nin 十四人 14 people
juzu⌐ 数珠 beads

— K —

ka 蚊 mosquito
ka⌐ 課, ...-ka ...課 section; lesson
ka-... 仮... temporary (tentative)
... ka ...か or; (the question) whether
...⌐-ka ...化 ...-ization; ~ shima⌐su ...化します ...-izes

kaban かばん・鞄 suitcase; briefcase
kabayaki 蒲焼き broiled eel
kabe 壁 wall (of house, room)
kabi かび・黴 mold, mildew; ~ ga haete ima⌐su かび [黴] が生 えています is moldy
kabin 花瓶 flower vase

kabocha かぼちゃ・南瓜 pump-kin

kabu 1. 株 stock (in a company) **2.** かぶ・蕪 = **kabura** かぶら・蕪 turnip

kaˈbu カーブ curve

kabuki 歌舞伎 a traditional style of Japanese theater; 〜-za 歌舞伎座 the Kabuki theater (building)

kabura かぶら・蕪 turnip

kaburimaˈsu かぶります・被ります, **kabuˈru** かぶる・被る wears on head

kabushiki-gaˈisha 株式会社 a corporation

kabuˈtte かぶって・被って → **kaburimaˈsu** かぶります・被ります; 〜 **ikimaˈsu/kimaˈsu** かぶって[被って]行きます/来ます wears it there/here

kaˈcha 勝ちゃ **1.** = **kaˈteba** 勝てば (if one win) **2.** 〜 **shinai** 勝ちゃしない = **kaˈchi ya/wa shinai** 勝ちや/はしない = **kataˈnai** 勝たない (not win)

kaˈchi 価値 value

kachiˈ 勝ち **1.** victory **2.** → **kachimaˈsu** 勝ちます [infinitive]

kaˈchi 勝ち → **kachimaˈsu** 勝ちます [infinitive]　「つ wins

kachimaˈsu 勝ちます, **kaˈtsu** 勝

ka-chō 課長 section manager

kaˈdo 角 (outside) corner, street corner

kaˈdo カード card

kae 1. 変え・買え → **kaemaˈsu** 変えます; 買えます (changes it; can buy) **2.** 買え → **kaimaˈsu** 買います [imperative] buy it!

kaˈe 飼え → **kaemaˈsu** 飼えます (can raise)

kaeˈ 飼え → **kaimaˈsu** 飼います [imperative] raise it!

kaeˈba 買えば → **kaimaˈsu** 買います (if one buy)

kaˈeba 飼えば → **kaimaˈsu** 飼います (if one raise)

kaede かえで・楓 maple

kaemaˈsu, kaeru 1. 変えます・換えます, 変える・換える changes it, exchanges **2.** 買います, 買える can buy

kaemaˈsu 飼えます, **kaeˈru** 飼える can raise

kaenai 変えない・買えない = **kaemaseˈn** 変えません; 買えません (not change it; cannot buy)

kaeˈnai 飼えない = **kaemaseˈn** 飼えません (cannot raise)

kaeˈre 帰れ → **kaeremaˈsu** 帰れます (can return) [infinitive]

kaˈere 帰れ → **kaerimaˈsu** 帰ります [imperative] return!

kaereˈba 変えれば・買えれば → **kaemaˈsu** 変えます; 買えます (if one change it; if one can buy)

kaeˈreba 飼えれば → **kaemaˈsu** 飼えます (if one can raise)

ka͞ereba 帰れば → **kaerima͞su** 帰ります (if one go home)

kaerema͞su 変えれます, **kaereru** 変えれる = **kaerarema͞su** 変えられます, **kaerareru** 変えられる can change it

kaerema͞su 帰れます, **kaere͞ru** 帰れる can go home

kaerenai 変えれない = **kaerarenai** 変えられない = **kae(ra)remase͞n** 変え(ら)れません (cannot change it)

kaere͞nai 帰れない = **kaeremase͞n** 帰れません (cannot go home)

kaeri͞ 帰り (the) return

ka͞eri 帰り → **kaerima͞su** 帰ります [infinitive]

kaerima͞su 帰ります, **ka͞eru** 帰る goes home, goes back, returns, leaves

kaero͞ 帰ろう = **kaerimasho͞** 帰りましょう (let's go home!)

kaeru 1. かえる・蛙 frog 2. 変える = **kaema͞su** 変えます (changes it)

kaeru 買える = **kaema͞su** 買えます (can buy)

kae͞ru 飼える = **kaema͞su** 飼えます (can raise)

ka͞eru 帰る = **kaerima͞su** 帰ります (goes home)

kaerya 変えりゃ・買えりゃ = **kaere͞ba** 変えれば; 買えれば (if one change it; if one can buy)

kae͞rya 飼えりゃ = **kae͞reba** 飼えれば (if one can raise)

ka͞erya 帰りゃ 1. = **ka͞ereba** 帰れば (if one go home) 2. ~ **shinai** 帰りゃしない = **ka͞eri ya/wa shinai** 帰りや/はしない = **kaera͞nai** 帰らない (not go home)

ka͞esha 返しゃ 1. = **ka͞eseba** 返せば (if one return it) 2. ~ **shinai** 返しゃしない = **ka͞eshi ya/wa shinai** 返しや/はしない = **kaesa͞nai** 返さない (not return it)

kaeshima͞su 返します, **ka͞esu** 返す returns it

ka͞eshite 返して → **kaeshima(͞)su** 返します

kaete 変えて・買えて → **kaema͞su** 変えます; 買えます (changes it; can buy)

ka͞ete 飼えて → **kaema͞su** 飼えます (can raise)

ka͞ette 1. かえって・却って contrary to expectations 2. 帰って → **kaerima͞su** 帰ります

kaeyo͞ 変えよう = **kaemasho͞** 変えましょう (let's change it!)

kafu͞n-sho͞ 花粉症 hay fever

ka͞fusu カフス cuff

ka͞gaku 1. 科学 = **sa͞iensu** サイエンス science; **kagaku-teki (na)** 科学的(な) scientific 2. 化学 = **bake͞gaku** 化け学・化学 chemistry; **kagaku-**

se˺ihin 化学製品 chemicals,
kagaku-ya˺kuhin 化学薬品
pharmaceuticals

kaga˺ku̳-sha 科学者 1. (=
sa˺iensu no ~ サイエンスの科
学者) scientist 2. 化学者 (=
bake◌gaku no ~ 化け学[化
学]の化学者) chemist

kagami˺ (o-kagami) 鏡(お鏡)
mirror

kaganai かがない・嗅がない =
kagimase˺n かぎません・嗅ぎ
ません (not smell it)

kagayakima˺su 輝きます,
kagaya˺ku 輝く shines,
gleams, glitters

kage かげ・嗅げ 1. → **kagema˺su**
かげます・嗅げます [infini-
tive] 2. → **kagima˺su** かぎます・
嗅ぎます [imperative] smell
it!

ka˺ge 影 shade; **ka˺ge-bo˺shi** 影法
師 shadow *(of a person)*

kage˺ba かげば・嗅げば →
kagima˺su かぎます・嗅ぎます
(if one smell it)

ka˺geki 歌劇 opera

kageki (na) 過激(な) excessive,
extreme, radical; **kageki-ha** 過
激派 the radicals, the extremists

kagema˺su かげます・嗅げます,
kageru かげる・嗅げる can
smell it

kagen (o-kagen) 加減(お加減)
(state of) one's health; flavor;

extent, degree; adjustment,
moderation; ~ **shima˺su** 加減
します adjusts, moderates,
makes allowance for, seasons,
flavors

kagenai かげない・嗅げない =
kagemase˺n かげません・嗅げ
ません (cannot smell it)

...-ka˺-getsu ...か月 (counts
months)

kagi かぎ・嗅ぎ → **kagima˺su** か
ぎます・嗅ぎます [infinitive]

kagi˺ 1. 鍵 key; **... no ~ ga
kakarima˺su** ...の鍵がかかり
ます it locks, **... no ~ o
kakema˺su** ...の鍵をかけます
locks it 2. 鉤 hook

kagi-ana 鍵穴 keyhole

kagima˺su かぎます・嗅ぎます,
kagu かぐ・嗅ぐ smells it

ka˺giri 限り limit

kagirima˺su 限ります, **kagi˺ru** 限
る limits (delimits) it; **... ni ~** ...
に限ります there is nothing
like (so good as, better than) ...

kago かご・籠 basket, (bird) cage

kagō かごう・嗅ごう =
kagimashō˺ かぎましょう・嗅
ぎましょう (let's smell it!)

kagu かぐ・嗅ぐ = **kagima˺su** か
ぎます・嗅ぎます (smells it)

ka˺gu 家具 furniture; **kagu-tsuki
(no)** 家具付き(の) furnished

ka˺gura 神楽 Shinto music and
dances

kagu˺-ya 家具屋 furniture store

kagya かぎゃ・嗅ぎゃ **1.** = **kage̅ba** かげば・嗅げば (if one smell it) **2.** ~ **shinai** かぎゃしない・嗅ぎゃしない = **kagi̅ya/wa shinai** かぎ[嗅ぎ]や/はしない = **kaganai** かがない・嗅がない (not smell it)

kai 買い → **kaima̅su** 買います (buys) [infinitive]

ka̅i 1. 貝 shellfish; (= **kai-gara** 貝殻) shell (of shellfish) **2.** 飼い → **kaima̅su** 飼います (raises) [infinitive]

... ka i? ...かい? (yes-or-no question)

...-kai ...階 (counts floors/stories)

...-ka̅i ...回 (counts times/occasions)

...-̅kai 1. ...会 society, association, club; social gathering, party **2.** ...海 sea

kaibutsu 怪物 monster

kaichū 1. ~ **(no)** 懐中(の) pocket(able) **2.** 海中 in the sea **3.** 回虫 (intestinal) worms

kaichu-de̅ntō 懐中電灯 flashlight

kaida かいだ・嗅いだ = **kagima̅shita** かぎました・嗅ぎました (smelled)

kaidan 階段 stairs, stairway

kaide かいで・嗅いで → **kagima̅su** かぎます・嗅ぎます

kaidō 会堂 an auditorium

kaidō̅ 街道 highway, main road/avenue

kaien 開演 starting a performance; ~**-chū** 開演中 during the performance; ~**-ji̅kan** 開演時間 curtain time

kaifuku 回復 recovery, recuperation; ~ **shima̅su** 回復します recovers, recuperates

ka̅igai 海外 overseas, abroad; **kaigai-de̅mpō** 海外電報 cable (telegram)

kaigan 海岸 seashore, coast, beach

kai-gara 貝殻 shell (of shellfish)

ka̅igi 会議 conference (formal); **kaigi-chū** 会議中 in conference; **kaigi̅-shitsu** 会議室 conference room

ka̅igun 海軍 navy

kaiheitai 海兵隊 marines, Marine Corps

kaihō 解放 liberation; ~ **shima̅su** 解放します liberates

kai̅i かいい = **kayu̅i** かゆい・痒い itchy

kai-in 会員 member

kaijō 開場 opening (of place/event); ~ **shima̅su** 開場します opens; ~**-ji̅kan** 開場時間 opening time; **kaijō̅-shiki** 開場式 opening ceremony

kaijū 怪獣 monster

kaikan 会館 a public hall, a building

kaikei 会計 **1.** (**o-kaikei** お会計) accounts; bill, check **2.** (= ~

-ga⌐kari 会計係), **kaike⌐i-shi** 会計士 accountant

kaiken 会見 interview

kaiketsu 解決 solution, settlement; **kaiketsu shima⌐su** 解決します solves, settles

ka⌐iko 解雇 dismissal (from employment), discharge; ～ **shima(⌐)su** 解雇します dismisses, discharges, disemploys, fires

ka⌐iko (o-ka⌐iko) 蚕（お蚕）silkworm

kaikyō 海峡 strait(s)

kaima⌐su 買います, **kau** 買う buys

kaima⌐su 飼います, **ka⌐u** 飼う raises, keeps (animals)

kaimen 海綿 sponge

kai-mono 買物 shopping

kaisatsu 改札 ticket examining/punching/collecting; **kaisatsu⌐-guchi** 改札口 (ticket) wicket

kaisatsu shima⌐su 改札します examines/punches/collects tickets

kaiseki 懐石 an assortment of elegant ceremonial-type Japanese foods

kaisetsu 解説 explanation, comment; **nyū⌐su o kaisetsu shima⌐su** ニュースを解説します comments on (explains) the news; **kaise⌐tsu⌐-sha** 解説者 commentator

kaisha 会社 a company, a business concern; "the office"; **kaisha⌐-in** 会社員 = **sha⌐-in** 社員 company employee

ka⌐ishaku 解釈 construal, interpretation, explanation, exposition; **ka⌐ishaku shima(⌐)su** 解釈します construes, interprets, explains, expounds

kaisō 1. 海藻 seaweed 2. 回送 (～-chū 回送中) in transit, out of service, off duty; **kaisō⌐-sha** 回送車 a car out of service, an off-duty taxi

kaisū⌐-ken 回数券 ticket book (for commuting), coupon ticket

kai-te 買い手 buyer

kaite 欠いて → **kakima⌐su** 欠きます (lacks)

ka⌐ite 書いて → **kakima⌐su** 書きます (writes)

kaiten 1. 回転 revolution, rotation; ～ **shima⌐su** 回転します revolves, rotates 2. 開店 opening a shop (for the first time or for the day); ～ **shima⌐su** 開店します opens shop/business

kai-torima⌐su 買い取ります, **-to⌐ru** 買い取る buys up

kaiwa 会話 conversation

kaizoku 海賊 pirate

ka⌐ji 1. 火事 a fire (accidental) 2. 舵 rudder

ka⌐jiki かじき swordfish

kajira゙nai かじらない =
  kajirimase゙n かじりません
  (not gnaw)

kajirima゙su かじります, **kaji゙ru**
  かじる gnaws, nibbles

kaji゙tte かじって → **kajirima゙su**
  かじります

kajō 過剰 glut, surplus, excess;
  ~ **(no)** 過剰(の) superfluous,
  surplus

kakaema゙su 抱えます,
  kakae⌐ru 抱える holds in
  one's arms (or under one's arm);
  keeps, retains, has; employs

kakanai 欠かない = **kakimase゙n**
  欠きません (not lack)

kaka゙nai 書かない = **kakimase゙n**
  書きません (not write)

kakara゙nai かからない =
  kakarimase゙n かかりません
  (not hang)

kaka゙ri かかり → **kakarima゙su**
  かかります [infinitive]

ka゙kari 係 = **kakari゙-in** 係員 attendant (in charge)

kakarima゙su かかり[掛り]ます,
  kaka゙ru かか[掛]る 1. it hangs
  2. it takes, requires 3. it weighs
  4. it begins, (engine) starts

kakato かかと・踵 heel

kaka゙tta かかった =
  kakarima゙shita かかりました

kaka゙tte かかって →
  kakarima゙su かかります

kake 欠け → **kakema゙su** 欠けま
  す (lacks) [infinitive]

kake゙ 1. 賭・かけ gambling; a
  bet; ~ **o shima゙su** 賭[かけ]を
  します bets, makes a bet 2. 掛
  け credit; ~ **de kaima゙su** 掛け
  で買います buys on credit

ka゙ke 1. かけ・賭け・駆け・書け
  → **kakema゙su** かけます; 賭け
  ます; 駆けます; 書けます
  (hangs; bets; runs; can write)
  [infinitive] 2. 書け →
  kakima゙su 書きます [impera-
  tive] write it!

kake゙ba 欠けば → **kakima゙su** 欠
  きます (if it lack)

ka゙keba 書けば → **kakima゙su** 書
  きます (if one write)

kake-bu゙ton 掛け布団・掛けぶと
  ん overquilt, top quilt

kake゙goto 賭け事・かけごと
  gambling

kake゙ji 掛け字, **kake゙jiku** 掛け軸
  scroll (hanging)

kakema゙su 欠けます, **kakeru** 欠
  ける lacks it, needs

kakema゙su, kake゙ru 1. かけます・
  掛けます, かける・掛ける
  hangs it; (… **ni denwa o** ~ …
  に電話をかけます) tele-
  phones; multiplies; begins it;
  (e゙**njin o** ~ エンジンをかけま
  す) starts (engine) 2. 賭けます,
  賭ける bets 3. 駆けます, 駆け
  る runs, gallops 4. 書けます,
  書ける can write

kake゙-mono 掛け物 scroll (hanging)

kakenai 欠けない = **kakemase`n** 欠けません (not lack it)

kake`nai** かけ[掛け]ない・賭けない・駆けない・書けない = **kakemase`n かけ[掛け]ません/賭けません/駆けません; 書けません (not hang/bet/run; can't write)

kake(ra)rema`su** かけ[掛け](ら)れます, **kake(ra)re`ru かけ[掛け](ら)れる can hang it, can telephone

kakere`ba** 欠ければ, **kakerya** 欠けりゃ → **kakema`su 欠けます (if one lack it)

kake`reba** かけ[掛け]れば, etc., **kake`rya かけ[掛け]りゃ, etc. → **kakema`su** かけます; etc. (if one hang it; if …)

kaketa 欠けた = **kakema`shita** 欠けました (lacked it)

ka`keta** かけ[掛け]た・賭けた・駆けた = **kakema`shita かけ[掛け]ました; 賭けました; 駆けました (hung; bet; ran)

kakete 欠けて → **kakema`su** 欠けます (lacks it)

ka`kete** かけ[掛け]て・賭けて・駆けて → **kakema`su かけ[掛け]ます; 賭けます; 駆けます (hangs; bets; runs); … ni ~ …にかけて (extending) through; … ni ~ wa …にかけては with respect to, as regards, as far as … is concerned

kake-uri 掛け売り = **uri-kake** 売り掛け credit sales

kake`-ya (san) 賭け屋(さん) bookie

kakeyo`** かけよう・掛けよう = **kakemasho` かけましょう・掛けましょう (let's hang it!)

kaki 1. 柿 (= **ki`no ~** 木の柿) persimmon 2. 欠き → **kakima`su** 欠きます (it lacks)

kaki`** 垣 = **kaki`ne 垣根 fence

ka`ki** 1. かき・牡蠣 (= **u`mi no ~ 海のかき[牡蠣]) oyster 2. 花器 flower vase 3. 夏期 summer (period/term) 4. 書き → **kakima`su** 書きます (writes) [infinitive]

kakiage かき揚げ a tangle of tidbits fried as tempura, fritters

kaki-atsumema`su** かき集めます, **-atsume`ru かき集める rakes (them up)

kaki-ga`kkō 夏期学校 summer school

kaki-irema`su** かき入れます, **-ire`ru かき入れる fill in (information)

kaki-kaema`su** 書き換えます, **-kae`ru 書き換える rewrites

kaki-ka`ta` 書き方 way of writing; spelling

kakima`su 欠きます, **kaku** 欠く it lacks, it is lacking/wanting

kakima`su, ka`ku 1. 書きます, 書く writes 2. 掻きます, 掻く scratches

kaki-mawashima`su かき回しま

す, **-mawasu** かき回す stirs

kaki-naoshima⌐su 書き直します, **-nao⌐su** 書き直す rewrites

kaki⌐ne 垣根 fence

kakitome 書留 registered mail

kakitori 書き取り dictation

kakkō 1. 格好 shape, form, appearance; ~ **ga i⌐i** 格好がいい shapely, ~ **ga waru⌐i** 格好が悪い unshapely 2. ~ **(na)** 格好 (な) suitable, moderate, reasonable (price)

ka⌐kkō かっこう・郭公 cuckoo

ka⌐ko 過去 the past

kakō 加工 processing (industrially treating); ~ **shima⌐su** 加工 します processes

kakō⌐ 書こう = **kakimashō⌐** 書きましょう (let's write it!)

kakō⌐-gan かこう［花崗］岩 granite

...-ka⌐koku ...か国 (counts countries)

kakomima⌐su 囲みます, **kakomu** 囲む surrounds

kaku 欠く = **kakima⌐su** 欠きます (it lacks)

kaku⌐ 角 1. = **shikaku** 四角 square 2. = **ka⌐kudo** 角度 angle

ka⌐ku 1. ~ **(no)** 核 (の) nuclear 2. 書く = **kakima⌐su** 書きます (writes)

ka⌐ku(-) ... (goto ni) 各...（ごと に・毎に) each

ka⌐kudo 角度 angle

ka⌐ku-eki 各駅 every station; **kakueki-te⌐isha (no re⌐ssha)** 各駅停車（の列車) local train

ka⌐ku⌐go 覚悟 resolution, premeditation, resignation; ~ **shima(⌐)su** 覚悟します is resolved (to do), is prepared for, is resigned to

kakujitsu 確実 certainty (= **kakujitsu-sei** 確実性); ~ **(na)** 確実 (な) certain, reliable, authentic

kakumei 革命 revolution (political, etc.)

kakunin 確認 confirmation; ~ **shima⌐su** 確認します confirms

kakurema⌐su 隠れます, **kakure⌐ru** 隠れる it hides

kakuse⌐i-ki 拡声器 loudspeaker

kakushima⌐su 隠します, **kaku⌐su** 隠す hides it

ka⌐kuteru カクテル cocktail (party)

kakuzai 角材 block of wood

kakya 欠きゃ 1. = **kake⌐ba** 欠け ば (if it lack) 2. ~ **shinai** 欠 きゃしない = **kaki⌐ ya/wa shinai** 欠きや/はしない = **kakanai** 欠かない (not lack)

ka⌐kya 書きゃ 1. = **ka⌐keba** 書け ば (if one write) 2. ~ **shinai** 書 きゃしない = **ka⌐ki ya/wa shinai** 書きや/はしない = **kaka⌐nai** 書かない (not write)

kama 1. かま・窯 oven 2. かま・ 釜 kettle, pot, cauldron, boiler

kamaboko かまぼこ steamed fish cake

kamachi かまち・框 frame

kamado かまど・竃 kitchen range, stove; oven; furnace

kamaimase n 構いません・かまいません, **kamawa nai** 構わない・かまわない it makes no difference; never mind

kamameshi 釜飯 rice (with chicken, crab, or shrimp) steamed in fish bouillon and served in a clay pot

kama nai かまない・噛まない = **kamimase n** かみません・噛みません (not chew/bite)

kamasu [¹] かます・魳 barracuda, saury-pike

kamawa nai 構わない・かまわない = **kamaimase n** 構いません・かまいません

kamban 看板 signboard; (o-kamban お看板) closing time; ～-se do 看板[かんばん]制度 the just-in-time inventory system

kam-bi iru 缶ビール canned beer

kamboku 潅木・灌木 bush

kame かめ・瓶 jar *(with large mouth)*

ka me 1. 亀 tortoise, turtle **2.** かめ[噛め] → **kamema su** かめ[噛め]ます [infinitive] **3.** かめ[噛め] → **kamima su** かみ[噛み]ます [imperative] chew!

ka meba かめば・噛めば →

kamima su かみ[噛み]ます (if one chew/bite)

kamei 1. 仮名 an assumed name; a temporary/tentative name **2.** 加盟 affiliation; ～ shima su 加盟します affiliates

ka mei 家名 family name

kamema su かめ[噛め]ます, **kame ru** かめる・噛める can chew/bite

kame nai かめ[噛め]ない = **kamemase n** かめ[噛め]ません (cannot chew/bite)

ka mera カメラ camera

kame rya かめりゃ・噛めりゃ → **kame reba** かめれば・噛めれば → **kamema su** かめ[噛め]ます (if one can chew/bite)

kami 1. 髪 hair (on head) **2.** 紙 paper

ka mi 1. 神 = **ka mi-sama** 神様 God **2.** かみ・噛み → **kamima su** かみ[噛み]ます (chews, bites)

kami-a bura 髪油 hair oil

kami-a rai 髪洗い shampoo

kami-ba sami 紙挟み **1.** file folder; file **2.** paperclip

kami-bu kuro 紙袋 paper bag

kami-dana 神棚 household altar *(Shinto)*

kamiku zu 紙くず・紙屑 wastepaper; **kamikuzu -kago** 紙くずかご・紙屑籠 wastepaper basket

kamima'su かみ[擤み]ます,
  kamu かむ: **hana o ~** 鼻をか
  みます blows one's nose
kamima'su かみ[噛み]ます,
  ka'mu かむ・噛む chews, bites
kamina'ri 雷 thunder; **~ ga
  narima'su** 雷が鳴ります it
  thunders
ka'mi-sama 神様 God; gods
kamiso'ri かみそり・剃刀 razor;
  ~ no ha かみそりの刃 razor
  blade
kami-tsukima'su かみつきます,
  -tsu'ku かみつく bites
kami-ya'suri 紙やすり sandpaper
ka'mo かも・鴨 1. wild duck
  2. sucker, dupe
... ka' mo (shiremase'n) ...かも
  (しれません) maybe, perhaps
kamo' かもう・噛もう (let's
  chew/bite it!)
kamoku 科目 subject, course (in
  school)
kā⁼-moku 火木 Tuesday-Thursday
kamome かもめ・鷗 seagull
kampai 乾杯 a toast, "bottoms
  up"
kampa⁼n 甲板 deck (of ship)
kampyō⁼ かんぴょう dried
  gourd strips
kamu かむ・擤む → **(hana o)
  kamima'su** (鼻を)かみます
  (blows nose)
ka'mu かむ・噛む → **kamima'su**

かみ[噛み]ます (chews, bites)
ka'mya かみゃ・噛みゃ 1. =
  ka'meba かめば・噛めば (if
  one chew it) 2. **~ shinai** か
  みゃ[噛みゃ]しない = **ka'mi
  ya/wa shinai** かみ[噛み]や/
  はしない = **kama'nai** かまな
  い・噛まない (not chew it)
ka'n 1. 缶 a can 2. 燗 (= **o-kan**
  お燗) heating rice wine; **~ o
  tsukema'su/shima'su** お燗を
  つけます/します warms the
  saké 3. 管 a tube
...⁼-kan ...間 for the interval of;
  between
kana かな・仮名 kana (Japanese
  syllabic writing)
... ka na ...かな I wonder
  (whether)
Ka'nada カナダ Canada;
  Kanada'-jin カナダ人 a Cana-
  dian
ka'nai 家内 my wife
kanaima'su, kana'u: (**... ni ~** ...
  にかないます) 1. かない[適
  い]ます, かなう・適う ac-
  cords/agrees (with); **dōri ni ~**
  道理にかないます it stands to
  reason; **mokuteki ni ~** 目的に
  かないます it serves the purpose 2. かない[敵い]ます, か
  なう・敵う is a match (for),
  matches, is equal (to); **aite' ni
  kanaimase'n** 相手にかないま
  せん is no match for the opponent 3. かない[叶い]ます, か

なう・叶う (= **dekima̶su** でき
ます) it is possible, can do it;
is accomplished, attained,
achieved, realized; **nozomi**⌐
ga ~ 望みがかないます a
desire is realized (fulfilled)

kanamono 金物 hardware; ~
-ya 金物屋 hardware store

kanarazu 必ず for sure; necessarily; inevitably

ka̶nari かなり fairly, rather

kanari(y)a カナリア[ヤ] canary

kanashii 悲しい sad

kanazuchi⌐ 金槌 hammer

kanchō 浣腸 enema

ka̶nchō 艦長 captain (of warship)

kandai (na) 寛大(な) generous

kanda̶n-kei 寒暖計 (room) thermometer

kande かんで → **(hana o)
kamima̶su** (鼻を)かみ[擤み]
ます (blows nose)

ka̶nde かんで・噛んで →
kamima̶su かみ[噛み]ます
(chews, bites)

kandō 感動 (strong) emotion,
(deep) feeling

kane 1. 金 money (= **o-kane** お
金); metal **2.** 鐘 bell *(large)*

... ka ne ...かね I wonder
(whether)

kane-bako 金箱 cashbox

kanema̶su 兼ねます, **kane̶ru** 兼
ねる combines, unites; dually/
concurrently serves as

kanemo̶chi̶ (no) 金持ち(の)
rich *(wealthy)*

...-ka̶nen ...か年 (counts years)
= **...⌐-nen** ...年

kan'en 肝炎 hepatitis

kanetsu̶-ki 加熱器 heater

kanga̶e 考え thought, idea, opinion; → **kangaema̶su** 考えま
す

kangaema̶su 考えます,
kanga̶e̶ru 考える thinks, considers

kangaerema̶su 考えられます,
kangaerare̶ru 考えられる can
think; it is thought

kange̶i-kai 歓迎会 reception
(welcome party)

kangeki 感激 (strong) emotion
(feeling)

kango 漢語 Chinese word/
vocabulary (in Japanese)

ka̶ngo 看護 nursing (a patient);
~ **shima**(⌐)**su** 看護します
nurses

kango̶-fu 看護婦 a nurse

kani かに・蟹 crab

kanja 患者 (medical) patient

kanji 1. 漢字 a Chinese character
(symbol) **2.** 感じ feeling
3. 感じ (**kan-ji** 感じ) → **kan-
jima̶su** 感じます

kan-jima̶su 感じます, **-jiru** 感じ
る feels

kanjō 1. 感情 emotion **2.** 環状
loop (shape); ~ **(no)** 環状(の)
ring-shaped, circular; ~**-sen** 環

状線 loop/belt line

kanjō⸍ 勘定, **o-kanjō** お勘定 bill, check, account; **kanjō-ga⸍kari** 勘定係 cashier

kankaku 1. 感覚 sense, sensibility, feeling **2.** 間隔 space, interval

kankei 関係 connection, relationship, interest, concern, relevance; **... no kanke⸍i-sha** ...の関係者 the people/authorities concerned with ..., the ... people

ka⸍nki 換気 ventilation; **kanki-so⸍chi** 換気装置 ventilation system

kan-ki⸍ri⸍ 缶切り can opener

kankō 観光 sightseeing, tour; **~-ba⸍su** 観光バス sightseeing bus; **~-re⸍ssha** 観光列車 sightseeing train

Ka⸍nkoku 韓国 *(preferred in South Korea)* Korea (= **Chōse⸍n** 朝鮮); **Kankoku-go** 韓国語 Korean *(language)*; **Kankoku⸍-jin** 韓国人 a Korean

kankō⸍-kyaku 観光客 tourist, sightseer

kankyō 環境 environment

kannu⸍ki⸍ かんぬき・閂 bolt *(of door)*

ka⸍nnushi 神主 priest *(Shinto)*

ka⸍no-jo 彼女 she/her; girlfriend, mistress

kanō (na) 可能(な) possible; **~-sei** 可能性 possibility

kanra⸍n-seki 観覧席 grandstand (seats)

kanre⸍isha 寒冷紗 cheesecloth

kanren 関連 relevance; **(... ni) ~ shima⸍sᴜ** (...に)関連します is relevant (to), is connected (with)

ka⸍nri 管理 control; **kanri⸍-nin** 管理人 custodian, janitor, manager, landlord (rental manager)

kansatsu 1. 観察 observation, watching; **kansatsu⸍-sha** 観察者 observer **2.** 監察 inspection; **kansatsu⸍-kan** 監察官 inspector **3.** 鑑札 license (tag); **inu⸍ no ~** 犬の鑑札 a dog (-license) tag

kansatsu shima⸍sᴜ (suru) 1. 観察します(する) observes, watches **2.** 監察します(する) inspects

kansei 完成 completion, perfection; **~ shima⸍sᴜ** 完成します completes, perfects

kansetsu 1. ~ (no) 間接(の) indirect; **~ ni** 間接に indirectly **2.** 関節 joint *(of two bones)*

ka⸍nsha 感謝 thanks, gratitude; **~ shima⸍sᴜ** 感謝します appreciates, thanks

kan-shima⸍sᴜ 関します, **-sᴜ⸍ru** する relates (to), concerns, is connected (with); **... ni ka⸍n-shite** ...に関して concerning, as regards, with respect to ...

kanshin 1. 関心 concern, interest **2.** 感心 admiration; ～ **shima͞su** 感心します admires

kanshō 干渉 interference, meddling; ～ **shima͞su** 干渉します interferes

kansoku 観測 observation; (= **i͞ken** 意見) opinion; **kansoku shima͞su** 観測します observes

kantan (na) 簡単(な) simple, brief

kante͞n 寒天 gelatin from *tengusa* seaweed

kantoku 監督 supervision; supervisor, superintendant, overseer, manager, director; **kantoku shima͞su** 監督します supervises, oversees, manages (a team), directs (a film)

kantō͞shi 間投詞 interjection

kantsū 姦通 adultery ⌊*(word)*

kanzei 関税 customs duty (tariff)

kanzen (na) 完全(な) perfect

kanzō 肝臓 liver

kan-zu͞me (no ...) 缶詰(の...) canned (food)

kao 顔 face; looks, a look; ... **(no) ～ o shite ima͞su** ...(の)顔をしています has/wears an expression of ...

kaō 買おう = **kaimashō͞** 買いましょう (let's buy it!)

kaō͞ 飼おう = **kaimashō͞** 飼いましょう (let's raise it!)

kao-iro 顔色 complexion

ka͞pe͞tto カーペット carpet

kappa かっぱ・河童 **1.** water imp **2.** [*sushi bar term*] cucumber (= **kyū͞ri** きゅうり・胡瓜) **3.** = **kappa-maki** かっぱ巻き seaweed-rolled sushi with cucumber in the center

kapparaima͞su かっぱらいます, **kappara͞u** かっぱらう swipes, steals, shoplifts

kappō かっぽう・割烹 Japanese cuisine; **kappō͞-ten** かっぽう〔割烹〕店 Japanese restaurant (with set menu)

ka͞ppu カップ a cup (with handle); **kōhii-～** コーヒーカップ coffee cup

ka͞puseru カプセル capsule

kara 1. 殻 shell, crust **2.** 空 (～ **no** 空の) empty = **karappo (no)** 空っぽ(の)

kara͞ から = **o-kara** おから (bean-curd lees)

... kara͞ ...から from; since; because; **... kara, ... ma͞de** ...から...まで from ... to ...

ka͞rā カラー **1.** collar **2.** color

karada 体・身体 body; one's health

kara͞i からい・辛い **1.** spicy, hot, peppery, pungent **2.** salty

karakaima͞su からかいます, **karaka͞u** からかう teases, pokes fun at

kara-ka͞sa 唐傘 umbrella *(oil-paper)*

karanai 刈らない = **karimase͞n**

刈りません (not mow)
karappo (no) 空っぽ(の) empty
karashi からし・芥子 mustard
ka⌐rasu からす・烏 crow
karate 空手 karate *(weaponless self-defense)*; **karate⌐-gi⌐** 空手着 karate outfit/suit
kare 枯れ・刈れ → **karema⌐su** 枯れます・刈れます
ka⌐re 彼 he/him; **ka⌐re-ra** 彼ら they/them
karē カレー curry; **~-ra⌐isu** カレーライス rice with curry
kare⌐ba 刈れば → **karima⌐su** 刈ります (if one mow)
ka⌐rei かれい・鰈 flatfish, turbot
karema⌐su, kareru 1. 枯れます, 枯れる withers; **karete ima⌐su** 枯れています is withered 2. 刈れます, 刈れる can mow/cut
karenai 枯れない = **karemase⌐n** 枯れません (not wither)
kare⌐ndā カレンダー calendar
karere⌐ba 枯れれば, **karerya** 枯れりゃ → **karema⌐su** 枯れます (if it wither)
ka⌐re-shi 彼氏 boyfriend, lover
karete 枯れて・刈れて → **karema⌐su** 枯れます・刈れます
kari 1. **~ (no)** 仮(の) temporary, tentative 2. 狩り → **karima⌐su** 狩ります hunts [infinitive]
ka⌐ri 狩り hunting; **~ o shima⌐su** 狩りをします hunts
kari⌐-chin 借り賃 rent *(charge)*

karima⌐su 刈ります, **karu** 刈る mows, cuts
karima⌐su 借ります, **kariru** 借りる: (**... ni** ...に) borrows/rents it (from ...)
karinai 借りない = **karimase⌐n** 借りません (not borrow)
kari(ra)rema⌐su 借り(ら)れます, **kari(ra)reru** 借り(ら)れる can borrow
karite 借りて → **karima⌐su** 借ります (borrows)
kari-te 借り手 the borrower/renter, the lessee, the tenant
kariyō 借りよう = **karimashō⌐** 借りましょう (let's borrow/rent it!)
karō 刈ろう = **karimashō⌐** 刈りましょう (let's mow!)
karu 1. 刈る = **karima⌐su** 刈ります mows, cuts 2. 借る [*dialect*] = **kariru** 借りる (borrows)
karui 軽い light (of weight)
karuishi 軽石 pumice
karya 刈りゃ 1. = **kare⌐ba** 刈れば (if one mow) 2. **~ shinai** 刈りゃしない = **kari⌐ ya/wa shinai** 刈りや/はしない = **karanai** 刈らない (not mow)
kasa⌐ かさ・嵩 bulk
ka⌐sa 1. 傘・かさ umbrella 2. 笠 bamboo hat; (mushroom) cap
ka⌐sai 火災 fire *(accidental)* = **ka⌐ji** 火事; **kasai-ke⌐ihō** 火災警報 fire alarm, **kasai-hōchi⌐ki**

火災報知器 fire alarm *(device)*, fire bell

kasanai 貸さない = **kashimase'n** 貸しません (not lend)

kasanarima'su 重なります, **kasanaru** 重なる they pile up

kasanema'su 重ねます, **kasaneru** 重ねる piles them up, puts one on top of another

kase 貸せ 1. → **kasema'su** 貸せます [infinitive] 2. → **kashima'su** 貸します [imperative] lend it!

kase'ba 貸せば → **kashima'su** 貸します (if one lend)

kasegima'su 稼ぎます, **kase'gu** 稼ぐ earns, works for (money)

kasei 1. 家政 housekeeping 2. 火星 Mars

kase'ide 稼いで → **kasegima'su** 稼ぎます

kase'i-fu 家政婦 housekeeper

kase'i-jin 火星人 a Martian

kasema'su 貸せます, **kaseru** 貸せる can lend

kasen 下線 underline; ～ **o** **hikima'su** 下線を引きます draws an underline

kasen 化繊 synthetic fiber

kasenai 貸せない = **kasemase'n** 貸せません (cannot lend)

kasha 貸しゃ 1. = **kase'ba** 貸せば (if one lend) 2. ～ **shinai** 貸しゃしない = **kashi'ya/wa shinai** 貸しや/はしない = **kasanai** 貸さない (not lend)

kashi 貸し → **kashima'su** 貸します [infinitive]

ka'shi 菓子 (= **o-ka'shi** お菓子) cakes, sweets, pastry, candy

kashikiri-ba'su 貸し切りバス chartered bus

kashiko'i 賢い wise

Kashikomarima'shita かしこまりました. I understand and will comply (with your request).

kashi-ma 貸間 rooms for rent; rented/rental room(s)

kashima'su 貸します, **kasu** 貸す lends; rents (it out to)

kashira' (o-kashira) 頭(お頭) head; chief, leader

... ka' shira ...かしら I wonder (whether)

kashi-te 貸し手 the lender/lessor, the landlord

kashite 貸して → **kashima'su** 貸します

kashi-ya 貸家 house for rent; rented/rental house

kashi'-ya 菓子屋 candy store

...-ka'sho ...か所・箇所・個所 (counter for places, installations, institutions)

kasō 貸そう = **kashimashō'** 貸しましょう (let's lend it!)

kasoku-pe'daru 加速ペダル gas pedal

kā⌐'soru カーソル cursor

kasu 貸す = **kashima'su** 貸します (lends)

ka͞su かす・滓 sediment, dregs

ka͞suka (na) かすか（な）・微か（な）faint, dim, slight

kasumema͞su かすめます・掠めます, **kasume͞ru** かすめる・掠める skims, grazes; (= **kasume-torima͞su** かすめ[掠め]取ります) robs, cheats

kasume-torima͞su かすめ[掠め]取ります, **-to͞ru** かすめ[掠め]取る skims off; robs (it of …), cheats (one out of …)

kasumi かすみ・霞 haze, mist

kasumima͞su かすみます・霞みます, **kasumu** かすむ・霞む gets dim, hazy, misty

kasutera カステラ (sponge)cake

kata͞ 型 1. form, shape, size, mold, pattern 2. type, model

ka͞ta 肩 shoulder

…-kata …方 manner of doing, way

… kata͞ (o-kata) …方（お方）(honored) person

katachi 形 form, shape

… kata͞-gata …方々 (honored) persons

katagi (na) 堅気（な）respectable, steady, honest

kata͞hō 片方, **kata͞ppō** 片っ方・かたっぽう, **kata͞ppo** 片っぽ・かたっぽ one of a pair; the other one (of a pair)

katai 固い・硬い・堅い hard, tight, tough, firm, solid; strong; upright; strict

kata͞kana カタカナ・片かな・片仮名 katakana *(the squarish Japanese letters)*

kataku͞riko 片栗粉 potato starch

katamari 1. 固まり・かたまり・塊 a lump, a clot, a mass; a loaf (of bread) 2. → **katamarima͞su** 固まります

katamarima͞su 固まります, **katamaru** 固まる it hardens, congeals, clots, (mud) cakes

katamema͞su 固めます, **katameru** 固める hardens it, congeals it; strengthens it

katamichi 片道 one-way; ～ **-ki͞ppu** 片道切符 one-way ticket

katamu͞ki͞ 傾き slant; inclination, tendency

katamukima͞su 傾きます, **katamu͞ku** 傾く leans (to one side), slants

katana͞ 刀 sword

kata͞nai 勝たない → **kachimase͞n** 勝ちません (not win)

kata͞ppo 片っぽ・かたっぽ → **kata͞ho** 片方

katarima͞su 語ります, **kataru** 語る relates, tells

… kata͞-tachi …方達 (honored) persons

kata͞wa かたわ・片輪 cripple

kata-yorima͞su 片寄ります・偏ります, **-yo͞ru** 片寄る・偏る

leans (to one side); is partial (to)

kata-zukema´su 片付けます, **kata-zuke´ru** 片付ける puts in order, straightens up, tidies, cleans up

kata-zukima´su 片付きます, **kata-zu´ku** 片付く it gets tidy (put in order)

ka´te 勝て 1. → **katema´su** 勝てます [infinitive] 2. → **kachima´su** 勝ちます [imperative] win!

katei 1. 家庭 home, household 2. 仮定 hypothesis, supposition 3. 課程 process (course, stage)

katei-yo´gu 家庭用具, **-yo´hin** 家庭用品 home appliances

katema´su 勝てます, **kate´ru** 勝てる can win

ka´ten カーテン curtain, drapes; **kāten-ro´ddo** カーテンロッド curtain rod

kate´nai 勝てない — **katemase´n** 勝てません (can't win)

kato´ 勝とう = **kachimasho´** 勝ちましょう (let's win!)

Katori´kku カトリック Catholic

ka´tsu 1. カツ a Japanese "cutlet" (fried in deep fat) 2. 勝つ = **kachima´su** 勝ちます (wins)

katsudō 活動 action, activity, movement

katsu-don カツ丼 a bowl of rice with sliced pork cutlet on top

katsu´gi 担ぎ → **katsugima´su** 担ぎます

katsugima´su 担ぎます, **katsu´gu** 担ぐ carries on shoulders

katsu´ide 担いで → **katsugima´su** 担ぎます

katsuji 活字 movable type; ~ **ni shima´su** 活字にします prints, puts in print

katsuo かつお・鰹 bonito; ~**-bushi** かつお[鰹]節 a dried bonito fish

katsura かつら・鬘 a wig

ka´tsute かつて, **ka´tte** かって at one time, formerly

katsuyaku 活躍 activity; **katsuyaku shima´su** 活躍します is active

katta 1. 買った; 飼った = **kaima´shita** 買いました; 飼いました (bought; raised) 2. 刈った = **karima´shita** 刈りました (mowed)

ka´tta 勝った = **kachima´shita** 勝ちました (won)

...ka´tta ...かった: ADJECTIVE ~ **(desu)** ...かった(です) was ...

...ka´ttara ...かったら: ADJECTIVE ~ ...かったら if/when it is

...ka´ttari ...かったり: ADJECTIVE ~ ...かったり being representatively/sometimes/alternately; ~ **...-ku na´kattari** ...かったり...くなかったり (is ...) off and on, sometimes is ... and sometimes isn't

katte 1. 勝手 kitchen **2.** ~ **(na/ni)** 勝手(な/に) selfish(ly), as one wishes **3.** 買って → **kaima゚su** 買います (buys) **4.** 刈って → **karima゚su** 刈ります (mows)

ka゚tte 1. かって = **ka゚tsute** かつて **2.** 勝って → **kachima゚su** 勝ちます (wins)

katte-do゚gu 勝手道具 kitchen utensils

katte-guchi 勝手口 kitchen door, back door

kau 買う = **kaima゚su** 買います (buys)

ka゚u 飼う = **kaima゚su** 飼います (raises)

kawa゚ 1. 川 river **2.** 皮・革 skin; leather; fur; (tree) bark; crust

kawai-garima゚su かわいがり[可愛がり]ます, **-ga゚ru** かわいがる・可愛がる treats with affection, loves

kawai゚i かわいい・可愛い, **kawairashi゚i** かわいらしい・可愛らしい cute, loveable, darling

kawai-so゚ (na) かわいそう・可愛そう(な) pitiful, poor

kawa゚ite 乾いて → **kawakima゚su** 乾きます

kawakashima゚su 乾かします, **kawaka゚su** 乾かす dries it (out)

kawakima゚su 乾きます, **kawa゚ku** 乾く gets dry

kawanai 買わない = **kaimase゚n** 買いません (not buy)

kawa゚nai 飼わない = **kaimase゚n** 飼いません (not raise)

kawara かわら・瓦 tile; ~**-buki (no)** かわら[瓦]ぶき(の) tile-roofed

kawaranai 変わらない = **kawarimase゚n** 変わりません (not change)

kawari 1. (o-kawari) 変わり(お変わり) change; 代わり(お代わり) substitute; **... no ~ ni ...** の代わりに instead of; **(... no) ~ ni su゚nde ima゚su** (...の)代わりに住んでいます is housesitting (for ...) **2. (o-ka゚wari)** 代わり(お代わり) a second helping (usually of rice) **3.** 変わり → **kawarima゚su** 変わります [infinitive]

kawarima゚su, kawaru: (... ni) ~ 1. 変わります, 変わる: (...に)変わる it changes (into ...) **2.** 代わります, 代わる: (...に)代わる it takes the place (of ...)

kawaru-ga゚waru 代わる代わる・かわるがわる alternately

kawase 為替 a money order

kawatta 変わった = **kawarima゚shita** 変わりました (changed; unusual, novel)

kawatte 変わって →
kawarima͞su 変わります; ～
ima͞su 変わっています is
unusual, novel

kaya 1. 蚊帳・かや mosquito net
2. 買や = **kae͞ba** 買えば (if
one buy) **3.** ～ **shinai** 買やし
ない = **ka͞i ya/wa shinai** 買い
や/はしない = **kawanai** 買わ
ない (not buy)

ka͞ya 飼や **1.** = **ka͞eba** 飼えば
(if one raise) **2.** ～ **shinai** 飼や
しない = **ka͞i ya/wa shinai** 飼
いや/はしない = **kawa͞nai** 飼
わない (not raise)

kayaku 火薬 gunpowder

Kayo͞bi 火曜日 Tuesday

kayoi 通い **1.** ～ **(no)** 通い(の)
commuting, live-out (help)
2. passbook, bankbook; chitbook **3.** → **kayoima͞su** 通いま
す [infinitive]

kayoima͞su 通います, **kayou** 通
う commutes, goes back and
forth, goes (regularly)

kayowanai 通わない =
kayoimase͞n 通いません (not
commute)

kayu (o-kayu) 粥・かゆ(お粥・お
かゆ) rice gruel, porridge

kayu͞i かゆい・痒い itchy

kaza͞m-bai 火山灰 volcanic ash

ka͞zan 火山 volcano

kazari 飾り **1.** = **kazari-mono** 飾
り物 **2.** → **kazarima͞su** 飾りま
す [infinitive]

kazarima͞su 飾ります, **kazaru** 飾
る decorates

kazari-mono 飾り物 ornament,
decoration

kaze 1. 風 wind; ～ **ga tsuyo͞i** 風
が強い is windy **2.** かぜ・風邪
a cold; ～ **o hikima͞su** かぜ[風
邪]をひきます catches (a)
cold

kaze-gu͞suri かぜ[風邪]薬 cold
medicine

kazo͞e 数え → **kazoema͞su** 数え
ます **1.** [infinitive] **2.** [impera-
tive] **kazoe͞ ro** 数えろ, **kazo͞e
yo** 数えよ count!

kazoe-kire͞nai 数え切れない
countless, innumerable

kazoema͞su 数えます, **kazoe͞ru**
数える counts

kazoe(ra)rema͞su 数え(ら)れま
す, **kazoe(ra)re͞ru** 数え(ら)れ
る can count

ka͞zoku 家族 family

ka͞zu 数 number

ke 毛 hair; wool; feathers

...͞ke ...家 clan, family

ke͞buru ケーブル cable; **kēburu͞-
kā͞** ケーブルカー cable car

kecha͞ppu ケチャップ ketchup

ke͞chi (na) けち(な) stingy

ke͞chimbo けちんぼ stingy person, skinflint

kedamono けだもの・獣 animal

ke͞do けど = **ke͞redo(-mo)** けれ
ど(も)

kega͞ (o-ke͞ga) けが・怪我(おけ

が・お怪我) injury, mishap; ~
o shima'su けが[怪我]をしま
す gets hurt
ke-gawa 毛皮 fur
...-kei ...系 **1.** type, model **2.** of ...
ancestry
keiba 競馬 horse racing/race;
~**-jō** 競馬場 racetrack
keibetsu 軽べつ・軽蔑 contempt,
despising; **keibetsu shima'su**
軽べつ[軽蔑]します despises
keiei 経営 management, operation; ~ **shima'su** 経営します
runs a business
keie'i-sha 経営者 manager,
operator, proprietor
keigo 敬語 honorific (word)
keihō 警報 alarm, alert, warning
keiji 繋詞 copula
keiji-ban 掲示板 bulletin board
keika 経過 course (of time), progress, development; ~
shima'su 経過します (time)
passes, elapses; lapses, expires
keikai 警戒 vigilance, watch,
guard; warning, caution; ~
shima'su 警戒します guards
against, watches out (for ...),
warns, cautions
keikaku 計画 plan, scheme, program; (... **no**) ~ **o tatema'su**
(...の)計画を立てます= (...
o) **keikaku shima'su** (...を)計
画します plans
keikan 警官 policeman, (police)
officer; ~**-tai** 警官隊 a con-

tingent of policemen
keiken 経験 experience; ~
shima'su 経験します experiences, undergoes
keiki 景気 business conditions,
prosperity, boom
ke'iki 計器 meter (device)
ke'iko (o-ke'iko) けいこ・稽古
（おけいこ・お稽古）exercise,
practice, drill
keikō 傾向 tendency, trend
keikō(-) 経口 oral; ~ **hini'n-
yaku** 経口避妊薬 oral contra-
ceptive
keikoku 警告 warning; **keikoku
shima'su** 警告します warns
keikō-tō 蛍光[螢光]灯 fluorescent light
keimu'-sho 刑務所 jail, prison
keireki 経歴 career (history)
keirin 競輪 bicycle race
keirō 敬老 respect for the aged;
~ **no hi'** 敬老の日 Respect-
for-the-Aged Day (15 September)
keiryaku 計略 plot, scheme
keisan 計算 calculation, computation; ~ **shima'su** 計算し
ます calculates, computes
keisa'n-ki 計算機 calculator
keisatsu 警察 police; **keisatsu-
sho**⌐ 警察署 police station
keishiki 形式 form, formality
keishoku 軽食 snack
keisotsu (na) 軽率(な) hasty,
rash

keiteki 警笛 horn *(of car)*

keito 毛糸 wool; yarn

keiyaku 契約 contract, agreement

keiyōˈshi 形容詞 adjective

... keˈⁿiyu (de/no) ...経由(で/の) by (way of) ... , via ...

keˈizai 経済 economics, finance; **keizaˈi-gaku** 経済学 (science of) economics; **keizai-teki (na)** 経済的(な) economical

keˈki ケーキ cake

kekka 結果 result, effect; as a result (consequence)

kekkaku 結核 tuberculosis

kekkō 欠航 cancelled flight; "flight cancelled"

keˈkkō 結構 1. ～ **(na)** 結構(な) splendid, excellent 2. fairly well; enough; **Keˈkkō desu** 結構です. No, thank you.

kekkon 結婚 marriage; (... **to**) ～ **shimaˈsu** (...と)結婚します marries; **kekkoˈn-shiki** 結婚式 wedding

kekkyoku' 結局 after all, in the long run

kembaˈi-ki 券売機 ticket vending machine

kembi-kyō 顕微鏡 microscope

kembutsu 見物 sightseeing; **kembutsu shimaˈsu** 見物します sees the sights

kemmei (na) 賢明(な) wise

kemono けもの・獣 ＝ **kedamono** けだもの・獣 animal

keˈmpei 憲兵 MP; shore patrol

keˈmpō 憲法 constitution; **Kempō-kineˈmbi** 憲法記念日 Constitution (Memorial) Day (3 May)

kemui けむい・煙い, **kemutai** けむたい・煙たい smoky

kemuri 煙 smoke

kemushiⁿ 毛虫 caterpillar

keˈn 県, ...ˈ**-ken** ...県 a Japanese prefecture (like a state)

...-ken 1. ...件 (counts buildings, shops) **2.** ...券 ticket

keˈnchi 見地 viewpoint

kenchiku 建築 construction; architecture; ～**-ka** 建築家 architect

keˈⁿchō 県庁 the prefectural government (office)

keˈndō 剣道 the art of fencing (with bamboo swords)

ken'etsu 検閲 censor(ship)

kengaku 見学 study by observation, field study/trip/work

keˈnji 検事 (public) prosecutor

kenjū 拳銃 pistol

kenka けんか・喧嘩 quarrel, argument; ～ **shimaˈsu** けんか[喧嘩]します quarrels, argues

keˈnka 堅果 nut

kenkō 健康 health; ～ **(na)** 健康(な) healthy; ～**-shoˈkuhin** 健康食品 health food(s)

Kenkoku-kiˈnen-no-hi 建国記念の日 National Foundation

Day (11 February)

kenkyū 研究 research, study; ~ **shima'su** 研究します studies, researches

kenkyū-jo[ ] 研究所 research room/laboratory/institute

ke'nri 権利 right *(privilege)*

kenri[ ]**-kin** 権利金 "key money" (to obtain rental lease)

kenritsu (no) 県立(の) prefectural

ke'nsa 検査 inspection, examination, check-up, test; **ke'nsa shima([ ])su** 検査します inspects, checks, tests

kensatsu 検札 ticket examining (on board); **kensatsu shima'su** 検札します examines tickets

kensetsu 建設 construction (work) *(building)*

kenson (na) 謙遜(な) humble *(modest)*

kentō 拳闘 boxing

kentō' 見当 aim; direction; estimate, guess; ~ **ga tsukima'su (tsuku')** 見当がつきます(つく) gets a rough idea (of it); ~ **o tsukema'su (tsuke'ru)** 見当をつけます(つける) makes a guess, takes aim

...-ke'ntō ...見当 roughly, approximately, about

ken'yaku 倹約 economy, thrift, economizing; ~ **(na)** 倹約(な)

thrifty, frugal; **ken'yaku shima'su** 倹約します economizes on, saves

ke'nzan 剣山 a frog (pinholder) for flowers

ke-o[ ]**ri**[ ]**mono** 毛織物 woolen goods

kera'nai け[蹴]らない = **kerimase'n** け[蹴]りません (not kick)

ke're け[蹴]れ → **kerema'su** け[蹴]れます (can kick) [infinitive]

ke'reba け[蹴]れば → **kerima'su** け[蹴]ります (if one kick)

ke'redo(-mo) けれど(も) however, though, but

kerema'su け[蹴]れます, **kere'ru** け[蹴]れる can kick

kere'nai け[蹴]れない = **keremase'n** け[蹴]れません (can't kick)

ke'rete け[蹴]れて → **kerema'su** け[蹴]れます (can kick)

ke'ri け[蹴]り → **kerima'su** け[蹴]ります (kicks) [infinitive]

kerima'su け[蹴]ります, **ke'ru** け[蹴]る kicks

kerō' け[蹴]ろう = **kerimashō'** け[蹴]りましょう (let's kick!)

ke'ro (yo) け[蹴]ろ(よ) kick! [irregular imperative of **kerima'su** け[蹴]ります]

ke'rya 1. け[蹴]りゃ = **ke'reba** け[蹴]れば (if one kick) **2.** ~

shinai け［蹴］りゃしない ＝
ke͞ri ya/wa shinai け［蹴］りや
/はしない ＝ **kera͞nai** け［蹴］
らない (not kick)

kesanai 消さない ＝ **keshimase͞n**
消しません (not extinguish)

kese 消せ 1. → **kesema͞su** 消せ
ます (can extinguish) [infini-
tive] 2. → **keshima͞su** 消しま
す [imperative] turn it off!,
put it out!

kese͞ba 消せば → **keshima͞su** 消
します (if one extinguish)

kesenai 消せない ＝ **kesemase͞n**
消せません (can't extinguish)

kesete 消せて → **kesema͞su** 消せ
ます (can extinguish)

kesha 消しゃ 1. ＝ **kese͞ba** 消せ
ば (if one extinguish) 2. ～
shinai 消しゃしない ＝ **keshi͞**
ya/wa shinai 消しや/はしな
い ＝ **kesanai** 消さない (not extinguish)

keshi 消し → **keshima͞su** 消しま
す [infinitive]

keshi-gomu 消しゴム (rubber)
eraser ⌈stamp

keshi-in 消印 cancellation mark/
ke͞shiki 景色 scenery, view

keshima͞su 消します, **kesu** 消す
extinguishes, puts out; turns
off; expunges, erases, deletes

keshite 消して → **keshima͞su** 消
します

kesho͞ (o-kesho͞) 化粧（お化粧）
cosmetics, make-up; **kesho͞[n]**-

hin 化粧品 cosmetics; **kesho͞-**
shitsu 化粧室 rest room, bathroom, toilet, lounge

keso͞ 消そう ＝ **keshimasho͞** 消し
ましょう (let's extinguish it!)

kessaku 傑作 masterpiece

ke͞ssan 決算 settling accounts

kesseki 欠席 absence (from
school, work); **kesse͞ki͞-sha** 欠
席者 absentee; **kesseki**
shima͞su 欠席します is absent

ke͞sshi͞n 決心 determination,
resolve; **(shiyo͞ to)** ～
shima(͞)su （しようと）決心し
ます resolves (to do)

kesshite 決して [+ NEGATIVE]
never

kesu 消す ＝ **keshima͞su** 消しま
す (puts out; turns off;
erases)

ke͞su ケース case *(a particular in-*
stance); **ke͞su-bai-ke͞su** ケース
バイケース case by case

keta けた・桁 1. (cross)beam,
girder; **keta-shita** けた下・桁下
under the beam/girder
2. abacus rod, (numerical)
column

ke͞tchae け［蹴］っちゃえ kick!

ke͞tchaima͞su け［蹴］っちゃいま
す, **ke͞tchau** け［蹴］っちゃう
kicks (＝ **ke͞tte shimaima͞su** け
［蹴］ってしまいます)

ke͞tchatta け［蹴］っちゃった,
ke͞tta け［蹴］った ＝
kerima͞shita け［蹴］りました

(kicked)

ke'tchatte け[蹴]っちゃって, **ke'tte** け[蹴]って → **kerima'su** け[蹴]ります (kicks)

ketsu けつ・穴 1. = **shiri** 尻 (buttock) 2. the tail end, the last (bottom)

ketsuatsu 血圧 blood pressure; ~ **ga taka'i/hiku'i** 血圧が高い/低い has high/low blood pressure; ~ **o hakarima'su** 血圧を計ります takes one's blood pressure

ketsuatsu-kei 血圧計 blood-pressure gauge; sphygmomanometer

ketsu⁻eki 血液 blood

ketsu⁻ron 結論 conclusion; ~ **to shite** 結論として in conclusion; ~ **shima'su** 結論します concludes

kettei 決定 determination, decision; ~ **shima'su** 決定します decides, determines (to do)

kette⁻n 欠点 flaw, defect, shortcoming

ketto⁻ ケット blanket

kewashi'i 険しい steep, precipitous; severe

kezurema'su 削れます, **kezureru** 削れる can sharpen

kezurima'su 削ります, **kezuru** 削る sharpens

ki 1. 気 spirit; feeling; mind, heart: see **ki ga** 気が, **ki ni** 気

に, **ki o** 気を 2. 着 → **kima'su** 着ます (wears) [infinitive]

ki 1. 木 tree; wood 2. 来 → **kima'su** 来ます (comes)

kibishi'i 厳しい strict, severe

kibō 希望 hope; **kibō-sha** 希望者 candidate, applicant; ~ **shima'su** 希望します hopes, aspires

ki'bun 気分 feeling, mood

kicha 来ちゃ = **kite' wa** 来ては

kicha'ima'su 来ちゃいます = **kite' shimaima'su** 来てしまいます (comes)

kicha'tta 来ちゃった = **kite' shimatta** 来てしまった; = **kita'** 来た (came)

kicha'u 来ちゃう = **kite' shimau** 来てしまう (comes)

ki'chi' 基地 military base

ki-chiga'i (no) 気違い(の) mad, insane

kichi'n-to きちんと punctually; precisely; neat(ly)

kichō 記帳 registration (at hotel, etc.); ~ **shima'su** 記帳します checks in, registers

kichō' 機長 captain (of an airplane)

kichō (na) 貴重(な) valuable; ~ **-hin** 貴重品 valuables

ki'do 木戸 entrance gate, wicket

kidorima'su 気取ります, **kidoru** 気取る・気どる puts on airs; **kidotte ima'su** 気取って[気どって]います, **kidotta ...** 気

取った・気どった... affected, stuck-up

kie 消え → **kiema̱'su** 消えます [infinitive]

kiema̱'su 消えます, **kieru** 消える is extinguished, goes out; fades, vanishes

ki ga 気が: ~ **mijika̱'i** 気が短い is impatient; ~ **omoi** 気が重い is depressed; ~ **tachima̱'su** 気が立ちます gets excited; ~ **tsukima̱'su** 気が付きます comes to one's senses

kigae 着替え a change of clothing

kigaema̱'su 着替えます, **kiga̱'e̱ru** 着替える changes (clothes) [newer form of **ki-kaema̱'su** 着替えます]

ki̱'geki 喜劇 comedy

kigen 機嫌・きげん (state of) health, mood: ~ **ga i̱'i** 機嫌 [きげん]がいい cheerful; ~ **ga waru̱'i** 機嫌[きげん]が悪い unhappy, moody **Go-kigen (wa) ika̱'ga desu ka** ご機嫌[きげん](は)いかがですか. How are you (feeling)? **Go-kigen yo̱'** ごきげんよう. Good-bye./ Hello.

ki̱'gen 1. 期限 term, period; deadline 2. 起源 origin

kigō 記号 sign, mark, symbol

ki̱'gu 器具 implement, fixture, apparatus

ki̱hon 基本 basis, foundation;

~ **-teki (na)** 基本的(な) basic, fundamental

ki̱'i キー key

kiiro (no) 黄色(の), **kiiroi** 黄色い・黄いろい yellow

kiita 聞いた → **ki̱kima̱'shita** 聞きました

kiite 聞いて → **ki̱kima̱'su** 聞きます

ki̱'-ito 生糸 raw silk

kiji きじ・雉 pheasant

ki̱'ji 1. 記事 article, news item, piece, write-up 2. 生地 material, cloth, fabric

ki̱'jitsu 期日 appointed day; deadline

ki̱-kaema̱'su 着替えます, **-ka̱'e̱ru** 着替える changes (clothes) [older form of **kigaema̱'su** 着替えます]

kika̱'i 機会 chance, opportunity, occasion

kika̱'i 機械 machine, machinery, instrument; **kikai-teki (na)** 機械的(な) mechanical

kikaku 1. 企画 plan(ning); **kikaku shima̱'su** 企画します plans 2. 規格 norm, standard; **kikaku̱'-ka** 規格化 standardization, ~ **-ka shima̱'su** 規格化します standardizes

kika̱'n 1. 期間 term, period 2. ~ **(no)** 季刊(の) quarterly; **kika̱'n-shi** 季刊誌 a quarterly 3. 機関 engine; instrument; agency, activity, organization; **kikan-jū** 機関銃 machine gun

kikanai 聞かない = **kikimase'n** 聞きません (not listen, not ask)

kikasema'su 聞かせます, **kikaseru** 聞かせる lets someone hear, tells, informs

kike 聞け 1. → **kikema'su** 聞けます [infinitive] 2. → **kikima'su** 聞きます [imperative] listen!

kike'ba 聞けば → **kikima'su** 聞きます (if one listen, ...)

kikema'su 聞けます, **kikeru** 聞ける can listen/hear, can ask

kiken 危険 danger, peril; ~ **(na)** 危険（な）dangerous

kikenai 聞けない = **kikemase'n** 聞けません (can't listen/hear/ask)

kikete 聞けて → **kikema'su** 聞けます

kiki 聞き → **kikima'su** 聞きます [infinitive]

ki'ki' 危機 crisis, critical moment, emergency

kikima'su, kiku 1. 聞きます, 聞く listens, hears; obeys; asks 2. 効きます, 効く takes effect, is effective, works

kiki-me 効き目 effect (effectiveness); ~ **ga arima'su** 効き目があります is effective

kiki-te 聞き手 hearer, listener

kikō 1. 気候 climate 2. 聞こう = **kikimashō'** 聞きましょう (let's listen/ask!)

kikoe 聞こえ → **kikoema'su** 聞こえます [infinitive]

kikoema'su 聞こえます, **kikoeru** 聞こえる can hear; is heard

kikoenai 聞こえない = **kikoemase'n** 聞こえません (not hear)

kikoku 帰国 returning to one's country (Japan); **kikoku shima'su** 帰国します returns from abroad

kiku 聞く・効く = **kikima'su** 聞きます・効きます

kiku' 菊 chrysanthemum

ki-ku'rage 木くらげ・木耳 tree-ears (an edible fungus)

kikya 聞きゃ; etc. 1. = **kike'ba** 聞けば (if one listen, ...) 2. ~ **shinai** 聞きゃしない = **kiki' ya/wa shinai** 聞きや/は しない = **kikanai** 聞かない, etc. (not listen, ...)

kikyū 気球 balloon

kimae ga i'i 気前がいい generous

kimari 1. 決まり settlement, arrangement; order; regulation 2. ~ **ga waru'i (desu)** きまり が悪い（です）is/feels embarrassed 3. 決まり → **kimarima'su** 決まります [infinitive]

kimarima'su 決まります, **kimaru** 決まる is settled, is arranged

kima'su 着ます, **kiru** 着る wears

kima'su 来ます, **ku'ru** 来る

comes

kimben (na) 勤勉(な) industrious, hardworking, diligent

kime きめ・肌理 grain, texture

kimema͏̀su 決めます, **kimeru** 決める settles, arranges, decides

kimi 1. 君・きみ you [*familiar*] **2.** 黄身 yolk (of egg)

kimi 気味 feeling, sensation; ~ **ga waru͏̀i** 気味が悪い nervous, apprehensive, weird(-feeling)

kim-ma͏̀kie 金蒔絵 gold lacquer

ki͏̀mmu 勤務 duty, service, work; ~ **shima(⌐)su** 勤務します works, is on duty

kimmu͏̄-sha 勤務者 worker, person(s) on duty

kimo͏̀ 肝 liver

kimochi 気持ち feeling, sensation; ~ **ga i͏̀i** 気持ちがいい it feels good, is comfortable; ~ **ga waru͏̀i** 気持ちが悪い is uncomfortable, is feeling bad/ unwell

ki-mono 着物 clothes; a kimono; ~ **-bu͏̀rashi** 着物ブラシ clothesbrush

kimpatsu (no) 金髪(の) blond

kimpira きんぴら・金平 fried burdock root and carrot strips served cold

ki-mu͏̀sume 生娘 virgin (female)

ki-muzukashi͏̀i 気難しい fussy

ki͏̀myō (na) 奇妙(な) strange, peculiar

ki͏̀n 金 gold

-⌐kin 金 money

ki͏̀na キナ quinine

kinai 着ない = **kimase͏̀n** 着ません (not wear)

ki͏̀nako 黄な粉 soybean meal/ flour

kinchō 緊張 strain, tension; ~ **shite ima͏̀su** 緊張しています is tense

kine͏̀m-bi 記念日 anniversary

kinen 記念 commemoration; **kine⌐n-hin** 記念品 souvenir; ~ **-ki͏̀tte/-gi͏̀tte** 記念切手/切手 commemorative stamp

kin'en 禁煙 smoking prohibited, no smoking; **kin'e⌐n-sha** 禁煙車 no(n)-smoking car

kingan (no) 近眼(の) nearsighted, shortsighted, myopic

ki͏̀ngyo 金魚 goldfish

ki ni 気に: **ki ni irima͏̀su (iru)** 気に入ります(入る) appeals to one, is pleasing; **(... ga) ki ni narima͏̀su** (...が)気になります worries (one); **(suru ~** する気に) gets in the mood (to do); **(... o) ki ni shima͏̀su** (...を)気にします worries about ... , minds

kini͏̀ine キニーネ quinine

ki-niku͏̀i 着にくい uncomfortable *(to wear)*

kin-iro (no) 金色(の) gold (color), golden

kin-jima͏̀su 禁じます, **-ji⌐ru** 禁じる forbids, prohibits

ki͡njo 近所 neighborhood, vicinity

kinka͡n きんかん・金柑 cumquat

ki͡nko 金庫 safe *(strongbox)*

ki͡nniku 筋肉 muscle

kinō͡ きのう・昨日 yesterday

ki-no-do͡ku 気の毒 pitiful, pitiable

ki͡ no ka͡ge 木の陰 shade *(of trees)*

ki͡ no kawa͡ 木の皮 bark *(of tree)*

ki͡noko きのこ・茸 mushroom

ki͡-no-me 木の芽 **1.** tree sprout **2.** pepper sprout

ki͡-no-mi 木の実 nuts, tree produce *(nuts, fruits, berries)*

kinō͡ no ban きのう［昨日］の晩 last night

Kinrō-ka͡nsha no hi͡ 勤労感謝の日 Labor Thanksgiving Day (23 November)

ki͡nryoku 筋力 muscle *(power)*

kinshi 1. 禁止 prohibition, ban; **kinshi shima͡su** 禁止します prohibits, bans **2.** 近視 = **kingan** 近眼 (nearsighted)

kinta͡ma͡ 金玉 testicle(s)

ki͡nu 絹 silk

Kin'yō͡bi 金曜日 Friday

kin'yū 金融 finance; **〜-shi͡jō** 金融市場 the money market

ki͡nzoku 金属 metal

ki o 気を: **〜 tsu͡kema͡su** 気を付けます (is) careful; **〜**

ushinaima͡su 気を失います loses consciousness, faints

kioku 記憶 memory; **kioku͡-ryoku** 記憶力 memory (capacity), retentiveness

kippa͡ri (to) きっぱり（と） definitely, firmly, flatly

kippu 切符 ticket; **kippu͡-uri** 切符売り ticket agent/seller; **kippu-u͡riba** 切符売り場 box office

kirai (na) 嫌い（な） is disliked; dislikes

kiraku (na) 気楽（な） carefree, comfortable; easygoing

kira͡nai 切らない = **kirimase͡n** 切りません (not cut)

ki(ra)rema͡su 着（ら）れます, **ki(ra)reru** 着（ら）れる can wear

kirasa͡nai 切らさない = **kirashimase͡n** 切らしません (not exhausts)

kirashima͡su 切らします, **kira͡su** 切らす exhausts the supply of, runs out of; **... o kira͡shite ima͡su** ...を切らしています is out of ... ; **shibire͡ o 〜** しびれを切らします loses patience

kira͡shite 切らして → **kirashima͡su** 切らします

kire͡ きれ・切れ a piece, a cut (of cloth)

ki͡re 切れ **1.** → **kirema͡su** 切れます, etc. (can cut, ...) [infinitive] **2.** → **kirima͡su** 切り

ます; etc. [imperative] cut it!

kire˺ba 着れば → **kima˺su** 着ます (if one wear)

ki˺reba 切れば → **kirima˺su** 切ります (if one cut)

ki˺rei (na) きれい［綺麗］(な) pretty; clean; neat, tidy; nice (-looking), attractive; ～ **ni shima˺su** きれいにします cleans/tidies it

-kiremase˺n 切れません, **-kire□nai** 切れない [verb infinitive +] cannot; **shi-kiremase˺n** し切れません, **-kire˺nai** し切れない cannot do it

kirema˺su 着れます, **kireru** 着れる = **ki(ra)rema˺su** 着(ら)れます, **ki(ra)reru** 着(ら)れる (can wear)

kirema˺su 切れます, **kire˺ru** 切れる 1. can cut; cuts (well) 2. runs out 3. breaks (off)

kire-me˺ 切れ目 a gap, a break, a pause

kire˺nai 切れない 1. dull(-edged), blunt 2. = **kiremase˺n** 切れません (cannot cut; not run out; not break)

kire˺reba 切れれば → **kirema˺su** 切れます; etc. (if one can cut; …)

ki˺rete 切れて → **kirema˺su** 切れます

kiri 1. 霧 fog, mist; ～ **ga fuka˺i** 霧が深い is foggy 2. 桐 pau-

lownia (tree or wood)

ki˺ri 1. 錐 a hole-punch, an awl, a drill 2. 切り → **kirima˺su** 切ります [infinitive]

kiri□-kabu 切り株 (tree) stump

kirima˺su 切ります, **ki˺ru** 切る cuts; cuts off, disconnects; hangs up (phone)

kirinuki 切り抜き clipping *(from newspaper, etc.)*

kirisame 霧雨 drizzle

Kirisuto キリスト Christ; ～ **-kyō** キリスト教 Christianity

ki□ritsu 規律 discipline

ki˺ro キロ 1. kilogram 2. kilometer 3. kilowatt 4. kiloliter

kirō˺ 切ろう = **kirimashō˺** 切りましょう (let's cut it!)

kiroku 記録 (historic) record; **kiroku shima˺su** 記録します records (an event)

kiru 着る = **kima˺su** 着ます (wears)

ki˺ru 切る = **kirima˺su** 切ります (cuts)

kirya 切りゃ 1. = **kire˺ba** 切れば 2. ～ **shinai** 切りゃしない = **ki˺ri ya/wa shinai** 切りや/はしない = **kira˺nai** 切らない; etc. (not cut; …)

ki˺ryō 器量 personal appearance, looks; ability

kisen 汽船 steamship

kise˺tsu 季節 season

kisha˺ 1. 汽車 (nonelectric/

steam) train **2.** 記者 = **shimbun-kí'sha** 新聞記者 newspaper reporter, journalist

kishi' 岸 shore, coast, bank

kishi'-men きしめん [Nagoya] = **himokawa(-u'don)** 紐革うどん

kishō-dai 気象台 weather observatory

kishu'ku'sha 寄宿舎 dormitory; boarding house

kiso' 基礎 foundation (base)

kisoima'su 競います, **kiso'u** 競う competes, vies; ... **o kiso'tte** ...を競って competing (in competition) for ...

kiso'ku 規則 rule, regulation

kissa'-ten 喫茶店 a tearoom, a coffee house, a café

ki'(s)su キ(ッ)ス kiss; ~ **shima'(')su** キ(ッ)スします kisses

kisu' きす・鱚 sillago (fish)

kita 着た = **kima'shita** 着ました (wore)

kita' 来た = **kima'shita** 来ました (came)

kita' 北 north; **kita-guchi** 北口 the north exit/entrance

Kita-A'merika 北アメリカ North America

kita'e 鍛え → **kitaema'su** 鍛えます [infinitive]

kitaema'su 鍛えます, **kitae'ru** 鍛える forges, tempers; drills, disciplines

kitai 1. 期待 expectation; ~ **shima'su** 期待します expects, anticipates **2.** 気体 vapor, a gas

ki-tai 着たい wants to wear

ki-ta'i 来たい wants to come

kitaku 帰宅 returning home; **kitaku shima'su** 帰宅します returns home

ki-taku 着たく wanting to wear; ~ **arimase'n** 着たくありません doesn't want to wear

ki-ta'ku 来たく wanting to come; ~ **arimase'n** 来たくありません doesn't want to come

kitana'i 汚い dirty; untidy, messy

kita-yori (no kaze) 北寄り(の風) northerly (wind)

kite 着て → **kima'su** 着ます (wears); ~ **ikima'su/kima'su** 着て行きます/来ます wears it there/here

kite' 来て → **kima'su** 来ます (comes)

kitei 規定 regulation, rule, stipulation; ~ **no ...** 規定の... regular, stipulated, compulsory; ~ **shima'su** 規定します prescribes, stipulates, requires

kite'i-shoku 規定食 diet

kiteki 汽笛 whistle (steam)

kitsuen 喫煙 smoking; **kitsue'n-sha** 喫煙者 smoker; **kitsue'n-**

shitsu 喫煙室 smoking room;
~ **shima'su** 喫煙します
smokes

kitsui きつい 1. tight 2. severe
3. bold

kitsune きつね・狐 fox

ki'tta' 切った = **kirima'shita** 切
りました (cut)

kitte⌐ 切手 (postage) stamp;
kitte-chō 切手帳 stamp album

ki'tte 切って → **kirima'su** 切り
ます (cut)

kitto きっと surely, doubtless,
no doubt, undoubtedly

kiwa' 際 brink, edge

kiwado'i きわどい・際どい
dangerous, delicate, ticklish

kiwamarima'su 極まります,
kiwama'ru 極まる comes to an
end; gets carried to extremes

kiwamema'su, kiwame'ru 1. 極
めます, 極める carries to ex-
tremes 2. 究めます, 究める
investigates thoroughly

kiwa'mete きわめて・極めて extremely

ki'ya shinai = **ki'wa shinai** 1. 着
やしない＝着はしない ＝
kinai 着ない (not wear) 2. 来
やしない＝来はしない ＝
ko'nai 来ない (not come)

kiyō 着よう = **kimashō'** 着まし
ょう (let's wear)

ki'yō (na) 器用(な) skillful, nimble, clever

kizamima'su 刻みます, **kizamu**

刻む chops fine; carves;
notches, nicks

kizu 傷 wound; scratch, crack,
flaw, blemish; fault, defect

kizu 着ず, **kizu ni** 着ずに =
kina'ide 着ないで (not wearing)

kizu-ato 傷跡 scar

ki-zu'ite 気付いて → **ki-
zukima'su** 気付きます

ki-zu'ka'i 気遣い・気づかい anxiety, concern, worry

ki-zuka'i 気遣い・気づかい → **ki-
zukaima'su** 気遣い[気づかい]
ます [infinitive]

ki-zukaima'su 気遣い[気づか
い]ます, **ki-zuka'u** 気遣う・気
づかう is anxious/worried
about, is concerned over

ki-zuka'tte 気遣って・気づかっ
て → **ki-zukaima'su** 気遣いま
す・気づかいます

ki-zukima'su 気付きます, **-zu'ku**
気付く notices

kizu-tsukema'su 傷付けます,
-tsuke'ru 傷付ける wounds, injures, damages

kizu-tsukima'su 傷付きます,
-tsu'ku 傷付く gets wounded,
injured, damaged

ko 子 child (= **kodomo** 子供);
person

ko' 粉 flour (= **kona'** 粉)

ko-... 小... little, small

...-ko ...個 (counts small objects)

...-ko ...湖 lake

kō こう (**kō** こう + PARTICLE or **de**su です) this way, so, like this

kō 香 incense

kō-... 高... high; **kō-ke**tsu**atsu** 高血圧 high blood pressure

...-kō 1. ...港 port (of ...); **Kōbe**-kō 神戸港 the port of Kobe **2.** ...校 school, branch (school); (bookish counter for schools); **hachi-jū sa**n-kō **mo no kokuritsu-da**igaku 83校もの国立大学 a good 83 national universities

kōba 工場 factory

kobamimasu 拒みます, **koba**mu 拒む refuses, rejects; opposes, resists

kōban 交番 police box

kobande 拒んで → **kobamima**su 拒みます

Kōbe 神戸 Kobe; **Kōbe**-Eki 神戸駅 Kobe Station; **Kōbe**-kō 神戸港 the port of Kobe

koboremasu こぼれます, **kobore**ru こぼれる it spills

koboshimasu こぼします, **kobo**su こぼす spills it; (**guchi o ~** 愚痴をこぼします) grumbles, complains

kobu こぶ・瘤 bump, knob, swelling

kobu こぶ・昆布 = **ko**mbu 昆布 (kelp)

kō-bun 子分 henchman, subordinate, follower

kobune 小舟 small boat

kobushi こぶし・拳 fist

kōcha 紅茶 (black) tea

kōchi こち・鯒 flathead *(fish)*

kōchi コーチ coach *(sports)*

kochira こちら **1.** this one (of two) **2.** here, this way **3.** I/me, we/us; **~ ko**so こちらこそ I am the one who should be expressing apology/gratitude.

kochira-gawa こちら側 this (my/our) side

kochō 誇張 exaggeration; **~ shima**su 誇張します exaggerates

kōchō 校長 principal/head of a school

kodai 古代 ancient times; **~ no** 古代の ancient

kodama こだま・木霊・谺 echo

kōdan 1. 公団 public corporation **2.** 講壇 lecture platform

kodo **1.** コード cord **2.** コード code **3.** 高度 high degree, altitude

kōdō 1. 公道 highway **2.** 行動 action, behavior **3.** 講堂 public (lecture) hall, auditorium

kodomo 子供 child; **kodomo**-tachi 子供達[たち] children; **~ no hi** こども[子供]の日 Children's Day (5 May)

koe 超え → **koema**su 超えます **1.** [infinitive] **2.** [imperative] **koe ro** 超えろ, **koe** yo 超えよ cross it!

ko̅e 1. 声 voice; cry; ~ **o da̅shi̅te** 声を出して aloud, out loud **2.** 肥え → **koema̅su** 肥えます (get fat) [infinitive]

koema̅su 超[越]えます, **koeru** 超[越]える crosses (a height, an obstacle)

koema̅su 肥えます, **koe̅ru** 肥える gets fat (= **futorima̅su** 太ります)

ko̅en 1. 公園 public park **2.** 講演 lecture, speech, talk **3.** 後援 support, backing

koenai 超[越]えない = **koemase̅n** 超[越]えません (not cross)

koe̅nai 肥えない = **koemase̅n** 肥えません (not get fat)

koe(ra)rema̅su 超[越]え(ら)れます, **koe(ra)reru** 超[越]え(ら)れる can cross

koeru 超[越]える = **koema̅su** 超[越]えます (crosses)

koe̅ru 肥える = **koema̅su** 肥えます (gets fat)

koete 超[越]えて → **koema̅su** 超[越]えます (crosses)

ko̅ete 肥えて → **koema̅su** 肥えます (gets fat)

ko̅fu 工夫 workman

ko̅fuku 1. 幸福 happiness; ~ **(na)** 幸福(な) happy **2.** 降伏 surrender; ~ **shima̅su** 降伏します surrenders

ko̅fun 興奮 excitement; ~ **shi̅te ima̅su** 興奮しています is excited

ko̅gai 公害 (environmental) pollution

ko̅gai 郊外 suburbs, suburbia

ko̅gaku 工学 engineering

ko̅gan 湖岸 lakeshore

ko̅gan 睾丸 testicle(s)

koga̅nai 漕がない = **kogimase̅n** 漕ぎません (not row)

kogashima̅su 焦がします, **koga̅su** 焦がす scorches it

kogata (no) 小型(の) small-size (model)

ko̅ge 1. 焦げ・漕げ → **kogema̅su** 焦げます・漕げます [infinitive] **2.** 漕げ → **kogima̅su** 漕ぎます [imperative] row!

ko̅geba 漕げば → **kogima̅su** 漕ぎます (if one row)

ko̅geki 攻撃 attack; **ko̅geki shima̅su** 攻撃します attacks

kogema̅su, koge̅ru 1. 焦げます, 焦げる gets scorched/burned **2.** 漕げます, 漕げる can row

koge̅nai 焦げない; 漕げない = **kogemase̅n** 焦げません; 漕げません (not get scorched; cannot row)

koge̅reba 焦げれば; 漕げれば, **koge̅rya** 焦げりゃ; 漕げりゃ → **kogema̅su** 焦げます; 漕げます (if it get scorched; if one can row)

ko̅gete 焦げて・漕げて → **kogema̅su** 焦げます・漕げます

kōgi 講義 lecture

kōˈgi 抗議 protest; ～ **shima(ˈ)su** 抗議します protests

kogimaˈsu 漕ぎます・こぎます, **koˈgu** 漕ぐ・こぐ rows (a boat)

kogiˈtte 小切手 (bank) check

kogōˈ 漕ごう ＝ **kogimashō** 漕ぎましょう (let's row!)

kōgo 口語 spoken language, colloquial (word); ～**-teki (na)** 口語的(な) colloquial

kogoe 小声 low voice, whisper

Kōgōˈ(-sama) 皇后(様) the Empress; **Kōgō-heˈika** 皇后陛下 Her Majesty the Empress

kogoto (o-koˈgoto) 小言・こごと (お小言) scolding, complaint

koˈgu 漕ぐ・こぐ ＝ **kogimaˈsu** 漕ぎます・こぎます (rows a boat)

koˈgya 漕ぎゃ 1. ＝ **koˈgeba** 漕げば (if one row) 2. ～ **shinai** 漕ぎゃしない ＝ **koˈgi ya/wa shinai** 漕ぎや/はしない ＝ **kogaˈnai** 漕がない・こがない (not row)

kōˈgyō 工業 industry

kohada こはだ shad

kōhai 後輩 one's junior (colleague, fellow student)

kohaku こはく・琥珀 amber

koˈhan 湖畔 lakeside

kōhei (na) 公平(な) fair, impartial

kōhiˈi コーヒー coffee; **kōhii-**

jaˈwan/-kaˈppu コーヒー茶碗 /カップ coffee cup; **kōhii-poˈtto** コーヒーポット coffee pot; **kōhiˈi-ten** コーヒー店, **kōhii-ya** コーヒー屋 coffee shop/house

ko-hiˈtsuˈji 小羊・子羊 lamb

kōhyō 好評 favorable criticism

koˈi 請い・乞い request

koˈi 1. こい・鯉 carp (fish) 2. 恋 love 3. ～ **(no)** 故意(の) deliberate; ～ **ni** 故意に deliberately 4. 濃い deep (color), strong (coffee, tea), well saturated; **koˈku arimaseˈn** 濃くありません is not strong 5. 来い → **kimaˈsu** 来ます [imperative] come!

kōˈi 1. 好意・厚意 goodwill, favor; ～ **o misemaˈsu** 好意・厚意を見せます does a favor 2. 行為 act, deed; behavior

koibito 恋人 sweetheart

koˈida 漕いだ ＝ **kogimaˈshita** 漕ぎました (rowed)

koˈide 漕いで → **kogimaˈsu** 漕ぎます・こぎます

koˈin コイン coin; **koin-roˈkkā** コインロッカー coin locker; **koiˈn-shō** コイン商 coin dealer

kōin 工員 factory worker

koi-noˈbori 鯉のぼり carp streamers (for the Boys' Festival)

koinu 小犬 puppy

koishi 小石 pebble

koitsu こいつ this damn one;
  koitsu-ra こいつら these
  damn ones

kōji 孤児 orphan; **koji-in** 孤児
  院 orphanage

kōji 工事 construction work;
  kōji-chū 工事中 under construction

kojiki こじき・乞食 beggar

kōjin 個人 an individual; **kojin-
  teki (na)** 個人的（な）individ-
  ual, personal

kojirema'su こじれます,
  kojire'ru こじれる gets
  twisted, complicated, entangled; *(illness)* worsens

kōjitsu 口実 excuse, pretext

kōjō 工場 = **kōba** 工場 factory, plant

kō'ka 1. 効果 effect 2. 硬貨 coin

kō'ka'ge 木陰 shade *(of trees)*

kō'kai 航海 voyage; ~
  shima'su 航海します makes a
  voyage, sails, navigates

kō'kai 後悔 regret; ~
  shima(')su 後悔します
  regrets

koka'in コカイン cocaine

kōkai (no) 公開（の）open to the
  public, open, public; ~
  shima'su 公開します opens it
  to the public

kōkan 交換 exchange; ~
  shima'su 交換します ex-
  changes, trades

kōka'n-shu 交換手 telephone
  operator

koke こけ・苔 moss

kō-ke'iki 好景気 prosperity,
  good business conditions

kō-ki'atsu 高気圧 high
  (barometric) pressure

kōki'shin 好奇心 curiosity, inquisitiveness

ko'kka 国家 nation

kokkai 国会 assembly, parliament, congress, Diet (=
  gi'kai 議会)

kokkei (na) こっけい［滑稽］（な）
  amusing, funny

kokki 国旗 (national) flag

ko'kku(-san) コック（さん）cook

kokkyō 国境 border *(of country)*

koko ここ here, this place

kō-kō 高校 senior high school

ko'ko'a ココア cocoa

kōkoku 広告 advertisement

ko'kona'ttsu ココナッツ coconut

kokonoka 九日 nine days; the
  9th day (of month)

koko'notsu 九つ nine; nine years
  old

koko'ro (o-kokoro) 心（お心）
  mind, heart, spirit, feeling; ~
  kara (no) 心から（の）heart-
  felt, sincere

kokoro-boso'i 心細い lonely

kokoro'mi' 試み trial, attempt, test

kokoro'mi 試み →
  kokoromima'su 試みます

kokoromimá su 試みます, **kokoromí ru** 試みる tries, attempts, tests

kokoro-mochi⌐ 心持ち feelings, spirit, mood

kokoro-zashi⌐ **(o-kokorozashi)** 志(お志) 1. mind; intention; purpose 2. ambition, hope 3. goodwill, kindness; gift

kokoro-zuke⌐ 心付け tip, gratuity

kōkō⌐**-sei** 高校生 (senior) high school student

...⌐**-koku** ...国 (name of) country; **koku-...** 国... national, state

kokuban 黒板 blackboard; **kokubá n-fuki** 黒板拭き eraser

kōkū⌐**-bin** 航空便, **kōkū-yū**⌐**bin** 航空郵便 airmail

kokubō 国防 national defense

kokudō 国道 highway

kōkū-gá isha 航空会社 airline (company)

kōkū⌐**-hei** 航空兵 airman

Kokujin 黒人 Negro, black (person)

kōkū⌐**-ki** 航空機 aircraft

kokumin 国民 a people, a nation; national(s), citizen(s)

koku motsu 穀物 grain (cereal)

koku nai (no) 国内(の) internal, domestic, inland

kokuritsu(-) 国立 national, government-established

koku rui 穀類 cereal(s), grain

kokusai 国際: ~**-dé nwa** 国際電話 international phone call; ~**-teki (na)** 国際的(な) international

Kokusai-ré ngō 国際連合 United Nations

kokusan (no) 国産(の) domestic(ally made), made in Japan

kokuseki 国籍 nationality

kōkū-shó kan 航空書簡 an air letter, aerogram

ko kyo 皇居 palace (in Tokyo); the Imperial Palace

ko kyō 故郷 hometown, birthplace

kōkyō-ryō kin 公共料金 utility bills/charges

kokyū 呼吸 respiration, breathing

kōkyū (na) 高級(な) high-class/-grade, high-ranking; fancy; **kōkyū**⌐**-hin** 高級品 fancy goods

ko ma こま・独楽 a toy top; **koma-má washi** こま[独楽]回し top-spinning

komaka i 細かい 1. fine, small 2. detailed, exact 3. thrifty 4. small (change); **komaká ku shimá su** 細かくします cashes it into smaller bills/coins

koma⌐**-mono** 小間物 notions, haberdashery, dime-store goods

komamo˺no˺-ya 小間物屋 dime store, haberdasher; ~ **o hirogema˺su** 小間物屋を広げます vomits

komarima˺su 困ります, **koma˺ru** 困る gets perplexed, embarrassed, troubled; is at a loss; is in need; **koma˺ru tokoro˺** 困るところ trouble *(difficulty)*; **koma˺tta koto˺** 困った事 predicament, mess, plight

ko˺mban 今晩 tonight; **Komban wa** こんばんは Good evening.

kombō 棍棒 club, billy-club, bludgeon

ko˺mbu 昆布 kelp (a kind of seaweed)

kome˺ 米, **o-kome** お米 rice *(hulled, uncooked)*

ko˺me 込め → **komema˺su** 込めます [infinitive]

ko˺meba 込めば・混めば → **komima˺su** 込みます・混みます (if it get crowded)

komema˺su 込めます, **kome˺ru** 込める includes

kome˺reba 込めれば, **kome˺rya** 込めりゃ → **komema˺su** 込めます (if one include)

ko˺mete 込めて → **komema˺su** 込めます

kome˺-ya 米屋, **o-komeya** お米屋 rice dealer/store

ko˺michi 小道 path, lane

komi-i˺tta 込み入った complicated, intricate

komima˺su 込みます・混みます, **ko˺mu** 込む・混む gets crowded

kōmoku 項目 item

ko˺mon 顧問 consultant, adviser

komo˺ri 子守 babysitter

kō˺mori こうもり・蝙蝠 1. bat 2. (= **kōmori-ga˺sa** こうもり傘) umbrella

ko˺mpasu コンパス compass *(for drafting)*

kompo˺n 根本 foundation, basis; **kompon-teki (na)** 根本的(な) fundamental, basic

kompyū˺tā コンピューター computer

komu˺gi 小麦 wheat

kōmu˺-in 公務員 government worker/employee

kōmurima˺su こうむります・被ります, **kōmu˺ru** こうむる・被る sustains, suffers, incurs

ko˺mya 込みゃ・混みゃ = **ko˺meba** 込めば・混めば (if it get crowded)

ko˺n 紺 = **kon-iro** 紺色 dark blue

kona˺ (o-ko˺na) 粉(お粉) powder; flour

kona-gu˺suri 粉薬 powdered medicine

ko˺nai 来ない = **kimase˺n** 来ません (does not come)

kō˺nai 構内 campus; ~ **(no)** 構内(の) intramural

konaida˺ こないだ = **kono-aida˺**

この間 the other day, lately

ko͡nakatta 来なかった＝ **kimase͡n deshi̱ta** 来ませんでした (didn't come)

kona-mi͡ruku 粉ミルク powdered milk, dry milk

konashima͞su こなします, **konasu** こなす 1. powders, pulverizes, grinds up; digests 2. (ful)fills, manages (to do it); **chū͡mon o ~** 注文をこなします fills an order; **ka͡zu de ~** 数でこなします relies on numbers (sales volume)

konchū 昆虫 insect

konda͡te͡ 献立 menu

ko͡nde 込んで・混んで → **komima͞su** 込みます・混みます; **~ ima͞su** 込んで[混んで]います is crowded

ko͡ndo 今度 this time; next time; last time

kondō͡mu コンドーム condom

ko͡ne コネ connection, "pull"; **(hi̱to ni) ~ o tsukema͞su (tsuke͡ru)** (人に)コネを付けます(付ける) establishes a connection, gets pull (with a person)

kone͡ko 小猫・子猫 kitten

kongetsu 今月 this month

ko͡ngo 今後 from now on, in the future

kongō͡-seki 金剛石 diamond

kōnin (no) 公認(の) authorized, certified; **kōnin-kaike͡ishi** 公

認会計士 certified public accountant (CPA), chartered accountant

kon-iro 紺色 dark blue

konkuri͡ito コンクリート concrete *(cement)*

konkū͡ru コンクール prize contest

ko͡nkyo 根拠 basis, grounds, authority, evidence

konna ... こんな... such a, this kind of; **~ ni** こんなに to this extent, this much

ko͡nnan 困難 difficulty, trouble, hardship; **~ (na)** 困難(な) difficult

Konnichi wa こんにちは・今日は Good afternoon; Hello!

konnya͡ku こんにゃく devil's-tongue root made into gelatin strips

kono ... この... this ... , these ...

kono-aida͡ この間 the other day, lately

kono-goro この頃 recently

kono ma͡e (no) この前(の) last time, the last (...)

ko͡nome 木の芽＝**ki͡-no-me** 木の芽 1. tree sprout 2. pepper sprout

konomi͡ (o-konomi) 好み(お好み) liking, taste; **~ no ...** 好みの... that one likes, that is to one's taste/liking, favorite ...

konomima͞su 好みます, **kono͡mu** 好む likes, is fond

of, prefers

kono̅nde 好んで → **konomima̅su** 好みます

kono-tsu̅gi̅ この次 next time

konran 混乱 mess *(disorder)*, confusion

ko̅nro こんろ・コンロ stove *(portable cooking)*

konsa̅rutanto コンサルタント consultant

konseki 痕跡 trace, mark, vestige; ～ **o nokoshima̅su (noko̅su)** 痕跡を残します(残す) leaves a mark

ko̅nse̅nto コンセント *(electricity)* outlet, (light) plug

konshi̅n-kai 懇親会 reception, get-together party

konshū 今週 this week

konsome コンソメ thin Western soup, consomme

kōn-suta̅chi コーンスターチ cornstarch

konta̅kuto コンタクト, **kontakuto-re̅nzu** コンタクトレンズ contact lenses

ko̅nte̅na コンテナ container *(for transporting goods)*

ko̅ntesuto コンテスト contest

ko̅n'ya 今夜 tonight

kon'yaku 婚約 engagement (to be married); (... **to) kon'yaku shite ima̅su** (...と)婚約しています is engaged (to ...)

kon'yoku 混浴 mixed bathing

ko̅nzatsu 混雑 confusion, jum-

ble, disorder

ko̅pii コピー copy *(photocopy)*

ko̅ppa̅ こっぱ・木っ端 chip *(of wood)*

koppu コップ a glass, a cup

kōra 甲羅 shell *(of tortoise, etc.)*

kōra コーラ cola

koraema̅su こらえます, **kora̅e̅ru** こらえる 1. stands, bears 2. controls, restrains, represses

kōranai 凍らない = **kōrimase̅n** 凍りません (not freeze)

korarema̅su 来られます, **korare̅ru** 来られる 1. can come (*also* **korema̅su** 来れます, **kore̅ru** 来れる) 2. [passive] has them come (to one's distress); [HONO-RIFIC] comes (= **irasshaima̅su** いらっしゃいます)

kōrasema̅su 凍らせます, **kōraseru** 凍らせる freezes it

kō̅rasu コーラス chorus, choir

kore これ this one; ～ **kara** これから from now on; ～ **to yū** ... これという... specific, particular

ko̅reba 凝れば → **korima̅su** 凝ります (if one get engrossed; if it get stiff)

korema̅su 来れます, **kore̅ru** 来れる = **korarema̅su** 来られます (can come)

kore̅nai 来れない = **korare̅nai** 来られない = **koraremase̅n**

来られません (cannot come)

kore-ra これら these

ko'rera コレラ cholera

kore'ru 来れる = **korema'su** 来
れます (can come)

kori' 凝り・こり **1.** stiffness,
hardening; **ka'ta (no)** ~ 肩
(の)凝り shoulder stiffness, a
stiff shoulder **2.** → **korima'su**
凝ります [infinitive]

kōri 1. 氷 ice **2.** 凍り →
kōrima'su 凍ります [infini-
tive]

ko'ri/ko'ri 行李/行李 wicker
trunk

korima'su 凝ります・こります,
ko'ru 凝る・こる **1.** gets
engrossed/absorbed (in)
2. (shoulder) gets stiff

kōrima'su 凍ります, **kōru** 凍る
it freezes

kōritsu (no) 公立(の) public,
municipal, prefectural

korobima'su 転びます, **korobu**
転ぶ falls down, tumbles

korogarima'su 転がります,
korogaru 転がる it rolls,
tumbles

korogashima'su 転がします,
korogasu 転がす rolls it

korosarema'su 殺されます,
korosareru 殺される gets
killed

koroshima'su 殺します, **korosu**
殺す kills

ko'ru 凝る・こる = **korima'su** 凝

りす・こります

kōru 凍る = **kōrima'su** 凍りま
す

ko'ruku コルク cork (=
koruku'-sen コルク栓);
koruku'-nuki コルク抜き
corkscrew

korya こりゃ = **kore wa** これは
(as for this)

ko'rya 凝りゃ = **ko'reba** 凝れば
(if one get engrossed; if it get
stiff)

ko'ryo 考慮 consideration, reflection, thought; ~ **ni irema'su**
(ireru) 考慮に入れます(入れ
る) takes into consideration/
account; ~ **shima'su** 考慮し
ます considers

ko'ryō' 香料 spice

koryōri-ya 小料理屋 small traditional Japanese restaurant

kōryu 交流 AC (alternating current)

ko'sa 濃さ strength (of saturation), deepness (of color)

kosaema'su こさえます, **kosaeru**
こさえる = **koshiraema'su** こ
しらえます・拵えます

kōsai 交際 social relations, company

ko-saji 小匙・小さじ teaspoon

kosame 小雨 light rain, drizzle

kōsan 降参 surrender; ~
shima'su 降参します surrenders

kosanai 越さない =

koshimase͡n 越しません, etc.
(not go over; not …)

kosasema͡su 来させます,
kosase͡ru 来させる has/lets
one come

kosase͡nai 来させない =
kosasemase͡n 来させません
(not have/let one come)

kosa͡sete 来させて →
kosasema͡su 来させます

kōsa͡-ten 交差点 an intersection (of streets), a crossing

kose 越せ・漉せ 1. → **kosema͡su**
越せます・漉せます [infinitive] 2. → **koshima͡su** 越します・漉します [imperative]

kose͡ba 越せば → **koshima͡su** 越
します, etc. (if it exceed; if
…)

kōsei 1. 構成 constituency, construction, composition 2. 更正
revival, reformation; regeneration 3. 公正 impartiality; ~
(na) 公正(な) impartial, fair
4. 校正 proofreading; ~
shima͡su 校正します proofreads

kōsei-bu͡sshitsu 抗生物質 antibiotic(s)

kōsei shima͡su 1. 構成します
constitutes 2. 更正します
reforms, starts a new life
3. 校正します proofreads

kosema͡su, koseru 1. 越せます,
越せる can go over 2. 漉せます, 漉せる can filter/strain it

3. 越せます, 越せる can move
(house)

kōsen 光線 ray, beam (of light),
light

kosenai 越せない = **kosemase͡n**
越せません ⌜せます
kosete 越せて → **kosema͡su** 越

kosha 越しゃ 1. = **kose͡ba** 越せ
ば, etc. (if it exceed; if …)
2. ~ **shinai** 越しゃしない =
koshi͡ ya/wa shinai 越しや/は
しない = **kosanai** 越さない,
etc. (not exceed; not …)

kōsha 後者 the latter

koshi 1. 腰 loin(s), hips, lower
part of back; (~ **no kubire** 腰
のくびれ) waist 2. 越し →
koshima͡su 越します

kō͡shi 講師 instructor, lecturer

Kōshi 孔子 Confucius

koshi-ka͡ke 腰掛け → **koshi-
kakema͡su** 腰掛けます [infinitive] ⌜bench
koshi-ka͡ke 腰掛け seat, chair,

koshi-kakema͡su 腰掛けます,
-kake͡ru 腰掛ける sits down

koshi-maki 腰巻き loincloth; petticoat

koshima͡su, kosu 1. 越します,
越す goes over; exceeds 2. こ
します・漉します, こす・漉す
filters/strains it 3. 越します,
越す = **hikkoshima͡su** 引っ越
します moves house

kōshin 1. 行進 march(ing) 2. 更
新 renewal

kōshin shima'su (suru) 1. 行進し
ます(する) marches **2.** 更新し
ます(する) renews (a contract
etc.)

koshi-o⌐¹bi 腰帯 girdle

koshiraema'su こしらえます・拵
えます, **koshiraeru** こしらえ
る・拵える makes, concocts

koshite 越して・こ[濾]して →
koshima'su 越します・こ[濾]し
ます

koshō 故障 **1.** breakdown,
something wrong; **~ shima'su**
故障します it breaks down
(gets inoperative) **2.** hindrance, impediment

koshō' こしょう・胡椒 pepper

kōshō 交渉 negotiations; connections

kōshoku (na) 好色(な) erotic;
lecherous

kōshū 公衆 the public, the
masses; (**~ no** 公衆の)
public; **~-de'nwa** 公衆電話
public telephone

... ko'so ...こそ precisely

kosō 越そう・こ[濾]そう =
koshimasho' 越しましょう・こ
[濾]しましょう (let's ... !)

kōsō (no) 高層(の) highrise; **~
-bi'ru** 高層ビル highrise
building, skyscraper

kōsoku 高速 high speed; **~
-dō'ro** 高速道路 expressway,
freeway; **~-gi'(y)a** 高速ギア
[ヤ] high gear

kosu 越す・こ[濾]す =
koshima'su 越します・こ[濾]
します

kō'su コース course; (traffic,
swim) lane; a set series of
chef's choices, a set meal

kōsui 香水 perfume

kosu'ri こすり → **kosurima'su**
こすります・擦ります [infini-
tive]

kosurima'su こすります・擦りま
す, **kosu'ru** こする・擦る rubs,
scrapes

kosu'tte こすって・擦って →
kosurima'su こすります・擦り
ます

kota'e 答え・応え an answer, a
response

kota'e 答え・応え → **kotaema'su**
答えます・応えます **1.** [infini-
tive] **2.** [imperative] **kotae'ro**
答えろ, **kotae'yo** 答えよ

kotaema'su 答えます・応えます,
kota'e'ru 答える・応える
answers, responds

kotai 固体 a solid

kōtai 交替 alternation; **~
shima'su** 交替します alter-
nates, shifts (with)

Kōta'ishi 皇太子, **Kōta'ishi-sama**
皇太子様 the Crown Prince

kotatsu (o-ko'tatsu, o-ko'ta)
こたつ・炬燵(おこたつ, おこ
た) traditional quilt-covered
heating arrangement (foot
warmer)

kotchí こっち = **kochira** こちら

kōtei 校庭 campus, school grounds

kōtetsu 鋼鉄 steel

koto 事 thing, matter; fact; words, sentence; case, circumstance, happening; experience; ... **suru koto ga arimásu** ...する事があります does it, does it sometimes; ... **suru koto wa arimasén** ...する事はありません never does it; ... **shita koto ga arimásu** ...した事があります has done it; ... **shita koto wa arimasén** ...した事はありません has never done it; ... **(suru/shinai) koto wa arimasén** ...(する/しない)事はありません it isn't that one (does/doesn't, will/won't do it); ... **(suru) koto ni shimásu** ...(する)事にします decides to (do it)

koto 琴 = **o-koto** お琴 Japanese harp

kōto コート 1. coat 2. (athletic) court

kotoba (o-kotoba) 言葉(お言葉) 1. word, words; sentence (spoken); remark 2. speech 3. language

kōtō-gakkō 高等学校 (senior) high school; ~ **no seíto** 高等学校の生徒 (= **kōkō-sei** 高校生) high school student

kotogára 事柄 affair, matter

koto-ji 琴柱 the bridges on a Japanese harp 「freeze

kōtōketsu-zai 抗凍結剤 anti-

kotonarimásu 異なります, **kotonáru** 異なる is different, differs; **kotonátte imásu** 異なっています is different; **kotonátta ...** 異なった... different

koto-ni ことに・殊に especially; moreover, what is more

kōtō (no) 口頭(の) oral, verbal; **kōtō-shímon** 口頭試問 oral examination

ko-tori 小鳥 bird

kotoshi 今年 this year

kotowári 断り refusal; notice, warning; permission; ~ **mo náku** 断りもなく without notice/permission/leave

kotowarimásu 断ります, **kotowáru** 断る 1. refuses, declines, begs off 2. makes excuses 3. gives notice 4. dismisses, lays off, fires

kotowaza ことわざ・諺 a proverb

kotozúke ことづけ・言付け, **kotozúte** ことづて・言づて a message (for someone)

kotsu こつ・コツ knack, trick

kōtsū 交通 traffic, transportation; communication(s); ~ **-hyóshiki** 交通標識 traffic signs; ~ **-jútai** 交通渋滞 traffic jam; ～-**kō᷇sha** 交通公社 Japan Travel Bureau; ～-**shi᷇ngō** 交通信号 traffic signal(s)

ko-tsu᷇zumi 小鼓 small hourglass-shaped drum

ko᷇tta 凝った ＝ **korima᷇shita** 凝りました (got stiff)

kōtta 凍った ＝ **kōrima᷇shita** 凍りました (it froze)

ko᷇tte 凝って ＝ **korima᷇su** 凝ります (gets stiff)

kōtte 凍って → **kōrima᷇su** 凍ります; ～ **ima᷇su** 凍っています is frozen ⌈tiques

kottō᷇-hin 骨董品 curios, an-

ko-uri 小売り retail; ～ **shima᷇su** 小売りします retails, sells retail

kowagarima᷇su こわがります・怖[恐]がります, **kowaga᷇ru** こわがる・怖[恐]がる fears, takes fright, is afraid

kowa᷇i こわい・怖[恐]い afraid; frightful; terrific

kowarema᷇su 壊れます, **koware᷇ru** 壊れる it breaks/smashes

kowaremo᷇no 壊れ物 fragile (article); **kowaremono-chū᷇i** 壊れ物注意 Handle With Care

koware-yasu᷇i 壊れやすい fragile, easily broken, breakable

kowashima᷇su 壊します, **kowa᷇su** 壊す breaks/smashes

it, destroys; **kuruma o** ～ 車を壊します wrecks a car; **karada o** ～ 体を壊します ruins one's health, **o-naka o** ～ おなかを壊します develops stomach trouble; **hito no ki᷇bun o** ～ 人の気分を壊します spoils a person's mood, makes a person feel bad

koya 小屋 hut, shed, cabin

koyama 小山 hill

koyō 雇用 employment (hiring)

koyō᷇ 来よう ＝ **kimashō᷇** 来ましょう (let's come!)

koyō᷇ji 小楊枝 toothpick

koyomi᷇ 暦 calendar

kō yū (iu) ... こうゆう（いう）... this kind/sort of ... , such ... (＝ **konna** こんな)

kōza 口座 an account; ～ **o hirakima᷇su** 口座を開きます opens an account

kō᷇zan 鉱山 a mine

ko᷇-zara (o-ko᷇zara) 小皿（お小皿） saucer

kōzen (no/to) 公然（の/と） open(ly), public(ly)

ko-zeni 小銭 small change

kozō᷇ 小僧・こぞう young monk (**kozō-san** 小僧さん); shopboy, apprentice; kid

kōzō 構造 structure, makeup, organization

ko᷇zu 来ず, **ko᷇zu ni** 来ずに ＝ **kona᷇ide** 来ないで (not coming)

ko͞ozuchi 小槌 a small hammer

kō͞ozui 洪水 flood

ko͞ozukai 1. 小使い janitor, custodian; attendant; servant 2. 小遣い (= **o-ko͞ozukai** お小遣い) pin money, pocket money

kozu͞otsumi 小包 package, parcel

ku͞o 1. 九 (= **kyū** 九) nine 2. 句 (= **mo͞onku** 文句) phrase

ku͞o 区, ...⁻**ku** ...区 a ward (in a city)

...⁻ku ...く: ADJECTIVE ～ being, so as to be, ...⁻ly; ～ **arimase͞on (na͞oi)** ...くありません(ない) is not

ku-bamme͞o 九番目 ninth

kubarima͞osu 配ります, **kuba͞oru** 配る distributes, allots; deals (cards)

ku͞obetsu 区別 difference, differentiation; discrimination

kubi 首 neck; ～ **ni shima͞osu** 首にします fires, lays off, disemploys; ～⁻**ka͞ozari** 首飾り necklace

kubire くびれ neck (of a bottle), constricted place, waist

kubi-wa 首輪 (dog) collar

kubomi くぼみ・窪み hollow, dent, depression

kuchi 口 1. mouth; ～ **(kara͞o) no** 口(から)の oral 2. words, speech 3. entrance; hole, opening, slot 4. cork, stopper 5. job opening

kuchi-beni 口紅 lipstick

kuchibiru 唇 lip

kuchi-bu͞oe 口笛 whistling *(with one's lips)*; ～ **o fukima͞osu** 口笛を吹きます whistles

kuchi-ge͞onka ロげんか[喧嘩] argument

kuchi͞o-hige ロひげ・ロ髭 mustache

kuchima͞osu 朽ちます, **kuchi͞oru** 朽ちる rots, decays

ku͞ochite 朽ちて → **kuchima͞osu** 朽ちます

ku͞oda 管 pipe, tube

kuda͞oita 砕いた = **kudakima͞oshita** 砕きました (broke it)

kuda͞oite 砕いて → **kudakima͞osu** 砕きます

kuda͞oke 砕け 1. → **kudakema͞osu** 砕けます [infinitive] 2. → **kudakima͞osu** 砕きます [imperative] break it!

kudakema͞osu 砕けます, **kudake͞oru** 砕ける 1. it breaks, smashes, crumbles 2. can break it

kuda͞okete 砕けて → **kudakema͞osu** 砕けます

kudakima͞osu 砕きます, **kuda͞oku** 砕く breaks it, smashes it, crumbles it

kuda͞omono 果物 fruit; **kudamo͞ono͞o-ya** 果物屋 fruit market

kudari 下り descent; outbound (from Tokyo), the down train

kudarimaꜜsu 下ります, **kudaru** 下る comes/goes down, descends; falls, drops

kudasaꜜi 下さい・ください give; (**shite ~** して下さい[ください]) please (do) [imperative of **kudasaꜜru** 下さる・くださる = **kudasaimaꜜsu** 下さいます・くださいます]

kudasaimaꜜshite 下さいまして・くださいまして = **kudasaꜜtte** 下さって・くださって

kudasaimaꜜsu 下さいます・くださいます, **kudasaꜜru** 下さる・くださる gives (he to you, you to me); does as a favor (he for you, you for me), kindly (does)

kudasaꜜri 下さり・くださり → **kudasaimaꜜsu** 下さいます・くださいます [infinitive]

kudasaꜜtta 下さった・くださった = **kudasaimaꜜshita** 下さいました・くださいました

kudasaꜜtte 下さって・くださって → **kudasaimaꜜsu** 下さいます・くださいます

kudashi 下し = **kudashi-guꜜsuri** 下し薬 a purgative, a laxative; = **mushi-kuꜜdashi** 虫下し a vermifuge

kudasuꜜtta 下すった・くださった = **kudasaꜜtta** 下さった・くださった = **kudasaimaꜜshita** 下さいました・くださいました gave (me)

kudasuꜜtte 下すって・くださって = **kudasaꜜtte** 下さって・くださって → **kudasaimaꜜsu** 下さいます・くださいます

kudatta 下った = **kudarimaꜜshita** 下りました

kudatte 下って → **kudarimaꜜsu** 下ります

kudoꜜi くどい **1.** long-winded, dull **2.** thick, greasy

kuꜜe 食え **1.** → **kuemaꜜsu** 食えます [infinitive] **2.** → **kuimaꜜsu** 食います [imperative] eat!

kuꜜeba 食えば → **kuimaꜜsu** 食います (if one eat)

kuemaꜜsu 食えます, **kueꜜru** 食える can eat

kueꜜreba 食えれば → **kuemaꜜsu** 食えます (if one can eat)

kufū 工夫 device, scheme

Kuꜜ-gatsu 九月・9月 September

kugi 釘 nail, peg

kugi-nuꜜkiꜜ 釘抜き claw hammer

kugiriꜜ 区切り punctuation

kūgun 空軍 air force; **~ -kiꜜchi** 空軍基地 air base

kuꜜi 1. 杭・くい post, stake, pile **2.** 食い → **kuimaꜜsu** 食います

kuꜜiki 区域 zone

kuimaꜜsu 食います, **kuꜜu** 食う eats [*inelegant*]

kuꜜi-shiꜜmbō (na) 食いしん坊・くいしんぼう(な) glutton(ous); greedy

kujaku くじゃく・孔雀 peacock

ku‾ji くじ・籤 a lot (in a lottery)

kuji‾ite 挫いて → **kujikima‾su** 挫きます

kujikema‾su 挫けます, **kujike‾ru** 挫ける **1. ashi‾ ga** ～ 足が挫けます gets a sprained ankle **2. ki ga** ～ 気が挫けます gets disheartened, discouraged **3.** (a plan) gets frustrated

kujikima‾su 挫きます, **kuji‾ku** 挫く **1.** sprains; **ashi‾ o** ～ 足を挫きます sprains an ankle **2. ki o** ～ 気を挫きます disheartens, discourages **3.** frustrates (a plan)

kujira くじら・鯨 whale

ku-jū‾ 九十・90 ninety

ku‾ki 茎 stalk, stem

kū‾ki 空気 air

kūkō 空港 airport

ku‾ma‾ 熊 bear *(animal)*

kumade 熊手 rake

kumanai 汲まない = **kumimase‾n** 汲みません (not scoop)

kuma‾nai 組まない = **kumimase‾n** 組みません (not braid)

kume‾ba 汲めば → **kumima‾su** 汲みます (if one scoop)

ku‾meba 組めば → **kumima‾su** 組みます (if one braid)

kumi 汲み → **kumima‾su** 汲みます (scoops) [infinitive]

kumi‾ 組 a set, suit, pack; a class, band, company

ku‾mi 組み → **kumima‾su** 組み ます (braids) [infinitive]

kumiai 組合 association, guild, union

kumi-awase 組み合わせ assortment, mixture

kumi-awa‾se 組み合わせ → **kumi-awasema‾su** 組み合わせ ます

kumi-awasema‾su 組み合わせます, **-awase‾ru** 組み合わせる assembles, puts together, teams them up

kumima‾su 汲みます, **kumu** 汲む scoops, draws, ladles; considers, sympathizes

kumima‾su 組みます, **ku‾mu** 組む braids; assembles, sets up, puts together; folds (arms), clasps (hands), crosses (legs); teams up (with)

kumi-tate 組み立て structure, setup, makeup, organization, framework

kumi-tatema‾su 組み立てます, **-tate‾ru** 組み立てる sets up, organizes; assembles, puts together

ku‾mo 1. 雲 cloud [*also* **kumo‾** 雲] **2.** くも・蜘蛛 spider

kumō 汲もう = **kumimashō‾** 汲みましょう (let's scoop!)

kumō‾ 組もう = **kumimashō‾** 組みましょう (let's braid!)

ku‾mo no su‾ くも[蜘蛛]の巣, **kumo-no-su** くも[蜘蛛]の巣 spiderweb, cobweb (= **ku‾mo**

no i̊to くも[蜘蛛]の糸 spider
threads)

kumori̊ 曇り cloudy weather

kumo̊ri 曇り → **kumorimåsu** 曇
ります [infinitive]

kumorimåsu 曇ります, **kumo̊ru**
曇る gets cloudy; **kumo̊tte**
imåsu 曇っています is cloudy

kumya 汲みゃ 1. = **kume̊ba** 汲
めば (if one scoop) 2. ~
shinai 汲みゃしない = **kumi̊**
ya/wa shinai 汲みや/はしな
い = **kumanai** 汲まない (not
scoop)

ku᷄mya 組みゃ 1. = **ku᷄meba** 組
めば (if one braid) 2. ~ shinai
組みゃしない = **ku᷄mi ya/wa
shinai** 組みや/はしない =
kumånai 組まない (not braid)

... **kun** ...君 [familiar title after
name of colleague or student,
usually male]

kunda 汲んだ = **kumimåshi̊ta**
汲みました (scooped)

ku᷄nda 組んだ = **kumimåshi̊ta**
組みました (braided)

kunde 汲んで → **kumimåsu** 汲
みます (scoops)

ku᷄nde 組んで → **kumimåsu** 組
みます (braids)

kuni (o-kuni) 国（お国）1. country, nation; ~ **no** 国の national, state, government
2. native place, home area

ku᷄nren 訓練 training, drill; ~
shima(᷄)su 訓練します trains,

drills

kuo̊ 食おう = **kuimasho̊** 食い
ましょう (let's eat!)

kurå 1. 鞍 saddle 2. 倉・蔵
warehouse storeroom (=
storehouse), cellar, godown

ku᷄rā クーラー air conditioner

kurabemåsu 比べます・較べま
す, **kuraberu** 比べる・較べる
compares, contrasts

ku᷄rabu クラブ club (group;
card suit)

ku᷄rage くらげ・水母 jellyfish

kurai 位 grade, rank ⌈(light)

kurai 暗い dark, gloomy; dim
... **ku᷄rai** ...くらい・位 = ...
gu᷄rai ...ぐらい・位

kuråkkā クラッカー crackers

kurånai 繰らない = **kurimase̊n**
繰りません (not wind)

kurashimåsu 暮らします,
kurasu 暮らす lives, gets by;
makes a living

ku᷄rasu クラス class (group)

kuråtchi クラッチ clutch (of
car); **kuratchi̊-pe̊daru** クラッ
チペダル clutch pedal

kure 1. 暮れ the dark; the end of
the year, (~ **no** 暮れの) year-
end 2. くれ・暮れ →
kuremåsu くれます; 暮れま
す (gives; gets dark) [infini-
tive] 3. くれ → **kuremåsu** く
れます (gives; does as a favor)
[imperative] gimme!

ku᷄re 繰れ 1.→ **kuremåsu** 繰れ

ます (can wind/reel) [infinitive] 2. → **kurima╢su** 繰ります [imperative] wind it!

ku╢reba 1. 来れば → **kima╢su** 来ます (if one come) **2.** 繰れば → **kurima╢su** 繰ります (if one wind/reel)

kurejitto-ka╢do クレジットカード credit card

kurema╢su, kureru 1. くれます、くれる gives (to me/us; he to you); **shite ~** してくれます does as a favor (for me/us; he for you) **2.** 暮れます、暮れる; **hi ga ~** 日が暮れます it gets dark

kurema╢su 繰れます、**kure╢ru** 繰れる can wind/reel

kure╢n クレーン crane *(machine)*

kurenai くれない = **kuremase╢n** くれません (not give)

kurere╢ba くれれば・暮れれば, **kurerya** くれりゃ・暮れりゃ → **kurema╢su** くれます; 暮れます (if one give; if it get dark)

kure╢reba 繰れれば, **kure╢rya** 繰れりゃ → **kurema╢su** 繰れます (if one can wind/reel)

kurete くれて・暮れて → **kurema╢su** くれます; 暮れます (gives; gets dark)

ku╢rete 繰れて → **kurema╢su** 繰れます (can wind/reel)

kuri╢ 栗 chestnut

ku╢ri 繰り → **kurima╢su** 繰ります [infinitive]

kuri╢imu クリーム cream

kuri╢ini╢ngu クリーニング cleaning; **kuriiningu-ya** クリーニング屋 (dry)cleaner(s); laundry

kuri-kaeshima╢su 繰り返します, **-ka╢esu** 繰り返す repeats

kurima╢su 繰ります, **ku╢ru** 繰る winds, reels

kuri╢ppu クリップ a clip

Kuri╢su╢masu クリスマス Christmas

ku╢ro (no) 黒(の) black

kuro╢ 繰ろう = **kurimasho╢** 繰りましょう (let's wind it!)

ku╢rō 苦労 difficulties, hardships; **(go-ku╢rō** ご苦労) hard work, effort

kuro-bi╢iru 黒ビール bock beer

kuro╢i 黒い black

kuro╢ku クローク cloakroom, check room

kuro-pan 黒パン brown bread

ku╢rō╢to くろうと・玄人 expert, professional

ku╢ru 1. 来る = **kima╢su** 来ます (comes) **2.** 繰る = **kurima╢su** 繰ります (winds, reels)

kuruima╢su 狂います, **kuru╢u** 狂う gets warped; gets out of order; **(ki ga ~** 気が狂います) goes mad (insane)

kuruma (o-ku╢ruma) 車(お車) car; taxi; vehicle, (hand)cart

kuruma╢-ebi 車えび[海老] prawn, jumbo shrimp ⌈nut

kurumi╢ くるみ・胡桃 walnut;

kurushi᷉i 苦しい painful; hard, heavy

kurushimema᷉su 苦しめます, **kurushime᷉ru** 苦しめる afflicts, pains, distresses, embarrasses

kurushi᷉mi᷉ 苦しみ affliction, agony, suffering, distress

kurushi᷉mi 苦しみ → **kurushimima᷉su** 苦しみます [infinitive]

kurushimima᷉su 苦しみます, **kurushi᷉mu** 苦しむ suffers; gets afflicted/distressed/embarrassed

ku᷉rya 1. 来りゃ・繰りゃ = **ku᷉reba** 来れば; 繰れば (if one come; if one wind/reel) **2. ~ shinai** 繰りゃしない = **ku᷉ri ya/wa shinai** 繰りや/は しない (not wind/reel)

kusa᷉ 草 grass; weed, herb; plant

kusa᷉i 臭い smelly, stinking; fishy, questionable

kusari 鎖 chain

kusari᷉ 腐り spoilage

kusa᷉ri 腐り → **kusarima᷉su** 腐り ます [infinitive]

kusarima᷉su 腐ります, **kusa᷉ru** 腐る goes bad, rots, decays, spoils, sours; **kusa᷉tte ima᷉su** 腐っています is spoiled/rotten

kuse᷉ 癖・くせ a (bad) habit, a quirk

kūsha 空車 vacant car, "(taxi)

available"

kusha᷉mi くしゃみ a sneeze

kushi᷉ 1. くし・櫛 a comb **2.** 串 a skewer, a spit

kūsho 空所 a blank (space)

kuso᷉ くそ・糞 dung, excrement, feces

kusugurima᷉su くすぐります, **kusuguru** くすぐる tickles

kusugutta᷉i くすぐったい ticklish

kusuri (o-kusu᷉ri) 薬(お薬) medicine, drug; **~-ya** 薬屋 drugstore, (**~ san** 薬屋さん) druggist

kutabirema᷉su くたびれます, **kutabire᷉ru** くたびれる gets tired

kutakuta くたくた, **kuttakuta** くったくた dead tired, utterly exhausted

...-kutatte ...くたって = **...-kute mo** ...くても even being ...

...-kute ...くて is and (also/so)

kutsu᷉ 靴 shoes

kutsu-be᷉ra 靴べら shoehorn

kutsu᷉-himo 靴紐・靴ひも shoelace

kutsu-mi᷉gaki 靴磨き shoeshine

kutsu-na᷉oshi 靴直し shoe-repair person/shop

kutsurogima᷉su くつろぎます, **kutsuro᷉gu** くつろぐ relaxes, gets comfortable

kutsu᷉-shita᷉ 靴下・くつ下 socks, stockings

ku̱tsu̱ˈ-ya 靴屋 shoe shop/store

ku̱tsu̱-zoko 靴底 shoesole

ku̱tsu̱-zu̱ˈre̱ˈ 靴擦れ・靴ずれ a foot sore *(from shoe rubbing)*

ku̱ˈtta̱ 1. 繰って = **ku̱rima̱ˈshi̱ta̱** 繰りました 2. 食って = **ku̱ima̱ˈshi̱ta̱** 食いました

ku̱ttaku̱ta̱ くったくた dead tired, utterly exhausted

ku̱ˈtte̱ 1. 繰って → **ku̱rima̱ˈsu̱** 繰ります 2. 食って → **ku̱ima̱ˈsu̱** 食います

...-ku̱tte̱ ...くって = **...-ku̱te̱** ...くて

ku̱ttsu̱kima̱ˈsu̱ くっつきます, **ku̱ttsu̱ˈku̱** くっつく sticks to

ku̱ˈu̱ 食う = **ku̱ima̱ˈsu̱** 食います (eats; bites)

ku̱wa̱ くわ・鍬 hoe

ku̱ˈwa̱ 桑 mulberry

ku̱wa̱da̱ˈte̱ˈ 企て plan, attempt, undertaking

ku̱wa̱da̱ˈte̱ 企て → **ku̱wa̱da̱te̱ma̱ˈsu̱** 企てます [infinitive]

ku̱wa̱da̱te̱ma̱ˈsu̱ 企てます, **ku̱wa̱da̱te̱ˈru̱** 企てる plans, attempts, undertakes

ku̱wa̱e̱ma̱ˈsu̱ 加えます, **ku̱wa̱e̱ˈru̱** 加える adds (on); imposes

ku̱wa̱ˈna̱i 食わない = **ku̱ima̱se̱ˈn** 食いません (not eat)

ku̱wa̱se̱ma̱ˈsu̱ 食わせます, **ku̱wa̱se̱ˈru̱** 食わせる feeds

ku̱wa̱shi̱ˈi 詳しい detailed, exact; (**... ni ~** ...に詳しい) is knowledgeable (about ...), is well versed (in ...); **~ koto̱ˈ** 詳しい事 details; **ku̱wa̱ˈshi̱ku̱** 詳しく in detail

ku̱ˈya̱ 食や 1. = **ku̱ˈe̱ba̱** 食えば (if one eat) 2. **~ shi̱na̱i** 食やしない = **ku̱iˈ ya̱/wa̱ shi̱na̱i** 食いや/はしない = **ku̱wa̱ˈna̱i** 食わない (not eat)

ku̱-ya̱ˈku̱sho 区役所 ward office

ku̱ya̱shi̱ˈi 悔しい humiliating, mortifying, vexatious

ku̱ˈzu̱ くず・屑 1. (= **ku̱zu̱ˈ-mono** くず物・屑物) waste, trash, rags, scrap, junk 2. くず・葛 arrowroot

ku̱zu̱-hi̱ˈroi くず拾い・屑拾い ragpicker

ku̱zu̱ˈ-kago くずかご・屑籠 wastebasket

ku̱zu̱ˈko̱ˈ 葛粉 powdered arrowroot

ku̱zu̱ˈ-mono くず物・屑物 waste, trash, rags, scrap, junk

ku̱zu̱re̱ma̱ˈsu̱ 崩れます, **ku̱zu̱re̱ˈru̱** 崩れる it crumbles, breaks (down); (weather) deteriorates

ku̱zu̱shi̱ma̱ˈsu̱ 崩します, **ku̱zu̱ˈsu̱** 崩す 1. cashes, changes, breaks (into small money) 2. breaks it down, demolishes 3. writes (a character) in cursive style

kya̱ˈba̱rē キャバレー cabaret,

nightclub

kya˥betsu キャベツ cabbage; **kyabetsu-sa˥rada** キャベツサ ラダ coleslaw

kyabure˥ta キャブレター car- buretor

kyaku 客 = **o-kyaku (o-kyaku- sa˥ma˥)** お客(お客様) visitor, guest, company; customer

kyakuma 客間 drawing room (parlor); guest room

kyakusha 客車 (railroad) passenger car, coach

kya˥mpasu キャンパス campus

kya˥mpu キャンプ camp(ing); ~ **o shima˥su** キャンプをします camps

kya˥nde キャンデー candy

kya˥ppu キャップ cap (of a pen)

kyarameru キャラメル caramel

kya˥tsu きゃつ・彼奴 = **aitsu** あ いつ that damn one; ~**-ra** きゃつ[彼奴]ら those damn ones

kyatto sakebima˥su きゃっと叫 びます, **sake˥bu** きゃっと叫ぶ screams

kyo˥ 今日・きょう today

...-kyō ...教 religion

kyōchō 強調 emphasis; ~ **shima˥su** 強調します empha- sizes

kyodai (na) 巨大(な) huge

kyo˥dai 兄弟・姉妹・きょうだい brothers and/or sisters; brother; sister

kyōdō 共同 union, cooperation, joint (activity)

kyōge˥n 狂言 traditional Noh farce

kyo˥gi˥ 協議 conference, discus- sion

kyo˥gi 競技 (athletic) game, match, contest, (game) event

kyōgi-jō 競技場 stadium

kyo˥hi 拒否 refusal, rejection, veto; **kyo˥hi shima(˥)su** 拒否 します refuses, rejects, vetoes

kyōiku 教育 education

kyōjin 巨人 giant; **Kyo˥jin** 巨人 the Giants [*baseball team*]

kyō˥ju 教授 professor

kyojū˥-sha 居住者 a resident

kyo˥ka 許可 permit, permission

kyōkai 1. 教会 church **2.** 協会 society, association **3.** 境界 border (*of district, etc.*)

kyōka˥-sho 教科書 text(book)

kyo˥ku 局, ...˥-kyoku ...局 of- fice, bureau

kyokuba 曲馬 horseback stunts; **kyokuba˥-dan** 曲馬団 = **sa˥kasu** サーカス circus

kyokuta˥n (na) 極端(な) ex- treme; ~ **ni** 極端に extremely

Kyokutō 極東 Far East

kyōkyū 供給 supply(ing), provi- sion; ~ **shima˥su** 供給します supplies

kyo˥mi 興味 interest (*pleasure*); **kyōmi-buka˥i** 興味深い inter- esting

kyo'nen 去年 last year

kyo'ri 距離 distance

kyō⌐ryoku 協力 cooperation

Kyō-ryo'ri 京料理 Kyoto-style cooking/dishes

Kyōsan-shu'gi 共産主義 Communism; **Kyōsanshugi'-sha** 共産主義者 a Communist

kyo'shi 教師 teacher, instructor, tutor

kyōshitsu 教室 classroom

kyōshuku shima'su 恐縮します feels grateful/obliged; feels sorry/ashamed

kyōsō 競争 competition, rivalry, contest, race; **~-a'ite** 競争相手 competitor; **~ shima'su** 競争します competes

kyōson 共存 = **kyōzon** 共存 co-existence

kyōten 経典 sutra (Buddhist scripture)

Kyō'to 京都 Kyoto; **Kyōto'-Eki** 京都駅 Kyoto Station; **Kyōto'-jin** 京都人 Kyotoite

kyōtsū (no) 共通(の) common, general

kyo'yo 供与 grant, allowance; **~ shima(⌐)su** 供与します grants it

kyōyō 1. **~(no)** 共用(の) for common use, for public use 2. 教養 culture, education, refinement

kyōzai 教材 teaching materials

kyōzon 共存 = **kyōson** 共存 co-existence

kyū 1. 灸・きゅう = **o-kyū** お灸・おきゅう moxibustion (burning moxa on the skin) 2. 急 crisis, emergency, danger; **~(na)** 急(な) sudden, urgent, precipitous, steep

kyū 1. 九・9 = **ku** 九・9 nine 2. 級 class, grade

kyū'(-) 旧... ... old

kyū'-dai 九台 nine (machines, vehicles)

kyūden 宮殿 palace

kyū'-do 九度 nine degrees

kyū'-do 九度 nine times

kyū'dō 弓道 (the traditional art of) archery

kyū'-he'n 九遍 nine times

kyū'-hon 九本 nine long things

kyū'-hyaku 九百・900 nine hundred

kyū'ji 給仕 waiter/waitress, steward, attendant, office-boy/-girl, factotum

kyūjitsu 休日 day off, holiday

kyū'jo 救助 rescue, relief; **~ shima(⌐)su** 救助します rescues

kyūjō 1. 球場 = **yakyū-jō** 野球場 ball park, (baseball) stadium 2. 宮城 palace *(in Tokyo)* → **kō'kyo** 皇居

kyū'-jū 九十・90 ninety

kyū⌐jutsu 弓術 archery

kyūka 休暇 vacation, furlough

kyū-kai 九階 nine floors/stories, ninth floor

kyū̄-ka¹i 九回 nine times

kyūkei 休憩 rest, recess, break

kyūke¹i-shi̱tsu 休憩室 lounge *(room)*

kyū̄-ko 九個 nine small things

kyūkō 急行 express (train, etc.); **kyūkō¹-ken** 急行券 express ticket

kyūkon 求婚 proposal of marriage; **～ shima¹su** 求婚します proposes *(marriage)*

kyū¹ku̱tsu (na) 窮屈（な） constrained, uncomfortable

kyūkyū̄-bako 救急箱 first-aid kit

kyūkyū̄-sha 救急車 ambulance

kyū̄-mai 九枚 nine flat things

kyū-ma¹n 九万・90,000 ninety thousand

kyū ni 急に suddenly

kyū¹ri きゅうり・胡瓜 cucumber

kyū̄ryō (o-kyū̄ryō) 給料（お給料） salary, pay; **kyūryō¹-bi** 給料日 payday

kyūryū 急流 (river) rapids

kyū̄-satsu 九冊 nine books

kyūsei (no) 急性（の） acute *(sudden)*

kyū-se¹n 九千・9,000 nine thousand

kyūshoku 求職 job hunting, seeking employment

Kyū¹shū 九州 Kyushu

kyūsu きゅうす・急須 teapot

kyūtei 宮廷 (imperial/royal) court

kyū̄-tō 九頭 nine (horses/oxen)

kyū̄-wa 九羽 nine (birds)

Kyū-yaku 旧約 the Old Testament

kyū¹yo 給与 allowance, grant, compensation

kyūyō 急用 urgent business

— **M** —

ma 間 1. room; space (available) 2. time, interval; (= **hima** 暇) leisure; **ma ni aima¹su** 間に合います → **ma-ni-aima¹su** 間に合います

mā¹ まあ 1. oh well; I should say; perhaps, I guess 2. dear me!; good heavens/grief!

ma-ba¹taki まばたき・瞬き wink(ing), blink(ing); **ma-** **ba¹taki shima(¹)su** まばたき ［瞬き］します winks, blinks

mabushi¹i まぶしい・眩しい dazzling, glaring

ma¹buta まぶた・瞼・目蓋 eyelid

machi¹ 町・街 town, city; **～ no** 町の local

ma¹chi 待ち → **machima¹su** 待ちます

machia¹i-shi̱tsu 待合室 waiting room

machidōshīi 待ち遠しい long awaited; waiting a long time

machigaᵈe 間違え → **machigaemaᵈsu** 間違えます

machigaemaᵈsu 間違えます, **machigaᵈeᵈru** 間違える mistakes

machigaᵈi 間違い 1. mistake, error 2. → **machigaimaᵈsu** 間違います

machigaimaᵈsu 間違います, **machigaᵈu** 間違う is mistaken, is wrong, is in error

machigaᵈtta 間違った wrong *(mistaken)*

machimaᵈsu 待ちます, **maᵈtsu** 待つ waits for, awaits, expects, anticipates

maᵈchiᵈnē マチネー matinee

maᵈda まだ (not) yet; still (to be)

madara まだら・斑 spots, speckles; ～ **(no)** まだら[斑] (の) spotted

... maᵈde ...まで (all the way) to, till, until

... maᵈde ni ...までに by, no later than, before (it gets to be a time)

... maᵈde ni wa ...までには by ... at the latest

maᵈdo 窓 window; **mado-gaᵈrasu** 窓ガラス windowpane; **madoᵈ-guchi** 窓口 window (opening), wicket; **madoᵈ-kake** 窓掛け curtain; **mado-waku** 窓枠 (window)sash

mae-moᵈtte 前もって (in) advance *(beforehand)*

mae-muki (no) 前向き(の) farsighted *(forward-looking)*

maᵈe (ni) 前(に) front; in front of; before, ago; ～ **no** 前の previous, former; **suru** ～ **ni** する前に before doing; **daibu** ～ **kara** だいぶ前から for quite a long time (now)

maeuri 前売り advanced sale; (= ～**-kiᵈppu** 前売り切符) advanced-sale ticket

magari 1. 曲がり a curve, a bend 2. 曲がり → **magarimaᵈsu** 曲がります [infinitive] 3. 間借り renting a room

magarimaᵈsu 曲がります, **magaru** 曲がる 1. turns, goes around 2. it bends, curves

magariᵈ-nin 間借り人 tenant *(of apartment, room)*

magemaᵈsu 曲げます, **mageru** 曲げる bends it, curves it

magiremaᵈsu 紛れます, **magireᵈru** 紛れる: (... **ni** ...に) gets distracted (by ...); gets confused (with ...), gets mixed up (with)

... maᵈgiwa ...間際 just before, right on the brink of (when) ...

magoᵈ (o-mago-san) 孫(お孫さん) grandchild

maguro まぐろ・鮪 tuna

magusa まぐさ・秣 hay

maᵈhi 麻痺 paralysis

mahōˈ-bin 魔法瓶 vacuum/thermos bottle

mai-... 毎... each, every

...ˈ-mai ...枚 (counts flat things)

maˈi-asa 毎朝 every morning

maⁿi-ban 毎晩 every night

maido 毎度 every time; **Maido ariˈgatō gozaimaˈsu** 毎度ありがとうございます。 We appreciate your (continuing) patronage.

maigetsu 毎月 every month; (～ **no** 毎月の) monthly

maˈigo 迷子 a lost child; ～ **ni narimaˈsu (naˈru, naˈtte)** 迷子になります(なる、なって)a child becomes lost

mai-kon マイコン microcomputer

mainasu マイナス less (minus); a minus, a disadvantage

mainen 毎年 every year

maˈinichi 毎日 every day; all the time; ～ **no yōˈ ni** 毎日のよう[様]に almost every day

mairimaˈsu 参ります, **maˈiru** 参る 1. [HUMBLE] I come/go 2. visits, calls on 3. is defeated, loses 4. is floored, stumped

maishū 毎週 every week

maisō 埋葬 burial

maite 巻いて → **makimaˈsu** 巻きます (rolls up)

maˈite まいて・蒔いて → **makimaˈsu** まきます・蒔きま

す (sows)

mai-toshi 毎年 every year

mai-tsuki 毎月 every month

Maˈitta! 参った・まいった! You've got me!

maⁿi-yo 毎夜 every night

māⁿjan マージャン・麻雀 mahjong; **mājan-ya** マージャン [麻雀]屋 mahjong parlor

majime (na) まじめ[真面目](な) serious, earnest, sober, conscientious, honest

majirimaˈsu 混じります, **majiˈru** 混じる it mixes

majiwarimaˈsu 交わります, **majiwaˈru** 交わる associates with

makanai 巻かない ＝ **makimaseˈn** 巻きません (not roll it up)

makaˈnai まかない・蒔かない ＝ **makimaseˈn** まきません・蒔きません (not sow)

makasemaˈsu 任せます, **makaseˈru** 任せる entrusts with

makashimaˈsu 負かします, **makasu** 負かす defeats

make 1. 負け defeat, loss **2.** 負け → **makemaˈsu** 負けます (loses): [infinitive]; [imperative] **make ro** 負けろ, **makeˈ yo** 負けよ **3.** 巻け → **makimaˈsu** 巻きます [imperative] roll it up!

maˈke まけ・蒔け → **makimaˈsu**

まきます・蒔きます [imperative] sow!

make̍ba 巻けば → **makima̍su** 巻きます (if one roll it up)

ma̍keba まけば・蒔けば → **makima̍su** まきます・蒔きます (if one sow)

makema̍su, makeru 1. 負けます, 負ける loses, is defeated; comes down on the price; is inferior 2. 巻けます, 巻ける can roll it up

makema̍su まけます・蒔けます, **make̍ru** まける・蒔ける can sow (seed)

makenai 負けない・巻けない = **makemase̍n** 負けません; 巻けません (not lose; cannot roll it up)

make̍nai まけない・蒔けない = **makemase̍n** まけません・蒔けません (cannot sow)

ma̍ke̍tto マーケット market

maki 1. まき・薪 firewood 2. 巻き a roll; a volume 3. (... -maki ...巻き) a bolt (of cloth)

maki 巻き → **makima̍su** 巻きます (rolls it up) [infinitive]

ma̍ki まき・蒔き → **makima̍su** まきます・蒔きます (sows) [infinitive]

maki⌐-e 蒔絵・蒔き絵 raised lacquer

makima̍su 巻きます, **maku** 巻く rolls up; winds; wraps

makima̍su まきます・蒔きます,

ma̍ku まく・蒔く sows (seed)

maki-mono 巻き物 scroll

maki-pan 巻きパン roll *(bread)*

maki-ta̍bako 巻きタバコ cigarette(s)

makka̍ (na) 真っ赤(な) crimson, deep red

makku̍ro (na) 真っ黒(な) jet black

makō 巻こう = **makimashō̍** 巻きましょう (let's roll it up!)

makō̍ まこう・蒔こう = **makimashō̍** まきましょう・蒔きましょう (let's sow!)

makoto (no) 誠[真]・まこと(の) sincere; faithful; true; genuine; ～ **ni** まことに・誠に・真に sincerely

maku 巻く = **makima̍su** 巻きます (rolls up)

maku̍ 幕 (stage) curtain; (play) act; ～ **no aida** 幕の間 between acts

ma̍ku まく・蒔く = **makima̍su** まきます・蒔きます (sows)

makuai 幕あい・幕間 intermission (between acts)

makuno̍uchi 幕の内 a riceball lunch(box)

ma̍kura まくら・枕 pillow

makya 巻きゃ 1. = **make̍ba** 巻けば (if one roll it up) 2. ～ **shinai** 巻きゃしない = **maki̍ya/wa shinai** 巻きや/はしない = **makanai** 巻かない (not roll it up) ma⌐kya まきゃ・蒔きゃ **1.** = ma⌐keba まけば・蒔けば (if one sow) **2.** ~ shinai まきゃ [蒔きゃ]しない = ma⌐ki ya/wa shinai まき[蒔き]や/はしない = maka⌐nai まかない・蒔かない (not sow)

ma⌐-mā まあまあ (just) so-so

mama-chichi まま[継]父 step-father

... mama⌐ (de/no) ...まま(で/の) intact, untouched/undisturbed; sono ~ de そのままで just as it is/was, ta⌐tta ~ de 立ったままで without sitting down   ⌐mother

mama-haha まま[継]母 step-

mama-ko まま[継]子 stepchild

ma⌐m-ba 万羽 = ichima⌐m-ba 一万羽 ten thousand birds

mam-bai 万倍 ten-thousandfold (10,000 times doubled)

ma⌐m-bai 万杯 = ichima⌐m-bai 一万杯 ten thousand cupfuls

mambi⌐ki⌐ 万引き shoplifting, shoplifter

ma⌐m-biki 万匹 = ichima⌐m-biki 一万匹 ten thousand animals/fish/bugs

ma⌐m-bon 万本 = ichima⌐m-bon 一万本 ten thousand long things

mame⌐ **1.** 豆 bean(s) **2.** まめ・肉刺 blister, corn, bunion

mame (na) まめ(な) healthy; diligent

mammaru 真ん丸・まんまる a perfect circle; ~ (na) 真ん丸・まんまる(な) perfectly round

ma-mo⌐-naku まもなく・間もなく soon, before long, shortly

mamorima⌐su 守ります, mamo⌐ru 守る defends, protects, guards

ma⌐n 万 ten thousand

man(-) ... 満... fully ...

manabima⌐su 学びます, manabu 学ぶ learns, studies

manai⌐ta⌐ まないた・俎・爼 chopping board

manande 学んで → manabima⌐su 学びます

mane まね・真似 imitation, mimicry; ... no ~ o shima⌐su ... のまね[真似]をします imitates, mimics

mane⌐ite 招いて → manekima⌐su 招きます

ma⌐nējā マネージャー manager

mane⌐ki 招き → manekima⌐su 招きます [infinitive]

manekima⌐su 招きます, mane⌐ku 招く invites

manema⌐su まね[真似]ます, maneru まね[真似]る imitates

manga 漫画 cartoon, comics; ~-bon 漫画本 comic book

ma-ni-aima⌐su 間に合います, -a⌐u 間に合う: (... ni) ~ (...に)間に合います is in time (for ...); -aimase⌐n (-awa⌐nai) 間に合いません(合わない) arrives too late (for ...), misses (the train/bus/plane)

ma-ni-awase 間に合わせ make-shift

ma-ni-awasema̅su 間に合わせます, **-awase̅ru** 間に合わせる: **(... de) ~** (...で)間に合わせます makes do (with ...)

ma̅n'ichi 万一 if by any chance

man'in 満員 full (of people)

Ma̅nira マニラ Manila

manjū̅ まんじゅう・饅頭 a steamed bun stuffed with ground pork (**niku-man** 肉まん) or bean jam (**am-man** あんまん)

mannaka 真ん中 the very middle, center; **~ no** 真ん中(の) central

manne̅n-hitsu 万年筆 fountain pen

ma̅nshon マンション a luxury apartment (house)

Ma̅nshū 満州 Manchuria

man-tan 満タン full tank; **~ ni shima̅su** 満タンにします fills the tank, fills it up

ma̅nto マント cloak

manukarema̅su まぬかれます・免れます, **manukare̅ru** まぬかれる・免れる escapes from, is exempt from

manza̅i 漫才 cross-talk comedy

ma̅n-zoku 万足 (*also* **ma̅n-soku** 万足) 10,000 pairs of footwear

ma̅nzoku (na) 満足(な) satisfac-

tory; **(... de) ma̅nzoku shima(̅)su** ...で満足します is satisfied/contented (with ...)

mara̅ まら penis

marason マラソン jog(ging); (= **~-kyō̅sō** マラソン競争) marathon; **~ o shima̅su** マラソンをします jogs, runs a marathon

mare̅ (na) まれ[稀](な) rare, infrequent; **~ ni** まれ[稀]に rarely

mari まり・鞠 ball

marifana マリファナ marijuana

maru 丸・まる circle, ring; zero

maru(-) ... 丸・まる... fully

maru de まるで perfectly, completely

marui 丸い・まるい round

maruta 丸太 log

ma̅saka まさか no kidding!; you don't say!; impossible!

masanai 増さない = **mashimase̅n** 増しません (not increase)

ma̅sa-ni まさに・正に exactly, just; certainly, really

masarima̅su 勝ります, **masa̅ru** 勝る surpasses, is superior

masatsu 摩擦 friction; **masatsu shima̅su** 摩擦します rubs, (**karada o ~** 体を摩擦します) rubs (oneself) down

mase 増せ 1. → **masema̅su** 増せます [infinitive] 2. →

mashima̅su 増します [imperative] increase (it!)

...-ma̅se ...ませ [imperative of polite auxiliary]

mase̅ba 増せば → **mashima̅su** 増します (if increase)

masema̅su 増せます, **maseru** 増せる can increase it

...-mase̅n ...ません does not; ~ **deshita** ...ませんでした did not

masenai 増せない = **masemase̅n** 増せません (cannot increase)

masha 増しゃ 1. = **mase̅ba** 増せば (if increase) 2. ~ **shinai** 増しゃしない = **mashi̅ ya/wa shinai** 増しや/はしない = **masanai** 増さない (not increase)

mashi 増し 1. an increase; a surcharge 2. → **mashima̅su** 増します [infinitive]

mashima̅su 増します, **masu** 増す increases, raises, swells

...-ma̅shite ...まして [gerund of polite auxiliary]

maso̅ 増そう = **mashimasho̅** 増しましょう (let's increase it!)

massa̅ji マッサージ massage; ~-**shi** マッサージ師 masseur

massa̅ka-sama ni 真っ逆さまに head over heels

masshi̅ro (na) 真っ白(な) snow white

massu̅gu (na) 真っすぐ・真っ直ぐ(な) straight

masu 増す = **mashima̅su** 増します (increases)

masu̅ 1. ます・鱒 trout 2. 升 a small measuring box (from which saké can be drunk)

masu-komi マスコミ mass communication (media)

ma̅suku マスク mask

masu̅-masu ますます・益々 more and more, increasingly

mata 1. また・又 again; moreover; **Mata do̅zo** また[又] どうぞ. Please come again. 2. 股 crotch, groin; fork

ma̅ta また・又 and also/ another/more (= ... **mo** ~ ... もまた[又])

matagarima̅su またがります・跨がります, **mataga̅ru** またがる・跨がる: ... **ni** ~ ...にまたがり[跨がり]ます straddles, sits astride, mounts, rides; stretches/extends over, spans

mata̅ge またげ・跨げ 1. → **matagema̅su** またげます・跨げます [infinitive] 2. → **matagima̅su** またぎます・跨ぎます [imperative] (stride over it!)

matagema̅su またげます・跨げます, **matage̅ru** またげる・跨げる can stride over

mata̅gi またぎ・跨ぎ → **matagima̅su** またぎます・跨ぎます [infinitive]

matagima͞su またぎます・跨ぎます, **mata͞gu** またぐ・跨ぐ strides over

mata͞ide またいで・跨いで → **matagima͞su** またぎます・跨ぎます

mata͞nai 待たない = **machimase͞n** 待ちません

ma-ta͞taki͞ 瞬き blink(ing); **ma-ta͞taki͞ shima(͞)su** 瞬きします blinks

ma͞ta͞-wa または・又は or, or else, on the other hand; also; and/or

matcha 抹茶 powdered green tea (for tea ceremony)

ma͞tchi マッチ 1. match(es) (for fire); **matchi͞-bako** マッチ箱 matchbox 2. matchbook

ma͞te 待て 1. → **matema͞su** 待てます (can wait) [infinitive] 2. → **machima͞su** 待ちます [imperative] wait!

matema͞su 待てます, **mate͞ru** 待てる can wait

mato 的 target, aim

mato͞ 待とう = **machimasho͞** 待ちましょう (let's wait!)

matomarima͞su まとまります, **matomaru** まとまる is settled, arranged, finished

matomema͞su まとめます, **matomeru** まとめる settles, arranges, finishes

ma͞tsu 松 pine tree (= ~ **no ki͞** 松の木)

ma͞tsu 待つ = **machima͞su** 待ちます (waits)

matsuba-zu͞e 松葉杖 crutch(es)

matsudake 松茸 = **matsutake** 松茸

ma͞tsuge まつげ・睫 eyelash(es)

matsuri⌐ (o-matsuri) 祭り（お祭り) festival

matsutake 松茸 a kind of mushroom (thumb-shaped)

matsu-yani 松やに・松脂 pine resin

mattaku 全く・まったく quite, completely, exactly; (~ **no** 全くの・まったくの) perfect

ma͞tte 待って → **machima͞su** 待ちます; ~ **ima͞su** 待っています is (or will be) waiting/awaiting

ma͞tto マット mat

mawari 周り: (... **no**) ~ (**ni/no**) (...の)周り（に/の) around ...

mawarima͞su, mawaru 1. 周ります, 周る goes around 2. 回ります, 回る turns, revolves, circulates

mawari⌐**-michi** 回り道 detour

mawashi まわし・回し sumo wrestler's belt (loincloth)

mawashima͞su 回します, **mawasu** 回す turns it around, passes it around, circulates it

mayaku 麻薬 narcotic(s), dope

mayoima͞su 迷います, **mayo͞u** 迷う gets lost; gets dazed; gets perplexed

ma-yo͞naka 真夜中 midnight

mayo͞tte 迷って → **mayoima͞su** 迷います

ma͞yu 1. 眉 = **ma͞yuge** 眉毛 eyebrow(s) 2. まゆ・繭 cocoon

maza͞ri 混ざり → **mazarima͞su** 混ざります [infinitive]

mazarima͞su 混ざります, **maza͞ru** 混ざる it mixes

ma͞ze 混ぜ → **mazema͞su** 混ぜます 1. [infinitive] 2. [imperative] **maze͞ ro** 混ぜろ, **ma͞ze yo** 混ぜよ

mazema͞su 混ぜます, **maze͞ru** 混ぜる mixes it

maze͞nai 混ぜない = **maze-mase͞n** 混ぜません (not mix it)

mazeyo͞ 混ぜよう = **mazemasho͞** 混ぜましょう (let's mix it!)

ma͞zu 1. まず・先ず first of all, before anything else 2. まず perhaps, nearly

mazu͞i まずい 1. まずい・不味い untasty, bad-tasting 2. まずい ・拙い awkward, poor 3. inadvisable 4. ugly

mazushi͞i 貧しい poor *(needy)*

me͞ (o-me) 1. 目（お目）eye; (... ～ **ni aima͞su** ...目に会います) (has/undergoes) an experience 2. 芽（お芽）bud

...-me ...め・奴 [*deprecates people*] damn (fool) ... ; **baka ～** ばかめ damn(fool) idiot

...-me ...目 NUMERAL-th;

itsutsu-me͞ 五つ目 fifth

me͞ate 目当て a guide (for the eye); aim

mechamecha めちゃめちゃ・目茶目茶 in pieces, all confused, in disorder

medachima͞su 目立ちます, **meda͞tsu** 目立つ stands out, becomes conspicuous

medama-yaki 目玉焼き fried egg(s)

meda͞tta ... 目立った... outstanding, conspicuous

meda͞tte 目立って outstandingly, conspicuously; ～ **ima͞su** 目立っています is outstanding, conspicuous

medeta͞i めでたい・目出度い 1. auspicious, happy 2. simple-minded

me͞do 1. 針孔 the eye of a needle 2. 目処・目途 (= **me͞ate** 目当て) aim

me͞do メード maid

megakema͞su 目がけ[目掛け]ます, **megake͞ru** 目がけ[目掛け]る aims at; ... **o mega͞kete** ...を目がけて (aiming) at, (going) toward

me͞gane めがね・眼鏡 (eye)-glasses; ～ **o kakema͞su** めがね[眼鏡]をかけます puts on (wears) glasses

megumarema͞su 恵まれます, **megumareru** 恵まれる gets blessed; ... **ni meguma͞rete ima(ˉ)su** ...に恵まれています

is blessed with …

megumi 恵み blessing, mercy, charity

megumima̲su 恵みます, **megumu** 恵む blesses with, gives mercifully (in charity)

megunde 恵んで → **megumima̲su** 恵みます

megurima̲su 巡ります, **meguru** 巡る centers on, surrounds, concerns

me-gu̲suri 目薬・眼薬 eye lotion, eye drops

megutte 巡って → **megurima̲su** 巡ります; **… o megutte** …を巡って centering on, surrounding, concerning

me̲i めい・姪 niece

…̲-mei …名 (counts people) [bookish] = **… (̲)-nin** …人

meibo 名簿 list (catalog) of names, directory, register, roll

me̲ibutsu 名物 a local specialty, a special attraction, a famous product

me⌐igo-san 姪子さん (your) niece

meihaku (na) 明白(な) clear, obvious, explicit; **~ ni** 明白に clearly, obviously, explicitly

mei-jima̲su 命じます, **-ji⌐ru** 命じる commands; appoints, nominates, orders

meiji̲n 名人 expert

me⌐i-jite 命じて → **mei-jima̲su** 命じます

meirei 命令 order, command

me̲-isha 目医者・眼医者 eye doctor, oculist

meishi 1. 名刺 calling card, visiting card, name card **2.** 名詞 noun

meishi̲-ire 名刺入れ calling-card case

me̲iwaku (go-me̲iwaku) 迷惑（ご迷惑）trouble, bother, nuisance; **~ (na)** 迷惑（な）troublesome; **(… ni) me̲iwaku o kakema̲su** （…に）迷惑をかけます causes (one) trouble

me̲iyo 名誉 prestige, honor, glory ⌐turer

mē̲kā メーカー maker, manufac-

mekake̲ (o-mekake) 妾（お妾）mistress, concubine

me-ka̲kushi 目隠し a blindfold

mekata 目方 weight

me-kya̲betsu 芽キャベツ Brussels sprouts

mēkya̲ppu メーキャップ makeup

me̲mbā メンバー member

me̲mo メモ note, memo(randum); **memo-chō** メモ帳 note pad, tablet

men 面 mask; face, front

me̲n 1. 綿 cotton (= **momen** もめん・木綿) **2.** めん・麺 noodles (= **me̲n-rui** めん類・麺類) **3.** 面 surface (= **hyōme̲n** 表面)

mendō̅ 面倒 trouble, bother, nuisance; ～ **(na)** 面倒(な), **mendō-kusa̅i** 面倒臭い bothersome

menjō̅ 免状 license; diploma

menkai 面会 interview, meeting; ～**-nin** 面会人 visitor

me̅nkyo 免許, **menkyo̅-shō/ -jō** 免許証/状 license, permit

me̅nseki 面積 area

me̅nyū メニュー menu

menzei (no) 免税(の) tax-free/ -exempt; **menze̅i-hin** 免税品 tax-free goods

meriken-ko メリケン粉 (wheat) flour ⌈goods

meriyasu メリヤス knitted

me̅ron メロン melon

mesa̅nai 召さない ＝ **meshimase̅n** 召しません

meshi̅ 飯 cooked rice; a meal

meshiagarima̅su 召し上がります, **meshiaga̅ru** 召し上がる [HONORIFIC] 1. eats 2. drinks

meshi̅-bitsu めしびつ・飯櫃 rice bucket/tub (＝ **o-hitsu** お櫃・おひつ ＝ **o-hachi** お鉢)

meshima̅su 召します, **me̅su** 召す [*in formal speech can replace such verbs as* **kima̅su** 着ます *(wears)*, **tabema̅su** 食べます *(eats)*, **nomima̅su** 飲みます *(drinks)*, **(kaze o) hikima̅su** (風邪を)ひきます *(catches cold), etc., that involve the body*]

meshi̅-mono 飯物 food boiled with (or poured over) rice

meshita̅ (no) 目下(の) inferior *(in status/rank/age)*

meshi-tsu̅kai 召し使い servant

me̅sseji メッセージ message

mesu̅ 雌・めす female animal; ... **no ～** ...の雌・めす a she-...

mē̅tā メーター meter *(device)*

mētoru メートル meter(s) *(of length)*

me̅-tsuki 目つき・目付き a look (in one's eye)

me̅tta (na) めった[滅多](な) reckless, rash

me̅tta ni めった[滅多]に ＋ NEGATIVE VERB seldom

meue̅ (no) 目上(の) superior *(in status/rank/age)*

me-yani̅ 目やに matter (gum, mucus) from the eye

me̅yasu 目安 1. a standard 2. (＝ **me̅ate** 目当て) guide; aim

meza̅mashi 目覚まし ＝ **mezamashi-do̅kei** 目覚まし時計 alarm clock

mezamema̅su 目覚めます, **mezame̅ru** 目覚める awake

mezashima̅su 目指します, **meza̅su** 目指す heads for (a destination); ... **o meza̅shite** ... を目指して heading for, aiming at

mezurashi̅i 珍しい rare, uncommon, novel, curious, unusual, unexpected (but welcome)

mezura⌐shiku 珍しく unusually

mi 1. 実 fruit, nut **2.** 身 body

mi⌐ 見 → **mi⌐ru** 見る **1.** [infinitive] **2.** [imperative] **mi⌐ ro** 見ろ, **mi⌐ yo** 見よ look!

miai 見合い (broker-arranged) meeting of prospective bride and groom; ~**-ke⌐kkon** 見合い結婚 an arranged marriage

mibō⌐-jin 未亡人 widow

mi⌐bun 身分 social standing

mi⌐[n]buri みぶり・身振り gesture, movement

mi⌐cha 見ちゃ = **mi⌐te wa** 見ては; ~ **dame⌐ (desu)** 見ちゃだめ（です) No peeking!

michi 道 way; street, road

michibata 道端 wayside, roadside

michibikima⌐su 導きます, **michibi⌐ku** 導く leads, guides

michima⌐su 満ちます, **michi⌐ru** 満ちる gets complete, full; **mi⌐chite ima⌐su** 満ちています is complete, full

midare⌐ 乱れ disorder

mida⌐re 乱れ → **midarema⌐su** 乱れます [infinitive]

midarema⌐su 乱れます, **midare⌐ru** 乱れる gets disturbed, disordered

midashi 見出し **1.** heading, caption, headline **2.** (= **midashi[n]-go** 見出し語) a dictionary entry; a headword **3.** (=

mokuji 目次) contents, (= **sakuin** 索引) index, (= **hyōdai** 標題・表題) title

mida⌐shi 乱し → **midashima⌐su** 乱します [infinitive]

midashima⌐su 乱します, **mida⌐su** 乱す throws into disorder, upsets, disturbs

mi⌐dori (no) 緑(の) green; ~ **no mado⌐-guchi** みどりの窓口 the Green Window (for special train tickets)

mie⌐ みえ・見栄 show, display; (dramatic) pose

mi⌐e 見え → **miema⌐su** 見えます [infinitive]

miemase⌐n 見えません, **mie⌐nai** 見えない is invisible, cannot be seen, does not appear; **mie⌐naku narima⌐su** 見えなくなります vanishes (from sight)

miema⌐su 見えます, **mie⌐ru** 見える **1.** is visible, can be seen **2.** appears; shows up, comes **3.** seems

mi⌐ete 見えて → **miema⌐su** 見えます

migaite 磨いて → **migakima⌐su** 磨きます

migakima⌐su 磨きます, **migaku** 磨く polishes, shines

migi 右 right *(not left)*; ~ **-do⌐nari** 右隣り next (door) on the right; ~**-kiki (no)** 右利き（の）right-handed; ~ **-ma⌐wari (ni)** 右回り(に)

clockwise

mi¯goto (na) 見事（な） splendid, admirable, beautiful

migurushi¯i 見苦しい unseemly, unsightly

mi¯-hako 三箱 three boxfuls

mihon 見本 a sample

Miichan-ha¯chan (Mi¯i-chan Ha¯-chan) ミーちゃんハーちゃん（みいちゃん　はあちゃん）, **Mii-Ha¯-zoku** ミーハー族 (every) Jane and Mary, silly girl(s)

mijika¯i 短い short *(not long)*; brief

miji¯ka¯ku shima[ ]su 短くします shortens

mikage¯-ishi 御影石 granite

mikake 見かけ・見掛け outward appearance; ～ **wa** 見かけは outwardly, seemingly

mi¯kan (o-mi¯kan) みかん・蜜柑（おみかん・お蜜柑） tangerine, mandarin (orange)

mikata 味方 a friend; an accomplice

mi-ka¯ta¯ 見方 a viewpoint

mi[ ]ki 1. 幹 trunk (of tree) **2.** 神酒 = **o-miki** おみき・御神酒 wine (saké) offered to the ⌐gods

mi¯kisā ミキサー blender

mikka 三日 three days; 3rd day (of month)

mikomi 見込み **1.** promise, hope **2.** outlook, expectation **3.** opinion, view

mi[ ]koshi (o-mi¯koshi) みこし・神輿（おみこし・お神輿） portable shrine (for festival parades)

mikuji みくじ・神籤 = **o-mikuji** おみくじ (written fortune)

mimai (o-mimai) 見舞い（お見舞い） a visit (of solicitude); **mima¯i-kyaku** 見舞い客 visitor

... mi¯man ...未満 less than, below (a quantity, an age)

mima¯su 見ます, **mi¯ru** 見る sees, looks, watches; tries doing

mimi¯ 耳 ear; ～ **ga tōi** 耳が遠い is hard of hearing

mimika¯ki 耳かき earpick

mimi-ka¯zari 耳飾り earring

mimiu[ ]chi[ ] shima¯su 耳打ちします whispers

mimi-wa 耳輪 earring

mi¯nai 見ない = **mimase¯n** 見ません (not see)

minami 南 south; ～**-guchi** 南口 the south exit/entrance; ～**-yori (no kaze)** 南寄り（の風） southerly (wind)

Minami-A¯merika 南アメリカ South America

mi-naraima¯su 見習います, **mi-nara[ ]u** 見習う follows (learns from) the example of

mina¯-san みなさん・皆さん you all, everybody; (you) ladies and gentlemen

minato 港 port

mine[ ] 峰 peak, summit

mingei 民芸, **minge⌐i-hin** 民芸品 folkcraft

mi⌐ ni 見に [goes] to see

miniku⌐i 醜い ugly

minkan (no) 民間(の) civil(ian), private (non-government)

minna⌐ みんな・皆 everybody, all; (= **ze⌐mbu** 全部) everything, all, completely; ~ **de** みんな[皆]で altogether

mi⌐no みの・簑 straw raincoat

minori 実り crop, harvest

minorima⌐su 実ります, **mino⌐ru** 実る bears fruit; ripens

minshū 民衆 the masses, the peo- ⌐ple

minshuku 民宿 tourist home, guest house, family inn, hostelry, bed-and-breakfast

minshu-shu⌐gi 民主主義 democracy

min'yō 民謡 folk song, ballad

mi⌐nzoku 民族 race

mi-okurima⌐su 見送ります, **-oku⌐ru** 見送る sees (them)

mi⌐rai 未来 future ⌐off

mi⌐reba 見れば → **mima⌐su** 見ます (if one see)

mirin みりん・味醂 sweet rice wine (for cooking)

mi⌐ ro 見ろ → **mima⌐su** 見ます [imperative] look!

mi⌐ru 見る → **mima⌐su** 見ます (sees)

miru⌐-gai みる貝 surf clam, geoduck

mi⌐ruku ミルク milk (= **gyūnyū** 牛乳); **miruku-se⌐ki** ミルクセーキ milkshake

mi⌐rya 見りゃ = **mi⌐reba** 見れば (if one see)

mi⌐ryoku 魅力 charm (attraction); **miryoku-teki (na)** 魅力的(な) charming

mi⌐sa ミサ (Catholic) mass

mi⌐saki 岬 cape, promontory, headland

mise⌐ 店 store, shop

mi⌐se 見せ → **misema⌐su** 見せます **1.** [infinitive] **2.** [imperative] **mise⌐ ro** 見せろ, **mi⌐se yo** 見せよ show it!

mise-kake (no) 見せかけ(の) sham, make-believe, pretend(ed)

misema⌐su 見せます, **mise⌐ru** 見せる shows

mise-mo⌐no⌐ 見せ物 show, exhibition, exhibit

mise⌐nai 見せない = **misemase⌐n** 見せません (not show)

mi⌐sete 見せて → **misema⌐su** 見せます

mi⌐shin ミシン sewing machine

mi⌐so (o-mi⌐so) みそ・味噌(お味噌) (fermented) bean paste

misoka みそか・晦日 last day of month

miso-shi⌐ru みそ汁・味噌汁 soup seasoned with miso

missetsu (na) 密接(な) thick, dense; close, intimate

misu みす・御簾 bamboo blind
mi‾su ミス a miss; = misute‾ku ミステーク a mistake
mi‾ta 見た = mima‾shita 見ました (saw)
mi-ta‾i 見たい wants to see
... mi‾tai desu ...みたいです = ... yo‾ desu (da/na, de, ni) ...よう [様]です(だ/な, で, に) seems/looks (like): NOUN ~ / NOUN datta ~ だったみたいです; VERB-(r)u/-ta ~ う(る) /たみたいです, ADJECTIVE-i/ -katta ~ い/かったみたいです
mitashima‾su 満たします, mita‾su 満たす fills up, satisfies
mi‾te 見て → mima‾su 見ます
mitomema‾su 認めます, mitomeru 認める recognizes, admits, acknowledges
mitōshi 見通し prospect, outlook
mi‾tsu‾ 三つ = mittsu‾ 三つ (three)
mi‾tsu 蜜 honey
mitsuba 三つ葉 trefoil leaves; honewort (stone parsley)
mitsu‾-bachi 蜜蜂 (honey) bee
mitsukarima‾su 見つかります, mitsukaru 見つかる is found, discovered; it turns up
mitsukema‾su 見つけます, mitsukeru 見つける finds, discovers

mi-tsumema‾su 見つめます, mi-tsume‾ru 見つめる gazes at, stares at
mi-tsumori 見積もり an estimate
mi-tsumo‾ri 見積もり → mi-tsumorima‾su 見積もります
mi-tsumorima‾su 見積もります, -tsumo‾ru 見積もる estimates, rates
mi‾tsu (na) 密(な) dense, thick
mitsurin 密林 jungle
mitsurō 蜜ろう・蜜臘 (bees)wax
mitsuyu 密輸 smuggling; ~ shima‾su 密輸します smuggles
mittsu‾ 三つ three; three years old; mittsu-me‾ 三つ目 third
mi-ukema‾su 見受けます, -uke‾ru 見受ける observes, happens to see; appears (to be)
mi-wakema‾su 見分けます, -wake‾ru 見分ける discriminates, distinguishes
miya 1. 宮 (o-miya お宮) Shinto shrine 2. 宮 prince
miyage (o-miyage, o-mi‾ya) みやげ・土産(おみやげ, おみや), miyage-mono みやげもの・土産物 a gift, a souvenir; miyagemono-ya みやげもの屋・土産物屋 gift shop
miyako 都 capital city
mi‾ ya shinai 見やしない = mi‾ wa shinai 見はしない = mi‾nai 見ない (not see)
mi-yasu‾i 見やすい clear (easy to see)

mi˺ yo 見よ = **mi˺ ro** 見ろ → **mima˺su** 見ます [imperative] look!

miyō˺ 見よう = **mimashō˺** 見ましょう (let's look!)

mizo 溝 drain, ditch

mizu 水 (cold) water (**o-mizu** お水); liquid

mizu-bu˺kure 水膨れ・水ぶくれ blister

mizu-bu˺soku 水不足 water shortage

mizu-de˺ppō 水鉄砲 water pistol

mizugi 水着 swim suit, bathing suit

mizu-ko˺shi˺ 水こし colander

mizumushi 水虫 athlete's foot

mizusa˺shi˺ 水差し water pitcher

mizutaki 水炊き chicken, bean curd, etc., dipped into hot broth till ready to eat

mizuu˺mi 湖 lake

mizuwari 水割り (highball of) whisky and water

mm(a/e/o)... = **um(a/e/o)...** うま/うめ/うも...

... mo ...も too, also, even; (not) ... either/even; indeed; NUMBER **mo** も + NEGATIVE not even (so much as), + AFFIRMATIVE as many/much as, all of

... mo ... mo ...も...も both ... and ... ; + NEGATIVE neither ... nor ...

mō˺ もう already; now; ~ **su˺gu** もうすぐ right away

mō もう more; (not) ... any more; ~ **hito˺ri** もう一人 another (one more) person; ~ **hito˺tsu** もう一つ another, one more, the other one; ~ **ichi-do˺/i˺k-ka˺i** もう一度／一回 one more time, again; ~ **suko˺shi** もう少し (a bit) more

mo˺cha 持ちゃ 1. = **mo˺teba** 持てば (if one have; if it last) 2. ~ **shinai** 持ちゃしない = **mo˺chi ya/wa shinai** 持ちや／はしない = **mota˺nai** 持たない (not have; not last)

mochi 餅・もち rice cake

mo˺chi 持ち → **mochima˺su** 持ちます [infinitive]

mochi-agema˺su 持ち上げます, **-age˺ru** 持ち上げる lifts

mochi-awase 持ち合わせ what is on hand (in stock); **... no ~** ...の持ち合わせ the stock of ...

mochi-awa˺se 持ち合わせ → **mochi-awasema˺su** 持ち合わせます

mochi-awasema˺su 持ち合わせます, **-awase˺ru** 持ち合わせる has on hand (in stock)

mochi-gome もち米・糯米 glutinous rice

mochiima˺su 用います, **mochii˺ru** 用いる = **tsukaima˺su** 使います (uses)

mochima˺su 持ちます, **mo˺tsu** 持つ has, holds, carries; it lasts mochi'-mono 持ち物 belongings

mochi'-nushi 持ち主 owner

mochi'ron もちろん of course, certainly

mōchō⌐-en 盲腸炎 appendicitis

mo'deru モデル model

mōdō-ken 盲導犬 seeing-eye dog

modorima'su 戻ります, modo'ru 戻る goes back, returns, reverts

modoshima'su 戻します, modo'su 戻す 1. vomits 2. sends back, returns

moe 燃え → moema'su 燃えます [infinitive]

moegara 燃え殻 cinder(s)

moema'su 燃えます, moeru 燃える (fire) burns

mō'fu 毛布 blanket

mogura もぐら・土竜 a mole (rodent)

moguri' 潜り diving; a diver

mogu'ri 潜り → mogurima'su 潜ります [infinitive]

mogurima'su 潜ります, mogu'ru 潜る dives (under); gets into (bed); goes under (ground)

mohan 模範 model, pattern

mo'ji 文字 letter, character, writing

mōji⌐n 盲人 blind person

mōkarima'su もうかります・儲かります, mōka'ru もうかる・儲かる is profitable, it makes money; Mōkarima'kka もうかりまっか・儲かりまっか (=

Mōkarima'su ka もうかりますか・儲かりますか) How are you doing? = Hello! (in Osaka)

mokei 模型 model, mold

mōkema'su, mōke'ru 1. もうけ[儲け]ます, もうけ[儲け]る makes money, profits 2. 設けます, 設ける prepares, sets up

Mō'ko 蒙古 Mongolia

mokuhan(-ga) 木版(画) wood-block print

mokuhyō 目標 target, goal

mokuji 目次 (table of) contents

mokuroku 目録 catalog, list, table, inventory

mokusō 黙想 meditation

mokuta'n 木炭 charcoal

mokuteki 目的 aim, objective, purpose, end, goal

mokutekī'-chi 目的地 destination, goal

Mokuyō'bi 木曜日 Thursday

mokuyoku 沐浴 bathing

moku⌐zai 木材 wood

momanai もまない・揉まない = momimase'n もみません・揉みません (not rub)

mo'mban 門番 gatekeeper, watchman, guard

Mombu'-shō 文部省 Ministry of Education

mome もめ・揉め 1. → momema'su もめます・揉めます [infinitive] 2. → momima'su もみます・揉みま

す [imperative] massage it!

mome¯ba もめば・揉めば → **momima¯su** もみます・揉みます (if one massage)

mome-goto もめごと・揉め事 discord, tiff, trouble

momema¯su もめます・揉めます, **momeru** もめる・揉める 1. is in discord/trouble; **ki ga** ～ 気が揉めます feels uneasy/troubled 2. can massage (rub with both hands)

momen もめん・木綿 cotton

momete もめて・揉めて → **momema¯su** もめます・揉めます

momi もみ・揉み → **momima¯su** もみます・揉みます [infinitive]

momi もみ・籾 unhulled rice

mo¯mi もみ・樅 fir (tree)

momigara もみ殻・籾殻 chaff

mo¯miji もみじ・紅葉 1. maple 2. autumn leaves

momima¯su もみます・揉みます, **momu** もむ・揉む massages, rubs with both hands

momo 桃 peach

mo¯mo もも・股 thigh

momō ももう・揉もう → **momima¯su** もみます・揉みます (let's massage it!)

momohiki ももひき・股引き tight-fitting workpants; (= **zubo¯n-shita** ズボン下) drawers

momo-iro (no) 桃色(の) pink, rosy

momya もみゃ・揉みゃ 1. = **mome¯ba** もめば・揉めば (if one massage) 2. ～ **shinai** 揉みゃしない = **momi¯ ya/wa shinai** 揉みや/はしない = **momanai** もまない・揉まない (not massage)

mo¯n もん = **mono¯** もの

mo¯n 1. 門 gate 2. 紋 = **monshō** 紋章 family crest

mondai 問題 question, problem, topic, subject; ～ **ni nara¯nai** 問題にならない unimportant

monde もんで・揉んで → **momima¯su** もみます・揉みます

monga¯i-kan 門外漢 outsider, nonspecialist, layman

mo¯nku 文句 phrase; complaint

mono¯ 1. 物・もの thing, object, article, something, stuff; … **shita mo¯n/mono¯ desu** …したもん/ものです used to do 2. 者 person, fellow

… mono …もの because

monoga¯tari 物語 tale, legend

mono¯goto 物事 things, everything

monohoshi-zuna 物干し綱 clothesline

mono-o¯boe 物覚え memory

mono-o¯ki 物置き shed *(storehouse)*

monorē¯ru モノレール monorail

monosashi 物差し ruler (= foot rule); measure; criterion

mono-sugo'i ものすごい・物凄い terrible, awesome

mono-su'go'ku ものすごく・物凄く terribly, extremely

mono'zuki' (na) 物好き(な) curious, inquisitive

monshō 紋章 family crest

mo'ppara もっぱら・専ら principally, chiefly

mo'ppu モップ mop

moraima'su もらいます, **morau** もらう receives, gets; has someone do it

mo'ra shima(')su (suru) 網羅します(する) includes, comprises, covers (all); **mo'ra shita** … 網羅した… exhaustive, complete

morashima'su 漏らします, **mora'su** 漏らす lets leak; reveals

moratta もらった = **moraima'shita** もらいました (got)

moratte もらって → **moraima'su** もらいます

morawanai もらわない = **moraimase'n** もらいません (not get)

more 盛れ → **morima'su** 盛ります [imperative] heap it up!

mo're 漏れ → **morema'su** 漏れます [infinitive]

morema'su 漏れます, **more'ru** 漏れる leaks out; is omitted; (=

morima'su 漏ります) it leaks

mori 1. 森 woods, forest **2.** 盛り・漏り → **morima'su** 盛ります・漏ります

moribana 盛り花 a flower arrangement in a low basin

morima'su 盛ります, **moru** 盛る heaps/piles it up

morima'su 漏ります, **mo'ru** 漏る it leaks

moro'i もろい・脆い brittle, frail

mo'ru モール lace

moruhine モルヒネ morphine

mo'shi (… shita'ra) もし(…したら) if, perchance

mōshi-agema'su 申し上げます, **-age'ru** 申し上げる [HUMBLE] I say

mōshi-de 申し出 proposal, offer; report, application; claim

mōshi-dema'su 申し出ます, **-de'ru** 申し出る proposes, offers; reports, applies for, claims

mōshi-ide 申し出 [old-fashioned] = **mōshi-de** 申し出

mōshi-ire 申し入れ (public) proposal, offering

mōshi-irema'su 申し入れます, **-ire'ru** 申し入れる (publicly) proposes, offers

mōshi-komi 申し込み application; reservation, subscription; proposal, offer

mōshi-komima'su 申し込みます,

-ko🜂mu 申し込む applies;
reserves, subscribes; proposes,
offers

mōshikomí-sha 申し込み者・申
込者 applicant

mōshimá su 申します, mō su 申
す [HUMBLE] 1. I say (=
mōshi-agemá su 申し上げま
す) 2. o-...-i / go-... ~ お...
い/ご...申します I humbly do
(= itashimá su 致します)

mo shi-moshi! もしもし! hello!
hey! say there!

mōshi-wake 申し訳 excuse; ~
arimase n/gozaimase n 申し訳
ありません/ございません
(What can I say? =) I am very
sorry.

mō shon モーション motion; sexual overture, pass; ... ni ~ o
kakemá su (kake ru) ...にモー
ションをかけます(かける)
makes a pass at, makes eyes at

Mo🜂sukuwa モスクワ Moscow

mō tā モーター motor

motá nai 持たない =
mochimase n 持ちません (not
have; not last)

motaremá su もたれます,
motare ru もたれる: (... ni)
~ (...に)もたれます leans
(against ...)

motasemá su 持たせます,
motase ru 持たせる lets one
have, provides (one with),
gives

mo tcha 持っちゃ = mo tte wa
持っては (having; lasting)

mo te 持て 1. → motemá su 持て
ます [infinitive] 2. →
mochimá su 持ちます [im-
perative] hold it!

mo teba 持てば → mochimá su
持ちます (if one have; if it
last)

motemá su 持てます, mote ru 持
てる 1. is popular, well liked
2. can hold

moto🜂 元 origin, source; cause
(of an effect)

moto もと・下 (at the) foot (of),
under

...-moto ...元 the source of an activity; shuppan ~ 出版元 the
publisher(s); hambai ~ 販売
元 sales agency; seizō ~ 製造
元 the maker(s); oroshi ~ 卸
元 the wholesaler

mo to (no) 元(の) former,
earlier; ~ kara 元から from
the beginning, always, all
along

motó 持とう = mochimashó 持
ちましょう (let's hold it!)

motomemá su 求めます,
motome ru 求める 1. wants,
looks for 2. asks for, demands
3. buys, gets

motomoto もともと・元々 from
the start, originally; by nature,
naturally; ...-te mo ~ de su ...
ても元々[もともと]です is

no worse off even if ..., it will
do no harm to ...

mo'to wa もとは・元は originally; earlier, before

mo'to'-yori もとより from the
beginning; by nature

motozukima'su 基づきます,
motozu'ku 基づく is based on;
conforms to

mo'tsu 持つ = **mochima'su** 持ち
ます (has, holds, carries)

motsure⌐ もつれ・縺れ tangle,
entanglement; complications

motsu⌐re もつれ・縺れ →
motsurema'su もつれます・縺
れます [infinitive]

motsurema'su もつれます・縺れ
ます, **motsure⌐ru** もつれる・
縺れる gets entangled/com-
plicated; **shita' ga ~** 舌がもつ
れ[縺れ]ます lisps

mottai-na'i もったいない
1. undeserving **2.** wasteful

motte 1. 盛って・漏って →
morima'su 盛ります・漏りま
す **2.** 持って = **mo'tte** 持って
(holding) [*before verbs of
movement*]

mo'tte 持って → **mochima'su** 持
ちます [*but* **motte** 持って
before verbs of movement]

motte ikima'su (iku) 持って行き
ます(行く) takes, carries;
brings (to you, there)

mo'tte ima'su (iru) 持っています
(いる) has, holds, owns,

possesses

motte itte 持って行って taking
it; **~ kudasa'i** 持って行って
下さい please take it with you

motte kima'su (ku'ru) 持って来
ます(来る) brings (to me,
here)

motte' kite 持って来て bringing
it; **~ kudasa(⌐)i** 持って来て
下さい please bring it here

motte ko'i 持って来い bring it
here!

motte-ko'i (no) もってこい[持っ
て来い](の) most desirable,
ideal; just the thing/ticket

mo'tto もっと more, still more;
longer, further; **~ i'i** もっと
いい better, **~ waru'i** もっと
悪い worse; **mo'tto takusa'n**
もっとたくさん[沢山] lots
more

mo'ttomo もっとも **1.** indeed, of
course **2.** but, however, to be
sure

mo'tto'mo 最も most; exceedingly

mo'ya もや・靄 mist, haze

moyashi⌐ もやし・萌やし bean
sprouts

moyō 模様・もよう pattern

moyōshima'su 催します,
moyō⌐su 催す holds/gives (an
event); feels

mubō (na) 無謀(な) reckless

mu-cha'kuriku (no) 無着陸(の)
non-stop (flight)

mu⌐cha (na) 無茶・むちゃ（な）
unreasonable; reckless; disorderly

mu⌐chi 鞭 a whip; ~ **de
uchima⌐su** 鞭で打ちます
whips

muchū 夢中 trance, ecstasy; ...
ni ~ ni narima⌐su ...に夢中に
なります gets entranced with
(engrossed in) ...

muda-ba⌐nashi 無駄[むだ]話
idle talk; gossip; hot air, bull;
~ **o shima⌐su** 無駄話をします
shoots the bull

muda (na) 無駄・むだ（な）futile,
no good, wasteful; useless

mu⌐dan de 無断で without
notice, without permission

muda ni 無駄に in vain; ~
shima⌐su 無駄にします wastes

muda-zu⌐kai 無駄使い、extrava-
gance; ~ **shima(⌐)su** 無駄使
いします wastes

mu⌐gi 麦 wheat, barley

mugi-wa⌐ra 麦わら・麦藁 straw

mugo⌐i むごい cruel, brutal

muika 六日 six days; the 6th day
(of month); ~**-me** 六日目 the
6th day

mu-i⌐mi (na) 無意味（な）mean-
ingless

mu-i⌐shiki (no/na) 無意識（の/な）
unconscious, involuntary

muite 向いて・むい[剥い]て →
mukima⌐su 向きます・むき[剥
き]ます

mu⌐jaki (na) 無邪気・むじゃき
（な）naive, innocent, un-
sophisticated

mu⌐ji (no) 無地（の）solid-color

mu-jō⌐ken (no) 無条件（の）un-
conditional; ~ **de** 無条件で
unconditionally

mujō (na) 無情（な）heartless,
unfeeling

mujun 矛盾 inconsistency, contradiction; ~ **shite ima⌐su** 矛
盾しています is inconsistent,
contradictory

mukade むかで・百足 centipede

mukae 迎え 1. a welcome 2. →
mukaema⌐su 迎えます [infini-
tive]

mukaema⌐su 迎えます, **mukaeru**
迎える meets; welcomes; in-
vites

mukai 向かい → **mukaima⌐su** 向
かいます [infinitive]

mukaima⌐su 向かいます, **mukau**
向かう: ... **ni ~** ...に向かいま
す opposes; heads for

mu⌐kamuka shima⌐su むかむか
[ムカムカ]します is queasy,
feels nauseated

mukanai 向かない =
mukimase⌐n 向きません (not
face)

mu-ka⌐nkaku (na) 無感覚（な）
numb

mu-ka⌐nkei (no) 無関係（の）: ...
to ~ ...と無関係（の）un-
related (unconnected, irrele-

vant) to …

mu-ka⌐nshin (na) 無関心（な）: … ni ~ …に無関心（な）indifferent to …, unconcerned with …

mukashi 昔 long ago; ancient days; (~ no 昔の) ancient, old(en); ~-ba⌐nashi 昔話 legend; mukashi kara⌐ no 昔からの old *(from way back)*

mukatte 向かって → mukaima⌐su 向かいます

muke 向け・むけ［剥け］→ mukema⌐su 向けます・むけ［剥け］ます [infinitive]

muke⌐ba 向けば → mukima⌐su 向きます (if one face)

mukema⌐su 向けます, mukeru 向ける turns (one's face/eyes/attention to), directs/points it (at)

…-muke (no) …向け（の） (bound/intended) for …

mukete 向けて → mukema⌐su 向けます

muki 向き・むき［剥き］→ mukima⌐su 向きます・むき［剥き］ます [infinitive]

mukima⌐su, muku 1. 向きます, 向く faces 2. むき［剥き］ます, むく・剥く (… no kawa⌐ o ~ … の皮をむき［剥き］ます) skins, pares, peels

…-muki (no) …向き（の）facing; (suitable) for …

mu⌐ko (o-mu⌐ko san) 婿（お婿さ

ん) son-in-law; bridegroom

mukō⌐ 向こう 1. (o-mu⌐kō お向こう) beyond; across the way, over there; ~ (no) 向こう（の) opposite, facing 2. = mukō-gawa 向こう側

mukō⌐ 向こう = mukimasho⌐ 向きましょう (let's face it!)

mukō-gawa 向こう側 the other side/party, the opposite side

mukō⌐-mizu (na) 向こう見ず（な) reckless, rash; ~ ni 向こう見ずに recklessly

mukō (na/no) 無効（な/の) invalid (= not valid)

muku⌐i 報い → mukuima⌐su 報い//ます [infinitive]

mukuima⌐su 報います, mukui⌐ru 報いる repays; compensates

mukui⌐nai 報いない = mukuimase⌐n 報いません (not repay/compensate)

muku⌐ite 報いて → mukuima⌐su 報います

mukya 向きゃ 1. = muke⌐ba 向けば (if one face) 2. ~ shinai 向きゃしない = muki⌐ ya/wa shinai 向きや/はしない = mukanai 向かない (not face)

mumei (no) 無名（の) nameless, anonymous; obscure

munashi⌐i むなしい・空しい・虚しい empty; futile, in vain

mune⌐ 棟 ridge (of roof)

mune⌐ 1. 胸 chest, breast; heart, mind 2. 旨 gist, purport, intent, effect

mura 村 village

muragarima su 群がります, **muraga ru** 群がる they flock/ throng together

mura saki 1. ~ **(no)** 紫(の) purple **2.** 紫 = **shōyu** しょうゆ・醤油 soy sauce

mure 群れ group, throng, flock

mu ri 1. 無理 strain, (undue) force, strain; ~ **o shima su** 無理をします overdoes, overworks, forces **2.** ~ **(na)** 無理(な) unreasonable, forced; violent; overdoing; (over)-demanding

mu ri ni sasema su 無理にさせます forces one (to do)

mu ri ni shima su 無理にします strains, forces; overdoes (it); demands too much

mu ri wa arimase n (na i) 無理はありません(ない): **... no mo** ~ ...のも無理はありません it is no wonder that ...

mu ryō (no) 無料(の) free of charge; **muryō-chū sha** 無料駐車 free parking

musa nai 蒸さない = **mushimase n** 蒸しません (not steam)

mu-se kinin (na) 無責任(な) irresponsible

mushi 虫 insect, bug; moth; worm; **mushi-ku dashi** 虫下し vermifuge

mu shi 蒸し → **mushima su** 蒸します (steams) [infinitive]

mushi-atsu i 蒸し暑い muggy, close, sultry, humid

mushi-ba 虫歯 decayed tooth

mushima su 蒸します, **mu su** 蒸す steams it; is sultry, humid

mushi -mono 蒸し物 steamed foods

mu shiro むしろ rather; preferably

mu shi shima(¬)su 無視します ignores, neglects, disregards

mu shite 蒸して → **mushima su** 蒸します

mushi-yo ke 虫よけ・虫除け insect repellent; mothballs

mushiyoke -ami 虫よけ網 window screen

musubi 1. むすび・結び (= **o-mu subi** おむすび・お結び) riceball **2.** 結び (= **musubi-me** 結び目) knot

musubima su 結びます, **musubu** 結ぶ ties, ties up, winds up; **ne kutai o** ~ ネクタイを結びます wears a tie

musuko 息子 son

musume 娘 daughter; girl

musū (no) 無数(の) innumerable, countless

musunde 結んで → **musubima su** 結びます

muto n-chaku/-jaku (na) 無頓着/着(な) careless

mutsu̠ 六つ = **muttsu̠** 六つ・6つ

mutsu̠kashii むつかしい・難しい = **muzukashii** むずかしい・難しい

muttsu̠ 六つ・6つ six; six years old

mu̠yami ni むやみ[無闇]に recklessly; indiscriminately; immoderately

mu[⌐]yō (no) 無用(の) unnecessary; useless; having no business

mu̠zai (no) 無罪(の) innocent, not guilty

muzō̠sa (na) 無造作・むぞうさ (な) effortless, easy; ～ **ni** 無造作[むぞうさ]に effortlessly, easily, readily; casually, carelessly

muzukashii むずかしい・難しい hard, difficult

mu̠zumuzu むずむず itchy, crawly, creepy

myaku̠ 脈, **myaku̠haku** 脈拍 pulse

myō̠ban 明晩 tomorrow night

myōchō 明朝 tomorrow morning

myōga みょうが・茗荷 Japanese ginger (buds)

myōgo[⌐]-nichi 明後日 day after tomorrow

myō̠ji 名字・苗字 family name [as written]

myō̠ (na) 妙(な) strange, queer, wondrous

myō̠nichi 明日 tomorrow

— N —

n̠ (''**un**'') ん(うん) uh-huh, yeah

...[⌐]n ......n... = **..[⌐] no ......の...**; **...[⌐] n desu̠ (da)** ...んです(だ) it's that ...

na (o-na) 名(お名) name

na̠ (o-na) 菜(お菜) = **na[⌐]ppa** 菜っ葉・なっぱ greens, vegetables; rape

... na ...な which is ... (→ **de[⌐]su̠** です, **da[⌐]** だ)

... na! ...な! Don't ... !

... na̠/nā̠ ...な/なあ = **... ne[⌐]/**

ne[⌐] ...ね/ねえ isn't it, don't you think/agree

na̠be (o-na[⌐]be) 鍋(お鍋) pan, pot

nabe[⌐]-mono 鍋物 food cooked and served in a pan

na-daka[⌐]i 名高い famous

nadamema̠su̠ なだめます, **nadame[⌐]ru** なだめる soothes, pacifies

nadare[⌐] 雪崩・なだれ avalanche; (= **yuki-na[⌐]dare** 雪なだれ) snowslide

na̅de なで・撫で → **nadema̅su** なでます・撫でます **1.** [infinitive] **2.** [imperative] **nade̅ ro** なでろ・撫でろ, **na̅de yo** なでよ・撫でよ

nadema̅su なでます・撫でます, **nade̅ru** なでる・撫でる strokes, smoothes, pats, pets

... na̅do ...など・等 and so forth/on, and what-not, and the like

na̅e 1. 苗 seedling **2.** なえ・萎え → **naema̅su** なえます・萎えます [infinitive] **3.** なえ・綯え → **naima̅su** ないます・綯います [imperative] twist it!

na̅eba なえば・綯えば → **naima̅su** ないます・綯います (if one twist it)

naema̅su, nae̅ru 1. なえます・萎えます, なえる・萎える droops, withers **2.** なえます・綯えます, なえる・綯える can twist it (into a rope)

nae̅reba 萎えれば・綯えれば, **nae̅rya** 萎えりゃ・綯えりゃ → **naema̅su** 萎えます; 綯えます (if it droop; if one can twist it)

nae̅ ya shinai 萎えやしない・綯えやしない = **nae̅ wa shinai** 萎えはしない・綯えはしない = **nae̅nai** 萎えない; 綯えない (not droop; cannot twist it)

nafuda 名札 name plate/tag; dog tag

nafuta▯rin ナフタリン (naphthalene) mothballs

naga-gutsu 長靴 boots

naga̅i 長い, **na̅gaku** 長く long

naga-isu 長椅子・長いす couch

nagame̅ 眺め view, scenery

naga̅me 眺め → **nagamema̅su** 眺めます [infinitive]

nagamema̅su 眺めます, **nagame̅ru** 眺める gazes/stares at, views

naga-ne▯gi 長ねぎ[葱] leek (*the regular* **ne̅gi** ねぎ・葱, *as contrasted with* **tama-ne̅gi** 玉ねぎ[葱] round onion)

... (-)na̅gara ...ながら while (= during/although)

nagare̅ 流れ a stream, a flow

naga̅re 流れ → **nagarema̅su** 流れます [infinitive]

nagare̅-boshi 流れ星 shooting star

nagarema̅su 流れます, **nagare̅ru** 流れる flows

nagare̅nai 流れない = **nagaremase̅n** 流れません (not flow)

naga̅rete 流れて → **nagarema̅su** 流れます

na▯gasa 長さ length

Naga̅saki 長崎 Nagasaki; **Nagasaki̅-ken** 長崎県 Nagasaki Prefecture; **Nagasaki̅-shi** 長崎市 Nagasaki City

nagasa̱nai 流さない = **nagashimase̱n** 流しません (not let flow)

nagashi̱ 流し kitchen sink

naga̱shi 流し → **nagashima̱su** 流します [infinitive]

nagashima̱su 流します, **naga̱su** 流す lets it flow

naga-ya 長屋 tenement house

na̱ge 投げ → **nagema̱su** 投げます 1. [infinitive] 2. [imperative] **nage̱ro** 投げろ, **na̱ge yo** 投げよ

nage-ire 投げ入れ a flower arrangement (in a tall vase)

nage̱ite 嘆いて → **nagekima̱su** 嘆きます

nageka̱nai 嘆かない = **nagekimase̱n** 嘆きません (not grieve)

nageki̱ 嘆き grief, lamentation

nage̱ki 嘆き → **nagekima̱su** 嘆きます [infinitive]

nagekima̱su 嘆きます, **nage̱ku** 嘆く grieves, weeps, moans, laments

nagema̱su 投げます, **nage̱ru** 投げる throws

nage̱nai 投げない = **nagemase̱n** 投げません (not throw)

nage-nawa 投げ縄 lasso

na̱gete 投げて → **nagema̱su** 投げます

nageyo̱ 投げよう = **nagemasho̱** 投げましょう (let's throw it!)

nagurima̱su なぐります・殴りま す, **nagu̱ru** なぐる・殴る knocks, beats, strikes

nagusame 慰め comfort, consolation

nagusamema̱su 慰めます, **nagusame̱ru** 慰める comforts, consoles

nagusami 慰み amusement, entertainment

nagu̱tte なぐって・殴って → **nagurima̱su** なぐります・殴り ます

na̱i 1. ない・無い = **arimase̱n** あ りません (there is no … , lacks, has no …) **2.** ない・綯い → **naima̱su** ないます・綯いま す [infinitive]

…-nai …内 within, in(side)

na̱ibu (no) 内部(の) internal

na̱ichi 内地 inside the country; ~ **(no)** 内地(の) inland, internal

…-na̱ide …ないで not [do] but instead, without [do]ing; → **shina̱ide** しないで

na̱ifu ナイフ knife

na̱igai 内外 inside and out; home and abroad

…-na̱igai …内外 approximately

na̱ikaku 内閣 a government cabinet

naima̱su ないます・綯います, **na̱u** なう・綯う twists (into a rope)

na̱in ナイン nine; baseball team

na̱iron ナイロン nylon

naisen 内線 extension *(phone line, inside)*

... na̅ishi ... ...ないし[乃至]... [bookish] **1.** and/or = **ma̅ta̅-wa** または・又は **2.** from ... to ... = **... kara ... ma̅de** ...から...まで

naisho (**no**) 内緒・内証(の) confidential, secret, private; **naisho** (**ˉ**) **no hanashi̅** 内緒[内証]の話, **naisho-ba̅nashi** 内緒[内証]話 a private talk

naita 泣いた = **nakima̅shita** 泣きました (cried)

na̅ita̅ ナイター night game (of baseball)

naite 泣いて → **nakima̅su** 泣きます

nai-teki (na) 内的(な) internal; ~ **sho̅ko** 内的証拠 internal evidence

naiyō 内容 contents

na̅ka 1. 中 inside; **... no** ~ **de/ni** ...の中で/に in ... **2.** 仲・なか relations, terms (between people); (**... to**) ~ **ga i̅i** (...と)仲[なか]がいい is on good terms (with ...)

naka **ba** 半ば middle

nakadachi̅ 仲立ち go-between, intermediary, broker

naka **gai** 仲買 broker

nakama̅ 仲間 friend, pal, companion (**o-nakama** お仲間)

naka̅mi 中身・中味 contents

nakanai 泣かない = **nakimase̅n** 泣きません (not cry)

nakanaka なかなか・仲々 extremely, very (long, hard, bad, etc.), more than one might expect

na̅katta なかった = **arimase̅n deshita** ありませんでした (was not, did not have)

...-na̅katta ...なかった = **...-mase̅n deshita** ...ませんでした (did not)

na̅kattara なかったら if/when there isn't (we don't have); unless there is (we have)

...-na̅kattara ...なかったら if/when one doesn't; unless one does

na̅kattari なかったり sometimes/alternately there isn't (we don't have)

...-na̅kattari (shima̅su, desu) ...なかったり(します, です) sometimes/alternately does not do

nake 泣け **1.** → **nakema̅su** 泣けます [infinitive] **2.** → **nakima̅su** 泣きます [imperative] cry!

nake̅ba 泣けば → **namima̅su** 泣きます (if one cry)

nakema̅su 泣けます, **nakeru** 泣ける can cry

nakere̅ba 泣ければ, **nakerya** 泣けりゃ if one can cry

na̅kereba なければ, **na̅kerya** なけりゃ unless there is, unless one has

...-na͡kereba ...なければ, **...-na͡kerya** ...なけりゃ unless one does; **~ narimase͡n** ...なければなりません has to (must) do ［す [infinitive]

naki 泣き → **nakima͡su** 泣きま

na͡ki ... なき・無き・亡き... [literary] = **na͡i ...** ない... (lacking, nonexistent); **i͡ma wa ~ ...** 今はなき[亡き]... the late ...

nakigara なきがら・亡骸 corpse

nakima͡su, naku 1. 泣きます, 泣く weeps; cries **2.** 鳴きます, 鳴く makes an animal sound

nakō 泣こう = **nakimashō͡** 泣きましょう (let's cry!)

nakō͡do 仲人 go-between (matchmaker)

na͡ku なく so that there isn't any (we don't have any); there not being; without

(...-)na͡kucha (...)なくちゃ = **(...-)na͡kute wa** (...)なくては

naku-narima͡su なくなります・亡くなります, **-naru** なくなる・亡くなる dies; gets lost

...-naku (narima͡su) ...なく(なります) (gets) so that one doesn't do (= **...-nai yō͡ ni ...** ないように)

na͡ku narima͡su (na͡ru) なく[無く]なります(なる) vanishes (from existence)

nakusanai なくさない = **nakushimase͡n** なく[無く]し

ません (not lose)

nakushima͡su なく[無く]します, **nakusu** なく[無く]す loses

na͡kute なくて without, lacking (→ **na͡i** ない = **arimase͡n** ありません)

...-na͡kute mo ...なくても even not doing, even if one not do; **shina͡kute mo i͡i** しなくてもいい need not do

...-na͡kute wa ...なくては not doing, if one not do; **shina͡kute wa ikemase͡n** しなくてはいけません must (ought to) do

nakya 泣きゃ = **nake͡ba** 泣けば (if one cry)

(...-)na͡kya (...)なきゃ = **(...-)na͡kerya** (...)なけりゃ = **(...-)na͡kereba** (...)なければ unless (there is)

nakya shimase͡n (shinai) 泣きゃしません(しない) = **naki͡ ya/wa shimase͡n** 泣きや/はしません = **nakimase͡n** 泣きません (not cry)

na͡ma 生 **1. ~ (no/de)** 生・なま (の/で) raw, uncooked, fresh **2.** (= **nama-bi͡iru** 生ビール) draft beer **3.** (= **gen-nama** 現なま) hard cash

namae (o-namae) 名前(お名前) name

nama-gomi 生ごみ garbage (kitchen waste)

namagusa͡i 生臭い fishy(-smelling)

namaiki (na) 生意気(な) impertinent

namakemasu 怠けます, **namakeru** 怠ける idles, is lazy

namake-mono no 怠け者 lazy *(person)*

nama-kurīimu 生クリーム whipping cream

nama-pan 生パン dough

namari 鉛 lead (metal)

namari なまり・訛り dialect, accent

namasu なます・鱠 raw fish tidbits with vegetables in vinegar

nama-yake (no) 生焼け(の) rare *(little cooked)*, underdone

namazu なまず・鯰 catfish

nám-ba 何羽 how many birds

nám-bā ナンバー = **nambā-purēto** ナンバープレート (car) license plate

nam-bai 何倍 how many times (doubled)

nám-bai 何杯 how many cupfuls

nám-ban 何番 what number

Nambei 南米 = **Minami-Amerika** 南アメリカ South America

nám-bén 何遍 how many times

nám-biki 何匹 how many animals/fish/bugs

námboku 南北 north and south

nám-bon 何本 how many long things

nám-bu 南部 the south, the southern part

námbyaku 何百 how many hundreds

nám-e なめ・嘗め → **namemásu** なめます・嘗めます 1. [infinitive] 2. [imperative] **name ro** なめろ・嘗めろ, **náme yo** なめよ・嘗めよ lick it!

namemásu なめます・嘗めます, **name ru** なめる・嘗める licks, tastes

name raka (na) 滑らか・なめらか(な) smooth

namí 波 wave

námida 涙 tear *(in eye)*

namiki 並木 row of trees

nami (no) 並(の) ordinary, common, average, regular

nami-no ri 波乗り surfing

naminori-ita 波乗り板 surfboard

nám-mai 何枚 how many flat things

nám-man 何万 how many tens of thousands

nampa 難破 shipwreck

nám-paku shimásu ka 何泊しますか How many nights will you stay?

nampō 南方 the south

nám-pun 何分 how many minutes

nan-... 南... south (= **minami no ...** 南の...)

nán-..., nám-... 何... how many ... ; ~ COUNTER **ka (no ...)** 何 COUNTER か(の...) a number (of ...)

na⌐n 何 (*before* **d, t, n**) = **na⌐ni** 何 what

na⌐na 七・7 seven

nana⌐-do 七度 seven degrees

nana⌐-do⌐ 七度 seven times

nana⌐-he⌐n 七遍 seven times

nana⌐-hyaku 七百・700 seven hundred

nana⌐-jū 七十・70 seventy

nana-kai 七階 seven floors/stories, seventh floor

nana⌐-ka⌐i 七回 seven times

nana-ma⌐n 七万・70,000 seventy thousand

nana⌐me (no/ni) 斜め(の/に) aslant, oblique, diagonal

nana⌐-nen 七年 the year 7; (= **nane⌐n-kan** 七年間) seven years

nana⌐-nin 七人 seven people

nana⌐-satsu 七冊 seven books

nana-se⌐n 七千・7,000 seven thousand

nana⌐tsu 七つ・7つ seven, seven years old; **nanatsu-me⌐** 七つ目 seventh

na⌐n-dai 何台 how many (*machines, vehicles*)

na⌐n da i 何だい = **na⌐n desu ka** 何ですか what is it

na⌐n de⌐ mo なんでも・何でも whatever it may be, anything (at all), everything

... na⌐n desu (da, de) ...なんです (だ, で) it's that it is ...

na⌐ndo (o-na⌐ndo) 納戸(お納戸) back room, closet

na⌐n-do 何度 how many times

na⌐n-gai/-kai 何階/階 how many floors/stories; what (number) floor

na⌐n-gatsu 何月 what month

na⌐n-gen 何軒 how many (*buildings, shops, ...*)

na⌐ni 何 what; ~ **(ga/o) ...-te⌐ mo** 何(が/を)...ても whatever

nani-... 何... what ... , which ... ; **nani-da⌐igaku** 何大学 what university

nanibun なにぶん・何分 anyway, anyhow

nanige-na⌐i 何気ない casual

nani-go 何語 what language

nani-iro 何色 what color

nani⌐-jin 何人 what nationality

na⌐ni ka なにか・何か something, anything

nani mo なにも・何も + NEGATIVE nothing, (not) anything

na⌐ninani 何々 something or other, so-and-so, what's-it(s-name)

na⌐ni-shiro なにしろ・何しろ anyway, anyhow

na⌐ni yori なにより・何より than what; ~ **mo** なによりも・何よりも more than anything

na⌐n-ji 何時 what time; **nan-ji⌐kan** 何時間 how many hours

... na⌐nka ...なんか and so forth/on, and what-not; the

likes of

nan-ka͞getsu 何か月 how many months

na͞n-kai 1. 何回 how many times **2.** 何階 = **na͞n-gai/-kai** 何階/階

nan-ka͞koku 何か国 how many countries

nan-ka͞kokugo 何か国語 how many languages

nan-ka͞sho 何個所・何箇所 how many places

Nanki͞n-mame 南京豆 peanut(s)

na͞n-ko 何個 how many little things

nan-na͞ra 何なら if you prefer, if you like, if you don't mind; if you don't want to

na͞n-nen 何年 what year; how many years

na͞n-nichi 何日 what day (of the month); how many days

nanni mo なんにも・何にも [emphatic] = **nani mo** なにも・何も

na͞n ni mo なんにも・何にも (= **na͞n no ... ni͞ mo** なんの[何の]...にも) + NEGATIVE not to/for/at anything

na͞n-nin 何人 how many people

na͞n no なんの・何の what (kind of); of what

nanoka 七日 seven days; the 7th day (of month)

... na͞ no ni ...なのに in spite of its being ... , despite that it is ...

na͞n-ra͞ ka no ... なんらかの・何らかの... some

na͞n-ra no ... なんらの・何らの... + NEGATIVE not any, not in any way ⌈old

na͞n-sai 何歳 how (many years)

na͞n-satsu 何冊 how many books

nansei 南西 southwest

na͞n-seki 何隻 how many boats

na͞n-shoku 何食 how many meals

na͞n-sō 何艘 how many ships

... na͞nte ...なんて = **... na͞ do to (yū) no) wa** ...などと(ゆうの)は; = **... na͞ do to yū** ...などとゆう; = **... na͞ do to (itte)** ...などと(言って)

na͞n to ... なんと[何と]... with what, what and ... ; (saying/ thinking/meaning) what

nantō 南東 southeast

na͞n-tō 何頭 how many large animals

na͞n to itte͞ mo なんと[何と]言っても eventually, come what may

na͞n to ka shite なんとかして・何とかして by some means (or other), somehow or other

nan to mo なんとも・何とも + NEGATIVE nothing (at all), not ... at all

na͞n to shite͞ mo なんとしても・何としても inevitably; at any cost

nan-yō͞bi 何曜日 what day (of

the week)

na⌐n-zoku 何足 (*also* **na⌐n-soku** 何足) how many pairs (of footwear)

na⌐o なお・尚 still more; moreover; ~ **i⌐i** なお[尚]いい still better

nao⌐ri 直り・治り → **naorima⌐su** 直ります・治ります [infinitive]

naorima⌐su 直ります・治ります, **nao⌐ru** 直る・治る is righted, cured, fixed, repaired; gets well, recovers; improves

na⌐o-sara なおさら・尚更 all the more, still more

nao⌐se 直せ → **naoshima⌐su** 直します [imperative] fix it!

naoshi⌐ 直し mending, repair-(ing), correcting, correction

nao⌐shi 直し・治し → **naoshima⌐su** 直します・治します [infinitive]

naoshima⌐su, nao⌐su 1. 直します・治します, 直す・治す makes it right, corrects, repairs, mends, fixes, cures, alters; improves it 2. ...直します, ...直す [INFINITIVE +] does it over (and better), re-does it

nao⌐tte 直って・治って → **naorima⌐su** 直ります・治ります

na⌐ppa 菜っ葉・なっぱ greens, vegetables; rape

na⌐puki⌐n ナプキン napkin

... **na⌐ra** ...なら, ... **na⌐ra-ba** ...ならば if it be, provided it is [*negative* ... **ja na⌐kereba/na⌐kerya** ...じゃなければ/なけりゃ]; VERB-**ru/-ta** ~ る/たなら, ADJ-**i/katta** ~ い/かったなら if (it be a matter of) ...

narabe 並べ 1. → **narabema⌐su** 並べます [infinitive]; [imperative] **narabe ro** 並べろ, **narabe⌐ yo** 並べよ line them up! 2. → **narabima⌐su** 並びます [imperative] line up!

narabema⌐su 並べます, **naraberu** 並べる arranges, lines them up

narabi 並び 1. row *(line)* 2. → **narabima⌐su** 並びます [infinitive]

narabima⌐su 並びます, **narabu** 並ぶ they line up, arrange themselves

nara⌐e 習え 1. → **naraema⌐su** 習えます [infinitive] 2. → **naraima⌐su** 習います [imperative] learn it!

naraema⌐su 習えます, **narae⌐ru** 習える can learn

naraima⌐su 習います, **nara⌐u** 習う learns

naranai 鳴らない = **narimase⌐n** 鳴りません (not sound)

nara⌐nai ならない = **narimase⌐n** なりません (not become)

narande 並んで → **narabima⌐su** 並びます; ~ **ima⌐su** 並んでいます are in a row, are lined up

narase 鳴らせ 1. → **narasemásu** 鳴らせます [infinitive] 2. → **narashimásu** 鳴らします [imperative] sound!

narasemásu 鳴らせます, **naraseru** 鳴らせる can sound

narasenai 鳴らせない = **narasemase̱n** 鳴らせません (cannot sound)

narashimásu 鳴らします, **narasu** 鳴らす sounds, rings it

narashimásu, narásu 1. 均します, 均す smoothes, averages 2. 馴らします, 馴らす domesticates, tames

narátta 習った = **naraimáshi̱ta** 習いました learned

narátte 習って → **naraimásu** 習います 「ます

naráu 習う → **naraimásu** 習い

narawánai 習わない = **naraimase̱n** 習いません (not learn)

nare 鳴れ → **narimásu** 鳴ります [imperative] sound!

náre 1. 慣れ・馴れ; なれ・成れ → **naremásu** 慣れます・なれ[成れ]ます [infinitive] 2. → **narimásu** なります・成れます [imperative]

naréba 鳴れば → **narimásu** 鳴ります (if it sound)

náreba なれば・成れば → **narimásu** なります・成ります (if it become)

naremásu, naréru 1. 慣れ[馴れ]ます, 慣れ[馴れ]る (... **ni** ...に) gets used to, grows familiar with 2. なれ[成れ]ます, なれ[成れ]る can become

naré̱nai 慣れない・なれ[成れ]ない = **naremase̱n** 慣れません; なれ[成れ]ません (not get used to; not become)

nari 鳴り → **narimásu** 鳴ります [infinitive]

narí̱ (o-ná̱ri) なり（おなり） form; personal appearance

ná̱ri なり・成り → **narimásu** なります・成ります [infinitive]

narimásu なります・成ります, **ná̱ru** なる・成る becomes, gets to be, turns into; is done, completed; amounts to, is; [HONORIFIC] **o-nari ni narimásu** おなりになります

... **ni** (ADJECTIVE-**ku**) ～ ...に（ADJECTIVE く）なります gets so it is ... , gets to be ... , turns into ...

... **suru koto ni** ～ ...する事になります it gets arranged/decided to (do) ...

narimásu 鳴ります, **naru** 鳴る it sounds, rings

nariyuki 成り行き・なりゆき process, development, course; result; ～ **o mimásu** 成り行きを見ます watches how things develop (turn out)

narṓ̱ なろう = **narimashṓ̱** なりましょう (let's become ... !)

naru-beᵓku ... なるべく... as ... as possible

naru-hodo なるほど・成る程 I see; quite so; you are so right; how true

narya 鳴りゃ 1. = **nare̍ba** 鳴れば (if it sound) 2. ~ **shinai** 鳴りゃしない = **nari̍ ya/wa shinai** 鳴りや/はしない = **naranai** 鳴らない (not sound)

na̍rya なりゃ 1. = **na̍reba** なれば (if it become) 2. ~ **shinai** なりゃしない = **na̍ri ya/wa shinai** なりや/はしない = **nara̍nai** ならない (not become)

nasa̍i なさい → **nasaima̍su** なさいます [imperative] please do it!

nasaima̍su なさいます, **nasa̍ru** なさる (someone honored) does

naᵓsakeᵓ (o-na̍sake) 情け(お情け) affection, feeling, tenderness, compassion, sympathy

nasake-na̍i 情けない wretched, miserable; shameful

nasa̍nai 成さない = **nashimase̍n** 成しません (not achieve)

nasa̍ri なさり → **nasaima̍su** なさいます [infinitive]

nasa̍tta なさった = **nasaima̍shita** なさいました (did)

nasa̍tte なさって → **nasaima̍su** なさいます

na̍se 成せ 1. → **nasema̍su** 成せます [infinitive] 2. → **nashima̍su** 成します [imperative] achieve it!

nasema̍su 成せます, **nase̍ru** 成せる can achieve it

nashi̍ 梨 pear

na̍shi 1. 成し → **nashima̍su** 成します [infinitive] 2. なし・無し [literary] = **na̍i** ない・無い (= **arimase̍n** ありません)

nashima̍su 成します, **na̍su** 成す achieves, forms, does

... na̍shi ni ...なし[無し]に = **... ga na̍ku(te)** ...がなく(て) without, lacking, not having

naso̍ 成そう = **nashimasho̍** 成しましょう (let's achieve it!)

na̍su 1. なす・茄子 (= **na̍subi** なすび) eggplant 2. 成す = **nashima̍su** 成します

nasu̍tta なすった = **nasa̍tta** なさった = **nasaima̍shita** なさいました (did)

nasu̍tte なすって = **nasa̍tte** なさって

nata なた・鉈 hatchet

natsu̍ 夏 summer

natsukashi̍i なつかしい・懐かしい dear(ly remembered)

natsume なつめ・棗 date (fruit)

natsu-mi̍kan 夏みかん・夏蜜柑 Japanese grapefruit (= pomelo)

natsu-ya゚sumi 夏休み summer vacation/holiday

natta 鳴った = **narima゚shita** 鳴りました (it sounded)

na゚tta 1. なった・成った = **narima゚shita** なりました・成りました (became) **2.** なった・綯った = **naima゚shita** ないました・綯いました (twisted it)

natte 鳴って → **narima゚su** 鳴ります (it sounds)

na゚tte 1. なって・成って → **narima゚su** なります・成ります (becomes …) **2.** なって・綯って → **naima゚su** ないます・綯います (twists it)

nattō゚ 納豆 fermented soy beans

nattoku 納得 understanding, compliance, assent; (… o) **nattoku shima゚su** (…を)納得します gets persuaded/convinced (of …), assents/consents to, complies with; **hito ni** (… o) **nattoku sasema゚su** 人に(…を)納得させます persuades/convinces one (of …)

na゚ttsu ナッツ nuts

na゚u なう・綯う = **naima゚su** ないます・綯います (twists it)

nawa゚ 縄 rope, cord

nawa゚nai なわない・綯わない = **naimase゚n** ないません・綯いません (not twist it)

na⌐ya 納屋 barn, shed

na゚ya なや・綯や **1.** = **na゚eba** なえば・綯えば (if one twist it)

2. ~ **shinai** なや[綯や]しない = **nai゚ ya/wa shinai** ない[綯い]や/はしない = **nawa゚nai** なわない・綯わない (not twist it)

nayami゚ 悩み suffering, distress, torment

naya゚mi 悩み → **nayamima゚su** 悩みます [infinitive]

nayamima゚su 悩みます, **naya゚mu** 悩む suffers

naya゚nde 悩んで → **nayamima゚su** 悩みます

na゚ze なぜ・何故 why; ~ **ka to yū to …** なぜかというと… the reason is that …

nazo なぞ・謎 riddle, mystery

nazu゚ke 名付け → **nazukema゚su** 名付けます: **1.** [infinitive] **2.** [imperative] ~ **yo** 名付けよ, **nazuke゚ ro** 名付けろ name it!

nazukema゚su 名付けます, **nazuke゚ru** 名付ける names, dubs

nazu゚kete 名付けて → **nazukema゚su** 名付けます

…゚ n desu (da) …んです(だ) it's that …

ne 1. 音 (= **oto゚** 音) sound **2.** 値 (= **nedan** 値段) price; **ne ga taka゚i** 値が高い is expensive **3.** 寝 (= **nemuri** 眠り) sleep-(ing) **4.** 寝 → **nema゚su** 寝ます [infinitive]; [imperative] **ne ro** 寝ろ, **ne yo** 寝よ sleep!

ne゚ 根 root

... ne͞/ne͞ ...ね/ねぇ isn't it, don't you think/agree

ne-age 値上げ price rise; raising the cost

ne͞baneba shima͞su ねばねばします is sticky

nebari͞ 粘り stickiness

ne-biki 値引き discount (of price)

ne-bu͞soku 寝不足 not enough sleep

necha 寝ちゃ = **nete͞ wa** 寝ては

nechaima͞su 寝ちゃいます = **nete shimaima͞su** 寝てしまいます

nedan (o-ne͞dan) 値段（お値段）price

nega͞i 願い 1. a request 2. → **negaima͞su** 願います [infinitive]

negaima͞su 願います, **nega͞u** 願う asks for, requests, begs

ne͞gi ねぎ・葱 onion (green)

ne-isu 寝椅子 couch, lounge (chair)

ne͞ji ねじ screw

neji-ma͞washi ねじ回し screwdriver

nejira͞nai ねじらない = **nejirimase͞n** ねじりません (not twist)

nejirima͞su ねじります, **neji͞ru** ねじる twists

neji͞tte ねじって → **nejirima͞su** ねじります

nekashima͞su 寝かします,

nekasu 寝かす puts to bed/ sleep; lays it on its side

ne͞kkuresu ネックレス necklace

ne͞ko 猫 cat

ne͞kutai ネクタイ necktie; **~ o musubima͞su (musubu)** ネクタイを結びます（結ぶ）puts on (wears) a necktie

ne-maki 寝巻き a yukata (kimono) to sleep in

nema͞su 寝ます, **neru** 寝る goes to bed, lies down, sleeps

nemmatsu 年末 the end of the year

ne-moto͞ 根元 (the part) near the root, the base (of a tree)

nemui 眠い sleepy

nemuri 眠り 1. sleep(ing) 2. → **nemurima͞su** 眠ります [infinitive]

nemurima͞su 眠ります, **nemuru** 眠る sleeps

nemutte 眠って → **nemurima͞su** 眠ります

ne͞n 1. 年 year 2. 念 sense, feeling; desire; caution, care, attention; **nen no tame͞ (ni)** 念のため（に）to make sure, to be on the safe side, as a precaution, as a (word of) caution; **(... ni) ~ o irema͞su** (...に)念を入れます pays attention (to ...), is careful (of/about ...), **~ o oshima͞su (osu)** 念を押します（押す）double-checks

nenai 寝ない = **nemase͞n** 寝ませ

ん (not go to bed)

nenchaku̱-tē̱pu 粘着テープ
adhesive tape

ne̱ndo 1. 粘土 clay 2. 年度 year
period, (fiscal) year

nenga⌐-jō 年賀状 New Year's
card

nenga̱ppi 年月日 date *(year
month day)*

nenkin 年金 pension

nenrei 年齢 (one's) age [bookish]
= **toshi⌐** 年

nenryō̱ 燃料 fuel

nerae 狙え 1. → **neraema̱su** 狙
えます [infinitive] 2. →
neraima̱su 狙います [impera-
tive] aim!

neraema̱su 狙えます, **neraeru** 狙
える can aim

nerai 狙い 1. an aim, object;
idea, intention, what one is
driving at 2. → **neraima̱su** 狙
います [infinitive]

neraima̱su 狙います, **nerau** 狙う
aims at, watches for, seeks

nera̱nai 練らない = **nerimase̱n**
練りません (not knead)

ne(ra)rema̱su 寝(ら)れます,
ne(ra)reru 寝(ら)れる can go
to bed, can lie down, can sleep

ne(ra)rete 寝(ら)れて →
ne(ra)rema̱su 寝(ら)れます

neratte 狙って → **neraima̱su** 狙
います

nerawanai 狙わない =
neraimase̱n 狙いません (not

aim at)

ne̱re 練れ 1. → **nerema̱su** 練れ
ます [infinitive] 2. →
nerima̱su 練ります [impera-
tive] knead!

nere̱ba 寝れば → **nema̱su** 寝ま
す (if one go to bed)

ne̱reba 練れば → **nerima̱su** 練
ります (if one knead)

nerema̱su 寝れます, **nereru** 寝れ
る = **nararema̱su** 寝られます
(can go to bed)

nerema̱su 練れます, **ne̱ru** 練
れる can knead; can drill,
train

nere̱reba 1. 練れれば →
nerema̱su 練れます (if one
can knead) 2. 寝れれば =
narare̱reba 寝られれば (if one
can go to bed)

nere̱ba 寝れれば, **nererya** 寝れ
りゃ → **ne(ra)rema̱su** 寝(ら)
れます (if one can go to bed)

nere̱reba 練れれば, **ne̱rerya** 練
れりゃ → **nerema̱su** 練れます
(if one can knead)

nerete 寝れて = **nararete** 寝られ
て (can go to bed)

ne̱ri 練り → **nerima̱su** 練ります
[infinitive]

neri-hami̱gaki 練り歯磨き toothpaste

neri̱-ko 練り粉 dough

nerima̱su 練ります, **ne̱ru** 練る
kneads; drills, trains

nerō̱ 練ろう = **nerimashō̱** 練り

ましょう (let's knead it!)

neru 寝る = **nema'su** 寝ます (goes to bed, lies down, sleeps)

ne'ru 1. ネル flannel 2. 練る = **nerima'su** 練ります

nerya 寝りゃ = **nere'ba** 寝れば (if one go to bed)

ne'rya 練りゃ 1. = **ne'reba** 練れば (if one knead) 2. ~ **shinai** 練りゃしない = **ne'ri ya/wa shinai** 練りや/はしない = **nera'nai** 練らない (not knead)

ne'-san (o-ne'-san) 姉さん（お姉さん） older sister; Miss!; Waitress!

nes-shima'su 熱します, **-su⌐ru** 熱する 1. gets hot, gets excited 2. heats it, warms it

ne'sshi'n (na) 熱心（な） enthusiastic; ~ **ni** 熱心に enthusiastically

neta 寝た = **nema'shita** 寝ました (went to bed; slept)

netamashi'i ねたましい・妬ましい envious; enviable

netamima'su ねたみます・妬みます, **neta'mu** ねたむ・妬む envies

nete 寝て → **nema'su** 寝ます

netsu' 熱 fever (**o-ne'tsu** お熱); heat

netsubō 熱望 ambition *(hope)*

ne'tta 練った = **nerima'shita** 練りました (kneaded)

nettai(-chi'ho') 熱帯（地方） tropic(s)

ne'tte 練って → **nerima'su** 練ります (kneads)

neuchi 値打ち value, worth

ne' ya shinai 寝やしない = **ne' wa shinai** 寝はしない = **nenai** 寝ない (not go to bed)

neyō 寝よう = **nemasho'** 寝ましょう (let's go to bed!)

nezumi ねずみ・鼠 mouse, rat

nezumi-iro (no) ねずみ色（の） gray

nezumi'-tori ねずみ捕り［取り］ mousetrap

ni 似 → **nima'su** 似ます [infinitive]

ni' 1. 二・2 two 2. 荷 load, burden

... ni(⌐) ...に 1. to/for (a person) 2. at/in (a place), at (a time) 3. = **... e(⌐)** ...へ to (a place) 4. as, so as to be, (turn/make) into being, being

ni-a'i 似合い → **ni-aima'su** 似合います [infinitive]

ni-aima'su 似合います, **ni-a'u** 似合う: **... ni ~** ...に似合います is becoming (to), suits

ni-bai 二倍 twice *(double)*

ni-bamme' (no) 二番目（の） second

nibu'i 鈍い dull, blunt

nicha 似ちゃ = **nite' wa** 似ては

Nichi-... 日..., **...-Nichi** ...日 Japan(ese); **Nichi-Ei** 日英 Japanese-English ⌐*days)*

...-nichi ...日 day *(counts/names*

nichibotsu 日没 sunset

Nichiyōbi 日曜日 Sunday

ni̅-dai 二台 two (machines, vehicles)

ni-do 二度 two times, twice; **nido-me** 二度目 the second time

ni̅-do 二度 two degrees

nie 煮え → **niema̅su** 煮えます [infinitive]

ni̅e にえ・沸・鎳 damascene

niema̅su 煮えます, **nieru** 煮える it boils, it cooks

niete 煮えて → **niema̅su** 煮えます

ni̅-fuda 荷札 (baggage/package) tag

niga̅i 苦い bitter; wry

nigashima̅su 逃がします, **niga̅su** 逃がす turns loose; lets one get away, lets it slip away

Ni-gatsu 二月・2月 February

ni̅ge 逃げ → **nigema̅su** 逃げます 1. [infinitive] 2. [imperative] **nige̅ ro** 逃げろ, **ni̅ge yo** 逃げよ run away!

nigema̅su 逃げます, **nige̅ru** 逃げる runs away, escapes, flees

ni̅geta 逃げた = **nigema̅shita** 逃げました (fled)

ni̅gete 逃げて → **nigema̅su** 逃げます

nigirima̅su 握ります, **nigiru** 握る grasps, grips, clutches

nigiri-meshi にぎりめし・握り飯 riceball (= **o-ni̅giri** おにぎり・

お握り)

nigiri̅-zushi にぎり[握り]ずし[寿司] sushi hand-packed into small balls (as traditional in Tokyo)

nigitte 握って → **nigirima̅su** 握ります

nigi̅yaka (na) にぎやか[賑やか] (な) merry, bustling, lively, flourishing

nigorima̅su 濁ります, **nigo̅ru** 濁る 1. gets muddy 2. (a voiceless sound) becomes voiced (**k > g, f/h > b, ch/sh > j, s > z, t/ts > z**)

ni̅gō (san) 二号(さん) mistress, concubine

ni̅-hai 二杯 two cupfuls

ni-he̅n 二遍 two times

Niho̅n 日本 Japan

  Nihon-fū 日本風 Japanese style

  Nihon-go 日本語 Japanese (language/word)

  Nihon-ji̅n 日本人 a Japanese

  Niho̅n-kai 日本海 the Sea of Japan

  Nihon-ma 日本間 Japanese-style room

  Nihon-ryo̅ri 日本料理 Japanese cuisine

  Nihon-sei 日本製 made in Japan

  Nihon-shu 日本酒 saké (rice wine)

ni̅-hon 二本 two long things

ni-hyakú 二百・200 two hundred

níi-san (o-níi-san) 兄さん（お兄さん）older brother

niji⁽ˉ⁾ 虹 rainbow

nijís-sai 二十歳 20 years old

ni-jū 二重 double, duplicate; **~-nábe** 二重鍋 double boiler

níi-jū 二十・20 twenty; **~ yokka** 二十四日 24 days, 24th day (of month); **nijū-bammé** 二十番目 20th

ni-kai 二階 second floor; upstairs (**o-níi-kai** お二階)

ni-káii 二回 (= **ni-dó** 二度) two times; **nikai-mé** 二回目 the second time

nikawa にかわ・膠 glue

ni-kayoimáisu 似通います, **-kayóu** 似通う: **... ni/to ~** ...に/と似通います closely resembles

níi-ken 二軒 two buildings

níikibi にきび pimple

Nikkei (no) 日系（の）(of) Japanese ancestry; **Nikkéii-jin** 日系人 person of Japanese ancestry

níikke(i) にっけ(い)・肉桂, **níikki** にっき cinnamon

nikki 日記 diary

níikkō 日光 sunshine; **Níikkō** 日光 Nikko (place)

níi-ko 二個 two small things

níikoniko にこにこ smiling; **~ shimáisu** にこにこします smiles

nikú (**o-níiku**) 肉（お肉）meat

niku-dáingo 肉団子 Chinese meatballs

nikúii 1. 憎い, dislikable, hated **2.** にくい・難い (**shi-~** しにくい) hard, difficult (to do)

nikukiri-bóichō 肉切り包丁 butcher/carving knife, meat cleaver

niku-man 肉まん steamed bun stuffed with ground pork

nikumimáisu 憎みます, **nikúimu** 憎む hates, detests

nikúinde 憎んで → **nikumimáisu** 憎みます

nikutai 肉体 flesh, the body

nikúi-ya 肉屋 butcher (shop)

níi-mai 二枚 two flat things

ni-máin 二万・20,000 twenty thousand

nimáisu, niru 1. 似ます, 似る resembles **2.** 煮ます, 煮る boils, cooks

níi-mei 二名 [bookish] = **fútari**⁾ 二人・ふたり two people

...-nimmae ...人前 (counts portions)

... níi mo ...にも also (even) at/in, to, as

ni-mono 煮物 boiled foods

níimotsu (o-níimotsu) 荷物（お荷物）baggage, load

níimpu 人夫 coolie, workman

...(ˉ)-nin ...人 person, people; **yo-níin** 四人 four people; **ichíi-nin** 一人 (is usually replaced by hito'ri 一人・ひとり one person), ni'-nin 二人 (*by* futari' 二人・ふたり two people)

nina'e 担え → ninaima'su 担います [imperative] carry it!

ninai 似ない・煮ない = nimase'n 似ません; 煮ません (not resemble; not boil/cook it)

nina'i 担い → ninaima'su 担います [infinitive]

ninaima'su 担います, nina'u 担う carries on shoulders

nina'tte 担って → ninaima'su 担います

ninawa'nai 担わない = ninaimase'n 担いません (not carry)

ni'-nen 二年 the year 2; (= nine'n-kan 二年間) two years; nine'n-sei 二年生 second-year student, sophomore

ningen 人間 human being

ningyō (o-ningyō) 人形（お人形） doll; ~-shi'bai 人形芝居 puppet show

ni'nja 忍者 a master of stealth(y espionage)

ninjin にんじん・人参 carrot

ni'njō 人情 human nature, human feelings, warmheartedness

ninki 人気 popularity; ~ ga arima'su 人気があります is popular

ninniku にんにく・大蒜 garlic

ninshin 妊娠 pregnancy; ~ shite ima'su 妊娠しています is pregnant

ninshin-chū'zetsu 妊娠中絶 abortion

ni'nsoku 人足 coolie, workman

ni'nzu 人数, ni'nzū 人数 number of people, population

nio'i 臭い・匂い 1. a smell; (... no) nio'i ga shima'su (...の)臭い[匂い]がします it smells (of ...) 2. → nioima'su 臭います・匂います [infinitive]

nioima'su 臭います・匂います, nio'u 臭う・匂う it smells, is fragrant

nio'tte 臭って・匂って → nioima'su 臭います・匂います

Nippo'n 日本 = Niho'n 日本 Japan

nira にら・韮 a leek; a green onion

niramima'su にらみます・睨みます, nira'mu にらむ・睨む glares, stares

nira'nde にらんで・睨んで → niramima'su にらみます・睨みます

nire にれ・楡 yew (tree)

nire'ba 似れば・煮れば → nima'su 似ます; 煮ます (if it resemble; if one boil/cook it)

ni ro 煮ろ → nima'su 煮ます [imperative] boil it!

niru 1. 似る = nima'su 似ます

(resembles) **2.** 煮る = **nima̶ su**
煮ます (boils, cooks)

nirya 似りゃ・煮りゃ = **nire̶ ba**
似れば; 煮れば (if it resem-
ble; if one boil/cook it)

ni̶ -sai 二歳 two years old

ni̶ -san (no) 二、三（の）several

ni̶ -satsu 二冊 two books

ni̶ -sei 二世 second generation
(Japanese emigrant); ... the
Second

nisema̶ su 似せます, **niseru** 似せ
る imitates, copies; counter-
feits (money), forges (a document, a signature)

nise-mono 偽物・にせもの a
fake, an imitation; a forgery

ni-se̶ n 二千・2,000 two thousand

nise (no) にせ・偽（の）false,
phony, fake, imitation

nise-satsu 偽札・贋札・にせ札
counterfeit bill (currency)

nishi 西 west; ～**-guchi** 西口 the
west exit/entrance; ～**-yori
(no kaze)** 西寄り（の風）wester-
ly (wind)

nishi-ka̶ igan 西海岸 west coast

ni̶ shiki にしき・錦 brocade

nishime (o-ni̶ shime) 煮しめ（お
煮しめ）boiled fish and
vegetables

ni̶ shin にしん・鰊 herring

nishoku-tsuki (no) 二食付き（の）
with two meals included

**nissu̶ ** 日数 the number of days

ni̶ su ニス = **wa̶ nisu** ワニス

(varnish)

nita ...似た... similar (= **nite iru**
... 似ている... → **nima̶ su** 似
ます)

nita 煮た = **nima̶ shita** 煮ました
(boiled)

nite 似て・煮て → **nima̶ su** 似ま
す・煮ます

... ni̶ te ...にて [literary] = **... de**
...で (at; ...)

ni-tō̶ ** 二等 second class; **nitō̶ -ken
二等券 second-class ticket;
nitō̶ -seki 二等席 second-class
seat; **nitō̶ -sha** 二等車 second-
class car; **nitō̶ -shō** 二等賞 the
second prize

nittei 日程 schedule, program,
itinerary

niwa (o-niwa) 庭（お庭）garden

ni̶ -wa 二羽 two (birds)

... ni̶ wa ...には to; at/in; as

ni̶ waka (no/ni) にわか（の/に）
sudden(ly), unexpected(ly);
niwaka-a̶ me にわか雨 sudden
shower

niwatori にわとり・鶏 chicken

ni̶ ya shinai 似やしない・煮やし
ない = **ni̶ wa shinai** 似はしな
い・煮はしない = **ninai** 似な
い; 煮ない (not resemble; not
boil/cook it)

ni yo 煮よ → **nima̶ su** 煮ます [im-
perative] boil it!

niyō 煮よう = **nimashō̶ ** 煮まし
ょう (let's boil it!)

ni-zu̶ kuri 荷造り packing

n͟n ("un-un") んん(うんうん)
huh-uh, uh-uh, nope

no͞ 野 = **no͞-hara** 野原 field
(dry)

... no ...の **1.** the one/time/
place that ... (= **hito͞** 人,
mono͞ 物, **toki͞** 時, **tokoro͞** 所)
2. the (specific) act/fact of ...
(*cf.* **koto͞** 事) **3.** which/that is ...
(→ **de͞su** です, **da͞** だ, **na** な)

nō͞⁅⁆ **(o-nō)** 能(お能) Noh
[Japanese classical theater]

nobashima͞su 伸ばします・延ば
します, **noba͞su** 伸ばす・延ば
す extends (lengthens,
stretches, defers) it

no͞be 述べ → **nobema͞su** 述べま
す **1.** [infinitive] **2.** [impera-
tive] **nobe͞ ro** 述べろ, **no͞be yo**
述べよ tell it!

nobema͞su 述べます, **nobe͞ru** 述
べる tells, relates

no͞bi 伸び → **nobima͞su** 伸びま
す [infinitive]

nobima͞su 伸びます, **nobi͞ru** 伸
びる it extends, reaches; it
spreads

nobori 1. 上り inbound (to
Tokyo), the up train **2.** 登り・
上り・昇り → **noborima͞su** 登
ります・上ります・昇ります
[infinitive]

noborima͞su, noboru 1. 登りま
す, 登る climbs **2.** 上ります,
上る goes up **3.** 昇ります, 昇
る rises

nochi⁅⁆ のち・後, **nochi-hodo** の
ちほど・後程 later = **a͞to (de)**
あと・後(で)

nō͞chi 農地 farm land

no͞do のど・喉 throat; ~ **ga
kawakima͞shita** のど[喉]が渇
きました is thirsty

no͞doka (na) のどか(な) tranquil, peaceful, quiet, calm

nō͞fu 農夫 farmer

nō͞gyō 農業 agriculture, farming

no͞-hara 野原 field

noite のいて・退いて →
nokima͞su のきます・退きま
す

nōjō⁅⁆ 農場 farm

nō͞ka 農家 farm house/family;
farmer

noke のけ・退け **1.** → **nokema͞su**
のけます・退けます [infini-
tive]; [imperative] **noke ro**
のけろ・退けろ, **noke͞ yo** のけ
よ・退けよ omit it! **2.** →
nokima͞su のきます・退きま
す [imperative] get out of the
way!

nokema͞su のけます・退けます,
nokeru のける・退ける
removes; omits

nokenai のけない・退けない =
nokemase͞n のけません・退け
ません (not remove/omit)

nokanai のかない・退かない =
nokimase͞n のきません・退き
ません (not get out of the
way)

nokete のけて・退けて → **nokema͡su** のけます・退けます

noki 1. 軒 eaves **2.** のき・退き → **nokima͡su** のきます・退きます [infinitive]

nokima͡su のきます・退きます, **noku** のく・退く gets out of the way

no͞kku shima(͞)su ノックします knocks (on door)

nokogi͞ri のこぎり・鋸 a saw

nokori͞ 残り the rest, the remainder, what is left, the leftover

nokorima͡su 残ります, **noko͞ru** 残る remains, is left behind/ over

nokori-mo͞no͞ 残り物 leftovers, remains, leavings

nokoshima͡su 残します, **noko͞su** 残す leaves behind/ over

noma͡nai 飲まない = **nomimase͞n** 飲みません (not drink)

no͞me 飲め **1.** → **nomema͡su** 飲めます [infinitive] **2.** → **nomima͡su** 飲みます [imperative] drink it!

no͞meba 飲めば → **nomima͡su** 飲みます (if one drink)

nomema͡su 飲めます, **nome͞ru** 飲める can drink; is (very) drinkable

nō-men 能面 mask (Noh drama)

nome͞nai 飲めない = **nomemase͞n** 飲めません (can't drink)

nome͞reba 飲めれば, **nome͞rya** 飲めりゃ → **nomema͡su** 飲めます (if one can drink)

no͞mete 飲めて → **nomema͡su** 飲めます

nomi͞ のみ・蚤 flea

no͞mi 1. のみ・鑿 chisel **2.** 飲み → **nomima͡su** 飲みます [infinitive]

... no͞mi ...のみ = **... dake͞** ...だけ only

nomi-komima͡su 飲み込みます, **-ko͞mu** 飲み込む swallows (ingests)

nomima͡su 飲みます, **no͞mu** 飲む drinks; smokes; takes (medicine)

nomi͞-mizu 飲み水 drinking water

nomi͞-mono 飲み物 beverage, something to drink, refreshments

nōmin 農民 the farmers

nō-mi͞so 脳みそ・脳味噌 brain

nomi͞-ya 飲み屋 tavern, neighborhood bar

no͞mi ya shimase͞n (shinai) 飲みやしません（しない） = **no͞mi wa shimase͞n** 飲みはしません = **nomimase͞n** 飲みません (not drink)

nomo͞ 飲もう = **nomimasho͞** 飲みましょう (let's drink!)

noˈmya 飲みゃ **1.** = **noˈmeba** 飲めば (if one drink) **2.** ~ **shinai** 飲みゃしない = **noˈmi wa shinai** 飲みはしない = **nomaˈnai** 飲まない (not drink)

noˈnda 飲んだ = **nomimaˈshita** 飲みました (drank)

noˈnde 飲んで → **nomimaˈsu** 飲みます

noˈnja 飲んじゃ = **noˈnde wa** 飲んでは; ~ **dameˈ (desu)** 飲んじゃだめ（です) don't drink it!

noˈnki (na) のん気・呑気（な) easygoing, happy-go-lucky, carefree

nonoshirimaˈsu ののしります・罵ります, **nonoshiˈru** ののしる・罵る reviles, abuses, swears at, curses

nonoshiˈtte ののしって・罵って → **nonoshirimaˈsu** ののしります・罵ります

nore 乗れ **1.** → **noremaˈsu** 乗れます [infinitive] **2.** → **norimaˈsu** 乗ります [imperative] get aboard!

noremaˈsu 乗れます, **noreru** 乗れる can ride/board

noren のれん・暖簾 shop curtain; credit

nori 乗り → **norimaˈsu** 乗ります [infinitive]

noriˈ 1. のり・海苔 seaweed (green) **2.** のり・糊 paste; starch

nori-ba 乗り場 boarding area/place; platform (at station); taxi station; bus stop

nori-kae 乗り換え change, transfer (of vehicle)

nori-kaemaˈsu 乗り換えます, **nori-kaˈeru** 乗り換える changes (vehicles)

nori-komi 乗り込み drive-in

noriˈ-maki のり巻き・海苔巻き sushi rice in a seaweed roll

norimaˈsu 乗ります, **noru** 乗る gets aboard, rides; is carried

nori-mono 乗り物・乗物 vehicle

nōˈritsu 能率 efficiency

norō 乗ろう = **norimashōˈ** 乗りましょう (let's get aboard!)

noroˈi のろい・呪い a curse

noroˈi 1. のろい slow, dull, sluggish **2.** のろい・呪い → **noroimaˈsu** のろいます・呪います [infinitive]

noroimaˈsu のろいます・呪います, **noroˈu** のろう・呪う curses, utters a curse

noroˈtte のろって・呪って → **noroimaˈsu** のろいます・呪います

noru 乗る = **norimaˈsu** 乗ります (gets aboard, rides; is carried)

nōˈryoku 能力 ability

nose 乗せ = **nosemaˈsu** 乗せます **1.** [infinitive] **2.** [imperative] **nose ro** 乗せろ, **noseˈ yo** 乗せよ load/carry it!

nosemaˈsu, noseru 1. 乗せます,

乗せる loads, puts aboard, ships, carries 2. 載せます, 載せる publishes

nosete 乗せて・載せて → nosema'su 乗せます・載せます

noten (de/no) 野天(で/の) outdoors; ～-bu'ro 野天風呂 outdoors bath

nō'to ノート, nōtobu'kku ノートブック notebook

notta 乗った = norima'shita 乗りました (got aboard) 「ます

notte 乗って → norima'su 乗り

notto'ri 乗っ取り → nottorima'su 乗っ取ります

nottori'-han 乗っ取り犯 hijacker

nottori-ji'ken 乗っ取り事件 a hijacking; (illegal) takeover, seizure

nottorima'su 乗っ取ります, notto'ru 乗っ取る hijacks; (illegally) takes over, seizes

notto'tte 乗っ取って → nottorima'su 乗っ取ります

nōzei 納税 payment of taxes

nozoite のぞいて・除いて → nozokima'su 除きます

nozoke のぞけ・覗け 1. → nozokema'su のぞけます・覗けます [infinitive] 2. → nozokima'su のぞきます・覗きます [imperative] peek!

nozokema'su, nozokeru 1. のぞけます・覗けます, のぞける・覗ける can peek/peep at 2. 除けます, 除ける can remove;

can omit

nozoki のぞき[覗き]・除き → nozokima'su のぞき[覗き]ます・除きます [infinitive]

nozoki'-ana のぞき穴・覗き穴 peephole

nozokima'su, nozoku 1. のぞき[覗き]ます, のぞ[覗]く peeks/peeps at 2. 除きます, 除く eliminates, removes; omits

nozoki-ya のぞき屋・覗き屋 peeping Tom

nozokō のぞ[覗]こう・除こう = nozokimashō のぞき[覗き]ましょう; 除きましょう (let's peek!; let's remove/omit it!)

nozomashi'i 望ましい desirable, welcome

nozomi' 望み a desire; a hope, an expectation

nozo'mi 望み・臨み → nozomima'su 望みます・臨みます [infinitive]

nozomima'su, nozo'mu 1. 望みます, 望む desires, looks to, hopes for 2. 臨みます, 臨む looks out on

nozo'nde 望んで・臨んで → nozomima'su 望みます・臨みます

nū'do ヌード a nude (model)

nu'e 縫え 1. → nuema'su 縫えます [infinitive] 2. → nuima'su 縫います [imperative] sew it!

nuema'su 縫えます, nue'ru 縫え

る can sew

nue nai 縫えない = **nuemase n**
縫えません (cannot sew)

nuga nai 脱がない = **nugimase n**
脱ぎません (not take it off)

nu ge 脱げ 1. → **nugema su** 脱げ
ます [infinitive] 2. →
nugima su 脱ぎます [impera-
tive] take it off!

nugema su 脱げます, **nuge ru** 脱
げる 1. it slips/comes off
2. can take it off

nuge nai 脱げない =
nugemase n 脱げません (not
slip off; cannot take it off)

nu geta 脱げた = **nugema shita**
脱げました (it slipped; could
take it off)

nu gete 脱げて → **nugema su** 脱
げます

nugima su 脱ぎます・ぬぎます,
nu gu 脱ぐ・ぬぐ takes off
(clothes, shoes)

nugo 脱ごう = **nugimasho** 脱
ぎましょう (let's take it off!)

nuguema su 拭えます, **nugue ru**
拭える can wipe it away

nugue nai 拭えない・ぬぐえない
= **nuguemase n** 拭えません
(cannot wipe it away)

nuguima su 拭います・ぬぐいま
す, **nugu u** 拭う・ぬぐう wipes
it away

nugu tta 拭った =
nuguima shita 拭いました
(wiped it away)

nugu tte 拭って → **nuguima su**
拭います (wipes it away)

nuguwa nai 拭わない =
nuguimase n 拭いません (not
wipe it away)

nu i 縫い → **nuima su** 縫います

nu i bari 縫い針 sewing needle

nu ida 脱いだ = **nugima shita** 脱
ぎました (took it off)

nu ide 脱いで → **nugima su** 脱ぎ
ます

nuima su 縫います, **nu u** 縫う
sews

nui-me 縫い目 seam

nuita 抜いた = **nukima shita** 抜
きました (uncorked/removed
it)

nuite 抜いて → **nukima su** 抜き
ます

nukashima su 抜かします,
nukasu 抜かす skips, leaves
out

nuke 抜け 1. → **nukema su** 抜け
ます [infinitive] 2. →
nukima su 抜きます [impera-
tive] uncork/remove it!

nukema su 抜けます, **nukeru** 抜
ける comes off; escapes; is
omitted

nukete 抜けて → **nukema su** 抜
けます

...-nuki (de/no) ...抜き(で/の)
without (omitting)

nukima su 抜きます, **nuku** 抜く
uncorks; removes; omits; surpasses; selects

nukō 抜こう = **nukimashō** 抜き
　ましょう (let's uncork/
　remove it!)

numa 沼 swamp, marsh

nuranai 塗らない = **nurimase⌐n**
　塗りません (not paint it)

nurashima⌐su ぬらします・濡ら
　します, **nurasu** ぬらす・濡ら
　す wets, dampens

nure 1. ぬれ[濡れ]・塗れ →
　nurema⌐su ぬれ[濡れ]ます・塗
　れます [infinitive] **2.** 塗れ →
　nurima⌐su 塗ります [impera-
　tive] paint it!

nure⌐ba 塗れば → **nurima⌐su** 塗
　ります (if one paint it)

nurema⌐su, nureru 1. ぬれ[濡
　れ]ます, ぬれる・濡れる gets
　wet, damp; **nurete ima⌐su** ぬれ
　て[濡れて]います is wet **2.** 塗
　れます, 塗れる can paint it

nurenai ぬれ[濡れ]ない・塗れな
　い = **nuremase⌐n** ぬれ[濡れ]
　ません; 塗れません (not get
　wet; cannot paint it)

nurere⌐ba ぬれ[濡れ]れば・塗れ
　れば, **nurerya** ぬれ[濡れ]りゃ
　・塗れりゃ → **nurema⌐su** ぬれ
　[濡れ]ます; 塗れます (if it
　get wet; if one can paint it)

nurete ぬれ[濡れ]て・塗れて →
　nurema⌐su ぬれ[濡れ]ます・塗
　れます

nuri 塗り **1.** lacquer, varnish,
　painting **2.** → **nurima⌐su** 塗り
　ます [infinitive]

nuri-gu⌐suri 塗り薬 ointment

nuri-kaema⌐su 塗り替えます,
　-ka⌐e⌐ru 塗り替える repaints

nurima⌐su 塗ります, **nuru** 塗る
　lacquers, paints, varnishes,
　stains

nuri-mono 塗り物 lacquerware

nurō 塗ろう = **nurimashō** 塗り
　ましょう (let's paint it!)

nuru 塗る = **nurima⌐su** 塗りま
　す (paints) 　　　　　　「tepid

nuru⌐i ぬるい・温い lukewarm,

nurya 塗りゃ **1.** = **nure⌐ba** 塗れ
　ば (if one paint it) **2.** ~ **shinai**
　塗りゃしない = **nuri⌐ya/wa
　shinai** 塗りや/はしない =
　nuranai 塗らない (not paint
　it)

nushi 主 master, owner

nusumi⌐ 盗み theft

nusumima⌐su 盗みます, **nusu⌐mu**
　盗む steals, swipes, robs

nutta 塗った = **nurima⌐shita** 塗
　りました (painted)

nu⌐tta 縫った = **nuima⌐shita** 縫
　いました (sewed)

nutte 塗って → **nurima⌐su** 塗り
　ます

nu⌐tte 縫って → **nuima⌐su** 縫い
　ます

nu⌐u 縫う = **nuima⌐su** 縫います
　(sews)

nuwa⌐nai 縫わない = **nuimase⌐n**
　縫いません (not sew)

nu⌐ya 縫や **1.** = **nu⌐eba** 縫えば
　(if one sew) **2.** ~ **shinai** 縫や

しない = **nu̅i ya/wa shinai** 縫
いや/はしない = **nuwa̅nai** 縫
わない (not sew)
... nya/nyā ...にゃ/にゃあ = ...
nỉ wa ...には
nyo̅bo 女房, **nyo̅bō** 女房 wife
nyūbai 入梅 the rainy season (in
Japan)
nyūgaku 入学 admission to a
school, entering a school;
nyūgaku-shike̅n 入学試験 entrance exam; **nyūgaku
shima̅su** 入学します enrolls
(in school)
nyū̅-gan 乳がん・乳癌 breast
cancer
nyūin 入院 entering a hospital,
hospital admission; ～ **shite
ima̅su** 入院しています is in
the hospital
Nyūjiira̅ndo ニュージーランド
New Zealand; **Nyūjiirando̅-
jin** ニュージーランド人 a
New Zealander

nyūjō 入場 admission *(to a
place)*; **nyūjō̅-ken** 入場券 admission ticket, platform (non-
passenger) ticket; **nyūjō̅-ryō**
入場料 admission fee
nyūkoku 入国 entering a country; immigration; **nyūkoku-
kanri-jimu̅sho** 入国管理事務
所 immigration control office
nyūkyo 入居 moving into an
apartment; ～ **shima̅su** 入居
します moves into an apart-
ment
nyūkyo̅-sha 入居者 tenant, resident (of an apartment)
nyūsha 入社 entering (joining) a
company; ～**-shike̅n** 入社試
験 employment selection exam
nyū̅su ニュース news
nyūyoku 入浴 bath, taking a ⌐bath
Nyūyō̅ku ニューヨーク New
York
nyūyō (na) 入用(な) necessary,
needed

— O —

o̅ 1. 尾 = **shippo̅** しっぽ・尻尾
tail **2.** 緒 = **hanao** 鼻緒 thong,
strap
o- お・御 HONORIFIC (personalizing) PREFIX: "your" or "that
important thing"
... o ...を PARTICLE: marks direct

object (gets WHAT, loves
WHOM) or path traversed (goes
through/along WHERE, using
WHAT PATH)
ō̅ 王 = **ō-sama** 王様 king
ō-... 大... big, great
o-aiso おあいそ・お愛想, **o-aisō**

お愛想 (restaurant) bill, check

ō-a῀me 大雨 heavy rain

o῀bā オーバー **1.** overcoat, (top) coat **2.** ~ **(na)** オーバー（な） exaggerated, over(ly), too much; **ji῀kan ga ~ shima(῀)su** 時間がオーバーします runs overtime

o-ba῀ke お化け・おばけ ghost

ōbako おおばこ・車前草 plantain

oba(-san) 1. おば［叔母・伯母］ （さん） aunt **2.** おばさん lady, woman

obā῀-san 1. おばあさん・お祖母さん grandmother **2.** おばあさん old lady/woman

ōbāshū῀zu オーバーシューズ overshoes

Ō῀-Bei 欧米 Europe and America

o῀bi 帯 girdle, sash, belt

obi-jō (no) 帯状（の） belt(-like), a narrow strip (of); **~-hō῀shin** 帯状疱疹 shingles, herpes zoster

obo῀e 覚え memory; consciousness

obo῀e 覚え → **oboema῀su** 覚えます [infinitive]

oboema῀su 覚えます, **oboe῀ru** 覚える remembers, keeps in mind; learns

oboko(-mu῀sume) おぼこ（娘） virgin *(female)*

o-bon お盆 tray

o-bo῀n お盆 the Bon Festival *(Buddhist All Saints Day)*

obore-jini shima῀su (suru) 溺れ死にします（する） drowns

o-bō-san お坊さん Buddhist monk

obu῀i 負ぶい・おぶい → **obuima῀su** 負ぶいます・おぶいます

obuima῀su 負ぶいます・おぶいます, **obu῀u** 負ぶう・おぶう carries on one's back

obu῀tte 負ぶって・おぶって → **obuima῀su** 負ぶいます・おぶいます

obuwa῀nai 負ぶわない・おぶわない = **obuimase῀n** 負ぶいません・おぶいません (not carry)

o-cha お茶 Japanese green tea; the tea ceremony

o῀chi 落ち → **ochima῀su** 落ちます

ochima῀su 落ちます, **ochi῀ru** 落ちる falls, drops; is omitted; fails; is inferior

o῀chite 落ちて → **ochima῀su** 落ちます

ochi-tsuite 落ち着いて calm(ly)

ochi-tsukanai 落ち着かない, **ochi-tsukimase῀n** 落ち着きません is restless

ochi-tsukima῀su 落ち着きます, **-tsuku** 落ち着く calms down, keeps cool, settles down, relaxes

o-cho̅ko おちょこ saké cup

o-chūgen お中元 midyear present, summer gift

O-daiji ni! お大事に！ Take care (of yourself)!

ō-da̅iko 大太鼓 large drum

ōdan 1. 黄疸 jaundice **2.** 横断 crossing, going across, intersecting

odate おだて → **odatema̅su** おだてます

odatema̅su おだてます, **odateru** おだてる coaxes

oda̅yaka (na) 穏やか（な）quiet, calm, peaceful, gentle

o-de̅n おでん assorted boiled foods

odokashima̅su 脅かします, **odokasu** 脅かす threatens

odoranai 踊らない ＝ **odorimase̅n** 踊りません (not dance)

odore 踊れ → **odorima̅su** 踊ります [imperative] dance!

odori 踊り **1.** dance, dancing; ~ **o shima̅su** 踊りをします dances, does a dance **2.** → **odorima̅su** 踊ります [infinitive]

ōdo̅ri 大通り main street, avenue

odorima̅su 踊ります, **odoru** 踊る dances

odoro̅ite 驚いて → **odorokima̅su** 驚きます

odorokashima̅su 驚かします,

odoroka̅su 驚かす surprises, scares, astonishes

odorokima̅su 驚きます, **odoro̅ku** 驚く is surprised, astonished

odoshi 脅し → **odoshima̅su** 脅します [infinitive]

odoshima̅su 脅します, **odosu** 脅す threatens

odotte 踊って → **odorima̅su** 踊ります

oe 1. 追え・終え → **oema̅su** 追えます; 終えます (can chase; end it) [infinitive]; → **oema̅su** 終えます [imperative] ～ **ro** 終えろ, **oe̅ yo** 終えよ end it! **2.** 追え → **oima̅su** 追います [imperative] chase it!

o̅e 負え, **1.** → **oema̅su** 負えます (can carry) [infinitive] **2.** → **oima̅su** 負います [imperative] carry it (on your back)!

ō̅e 覆え・おおえ **1.** → **ōema̅su** 覆えます・おおえます (can cover) [infinitive] **2.** → **ōima̅su** 覆います・おおいます [imperative] cover it!

oe̅ba 追えば → **oima̅su** 追います (if one chase)

o̅e̅ba 負えば → **oima̅su** 負います (if one carry)

ō̅e̅ba 覆えば・おおえば → **ōima̅su** 覆います・おおいます (if one cover)

oema̅su, oeru 1. 終えます, 終える ends it, finishes, completes

2. 追えます, 追える can chase, can pursue

oemaˈsu 負えます, **oeˈru** 負える can carry on one's back

ōemaˈsu 覆えます・おおえます, **ōeˈru** 覆える・おおえる can cover

oereˈba 終えれば; 追えれば → **oemaˈsu** 終えます; 追えます (if one end it; if one can chase)

oeˈreˈba 負えれば → **oemaˈsu** 負えます (if one can carry)

ōeˈreˈba 覆えれば・おおえれば → **ōemaˈsu** 覆えます・おおえます (if one can cover)

oeta 終えた・追えた = **oemaˈshita** 終えました; 追えました (ended it; could chase)

oˈeta 負えた = **oemaˈshita** 負えました (could carry)

ōˈeta 覆えた・おおえた = **ōemaˈshita** 覆えました・おおえました (could cover)

oete 終えて・追えて → **oemaˈsu** 終えます; 追えます (ends it; can chase)

oˈete 負えて → **oemaˈsu** 負えます (can carry)

ōˈete 覆えて・おおえて → **ōemaˈsu** 覆えます・おおえます (can cover)

ō-fuˈbuki 大吹雪 blizzard

ōfuku 往復 round trip; ~ **-kiˈppu** 往復切符 round-trip ticket

ofukuro おふくろ・お袋

(familiar, usually male) my mother

o-fuˈro お風呂 bath

ogamimaˈsu 拝みます, **ogaˈmu** 拝む worships, looks at with respect

ogaˈnde 拝んで → **ogamimaˈsu** 拝みます

ōgata 大型・大形 large-size (model)

ogawa 小川 brook

ōgesa (na) 大げさ(な) exaggerated

oˈgi 荻 a reed

ōgiˈ 扇 a folding fan

oginaˈi 補い supplement

oginaˈi 補い → **oginaimaˈsu** 補います [infinitive]

oginaimaˈsu 補います, **oginaˈu** 補う completes; complements, makes good, makes up for

ōˈgoˈe de 大声で in a loud voice

ogorimaˈsu, ogoru 1. おごります・驕ります, おごる・驕る is extravagant **2.** おごる・奢る treats *(pays the bill)*

ogotte おごって → **ogorimaˈsu** おごります

o-hachi お鉢 rice bucket/tub (= **o-hitsu** お櫃 = **meshiˈ-bitsu** 飯櫃)

ohako おはこ・十八番 one's hobby; one's "thing", specialty, (favorite) trick

o-hana 1. お花 flower; flower arrangement **2.** お鼻 (your) nose

o-haˈshi お箸・おはし chopsticks

O-hayō (gozaima⟨su)! おはよう
［お早う］（ございます）! Good
morning!

o-hi⟨na sama おひな［雛］さま
(Dolls Festival) dolls

o-hi-sama お日様 sun

o-hita⟨shi お浸し・おひたし
boiled greens (usually spinach,
served cold with seasoning)

o-hitsu お櫃 rice bucket/tub (=
o-hachi お鉢 = **meshi⟨‐bitsu**
飯櫃)   「water

o-hi⟨ya お冷や・おひや cold

oi 1. 甥・おい nephew 2. 追い →
oima⟨su 追います (chase)

o⟨i 負い → **oima⟨su** 負います
(carry on back) [infinitive]

o⟨i おい hey!

ō⟨i 多い (= **oo⟨i** 多い), **ō⟨ku** 多く
many, numerous; lots

ō⟨i 覆い・おおい (= **oo⟨i** 覆い・
おおい) → **ōima⟨su** 覆います・
おおいます [infinitive]

oide (ni narima⟨su) おいで（にな
ります）= **irasshaima⟨su** いら
っしゃいます [HONORIFIC]
1. comes 2. goes 3. is, stays

oigo-san 甥子さん your nephew

oi-ka⟨ke 追い掛け → **oi-**
kakema⟨su 追い掛けます [in-
finitive]

oi-kakema⟨su 追い掛けます,
-kake⟨ru 追い掛ける chases

oi-koshi kinshi 追い越し禁止 No
Passing

oi-koshima⟨su 追い越します,

-ko⟨su 追い越す (overtakes
and) passes

o-ikura (de⟨su ka) おいくら（で
すか） Check (please)! What's
the bill/tab/price? How much
is this?

o-ikutsu (de⟨su ka) おいくつ（で
すか） How old (are you)?

oima⟨su 追います, **ou** 追う
chases, pursues

oima⟨su 負います, **o⟨u** 負う carries on one's back

ōima⟨su 覆います・おおいます,
ō⟨u 覆う・おおう (= **oo⟨u** 覆
う・おおう) covers, shields

o-imōto-san お妹さん your
younger sister

o⟨iru オイル oil (for car engine)

o-isha (san) お医者（さん）doc-
tor

oishi⟨i おいしい・美味しい
tasty, nice, delicious

ō-i⟨sogi (no/de) 大急ぎ（の/で）
(in) a great rush, a big hurry

oita 置いた = **okima⟨shita** 置き
ました (put) [**o⟨ita** おいた・置
いた *after atonic* **...-te** ...て]

oita⟨ra 置いたら → **okima⟨su** 置
きます (if/when one puts)
[**o⟨itara** おいたら・置いたら
after atonic **...-te** ...て]

oita⟨ri 置いたり → **okima⟨su** 置
きます (sometimes putting)
[**o⟨itari** おいたり・置いたり
after atonic **...-te** ...て]

oite 置いて → **okima⟨su** 置きま

す (puts) [o̖ite おいて・置いて
after atonic ...-te ...て]

oite おいて・於いて: **... ni ~** ...
において[於いて] [bookish]
= **... de** ...で (at/in)

o-itoko-san おいとこさん your
cousin

o-itoma おいとま・お暇 leave-
taking, farewell; **~
(ita)shima̖su** お暇(致)します
I will take my leave.

oi-tsukima̖su 追い付きます,
-tsuku̖ 追い付く (**... ni** ...に)
catches up (with), overtakes

o-jama おじゃま・お邪魔 →
jama じゃま・邪魔; **O-jama
desho̖ ga** おじゃま[邪魔]で
しょうが Excuse me for inter-
rupting/bothering you; **O-
jama shima̖shita** おじゃま[邪
魔]しました. Excuse me for
having interrupted/bothered
you; **Ashita o-jama shima̖su**
明日おじゃま[邪魔]します. I
will visit you tomorrow.

o-jigi おじぎ・お辞儀 a polite
bow; **~ o shima̖su** おじぎ[お
辞儀]をします bows

oji̖i-san 1. おじいさん・祖父さ
ん grandfather **2.** おじいさん
old (gentle)man

ō-jima̖su 応じます, **ō-ji̖ru** 応
じる responds (to), accedes
(to), complies (with)

oji(-san) 1. おじ[叔父・伯父]
（さん）uncle **2.** おじさん

(gentle)man

ō-jite 応じて → **ō-jima̖su** 応じ
ます; **... ni ~** ...に応じて in
accordance/compliance with ...

ojoku 汚辱 disgrace, shame,
scandal

ojo̖-san お嬢さん a young lady;
your daughter; Miss

o-ju̖ お重 = **jūbako** 重箱

oka 丘 hill; 陸 dry land

okabu お株 = **ohako** おはこ・十
八番 (hobby)

O-kaeri nasa̖i! お帰りなさい!
Welcome back!

okage おかげ・お蔭・お陰: **... no
okage de** ...のおかげ[お蔭・お
陰]で thanks to ...

okage-sama de おかげさま[お蔭
様]で thanks to your sol-
icitude; thank you (I'm very
well *or* it's going very nicely).

O-kamai na̖ku お構いなく・おか
まいなく. Don't go to any
trouble.

oka̖me おかめ・お亀 moon
faced/ugly woman

oka̖mi 1. 御上・お上 the authorities, the government
2. おかみ・女将 = **okami-san**
おかみ[女将]さん landlady;
内儀 married woman, wife

o̖kami おおかみ・狼 wolf

o-kan お燗 = **ka̖n** 燗 (heating
saké)

ōkan 王冠 **1.** crown **2.** (**bin no ~**
瓶の王冠) bottle cap

okanai 置かない = **okimase̍n** 置きません (not put)

o-kane お金 money

o-kara おから bean-curd lees

okā̍-san お母さん・おかあさん mother

okasa̍nai 犯さない・侵さない = **okasimase̍n** 犯しません・侵しません (not violate)

oka̍shi 犯し・侵し → **okashima̍su** 犯します・侵します [infinitive]

o-ka̍shi お菓子 confections, sweets, pastry, candy; (= **wa̍ga̍shi** 和菓子) Japanese cakes

okashi̍i おかしい, **oka̍shi-na** (...) おかしな(...) amusing, funny; strange, peculiar, queer

okashima̍su 犯します・侵します, **oka̍su** 犯す・侵す commits, perpetrates; violates, encroaches upon

ōkata おおかた・大方 1. for the most part 2. probably

o-kawari お変わり change (in health)

o-ka̍wari お代わり a second helping (usually of rice)

o-kayu お粥・おかゆ gruel *(rice)*

ō-ka̍ze̍ 大風 strong wind

okazu おかず・お数 side dish (to go with the rice)

oke 置け 1. → **okema̍su** 置けます [infinitive] 2. → **okima̍su** 置きます [imperative]; (**koko ni**) ~ （ここに）置け put it (here)!

o̍ke 桶 tub, wooden bucket

oke̍ba 置けば → **okima̍su** 置きます (if one put)

o-ke̍iko おけいこ・お稽古 practice *(artistic)*

okema̍su 置けます, **okeru** 置ける can put

okenai 置けない = **okemase̍n** 置けません (cannot put)

okere̍ba 置ければ, **okerya** 置けりゃ → **okema̍su** 置けます (if one can put)

oki 1. 沖 offshore, offing; **Naga̍saki no** ~ 長崎の沖 off Nagasaki 2. 置き → **okima̍su** 置きます (puts) [infinitive]

o̍ki 起き → **okima̍su** 起きます (gets up) 1. [infinitive] 2. [imperative] **oki̍ ro** 起きろ, **o̍ki yo** 起きよ get up!

oki-ba 置き場 a place (to put something)

ōki̍i 大きい, **o̍ki-na** (...) 大きな(...) big, large; loud

o̍kiku 大きく greatly, much(ly), loudly; so as to be big/loud; ~ **na̍i (arimase̍n)** 大きくない（ありません）small, modest

okima̍su 置きます, **oku** 置く puts (aside), places, sets, lays; **shite** ~ しておく［置く］does for later, does for now (for the time being)

okima̍su 起きます, **oki̍ru** 起き

る gets up; arises

oki-mono 置き物 an ornament; bric-a-brac

oki'nai 起きない = **okimase'n** 起きません (not get up; not arise)

oki(ra)rema'su 起き(ら)れます, **oki(ra)re'ru** 起き(ら)れる can get up

oki'reba 起きれば, **oki'rya** 起きりゃ → **okima'su** 起きます (if one get up; if it arise)

oki'ru 起きる = **okima'su** 起きます (gets up; arises)

ōkisa 大きさ size

o'kita 起きた = **okima'shita** 起きました (got up)

o'kite 起きて → **okima'su** 起きます (gets up)

o'ki ya shinai 起きやしない = **o'ki wa shinai** 起きはしない = **oki'nai** 起きない (not get up; not arise)

okiyo' 起きよう = **okimashō'** 起きましょう (let's get up!)

okko'chi 落っこち → **okkochima'su** 落っこちます [infinitive]

okkochima'su 落っこちます, **okkochi'ru** 落っこちる falls

okō 置こう = **okimashō'** 置きましょう (let's put it!)

o-kome お米 rice (hulled, uncooked)

okonai 行い 1. act(ion), deed, conduct 2. → **okonaima'su** 行

います [infinitive]

okonaima'su 行います, **okonau** 行う acts, does, carries out, performs

okonatte 行って → **okonaima'su** 行います

okonawanai 行わない = **okonaimase'n** 行いません (not act)

okonomi-yaki お好み焼き seasoned pancake

okori 1. 起こり origin, source 2. おこり ague, the shakes

oko'ri 起こり・怒り → **okorima'su** 起こります・怒ります [infinitive]

okorima'su, oko'ru 1. 起こります, 起こる happens, occurs, arises 2. 起こります, 起こる springs from 3. 怒ります, 怒る gets mad/angry

o-ko-san お子さん your child

okoshima'su, oko'su 1. 起こします, 起こす raises; establishes; gets a person up, rouses 2. 興します, 興す gives rise to, brings about

okotarima'su おこたります・怠ります, **okotaru** おこたる・怠る neglects, shirks; is lazy about

oko'tta 起こった・怒った = **okorima'shita** 起こりました; 怒りました (happened; got mad)

oko'tte 起こって・怒って →

okorima̱su 起こります・怒ります 「(put)
oku 置く = **okima̱su** 置きます
o̱ku 1. 億 a hundred million 2. 奥 the back or inside part
okubi おくび belch
okubyō̱ 憶病・臆病 cowardice; ～ **(na)** 憶病・臆病（な） cowardly, timid; **okubyō-mo̱no̱** 憶病［臆病］者 coward
okujō 屋上 roof(top), rooftop floor 「mostly
o̱ku (no) 多く（の） lots (of);
okuranai 送らない = **okurimase̱n** 送りません (not send)
Ōkura̱-shō 大蔵省 Ministry of Finance
okure 1. 後れ・遅れ a lag; ～ **o torima̱su** 後れを取ります falls behind, gets defeated 2. 遅れ → **okurema̱su** 遅れます [infinitive] 3. 送れ → **okurima̱su** 送ります [imperative] send it!
o-kure おくれ [honorific infinitive of **kurema̱su** くれます, used as a command] please give (it to me)
okurema̱su, okureru 1. 遅れます, 遅れる is late, gets delayed; lags, falls behind; runs slow 2. 送れます, 送れる can send; can spend (time) 3. 贈れます, 贈れる can present/award

okurenai 遅れない・送れない = **okuremase̱n** 遅れません; 送れません (is not late; cannot send)
okurete 遅れて・送れて → **okurema̱su** 遅れます・送れます
okuri 送り・贈り → **okurima̱su** 送ります・贈ります [infinitive]
okurima̱su, okuru 1. 送ります, 送る sends; sees a person off; spends (time) 2. 贈ります, 贈る presents, awards
okuri-mono 贈り物 gift, present
okurō 送ろう = **okurimashō̱** 送りましょう (let's send it!)
o̱ku-san/-sama 奥さん/様 wife, your wife; lady, Madam
okutte 送って・贈って → **okurima̱su** 送ります・贈ります
okya 置きゃ 1. = **oke̱ba** 置けば (if one put) 2. ～ **shinai** 置きゃしない = **oki̱ ya/wa shinai** 置きや/はしない = **okanai** 置かない (not put)
o-kyaku お客, **o-kyaku-san/-sa̱ma̱** お客さん/様 visitor; customer, patron 「ture)
o-kyō お経 sutra (Buddhist scrip-
o-kyū お灸・おきゅう = **kyū** 灸・きゅう
ōkyū-te̱ate 応急手当て first aid
O-machidō-sama de̱shita お待ちどうさまでした. Sorry to be

so late.

omae お前・おまえ *(condescending, usually male)* you

omake おまけ extra, bonus, premium; ~ **ni** おまけに to boot, in addition

o-mamori お守り・おまもり amulet, charm, good-luck piece

omaⁿru おまる bedpan; cham- ⌐berpot

O-matase itashimaˈshita お待た せ致しました. Sorry to have made you wait.

omaˈwari-san お巡りさん・おま わりさん policeman, (police) officer

oˈmbu shima(ˈ)su (suru) おんぶ します(する) carries baby on back; rides on back

o-me お目: ~ **ni kakarimaˈsu (kakaˈru)** お目にかかります （かかる）I meet/see you; ~ **ni kakemaˈsu (kakeˈru)** お目に かけます（かける）I show it to you

o-medetō (gozaimaˈsu) おめでと う［お目出度う］（ございます） congratulations; (= **shiˈnnen/ akemaˈshite** ~ 新年/明けまし ておめでとう（ございます）) Happy new year!

o-meshi ni narimaˈsu お召しに なります **1.** wears **2.** buys **3.** in- vites **4. kaze o** ~ 風邪［かぜ］ をお召しになります catches a cold

o-mi- おみ (for a few words) = **o-** お・御 → HONORIFIC PREFIX

o-miki おみき・御神酒 = **miki** 神 酒 ⌐神輿

o-miˈkoshi お神輿 = **miⁿkoshi**

o-mikuji おみくじ・御神籤 for- tune *(written)*

ō-miˈsoka 大みそか・大晦日 last day of year; New Year's eve

o-miya お宮 shrine *(Shinto)*

o-miˈya おみや [baby talk] = **o- miyage** おみやげ・お土産 gift

o-miyage おみやげ・お土産 gift, present *(as souvenir)*

ōˈmiˈzu 大水 flood

omoˈcha おもちゃ・玩具 toy

omoˈe 思え **1.** → **omoemaˈsu** 思 えます [infinitive] **2.** → **omoimaˈsu** 思います [impera- tive] think!

omoˈeba 思えば → **omoimaˈsu** 思います (if one think)

omoemaˈsu 思えます, **omoeˈru** 思える **1.** can think **2.** = **omowaremaˈsu** 思われます (is thought)

omoi 重い heavy; grave, serious; important

omoˈi 思い **1.** thought, idea; feel- ing, mind, heart; desire, will **2.** → **omoimaˈsu** 思います [in- finitive]

omoi-dashimaˈsu 思い出します, **omoⁿi-daⁿsu** 思い出す re- members, recalls

omoide 思い出 memory *(a recol-*

lection)

omoima̱su 思います, **omo̱u** 思う thinks, feels

omoi-yari 思いやり・思い遣り consideration *(being kind)*, solicitude

o̱mo na 主な principal, main; **o̱mo ni** 主に mainly

omo-ni 重荷 burden (on one's mind)

ō-mono 大物 a big shot

omosa 重さ weight

omoshi 重し a weight *(object)*

omoshiro̱i おもしろい・面白い interesting, pleasant, amusing, fun

omote̱ 表 front (side), surface, outer side/surface

omote-mon 表門 (front) gate

omo̱tta 思った = **omoima̱shita** 思いました (thought)

omo̱tte 思って → **omoima̱su** 思います

omo̱u 思う = **omoima̱su** 思います (thinks)

omowa̱nai 思わない = **omoimase̱n** 思いません (not think)

omowa̱nu ... 思わぬ... unexpected, unanticipated

omowa̱re 思われ → **omowarema̱su** 思われます [infinitive]

omowarema̱su 思われます, **omoware̱ru** 思われる is thought; seems, appears

omowasema̱su 思わせます, **omowase̱ru** 思わせる reminds one of, makes one think of

omo̱ya 思や 1. = **omo̱eba** 思えば (if one think) 2. ~ **shinai** 思やしない = **omo̱i ya/wa shinai** 思いや/はしない = **omowa̱nai** 思わない (not think)

ōmu おうむ・鸚鵡 parrot

ō-mu̱gi 大麦 barley

omu-ra̱isu オムライス omelet wrapped around rice mixed with tidbits

omuretsu オムレツ omelet

omu̱tsu おむつ diapers

on 音 sound; pronunciation

on- 御 (for a few words) = **o-** お・御 → HONORIFIC PREFIX

o̱n (go-o̱n) 恩(ご恩) obligation; kindness

onaji (...) 同じ(...) the same (...); ~ **yo̱ (na)** 同じよう(な) alike, similar

o-naka おなか・お腹 stomach; ~ **ga sukima̱shita** おなかがすきました is hungry; ~ **no guai ga waru̱i** おなかの具合いが悪い has an upset stomach; ~ **o kowashima̱su** おなかを壊します develops stomach trouble

onara おなら flatulence, fart

o̱ndo 温度 temperature; **ondo̱-kei** 温度計 thermometer

o-ne̱ba おねば sticky water from

boiling rice

o-negai お願い favor (requested), request; ~ **shima⌝sụ** お願いします please

o⌝ngaku 音楽 music; **ongak(ụ)-ka** 音楽家 musician; **onga⌝k(ụ)-kai** 音楽会 concert

oni⌝ 鬼 devil, ogre

o-ni⌝kai お二階 upstairs

onkyō 音響 sound

onna⌝ 女, **onna no hịto⌝/kata⌝** 女の人/方 woman, female; **onna no kyō⌝dai** 女のきょうだい［兄弟］sister(s)

onna-gata 女形 = **oya⌝ma** おやま·女形 female impersonator (in Kabuki)

onna-mono 女物 womenswear

onna⌝-no-ko 女の子 girl

onna-shu⌝jin 女主人 hostess

onna-ta⌝rashi 女たらし womanizer, Don Juan, Casanova, ladies' man, ladykiller, seducer

onna-yu 女湯 women's (section of the) bath

o⌝no 斧 ax, hatchet

o-nō お能 = **nō**[⌝] 能

ono⌝ono 各々·おのおの each, respectively, severally; ~ **no ...** 各々の... respective ...

onore 己·おのれ self

onozukara おのずから·自ずから automatically, spontaneously

o⌝nrii オンリー mistress (of an American serviceman)

onsen 温泉 hot spring; spa

onsetsu 音節 syllable

oō 追おう = **oimashō⌝** 追いましょう (let's chase!)

oō[⌝] 負おう = **oimashō⌝** 負いましょう (let's carry it!)

ōō[⌝] 覆おう·おおおう = **ōimashō⌝** 覆いましょう·おおいましょう (let's cover it!)

ōo⌝toko 大男 a giant (of a man)

o⌝pera オペラ opera

o⌝ppai おっぱい [baby talk, slang] = **chịchi⌝** 乳 (breast; milk)

ō⌝pun オープン **1.** ~ **shima(⌝)sụ** オープンします (a shop, an event) opens **2.** ~**(na)** オープン(な) open, candid; ~ **ni hanashi-aima⌝sụ** オープンに話し合います talk openly

ōrai 往来 traffic; communication; thoroughfare

ō⌝rai オーライ "all right! OK!" (= all clear, go ahead)

ora⌝nai おらない［居らない］·折らない·織らない = **orimase⌝n** おりません; 折りません; 織りません (not stay; not break/fold/bend; not weave)

Ora[⌝]**nda** オランダ Holland; (~ **no** オランダの) Dutch; **Oranda-go** オランダ語 Dutch *(language)*; **Oranda⌝-jin** オランダ人 Dutch *(person)*

ore おれ·俺 *(male, unrefined)* I/me

o͞re 1. 折れ・おれ[居れ]・織れ → **orema͞su** 折れます・おれ[居れ]ます・織れます [infinitive] **2.** 折れ・織れ → **orima͞su** 折ります・織ります [imperative] break/fold/bend it!; weave it!

o͞reba おれ[居れ]ば・折れば・織れば → **orima͞su** おり[居り]ます; 折ります; 織ります (if one be/stay; if one break it; if one weave)

o-rei お礼 an acknowledgment, a thank-you, a present (of appreciation); (... **ni**) ~ **o iima͞su** (...に)お礼を言います thanks

orema͞su, ore͞ru 1. 折れます, 折れる it breaks; it folds **2.** おれ[居れ]ます, おれ[居れ]る can stay **3.** 折れます, 折れる can break/fold/bend it **4.** 織れます, 織れる can weave it

ore͞nai 折れない・おれ[居れ]ない・織れない = **oremase͞n** 折れません; おれ[居れ]ません; 折れません; 織れません (not break/fold; cannot stay; cannot break it; cannot weave it)

ore͞nji オレンジ orange; **orenji-ju͞u͞su** オレンジジュース orange juice/drink

ore͞reba 折れれば・おれ[居れ] れば・織れれば, **ore͞rya** 折れりゃ・おれ[居れ]りゃ・織れりゃ → **orema͞su** 折れます; おれ[居れ]ます; 折れます; 織れます (if it break; if one can stay; if one can break it; if one can weave it)

o͞rete 折れて・おれ[居れ]て・織れて → **orema͞su** 折れます・おれ[居れ]ます・織れます

o͞re ya shinai 折れやしない・おれ[居れ]やしない・織れやしない = **o͞re wa shinai** 折れはしない・おれ[居れ]はしない・織れはしない = **ore͞nai** 折れない・おれ[居れ]ない・織れない (not ...)

ori おり・澱 dregs, sediment

ori͞ 1. 檻 cage; jail **2.** 折 time, occasion

o͞ri 1. おり[居り]・折り・織り・下り → **orima͞su** おり[居り]ます; 折ります; 織ります; 下ります [infinitive] (is; breaks/folds/bends it; weaves it; gets down) **2.** 下り [imperative] **ori͞ ro** 下りろ, **o͞ri yo** 下りよ get down!

ori͞gami おりがみ・折り紙 paper-folding (art)

ori͞ibu オリーブ olive

orima͞su, o͞ru 1. おり[居り]ます, おる・居る [DEFERENTIAL/HUMBLE] is, stays (= **ima͞su** い[居]ます, **iru** いる・居る) **2.** 折ります, 折る breaks (folds, bends) it **3.** 織ります, 織る weaves it

orimaꞋsu 下ります・降ります, **oriꞋru** 下りる・降りる gets down, gets off (a ship/plane), gets out (of a car)

ori-meꞋ 折り目 fold, crease, pleat

oriꞋ-moꞋno 織物 cloth, textile, fabric

oriꞋnai 下りない・降りない = **orimaseꞋn** 下りません・降りません (not get down)

ori(ra)remaꞋsu 下り[降り](ら)れます, **ori(ra)reꞋru** 下り[降り](ら)れる can get down

oriꞋreba 下りれば・降りれば, **oriꞋrya** 下りりゃ・降りりゃ → **orimaꞋsu** 下ります・降ります (if one get down)

oriꞋrete 下りれて・降りれて, **oriraꞋrete** 下りられて・降りられて → **ori(ra)remaꞋsu** 下り[降り](ら)れます

oꞋrita 下りた・降りた = **orimaꞋshita** 下りました・降りました (got down)

ori-tatamimaꞋsu 折り畳みます, **-tataꞋmu** 折り畳む folds up

oꞋrite 下りて・降りて → **orimaꞋsu** 下ります・降ります (gets down)

oꞋri ya shinai = **oꞋri wa shinai** 1. 下り[降り]やしない = 下り[降り]はしない = **oriꞋnai** 下りない・降りない (not get down) 2. おり[居り]やしない・折りやしない・織りやしない = おり[居り]はしない・折り

はしない・織りはしない = **oraꞋnai** おら[居ら]ない; 折らない; 織らない (not be/stay; not break/fold/bend it; not weave it)

oriyoꞋ 下りよう・降りよう = **orimashoꞋ** 下りましょう・降りましょう (let's get down)

oroꞋ 折ろう・織ろう = **orimashoꞋ** 折りましょう; 織りましょう (let's break/fold/bend it!; let's weave it!)

oroꞋse 下ろせ・降ろせ → **oroshimaꞋsu** 下ろします・降ろします [imperative] lower it!

oroꞋsha 下ろしゃ・降ろしゃ 1. = **oroꞋseba** 下ろせば・降ろせば (if one lower) 2. ~ **shinai** 下ろ[降ろ]しゃしない = **oroꞋshi ya/wa shinai** 下ろ[降ろ]しや/はしない = **orosaꞋnai** 下ろさない・降ろさない (not lower)

oroshiꞋ 下ろし 1. (= **oroshiꞋ-gane** 下ろし金) a grater 2. (something) grated; (= **daikon-oꞋroshi** 大根下ろし[おろし]) grated radish

oroꞋshi 下ろし・降ろし → **oroshimaꞋsu** 下ろします・降ろします [infinitive]

oꞋroshiꞋ (de/no) 卸(で/の) wholesale

oroshiꞋ-gane 下ろし金 grater

oroshimaꞋsu, oroꞋsu 1. 下ろします・降ろします, 下ろす・降ろす takes down, lowers; unloads;

(yokin o ～ 預金を下ろします) withdraws (deposited money); invests; lets one off (a ship/plane), drops off (from a car), lets out (of a car); **... no jō o ～** ...の錠を下ろします locks up 2. 堕ろします, 堕ろす aborts, has an abortion

oroshi⁻-uri 卸し売り (selling) wholesale; ～ **shima⁻su** 卸し売りします sells wholesale, wholesales

orosō⁻ 下ろそう・降ろそう = **oroshimashō⁻** 下ろ[降ろ]しましょう (let's take it down!)

o⁻ru おる[居る]・折る・織る = **orima⁻su** おり[居り]ます・折ります・織ります

o⁻rya おりゃ・折りゃ・織りゃ **1.** = **o⁻reba** おれ[居れ]ば・折れれば・織れば (if one be/stay; if one break it; if one weave) **2.** ～ **shinai** おりゃしない・折りゃしない・織りゃしない = **o⁻ri ya/wa shinai** おりや/はしない・折りや/はしない・織りや/はしない = **ora⁻nai** おら[居ら]ない・折らない・織らない (not stay; not break/fold/bend; not weave)

osaema⁻su 押さえます・抑えます, **osa⁻e⁻ru** 押さえる・抑える represses, restrains, controls

o-sai お菜 side dish (to go with the rice)

o-sa⁻ji お匙 = **sa⁻ji⁻** さじ・匙

ō-saji 大匙・大さじ tablespoon

Ōsaka 大阪 Osaka; **Ōsaka⁻-Eki** 大阪駅 Osaka Station; **Ōsaka⁻-jin** 大阪人 an Osakan

o-sake お酒 saké (Japanese rice wine)

o-saki ni お先に excuse me for going first; **dō⁻zo** ～ どうぞお先に, ～ **dō⁻zo** お先にどうぞ please go first; ～ **shitsu⁻rei shima⁻su** お先に失礼します Excuse me for being the first to leave

ō-sama 王様 king.

osamarima⁻su, osama⁻ru 1. 収まります, 収まる gets reaped (collected, brought in) **2.** 納まります, 納まる is paid **3.** 治まります, 治まる settles (down/in)

osa⁻me 収め・納め・治め → **osamema⁻su** 収めます・納めます・治めます [infinitive]

osamema⁻su, osame⁻ru 1. 収めます, 収める reaps, harvests, collects; gets **2.** 納め[収め]ます, 納め[収め]る pays; finishes **3.** 治めます, 治める governs; pacifies

osana⁻i 幼い infant(ile), very young; childish, green *(inexperienced)* ⌈noon⌉

o-sa⁻nji お三時 snack *(mid-after-*

o-san shima⁻su お産します gives birth to ⌈ance⌉

ō-sa⁻wagi 大騒ぎ fuss, disturb-

ose 押せ → **oshima˺su** 押します [imperative] push!

ose˺ba 押せば → **oshima˺su** 押します (if one push)

o-se˺chi おせち・お節, **osechi-ryo˺ri** おせち[お節]料理 festival cookery (for New Year's)

o-seibo お歳暮 year-end present, winter gift

o-seji お世辞・おせじ compliment, flattery; ～ **o iima˺su (yū)** お世辞[おせじ]を言います(言う) pays compliments, flatters

o-se˺kkai おせっかい・お節介 meddling; ～ **o shima˺su** おせっかい[お節介]をします meddles; ～**(na)** おせっかい・お節介(な) meddlesome

osen 汚染 contamination; (= **osen-ko˺gai** 汚染公害) pollution

o-se˺n おせん・お煎 rice crackers = **se˺mbe(i)** せんべ(い)・煎餅

o-se˺wa お世話 = **sewa˺** 世話

o-sewa-sama お世話さま・お世話様 (thank you for) your help/attention

osha 押しゃ 1. = **ose˺ba** 押せば (if one push) 2. ～ **shinai** 押しゃしない = **oshi˺ ya/wa shinai** 押しや/はしない = **osanai** 押さない (not push)

osha˺beri おしゃべり chatterbox, gossip

osha˺buri おしゃぶり teething ring, pacifier

osha˺re おしゃれ dandy, dude, fancy dresser

oshi 1. おし・唖 a (deaf-)mute 2. 押し → **oshima˺su** 押します [infinitive]

o-shi˺bori おしぼり・お絞り damp hand-towel

oshie 教え 1. instruction, teaching(s) 2. → **oshiema˺su** 教えます [infinitive]; [imperative] **oshie ro** 教えろ, **oshie˺ yo** 教えよ teach!

oshie⌐ᴵgo 教え子 a student (of a teacher's)

oshiema˺su 教えます, **oshieru** 教える teaches, shows, tells, informs

oshieta 教えた = **oshiema˺shita** 教えました (taught, told)

oshiete 教えて → **oshiema˺su** 教えます

oshieyō 教えよう = **oshiemashō** 教えましょう (let's teach!)

oshi˺i 惜しい 1. regrettable 2. precious

oshi-ire 押し入れ closet, cupboard

o-shimai おしまい the end

oshima˺su 押します, **osu** 押す pushes, presses (on)

oshi˺me おしめ diapers

o-shinko おしんこ・お新香 radish (etc.) pickles

o-shirase お知らせ = shirase 知らせ

o-shiro お城 castle

oshiroi おしろい・白粉 face powder 「ます

oshite 押して → oshima'su 押し

oshi[ⁿ]-zushi 押し鮨 sushi rice and marinated fish pressed in squarish molds (Osaka style)

Ō'shū 欧州 = Yōro'ppa ヨーロッパ Europe

osō 押そう = oshimashō' 押しましょう (let's push!)

o-soba おそば = so'ba そば・側

o-so'ba おそば・お蕎麦 buckwheat (noodles)

o-sobaya おそば[蕎麦]屋 = soba'-ya そば[蕎麦]屋

osoi 遅い, osoku 遅く late; slow; oso'ku-tomo 遅くとも at the latest

o-so'matsu-sama お粗末さま Please excuse the poor fare (reply to gochisō-sama ご馳走さま・ごちそうさま)

oso'raku おそらく・恐らく probably

osore' 恐れ fear 「ably

oso're 恐れ → osorema'su 恐れます [infinitive]

oso're-irimasu 恐れ入ります 1. excuse me 2. thank you

osorema'su 恐れます, osore'ru 恐れる fears

osoroshi'i 恐ろしい fearful, dreadful, awful, terrible, horrible

osoro'shiku 恐ろしく terribly

o-sō'shiki お葬式 funeral

osowarima'su 教わります, osowaru 教わる is taught, studies, learns

osowatte 教わって → osowarima'su 教わります

ossha'i おっしゃい = osshaima'su おっしゃいます [imperative] say it!

osshaima'su おっしゃいます, ossha'ru おっしゃる (someone honored) says; is called

ossha'tta おっしゃった = osshaima'shita おっしゃいました (said)

ossha'tte おっしゃって → osshaima'su おっしゃいます

osu 押す = oshima'su 押します

o-su お酢 = su' 酢 「(pushes)

osu' 雄・おす male animal; ... no ~ ...の雄 a he-...

osui 汚水 sewage

osui-dame 汚水溜め cesspool

o-sumō-san お相撲さん sumo wrestler

o-su'shi おすし・お寿司・お鮨 = su'shi すし・寿司・鮨

o-sushiya おすし[お寿司・お鮨]屋 = sushi'-ya すし[寿司・鮨]屋

Ōsutora'ri(y)a オーストラリア[ヤ] Australia; Ōsutorari-(y)a'-jin オーストラリア[ヤ]人 an Australian

o-tagai (no) お互い(の) mutual,

reciprocal; ~ **(ni)** お互い(に) mutually, reciprocally

o-taku お宅 your house; (= **o-takˌu sama** お宅さま) you

o-teaˈrai お手洗い washroom, toilet

o-teˈmae お手前・お点前 = **temae** 手前・点前

o-teˈnki お天気 = **teˈnki** 天気

o-teˈnto-sama おてんとさま・お天道様 the sun

o-tera お寺 Buddhist temple

oteˈtsudai (san) お手伝い(さん) household helper, maid (-servant)

otoˈ 音 sound, noise; ~ **ga shimaˈsu** 音がします it makes a noise, there is a noise

ōtoˈbai オートバイ motorcycle

otokoˈ 男, **otoko no hiˌtoˈ**/**kataˈ** 男の人/方 man, male, boy; **otoko no kyoˈdai** 男の兄弟 brother(s)

otoko-mono 男物 menswear

otokoˈ-no-ko 男の子 boy

otoko-taˈrashi 男たらし seductress, mankiller, a Cleopatra

otoko-yaˈmome 男やもめ widower

otoko-yu 男湯 men's (section of the) bath

ōtokuchˌuˈru オートクチュール haute couture, high fashion

o-toˈmo shima(ˈ)su お伴します (I will) accompany (you)

otona 大人・おとな adult

otonashiˈi おとなしい gentle,

well-behaved, polite

otonaˈshiku おとなしく gently, politely

otori おとり・囮 decoy; lure

otorimaˈsu 劣ります, **otoˈⁿru** 劣る is inferior, worse

otoroemaˈsu 衰えます, **otoroˈⁱeru** 衰える declines, fades, grows weak

otoˈsan お父さん・おとうさん father

otosaˈnai 落とさない = **otoshimaseˈn** 落としません (not drop it)

ōto-saˈnrin オート三輪 three-wheeled truck

otoˈse 落とせ → **otoshimaˈsu** 落とします [imperative] drop it!

otoˈseba 落とせば → **otoshimaˈsu** 落とします (if one drop it)

otoˈsha 落としゃ 1. = **otoˈseba** 落とせば 2. ~ **shinai** 落としゃしない = **otoˈshi ya/wa shinai** 落としや/はしない = **otosaˈnai** 落とさない (not drop it)

o-toshi お年 your age

otoshimaˈsu 落とします, **otoˈsu** 落とす drops; omits

otoshi-taˈmago 落とし卵 poached eggs

otoˈshite 落として → **otoshimaˈsu** 落とします

otōtoˈ 弟 younger brother; **otōto-san** 弟さん your younger brother

ototo'i おととい・一昨日 day before yesterday

oto'toshi おととし・一昨年 year before last

o-tsukai (san) お使い(さん) errand runner, messenger

O-tsukare-sama (de'shita) お疲れさま[様](でした). You must be weary (tired, exhausted).

o'-tsuki-sama お月さま・お月様 moon

o-tsu'mami おつまみ・お摘み = **tsumami** つまみ

otsu (na) おつ[乙](な) chic, stylish

o-tsuri おつり・お釣り change *(money returned)*

o-tsutome お勤め・お務め = **tsutome** 勤め・務め

otta 追った = **oima'shita** 追いました (chased)

o'tta 負った = **oima'shita** 負いました (carried on back)

o'tta 織った・折った・おった[居った] = **orima'shita** 織りました; 折りました; おり[居り]ました (wove; broke; stayed)

ō'tta 覆った・おおった = **ōima'shita** 覆いました・おおいました (covered)

otte 追って → **oima'su** 追います (chases)

o'tte 負って → **oima'su** 負います (carries on back)

o'tte 織って・折って・おって[居って] → **orima'su** 織ります; 折ります; おり[居り]ます (weaves; breaks; stays)

ō'tte 覆って・おおって → **ōima'su** 覆います・おおいます (covers)

otto 夫 (my) husband

ou 追う = **oima'su** 追います (chases, pursues)

o'u 負う = **oima'su** 負います (carries on one's back)

ō'u 覆う・おおう (= **oo'u/oou** 覆う/覆う) = **ōima'su** 覆います・おおいます (covers, shields)

o-ukagai お伺い = **ukagai** 伺い

o-u'su お薄 = **usu-cha** 薄茶

o-wakare お別れ = **wakare'** 別れ

owanai 追わない = **oimase'n** 追いません (not chase)

owa'nai 負わない = **oimase'n** 負いません (not carry on back)

ōwa'nai 覆わない・おおわない = **ōimase'n** 覆いません・おおいません (not cover)

oware 1. 追われ・終われ → **owarema'su** 追われます・終われます [infinitive] **2.** 終われ → **owarima'su** 終わります [imperative] end it!

owarema'su, owareru 1. 終われます, 終われる can end it **2.** 追われます, 追われる gets

chased
owari 終わり 1. the end; ~ no ...
終わりの... the last, final
2. → owarima˥su 終わります
[infinitive]
owarima˥su 終わります, owaru
終わる it ends; ends it
owarō 終わろう = owarimashō˥
終わりましょう (let's end it!)
owatta 終わった = owarima˥-
shịta 終わりました (ended)
owatte 終わって → owarima˥su
終わります
oya 追や 1. = oe˥ba 追えば (if
one chase) 2. ~ shinai 追やし
ない = oi˥ya/wa shinai 追い
や/はしない = owanai 追わ
ない (not chase)
oya˥ 親 parent; oya-kō˥kō 親孝行
filial piety (honoring one's
parents)
o⌐ya おや Gee whiz! I say! How
(a)bout that!
o⌐ya 負や = o⌐e˥ba 負えば (if
one carry)
ō⌐ya 覆や・おおや 1. = ō⌐e˥ba
覆えば・おおえば (if one
cover) 2. ~ shinai 覆やしない
= ō⌐i˥ya/wa shinai 覆いや/は
しない = ōwa⌐nai (not
cover)
o˥ya-bun 親分 boss, ringleader,
chief
oyago-san 親御さん your parent
ōyake (no/ni) 公（の/に) public-
(ly), open(ly), official(ly)

o˥yako 親子 parent and child
oyako-do⌐mburi 親子丼 rice
topped with chicken and
onion cooked in egg
o˥ya˥ma おやま・女形 female im-
personator
o˥yaoya おやおや Dear dear!
ō˥ya (san) 大家（さん） landlord
o-yasumi お休み = yasumi˥ 休み
O-yasumi nasa˥i おやすみ［お休
み］なさい. Good night.
o-ya˥tsu おやつ = o-sa˥nji お三
oya-yubi 親指 thumb   └時
ōyō 応用 application, putting to
use; ~ shima˥su 応用します
applies it, puts it to use
oyobanai 及ばない =
oyobimase˥n 及びません (not
reach)
oyobi 及び → oyobima˥su 及び
ます [infinitive]
o⌐yobi および・及び and also
oyobima˥su 及びます, oyobu 及
ぶ reaches, extends to, equals
oyo˥ge 泳げ 1. → oyogema˥su 泳
げます [infinitive] 2. →
oyogima˥su 泳ぎます [impera-
tive] swim!
oyogema˥su 泳げます, oyoge˥ru
泳げる can swim
oyo˥gete 泳げて → oyogema˥su
泳げます
oyogi˥ 泳ぎ swimming
oyo˥gi 泳ぎ → oyogima˥su 泳ぎ
ます [infinitive]
oyogima˥su 泳ぎます, oyo˥gu 泳

ぐ swims
oyogō 泳ごう = **oyogimashō**
泳ぎましょう (let's swim!)
oyoida 泳いだ = **oyogimashita**
泳ぎました (swam)
oyoide 泳いで → **oyogimasu** 泳
ぎます
oyonda 及んだ = **oyobimashita**
及びました (reached)
oyonde 及んで → **oyobimasu** 及
びます ⌜great delight
ō-yorokobi de 大喜びで with
oyoso およそ, **ōyoso (no)** おおよ
そ(の) about, roughly

o-yu お湯 hot water; ～ **o**
wakashimasu お湯を沸かし
ます boils water
ō-yuki 大雪 heavy snow
ōzei 大勢 large crowd, throng;
～ **no** 大勢の many; ～ **de** 大
勢で in large numbers
ō-zeki 大関 champion sumo
wrestler
o-zen お膳 dining tray
o-zōni お雑煮・おぞうに =
zōni 雑煮・ぞうに
ō-zumō 大相撲 a grand sumo
tournament; an exciting match

— P —

pachinko パチンコ pinball
(machine); ～-**ya** パチンコ屋
pachinko parlor
pai パイ 1. pie 2. a mahjong tile
pai-kan パイ缶 canned pineapple
painappuru パイナップル pineapple
paipu パイプ pipe; cigarette
holder
...-paku ...泊 → **...-haku** ...泊
pāma パーマ permanent wave
pan パン bread
panfuretto パンフレット
pamphlet
pan-ko パン粉 1. bread crumbs
2. bread flour

panku パンク puncture, blowout; ～ **o shimasu** パンクをし
ます gets a flat tire
pan-kuzu パンくず (bread)
crumbs
pantaron パンタロン (women's)
slacks, pantaloons
pantii パンティー underwear
(*panties*)
pantsu パンツ underwear
(*underpants*); slacks, pants
pan-ya パン屋 bakeshop,
bakery; (～ **san** パン屋さん)
baker
Pari(i) パリ(ー) Paris
paripari (no) ぱりぱり(の)
crisp; first-rate

pāse'nto パーセント percent

paso-kon パソコン personal computer

pa'su パス pass(ing); **pa'su shimasu** パスします passes (an exam)

pasupo'to パスポート passport

pata'n パターン, **pata'n** パタン pattern

pā'tii パーティー party

pa'zuru パズル puzzle

pe'daru ペダル pedal

pēji ページ page

Pe'kin ペキン・北京 Peking

pe'n ペン pen

...-pe'n ...遍 = **...-he'n** ...遍 (counts times)

pe'nchi ペンチ pliers, pincers

pe'nisu ペニス penis

penki ペンキ paint; **(... ni) ~ o nurima'su** (...に)ペンキを塗ります paints

penki-ya ペンキ屋 painter *(housepainter)*

pe'tto ペット pet

pi'iman ピーマン green/bell pepper

pi'ina'tsu ピーナツ peanut(s)

pika'pika ぴかぴか flashing, glittering; **~ shima'su** ぴかぴかします flashes

pi'kuni'kku ピクニック picnic

pi'n ピン pin *(for hair)*

pi'nku ピンク 1. pink 2. pornographic; **pinku-e'iga** ピンク映画 a porno film

pin-to ぴんと (stretched) taut; **~ kima'su (ku'ru)** ぴんと来ます(来る) hits home with one, comes home to one, appeals to one

pi'nto ピント focus

pisutoru ピストル revolver, pistol

pitta'ri ぴったり exactly, perfectly, closely; just right

pi'za ピザ pizza

po'chi ぽち a dot

poke'tto ポケット pocket

pomā'do ポマード pomade, hair oil

po'mbiki ぽん引き, **po'mpiki** ぽん引き a pimp

po'mpu ポンプ pump

po'ndo ポンド pound *(weight or money)*

po'nsu ポン酢, **ponzu'** ポン酢 juice of bitter orange (**daidai** 橙)

poppuko'n ポップコーン popcorn

pori(-) ポリ poly(ethylene); plastic

pori-bu'kuro ポリ袋 (plastic) bag

po'runo ポルノ pornography

po'suto ポスト mail box

pō'tā ポーター porter

potā'ju ポタージュ potage, thick Western soup

po'te'to ポテト potato

po'tsu ぽつ = **po'chi** ぽち a dot

pu⌐ra⌐gu プラグ (electric) outlet, plug

puranetaryū mu プラネタリューウム planetarium

pura suchi kku プラスチック plastic(s)

purē-ga ido プレイガイド a "Play Guide" theater ticket agency

puretapo rute プレタポルテ (ready to wear) off the rack, prêt à porter, not custom-tailored

pure zento プレゼント present

pu ri n プリン a small custard; crème brûlée

pu ro プロ pro(fessional)

purogura mā プログラマー programmer

purogu ramu プログラム program

puro pan プロパン propane; puropan-ga su プロパンガス propane gas

puro-resu プロレス professional wrestling

pu ru プール 1. swimming pool 2. motor pool, parking lot

— R —

...⌐-ra ...ら and others; all of

ra bo ラボ lab

raifuru -jū ライフル銃 rifle

ra igetsu 来月 next month

raikyaku 来客 guest, caller, visitor, company

ra imu ライム lime (fruit)

rainen 来年 next year

ra⌐ion ライオン lion

raishū 来週 next week

ra isu ライス rice (served on plate)

ra ita ライター lighter (cigarette)

rajie tā ラジエーター radiator (car)

ra⌐jio ラジオ radio

rakkan 楽観 optimism; ～-teki

(na) 楽観的(な) optimistic

raku 楽 ease, comfort; ～(na) 楽(な) comfortable; Dō zo o-raku ni どうぞお楽に. Please make yourself comfortable.

rakuda らくだ・駱駝 camel

rakudai 落第 failure (in a test); ～ shima su 落第します fails

rakugaki 落書き scribbling; doodling

rakugo 落語 comic storytelling; ～-ka 落語家 a comic story-teller

rambō 乱暴 violence, outrage; ～ (na) 乱暴(な) violent, wild, rough, disorderly

ra men ラーメン Chinese

noodles (in broth)

ramma 欄間 transom window (opening)

raᷓmpu ランプ 1. lamp 2. ramp

ramune ラムネ lemon soda

raᷓn 1. 蘭 orchid 2. 欄 column 3. 乱 disturbance; war

raᷓnchi ランチ 1. lunch 2. launch *(boat)*

ranchi-saᷓbisu ランチサービス special lunch, a luncheon special

randoᷓseru ランドセル knapsack

rappa ラッパ・らっぱ trumpet, bugle

... rashiᷓi ...らしい (seems) like, apparent, seems to be

rashim-ban 羅針盤 compass *(for directions)*

rasshu-aᷓwā ラッシュアワー rush hour

ratai (no) 裸体(の) nude; **~-ga** 裸体画 a nude (picture)

Raten-go ラテン語 Latin

reᷓa レア rare (beef)

reᷓbā レバー 1. liver (to eat) 2. lever

rei 礼 (= **sharei** 謝礼) remuneration, reward, fee

reᷓi 1. 礼 (= **o-rei** お礼) greeting; thanks; gift 2. 零 (= **maru** 丸) zero 3. 例 precedent (= **zenrei** 前例), example (= **ichi-rei** 一例); **reᷓi no ...** 例の... the ... in question, the said ... ; the usual/customary ...

reibō(-soᷓchi) 冷房(装置) air conditioning

reigai 例外 exception (to the rule)

reigiᷓ 礼儀 courtesy, etiquette; **reigi-tadashiᷓi** 礼儀正しい polite

reᷓi-ji 零時 zero o'clock = twelve o'clock

rei-kin 礼金 "thank-you money" (to obtain rental)

reizoᷓko 冷蔵庫 refrigerator, icebox

reᷓjā レジャー leisure, recreation

reᷓji レジ cashier

rekishi 歴史 history

rekishi-ka 歴史家 historian

reᷓkkā レッカー, **rekkaᷓ-sha** レッカー車 wrecker *(tow truck)*

rekoᷓdo レコード a record *(phonograph)*

rekurieᷓshon レクリエーション recreation

reᷓmon レモン lemon; **remoᷓn-sui** レモン水 lemonade

remoneᷓdo レモネード lemonade

ren'ai 恋愛 love; **~-kaᷓnkei** 恋愛関係 a love affair; **~-keᷓkkon** 恋愛結婚 a love marriage

reᷓnchi 1. レンチ wrench 2. 廉恥 one's honor; **renchiᷓ-shin** 廉恥心 sense of honor/shame

renchū 連中, **renjū** 連中 gang, crowd, clique

reᷓnga れんが・煉瓦 brick

rengō 連合 union, alliance, Allied; **rengō-koku** 連合国 the Allies

renji レンジ cooking stove, kitchen range

renjū 連中, **renchū** 連中 gang, crowd, clique

renkon れんこん・蓮根 lotus root

rennyū 練乳 condensed milk

renraku 連絡 connection, liaison; relevance; **(... to) renraku shimasu** (...と)連絡 します gets in touch (with), contacts

renraku-saki 連絡先 address of contact

renshū 練習 training, practice, drill

rentakā レンタカー rental car

rentogen レントゲン = **rentogen-sen** レントゲン線 X-ray

renzu レンズ lens

resepushon レセプション a reception

ressha 列車 a train; **ressha-jiko** 列車事故 train accident/wreck

rēsu レース lace; a race

resuringu レスリング wrestling

resutoran レストラン restaurant

retasu レタス lettuce

retsu 列 row, line; queue

retteru レッテル label

rettō 列島, **...-rettō** ...列島

archipelago, chain of islands

ri 利 advantage, profit, interest

ribon リボン ribbon

rieki 利益 benefit, advantage, profit

rihatsu 理髪 haircut(ting); **rihatsu shimasu** 理髪します gets/gives a haircut

rihatsu-ten 理髪店 barbershop

rikai 理解 understanding, comprehension; ~ **shimasu** 理解 します understands, comprehends

rikai-ryoku 理解力 comprehension *(ability)*

rikon 離婚 divorce; **(... to) ~ shimasu** (...と)離婚します gets divorced (from ...), divorces

rikō (na) 利口(な) clever, sharp, smart, intelligent; ~ **ni** 利口 に cleverly

riku 陸 land, dry land

rikugun 陸軍 army

rikusentai 陸戦隊 marines

rikutsu 理屈 reason, logic, argument

rimbyō 淋病 gonorrhea

rimo-kon リモコン remote control

rin 鈴 a bell, a doorbell

ringo りんご apple

rinji (no) 臨時(の) extraordinary, special, emergency; temporary

rinki 臨機 expediency; ~ **(no)**

臨機(の) expedient
rinneru リンネル linen
rị̄nri 倫理 ethics
rippa (na) 立派(な) fine, splendid, admirable; 〜 **ni** 立派に admirably, splendidly, well
rireki 履歴, **rire̅kị-sho̅** 履歴書 one's personal history, career summary
ririku 離陸 take-off (of airplane); **ririkụ shima̅sụ** 離陸します takes off
ri̅ron 理論 theory
rị̄shi 利子 interest (on money)
risō 理想 an ideal; 〜**-teki (na)** 理想的(な) ideal
risoku 利息 interest (on money)
rị̄su りす・栗鼠 squirrel
rị̄sụto リスト list
rị̄tsu 率 1. rate, proportion 2. a cut, a percentage
rittai 立体 solid; 3-D, stereo(phonic/scopic)
ri̅ttoru リットル liter(s)
riyō 利用 use, utilization; 〜 **shima̅sụ** 利用します utilizes, makes use of
riyū 理由 reason, cause, grounds; … **to iu** 〜 **de** …という理由で for the reason that …
ro 炉 furnace
… **ro** …ろ, … **ro̅ yo** …ろよ [eastern Japan] = … **yo** …よ (imperative of …**i-** …い and …**e-** …え verb stems)
rō-… 老… old (not young)

rō̅ ろう・蠟 wax; = **mitsurō** 蜜ろう・蜜蠟 beeswax
ro̅ba ろば・驢馬 donkey
ro̅bii ロビー lobby
ro̅ddo ロッド rod (curtain, etc.)
rōdō 労働 labor; 〜**-kụmiai** 労働組合 labor union; **rōdō̅-sha** 労働者 worker, laborer
rōdo-shō̅ ロードショー road-show attraction, first-run movie
rōgan (no) 老眼(の) farsighted (presbyopic)
rōgoku 牢獄 jail
rō̅hi 浪費 extravagance (= **muda-zụ̅kai** 無駄使い); **rō̅hị shima̅sụ** 浪費します wastes
ro̅ji 路地 alley
rōji̅n 老人 old person
rōka 廊下 passage(way), corridor, aisle
rok-ka̅i 六回 six times
rokụ̅ 六・6 six
rokụ̅-do 六度 six times
rokụ̅-do 六度 six degrees
Roku-gatsu 六月・6月 June
roku-jū̅ 六十・60 sixty
roku-ma̅n 六万・60,000 sixty thousand
rokuon 録音 record(ing sound); 〜 **shima̅sụ** 録音します records (sound)
rokuo̅n-ki 録音機 a (tape) recorder
ro̅kuro ろくろ・轆轤 potter's wheel
rokụ-satsụ 六冊 six books

rokụ-sḛn 六千・6,000 six thousand

Rō̄ma ローマ Rome

rōmạ̄-ji ローマ字 romanization, Latin letters

rombun 論文 treatise; (**gakui-rọmbun** 学位論文) dissertation, thesis

rọn 論 argument, discussion; treatise; theory

Rọndon ロンドン London

rōnen 老年 old age

rōnin 浪人 an unemployed samurai; a student between schools; a man without a job

ron-jimạsụ 論じます, **-jị̄ru** 論じる discusses, argues, debates

rọnri 論理 logic; **ronri-teki (na)** 論理的(な) logical

ronsō 論争 controversy, dispute, argument, debate, discussion

rop-pḛn 六遍 six times

rọp-pun 六分 six minutes

rop-pyakụ 六百・600 six hundred

rō̄rā ローラー roller; **rōrā-sụkḗto** ローラースケート roller-skates/-skating

rō̄ru ロール 1. (= **rōru-paạn** ロールパン) roll; **batā-~** バターロール (butter) roll 2. roller

Rosanzeụrusu ロサンゼルス Los Angeles

Rọshi(y)a ロシア[ヤ] Russia; **Roshi(y)a-go** ロシア[ヤ]語 Russian *(language)*; **Roshi(y)ạ-jin** ロシア[ヤ]人 a Russian

rōsọ̄kụ ろうそく・蠟燭 candle

rō̄su ロース roast (cut of meat)

Rọsu ロス Los Angeles

rō̄suto ロースト roast; **rōsuto-bị̄fu/-chị̄kin** ローストビーフ/チキン roast beef/chicken

rō̄tarii ロータリー traffic circle, rotary

rō̄to ろうと・漏斗 [*bookish*] = **jọ̄go** じょうご funnel

rō̄zu ローズ・蘆頭 waste, refuse; shopworn goods

...ʾ-rui ...類 kinds, (different) species of ...

ruiji 類似 resemblance, similarity; analogy; **... ni/to ~ shimạsụ** ...に/と類似します resembles, is similar to

rụmpen ルンペン tramp, hobo, bum

rūmu-sạ̄bisu ルームサービス room service

rụ̄su (o-rụ̄su) (no) 留守(お留守)(の) absent, away from home

rusu-ban 留守番 caretaking/caretaker; someone to take care of the house in one's absence

...rya ...りゃ = **...rḛba** ...れば (if)

ryakugo 略語 abbreviation

ryakusạnai 略さない = **ryakushimasḛn** 略しません

(not abbreviate)

ryakushima´su 略します, **ryaku´su´** 略す abbreviates, shortens; omits

ryō´ 1. 猟 hunting; 漁 fishing (as sport); ～ **o shima´su** 猟[漁]をします hunts, fishes **2.** 寮 dormitory, boarding house **3.** 陵 mound, mausoleum **4.** 領 territory **5.** 量 quantity, volume

ryō-... 両... both

...´-ryō ...料 fee, charge

ryō´chi 領地 territory

ryo´dan 旅団 brigade

ryō´do 領土 territory

ryō[ ]gae 両替 money exchange/changing; ～ **shima´su** 両替します changes (money)

ryōgae´-ki 両替機 money-changing machine, money-changer

ryō-gawa 両側 both sides

ryōhō[ ] 両方 both

ryō´ji 領事 consul; **ryōji´-kan** 領事館 consulate

ryokaku 旅客 = **ryokyaku** 旅客

ryokan 旅館 inn (traditional)

ryoken 旅券 passport

ryō[ ]kin 料金 fee, charge, fare, rate; ～ **saki-ba´rai no denwa** 料金先払いの電話 a collect call

ryokō 旅行 travel, trip; ～ **shima´su** 旅行します travels, takes a trip

ryokō´-sha 旅行者 traveler;

ryokōsha-yō kogi´tte 旅行者用小切手 = **ryokō-kogi´tte** 旅行小切手 traveler's check

ryoku-cha 緑茶 green tea   「ger

ryokyaku 旅客 traveler, passen-

ryōme[ ]n 両面 both sides/directions, **ryōmen-tsu´kō** 両面通行 two-way traffic

ryō´ri 料理 cooking; ～ **shima(´)su** 料理します cooks/prepares it

ryōri[ ]-nin 料理人 cook

ryōri´-ten 料理店, **-ya** 料理屋 a restaurant

ryō´shi 漁師 fisherman

ryō´shin 1. 両親 (both) parents **2.** 良心 conscience; **ryōshin-teki (na)** 良心的(な) conscientious

ryōshū[ ]-sho[ ] 領収書 receipt

ryō-teki (na) 量的(な) quantitative; ～ **ni´ mo shitsu-teki ni´ mo** 量的にも質的にも both quantitatively and qualitative-

ryū´ 竜・龍 dragon   └ly

ryū´chō (na) 流ちょう・流暢(な) fluent

ryu´kku リュック, **ryukkusa´kku** リュックサック knapsack

ryūkō 流行 popularity, vogue, fashion; ～ **(no)** 流行(の) fashionable; ～**-byō** 流行病 an epidemic

Ryūkyū´ 琉球 the Ryukyus (Okinawa, etc.)

ryū´zan 流産 miscarriage

— S —

sa⌐¹⌐ 差 difference, discrepancy

...-sa ...さ ...ness *(abstract noun from adjective)*

sā⌐ さあ well; come on; let me see

saba さば・鯖 mackerel

sa⌐baku 砂漠 desert

sa⌐betsu 差別 discrimination

sabi⌐ さび・錆 rust

sa⌐bi さび・錆び → **sabima⌐su** さ びます・ びます [infinitive]

sabima⌐su さびます・錆びます, sabi⌐ru さびる・錆びる it rusts

sabi⌐nai さびない・錆びない rustproof

sabishi⌐i 寂しい・淋しい lonely

sā⌐bisu サービス service; free (as part of the service); **sābisu- ryō** サービス料 service charge, cover charge

sa⌐bite さびて・錆びて → **sabima⌐su** さびます・錆びます

sabo⌐ri さぼり・サボリ → **saborima⌐su** さぼります・サボ ります [infinitive]

saborima⌐su さぼります・サボリ ます, sabo⌐ru さぼる・サボる loafs (on the job); cuts class, plays hookey

saboten サボテン, **shaboten** シ ャボテン cactus

sabo⌐tte さぼって →

saborima⌐su さぼります・サボ ります

sadamarima⌐su 定まります, sadama⌐ru 定まる is settled, fixed

sadamema⌐su 定めます, sadame⌐ru 定める settles it, fixes it

sa⌐dō 茶道 tea ceremony

saga⌐ri 下がり → **sagarima⌐su** 下 がります [infinitive]

sagarima⌐su 下がります, saga⌐ru 下がる it hangs down; goes down

sagashi 探し・捜し → sagashima⌐su 探します・捜し ます [infinitive]

sagashima⌐su 探します・捜しま す, sagasu 探す・捜す looks for

sagashite 探して・捜して → sagashima⌐su 探します・捜し ます

saga⌐tte 下がって → **sagarima⌐su** 下がります

sa⌐ge 下げ → **sagema⌐su** 下げま す **1.** [infinitive] **2.** [impera- tive] **sage⌐ ro** 下げろ, **sa⌐ge yo** 下げよ

sagema⌐su, sage⌐ru **1.** 下げます, 下げる hangs it, lowers it,

brings it down, clears from the
table 2. さげます・提げます,
さげる・提げる carries (dangl-
ing from hand)

sa⌐gete 下げて・さげて・提げて
→ sagema⌐su 下げます・さげ
ます・提げます

sa⌐gi 詐欺・サギ fraud

sagu⌐ri 探り → sagu26ma⌐su 探
ります [infinitive]

sagurima⌐su 探ります, sagu⌐ru
探る gropes

sagu⌐tte 探って → sagurima⌐su
探ります

sa⌐gyō 作業 work, operations;
sagyō-ji⌐kan 作業時間 work-
ing hours

sa⌐hō 作法 manners, etiquette

sai 菜 = o-sai お菜 side dish (to
go with the rice)

sa⌐i 1. 才 talent, ability 2. 際
time, occasion 3. 妻 (my) wife
4. 差異・差違 (= sa⌐-i 差異) difference

...⌐-sai ...歳 years of age (ni⌐ji⌐s-
sai 二十歳 = ha⌐tachi 二十歳・
はたち 20, sa⌐nji⌐s-sai 三十歳
= sa⌐njū 三十 30)

sai-... 再... re-(doing)

saiaku (no) 最悪(の) the worst

sa⌐iban 裁判 trial; saiba⌐n-kan 裁
判官 judge; saiban-sho⌐⌐ 裁判
所 court

sa⌐ichū 最中 midst

sa⌐idā サイダー ''cider'' (fizzy
lemon soda)

saidai (no) 最大(の) the largest,

the most; maximal, maxi-
mum; ~-ge⌐ndo 最大限度 the
maximum (degree)

saidan 祭壇 altar

saido-burē⌐ki サイドブレーキ
handbrake

sa⌐iensu サイエンス science

saifu 財布 purse, wallet

sa⌐igo (no) 最後(の) last, final

saijitsu 祭日 holiday (official)

saijō (no) 最上(の) best, highest, topmost

sai-ka⌐kunin 再確認 reconfirmation; ~ shima(⌐)su 再確認し
ます reconfirms

sa⌐ika (no) 最下(の) lowest
(minimum, minimal)

saiken 債券 bond (debenture)

saikin 細菌 germ

saikin (ni) 最近(に) recently,
lately; ~ no 最近の recent

saikō (no) 最高(の) the highest,
the best, tops; ~-ge⌐ndo 最高
限度 the highest (degree)

saiko⌐ro さいころ dice, a die

saiku⌐⌐ 細工 work(manship), (=
te-za⌐iku 手細工) handiwork,
ware(s)

saina⌐n 災難 calamity, disaster

sa⌐⌐inō 才能 talent

sai-nyū⌐⌐koku 再入国 reentry (into the country)

sairyō (no) 最良(の) the best

saise⌐⌐n (o-saisen) さい銭・賽銭
(お賽銭) money offering (at
a shrine); saise⌐n-bako さい銭

箱・賽銭箱 offering box

sai-shiḳe̅n 再試験 makeup exam

saishin (no) 最新(の) newest, up-to-date

sa̅i-shite 際して: **... ni ~** ...に際して on the occasion of, at the time of, when, in case of

saisho 最初 the very beginning, the outset; **~ no ...** 最初の... the first ...

saishoku̅-sha 菜食者 vegetarian

saishō (no) 最小・最少(の) smallest, least, minimal, minimum; **~-ge̅ndo** 最小限度 the minimum (degree)

saishū (no) 最終(の) final, the very end (last)

saita 咲いた = **sakima̅shita** 咲きました (bloomed)

sa̅ita 裂いた = **sakima̅shita** 裂きました (split it)

saite 咲いて → **sakima̅su** 咲きます (blooms)

sa̅ite 裂いて → **sakima̅su** 裂きます (splits it)

saitei (no) 最低(の) lowest, worst, bottom(most); minimum

saiwai 幸い・さいわい good fortune; **~ (na)** 幸い・さいわい (な) fortunate, **~ ni** 幸いに fortunately

saizen 最善 the best; one's best/ utmost; **~ o tsukushima̅su** 最善を尽くします does one's best/utmost

sa̅izu サイズ size

sa̅ji̅ (o-sa̅ji) さじ・匙(お匙) spoon

saka 坂 hill, slope 「ing)

saka-ba̅ 酒場 bar *(for drink-*

saka̅e 栄え → **sakaema̅su** 栄え ます [infinitive]

sakaema̅su 栄えます, **saka̅e̅ru** 栄える thrives, flourishes, prospers

saka̅i 境 boundary, border

sakan (na) 盛ん(な) flourishing, prosperous; splendid, vigorous, lively

sakana (o-sakana) 1. 魚(お魚) fish **2.** 肴(お肴) appetizers to go with drinks

sakanai 咲かない = **sakimase̅n** 咲きません (not bloom)

saka̅nai 裂かない = **sakimase̅n** 裂きません (not split)

sakana̅-tsuri 魚釣り fishing *(as sport)*

sakana-ya 魚屋 fish dealer/ market

sakanoborima̅su さかのぼりま す・遡ります・溯ります, **sakanobo̅ru** さかのぼる・遡る ・溯る: **... ni ~** ...にさかのぼ り[遡り・溯り]ます goes against (the stream), goes upstream; goes back (in time) to; **sore o ... ni ~** それを... さかのぼり[遡り・溯り]ます traces it back to ... ; is retro-active to

sakaraima̍su 逆らいます,
sakara̍u 逆らう: ... **ni ~** ...に
逆らいます defies, opposes,
contradicts, acts contrary to

sakasa(ma) (no/ni) さかさま・逆
さ(ま)(の/に) upside down

sa̍kasu サーカス circus

sakazuki (**o-sakazuki**) 杯(お杯)
wine cup, saké cup

sake 酒 = **o-sake** お酒 saké
(Japanese rice wine)

sa̍ke 1. 鮭 (= **sha̍ke** しゃけ・鮭)
salmon **2.** 避け・裂け →
sakema̍su 避けます・裂けます

sake̍ba 咲けば → **sakima̍su** 咲
きます (if it bloom)

sa̍keba 裂けば → **sakima̍su** 裂
きます (if one split/tear it)

sakebima̍su 叫びます, **sake̍bu**
叫ぶ cries out, shouts

sakema̍su, sake̍ru 1. 避けます,
避ける avoids **2.** 裂けます, 裂
ける it splits, it tears **3.** 裂け
ます, 裂ける can split/tear it

sake̍nai 避けない・裂けない =
sakemase̍n 避けません; 裂け
ません (not avoid; not split;
cannot split/tear it)

sake̍nda 叫んだ =
sakebima̍shita 叫びました
(shouted)

sake̍nde 叫んで → **sakebima̍su**
叫びます (shouts)

sake(ra)rema̍su 避け(ら)れます,
sake(ra)re̍ru 避け(ら)れる
can avoid

sa̍keta 避けた・裂けた =
sakema̍shita 避けました; 裂
けました (avoided; it tore)

sa̍kete 避けて・裂けて →
sakema̍su 避けます・裂けます

sakeyo̍ 避けよう = **sakemasho̍**
避けましょう (let's avoid it!;
...)

saki (**o-saki**) 先(お先) **1.** front;
future; ahead; first (ahead of
others); **kono ~** この先 ahead
of here; → **o saki ni** お先に
2. point, tip **3.** address, destination

saki 咲き → **sakima̍su** 咲きます
(blooms) [infinitive]

sa̍ki 裂き → **sakima̍su** 裂きま
す (splits it) [infinitive]

saki-hodo 先程・さきほど a little
while ago

sakima̍su 咲きます, **saku** 咲く
blooms, blossoms

sakima̍su 裂きます, **sa̍ku** 裂く
splits it; tears it

saki-ototo̍i さきおととい・一昨
々日 three days ago

saki-oto̍toshi さきおととし・一
昨々年 three years ago

sa̍kka 作家 writer; novelist

sa̍kkā サッカー soccer

sa̍kki さっき = **saki-hodo** 先程

sa̍kku サック condom

sako̍ 裂こう = **sakimasho̍** 裂き
ましょう (let's split/tear it!)

saku 咲く = **sakima̍su** 咲きます
(blooms)

sa̅ku 裂く = sakima̅su 裂きます (splits/tears it)

saku̅ban 昨晩 last night

sakubun 作文 writing a composition (a theme)

sakuhin 作品 a work (of literature or art)

sakuin 索引 index

sakura 桜 cherry tree; ～ no hana̅ 桜の花 cherry blossoms

sakurambo さくらんぼ・桜ん坊・桜桃 a cherry

sakya 咲きゃ 1. = sake̅ba 咲けば (if it bloom) 2. ～ shinai 咲きゃしない = saki̅ ya/wa shinai 咲きや/はしない = sakanai 咲かない (not bloom)

sa̅kya 裂きゃ 1. = sa̅keba 裂けば (if one split/tear it) 2. ～ shinai 裂きゃしない = sa̅ki ya/wa shinai 裂きや/はしない = saka̅nai 裂かない (not split/tear it)

sakyū 砂丘 sand dune

sam-... さん... = san-... さん... (before m b p)

... (-)sama ...様・さま [formal] = ... (-)san ...さん Mr., Ms., Mrs., Miss

samatagema̅su 妨げます, samatage̅ru 妨げる obstructs, hinders

samayoima̅su さまよいます・彷徨います, samayo̅u さまよう・彷徨う wanders about

sama̅za̅ma (na/no) さまざま [様々](な/の) diverse, (of) all kinds

sa̅m-ba 三羽 three birds

sam-bai 三倍 triple

sa̅m-bai 三杯 three glassfuls

sam-bamme̅ 三番目 third

sambashi 桟橋 pier

sa̅m-be̅n 三遍 three times

sa̅m-biki 三匹 three animals/fish/bugs

sa̅m-bon 三本 three long things

sambutsu 産物 product, produce; fruit, outcome

sa̅m-byaku 三百・300 three hundred

same さめ・鮫 shark

sa̅me 覚め・冷め・褪め → samema̅su 覚めます・冷めます・さめ[褪め]ます [infinitive]

samema̅su, same̅ru 1. 覚めます, 覚める wakes up, comes to one's senses 2. 冷めます, 冷める gets cold, cools off 3. さめ[褪め]ます, さめ[褪め]る it fades, loses color

same̅nai 覚めない, etc. = samemase̅n 覚めません, etc. (not wake up; not ...)

samma さんま・秋刀魚 mackerel pike

sa̅m-mai 三枚 three flat things

sa̅m-mei 三名 [bookish] = san-ni̅n 三人 three people

sammon 山門 temple gate

sammyaku 山脈 mountain range

saˈ-mo naˈkereba さもなければ otherwise

sam-paku 三泊 three nights lodging

sampatsu 散髪 haircut; **～-ya** 散髪屋 a barber(shop); **sampatsu shimaˈsu** 散髪します gets/gives a haircut

sampo 散歩 a walk, a stroll; **～ shimaˈsu** 散歩します takes a walk

saˈm-pun 三分 three minutes

samuˈi 寒い cold, chilly

samurai 侍 samurai (warrior)

san 三・3 three

saˈn 酸 acid

... (-)san ...さん Mr., Ms., Mrs., Miss

...ˈ-san ...山 mountain

saˈnchi 産地 home (of a product/crop)

saⁿndaru サンダル sandal

san-diikeˈ 3DK three rooms and "DK" (eat-in kitchen)

saˈn-doˈ 三度 three times

saˈn-do 三度 three degrees

...-saˈndo ...サンド sandwich

sandō 参道 approach to a shrine; **omote-saˈndō** 表参道 main road to a shrine

sandoiˈtchi サンドイッチ sandwich

sando-meˈ 三度目 the third time

sandopeˈpā サンドペーパー sandpaper

Sanfuranshiˈsuko サンフランシ

スコ San Francisco

san-gai 三階 three floors/stories; third floor

sangaⁿnichi 三が日 the first three days of the New Year

Saˈn-gatsu 三月・3月 March

saˈn-gen 三軒 three buildings

saˈngo さんご・珊瑚 coral

sangyō 産業 industry

saˈn-jū 三十・30 thirty

saⁿnka 参加 participation; (...ni) **～ shimaˈsu** (...に)参加します participates (in)

saˈn-kaˈi 三回 three times; **sankai-meˈ** 三回目 the third time

saˈnkaku 三角 triangle

sankaˈ-sha 参加者 participant

san-nen 三年 the year 3; (= **sanneˈn-kan** 三年間) three years; **sanneˈn-sei** 三年生 third-year student, junior

san-niˈn 三人 three people

sanriˈn-sha 三輪車 tricycle

saˈn-sai 三歳 three years old

saˈn-satsu 三冊 three books

sansei 賛成 approval, support; **～ shimaˈsu** 賛成します agrees, approves

saˈn-sei 三世 third generation (of emigrant Japanese); ... the Third

san-shi-... 三,四... 3 or 4 (but **san-yo-** 三,四 ＋ **-bai** 倍, **-bammeˈ** 番目, **-do** 度, **ˈ-en** 円, **-jiˈkan** 時間, **-nen** 年, **-nimmae**

人前, **-ni̱n** 人; **sa̱n-yokka** 三，
四日 3 or 4 days)
sanshō さんしょう・山椒
Japanese pepper *(mild)*
sa̱n-shoku 三食 three meals
sa̱nso 酸素 oxygen
san-tō 三等 third class
sa̱n-tō 三頭 three horses/oxen
san-yo- 三，四 three or four; ～
-bai 三，四倍 times as much, ～
-bamme̱ 三，四番目 third or
fourth, **～-do** 三，四度 times,
～-en 三，四円 yen, **～-ji̱kan**
三，四時間 hours, **～-man** 三，
四万 thirty or forty thousands,
～-ni̱n 三，四人 people, ～
-nimmae 三，四人前 servings
san-yokka 三，四日 three or four
days; half a week
san-ze̱n 三千・3,000 three thousand
sa̱n-zoku 三足 *(also* **sa̱n-soku** 三
足) three pairs (of footwear)
sao̱ さお・竿・棹 pole, rod
sapo̱tā サポーター jockstrap,
(athletic) supporter
sappa̱ri さっぱり not at all; ～
shi̱ta さっぱりした clean,
fresh; frank
sara (o-sara) 皿（お皿）plate,
dish; saucer; ashtray
sara-arai-o̱ke 皿洗い桶 dishpan
sa̱rada サラダ salad
sara̱igetsu 再来月 month after
next
sarainen 再来年 year after next

saraishū 再来週 week after next
sa̱ra-ni 更に・さらに anew;
(some) more; further
sa̱rarii サラリー salary
sare され → **sarema̱su** されます
[infinitive]
sarema̱su されます, **sareru** され
る 1. has it done to one (unwantedly) 2. is done; **hakai** ～
破壊されます is destroyed
3. = **nasaima̱su** なさいます
sa̱ri 去り → **sarima̱su** 去りま
す [infinitive]
sarima̱su 去ります, **sa̱ru** 去る
leaves, goes away; removes it
sa̱ru 去る 1. = **sarima̱su** 去り
ます 2. さる・去る (+ DATE)
last … , most recent, (past
day) of this month
sa̱ru (o-saru) 猿（お猿）monkey
sarumata さるまた・猿股 loincloth
sasa̱e 支え → **sasaema̱su** 支え
ます [infinitive]; **sasa̱e̱** 支
え a support, a prop
sasaema̱su 支えます, **sasae̱ru**
支える supports, props (up)
sa̱sai (na) ささい［些細］(な) petty, trifling, trivial; **sa̱sai na
kane** ささい［些細］な金 petty
cash
sasa̱yaka (na) ささやか（な）
small(-scale), petty
sasayaki̱ ささやき・囁き a
whisper, murmur
sasaya̱ki ささやき・囁き →

sasayakima'su ささやきます・
囁きます [infinitive]

sasayakima'su ささやきます・囁
きます, sasaya⌐ku ささやく・
囁く whispers

sase させ → sasema'su させます
(make/let do) 1. [infinitive]
2. [imperative] sase ro させろ,
sase' yo させよ let them do it!

sa'se 刺せ 1. → sasema'su 刺せ
ます (can stab) [infinitive]
2. → sashima'su 刺します
[imperative] stab!

sa'seba 指せば・刺せば →
sashima'su 指します; 刺しま
す (if one point to; if one stab)

sasema'su させます, saseru させ
る makes/has/lets one do

sasema'su, sase'ru 1. 指せます,
指せる can point to 2. 刺せま
す, 刺せる can stab

sasenai させない = sasemase'n
させません (not make/have/
let one do)

sase'nai 指せない・刺せない =
sasemase'n 指せません; 刺せ
ません (cannot point to; cannot stab)

sasere'ba させれば, saserya させ
りゃ → sasema'su させます (if
one make/have/let them do)

sase'reba 指せれば・刺せれば,
sase'rya 指せりゃ・刺せりゃ
→ sasema'su 指せます; 刺せ
ます (if one can point to/stab)

sasete させて → sasema'su させ

ます (makes/has/lets one do)

sa'sete 指せて・刺せて →
sasema'su 指せます; 刺せま
す (can point to; can stab)

saseyō させよう = sasemashō'
させましょう (let's make/let
them do it!)

sa'sha 指しゃ・刺しゃ 1. =
sa'seba 指せば; 刺せば (if one
point to; if one stab) 2. ～
shinai 指しゃしない・刺しゃ
しない = sa'shi ya/wa shinai
指しや/はしない; 刺しや/は
しない (not point to; not stab)

sa'shi 指し・刺し → sashima'su
指します・刺します [infini-
tive]

sashi-agema'su 差し上げます・さ
しあげます, -age⌐ru 差し上
げる・さしあげる [HUMBLE,
DEFERENTIAL] presents, give
(I give you, you give them);
holds up

sashide⌐guchi 差し出口 un-
called-for remark; ... no
hanashi' ni ～ o shima'su ...の
話に差し出口をします inter-
rupts

sashi-komi 差し込み plug (electricity outlet)

sashi-ko⌐mi 差し込み → sashi-
komima'su 差し込みます

sashi-komima'su 差し込みます,
-ko⌐mu 差し込む inserts

sashima'su, sa'su 1. 指します,
指す points to, indicates 2. 差

します, 差す holds umbrella
3. 刺します, 刺す stabs,
stings
sashimi (o-sashimi) 刺身・さしみ
（お刺身）sliced raw fish
sashitsukae 差し支え・さしつか
え 1. hindrance, impediment
2. previous appointment/
engagement
sa shizu 指図 directions, instructions, commands 「ザ visa
sashō 査証 [bookish] = **bi za** ビ
sasō 刺そう = **sashimashō** 刺し
ましょう (let's stab!)
sasoi 誘い 1. invitation; temptation 2. → **sasoima su** 誘いま
す [infinitive]
sasoima su 誘います, **sasou** 誘う
invites; tempts
sasoō 誘おう = **sasoimashō** 誘
いましょう (let's invite/tempt
them!) 「います
sasotte 誘って → **sasoima su** 誘
sasou 誘う → **sasoima su** 誘いま
す
sasowanai 誘わない =
sasoimase n 誘いません (not
invite/tempt)
sas-shi (o-sasshi) 察し（お察し）
conjecture, guess; perception,
understanding; sympathy; ~
ga tsukima su 察しがつきます
perceives, guesses (correctly)
sa s-shi 察し → **sas-shima su** 察
します [infinitive]
sas-shima su 察します, **-su ru**

察する perceives, under-
stands; conjectures, guesses;
sympathizes
sa s-shite 察して → **sas-
shima su** 察します
sa sshu サッシュ, **sa sshi** サッシ
sash (windowsash)
sassoku さっそく・早速 at once,
right away, promptly, im-
mediately; ~ **(no)** さっそく
[早速]（の）immediate,
prompt
sa su 指す・差す・刺す →
sashima su 指します・差しま
す・刺します
sasuga さすが: ~ **(ni/wa)** さす
が（に/は）as we might expect,
indeed; ~ **no ...** さすがの...
itself, being what it is; oneself,
being who one is
sa ta (go-sa ta) 沙汰（ご沙汰）
news, message; command;
affair
sa -te さて well now/then, and
now/then, now then; as to the
matter at hand
sa ten サテン satin
sato 里 village; home (town)
satō (o-satō) 砂糖（お砂糖）
sugar
sato-oya 里親 foster parent
satori 悟り 1. enlightenment
2. → **satorima su** 悟ります
[infinitive]
satorima su 悟ります, **sato ru**
悟る realizes (comprehends)

satsu (o-satsu) 札（お札）folding money, currency bill/note

…-satsu˥ …冊 (counts books, magazines)

…˥-satsu …札 (currency) bill; **hyakudoru̱˥-satsu ni̱˥-mai** 百ド ル札二枚 two $100 bills

satsu-i˥re˥ 札入れ billfold, **satsujin** 殺人 murder ⌐wallet

Satsuma˥-age さつま［薩摩］揚げ deep-fried fish cake

Satsuma-imo さつま［薩摩］芋 sweet potato

satsu-ta˥ba 札束 a roll/wad of (currency) bills

sawagashi̱˥i 騒がしい boisterous

sa˥wagi 騒ぎ 1. noise *(boisterous)*, clamor 2. → **sawagima˥su̱** 騒ぎます [infinitive]

sawagima˥su̱ 騒ぎます, **sawa˥gu̱** 騒ぐ makes lots of noise, clamors ⌐騒ぎます

sawa˥ide 騒いで → **sawagima˥su̱**

sawara さわら・鰆 mackerel

sawarima˥su̱ 触ります, **sawaru̱** 触る touches

sawatte 触って → **sawarima˥su̱** 触ります

sawa˥yaka (na) さわやか（な） refreshing, bracing; fluent

sa˥ya 1. さや・莢 sheath; pod 2. さや・鞘 price difference/differential, margin, brokerage (fee), commission

sayō さよう [DEFERENTIAL] =

sō˥ そう (like that): **Sayō de gozaima˥su̱.** さようでございま す. = **Sō˥ desu̱** そうです. Yes; That's right.

sayona˥ra さよなら, **sayōna˥ra** さようなら good-bye

sa˥yori さより halfbeak (fish)

sa˥zae さざえ・栄螺 wreath shell, turban shell, turbo

se˥ 背 (height); ~ **ga taka˥i/ hi̱ku̱˥i** 背が高い/低い is tall/ short

sebiro 背広 business suit

sebone 背骨 backbone, spine

se˥bun セブン seven

se˥i 1. せい・背 = **se˥** 背 height, stature 2. 性 nature; sex; gender 3. 姓 family name

sei- 西 west

… se˥i …せい cause, effect, influence, fault; ~ **de** …せいで owing to … , on account of … ; ~ **ka** …せいか perhaps because of …

…˥-sei 1. …生 student 2. …製 made in …

seibo 歳暮 = **o-seibo** お歳暮 year-end gift

se˥ibu 西部 the west, the western part ⌐nent

se˥ibun 成分 ingredient, compose-

se˥ibutsu 生物 a living thing, a creature

seibutsu˥-gaku 生物学 biology

seibutsuga˥ku̱-sha 生物学者 biologist

seibutsugaku-teki (na) 生物学的（な）biological

seibyō 性病 venereal disease

seichō 成長 growth; ～ **shima`su** 成長します grows; grows up

se`ido 制度 system

seidō 青銅 bronze

se`ifu 政府 government

seifuku 制服 uniform *(attire)*

seige`n** 制限 limit, restriction; ～ **shima(`)su 制限します limits, restricts

seihin 製品 product, manufactured goods

seihō 西方 the west

seiji 政治 politics

se`ijin** 成人 adult (= **otona** 大人・おとな); ～ **no hi` 成人の日 Coming-of-Age Day [honoring 20-year-olds] on 15 January

seijitsu (na) 誠実（な）sincere

seijuku 成熟 ripening, maturing; **seijuku shima`su** 成熟します ripens, matures

se`ika 1. 成果 result, outcome 2. 正価 net price

seikaku 1. 性格 character *(personal traits)* 2. ～ **(na)** 正確・精確（な）exact, accurate, correct

seikatsu 生活 life, (daily) living; **seikatsu`-hi** 生活費 living costs

seiketsu (na) 清潔（な）clean, pure

se`iki 世紀 century

seikō 1. 成功 success; ～

shima`su 成功します succeeds 2. 性交 (sexual) intercourse

seikyū 請求 claim, demand, request; ～ **shima`su** 請求します claims, demands, requests

se`ime`i 生命 life

seimitsu (na) 精密（な）precise, detailed, minute, thorough

seimon 正門 the front (main) gate

seinen 青年 young person, youth, adolescent

seinen-ga`ppi 生年月日 date of birth

seine`n-ki** 青年期 (one's) youth; (= **seishu`n-ki 青春期) adolescence

seireki 西暦 the Western (Christian) calendar; ～ **...`-nen** 西暦...年 the year ... A.D.

se`iri** 生理 physiology; ～**-teki (na)** 生理的（な）physiological; ～**-yō no na`puki`n 生理用のナプキン sanitary napkin

se`iri** 整理 adjustment, arrangement; ～ **shima(`)su 整理します adjusts, arranges, (re)orders, (re)organizes

seiritsu 成立 formation, finalization, conclusion; **seiritsu shima`su** 成立します gets formed (organized), comes into being, gets finalized/concluded

Se`iron セイロン Ceylon =

Surira⌐nka スリランカ Sri Lanka

se⌐iryoku 勢力 power, energy; influence

seisaku 1. 政策 (political) policy **2.** 制作・製作 manufacture, production; ～ **suru** 制作する・製作する manufactures, produces ⌐ture

seisan 生産 production, manufac-

seiseki 成績 results, marks, grades, record; **seiseki-hyō** 成績表 report card

seishiki (no/na) 正式(の/な) formal, formality

se⌐ishin 精神 soul, mind, spirit, psyche; ～ **(no)** 精神(の) mental

seishitsu 性質 character, quality, disposition, nature

Se⌐isho 聖書 Bible

seishu⌐n-ki 青春期 adolescence

sei-teki (na) 性的(な) sexual

se⌐ito 生徒 pupil, student

seitō 政党 political party

Se⌐iyō 西洋 the West, the Occident, Europe and America; ～**-fū (no)** 西洋風(の) Western-style

seiyu-sho⌐ 製油所 (oil) refinery

se⌐izei せいぜい at most, at best

seizō 製造 production, manufacture; ～**-moto** 製造元 maker *(manufacturer)*; ～ **shima⌐su** 製造します manufactures, produces

seizon 生存 existence; ～ **shima⌐su** 生存します exists

seji 世辞・せじ = **o-seji** お世辞・おせじ

se⌐kai 世界 world; **sekai-jū** 世界中 throughout the world, worldwide; **sekai-teki (na)** 世界的(な) worldwide, international ⌐(ting)

sekem-ba⌐nashi 世間話 chat-

se⌐ken 世間 the public, people, the world

seki⌐ せき・咳 cough; ～ **o shima⌐su** せき[咳]をします coughs

se⌐⌐ki (o-se⌐ki) 席(お席) seat, (assigned) place

…-seki …隻 (counts boats)

sekiha⌐n (o-se⌐kihan) 赤飯(お赤飯) rice boiled with red beans

Sekijū⌐ji 赤十字 Red Cross

sekinin 責任 responsibility, obligation; **sekini⌐n-sha** 責任者 responsible person

se⌐kiri 赤痢 dysentery

seki⌐-ryō 席料 cover charge

sekita⌐n 石炭 coal

sekitan-san 石炭酸 carbolic acid

sekito⌐ri 関取 a (ranking) sumo wrestler

sekiyu 石油 petroleum, oil, kerosene; ～**-suto⌐bu** 石油ストーブ kerosene heater

se⌐kkai 石灰 lime *(mineral)*

sekkaku⌐ せっかく especially;

with much effort/devotion (but); on purpose, taking the trouble **Sekkaku¹ desu ga ...** せっかくですが... It is kind of you (to ask), but ...

sekken 石けん・石鹸 soap

sekkin 接近 approach(ing); **... ni ~ o hakarima¹su** ...に接近を図ります seeks access to ... ; **... ni ~ shima¹su** ...に接近します approaches, draws near

sekkō 石こう・石膏 plaster

sekku⁽ⁿ⁾ 節句; **Ta¹ngo no ~** 端午の節句 Boys' Festival (5 May)

se¹kkusu セックス sex; **~ o shima¹su** セックスをします has sex

se⁽ⁿ⁾**kkyō**⁽ⁿ⁾ 説教 sermon; **~ shima¹su** 説教します preaches

sekkyoku-teki (na) 積極的(な) positive, energetic, vigorous

sema¹i 狭い narrow, tight

se¹m-ba 千羽 1,000 birds

sem-bai 千倍 a thousandfold (1,000 times doubled)

se¹m-bai 千杯 1,000 cupfuls

se¹mbe せんべ = **se¹mbei (o-se¹n)** せんべい・煎餅(お煎) rice crackers

se¹m-biki 千匹 1,000 animals/fish/bugs

se¹m-bon 千本 1,000 long things

se¹me 攻め・責め → **semema¹su** 攻めます・責めます [infinitive]

semema¹su, seme¹ru 1. 攻めます, 攻める attacks, assaults **2.** 責めます, 責める censures, reproaches, criticizes

semen(to) セメン(ト) cement

se¹mete 1. せめて at least; at most **2.** 攻めて・責めて → **semema¹su** 攻めます・責めます

semmen-jo⁽ⁿ⁾ 洗面所 lavatory (to wash up at/in)

semme¹n-ki 洗面器 wash basin

semmon 専門 specialty, major (line/field/study); **~-go** 専門語 technical term, jargon; **~ no hito¹** 専門の人, **~-ka** 専門家 specialist; **semmo¹n-i** 専門医 (medical) specialist

sempai 先輩 one's senior (colleague, fellow student)

sempō 先方 the other side

sempū⁽ⁿ⁾ 旋風 whirlwind

sempū¹-ki 扇風機 electric fan

se¹n 1. 千・1,000 (= **is-se¹n** 一千・1,000) thousand **2.** 線 (= **se¹nro** 線路) line, route **3.** 栓・せん plug, cork, stopper

...¹-sen ...船 ship

senaka 背中 back (of body)

(...-)se¹nchi (...)センチ, **senchi-mē¹toru** センチメートル centimeter

senchime¹ntaru (na) センチメンタル(な) sentimental

se¹nchō 船長 captain (of ship)

sendatte¹ 先立って a few days ago, recently

senden 宣伝 propaganda, publicity

sen-en 千円 a thousand yen

se⌐ngetsu 先月 last month

se⌐ngo 戦後 postwar, after/since the war

se⌐n'i 繊維 fiber

sen'in 船員 ship's crew (member), sailor

se⌐nji 戦時 wartime; **senji-chū** 戦時中 during the war

senjitsu 先日 a few days ago, recently, the other day

se⌐nko 線香, **se⌐nkō (o-se⌐nkō)** 線香(お線香) incense, joss stick

senkō 専攻 major (study); ~ **shima⌐su** 専攻します majors (specializes) in

se⌐nkyo 選挙 election

senkyo⌐shi 宣教師 missionary

sen-nu⌐ki⌐ 栓抜き corkscrew, bottle opener

senrei 先例 precedent, prior example

se⌐nro 線路 railroad track/line

senryō 占領 military occupation

sense⌐i 先生 teacher; doctor; maestro, master (artisan/artist)

sense⌐n-getsu 先々月 month before last, two months ago

sense⌐n-shū 先々週 week before last

sense⌐shon センセーション a sensation (excitement)

se⌐nshu 選手 athlete; player

senshū 先週 last week

sensō 戦争 war

sensu (o-sensu) 扇子(お扇子) fan (folding)

se⌐nsu センス sense

sensu⌐i-kan 潜水艦 submarine

sentaku 1. 洗濯 (o-se⌐ntaku お洗濯) laundry, washing (= **sentaku-mono** 洗濯物) 2. 選択 selection, choice

senta⌐ku⌐-ki 洗濯機 washer (washing machine)

sentakumono-ire 洗濯物入れ clothesbag (for laundry)

sentaku shima⌐su (suru) 1. 洗濯します(する) launders, washes 2. 選択します(する) selects

sentaku-ya 洗濯屋 a laundry

se⌐ntensu センテンス sentence (linguistic)

(...-)se⌐nto (...)セント cent(s)

sentō 戦闘 battle

se⌐ntō 銭湯 public bath

sen'yaku 先約 previous appointment/engagement

senzen (no) 戦前(の) prewar, before the war

se⌐nzo 先祖 ancestor

se⌐n-zoku 千足 (also **se⌐n-soku** 千足) 1,000 pairs of footwear

senzuri o kakima⌐su (ka⌐ku) せんずりをかきます(かく) masturbates

seppuku 切腹 harakiri

seppun 接吻 kiss; ~ **shima⌐su** 接

吻します kisses

seri¹ 1. 競り・せり auction 2. せり・芹 Japanese parsley

seri⌐fu せりふ・台詞 one's lines (in a play), dialogue

se¹rohan セロハン cellophane

se⌐ron 世論 public opinion

se¹rori セロリ celery

se̅ru セール sale

se¹sse-to せっせと diligently, hard (laboriously); frequently, often

ses-shima¹su 接します, -su⌐ru 接する: (… ni) ~ (…に)接します 1. comes in contact (with), borders (on), is adjacent/contiguous (to) 2. encounters, meets, receives, treats, handles

sesshoku 接触 contact, touch; … ni sesshoku shima¹su …に接触します touches, comes into contact with

se̅ta̅ セーター sweater

sctomono 瀬戸物 porcelain, china(ware)

Seto-na¹ikai 瀬戸内海 the Inland Sea

se¹tsu 節 occasion (time or event)

se¹tsubi 設備 equipment, facilities, accommodations

setsubi⌐-go/-ji 接尾語/辞 suffix

setsumei 説明 explanation, description; ~ shima¹su 説明します explains, describes

setsumei⌐-sho⌐ 説明書 written

explanation, instructions

se¹tsuna 利那 moment, instant

setsuyaku 節約 economizing; setsuyaku shima¹su 節約します saves (economizes on), conserves ⌐tion

setsuzo⌐ku-shi 接続詞 a conjuncse̅tto セット 1. set (hair, etc.) 2. a set meal

settō⌐-go/-ji 接頭語/辞 prefix

settoku 説得 persuasion; settoku shima¹su 説得します persuades

sewa¹ (o-se̅wa, o-sewa-sama) 世話（お世話, お世話さま） 1. care, trouble, assistance, help; (… no) ~ ni narima¹su (…の)世話になります becomes obliged (to one for help); → o-sewa-sama お世話さま 2. meddling, minding other people's business

sewashi̅i せわしい busy

sezu せず, sezu ni せずに = shina¹ide しないで not doing

…¹-sha 1. …社 company 2. …者 person

…⌐-sha …車 vehicle

shabera¹nai しゃべらない = shaberimase¹n しゃべりません (not chatter)

shaberima¹su しゃべります・喋ります, shabe¹ru しゃべる・喋る chatters

sha¹beru シャベル a shovel

shabe¹tte しゃべって →

shaberima⌐su しゃべります

shabon シャボン = **sekken** 石けん・石鹸 soap

shabon-dama シャボン玉 soap bubble

shaboten シャボテン, **saboten** サボテン cactus

shaburanai しゃぶらない = **shaburimase⌐n** しゃぶりません (not suck)

shaburima⌐su しゃぶります, **shaburu** しゃぶる sucks, chews

shabu-shabu しゃぶしゃぶ beef slices dipped in hot broth till ready to eat; (Mongolian) chimney pot

shabutte しゃぶって → **shaburima⌐su** しゃぶります

shachō 社長 president of a company, boss

shadan 遮断 interruption

sha⌐dan 社団 corporation

shadō 車道 road(way), drive-(way), street

shagamima⌐su しゃがみます, **shagamu** しゃがむ squats, crouches on heels

shagande しゃがんで → **shagamima⌐su** しゃがみます

sha⌐-in 社員 employee (of a company)

Sha⌐ka 釈迦 = **o-Shaka-sa⌐ma⌐** お釈迦様 Buddha (Sakya-muni)

sha⌐kai 社会 society, (~ no 社会

の) social; ~ **no ma⌐do ga aite ima⌐su** 社会の窓が開いています. Your fly is open (un-zipped/unbuttoned).

shakai-ka⌐gaku 社会科学 social science(s)

shakai-shu⌐gi 社会主義 social-ism; **shakai-shugi⌐-sha** 社会主義者 a socialist

sha⌐ke しゃけ・鮭 salmon (= **sa⌐ke** さけ・鮭)

shakki⌐n 借金 debt

sha⌐kkuri しゃっくり hiccup

sha⌐ko 1. 車庫 garage, car barn **2.** しゃこ squilla, mantis shrimp

shakō 社交 social intercourse, socializing

shaku (o-shaku) 酌（お酌） serv-ing/pouring the rice wine; ~ **o shima⌐su** 酌をします serves the saké

shaku ni sawarima⌐su (sawaru) しゃく［癪］に障ります（障る） takes offense, gets irritated/provoked; ... **ga ~** ...がしゃく［癪］に障ります is offen-sive, irritating, provoking

shaku⌐hachi 尺八 vertical bam-boo flute

sha⌐kushi 杓子 ladle (large wooden)

shamisen 三味線 a three-stringed banjo

shampa⌐n シャンパン, **shampe⌐n** シャンペン champagne

sha'mpū シャンプー, sha'mpu シャンプ shampoo

sha'nai (no) 社内(の) within the office/company, internal

Sha'nha'i シャンハイ・上海 Shanghai

share しゃれ・洒落 joke, pun

sharei 謝礼 remuneration, reward, fee

sharin 車輪 wheel

shasen 斜線 a slant line (such as "/")

shashin 写真 photo, picture; ~ -chō 写真帳 photo album; ~ -ka 写真家 photographer

shashi'n-ki 写真機 camera

shashō 車掌 conductor

sha'tsu シャツ undershirt

sha'ttā シャッター shutter (camera, etc.)

sha'wā シャワー shower; ~ o abima'su (abiru) シャワーを浴びます(浴びる) takes a shower

shi 1. 詩 poetry, poem, verse 2. し → shima'su します [infinitive]

... shi ...し and, and so, what with (the fact that) ...

shi' 1. 死 death 2. 四 (= yo'n 四) four 3. 市 (= to'shi 都市) city

shiage 仕上げ the finish(ing touch)

shia'ge 仕上げ → shiagema'su 仕上げます [infinitive]

shiagema'su 仕上げます,

shiage'ru 仕上げる finishes up

shiage'nai 仕上げない = shiagemase'n 仕上げません (not finish up)

shia'gete 仕上げて → shiagema'su 仕上げます

shiai 試合 match, contest, meet

shiasa'tte しあさって・明々後日 three days from now

shiawase 幸せ・しあわせ・仕合わせ luck, fortune, happiness; ~ (na) 幸せ・しあわせ(な) lucky, happy

shiba 1. 芝 turf, lawn 2. 柴 brushwood

Shi'ba 芝 Shiba; Shiba-Kō'en 芝公園 Shiba Park

shiba□-ebi 芝えび[海老] tiny shrimp

shibafu 芝生 lawn, grass

shibai 芝居 a play (drama)

shibakari'-ki 芝刈り機 lawn mower

shiba'raku しばらく・暫く (for) a while; ~ shite しばらくして after a while

Shiba'raku desu ne しばらくですね。It's nice to see you again.

shibara'nai 縛らない = shibarimase'n 縛りません (not tie up)

shibarima'su 縛ります, shiba'ru 縛る ties up

shi'bashiba しばしば often, repeatedly

shiba̱tte 縛って → shibarima̱su 縛ります [infinitive]

Shiberi(y)a シベリア［ヤ］ Siberia

shibin しびん bedpan (urinal)

shibire̱ しびれ・痺れ numbness; ~ o kirashima̱su (kira̱su) し びれを切らします(切らす) loses patience

shibi̱re しびれ・痺れ → shibire-ma̱su しびれます・痺れます

shibirema̱su しびれます・痺れま す, shibire̱ru しびれる・痺れ る gets numb, (a leg, etc.) goes to sleep

shibō 脂肪 fat (lard, blubber)

shibora̱nai 絞らない = shiborimase̱n 絞りません not wring it

shibori̱ 絞り, o-shi̱bori おしぼ り・お絞り a damp hand-towel

shibo̱ri 絞り → shiborima̱su 絞 ります [infinitive]

shiborima̱su 絞ります, shibo̱ru 絞る wrings (out), squeezes, strains (through cloth)

shibo̱tte 絞って → shiborima̱su 絞ります

shibu̱i 渋い 1. puckery, astrin-gent 2. wry; glum 3. severely simple, tastefully bare/restrained

Shibuya 渋谷 Shibuya; Shibuya̱-Eki 渋谷駅 Shibuya Station

shi̱cha しちゃ = shi̱te̱ wa して は

shichaima̱shita しちゃいました = shite shimaima̱shita してし まいました = shima̱shita し ました (did)

shichaima̱su しちゃいます = shite shimaima̱su してしまい ます

shichatta しちゃった = shite shimatta してしまった = shi̱ta した (did)

shichau しちゃう = shite shimau してしまう

shichi̱ 1. 七・7 (= na̱na 七・7) seven 2. 質 a pawn (something pawned)

Shichi-gatsu̱ 七月・7月 July

Shichi-go̱-san 七五三 the "seven-five-three" day when children of those ages visit shrines (15 November)

shichi-ju̱ 七十・70 seventy (= nana̱-jū 七十・70)

shichimen-chō 七面鳥 turkey

shichi̱-ya̱ 質屋 pawnbroker, pawnshop

shicho̱ 市長 mayor

shichū̱ シチュー stew

shi̱da しだ・羊歯 fern

shidai 次第・しだい circum-stances; (NOUN, VERB-i い) shi̱dai desu 次第です it depends on … ; (VERB-i い)-shi̱dai (ni) 次第(に) as soon as

shi̱dan 師団 army division

shidashi-ya 仕出し屋 caterer, catering shop

shidō 指導 guidance, direction, leadership, counsel(ing), coaching; ～ **shimaˈsu** 指導します guides, directs, leads, counsels, coaches

shidōˈ-sha 指導者 guide, director, leader, counsel, coach

shifuku 私服 plain clothes; civilian clothes, civies

shiˈgā シガー cigar

shi-gachi (na) しがち(な) apt to do

shigai 死骸 corpse

shiˈgai 市外 outskirts of city, suburbs

shiˈgareˈtto シガレット cigarette(s)

Shi-gatsuˈ 四月・4月 April

shigeki 刺激 stimulation

shigerimaˈsu 茂ります, **shigeˈru** 茂る it grows thick(ly)/luxuriant(ly)

shi-go-... 四,五... four or five ...

shiᒣgoku しごく・至極 extremely

shigoto (o-shiˈgoto) 仕事(お仕事) job, work, task, undertaking, business; ～ **o shimaˈsu** 仕事をします works

shigure 時雨・しぐれ an on-and-off drizzle (in November or December)

shihaˈi 支配, **shiˈhai** 支配 management, control; **shihaˈi-nin** 支配人 manager; **shihaˈi-sha** 支配者 ruler; **shiˈhai shimaˈsu**

支配します rule, control

shiharai 支払い paying out, payment, disbursement

shihei 紙幣, **shiˈhei** 紙幣 paper money, currency (bill)

shihoˈ 四方, **shiˈhō** 四方 all sides/directions

shihon 資本 capital, funds; ～ **-ka** 資本家 capitalist; ～ **-shuˈgi** 資本主義 capitalism

shiieˈmu シーエム・CM CM = commercial (message)

shi-iˈi しいい easy to do

shiin 子音 consonant

shiˈin シーン scene

shiˈitake しいたけ・椎茸 large brown mushrooms (often dried)

shiite 敷いて → **shikimaˈsu** 敷きます (spreads it)

shiˈite 強いて・しいて forcibly; ～ **sasemaˈsu** 強いてさせます forces one to do

shiˈito シート 1. sheet 2. seat; **shiito-beˈruto** シートベルト seatbelt

shiˈitsu シーツ sheet (for bed)

shiˈizun シーズン the season

shiˈji 支持 support, maintenance; ～ **shima(ᒣ)su** 支持します supports, endorses

shiˈji 指示, **shiˈshi** 指示 indication, instruction, directions; ～ **shima(ᒣ)su** 指示します indicates, points out

shijin 詩人 poet

shi□**jō** 市場 market

shi-jū' 四十・40 forty (= **yo'n-jū** 四十・40)

shī'jū 始終・しじゅう all the time

shika□ しか・鹿 deer

shika' 歯科 dentistry; (= **shika'-i** 歯科医) dentist

... □**shika** ...しか + NEGATIVE (nothing) but, except for; (= ... **dake'** ...だけ + POSITIVE) only, just

shika'-i 歯科医 dentist (= **ha'-isha** 歯医者)

shikake 仕掛け・しかけ device *(gadget)*

shikaku 資格 qualification(s), competency; **zairyū** ~ 在留資格 status of residence

shikaku' (**no**) 四角(の) square

shikaku'i 四角い square

shika'-mo しかも moreover; and yet

shikanai 敷かない = **shikimase'n** 敷きません (not spread it)

shikaranai 叱らない = **shikarimase'n** 叱りません (not scold)

shikari 叱り → **shikarima'su** 叱ります [infinitive]

shikarima'su 叱ります, **shikaru** 叱る scolds

shikarō' 叱ろう = **shikarimashō'** 叱りましょう (let's scold!)

shika'shi しかし but, however

shi-kata 仕方・しかた way (of do-

ing), manner, method, means; ~ **ga arimase'n** (**na'i**) 仕方[しかた]がありません(ない) there's nothing we can do about it

shika'tte 叱って → **shikarima'su** 叱ります

shike'ba 敷けば → **shikima'su** 敷きます (if one spread it)

shike'n (**o-shike'n**) 試験(お試験) examination, test, trial, experiment

shiken-jo□ 試験所 (testing) laboratory

shiken-jō 試験場 exam room/place

shike□**n-kan** 試験管 test tube

shiki' 式 ceremony

shiki 敷き → **shikima'su** 敷きます [infinitive]

shikibetsu 識別 discriminating; **shikibetsu shima'su** 識別します discriminates, discerns, distinguishes

shiki-bu'ton 敷布団 bottom quilt

shiki-chi 敷地 building lot; (house)site

shikifu 敷布 (bed) sheet

shikii 敷居 sill; threshold

shiki'-kin 敷金 security deposit *(for rental)*

shikima'su 敷きます, **shiku** 敷く spreads (a quilt, etc.); sits on

shiki-mono 敷物 a spread; rug, mat, cushion

shiki'n 資金 fund

shi̱-kiremase̱n し切れません・し
きれません, **-kire̱nai** し切れ
ない・しきれない cannot do it
(= **dekimase̱n** できません,
deki̱nai できない)

shi̱kiri 仕切り partition

shi̱kiri-ni しきりに incessantly;
intently, hard

shi̱kī-sha 指揮者 conductor (orchestra)

shi̱kka̱ri しっかり firmly,
resolutely

shikke̱[ŋ] 湿気 = **shikki**[ŋ] 湿気

shi̱kki 漆器 lacquer(ware)

shikki[ŋ] 湿気, **shikke̱**[ŋ] 湿気
dampness, humidity

shi̱kko しっこ = **o-shi̱kko** おし
っこ [baby talk] urine, urinating

shi̱kkui しっくい・漆喰 plaster,
stucco

shi̱kkusu シックス six

shi̱kō 嗜好 liking, fancy, taste; ...
ni ~ ga arima̱su ...に嗜好が
あります has a taste/liking for
...

Shi̱ko̱ku 四国 Shikoku

shi̱ku 敷く = **shikima̱su** 敷きま
す (spreads it)

shi̱kya 敷きゃ 1. = **shike̱ba** 敷
けば (if one spread it) 2. ~
shinai 敷きゃしない = **shiki̱**
ya/wa shinai 敷きや/はしな
い = **shikanai** 敷かない (not
spread it)

shi̱kyū 至急 urgency; ~ **(no)** 至

急(の) urgent; ~ **ni** 至急に
urgently

shima̱ 1. 島 island 2. しま・縞
stripes

shimai 1. しまい・終い the end;
~ **(no)** しまい(の) the final/
last 2. しまい → **shimaima̱su**
しまいます [infinitive]

shimaima̱su しまいます,
shimau しまう puts away,
finishes; **shite ~** してしまう
finishes doing, ends up by doing (after all), does anyway,
does it all

shimaō しまおう =
shimaimashō̱ しまいましょう
(let's put it away; let's finish)

shimara̱nai 閉まらない =
shimarimase̱n 閉まりません
(not shut; not ...)

shimarima̱su, shima̱ru 1. 閉ま
ります, 閉まる it shuts,
closes, locks 2. 締まります,
締まる gets steady, braces
oneself 3. 締まります, 締まる
gets thrifty, frugal

shimase̱n しません, **shinai** しな
い doesn't

shimase̱n deshi̱ta しませんでし
た, **shina̱katta** しなかった
didn't

shima̱shi̱ta しました, **shi̱ta** した
did

shimashō̱ しましょう, **shiyō̱** し
よう let's do it; ~ **ka** しまし
ょうか Shall we do it?

shima͞su します, **suru** する does (it); it happens; wears
... ni (ADJECTIVE-ku) ～ ...に (ADJECTIVE く)します makes it so that (it is), makes it into; decides on (= **... ni kimema͞su** ...に決めます)
... (shiyō) to ～ ...（しよう）と します goes (tries, is about) to do
... (suru) koto ni ～ ...（する）事にします decides to (do)
... to shite(͞ mo) ...として（も）(even) as a ...

shi͞matsu 始末・しまつ managing, dealing with; outcome, upshot, climax; **shi͞matsu shima(͞)su** 始末［しまつ］します deals with, manages, settles, disposes of

shimatta しまった = **shimaima͞shita** しまいました (finished)

shima͞tta 1. 閉まった・絞まった = **shimarima͞shita** 閉まりました・締まりました **2.** しまった！ Damn!

shimau しまう = **shimaima͞su** しまいます

shima͞uma, shima͞mma しまうま・縞馬 zebra

shimawanai しまわない = **shimaimase͞n** しまいません (not put away)

Shi͞mbashi 新橋 Shimbashi;

Shimbashi͞-Eki 新橋駅 Shimbashi Station

shi͞mbō 辛抱 endurance, patience, forbearance; ～ **shima(͞)su** 辛抱します endures, bears, stands, puts up with

shimbun 新聞 newspaper; ～ **-ki͞sha** 新聞記者 reporter; ～ **-u͞riba** 新聞売り場 newsstand; ～**-u͞riko** 新聞売り子 news vendor

shimbu͞n-dai 新聞代 (news) paper bill

shimbu͞n-sha 新聞社 newspaper (company)

shi͞me 閉め・締め → **shimema͞su** 閉めます・締めます [infinitive]

shime͞-gane 締め金 buckle

shimei-tsu͞wa 指名通話 person-to-person call

shimekiri 締め切り closing; "Closed"; ～**-ki͞gen** 締め切り期限, ～**-ki͞jitsu** 締め切り期日 deadline

shimema͞su, shime͞ru 1. 閉めます, 閉める shuts (closes, locks) it **2.** 締めます, 締める ties, fastens, tightens it; puts on, wears (a necktie, a belt); tightens up on, economizes on

shime͞nai 閉めない = **shimemase͞n** 閉めません (not shut it) ⌈humid

shimeppo͞i 湿っぽい damp;

shimeri 湿り → **shimerima͞su** 湿

りします [infinitive]

shimerima'su 湿ります, **shimeru** 湿る gets damp

shimeru 湿る = **shimerima'su** 湿ります (gets damp)

shime'ru 閉める・締める = **shimema'su** 閉めます; 締めます (closes it; wears it)

shimeshima'su 湿します, **shimesu** 湿す moistens/ dampens it, wets it

shimeshima'su 示します, **shime⌐su** 示す shows, indicates

shi'meta 閉めた・締めた = **shimema'shita** 閉めました; 締めました (closed it; wore it)

shi'mete 閉めて・締めて → **shimema'su** 閉めます・締めます

shimetta 湿った = **shimerima'shita** 湿りました (got damp)

shimette 湿って → **shimerima'su** 湿ります; ~ **ima'su** 湿っています is damp

shimi 染み・しみ 1. stain, blot, blotch, spot 2. → **shimima'su** 染みます [infinitive]

shi⌐mi 衣魚 clothes moth

shimiji'mi (to) しみじみ(と) keenly/deeply (feels), fully (appreciates)

shimima'su 染みます, **shimiru** 染みる penetrates, smarts

shi'min 市民 citizen, civilian

shimi-yo⌐ke⌐ 衣魚よけ mothballs

shimo' 霜 frost

shi'mo しも; ~ **shimase'n (shinai)** しもしません(しない) nor do, not do either/even

shimon 1. 指紋 fingerprint 2. 試問 question, interviewing, examination; **kōtō-shi'mon** 口頭試問 oral examination

shimpai 心配 worry, uneasiness, concern, anxiety, fear; ~ **(na)** 心配(な) uneasy; (... **ni**) ~ **o kakema'su** (...に)心配をかけます causes (one) worry/concern; ~ **shima'su** 心配します worries about, fears

shi'mpi 神秘 mystery; **shimpi-teki (na)** 神秘的(な) mysterious, esoteric, miraculous

shi'mpo 進歩 progress; ~ **shima(⌐)su** 進歩します makes progress

shi'mpu 神父 priest (Christian), Father, Reverend

shi'mpuru (na) シンプル(な) simple

shi'n 1. 芯・しん core, pith, heart 2. 心 heart, spirit

shi'n(-) 新... ... new; ~ **...⌐-Eki** 新...駅 Shinkansen (bullet train) ... station

shina 品 articles, goods; quality

Shi'na 支那 China

shi-nagara しながら while doing

shinai しない = **shimase'n** しま

せん doesn't do it

shi⌐nai 市内 within the city; urban, city, municipal

shina⌐ide しないで not doing it, instead of doing it; ～ **ima⌐su** しないでいます keeps on not doing it; ～ **kudasai** しないで下さい don't do it!; ～ **okima⌐su** しないでおきます neglects to do it, leaves it undone; ～ **mima⌐su** しないでみます tries not doing it; ～ **sumima⌐su** しないで済みます gets by without doing it

shinai-de⌐nwa 市内電話 local telephone call

shinai to しないと = **shina⌐kereba** しなければ (unless one does it)

shina⌐katta しなかった = **shimase⌐n deshita** しませんでした (didn't do it)

shina⌐kereba しなければ, **shina⌐kerya** しなけりゃ unless one does it; ～ **narimase⌐n** しなければなりません must do it

shina⌐kute mo しなくても even not doing it; ～ **i⌐i desu** しなくてもいいです needs not do it, doesn't have to do it

shina⌐kya しなきゃ = **shina⌐kerya** しなけりゃ = **shina⌐kereba** しなければ

shina-mono 品物 goods

shinanai 死なない =

shinimase⌐n 死にません (does/will not die)

shinana⌐katta 死ななかった = **shinimase⌐n deshita** 死にませんでした (didn't die)

shi-naoshima⌐su し直します, **-nao⌐su** し直す redoes it, fixes/improves it

shinchū しんちゅう・真鍮 brass

shi⌐nchū 心中 (the bottom of) one's heart

shinda 死んだ = **shinima⌐shita** 死にました (died)

shindai 寝台 bed, berth, bunk; **shinda⌐i-ken** 寝台券 berth ticket; **shinda⌐i-sha** 寝台車 sleeping car

shinde 死んで → **shinima⌐su** 死にます; ～ **ima⌐su** 死んでいます is dead

shinden 神殿 the sanctuary of a shrine

shindō 振動 vibration

shingeki 新劇 modern drama

shingō 信号 signal

shi⌐ngu 寝具 bedding

shi⌐nguru シングル = **shinguru-rū⌐mu** シングルルーム a single (room)

shinima⌐su 死にます, **shinu** 死ぬ dies

shinin 死人 dead person

shi⌐nja⌐ 信者 a believer; (= **Kirisuto-kyō no** ～ キリスト教の信者) a Christian

shi⌐n-ji 信じ → **shin-jima⌐su** 信

じます [infinitive]

Shinjiku 新宿 = **Shinjuku** 新宿

shin-jima´su 信じます, **-ji´ru** 信
じる believes in, trusts

shin-ji´nai 信じない = **shin-jimase´n** 信じません (doesn't
believe/trust)

shin-ji´na´katta 信じなかった =
shin-jimase´n deshita 信じま
せんでした (didn't believe/
trust)

shi´njitsu 真実 truth

shinju 真珠 pearl; **Shinju´-wan**
真珠湾 Pearl Harbor

shinjū 心中 double suicide,
lovers' suicide

Shinjuku 新宿, **Shinjuku** 新宿
Shinjuku; **Shinjuku´-Eki** 新宿
駅 Shinjuku Station

shinka´nsen 新幹線 bullet train
(line), Shinkansen

shi´nkei 神経 nerve; ~ **ni
sawarima´su** 神経に障ります
gets on one's nerves; **shinke´i-shitsu (na)** 神経質(な) nervous

shinko しんこ・新香, **o-shinko**
おしんこ・お新香 radish (etc.)
pickles

shinkoku (na) 深刻(な) serious,
grave

shi´nnen 新年 new year; ~ **o-
medetō (gozaima´su)** 新年おめ
でとう[お目出度う](ござい
ます)! Happy new year!

shinō 死のう = **shinimashō´** 死

にましょう; ~ **to omo´tte
ima´shita** 死のうと思っていま
した. I thought I would die.

shinoba´nai 忍ばない =
shinobimase´n 忍びません

shinobima´su 忍びます,
shino´bu 忍ぶ bears, puts up
with

shino´nde 忍んで →
shinobima´su 忍びます

shinrai 信頼 trust, confidence,
reliance

shinrai-sei 信頼性 reliability; ~
ga taka´i 信頼性が高い highly
reliable

shi´nri 1. 心理 psychology, mentality 2. 真理 truth

shinri´-gaku 心理学 (science/
study of) psychology;
shinriga´ku´-sha 心理学者
psychologist

shi´nrui 親類 a relative

shinryaku 侵略 aggression

shinsatsu 診察 medical examination

shinsei-sho´ 申請書 application
(for a permit)

shinseki 親戚 a relative

shinsen (na) 新鮮(な) fresh

shi´nsetsu (go-shi´nsetsu) 親切
(ご親切) kindness, goodwill,
favor; ~ **(na)** 親切(な) kind,
cordial

shi´nshi 紳士 gentleman

shinshitsu 寝室 bedroom

shi´ntai (no) 身体(の) physical;

shintai-ke'nsa 身体検査 physical exam; **shintai-shōga'i-sha** 身体障害者 handicapped person

Shi'ntō 神道, **Shi'ndō** 神道 Shinto(ism)

shinu 死ぬ = **shinima'su** 死にます (dies)

shinwa 神話 myth

shi'n'ya 深夜 late at night

Shin-yaku 新約 the New Testament

shin'yō 信用 trust, confidence; credit; ～ **shima'su** 信用します trusts

shinzō 心臓 heart

shio' 1. (o-shi'o) 塩(お塩) salt 2. 潮 tide

shio-kara'i 塩辛い salty

shion 子音 consonant

shiori□ しおり bookmark

shio-ya□**ki**□ 塩焼き broiled salt-coated fish

shippai 失敗 failure, blunder, defeat; ～ **shima'su** 失敗します fails, misses

shippo' しっぽ・尻尾 tail

shirabe' (o-shirabe) 調べ(お調べ) investigation

shira'be 調べ → **shirabema'su** 調べます 1. [infinitive] 2. [imperative] **shirabe ro** 調べろ, **shirabe'** **yo** 調べよ investigate!

shirabema'su 調べます, **shirabe'ru** 調べる investigates, examines, checks

shirabe'nai 調べない = **shirabemase'n** 調べません (not investigate)

shira'beta 調べた = **shirabema'shita** 調べました (investigated)

shira'bete 調べて → **shirabema'su** 調べます

shiraga' 白髪・しらが gray hair

shirami しらみ・虱 louse, lice

shiranai 知らない = **shirimase'n** 知りません (not know); ～ **hito** 知らない人 a stranger

shirarema'su 知られます, **shirareru** 知られる gets (widely) known; becomes famous

shirase 知らせ 1. (o-shirase) お知らせ report, notice, information 2. → **shirasema'su** 知らせます [infinitive]; [imperative] **shirase ro** 知らせろ, **shirase'** **yo** 知らせよ let them know!

shirasema'su 知らせます, **shiraseru** 知らせる announces *(informs of)*, lets one know, notifies

shi□**rasu** しらす・白子 whitebait; baby sardines

shira'taki しらたき・白滝 fine white threads of *konnyaku* こんにゃく

shire'ba 知れば → **shirima'su** 知ります (if one learn/know)

shire'i-bu 指令部 headquarters

shire'i-kan 指令官 commander

shirema'su 知れます, **shireru** 知

れる gets known; is identified;
becomes clear/evident

shirenai 知れない = **shiremase̱n**
知れません (not get known;
not be clear)

shiri 知り → **shirima̱su** 知りま
す [infinitive]

shiri̱ (o-shiri) 尻(お尻) butt-
(ock), hip, bottom, seat

shiriai 知り合い acquaintance

shirimase̱n 知りません, **shiranai**
知らない does not know

shirima̱su 知ります, **shiru** 知る
acquaints oneself with, finds
out, learns; **shi̱tte ima̱su** 知っ
ています knows

shiri-tai 知りたい curious about,
want(ing) to know

shi̱ritsu (no) 1. 市立(の)
municipal 2. 私立(の) (=
wataku̱shi̱-ritsu 私立) private-
(ly established)

shirizo̱ita 退いた =
shirizokima̱shita 退きました
(retreated)

shirizo̱ite 退いて →
shirizokima̱su 退きます

shirizoka̱nai 退かない =
shirizokimase̱n 退きません
(not retreat)

shirizo̱ki 退き → **shirizokima̱su**
退きます [infinitive]

shirizokima̱su 退きます,
shirizo̱ku 退く retreats,
withdraws, retires

shiro 城 castle (= **o-shiro** お城)

shi̱ro (no) 白(の) white

shi ro しろ, **shi ro̱ yo** しろよ do
it! (= **se̱ yo** せよ)

shirō 知ろう = **shirimashō̱** 知り
ましょう (let's find out!)

shiro̱i 白い white

shi̱ro̱mi 白身 white (of an egg),
albumen; white meat

shi̱ro̱ppu シロップ syrup

shi̱rō̱to しろうと・素人 an
amateur, a novice

shiru 知る = **shirima̱su** 知りま
す (learns; knows)

shi̱ru 汁 juice, gravy; broth,
soup

shirubā-ui̱iku/-wi̱iku シルバー
ウイーク/ウィーク Silver
Week (around 3 November)

shiruko̱ (o-shiruko) しるこ・汁
粉(おしるこ・お汁粉) a sweet
redbean-paste soup

shirushi (o-shirushi) しるし・印・
徴(お印・お徴) indication,
token, sign, symptom; effect-
(iveness)

shirya 知りゃ 1. = **shire̱ba** 知れ
ば (if one learn/know) 2. ～
shinai 知りゃしない = **shiri̱**
ya/wa shinai 知りや/はしな
い = **shiranai** 知らない (not
know)

shi̱ryo 思慮 consideration,
thought(fulness)

shi̱ryō 資料 materials; data

shi̱ryoku 視力 vision, eyesight,
visual acuity

shisei 姿勢 posture; attitude

shisen 支線 branch *(of rail line)*

shisetsu 私設 = **watakushī-setsu** 私設 private

shi⌐se⌐tsu 施設 facility, institution, establishment, installation

shi⌐shi 1. しし・獅子 lion **2.** = **shi⌐ji** 指示 (indication)

shishō⌐-sha 死傷者 casualties *(dead and wounded)*

shishū 刺しゅう・刺繍 embroidery

shishu⌐n-ki 思春期 adolescence

shiso しそ・紫蘇 perilla, beefsteak plant

shisō 思想 thought, concept

shi⌐son 子孫 descendants; posterity

shi-sō (na) しそう（な）likely/about to do it; **~ mo na⌐i** しそうもない unlikely to do it

shi⌐sso (na) 質素（な）simple, plain, frugal

shi-su⌐gi し過ぎ・しすぎ → **shi-sugima⌐su** し過ぎます・しすぎます [infinitive]

shi-sugima⌐su し過ぎます・しすぎます, **-sugi⌐ru** し過ぎる・しすぎる over(does)

shita した = **shima⌐shita** しました (did, has done); **~ a⌐to de** した後で after doing; **~ ba⌐kari desu** したばかりです just (now) did it; **~ hō⌐ ga i⌐i** した方[ほう]がいい ought to do it, better do it; **~ koto⌐ ga arimase⌐n** したことがありません has never done it; **~ mono⌐ desu** したものです used to do it

shita 下, **... shita⌐** ...下 below, under, bottom, lower; (= **toshi-shita** 年下) younger, youngest

shita⌐ 舌 tongue

shita-baki 1. 下穿き・下ばき underwear, underpants **2.** 下履き・下ばき (outdoor) shoes

shita-bi⌐rame したびらめ・舌平目 sole *(fish)*

shitagaima⌐su 従います, **shitaga⌐u** 従う: **... ni ~** ...に従います conforms to ... , accords with ...

shi-tagarima⌐su したがります, **shi-taga⌐ru** したがる wants (is eager) to do

shitaga⌐tte 1. したがって・従って accordingly, therefore; **... ni ~** ...に従って[したがって] according to ... , in conformity with/to ... **2.** **shi-taga⌐tte** したがって → **shi-tagarima⌐su** したがります

shita-gi 下着 underwear

shitai 死体 corpse

shi-tai したい wants to do it

shi-ta⌐katta したかった wanted to do it

shitaku 支度 preparation, arrangement

shi̱-taku したく: ~ **arimase̱n (na̱i)** したくありません(ない) is unwilling to do it; ~ **narima̱su (na̱ru)** したくなります(なる) gets so one wants to do it

shi̱ta-machi 下町 downtown 「it

shi̱ta̱ra したら if/when one does

shi̱ta̱ri (... shima̱su) したり(... します) does/is such things as; sometimes does/is; does/is intermittently (off and on)

shi̱tashi̱i 親しい intimate, familiar, dear

shi̱tate-ya 仕立屋 tailor

shi̱ta̱tte したって = **shi̱te̱ mo** してても even doing, even if it does

shi̱te して doing; does and; **shi̱te̱ kara** してから (next) after doing; **shi̱te̱ mo i̱i** してもいい may do it, it is OK to do it; **shi̱te̱ wa ikemase̱n/ikenai/ dame̱** してはいけません/いけない/だめ mustn't do it, don't do it!

shi̱tei 指定 designation, appointment; ~ **shima̱su** 指定します designates, appoints

shi̱te̱i-seki 指定席 reserved seat(s)

shi̱te̱i-shi 指定詞 the copula (**de̱su, da̱, na̱, no̱, ni̱, de̱, ...** です, だ, な, の, に, で,...)

shi̱teki shima̱su (suru) 指摘しま

す indicates, points out

shi̱ten 支店 branch shop

shi̱tetsu 私鉄 private railroad

shi̱tsu⌐ 質 quality, nature

...⌐-shi̱tsu ...室 room

shi̱tsubō 失望 disappointment

shi̱tsu̱do 湿度 humidity

shi̱tsugyō 失業 unemployment; **shi̱tsugyō̱-sha** 失業者 unemployed person

shi̱-tsuke しつけ・躾 training (of children, ...), discipline, upbringing

shi̱-tsuke 仕付け basting, tacking (with thread); **shitsuke-i̱to** 仕付け糸 basting/tacking thread

shi̱tsukema̱su, shi̱tsuke̱ru しつけ[躾け]ます, しつけ[躾け]る trains (children, ...), disciplines, brings up

shi̱-tsukema̱su, shi̱-tsuke̱ru 仕付けます, 仕付ける bastes, tacks (with thread)

shi̱tsumon 質問 question; ~ **shima̱su** 質問します asks a question

shi̱tsu̱rei 失礼 discourtesy; ~ **(na)** 失礼(な) impolite; ~ **shima(⌐)su** 失礼します does a discourtesy, excuses oneself (= leaves)

shi̱tsuren 失恋 disappointment in love; ~ **shima̱su** 失恋します gets brokenhearted

shi̱tsuteki (na) 質的(な) qualitative

shitta 知った = **shirimashita** 知りました (learned, found out)

shitte 知って → **shirimasu** 知ります; **~ imasu** 知っています knows

shitto しっと・嫉妬 jealousy

shiwa しわ・皺 wrinkle, crease, fold; **~ ga dekimasu (dekiru)** しわ[皺]ができます(できる) it wrinkles

shi-wa 四羽 four birds (= **yon-wa** 四羽)

shi wa shimasen (shinai) しはしません(しない) = **shimasen** しません (not do)

shiwaza しわざ・仕業 act, deed

shi-yakusho 市役所 city office

shi ya shimasen (shinai) しやしません(しない) = **shi wa shimasen** しはしません (not do)

shi-yasui しやすい 1. easy to do 2. likely to do it, tends to do it

shi-yō しよう・仕様 = **shi-kata** 仕方・しかた (method, means, way); **~ ga nai** しようがない hopeless, beyond remedy (= **shō ga nai** しょうがない)

shiyō 1. 使用 use, employment; **~-chū** 使用中 in use, occupied *(toilet, etc.)*; **shiyō-nin** 使用人 servant; **shiyō-sha** 使用者 user; **~ shimasu** 使用します uses, employs 2. 私用 = **jibun-yō** 自分用 private use/business; **~ no** 私用の private

shiyō しよう = **shimashō** しましょう (let's do it); **~ to shimasu** しようとします tries/starts to do it

shizen 自然 nature; **~ (no)** 自然(の) natural; **~ (na)** 自然(な) natural, spontaneous

shizuka (na) 静か(な) quiet, still

shizumanai 沈まない = **shizumimasen** 沈みません (not sink)

shizumaranai 静まらない・鎮まらない = **shizumarimasen** 静まりません・鎮まりません (not get quiet)

shizumarimasu 静まります・鎮まります, **shizumaru** 静まる・鎮まる gets quiet/calm, quiets/calms down

shizumatte 静まって・鎮まって → **shizumarimasu** 静まります・鎮まります (gets quiet)

shizumemasu 静めます・鎮めます, **shizumeru** 静める・鎮める soothes, quiets, calms, pacifies, suppresses

shizumemasu 沈めます, **shizumeru** 沈める sinks it

shizumenai 静めない・鎮めない = **shizumemasen** 静めません・鎮めません (not soothe it)

shizumenai 沈めない = **shizumemasen** 沈めません (not sink it)

shizumete 沈めて → **shizumema'su** 沈めます (sinks it)

shizumete 静めて・鎮めて → **shizumema'su** 静めます・鎮めます (soothes)

shizumima'su 沈みます, **shizumu** 沈む it sinks

shizunde 沈んで → **shizumima'su** 沈みます (it sinks)

sho- 諸 [*makes definite plurals of certain nouns*]: **sho-ho'gen** 諸方言 the dialects

shō 1. 性 nature, disposition, quality 2. 賞 prize 3. しょう・笙 17-reed mouth organ

...'-shō 1. ...省 Ministry of ... 2. ...商 dealer (*seller of ... *)

shō しょう: ～ **ga na'i** しょうがない = **shi-yō ga na'i** しようがない hopeless, beyond remedy; **...-kute ～ ga na'i** ...くてしょうがない, **... de ～ ga na'i** ...でしょうがない is ever so ... , is terribly ...

shōa'tsu'-ki 昇圧機 booster (*of current*)

shō'bai 商売 trade, business

shō'-batsu 賞罰 rewards and punishments

shōbe'n 小便 urine, urinating; ～ **shima(')su** 小便します urinates

shōben-jo[ㄱ] 小便所 urinal (*place*), pissoir

shōbe'n-ki 小便器 urinal (*receptacle*)

shōbō 消防 fire fighting; **shōbō'-sha** 消防車 fire engine; **shōbō'-shi/-fu** 消防士/夫 fire fighter, fireman; **shōbō-sho**[ㄱ] 消防署 fire house/station, fire department

shō'bu 1. 勝負 match, contest 2. しょうぶ・菖蒲 iris

shō'bun 処分 disposition, dealing with; **shō'bun shima(')su** 処分します disposes of, deals with

shō'chi 処置 disposition, dealing with; **shō'chi shima(')su** 処置します disposes of, deals with

shōchi 承知 agreement, understanding; **shōchi shima'su** 承知します understands (and consents); **Shōchi shima'shita** 承知しました. Yes, sir/ma'am.

shochō 所長 institute director

shōchō 象徴 symbol

shōchū' 焼酎・しょうちゅう distilled liquor made from yam or rice

shō'dai 招待 = **shō'tai** 招待 invitation; ～ **shima(')su** 招待します invites

shōda'i-jō 招待状 = **shōta'i-jō** 招待状 invitation card

shōdaku 承諾 consent, acceptance; **shōdaku shima'su** 承諾します consents, accepts

sho⌐dō 書道 calligraphy

shōdoku⌐-yaku/-zai 消毒薬/剤 disinfectant

shoe̅ba しょえば → **shoima̅su** しょいます (if one shoulder it)

shō-fuda⌐ 正札 price tag

shōga しょうが・生姜 ginger

shōgai 障害 impediment, obstacle, hindrance; **shōga̅i-sha** 障害者 handicapped person

shō̅gai 生涯 life(long), for all one's life(time)

shōga̅kkō 小学校 primary (elementary) school

shōga̅ku-sei 小学生 primary school student

Shōgatsu̅ 正月 January; New Year (**o-Shōgatsu** お正月)

shōgi 将棋 chess; ~**-ban** 将棋盤 chessboard

shō̅go 正午 noon (exactly)

shō̅gyō 商業 commerce, trade, business

shōhi 消費 consumption; **shōhi̅-sha** 消費者 consumer

shōhin 賞品 prize (*object*)

shō⌐hin 商品 goods, merchandise, (sales) product

shohō 処方 prescription, prescribing; ~ **shima̅su** 処方します prescribes (medicine)

shohō-sen 処方箋 prescription (slip)

shoi しょい → **shoima̅su** しょいます・背負います [infinitive]

shō̅i 少尉 2nd lieutenant; ensign

shoima̅su しょいます・背負います, **shou** しょう・背負う carries on the back, shoulders it

shōji (o-shō̅ji) 障子(お障子) translucent sliding panel/door

shōji̅ki̅ (na) 正直(な) honest; ~ **ni** 正直に honestly

shō-jima̅su 生じます, **-ji̅ru** 生じる 1. produces, brings about 2. arises, happens

shōjin-ryō̅ri 精進料理 vegetarian cuisine

sho̅jo 処女 virgin (*female*)

shō̅jo 少女 young girl

shōjū 小銃 rifle

shōka 消化 digestion; ~ **shima̅su** 消化します digests

shōka-fu̅ryō 消化不良 indigestion

shōkai (go-shōkai) 紹介(ご紹介) introduction (of a person); ~ **shima̅su** 紹介します introduces

shōka̅-ki 消火器 fire extinguisher

shōka̅-sen 消火栓 fireplug, hydrant

shō⌐ken 証券 security (*stock, bond*)

shō̅ki 書記 secretary

shō⌐ki (no) 正気(の) sober, sane; in one's right mind

shōkin 1. 正金 hard cash 2. 賞金 prize money; reward 3. 償金 → **baishō⌐-kin** 賠償金 (indemnity, reparation)

shokken 食券 meal ticket

shokki 食器 tableware, dish, plate; **shokki-dana** 食器棚 dish rack; **shokki-to dana** 食器戸棚 cupboard; **shokki-shitsu** 食器室 pantry

shokkō 職工 = **kōin** 工員 factory worker; workman

sho kku ショック shock; **oiru-~** オイルショック the oil shock

shōko 証拠 proof, evidence

shō kō 将校 military officer

shoku 1. 職 office, occupation 2. (...-**shoku** ...食) food; (counts meals)

shoku butsu 植物 (botanical) plant; **shokubutsu-en** 植物園 botanical garden

shokudō 食堂 dining room; restaurant

shokudō-sha 食堂車 dining car, diner

shoku en 食塩 table salt

shokugo 食後 after a meal (= **ta beta a to de** 食べた後で)

shoku gyō 職業 occupation, vocation, job, profession

shokuhin 食品 foodstuffs, groceries

shokuji (o-shokuji) 食事(お食事) a meal; eating, having a meal; **~ shima su** 食事します dines, eats (a meal)

shokumi n-chi 植民地 colony

shoku motsu 食物 food(s)

shoku-pa n 食パン bread

shokureki 職歴 professional experience

shokuryō-hin 食料品 foodstuffs, groceries

shokuryōhi n-ten 食料品店 grocery store

shokutaku 食卓 dinner table; **shokutaku-en** 食卓塩 table salt

shoku-tsuki (no) 食付き(の) with meals (included)

shoku yoku 食欲 appetite

shokuzen 1. 食膳 (low) individual meal table 2. 食前 before a meal (= **tabe ru ma e ni** 食べる前に)

shōkyoku-teki (na) 消極的(な) negative; conservative

shomei 署名 signature; **~ shima su** 署名します signs one's name

shōmei 1. 証明 proof, verification, attestation, certification; **~ shima su** 証明します proves, verifies, attests, certifies 2. 照明 lighting, illumination; **~-ki gu** 照明器具 lighting fixtures

shōme i-sho 証明書 certificate; note of authentication

shōme n 正面 the face (front side)

sho motsu 書物 [bookish] = **ho n** 本 book

shō myō 声明 chanting of

Buddhist scriptures

shōnen 少年 boy, lad, youngster

shōˈni 小児 infant, child; **shōni-maˈhi** 小児麻痺 infantile paralysis, polio

shōni-ka 小児科 pediatrics; (= **shōnikaˈ-i** 小児科医) pediatrician

shōnin 証人 a witness

shōˈnin 商人 merchant, trader

shoppaˈi しょっぱい salty

shoˈppingu ショッピング shopping; **shoppingu-baˈggu** ショッピングバッグ shopping bag; **shoppingu-seˈntā** ショッピングセンター shopping center

shōˈrai 将来 future

shōrei 奨励 encouragement, promotion

shoˈri 処理 managing, disposing of, transacting, dealing with; ~ **shima(ˈ)su** 処理します manages, handles, takes care of, deals with

shōˈri 勝利 victory; **shōriˈ-sha** 勝利者 winner, victor

shori-jō 処理場 [sewage] treatment plant

shoˈrui 書類 form, document, paper(s)

shōryaku 省略 abbreviation

shōsa 少佐 major; lieutenant commander

shosai 書斎 a study, library (room)

shōsai 詳細 details

shoˈseki 書籍 books, publications

shōsetsu 小説 fiction, a novel

shōˈshō 少々 = **choˈtto** ちょっと (a little) [DEFERENTIAL]

shōˈshō 少将 major general; rear admiral

shōshū 召集・招集 conscription, (military) draft; ~ **saremaˈsu** 召集[招集]されます gets drafted; ~ **shimaˈsu** 召集[招集]します drafts, conscripts

shōsoku 消息 news, word (from/ of ...)

shotaˈi 所帯・世帯 a household; housekeeping

shōˈtai 招待, **shōˈdai** 招待 invitation; ~ **shima(ˈ)su** 招待します invites

shōtaˈi-jō 招待状, **shōdaˈi-jō** 招待状 invitation (card)

shoˈtchū しょっちゅう all the time

shoˈten 書店 bookshop

shōˈten 焦点 focus, focal point

shōˈten 商店 shop, store

shōteˈn-gai 商店街 shop street(s), shopping area

shōˈto ショート a short (circuit); short story; shortstop

...-shoˈtō ...諸島 ... Islands

shoˈtoku 所得 income; **shotokuˈ-zei** 所得税 income tax

shōtotsu 衝突 collision; **shōtotsu shimaˈsu** 衝突します collides shotte しょって → **shoima¹su** しょいます・背負います (carries on the back)

shou しょう・背負う = **shoima¹su** しょいます・背負います (carries on the back)

showanai しょわない = **shoimase¹n** しょいません (not carry on the back)

shoya しょや 1. = **shoe¹ba** しょえば (if one carry on the back) 2. ~ **shinai** しょやしない = **shoi¹ya/wa shinai** しょいや/はしない = **showanai** しょわない (not carry on the back)

shō¹yo 賞与 bonus; **shōyo⁽¹⁾-kin** 賞与金 bonus money

shoyū (no) 所有(の) possessed, owned, belonging; one's own

shōyu (o-shōyu) 醤油・しょうゆ (お醤油) soy sauce

shoyū¹-butsu/-hin 所有物/品 belongings, possessions

shoyū¹-sha 所有者 owner

shozai 所在 whereabouts

shōzō-ga 肖像画 portrait

shū¹, ...¹-shū 1. 州, ...州 state (U.S., Australia); province (Canada); county (Britain) 2. 週, ...週 = **shūkan** 週間 week

shūbun 秋分 autumnal equinox; ~ **no hi¹** 秋分の日 Autumnal Equinox Day

shuchō 主張 assertion; ~ **shima¹su** 主張します asserts, claims, maintains

shūchū 集中 concentration; ~ **shima¹su** 集中します concentrates, centers (on)

shu¹dan 手段 ways, means, measures, steps

shūdan 集団 group, collective body

shūdō¹-in 修道院 convent

shu¹fu 1. 主婦 housewife 2. 首府 capital city

shūgeki 襲撃 attack, charge, raid; **shūgeki shima¹su** 襲撃します attacks, charges, raids

shu¹gi 主義 principle, doctrine, -ism

shu¹go 主語 subject (of a sentence)

shūgō 集合 assembly, gathering; ~ **shima¹su** 集合します congregate, gather, meet (as a group)

shugyō 修行・修業 (getting one's) training, ascetic practices, meditation; ~ **shima¹su** 修行します・修業します gets training

shūgyō 就業 starting one's work-(day); ~**-ji¹kan** 就業時間 working hours; ~ **shima¹su** 就業します goes to (starts) work

shū⁽¹⁾ha 宗派 sect

shūhen 周辺 circumference; environs, (to¹shi no ~ 都市の周辺) outskirts (of city); ~ **no ...** 周辺の... the surrounding ...

shūˈi 周囲 circumference; surroundings

shuin 手淫 masturbation; **～ o shimaˈsu** 手淫をします masturbates

shūji (o-shūˈji) 習字（お習字） calligraphy (handwriting) practice

shuˈjin 主人 **1.** husband; **go-shuˈjin** ご主人 your husband **2.** master, owner, landlord, boss, host

shuˈju (no) 種々（の） all kinds of

shuˈjutsu 手術 surgical operation, surgery; **shuˈjutsu shima(ˈ)su** 手術します performs an operation, operates

shūkaku 収穫 harvest, crop; **shūkaku shimaˈsu** 収穫します harvests, reaps

shukan 主観 subjectivity; **～ -teki (na)** 主観的（な） subjective

shūkan 1. 週間 week **2.** 習慣 custom, practice, habit

shūˈki 秋期 autumn (period/term)

shūki-dome 臭気止め deodorant (*household, etc.*)

shukkin 出勤 office attendance; **～ shimaˈsu** 出勤します reports for work

shukudai 宿題 homework

shukuˈga 祝賀 congratulation

shū-kuriˈimu シュークリーム a cream puff, an éclair

shūˈkyō 宗教 religion

shūmai シューマイ pork meatballs steamed in thin pastry

shūmatsu 週末 weekend

shumbun 春分 vernal equinox; **～ no hiˈ** 春分の日 Vernal Equinox Day

shuˈmi 趣味 taste, interest, liking, hobby

shuˈmoku 種目 item, (competition) event

shunga 春画 pornography

shuˈngiku 春菊 (tasty leaves of) garland chrysanthemum

shunkan 瞬間 a moment, an instant

shūnyū 収入 earnings, income; **～-iˈnshi** 収入印紙 tax (revenue) stamp

shuppan 出版 publishing; **～ shimaˈsu** 出版します publishes

shuppaˈn-butsu 出版物 publication(s)

shuppaˈn-sha 出版社・出版者 publishing company, publisher

shuppatsu 出発 departure; **shuppaˈtsu-ten** 出発点 point of departure

shuppin 出品 exhibit(ing); **～ shimaˈsu** 出品します exhibits; **shuppiˈn-sha** 出品者 exhibitor

shūˈri 修理 repair; **～ shima(ˈ)su** 修理します repairs

shūrí-kō 修理工 repairman, mechanic

shūrui 種類 type, sort, kind, variety

shūsatsu 集札 ticket collecting; **shūsatsu shima'su** 集札します collects tickets

shūsen 終戦 the end of a war; ~ **ni narima'su** 終戦になります the war ends; ~**-go** 終戦後 after the war

shū'shi 修士 master's degree; **shūshi-ro'mbun** 修士論文 master's thesis

shūshi'-fu 終止符 period, full stop *(punctuation)*

shū'shin 修身 ethics, morals

shushō 首相 prime minister

shūshoku 就職 getting a job, finding employment

shūshū 収集 collecting, collection; ~**-ka** 収集家 collector; ~ **shima'su** 収集します collects

shusse 出世 making a success in life

shussei 出生 [bookish] = **umare** 生まれ birth

shusseki 出席 attendance, presence; **shusseki shima'su** 出席します attends, is present

shusse'ki'-sha 出席者 those present

shusshin 出身 alumnus (of …); coming (from …)

shu'su しゅす・繻子 satin

shutchō 出張 business trip, official tour; ~ **shima'su** 出張し ます makes a business trip

shūten 終点 terminus, end of the line, last stop, destination

shuto' 首都, **shu'to** 首都 capital city

shuyō (na) 主要(な) leading, chief; **shuyō-to'shi** 主要都市 major city

shūzen 修繕 repair; ~ **shima'su** 修繕します repairs; **shūze'n-kō** 修繕工 repairman

si… → **shi…**

sō' (**desu, ja arimase'n, wa**) そう (です, じゃありません, は) / **sō** (**shima'su, …**) そう(しま す, …) that way, like that, so; that's right, yes

sō' 僧 = **sōryo** 僧侶 Buddhist priest

sō' そう [hearsay]: … (**suru, shita; da', da'tta**) **sō'** (**desu, da/na, de, ni**) …(する, した; だ, だった)そう(です, だ/な, で, に) it is reported (said/ written) that, I hear that, they say that … ; reportedly …

…-sō …そう, **…-sō'** …そう: **shi-sō** (**de'su, da'/na, de', ni'**) しそ う(です, だ/な, で, に) look-ing (as though), about to (hap-pen); will at any moment; **abuna-sō** (**de'su, ni miema'su**) 危なそう(です, に見えます) looks dangerous, **jōbu-sō ni' wa miemase'n** 丈夫そうには見 えません doesn't look sturdy;

ochi-sō̍ desu̥ 落ちそうです is about to fall

…-sō …艘 (counts ships; commonly replaced by **…-seki** …隻)

so̍ba 1. (o-soba) そば・側（おそば） near/close(-by), (be)side **2.** そば・蕎麦 = **o-so̍ba** おそば・お蕎麦 buckwheat noodles

soba-gara そばがら・蕎麦殻 buckwheat chaff (used as pillow stuffing)

soba̍-ya そば［蕎麦］屋, **o-sobaya** おそば［蕎麦］屋 noodle shop

sōbetsu 送別 farewell; send-off; **sōbe̍tsu̥-kai** 送別会 farewell party (reception)

sobiema̍su̥ そびえます・聳えます, **sobie̍ru** そびえる・聳える rises, looms

So̍bi̍e̍to ソビエト Soviet, the Soviet (Union)

so̍bo 祖母 grandmother

soboku (na) 素朴・そぼく（な） simple, naive, unsophisticated

soboro そぼろ parched minced fish; fish meal

so̍chi 装置 equipment, apparatus

sochira そちら **1.** there, that way **2.** that one (of two) **3.** you

sochira-gawa そちら側 your side

so̍da ソーダ = **sōda̍-sui** ソーダ水 soda water

so̍ da そうだ = **sō̍ desu̥** そうで

す (that's right, yes)

sodachi̍ (o-sodachi) 育ち（お育ち） growing up, one's early years

soda̍chi 育ち → **sodachima̍su̥** 育ちます [infinitive]

sodachima̍su̥ 育ちます, **soda̍tsu** 育つ grows up, is raised (reared)

sōdai (na) 壮大（な） magnificent, grand

sōdan 相談 conference (personal), talk, consultation, advice; **(… to) ~ shima̍su̥** （…と）相談します consults (with), discusses, talks it over

sōda̍-sui ソーダ水 soda water

sodata̍nai 育たない = **sodachimase̍n** 育ちません (not grow up)

soda̍te 育て **1.** → **sodatema̍su̥** 育てます [infinitive]; [imperative] **sodate̍ ro** 育てろ, **soda̍te yo** 育てよ raise them! **2.** → **sodachima̍su̥** 育ちます [imperative] grow up!

sodatema̍su̥ 育てます, **sodate̍ru** 育てる raises, rears, educates

sodate̍nai 育てない = **sodatemase̍n** 育てません (not raise)

sodate-no-oya̍ 育ての親 a foster parent

sodate̍ru 育てる = **sodatema̍su̥** 育てます

soda̍tete 育てて → **sodatema̍su̥**

育てます

soda`tsu** 育つ = **sodachima`su 育ちます

soda`tte** 育って → **sodachima`su 育ちます

sode (o-sode) 袖(お袖) sleeve

Sō` desu ka そうですか. **1.** Oh? How interesting! **2.** Is that right/so?

Sō` desu ne そうですね. Well, now; Let me see.

so`dō 騒動 unrest, disturbance, tumult, strife; (= **bōdō** 暴動) riot

soe 添え → **soema`su** 添えます **1.** [infinitive] **2.** [imperative] **soe ro** 添えろ, **soe` yo** 添えよ add it!

soe`ba** 沿えば → **soima`su 沿います (if it follow)

soema`su 添えます, **soeru** 添える adds, throws in extra, attaches

soenai 添えない = **soemase`n** 添えません (not add)

soeru 添える = **soema`su** 添えます

soete 添えて → **soema`su** 添えます

soe` ya shinai** 添えやしない = **soe` wa shinai 添えはしない = **soenai** 添えない (not add)

soeyō 添えよう = **soemashō`** 添えましょう (let's add it!)

so`fu 祖父 grandfather

so`futo** ソフト, **sofuto-kuri`imu

ソフトクリーム soft ice cream

sofutowe`a ソフトウェア (computer) software

sōgan-kyō 双眼鏡 binoculars

sōgi-ya 葬儀屋 undertaker *(funeral director)*

sōgō 総合 synthesis; **~-teki (na)** 総合的(な) composite, comprehensive, overall, synthesized

sō`go (no) 相互(の) mutual, reciprocal; **~ ni** 相互に mutually, reciprocally (= **o-tagai ni** お互いに)

soi 沿い → **soima`su** 沿います [infinitive]

sōi 相違 discrepancy, difference

soima`su 沿います, **sou** 沿う runs along, follows

soitsu そいつ that damn one; **soitsu`-ra** そいつら those damn ones

sō` ja na`i to そうじゃないと, **sō` ja na`kereba/na`kerya** そうじゃなければ/なけりゃ otherwise

sōji (o-sō`ji)** 掃除·そうじ(お掃除) cleaning, sweeping; **sōji`-fu 掃除夫 cleaning person (man/woman); **sōji`-ki** 掃除機 a sweeper; **~ shima`su** 掃除します cleans, sweeps

sōjū 操縦 handling, operation; **~ shima`su** 操縦します manipulates, handles, controls, operates

sōkei 総計 the grand total

soke̲tto ソケット socket, plug

sōkin 送金 remittance; ～ **shima̲su** 送金します remits

sokki 速記 shorthand

sokkō-jo 測候所 weather observatory/station

sokku̲ri そっくり entirely, completely; ～ **(no)** そっくり(の) just like

so̲kkusu ソックス anklets, socks

soko 1. そこ there, that place **2.** 底 bottom

sō̲ko 倉庫 warehouse

so̲koku 祖国 homeland, mother country

soko-mame 底まめ bunion, corn, blister

sokonaima̲su 損ないます, **sokona̲u** 損なう harms, injures, hurts; [VERB INFINITIVE +] fails in doing; **yari-～** やり損ないます botches, misses

...-soku̲ ...足 (counts pairs of footwear)

so̲kudo 速度, **soku̲ryoku** 速力 speed; "**So̲kudo oto̲se**" 速度落とせ Reduce Speed.

sokutatsu 速達 special delivery

so̲matsu (na) 粗末(な) crude, coarse; **o-so̲matsu-sama** お粗末さま Please excuse the poor fare (*reply to* **gochisō-sama** ご馳走さま・ごちそうさま)

some 染め → **somema̲su** 染めま

す **1.** [infinitive] **2.** [imperative] **some ro** 染めろ, **some̲ yo** 染めよ dye it!

somema̲su 染めます, **someru** 染める dyes

sō̲men そうめん・素麺 thin white wheat-flour noodles (*cf.* **hiyamu̲gi** 冷や麦・ひやむぎ)

somete 染めて → **somema̲su** 染めます

somu̲ite 背いて → **somukima̲su** 背きます

somukima̲su 背きます, **somu̲ku** 背く: **(... ni) ～** (...に)背きます disobeys, goes against, violates; rebels, revolts

so̲n 損 damage, loss; disadvantage

...-son ...村 village

sona̲e 備え preparations, provisions; defenses

sona̲e 備え → **sonaema̲su** 備えます **1.** [infinitive] **2.** [imperative] **sona̲e ro** 備えろ, **sona̲e yo** 備えよ prepare it!

sonaema̲su 備えます, **sona̲eru** 備える prepares, fixes, installs, furnishes; possesses

sona̲enai 備えない = **sonaemase̲n** 備えません (not prepare it)

sona̲ete 備えて → **sonaema̲su** 備えます

sōnan 遭難 disaster, accident, shipwreck, train wreck; ～ **shima̲su** 遭難します has an accident (a disaster); (a ship/ train) is wrecked

songai 損害 damage, harm, loss

sonkei 尊敬 respect, esteem; ~ **shima̱su** 尊敬します respects, esteems

sonna ... そんな... such (a) ... , that kind of ... ; ~ **ni** そんなに to that extent, that much, so (very/much)

sonna̱ra そんなら then, in that case

sono ... その... that ... ; **sono a̱to** その後, **sono-go** その後 since then; **sono mama̱ (de/ ni/no)** そのまま(で/に/の) intact

sono̱-hoka その他[外] and others

... sono-mo̱no̱ ...そのもの (in) itself, the very ...

sono̱-ta その他 [*bookish*] = **sono̱-hoka** その他[外] and others

sono to̱ki その時 at that time, then

sono-uchi (ni) そのうち(に) meanwhile

sono uchi(⌐ ni) そのうち(に) among them; in that house

sono ue(⌐ ni) そのうえ[上](に) moreover, also, besides

sono yo̱ na そのよう[様]な such(-like); **sono yo̱ ni** そのよう[様]に like that, that way

son-shima̱su 存します, **son-**

su̱ru 存する [*bookish*] exists

sonshitsu 損失 a loss

sonzai 存在 existence; being/person (in existence), personage, figure; ~ **shima̱su** 存在します exists

sōon 騒音 noise

so̱ppa 反っ歯 bucktooth

so̱ra 空 sky

so̱ra de そらで by heart, from memory

sora̱nai 剃らない・反らない = **sorimase̱n** 剃りません; 反りません (not shave; not bend/ curve)

sorasa̱nai そらさない・逸らさない = **sorashimase̱n** そらしません・逸らしません (not dodge/warp)

sora̱shi そらし・逸らし → **sorashima̱su** そらします・逸らします

sorashima̱su そらします・逸らします, **sora̱su** そらす・逸らす **1.** dodges, turns aside **2.** warps it

sora̱shite そらして・逸らして → **sorashima̱su** そらします・逸らします

sore それ that one, it

so̱re 1. 逸れ・剃れ・反れ → **sorema̱su** 逸れます・剃れます・反れます [*infinitive*] **2.** 剃れ・反れ → **sorima̱su** 剃ります/反ります [*imperative*] shave!; bend!

so⌐reba 剃れば・反れば →
sorima⌐su 剃ります/反ります
(if one shave/bend)

sore da⌐tte それだって = sore
de⌐ mo それでも

sore de それで and (then/so/
also)

sore de⌐ mo それでも still, yet,
even so

sore de⌐ wa それでは, sore ja/jā
それじゃ/じゃあ well, well
now/then; in that event; (=
~ shitsu⌐rei shima⌐su それで
は失礼します excuse me but
I'll be on my way) good-bye

sore ji⌐shin/ji⌐tai それ自身/自体
itself

sore kara それから and (then);
after that, since then

sorema⌐su, sore⌐ru 1. それます・
逸れます, それる・逸れる
deviates, strays, digresses
2. それます・剃れます, それ
る・剃れる can shave 3. 反れ
ます, 反れる can bend/warp

So⌐ren ソ連 Soviet Union;
Sore⌐n-jin ソ連人 a Soviet
(citizen)

sore na⌐ no ni それなのに nevertheless, nonetheless, and yet

sore na⌐ra それなら then, in that
case

sore ni それに on top of that,
moreover, in addition, plus

sore⌐-ra それら those, they/them

sore⌐ru 逸れる・剃れる・反れる

= sorema⌐su 逸れます・剃れ
ます・反れます

so⌐rete 逸れて・剃れて・反れて
→ sorema⌐su 逸れます・剃れ
ます・反れます

sore-to⌐mo それとも or else

sore wa sore wa それはそれは
My my! My goodness!

sore⌐zo⌐re それぞれ respectively,
severally

sori⌐ 1. そり・反り a warp, curve,
bend 2. そり・剃り shaving

so⌐ri 1. そり・橇 sled 2. 剃り・反
り → sorima⌐su 剃ります・反
ります [infinitive]

sōri-da⌐ijin 総理大臣 prime minister

sorima⌐su, so⌐ru 1. 剃ります, 剃
る shaves 2. 反ります, 反る
bends (back), warps

sōritsu 創立 establishment

soroban そろばん・算盤 abacus,
counting beads

soro⌐e 揃え・そろえ an array

soro⌐e 揃え・そろえ →
soroema⌐su 揃えます・そろえ
ます [infinitive]

soroema⌐su 揃えます・そろえま
す, soroe⌐ru 揃える・そろえる
puts in order; collects; completes a set

soro⌐i 揃い・そろい a set (of ...)

soro⌐i 揃い・そろい →
soroima⌐su 揃います・そろい
ます [infinitive]

sō⌐ron 1. 争論 quarrel, dispute

2. 総論 general remarks, outline, introduction

so̱rosoro そろそろ little by little, gradually; (leave) before long

so̱ru 剃る・反る = **sorima̱su** 剃ります; 反ります (shaves; bends, warps)

sorya そりゃ = **sore wa** それは (as for that)

so̱rya 剃りゃ・反りゃ **1.** = **so̱reba** 剃れば/反れば (if one shave/bend) **2.** ~ **shinai** 剃りゃしない・反りゃしない = **sori̱ ya/wa shinai** 剃りや/はしない・反りや/はしない = **sora̱nai** 剃らない/反らない (not shave/bend)

so̱ryo 僧侶 Buddhist priest

sō-ryo̱ji 総領事 consul general

so̱sē̱ji ソーセージ sausage

so̱sen 祖先 ancestor

so̱shiki 組織 system, structure, setup, organization

sōshiki (o-sōshiki) 葬式(お葬式) funeral

soshite そして, **sōshite** そうして and then

soshō 訴訟 lawsuit

sōshoku 装飾 ornament, decoration

sosogima̱su 注ぎます, **soso̱gu** 注ぐ pours (into)

sosoide 注いで → **sosogima̱su** 注ぎます

so̱su (o-so̱su) ソース(おソース)

sauce, gravy

sotchi̱ そっち = **sochira** そちら

sotchoku (na) 率直(な) frank

so̱to 外 outside, outdoors

sōtō 相当 **1.** rather, quite, fairly **2.** suitable, proper

soto-bori 外堀 outer moat

soto-gawa 外側 the outside; ~ **(no)** 外側(の) external

sotsugyō 卒業 graduation; ~ **shima̱su** 卒業します graduates

sotsugyō̱-sei 卒業生 a graduate

sotsugyō̱-shiki 卒業式 commencement, graduation ceremony

sotta 沿った = **soima̱shita** 沿いました (followed)

so̱tta 剃った・反った = **sorima̱shita** 剃りました; 反りました (shaved; bent, warped)

sotte 沿って → **soima̱su** 沿います (follow)

so̱tte 剃って・反って → **sorima̱su** 剃ります; 反ります (shave; bend, warp)

sou 沿う = **soima̱su** 沿います (it runs along, follows)

So̱uru ソウル Seoul

sowanai 沿わない = **soimase̱n** 沿いません (not follow)

soya 沿や **1.** = **soe̱ba** 沿えば (if it follow) **2.** ~ **shinai** 沿やしない = **soi̱ ya/wa shinai** 沿いや/はしない = **sowanai** 沿わ

ない (not follow)

sō yū ("iu") ... そうゆう（いう）... that kind/sort of ... ; such ... (= **sonna** そんな)

sōzō 想像 imagination; ~ **shima'su** 想像します imagines

sōzōshi'i 騒々しい noisy

su⁽ⁿ⁾ 巣 nest

su' 酢 = **o-su** お酢 vinegar

sū 吸う = **suu** 吸う (sips; smokes)

sū 数 number (= **ka'zu** 数), numeral (= **sūji** 数字); **sū-...** 数... several

subarashi'i すばらしい・素晴らしい wonderful, splendid; **subara'shiku** すばらしく・素晴らしく splendidly

subekko'i すべっこい・滑っこい slippery, slick, smooth

suberi'-dai すべり台・滑り台, **o-su'beri** お滑り a slippery-slide

suberima'su 滑ります, **sube'ru** 滑る slides, slips, skates

su'bete すべて・全て all

sube'tte 滑って → **suberima'su** 滑ります

su⁽ⁿ⁾**-buta** 酢豚 sweet and sour pork

suchuwā'desu スチュワーデス stewardess

suchuwā'do スチュワード steward

sudare すだれ・簾 curtain *(bamboo)*

su'de-ni すでに・既に already (=

mō' もう); long before/ago

sue 1. 末 end, close; **kongetsu sue ma'de** 今月末まで until the end of this month **2.** 末 future **3.** 吸え → **suema'su** 吸えます (sets it up; can sip) [infinitive] **4.** 吸え → **suima'su** 吸います [imperative] sip!; smoke!

su'e すえ・饐え → **suema'su** すえます・饐えます (it spoils)

sue'ba 吸えば → **suima'su** 吸います (if one sip/suck/smoke)

suema'su, sueru 1. 据えます・すえます, 据える・すえる sets it up **2.** 吸えます, 吸える can sip (suck, smoke)

suema'su すえます・饐えます, **sue'ru** すえる・饐える it spoils, goes bad

suete 据えて・吸えて → **suema'su** 据えます; 吸えます (set it up; can sip)

su'ete すえて・饐えて → **suema'su** すえます・饐えます (it spoils)

su'fu スフ staple fiber

sūgaku 数学 mathematics; **sūga'ku-sha** 数学者 mathematician

su'gata (o-su'gata) 姿（お姿） form, figure, shape

sugi 杉 cryptomeria, Japanese cedar

su'gi 過ぎ → **sugima'su** 過ぎます

...-sugi ...過ぎ past *(the hour)*

sugima̅su 過ぎます, **sugi̅ru** 過ぎる passes, exceeds; **(shi-)～** (し)過ぎ［すぎ］ます overdoes, **(ADJ-)～** 過ぎます・すぎます is overly/excessively/too

sugi̅nai 過ぎない ＝ **sugimase̅n** 過ぎません (not pass; not exceed); **(... ni) ～** (...に)過ぎ［すぎ］ない is nothing more/other than, only

sugo̅i すごい・凄い **1.** swell, wonderful, marvelous, terrific **2.** fierce, dreadful, ghastly, weird, uncanny

su̅go̅ku すごく awfully, terribly

sugoshima̅su 過ごします, **sugo̅su** 過ごす passes (time); **do̅ o ～** 度を過ごします goes too far (to excess)

su̅gu (ni) すぐ(に) at once, right away, immediately; in a minute; directly, right (there)

sugurema̅su 優れます・すぐれます, **sugure̅ru** 優れる・すぐれる excels, **(... ni/yo̅ri) ～** (...に/より)優れ［すぐれ］ます surpasses, is superior (to); **sugu̅rete ima̅su** 優れ［すぐれ］ています is excellent, **sugu̅reta ...** 優れ［すぐれ］た... excellent ...

su̅gu so̅ba すぐそば right near (at hand)

sui 吸い, → **suima̅su** 吸います [infinitive]

suichoku (no) 垂直(の) vertical; perpendicular

suidō 水道 waterworks, water service, running water; plumbing

suidō̅-kyoku 水道局 the Waterworks Bureau; plumbing service

suidō-ya (san) 水道屋（さん） plumber

suiei 水泳 swimming; **suiei-jō** 水泳場 swimming pool

suie̅i-gi̅ 水泳着 swim suit

su̅ifu 水夫 seaman, sailor

suigara 吸い殻 cigarette/cigar butt

su̅ihei 水平 navy enlisted person, sailor, seaman

suihei (no) 水平(の) horizontal, level; **～-sen** 水平線 (sea) horizon

suijun 水準 water level; standard

suika すいか・西瓜 watermelon

sui-kuchi 吸い口 cigarette holder

suima̅su 吸います, **suu** 吸う sips, sucks, smokes, breathes in

suimin 睡眠 sleep; **suimi̅n-zai** 睡眠剤, **suimi̅n-yaku** 睡眠薬 sleeping pill(s)

sui-mono 吸い物 clear soup

suisen 1. 推薦 recommendation; **～ shima̅su** 推薦します recommends **2.** 水洗 flushing; **-be̅njo** 水洗便所, **～-to̅ire** 水洗トイレ flush toilet; **(to̅ire o) ～ shima̅su** (トイレを)水洗

します flushes (the toilet)

suise⌐n-jō 推薦状 letter of recommendation

suˈiso 水素 hydrogen

suisoku 推測 conjecture, guess, surmisal, supposition; **suisoku shimaˈsu** 推測します guesses, surmises

Suˈisu スイス Switzerland; **〜 no** スイスの Swiss; **Suisuˈ-jin** スイス人 a Swiss

suiˈtchi スイッチ switch; ignition switch; **〜 o iremaˈsu** スイッチを入れます turns/switches it on, turns on the ignition; **〜 o kirimaˈsu** スイッチを切ります turns/switches it off

suitei 推定 inference, presumption, estimation; **〜 shimaˈsu** 推定します infers, presumes, estimates

suitō-gaˈkari 出納係 cashier

suitoriˈ-gami 吸い取り紙 blotter

Suiyōˈbi 水曜日 Wednesday

suizōˈk-kan 水族館, **suizōkuˈ-kan** 水族館 aquarium

suˈji 筋 tendon; muscle; fiber; line; plot

sūji 数字 numeral, figure

sujiⁿkoⁿ すじこ・筋子, **suzuⁿkoⁿ** すずこ salmon roe

sūⁿ-jitsu 数日 several days

sukaˈfu スカーフ scarf; *(military)* sash

sukaˈto スカート skirt

sukeˈbē (na) 助平・すけべえ（な） lecherous; lewd

sukeˈto スケート skate(s); skating; **〜 o shimaˈsu** スケートをします skates

suki すき・透き ＝ **suki-ma** すきま・透き間・隙間 crack; opening; opportunity

sukiˈi 1. 〜 (o-suki) (na) 好き（お好き）（な） is liked; likes **2.** すき・鋤き・梳き → **sukimaˈsu** すき［空き］ます・鋤きます・梳きます [infinitive]

sukiˈi スキー ski, skiing; **〜 o shimaˈsu** スキーをします skis

suki-ma すきま・透き間・隙間 crack; opening; opportunity

sukimaˈsu, suku 1. すき［空き］ます, すく・空く gets empty/clear **2.** 鋤きます, 鋤く plows **3.** 梳きます, 梳く combs

sukimaˈsu 好きます, **sukuˈ** 好く likes

sukimu-miˈruku スキムミルク skim milk

sukiyaki すき焼き・すきやき thin-sliced beef cooked in an iron pan with leeks, mushrooms, bean curd, etc.

sukkaˈri すっかり completely, all

sukoˈshi 少し a little, a bit; **〜 (no)** 少し（の） some, a few; somewhat; **〜 mo** 少しも ＋ NEGATIVE not in the least; **sukoshiˈ-zuˈtsu** 少しずつ bit

by bit, a bit of/for each, a little at a time, gradually

sụkuima῾sụ, sụkuu 1. 救います,
救う helps, rescues, saves
2. すく[掬]います, すく[掬]
う scoops

sụkunai 少ない few, meager,
scarce, little; (yori ～ より少
ない) fewer, less

sụkụnaku 少なく (so as to be)
few, little; sụkụnaku
shima῾sụ 少なくします lessens

sụkụnakụ-tomo 少なくとも at
(the) least

sụkuramburu-e῾ggu スクランブ
ルエッグ scrambled eggs

sụkuriin スクリーン (movie)
screen

sụkutte 救って・すく[掬]って
→ sụkuima῾sụ 救います・すく
[掬]います

sụkuu 救う・すく[掬]う →
sụkuima῾sụ 救います・すく
[掬]います

sụkya῾ndaru スキャンダル scan-
dal

sụ῾mai (o-sụ῾mai) 住まい(お住
まい) residence

suma῾nai すまない・済まない ＝
sumimase῾n すみません・済み
ません (it never ends; thank
you, excuse me); ～ koto῾ o
shima῾shita すまないこと[済
まない事]をしました. I
apologize (for what I did).

sumasema῾sụ 済ませます・すま

sumasema῾sụ 済ませます・すま
せます, sumase῾ru 済ませる・
すませる finishes, concludes it

sumashima῾sụ 済まします・すま
します, suma῾sụ 済ます・すま
す 1. finishes, concludes it
2. puts up with (things as they
are)

suma῾to (na) スマート(な)
smart, stylish, fashionable

sụ῾mi 隅 an inside corner

sumi 1. 炭 charcoal 2. 墨 India
ink, ink stick 3. 済み・すみ →
sumima῾sụ 済みます・すみま
す [infinitive]

sumi[ⁿ]-e 墨絵 India ink painting

sumimase῾n すみません・済みま
せん. 1. Excuse me. Sorry.
2. Thank you.

sumima῾sụ, su῾mu 1. 済みます・
すみます, 済む・すむ comes
to an end 2. 住みます, 住む
lives, takes up residence,
resides

sumire すみれ・菫 violet

sumō 相撲・すもう Japanese
wrestling, sumo

sumō῾ 住もう ＝ sumimashō῾ 住
みましょう (let's reside!)

su-momo すもも・李 plum

su῾mon スモン ＝ sumon-byō῾ ス
モン病 SMON (subacute
myelo-optico neuropathy)

sumō῾-to῾ri 相撲[すもう]取り a
sumo wrestler

sumpō 寸法 measurements

su῾mu 済む・住む ＝ sumima῾sụ

済みます・住みます
(…-)suˉn (…)寸 inch *(Japanese)*
suna 砂 sand   「zard
suna-buˊkuro 砂袋 sandbag; giz-
sunaˊkku スナック 1. a snack-
　shop 2. an after-hours bar
suˊnao (na) すなお[素直](な)
　docile, gentle, obedient, sub-
　missive, meek
sunaˊwachi すなわち・即ち name-
　ly, to wit; that is to say; in
　other words
suˊnda 済んだ・住んだ =
　sumimaˊshita 済みました; 住
　みました (ended; lived)
suˊnde 住んで → sumimaˊsu 住
　みます; ～ imaˊsu 住んでいま
　す lives, resides
suneˊ すね・脛 shin, leg
suˉ⁽¹⁾-nen 数年 several years
suˉ⁽¹⁾-nin 数人 several people
su-no-mono 酢の物 vinegared
　dishes; a small dish of relish
suˉˊpā スーパー, sūpā-maˊketto
　スーパーマーケット super-
　market
supaˊi スパイ spy
supaˊna スパナ wrench
Supein スペイン Spain; Supein-
　go スペイン語 Spanish;
　Supeiˊn-jiˊn スペイン人 Spani-
　ard
supeˊringu スペリング spelling
supiˊido スピード speed
supiˊikā スピーカー (loud)
　speaker

suponji スポンジ sponge; swab
supoˉ̌tsu スポーツ sport(s),
　athletics
suppaˊi 酸っぱい sour
suppon すっぽん snapping turtle
suˉˊpu スープ soup
supuˉˊn スプーン spoon
suraˊkkusu スラックス slacks
suraˊnai すらない = surimaseˊn
　すりません・擦りません (not
　rub; not …)
sure すれ → suremaˊsu すれます
　・擦れます [infinitive]
suˊre すれ → surimaˊsu すります
　・擦ります [imperative] rub!; …!
sureˊba すれば → shimaˊsu しま
　す (if one do)
suˊreba すれば → surimaˊsu す
　ります・擦ります (if one rub;
　…)
suremaˊsu, sureˊru 1. すれます・
　擦れます, すれる・擦れる it
　rubs/grazes 2. すれます・擦れ
　ます, すれる・擦れる can
　rub/file/grind 3. 刷れます,
　刷れる can print
sureˊnai すれない = suremaseˊn
　すれません・擦れません・刷れ
　ません (not …; cannot …)
sureˊreba すれれば・擦れれば,
　sureˊrya すれりゃ・擦れりゃ
　(if it rub; if one can …)
suriˊ 刷り print(ing)
suˊri 1. すり・スリ・掏り pick-
　pocket 2. すり・刷り・掏り
　→ surimaˊsu すります・刷りま

す・すり[掏り]ます [infinitive]

suri̇̀bachi すり鉢 earthenware kitchen-mortar with wooden pestle

suri̇̀i スリー three

surima̍su, su̍ru 1. すり[擦り]ます, する・擦る rubs; 摺[摩]り ます, 摺[摩]る files; grinds **2.** 刷ります, 刷る prints **3.** すり[掏り]ます, す[掏]る picks one's pocket

suri̇̀ppa スリッパ slippers

suri̇̀ppu スリップ slip(ping); **surippu-ji̍ko** スリップ事故 slipping accident; **"Surippu-ji̍ko o̍shi/o̍i"** スリップ事故 多し/多い Slippery (Area)

Surira̍nka スリランカ Sri Lanka

su̍ri̍ru スリル thrill

suro̍ 1. す[擦]ろう・摺[摩]ろ う・刷ろう・す[掏]ろう = **surimasho̍** すり[擦り]ましょ う/摺りましょう/摩りましょ う; 刷りましょう (let's rub/ file/grind it!; let's print it!) **2.** ~ **(na)** スロー(な) slow

suro̍gan スローガン slogan

suro̍pu スロープ ramp

suru する = **shima̍su** します (does)

su̍ru す[擦]る・摺る・刷る・す [掏]る = **surima̍su** すり[擦 り]ます, 摺ります, 摩ります; 刷ります; すり[掏り]ます

(rubs; files, grinds; prints; picks one's pocket)

surudo̍i 鋭い sharp, acute

surume するめ dried cuttlefish

surya すりゃ = **sure̍ba** すれば (if one do)

su̍rya すりゃ **1.** = **su̍reba** すれ ば・擦れば (if one rub; if …) **2.** ~ **shinai** すりゃしない = **su̍ri ya/wa shinai** すりや/は しない = **sura̍nai** すらない・ 擦らない (not rub; not …)

su̍shi すし・寿司・鮨, **sushi̍ (o-su̍shi)** すし・寿司・鮨(おすし・ お寿司・お鮨) rice seasoned with sweetened vinegar (often with raw fish)

sushi̍-ya すし[寿司・鮨]屋, **o-sushiya** おすし[お寿司・お鮨] 屋 a sushi bar

su-sho̍ga 酢生姜 pickled ginger slices (= **gari** がり・ガリ)

suso すそ・裾 skirt (of mountain); hem

su̍su すす・煤 soot

susume 1. 進め・勧め → **susumema̍su** 進めます・勧め ます [infinitive] **2.** 進め → **susumima̍su** 進みます [im-perative] forward!

susumema̍su, susumeru 1. 進め ます, 進める furthers, ad-vances **2.** 勧めます, 勧める en-courages, recommends, ad-vises, counsels; persuades, urges

susumima'su 進みます, **susumu** 進む goes forward, progresses; goes too fast, gets ahead

susumō 進もう = **susumimashō** 進みましょう (let's go forward!)

susunde 進んで → **susumima'su** 進みます; ~ **ima'su** 進んでいます is advanced, (clock) is fast

sutā' スター star (actor)

suta[ ]jio スタジオ studio

sutando スタンド 1. stand (selling things) 2. (= **denki-suta'ndo** 電気スタンド) desk/floor lamp

sute 捨て → **sutema'su** 捨てます 1. [infinitive] 2. [imperative] **sute ro** 捨てろ, **sute' yo** 捨てよ throw it away!

sute-ba 捨て場 dump site

suteki (na) すてき[素敵](な) fine, splendid, swell

sute'ki ステーキ steak

sute'kki ステッキ walking stick, cane

sutema'su 捨てます, **suteru** 捨てる throws away, abandons, dumps

sute-mono 捨て物 scrap, refuse, junk; a throwaway

sutereo ステレオ stereo (sound/player)

sutē[ ]shon ステーション railroad station

suto' スト = **sutora'iki** ストライキ strike (job action)

suto'bu ストーブ stove, heater

sutora'iki ストライキ strike (job action)

sutora'iku ストライク strike (baseball)

sutori'ppu ストリップ striptease, strip show, burlesque

suto'rō ストロー straw (to drink with)

sū'tsu スーツ suit (especially woman's)

sūtsuke'su スーツケース suitcase

sutte 吸って → **suima'su** 吸います

suu 吸う = **suima'su** 吸います (sips, sucks, smokes, breathes in)

suwanai 吸わない = **suimase'n** 吸いません (not sip, …)

suwarema'su 座れます・すわれます, **suwareru** 座れる・すわれる can sit; seats are available

suwarikomi(-su'to) 座り込み(スト) sit-in (strike)

suwarima'su 座ります・すわります, **suwaru** 座る・すわる sits (especially Japanese style)

suwatte 座って・すわって → **suwarima'su** 座ります・すわります

suya 吸や 1. = **sue'ba** 吸えば (if one sip/suck/smoke) 2. ~ **shinai** 吸やしない = **sui' ya/wa shinai** 吸いや/はしない =

suwanai 吸わない (not sip/suck/smoke)
suzu 鈴 little bells
su˺zu すず・錫 tin
suzuki すずき・鱸 sea bass
suzu˺ko すずこ, **suji˺ko** すじこ・筋子 salmon/trout roe

suzume すずめ・雀 sparrow
suzume˺-bachi 雀蜂 hornet
suzuri˺ すずり・硯 inkstone; ~-**bako** すずり[硯]箱 inkstone case
suzushi˺i 涼しい cool
sy... → sh..

— T —

ta˺ 他 = **hoka** 他・外 other(s)
ta˺ 田 rice field
...-ta ...た = **...-ma˺shita** ...ました did
ta˺ba 束 bundle, bunch
tabako たばこ・タバコ tobacco; cigarettes; ~-**ya** たばこ[タバコ]屋 tobacco shop, cigar store
tabako˺-ire たばこ[タバコ]入れ cigarette case
tabako˺-nomi たばこ[タバコ]飲み smoker
ta˺be 食べ → **tabema˺su** 食べます **1.** [infinitive] **2.** [imperative] **tabe˺ ro** 食べろ, **ta˺be yo** 食べよ eat!
tabema˺su 食べます, **tabe˺ru** 食べる eats
tabe˺-mo˺no 食べ物 food
tabe(ra)rema˺su 食べ(ら)れます, **tabe(ra)re˺ru** 食べ(ら)れる can eat
tabesasema˺su 食べさせます,

tabesase˺ru 食べさせる feeds
ta˺bete 食べて → **tabema˺su** 食べます
tabeyo˺ 食べよう = **tabemashō˺** 食べましょう (let's eat!)
ta˺bi たび・足袋 split-toe socks
tabi˺ **1.** 旅 journey **2.** 度・たび time, occasion; **... tabi˺ (ni)** ...度[たび](に) every time that ...
tabitabi たびたび・度々 often
tabō (na) 多忙(な) busy [bookish] = **isogashi˺i** 忙しい
ta˺bu タブ a tab
ta˺bun 多分・たぶん probably, likely; perhaps (~ **... deshō˺** 多分...でしょう, ~ **... ka˺ mo shiremase˺n** 多分...かも知れません)
tabun (ni) 多分(に) a lot, much
ta˺cha 立ちゃ **1.** = **ta˺teba** 立てば (if one stand) **2.** ~ **shinai** 立ちゃしない = **ta˺chi ya/wa shinai** 立ちや/はしない = **tata˺nai** 立たない (not stand)

ta'chi 1. たち・質 nature, disposition **2.** 立ち・経ち・断ち → **tachima'su** 立ちます・経ちます・断ちます

...'-tachi ...達・たち [animate plural]; and others

tachi-agarima'su 立ち上がります, **-aga'ru** 立ち上がる rises, stands up

tachi-ba 立場 viewpoint, standpoint, situation

tachi-ba'nashi 立ち話 a (wayside) chat; ~ o shima'su 立ち話をします chats

tachi-domarima'su 立ち止まります, **-doma'ru** 立ち止まる stops, stands still

"Tachiiri kinshi" 立ち入り禁止. No Trespassing. Off Limits.

tachimachi たちまち immediately, instantly, suddenly

tachima'su, ta'tsu 1. 立ちます, 立つ stands up; 発ちます, 発つ leaves (for a far place) **2.** 経ちます, 経つ elapses **3.** 断ちます, 断つ cuts off

tachimi 立ち見 standing to see; ~ no kyaku 立ち見の客 standee; ~ shima'su 立ち見します sees as a standee

tachimi'-seki 立ち見席 the gallery, standing room

ta'dachi-ni 直ちに immediately

tada'ima ただ今・只今 = **tatta-i'ma** たった今 just now; in a minute

Tadaima (kaerima'shita) ただ今 (帰りました). I'm back! *(said on returning to one's residence)*

ta'da (no) ただ(の) **1.** only, just **2.** (for) free, gratis, no fee/charge **3.** ordinary

ta'dashi ただし・但し however; provided

tadashi'i 正しい proper, right, correct, honest; **tada'shiku** 正しく properly, correctly

tadō'-shi 他動詞 transitive verb

ta'e 堪え・絶え → **taema'su** 堪えます・絶えます [infinitive]

taema-na'ku 絶え間なく (= **ta'ezu** 絶えず) continuously, without interruption

taema'su, tae'ru 1. 堪えます, 堪える bears, puts up with **2.** 絶えます, 絶える ceases

tae'nai 堪えない・絶えない = **taemase'n** 堪えません; 絶えません (not bear; not cease)

tae(ra)rema'su 堪え(ら)れます, **tae(ra)re'ru** 堪え(ら)れる (can bear)

tae(ra)re'nai 堪え(ら)れない = **tae(ra)remase'n** 堪え(ら)れません (cannot bear)

tae'ru 堪える・絶える = **taema'su** 堪えます・絶えます

ta'ete 堪えて・絶えて → **taema'su** 堪えます・絶えます

ta'ezu 絶えず (= **taema-na'ku** 絶え間なく) continuously,

without interruption

taga⌐ たが・箍 a barrel hoop

tagai (no/ni) 互い(の/に) = **o-tagai (no/ni)** お互い(の/に)

…-tagarima⌐su …たがります, **-tagaru / -taga⌐ru** …たがる/…たがる wants to … , is eager to …

tagayashima⌐su 耕します, **tagaya⌐su** 耕す plows

tahō⌐ 他方 a different direction, another place; ～ **de wa** 他方では on the other hand

ta⌐i 1. たい・鯛 sea bream, red snapper **2.** 体 form, style; body **3.** 帯 belt; zone

tai-… 対…, **…⌐-tai** …対 versus, towards, against; **roku⌐-tai yo⌐n** 六対四, 6 対 4 4 to 6 *(score)*

…-tai / …-ta⌐i …たい/…たい wants to, is eager to

taibetsu shima⌐su (suru) 大別します(する) divides roughly (into main categories)

ta⌐ido 態度 attitude, disposition, behavior

taifū⌐ 台風 typhoon

taigai 大概・たいがい **1.** in general; for the most part; practically **2.** probably, like(ly), like as not

taigū 待遇 treatment, reception

Taihe⌐iyō 太平洋 Pacific Ocean

taihen 大変 **1.** very, exceedingly, terribly **2.** ～ **(na)** 大変(な)

serious; disastrous; enormous

ta⌐ihi 対比 contrast, comparison; **ta⌐ihi shima⌐su** 対比します contrasts, compares

ta⌐iho 逮捕 arrest(ing); ～ **shima(⌐)su** 逮捕します arrests

taihō 大砲 cannon

ta⌐ii 大尉 army captain; *(usually* **da⌐ii** 大尉*)* navy lieutenant

ta⌐iiku 体育 physical education, athletics; ～ **no hi⌐** 体育の日 Sports Day (10 October)

tai⌐ku-kan 体育館 gymnasium

taijū 体重 body weight

ta⌐ika 大家 authority

taikai 大会 mass meeting; convention, conference; tournament

taika⌐i 大海 *(also* **daika⌐i** 大海*)* ocean, high sea

taikaku 体格 body build, physique

taikei 体系 a system

taiken 体験 personal experience

taiko 太鼓 drum

taikō 対抗 confrontation, opposition; **… ni** ～ **shima⌐su** …に対抗します opposes, stands against, confronts; **… ni** ～ **shite** …に対抗して in opposition to, against, in rivalry with

taiku̯tsu (na) 退屈(な) boring, dull

taiman (na) 怠慢(な) negligent, careless, neglectful

ta⌐imatsu たいまつ・松明 torch

taimen 対面 interview

taime⌐n 体面 one's dignity, sense of honor, "face"

taiō 対応 symmetry, correspondence; (... **ni**) ~ **shima⌐su** (...に)対応します corresponds (to), is equivalent (to)

taion 体温 body temperature; **taio⌐n-kei** 体温計, **taio⌐n-ki** 体温機 (clinical) thermometer

ta⌐ipu タイプ type; (= **taipu-ra⌐itā** タイプライター) typewriter

taira⌐-gai 平貝, **taira-gi** たいらぎ・玉珧 pin/razor/fan shell (a kind of scallop)

taira (na) 平ら(な) even, smooth, flat

tairiku 大陸 continent

tairitsu 対立 confronting, opposing; **tairitsu shima⌐su** 対立します confronts, opposes

ta⌐iru タイル tile (floor, wall)

tairyō⌐ 大量 large quantity

taisa 大佐 army colonel; (usually **daisa** 大佐) navy captain

ta⌐isa 大差 a great difference

Taise⌐iyō 大西洋 Atlantic Ocean

taisen 大戦 a great war, a world war

taisetsu (na) 大切(な) important; valuable, precious

ta⌐ishi 大使 ambassador; **ta⌐i-shi** 対し → **tai-shima⌐su** 対します [infinitive]

taishi⌐-kan 大使館 embassy

tai-shima⌐su 対します, **-su⌐ru** 対する: (... **ni**) ~ (...に)対します confronts, opposes; ... **ni ta⌐i-shite** ...に対して **1.** against; toward; as against, as compared with, in contrast to **2.** with respect to, in regard to

ta⌐i-shita ... 大した... important; serious; immense

taishitsu 体質 (physical) constitution

taishō 1. 対象 object **2.** 対照 contrast; ~ **shima⌐su** 対照します contrasts

ta⌐ishō 大将 general; admiral

taishoku 退職 retirement; **taishoku shima⌐su** 退職します retires

taisho⌐ku⌐-kin 退職金 retirement allowance

taishoku-ne⌐nkin 退職年金 (retirement) pension

taishū 大衆 the general public, the masses; ~ **(no)** 大衆(の) popular

taisō 体操 calisthenics, physical exercises

ta⌐isō たいそう・大層 very; ~ **(na)** たいそう[大層](な) a great many/much; (= **go-~** ごたいそう・ご大層) exaggerated

taita 炊いた = **takima⌐shita** 炊きました (cooked)

taite 炊いて・焚いて → **takima⌐su** 炊きます・焚きます

taitei たいてい・大抵 usually; 〜 **no** ... たいていの... the usual ... , most ...

taitō (no) 対等(の) equal, equivalent

ta⌐itoru タイトル title

Taiwa⌐n 台湾 Taiwan, Formosa; **Taiwan-ji⌐n** 台湾人 a Taiwanese

ta⌐iya タイヤ a tire

taiyō 1. 大洋 ocean 2. 大要 summary

ta⌐iyō 太陽 sun

taizai 滞在 a stay (away from home), a sojourn; 〜 **shima⌐su** 滞在します stays (away from home), sojourns

taka たか・鷹 hawk

ta⌐ka⌐ 高 quantity

taka⌐i 高い high, tall; costly, expensive; loud

takanai 炊かない = **takimase⌐n** 炊きません (not cook)

takara⌐ (o-takara) 宝(お宝) a treasure

takara⌐-kuji 宝くじ lottery

takara-mo⌐no⌐ 宝物 a treasure

ta⌐kasa 高さ height

take 1. 竹 bamboo 2. [compounds/dialect] 茸 = **ki⌐noko** きのこ mushroom 3. 炊け・焚け → **takema⌐su** 炊けます・焚けます [infinitive] 4. 炊け → **takima⌐su** 炊きます [imperative] cook it!

take⌐ba 焚けば・炊けば →

takima⌐su 焚きます; 炊きます (if one make a fire; if one cook/burn it)

take-fū⌐rin 竹風鈴 bamboo wind-chimes

takema⌐su, takeru 1. 焚けます, 焚ける can make a fire 2. 炊けます, 炊ける can cook; can burn it

take-no-ko たけのこ・竹の子・筍 bamboo shoot

take-za⌐iku 竹細工 bambooware

taki 1. 滝 waterfall 2. 炊き・焚き → **takima⌐su** 炊きます・焚きます [infinitive]

taki-bi 焚き火 bonfire

taki-gi たきぎ・薪 firewood, fuel

takima⌐su, taku 1. 焚きます, 焚く makes a fire 2. 炊きます, 炊く cooks; burns it

taki-tsuke 焚き付け kindling

ta⌐ko 1. たこ・蛸・章魚 octopus 2. 凧・たこ kite; 〜 **o agema⌐su** 凧[たこ]を揚げます flies a kite 3. たこ・胼胝 callus, corn

takō 焚こう・炊こう = **takimashō⌐** 焚きましょう; 炊きましょう; 焚きましょう (let's make a fire!; let's cook!; let's burn it!)

tako⌐-a⌐ge 凧揚げ・たこあげ kite-flying

tako-yaki たこ焼き griddled dumplings with octopus bits inside

taku 1. (o-taku) 宅(お宅) house;

my (your) husband **2.** 焚く・炊く = **takima̱su** 焚きます・炊きます (makes a fire; cooks; burns)

ta⌐ku 卓 table, desk

taku̱an たくあん = **taku̱(w)an** たくあ(わ)ん 「desk

takujō 卓上 desk-top; on one's

ta⌐kumi 巧み skill; ~ **(na)** 巧み(な) skillful, ~ **ni** 巧みに skillfully 「plot

takurami⌐ 企み plan, scheme,

takura̱mi 企み → **takuramima̱su** 企みます [infinitive]

takuramima̱su 企みます, **takura̱mu** 企む plans, schemes, plots

takura̱nde 企んで → **takuramima̱su** 企みます; intentionally, on purpose, with forethought; **... to ~** ...と企んで in collusion/cahoots with ...

takṵsa̱n (no) たくさん[沢山](の) lots (of), much/many, a lot (of)

ta̱kushii タクシー taxi

takuwa⌐e⌐ 蓄え savings, a reserve, a stock

takuwa⌐e 蓄え → **takuwaema̱su** 蓄えます [infinitive]

takuwaema̱su 蓄えます, **takuwa⌐e⌐ru** 蓄える saves up, hoards

taku̱(w)an たくあ(わ)ん yellow pickles made from sliced daikon

takya 焚きゃ・炊きゃ **1.** = **take̱ba** 焚けば・炊けば (if one make a fire; if one cook/burn it) **2.** ~ **shinai** 焚きゃしない・炊きゃしない = **taki̱ ya/wa shinai** 焚き[炊き]や/はしない = **takanai** 焚かない・炊かない (not make a fire; not cook/burn it)

tama たま: ~ **no** たまの occasional, infrequent; ~ **ni** たまに occasionally, now and then, at times, once in a while, infrequently

tama̱ 1. 玉 ball; 球 globe; bulb; 弾 bullet **2.** 玉・珠 jewel; bead; drop **3.** 玉 round thing; coin; slug

tama⌐go (o-ta̱mago, o-ta̱ma) 卵・玉子(お卵・お玉子, お玉) egg; ~ **no kara** 卵の殻 egg-shell

tama-ne̱gi 玉ねぎ・玉葱 onion *(round bulb)*

tamaranai = **tamarimase̱n 1.** たまら[溜ら]ない=たまり[溜り]ません does/will not accumulate **2.** たまら[堪ら]ない=たまり[堪り]ません is intolerable, insufferable, unbearable; (**...-te** ~ ...てたまらない does/is) unbearably, insufferably

tamari 1. たまり・溜まり =
   tamari-ba 溜まり場 **2.** たまり
   ・溜まり・貯まり →
   tamarima̱su たまり[溜まり・
   貯まり]ます [infinitive]
tamari-ba 溜まり場 a gathering
   place (waiting room, hangout,
   haunt, taxi stand, motor pool)
tamarima̱su たま[溜ま・貯ま]り
   ます, **tamaru** たま[溜ま・貯
   ま]る it accumulates
ta̱mashii 魂 soul, spirit
tamatama たまたま occasionally
tama̱-tsuki̱ 玉突き billiards
tamatte たまって・貯まって・溜
   まって → **tamarima̱su** たまり
   ます・貯まります・溜まります
... tambi̱ (ni) ...たんび(に) =
   tabi̱ (ni) 度[たび](に) every
   time that ...
tambo 田んぼ rice field
tame ため・溜め・貯め →
   tamema̱su ため[溜め・貯め]
   ます **1.** [infinitive] **2.** [impera-
   tive] **tame ro** ため[溜め・貯
   め]ろ, **tame̱ yo** ため[溜め・貯
   め]よ amass it!
... tame̱ ...為・ため **1.** (**o-tame** お
   為・おため) for the sake (good,
   benefit) of **2.** for the purpose
   of **3.** because (of)
tamema̱su ため[溜め・貯め]ま
   す, **tameru** ため[溜め・貯め]
   る amasses/accumulates
tameraima̱su ためらい[躊躇い]
   ます, **tamera̱u** ためらう・躊躇

   う hesitates
tameshi̱ 試し trial, test, experiment; ～ **ni** 試しに as a trial/
   test
tame̱shi 試し → **tameshima̱su**
   試します [infinitive]
tameshima̱su 試します, **tame̱su**
   試す tries, attempts, experi-
   ments with
tamete ため[溜め・貯め]て →
   tamema̱su ため[溜め・貯め]
   ます
tam-mono 反物 draperies, dry
   goods
tamo̱chi 保ち → **tamochima̱su**
   保ちます [infinitive]
tamochima̱su 保ちます,
   tamo̱tsu 保つ keeps, preserves
tamota̱nai 保たない =
   tamochimase̱n 保ちません
   (not keep)
tamoto̱ たもと・袂 sleeve; edge,
   end
tamo̱tte 保って →
   tamochima̱su 保ちます
tampaku̱-shi̱tsu 蛋白質・たんぱ
   く質 protein
ta̱mpopo たんぽぽ・蒲公英
   dandelion
tamushi̱ 田虫 ringworm;
   athlete's foot
...̱-tan ...反 bolt *(of cloth)*
tana 棚 shelf, rack
Tanabata 七夕・たなばた the
   Festival of the Weaver Star (7
   July)

ta︎ne 種 **1.** seed **2.** source, cause **3.** material **4.** secret, trick to it **5.** subject, topic

tango 単語 word(s), vocabulary

Ta︎ngo no sekku⁼ 端午の節句 Boys' Festival (5 May)

tani 谷 = **tani-ma**⁼ 谷間 valley

ta︎ ni 他に = **hoka ni** 他に・外に to/for/as others, additionally

ta︎n'i 単位 unit

tanin 他人 outsider, stranger; others

tanjo︎ bi (o-tanjo︎ bi) 誕生日（お誕生日） birthday

tanjun (na) 単純（な） simple; simplehearted, simpleminded

ta︎nka 1. 短歌 31-syllable poem **2.** 担架 stretcher, litter

tanki-da︎ igaku 短期大学 junior college, two-year college

tankō 炭鉱 coal mine

ta︎n naru ... 単なる... only, mere [*bookish*] = **honno ...** ほんの..., **... dake︎** ...だけ, **... ni sugimase︎ n (sugi︎ nai)** ...に過ぎません（過ぎない）

ta︎n ni 単に・たんに merely, only, [*bookish*] = **ta︎ da** ただ

tannin 担任 (teacher) in charge; **... o ~ shima︎ su** ...を担任します takes charge (is in charge) of ...

ta︎ no ... 他の... = **hoka no ...** 他の・外の... other

tanomi︎ 頼み a request

ta︎nomi 頼み confidence, trust, reliance

tano︎ mi 頼み → **tanomima︎ su** 頼みます [infinitive]

tanomima︎ su 頼みます, **tano︎ mu** 頼む **1.** requests, begs **2.** relies upon, entrusts with **3.** hires, engages (a professional)

tano︎ nde 頼んで → **tanomima︎ su** 頼みます

tanoshi︎ i 楽しい pleasant, enjoyable

tanoshi︎ mi︎ (o-tanoshimi) 楽しみ（お楽しみ） a pleasure, an enjoyment; **... (suru︎ no) o ~ ni shima︎ su** ...（するの）を楽しみにします takes pleasure in (doing)

tanoshimima︎ su 楽しみます, **tanoshi︎ mu** 楽しむ enjoys, takes pleasure in

tanoshi︎ nde 楽しんで → **tanoshimima︎ su** 楽しみます

tansan 炭酸 carbonic acid

tansa︎ n-sui 炭酸水 soda water

ta︎nsho 短所 shortcoming, fault, weak point

tansu たんす・箪笥 chest of drawers

tantei 探偵 detective

tantō 担当 responsibility, charge; **~ shima︎ su** 担当します takes charge of

tantō︎ -sha 担当者 person in charge, responsible person

ta︎nuki たぬき・狸 **1.** raccoon-

dog (*not* badger **anaguma** 穴
熊) 2. sly person

taˈnzeˈn 丹前 = **dotera** どてら
padded bathrobe

taoˈre 倒れ → **taoremaˈsu** 倒れ
ます [infinitive]

taoremaˈsu 倒れます, **taoreˈru** 倒
れる falls down, tumbles, col-
lapses

taˈoru タオル towel

taoˈse 倒せ → **taoshimaˈsu** 倒し
ます [imperative] knock it
down!

taoˈshi 倒し → **taoshimaˈsu** 倒し
ます [infinitive]

taoshimaˈsu 倒します, **taoˈsu** 倒
す knocks down, overthrows

tappuˈri たっぷり fully, more
than enough

taˈra たら・鱈 cod (fish)

...-taˈra ...たら if, when

tarai たらい tub, basin

taraˈ「」koˈ「」 たらこ・鱈子 cod roe

taraˈppu タラップ gangway

tarashimaˈsu, taraˈsu 1. 垂らし
ます, 垂らす dangles; drops,
spills 2. たらします, たらす
= **tarashi-komimaˈsu** たらし
[誑し]込みます, **-koˈ「」mu** た
らし[誑し]込む seduces;
wheedles

tareˈ たれ・垂れ gravy, (cooking)
sauce

taremaˈsu 垂れます, **tareˈru** 垂れ
る hangs down, dangles; drips

taˈ「」rento タレント a personali-

ty, (person of) talent

tari 足り → **tarimaˈsu** 足ります
[infinitive]

...-taˈri (shimaˈsu/desu) ...たり
(します/です) doing represen-
tatively/sometimes/alternate-
ly; ~ **...-naˈkaˈttari** ...たり...
なかったり doing off and on,
sometimes does and some-
times doesn't

tarimaˈsu 足ります, **tariru** 足り
る is enough/sufficient, suf-
fices

tarinai 足りない = **tarimaseˈn** 足
りません (is not enough, is insufficient)

tariru 足りる = **tarimaˈsu** 足り
ます

tarite 足りて → **tarimaˈsu** 足り
ます

taru 1. たる・樽 barrel, keg, cask
2. 足る [*dialect, literary*] =
tariru 足りる

tarumi 弛み・たるみ →
tarumimaˈsu 弛みます・たるみ
ます [infinitive]

tarumimaˈsu 弛みます・たるみま
す, **tarumu** 弛む・たるむ gets
slack (loose), relaxed

tarunde 弛んで・たるんで →
tarumimaˈsu 弛みます・たるみ
ます

taryō 多量 large quantity

tasanai 足さない = **tashimaseˈn**
足しません (not add)

tase 足せ → **tashimaˈsu** 足しま

す [imperative] add!

tase⌐ba 足せば → tashima⌐su 足
します (if one add)

tasha 足しゃ 1. = tase⌐ba 足せば
(if one add) 2. ~ shinai 足し
ゃしない = tashi ya/wa
shinai 足しや/はしない =
tasanai 足さない (not add)

ta⌐sha 他社 other companies;
other newspapers (= news-
paper companies)

tashi 足し → tashima⌐su 足しま
す [infinitive]

ta⌐shika 確か 1. if I remember
rightly, probably 2. ~ ni 確か
に for sure, surely, undoubtedly; ~ (na) 確か(な) safe,
sure, certain

tashikamema⌐su 確かめます,
tashikame⌐ru 確かめる makes
sure, ascertains

tashima⌐su 足します, tasu 足す
1. adds; ni⌐ ni san o ~ 二に三
を足します adds three to two,
adds three and two 2. yō⌐ o ~
用を足します does one's
business, relieves oneself, goes
to the bathroom

tashite 足して → tashima⌐su 足
します

tashō 多少 1. (large and/or
small) number, quantity,
amount 2. ~ (no) 多少(の)
more or less; somewhat; some

tassha (na) 達者(な) healthy;
skillful, expert, good at

tas-shima⌐su 達します, -su⌐ru
達する accomplishes; reaches

tas-shi⌐nai 達しない = tas-shi-
mase⌐n 達しません (not ac-
complish/reach)

tasū⌐ 多数 large number; majority

tasukarima⌐su 助かります,
tasuka⌐ru 助かる is saved; is
relieved

tasuke⌐ 助け → tasukema⌐su 助
けます 1. [infinitive] 2. [im-
perative] tasuke⌐ ro 助けろ,
tasuke⌐ yo 助けよ help!

tasukema⌐su 助けます, tasuke⌐ru
助ける 1. helps 2. saves

tasuke⌐nai 助けない →
tasukemase⌐n 助けません (not
help/save)

tasuke⌐te 助けて → tasukema⌐su
助けます

tasuki⌐ たすき・襷 a sleeve cord

tata⌐ite 叩いて → tatakima⌐su 叩
きます

tatakaema⌐su 戦えます,
tatakae⌐ru 戦える can fight

tatakaenai 戦えない =
tatakaemase⌐n 戦えません
(cannot fight)

tatakaete 戦えて →
tatakaema⌐su 戦えます

tatakaima⌐su 戦います・闘いま
す, tatakau 戦う・闘う fights

tataka⌐nai 叩かない =
tatakimase⌐n 叩きません (not
strike)

tataka¯tte 戦って → **tatakaima¯su** 戦います・闘います

tatakau 戦う・闘う = **tatakaima¯su** 戦います・闘います (fights)

tatakawanai 戦わない = **tatakaima¯se¯n** 戦いません (not fight)

tatakema¯su 叩けます, **tatake¯ru** 叩ける can strike (hit, knock, clap)

tatake¯nai 叩けない = **tatakema¯se¯n** 叩けません (cannot strike)

tata¯kete 叩けて → **tatakema¯su** 叩けます

tataki¯ 1. たたき・叩き pounding; bashing; mincing; **Nihon-ta¯taki** 日本たたき[叩き] Japan-bashing 2. たたき・三和土 concrete/cement floor

tatakima¯su 叩きます・たたきます, **tata¯ku** 叩く・たたく strikes, hits, knocks; (**te¯ o ~** 手を叩きます) claps; pounds (fish/meat to tenderize or mince it), minces

tatami 1. 畳 floor mat(ting), matted floor 2. 畳み → **tatamima¯su** 畳みます [infinitive]

tatamima¯su 畳みます, **tatamu** 畳む folds up

tata¯nai 立たない = **tachimase¯n** 立ちません (not stand)

tatanda 畳んだ = **tatamima¯shita** 畳みました (folded up)

tatande 畳んで → **tatamima¯su** 畳みます

ta¯te 1. 盾・楯 shield 2. ~ (no) 縦（の）vertical; ~ ni 縦に vertically, lengthwise 3. 建て・立て → **tatema¯su** 建てます・立てます [infinitive]; [imperative] **tate¯ ro** 建てろ, **ta¯te yo** 建てよ build it! 4. 立て → **tachima¯su** 立ちます [imperative] stand up!

...-tate (no) ...たて（の）fresh from ...

ta¯teba 立てば → **tachima¯su** 立ちます (if one stand)

tate¯-fuda 立て札・立札 signboard

tate-ito 縦糸 warp (vertical threads)

tate¯mae 建て前 principle, policy; ... o ~ to shima¯su ...を建て前とします makes ... one's policy

tate-mashi 建て増し house addition/extension, annex

tatema¯su, tate¯ru 1. 建てます, 建てる erects, builds, raises; sets up, establishes 2. 立てます, 立てる can stand

tate¯-mo¯no 建て物・建物 building

tate¯nai 建てない = **tatemase¯n** 建てません (not build)

tate(ra)rema͘su 建て(ら)れます, **tate(ra)re͞ru** 建て(ら)れる can build it

tate(ra)re͞reba 建て(ら)れれば → **tate(ra)rema͘su** 建て(ら)れます (if one can build)

tate͞reba 建てれば・立てれば, **tate͞rya** 建てりゃ・立てりゃ → **tatema͘su** 建てます; 立てます (if one build; if one can stand)

tate͞-tsubo 建て坪 floor space

ta͞te ya 建てや = **ta͞te wa** 建ては; **~ shimase͞n (shinai)** 建てやしません(しない) = **tatemase͞n** 建てません doesn't build

ta͞te yo [imperative] **1.** 建てよ = **tate͞ro** 建てろ build it! **2.** 立てよ stand up!

tateyo͞ 建てよう = **tatemasho͞** 建てましょう (let's build it!)

tato͞ 立とう = **tachimasho͞** 立ちましょう (let's stand!)

tato⁻e 例え・たとえ, **tato⁻i** 例い・たとい an example, an instance; a simile, an analogy

tato͞e 例え・たとえ → **tatoema͘su** 例えます・たとえます [infinitive]

tato͞eba 例えば・たとえば for example, for instance

tatoema͘su 例えます・たとえます, **tatoe͞ru** 例える・たとえる gives an example, compares (draws a simile to)

ta͞tsu 立つ・発つ・経つ・断つ → **tachima͘su** 立ちます・発ちます・経ちます・断ちます

tatta たった just, merely, only

ta͞tta 立った = **tachima͘shita** 立ちました; etc. (stood up; …)

tatta-i͞ma たった今 just now; in (just) a minute

ta͞tte 立って → **tachima͘su** 立ちます; **~ ima͘su** 立っています is standing

taue͞ 田植え rice planting

tawara͞ たわら・俵 straw bag; bale

tawashi たわし scrub(bing) brush; swab

taya⁻su⁻ku たやすく easily

tayora͞nai 頼らない = **tayorimase͞n** 頼りません (not rely on)

tayo͞ri 頼り → **tayorima͘su** 頼ります [infinitive]

ta͞yori 便り communication, correspondence, a letter, word (from someone), news

tayorima͘su 頼ります, **tayo͞ru** 頼る relies on, depends on

tayo͞tte 頼って → **tayorima͘su** 頼ります

tazuna 手綱 reins

tazu͞ne 尋ね・訪ね → **tazunema͘su** 尋ねます・訪ねます **1.** [infinitive] **2.** [imperative] **tazune͞ro** 尋ねろ, **tazu͞ne yo** 尋ねよ ask!; … !

tazunema͘su, tazune͞ru 1. 尋ね

ます, 尋ねる asks (a question)
2. 訪ねます, 訪ねる visits
3. 尋ねます, 尋ねる looks for

te┐ 手 hand, arm; trick, move;
kind; person

...-te ...て (does/did) and, and
then, and so; doing; [+ aux-
iliary] *see* **shi̱te** して

tea┐rai 手洗い, **o-tea┐rai** お手洗
い washroom, rest room,
toilet

te┐ate (o-te┐ate) 1. 手当て(お手当
て) treatment; reparation, provision **2.** 手当(お手当) allowance

tebu┐kuro 手袋 gloves

tēburu テーブル table; **tēburu┐-
kake** テーブル掛け tablecloth

tefuki┐ (o-te┐fuki) 手拭き(お手拭
き) hand towel

tega┐kari 手掛かり・てがかり a
hold, a place to hold on; a clue

tegami (o-te┐gami) 手紙(お手紙)
letter

tegata 手形 a note, a bill

te-gata⌐i 手堅い safe; reliable;
steady

tego┐koro 手心 discretion

te┐guchi 手口 way (of doing bad
things), trick

te-gu┐ruma 手車 (hand)cart

te┐hai 手配 (setting up) a search
for a criminal, a dragnet; ~
shima(⌐)su 手配します sets up
a dragnet; **tehai-sha┐shin** 手配
写真 photograph of a wanted

criminal

te┐hazu 手はず・手筈 arrangements

teho┐n (o-tehon) 手本(お手本)
model, pattern

tei-... 1. 定... fixed, appointed
2. 低... low; **tei-ke┐tsu̱atsu** 低
血圧 low blood pressure

...-te i ...てい → **...-te ima┐su** ...
ています [infinitive]

teian 提案 proposal, suggestion;
~ **shima┐su** 提案します pro-
poses

teibō 堤防 dike, embankment

teiden 停電 power failure/out-
age

te┐ido 程度 degree, extent, level

teika 定価 the set price

te┐iki 定期 **1.** ~ **(no)** 定期(の)
fixed, regular, periodic,
scheduled **2.** = **teiki┐-ken** 定期
券

tei-ki┐atsu 低気圧 low (barometric) pressure

teiki┐-ken 定期券 pass *(commuter ticket)*, season ticket

teiki-yo┐kin 定期預金 time
deposit

teikō 抵抗 resistance; ~
shima┐su 抵抗します resists

te┐ikoku 帝国 empire, ~ **(no)** 帝
国(の) imperial; **teikoku-
shu┐gi** 帝国主義 imperialism

te┐inei (na) ていねい[丁寧](な),
go-te┐inei (na) ごていねい[丁
寧](な) polite; careful

te-ire 手入れ repair; upkeep, care

teiryū-jo 停留所 (bus) stop

teisai 体裁 appearance, get-up, form, format, layout

teisetsu (na) 貞節(な) chaste

teisha 停車 stopping (of a vehicle)

teishi 停止 suspension, interruption

teishoku 定食 a set meal, table d'hôte; a complete meal

te̅ishu 亭主 host; landlord; husband

teisoku-gi̅(y)a 低速ギア(ヤ) low gear

te̅jina 手品 jugglery, magic (tricks); **tejina̅-shi** 手品師 juggler, magician

te̅jun 手順 order, procedure, program

…-te̅ kara …てから after (do)-ing, after one does/did, does/did and then (next)

te̅ka̅zu 手数 trouble (taken), inconvenience

teki 敵 enemy, opponent, rival

te̅ki テキ (beef)steak (= **bifu-teki** ビフテキ)

…-teki 1. …滴 a drop **2.** ~ **(na)** …的(な) …ic, …ical, …al, …ly; ~ **ni** …的に …ically, …ally

te̅kido 適度 moderation

te̅kigi (no) 適宜(の) suitable, fit, proper

teki-sa̅nai 適さない = **teki-**

shi̅nai 適しない = **teki-shimase̅n** 適しません (is not suitable)

teki-sa̅ndo テキサンド steak sandwich

teki̅setsu (na) 適切(な) appropriate, to the point

teki-shima̅su 適します, **teki-su̅ru** 適する is suitable, qualified

teki-shi̅nai 適しない = **teki-shimase̅n** 適しません (is not suitable)

teki̅-shite 適して → **teki-shima̅su** 適します

te̅ki̅suto テキスト text(book)

tekitō (na) 適当(な) suitable, proper; ~ **ni** 適当に suitably, properly

tekka(-maki) 鉄火(巻き) seaweed-rolled sushi with tuna inside

tekki 鉄器, **tekki̅-rui** 鉄器類 hardware (items)

tekkyō 鉄橋 iron bridge

teko てこ・挺・挺子 lever

te̅-kubi 手首 wrist

…-te kudasa̅i …て下さい please (do)

tema̅ (o-te̅ma) 手間(お手間) time (taken up); one's trouble

te̅ma テーマ theme, topic

temae 1. 手前・てまえ this side (of …); I/me **2. (o-te̅mae)** 手前(お手前) prowess, skill, ability; 点前(お点前) tea-ceremony procedures te͞ mane 手まね・手真似 gesture

tema͞ neki 手招き beckoning

te͞ -mari 手まり・手毬 (decorated) handball

...-tema͞ su ...てます ＝ ...-te ima͞ su ...ています

tema͞ wari 手回り, temawari⌐-hin 手回り品 personal effects; luggage

tembō-dai 展望台 (sightseeing) observatory

temmon-dai 天文台 (astronomical) observatory

temmo͞ n-gaku 天文学 astronomy

...-te͞ mo ...ても even doing/being, even if (one does/is); shite͞ mo i͞ i してもいい it is OK to do, one may do

te͞ mpi 天火 oven

tempura 天ぷら・天麩羅 food fried in batter, especially shrimp

ten 点 point, dot, spot; score (points)

te͞ n 1. 天 sky, heaven 2. 天 ＝ tempura 天ぷら・天麩羅 3. テ ン ten; besuto͞ -te͞ n ベストテ ン the best ten

...⌐-ten ...店 shop

ten-don 天丼 a bowl of rice with tempura shrimp on top

te͞ ngoku 天国 paradise, heaven

tengu 天狗 1. (＝ tengu-sa͞ ma͞ 天 狗様) a long-nosed goblin 2. conceited person

te͞ ni 手に: sore ga te͞ ni hairima͞ su それが手に入りま す ＝ sore o te͞ ni irema͞ su そ れを手に入れます obtains, gets it

te-ni͞ motsu 手荷物 hand luggage

ten'in 店員 shop clerk, sales-clerk, salesperson (salesgirl/ saleswoman/salesman)

te͞ nisu テニス tennis

tenji͞ -kai 展示会 exhibition

ten-jima͞ su 転じます, -ji⌐ru 転 じる changes, shifts; gets trans-ferred

tenjō 天井 ceiling

te͞ nki 天気 (＝o-te͞ nki お天気) 1. weather; tenki-yo͞ hō 天気予 報 weather forecast 2. fair weather

tenkin 転勤 job transfer; ～ shima͞ su 転勤します changes posts, gets transferred

te⌐nnen (no) 天然(の) natural

tennentō 天然痘 smallpox

tennin 転任 job transfer; ～ shima͞ su 転任します gets transferred

Tennō͞ (-sama) 天皇(様) the Emperor; Tennō-he͞ ika 天皇 陛下 His Majesty the Emperor

Tennō-tanjō͞ bi 天皇誕生日 the Emperor's Birthday (23 December)

te͞ -no͞ -hira 手のひら[平] palm (of hand)

tenra͞ n-kai 展覧会 exhibition

tensai 天才 genius

te⌐nsei 天性 disposition, temperament

te⌐nshi 天使 angel

tenshō⌐gi 天象儀 planetarium

tensū⌐ 点数 score, points

te⌐nto テント tent

te-nugui (o-te⌐nugui) 手拭い(お手拭い) hand towel

te⌐-o⌐no 手斧 hatchet

teppan-yaki 鉄板焼き sliced meat, etc. grilled at table

teppe⌐n てっぺん top, highest part

teppō 鉄砲 gun, rifle

te⌐pu テープ tape; **tēpu-rekō⌐dā** テープレコーダー tape recorder

tera⌐ (o-tera) 寺(お寺) Buddhist temple

tera⌐nai 照らない = **terimase⌐n** 照りません (not shine)

terashi-awase⌐masu 照らし合わせます, **terashi-awase⌐ru** 照らし合わせる collates

terashima⌐su 照らします, **tera⌐su** 照らす illuminates, lights it up, shines on; compares, collates, checks; **... ni tera⌐shite** …に照らして in the light of …, in view of …

te⌐re 照れ → **terema⌐su** 照れます [infinitive]

...-tere⌐ba …てれば = **...-te ire⌐ba** …ていれば

te⌐reba 照れば → **terima⌐su** 照ります

ます (if it shine)

te⌐rebi テレビ, **terebi⌐jon** テレビジョン television

terema⌐su 照れます, **tere⌐ru** 照れる feels embarrassed, awkward, flustered

tere⌐nai 照れない = **teremase⌐n** 照れません (not feel embarrassed)

tere⌐reba 照れれば → **terema⌐su** 照れます (if one feel embarrassed)

te⌐rete 照れて → **terema⌐su** 照れます

te⌐ri 照り → **terima⌐su** 照ります [infinitive]

terima⌐su 照ります, **te⌐ru** 照る it shines

teriyaki 照り焼き (fish, chicken, etc.) broiled with soy sauce and sweeteners

te⌐ro テロ terrorism, terrorist

...-teru …てる = **...-te iru** …ている = **...-te ima⌐su** …ています

...-terya …てりゃ = **...-te irya** …ていりゃ = **...-te ire⌐ba** …ていれば

te⌐rya 照りゃ 1. = **te⌐reba** 照れば (if it shine) 2. ~ **shinai** 照りゃしない = **te⌐ri ya/wa shinai** 照りや/はしない = **tera⌐nai** 照らない (not shine)

tesage⌐ 手提げ・手さげ handbag

tesei (no) 手製(の) homemade, handcrafted

tesū˥ (o-tesū) 手数(お手数) trouble (taken), inconvenience; **tesū˥-ryō** 手数料 handling/service charge
te˥sụto テスト test
...-te˥ta ...てた = **...-te ita** ...ていた = **...-te ima˥shịta** ...ていました
...-te˥te ...てて = **...-te ite** ...ていて
tetsu 鉄 iron, steel
tetsu-bō 鉄棒 iron bar
tetsuda˥e 手伝え → **tetsudaima˥sụ** 手伝います [imperative] help!
tetsuda˥i 手伝い **1.** **(o-te˥tsudai** お手伝い) assistance, help **2.** → **tetsudaima˥sụ** 手伝います [infinitive]
tetsudaima˥sụ 手伝います, **tetsuda˥u** 手伝う helps
tetsudaō˥ 手伝おう = **tetsudaimashō˥** 手伝いましょう (let's help!)
tetsuda˥tte 手伝って → **tetsudaima˥sụ** 手伝います
tetsudō 鉄道 railroad, railway
tetsu[˥]gaku 哲学 philosophy; **tetsuga˥kụ˥-sha** 哲学者 philosopher
tetsuya shima˥sụ 徹夜します stays up all night
te-tsu˥zuki 手続き formalities, procedure
te˥tte 照って → **terima˥sụ** 照ります
tettei-teki (na) 徹底的(な) thorough
...-te˥ wa ...ては doing/being, if one do/be; ~ **ikemase˥n (ikenai)** ...てはいけません(いけない) mustn't
...-te˥ ya imase˥n (inai) ...てやいません(いない) = **...-te˥ wa imase˥n (inai)** ...てはいません(いない)
te-za˥iku 手細工 handiwork
tezu˥kuri (no) 手作り(の) homemade, made by hand
ti... → **chi...**
tisshụ-pē˥pā ティッシュペーパー tissue(s)
to 戸 door
... to ...と **1.** with **2.** and [*concatenates a noun*]
... to ...と (said/thought/seemed) that ... ; " ... " (quote-)unquote
... to ...と **1.** **(su)-ru to** (す)ると when(ever), if; ... and thereupon, ... whereupon **2.** **(shi)-nai to** (し)ないと unless
tō˥ **1.** 十 ten **2.** 籐 rattan, cane **3.** 塔 tower, pagoda
...˥-tō ...頭 (counts large animals) [5 **go-tō** 五頭 *unaccented*]
...-tō ...等 class
Tō˥a 東亜 East Asia = **Higashi-A˥ji(y)a** 東アジア[ヤ]
tobaku 賭博·とばく gambling; **(jidō-)tobaku˥-ki** (自動)賭博

機 slot machine

tōˈban (o-tōˈban) 当番（お当番） person on duty

tobanai 跳ばない・飛ばない = **tobimaseˈn** 跳びません/飛びません (not jump/fly)

tobashimaˈsu 飛ばします, **tobasu** 飛ばす lets fly; skips, omits; hurries

tobe 跳べ・飛べ **1.** → **tobemaˈsu** 跳べます/飛べます (can jump/fly) [infinitive] **2.** → **tobimaˈsu** 飛びます [imperative] jump!; fly!

tobeˈba 跳べば・飛べば → **tobimaˈsu** 跳びます/飛びます (if one jump/fly)

tobemaˈsu, toberu 1. 跳べます, 跳べる can jump **2.** 飛べます, 飛べる can fly

tobete 跳べて・飛べて → **tobemaˈsu** 跳べます・飛べます

tobi 跳び・飛び → **tobimaˈsu** 跳びます・飛びます [infinitive]

tobi-dashimaˈsu, tobi-daˈsu 1. 跳び出します, 跳び出す jumps out **2.** 飛び出します, 飛び出す runs/bursts out; it sticks out, protrudes; (**uchi o ~** 家を飛び出します) runs away (from home)

tobimaˈsu, tobu 1. 跳びます, 跳ぶ jumps **2.** 飛びます, 飛ぶ flies

tobira 扉 **1.** a door wing, a door of a gate **2.** title page

toboshiⁿˈi 乏しい scarce, meager, scanty

tobu 跳ぶ・飛ぶ = **tobimaˈsu** 跳びます; 飛びます (jumps; flies) ⌐part

tōˈbu 東部 the east, the eastern

tōbun 当分 for the time being

tobya 跳びゃ・飛びゃ **1.** = **tobeˈba** 跳べば/飛べば (if one jump/fly) **2.** **~ shinai** 跳びゃしない・飛びゃしない = **tobiˈya/wa shinai** 跳びや/はしない・飛びや/はしない = **tobanai** 跳ばない/飛ばない (not jump/fly)

tōchaku 到着 arrival; **tōchaku shimaˈsu** 到着します arrives

tochi 土地 ground, earth, soil; a piece of land

tochū (de/no) 途中（で/の） on the way

tōdai 1. 燈台 lighthouse **2. (Tōdai)** 東大 Tokyo University

to-dana 戸棚 cupboard, enclosed shelves ⌐trains

toden 都電 Tokyo Metro (line/

todoˈite 届いて → **todokimaˈsu** 届きます

todokeˈ (o-todoke) 届け（お届け） notification, notice, report

todoˈke 届け → **todokemaˈsu** 届けます **1.** [infinitive] **2.** [imperative] **todokeˈ ro** 届けろ, **todoˈke yo** 届けよ deliver! notify!

todokema'su 届けます,
　todoke'ru 届ける 1. delivers
　2. reports it (to), notifies

todoke(ra)rema'su 届け(ら)れま
　す, todoke(ra)re'ru 届け(ら)
　れる can deliver

todoke-saki 届け先 address (for
　delivery)

todo'kete 届けて →
　todokema'su 届けます

todo'ki 届き → todokima'su 届
　きます [infinitive]

todokima'su 届きます, todo'ku
　届く reaches; arrives; gets
　delivered

todoma'ri とどまり →
　todomarima'su とどまります
　[infinitive]

todomarima'su とどまります,
　todoma'ru とどまる it stops;
　it remains

todoma'tte とどまって →
　todomarima'su とどまります

todo'me とどめ → todomema'su
　とどめます 1. [infinitive]
　2. [imperative] todome'ro と
　どめろ, todo'me yo とどめよ
　stop it!

todomema'su とどめます,
　todome'ru とどめる stops it

todo'mete とどめて →
　todomema'su とどめます

todoro'ite 轟いて →
　todorokima'su 轟きます

todoro'ki 轟き → todorokima'su
　轟きます [infinitive]

todorokima'su 轟きます,
　todoro'ku 轟く roars, rumbles

to'e 問え 1.→ toema'su 問えま
　す [infinitive] 2. → toima'su
　問います [imperative] inquire!

to'e'ba 問えば → toima'su 問い
　ます (if one inquire)

toei 都営 metropolitan (run by
　Tokyo), metro; Toei-sen 都営
　線 Tokyo Metro Line

toema'su 問えます, toe'ru 問え
　る can inquire

toe'nai 問えない = toemase'n
　問えません (cannot inquire)

tōfu' (o-tōfu) 豆腐(お豆腐)
　bean curd

togame' (o-togame) とがめ・咎め
　(おとがめ・お咎め) rebuke,
　censure, blame

toga'me とがめ・咎め →
　togamema'su とがめます・咎
　めます [infinitive]

togamema'su とがめます・咎め
　ます, togame'ru とがめる・咎
　める blames, rebukes, re-
　proves, finds fault with

togarashima'su とがらします・
　尖らします, togara'su とがら
　す・尖らす sharpens, points

togarima'su とがります・尖りま
　す, toga'ru とがる・尖る gets
　sharp (pointed)

toge とげ・刺・棘 thorn

to'ge 1. 遂げ・研げ → togema'su
　遂げます・研げます [infini-
　tive] 2. 研げ → togima'su 研ぎ

ます [imperative] sharpen it!

tōge' 峠 mountain pass; **...-tō'ge** ... 峠 ... Pass

tōgei 陶芸 ceramic art, ceramics

togema'su, toge'ru 1. 遂げます, 遂げる achieves, accomplishes **2.** 研げます, 研げる can sharpen (grind, polish)

to'gete 遂げて・研げて → **togema'su** 遂げます・研げます

to'gi 研ぎ → **togima'su** 研ぎます [infinitive]

togima'su 研ぎます, **to'gu** 研ぐ sharpens, grinds, polishes

tōhō 東方 the east

tōhyō 投票 ballot, vote

to⌐i 問い → **toima'su** 問います [infinitive]

to'i とい・樋 drain pipe, gutter

tōi 遠い far-off, distant; (**mimi'** / **denwa ga** ~ 耳/電話が遠い) hard to hear

toiawase (o-toiawase) 問い合わせ(お問い合わせ) inquiry

to'ida 研いだ = **togima'shita** 研ぎました (sharpened it)

to'ide 研いで → **togima'su** 研ぎます

toima'su 問います, **to⌐u** 問う inquires

to'ire トイレ, **to'ire'tto** トイレット toilet, bathroom

toiretto-pē'pā トイレットペーパー toilet paper

to'ita 解いた → **tokima'shita** 解きました (undid; ...)

...-to'ita ...といた = **...-te o'ita** ...ておいた (= **okima'shita** おきました)

...-to'itara ...といたら = **...-te o'itara** ...ておいたら

...-to'itari ...といたり = **...-te o'itari** ...ておいたり

to'ite 解いて → **tokima'su** 解きます

...-to'ite ...といて = **...-te o'ite** ...ておいて

tōitsu 統一 unification, standardization; **tōitsu shima'su** 統一します unifies, standardizes

to'ji 閉じ → **tojima'su** 閉じます [infinitive]

tōji 1. 冬至 winter solstice **2.** 湯治 hot-spring cure; ~**-ba** 湯治場 spa; ~ **shima'su (ni ikima'su)** 湯治します(に行きます) takes (goes for) the baths

tō'ji 当時 (at) that time, then, (in) those days

tojima'su 閉じます, **toji'ru** 閉じる closes (a book, door wings, ...)

toji'nai 閉じない = **tojimase'n** 閉じません (not close)

to'jite 閉じて → **tojima'su** 閉じます

tōjitsu 当日 the day in question, that very day

tōjō 1. 搭乗 boarding a plane; ~**-chū** 搭乗中 (in the midst

of) boarding; ～ **shima'su** 搭
乗します boards 2. 登場 entry
upon the stage; ～ **shima'su** 登
場します appears on stage

tōjō-ken 搭乗券 boarding pass

... to ka ...とか or something
(like it)

tōka 十日 ten days; 10th day (of
month)

tokage とかげ・蜥蜴 lizard

tokai 都会 city, town; **toka'i-jin**
都会人 city dweller, urbanite

tokaku (... shima'su) とかく(...
します) apt/liable (to do); ～
(... **no**) とかく(...の) various
(and nefarious), ～ **no uwasa**
とかくのうわさ[噂] unsavory
rumors

toka'nai 解かない ＝ **tokimase'n**
解きません (not undo it; not
...)

tokasa'nai 溶かさない・梳かさな
い ＝ **tokashimase'n** 溶かしま
せん; 梳かしません (not
melt/dissolve; not comb)

toka'se 溶かせ・梳かせ 1. →
tokasema'su 溶かせます・とか
[梳か]せます [infinitive] 2. →
tokashima'su 溶かします・と
か[梳か]します [imperative]
melt it!; comb it!

tokasema'su, tokase'ru 1. 溶かせ
ます, 溶かせる can melt/
dissolve it 2. とか[梳か]せま
す, とか[梳か]せる can comb
it

tokase'nai 溶かせない・梳かせな
い ＝ **tokasemase'n** 溶かせま
せん; 梳かせません (cannot
melt/dissolve; cannot comb)

toka'shi 溶かし・梳かし →
tokashima'su 溶かします・と
か[梳か]します [infinitive]

tokashima'su, toka'su 1. 溶かし
ます, 溶かす melts/thaws/
dissolves it 2. とか[梳か]しま
す, とか[梳か]す combs

to'ke 溶け・解け → **tokema'su**
溶けます・解けます [infini-
tive] 2. 解け → **tokima'su** 解
きます [imperative] undo!; ...!

to'keba 解けば → **tokima'su** 解
けます, etc. (if one undo it; if
...)

tokei 時計 timepiece; clock;
watch

tōkei 統計 statistics

tokema'su, toke'ru 1. 溶けます,
溶ける it melts/thaws/dis-
solves 2. 解けます, 解ける
comes undone; gets solved

to'kete 溶けて・解けて →
tokema'su 溶けます・解けます

toki' 時, ... **to'ki'** ...時 time; ...
～ **(ni)** ...時(に) at the time
that ... , when ...

to'ki 1. とき・朱鷺・鴇 crested ibis
(bird) 2. 解き・説き・梳き →
tokima'su 解きます・説きま
す・梳きます [infinitive]

tō'ki 1. 陶器 pottery, ceramics
2. 登記 registration 3. 冬期

winter (period/term)

tokidoki 時々・ときどき sometimes

tokima̱ su, to̱ ku 1. 解きます, 解く undoes, unties; solves 2. 説きます, 説く explains, persuades, preaches 3. 梳きます, 梳く combs

...-tokima̱ su ...ときます = ...-te okima̱ su ...ておきます

toki̱ ni ときに・時に by the way, incidentally; sometimes

tokkuri とっくり・徳利 saké bottle/pitcher, ceramic decanter for serving saké

tokkyū 1. 特急 special express (train); **tokkyū-ken** 特急券 special-express ticket 2. 特級 special class; (best) quality

toko (o-toko) 床(お床) bed; ~ **ni tsukima̱ su (tsuku̱)** 床に就きます(就く) takes to one's bed, goes to bed

... toko̱ ...とこ place (= ... **tokoro̱** ...所)

tokonoma 床の間 alcove in Japanese room

tokoro, ... tokoro̱ 1. 所, ...所 place 2. 所, ...所 address 3. ところ, ...ところ circumstance, time
  shi̱ta tokoro̱ desu̱ したところです has just done it
  shi̱te iru tokoro̱ desu̱ しているところです is (in the midst of) doing it

suru tokoro̱ desu̱ するところです is about to do it

tokoro̱-de ところで by the way; well now

tokoro-do̱ koro ところどころ・所々 various places, here and there

tokoro̱-ga ところが but, however

... tokoro̱ ga ...ところが but; whereupon

tokoro-gaki 所書き address *(written)*

tokoroten ところてん seaweed-gelatin strips served cold in a tangy soy sauce

tokoya 床屋 barber(shop)

toku-... 特... special (= **toku-betsu** 特別)

toku 1. 徳 virtue 2. (o-toku) 得 (お得) profit, advantage, gain; ~ **(na)** 得(な) profitable, advantageous

to̱ku 解く・説く・梳く = **tokima̱ su** 1. 解きます undoes, unties; solves 2. 説きます explains, persuades, preaches 3. ときます・梳きます combs

...-toku ...とく = ...-te oku ...ておく (= **okima̱ su** おきます)

tōku̱ 遠く 1. the distance, far off 2. so as to be far/distant (→ **tōi** 遠い)

tokubetsu (no) 特別(の) special, particular, extra; ~ **ni** 特別に especially

tokuchō 特徴 special feature/ quality, (a distinguishing) characteristic

tokuhon 読本 reader, reading book

toku⌐i 1. 得意 pride; ～ (na) 得意(な) proud, exultant 2. 特異・得意 specialty *(forte)*; ～ (na/no) 特異・得意(な/の) special, favorite 3. 得意 (o-tokui お得意) (regular) customer, patron 4. 得意 prosperity

to⌐ku-ni 特に in particular

toku-ni⌐tō 特二等 special second class

tokushoku 特色 special feature, characteristic

to⌐kushu (na) 特殊(な), **tokuyū (no)** 特有(の) special, particular ⌐score

tokute⌐n 得点 points obtained,

to⌐kya 解きゃ 1. = **to⌐keba** 解ければ, etc. (if one undo it; if …) 2. ～ **shinai** 解きゃしない = **to⌐ki ya/wa shinai** 解きや/はしない = **toka⌐nai** 解かない (not undo it)

Tōkyō 東京 Tokyo; **Tōkyō⌐-Eki** 東京駅 Tokyo Station; **Tōkyō⌐-jin** 東京人 a Tokyoite; **Tōkyō⌐-to** 東京都 the metropolis of Tokyo

tō⌐kyoku 当局 the authorities

toma⌐nai 富まない = **tomimase⌐n** 富みません (not abound)

tomare 止まれ・泊まれ 1. → **tomarema⌐su** 止まれます・泊まれます [infinitive] 2. → **tomarima⌐su** 止まります・泊まります [imperative] stop!; stay overnight!

tomarema⌐su, tomareru 1. 泊まれます, 泊まれる can stay overnight 2. 止まれます, 止まれる can stop

tomarete 泊まれて・止まれて → **tomarema⌐su** 泊まれます・止まれます

tomari 1. 泊まり staying overnight; night duty 2. 止まり・泊まり → **tomarima⌐su** 止まります・泊まります [infinitive]

tomarima⌐su, tomaru 1. 止まります, 止まる it stops 2. 泊まります, 泊まる stays overnight

tomarō 泊まろう = **tomarimashō** 泊まりましょう (let's stay overnight!)

tomaru 泊まる = **tomarima⌐su** 泊まります; ～ **tokoro** 泊まる所 accommodation(s), place to stay

tomatte 止まって・泊まって → **tomarima⌐su** 止まります・泊まります

tōma⌐wari 遠回り detour

tombo とんぼ・蜻蛉 dragonfly

tome 止め・泊め・留め → **tomema⌐su** 止めます・泊めま

す・留めます [infinitive]

tō-me｣ 十目（の）(no) = jū-
bamme｣ 十番目 tenth

to｣meba 富めば → tomima｣su 富
みます (if it abound)

tome-ba｣ri 留め針 pin 「clear

tōmei (na) 透明（な）transparent,

tomema｣su, tomeru 1. 止めます,
止める stops it 2. 泊めます,
泊める puts one up overnight
3. 留めます, 留める fastens
(firmly attaches)

tomenai 止めない =
tomemase｣n 止めません, etc.
(not stop it; ...)

tome(ra)re 止め（ら）れ・泊め
（ら）れ → tome(ra)rema｣su 止
め（ら）れます・泊め（ら）れま
す [infinitive]

tome(ra)rema｣su, tome(ra)reru
1. 止め（ら）れます, 止め（ら）
れる can stop it 2. 泊め（ら）れ
ます, 泊め（ら）れる can put
one up overnight

tome(ra)renai 止め（ら）れない
= tome(ra)remase｣n 止め（ら）
れません, etc. (cannot stop it;
...)

tomeyō 止めよう = tomemashō｣
止めましょう (let's stop it!;
...)

to｣mi 1. 富 wealth, fortune,
riches, abundance 2. 富み →
tomima｣su 富みます [infini-
tive]

tomima｣su 富みます, to｣mu 富む

is rich; abounds

to｣mma とんま・頓馬 idiot, fool

to｣mo (o-to｣mo) 伴（お伴）・友（お
友）together; company; friend

... to｣-mo! ...とも! of course ... !

tomodachi (o-tomodachi) 友達
（お友達）friend

to｣-mo-kaku ともかく anyway,
anyhow, at any rate

tomonaima｣su 伴います,
tomona｣u 伴う: ... ni ~ ...に
伴います accompanies

to｢mo ni 共に together

tō-mo｣rokoshi とうもろこし
corn (on the cob);
tōmorokoshi｣-ko とうもろこ
し粉 cornstarch

tomoshima｣su ともします・灯し
ます, tomo｣su ともす・灯す
burns (a light)

to｣mu 富む = tomima｣su 富みま
す (is rich; abounds)

to｣mya 富みゃ 1. = to｣meba 富
めば (if it abound) 2. ~ shinai
富みゃしない = to｣mi ya/wa
shinai 富みや/はしない =
toma｣nai 富まない (not
abound)

tona｣e 唱え → tonaema｣su 唱え
ます 1. [infinitive] 2. [impera-
tive] tona｣e｣ ro 唱えろ, tona｣e
yo 唱えよ

tonaema｣su 唱えます, tona｣e｣ru
唱える advocates; shouts;
recites; calls; claims

tona｣ete 唱えて → tonaema｣su

唱えます

to͞nai 都内 within the metropolis (of Tokyo)

tōnan 1. 東南 southeast 2. 盗難 (suffering) theft

tonari 隣 next-door, neighbor-(ing)

tonda 1. とんだ outrageous, terrible, shocking 2. 跳んだ・飛んだ = **tobima͞shita** 跳びました・飛びました (jumped; flew)

to͞nda 富んだ = **tomima͞shita** 富みました (was rich; abounded)

tonde 跳んで・飛んで → **tobima͞su** 跳びます・飛びます

to͞nde 富んで → **tomima͞su** 富みます; ～ **ima͞su** 富んでいます is rich, abundant

tonde-mo arimase͞n (na͞i) とんでもありません(ない) Oh, no. No way.

tonde-mo na͞i とんでもない 1. = **tonde-mo arimase͞n** とんでもありません 2. = **tonda** とんだ outrageous, terrible, shocking

to͞-ni-kaku とにかく nevertheless, anyway, anyhow

ton-katsu 豚カツ・トンカツ pork cutlet

tonneru トンネル tunnel

tōnyō-byō 糖尿病 diabetes

toppatsu 突発 outbreak

tora 虎 tiger

tora͞e 捕らえ → **toraema͞su** 捕らえます [infinitive]

toraema͞su 捕らえます, **tora͞eru** 捕らえる catches, seizes, captures, arrests

tora͞kku トラック 1. truck 2. track (for running)

torampe͞tto トランペット trumpet

tora͞mpu トランプ playing cards

tora͞nai 取らない = **torimase͞n** 取りません, etc. (not take; not ...)

tora͞nku トランク (clothes/car) trunk

to͞re 取れ 1. → **torema͞su** 取れます [infinitive] 2. → **torima͞su** 取ります [imperative] take it!; ... !

to͞reba 取れば → **torima͞su** 取ります (if one take)

torema͞su 取れます, **tore͞ru** 取れる 1. (button, etc.) comes off 2. can take

tore͞nai 取れない = **toremase͞n** 取れません (not come off; cannot take)

torepe トレペ tracing paper (= **torēshingu-pe͞pā** トレーシングペーパー)

tore͞reba 取れれば, **tore͞rya** 取れりゃ → **torema͞su** 取れます (if it come off; if one can take)

to͞rete 取れて → **torema͞su** 取れます

tori 1. 鳥 bird 2. とり・鳥・鶏 (=

niwa-tori 鶏・にわとり)
chicken

toʻri 取り・撮り → torimaʻsu 取
ります・撮ります [infinitive]

tori-... 取り... [VERB PREFIX]:
takes and ...

tōriʻ 通り street, avenue; passage

tōʻri 通り 1. way (of doing), manner; ... no ~ ni ...の通り[と
おり]に like ... 2. →
tōrimaʻsu 通ります [infinitive]

tori-agemaʻsu 取り上げます,
-ageʻru 取り上げる takes up;
takes away

tori-atsukai 取り扱い, handling,
treatment, management, transaction

tori-atsukaʻi 取り扱い → tori-
atsukaimaʻsu 取り扱います
[infinitive]

tori-atsukaimaʻsu 取り扱います,
-atsukaʻu 取り扱う handles,
deals with, manages

tori-awase 取り合わせ assort-
ment

toriʻ-gai 鳥貝 cockle

toʻri-hiki 取り引き・取引 transaction, deal, business, trade

torii 鳥居 the gate to a Shinto
shrine

torikae 取り替え 1. change,
replacement 2. → tori-
kaemaʻsu 取り替えます [infini-
tive]; [imperative] torikae ro
取り替えろ, torikaeʻ yo 取り
替えよ replace it!

torikaemaʻsu 取り替えます,
torikaeru 取り替える replaces
it

torikaenai 取り替えない =
torikaemaseʻn 取り替えませ
ん (not replace it)

torikae(ra)re 取り替え(ら)れ →
torikae(ra)remaʻsu 取り替え
(ら)れます

torikae(ra)remaʻsu 取り替え
(ら)れます, torikae(ra)reru 取
り替え(ら)れる can replace it

torikae(ra)renai 取り替え(ら)れ
ない = torikae(ra)remaseʻn 取
り替え(ら)れません (cannot
replace it)

tori-kago 鳥かご・鳥籠 bird cage

tori-kesaʻnai 取り消さない =
tori-keshimaseʻn 取り消しま
せん (not cancel)

tori-keshi 取り消し cancellation,
revocation; deletion, erasure

tori-keʻshi 取り消し → tori-
keshimaʻsu 取り消します

tori-keshimaʻsu 取り消します,
-keʻsu 取り消す cancels,
revokes; deletes, erases

tori-keʻshite 取り消して →
tori-keshimaʻsu 取り消します

tori-kesōʻ 取り消そう = tori-
keshimashōʻ 取り消しましょ
う (let's cancel it!)

tori-kumi 取り組み・取組み
wrestling match/bout/pro-
gram

torimaʻsu, toʻru 1. 取ります, 取

る takes; takes away, removes
2. 取ります, 取る hands it
(to), passes *(the salt, sugar,
etc.)* **3.** 撮ります, 撮る takes
(a picture) **4.** 取ります, 取る
takes (a course)

tōrima⌐su, tō⌐ru 1. 通ります, 通
る passes by, passes through
2. 透ります, 透る penetrates

torishimari 1. 取り締まり・取締
り control, management,
supervision **2.** 取締り (=
torishimari⌐-yaku 取締役)
managing director

tori-shima⌐ri 取り締まり →
tori-shimarima⌐su 取り締まり
ます

tori-shimarima⌐su 取り締まりま
す, **-shima⌐ru** 取り締まる
controls, manages, supervises,
directs

toritsugi 1. 取り次ぎ・取次ぎ
answering the door **2.** 取次 an
usher **3.** 取次 agency

toriwake とりわけ especially, in
particular

to⌐ro とろ・トロ fatty tuna
(*cf.* **chū-toro** 中とろ・中トロ,
aka-mi 赤身)

torō⌐ 取ろう = **torimashō⌐** 取り
ましょう (let's take it!)

tōrō とうろう・灯籠 a stone
lantern

tōroku 登録 registration; **tōroku
shima⌐su** 登録します registers,
enrolls

tō⌐ron 討論 debate, discussion,
dispute

tororo とろろ grated yam;
tororo-ko⌐mbu とろろ昆布
kelp flakes

to⌐ru 取る = **torima⌐su** 取ります
(takes; takes away)

tō⌐ru 通る・透る = **tōrima⌐su** 通
ります; 透ります (passes by,
passes through; penetrates)

To⌐ruko トルコ **1.** Turkey
2. = **sauna-bu⌐ro** サウナ風
呂 sauna

to⌐rya 取りゃ **1.** = **to⌐reba** 取れ
ば (if one take) **2.** ~ **shinai** 取
りゃしない = **to⌐ri ya/wa
shinai** 取りや/はしない =
tora⌐nai 取らない (not take)

tōsan 倒産 = **hasan** 破産 bankruptcy

tōsa⌐nai 通さない = **tōshimase⌐n**
通しません (not let through/
in)

tō⌐se 通せ **1.** → **tōsema⌐su** 通せ
ます [infinitive] **2.** →
tōshima⌐su 通します [impera-
tive] let them through/in!

tōsei 統制 control (*of prices,
etc.*)

tōsema⌐su, tōse⌐ru 1. 通せます,
通せる can let through/in
2. 透せます, 透せる can
pierce/penetrate

tōse⌐nai 通せない = **tōsemase⌐n**
通せません (cannot let
through/in)

toshi⌐ (o-toshi) 1. 年(お年) year **2.** 年・歳(お年・お歳) age; ~ **o torima⌐su** 年を取ります gets old

to⌐shi 都市 city

tōshi⌐ (no) 通し(の) direct, through (to destination); ~ **de ikima⌐su** 通しで行きます goes direct (through to destination); **tōshi-gi⌐ppu** 通し切符 a through ticket

tō⌐shi 投資 investment, investing; **tō⌐shi shima⌐su** 投資します invests

tō⌐shi 通し・透し → **tōshima⌐su** 通します・透します [infinitive]

tōshima⌐su, tō⌐su 1. 通します, 通す lets through/in, admits; shows in **2.** 通し[透し]ます, 通す・透す pierces, penetrates

toshi-shita (no) 年下(の) younger, junior

tō⌐shi shite 投資して → **tō⌐shi shima⌐su** 投資します (invests)

tō⌐shite 通して → **tōshima⌐su** 通します

toshi-ue (no) 年上(の) older, senior

toshiyo⌐ri⌐ (o-toshiyori) 年寄り (お年寄り) an old person

to⌐sho 図書 library (= book collection); ~**-ga⌐kari** 図書係 the librarian (in charge), (book) custodian

tosho⌐-kan 図書館 library

(building); **toshoka⌐n-in** 図書館員 a librarian; **toshoka⌐n-chō** 図書館長 the (head) librarian, the head of the library

tosho⌐-shitsu 図書室 library (= book room)

to⌐so (o-to⌐so) とそ・屠蘇(おとそ・お屠蘇) spiced saké drunk at New Year's

tossa (no) とっさ(の) prompt, immediate, imminent; ~ **ni** とっさに in an instant, promptly, immediately

tō⌐su 通す・透す = **tōshima⌐su** 通します・透します (lets through /in, admits; shows in; pierces, penetrates)

tō⌐sutā トースター toaster

tō⌐suto トースト toast

... totan ni ...とたん[途端]に (at) the instant/moment that ...

tōtei 到底・とうてい + NEGATIVE absolutely not

totemo とても very

tō⌐tō とうとう at last, finally; after all

totonoe 整え → **totonoema⌐su** 整えます

totonoema⌐su 整えます, **totono⌐e⌐ru** 整える regulates, adjusts; prepares

totonoe⌐nai 整えない = **totonoemase⌐n** 整えません

totono⌐i 整い → **totonoimase⌐n** 整いません

totonoima'su 整います, **totono'u** 整う is in order; is ready

totonowa'nai 整わない = **totonoimase'n** 整いません (is not ready)

tō'ta 問うた = **toima'shita** 問いました (inquired)

tō'te 問うて → **toima'su** 問います (inquires)

tō'te'mo 問うても even inquiring

totsuzen 突然 suddenly; ~ **no** 突然の sudden, abrupt

to'tta 取った = **torima'shita** 取りました (took)

totte 取って = **to'tte** 取って (taking) [*before verbs of movement*]

totte' 取っ手・把っ手 a handle

to'tte 取って → **torima'su** 取ります (takes) [*but* **totte** 取って *before verbs of movement*]; ... **ni** ~ ...にとって (with reference) to, for

totte ikima'su (iku) 取って行きます(行く) takes, brings it there

totte kima'su (ku'ru) 取って来ます(来る) brings it (here)

tottemo とっても terribly, extremely, completely

to'tte mo 取っても even taking

to'tte okima'su (oku) 取っておきます(おく) puts aside, reserves, holds

to'u 問う = **toima'su** 問います (inquire)

tōwaku 当惑 embarrassment, dilemma

towa'nai 問わない = **toimase'n** 問いません (not inquire)

to'ya 問や 1. = **to'e'ba** 問えば (if one inquire) 2. ~ **shinai** 問やしない = **toi'ya/wa shinai** 問いや/はしない = **towanai** 問わない (not inquire)

Tō'yō 東洋 the East, the Orient

... to yū (iu) ...とゆう(いう) which says; which is (called), called; which is (in effect)

To yū' [= **yuu'**] **no wa ...** とゆう[ゆう]のは... What that means (What that amounts to) is that ...

tōza 1. ~ **(no)** 当座(の) temporary 2. 当座 = **tōza-yo'kin** 当座預金 current deposit, checking account

to'zan 登山 mountain-climbing

toza'n-sha 登山者 mountain-climber

tōzen 当然 naturally; (~ **no** 当然の) proper, deserved

tsū 1. 通 an authority, an expert 2. ツー two

tsū'ā ツアー tour

tsu'ba つば・唾 spit, saliva

tsu'ba つば・鍔 sword-guard

tsubaki' つばき・唾 = **tsu'ba** つば・唾 spit

tsu'baki つばき・椿 camellia

tsubame つばめ・燕 swallow

tsu⌐basa 翼 wing ⌊(bird)

tsubo 1. つぼ・壺・壷 jar, crock
2. 坪 tsubo (6 sq. ft.)

tsubomarima͞su つぼまります,
tsubomaru つぼまる it
puckers up; gets puckered up,
is shut; it narrows

tsubome つぼめ → **tsubomeru**
つぼめる 1. [infinitive] 2. [im-
perative] **tsubome ro** つぼめろ,
tsubome͞ yo つぼめよ pucker
it!

tsubomema͞su つぼめます,
tsubomeru つぼめる puckers
it; shuts it; narrows it

tsubomi つぼみ・蕾 flower bud

tsubo-yaki つぼ焼き・壺[壷]焼
き turbo (**sa͞zae** さざえ・栄螺)
cooked in its shell

tsu⌐bu 粒 grain; drop

tsuburema͞su, tsubureru 1. 潰れ
ます, 潰れる it collapses/
smashes 2. つぶ⌊瞑⌋れます,
つぶ[瞑]れる can shut/close
one's eyes

tsuburima͞su つぶ[瞑]ります,
tsuburu つぶ[瞑]る: **me͞ o ~**
目をつぶ[瞑]ります shuts/
closes one's eyes

tsubushima͞su 潰します,
tsubusu 潰す smashes
(crushes, squeezes) it

tsuchi͞ 1. 土 earth, ground 2. 槌
hammer (= **ha͞mmā** ハンマー,
ha͞mma ハンマ)

tsūchi 通知 report, notice, notification

tsūchō 通帳 = **kayoi** 通い passbook, bankbook

tsu͞e 杖 cane, walking stick

tsuganai 注がない =
tsugimase͞n 注ぎません; etc,
(not pour it; not ...)

tsuge 1. つげ・柘植 boxwood
2. 告げ → **tsugema͞su** 告げま
す [infinitive]; [imperative]
tsuge ro 告げろ, **tsuge͞ yo** 告げ
よ tell it! 3. 注げ →
tsugima͞su 注ぎます [impera-
tive] pour it!

tsugema͞su, tsugeru 1. 告げます,
告げる tells, informs 2. 注げま
す/継げます/接げます, 注げ
る/継げる/接げる can pour/
inherit/join it

tsugenai 告げない・注げない =
tsugemase͞n 告げません; 注
げません/etc. (not tell; cannot
pour/...)

tsugi 継ぎ patch; (... **ni**) ~ **o**
atema͞su (...に)継ぎを当てま
す patches it

tsugi͞ 1. 次 (**o-tsu⌐gi** お次) next,
the following; (− **tsugi͞ no** 次
の) the next one 2. 注ぎ・継ぎ・
接ぎ → **tsugima͞su** 注ぎます・
継ぎます・接ぎます [infini-
tive]

tsugima͞su, tsugu 1. 注ぎます,
注ぐ pours it 2. 継ぎます, 継
ぐ inherits, succeeds to 3. 接ぎ

ます, 接ぐ joins it, grafts,
glues

tsugi-me 継ぎ目・接ぎ目 joint,
seam

tsugitashi-ko̅do 継ぎ足しコード
extension cord

tsugi̅-tsugi (ni) 次々（に）one
after another

tsugō (go-tsugō) 都合（ご都合）
circumstances, convenience,
opportunity; ～ **ga i̅i/waru̅i**
都合がいい/悪い (it is) conve-
nient/inconvenient

tsui 対 a pair; ～ **ni narima̅su
(na̅ru)** 対になります（なる）
become/make/form a pair

tsu̅i つい 1. unintentionally, inadvertently 2. just (now); ～
imashi̅gata つい今しがた just
now; ～ **saki-hodo** つい先程
just a little while ago

tsui-... つい... follow-up, sup-
plementary

tsuide 1. ついで・序で opportunity, occasion, convenience; **o-
tsuide no se̅tsu** おついでの節
= **o-tsuide no toki̅ ni** おつい
での時に at your convenience;
～ **ga arima̅su** ついで[序で]
があります has occasion to ...
2. 次いで order 3. 注いで・継
いで・接いで **tsugima̅su** 注
ぎます・継ぎます・接ぎます

tsu̅[ ]ide 次いで next, in succession, subsequently; **... ni** ～ ...
に次いで next after/to ... (in

importance)

... tsuide ...ついで・序で occasion; ～ **ni** ...ついでに on the
occasion of/that ... , incidentally to ... ; while ...

tsuide ni ついでに・序でに by the
way, incidentally

tsuihō 追放 purge

tsu̅in ツイン, **tsuin-ru̅mu** ツイ
ンルーム twin(-bed) room

tsuin-be̅ddo ツインベッド twin
beds ⌈all

tsu̅i-ni ついに・遂に at last; after

tsuiraku 墜落 plane crash;
tsuiraku shima̅su 墜落します
(a plane) crashes

tsui-shike̅n 追試験 makeup exam

tsuitachi̅ 一日・ついたち first
day of month

tsuite 突いて → **tsukima̅su** 突き
ます (stabs, ...)

tsu̅ite 1. ついて ... **ni** ～ **(no)** ...
について（の）about, concern-
ing 2. 付いて → **tsukima̅su** 付
きます (comes in contact; ...)
3. ～ **imase̅n** ついて[付いて]
いません is unlucky, fails to
strike it lucky

tsuji 辻 crossroads; road(side),
street

tsu̅-ji 通じ 1. (**o-tsu̅-ji** お通じ)
bowel movement; ～ **ga
tsukima̅su (tsuku̅)** 通じがつ
きます（つく）has a bowel
movement 2. effect 3. → **tsu̅-**

jima̍su 通じます [infinitive]
tsū-jima̍su 通じます, **-jiru** 通じ
る gets through, communi-
cates; transmits; connects,
runs; is understood; is well
versed in; one's bowels move;
(... o) tsū-jite (...を)通じて
through (the medium of)
tsūji¯n 通人 an expert, an
authority; a man of the world
tsūjō (no) 通常(の) usual, ordinary   ⌐hilt
tsuka¯ 1. 塚 mound 2. つか・柄
tsukae 使え 1. → **tsukaema̍su**
使えます [infinitive] 2. →
tsukaima̍su 使います [impe-
rative] use it!
tsuka¯e つかえ obstruction
tsukaeba 使えば → **tsukaima̍su**
使います (if one use it)
tsukaema̍su 使えます, **tsukaeru**
使える can use it; be useful
tsukaema̍su つかえ[支え]ます,
tsuka¯e¯ru つかえ[支え]る
gets clogged up, obstructed,
busy
tsukaenai 使えない =
tsukaemase¯n 使えません (cannot use it)
tsuka¯e¯nai つかえない =
tsukaemase¯n つかえ[支え]ま
せん (not get obstructed)
tsukaere¯ba 使えれば →
tsukaema̍su 使えます (if one
can use it)
tsukae¯reba つかえれば →

tsukaema̍su つかえ[支え]ま
す (if it is obstructed)
tsukaete 使えて → **tsukaema̍su**
使えます (can use it)
tsuka¯ete つかえて →
tsukaema̍su つかえ[支え]ま
す (gets obstructed)
tsukai 使い 1. message, errand
2. messenger 3. → **tsukaima̍su**
使います [infinitive]
tsukaima̍su 使います, **tsukau** 使
う uses; spends; employs;
handles
tsukamae 捕まえ →
tsukamaema̍su 捕まえます
1. [infinitive] 2. [imperative]
tsukamae ro 捕まえろ,
tsukamae¯ yo 捕まえよ catch!
tsukamaema̍su 捕まえます,
tsukamaeru 捕まえる catches,
seizes, arrests
tsukamaenai 捕まえない =
tsukamaemase¯n 捕まえませ
ん (not catch)
tsukama¯nai つかまない =
tsukamimase¯n つかみません
(not seize)
tsukamema̍su つかめます,
tsukame¯ru つかめる can scize
tsukame¯nai つかめない =
tsukamemase¯n つかめません
(cannot seize)
tsuka¯mete つかめて →
tsukamema̍su つかめます
(can seize)
tsukamima̍su つかみます,

tsuka⌐mu つかむ seizes, grasps, clutches

tsukamō⌐ つかもう = **tsukamimashō⌐** つかみましょう (let's seize it!)

tsukanai 突かない = **tsukimase⌐n** 突きません (not stab, …)

tsuka⌐nai 付かない = **tsukimase⌐n** 付きません (not come in contact, …)

tsuka⌐nde つかんで → **tsukamima⌐su** つかみます (seizes)

tsukaō 使おう = **tsukaimashō⌐** 使いましょう (let's use it!)

tsukarema⌐su 疲れます, **tsukare⌐ru** 疲れる gets tired

tsukatte 使って → **tsukaima⌐su** 使います (uses)

tsukau 使う = **tsukaima⌐su** 使います (uses)

tsukawanai 使わない = **tsukaimase⌐n** 使いません (not use)

tsuke 漬け・突け・付け → **tsukema⌐su** 漬けます・突けます・付けます **1.** [infinitive] **2.** 漬け [imperative] **tsuke ro** 漬けろ, **tsuke⌐ yo** 漬けよ soak it! **3.** 突け → **tsukima⌐su** 突きます [imperative] stab it!

tsuke⌐ 1. 付け bill, account; ~ **de kaima⌐su** 付けで買います buys it on credit **2.** 付け・着け → **tsukema⌐su** 付けます; 着

けます (attach; can arrive) [infinitive]; 付け [imperative] **tsuke⌐ ro/yo** 付けろ/よ attach it! **3.** 着け → **tsukima⌐su** 着きます [imperative] arrive!

tsuke⌐ba 突けば・付けば → **tsukima⌐su** (**1.** 突きます if one stab, … **2.** 付きます if it come in contact, …)

tsukema⌐su, tsukeru 1. 漬けます, 漬ける pickles; soaks **2.** 突け ます, 突ける can stab, thrust, poke, push

tsukema⌐su, tsuke⌐ru 1. 付けます, 付ける attaches, sticks on, adds **2.** つけます・点けます, つける・点ける turns on (lights) **3.** 着けます, 着ける puts on, wears **4.** 付けます, 付ける applies

tsuke-mono 漬物 pickles

tsukenai 漬けない・突けない = **tsukemase⌐n** 漬けません; 突 けません, etc. (not pickle/soak; cannot stab, …)

tsuke⌐nai 付けない = **tsukemase⌐n** 付けません, etc. (not attach, …)

tsukete 漬けて・突けて → **tsukema⌐su** 漬けます; 突けま す, etc. (pickles, soaks; can stab, …)

tsuke⌐te 付けて → **tsukema⌐su** 付 けます, etc. (attaches, …)

tsukeyō 漬けよう = **tsukemashō⌐** 漬けましょう

(let's pickle/soak it!)

tsukeyō 付けよう =
tsukemashō 付けましょう,
etc. (let's attach/ … it!)

tsuki 突き → **tsukima'su** 突きま
す (stabs) [infinitive]

tsuki[⌐] 着き → **tsukima'su** 着き
ます (comes to an end) [in-
finitive]

tsuki[⌐] 1. 月 moon; month 2. 付き
→ **tsukima'su** 付きます
(comes in contact, …) [in-
finitive]

…-tsuki (no) …付き(の) with (…
attached)

tsuki-ai 付き合い 1. (o-tsuki'ai
お付き合い) association,
social company, friendship
2. → **tsuki-aima'su** 付き合い
ます [infinitive]

tsuki-aima'su 付き合います, -a'u
付き合う associates (with), enjoys the company of (… to ~ …
と付き合います)

tsuki-atari 突き当たり 1. the end
of a street/corridor 2. →
tsuki-atarima'su 突き当たり
ます [infinitive]

tsuki-atarima'su 突き当たりま
す, -ata'ru 突き当たる runs in-
to; comes to the end of (a
street)

tsuki-dashima'su 突き出します,
-da'su 突き出す makes it pro-
trude, sticks it out

tsuki-dema'su 突き出ます,

-de'ru 突き出る protrudes,
sticks out

tsukima'su 突きます, **tsuku** 突く
stabs, thrusts, pokes, pushes

tsukima'su, tsuku[⌐] 1. 付きます,
付く comes in contact 2. 付き
ます, 付く sticks to; joins;
follows; touches 3. 着きます,
着く arrives 4. つきます・点き
ます, つく・点く burns, is
turned (on), is lit

tsukima'su 尽きます, **tsuki**[⌐]**ru**
尽きる comes to an end, runs
out

tsuki-mi[⌐] (o-tsukimi) 月見(お月
見) moon viewing

tsūkin 通勤 commuting to work;
~-ji'kan 通勤時間 commut-
ing time; ~ shima'su 通勤しま
す commutes to work

tsuki[⌐]**nai** 尽きない =
tsukimase'n 尽きません (not
come to an end)

tsuki[⌐]**ru** 尽きる = **tsukima'su**
尽きます (comes to an end)

tsuki-sa'shi 突き刺し → **tsuki-**
sashima'su 突き刺します

tsuki-sashima'su 突き刺します,
-sa'su 突き刺す stabs

tsu[⌐]**ki**[⌐]**te** 尽きて → **tsukima'su**
尽きます (comes to an end)

tsuki'yo 月夜 moonlight (night)

tsukiyō[⌐] 尽きよう →
tsukima'su 尽きます; ~ to
shima'su 尽きようとします is
about to come to an end

tsukō 付こう → **tsukima'su** 付きます; ~ **to shima'su** 付こうとします is about to come in contact, …

tsukō 突こう = **tsukimashō** 突きましょう (let's stab/poke/thrust!)

tsūkō 通行 passing, passage, transit; ~**-dome** 通行止め closed to traffic, No Passage; ~**-nin** 通行人 passer-by; ~ **shima'su** 通行します = **tōrima'su** 通ります passes (by/through)

Tsuku'ba つくば・筑波 Tsukuba; **Tsukuba-Da'igaku** 筑波大学 Tsukuba University

tsukuda-ni つくだに・佃煮 conserves boiled down from fish or seaweed

tsukue 机 desk

tsukura'nai 作らない = **tsukurimase'n** 作りません (not make it)

tsuku're 作れ 1. → **tsukurema'su** 作れます (can make) [infinitive] 2. → **tsukurima'su** 作ります (makes) [imperative] make it!

tsuku'reba 作れば → **tsukurima'su** 作ります (if one make it)

tsukurema'su 作れます, **tsukure'ru** 作れる can make it

tsukure'nai 作れない = **tsukuremase'n** 作れません (cannot make it)

tsukure'reba 作れれば → **tsukurema'su** 作れます (if one can make it)

tsuku'rete 作れて → **tsukurema'su** 作れます

tsukuri 1. 造り a structure, build 2. 作り makeup, toilette 3. 作り artistically arranged slices of raw fish

tsuku'ri 作り・造り → **tsukurima'su** 作ります・造ります [infinitive]

tsukurima'su 作ります・造ります, **tsuku'ru** 作る・造る makes, forms, creates, produces, grows, manufactures, prepares (fixes); builds; writes; **jikan o** ~ 時間を作ります makes (sets aside) time, sets up a time

tsukuro'e 繕え 1. → **tsukuroema'su** 繕えます (can mend it) [infinitive] 2. → **tsukuroima'su** 繕います [imperative] mend it!

tsukuro'eba 繕えば → **tsukuroima'su** 繕います (if one mend it)

tsukuroe'nai 繕えない = **tsukuroemase'n** 繕えません (cannot mend it)

tsukuroe'reba 繕えれば → **tsukuroema'su** 繕えます (if one can mend it)

tsukuro'i 繕い 1. mending,

repair **2.** → **tsukuroima'su** 繕
います [infinitive]
tsukuroima'su 繕います,
tsukuro'u 繕う mends, repairs
tsukuroo' 繕おう =
tsukuroimashō' 繕いましょう
(let's mend it!)
tsukurowa'nai 繕わない =
tsukuroimase'n 繕いません
(not mend)
tsukusa'nai 尽くさない =
tsukushimase'n 尽くしません
(not exhaust)
tsuku'se 尽くせ →
tsukushima'su 尽くします [im-
perative] exert yourself!
tsuku'seba 尽くせば →
tsukushima'su 尽くします (if
one exhaust)
tsukusema'su 尽くせます,
tsukuse'ru 尽くせる can exhaust
tsukuse'nai 尽くせない =
tsukusemase'n 尽くせません
(cannot exhaust)
tsukuse'reba 尽くせれば →
tsukusema'su 尽くせます (if
one can exhaust)
tsuku'sete 尽くせて →
tsukusema'su 尽くせます (can
exhaust)
tsuku'shi 尽くし →
tsukushima'su 尽くします (exhausts) [infinitive]
tsukushima'su 尽くします,
tsuku'su 尽くす exhausts, runs

out of; exerts oneself, strives
tsuku'shite 尽くして →
tsukushima'su 尽くします (exhausts)
tsukusō' 尽くそう =
tsukushimashō' 尽くしましょ
う (let's exert ourselves!)
tsuku'tta 作った =
tsukurima'shita 作りました
(made it)
tsuku'tte 作って → **tsukurima'su**
作ります (makes)
tsukya 突きゃ・付きゃ **1.** =
tsuke'ba 突けば; 付けば, etc.
(if one stab, …; if it come in
contact, …) **2.** ~ **shinai** 突
きゃしない = **tsuki' ya/wa**
shinai 突きや/はしない =
tsukanai 突かない, etc. (not
stab, …), = **tsuka'nai** 付かな
い, etc. (not come in contact,
…)
tsu'ma 妻 wife
tsuma' **1.** つま・褄 skirt **2.** つま
sashimi garnishings
tsumamanai 摘まない =
tsumamimase'n 摘みません
(not pinch)
tsumami 摘み・つまみ **1.** a knob;
a pinch **2.** つまみ ー **tsumami-**
mono 摘み物, **o-tsu'mami** お
つまみ・お摘み things to nib-
ble on while drinking **3.** →
tsumamima'su 摘みます [in-
finitive]
tsumamima'su 摘みます・つまみ
ます, **tsumamu** 摘む・つまむ

pinches, picks; summarizes

tsumanai 積まない・摘まない =
tsumimase⌐n 積みません; 摘
みません (not pile it up; not
gather/pluck)

tsuma⌐nnai つまんない =
tsumara⌐nai つまらない

tsumara⌐nai 1. つまらない
worthless, no good, boring,
trivial 2. 詰まらない =
tsumarimase⌐n 詰まりません
(is not clogged)

tsuma⌐ri 詰まり → **tsumarima⌐sụ**
詰まります [infinitive]

tsu⌐mari つまり after all; in
short; more or less

tsumarima⌐sụ 詰まります,
tsuma⌐ru 詰まる is clogged up,
choked; is stuck; is shortened;
is crammed

tsuma⌐ru tokoro つまるところ
= **tsu⌐mari** つまり

tsumasaki つま先・爪先 toe,
toetip(s)

tsumashi⌐i つましい・倹しい is
thrifty, frugal

tsuma⌐tte 詰まって →
tsumarima⌐sụ 詰まります

tsuma-yō⌐ji つまようじ・爪楊枝
toothpick

tsuma-zuite つまずいて・躓いて
→ **tsuma-zukima⌐sụ** つまずき
ます・躓きます

tsuma-zuka⌐nai つまずかない・
躓かない = **tsuma-zukimase⌐n**
つまずきません・躓きません

(not stumble)

tsuma-zukima⌐sụ つまずきます・
躓きます, **-zuku** つまずく・躓
く stumbles

tsume 1. 爪 claw, nail, hoof 2. 積
め・摘め → **tsumima⌐sụ** 積みま
す・摘みます [imperative] pile
it up!; pluck it!

tsu⌐me 積め・詰め → **tsumema⌐sụ**
積めます・詰めます 1. [infini-
tive] 2. [imperative] **tsume⌐ ro**
詰めろ, **tsume⌐ yo** 詰めよ stuff
it!

tsumeki⌐ri⌐ 爪切り nail clippers

tsumema⌐sụ, tsumeru 1. 積めま
す, 積める can pile it up 2. 摘
めます, 摘める can gather/
pluck it

tsumema⌐sụ, tsume⌐ru 1. 詰めま
す, 詰める stuffs, crams 2. 積
めます, 積める accumulates
3. 詰めます, 詰める cans

tsumenai 積めない・摘めない =
tsumemase⌐n 積めません; 摘
めません (cannot pile it up;
cannot gather/pluck it)

tsume⌐nai 詰めない・積めない・
詰めない = **tsumemase⌐n** 詰め
ません/積めません; 詰めま
せん (not stuff/cram/accu-
mulate; not can it)

tsume(ra)rema⌐sụ 詰め(ら)れま
す/積めれます/詰め(ら)
れます, **tsume(ra)re⌐ru** 詰め
(ら)れる/積め(ら)れる/詰め
(ら)れる can stuff/accumu-

late/can it

tsume(ra)re̠nai 詰め（ら）れない
= **tsume(ra)remase̠n** 詰め
（ら）れません/etc. (cannot
stuff/...)

tsumera̠rete 詰められて、
tsume̠rete 詰めれて →
tsume(ra)rema̠su 詰め（ら）れ
ます

tsumeru 積める・摘める =
tsumema̠su 積めます；摘めま
す (can pile it up; can gather/
pluck it)

tsume̠ru 詰める = **tsumema̠su**
詰めます, etc. (stuffs, ...)

tsumeta 積めた =
tsumema̠shita 積めました；
etc. (could pile it up; ...)

tsu̠meta 詰めた =
tsumema̠shita 詰めました,
etc. (stuffed, ...)

tsumetai 冷たい cold (to the
touch)   ⌈it

tsume-ta̠i 詰めたい wants to can

tsumete 積めて → **tsumema̠su**
積めます；etc. (can pile it up;
...)

tsu̠mete 詰めて → **tsumema̠su**
詰めます, etc. (stuff, ...)

tsume-ya̠suri 爪やすり nail file,
emery board

tsumeyo̠ 詰めよう =
tsumemasho̠ 詰めましょう
(let's stuff it!)

tsumi 積み → **tsumima̠su** 積み
ます [infinitive]

tsu̠mi 罪 crime, sin, guilt, fault

tsumi-(i)re つみれ・摘みれ（つみ
いれ・摘み入れ) fishballs (for
soup)

tsumima̠su, tsumu 1. 積みます，
積む piles it up, accumulates
it; deposits; loads **2.** 摘みます，
摘む gathers, plucks, clips,
picks

tsumi-ta̠i 積みたい wants to pile
it up (to accumulate it)

tsumitate□-kin 積立金 reserve
fund; = **tsumitate-cho̠kin** 積
立貯金 installment savings

tsumō 積もう・摘もう =
tsumimasho̠ 積みましょう；
摘みましょう (let's pile it up!;
let's pluck it!)

tsumori (o-tsumori) つもり（お
つもり) intention, plan, (what
one has in) mind, purpose, expectation

tsumu 積む・摘む = **tsumima̠su**
積みます・摘みます

tsumuji̠-kaze つむじ風・旋風
whirlwind

tsuna̠ 綱 rope, cord, cable

tsu̠na ツナ tuna(fish) *(canned)*

tsunagari つながり・繋がり
1. connection, relation **2.** →
tsunagarima̠su つながります
[infinitive]

tsunagarima̠su つながります・
繋がります, **tsunagaru** つなが
る・繋がる is connected,
linked

tsunagatte つながって → **tsunagaru** つながる; in a string (line, chain), in succession, in a row

tsunage つなげ 1. → **tsunagema̱su** つなげます [infinitive] 2. → **tsunagima̱su** つなぎます [imperative] link them!

tsunagema̱su つなげます・繫げます, **tsunageru** つなげる・繫げる can connect, link, tie

tsunagete つなげて → **tsunagema̱su** つなげます

tsunagi つなぎ・繫ぎ 1. a connection, a link 2. → **tsunagima̱su** つなぎます [infinitive]

tsunagima̱su つなぎます・繫ぎます, **tsunagu** つなぐ・繫ぐ connects, links, ties

tsunaide つないで → **tsunagima̱su** つなぎます

tsuna-sa̱ndo ツナサンド tunafish sandwich

tsunda 積んだ = **tsumima̱shita** 積みました (piled it up; …)

tsunde 積んで・摘んで → **tsumima̱su** 積みます・摘みます

tsu̱ne (no) 常(の) usual, ordinary

tsunerima̱su つねります, **tsune̱ru** つねる pinches

tsune̱zu̱ne つねづね・常々 all the time, usually

tsuno̱ 角 horn (of an animal)

tsū-pi̱isu ツーピース a two-piece woman's suit

tsura̱ 面・つら face

tsurai つらい・辛い painful, cruel, hard, trying

tsuranai 吊らない・釣らない → **tsurimase̱n** 吊りません; 釣りません (not hang it; not fish)

tsurara つらら・氷柱 icicle

tsure 1. **(o-tsure)** 連れ(お連れ) company, companion 2. 連れ・吊れ・釣れ → **tsurema̱su** 連れます・吊れます・釣れます [infinitive] 3. 吊れ・釣れ → **tsurima̱su** 吊ります・釣ります [imperative] hang it!; fish!

tsure̱ba 吊れば・釣れば → **tsurima̱su** 吊ります/釣ります (if one hang/fish)

tsurema̱su, tsureru 1. 連れます, 連れる brings along, is accompanied by (= brings one along) 2. 吊れます, 吊れる can hang it 3. 釣れます, 釣れる can fish

tsurenai 連れない・吊れない・釣れない = **tsuremase̱n** 連れません; 吊れません/ 釣れません (not bring along; cannot hang/fish)

tsurena̱i つれない coldhearted, cruel

tsurerarema̱su 連れられます, **tsurerareru** 連れられる: 1. (… ni) ～ (…に)連れられます gets brought along (by …)

2. = **tsurerema̱su̱** 連れれます, **tsurereru** 連れれる can bring one along

tsurere̱ba 連れれば・吊れれば・釣れれば → **tsurema̱su̱** 連れます; 吊れます/ 釣れます (if one bring along; if one can hang/fish)

tsurete 連れて・吊れて・釣れて → **tsurema̱su̱** 連れます・吊れます・釣れます

tsureyō 連れよう = **tsuremashō** 連れましょう (let's bring him along!)

tsuri 1. つり・釣り = **o-tsuri** おつり・お釣り, **tsuri⌐-sen** つり銭・釣り銭 (small) change **2.** 釣り fishing **3.** 釣り → **tsurima̱su̱** 釣ります [infinitive]

tsuriai 釣り合い・つりあい balance, equilibrium, symmetry

tsuriba⌐ri 釣り針 fishhook
tsurigane 吊り鐘 temple bell
tsuri-kawa 吊り革 strap (to hang on to)

tsurima̱su̱, tsuru 1. 吊ります, 吊る hangs it (by a line), suspends, strings up **2.** 釣ります, 釣る fishes

tsū̱ro 通路 passage(way), aisle, thoroughfare

tsuru 吊る・釣る = **tsurima̱su̱** 吊ります; 釣ります (hangs it; fishes)

tsuru⌐ 1. つる・蔓 vine **2.** つる・蔓 earpieces of a glasses frame **3.** つる・弦 string (of bow or violin) **4.** つる・鉉 handle

tsū̱ru 鶴 crane (bird)
tsurugi⌐ 剣・つるぎ sword
tsurya 吊りゃ・釣りゃ **1.** = **tsure̱ba** 吊れば; 釣れば (if one suspend it; if one fish) **2.** ~ **shinai** 吊りゃしない・釣りゃしない = **tsuri⌐ ya/wa shinai** 吊りや/はしない・釣りや/はしない = **tsuranai** 吊らない; 釣らない (not suspend it; not fish)

tsūshin 通信 correspondence; news; communications

Tsūshō-sangyō⌐-shō 通商産業省 Ministry of Trade and Industry

tsuta⌐ つた・蔦 ivy
tsutae⌐ (o-tsutae) 伝え（お伝え） message, report

tsuta⌐e 伝え → **tsutaema̱su̱** 伝えます **1.** [infinitive] **2.** [imperative] **tsuta⌐e⌐ro** 伝えろ, **tsuta̱e⌐ yo** 伝えよ transmit!

tsutaema̱su̱ 伝えます, **tsuta⌐e⌐ru** 伝える passes it on to someone else; reports, communicates; transmits; hands down

tsutae⌐nai 伝えない = **tsutaemase̱n** 伝えません (not transmit)

tsutae(ra)rema̱su̱ 伝え（ら）れま

す, **tsutae(ra)re**⌐**ru** 伝え（ら）
れる can transmit it

tsutae(ra)renai 伝え（ら）れない
= **tsutae(ra)remase**⌐**n** 伝え
（ら）れません (cannot trans-
mit it)

tsutaera⌐**rete** 伝えられて、
tsutae⌐**rete** 伝えれて →
tsutae(ra)rema⌐**su** 伝え（ら）れ
ます (can transmit it)

tsutaere⌐**ba** 伝えれば →
tsutaema⌐**su** 伝えます (if one
transmit it)

tsuta⌐**ete** 伝えて → **tsutaema**⌐**su**
伝えます

tsutawara⌐**nai** 伝わらない =
tsutawarimase⌐**n** 伝わりませ
ん (not get transmitted)

tsutawa⌐**re**⌐**ba** 伝われば →
tsutawarima⌐**su** 伝わります (if
it be transmitted)

tsutawa⌐**ri** 伝わり →
tsutawarima⌐**su** 伝わります [in-
finitive]

tsutawarima⌐**su** 伝わります,
tsutawa⌐**ru** 伝わる is passed
on; is reported, communi-
cated; is transmitted; is
handed down

tsutawa⌐**tte** 伝わって →
tsutawarima⌐**su** 伝わります

tsuto⌐ つと・苞 straw wrapping,
straw-wrapped package

tsutome⌐ (o-tsutome) **1.** 勤め（お
勤め) work(ing), job (post)
2. 務め（お務め) duty, role

tsuto⌐**me** 勤め・努め →
tsutomema⌐**su** 勤めます・努め
ます **1.** [infinitive] **2.** [impera-
tive] **tsutome**⌐ **ro** 勤めろ・努め
ろ, **tsuto**⌐**me yo** 勤めよ・努め
よ

tsutomema⌐**su, tsutome**⌐**ru 1.** 勤
めます, 勤める is employed,
works; works as; **ginkō**⌐**-in o**
～ 銀行員を勤め［務め］ます
works as a bank clerk **2.** 努め
ます, 努める exerts oneself,
strives, endeavors

tsutome-saki 勤め先 place of
employment, one's office

tsuto⌐**mete** 勤めて・努めて →
tsutomema⌐**su** 勤めます・努め
ます

tsutomeyō⌐ 努めよう =
tsutomemashō⌐ 努めましょう
(let's exert ourselves!)

tsutsu⌐ 筒 cylinder, pipe

...⌐**-tsu**⌐**tsu** ...つつ [literary] **1.** = ...
-na⌐**gara** ...ながら (while
doing) **2.** ～ **arima**⌐**su** ...つつ
あります is doing (= **...-te**
ima⌐**su** ...ています)

tsutsu⌐**ji** つつじ azalea

tsutsukima⌐**su** つつきます →
tsu(t)tsukima⌐**su** つ（っ）つきま
す

tsutsuma⌐**nai** 包まない =
tsutsumimase⌐**n** 包みません
(not wrap it up)

tsutsu⌐**me** 包め **1.** → **tsutsume-**
ma⌐**su** 包めます [infinitive]

2. → **tsutsumima͞su** 包みます [imperative] wrap it up!

tsutsu͞meba 包めば → **tsutsumima͞su** 包みます (if one wrap it up)

tsutsumema͞su 包めます, **tsutsume͞ru** 包める can wrap it up

tsutsume͞nai 包めない = **tsutsumemase͞n** 包めません (cannot wrap it up)

tsutsume͞reba 包めれば → **tsutsumema͞su** 包めます (if one can wrap it up)

tsutsu͞mete 包めて → **tsutsumema͞su** 包めます

tsutsumi͞ 1. 包み package, bundle 2. 堤 dike, embankment

tsutsu͞mi 包み → **tsutsumima͞su** 包みます [infinitive]

tsutsumima͞su 包みます, **tsutsu͞mu** 包む wraps it up

tsutsumo͞ 包もう = **tsutsumimasho͞** 包みましょう (let's wrap it up!)

tsutsu͞nde 包んで → **tsutsumima͞su** 包みます

tsutsushimi[1] 慎み・つつしみ prudence, discretion

tsutsushi͞mi 慎み・謹み → **tsutsushimima͞su** 慎みます・謹みます [infinitive]

tsutsushimimasu, tsutsushimu 1. 慎みます, 慎む be discreet, be careful; refrain from 2. 謹

みます, 謹む be humble, be reverent

tsutsushi͞nde 慎んで・謹んで → **tsutsushimima͞su** 慎みます・謹みます

tsutte 吊って・釣って → **tsurima͞su** 吊ります・釣ります

tsu(t)tsu͞ite つ(っ)ついて → **tsu(t)tsukima͞su** つ(っ)つきます

tsu(t)tsukima͞su つ(っ)つきます, **tsu(t)tsu͞ku** つ(っ)つく pecks at

tsuya つや・艶 gloss, shine

tsu͞yaku 通訳 interpreter; interpreting

tsuyo͞i 強い strong; brave; **tsu[¬]yosa** 強さ strength

tsuyu つゆ・梅雨 rainy season (in Japan)

tsu͞yu 1. 露 dew 2. つゆ・汁 (= **o-tsu͞yu** おつゆ・お汁) light (clear) soup

tsuzuite 続いて → **tsuzukima͞su** 続きます

tsuzukanai 続かない = **tsuzukimase͞n** 続きません (it does/will not continue)

tsuzuke 続け → **tsuzukema͞su** 続けます [infinitive]

tsuzukema͞su 続けます, **tsuzukeru** 続ける continues it, goes on (with it)

tsuzukenai 続けない = **tsuzukemase͞n** 続けません (does not continue it)

tsuzuke(ra)renai 続け（ら）れない = **tsuzuke(ra)remaseˉn** 続け（ら）れません (cannot continue it)

tsuzuke(ra)rete 続け（ら）れて = **tsuzuke(ra)remaˉsu** 続け（ら）れます

tsuzukete 続けて continuously, in succession, going on (to the next); → **tsuzukemaˉsu** 続けます

tsuzukeyō 続けよう = **tsuzukemashōˉ** 続けましょう (let's continue!)

tsuzuki 続き continuation, sequel, series

tsuzukimaˉsu 続きます, **tsuzuku** 続く it continues (will continue); adjoins

tsuzumarimaˉsu つづまります・約まります, **tsuzumaˉru** つづまる・約まる it shrinks, gets shortened

tsuzumaˉtte つづまって → **tsuzumarimaˉsu** つづまります

tsuzumemaˉsu つづめます・約めます, **tsuzumeˉru** つづめる・約める reduces, cuts down, summarizes

tsuzuˉmete つづめて → **tsuzumemaˉsu** つづめます

tsuzumiˉ 鼓・つづみ drum *(hourglass-shaped)*

tsuzuraˉnai 綴らない = **tsuzurimaseˉn** 綴りません (not spell/ … it)

tsuzure 綴れ 1. rags 2. hand-woven brocade

tsuzuˉre 綴れ 1. → **tsuzurema-ˉsu** 綴れます [infinitive] 2. → **tsuzurimaˉsu** 綴ります [imperative] spell/ … it!

tsuzuremaˉsu 綴れます・つづれます, **tsuzureˉru** 綴れる・つづれる can spell; can compose; can patch, bind, sew (together)

tsuzureˉnai 綴れない = **tsuzuremaseˉn** 綴れません (cannot spell/ … it)

tsuzuriˉ 綴り・つづり spelling; binding, bound (sewn) pages

tsuzuˉri 綴り → **tsuzurimaˉsu** 綴ります

tsuzurimaˉsu 綴ります・つづります, **tsuzuˉru** 綴る・つづる 1. spells 2. composes, writes 3. patches; binds; sews (together/up)

tsuzurōˉ 綴ろう = **tsuzurimashōˉ** 綴りましょう (let's spell/compose/bind it!)

tsuzuˉtte 綴って → **tsuzurimaˉsu** 綴ります

tu… → **tsu…**

ty… → **ch…**

— U —

u 鵜 cormorant *(fishing bird)*

ubaima⌐su 奪います, **uba⌐u** 奪う
seizes, robs, plunders

uba⌐tte 奪って → **ubaima⌐su** 奪
います

ubawa⌐nai 奪わない =
ubaimase⌐n 奪いません (not
seize)

u⌐cha 打ちゃ **1.** = **u⌐teba** 打てば
(if one hit) **2.** ~ **shinai** 打ちゃ
しない = **u⌐chi ya/wa shinai**
打ちや/はしない = **uta⌐nai** 打
たない (not hit)

uchi 内・家, ... **uchi⌐** ...うち
1. 内・家 (**o-uchi** お家) house,
home; family; ~ **no na⌐ka de/
ni** 家の中で/に indoors **2.** う
ち we/us; I/me **3.** ... **no uchi⌐**
(**de**) ...の内（で） inside;
among; (**shi**)-**nai uchi⌐ ni**（し）
ないうちに before it happens
(while it has not yet happened)

u⌐chi 打ち → **uchima⌐su** 打ちま
す [infinitive]

uchi- 打ち [VERB PREFIX]: hits
and, takes and

uchi-akema⌐su 打ち明けます,
-ake⌐ru 打ち明ける con-
fesses, frankly reveals

uchi-awase 打ち合わせ・打合せ
prior arrangement, appointment, consultation, meeting
(by appointment)

uchi-awasema⌐su 打ち合わせま
す, **-awase⌐ru** 打ち合わせる
prearranges, arranges (a meet-
ing/consultation)

uchi-bori 内堀 inner moat

uchi-gawa 内側 the inside

uchi-keshi 打ち消し denial; negation, negative

uchi-keshima⌐su 打ち消します,
-ke⌐su 打ち消す denies

uchiki (na) 内気（な）shy, timid

uchi⌐-ki⌐zu 打ち傷 bruise

uchi-koroshima⌐su 撃ち殺しま
す, **-koro⌐su** 撃ち殺す shoots
to death

uchima⌐su, u⌐tsu 1. 打ちます, 打
つ hits, strikes, hammers;
sends a telegram **2.** 撃ちます,
撃つ fires, shoots (a gun)

uchi⌐-mi⌐ 打ち身 bruise

uchiwa 内輪 **1.** the family circle;
the inside; ~ (**no**) 内輪（の）
private **2.** ~ (**na**) 内輪（な）
moderate, modest, conservative

uchi⌐wa うちわ・団扇 a flat fan

u⌐chū 宇宙 universe, (outer)
spacc

ude⌐ 腕 arm

ude-do¹kei 腕時計 wristwatch

ude¹-kubi 腕首 wrist

udema⁻e⁻ 腕前 prowess, skill, ability

ude-wa 腕輪 bracelet

u¹do うど・独活 Japanese celery

udon (o-u¹don) うどん（おうどん） Japanese wheat-flour noodles; ～-ya うどん屋 noodle shop

ue 上, ... **ue¹** ...上 above, upper; ... **no ue¹ (de/ni/no)** ...の上（で/に/の）on, on top of; (= **toshi-ue** 年上) older, oldest

ue 植え → **uema¹su** 植えます (plants) [infinitive]

u¹e 飢え → **uema¹su** 飢えます (starves) [infinitive]

ueki 植木 garden/potted plant; **ueki¹-bachi** 植木鉢 flowerpot; **ueki-ya** 植木屋 gardener

uema¹su 植えます, **ueru** 植える plants, grows

uema¹su 飢えます, **ue¹ru** 飢える starves (hungers)

uenai 植えない = **uemase¹n** 植えません (not plant)

ue¹nai 飢えない = **uemase¹n** 飢えません (not starve)

Ueno 上野 Ueno; **Ueno¹-Eki** 上野駅 Ueno Station; **Ueno-Kō¹en** 上野公園 Ueno Park

ue(ra)re 植え（ら）れ → **ue(ra)rema¹su** 植え（ら）れます [infinitive]

ue(ra)rema¹su 植え（ら）れます,

ue(ra)reru 植え（ら）れる can plant

uere¹ba 植えれば → **uema¹su** 植えます (if one plant)

ue¹reba 飢えれば → **uema¹su** 飢えます (if one starve)

ue¹rudan ウエルダン well-done (beef)

ueta 植えた = **uema¹shita** 植えました (planted)

u¹eta 飢えた = **uema¹shita** 飢えました (starved)

uē¹tā ウェーター waiter

uete 植えて → **uema¹su** 植えます (plants)

u¹ete 飢えて → **uema¹su** 飢えます (starves)

uē¹toresu ウエートレス waitress

ueyō 植えよう = **uemashō¹** 植えましょう (let's plant it!)

ugo¹ita 動いた = **ugokima¹shita** 動きました (it moved)

ugo¹ite 動いて → **ugokima¹su** 動きます (it moves)

ugoka¹nai 動かない = **ugokimase¹n** 動きません (not move)

ugokasa¹nai 動かさない = **ugokashimase¹n** 動かしません (not move it)

ugoka¹se 動かせ 1. → **ugokasema¹su** 動かせます [infinitive] 2. → **ugokashima¹su** 動かします [imperative] move it!

ugokasema¹su 動かせます,

ugokaseˈru 動かせる can move it

ugokaseˈnai 動かせない = **ugokasemaseˈn** 動かせません (cannot move it)

ugokaˈsete 動かせて → **ugokasemaˈsu** 動かせます (can move it)

ugokashimaˈsu 動かします, **ugokaˈsu** 動かす moves it

ugokaˈshite 動かして → **ugokashimaˈsu** 動かします (moves it)

ugoˈke 動け 1. → **ugokemaˈsu** 動けます [infinitive] 2. → **ugokimaˈsu** 動きます [imperative] move!

ugokemaˈsu 動けます, **ugokeˈru** 動ける it can move

ugokeˈnai 動けない = **ugokemaseˈn** 動けません (cannot move)

ugoˈkete 動けて → **ugokemaˈsu** 動けます (can move)

ugokiˈ 動き movement, motion; trend

ugoˈki 動き → **ugokimaˈsu** 動きます [infinitive]

ugokimaˈsu 動きます, **ugoˈku** 動く it moves

uguˈisu うぐいす・鴬・鶯 bush warbler

uiˈnku ウインク, **wiˈnku** ウィンク wink(ing); **uiˈnku shima(ˈ)su** ウインクします winks

uiˈsuˈkiˈi ウイスキー, **wiˈsukii** ウィスキー whisky

uita 浮いた = **ukimaˈshita** 浮きました (floated)

uite 浮いて → **ukimaˈsu** 浮きます (float)

uˈji 氏 clan, family; family name

ujiᴺ-gaᴺmi 氏神 tutelary deity (= guardian spirit)

ukabanai 浮かばない = **ukabimaseˈn** 浮かびません (not float)

ukabe 浮かべ 1. → **ukabemaˈsu** 浮かべます [infinitive]; [imperative] **ukabe ro** 浮かべろ, **ukabeˈ yo** 浮かべよ float it! 2. → **ukabimaˈsu** 浮かびます [imperative] float!

ukabeˈba 浮かべば → **ukabimaˈsu** 浮かびます (if it float)

ukabemaˈsu 浮かべます, **ukaberu** 浮かべる lets/makes it float, floats it; shows (a look); brings to mind

ukabenai 浮かべない = **ukabemaseˈn** 浮かべません (not float it)

ukabereˈba 浮かべれば → **ukabemaˈsu** 浮かべます (if one float it)

ukabete 浮かべて → **ukabemaˈsu** 浮かべます (floats it)

ukabimaˈsu 浮かびます, **ukabu** 浮かぶ floats

ukagae 1. 伺え・窺え →
ukagemásu 伺えます・窺え
ます [infinitive] **2.** 伺え →
ukagaimásu 伺います [im-
perative] visit!; ... !

ukagemásu, ukagaeru 1. 伺え
ます, 伺える can visit; can inquire **2.** 窺えます, 窺える can
watch for

ukagaenai 伺えない・窺えない
= **ukagemasén** 伺えません;
窺えません (cannot visit/in-
quire; cannot watch for)

ukagaete 伺えて・窺えて →
ukagemásu 伺えます・窺え
ます

ukagai 1. (o-ukagai) 伺い（お伺
い）visit; inquiry, consultation
2. 伺い・窺い → **ukagaimásu**
伺います・窺います [infini-
tive]

ukagaimásu, ukagau 1. 伺いま
す, 伺う [HUMBLE] I visit
(you); I inquire; I hear **2.** 窺い
ます・うかがいます, 窺う・う
かがう keeps a watchful eye
on (the situation); (**kikái o ～**
機会を窺い［うかがい］ます)
watches for (an opportunity)

ukagatte 伺って・窺って →
ukagaimásu 伺います・窺いま
す

ukagawanai 伺わない・窺わない
= **ukagaimasén** 伺いません;
窺いません (not visit/inquire;
not watch for)

ukai 迂回・う回 detour

u⌐kai 鵜飼い・う飼い cormo-
rant fishing

ukanai 浮かない = **ukimasén** 浮
きません (not float)

ukande 浮かんで → **ukabimásu**
浮かびます (floats)

uke 浮け **1.** → **ukemásu** 浮けま
す (can float) [infinitive] **2.** →
ukimásu 浮きます [impera-
tive] float!

u⌐ke 受け → **ukemásu** 受けます
(accepts) **1.** [infinitive] **2.** [im-
perative] **uke⌐ ro** 受けろ, **u⌐ke
yo** 受けよ accept it!

uke⌐ba 浮けば → **ukimásu** 浮き
ます (if one float)

ukemásu 浮けます, **ukeru** 浮け
る can float

ukemásu 受けます, **uke⌐ru** 受け
る accepts; receives; takes;
gets; suffers, incurs

ukenai 浮けない = **ukemasén**
浮けません (cannot float)

uke⌐nai 受けない = **ukemasén**
受けません (not accept)

ukeoe 請け負え **1.** → **ukeoemásu** 請け負えます (can
contract) [infinitive] **2.** →
ukeoimásu 請け負います [im-
perative] contract to do it!

ukeo⌐eba 請け負えば →
ukeoimásu 請け負います (if
one contract to do it)

ukeoemásu 請け負えます,
ukeoe⌐ru 請け負える can con-

tract to do it

ukeoe‾nai 請け負えない =
ukeoemase‾n 請け負えません
(cannot contract to do it)

ukeoe‾reba 請け負えれば →
ukeoema‾su 請け負えます (if
one can contract to do it)

ukeo‾ete 請け負えて →
ukeoema‾su 請け負えます
(can contract to do it)

ukeo□i 請負・請け負い, a contract (to undertake work)

ukeo‾i 請け負い → **ukeoima‾su**
請け負います [infinitive]

ukeoima‾su 請け負います,
ukeo‾u 請け負う contracts (to
undertake work)

ukeoi-nin 請負人 contractor

ukeoō‾ 請け負おう =
ukeoimashō‾ 請け負いましょ
う (let's contract to do it!)

ukeo‾tte 請け負って →
ukeoima‾su 請け負います

ukeowa‾nai 請け負わない =
ukeoimase‾n 請け負いません
(not contract to do it)

uke(ra)rema‾su 受け（ら）れます,
uke(ra)re‾ru 受け（ら）れる can
accept; can receive; …

uke(ra)re‾nai 受け（ら）れない =
uke(ra)remase‾n 受け（ら）れま
せん (cannot accept)

ukera‾rete 受けられて, **uke‾rete**
受けれれて → **uke(ra)rema‾su**
受け（ら）れます

ukere‾ba 浮ければ, **ukerya** 浮け

りゃ → **ukema‾su** 浮けます (if
one can float)

uke‾reba 受ければ, **uke‾rya** 受け
りゃ → **ukema‾su** 受けます (if
one accept)

ukeru 浮ける = **ukema‾su** 浮け
ます (can float)

uke‾ru 受ける = **ukema‾su** 受け
ます (accepts)

uketamawarima‾su 承ります,
uketamawa□ru 承る I [hum-
bly] hear/listen/consent

ukete 浮けて → **ukema‾su** 浮け
ます (can float)

u‾kete 受けて → **ukema‾su** 受け
ます (accepts)

uke-tora□nai 受け取らない =
uke-torimase‾n 受け取りませ
ん (not accept)

uke-to□re 受け取れ → **uke-
torema‾su** 受け取れます [in-
finitive]

uke-to□reba 受け取れば →
uke-torima‾su 受け取ります
(if one accept)

uke-torema‾su 受け取れます,
-tore□ru 受け取れる can ac-
cept/take

uke-tore□nai 受け取れない =
uke-toremase‾n 受け取れませ
ん (cannot accept)

uke-tore‾re‾ba 受け取れれば →
uke-torema‾su 受け取れます
(if one can accept)

uke-tori 受け取り・受取 receipt

uke-to□ri 受け取り → **uke-**

torima̍su 受け取ります [in-
finitive]
uke-torima̍su 受け取ります,
-to⌐ru 受け取る accepts,
receives, takes; takes it (=
understands it)
uke-torō⌐ 受け取ろう = **uke-
torimashō̍** 受け取りましょう
(let's accept it!)
uke-to⌐tte 受け取って → **uke-
torima̍su** 受け取ります
uke-tsuke 受付 acceptance; information desk; receptionist
uke-tsukema̍su 受け付けます,
-tsuke⌐ru 受け付ける ac-
cepts, receives
uke̍ ya shinai 浮けやしない =
uke̍ wa shinai 浮けはしない
= **ukenai** 浮けない (cannot
float)
u̍ke ya shinai 受けやしない =
u̍ke wa shinai 受けはしない
= **uke̍nai** 受けない (not accept)
ukeyō̍ 受けよう = **ukemashō̍**
受けましょう (let's accept it!)
uke̍-zara 受け皿 saucer (for cup)
ukima̍su 浮きます, **uku** 浮く
floats 「ly
ukka̍ri うっかり absentminded-
ukō 浮こう = **ukimashō̍** 浮きま
しょう (let's float!)
ukya 浮きゃ 1. = **uke̍ba** 浮けば
(if one float) 2. ~ **shinai** 浮き
ゃしない = **uki̍ ya/wa shinai**
浮きや/はしない = **ukanai** 浮

かない (not float)
uma̍/mma̍ 馬 horse
uma̍i/mma̍i 1. うまい・旨い tasty, delicious 2. うまい・上手い
skillful, good 3. うまい successful; profitable
u̍maku うまく skillfully, successfully; so as to be tasty
umanai/mmanai 産まない =
umimase̍n 産みません (not
bear)
uma̍nai/mma̍nai うまない・膿
まない = **umimase̍n** うみま
せん・膿みません (not fester)
umare/mmare 生まれ・産まれ
1. birth 2. → **umarema̍su** 生
まれます・産まれます [infini-
tive]
umarema̍su/mmarema̍su 生ま
れ[産まれ]ます, **umareru/
mmareru** 生まれ[産まれ]る is
born
umarima̍su/mmarima̍su 埋まり
ます, **umaru/mmaru** 埋まる
gets buried (= **uzumarima̍su**
うずまり[埋まり]ます)
ume/mme 1. 梅 Japanese apricot
("plum") 2. 埋め・産め →
umema̍su 埋めます・産めます
[infinitive] 3. 産め →
umima̍su 産みます (bear) [im-
perative]
ume̍ba/mme̍ba 産めば →
umima̍su 産みます (if one
bear)
u̍meba うめば・膿めば →

umima͞su うみます・膿みます
(if it fester)

ume-boshi/mme-boshi 梅干し
pickled plum/apricot

umeite/mme͞ite うめいて・呻い
て → umekima͞su うめきます
・呻きます   ⌈groan

umeki͞/mmeki͞ うめき・呻き a

umekima͞su/mmekima͞su うめ
きます・呻きます, ume͞ku/
mme͞ku うめく・呻く groans

umema͞su/mmema͞su, umeru/
mmeru 1. 埋めます, 埋める
(= uzumema͞s u うずめます・
埋めます) buries 2. 生め[産
め]ます, 生め[産め]る can
give birth to, can bear (a baby)

umenai/mmenai 埋めない・生め
[産め]ない = umemase͞n 埋
めません; 生め[産め]ません
(not bury; cannot bear)

umereba/mmere͞ba 埋めれば・生
め[産め]れば, umerya/
mmerya 埋めりゃ・生め[産
め]りゃ → umema͞su 埋めま
す; 生め[産め]ます (if one
bury, if one can bear)   ⌈wine

ume-shu/mme-shu 梅酒 apricot

umete/mmete 埋めて・生め[産
め]て → umema͞su 埋めます・
生め[産め]ます

umeyō/mmeyō 埋めよう =
umemashō͞ 埋めましょう
(let's bury it!)

umi 生み・産み 1. birth; ~ (no)
生み・産み(の) (by giving)

birth, natal 2. → umima͞su 生
みます・産みます (bears baby)
[infinitive]

umi͞ うみ・膿 pus

u͞mi 1. 海 sea 2. うみ・膿み →
umima͞su うみます・膿みます
(festers) [infinitive]

umibe 海辺 (sea)shore, seaside

umima͞su 生みます・産みます,
umu 生む・産む gives birth to,
bears

umima͞su うみます・膿みます,
u͞mu うむ・膿む festers

u͞mmei 運命 destiny; one's lot/
luck (in life)

umō/mmō 生もう・産もう =
umimashō͞ 生み[産み]ましょ
う (let's give birth!)

umpan 運搬 transport(ation)

umu 生む・産む = umima͞su 生
みます・産みます (gives birth)

u͞mu 1. 有無 existence (or nonexistence) 2. うむ・膿む =
umima͞su うみます・膿みます
(festers)

umya 生みゃ・産みゃ = ume͞ba
生めば・産めば (if one bear)

u͞mya うみゃ・膿みゃ = u͞meba
うめば・膿めば (if it fester)

umya shimase͞n (shinai) 生みゃ
[産みゃ]しません(しない) =
umi͞ ya/wa shimase͞n 生み[産
み]や/はしません =
umimase͞n 生みません・産み
ません (not bear)

u͞mya shimase͞n (shinai) うみゃ

[膿みゃ]しません(しない) =
u͞mi ya/wa shimase͞n うみ[膿
み]や/はしません =
umimase͞n うみません・膿み
ません (not fester)

u͞n 1. 運 fate, luck **2.** うん = **n**
ん yeah, yes

"un" うん = **n͞** ん

una-don うな丼 a bowl of rice
topped with broiled eel

unagashima͞su 促します,
unaga͞su 促す stimulates,
urges (on)

unagi (o-u͞na) うなぎ・鰻(おう
な) eel

una͞-jū うな重 broiled eel on rice
in a lacquered box

unari͞ 唸り・うなり a roar; a
growl; (= **umeki͞** うめき・呻
き) a groan

unarima͞su 唸ります・うなりま
す, **una͞ru** 唸る・うなる roars;
growls; (= **umekima͞su** うめ
きます・呻きます) groans

unazukima͞su うなずきます・頷
きます, **unazu͞ku** うなずく・
頷く nods   「tion.)

u͞nchin 運賃 fare (transporta-

unda 生んだ・産んだ =
umima͞shita 生みました・産み
ました (gave birth)

u͞nda うんだ・膿んだ =
umima͞shita うみました・膿み
ました (festered)

unde 生んで・産んで →
umima͞su 生みます・産みます

(gives birth)

u͞nde うんで・膿んで →
umima͞su うみます・膿みます
(festers)

undō 運動 **1.** movement **2.** exercise; sports; athletics; ~**-ba** 運
動場, ~**-jō** 運動場 athletic
field, gymnasium; ~**-ka** 運動
家 athlete; ~**-pa͞ntsu** 運動パ
ンツ gym pants

u͞nga 運河 canal

u͞n ga i͞i 運がいい lucky

u͞ni うに・雲丹 sea urchin (roe)

unsō 運送 transport(ation)

unsō-ya 運送屋 **1.** express/for-
warding agent **2.** = **hi̱kkoshi-
ya** 引っ越し屋 (house) mover

unten 運転 operation, operating,
running, working, driving; ~
shima͞su 運転します operates
(a vehicle), drives   「driver

unte͞n-shu 運転手 operator,

u͞nto うんと much, a good
deal, greatly

unubore ga tsuyo͞i うぬぼれが強
い vain, conceited

"un-un" うんうん = **n͞n** んん

u͞n-waruku 運悪く unluckily

u͞n-yoku 運良く luckily

uo 魚 fish

ura͞ 1. 裏 reverse (side), back; lining; what's behind it; the alley
2. 裏 sole (of foot/shoe) **3.** 浦
bay

ura͞bon うら[盂蘭]盆 = **(o-)
bo͞n** (お)盆 the Bon Festival

ura-dōri 裏通り back street, alley

ura-gi⌐ri 裏切り a double-cross, betrayal, treachery

ura-girima⌐su 裏切ります, **-gi⌐ru** 裏切る betrays, double-crosses

ura-guchi 裏口 back door

ura-ji 裏地 lining (material)

urami⌐ 恨み grudge, resentment, ill will

uramima⌐su 恨みます, **ura⌐mu** 恨む begrudges, resents; regrets

ura-mon 裏門 back gate

uranai 売らない = **urimase⌐n** 売りません (not sell)

urana⌐i 占い fortunetelling; (= **urana⌐i-sha** 占い者) fortune-teller

urayamashi⌐i 羨ましい・うらやましい enviable; envious

urayamima⌐su 羨みます・うらやみます, **uraya⌐mu** 羨む・うらやむ envies

ure 売れ 1. → **urema⌐su** 売れます [infinitive] 2. → **urima⌐su** 売ります [imperative] sell it!

ure⌐ba 売れば, **urya** 売りゃ → **urima⌐su** 売ります (if one sell)

ure-kuchi 売れ口 sales outlet

urema⌐su 売れます, **ureru** 売れる 1. it sells, is in demand; thrives; is popular 2. can sell

urenai 売れない = **uremase⌐n** 売れません (not sell; cannot sell)

urere⌐ba 売れれば, **urerya** 売れ

りゃ → **urema⌐su** 売れます (if it sell; if one can sell)

ureshi⌐i うれしい・嬉しい glad, delightful, pleasant, wonderful   「す

urete 売れて → **urema⌐su** 売れま

ure⌐ ya shinai 売れやしない → **ure⌐ wa shinai** 売れはしない = **urenai** 売れない (it doesn't sell; one can't sell)

uri 売り → **urima⌐su** 売ります [infinitive]

u⌐ri 瓜 melon

uri-ba 売り場 (shop) counter, stand; shop, store

uri-dashi 売り出し (special) sale

uri-kake 売り掛け credit sales

uri-kire 売り切れ sellout; sold out

uri-ki⌐re 売り切れ → **uri-kirema⌐su** 売り切れます [infinitive]

uri-kirema⌐su 売り切れます, **-kire⌐ru** 売り切れる sells out, runs out of

uriko 売り子 salesclerk (salesgirl/saleswoman/salesman); shopgirl; (**shimbun-u⌐riko** 新聞売り子) news vendor (newsboy/newsgirl)

urima⌐su 売ります, **uru** 売る sells

uri-mono 売り物 sales goods/item, (something) for sale

uri-te 売り手 seller

urō 売ろう = **urimashō** 売りま

しょう (let's sell!)

u⌐roko⌐ うろこ・鱗 scales (on a

u⌐ru ウール wool ⌐fish)

urū⌐-doshi うるう［閏］年 leap year

urume(-i⌐washi) うるめ（いわし）・潤目（鰯）large (and usually dried) sardine

urusa⌐i うるさい annoying, noisy

urushi うるし・漆 lacquer

urya 売りゃ 1. = **ure⌐ba** 売れば (if one sell) 2. ~ **shinai** 売りゃしない = **uri⌐ ya/wa shinai** 売りゃ/はしない = **uranai** 売らない (not sell)

usagi うさぎ・兎 rabbit, hare

ushi 牛 ox, oxen; cow, cattle

ushinai 失い → **ushinaima⌐su** 失います [infinitive]

ushinaima⌐su 失います, **ushinau** 失う loses

ushinatte 失って → **ushinaima⌐su** 失います

ushiro 後ろ behind; (in) back

u⌐so うそ・嘘 lie, fib, false(hood); **uso⌐-tsuki** うそつき・嘘つき liar

usu-cha (o-u⌐su) 薄茶（お薄）weak powdered tea

usui 薄い thin, pale, weak

uta⌐ (o-uta) 歌（お歌）song; poem

utaema⌐su 歌えます, **utaeru** 歌える can sing

utaenai 歌えない = **utaemase⌐n** 歌えません (cannot sing)

utagaema⌐su 疑えます, **utagaeru** 疑える can doubt

utagaenai 疑えない = **utagaemase⌐n** 疑えません (cannot doubt)

utagai 疑い 1. a doubt; ~ **na⌐ku** 疑いなく undoubtedly, doubtless 2. → **utagaima⌐su** 疑います [infinitive]

utagaima⌐su 疑います, **utagau** 疑う doubts

utagawanai 疑わない = **utagaimase⌐n** 疑いません (not doubt)

utai 1. 謡 (o-u⌐tai お謡) chanting a Noh libretto 2. 歌い → **utaima⌐su** 歌います [infinitive]

utaima⌐su, utau 1. 歌います, 歌う sings; recites, chants 2. うたい［謳い］ます, うたう・謳う expressly states; extols

uta⌐nai 打たない = **uchimase⌐n** 打ちません (not hit)

utaō 歌おう = **utaimashō⌐** 歌いましょう (let's sing!)

utawanai 歌わない = **utaimasen** 歌いません (not sing)

u⌐tcha 打っちゃ = **u⌐tte wa** 打っては (hitting)

u⌐te 打て 1. → **utema⌐su** 打てます [infinitive] 2. → **uchima⌐su** 打ちます [imperative] hit it!

u⌐teba 打てば, **u⌐cha** 打ちゃ →

uchima̖su 打ちます (if one hit)

utema̖su, ute̖ru 1. 打てます, 打てる can hit; can send (a telegram) **2.** 撃てます, 撃てる can shoot (a gun)

ute̖nai 打てない = **utemase̖n** 打てません (can't hit)

ute̖reba 打てれば, **ute̖rya** 打てりゃ → **utema̖su** 打てます (if one can hit)

uto̖ 打とう = **uchimashō** 打ちましょう (let's hit!)

uto̖i うとい・疎い: ... **ni ~** ...に疎い[うとい] out of touch with ... , not abreast of ... ; estranged from ...

u̖touto うとうと drowsing (off); **~ shima̖su** うとうとします drowses, dozes

u̖tsu 打つ = **uchima̖su** 打ちます (hits)

utsukushi̖i 美しい beautiful

utsumukema̖su うつむけます, **utsumuke̖ru** うつむける: **kao o ~** 顔をうつむけます turns one's face down

utsumukima̖su うつむきます, **utsumu̖ku** うつむく lowers one's eyes, looks down, hangs one's head

utsuri̖ 映り reflection, picture quality; (a becoming) match

utsu̖ri 移り・映り → **utsurima̖su** 移ります・映ります [infinitive]

utsurima̖su, utsu̖ru 1. 移ります, 移る it moves, shifts, changes; moves house/residence **2.** 映ります, 映る is reflected; can be seen (through); is becoming

utsuro (na) うつろ・虚ろ(な) hollow, empty, vacant; **~ na hyōjō o mi̖sete** うつろな表情を見せて with a blank look

utsu̖se 移せ = **utsushima̖su** 移します [imperative] move it!

utsu̖shi 移し・写し・映し → **utsushima̖su** 移します・写します・映します [infinitive]

utsushima̖su, utsu̖su̖ 1. 移します, 移す moves/transfers it **2.** うつします, うつる infects, gives another person a disease **3.** 写します, 写す copies; takes a picture of; projects a picture **4.** 映します, 映す reflects, mirrors

utsu̖shite 移して・写して・映して → **utsushima̖su** 移します・写します・映します

utsu̖tte 移って・映って → **utsurima̖su** 移ります・映ります

utsuwa 器 **1.** receptacle, utensil **2.** tool **3.** ability

utta 売った = **urima̖shita** 売りました (sold)

u̖tta 打った = **uchima̖shita** 打ちました (hit)

uttae 訴え complaint, lawsuit

uttaema̖su 訴えます,

utta⌐e⌐ru 訴える accuses, sues 「す (sell)

utte 売って → **urima̍su** 売りま

u̍tte 打って → **uchima̍su** 打ちます (hit)

uttetsuke (no) うってつけ(の) the most suitable; just right, just the ... , just the one/ticket

utto̍ri (to) うっとり(と) absorbed, fascinated; ~ **shima̍su** うっとりします is fascinated, spellbound

uttōshi̍i うっとうしい・鬱陶しい gloomy, dismal, dreary

uwabaki 上履き・上ばき slippers, indoor shoes

uwabe 上辺・うわべ surface; outer appearances

uwagaki 上書き address (written on envelope, etc.)

uwagi 上着 coat, jacket, blouse

uwagoto うわごと・うわ言 raving, delirium

uwaki 浮気 1. ~ **(na)** 浮気(な) fickle 2. ~ **o shima̍su** 浮気をします is unfaithful, has an (extramarital) affair

uwasa うわさ・噂 rumor, gossip

uyama⌐i 敬い reverence, respect

uyama̍i 敬い → **uyamaima̍su** 敬います [infinitive]

uyamaima̍su 敬います, **uyama̍u** 敬う reveres, respects

uyama̍tte 敬って → **uyamaima̍su** 敬います

u̍zu 渦, **uzu̍-maki** 渦巻き whirlpool

uzumarima̍su うずまります・埋まります, **uzumaru** うずまる・埋まる gets buried

uzumema̍su うずめます・埋めます, **uzumeru** うずめる・埋める buries

uzura うずら・鶉 quail

— W —

wa̍ 輪 circle; wheel; link; ring; loop

wa-... 和... Japanese

... wa ...は as for ... , speaking of ... , let's talk about (change the subject to) ... ; ... , guess what —; if it be (= **... de̍ wa** ... では = **... na̍ra** ...なら)

... wa! ...わ! (mostly female) indeed, you see

wabi (o-wabi) 詫び(お詫び) apology

wabi⌐ 1. わび・侘び a liking for simple things; simple (modest) tastes 2. わび・詫び → **wabima̍su** 詫びます [infinitive]

wabima̍su 詫びます, **wabiru** 詫びる apologize

wabi¹nai 詫びない ＝
  wabimase¹n 詫びません (not
  apologize)

wabishi¹i わびしい・侘しい
  miserable; lonely

wa¹bite 詫びて → **wabima¹su** 詫
  びます

wa⌐ʼ-dachi わだち・轍 rut

wadai 話題 topic of conversation,
  subject (of talk)

wa-dome¹ 輪止め brake

wa-ei 和英 Japanese-English;
  waei-ji¹ten 和英辞典 Japanese-
  English dictionary

wa-fuku 和服 Japanese clothes

wa¹-ga ... 我が・わが... my, our;
  ～ kuni 我が国・わが国 Japan

waga-ma¹ma¹ (na) わがまま(な)
  selfish

wa-ga¹shi 和菓子 Japanese
  cakes/sweets

wa-gomu 輪ゴム rubber band

wa¹in ワイン wine

wa¹ipā ワイパー windshield
  wiper　　　　　　　　　 ⌐graft

wa¹iro わいろ・賄賂 bribe(ry);

waisetsu わいせつ・猥褻 obscenity;
  ～ (na) わいせつ[猥褻](な)
  obscene

wai-shatsu ワイシャツ shirt

waita 沸いた・湧いた ＝
  wakima¹shita 沸きました; 湧
  きました (boiled; gushed)

waite 沸いて・湧いて →
  wakima¹su 沸きます・湧きま
  す

wa¹ka 和歌 31-syllable poem

waka¹i 若い young

waka¹me わかめ・若布 a kind of
  seaweed

waka-mono 若者 young person,
  youth

wakanai 沸かない・湧かない ＝
  wakimase¹n 沸きません; 湧き
  ません (not boil/gush)

wakara¹nai わからない・分から
  ない → **wakarimase¹n** わかり
  ません・分かりません (not
  understand)

wakare¹ 1. 別れ (**o-wakare** お別
  れ) parting, farewell **2.** 分かれ
  branch(ing), fork(ing), division

waka¹re 1. 別れ → **wakarema¹su**
  別れます [infinitive]; [imperative] **wakare¹ ro** 別れろ,
  waka¹re yo 別れよ part! **2.** 分
  かれ・分かれ → **wakarima¹su**
  わかります・分かります [imperative] understand!

wakarema¹su, wakare¹ru 1. 別れ
  ます, 別れる they part,
  separate **2.** 分かれます, 分か
  れる it branches off, splits

wakare¹nai 別れない →
  wakaremase¹n 別れません
  (not part)

wakari¹ わかり・分かり comprehension; **～ ga haya¹i** わかり
  [分かり]が早い quick-witted,
  ～ ga i¹i わかり[分かり]がい
  い intelligent; **～ ga waru¹i**

わかり［分かり］が悪い dull
(-witted), stupid

waka'ri わかり・分かり →
wakarima'su わかります・分か
ります [infinitive]

Wakarima'shita わかりました・
分かりました. 1. Yes, I see.
2. Yes, I will (comply with
your request).

wakarima'su わかります・分かり
ます, **waka'ru** わかる・分かる
it is clear (understood); understands; finds out; has good
sense; **da're ga(/ni) na'ni ga
wakarima'su ka** 誰が(/に)何
が分かりますか who under-
stands what?

wakari-yasu'i わかり［分かり］や
すい clear, easy to understand

wakashima'su 沸かします,
wakasu 沸かす boils it

wakate⌐¹ 若手 young person;
wakate-sa'kka 若手作家
young writer

waka'tta 分かった =
wakarima'shita 分かりました
(understood)

waka'tte 分かって →
wakarima'su 分かります; ～
ima'su 分かっています it is
understood, it is (now) clear

wa'ke 1. わけ・訳 reason 2. 訳
meaning 3. わけ case, cir-
cumstance 4. 分け →
wakema'su 分けます [infini-
tive]; [imperative] **wake' ro** 分

けろ, **wa'ke yo** 分けよ divide
it!

wake'ba 沸けば・湧けば →
wakima'su 沸きます; 湧きま
す (if it boil/gush)

wakema'su 分けます, **wake'ru** 分
ける divides (splits, distributes) it; separates them

wake-me' 分け目 dividing line,
part(ing) (in hair)

wa'ke mo arimase'n (na'i) 訳も
ありません(ない) is no prob-
lem, is a cinch; easy

wake'nai 分けない =
wakemase'n 分けません (not
divide it; not separate them)

wa'ke-nai 訳ない easy, simple,
ready; **-naku** 訳なく easily,
simply, readily

wakerarema'su 分けられます,
wakerare'ru 分けられる 1. it
gets divided; they get separated 2. = **wake(ra)rema'su** 分
け(ら)れます, **wake(ra)re'ru** 分
け(ら)れる can divide it

wakerare'reba 分けられれば →
wakerarema'su 分けられます
(if it get divided; if we can
divide it)

wakera'rete 分けられて →
wakerarema'su 分けられます
(it gets divided; can divide it)

wakere'nai 分けれない =
wakerare'nai 分けられない =
wake(ra)remase'n 分け(ら)れ
ません (cannot divide it)

wakere͡reba 分けれれば =
　wakerare͡reba 分けられれば
　→ **wake(ra)rema͡su** 分け（ら）
　れます (if we can divide it)

wake͡rete 分けれて =
　wakera͡rete 分けられて →
　wake(ra)rema͡su 分け（ら）れ
　ます (can divide it)

wa͡kete 分けて → **wakema͡su** 分
　けます (divides it; separates
　them)

wakeyo͡ 分けよう =
　wakemasho͡ 分けましょう
　(let's divide it!)

waki͡ わき・脇・腋 side (of the
　body); **waki-no͡-shita** わき［脇
　・腋］の下 armpit

waki 沸き・湧き → **wakima͡su** 沸
　きます・湧きます [infinitive]

waki⌐-ga わきが・腋臭 armpit
　smell, body odor

wakima͡su, waku 1. 沸きます,
　沸く it boils **2.** 湧きます, 湧
　く it gushes, springs forth

waku 沸く・湧く = **wakima͡su**
　沸きます・湧きます

waku͡ 枠 **1.** frame; crate **2.** reel

wa⌐kuchin ワクチン vaccine

wakya 沸きゃ・湧きゃ **1.** =
　wake͡ba 沸けば; 湧けば (if it
　boil; if it gush) **2. ~ shinai** 沸
　きゃしない・湧きゃしない =
　waki͡ ya/wa shinai 沸きや/は
　しない・湧きや/はしない =
　wakanai 沸かない; 湧かない
　(not boil; not gush)

wame͡ite わめいて・喚いて →
　wamekima͡su わめきます・喚
　きます

wamekima͡su わめきます・喚き
　ます, **wame͡ku** わめく・喚く
　yells

wa͡m-man ワンマン **1.** one-man,
　operator-only (bus) **2.** dictator

wampaku-kozo͡ 腕白小僧 brat

wampaku(-mono⌐) 腕白（者）
　mischievous child

wa⌐mpaku (na) 腕白・わんぱく
　（な）naughty, mischievous

wam-pi͡isu ワンピース (one-
　piece) dress

wan (o-wan) 碗（お碗）bowl

wa͡n 1. 湾 bay, gulf **2.** ワン one

wa͡na わな・罠 trap; lasso; **~ ni
　kakarima͡su (kaka͡ru)** わな
　［罠］にかかります（かかる）
　gets trapped/snared

wa͡ni わに・鰐 crocodile, alli-
　gator

wani͡-ashi (no) わに足・鰐足（の）
　bowlegged

wa͡nisu ワニス varnish

wan-ru͡mu ワンルーム one-
　room (studio) apartment

wa͡n-wan ワンワン bow-wow!

wappu 割賦 allotment, install-
　ment

wā-puro ワープロ word pro-
　cessor

wa͡ra わら・藁 rice straw

warae 笑え **1.** → **waraema͡su** 笑
　えます [infinitive] **2.** →

waraima'su 笑います [imperative] laugh!

warae'ba 笑えば → **waraima'su** 笑います (if one laugh)

waraema'su 笑えます, **waraeru** 笑える can laugh

waraenai 笑えない = **waraemase'n** 笑えません (cannot laugh)

warae'reba 笑えれば → **waraema'su** 笑えます (if one can laugh)

warai 笑い 1. a laugh, laughter 2. → **waraima'su** 笑います [infinitive]

waraima'su 笑います, **warau** 笑う laughs; laughs at

waranai 割らない = **warimase'n** 割りません (not break/divide/dilute it)

waraō 笑おう = **waraimashō'** 笑いましょう (let's laugh!; about to laugh)

warawanai 笑わない = **waraimase'n** 笑いません (not laugh)

waraware 笑われ → **warawarema'su** 笑われます [infinitive]

warawarema'su 笑われます, **warawareru** 笑われる gets laughed at

warawarenai 笑われない = **warawaremase'n** 笑われません (not get laughed at)

warawarere'ba 笑われれば →

warawarema'su 笑われます (if one gets laughed at)

warawarete 笑われて → **warawarema'su** 笑われます

waraya 笑や 1. = **warae'ba** 笑えば (if one laugh) 2. ~ **shinai** 笑やしない = **warai' ya/wa shinai** 笑いや/はしない = **warawanai** 笑わない (not laugh)

wa're 我 oneself; I/me

ware 割れ 1. → **warema'su** 割れます [infinitive] 2. → **warima'su** 割ります [imperative] divide it!

warema'su 割れます, **wareru** 割れる 1. it cracks, it splits 2. can divide/break/dilute it

ware-me 割れ目 crack, crevice, gap

warenai 割れない = **waremase'n** 割れません (not crack; cannot divide/break/dilute)

warete 割れて → **warema'su** 割れます

ware-ware 我々・われわれ we; us

wari 割 1. (...-wari ...割) tens of percent; percentage; **sa'n-wari** 三割 = **sanjip-pāse'nto** 三十パーセント・30% thirty percent 2. profit(ability); ~ **ni aimase'n (awa'nai)** 割に合いません（合わない）it doesn't pay (off); ~ **ga i'i** 割がいい profitable, ~ **ga waru'i** 割が悪い unprofitable

wariai 割合 rate, percentage; ~
  (ni) 割合(に) comparatively,
  relatively   ⌐ment
wariate 割り当て quota, allot-
wari-ba⌐shi 割りばし[箸]
  throwaway chopsticks
wari-biki 割引 discount
wari-kan 割り勘 splitting the
  bill; (going) Dutch treat
wari-mae 割り前 share, portion
warima⌐su 割ります, **waru** 割る
  divides/splits it, breaks it,
  dilutes it
wari ni わりに·割に = **wariai ni**
  割合に relatively, comparatively
warō 割ろう = **warimashō⌐** 割り
  ましょう (let's divide/break/
  dilute it!)
waru⌐i 悪い 1. bad, poor; wrong;
  vicious 2. at fault
waru⌐-kuchi/-guchi 悪口/口
  abuse, scolding, slander
wa⌐sabi わさび·山葵 horse-
  radish
washi 1. わし·鷲 eagle 2. わし
  (mostly male) I/me =
  wata(ku)shi わた(く)し·私
wa⌐shi 和紙 Japanese paper
Washi⌐nton ワシントン
  Washington
wa-shitsu 和室 Japanese-style
  room
wa-shoku 和食 Japanese food
wasure 忘れ → **wasurema⌐su** 忘
  れます 1. [infinitive] 2. [im-

perative] **wasure ro** 忘れろ,
  wasure⌐ yo 忘れよ forget it!
wasurema⌐su 忘れます,
  wasureru 忘れる forgets
wasure-mono 忘れ物 1. leaving
  something behind 2. a thing
  left behind (forgetfully)
wasurena⌐ide (… shite) kudasa⌐i
  忘れないで(…して)下さい
  don't forget (to do …)
wasure(ra)rema⌐su 忘れ(ら)れま
  す, **wasure(ra)reru** 忘れ(ら)れ
  る can forget
wasure(ra)renai 忘れ(ら)れない
  = **wasure(ra)remase⌐n** 忘れ
  (ら)れません (cannot forget)
wasure(ra)rere⌐ba 忘れ(ら)れれ
  ば → **wasure(ra)rema⌐su** 忘れ
  (ら)れます (if one can forget)
wasurere⌐ba 忘れれば →
  wasurema⌐su 忘れます (if one
  forget)
wasurerere⌐ba 忘れれれば =
  wasure(ra)rere⌐ba 忘れ(ら)れ
  れば (if one can forget)
wasureta 忘れた =
  wasurema⌐shita 忘れました
  (forgot)
wasurete 忘れて → **wasurema⌐su**
  忘れます
wasureyō 忘れよう =
  wasuremashō⌐ 忘れましょう
  (let's forget it!)
wata⌐ 1. 綿 cotton 2. 腸 = **hara-
  wa⌐ta⌐** 腸 guts, intestines
wata-i⌐re⌐ 綿入れ (cotton-)pad-

ded garment

watakushi わたくし・私, watashi わたし・私 I/me; watakushi̱-tachi わたくし[私]達, wata̱shi̱-ta̱chi わたし[私]達 we/us

watakushi̱-ritsu (no) 私立(の) private(ly established)

wataranai 渡らない = watarimase̱n 渡りません (not cross over)

watare 渡れ 1. → waterema̱su 渡れます [infinitive] 2. → watarima̱su 渡ります [imperative] cross over!

waterema̱su 渡れます, watareru 渡れる can cross over

watarenai 渡れない = wataremase̱n 渡れません cannot cross over

waterete 渡れて → waterema̱su 渡れます

watari 渡り 1. crossing, ferry (place); ~ o tsukema̱su (tsuke̱ru) 渡りをつけます(つける) forms an understanding with, gets in touch with; ~ ni fu̱ne 渡りに舟 a timely rescue, a convenient escape/excuse 2. → watarima̱su 渡ります [infinitive]

watarima̱su 渡ります, wataru 渡る crosses over

watarō 渡ろう = watarimashō̱ 渡りましょう (let's cross over!)

watasanai 渡さない = watashimase̱n 渡しません (not hand it over; not ferry)

watase 渡せ 1. → watasema̱su 渡せます [infinitive] 2. → watashima̱su 渡します [imperative] hand it over!

watase̱ba 渡せば → watashima̱su 渡します (if one hand it over; if one ferry)

watasema̱su 渡せます, wataseru 渡せる can hand it over; can ferry

watasenai 渡せない = watasemase̱n 渡せません (cannot hand it over; cannot ferry)

watasere̱ba 渡せれば → watasema̱su 渡せます (if one can hand it over; if one can ferry)

wata̱sete 渡せて → watasema̱su 渡せます

watashi 1. 私・わたし = watakushi 私・わたくし I/me 2. 渡し → watashima̱su 渡します [infinitive]

watashi-bu̱ne 渡し舟 ferryboat

watashima̱su 渡します, watasu 渡す hands it over; ferries

wata̱shi̱-ta̱chi わたし[私]達 we, us

watashite 渡して → watashima̱su 渡します

watasō 渡そう = watashimashō̱ 渡しましょう (let's hand it over!; let's ferry them!)

watasu 渡す → **watashima̅su** 渡
します
watatte 渡って → **watarima̅su**
渡ります
watta 割った = **warima̅shita** 割
りました (divided/ … it)
watte 割って → **warima̅su** 割り
waza 業 trick, feat   ⌊ます
wa̅za-to わざと, **wa̅zawaza** わざ
わざ deliberately, on purpose
wazawai 災い misfortune, mishap, disaster, calamity
wazurai 1. 煩い・わずらい trouble, worry; 患い (= **byōki** 病
気) illness **2.** 煩い・患い →
wazuraima̅su 煩います・患い

ます [infinitive]
wazuraima̅su, wazurau 1. 煩い
ます, 煩う worries about, is
troubled by **2.** 患います, 患う
(**me̅ o ∼** 目を患います) has
trouble with (one's eyes), suffers from (an ailment)
wazuratte 煩って・患って →
wazuraima̅su 煩います・
患います
wazurawanai 煩わない =
wazuraimase̅n 煩いません
(not worry …)
wazurawashi⌐i 煩わしい
troublesome; complicated
wi̅sukii ウィスキー whisky

— Y —

ya̅ 矢 arrow
... ya ... ...や... and … and …
(choosing typical items)
...ya ...や **1.** = **...i ya** ...いや = **...i
wa** ...いは **2.** = **...eba** ...えば
(if)
...-ya ...屋 shop, shopkeeper,
dealer; house
ya̅ やあ hi!, hello!
yaba̅i やばい dangerous (will get
you into trouble)
yaban (na) 野蛮(な) barbarous,
barbarian, savage; **∼-ji̅n** 野
蛮人 a barbarian, a savage
ya̅bo (na) 野暮(な) stupid,

rustic
yabu やぶ・薮 bush, thicket
yabu̅ite 破いて → **yabukima̅su**
破きます
yabuka̅nai 破かない =
yabukimase̅n 破きません (not
tear it)
yabu̅ke 破け **1.** → **yabukema̅su**
破けます [infinitive] **2.** →
yabukima̅su 破きます [imper-
ative] tear it!
yabukema̅su 破きます,
yabuke̅ru 破ける =
yaburema̅su 破れます
yabuke̅nai 破けない =

yabukemase꜒n 破けません (it does not tear)

yabu꜒kete 破けて → **yabukema꜒su** 破けます

yabu꜒ki 破き → **yabukima꜒su** 破きます [infinitive]

yabukima꜒su 破きます, **yabu꜒ku** 破く = **yaburima꜒su** 破ります

yabura꜒nai 破らない = **yaburimase꜒n** 破りません (not tear it)

yabu꜒re 破れ 1. → **yaburema꜒su** 破れます [infinitive] 2. → **yaburima꜒su** 破ります [imperative] tear it!

yaburema꜒su 破れます, **yabure꜒ru** 破れる 1. it tears, bursts; is frustrated 2. can tear/burst it

yabure꜒nai 破れない = **yaburemase꜒n** 破れません (it does not tear)

yabu꜒rete 破れて → **yaburema꜒su** 破れます

yaburima꜒su 破ります, **yabu꜒ru** 破る tears (bursts) it; frustrates; violates; defeats

yabu꜒tte 破って → **yaburima꜒su** 破ります

ya꜒-chin 家賃 house rent

ya꜒do (o-yado) 宿（お宿）, **yado-ya** 宿屋 inn

yaei 野営 camp, bivouac

ya▯gai 野外 out in the country, outdoors, in the field

yagate▯ やがて before long; in time

ya꜒gi やぎ・山羊 goat

ya꜒gu 夜具 bedclothes; top quilt

yaha꜒ri やはり also; either; after all

yaiba やいば・刃 blade; sword

yaite 焼いて → **yakima꜒su** 焼きます

ya꜒ji やじ・野次 heckling

yakamashi꜒i やかましい noisy, boisterous, clamorous; annoying; overly strict, demanding

yakan やかん teakettle

ya▯kan 夜間 (at) night

yakanai 焼かない = **yakimase꜒n** 焼きません (not burn it)

yake 焼け 1. → **yakema꜒su** 焼けます [infinitive] 2. → **yakima꜒su** 焼きます [imperative] burn/broil it!

ya꜒ke やけ・自棄 desperation; ～ **ni** やけに excessively, unbearably, terribly; ～ **ni na꜒tte** やけになって desperately, from (out of) despair

yake꜒ba 焼けば → **yakima꜒su** 焼きます (if one burn/broil it)

yakedo やけど・火傷 burn, scald (on the skin)

yakema꜒su 焼けます, **yakeru** 焼ける 1. it burns; it is baked 2. can burn it

yakenai 焼けない = **yakemase꜒n** 焼けません (it does not burn; cannot burn it)

yakete 焼けて → **yakema꜒su** 焼

けます

yaki 焼き **1.** baking, burning, broiling; tempering; exposure **2.** → **yakima͞sṳ** 焼きます [infinitive]

yaki-... 焼き... roast; **yaki⌐-guri** 焼き栗 roasted chestnuts; **(ishi-)yaki-imo** (石)焼き芋 (stone-)baked yam

...-yaki ...焼 (ceramic) ware from ... ; **Imari-yaki** 伊万里焼 Imari (ware), **Kutani-yaki** 九谷焼 Kutani (ware)

yaki-dō͞fu 焼き豆腐 broiled bean curd

yaki-gushi 焼き串 skewer, spit

yakima͞sṳ, yaku 1. 焼きます, 焼く burns/broils it, bakes (roasts, toasts) it **2.** 妬きます, 妬く is jealous

yaki-meshi 焼き飯 fried rice

yaki-mo͞chi⌐ やきもち・焼き餅 **1.** toasted rice-cake **2.** jealousy

yaki-mono 焼き物 **1.** pottery **2.** broiled food/dishes

yaki-niku 焼き肉・焼肉 grilled slices of meat

yaki-soba 焼きそば・やきそば chow mein

yaki-tori 焼き鳥・やきとり chicken shishkebab (skewers); ～-ya 焼き鳥屋 a *yakitori* shop/stand

ya⌐kkai (go-ya⌐kkai) 厄介・やっかい(ご厄介) trouble, bother; ～ **(na)** 厄介・やっかい(な) troublesome, annoying

yakko やっこ・奴 **1.** servant, slave; ～ **san** やっこ[奴]さん that guy, he/him **2.** = **yakko-dō͞fu** やっこ[奴]豆腐 (parboiled) bean-curd cubes

yakkyoku 薬局 pharmacy, drugstore

yaku 焼く = **yakima͞sṳ** 焼きま

yaku⌐ (o-yaku) 役(お役) **1.** office, post, duty **2.** part, role **3.** use, service

ya⌐ku ... 約... approximately, about ...

yaku-dachima͞sṳ 役立ちます, **-da⌐tsu** 役立つ serves a purpose, is useful

yaku-data⌐nai 役立たない = **yaku-dachimase⌐n** 役立ちません (not ...)

yakuhin 薬品 drugs; chemicals

yakume⌐ (o-yakume) 役目(お役目) duty, function

yakunin 役人 government official

yaku⌐ ni tachima͞sṳ (ta⌐tsu) 役に立ちます(立つ) serves a purpose, is useful

yaku⌐ ni tatema͞sṳ (tate⌐ru) 役に立てます(立てる) puts it to use

yakusa⌐nai 訳さない = **yakushimase⌐n** 訳しません (not translate)

yaku͞se 訳せ **1.** → **yakusema͞sṳ** 訳せます [infinitive] **2.** =

yakushima'su 訳します [imperative] translate!

yakusema'su 訳せます, yakuse'ru 訳せる can translate

yakuse'nai 訳せない = yakusemase'n 訳せません (cannot translate)

yaku'sete 訳せて → yakusema'su 訳せます

yakusha 役者 actor

yaku'shi 訳し → yakushima'su 訳します

yakushima'su 訳します, yaku'su 訳す translates

yaku'shite 訳して → yakushima'su 訳します

yakusho (o-yakusho) 役所(お役所) government office

yakusō' 訳そう = yakushimashō' 訳しましょう (let's translate!)

yakusoku (o-yakusoku) 約束(お約束) promise, agreement; appointment, engagement, date, commitment; ~-goto 約束事 a promise; yakusoku shima'su 約束します promises, agrees

yakuwa'ri' 役割 role, part; (cast of) players

ya'kuza やくざ 1. ~ (na) やくざ(な) no-good, worthless; coarse 2. gangster, hoodlum

yaku'zai 薬剤 pharmaceuticals, medicines

yakya 焼きゃ 1. = yake'ba 焼けば (if one burn/broil it) 2. ~

shinai 焼きゃしない = yaki' ya/wa shinai 焼きや/はしない = yakanai 焼かない (not burn)

yakyū 野球 baseball; ~-jō 野球場 ball park, (baseball) stadium

yama' 山 1. mountain; (~ no 山の) wild, uncultivated 2. heap, pile, bunch 3. climax 4. speculation, venture

yama-goya 山小屋 cabin, mountain lodge

yamanai やまない = yamimase'n やみません (not stop) 「climbing

yama-no'bori 山登り mountain-

yamashi'i やましい・疚しい ashamed of oneself; guilty-feeling

ya'ma-te' 山手, yama-no'-te 山手・山の手 uptown; the Ya'mato 大和 Japan 「bluff

yame やめ → yamema'su やめます 1. [infinitive] 2. [imperative] yame ro やめろ, yame' yo やめよ stop it!

yame'ba やめば → yamima'su やみます (if it stop)

yamema'su, yameru 1. やめ[止め]ます, やめ[止め]る stops it; abolishes, abstains from, gives up 2. 辞めます・やめます, 辞める・やめる resigns, quits

yamenai やめない =

yamemase'n やめません (not stop it)

yame(ra)rema'su やめ(ら)れます, **yame(ra)reru** やめ(ら)れる can stop it

yame(ra)renai やめ(ら)れない = **yame(ra)remase'n** やめ(ら)れません (cannot stop it)

yamere'ba やめれば, **yame'rya** やめりゃ → **yamema'su** やめます (if one stop it)

yamete やめて → **yamema'su** やめます

yameyō やめよう = **yamemashō'** やめましょう (let's stop it!)

yami やみ → **yamima'su** やみます [infinitive]

yami' 闇 1. darkness 2. disorder 3. black market 4. anything illicit, the dark

yami⁻i⁻chi 闇市, **yami-i'chiba** 闇市場 black market

yamima'su やみ[止み]ます, **yamu** や[止]む it stops

yamō やもう → **yamima'su** やみます (about to stop); ~ **to shita tokoro'** やもうとしたところ just as it was about to stop

yamome やもめ widow

ya'mori やもり・守宮 gecko

yamu やむ・止む = **yamima'su** やみ[止み]ます (it stops)

yamu-o-e'nai やむ[止む]を得ない unavoidable

yamya やみゃ 1. = **yame'ba** やめば (if it stop) 2. ~ **shinai** やみゃしない = **yami'** ya/wa **shinai** やみや/はしない = **yamanai** やまない (not stop)

yanagi 柳 willow

yanda やんだ = **yamima'shita** やみました (it stopped)

yande やんで → **yamima'su** やみます

ya'ne 屋根 roof

yani' やに・脂 resin, gum; → **me-yani'** 目やに・目脂

ya⁻nushi 家主 landlord

yaoya 八百屋 greengrocer, vegetable market

yappa'ri やっぱり, **yappa'shi** やっぱし also; either; after all; as I thought

yarakashima'su やらかします, **yaraka⁻su** やらかす does it [*demeans the object*]; **he'ma o** ~ へまをやらかします makes a damn mess of it

yaranai やらない = **yarimase'n** やりません (not give/ …)

yararema'su やられます, **yarareru** やられる gets had/ hit = beaten, outwitted, robbed, ripped off, beset (by illness), wounded, killed, …

yare やれ 1. → **yarema'su** やれます [infinitive] 2. → **yarima'su** やります [imperative] give/ … !

yarema'su やれます, **yareru** やれる 1. can give 2. can send

3. can do

yarenai やれない = **yaremase'n** やれません (cannot give/ ...)

yarete やれて → **yarema'su** やれます

yari 1. やり・槍 spear **2.** やり → **yarima'su** やります [infinitive]

yari-kata やり方 way, method, process, manner

yarima'su やり[遣り]ます, **yaru** やる・遣る **1.** gives **2.** sends **3.** does **4.** (**i'p-pai** ~ 一杯やります) has a drink **5.** has sex

yari-naoshima'su やり直します, **-nao'su** やり直す redoes it, does it over (again)

yari-sokonaima'su やり損ないます, **-sokona'u** やり損なう botches, misses

yarō やろう = **yarimashō'** やりましょう (let's give/send/do/ ... !)

yarō' 野郎 scoundrel, so-and-so

yaru やる = **yarima'su** やります (gives, etc.)

yarya やりゃ **1.** = **yare'ba** やれば (if one do) **2.** ~ **shinai** やりゃしない = **yari'ya/wa shinai** やりや/はしない = **yaranai** やらない (not do)

yasai (o-ya'sai) 野菜 (お野菜) vegetables

yasashii 優しい gentle; easy

yasashiku 優しく gently; politely

yase やせ・痩せ → **yasema'su** や

せます・痩せます (gets thin) [infinitive]

yasei (no) 野生 (の) wild, not cultivated

yasema'su やせます・痩せます, **yaseru** やせる・痩せる gets thin; **yasete ima'su** やせて[痩せて]います is thin

ya'shi やし・椰子 (coconut) palm

ya'shin 野心 ambition; treachery

yashinai 養い **1.** foster(ing) **2.** → **yashinaima'su** 養います [infinitive]

yashinaima'su 養います, **yashinau** 養う brings up, rears; fosters; nourishes

yashinatte 養って → **yashinaima'su** 養います

yashinawanai 養わない = **yashinaimase'n** 養いません (not rear)

...'-yasu ...安 cheap(er/lower) by ... ; **hyakue'n-yasu** 百円安 down/off ¥100

yasu'i 1. 安い cheap, low (-priced) **2.** やすい・易い (**shi-** ~ しやすい) easy (to do) **3.** やすい (**shi-** ~ しやすい) likely/apt to (do)

yasu'me 休め **1.** → **yasumema'su** 休めます [infinitive] **2.** → **yasumima'su** 休みます [imperative] rest!

yasu'meba 休めば → **yasumima'su** 休みます (if one rest)

yasumemásu 休めます,
yasuméru 休める **1.** rest/relax
it, let it rest; ease it **2.** can rest

yasuméreba 休めれば →
yasumemásu 休めます (if we
let it rest)

yasumeyṓ 休めよう =
yasumemashṓ 休めましょう
(let's let it rest!)

yasumí (o-yasumi) 休み(お休み)
rest, break, pause, time off, recess; vacation; holiday

yasu̇mi 休み → **yasumimásu** 休
みます [infinitive]

yasumimásu 休みます, **yasu̇mu**
休む rests, relaxes, takes time
off; stays away (from school);
goes to bed, sleeps

yasumṓ 休もう =
yasumimashṓ 休みましょう
(let's rest!)

yasu̇nde 休んで → **yasumimásu**
休みます

yasuri⌐ やすり file, rasp

yasurí-gami やすり紙 sandpaper
(= **kami-yásuri** 紙やすり)

yatara やたら: 〜 **na** やたらな indiscriminate, reckless, random; 〜 **ni** やたらに indis-
criminately, randomly, recklessly, blindly, unduly

yatóe 雇え **1.** → **yatoemásu** 雇
えます [infinitive] **2.** →
yatoimásu 雇います [impera-
tive] hire them!

yato̓eba 雇えば → **yatoimásu**

雇います (if one hire)

yatoe̓reba 雇えれば →
yatoemásu 雇えます (if one
can hire)

yatoe̓ru 雇える = **yatoemásu**
雇えます (can employ/hire)

yatói 雇い **1.** (**o-yatoi** お雇い)
employment **2.** → **yatoimásu**
雇います [infinitive]

yatoimásu 雇います, **yato̓u** 雇
う employs, hires　「います

yato̓tte 雇って → **yatoimásu** 雇

yato̓u 雇う = **yatoimásu** 雇い
ます (employs)

yatowa̓nai 雇わない = **yatoi-
mase̓n** 雇いません (not hire)

yatsú 八つ = **yattsú** 八つ
(eight)

ya̓tsu やつ・奴 **1.** guy, fellow,
wretch, (damn) person/one;
(damn) thing/one **2.** he/him

yatto やっと at last; barely, with
difficulty

yattoko やっとこ pincers, pliers

yattsú 八つ eight; eight years old

yawaraka̓i 軟らかい・柔らかい
soft, mild

ya̓ya やや a little, slightly; 〜
a̓tte ややあって after a little
while

yaya(k)koshī̓i やや(っ)こしい
complicated; puzzling; tangled

ye... → **e...**

yo⌐ **1.** 世 the world at large, the
public **2.** 代 the age, the times;
one's lifetime

yo' 夜 (= **yo'ru** 夜) night

yo-... 四 four

... yo ...よ **1.** indeed, mind you, I tell/warn/alert you **2.** (reinforces imperative)

yo' 要 (= **yo'shi** 要旨, **yōryō'** 要領) gist

yō' (**go-yō'**) 用 (ご用) **1.** (= **yōji** 用事) business; errand **2.** use, service **3.** going to the bathroom

yō-... 洋... Western, Occidental, American, European

yoake' 夜明け dawn

yo-bai 四倍 = **yom-bai** 四倍 (fourfold)

yo-bamme' (**no**) 四番目(の) fourth

yo-ban 四番 number four (*also* **yo'm-ban** 四番)

yobanai 呼ばない = **yobimase'n** 呼びません (not call/invite)

yobe 呼べ **1.** → **yobema'su** 呼べます [infinitive] **2.** → **yobima'su** 呼びます [imperative] call!

yobe'ba 呼べば → **yobima'su** 呼びます (if one call/invite)

yobema'su 呼べます, **yoberu** 呼べる **1.** can call **2.** can invite

yobenai 呼べない = **yobemase'n** 呼べません (cannot call/invite)

yobete 呼べて → **yobema'su** 呼べます

yobi 呼び → **yobima'su** 呼びま

す [infinitive]

yo'bi 予備 preparation; ～ (**no**) 予備(の) reserve, spare

yobi-kō 予備校 prep school

yobima'su 呼びます, **yobu** 呼ぶ **1.** calls; names; summons **2.** invites

yobi-se'nkyo 予備選挙 a primary election

yobi-tai 呼びたい wants to call/invite

yobi-tai 予備隊 reserve forces, reserves

yobō 呼ぼう = **yobimashō'** 呼びましょう (let's call/invite!)

yobō 予防 precaution, prevention; ～-**chū'sha** 予防注射 inoculation; ～ **shima'su** 予防します prevents, wards off

yobun (**no/ni**) 余分(の/に) extra, excess

yobya 呼びゃ **1.** = **yobe'ba** 呼べば (if one call/invite) **2.** ～ **shinai** 呼びゃしない = **yobi' ya/wa shinai** 呼びや/はしない = **yobanai** 呼ばない (not call/invite)

yo⌐chi 余地 room, space, margin, leeway

yōchi'-en 幼稚園 kindergarten

yo'do ヨード iodine

yo'eba 酔えば → **yoima'su** 酔います (if one get drunk)

yo'-en 四円 (*also* **yo'n-en** 四円) four yen

yo-fu̯ka'shi 夜更かし staying up

late; ～ **o shima'su** 夜更かし
をします stays up late
yō-fuku (o-yṓfuku) 洋服（お洋
服）Western-style clothes, a
suit, a dress; ～-**ya** 洋服屋
tailor, clothing shop
yō⁻gan 溶岩 lava
yō-ga'sa 洋傘 (Western-style) umbrella
yogen 予言 prediction; ～
shima'su 予言します predicts
yo'gi'sha 夜汽車 a night train
yōgi'-sha 容疑者 a suspect
... yōgo ...用語 term *(technical
word)*
yogore 汚れ 1. dirt, smudge,
blot, blotch 2. → **yogorema'su**
汚れます [infinitive]
yogorema'su 汚れます, **yogoreru**
汚れる gets soiled, smudged;
yogorete ima'su 汚れています
is dirty
yogorenai 汚れない =
yogoremase'n 汚れません (not
get soiled)
yogosanai 汚さない =
yogoshimase'n 汚しません
(not soil)
yogoshi 汚し → **yogoshima'su**
汚します [infinitive]
yogoshima'su 汚します, **yogosu**
汚す soils, dirties, stains
yō'gu 用具 tools, implements, in-
struments, kit; **yōgu-bu'kuro**
用具袋 kit bag; **yōgu⁻-bako**
用具箱 tool box

yohaku 余白 margin, blank
(space)
yōhin 1. 用品 = **...-yō'hin** ...用
品 utensils, appliances, supplies 2. 洋品 haberdashery
yohō 予報 forecast, prediction
yohodo よほど・余程 considerably, a good deal
yoi 1. 宵 evening 2. 酔い intoxication; motion sickness
yo'i 1. 良い・よい = **i'i** いい good
2. 酔い → **yoima'su** 酔います
[infinitive]
yō'i 用意 preparation; caution; ...
no yō'i o shima'su ...の用意を
します prepares ...
yōiku 養育 bringing up, education
yoima'su 酔います, **yo'u** 酔う
gets drunk; gets seasick, carsick, airsick
yo'-ji 四時 four o'clock
yōji 1. 用事 business, errand
2. 楊枝 (= **tsuma-yō'ji** つまよ
うじ・爪楊枝) toothpick
yō'ji 幼児 infant
yōjim-buka'i 用心深い cautious,
careful
yō'jin 用心 precaution, caution,
care
yō'jo 養女 adopted daughter; (...
o) ～ **ni shima'su** (...を)養女
にします adopts (a girl)
yojṓ-han 四畳半 four-and-a-
half mat area, a small
Japanese room

yōka 八日 eight days; 8th day (of month)

yokan 予感 premonition, foreboding

yōkan 洋館 Western-style building

yōˈkan ようかん・洋羹 sweet bars of bean paste and agar-agar flavored with chestnut, plum, etc.

yoˈke よけ・避け → **yokemaˈsu** よけます・避けます [infinitive]

yokei (na) 余計(な) superfluous, unnecessary, uncalled-for; ～ **ni** 余計に unnecessarily

yokemaˈsu よけます・避けます, **yokeˈru** よける・避ける avoids, keeps away from

yokeˈnai よけない・避けない = **yokemaseˈn** よけません・避けません (not avoid)

yokeyoˈ よけよう・避けよう = **yokemashoˈ** よけましょう・避けましょう (let's avoid!)

yōˈki 容器 container, receptacle

yokin 預金 deposit (of money); ～**-koˈza** 預金口座 bank account; ～**-tsuˈchō** 預金通帳 bankbook; ～ **shimaˈsu** 預金します deposits (money)

yōki (na) 陽気(な) cheerful, bright, lively

yokka 四日 four days; 4th day (of month)

yoko 横 side; the width; sideways, sidewise

yokochō 横町 sidestreet, alley

yoko-girimaˈsu 横切ります, **-giˈru** 横切る crosses, cuts across, intersects

Yokohama 横浜 Yokohama; **Yokahamaˈ-Eki** 横浜駅 Yokohama Station; **Yokohamaˈ-kō** 横浜港 the port of Yokohama

yoko-ito 横糸 woof (horizontal threads)

yokoshimaˈsu よこします・寄越します, **yokoˈsu** よこす・寄越す sends (here), hands over to me

Yoˈ koso. ようこそ Welcome!

yokozuna 横綱 grand champion sumo wrestler

yokuˈ 欲 greed

yoˈku 良く・よく 1. well; better 2. lots, much 3. lots, often

yoˈku(-) ... 翌... the next (day, night, month, year; DATE)

yokubaˈri 1. ～ **(na)** 欲張り(な) greedy 2. 欲張り a greedy person

yokubaˈri 欲張り → **yokubarimaˈsu** 欲張ります [infinitive]

yokubarimaˈsu 欲張ります, **yokubaˈru** 欲張る is greedy

Yoˈku irasshaimaˈshita. よくいらっしゃいました. Welcome!

yokujō 浴場 bathroom; public bath

yokusō 浴槽 bathtub

yōkyū 要求 requirement, demand, claim, request

yō-ma 洋間 Western-style room

yo-mai 四枚 = **yo'm-mai** 四枚

yo-ma'wari 夜回り night watchman

yom-bai 四倍, **yo-bai** 四倍 fourfold, four times (doubled)

yom-bamme' 四番目 = **yo-bamme'** 四番目 (fourth)

yo'm-ban 四番 = **yo-ban** 四番 (number four)

yome (o-yome) 嫁（お嫁）bride

yo'meba 読めば → **yomima'su** 読みます (if one read)

yomima'su 読みます, **yo'mu** 読む reads

yo'm-mai 四枚 four flat things (*also* **yo-mai** 四枚)

yom-ma'n 四万・40,000 forty thousand

yōmo 羊毛 wool

yo'm-pun 四分 four minutes (*also* **yo'n-fun** 四分)

yōmu'-in 用務員 custodian, janitor, servant

yo'mya 読みゃ 1. = **yo'meba** 読めば (if one read) 2. ~ **shinai** 読みゃしない = **yoma'nai** 読まない (not read)

yo'n 四・4 four

... **yō'** (na) ...よう［様］(な) seem(ing) to be; ~ **ni** ...よう［様］に (so as to be) like ... ; **suru** ~ **ni iima'su** するよう

［様］に言います tells one to do it

yonaka' 夜中 middle of the night

yo'n-dai 四台 four (machines, vehicles)

yo'n-do 四度 four degrees

yo'n-do' 四度 four times

yondokoro-na'i よんどころない inevitable

yondo-me' 四度目 the fourth time

yo-nen 四年 the year 4; (= **yone'n-kan** 四年間) four years; **yone'n-sei** 四年生 fourth-year student, senior

yo'n-en 四円 = **yo'-en** 四円 four yen

yo'n-fun 四分 = **yo'm-pun** 四分 four minutes

yo'n-hai 四杯 four cupfuls

yo'n-he'n 四遍 four times

yo'n-hiki 四匹 four animals/ fish/bugs

yo'n-hon 四本 four long objects

yo'n-hyaku 四百・400 four hundred

yōniku 羊肉 lamb (*meat, includes mutton*)

yo-ni'n 四人 four people

yo'n-jū 四十・40 forty

yon-ka'getsu 四か月 four months

yon-kai 四階 four floors/stories; fourth floor

yo'n-ka'i 四回 four times; **yonkai-me'** 四回目 the fourth

time

...-yō (no) ...用(の) for the use of ...

yo-no'-naka 世の中 the world at large, society

yo'n-satsu 四冊 four books

yon-se'n 四千・4,000 four thousand

yo'n-wa 四羽 four birds (= **shi'-wa** 四羽)

yopparaima'su 酔っ払います, **yopparau** 酔っ払う gets drunk

yoppodo よっぽど = **yohodo** よほど・余程 considerably, a good deal

yoranai 寄らない・よら[拠ら]ない = **yorimase'n** 寄りません; より[拠り]ません (not drop in; not rely)

yora'nai よらない・撚らない = **yorimase'n** よりません・撚りません (not twist)

yore 寄れ 1. → **yorema'su** 寄れます (can drop in) [infinitive] 2. → **yorima'su** 寄ります・よります [imperative] **yore** 寄れ drop in!

yo're よれ・撚れ 1. → **yorema'su** よれます・撚れます (can twist) [infinitive] 2. → **yorima'su** よります・撚ります [imperative] twist it!

yore'ba よれ[拠れ]ば・寄れば → **yorima'su** よります・拠ります; 寄ります (if one rely; if one drop in)

yo'reba よれば・撚れば → **yorima'su** よります・撚ります (if one twist)

yorema'su 寄れます, **yoreru** 寄れる can drop in; can approach

yorema'su よれます・撚れます, **yore'ru** よれる・撚れる can twist/twine

yorenai 寄れない = **yoremase'n** 寄れません (cannot drop in)

yore'nai よれない・撚れない = **yoremase'n** よれません・撚れません (cannot twist)

yorere'ba 寄れれば → **yorema'su** 寄れます (if one can drop in)

yore'reba よれれば・撚れれば → **yorema'su** よれます・撚れます (if one can twist)

yorete 寄れて → **yorema'su** 寄れます (can drop in)

yo'rete よれて・撚れて → **yorema'su** よれます・撚れます (can twist)

yori 寄り・より[拠り] → **yorima'su** 寄ります; より[拠り]ます (drops in; relies) [infinitive]

yo'ri より・撚り → **yorima'su** よります・撚ります (twists) [infinitive]

yori-... より... (+ ADJECTIVE) more ... , ...-er [bookish]

... yo'ri ...より (more/rather/other) than ...

yorigo'nomi より好み・選り好み choosiness; ~ **o shima'su** より好みをします is choosy

yorima'su, yoru 1. 寄ります, 寄る drops in; approaches, comes near; meets **2.** より[拠り]ます, よる・拠る relies on; ... **ni yotte** ...によって, ... **ni yoru to** ...によると, ... **ni yore'ba** ...によれば according to ...

yorima'su よります・撚ります, **yo'ru** よる・撚る twists, twines

yorō 寄ろう = **yorimashō'** 寄りましょう (let's drop in!; let's approach!)

yorō' よろう・撚ろう = **yorimashō'** よりましょう・撚りましょう (let's twist it!)

yoroi[¹]-do よろい戸・鎧戸 shutter *(house)*

yoroko[¹]bi[¹] 喜び **1.** joy **2.** → **yorokobima'su** 喜びます [infinitive]

yorokobima'su 喜びます, **yoroko'bu** 喜ぶ is glad, happy, delighted; rejoices

yoroko'nde 喜んで → **yorokobima'su** 喜びます; gladly

yoro-meki[¹] よろめき an (extramarital) affair

yoro-mekima'su よろめきます, **-me'ku** よろめく totters, falters, staggers; has an (extramarital) affair

yo'ron 世論 public opinion

Yōro'ppa ヨーロッパ Europe

yoroshii よろしい・宜しい very well; satisfactory

yoroshika'ttara よろしかったら if you don't mind; if you like

yoroshiku よろしく・宜しく **1. (** ... **ni) ~ (itte kudasa'i, o-tsutae kudasa'i)** (...に)よろしく(言って下さい, お伝え下さい) Give my regards to ... **2.** → **yoroshii** よろしい・宜しい **Dō'zo yoroshiku.** どうぞよろしく. **1.** How do you do? **2.** Please favor [my request, me, mine].

yo'royoro (to) よろよろ(と) tottering, faltering, staggering; having an affair; ~ **shima'su** よろよろします = **yoro-mekima'su** よろめきます

yoru 寄る・よる[拠る] = **yorima'su** 寄ります; より[拠り]ます (drops in; relies); ... **ni ~ to** ...によると according to ...

yo'ru 1. 夜 night **2.** よる・撚る = **yorima'su** より[撚り]ます (twists)

yorya よ[拠]りゃ・寄りゃ **1.** = **yore'ba** よれ[拠れ]ば; 寄れば (if one rely; if one drop in) **2.** ~ **shinai** よ[拠]りゃしない・寄りゃしない = **yori' ya/wa shinai** よ[拠]りや/はしない・寄りや/はしない = **yoranai**

よら［拠ら］ない; 寄らない
(not rely; not drop in)

yo̅rya よりゃ・撚りゃ **1.** =
yo̅reba よれば・撚れば (if one
twist it) **2.** ~ **shinai** よりゃ［撚
りゃ］しない = **yo̅ri ya/wa
shinai** より［撚り］や/はしな
い = **yora̅nai** よらない・撚ら
ない (not twist)

yo̅ryo̅ 要領 gist; knack

yo̅sai 洋裁 dressmaking; **yo̅sa̅i-
shi** 洋裁師 dressmaker

yosan 予算 budget

yo̅san 養蚕 raising silkworms,
silk farming, sericulture

yose 1. 寄席 vaudeville (theater)
2. 寄せ → **yosema̅su** 寄せま
す [infinitive]; [imperative]
yose ro 寄せろ, **yose̅ yo** 寄せ
よ let them approach!

yo̅se よせ **1.** → **yosema̅su** よせ
ます (can stop it) [infinitive]
2. → **yoshima̅su** よします
[imperative] stop doing it!

yo̅seba よせば → **yoshima̅su** よ
します (if they stop doing it)

yosema̅su 寄せます, **yoseru** 寄
せる **1.** lets approach, brings
near **2.** collects, gathers
3. adds **4.** sends

yosema̅su よせます, **yose̅ru** よ
せる can stop doing it

yose-nabe 寄せ鍋 chowder

yosenai 寄せない = **yosemase̅n**
寄せません (not let approach;
…)

yose̅nai よせない = **yosemase̅n**
よせません (cannot stop do-
ing it)

yose-nami 寄せ波 surf

yosere̅ba 寄せれば, **yoserya** 寄
せりゃ → **yosema̅su** 寄せます
(if we let them approach; …)

yose̅reba よせれば, **yose̅rya** よ
せりゃ → **yosema̅su** よせます
(if they can stop doing it)

yosete 寄せて → **yosema̅su** 寄せ
ます (lets approach; …)

yo̅sete よせて → **yosema̅su** よ
せます (can stop doing it)

yo̅shi 1. 由 reason; meaning; circumstance; means **2.** よし →
yoshima̅su よします [infini-
tive]

Yo̅shi! よし! OK; very well

yo̅shi 1. 洋紙 (yo̅-shi 洋紙)
Western paper **2.** 養子
adopted son; (… **o**) **yo̅shi ni
shima̅su** (…を)養子にします
adopts (as a son)

yo̅⁽ⁿ⁾shi 用紙 forms, blanks,
papers

yo̅shi 要旨 summary, abstract
(*gist*)

yoshima̅su よします, **yo̅su** よす
stops doing it (= **yamema̅su**
やめます)

yo̅-shima̅su 要します, **-su̅ru** 要
する needs, requires, takes,
costs; summarizes, sums it up

yo̅-shoku 洋食 foreign (Western)
food

yōshoku-shi'nju 養殖真珠 cultured pearls

yoshū 予習 preparatory study; ~ **shima'su** 予習します prepares, studies (ahead)

yōshu 洋酒 liquor (Western)

yoso' よそ・余所 somewhere else; alien, strange; ~ **no hito'** よその人 outsider, stranger

yosō 予想 expectation, presumption; ~ **i'jō** 予想以上 above/beyond expectations; ~ **shima'su** 予想します expects, anticipates, presumes

yosō' よそう = **yoshimashō'** よしましょう (let's stop doing it!)

yo'so 要素 element

yosoku 予測 forecast, prediction, estimate; **yosoku shima'su** 予測します forecasts, predicts, estimates

yoso-mono よそ者・余所者 outsider

yo'su よす = **yoshima'su** よします (stops doing it)

yōsu 様子・ようす circumstances; aspect; appearance, look

yo-su'ru 要する = **yō-shima'su** 要します: ~ **ni** 要するに in summary, to sum it up, in short; in effect, what it amounts to (boils down to) is … ; after all

yotamono よた者・与太者 hoodlum

yō-ta'shi 用足し business, errand

yotei 予定 expectation, plan; ~ **shima'su** 予定します schedules, plans

yōte[]n 要点 gist, point

yotsu-kado 四つ角 intersection (of two streets), crossroads

yotta 寄った・よ[拠]った = **yorima'shita** 寄りました; より[拠り]ました (dropped in; relied)

yo'tta 1. よった・撚った = **yorima'shita** よりました・撚りました (twisted) 2. 酔った = **yoima'shita** 酔いました (got drunk)

yotte 寄って・よ[拠]って → **yorima'su** 寄ります; より[拠り]ます (drops in; relies)

yo'tte 1. よって・撚って → **yorima'su** よります・撚ります (twists) 2. 酔って → **yoima'su** 酔います (gets drunk)

yottsu' 四つ four

yo'u 酔う = **yoima'su** 酔います (gets drunk; gets seasick, etc.)

yowa'i 弱い weak; frail; poor at *(math, etc.)*; (**sake ni** ~ 酒に弱い) easily intoxicated

yowa'nai 酔わない = **yoimase'n** 酔いません (not get drunk)

yowasema'su 酔わせます, **yowase'ru** 酔わせる gets one drunk, lets one get drunk

yo'ya 酔や = **yo'eba** 酔えば (if

one get drunk)

yoyaku 予約 reservation, subscription, booking, appointment

yōyaku 1. ようやく gradually; at last; barely **2.** 要約 a summary; **yōyaku shima̱su** 要約します summarizes

yo̱ya shinai 酔やしない = **yo̱i ya/wa shinai** 酔いや/はしない = **yowa̱nai** 酔わない (not get drunk)

yoyū 余裕 room, leeway, margin, excess, surplus

yu̱ 湯 = **o-yu** お湯 hot water, bath; hot tea

yū 1. ゆう・言う = **iu** 言う = **iima̱su** 言います (says) **2.** 結う = **yuu** 結う = **yuima̱su** 結います does up one's hair

yūbe̱ ゆうべ・昨夕 = **kinō no ban** きのう[昨日]の晩 last night

yubi̱ 指 finger; toe

yūbi̱m-bako 郵便箱 mailbox

yūbim-ba̱ngō 郵便番号 zip code; ZIP Code

yūbin 郵便 mail; ~**-cho̱kin** 郵便貯金 postal savings; ~**-fu̱rikae** 郵便振替 postal transfer; ~**-ga̱wase** 郵便為替 (postal) money order

yū̱bi (na) 優美(な) elegant, graceful

yūbi̱n-kyoku 郵便局 post office

yubi-nu̱ki̱ 指貫き thimble

yūbin-ya (san) 郵便屋(さん) mail deliverer, mailman, postman

yubi-wa 指輪 ring

yu̱bune 湯船 bathtub

yūdachi 夕立 a sudden shower

yudan 油断 negligence, carelessness, remissness

yuda̱ne 委ね → **yudanema̱su** 委ねます **1.** [infinitive] **2.** [imperative] **yudane̱ ro** 委ねろ, **yuda̱ne yo** 委ねよ entrust it!

yudanema̱su 委ねます, **yudane̱ru** 委ねる entrusts, commits

Yudaya̱-jin ユダヤ人 Jew; **Yudaya-kyō** ユダヤ教 Judaism

yudema̱su ゆでます・茹でます, **yude̱ru** ゆでる・茹でる boil (food)

yude-ta̱mago ゆで卵・茹で卵 boiled egg

yu̱dete ゆでて・茹でて → **yudema̱su** ゆでます・茹でます

yu-dō̱fu 湯豆腐 bean-curd squares boiled in an earthenware pot

yue 結え **1.** → **yuema̱su** 結えます [infinitive] **2.** → **yuima̱su** 結います [imperative] do up your hair!

yue̱ 故・ゆえ reason, grounds; ... ~ **ni** ...故に・ゆえに for the reason that ... , because ...

yueˉba 結えば → **yuimaˉsu** 結い
ます (if one do up one's hair)

yuemaˉsu 結えます, **yueru** 結え
る can do up one's hair

yuenai 結えない = **yuemaseˉn** 結
えません (cannot do up one's
hair)

yuereˉba 結えれば → **yuemaˉsu**
結えます (if one can do up
one's hair)

yūⁿfuku (na) 裕福(な) rich,
wealthy

yugamaⁿnai 歪まない・ゆがま
ない = **yugamimaseˉn** 歪みま
せん・ゆがみません (not get
distorted/warped)

yugamemaˉsu 歪めます・ゆがめ
ます, **yugameⁿru** 歪める・ゆ
がめる distorts, warps

yugameⁿnai 歪めない・ゆがめ
ない = **yugamemaseˉn** 歪めま
せん・ゆがめません (not dis-
tort/warp)

yugaⁿmete 歪めて・ゆがめて →
yugamemaˉsu 歪めます・ゆが
めます

yugamiⁿ 歪み・ゆがみ distortion, warp

yugaⁿmi 歪み・ゆがみ →
yugamimaˉsu 歪みます・ゆが
みます [infinitive]

yugamimaˉsu 歪みます・ゆがみ
ます, **yugaⁿmu** 歪む・ゆがむ
gets distorted/warped

yugaⁿnde 歪んで・ゆがんで →
yugamimaˉsu 歪みます・ゆが

みます

yūgata 夕方 evening

yuⁿge 湯気 steam

yū-han 夕飯 supper, dinner

yui 結い → **yuimaˉsu** 結います
[infinitive]

yuigon 遺言 will, testament

yuˉiitsu (no) 唯一(の) the only,
unique

yuimaˉsu 結います, **yuu** 結う
does up one's hair

yuka 床 floor

yuⁿkai (na) 愉快(な) merry, happy, gay; funny, droll

yūkai 誘拐 kidnap(ping); ~
shimaˉsu 誘拐します kidnaps

yūkan 1. 夕刊 evening paper
2. ~ **(na)** 勇敢(な) brave

yukata 浴衣・ゆかた (light) bathrobe

yuki 行き・ゆき [literary] = **iki**
行き (goes) [infinitive]

yukiˉ 雪 snow; ~ **ga furimaˉsu**
雪が降ります it snows

yukimaˉsu 行きます・ゆきます
[literary] = **ikimaˉsu** 行きます
(goes)

yuki-naˉdare 雪なだれ snowslide, avalanche

yukkuˉri ゆっくり slowly; at
ease

yūkō (na) 有効(な) effective,
valid

yuku 行く・ゆく [literary] = **iku**
行く (goes)

yumeˉ 夢 dream; (… **no**) ~ **o**

mima'su (...の)夢を見ます dreams (of ...)

yūmei (na) 有名(な) famous

yū-meshi 夕飯 supper, dinner

yumi' 弓 bow (for archery or violin)

yumi-gata 弓形 curve, arch, bow

yū'moa ユーモア humor, wit

yunomi' 湯飲み, **yunomi-ja'wan** 湯飲み茶碗 teacup

yunyū 輸入 import(ing); ～ shima'su 輸入します imports

yunyū⌐-hin 輸入品 imported goods

yunyū'-zei 輸入税 (import) duty

yūran 遊覧 excursion

yuranai 揺らない = **yurimase'n** 揺りません (not shake it)

yure 揺れ 1. tremor, shock 2. → **yurema'su** 揺れます [infinitive] 3. → **yurima'su** 揺ります [imperative] shake it!

yure'ba 揺れば → **yurima'su** 揺ります (if one shake it)

yū'rei 幽霊 ghost

yurema'su 揺れます, **yureru** 揺れる it shakes, sways, swings, rocks, rolls

yurenai 揺れない = **yuremase'n** 揺れません (not shake it)

yurere'ba 揺れれば (if it shake)

yurete 揺れて → **yurema'su** 揺れます

yū⌐retsu 優劣 relative merits (superiority or inferiority)

yuri ゆり・百合 lily

yuri 揺り → **yurima'su** 揺ります [infinitive]

yuri-kago 揺りかご・揺り籠 cradle

yurima'su 揺ります, **yuru** 揺る shakes (sways, swings, rocks) it

yū'ri (na) 有利(な) profitable, advantageous

yurō 揺ろう = **yurimashō'** 揺りましょう (let's shake it!)

yuru'i 緩い・ゆるい loose, slack; lax, lenient; slow

yurushima'su 許します, **yuru'su** 許す allows, permits, lets; pardons, forgives

yurya 揺りゃ = **yure'ba** 揺れば (if one shake it)

yurya shinai 揺りゃしない = **yuri'ya/wa shinai** 揺りや/はしない = **yuranai** 揺らない (not shake it)

yūryoku (na) 有力(な) strong, powerful, influential

yūryō (no) 有料(の) pay *(not free)*, charge, fee; ～-chū'sha 有料駐車 pay parking

yūshi-te'ssen 有刺鉄線 barbed wire

yūshō 優勝 (winning) the victory/championship; ～ shima'su 優勝します wins (the victory); **yūshō'-sha** 優勝者 the winner, victor

yūshoku 夕食 evening meal (supper, dinner)

yushutsu 輸出 export(ing); ~ **shima⌐su** 輸出します exports

yushutsu⌐-hin 輸出品 export goods

yusō 輸送 transport(ation)

yūsō⌐-ryō 郵送料 postage

yusuburima⌐su 揺すぶります, **yusuburu** 揺すぶる shakes (sways, swings, rocks) it

yūsu-ho⌐suteru ユースホステル youth hostel

yusuri ゆすり・強請り blackmail, extortion

yu⌐taka (na) 豊か(な) abundant, plentiful; wealthy

yu-ta⌐mpo 湯たんぽ hot-water bottle

yū-ta⌐n ユー[U]ターン U-turn; ~ **shima(⌐)su** ユー[U]ターンします makes a U-turn

yutte 1. 結って → **yuima⌐su** 結います (does up one's hair) **2.** 揺って → **yurima⌐su** 揺ります (shakes it) **3.** ゆって・言って = **itte** 言って (saying, says and)

yuu 結う (= **yū** 結う) = **yuima⌐su** 結います (does up onc's hair)

yūutsu (na) 憂うつ・憂鬱(な) melancholy, gloom

yu-wa⌐kashi 湯沸かし teakettle, boiler *(for heating water)*

yūwaku 誘惑 temptation; seduction; **yūwaku shima⌐su** 誘惑します seduces

yuwanai 1. 結わない = **yuimase⌐n** 結いません (not do up one's hair) **2.** ゆわない・言わない = **iwanai** 言わない (not say)

yuya 結や 1. = **yue⌐ba** 結えば (if one do up one's hair) **2.** ~ **shinai** 結やしない = **yui⌐ ya/ wa shinai** 結いや/はしない = **yuwanai** 結わない (not do up one's hair)

yu-za⌐mashi 湯冷まし boiled water *(cooled for drinking)*

yu⌐zu ゆず・柚子 citron

yūzū 融通 **1.** financing; ~ **shima⌐su** 融通します finances, lends/advances money **2.** adaptability, versatility; ~ **no/ga kiku** 融通の/がきく adaptable, versatile

yuzuranai 譲らない = **yuzuri- mase⌐n** 譲りません (not cede)

yuzure 譲れ **1.** → **yuzurema⌐su** 譲れます [infinitive] **2.** → **yuzurima⌐su** 譲ります [imperative] cede!

yuzure⌐ba 譲れば → **yuzurima⌐su** 譲ります (if one cede)

yuzurema⌐su 譲れます, **yuzureru** 譲れる can give up/in; can cede

yuzurenai 譲れない = **yuzuremase⌐n** 譲れません (cannot cede)

yuzure⌐reba 譲れれば →

yuzurema̅su 譲れます (if we
can cede)
yuzuri 譲り 1. → **yuzurima̅su** 譲
ります [infinitive]
2. (**o-yu̅zuri** お譲り) inheritance;
... ～ **no** ...譲りの inherited
from ...

yuzurete 譲れて → **yuzurema̅su**
譲れます (can cede)
yuzurima̅su 譲ります, **yuzuru**
譲る gives up; gives in; yields;
cedes; is inferior
yuzutte 譲って → **yuzurima̅su**
譲ります (cedes)

— Z —

za⁼ 座 1. theater 2. seat
zabu̅ton 座布団・ざぶとん
cushion to sit on
zadan 座談 chat; **zada̅n-kai** 座談
会 roundtable discussion
za̅i 材 1. (= **zaimoku** 材木)
lumber 2. 材 (= **zairyo̅** 材料)
material 3. 財 (= **za⁼isan** 財
産) wealth
zai-... 在... (resident) in
zaibatsu 財閥 a big financial
group
zaidan 財団 a foundation (non-
profit)
zaikai 財界 financial circles
zaimoku 材木 lumber, wood
za̅iru ザイル a mountain-climbing rope
zairyo̅ 材料 raw material(s), in-
gredient(s)
zairyū 在留 residing, residence;
～**-shi̅kaku** 在留資格 status
of residence
za⁼isan 財産 wealth, property,

fortune
zaisei 財政 finance
za-isu 座椅子 backrest (= legless
chair)
zakka 雑貨 miscellaneous goods,
sundries
zama̅-miro ざあ見ろ (=
zama̅ o mi̅ ro ざまを見ろ) It
serves you/them right!
zangai 残骸 wreck(age)
za̅nge̅ ざんげ・懺悔 confession
(of sins)
zangyaku (na) 残虐(な) cruel,
brutal, atrocious; **zangyaku̅-
ko̅i** 残虐行為 an atrocity
zangyō 残業 overtime (work)
zankoku (na) 残酷(な) cruel,
brutal, harsh
zanne̅n (na) 残念(な) regrettable, disappointed; too bad, a
pity; **zannen-na⁼gara** 残念な
がら regrettably
zannin (na) 残忍(な) brutal
zara-ni ざらに found every-

where, very common

za̅razara (shita) ざらざら(した) rough(-textured)

zaru̅ ざる・笊 a bamboo sieve/colander

zāsai ザーサイ・搾菜 Chinese pickles

zaseki 座席 seat; ～-ba̅ngō 座席番号 seat number; ～-be̅ruto 座席ベルト seatbelt

zasetsu 挫折 frustration; zasetsu̅-kan 挫折感 feeling of frustration; zasetsu shima̅su 挫折します gets frustrated; zasetsu sasema̅su 挫折させます frustrates

zashiki̅ (o-zashiki) 座敷(お座敷) room, living room; tatami room

zasshi 雑誌 magazine, periodical

zassō 雑草 weeds

zatsu (na) 雑(な) coarse, crude

zatsuon 雑音 noise(s), static

zatta (na) 雑多(な) sundry, miscellaneous

zatto ざっと roughly; briefly

zaze̅n 座禅 meditation (Zen)

... ze ...ぜ (mostly male) indeed, I tell you

ze̅-hi ぜひ・是非 1. without fail, for sure 2. right or wrong

ze̅i 税 tax, customs

zeikan 税関 customs, custom house

zeikin 税金 tax

zeita̅ku̅ ぜいたく・贅沢 luxury,

extravagance; ～ (na) ぜいたく・贅沢(な) luxurious

zeitaku̅-hin ぜいたく[贅沢]品 luxury (goods), luxuries

ze̅kken ゼッケン an athlete's number; ～ o tsu̅kema̅su ゼッケンを付けます attaches/assigns a number (to an athlete)

ze̅mbu 全部 all, everything, completely; ～ de 全部で altogether

ze̅mi ゼミ, zeminā̅ru ゼミナール seminar

zemmai 1. ぜんまい・発条 a spring, hairspring, clockspring 2. ぜんまい・薇 royal fern, osmund

zemme̅n 1. 全面 the entire surface 2. 前面 the front side

zemmetsu 全滅 annihilation

zempō̅ 前方 the front

zen 膳 (traditional individual low) meal table, dining tray (o-zen お膳, go̅-zen 御膳)

ze̅n(-) ... 全... all, total, whole, complete, the whole

ze̅n(-) ... 前... former, earlier [bookish = ma̅e no ... 前の...]

zenchō 前兆 omen, sign

ze̅ngo 前後 1. before and after; ahead and behind; back and forth 2. sequence, order

...-ze̅ngo ...前後 approximately, around, about ⌜wide

ze̅nkoku (no) 全国(の) nation-

zenrei 前例 precedent, prior example

ze̅nsha 前者 the former

Ze̅nsho shima(ꞋꞋ)su̱. 善処します. "I will do my best" = Don't expect me to do anything.

zensoku ぜんそく・喘息 asthma

zentai 全体 the whole body, the entirety; ～ **no** 全体の entire, whole; ～ **ni** 全体に wholly, generally

ze̅ntai 全体 originally, primarily (= **ga̅nrai** 元来)

ze̅nto 前途 the future, prospects

ze̅n'ya 前夜 the night before

zenzen 全然・ぜんぜん completely, utterly, entirely, altogether; (not) at all, (not) ever

zeppeki 絶壁 precipice

zera̅chin ゼラチン gelatine

ze̅rii ゼリー jelly

ze̅ro ゼロ zero

zetsubō 絶望 despair; ～ **shima̅su** 絶望します despairs

zetsuen shima̅su 絶縁します insulates

zettai (no) 絶対(の) total, absolute; ～ **ni** 絶対に totally, absolutely

zi... → **j...**

... zo ...ぞ *(mostly male)* indeed, I tell you

zo̅ 1. 像 statue, image, portrait 2. 象 elephant

zōdai 増大 enlargement, increase

zōga̅n 象眼 inlaid work; dama-scene

zōge̅ 象牙 ivory

zō̅ho 増補 supplement

zō̅ka 増加 increase, growth

zōkin ぞうきん・雑巾 rag, dustcloth

zoku 賊 robber, bandit, thief

...-zoku ...族 the tribe/gang/group of ... ; the ...s

zokugo 俗語 slang

zoku (na) 俗(な) common, vulgar; popular

zoku̱sa̅nai 属さない = **zoku̱shimase̅n** 属しません (not belong)

zoku̱shima̅su 属します, **zoku̱̅su** 属す belongs

zoku-shima̅su 属します, **zoku̱-su̅ru** 属する belongs

zoku̱-shi̅nai 属しない = **zoku̱(-)shimase̅n** 属しません (not belong)

zoku̱̅(-)shi̱te 属して → **zoku̱(-)shima̅su** 属します

zo̅kuzoku ぞくぞく・続々 one right after another, in rapid succession

zombu̅n (ni) 存分(に) as much as one likes

zo̅ngai 存外 beyond expectations

zōni̅ 雑煮・ぞうに (= **o-zōni** お雑煮・おぞうに) rice cakes boiled with vegetables (eaten as New Year's soup)

zo̅n-ji 存じ → **zon-jima̅su** 存

じます [infinitive]; → **go-zo'n-ji** ご存じ

zon-jima'su 存じます, **-ji'ru** 存じる [HUMBLE/DEFERENTIAL] thinks, feels; knows

zon-ji'nai 存じない = **zon-jimase'n** 存じません (not think/feel/know)

zo'n-jite 存じて → **zon-jima'su** 存じます

zonza'i (na) ぞんざい(な) slovenly, rough, careless, sloppy

zōri (o-zō'ri) 草履(お草履) straw sandals

zo'rozoro ぞろぞろ in streams/crowds, in large numbers

zōsen 造船 ship building; **zōsen-jo'** 造船所 shipyard

zōshin 増進 promotion, betterment, increase

zōsho 蔵書 book collection, library

zōsui 雑炊 rice boiled in a soup

zotto ぞっと with a shudder/shiver; ~ **shima'su** ぞっとします shudders, shivers, thrills (is thrilled)

zu 図 picture, drawing, chart, map, diagram, figure; ~ **ni norima'su (noru)** 図に乗ります(乗る) pushes a good thing too far, takes advantage of a person

...-zu ...ず, **...-zu ni** ...ずに = **...-na'ide** ...ないで (not doing, instead of doing)

zuan 図案 sketch, design

zubo'n ズボン trousers, pants

zubo'n-shita ズボン下 underpants, shorts, drawers

zubo'n-tsuri ズボン吊り suspenders

zuhyō 図表 chart, diagram

zu'ibun 随分・ずいぶん 1. fairly, rather 2. very, quite, extremely

zuihitsu 随筆 essays

zu'ii (no) 随意(の) voluntary, optional

zukai 図解 illustration, diagram

...-zuki ...好き a lover of ... , a great ... fan

zu'kku ズック canvas; duck (*fabric*)

zukku'-gutsu ズック靴 = **zu'kku no kutsu'** ズックの靴 canvas shoes, sneakers

...-zu'kuri ...造り made of ...

zu'nō 頭脳 brains, head

zure' ずれ discrepancy, lag, gap

zu're ずれ → **zurema'su** ずれます [infinitive]

zurema'su ずれます, **zure'ru** ずれる slips out of place, gets loose

zure'nai ずれない = **zuremase'n** ずれません (not get loose)

zu'rereba ずれれば → **zurema'su** ずれます (if it get loose)

zu'rete ずれて → **zurema'su** ずれます

zurō'su ズロース panties; drawers

zu̅ru ずる cheating

zuru̅i ずるい・狡い sly, cunning, tricky

zurukema̅su ずるけます, zuruke⌐ru ずるける shirks; skips school

zuru-ya̅sumi ずる休み skipping school, playing hookey; ～ shima̅su ずる休みします skips school, plays hookey

zusan (na) ずさん・杜撰(な) sloppy, slipshod, careless

...zu̅tsu ...ずつ (of/for) each, apiece, at a time

zutsū 頭痛 headache; ～ no ta̅ne 頭痛の種 one's biggest headache; ～ ga shima̅su 頭痛がします has a headache

zutto ずっと 1. directly 2. by far, much (more); ～ ma̅e ずっと前 way back (before), a long time ago 3. all the way through, all the time

zūzūshī̅i ずうずうしい・図々しい brazen, shameless, pushy

zy... → j...

OTHER TITLES IN THE TUTTLE LANGUAGE LIBRARY

A REFERENCE GRAMMAR OF JAPANESE *by Samuel E. Martin*
"This grammar . . . is by far the most comprehensive reference grammar of Japanese in the English language (and perhaps in any language)."

—Journal of Linguistics

COMPLETE JAPANESE EXPRESSION GUIDE *by Mizue Sasaki*
"Studying Japanese idiomatic expressions doesn't have to be a futile exercise in hitori-zumo (one-man sumo) any longer."

—The Japan Times

THE COMPLETE JAPANESE VERB GUIDE *compiled by the Hiroo Japanese Center*
" . . . a real charmer for people who want to liven up their Japanese."

—The Nippon View

A GUIDE TO READING & WRITING JAPANESE *edited by Florence Sakade*
"Invaluable to anyone eager to acquaint himself with an elementary knowledge of written Japanese."

—Asian Student

JAPANESE FOR ALL OCCASIONS *by Anne Kaneko*
". . . a godsend to all non-native speakers."

—Nikkei Weekly

KANJI POWER *by John Millen*
"Clear, straightforward, and easy to use. The definitive tool for kanji beginners."

—Mizue Sasaki, columnist, Asahi Evening News

THE MODERN READER'S JAPANESE-ENGLISH CHARACTER DICTIONARY (2nd Revised Edition) *by Andrew N. Nelson*
"The new compilation offers many advantages: a larger number of characters . . ., more readings still in current use . . ., and a greatly expanded list of compounds . . ."

—Harvard Journal of Asiatic Studies